Television Character and Story Facts

Television Character and Story Facts

*Over 110,000 Details from
1,008 Shows, 1945–1992*

by
Vincent Terrace

McFarland & Company, Inc., Publishers
Jefferson, North Carolina, and London

British Library Cataloguing-in-Publication data are available

Library of Congress Cataloguing-in-Publication Data

Terrace, Vincent, 1948–
Television character and story facts : over 110,000 details from
1,008 shows, 1945–1992 / by Vincent Terrace.
p.   cm.
Includes index.
ISBN 0-89950-891-X (lib. bdg. : 50# alk. paper) ∞
1. Television serials—United States.   2. Television pilot
programs—United States.   3. Television programs—United States—
Plots, themes, etc.   I. Title.
PN1992.8.S4T48   1993
791.45'097309045—dc20
92-51095
CIP

Manufactured in the United States of America

McFarland & Company, Inc., Publishers
Box 611, Jefferson, North Carolina 28640

Acknowledgments

The author would like to thank the following people for their help in making this book possible:

Steven Eberly   Alvin H. Marill
Lloyd Friedman   James Robert Parish
Barry Gillam   Robert ("Bob") Reed
Steven Lance   Laura Stuart

and especially Debbie Milano, who made her collection of aired and unaired pilot films available to the author.

Table of Contents

Preface

In thirteenth-century Italy a woman named Clare founded the Order of the Poor Clares. Clare, who would later be canonized as a saint by the Roman Catholic Church, took a vow of strict poverty. Her order flourished and spread to France and Germany. It is reported that one Sunday extreme illness prevented Clare from attending a mass presided over by the pope. Nevertheless, Clare saw the entire mass, as it happened, in a vision on the wall of her convent room. For this reason, she has been named the patron saint of television.

This is the first known television fact. On June 13, 1925, the first known motion picture (a Charles Jenkins experiment) was telecast. Three years later, on August 21, 1928, WOR in New York telecast the first known drama (done with puppets) from Bamberger's department store. Later that year, on September 11, WGY in Schenectady, New York, telecast the first live drama: "The Queen's Messenger."

In August 1931, CBS experimental TV station W2XAB broadcast the first known musical variety series, "Half-Hour on Broadway." This was followed by the first known dramatic series, "The Television Ghost," and by the first musical comedy series, "Ned Wayburn's Musical Comedy Show" (both over W2XAB and both premiering on August 27, 1931).

The Return of the Scarlet Pimpernel became the first motion picture to be seen on American television (over NBC's New York station, W2XBS on May 31, 1938). The first televised soap opera was "Vine Street," broadcast over W6XAO in Los Angeles in January 1939. "The World's Fair Beauty Show," broadcast by NBC on June 21, 1939, is the first example of a televised beauty pageant. TV's first Western, "Missouri Legend," was broadcast by W2XBS on July 18, 1939. In January 1945, NBC telecast the first known miniseries, "The Black Angel" (shown over four nights), with Mary Patton, Richard Keith and Phil Foster.

Facts like these can be found in various sources, like

Variety. Unfortunately, the actual programs appear to have been lost forever and what information is available has basically been reported here. This book is just the opposite. The actual episodes of well known as well as lost and forgotten series were found and watched to compile television information that has never before appeared in print. You'll find a veritable gold mine of television information here, information that simply cannot be found in any other source—not in *TV Guide*, newspapers, magazines, libraries or even from the show's production companies. In many cases, the factual information that appears in this book is the only record of such information that exists in print; in other cases it is the only source of such information that is available to the general public.

This is *not* a book of opinions or essays about specific programs; it is a narrative of the facts associated with each of the 1,008 series and pilots that are represented here in 781 numbered entries covering the period September 26, 1945, to December 31, 1992. While all the basic information about these series wil be found here, you'll also find information you never knew existed or never could find before—from addresses, phone numbers and license plate numbers, to maiden names, nicknames and pet names, to clothing sizes and favorite foods.

All entries include a principal cast (those directly involved with the factual information), networks, broadcast dates and theme song credits. Most entries (where such information was given) also include relatives (the aunts, uncles, brothers, sisters, parents, and so forth, of the regular cast), flashbacks (the performers who played a regular cast member as a younger person) and flash forwards (performers who played cast members in a future time). Where possible (when the film could be found), the unaired pilot information has been included with a series. For example, you'll discover that Ellie Wood Walker was the first "Wonder Woman"; Alan Young the first "Mr. Terrific"; and that "How to Marry a Millionaire" and "Mister Ed" had different casts.

Not every series that was ever made could be found and included in this work (some seem not to exist anymore). There was as much difficulty in finding shows from 1987 as there was with those made in 1950. Information (facts) about many of the shows that appear here come from collectors; the shows themselves haven't been seen since their initial broadcasts (for example, "The Bickersons," "A Date with Judy," "The Halls of Ivy," "Johnny Jupiter," "N.O.P.D." and "Rod Brown of the Rocket Rangers"). Many more series were watched than are actually listed here: not all series are created equal and while some have tremendous amounts of information, others have barely enough facts to qualify for an entry. The end result, however, is a listing of more than 111,000 screen facts, encompassing the early and lost series of television (for example, "Life with Luigi," "Meet Corliss Archer," "Two Girls Named Smith" and "Mysteries of Chinatown"), the cult shows (for example, "Doctor Who," "Dobie Gillis" and "My Mother the Car") and programs as recent as fall 1992 (for example, "Beverly Hills, 90210," "Married . . . with Children" and "Murphy Brown").

Most of the dates listed for series include the complete runs (from first broadcast to last rerun broadcast). However, in recent years, shows have been taken off the air so quickly that they were still listed as being on in *TV Guide* and other printed sources even though they were not on (for example, "Heartland" ended 7/24/89 even though a repeat episode, listed for 7/31/89 in *TV Guide* never aired). If a network ran a series commitment of episodes then dropped the program (for example, "Married People") and then returned it months later for repeats, only the first run dates are listed. If, however, a series was dropped after one or two episodes (for example, "Melba") and returned months later to complete the run, then the various dates will be listed. Since all the information in his book was based on watching programs, it makes only sense to compile date information in the same manner. Thus, dates listed for some shows from 1986 to 1993 will conflict with other sources that used printed sources like *TV Guide* or press releases.

From the population of Bedrock ("The Flintstones") to Herman Munster's blood pressure reading ("The Munsters") to Ginger's measurements on "Gilligan's Island," you'll find an incredible wealth of television information that simply cannot be found anyplace else.

Television Character and Story Facts

1. *The A-Team*

NBC, 1/23/83 to 3/8/87

Cast: George Peppard *(Hannibal Smith)*, Dirk Benedict *(Templeton Peck)*, Mr. T *(B.A. Baracus)*, Dwight Schultz *(H.M. Murdock)*, Melinda Culea *(Amy Allen)*, Marla Heasley *(Tawnia Baker)*, Robert Vaughn *(Hunt Stockwell)*.

Facts: In Vietnam on Sunday morning, January 27, 1971, Colonel John ("Hannibal") Smith, Lieutenant Templeton Peck, Sergeant Bosco ("B.A.") Baracus and Captain H.M. Murdock, members of the U.S. Armed Services A-Team, receive orders from a Colonel Samuel Morrison to rob the Bank of Hanoi. The team members believe they are performing a mission to help end the Vietnam War; in reality, however, they are unknowingly helping Morrison, who is a Vietnamese supporter. The robbery nets Morrison 100 million yen (another episode mentions ten million pesetas; about one million dollars). Shortly after, Morrison alerts officials to the robbery, then stages his own death. The A-Team is captured by Colonel Roderick Decker (Lance Le Gault) and imprisoned for murder and robbery. Before the team can be tried, they escape from Fort Bragg and retreat to the Los Angeles underground where they become soldiers of fortune and help people who are unable to turn to the police for help. (Military brass believes that only Hannibal, Peck and Baracus compose the A-Team; Murdock, a pilot, was on another mission when the team was captured. Murdock now secretly aids the A-Team.)

Members of the A-Team, Military File Number 1-HG-4227, are branded fugitives, and $20,000 is offered for their capture. Colonel Decker, later replaced by Colonel Lynch (William Lucking), was the most persistent of the military brass seeking the A-Team. In the last season's episodes, the A-Team, including Murdock, is captured by General Hunt Stockwell and tried in California at Fort Owen. The team is convicted of murder and robbery and sentenced to death by firing squad—but they are given a chance to redeem themselves by performing hazardous missions for Stockwell. The team is given a base—a home in Langley, Virginia, and it now operates under the code name Empress 6 (Stockwell's code is Empress 1). The A-Team's mobile phone number is 555-6162, and Stockwell's limo license plate reads NRB 729.

Colonel John ("Hannibal") Smith is the head of the A-Team (in Vietnam, he was commander of the 5th Special Forces Group). His Social Security number is 844-31-3142, and his FBI file number (he is wanted as a fugitive) is 61-5683-1. Before he accepts an assignment, a client must meet with Mr. Lee (Hannibal in disguise), the Chinese owner of Mr. Lee's Laundry Shop on Sixth Street in Los Angeles. (Hannibal finds this deception necessary to evaluate a case and determine that it is not a military trap.) When time permits, Hannibal plays the Aquamaniac or the Slime Monster in horror movies. Hannibal is famous for his expression "I love it when a plan comes together" and has an M-60 gun he calls "Baby." He gets "on the jazz" (a feeling of excitement during each assignment).

Lieutenant Templeton Peck, known as "Face" and "The Faceman," is a master con artist and the team's means of getting what it needs without paying for it. His Social Security number is 522-70-5044, and 61-5683-2 is his FBI file number. Face was orphaned at the age of five; he wandered into and was raised at the Guardian Angels Orphanage in Los Angeles. He learned most of his cons from his favorite TV show—"Dragnet." Face is an expert at bending the rules. "He's a great liar," Hannibal says, "and he has such a face that everybody believes what he is saying." Peck's favorite scam is Miracle Films ("If it's a good picture, it's a Miracle"), and he has a script called "The Beast of the Yellow Night" ready for production. (In the pilot episode, his scam was a film called "Boots and Bikinis" for 20th Century-Fox; it was to star Loni Anderson, Bo Derek and Farrah Fawcett.) Face's license plate reads IHG 581. His address (a beach house he scams) is 1347 Old Balboa Road. Tim Dunigan played Face in the pilot episode (he was considered too young to have served in Vietnam and was replaced).

Sergeant B.A. Baracus is the toughest and meanest member of the team ("B.A." stands for Bad Attitude). His Social Security number is 554-04-3106, and 61-5683-3 is his FBI file number. B.A. loves children (he runs a day care center in his spare time) and gold jewelry. His biggest fear is flying. To rid B.A. of this fear, Hannibal does one of three things: spikes his milk (his favorite drink), injects him with a tranquilizer, or gives him his "beddy-bye drink" (a conk on the head with a two-by-four). B.A.'s nickname (from his mother) is "Scooter"; his real first name is Elliott. B.A.'s black-with-red trim GMC van's license plate numbers are 218 3000, S96 7238, 2A22029 and 2E14859. B.A. lives in an apartment at the Hotel Regina. Mr. T's real name is Lawrence Tero.

Captain H.M. ("Howling Mad") Murdock was a pilot for the Thunderbirds before the Vietnam War, and he performed heroic missions in Vietnam. He now pretends to be insane and resides in Building 16 of the V.A. Hospital in Los Angeles. While the military suspects Murdock is a member of the A-Team, they can't prove it. Living in the ward provides him with the perfect cover.

Murdock shares the same blood type with B.A. (AB-negative) and has an invisible dog (Billy), an alligator (Wally Gator) and a plant ("The Little Guy"). "The Range Rider" (from the old TV show) and Captain Bellybuster of the Burger Heaven Food Chain are his heroes. Murdock has been diagnosed with paranoid delusions and ammonia is the key word that triggers his aggression. In the last season's episodes, Murdock is pronounced sane and released from the hospital; he then resides with the team in Virginia.

Amy Amanda Allen, called "Triple A" by Hannibal, is a reporter for the Los Angeles *Courier-Express*. She assists the team when a beautiful girl is needed to help in a scam. Amy became part of the team when she hired it to find a missing reporter and became actively involved in the case. Amy's license plate numbers are 1FH 480, 1FHJ 484 and ILBJ 1247.

Tawnia Baker is Amy's friend, and is also a reporter for the *Courier-Express* (she became a part of the team when

Amy was transferred overseas). Like Amy, Tawnia helps the team when needed. (Before taking the role of Tawnia, Marla Heasley played Charise, a bikini-clad student in the episode "Bad Time on the Border"). Tawnia left the team to marry archaeologist Brian Lefcourt (Barry Van Dyke) in the episode "Bend in the River." Tawnia's license plate numbers are 1JFY 515 and 854 022.

In the last season's episodes, Eddie Velez joins the team as Frankie Santana, a Hollywood special-effects man, and Judith Ledford plays Carla, Stockwell's aide.

Relatives: Della Reese (B.A.'s mother, *Mrs. Baracus*; she lives at 700 Foster Avenue in Chicago), Clare Kirkconnell (Face's half sister, *Ellen Bancroft*), Ken Olandt (Hannibal's nephew, *Kid Harmon*), Stuart Whitman (Kid's father, *Jack Harmon*), Toni Hudson (Kid's wife, *Dana Harmon*).

Theme: "The A-Team," by Mike Post and Pete Carpenter.

2. *The Abbott and Costello Show*

Syndicated, 1952 to 1954

The Fields Rooming House at 214 Brookline Avenue in Hollywood, California, is owned by Sidney Fields (himself), a man whose patience is tried by his worst tenants, Bud Abbott and Lou Costello (themselves), former movie and radio stars who are now out of work and down on their luck.

Bud and Lou's rent is seven dollars a week, and their phone number is Alexander 4444 (also given as Alexander 2222). The boys live day by day and try to find what work they can (that is, Bud tries to find Lou work). Most notable of their jobs were those of door-to-door salesmen selling NO PEDDLERS ALLOWED signs; delivery boys for the Susquehanna Hat Company on Flugel Street; discount roller skate salesmen ("Abbott & Costello Cheap Skates"); and owners (for one episode) of "Abbott and Costello Pest Exterminators." They also appeared on the TV stunt game show "Hold That Cuckoo" (where Lou held that cuckoo and won the grand prize—a box of bubble gum). Lou mentioned that he was born in Paterson, New Jersey, and helps support his sister and three nieces. Bud mentioned he was a professional loafer (one who makes bread; not, as Lou thought, one who gets paid for sitting around and doing nothing).

Hillary Brooke (herself) is a tenant and Lou's girlfriend. Her job depends on what the episode calls for (for example, she was Nurse Brooke when Lou had insomnia; a dental assistant when Lou had a toothache and a secretary when the boys sought legal help). Hillary moved to Texas in one episode when she inherited the B-Bar-B Ranch from a relative; in another episode, she inherited a haunted castle from the late Montague Brooke at Goblins Knob.

Mike Kelly (Gordon Jones), called "Mike the Cop," is the not too bright police officer plagued by Lou; Stinky Davis (Joe Besser) is a mischievous "30-year-old kid" who lives in the rooming house (as does Mike) and plays games with Lou (for example, jump rope, cops and robbers). Mr. Bachagalupe (Joe Kirk) is the enterprising businessman; he owns various businesses, such as Bachagalupe's Vegetable Stand and Bachagalupe's Ice Cream Wagon. Second season episodes feature Lou's pet chimpanzee, Bingo the Chimp (who eats watermelon for breakfast and 50 pounds of bananas a week).

Raoul Kraushaar composed "The Theme from the Abbott and Costello Show."

3. *The Addams Family*

ABC, 9/18/64 to 9/2/66

Cast: John Astin *(Gomez Addams)*, Carolyn Jones *(Morticia Addams)*, Jackie Coogan *(Uncle Fester)*, Lisa Loring *(Wednesday Addams)*, Ken Weatherwax *(Pugsley Addams)*, Ted Cassidy *(Lurch)*, Blossom Rock *(Grandmama Addams)*.

Facts: The Victorian home at 000 Cemetery Lane in the town of Cemetery Ridge is owned by the Addams family. Deadly nightshade, poison sumac and weeds grow in the backyard; quicksand and a swamp can also be found there. The family enjoys gloomy weather, thunderstorms, moonbathing and exploring caves. The second *d* in their name distinguishes them from "the embarrassingly famous and historic John Adams and family."

Gomez Addams is the father. He is an attorney (for the defense) and is responsible for putting more men behind bars than any other lawyer in the United States. He dabbles in the stock market (Consolidated Fuzz is his favorite stock) and owns an elephant herd in Africa, a nut plantation in Brazil, a salt mine and an animal preserve in Nairobi (for its subterranean bat caves). Gomez is a member of the Zen Yoga Society, and Ivan the Terrible is his favorite person in history. His ancestors date back to Egypt in the year A.D. 270 when Maumud Kali Pashu Addams set fire to the library at Alexandria. For relaxation, Gomez enjoys running Lionel "O-Gauge" electric trains (for the thrill of collisions and explosions).

Gomez and the former Morticia Frump were both 22 years old when they met and married (Gomez only dropped Morticia once while carrying her across the threshold). Their first night in the house held an unexpected thrill when they thought the house was haunted. Fried eyes of newt, fried yak and barbecued turtle tips are their favorite foods. Blue eyed Morticia's favorite color is black ("It's so soothing and mysterious"). She always wears the same tight, floor length black dress (on their wedding day, Gomez was driven wild by it; "I'll never wear another," she told him).

Morticia's ancestry dates back to the early colonial days of Salem, Massachusetts. Morticia loves to paint, smokes (literally) and is famous for her dwarf's hair pie and animal imitations (especially the bullfrog, which drives Gomez wild). Gomez also becomes romantic when Morticia speaks French (when she first spoke it, it cleared up a sinus condition that Gomez had for 22 years). Morticia has a carnivorous plant (an African Strangler) named Cleopatra (who loves zebra burgers), and she strives to keep the house nice and bleak. Gomez calls Morticia "Tish," "Cara Mia" and Caita"; she calls Gomez "Bubala." As a child Morticia had a doll named Anne Boleyn.

Wednesday and Pugsley are Gomez and Morticia's children; they attend the Sherwood Elementary School. Wednesday has a doll named Marie Antoinette (who is missing her head) and a pet spider named Homer. Pugsley has an octopus named Aristotle and a jaguar named Fang. He likes to play with dynamite caps and shocked his family when he joined the Boy Scouts.

Morticia's Uncle Fester also lives with the family, as does Gomez's mother, Grandmama, and Lurch, the zombie-like butler. Uncle Fester thrives on electricity and needs to be recharged when he runs low. He once worked as an advice-to-the-lovelorn columnist but quit when everybody started suing him. He has a Revolutionary War rifle named Genevieve (his philosophy is "Shoot 'em in the back") and cures his headaches by forcing the pain out with vises.

Grandmama attended Swamp Town High School and first voted in 1906—even before women's suffrage ("It didn't stop me"). She uses love dust to spark romances. Lurch stands six feet nine inches tall and loves to play the harpsichord. When he is summoned by a gong, he responds with, "You rang?"

Gomez's childhood companion, a human right hand named Thing, lives in a box and acts as a family servant. BEWARE OF THE THING is posted on the front of the iron gate that surrounds the house.

Ophelia Frump (Carolyn Jones) is Morticia's attractive but flakey sister. She cooks all day so she can do the dishes. "She loves to do dishes. She loves water. She is forever jumping into fountains and brooks, even tubs and sinks." Cousin Itt (Felix Silla) is the family intellectual who speaks a language all his own. He is a ladies' man, covered with hair from head to foot, and the chimney or broom closet are his favorite nooks. When Gomez asked Itt what was under all that hair, he replied, "Roots."

The family pet is Kit Kat (a cowardly lion). Al Smith, Alf Landon, Wendell Willkie and Thomas E. Dewey were some of the candidates for president backed by the Addams family. Pierre is the lopsided moose head on the living room wall; the leg sticking out of the shark's mouth on the wall belongs to Cousin Ferouke. In one episode, Thing fell in love with Lady Fingers, a human left hand who serves as the handmaiden of Gomez's Aunt Millicent (Elvia Allman).

Relatives: Margaret Hamilton (Morticia's mother, *Esther Frump*), Ellen Corby *(Mother Lurch)*. Roger Arravo also played Cousin Itt, and Nat Perrin provided Itt's voice. Other relatives (not seen) are Uncle Droop and Aunt Drip, Uncle Tick (has two left feet), Aunt Phobia (has two right feet), Aunt Trivia, Great-Grandfather Blob, Cousin Bleek (has three eyes), Grandpa Slurp, Cousin Kurdle, Cousin Cackle, Great Uncle Grizzly, Aunt Blemish and Uncle Crimp.

Theme: "The Addams Family," by Vic Mizzy.
Note: With the exception of Blossom Rock, the original cast was reunited to celebrate their favorite holiday, Halloween, in the NBC TV movie *Halloween with the Addams Family* (10/30/77). Jane Rose portrayed Grandmama, and Henry Darrow played Gomez's brother, Pancho Addams.

4. *Adventures in Paradise*
ABC, 10/5/59 to 4/1/62

Cast: Gardner McKay *(Adam Troy)*, Weaver Levy *(Oliver Wendell Key)*, James Holden *(Clay Baker)*, Guy Stockwell *(Chris Parker)*.

Facts: Adam Troy, a graduate of Yale University (class of '54, and a member of the Omega fraternity) is a Korean War veteran who now owns the *Tiki*, a 60-foot schooner he hires out to transport cargo and passengers in the South Pacific. Adam, who possesses the rare blood type AB-negative, has the wanderlust but hopes one day to return to America to buy his own ranch ("but not right now"). The *Tiki* is anchored in the Papeete Harbor in Tahiti (the address given for Troy is The Schooner Tiki).

The *Tiki* has two masts and five sails (two large, three small) and a temperamental engine that Adam and his crew call "The Lady." Adam paid $750 for the schooner's transmitter (call letters KQR); for guidance when sailing at night, Adam follows the constellation called the Southern Cross ("Find those stars and you'll never lose your way in the South Pacific"). Adam's Jeep (in the Tahiti-based episodes) has the license plate 3134A.

Oliver Wendell Key was Adam's first mate, cook and lawyer ("he handles all the deals") during first season episodes. Prior to acquiring the *Tiki*, Adam was the skipper of a barge in Pusong; it was there that Oliver first came to work for him.

Tennessee born Clay Baker became Adam's first mate the following season, and Chris Parker was Adam's first mate during the final season.

When Chris signed on, Clay became the innkeeper of the Bali Miki, a hotel originally owned by Trader Penrose (George Tobias). Clay renamed the inn the Bali Miki Baker and was famous for two exotic drinks he concocted: Tahitian Madness and the Polynesian Rainmaker ("two of these and you'll swear it rained"). Before the inn became a "regular," it was called the Hotel DuJour.

To provide storylines, Adam had to become involved with the lives of his passengers. When police help was needed, Inspector Marcel Bouchard (Marcel Hillaire) of the Tahitian Policia was most often there to help him. Kelly (Lani Kai), who doubled as Clay's lounge singer, and Bulldog Lovey (Henry Slate) also served as Adam's shipmates in various episodes. Bulldog, who claimed Adam lived by a code ("There are certain things Adam will do and there are certain things he won't do"), was a master at predicting when night would fall by simply looking at the sky ("I can give you the exact hour and minute, but don't hold me to the seconds").

The series' official screen title is "James A. Michener's Adventures in Paradise," but through *TV Guide* and newspaper listings, it became known as "Adventures in Paradise." In 1956, an unaired pilot called "James A. Michener Presents a South Pacific Adventure" was produced. It was written by Michener and starred Lyle Bettger as a trading schooner captain in the South Pacific.

Theme: "Adventures in Paradise," by Lionel Newman.

5. *The Adventures of Superboy*

Syndicated, 10/8/88 to 5/16/92

Cast: John Haymes Newton and Gerard Christopher (*Clark Kent/Superboy*), Stacy Haiduk (*Lana Lang*), Jim Calvert (*T.J. White*), Scott Wells and Sherman Howard (*Lex Luthor*), Tracey Roberts (*Darla*), Peter Jay Fernandez (*Matt Ritter*), Robert Levine (*Dennis Jackson*).

Facts: "Rocketed from a distant planet to a bold new destiny on Earth. Found by a Kansas family and raised as Clark Kent, he learned he possessed the strength of steel, the speed of light and the desire to help all mankind. He is Superboy."

This simple narration from the opening theme introduced viewers to Clark Kent, who, as the baby Kal-El, escaped the destruction of his planet (Krypton) when his parents (Jor-El and Lara) placed him in an experimental rocket that was programed to land on Earth. The ship landed in Smallville (a small town in Kansas), and the baby was raised by a farm couple named Jonathan and Martha Kent.

First and second season episodes are set at Schuster University, where Clark is studying to become a journalist (he writes for the school newspaper, the *Herald*). Lana Lang and T.J. White are his Lois Lane– and Jimmy Olsen–like friends; Lex Luthor, his most diabolical enemy, is the man determined to destroy Clark's alter ego, Superboy.

When the series returned for its third season (10/7/90), Clark and Lana graduate from Schuster University and begin jobs as interns with the Bureau of Extra-Normal Matters at 101 North Siegel Street, 6th Floor, in Capitol City, Florida (the agency investigates strange phenomena). T.J. White was dropped from the series; added were Dennis Jackson, the head of the bureau; Matt Ritter, an investigator; and Darla, Lex's sensuous assistant. Bizarro (Barry Meyers), an imperfect and indestructible copy of Superboy who was created at Schuster University, became a threat to Superboy in several episodes. Roger Corbin (Michael Callan), an evil criminal known as Metallo, was also out to destroy Superboy.

Clark's alarm clock rings at 6:30 A.M. (Lana's awakes her at 6:00 A.M.). Clark lives in Apartment 307 and takes the number 7 bus to work. The Shift Military Institute has the only known supply of Kryptonite, the green metal remnants of Krypton, which can destroy Clark. In the episode "The Lair" (10/21/90), Clark mentions that he hopes one day to move to Metropolis and become a reporter. In advertisements for the series, Clark says "I have three passions—

truth, justice and the American way." Clark becomes Superboy by either twirling rapidly or running at supersonic speed. When Lex has a problem he can't solve, he kidnaps Lana. People who believe they have seen the abnormal, file form C-29 at the bureau.

When Clark stumbles into a series of parallel worlds, he meets his elder self (Ron Ely) and his future self as a young boy (Robert Allen Shippy) in the episode "The Road to Hell" (5/25/91). The episode of 11/8/91 ("Paranoia") reunited "Adventures of Superman" co-stars Jack Larson (as Lew Lamont) and Noel Neill (as Alexis)—both of whom work for the bureau as investigators. The building that houses the bureau was formerly a night club called the Trocadel.

Relatives: Stuart Whitman (Clark's Earth father, *Jonathan Kent*), Salome Jens (Clark's Earth mother, *Martha Kent*), Elizabeth Peach (Clark's aunt, *Cassandra*).

Flashbacks: Edan Gross (*Clark as a young boy*), George Lazenby and Jacob Wilkin (Clark's Krypton father, *Jor-El*), Britt Ekland and Kathy Polin (Clark's Krypton mother, *Lara*), Jennifer Hawkins (Lex's sister, *Lena Luthor*), Kathy Gustafson-Hilton (*Lex's mother*), Edgar Allan Poe IV (*Lex's father*).

Theme: "Superboy," by Kevin Kiner.

6. *The Adventures of Superman*

Syndicated, 1953 to 1957

Cast: George Reeves (*Clark Kent/Superman*), Phyllis Coates and Noel Neill (*Lois Lane*), Jack Larson (*Jimmy Olsen*), John Hamilton (*Perry White*), Robert Shayne (*Bill Henderson*).

Facts: Jor-El (Robert Rockwell), a scientist on the distant planet Krypton, believes that the planet is being drawn closer to the sun and is on the brink of destruction. He is unable to convince members of the Scientific Council.

Believing that there is only a short time left before his planet begins to explode, Jor-El begins preparations to save his family, his wife, Lara (Aline Towne), and their infant son, Kal-El, from the impending doom. Shortly after he finishes a small, experimental rocket, the planet begins to explode. Jor-El and Lara decide to save their infant son and place him inside the rocket. Jor-El programs the rocket to head for Earth, a planet he knows to be inhabited. Krypton explodes and scatters billions of particles of Kryptonite, the only substance that can harm Kal-El, into the universe. The rocket, with its infant passenger, crash-lands near the Jones farm in Smallville, U.S.A., on April 10, 1926.

Eben and Sarah Kent (Tom Fadden and Dina Nolan), a childless farm couple, witness the landing. Eben risks his life and rescues Kal-El from the rocket. The baby, wrapped in red and blue blankets, is miraculously unharmed. The rocket, which explodes seconds later, destroys all evidence of its ever having been there.

Realizing that no one would ever believe their fantastic story, Eben and Sarah decide to raise the baby as their own and name him Clark. Each year brings to light evidence of Clark's amazing powers (for example, X-ray vision, incredible strength and the ability to fly). Twenty-five years later, following Eben's death from a heart attack, Sarah urges Clark to use his great abilities to help mankind. Before Sarah moves in with her cousin, Louise, she makes Clark a costume from the blankets that were originally wrapped around him (how she managed to cut and sew the indestructible material was not explained).

To keep his true identity secret, Clark maintains the alias of mild-mannered Clark Kent and moves to Metropolis, where he becomes a reporter for the *Daily Planet,* a crusading newspaper (it sells for five cents).

Clark lives in Apartment 5H of the Standish Arms Hotel (West 3-0963 is his phone number). Lois Lane, the reporter who is always in distress, lives in Apartment 6A of an unnamed building. She was born in the small town of Clifton-by-the-Sea and drives a car with the license plate ZN 18683. James ("Jimmy") Bartholomew Olsen, the young cub reporter-photographer, lives with his mother (address not given). Jimmy constantly annoys Perry White, the editor of the *Planet,* by calling him "Chief" ("Don't call me Chief!" is Perry's response). Perry (mobile car phone number MX31962) was a top-notch reporter and then the mayor of Metropolis before he became the paper's editor (he is also a member of the Amateur Magicians' Society). When Perry becomes angry, he yells, "Great Caesar's ghost!" William ("Bill") Henderson is an inspector with the Robbery Division of the Metropolis Police Department. The mischievous Professor J.J. Pepperwinkle (Phillips Tead) lives at 64 Hope Street (his phone number is Greenleaf 8975). The Professor believes that there are two kinds of Kryptonite: Kryptonite Negative, which takes away Superman's powers, and Kryptonite Positive, which gives him his powers.

Metropolis 6-0500 is the telephone number of the *Daily Planet.* The building seen in the opening sequence is actually Los Angeles City Hall. The diesel locomotive seen in the opening sequence is owned by the Southern Pacific Railroad. The series is based on the comic strip by Jerry Siegel and Joe Schuster.

Relatives: Sarah Padden (Jimmy's aunt, *Louisa Horne*), Mabel Albertson (Perry's sister, *Kate White*), Lane Bradford (Perry's nephew, *Chris White*). Stuart Randall played Clark as a boy in the pilot episode.

Theme: "The Adventures of Superman," by Leon Klatzkin.

Note: See also "The Adventures of Superboy." Prior to this 1988 series, two attempts were made to revise the original concept: "Superpup" and "Superboy."

"Superpup" is an unaired 1958 pilot film that portrayed characters in costumes as dogs. Billy Curtis played Bark Bent, reporter for the *Daily Beagle*; Ruth Delfino was reporter Pamela Poodle; Angelo Rossitto was editor Perry Bite; and Harry Monty was the villain, Professor Sheepdip.

"Superboy" is a 1961 unaired pilot that dealt with the exploits of Clark Kent as a teenager attending Smallville High School (he battled evil as Superboy). Johnny Rockwell played Clark Kent/Superboy; Bonnie Henning was his girlfriend, Lana Lang; and Monty Margetts was Clark's mother, Martha.

7. *The Adventures of Tugboat Annie*

Syndicated, 1957

Annie Brennan (Minerva Urecal) is a 50-years-young old salt who captains the *Narcissus,* a tugboat owned by the Severn Tugboat Company. Annie, who previously worked as the skipper of a garbage scow, is a sympathetic soul who tries to help people in trouble (her "adventures" are the comical situations she encounters). Annie mentioned that she got her late husband to propose to her by telling him that Francis X. Bushman was after her.

Fogerty's Beanery (where "Honesty Is the Best Policy") is the dive of a café where Annie and her crew eat. Shiftless (Eric Clavering) is her deckhand, and Pinto (Don Orlando) is the tug's cook. When Pinto temporarily lost his job, Annie helped him start Pinto's Hotcake Heaven, a diner that failed to find paying customers.

Horatio Bullwinkle (Walter Sande) is a rival tugboat captain who calls Annie "The Old Petticoat." Murdock Severn (Stan Francis) is the tugboat company owner.

The series is based on the stories by Norman Reilly Raine.

8. *Airwolf*

CBS, 1/22/84 to 7/23/86

Cast: Jan-Michael Vincent (*Stringfellow Hawke*), Ernest Borgnine (*Dominic Santini*), Jean Bruce Scott (*Caitlin O'Shaughnessy*), Alex Cord (*Michael Archangel*).

Facts: Airwolf is an awesome attack helicopter that was built by Dr. Moffet (David Hemmings) for the Firm, an agency of the U.S. government. When Moffet steals Airwolf and tries to sell it to a foreign power, Michael Archangel, the head of the Firm, recruits a former employee named Stringfellow Hawke to retrieve it. In return Michael promises Stringfellow that the government will look for his brother, Saint John (pronounced Sin-Jin), who is listed as missing in Vietnam. Hawke accomplishes his mission but decides to hold on to Airwolf to force the government to keep its promise. In the meantime, Hawke uses Airwolf to help Michael when the need arises.

Stringfellow ("String") Hawke, a one-time pilot for the Firm, is 34 years old. He served with the 328 AHC unit in Vietnam. String was orphaned at the age of 12 and raised by his brother, Saint John, and his friend, Dominic Santini (for whom he now works). Hawke has a dog named Tet and lives in a remote, wooded area of California. String has hidden Airwolf deep in "The Valley of the Gods" (a secret mountain location in the California desert).

Dominic ("Dom") Santini runs the Santini Air Charter Service from the Van Nuys Airport (also given as the Municipal Airport) in California. Dom's copters are red, white and blue, and he is equipped for motion picture stuntwork. Dom, who was born on the island of San Remo, calls Airwolf "The Lady." His Jeep's license plate is 1-BOX-070; IDT 0406 is his station wagon's license plate; and 2G 15626 is the license plate of the Santini Air gas truck.

Caitlin O'Shaughnessy is a pilot for Santini Air. She was originally a deputy with the Texas Highway Patrol, Aerial Division (helicopter pilot). She was a member of the Kappa Lambda Chi sorority in college.

Michael Coldsmith Briggs III, code name Michael Archangel, is the head of the Firm. Angel One is Michael's code to Airwolf. FIRM-1 is his limo license plate, and he was assisted by several beautiful women throughout the series' run: Belinda Bauer (as Gabrielle in the pilot), Deborah Pratt (Gabrielle, in the series), Sandra Kronemeyer (Lydia), Kandace Kuehl (Amanda) and Leigh Walsh (Rhonda).

Airwolf, which has the government file A56-7W, is a black with white underbellied Bell 222 helicopter with a cruising speed of 300 knots and a maximum speed of 662-plus miles with the main rudder disengaged. In some episodes the top speed is mentioned as Mach 2, and it can travel up to 82,000 feet. Ranger 276 is Airwolf's Coast Guard code. In addition to a sophisticated computer control system, Airwolf has radar scanners (to identify objects), turbos for fast flight, and movie and infrared cameras. When an unauthorized person attempts to touch Airwolf, he or she receives an electrical shock.

Airwolf armaments include four 30mm chain guns (in the wings) and two 40mm wing cannons. It also has a series of missiles. Air-to-air missiles include Redeye (short range), Sidewinder and Sparrow (radar homing) and Phoenix (programable, radar homing). Air-to-surface missiles include Hellfire (short range), Copperhead (long range), Maverick (infrared radio imaging) and Shrike (electromagnetic homing). Airwolf also has two warheads: the Bullpup (radio command) and Harpoon (radio homing, anti-sky).

Relatives: Christopher Connelly (Hawke's brother, *Saint John*), Richard Harrah III (Hawke's nephew, *Le Van Hawke*), Barbara Howard (Dom's niece, *Holly Matthews*), Diane McBain (Dom's ex-wife, *Lila Morgan*). Not seen was Dom's daughter, Sally Ann, who died from a drug overdose.

Theme: "Airwolf," by Sylvester Levay.

Theme Narration: Lance LeGault (network version only; cut from syndicated version).

Note: The USA cable network aired a revised version of the series called "Airwolf" (1/23/87 to 7/15/88). The new version begins by introducing Dom's niece, Jo Ann ("Jo") Santini (Michele Scarabelli), as a pilot for Santini Air. Michael Archangel has been transferred to the Far East and Jason Locke (Anthony Sherwood) now heads the Company (not the Firm as in the earlier series).

Stringfellow Hawke acquires positive proof that Saint John is alive. Before he can organize a rescue mission, he is seriously injured in a helicopter explosion that kills Dom. As Jo readies Airwolf for a rescue attempt, she is surprised by two strangers in the copter's hideout—Jason Locke and U.S. Air Force pilot Mike Rivers (Geraint Wyn Davies), who tracked Airwolf through high-resolution photography.

When Jason is told about Saint John, he allows Jo to proceed with the rescue. When Saint John is rescued, Jason decides to keep Airwolf a secret and forms a new Airwolf team: himself, Jo, Saint John (Barry Van Dyke) and Mike (Jason fears the copter may fall into enemy hands if it is returned to the government). Episodes relate the team's dangerous missions for Jason and the Company.

Company officials call Jo "Little Lady"; the team's code for Airwolf's hideout is Wolf (also called "The Company Store"); their code for Santini Air is Cubs (for example, "Wolf to Cubs"); during assignments, Saint John often uses "Plan B" (make it up as you go along).

Donnelly Rhodes appeared as Jo's father, Tony Santini; Saint John mentioned that his late father's name was Alan B. Hawke.

Sylvester Levay composed the "Airwolf" theme (adapted by Dan Milner for the series).

The Alaskans see *Klondike*

9. *ALF*

NBC, 9/22/86 to 6/18/90

Cast: Max Wright *(Willie Tanner)*, Anne Schedeen *(Kate Tanner)*, Andrea Elson *(Lynn Tanner)*, Benji Gregory *(Brian Tanner)*, Paul Fusco *(ALF's voice)*.

Facts: William ("Willie") Tanner, his wife, Kate, and their children, Lynn, Brian and infant son Eric (J.R. and Charles Nickerson), live at 167 Hemdale Street in Los Angeles (the locale is also given as San Francisco). Their phone number is given as 555-8531, 555-7787 and 555-4044. Willie works for the Los Angeles Department of Social Services and enjoys communicating with people around the world via his shortwave radio (call letters KC276XAA). One night, while he is operating the radio, the frequencies interfere with those of an alien's spacecraft. The alien pilot loses control of his craft and crashes into the Tanners' garage roof. Willie rescues the Alien Life Form (ALF) and finds he has a new family member when ALF tells him that the parts he needs to repair his ship are unknown on Earth. Stories follow ALF's attempts to adjust to life on Earth.

ALF is short and furry (burnt sienna color) with off-black eyes, a large snout, four teeth and an enormous appetite (his favorite food is "everything with everything on it"; but he prefers Siamese cats).

ALF was born on the planet Melmac 229 years ago. He first mentions he was born on the twenty-eighth of Nathanganger, then to parents Bob, Biff and Flo on August 12 and October 2, 1757. ALF's body temperature is 425 degrees; he has eight stomachs and a craving for cats (his favorite breakfast on Melmac was Cats Benedict; on Earth he enjoys spaghetti, Jell-O and eggs for breakfast).

ALF holds degrees in software and pedestrian crossing; he

attended Melmac High School for 122 years and Melmac State College for two years. He was known as Mr. Science and held the following jobs: the bearded lady in the circus, a TV show host, a car salesman and an orbit guard. He became a male model at the age of 150 and later co-captained the Codsters, a bouillabaisseball team, for three years (played like Earth baseball but with fish parts as the ball; fish gills are sold at concession stands). Their "baisseball" cards feature such players as Mickey Mackerel and come in packages with tabby and Persian-flavored gum. ALF believes Earth TV cartoons reflect real life. "Gilligan's Island" and the mythical "Polka Time" are his favorite TV shows. *Shana, Mistress of the Universe* is his favorite comic book. He orders pizza via the house account at the Pizza Barge.

When ALF first moved in with the Tanners, he lived in the laundry basket next to the washing machine; he later resides in the attic (he hides under the kitchen table when the doorbell rings).

Dieting causes a strange reaction: when ALF goes without food, it causes an enzyme imbalance and he becomes Wolf, a primitive Melmacian hunting machine. Melmacians gain weight from the inside and have a tendency to explode if they are not careful.

The motto of the planet Melmac, since destroyed by an explosion, is "Are you going to finish that sandwich?" It had a purple moon, and its good luck charms were a mouse and a Tupperware lid. On Melmac, the monetary system was based on foam, and the word *stupid* translated as slang for a rich person. The motto of the Orbit Guards (of which ALF was a member) was "To Guard the Orbits—Whether They Want It or Not." When ALF talks on the phone he uses the name "Alf Tanner"; when he became interested in ventriloquism, he ordered a dummy (for $29.95) that he named Paul.

Willie has an '82 Ford and considers ALF "my own personal hell" (ALF is very mischievous and forever getting Willie into trouble). Willie, a social science major, and Kate, an art history major, met at Amherst College in Massachusetts. They married on July 11, 1967, and honeymooned in Niagara Falls at the Duke of Mist Hotel. Lynn attends South Bay High School. She wanted to attend Amherst College, but was unable (because of the extra expenses required to care for ALF); she chose to attend State University. When Lynn believed she was not as pretty as the other girls in her high school class, ALF entered her in the Miss Southland Beauty Pageant to boost her confidence (he listed her talent as clog dancing). Though pretty, Lynn lost. (On Melmac, the judges wear swimsuits in beauty pageants and the contestants rate the judges.) Brian attends Franklin Elementary School. Lynn wears a locket that has a picture in it of Mary Tyler Moore and Elvis Presley from the film *A Change of Habit*.

Lucky the cat was the original family pet (whom ALF tried to hypnotize into believing he was a bagel so ALF could eat him). When Lucky passed away, the Tanners got another cat, whom they named Lucky II (ALF called him Flipper).

Relatives: Anne Meara (Kate's mother, *Dorothy Halligan*), JM J. Bullock (Willie's brother, *Neal Tanner*), Elisha Cook, Jr. (Willie's uncle, *Albert*), Allyce Beasley (Neal's ex-wife, *Barbara*), Lisa Buckley (ALF's girlfriend, *Rhonda*), Bob Fappiano (ALF's friend, *Skip*).

Flash Forwards: Andrea Elson *(adult Lynn)*, Edward Edwards *(adult Brian)*, Mark Blankfield *(adult Eric)*.

Theme: "ALF," by Alf Clausen and Tim Kramer.

10. *Alice*

CBS, 9/29/76 to 3/19/85

Mel's Diner is a roadside eatery located at 1030 Bush Highway in Phoenix, Arizona. Melvin ("Mel") Emory Sharples (Vic Tayback) is the owner, an always yelling cheapskate who is the diner's only cook (and famous for his special dish, Mel's Chili). He lives at 634 Plainview Drive.

Alice Spevack Hyatt (Linda Lavin), Vera Louise Gorman (Beth Howland), Florence Jean ("Flo") Castleberry (Polly Holliday), Belle DuPree (Diane Ladd) and Jolene Hunnicutt (Celia Weston) are the waitresses Mel employs during the series run. The girls wear pink uniforms and earn $2.90 an hour.

Alice is a widow (Donald Hyatt was her late husband) and the mother of a young boy named Tommy (Philip McKeon). She moved to Arizona to begin a new life and hopes eventually to become a singer. She first lived at the Desert Sun Apartments, then at the Phoenix Arms (Apartment 108).

Vera, who lives at the Sun Rise Apartments, has a pet cat (Mel) and two hamsters (Harold and Mitzi). She is a bit klutzy and always getting on Mel's nerves. She married police officer Elliott Novack (Charles Levin) and has a very famous cousin—Art Carney.

The wisecracking Flo, who is famous for her comeback line "Kiss my grits," was the first waitress to leave. Flo lived in a mobile home (parked in the Desert Trailer Court) and left to open Flo's Golden Rose, a bar in her hometown of Cowtown, Texas (in the spinoff series "Flo"; CBS 3/24/80 to 7/21/81).

Belle DuPree, who lived at 1112 Ashton Drive, replaced Flo. She was a bit older than the others and was soon replaced by the young and bubbly Jolene Hunnicutt, a small town girl from a large family. Jolene had a room at the Pine Valley Apartments and a dream of opening her own beauty shop.

The last episode ("Th-Th-Th-Th-That's All, Folks") found Mel selling the diner (which he had owned for 27 years) to the Ferguson brothers (who plan to tear it down). Alice finally got a break and moved to Nashville to sing with Travis Marsh; Vera discovered she was pregnant at the same time Elliott got a promotion; and Jolene opened her own beauty shop with money inherited from her grandmother.

In the original pilot episode (CBS, 8/31/76), Alfred Lutter played the role of Tommy Hyatt. Although his character was not in the pilot, Marvin Kaplan appears almost regularly as Henry, the always complaining, henpecked diner customer. (He works for the phone company, and his wife is named Chloe.)

Relatives: Doris Roberts (Alice's mother, *Mona Spevack*), Eileen Heckart (Alice's mother-in-law, *Rose Hyatt*), Martha Raye (Mel's mother, *Carrie Sharples*), David Rounds (Mel's cousin, *Wendel*), Merie Earle (Mel's *Grandma Sharples*), Forrest Tucker (Flo's father, *Edsel Jarvis Castleberry*), Mildred Natwick (Vera's aunt, *Agatha*), Art Carney (Vera's cousin, *Art Carney*), Gregory Walcott (Jolene's father, *Big Jake Hunnicutt*), Trevor Henley (Jolene's brother *Jesse*), Kent Parkins (Jolene's brother *Jasper*), Grant Wilson (Jolene's brother *Jeremy*), Robin Eurich (Jolene's brother *Jimmy*), Steve McGriff (Jolene's brother *Jake Jr.*), Gurich Koock (Jolene's brother *Jonas*), Natalie Masters (Jolene's *Granny Gumms*), Ruth Buzzi (Henry's wife, *Chloe*).

Theme: "There's a New Girl in Town," vocal by Linda Lavin.

11. *Alien Nation*

Fox, 9/18/89 to 9/17/90

The series is set in Los Angeles in 1995. Little Tencton is a special area where aliens from the planet Tencton now live. Five years earlier, a slave ship from another galaxy landed in a remote section of the Mojave Desert. Aboard the craft were 250,000 workers bred to survive in any environment. When it is learned that the craft is inoperable and impossible to fix (needed materials do not exist on Earth), the government assimilates them into Los Angeles society. Stories follow the experiences of one such family — the Franciscos, who live in house number 1377: George (Eric Pierpont), his wife, Susan (Michele Scarabelli), and their children, Emily (Lauren Woodland), Buck (Sean Six) and infant Vessna.

George, whose alien name is Neemo, is a detective with the Central Homicide Division of the L.A.P.D. He works with Earth detective Matthew Sikes (Gary Graham). George won the Kareem Abdul-Jabbar Standing Tall Citizenship Award and earns $100 a week more than Sikes (George is the first alien to become a detective, second grade). Their car code is 1-William-52.

Matthew lives in Apartment 203 of an unnamed building. He is president of the Tenants' Association and is hooked on instant-win lottery tickets (he buys three scratch-off tickets each day. He has spent $750 since George has known him and only won $25). His car license plate reads 21MU684.

Cathy Frankel (Terri Treas) is Matthew's neighbor, a beautiful alien who lives in Apartment 204. Her alien name is Gelana, and she works as a biochemist at the Newcomers' Behavioral Center.

The aliens are referred to both as the Newcomers and by the slang term *Slags*. They have two hearts and require ultraviolet light for energy. The aliens fear salt water (which burns) and cannot eat Earth foods made from meat or animal fat. They speak the Tenctonese language and cele-

brate a special day called the Day of Descent (the day they landed on Earth). The backs of an alien's knees are especially sensitive; a male alien finds the female's ear valley (that forms the shape of the letter *S*) to be most sexy. A special mating alien called a Binon is required when an alien husband and wife decide to have a baby (it is the male who becomes pregnant). When an alien is born, it requires "the Touch" to be comforted (touching the temples allows feelings of love to flow through the body). Newcomer women are sexually aroused by the piercing tone (F sharp above high C) of an earth TV station's Emergency Broadcast System test. The Palace Theater shows American films dubbed in Tenctonese; in the opening sequence, marquees show *Back to the Future 5* and *Rambo 6*. The show is based on the 1988 feature film of the same title.

Joe Harnell composed the "Alien Nation" theme.

12. *All in the Family*

CBS, 1/21/71 to 9/16/79

Cast: Carroll O'Connor (*Archie Bunker*), Jean Stapleton (*Edith Bunker*), Sally Struthers (*Gloria Stivic*), Rob Reiner (*Mike Stivic*), Danielle Brisebois (*Stephanie Mills*), Allan Melvin (*Barney Hefner*), Liz Torres (*Teresa Betancourt*).

Facts: The house at 704 Houser Street in Queens, New York, is "the only house on the block with a paid-up mortgage," says its owner, Archibald ("Archie") Bunker, a bigoted and uncouth conservative who has lived there for 25 years. Also living with him are his dim-witted wife, Edith; their liberated daughter, Gloria; and Gloria's liberal husband, Mike (called "Meathead" by Archie). Archie believes that credit is "the American way" ("That way you can buy anything you can't afford"). He reads the *Daily News* and bowls on Tuesday nights. "Whoop-dee-doo" is his catchphrase.

Archie first met Edith at the Puritan Maid Ice Cream Parlor. During World War II ("The Big One," as Archie calls it), Archie was first stationed at Fort Riley in Kansas. He later served 22 months in Italy with the Air Corps; he was second-in-charge of the motor pool. For his efforts, he received the Purple Heart, the good-conduct medal and "a butt full of shrapnel—which is why I ain't danced with my wife for 30 years." In 1944, when Gloria was born at Bayside Hospital, the bill for her delivery was $131.50. With the advent of TV in 1948, Archie and Edith, who couldn't afford a set, would watch "The Milton Berle Show" in the window of Tupperman's Department Store. Two years later they got their first set—a console with a six inch screen.

Archie works as a dock foreman for the Prendergast Tool and Die Company. He drives a cab on the side to make extra money. When Archie is laid off, he buys his favorite hangout (Kelsey's Bar) and reopens it as Archie Bunker's Place (a bar-restaurant in Astoria, Queens).

Archie's blood pressure varies between 168/95 and 178/90. He drinks Schlitz beer and is a member of the Royal Brotherhood of the Kings of Queens Lodge (phone number 555-4378). As a kid, Archie was called "Shoebootie"

Archie Bunker's Place. Danielle Brisebois, Denise Miller and Carroll O'Connor.

(he once wore one shoe and one bootie when his Depression-poor family couldn't afford to buy him a new pair of shoes).

Although Archie calls Edith "Dingbat" and tells her to "stifle it" for talking too much, he loves her very much and strayed only once—nearly having an affair with a woman named Denise (Janis Paige). Archie considers the day Sammy Davis, Jr., came to his house to be the greatest thing that ever happened to him (he let Sammy sit in his favorite easy chair by the TV—a privilege few can claim).

Edith, whose maiden name is Baines, is a simple housewife who takes life as it comes and sees only the good in people. She attended Millard Fillmore High School (class of '43); in 1946 she held a job with the Hercules Plumbing Company. Buck Evans was her boyfriend in high school, and her most "despicable act" occurred when she was six years old—she stole a five-cent O'Henry bar from the candy counter at F.W. Woolworth (she later went back to make restitution—but had to pay a dime as the price had gone up).

Edith's favorite TV soap opera is "As the World Turns." She buys her meat at Klemer's Butcher Shop and earns $2.65 an hour as a Sunshine Lady at the Sunshine Home for the Elderly (she received the Citizen of the Week Award for saving the life of an elderly man). At the First Friendly Bank of Queens, Archie and Edith have joint checking and savings accounts. In addition, Edith has three accounts of her own (that total $78): the Magic Potato Cutter account, a Christmas Club account and her grandson Joey's education account. When Edith went through menopause, the doctor prescribed pills for Archie, the nervous type, to take three times a day.

Gloria, a perfume salesgirl at Kresler's Department Store, earns $80 a week. Her husband, Mike, is first a college student and later a college teacher (school not named). After the birth of their son, Joey (Corey and Jason Drager), Mike moves his family to California when a better paying job comes his way. (Before Joey's birth, Mike and Gloria planned to name him Stanislaus—but Archie objected and put up a fuss: "Kids are mean. They're gonna call him Louse.") When Mike and Gloria moved to California, the spinoff series, "Gloria" (CBS, 9/26/82 to 9/21/83) evolved.

In the "Gloria Comes Home" episode of "Archie Bunker's Place" (2/28/82), Gloria returns to Queens with Joey (Christian Jacobs) when Mike deserts them and moves to a commune in Humboldt, California. Shortly after, Gloria finds a job in Fox Ridge (Dutchess County, New York) as the assistant to Dr. Willard Adams (Burgess Meredith), an aging veterinarian. Joey, played by Christopher Johnston in the pilot, has a dog named Archie and a turtle named Murphy.

Stephanie Mills, Archie's ward, is the daughter of Edith's "no-good cousin," Floyd Mills (with whom she went to live after her mother was killed in a car accident; Floyd is a drunk and unable to care for her). She became a member of the family when Edith took pity on her and gave her the opportunity to grow up in a decent environment. She is Jewish and a member of the Temple Beth Shalom (Edith is Episcopalian; Archie mentions that he is a Christian).

Teresa Betancourt, the nurse who comes to live with the Bunkers (in Gloria's old room), calls Archie "Mr. Bunkers" (with her Spanish accent it comes out "Mr. Bonkers") and pays $100 a month rent.

Barney Hefner is Archie's friend and neighbor. He works as a bridge inspector for the city of New York and has a dog named Rusty; he is also one of Archie's best customers at the bar.

When Edith passes away in 1979, the spinoff series "Archie Bunker's Place" (9/23/79 to 9/21/83) begins. Archie is now a widower and guardian to two beautiful girls: his niece, Barbara Lee ("Billie") Bunker (Denise Miller), and his ward, Stephanie Mills (Danielle Brisebois). Archie still resides at 704 Houser Street and is now a partner with Murray Klein (Martin Balsam) in the Archie Bunker's Place bar-restaurant. (In 1981 Archie buys out Murray's share of the bar when he leaves to marry Marcie Phillips [Cynthia Harris]).

Billie, who works as a waitress at the bar, is the daughter of Archie's brother, Fred (Richard McKenzie). She came to live with Archie when Fred was no longer able to care for her. Stephanie, whose birthday is in May, attends Ditmars Junior High School (her mother, Marilyn, was killed in a car accident).

Harry Snowden (Jason Wingreen) is Archie's bartender; Veronica Rooney (Anne Meara) is the bar's cook; and Edgar Van Ranseleer (Bill Quinn) is the blind bar regular.

"The Jeffersons" (see entry) and "Maude" were also spinoffs. In "Maude" (9/12/72 to 8/29/78), Bea Arthur played Edith's liberal cousin, Maude Findlay, an outspoken woman who lives with her husband, Walter (Bill Macy), and divorced daughter, Carol Traynor (Adrienne Barbeau) at 30 Crenshaw Street (later 271 Elm Street) in Tuckahoe, New York. Walter owns Findlay's Friendly Appliance Store; Carol was originally played by Marcia Rodd on "All in the Family." Conrad Bain and Rue McClanahan are their neighbors, Dr. Arthur Harmon and his wife, Vivian.

Relatives: Elizabeth Wilson and Rae Allen (Edith's cousin, *Amelia*), Nedra Volz (Edith's aunt, *Iola*), Tim O'Connor (Edith's cousin, *Roy*), Ruth Manning (Edith's cousin, *Clara*), Peggy Rea (Edith's cousin, *Bertha*), Marty Brill and Ben Slack (Stephanie's father, *Floyd Mills*), Michael Conrad (Mike's father, *Casimir Stivic*), Estelle Parsons (Barney's wife, *Blanche Hefner*).

Themes: "Those Were the Days" (opening theme; vocal by Carroll O'Connor and Jean Stapleton; written by Lee Adams and Charles Strouse) and "Remembering You" (closing theme by Carroll O'Connor and Roger Kellaway).

Note: Two unaired pilots were made prior to the series. "Those Were the Days" was produced in 1968 with Kelly Jean Peters as Gloria and Tim McIntire as Mike. A second pilot was taped in 1969 with Candace Azzara as Gloria and Chip Oliver as Mike. (Carroll O'Connor was Archie and Jean Stapleton played Edith in both of these pilots, which were based on the British series "Till Death Do Us Part.") Archie was originally conceived as an elevator operator and had the name Archie Justice ("And Justice for All" was the proposed series title). After the second pilot was shot, Sally Struthers beat out Penny Marshall for the role of Gloria.

Aloha Paradise. Debbie Reynolds and guest Van Johnson.

Archie Bunker received one vote for the vice presidency at the 1972 Democratic Convention; Archie's living room chair and Edith's simple easy chair are on display at the Smithsonian Museum.

13. *Aloha Paradise*

ABC, 2/18/81 to 4/29/81

The Paradise Village is a secluded resort for lovers on the Kona Coast in Hawaii. Sydney Chase (Debbie Reynolds) is the resort's charming manager; Curtis Shaw (Bill Daily) is the harried assistant manager; Fran Linhart (Patricia Klous) is the stunning social director; Everett DeGroot (Charles Fleischer) is the rather strange groundskeeper who lives in a world all his own; and Richard Bean (Stephen Shortridge) is the resort's handsome lifeguard. The eight episode anthology series, which focused on the lives of the people who vacationed at the resort, was produced by Aaron Spelling and was an obvious (but failed) attempt to transpose the magic of "The Love Boat" (see entry) from sea to land. Stephen Lawrence sang the theme, "Aloha Paradise."

Prior to "Aloha Paradise," NBC tried the idea in a failed pilot called "Pleasure Cove" (1/3/79), in which Henry Sinclair (James Murtaugh) managed Pleasure Cove, a posh resort that is part of the Xavier Hotel chain. Julie (Melody Anderson) was the reservations clerk; Kim Parker (Constance Forslund) assisted Henry; and Osaki (Ernest Harada) was the desk clerk.

A year later, NBC aired another failed pilot, "Magic on Love Island" (2/15/80). Janis Paige played Madge (no other name given), a beautiful but mysterious woman who runs a tropical resort called Love Island. While it is not made perfectly clear, Madge is presumed to be a good witch who uses her magical charm to help the attractive singles who have come to Love Island to find one another. She is assisted by her pretty niece, Cheryl (Dominique Dunne), and by Cheryl's brother, Jimmy (Christopher Knight). Bernard Ighner sang the theme, "Love Island, Our Island of Love."

Still with a hope of presenting the private lives of vacationers, ABC aired another failed pilot called "For Lovers Only" on 10/15/82 (had it sold, the series would have been called "Honeymoon Hotel"). In it, Andy Griffith played Vernon Bliss, the owner of the Bliss Cove Haven, a resort for newlywed couples in Pennsylvania's Pocono Mountains. Katherine Helmond played his wife, Bea; Anna Garduno was Cindy, the resort photographer; and Christopher Wells was Flip Leonard, the social director. Thea and Company performed the theme, "On Our Honeymoon."

14. *The Amazing Spider-Man*

CBS, 4/5/78 to 7/6/79

Peter Parker (Nicholas Hammond), a graduate student in physics at Empire State University in New York City, is also a freelance photographer for the *Daily Bugle,* a local newspaper founded in 1890 and housed in the Bugle Building. One day, during an experiment on radioactivity, Peter is bitten by a spider that was exposed to the deadly effects of the experiment. Peter later absorbs the proportionate powers and abilities of a living spider. In response to his newfound powers, Peter creates a special red and blue costume to conceal his true identity while he battles crime as the mysterious Spider-Man.

Peter lives at 1231 Maple Drive with his aunt, May Parker (Irene Tedrow); their phone number is 555-1834. J. Jonah Jameson (Robert F. Simon) is the editor of the *Bugle* (his Rolls Royce license plate reads 49NEJJ). Julie Masters (Ellen Bry) is a reporter for the rival paper, the *Register* (her car license plate reads 376 KNP). Rita Conway (Chip Fields) is Jonah's administrative assistant; and police captain Barbera (Michael Pataki) is headquartered at One Police Plaza in Manhattan. In stunt sequences, Fred Waugh plays Spider-Man.

In the pilot episode, David White was J. Jonah Jameson and Jeff Donnell played Aunt May. The series is based on the comic strip by Stan Lee. Dana Kaproff and Stu Phillips composed the theme.

In 1969 ABC presented the animated adventures of "Spider-Man" (8/30/69 to 9/9/72) in the first TV adaptation of the Marvel comic book character. In this version, Peter Parker (voice of Peter Soles) is a student at Central High School and a reporter for the *Bugle.*

Jessica Drew (voice of Joan Van Ark) became the next victim of a spider in the animated series "Spider-Woman" (ABC, 9/22/79 to 3/1/80). Jessica, the daughter of a famous scientist, is bitten by a poisonous spider. To save his daughter's life, Dr. Drew injects her with an experimental spider serum. The serum saves Jessica's life and endows her with amazing spider-like powers. Jessica, who publishes *Justice* magazine, creates a red and blue costume to conceal her true identity when she battles crime as Spider-Woman.

15. *Amen*

NBC, 9/27/86 to 7/27/91

Cast: Sherman Hemsley *(Ernest Frye),* Clifton Davis *(Reuben Gregory),* Anna Maria Horsford *(Thelma Frye).*

Facts: When the pastor of the First Community Church of Philadelphia quits (Deacon Ernest J. Frye commented, "The collection is down 33 percent, attendance is down 12 percent and your weight is up 80 percent."), the directors hire the Reverend Reuben Gregory, a young minister with progressive ideas, to replace him. Ernest's father founded the church; he is set in his ways as to how the church should be run. Reuben feels the church is behind the times and seeks ways to improve it. Hence the conflict and the efforts of each man to do what he thinks is best for the church and its parishioners.

Besides his duties as the deacon, Ernest is also an attorney and later a judge. He has a law office (Room 203) on 56th Street, and his shingle reads ATTORNEY-AT-LAW, ERNEST FRYE — WHERE WINNING IS EVERYTHING. Ernest has A-positive blood, reads *Popular Gospel* magazine and drives a sedan with the license plate KNC 481. He buys one lottery ticket each week, and when he ran for state senator, he used the slogan "Vote for Frye and Get a Piece of the Pie." He lost against a jailed incumbent 19,372 to 43. In the opening sequence, two girls are seen jumping rope. Ernest joins in and jumps 11 times. Ernest's parking space has a sign that reads DON'T EVEN THINK ABOUT PARKING HERE. His late wife was named Laraine. During the Korean War, Laraine Tillman was a nurse at County General Hospital; Ernest was studying to become a lawyer and was working for Al's Delivery Service. One day he delivered flowers to a patient, saw Laraine and it was love at first sight. They married, had a child they named Thelma and lived happily for five years, and then Laraine passed away. Ernest is deathly afraid of snakes and his favorite pizza is meatball-topped pizza.

Reuben has a B.A. from Morehouse College, a master's degree in religious education from Yale Divinity School, and a doctorate in Christian studies from Union Theological Seminary. He started preaching in Cleveland, where he did "Sunrise Semester" on television. He now holds a weekly "Pastor's Pow Wow" to discuss church matters with his parishioners. He lives in Apartment 931 (address not given) and married Ernest's daughter, Thelma, after a rocky courtship (they married in February 1990 and had a baby boy in May 1991). To experience Thelma's pregnancy, Reuben wore a 35-pound "Daddy Tummy." In 1991 Reuben taught theology at Baxter Women's College. Charlotte (Telma Hopkins) and Roger (William Allen Young) Holloway were the first couple Reuben married in Cleveland ten years ago.

Thelma attended West Holmes High School, where she was called "The Undateable" (in the pilot, Ernest said she was jilted 20 times in ten years; in the third episode he says 16 times in ten years). Thelma also won the 100 yard dash for girls with flat feet when she joined the high school track team. After marrying Reuben, Thelma studied real estate and acquired a job with the firm of Underwood-Baines. Her favorite subjects in school were science, English and home economics. Even though she can't cook, Thelma did a television commercial for Bake Rite Flour and was given her own television show, "Thelma's Kitchen" (which folded before the first episode finished airing — Thelma and her assistants, Ernest and Reuben, managed to destroy the set while preparing a meal). Thelma calls Reuben "Sweet Potato." Before the birth of their son, Thelma attempted to adopt a child named Jeanette (Gloria Briscoe) through the Women's Christian Alliance (the girl stayed with Thelma for three weeks until her aunt and uncle came for her).

Other Regulars: Jester Hairston (*Rolly Forbes,* the older church board member who insults Ernest with one-liners at every opportunity; he is Thelma's godfather and married Thelma's aunt, Leola); Roz Ryan (*Amelia Hetebrink*) and Barbara Montgomery (*Casietta Hetebrink*) are two spinster sisters who are also members of the church board (and choir; their phone number was given as 555-1765). The church also has a volunteer teen hot line (295-TEEN).

Relatives: Jane White (Reuben's mother, *Josephine Gregory*), Vivian Bonnell (Reuben's aunt, *Martha*), Moses Gunn (Ernest's estranged father-in-law, *Ben Tillman*; he deserted Laraine when she married Ernest), Rosetta Le Noir (Thelma's aunt, *Leola*).

Flashbacks: Anna Maria Horsford (Thelma's mother, *Laraine Tillman*), Alexandria Simmons (*Thelma age five*).

Theme: "Shine on Me," vocal by Vanessa Bell Armstrong.

16. *American Dreamer*

NBC, 9/20/90 to 12/22/90
NBC, 5/25/91 to 6/22/91

Cast: Robert Urich (*Tom Nash*), Chay Lentin (*Rachel Nash*), Johnny Galecki (*Danny Nash*), Carol Kane (*Lillian Abernathy*), Jeffrey Tambor (*Joe Barnes*), Margaret Welsh (*Holly Baker*).

Facts: In 1972, after graduating from college (NYU), Tom Nash becomes a stringer for an unnamed, low-rated TV news program. At a later date, he becomes a reporter and falls in love with and marries Elizabeth, his field cameraperson. Although they both continue to work, they manage to have two children (Rachel and Danny). Fourteen years later, when they are both working for UPI, Elizabeth is killed while covering the war in Lebanon. Tom quits his job and moves to a small Wisconsin town to raise his children.

There, Tom acquires a job as a columnist for the *Chicago American* (a.k.a. the *Chicago Metro*), a Chicago-based newspaper. Joe Barnes, the editor, visits Tom on a weekly basis to pick up his columns and complain about "the fresh air and general decency of the people," which appalls him.

Tom writes about "things he worries about, things that touch his life and things he wonders about." When Tom was a reporter (for 12 years), he had two embarrassing moments: spilling red wine on Margaret Thatcher's dress while interviewing her, and reporting live from the White

House with his fly open. Tom attended Madison High School in St. Louis (where he was born). His girlfriend at the time was Jessica Rhodes (Lisa Barnes), whom he stood up on prom night. Tom wears a Green Bay Packers sweatshirt and is a Pisces. As a kid, Tom had a dog named Pete.

Rachel Nash, Tom's 15-year-old daughter, attends Mission West High School. She is one of the prettiest girls in her school, "always having boy trouble" and constantly in a dither about the attention she keeps getting but apparently can't handle. Though her father and brother are Catholic, Rachel became an Episcopalian. She plans to marry a blond rock star when she is 24. Rachel now works after school as a waitress at Baker's Corner, the local diner.

Danny Nash, Tom's 12-year-old son, attends Wisconsin Junior High School. He is a member of the Leopards, the baseball team.

Lillian ("Lilly") Abernathy is Tom's flakey secretary. She attended Mission West High School and later spent 12 years in night school to obtain her B.A. in journalism. As a kid, she imagined she attended her dream school, Fairpoint Academy. Lillian is a Libra and has been distrustful of men since her divorce from Bill (she has trouble walking past the men's room). She once attended a bachelor party ("I jumped out of the cake") and knew her first marriage was over when Bill said "Lilly, it's over." Lillian played a shrub in her ninth grade school play of "A Midsummer Night's Dream" (the role got her three curtain calls and a wet shoe when a dog decided to relieve himself).

Holly Baker is the owner of the local hangout, a diner called Baker's Corner. Her favorite meal to cook and serve is brussels sprouts casserole. When she was a kid, Holly and her sister, Drew, performed as the singing group Holly and the Pip for the Girl Scout Jamboree.

Relatives: DeLane Matthews (Holly's sister, *Drew Baker*), Kiersten Warren (Joe's daughter, *Lisa Barnes*; she attends Blessed Sacrament Academy), John Glover (Lillian's ex-husband, *Bill Abernathy*), Eileen Brennan (Lillian's mother, *Beatrice Pfeiffer*), Brice Beckham (Lillian's son, *Nelson Abernathy*).

Relatives Not Seen: Lillian's aunt, Sylvia; Joe's ex-wife, Barbara.

Flashbacks: Heather Menzies (Tom's wife, *Elizabeth Nash*), Michael Alldredge (*Tom's father*).

Theme: "American Dreamer," by Peter Leinheiser.

17. *The American Girls*

CBS, 9/23/78 to 11/10/78

Rebecca Tomkins (Priscilla Barnes) and Amy Waddell (Debra Clinger) are roving reporters for "The American Report," a New York–based television newsmagazine series hosted by Jason Cook (William Prince) and produced by Francis X. Casey (David Spielberg). Rebecca is a sophisticated blonde who was formerly the anchor of the "10 O'Clock News Hour" at KSF-TV, Channel 6, in San Francisco; Amy, a cunning brunette, is a recent college graduate

The American Girls. Debra Clinger, David Spielberg and Priscilla Barnes.

and did her internship at WREF-TV, Channel 36, in Washington, D.C. The reporters drive around the country in a van (mobile phone number 456-2114; later 555-2114) and investigate stories given to them by Casey. Lisa Lyke played Amy as a young girl in a flashback sequence.

Jerrold Immel composed "The American Girls Theme."

18. *The Amos 'n' Andy Show*

CBS, 6/28/51 to 6/11/53

Cast: Alvin Childress (*Amos Jones*), Spencer Williams, Jr. (*Andrew H. Brown*), Tim Moore (*George Stevens*), Jane Adams (*Ruby Jones*), Ernestine Wade (*Sapphire Stevens*), Amanda Randolph (*Mama*).

Facts: Amos Jones, Andrew ("Andy") Halt Brown and George ("Kingfish") Stevens are three friends who live in New York City. Amos lives with his wife, Ruby, in an apartment at 134th Street and Lenox Avenue. Andy is single

and lives in a small apartment on 134th Street. George, a con artist, is married to the always nagging Sapphire and lives with her and her mother, "Mama," at 134 East 145th Street (there are no numbers on any of the apartment doors).

Amos and Andy lived previously in Marietta, Georgia. With a dream of beginning a new life "up north," the boys came to New York in 1932. It was the somewhat naive and easily manipulated Andy who first met George. While watching the construction of a skyscraper in Manhattan, Andy catches George attempting to pick his pocket. As George explains that "one of my solid gold cufflinks must of gotten caught on your jacket sleeve," he learns that Andy and his partner, Amos, have $340 to invest in a business. George just happens to have a cab and before he realizes he has been taken, Andy becomes its owner. Amos and Andy make the best of their investment and begin a service called the Fresh Air Taxi Cab Company of America, Inc. (Amos drives the cab; Andy oversees its operation).

George, Amos and Andy are members of the Mystic Knights of the Sea, a lodge that is located at 127th Street

The Amos 'n' Andy Show. Spencer Williams, Jr., Tim Moore (center) and Alvin Childress.

and Lenox Avenue. George is the "Kingfish" and Andy is its entertainment chairman.

George is a schemer and lives on cons. He tries to find work, "but there ain't no jobs around for a man like me." His favorite activity is sleeping (which he does whenever he can), and he is the owner of a lot that he bought for $1,000 in New Jersey (he acquired it in 1932 "figurin' New York would spread to New Jersey" and that he would become rich). Sapphire works as a secretary at the Superfine Brush Company and is treasurer of the neighborhood Women's Club of Lenox Avenue. She and George have been married for 20 years in 1951.

Amos is the most stable member of the group. He met Ruby Taylor after a Sunday mass and married her shortly after. Andy, on the other hand, considers himself a ladies' man and supposedly had many girlfriends. He is most famous for his romantic involvement with Madame Queen (Lillian Randolph), the woman who stole his heart, then sued him for breach of promise when she caught him with another woman.

Andy smokes two cent cigars and hopes one day to be able to afford the five cent ones. Andy's net worth, taking into account his life insurance policy, investments, Christmas Club, savings and checking accounts, amounts to nine dollars. George and Andy eat lunch at the Beanery, the diner next to the lodge hall; they have accounts at both the Lenox Savings Bank and the New Amsterdam Savings Bank.

Other characters include the inept lawyer Algonquin J. Calhoun (Johnny Lee) and Lightnin' (Nick O'Demus), the slow-moving cab company/lodge hall janitor (he calls George "Mr. Kingfish" and Andy "Mr. Andy"). George's interest in money began when he was a boy in Georgia. He attended a christening and noticed that his uncle, Clarence, gave $500 to the parents when a baby was born into the family. Watching other people acquire Uncle Clarence's money gave George the idea that he too could acquire other people's money by being clever.

Theme: "The Perfect Song," by Clarence Lucas and Joseph Breil.

19. *The Andy Griffith Show*

CBS, 10/3/60 to 9/16/68

Cast: Andy Griffith (*Andy Taylor*), Don Knotts (*Barney Fife*), Ronny Howard (*Opie Taylor*), Frances Bavier (*Bee Taylor*).

Facts: Mayberry is a sleepy little town in North Carolina. Sheriff Andrew Jackson ("Andy") Taylor and Deputy Bernard Milton ("Barney") Fife uphold the law (which consists mainly of helping children across the street, handing out parking tickets and replacing lids on garbage cans). Andy's office is a bit behind the times. There are no submachine guns or tear gas grenades, though the office does boast a wall rack with five to seven rifles and some emergency equipment—a rake and a shovel that Andy carries in the trunk of his squad car (license plate JL 327).

Andy does not carry a gun (he is called "The Sheriff Without a Gun" in the national sheriff's magazine). Barney is allowed to wear a gun, but can carry one bullet (which he cannot use unless there is a real emergency).

Andy and Barney, 1945 graduates of Mayfield Union High School (the school colors are blue and orange), are actually cousins. Andy is also the justice of the peace, and Barney has been a deputy for five of the 12 years Andy has been sheriff. Andy's address was given as both 322 Maple Road and 14 Maple Street; Barney lives at 411 Elm Street. Andy and Barney, whose birthstone is the ruby, eat at the Junction Café (Juanita Beasley is the talked about but unseen waitress).

Andy's favorite pastime is playing the guitar; Barney struggles to uphold the law as best he can but fears "Mayberry is going to turn into a sin town." Barney left in 1965 for a job in state traffic with the Raleigh Police Department. He was replaced by Deputy Warren Ferguson (Jack Burns). Raleigh and Mt. Pilot are Mayberry's neighboring towns.

Beatrice Taylor, affectionately called "Aunt Bee," cares for Andy (a widower) and his young son, Opie. Aunt Bee raised Andy and claims that "Andy is meaner than a bear that backed into a beehive when he doesn't eat supper." Aunt Bee is noted for her cooking and ability to maintain a garden. She is famous for her homemade pickles and pies (apple and butterscotch pecan being Andy and Opie's favorites). She received a trip to Mexico for winning the Tampico Tamale Contest and won assorted prizes for her cooking knowledge on the television game show "Win or Lose." Aunt Bee is a member of the garden club, the church choir and the Greater Mayberry Historical Society and Tourist Bureau. She and her friend Clara Edwards (Hope Summers) wrote the town's sentimental song "Mayberry, My Hometown." Aunt Bee's catchphrase is "Oh, fiddle-faddle." Rose (Mary Treen) was Andy's original housekeeper; she left to marry Wilbur (Frank Ferguson).

Opie has a dog named Gulliver, a lizard (Oscar) and a parakeet (Dinkie). He attends the Mayberry School and enjoys fishing with his father at Meyer's Lake (where they are seen in the opening sequence and where Andy has a small rowboat he calls *Gertrude*).

Eleanor ("Ellie") Walker (Elinor Donahue) was Andy's original girlfriend. Andy called her "Miss Ellie," and she was the pharmacist at the Walker Drug Store (which was owned by her uncle, Fred Walker). Andy later falls for and marries Helen Crump (Aneta Corsaut), the town's grade school teacher. Thelma Lou (Betty Lynn) is Barney's longtime girlfriend.

Gomer and Goober Pyle (Jim Nabors and George Lindsey) are cousins who work at a gas station called Wally's Filling Station. Goober is deputized yearly to guard the cannon in the park on Halloween "to prevent kids from putting orange peels, taters and rotten tomatoes in it." Gomer left the series in 1964 to join the Marines (see "Gomer Pyle, U.S.M.C." for information).

Floyd Lawson (Howard McNear) is the proprietor of Floyd's Barber Shop (he is deputized so he can carry the flag in the Veterans' Day parade). Emmett Clark (Paul Hartman) owns Emmett's Fix-It Shop. Otis Campbell (Hal Smith) is the town drunk and has jail privileges (he locks himself up when he gets intoxicated and lets himself out when he is sober again). Howard Sprague (Jack Dodson) is the county clerk, and Ernest T. Bass (Howard Morris) is the trouble making hillbilly.

Sam Jones (Ken Berry) is a widowed farmer who becomes a city councilman. Millie Swanson (Arlene Golonka) is his girlfriend, and Mike (Buddy Foster) is his son; these characters were spun off into the series "Mayberry, R.F.D." (CBS, 9/23/68 to 9/6/71).

The original pilot aired on "The Danny Thomas Show" on 2/15/60. In it, Andy was the sheriff, justice of the peace and newspaper editor in a small southern town called Mayberry. Ronny Howard was his son, Opie; Frances Bavier was a citizen named Henrietta Perkins; and Frank Cady was Will Hoople, the town drunk. The series is also known as "Andy of Mayberry."

In the television movie, *Return to Mayberry* (NBC, 4/13/86), Mayberry and its citizens have remained virtually unchanged. Andy, who has been married to Helen (since 1968) returns to run for sheriff—without knowing the race is against Barney Fife, the acting sheriff (who, after 25 years, is still engaged to Thelma Lou). Opie has married a girl named Eunice (Karlene Crockett) and is now editor of the Mayberry *Gazette*; Gomer and Goober own the G&G Garage. (The movie ends with Andy becoming sheriff and Barney his deputy.)

Relatives: Candace Howard (Bee's niece, *Martha*), Joe Connell (Martha's husband, *Darryl*), Mary Lansing (Emmett's wife, *Martha Clark*), Mabel Albertson (Howard's mother, *Mrs. Sprague*), Dub Taylor (Emmett's brother-in-law, *Ben*), Elizabeth Harrower (Millie's mother), Steve Pendleton (Millie's father), Jan Shutan (Andy's cousin, *Gloria*), Mary Ann Durkin (Helen's niece, *Cynthia*).

Theme: "The Andy Griffith Show Theme: The Fishin' Hole," by Earle Hagen.

Note: See also "Gomer Pyle, U.S.M.C.," a spinoff series.

20. *Andy's Gang*

NBC, 8/20/55 to 6/28/58

A revised version of "Smilin' Ed's Gang" (see title). Our genial host, Andy Devine, first appeared to say, "Hiya, kids, it's Andy's Gang." Andy and his gang (the studio audience) then sang the theme: "I got a gang, you got a gang, everybody's gotta have a gang; but there's only one gang for me—good old Andy's Gang."

Children of all ages were then led into a world where the unreal became real. Andy usually began each program with Andy's Storytime. Seated on stage in a large easy chair, he opened a rather big book called *Andy's Stories*. As he read a chapter, a filmed segment was shown. Most often, Andy's stories related the thrilling, serialized adventures of "Gunga, the Elephant Boy" (originally Ghanga Rama on "Smilin' Ed's Gang"). These tales, set in Bakore, India, followed the

exploits of Gunga (Nino Marcel) and his friend Rama (Vito Scotti) as they performed hazardous assignments for the Maharajah (Lou Merrill; later Lou Krugman).

Segments about either Grandie the Talking Piano (voice of June Foray) or Midnight the Cat and Squeaky the Mouse followed. The talented cat (voice of June Foray) and mouse performed like a vaudeville team (for example, while Squeaky played his ukulele, Midnight would dance on her hind legs; as Midnight attempted to play the tamborine, Squeaky would ride his bicycle and annoy her).

Finally came the most popular segment. Andy, standing next to a grandfather clock, would say, "North or south, east or west, wherever you are, Froggie the Gremlin, we want you to become visible. Plunk your magic twanger, Froggie." A puff of smoke and the magical and mischievous Froggie the Gremlin (a rubber frog toy) would appear ("How are ya, kids? How are ya, how are ya? Ha ha ha!"). After a brief chat with Andy, the show's weekly guest would appear, and Froggie (voice of Frank Ferrin) would do his best to annoy him (for instance, guest Alan Reed would say, "Greetings and salutations, everyone, it is I, Algernon Archibald Percival Shortfellow the poet." Froggie would immediately interrupt: "He's crazy, he is, he is." The poet would respond, "Yes, I'm crazy I am, I am. No, no, no . . ." Total chaos followed as the poet tried to recite his poems.)

With the conclusion of Froggie's segment also came the end of our Saturday half-hour stay at Andy's clubhouse. Andy appeared one last time to say, "Yes, sir, we're pals and pals stick together. And now, don't forget church or Sunday school. And remember, Andy's Gang will get together right here at this same time next week. So long, fellows and gals."

21. *Angel Street*

CBS, 9/15/92 to 10/3/92

Anita Wellman King (Robin Givens) and Dorothy ("Dotty") Paretsky (Pamela Gidley) are detectives with the Homicide Division of the Violent Crimes Unit of the Chicago Police Department. Anita is ambitious and wants to work her way up in the department (she is eager to become a lieutenant). Dorothy is streetwise and satisfied where she is; she refuses to work with Anita on other cases—"We're homicide; no body, no case."

Anita and Dorothy first met when they were teamed by the department. Anita is a glamorous black woman who "overdresses" (as Dotty says) for the job. She wears skirts and heels and gets angry when she ruins her expensive pantyhose ($15 a pair) chasing suspects. Anita is a Catholic and grew up in the poor South Side of Chicago (she now lives in a better neighborhood at 311 Ashford Drive). Her phone number is 555-6616 and M9640 is her car license plate number.

Dorothy began her career with the narcotics department (Anita was previously with Internal Affairs). She is a

Catholic and attended Francis Xavier Elementary School. Dorothy grew up in the Polish Hill section of Chicago, a well-to-do area that is also called Angel Street. She smokes Marlboro cigarettes and drives a car with the license plate 3X4 919. Dorothy is the mother of a young daughter named Jennifer (Christiana Robinson) and lives with her grandfather, "Pobby" (Everett Smith, then Jan Rubes), at 9034 Mid-Valley Road on Polish Hill. (Dorothy refuses to talk about Jennifer's father or whether she was married to him or just had an affair).

The Roll Call is the local watering hole. Detective Ken Brannigan (Ron Dean) is the senior detective in the unit. He has an unseen wife named Marjorie (whom he calls "Mrs. B"). Ken's first case was an unsolved Jane Doe called "Blonde in the Pond" ("A girl was found in a lake. No one claimed the body; no suspects."). The series was originally titled "Polish Hill."

Anthony Marinelli composed the "Angel Street" theme.

22. *Angie*

ABC, 2/8/79 to 10/23/80

Angela ("Angie") Falco (Donna Pescow) is a waitress at the Liberty Coffee Shop in Philadelphia. She lives with her mother, Theresa Falco (Doris Roberts), and her sister, Marie Falco (Debralee Scott), at 421 Vermont Street, Apartment 1. Theresa operates the Falco Newsstand; she later purchases a beauty shop called Rose's House of Beauty.

Life changes for Angie also. One day she meets a wealthy doctor named Bradley ("Brad") Benson (Robert Hays). They fall in love, marry and set up housekeeping in a luxurious home at 76 Clinton Street. Stories follow Angie's efforts to live the good life, despite the objections of Joyce Benson (Sharon Spelman), Brad's divorced sister, who objects to his marriage and to having someone of lower social status in the family. Joyce lives with her daughter, Hilary (Tammy Lauren), at 101 Willow Pond Avenue.

John Randolph played Brad's father, Randall Benson (who is delighted to have Angie as a daughter-in-law); Carlo Imperato played Angie's cousin, Pete Fortunato.

Maureen McGovern sings the theme, "Different Worlds."

23. *Ann Jillian*

NBC, 11/30/89 to 1/20/90
NBC, 8/5/90 to 8/19/90

Cast: Ann Jillian *(Ann McNeil)*, Lisa Rieffel *(Lucy McNeil)*, Amy Lynne *(Robin Walker)*, Chantal Rivera-Batisse *(Melissa Santos)*, Cynthia Harris *(Sheila Hufnagel)*, Zachary Rosencrantz *(Kaz Sumner)*, Noble Willingham *(Duke)*.

Facts: Ann McNeil, her husband, Eddie (not seen) and their daughter, Lucy, live at 1027-64 South Ferry Street in

Queens, New York. Ann is a Radio City Music Hall Rockette; Lucy attends St. Michael's High School; and Eddie is a fireman for the city of New York. When Eddie is killed in the line of duty, Ann decides to leave the city and begin a new life in Marvel, California.

Ann and Lucy now live in a small house at 805 Etchfield Street. Ann, who has a bank account at the Fidelity Mutual Bank, now works as the manager of Aunt Betty's Coffee and Bean Shop, a quaint eatery owned by Sheila Hufnagel. Fifteen-year-old Lucy attends Marvel High School. She has a dog named Corkey (whom Ann calls "the puppy from hell") and eats Dipples brand potato chips as a bedtime snack.

Robin Walker is Lucy's schoolmate and Ann's not too bright assistant at the shop. Melissa Santos, a conceited high school bombshell, is a beauty pageant winner who holds the titles Miss Teen Avocado and Miss Teenage Tomato. Kaz Sumner is Ann's neighbor, a kid who apparently lives with his grandfather, Duke.

Ann and her husband first met as teenagers. They saw a play and took a hansom cab ride through Central Park on their first date. To neck, they would go to Montague Point "to watch for Halley's Comet—which wasn't due for 30 years." (In Marvel, the makeout spot is Paradise Point, "where the kids go to watch for UFOs.") Before a date, Ann would hang upside down to get color in her cheeks. Thunderstorms still frighten Ann; to feel secure, she snuggles up in bed with Lucy.

The episode of 8/19/90 introduced a new format in an effort to save the series. When Ann makes a pastry delivery from Aunt Betty's to Marsh Pearson, president of the Merchants Association of the Marvel Mall, she suggests a way to improve the mall—to make it a happy place. Marsh finds the idea terrific and hires Ann as its activities director.

Ann's license plate is 2DDL 274. There are 317 mannequins in the mall. The town of Marvel was founded by Jacob Sweeney in 1921. (While driving to San Francisco, Jacob's model-T Ford got a flat tire. Rather than fix the flat, he decided to stay where he was.)

The revised format cast added Bruce Kirby as Marsh Pearson; Adam Biesk as Tad Pearson, Marsh's son and Ann's assistant; and James Henriksen as Russ, the security guard. Only the new pilot episode aired.

Theme: "Ann Jillian," vocal by Ann Jillian and Stan Harris.

Note: In the original, unaired pilot (produced in 1989 as "The Ann Jillian Show"), Ann and Lucy had the last name Morgan.

24. *The Ann Sothern Show*

CBS, 10/6/58 to 9/25/61

The Bartley House at 36 East 56th Street in Manhattan is a fashionable New York City hotel. Kathleen ("Katy") O'Connor (Ann Sothern) is its assistant manager. She lives at 21 East 10th Street in Greenwich Village (address also given as 15 Greenwich Place). She shares Apartment 3B with her best friend, Olive Smith (Ann Tyrrell); Olive works for Katy as her secretary at the hotel.

Tom Bartley, Sr. (Lester Matthews), owns the hotel. The henpecked Jason Macauley and his domineering wife, Flora (Ernest Truex and Reta Shaw), manage the hotel. In 1959 they are transferred to the Calcutta Bartley House. Jason called Katy "the best darned assistant manager I ever had." Bartley then hired James Arlington Devery (Don Porter) to manage the hotel. Devery, whose middle name was also given as Aloysius, was born in Ohio on August 23, 1916. He graduated from Harvard in 1939 and began his career as a bellboy for the Bartley chain. Woodrow ("Woody") Hamilton (Ken Berry) and Johnny Wallace (Jack Mullaney) are the hotel bellboys; Dr. Delbert Gray (Louis Nye) is the hotel dentist.

Relatives: Terence deMarney (Katy's uncle, *Terence*), Cecil Kellaway (Katy's uncle, *Sean*), Frederick Ford (Tom's son, *Tom Bartley, Jr.*), Christine White (Tom's niece, *Margaret Finchley*), Gladys Hurlbut (Delbert's mother, *Dr. Gray*; a dentist also), Frances Bavier (*Johnny's mother*).

Theme: "Katy," by Ann Sothern and Bonny Lake.

25. *Anne of Green Gables*

PBS, 2/16/86 to 3/2/86

Cast: Megan Follows (*Anne Shirley*), Colleen Dewhurst (*Marilla Cuthbert*), Richard Farnsworth (*Matthew Cuthbert*), Schuyler Grant (*Diana Barry*), Jonathan Crombie (*Gilbert Blythe*).

Facts: "The prettiest acreage on the North Shore" of Prince Edward Island in Canada (early 1900s) is Green Gables, a farm owned by Marilla and Matthew Cuthbert. Anne Shirley is a very pretty, 13-year-old, red haired orphan girl who yearns for a home and love. Anne was born in Fairfax, Canada, and orphaned at age three months when her parents, Walter and Bertha, died of "the fever." Anne was sent to and raised at the Fairview Orphanage in Nova Scotia. "My life is a graveyard of buried hopes," Anne would say of her days at Fairview; her only friend was Katie Moore, her "imaginary window friend" (Anne's reflection in the window).

Matthew and Marilla are an elderly brother and sister. When they decide they need help in running Green Gables, they agree to adopt an orphan boy; they are sent a girl instead—Anne. Marilla, who never married, is a very bitter and stern woman. Matthew, who remained a bachelor, is very kind and gentle. Anne is full of life, has a vivid imagination and a special gift for overcoming obstacles and bringing out the best in people. "We wanted a boy," Marilla says, "but it was Providence that brought her to us. It was He who knew that we needed her." Anne's growth from teenager to young woman is the focal point of this beautifully enacted and heartwarming television adaptation of the books by Lucy Maud Montgomery.

In describing herself, Anne remarks, "I'm skinny, a little freckled and have green eyes. I'm blessed with a wonderful imagination and want to be beautiful when I grow up." She has ambitions to be a writer and insists that her first name be spelled "Anne with an *e* ("It's more distinguished and vibrant than plain old Ann without an *e*"). Anne feels that her downfall is her temper, which she attributes "to the curse of my red hair" (she gets highly charged when someone remarks negatively about her hair). When Anne promises to keep a secret, "Wild horses couldn't drag it from me," and her philosophy is "Tomorrow is always fresh, with no mistakes in it."

Anne's greatest wish "is to have a bosom friend, a really kindred spirit." Through Marilla, Anne meets Diana Barry, the teenage girl living on Orchid Slope, who becomes her best friend (their oath: "I solemnly swear to remain faithful to my bosom friend for as long as the sun and the moon shall endure"). Diana believes Anne has "more nerve than a fox in a henhouse," while Marilla contends that Anne has a genius for trouble.

On her first day at the Avonlea Public School, Anne encounters Gilbert Blythe, the boy she takes a dislike to when he calls her "Carrots." (Anne felt "excruciatingly embarrassed" and vowed never to associate with him again. They became rivals at everything. Although Anne never really forgave Gilbert, she allowed herself to grow close to him. Their friendship bonded in the sequel series, "Anne of Avonlea" [PBS, 4/5/88 to 4/12/88], in which Gilbert helped Anne achieve her goals.)

After graduating from the Avonlea School, Anne enrolls at Queen's College in a one year course to get her teaching license. Following her year of study, Anne receives a scholarship to continue at the Redmond College. Matthew's sudden death at this time leaves Marilla with no choice but to sell her beloved Green Gables. In an attempt to prevent this from happening, Anne gives up her scholarship to teach at the Avonlea Public School and help Marilla run Green Gables.

Information is now based on "Anne of Avonlea." When Diana learns that Anne's short story "Avaral's Atonement" has been rejected by *Women's Home Journal* magazine, she reworks the copy Anne gave to her and submits it to the Rollings Reliable Baking Powder Story competition. While Anne did not intend for her main character to praise baking powder, she wins the first prize of $100.

Anne next receives a letter from Miss Stacey (Marilyn Lightstone), her former teacher at the Avonlea School (now head of the Kingspoint Ladies College) informing her that a position has become available in the English Department. Anne is about to reject the offer when the husband of Marilla's friend of 45 years, Rachel Lynde (Patricia Hamilton), dies. When Marilla asks Rachel to move in with her, Anne accepts the teaching job in Charlotts Town, New Brunswick (her greatest challenge is to overcome the hostility of the blue-blooded Pringle girls, especially Jen Pringle [Susannah Hoffman], who is determined to discredit her). It is during this time that Anne has her first book published, *Avonlea Vignettes* (for which she received a $250 advance) and has a brief romance with Morgan Harris (Frank Converse), the wealthy father of her favorite student, Emmaline Harris (Genevieve Appleton). Morgan lives on an estate called Maplehurst.

Marilla was famous for her currant wine; Anne was first seen by Matthew, who convinced Marilla to let her stay, at the Bright River Train Station. Anne had a mischievous cow named Dolly, was gentle and kind to her students and remarked that "Green Gables is a beautiful dream that will always haunt me" whenever she had to leave it.

Theme: "Anne of Green Gables," by Hagood Hardy.

26. *Annette*

ABC, 2/6/58 to 3/6/58

In 1943 in the farming community of Beaver Junction, Nebraska, a girl (Annette) is born to Brice and Blanche McCleod. Fifteen years later, after her parents' deaths, Annette (Annette Funicello) moves to the town of Ashford to live with her uncle, Dr. Archie McCleod (Richard Deacon), and her aunt, Lila McCleod (Sylvia Field), Brice's brother and sister. Archie and Lila live with a housekeeper named Katie (Mary Wickes).

Annette first befriends Jet Maypen (Judy Nugent), the farm girl who delivers eggs and chickens to the families in town. Through Jet, Annette meets Steve Abernathy (Tim Considine), the most popular boy in town; Val Abernathy (Doreen Tracy), Steve's sister; Mike Martin (David Stollery), a high school senior who is the soda jerk at the Malt Shop; and their friends Omstead ("Steady") Ware (Ruby Lee), Madge Markham (Cheryl Holdridge), Kitty Bleylock (Sharon Baird) and Moselle Corey (Shelley Fabares).

Laura Rogan (Roberta Shore) is the richest and prettiest girl at Old South High School (where Annette is in tenth grade). Although the girls say "Laura is loaded with talent and has every boy in town jumping through hoops," she takes an instant dislike to Annette when she sees Steve (her boyfriend) being kind to her.

When Annette is invited to a party given by Val, trouble starts. Before she sings "Readin', 'Ritin' and Rhythm," Laura places her necklace on the piano (which she forgets to retrieve when she finishes singing). As part of the "punishment" in a party game, Annette must sing "How Will I Know My Love?" Before she is able to complete it, dinner is announced. The kids clear the room, leaving Annette to follow seconds later. When Annette departs to keep her 11:00 P.M. curfew, Laura remembers leaving her necklace on the piano and goes for it, but it's missing. Laura immediately accuses Annette ("That McCleod girl was in here alone when we were all at dinner"). Jet immediately defends Annette, saying she would never take it, but Laura's mind cannot be changed.

At a Thanksgiving party rehearsal for school at Val's house, the gang—including Annette and Laura—get together. When Laura goes to the piano to rehearse a song, she finds the piano is out of tune. Steve looks inside and sees the missing necklace wedged between the strings. Laura makes the first move: "I guess I owe you an apology, Annette. I'm sorry, really I am . . . Is it too late for us to be

friends?" "I'd like to be your friend if you'd let me," responds Annette. "Try me" is Laura's response and the two become friends.

The McCleods live at 149 Elm Street. Annette sleeps in the room next to Lila's (which was Lila's grandmother's room) and at Old South High, Annette is program chairman of the activities committee. Archie, a doctor of philosophy, has a Ph.D. and is fond of Katie's chicken soup (as is Annette). He was the last subscriber to a magazine called *Philosophical Review*—which ceased publication after he paid for a five year subscription. Annette's "ultra favorite" meal is burgers with pickle relish, mustard and chips. Laura is called "the slickest chick that ever hit this old town" by the boys. Jet, who has a pig named Queenie, lives on a ranch at Spring Branch (which is next to Highway 26). Katie, who has been with the McCleods for 20 years, orders groceries from the Main Street Market.

Theme: "Annette," by Jimmie Dodd.

Note: Aired as 19 segments (plus an introduction episode) on "The Mickey Mouse Club."

27. *Annie McGuire*

CBS, 10/26/88 to 12/28/88

At 235 West Perry Street in Bayonne, New Jersey, live newlyweds Annie Block-McGuire (Mary Tyler Moore), the deputy coordinator of community relations for the city of New York, and her husband of five weeks, Nicholas ("Nick") McGuire (Denis Arndt), a structural engineer with the firm of McGuire and Conrad in Bayonne. Annie is divorced and the mother of 12-year-old Lewis (Bradley Warden); Nick is a widower and the father of 14-year-old Lenny (Adrien Brody) and nine-year-old Debbie (Cynthia Marie King). Annie is a bleeding heart liberal who will help anyone with a problem; she believes children should not be forced to do anything ("If you force them, they will hate it later in life"). Nick, a Republican, believes just the opposite: "You have to force them, it's the only way to get them to do something." Their phone number is 555-5551; schools for the children are not mentioned.

Annie takes the ferry from Bayonne to New York and works in the Municipal Building (Room 805) in Manhattan. In the original concept of the series, titled "Mary Tyler Moore," Mary's "Annie" character lived in Manhattan and worked for the city. When Denis Arndt replaced Edward J. Moore (no relation to Mary) as her husband and the home locale switched to New Jersey, Annie would not have been permitted to work for New York (city workers must live in the city); it was not explained how Annie was able to work for New York when she lived in New Jersey.

Relatives: Eileen Heckart (Annie's mother, *Emma Block*), Stephen Elliott (Annie's father, *Phil Block*), John Randolph (Nick's father, *Red McGuire*, owner of Red's All American Grill in Bayonne).

Theme: "Annie McGuire," by J.A.C. Redford.

28. *Annie Oakley*

Syndicated, 1/54 to 2/57

Annie Oakley (Gail Davis) is a pretty, expert sharpshooter who helps Deputy Lofty Craig (Brad Johnson) uphold the law in Diablo County, Arizona, during the early 1900s. In the opening theme, Annie shoots a hole in the center spade of the nine of spades playing card. "It's easy to hit the bull's-eye every time," she says. "Once you learn to see just the bull's-eye and nothing else, all you have to do is point your gun and pull the trigger." Annie, television's earliest heroine, never shoots to kill; what she aims at she hits ("Once Annie aims at something, it's a bull's-eye"). Annie often plays detective to uncover evidence against outlaws.

Orphaned when her parents died, Annie now cares for her kid brother, Tagg Oakley (Jimmy Hawkins). Their uncle, Luke McTavish (Kenneth MacDonald) is the sheriff of Diablo County. Target and (later) Daisy were Annie's horses; Pixie was Tagg's horse. Tagg also had a frog named Hector and a rabbit called Mr. Hoppity (who lived on a game preserve Annie called "Annie's Ark").

Judy Nugent played Lofty's niece, Penny; Nan Martin, a remarkable Gail Davis look-alike, was Annie's outlaw double, Alias Annie Oakley. Fess Parker (as Tom Conrad) was editor of the *Diablo Courier* (the position is later played by Stanley Andrews as Chet Osgood, editor of the *Diablo Bugle*). Other townspeople are Tom Jennings (William Fawcett), the postal clerk; Gloria Marshall (Sally Fraser), owner of the Diablo General Store; Curley Dawes (Roscoe Ates), the telegraph operator; George Lacey (Stanley Andrews), the owner of the Diablo Hotel; and the Diablo County schoolteachers: Marge Hardy (Virginia Lee), Mary Farnsworth (Wendy Drew) and Deborah Scott (Nancy Hale). In the original, unaired pilot version, titled "Bull's Eye," Billy Gray plays Tagg Oakley.

Ben Weisman and Fred Wise composed the theme. Gail Davis sings the "Annie Oakley" theme on the record album *Hooray for Cowboys*.

29. *Anything but Love*

ABC, 3/7/89 to 4/11/89
ABC, 9/27/89 to 9/5/90
ABC, 2/6/91 to 6/17/92

Cast: Jamie Lee Curtis *(Hannah Miller)*, Richard Lewis *(Marty Gold)*, Holly Fulger *(Robin Duliteski)*, Ann Magnuson *(Catherine Hughes)*.

Facts: Hannah Miller and Marty Gold are writers for *Chicago Monthly* magazine (later called *Chicago Weekly*). Hannah, formerly a Los Angeles schoolteacher, was first a researcher for the magazine. Marty previously worked as a reporter for the Chicago *Tribune*. Stories were originally a depiction of their platonic relationship; as the series progressed, they became lovers.

Hannah was born on March 28, 1960, and now lives at 415 Van Nest Avenue (although the house number reads 223). Hannah knows she is a very attractive woman and struggles to maintain her figure. She is especially proud of her breasts and calls them "The Girls." Hannah's best friend is Robin, whom she has known since she was five years old. "How long have we been friends?" asks Hannah. "Forever," says Robin, "and how long are we going to be friends?" "Forever," says Hannah. Robin is a dental hygienist, and she and Hannah call each other "Mrs. Schmenkman." In the eleventh grade Hannah and Robin made a pact that if neither of them was married by age 30, they both would tell people their husbands were with the witness protection program. Lani O'Grady was heard as Hannah's inner voice in several episodes.

Martin E. ("Marty") Gold enjoys watching women mud-wrestle at Dick and Dee's International House of Mud. He lives in Apartment 3K (no address given), and Mark Twain is his hero. His and Hannah's favorite restaurant is Marino's. Hannah and Marty became romantically involved in the episode of 2/6/91 ("Say It Again, Han") and lovers in the episode of 3/14/91 ("Long Day's Journey into What?"). Hannah envisions herself and Marty married with two children: Anna (Katie Jane Johnson) and Artie (Josh C. Williams).

The editorial offices of the *Chicago Weekly* are in Room 702. Norman Kiel (Louis Giambalvo) was the original editor; he was replaced by the outlandish and unconventional Catherine Hughes. Jules Bennett (Richard Frank) is Catherine's mousey assistant, and Mike Urbanek (Bruce Weitz) is a columnist. Brian Allquist (Joseph Maher) was the television critic in the first season episodes (pressures from the job caused him to go to Marshall's Department Store and smash all the television screens in the video department; he is now in a mental hospital).

Relatives: Bruce Kirby (Hannah's father, *Leo Miller*), Lindsey Haun (Hannah's five-year-old niece, *Nicky*), Tia Carrere (Marty's foster daughter, *Cey*), Susie Duff (Marty's sister, *Jo Levin*), Jeff Silverman (Jo's husband, *Philip Levin*), Doris Belack (Marty's original mother, *Dorothy Gold*), Anna Berger (Marty's mother, *Sylvia Gold,* in later episodes). Marty mentioned his late father's name as Sam; Robin has an ex-husband named Kenny.

Flashbacks: Emily Ann Lloyd *(Hannah, age seven)*, Gina Tuttle *(Hannah as a teenager)*, Bradley Michael Pierce *(Marty, age seven)*, Jason Marsden *(Marty as a teenager)*.

Theme: "Anything but Love," by John David Souther.

30. *Apple Pie*

ABC, 9/23/78 to 10/7/78

"March the fourth, nineteen and thirty-three. Mercy, what times these are. Nobody in this whole country has money to buy dirt. Luckily, though, we live here in Kansas City, Kansas, where there is plenty of dirt for free. Just everything else we can't afford." These words are spoken by

Ginger-Nell Hollyhock (Rue McClanahan) in the opening theme. Ginger-Nell is a lonely woman who is longing for a family; to resolve her problem, she advertises in the *Gazette* for a family: a husband, two children and a grandfather.

When the series begins, Ginger-Nell has a beautiful daughter named Anna Marie (Caitlin O'Heaney), a son named Junior (Derrel Maury), a somewhat senile and blind grandfather (called only Grandpa Hollyhock and played by Jack Gilford) and a handsome "husband" named "Fast" Eddie Barnes (Dabney Coleman), a bank robber on the run who finds refuge by posing as a family man.

The family lives at 93600 Morning Glory Road. Ginger-Nell owns the Hollyhock Beauty Salon and pays a home mortgage of $43 a month to the First National Bank of Kansas City. Anna Marie, who knows she is very sexy, titillates the boys by revealing her gorgeous legs (dubbed "leggy sexuality" by *Variety*). She attends Kansas City University—as does Junior. Grandpa is a loudmouth who constantly complains about the Roosevelt administration and having to "smell the funnies" (the newspaper is not printed in braille). Based on the play *Nourish the Beast*, by Steve Tesich.

No credit is given for the theme, a 1930s jazz-style version of the song "Happy Days Are Here Again."

Archie Bunker's Place see All in the Family

31. *Arnie*

CBS, 9/19/70 to 9/9/72

Arnold ("Arnie") Nuvo (Herschel Bernardi), his beautiful wife, Lillian (Sue Ane Langdon), and their teenage children, Andrea (Stephanie Steele) and Richard (Del Russel), live at 4650 Liberty Lane in Los Angeles (555-6676 is their phone number). Arnie works as a loading dock foreman for Continental Flange, Inc. (located at 36 West Pico Boulevard). After 12 years of faithful service on Arnie's part, Hamilton Majors, Jr. (Roger Bowen), the company president, gives him a promotion and makes him an executive—the head of New Product Improvement. Arnie now makes $20,000 a year and feels that for the first time in his life he may become self-sufficient—until he sees his deductions. Each week: $81.26 (federal withholding), $22.07 (Social Security), $4.21 (state withholding), and $25 for the company pension fund. Each month there is $10 for the secretaries' coffee fund, $25 for the executive dining table fund and $100 yearly for the company's favorite charity, Pals of the Poor. Added to this is $40 weekly for the family grocery bill and $200 a month for the payment of bills. What Arnie has left ("which ain't much") makes him

realize that there is a long road ahead as he struggles to become self-sufficient.

Lillian purchases ten pounds of peanut butter every week (on Thursday, which is her grocery shopping day). She buys her dresses at Helen's Dress Shop and held a job as a Perfect Figure lingerie model. Andrea, who loves to play the guitar, and Richard attend Westside High School.

Hamilton Majors, Jr., runs the company for "Dad." His favorite letters are S-A-V-E. He babies his right hand (his mallet hand) for matches at the Bayshore Polo Club and will only shake hands with his left hand. It is a 26-second walk from Arnie's office to the boardroom, where he and Hamilton attend daily meetings.

Randolph ("Randy") Robinson (Charles Nelson Reilly) is Arnie's neighbor, the host of television's "The Giddyap Gourmet." Felicia Farfas (Elaine Shore) is Arnie's secretary, and Neil Ogilvie (Herb Voland) is the plant supervisor.

Harry Geller composed the theme song, "Arnie."

32. *The Avengers*

ABC, 3/28/66 to 7/1/66
ABC, 1/20/67 to 9/1/67
ABC, 1/10/68 to 9/15/69

Cast: Patrick Macnee (*John Steed*), Diana Rigg (*Emma Peel*), Linda Thorson (*Tara King*), Honor Blackman (*Catherine Gale*), Patrick Newell (*Mother*).

Facts: John Steed, Catherine Gale, Emma Peel and Tara King are agents for the British government who "avenge crimes perpetrated against the people and the state."

John Steed is a suave and sophisticated ministry agent who exudes Old World charm and courtesy. He originally lived at 5 Westminster Mews, then at 3 Stable Mews in London. Steed's first car was a yellow 1926 vintage Rolls Royce Silver Ghost, then a dark green vintage 4.5-litre Bentley (license plate YT 3942; later RX 6180 and VT 3942). Steed takes three sugars in his coffee, and his Achilles' heel is the opposite sex. When first introduced in 1961, Steed had no first name and his cover was that of a dilettante man-about-town. In these early British-broadcast episodes, Steed works with Dr. David Keel (Ian Hendry) and has a dog named Juno.

Catherine Gale is a beautiful blonde with a Ph.D. in anthropology. When her husband is killed during a Mau Mau raid in Kenya, Catherine returns to England to work at the British Museum. Catherine is not as professional as Steed, but possesses scientific knowledge and martial arts skills. They make the perfect crime-solving duo when they are teamed by the government. Cathy, as Steed sometimes calls her, has a Triumph motorcycle with the license plate 987 CAA. Steed has a dog named Sheba. During this era (1962–65), Steed also worked with Venus Smith (Julie Stevens), a nightclub singer who was fascinated by him, and Martin King (Jon Rollason), a doctor who had a private practice at 12 Marshback Terrace.

Opposite: *Apple Pie.* **Rue McClanahan and Dabney Coleman.**

A slight car accident unites Steed with the totally emancipated Emma Peel, the beautiful, wealthy widow of a test pilot (Peter Peel). She joins Steed (1966–68) for the sheer love of adventure. Emma drives a 1966 Lotus Elan (license plate JJH 4990; later HNK 999C and HN 9996).

Emma's maiden name is Knight; her father, Sir John Knight, owned Knight Industries, a business located in the Knight Building in London. When her father passed away, Emma was 21 years old and became the head of the company. She is interested in anthropology and loves to play bridge (she wrote the article "Better Bridge with Applied Mathematics" for the June issue of *The Bridge Players International Guide*). Emma's least favorite assignment was posing as Emma, Star of the East, a beautiful (but dense) harem dancer in "Honey for the Prince." Emma, who loves to wear sexy black outfits ("The Emmapeeler"), lives in London, but an address was never given.

"Always keep you bowler on in times of stress and watch out for diabolical masterminds" are the final words Emma speaks to Steed as she prepares to join her husband. (Peter was an air ace who was believed to have been killed; he was found alive, however, in the Amazonian jungle.) "I'll remember, Emma, thanks," are Steed's parting words to Emma. As Emma returns to Peter (a man who looks much like Steed), Steed is teamed with Tara King, a shapely brunette who had just completed her agent's training. (She was recruit no. 69 and first encountered Steed when she tackled him by mistake during a training exercise. Emma and Tara meet on Steed's staircase. Emma approves and tells her, "Steed likes his tea stirred anti-clockwise." When Tara enters apartment no. 3 she tells Steed, "Mother sent me.") Mother, a man, is Steed's wheelchair-bound superior in these episodes. Tara lives at 9 Primrose Crescent in London and drives a red Lotus Europa (license plate NPW 99F). Tara loves to wear miniskirts and tight blouses. She loves music and fashion; car racing and skiing are her hobbies.

Relatives: Joyce Carey (Mother's aunt, *Harriet*), Mary Merrill (Mother's aunt, *Georgina*).

Theme: "The Avengers," by Johnny Dankworth (1962–65) and Laurie Johnson (1966–69).

Note: Patrick Macnee reprised his role as John Steed in "The New Avengers" (CBS, 9/15/78 to 3/23/79), in which he was teamed with a beautiful agent named Purdy (Joanna Lumley) and a two-fisted agent named Mike Gambit (Gareth Hunt).

33. *Babes*

Fox, 9/13/90 to 6/6/91

Cast: Wendie Jo Sperber (*Charlene Gilbert*), Lesley Boone (*Marlene Gilbert*), Susan Peretz (*Darlene Gilbert*).

Facts: "The ground just shook and everywhere you look all you see is babes..." The theme is referring to the Gilbert sisters, Charlene, Marlene, and Darlene, three full-figured women who live together and stick together through thick and thin. (They have a pact never to say the word *overweight*.)

Charlene, the middle sister, is the most adjusted to the fact that they will always be heavy (each weighs over 200 pounds). She works as a commercial makeup artist (she was the makeup artist to Dolly Parton in the episode of 2/7/91). In 1970 Charlene took tap dancing lessons at Madame McNair's School of Dance. She was the fourth dancing teapot in "Madame McNair's Winter Recital" (Gretchen Wyler played Madame McNair). Charlene's boyfriend, Ronnie Underwood (Rick Overton) owns Ronnie's Ribs Take Out Food.

Marlene is the youngest, prettiest and most sensitive of the sisters. She also possesses the least self-confidence and is having a difficult time accepting the fact that she will never be thin. Marlene was first a model for the Merit, Barrett and Cole Ad Agency (she was "The Hefty Hose Girl") and later a video photographer at a dating service called Ideal Mates, Inc. Before the series began, Marlene was a toll collector. She was "Miss Exact Change" three years in a row and lost her job to automation. As a kid, Marlene dreamed of being an actress (she desperately wanted to be Susan Dey's "Laurie Partridge" character on "The Partridge Family" television series). She twirled a baton and sang "You Light Up My Life" for her fourth grade music recital, and in high school she played the mother in the school's production of "Our Town." As a kid Marlene loved to play with building blocks; they called her "Block Head."

Darlene is the oldest and nastiest of the sisters; she is also fully aware that thin will never be in for her. She works as a dog groomer and has a puppy named Big Mike (whom she calls a "miniature Cujo"). Darlene loves impressionist art and catching snowflakes on her tongue. She is the only sister who married (she is now divorced after 14 years). While she was married, she had a pet hamster named Potsie.

The girls live in Apartment 410 at 362 East 7th Street in Manhattan. They went to Camp Tamarack as kids and attended Edgar Allan Poe High School. They dine frequently at Stein's Restaurant and attempted a business venture designing dresses for the fuller figured woman (it failed when their store contact was fired).

Relatives: Barbara Barrie (*"Mom" Gilbert*; she lives in Delray Beach, Florida, and is thin; the girls take after their father), Rhoda Gemignani (the girls' aunt, *Marion*), Brandon Maggart (Darlene's ex-husband, *Wilbur Heckley*), Dena Dietrich (Ronnie's mother, *Doris Underwood*).

Theme: "Babes," by Jay Gruska.

34. *Baby Boom*

NBC, 9/10/88 to 1/4/89
NBC, 7/13/89, 8/14/89, 9/10/89

A television adaptation of the feature film of the same title, the show tells the story of J.C. Wiatt (Kate Jackson), a high powered executive, and her efforts to care for Elizabeth (Michelle and Kristina Kennedy), a baby she inherited from a distant cousin. J.C., nicknamed "The Tiger Lady" at work, is a management consultant for the Sloane-Curtis Company in New York City (located at 631 East 56th Street). J.C. lives in Apartment 15D (address not given); Elizabeth has a plush kangaroo (Cuppy) and four goldfish J.C. named Goldie, Frank, Ernie and Hector.

Sam Wanamaker plays J.C.'s boss, Fritz Curtis; Tippi Hedren is Fritz's wife, Laura Curtis; and Norman Parker appeared as J.C.'s father, J.C. Wiatt, Sr.

Nikki Feemster played J.C. as a girl and Jill Whitlow was J.C. as a teenager in a flashback sequence. Steve Tyrell composed the "Baby Boom" theme.

35. *Baby, I'm Back!*

CBS, 1/30/78 to 8/12/78

On February 13, 1963, Raymond Ellis (Demond Wilson) and Olivia Carter (Denise Nicholas) married. Seven years later, when he felt unable to cope with the responsibility of raising a family, Ray deserted Olivia and their children, Angie (Kim Fields) and Jordan (Tony Holmes). To support her family, Olivia, who lives at 1684 Richmond Drive in Washington, D.C., acquires a job at the Pentagon as an assistant to Wallace Dickey (Ed Hall), an army colonel. As the years pass, Olivia and Wallace fall in love and plan to marry. In 1977 Olivia has Ray pronounced legally dead so she can marry Wallace.

When Ray hears that he is "dead," he appears on the scene to claim his legal right to be alive and to convince Olivia that he has changed and that they should pick up where they left off. Olivia refuses and sets her goal as marrying Wallace before Ray can have himself declared "alive." She is ably abetted by her mother, Luzelle Carter (Helen Martin), who has always considered Ray a dead issue as a husband. Stories relate the legal race for the matrimonial wire, with Ray attempting to maneuver his way back into Olivia's life before the "I do's" with Wallace.

The series has very little additional trivia: Angie, who is eight years old, and 12-year-old Jordan attend the Richfield Elementary School. Angie played Ruth in her Sunday school play based on the Bible story of Ruth; Jordan is a member of a rock group called Big News; and to win a bet with Ray that Wallace (whom Ray considers a "square") could not be tempted by another woman, Olivia pretended to be a sensual French temptress to win the wager.

Jeff Berry composed the "Baby, I'm Back" theme.

36. *Baby Talk*

ABC, 3/8/91 to 5/24/91
ABC, 9/20/91 to 7/3/92

Cast: Julia Duffy and Mary Page Keller *(Maggie Campbell)*, Tony Danza *(voice of Mickey)*.

Facts: Margaret ("Maggie") Eunice Campbell is a single mother and lives in an apartment at 46 Bleeker Street in Manhattan (next to the Goodall Rubber Company). Her infant son, Mickey, was born after an affair with a man named Nick—"A selfish, inconsiderate louse who wasn't fit to be a husband, a father or a human." Maggie works out of her apartment as an accountant; Cecil Fogarty (William Hickey) and Howard (Lenny Wolpe) are the carpenters Maggie hires to convert her loft into a baby-safe apartment. Stories focus on Maggie's life as seen through the eyes of eight-month-old Mickey Campbell (Paul and Ryan Jessup); his thoughts (voiceover dubbing) are heard by viewers and other infants. Based on the film *Look Who's Talking*.

Mickey has type AB blood. "Muskrat Love" is his favorite song, and red Jell-O is his favorite food. His rubber ducky is named Ralphie, and Maggie named him after her uncle, Mickey O'Brien, a dry cleaner. When Maggie thought Mickey was a genius at ten months, she enrolled him in the Academy for Gifted Babies. He is also on the waiting list for the Sheridan Academy. In the episode of 3/15/91, Mickey auditioned for a television commercial for the tropical line of Beacon Baby Foods.

Maggie and Mickey are members of the Mommy and Me Group (which meets on Friday afternoons at 2:00 P.M.). Members of the group are Claire (Paula Kelly), Stella (Jackie Swanson), Regina (Sue Grosa) and Paul (Paul Sand).

Elliott Fleischer (Tom Alan Robbins) is Mickey's doctor; he has an office at the Museum West Medical Center; Andrea (Michelle Ashlee) is his office nurse.

When the series returned for its second season, Maggie Campbell (now played by Mary Page Keller) moves to a new apartment (3A) in Brooklyn Heights and acquires a job with Coleman Accounting in the World Trade Center building in Manhattan. She works at the office two days a week (from 11:00 A.M. to 3:00 P.M.); the rest of the time she works out of her apartment.

New to the cast are James Halbrook (Scott Baio), Maggie's romantic interest; Anita Craig (Francesca P. Roberts), Maggie's neighbor (Apartment 3B); Susan Davis (Jessica Lundy), Maggie's co-worker; and Doris Campbell (Polly Bergen), Maggie's mother. Anita's infant daughter, Danielle, is played by Alicia and Celicia Johnson; she is voiced by Vernee Watson.

Maggie loves to shop ("I have great credit lines; it was passed down from my mother"). Maggie attended Penn State College, and when something upsets her she says, "The universe is expanding." James is an aspiring songwriter (he wrote the Peachy Time Gum jingle) who is also the building's janitor (he took the job so he could get Apartment 1A free). He calls Mickey "The Mickster" and he attended Berkley College. Mickey's favorite television show is "Mr. Duck's Jamboree," and his first word was *Daddy* (which he said when looking at James). Mickey also has a plush bear named Bo Bo. In the episode of 5/8/92 ("The Wedding"), Maggie and James marry.

In the original, unaired pilot version, Connie Sellecca played Mollie Campbell. She was replaced by Alison LaPlaca as Maggie Campbell in a second, unaired pilot. Julia Duffy replaced her in the first aired pilot, and Mary Page Keller replaced Duffy in the revamped version. Tony Danza was Mickey's voice in all versions. The Julia Duffy version also featured George Clooney as Joe, the contractor Maggie originally hired to redo her apartment. Joe resurfaced in the episode of 5/17/91 to marry Robin (Nana Visitor), Maggie's sorority sister.

Relatives: Tony Danza (Mickey's father, *Nick Miller*), Charlotte Rae (Maggie's aunt, *Beverly*), Donnelly Rhodes (Maggie's father-in-law, *Nick Miller, Sr.*), Georgia Brown (James's mother, *Gina Halbrook*), Tom Troupe (James's father, *Warren Halbrook*).

Flash Forwards: Sean O'Bryan *(adult Mickey)*.

Theme: "Bread and Butter," vocal by Gene Miller (written by Jay Turnbow and Larry Parkes).

Note: Prior to *Look Who's Talking* and "Baby Talk," there was the NBC series "Happy" (6/6/60 to 9/2/60; 1/31/61 to 9/8/61). In 1957 Sally Dooley (Yvonne Lime) and Chris Day (Ronnie Burns) married. They spent their honeymoon in Palm Springs and stayed in Room 7 of the Desert Palms Hotel. In the room were two dozen white roses, two dozen yellow roses, a bowl of floating gardenias and a wedding cake with a bride and groom on the top. When Chris learns that the owner, Clara Mason (Doris Packer) is looking for someone to run the hotel, he and Sally take the job. Gradually, they are allowed to buy 10 percent of the hotel—which they have when the series begins.

Sally and Chris also have an infant son in 1960 whom they name Christopher Hapgood ("Happy") Day (David and Steven Born). As Chris and Sally attempt to run the hotel, Happy comments on adult activities via voiceover dubbing. Lloyd Corrigan played Sally's uncle, Charley Dooley. There is no credit for the off-screen voice for Happy; the credit reads "And Happy (of course)."

37. *Bachelor Father*

CBS, 9/15/57 to 6/11/58
NBC, 6/18/58 to 6/19/61
ABC, 10/3/61 to 9/25/62

Cast: John Forsythe *(Bentley Gregg)*, Noreen Corcoran *(Kelly Gregg)*, Sammee Tong *(Peter Tong)*, Bernadette Withers *(Ginger)*, Jimmy Boyd *(Howard Meechim)*.

Facts: Kelly Gregg is a very pretty 13-year-old girl who lives with her uncle, Bentley Gregg, and his houseboy, Peter Tong, at 1163 Rexford Drive in Beverly Hills, California. Bentley is a suave and sophisticated ladies' man whose life suddenly changes when his sister and brother-in-law are killed in a car accident and he decides to take on the responsibility of raising their only child. Stories follow Bentley and Peter's efforts to provide and home and love for Kelly.

Bentley is a private practice attorney with an office (Room 106) in the Crescent Building on Crescent Drive in Los Angeles. The Coconut Grove is his favorite nightclub; his

dates prefer dancing at the Ambassador Room. Bentley's license plate reads RXR 553.

Kelly and her friends, Ginger and Howard, are enrolled in Beverly Hills High School (Kelly's favorite subject is math). The afterschool hangout is Bill's Malt Shop. Kelly first worked as a secretary for her Uncle Bentley (she became the first secretary he ever kissed when she solved a complicated case for him). In the last season episodes, Kelly's boyfriend, Warren Dawson (Aaron Kincaid), joins Bentley's law practice as a junior partner.

The Gregg family dog is Jasper (who has a "girlfriend" named Sheila; Sheila is owned by Bentley's gorgeous neighbor, Phyllis Wentworth, played by Elaine Davis).

Peter, who attends night school to improve his knowledge of America, has dinner ready for the Greggs every night at 7:00. He calls Bentley "Mr. Gregg" and Kelly "Niece Kelly." Peter also has many relatives, two of whom appear several times: Grandpa Ling (Beal Wong), "a 70-year-old juvenile delinquent" who believes in the barter system and knows only three words of English—"Hello, Joe" and "Nice"—and Cousin Charlie Fong (Victor Sen Yung), "the beatnik of the family" and con artist whose schemes often backfire (when first introduced, the character was named Charlie Ling).

For unexplained reasons (perhaps because of network changes), Ginger has three last names: Farrell (1957–58), with a widowed mother named Louise (Catherine McLeod); Loomis (1958–61), with Whit Bissell and Florence Mac-Michael as her parents, Bert and Amy Loomis; and Mitchell (1961–62), with Evelyn Scott and Del Moore as her parents, Adelaide and Cal Mitchell.

Bentley Gregg had four secretaries throughout the series run: Vickie (J.D. Thompson in the pilot; Alice Backus for the series), Kitty Devereaux (Shirley Mitchell and Jane Nigh), Kitty Marsh (Sue Ane Langdon), and Connie (Sally Mansfield).

Relatives: Cherylene Lee (Peter's niece, *Blossom Lee*), Beulah Quo (Peter's aunt, *Rose*), Kristina Hanson (Ginger's cousin, *Norma*), Joan Vohs (Howard's sister, *Elaine*), David Lewis (Warren's father, *Horace Dawson*), Sheila Bromley (Warren's mother, *Myrtle Dawson*).

Theme: "Bachelor Father," by Johnny Williams.

Note: The original pilot, "New Girl in His Life," aired on "G.E. Theater" on 5/26/57 (the proposed series title at the time was "Uncle Bentley"). John Forsythe, Noreen Corcoran and Sammee Tong played the same roles.

38. *B.A.D. Cats*

ABC, 1/4/80 to 2/8/80

Nicholas ("Nick") Donovan (Asher Brauner), Ocee James (Steven Hanks) and Samantha ("Sunshine") Jensen (Michelle Pfeiffer) are undercover officers with the Burglary Auto Detail, Commerical Auto Thefts Division (B.A.D. Cats) of the Los Angeles Police Department. Nick and Ocee's car code is Cat-1 (also given as Stray Cat-1); Samantha's code is

Cat-2. Samantha resides at 701 Figueroa Street; Nick lives at 1324½ Los Palmas and Ocee has an apartment on Bergen Street. Nick's license plate reads 938 LYN. Ma's Place, a restaurant owned by Ma (LaWanda Page), is their favorite hangout. Eugene Nathan (Vic Morrow) is their stern captain. He has the nickname "Skip" and his license plate reads 264 PPA.

Barry DeVorzon composed the "B.A.D. Cats" theme.

39. *Bagdad Cafe*

CBS, 3/30/90 to 11/30/90

The Bagdad Cafe is a rundown diner, hotel and truck stop that makes up the one-building town of Bagdad in the Mojave Desert. It is run by a feisty woman named Brenda (Whoopi Goldberg). Brenda is divorced from Sal (Cleavon Little) and is the mother of two grown children: Debbie (Monica Calhoun) and Juney (Scott Lawrence).

Jasmine (Jean Stapleton) is a retired schoolteacher who left her husband after 25 years of marriage to become her own woman (she left her husband when their car stalled while crossing the desert. She took her bags, started walking and stumbled across the town. She befriended Brenda and now works as her helper in the diner).

Rooms at the hotel cost $25 a day, or $127 a week. Brenda, a former rodeo clown, was in labor for 96 hours with Debbie (who resides in Room 104; Brenda lives in Room 101). Jasmine, who lives in Room 102, was named "after my cousin Mildred. When Mildred was born she was going to be named Jasmine, but she looked more like a Mildred." The series is based on the feature film of the same title.

JeVetta Steele sings the theme, "Calling You."

40. *Banacek*

NBC, 9/13/72 to 9/3/74

Thomas Banacek (George Peppard) is a Boston-based freelance insurance company investigator who recovers lost or stolen objects for 10 percent of their insured value. He has a 66 percent success rate, and companies find that it is cheaper to hire Banacek than to assign their own agents to a case—"let's face it, he's good. And that 66 percent is better than we do."

Banacek's official business is restoring antiques (his one-man operation is called "T. Banacek—Restorations"). His research material is a paper called *The Assurance Reports*. The recovery and rewards section lists current and unsolved insurance company cases. If a case is more than 60 days old, it becomes public domain and anyone can attempt to solve it (these are the cases he likes to take); he can't, however, tackle other cases unless he is hired to do so.

Thomas's father was born in Warsaw, Poland, and was a

research scientist. He came to America and worked as a mathematician for an insurance company. After 20 years he was replaced by a computer. Because of this, Thomas will not work a nine to five job for any insurance company—"I don't work for anybody, I work for myself." When he is hired to solve a case, he gets, in addition to the 10 percent, $100 a day plus expenses. And what does he get if he can't solve a case—"I get a little bit older."

Banacek, who was born on Scully Square in Boston, has a saying for all occasions (for example, "There's an old Polish proverb that says, 'Only someone with nothing to be sorry about smiles at the rear of an elephant'").

Caroline Kirkland (Christine Belford), who prefers to be called "Carlie," works for the National Meridian Insurance Company (in the pilot) and the Boston Insurance Company (in the series) in the Property Recovery Division (the company is located on Government Square). Carlie, who was married for two years (1967–69), is determined to solve cases before Thomas does.

Felix Mulholland (Murray Matheson) is Banacek's friend and information man. He runs Mulholland's Book Store and considers himself very intelligent ("I'm a walking compendium of all man's knowledge").

Jay Drury (Ralph Manza) owns Jay's Executive Limo Service and works as Banacek's chauffeur. His real name is Dunicello, and he is thinking of legally changing his last name to Drury. Jay mentioned that his father was a music teacher.

The pilot episode aired on 3/20/72; Eliot Kaplan composed the theme.

41. *The Barbary Coast*

ABC, 9/8/75 to 1/9/76

The series is set in the 1880s. Cash Conover (Doug McClure) is a slick riverboat gambler. One night during a poker game in New Orleans, Cash accuses the governor's son of cheating. A duel to defend honor ensues, and Cash kills his opponent in self-defense. Fearing that he would never get a fair trial because he killed the governor's son, Cash flees to San Francisco to begin a new life. He wins the Golden Gate Casino in a card game and becomes the respected owner of the casino.

Jeff Cable (William Shatner), a California police officer, is recruited by the governor of California to battle the rising tide of crime. While looking through wanted posters, Jeff recognizes Cash as a man wanted for murder in Louisiana. But instead of turning Cash in, Jeff decides Cash is more important where he is and recruits Cash to help him. Jeff sets up headquarters in a secret room in the casino and spreads the word that criminals can find refuge at the Golden Gate. Stories chronicle Jeff's adventures as he and Cash battle crime on the notorious Barbary Coast.

A West Point graduate, Jeff uses various disguises to apprehend criminals. Cash knocks three times on wood for luck, and lives by his motto "Cash Makes No Enemies"

Bachelor Father. **Sammee Tong, John Forsythe and Noreen Corcoran.**

(meaning he pays cash for anything he wants; nobody knows for sure whether Cash is Conover's real name or his religion). Jeff's base of operations is a secret room behind the fireplace in Cash's office.

Flame (Bobbi Jordan) is the casino croupier; Moose Moran (Richard Kiel) is the bouncer; and Thumbs (David Turner) is the casino's piano player. Dennis Cole played Cash Conover in the pilot episode (5/4/75), and the series was originally called "Cash and Cable." John Andrew Tartaglia composed the theme, "The Barbary Coast."

42. *Bare Essence*

CBS, 10/4 and 10/5/82 (pilot)
NBC, 2/15/83 to 6/13/83

Patricia Louise ("Tyger") Hayes (Genie Francis) was six years old when her mother, Roberta ("Bobbi") Hayes (Linda Evans, then Jennifer O'Neill) left her and her father, Jack (not seen). Tyger cried so hard she had the hiccups for two days. When she went back to school, she told everyone that her mother had died. Jack, a low budget Hollywood horror film maker, raised Tyger alone. When Tyger graduated from high school, she enrolled at UCLA. She attended classes for four years but never graduated; the reason: assisting her father on such films as *Halloween Sorority Massacre, Flight Inferno, The Wolfman of Tucson* and *Scream Blood, Mama*. In 1982, when Tyger turned 21, Jack died from a heart attack.

At the funeral, Tyger is reunited with her estranged mother, now married for the fourth time and known as Lady Bobbi Rowan (she is considered one of the world's most beautiful women; Lord Rowan, from whom Bobbi is later divorced, is not seen). Bobbi extends an invitation to Tyger to visit her in New York (she lives in a brownstone on Gramercy Park).

Shortly after, Tyger learns that Kellerco, a low profile, privately owned New York conglomerate, had backed her

B.A.D. Cats. Steven Hanks, Michelle Pfeiffer and Asher Brauner.

father's films. Hoping to continue the project Jack started, Tyger decides to approach Kellerco.

Bobbi arranges for Tyger to meet the company owner, Hadden Marshall (John Dehner). Hadden tells her that the film has been declared a tax loss and he can do nothing to help her continue it. He does, however, offer her a job. "What can you do?" he asks. Tyger surprises him by her response: "I can drive a truck, an 18-wheeler; keep books— accurate too. Talk to teamsters and get them to do what I want; play poker and win. Work all night and the next day too. I'm a horse, I never get sick. I cook, simple food but good; and I can outtalk and outrun any sheriff in three Southern states." They shake hands. "Good grip," says Hadden. "Touch football," replies Tyger. "I always play quarterback."

Hadden then sets Tyger up with his grandson, Chase Marshall (Bruce Boxleitner, then Al Corley), a racing car driver whom Hadden has just made an executive in the hope of getting him into the business. When Tyger discovers that Kellerco is in financial trouble, she convinces Chase to begin a perfume company (at a low inventory and a 1,000 percent markup). Hadden advances them $250,000 to start the company. They hire Armand Habib (François-Marie Benard) of the DeHavilland Fragrances in Grosse, France, to create the new perfume.

"My mother always says women dress for other women, but I know they smell good for men," says Tyger as she samples the new perfume. "It's so basic, so primitive. It's breathtaking, romantic and personal. It's got to be . . . Bare Essence." With the Kellerco Perfume Company established, serial-like stories relate the power plays, love affairs and intrigues behind big business. (When Tyger first inhaled the new perfume, she called it "Sexy Smelly Good.")

Other Regulars: Ava Marshall (Lee Grant, then Jessica Walter), Chase's evil stepmother (married to his late father, Hugh) who seeks to destroy Tyger so her son, Marcus Marshall (Jonathan Frakes) can inherit the Marshall empire (the tension builds after Chase is killed in a racing car accident in Europe); Margaret Benedict (Susan French), Hadden's sister; Sean Benedict (Michael Woods), Margaret's son; and Kathy (Laura Bruneau), Hadden's granddaughter.

Theme: "In Finding You I Found Love," vocal by Sarah Vaughan.

43. *Baretta*

ABC, 1/17/75 to 6/1/78

Anthony ("Tony") Baretta (Robert Blake) is a police detective with the 53rd Precinct in an eastern city that is presumed to be in New Jersey. Tony's badge number is 609, and he drives a car called "The Blue Ghost" (license plate 532 BEN). He lives in Apartment 2-C of the King Edward Hotel and has a talented pet cockatoo named Fred (played by Lala), who likes a little nip now and then and thinks he is a chicken. Tony's best weapon against crime is his ability to go undercover as various characters. Billy Truman (Tom

Ewell) is his elderly friend, the house detective at the King Edward Hotel, and inspectors Shiller (Dana Elcar) and Hal Brubaker (Ed Grover) are Tony's superiors.

Sammy Davis, Jr., sings the theme, "Keep Your Eye on the Sparrow."

44. *Barney Miller*

ABC, 1/23/75 to 9/9/82

Captain Barney Miller (Hal Linden) is the chief of detectives of the 12th Precinct in New York's Greenwich Village. His squad: Sergeant Stan Wojehowicz (Max Gail), Sergeant Phil Fish (Abe Vigoda), Detective Chano Amengual (Gregory Sierra), Sergeant Nick Yemana (Jack Soo), Detective Ron Harris (Ron Glass), Sergeant Arthur Dietrich (Steve Landesberg) and Officer Carl Levitt (Ron Carey).

Bernard ("Barney") Miller first lived at 617 Chestnut Street in Manhattan with his wife, Elizabeth (Abby Dalton, then Barbara Barrie), their 21-year-old daughter, Rachel (Anne Wyndham), and their 12-year-old son, David (Michael Tessier). Elizabeth held a job as a social worker for the New York Department of Social Services, and when she and Barney separated, Barney moved to an apartment (Room 45) at the Hotel Greenwich.

Stanley ("Stan") Tadeusz Wojehowicz, called "Wojo" for short, lives in Apartment 12 of an unidentified building with a parrot named Crackers (for which he paid $225). It took him eight years to attain the rank of sergeant; he served with the Marines in Vietnam.

Arthur P. Dietrich, who was born 10/12/47 in St. Mary's Hospital in Allentown, Pennsylvania, said he had no idea what the *P* in his name stands for. He joined the ranks of the N.Y.P.D. on 11/2/73. In another episode, his birth year was given as 1943. His favorite comedy team is the Three Stooges.

Ronald ("Ron") Harris is the author of the novel *Blood on the Badge*. He refers to his book, which bore the working title *Precinct Diary,* as "B.O.B." It was released by Wainwright Publishers. Ron's great-grandfather, Ezekiel, ran a liquor store in Cleveland, Ohio. His great-great-great-great-great-grandfather was a commander of the Scottish Dragoons in fifteenth century Scotland. Ron's family crest is a bagpipe on a field of tweed. Ron paid $35 for the genealogical survey.

Carl Levitt was born in 1942 in New Brunswick, New Jersey; at age two, he and his parents moved to Rutherford, New Jersey. Nick Yemana was born in April in Omaha, Nebraska.

Other Roles: Detective Janet Wentworth (Linda Lavin), one of the few female detectives featured in the squad room; Frank Luger (James Gregory), the police inspector; and Arnold Ripner (Alex Henteloff), the rather disreputable lawyer.

The bulletin board at the 12th Precinct featured a photo of David Sylvan Fine. (He was one of several people charged with a bombing at the University of Wisconsin in Madison in which researcher Robert Fassnacht was killed. This really happened as part of the antiwar protests.) The legend NEVER GIVE A THIEF AN EVEN BREAK also appears on the bulletin board. One episode placed the often mentioned Bellevue Hospital at 27th Street and First Avenue (the actual address); corpses were often sent to Hubbard's Mortuary on 9th Street. In another episode, the names of two major companies were edited out just prior to air time. A prisoner, inquiring about the war in Vietnam, mentioned Dow Chemical and DuPont. ABC, afraid of angering sponsors, ordered their names deleted to avoid the possibility of lawsuits. The pilot, "The Life and Times of Captain Barney Miller," aired on ABC on 8/22/74.

"Who can fill a uniform out like no man can ... Who's the cop who makes traffic stop when she goes by ... My, oh my, Sergeant Ann..." These are the opening theme lyrics to an unsold female version of "Barney Miller" called "Ann in Blue" (ABC, 8/8/74). Penny Fuller was Ann Neal, a sergeant with the N.Y.P.D.'s 27th Precinct and head of a special squad of policewomen called the Neighborhood Police Team. Her squad: Officers Bea Russo (Mary Elaine Monte), Elizabeth Jensen (Mary-Beth Hurt) and Jessie Waters (Hattie Winston). "Ann in Blue" was made before "Barney Miller" and had the same production team (producer Danny Arnold; director Theodore J. Flicker; and musicians Jack Elliott and Allyn Ferguson, who composed both the "Ann in Blue" and "Barney Miller" themes).

See also "Fish," the "Barney Miller" spinoff series.

45. *Batman*

ABC, 1/12/66 to 3/14/68

Cast: Adam West *(Bruce Wayne/Batman)*, Burt Ward *(Dick Grayson/Robin)*, Yvonne Craig *(Barbara Gordon/Batgirl)*, Neil Hamilton *(Commissioner Gordon)*, Stafford Repp *(Chief O'Hara)*, Alan Napier *(Alfred)*, William Dozier *(Narrator)*.

Facts: Bruce Wayne is the ten-year-old son of millionaire Thomas Wayne and his wife, Martha. They live at Stately Wayne Manor in Gotham City. One summer night while walking home from a dinner party, Bruce and his parents are approached by a thief. A scuffle ensues when Thomas refuses to give the thief Martha's jewels. The thief shoots Thomas, then Martha. He is about to shoot Bruce when his gun jams. The sound of approaching police officers scares the thief off. Suddenly Bruce is orphaned—and determined to get even: "I swear by the spirits of my parents to avenge their deaths by spending the rest of my life fighting criminals. I will make war on crime!"

Backed by his family's vast wealth, Bruce works in almost total isolation to become a master scientist and to perfect his mental and physical skills. With the help of Alfred Pennyworth, the Wayne family butler (who now cares for Bruce), Bruce creates the world's greatest crime lab (later to be called the Batcave) beneath Wayne Manor.

Ten years later, on the anniversary of that tragic night, Bruce decides it is time for him to fulfill the promise he made. "I must have a disguise," he tells Alfred. "Criminals are a superstitious, cowardly lot. So my disguise must be able to strike terror in their hearts. I must be a creature of the night. Black, mysterious." Suddenly, Bruce and Alfred hear a noise at the window. They see a bat that has been attracted by the light. "That's it," Bruce says. "It's an omen; the perfect disguise. I shall become a bat!" Bruce then develops his costume, his special utility belt and the Batmobile. Soon Batman becomes a legend ("The Caped Crusader") and the police are quick to use his help to apprehend criminals.

Sometime later Bruce establishes the Wayne Foundation, an organization that sponsors worthwhile projects. One such project with which Bruce becomes involved is taking a group of orphans to the circus.

A high-wire act called the Flying Graysons is performing high above the ground without a net when the rope snaps. The ensuing fall kills the parents of young Dick Grayson. Batman investigates and discovers that racketeers sabotaged the rope to force the circus owner to pay protection money. Batman approaches Dick and tells him what has happened. He also tells him about the circumstances that led to his becoming a crime fighter. "If only I could do something like that," Dick says, "it will help avenge their deaths. Let me join you, please." "With your acrobatic skills plus what I could teach you, maybe you can make the grade," says Batman.

Bruce takes on the responsibility of raising Dick and eventually becomes his legal guardian. Dick perfects his mental and physical skills and adopts the alias of Robin, the Boy Wonder. The Dynamic Duo was thus born. (Robin attends Woodrow Roosevelt High School.)

When Barbara Gordon, the beautiful daughter of Police Commissioner Gordon, finishes college, she returns home and begins work at the Gotham City Library. Feeling the need to help her father battle crime, she adopts the disguise of Batgirl—and, though she usually operates independently of Batman and Robin, they form the Terrific Trio when working together.

At Wayne Manor, the button used to gain access to the Batcave is located in the bust of Shakespeare in Bruce's den. When the button is pressed, a secret entrance is revealed, and Bruce and Dick become Batman and Robin as they descend their respective Batpoles (when they ascend, they don their street clothes again). In the Batcave, located 14 miles from Gotham City, are various Batcomputers and the black with red trim Batmobile (license plate 2F 3567; later B-1), Batman and Robin's main mode of transportation. The Batmobile is powered by atomic batteries, uses turbines for speed, and has controls such as the Bat Ray Projector, a Bat Homing/Receiving Scope, the Bat Ram, the Bat Parachute (to stop the car at high speeds) and the start-decoy button (which fires rockets if an unauthorized person tries to start the car). Batman also has the Batcopter (I.D. number N3079; later N703) and the Batman Dummy Double (which Bruce stores in the Bat Dummy Closet). After an assignment, Alfred serves Bruce and Dick milk and sandwiches in the study (however, Bruce never mixes crime fighting with eating). According to the villain King Tut (a.k.a. William Omaha McElroy), there is a supply of Nilanium, the world's hardest metal (after it is refined), under the Batcave.

Barbara, who lives in midtown Gotham City in Apartment 8A (address not given) with her pet bird, Charlie, conceals her Batgirl costume in a secret closet behind her bedroom wall (she activates the wall with a hidden button on her vanity table). Her mode of transportation, the Batgirl Cycle, is hidden in a secret freight elevator in the back of her building.

Barbara is also the chairperson of the Gotham City Anti-Littering Committee. Her favorite opera is *The Marriage of Figaro*. Batgirl received the first Gotham City Female Crime Fighter and Fashion Award, "The Battie," for her crusade against crime in her sexy costume. In one episode, Batgirl rode Bruce's horse, Waynebow, in the Bruce Wayne Foundation Handicap. Millionaire Bruce Wayne, as he is called, has an office in the Wayne Foundation Building in downtown Gotham City; he is also the chairman of the Gotham City Boxing Commission. An attempt was made to spin "Batgirl" off into her own series, but only a short, unaired pilot was developed. In it, Barbara is still Commissioner Gordon's daughter and she still works as a librarian. Barbara has a secret room in the Gotham City Library that conceals her Batgirl costume (which she patterned after that of her idol, Batman). In addition to the Batgirl Cycle, Barbara has an electronic compact equipped with a deadly laser beam. As in the series, Batgirl disappears from the scene as mysteriously as she appeared. In the pilot story, Batgirl helps Batman and Robin defeat the evil Killer Moth and his Moth Men (who planned to kidnap Bruce's wealthy friend, Roger Montgross). There are no screen credits listed on the film; Adam West, Burt Ward and Neil Hamilton appeared in their "Batman" roles to help Yvonne Craig launch her own series. "Is the Dynamic Duo destined to become the Triumphant Trio? Only time will tell us more about this dazzling dare doll—Batgirl."

Gotham City's Police Commissioner Gordon has two means of contacting Batman: the red Bat Phone in his office, and the Bat Signal, which is flashed from the roof of city hall. Commissioner Gordon is assisted by Police Chief O'Hara (Stafford Repp; his catchphrase is "Saints preserve us," which he utters when a criminal is on the loose). Alfred answers the Wayne Mansion phone with "Stately Wayne Manor." He can contact Batman via his emergency Bat Buckle Signal Button (he also assists Batman in the field by donning various disguises). Batman wears a gray/black costume with a black cape and black hoodlike mask; Robin has a red and green costume with a gold cape and black mask; Batgirl wears a tight purple costume with a dark purple hoodlike mask and a gold and purple cape. She also wears a red wig to conceal Barbara's natural black hair. Bruce and Dick have spare costumes in their limo; Batman invented a dance called "The Batusi"; and Batman can't abide being called a coward. Robin's catchphrase is the word *Holy* followed by a term (for example, "Holy Crucial Moment" or "Holy Strawberries Batman, We're in a Jam"—the one phrase Burt Ward wanted to use but was never allowed to). The series is based on the comic by Bob Kane.

Principal Villains: The Joker (Cesar Romero), The Penguin (Burgess Meredith), Catwoman (Julie Newmar, Lee Meriwether and Eartha Kitt), The Riddler (Frank Gorshin and John Astin), Lola Lasagne (Ethel Merman), The Archer (Art Carney), Louie the Lilac (Milton Berle), King Tut (Victor Buono), The Siren (Joan Collins), Marsha, Queen of Diamonds (Carolyn Jones), Mr. Freeze (Eli Wallach, George Sanders and Otto Preminger), Minerva (Zsa Zsa Gabor), Egghead (Vincent Price), The Mad Hatter (David Wayne), The Clock King (Walter Slezak).

Themes: "Batman," by Neil Hefti; and "Batgirl," by Billy May and Wally Mack.

46. *Battlestar Galactica*

ABC, 9/17/78 to 4/20/79

Cast: Lorne Greene (*Adama*), Dirk Benedict (*Starbuck*), Richard Hatch (*Apollo*), Maren Jensen (*Athena*), Laurette Spang (*Cassiopea*), John Colicos (*Baltar*), Patrick Macnee (*Voice of Imperious Cylon Leader*).

Facts: In a galaxy far beyond our own, 12 colony planets evolved from a mother planet called Cobor: Aries, Taura, Gemins, Canca, Lea, Vargus, Libra, Scorpios, Sagitari, Caprica, Aquara and Picon (named after the signs of the zodiac). In this same galaxy, on the planet Cylon, the inhabitants (reptilian creatures) create a race of highly sophisticated robots, patterned after the human form, called Cylons. It is not explained how, but the live Cylon race died off, leaving the robots to live on and become a mortal threat to the 12 colony planets.

When the series begins, it is the seventh millennium of time. The Colonials (the inhabitants of the 12 planets) and the Cylons have been engaged in a thousand year war that erupted when the Imperious Leader of the Cylon Empire began the subjugation of the human race. The Cylons detest the human race and its principles of freedom and independence and the ability to resist repression. To them, it is an alien way of existing and can never be accepted. Although they are highly advanced and can function far better than any human, the Cylons operate by a programed code; they fear humans because they can do the unexpected.

In a final attempt to end the war, the Imperious Leader recruits Baltar, commander of the planet Vargus, with a promise to make him the leader of the entire human race once the Cylons conquer it. Baltar betrays the Colonials. He arranges a special meeting of the colony planet leaders, the Forum of the Twelve.

The leaders gather aboard the presidential battlestar ship, the *Atlantia*. The *Atlantia* is under heavy protection, with all the colony planet spaceships and battlestars surrounding it. As Baltar presents the Cylons' proposals to the forum (to surrender their weapons and live in peace), Adama, commander of the planet Caprica, becomes distrustful of Baltar. Adama, however, is unable to convince the other members of the forum.

Just as Adama returns to the command of his battlestar

Battlestar Galactica. Maren Jensen, Dirk Benedict, Richard Hatch and Lorne Greene.

ship, the *Galactica,* he receives reports of approaching Cylon warships. The Cylons' devious plan has been put into action: to attack both the star fleet ships and the unprotected colony planets. The humans launch a counterattack, but it is too late. The 1,000 Cylon ships destroy the *Atlantia* (Baltar escapes "just in time"), most of the colonial fighters—and the 12 home planets.

The *Galactica* is the only surviving battlestar ship, and only 67 star fighters remain intact. Adama returns to Caprica. As he surveys the destruction, he tells his sons, Starbuck and Apollo, that "we are going to fight back, but not here, not in this star system." As a group of survivors gathers around, Adama tells them, "Spread the word. Tell every man, woman and child to set sail on anything that will carry them." Within hours, 220 ships, representing every creed and color in the star system, band together to follow the *Galactica* to begin a new life.

On the *Galactica,* Adama, now the supreme ruler, tells his people that they have a chance for survival—on their thirteenth colony: "Our recorded history tells us that we descended from another civilization, a world outside of our civilization, a world called Earth." Stories follow the Colonials (also called Galacticans) on a hazardous journey across the universe, seeking to avoid the Cylons as they search for Earth.

Rising Star and *Colonial Movers* are two of the ships that follow the *Galactica.* Adama's shuttlecraft is *GAL 35*; his late wife (killed in the war but seen only in a photo) was named Lila.

Captain Apollo is Adama's first-born child and leader of the fighter squadron; Lieutenant Starbuck, Adama's second-born son, is an ace fighter pilot who is also a con artist, Romeo and gambler ("If there is a game going on, Starbuck will know about it"). They are both Colonial Warriors. Adama's youngest son, Zack, was killed in the initial battle; his beautiful daughter, Athena, now works by his side.

Cassiopea, whose name means "Fairy Queen," is Starbuck's romantic interest. She was a socialator (a high class call-girl) and objects to Starbuck's smoking cigars ("Do you have to smoke those weeds?"). Young Boxey (Noah Hathaway) and his mother (Jane Seymour) are two survivors who are now part of the *Galactica*'s crew; Boxey has a doglike drone called Muffet. Lieutenant Boomer (Herb Jefferson, Jr.), Flight Sergeant Jolly (Tony Swartz) and Colonel Tigh (Terry Carter) are the other crew members.

Cathy Pine is the voice of Cora, the *Galactica*'s computer; and Jonathan Harris supplies the voice for Lucifer, Baltar's Cylon aide.

The first planet the Colonials encountered was Carolon, which supplied them with a needed mineral called Tylium. Before the final war, trained Daggets stood watch for Colonial Warriors while they slept. A hand-held device called a Lanatran translates alien tongues into English for the Galacticans. "Alpha" is the code name used from Star Fighters to the *Galactica*. Laser torpedoes are the main defense weapons of Star Fighters and Interceptor ships.

Cylon warriors, named Raiders, pilot ships called Vipers. Baltar must now deliver the *Galactica* to the Imperioius Leader (portrayed by Dick Durock) or forfeit his life.

After many years in space, the *Galactica* reaches Earth in the year 1980. Thus was born the series "Galactica 1980" (ABC, 1/27/80 to 5/4/80). The Galacticans, are unable to land, however, fearing they will bring with them their enemies, the Cylons, and destruction. Stories focus on the Galacticans' attempts to advance Earth's technology to a point where the planet can fend off alien invaders; and on Galacticans Troy and Dillon, and a group of Galactican children who are sent to Earth as scouts to pave the way for the rest of the population to settle on the planet.

The plot was advanced by 30 years, and young Boxey is now the adult Troy. Lorne Greene (as Commander Adama) and Herb Jefferson, Jr. (as Colonel Boomer), reprised their roles. New to the cast were Kent McCord as Captain Troy; Barry Van Dyke as Lieutenant Dillon; Robbie Rist (later, Patrick Stuart) as Dr. Zee, the scientific genius; Robyn Douglass as Jamie Douglas, the United Broadcasting Company TV reporter who helps Troy and Dillon; and Allan Miller as Colonel Sydell, the Air Force agent seeking Troy and Dillon.

Tori Spelling, Georgi Irene, Lindsay Kennedy, Tracy Justrich, Jerry Supiran, Michael Larson and Jeff Cotler were among the actors playing the Galactican children.

Theme: "Galactica" (original series), by Glen A. Larson; "Galactica Song" (spinoff), by John Andrew Tartaglia.

47. *Baywatch*

NBC, 9/22/89 to 6/29/90
Syndicated, 9/23/91 to the present

Cast: David Hasselhoff *(Mitch Buchannon),* Shawn Weatherly *(Jill Riley),* Erika Eleniak *(Shauni McClain),* Parker Stevenson *(Craig Pomeroy),* Billy Warlock *(Eddie Kramer),* Nicole Eggert *(Summer Quinn),* Alexandra Paul *(Stephanie Holden),* David Charvet *(Matt Brody).*

Facts: Mitch Buchannon, Jill Riley, Shauni McClain, Craig Pomeroy and Eddie Kramer are Los Angeles County lifeguards stationed at Malibu Beach (also called Sunset Beach) in California. Their daily adventures as they patrol and protect the beach are the focal point of the series.

Mitch and Jill share Outpost Tower 27; 208 Lincoln is Mitch's mobile code, and 200T 456 is his license plate number. Mitch met his now ex-wife Gayle (Wendie Malick) when they were students at Palisades High School. When they broke up, Gayle burned Mitch's surfer dude cap; Mitch crushed Gayle's ceramic duck. Their son, Hobie (Brandon Call), lives with Mitch and has a dog named Rocky. Gayle now works as a restaurant consultant for Captain Cluck's Chicken and Fixin' franchieses in Columbus, Ohio. Amanda (Sherilyn Wolter) is Mitch's new romantic interest. Mitch and Gayle have an unseen uncle who lives at Loon Lake.

At age 15, Jill found a love for fishing. She would take a rowboat out on Lake Motawanakeg and read while fishing. Halfway through the book *Wuthering Heights,* she got a nibble, then a bite and reeled in a large striped bass—

which she gutted and ate for supper that night. As a lifeguard years later, Jill attempted to rescue some children during a shark sighting. She was attacked, lost a great deal of blood and suffered massive internal injuries. Jill was taken to Webster Memorial Hospital and received more than 200 stitches. She appeared to be recovering but later died from complications (a blood embolism). Jill never had the opportunity to finish reading *Wuthering Heights.*

Shauni, the daughter of wealthy parents, attended South Central High School and now lives at 3360 North Canyon Drive; she uses Bohemian Love sunblock lotion. Craig's favorite television show is "Sea Hunt." Eddie, who was born in Philadelphia, went through 17 foster families. He had a sister named Lonnie (who drowned in a swimming pool at age seven); during the great Los Angeles earthquake, Eddie delivered twins when he came across a woman in labor.

Captain Don Thorpe (Monte Markham) is the head of Baywatch (he was stationed in Tower 21 when he was a rookie). He ex-wife was named Doris; when she left him, he bought himself a red Miata sports car.

The radio call letters for Baywatch headquarters are KMF 295; Sam's Surf and Dive is the area beach store; Bucky's Ocean Grill is the hangout.

Holly Gagnier (series) and Gina Hecht (pilot) played Craig's wife, Gina; Pamela Bowen played Jill Riley in the original pilot ("Baywatch: Panic at Malibu Pier," NBC, 4/23/89).

New episodes were produced for syndication beginning in September of 1991. David Hasselhoff, Erika Eleniak, Billy Warlock and Monte Markham reprised their former roles. New to the cast were Richard Jaeckel as Lieutenant Ben Edwards and Jerry Jackson as Mitch's son, Hobie. Mitch, Shauni and Eddie are lifeguards with the Beach and Harbors Unit of the L.A. County Lifeguards. Mitch drives truck number 18903 (license plate 3E9 1063; later 4J06197); Shauni, now based in Tower 17, also pilots *Rescue Boat One.* Here, Shauni attended Valley High School (her parents gave her $50 for every *A* on her report card). Eddie, who has a dog named Buck, drives a patrol car with the I.D. number 48327; "Gilligan's Island" is his favorite television show. The Beach Hut is the local hangout (in some episodes it's Bruce's Beach Burgers: $3 for a regular hamburger; $3.75 for a cheeseburger). Santa Monica Bay is also mentioned as the beach they are patrolling. Wendie Malick recreated her role as Mitch's ex-wife, Gayle.

Additional changes occurred in second season syndicated episodes. Roberta ("Summer") Quinn is a beautiful lifeguard trainee who replaced Shauni when Shauni and Eddie married and moved to Australia to begin a family (Shauni discovered she was pregnant in the episode of 9/26/92, "River of No Return"). Summer, as Roberta likes to be called, was born in Pittsburgh; in the third episode, "Rookie of the Year" (10/10/92), Summer becomes a lifeguard at Baywatch (her greatest fear during training was diving off the 100-foot pier; she is assigned to Tower 26). Lifeguard trainee Matt Brody is also introduced in the "River of No Return" episode as Eddie's replacement and Summer's romantic interest (Matt won the "Rookie of the

Year" award and 853 DTS is his license plate number). Summer attends Malibu Beach High School.

Lieutenant Stephanie Holden replaced Don Thorpe (who received a promotion to captain) as the new head of Baywatch headquarters (in the episode of 10/3/92, "Tequila Bay"). Mitch remains the supervisor of beach operations (he is now in Tower 2 and his mobile code is KMF 295).

Stephanie shares a room with C.J. (Pamela Denise Anderson), a lifeguard who pilots the rescue boat *Lifeguard One* (her radio code is Rescue One). Stephanie appeared on the earlier NBC series as Mitch's girlfriend, a lifeguard at the time (Mitch walked into the men's locker room and saw Stephanie, who had mistaken it for the women's locker room, changing into her swimsuit. The two became friends and dated. When the relationship became serious, Stephanie broke it off by leaving Mitch. Stephanie was married and only separated from her husband).

Relatives: Susan Anton (Summer's mother, *Jackie Quinn*), Dirk Benedict (Matt's father, *Aaron Brody*), Josette Prevost (Matt's mother, *Vivian Brody*).

NBC Theme: "The Theme from Baywatch," vocal by Peter Catera.

Syndicated Theme: "I'm Always Here" (opening vocal by Jim Jamison); and "Current of Love" (closing vocal by David Hasselhoff).

48. *The Beany and Cecil Show*

ABC, 1/5/63 to 9/3/67

"So come on kids, let's flip our lids, higher than the moon, 'cause now it's Beany and Cecil in a whole half hour of Bob Clampett Cartoo-OOO-ooons." The *Leakin' Lena* is a one mast sailing ship captained by Horatio K. Huffenpuff, who has a trophy for being the world's greatest liar. His nephew, Beany, a freckle-faced young boy who wears a "Flip Lid Cap" (a cap with a propellor on top), and Cecil, the affectionate sea serpent who becomes seasick in wavy water, are the crew accompanying the intrepid explorer on various assignments (such as getting the spots off a leopard, and capturing Venus the Menace, the robot from Venus). Hindering their efforts is Dishonest John, "the do-badder who hates do-gooders." Voted "Villain of the Year" and famous for his catchphrase "Nya ha ha," D.J. (as he is often called) seeks to beat the captain to the fame and fortune that is associated with each assignment.

Cecil calls himself "tall, green and gruesome" and mentioned that Dinah Shore was his favorite television personality. "Beany Boy, Beany Boy's in trouble" was Cecil's cry, and "I'm coming, Beany Boy, I'm coming" was Cecil's reply when he rushed to Beany's aid. When Cecil finally saved Beany, he would say, "Hang on, Beany Boy," as they scrambled to escape. When Cecil discovered that Dishonest John was behind a scam, he would say, "D.J., you dirty guy." Beany called Horatio "Uncle Captain" and "Uncle Admiral Sir"; he called Cecil "Ceese." Cecil's song about

Beany went, "Beany Boy, you're my buddy through and through. I want you to know, wherever you go, I will stick with you."

Crowy is the *Leakin' Lena*'s lookout bird; Pop Gun is the old-time Western Indian fighter (he uses popguns and "is the best Indian fighter east and west of the Mr. and Mississippi River"); Cecelia McCoy, the she serpent, is the love of Cecil's life; Baby Ruth is Beany's girlfriend.

Bob Clampett (the creator) and Sody Clampett, Jim MacGeorge, Erv Shoemaker, Eddie Brandt and Mike Sweet are the voices for the characters; however, voice-character matchups are not given on the screen, in *TV Guide*, on press releases, or in any other known source.

Bob Clampett and Sody Clampett (his wife) composed the theme.

The Bob Clampett–created series actually began in 1950 as the syndicated "Time for Beany." Like the animated series, this version also dealt with the worldwide adventures of Beany, Cecil and Captain Huffenpuff. Beany and the captain were rubber hand puppets with immobile expressions (Beany always had a large smile; the captain was always jolly). Cecil was a cloth hand puppet; only his neck and head were seen, and his mouth moved when speaking. With the addition of clever dialogue, imaginative painted backgrounds and music and sound effects, a primitive but effective series was sustained for four years. The cast was credited verbally (with no matchups) as "starring Herb Shoemaker, Walker Edmiston, Jimmy MacGeorge and Bill Oberlon." Music and theme by Paul Sells.

The animated Beany and Cecil next appeared on "Matty's Funday Funnies" (ABC, 1/6/62 to 9/22/62). Beany, Cecil and Captain Huffenpuff set sail again on the *Leakin' Lena* on the short-lived animated version called "Beany and Cecil" (ABC, 9/10/88 to 10/8/88). Voices (not matched to characters) were by Billy West, Jim MacGeorge, Maurice LaMarche, Mark Hildreth, Cree Summer Francs and Laura Harris.

49. *Bearcats*

CBS, 9/16/71 to 12/30/71

The series is set in the Southwest in 1914. Hank Brackett (Rod Taylor) is a former army captain; Johnny Reach (Dennis Cole) was orphaned as a child and raised by the Chiricahua Apache Indians. They are now freelance troubleshooters who help people in desperate need. They drive a white Stutz Bearcat (license plate 4596 NYD), and their payment varies: they ask for a blank check and fill in the amount based on what they feel the case is worth. Fernando Raoul Estevan (Henry Darrow) is their friend, the head of the one-plane Mexican Air Force. The pilot film, "Powderkeg," aired on CBS on 4/16/71.

John Andrew Tartaglia composed the theme, "The Bearcats."

50. *Beauty and the Beast*

CBS, 9/25/87 to 8/4/90

Cast: Ron Perlman *(Vincent)*, Linda Hamilton *(Catherine Chandler)*, Roy Dotrice *(Father)*, Jo Anderson *(Diana Bennett)*.

Facts: In the 1950s, Dr. Jacob Wells (I.D. number 1-7), was a scientist with the Chittenden Research Institute in New York City. When Jacob questioned the Atomic Energy Commission about its activities (he called for the abolition of atomic weapons), he was blacklisted by the House Un-American Activities Committee in November 1952. At this time Jacob was married to a woman named Margaret Chase (Diana Douglas), but the marriage ended when her father had it annulled. Shortly thereafter, Jacob fled to a forgotten subterranean world beneath New York's subways and became "Father," the leader of a group of misfits who are living there. Sometime later, Father finds an abandoned infant in front of St. Vincent's Hospital. The misfit baby, whom he names Vincent, grows to become the beast of the series title.

Vincent's world is mysterious and beautiful, untouched by the crime of the big city. Its tunnels lead to all areas of the city, allowing access to the outside world. The most dangerous part of the city for these people is Prince Street on Manhattan's Lower East Side; there are only two tunnels in this area and they are rarely used. The people live as one, looking to Father for leadership and keeping in constant communication with each other by tapping on the main pipes that run throughout the underworld city.

Beauty is Catherine Chandler, a woman who was mistaken by thugs for someone else and brutally beaten and slashed across the face. Her body is dumped on the street, and she is left for dead. She is found by Vincent, who takes her to his world. There, she is saved by Father. Before she leaves, Catherine promises Vincent that she will keep his world a secret.

Plastic surgery restores Catherine's scarred face to normal, and she takes a job with the D.A.'s office to battle crime. She has the secret help of Vincent, who can sense when she is in danger (and, via the tunnels, comes to her aid). (Although Catherine was left with a large scar on the right side of her chin and neck following the surgery, it is "mysteriously" healed in some episodes but not in others.)

Catherine, who is 30 years old, lives in Apartment 21E off Central Park West (her license plate reads CLO 426). Catherine previously worked for her father, Charles Chandler (John McMartin), the owner of a law firm. The only time Vincent can roam freely is on Halloween. Elliott Burch (Edward Albert), the owner of the Burch Development Corporation, threatened to destroy Vincent's world when he planned to build Burch Towers, a 152 story, three billion dollar skyscraper. (The blasting would have destroyed the underworld city. Catherine exposed Burch as a crook, and the project was canceled.) The underworld people have contacts in the above-world who are called Helpers. Vincent was touched by the writings of Bridget O'Donnell (Caitlin

O'Heaney), whose books helped him "through dark times" and made him think. Vincent's face is described as "a mask of a cat's face with long hair." Paracelsus (Tony Jay), who helped Father establish the city, is now an enemy of Vincent's. Paracelsus tried to control the people for his own evil purposes and was banished by Father. He now seeks to regain his world by killing Vincent and destroying Father.

In the episode of 12/12/89 ("Though Lovers Be Lost"), Catherine, pregnant by Vincent and about to give birth, is kidnapped by Gabriel (Stephen McHattie), a tycoon who heads a criminal empire. Shortly after Catherine gives birth to a boy, Gabriel orders Catherine to be killed by a drug overdose. Catherine's death enrages Vincent, who vows to find his son and destroy Gabriel.

While investigating Catherine's death, detective Diana Bennett comes to know and help Vincent in his quest. In the last episode, Diana confronts Gabriel and shoots him dead at point-blank range. Though technically unjustified, it was Diana's way of releasing the anger and hatred she felt for what Gabriel did to Vincent. When Vincent is reunited with his son, he names him Jacob.

Flashbacks: Kelly Kehoe *(young Catherine)*, Caryn West *(Catherine's mother)*.

Theme: "Beauty and the Beast," by Lee Holdridge.

51. *Benson*

ABC, 9/13/79 to 8/30/86

Benson DuBois (Robert Guillaume) first appeared on the television series "Soap" (ABC, 1977–81) as butler to the wealthy Tate family. When her cousin, Gene Gatling (James Noble) is elected governor of Capitol City, Jessica Tate (Katherine Helmond) loans him Benson to help him organize his household. Gene, a paper mill industrialist who entered politics to give people an honest government, is incapable of running the government; Benson soon becomes indispensable when his suggestions help Gene attain his goal. Benson leaves the Tate household and takes up permanent residence in Capitol City. Stories relate his misadventures as the governor's aide.

As the series progressed, Benson became the budget director, then Gene's executive secretary and finally the lieutenant governor. When the state instituted its first Lotto game, Benson won $50,000 with the ticket number 000-0051. His fondest memory of Christmas at home was the smell of caramel swirl coffee cake freshly baked by his mother.

Gene, who resides in the governor's mansion in Lawrence County, is six feet three inches tall, loves fishing, is a Sagittarius and a widower. He attended Crandall High School and at age 14 entered his first log rolling competition. He took his sister to the prom two years in a row and is famous for his "Bunkhouse Biscuits" (which he made when he worked in the mill). Gene gives Benson a wallet for Christmas.

Kathryn ("Katie") Gatling (Missy Gold) is Gene's

daughter (nine years old when the series begins). She first attended Capitol City Grammar School (where she played cello in the school orchestra) and later Crandall High. Benson calls her "Sugar" and she is a member of the Capitol City Girls' Softball League. Katie's favorite part of Christmas is picking out the tree with Benson.

Gretchen Krauss (Inga Swenson) is the head of household affairs and Benson's nemesis (she and Benson just don't get along). She was born in Bulgaria and came to America when she was a young girl.

Marcie Hill (Caroline McWilliams) is Gene's secretary; she married Dan Slater (Ted Danson) on 2/20/81 and was replaced by Denise Stevens (Didi Conn). Denise married Peter Downey (Ethan Phillips), Gene's press secretary, on 9/16/83. Peter attended forestry school before his current job. He eats at Fatso's, a hamburger joint, and works out at Morry's Gym. Denise calls him "Bunny Wabbitt Face."

Clayton Endicott (René Auberjonois) is Gene's right-hand man, the chief of staff; he is a member of the indoor polo team.

The motto of the state is "If it's not broken, don't fix it." In the 1984 Christmas episode, Benson is injured in an accident and has an out-of-body experience. He envisioned what life would be like in 1991: Katie is a Madonna-like sexpot who dropped out of college to marry a football player named Lunkhead; they divorced 25 weeks later. Gretchen is now a bag lady and is called "Miss Nuts and Fruit Cake"—"She got off at the wrong exit on the interstate of life and sells nuts, fruit cakes and Christmas candy door to door."

Clayton is the state's mean governor and Gene is now his butler. Without Benson to keep him in check, Clayton lost all sense of human kindness. And, without Benson to watch out for Gene, his political enemies impeached him and removed him from office. Clayton, elected the new governor, felt sorry for Gene and made him his personal valet.

Relatives: Beah Richards (Benson's mother, *Lois DuBois*), Tim Reid (Benson's brother, *Russell DuBois*), Kene Holliday (Benson's brother, *Earl DuBois*), Keenen Ivory Wayans (Benson's nephew, *Chester*), Helen Martin (Benson's aunt, *Lil*), Julius Harris (Benson's uncle, *Buster*), Vernee Watson (Benson's sister, *Elaine DuBois*), Alva Petway (Benson's cousin, *Saundra*), Dorothy Green (Gene's sister, *Libby*), Sandy McPeak (Gene's brother, *Jack Gatling*), Tracey Gold (Katie's cousin, *Laura*), Stephen Elliott (Clayton's father, *Whitney Endicott*), Billie Bird (Clayton's mother, *Harriett Endicott*), Ernestine Mercer (Clayton's aunt, *Carney*), Allyn Ann McLerie (Marcie's mother, *Mrs. Hill*), Sudie Bond (Gretchen's mother, *Fritzie Krauss*).

Theme: "Benson," by George Aliceson Tipton.

52. *Best of the West*

ABC, 9/10/81 to 2/26/82

During the Civil War, Union captain Samuel ("Sam") Best (Joel Higgins) meets Southern belle Elvira Devereaux

Benson. Back, left to right: Caroline McWilliams, James Noble, René Auberjonois. Front, left to right: Ethan Phillips, Robert Guillaume, Inga Swenson and Missy Gold.

Ad for *Best of the West*. Seated, left to right: Valri Bromfield, Meeno Peluce, Carlene Watkins. Back, left to right: Leonard Frey, Tracey Walter, Joel Higgins, Tom Ewell.

(Carlene Watkins) when his troops begin burning her father's Georgia plantation. Though it appears to be an unlikely match, Sam, a widower and the father of ten-year-old Daniel (Meeno Peluce), and Elvira marry shortly after. With a dream of beginning a new life out West, the Bests move from their home in Philadelphia to Copper Creek, Montana, to become shopkeepers. Shortly after Sam opens the Copper Creek General Store, he is elected marshal when he stands up to a feared gunfighter named the Calico Kid (Christopher Lloyd). Stories relate Sam's fumbling attempts to uphold the law.

The Montana Overland Stage Lines services the area. Sam was on the regimental boxing team in the army. Because of his moves in the ring, he was called "The Dancer" (he also lost the only three fights he had). Since Sam has been marshal, he has only shot himself once. Sam sort of stumbles upon crimes and solves them by accident. He and his family live in a small, freezing-in-the-winter, hot-in-the-summer cabin and seem to enjoy life out West. Daniel attends the Copper Creek School.

Parker Tillman (Leonard Frey) is the crooked owner of the town. He runs his business empire from the Square Deal Saloon and is assisted by the dim-witted Frog Rothchild, Jr. (Tracey Walter). Parker, considered "a crook, liar and a cheat" by the citizens, also runs the First Bank of Copper Creek from the back of the saloon (Frog is the teller; "a free, complimentary soup bone" is given to new depositors).

Jerome ("Doc") Kullens (Tom Ewell) is the intoxicated, elderly town doctor. Doc can't shoot straight, can barely see and has "the shakes in both hands." He doesn't ride with posses because "I better stay here in case someone needs surgery." Laney Gibbs (Valri Bromfield) is a fur trapper who assists Sam as a deputy when she is needed.

Andy Griffith and Eve Brent Ashe played Elvira's parents, Lamont and Lily Devereaux.

Rex Allen performs the theme, "Best of the West."

53. *The Betty Hutton Show*

CBS, 10/1/59 to 6/30/60

Goldie Appleby (Betty Hutton) is a onetime vivacious showgirl turned manicurist. She lives with her two best friends, Lorna Peterson (Joan Shawlee) and Rosemary Zandt (Jean Carson) in Apartment 18A at 346 West 41st Street in Manhattan. One day, Goldie accepts a dinner invitation from a lonely but wealthy customer named Mr. Strickland (David White). Later that night, Strickland's sudden death makes her the beneficiary of his will, the head of the $60 million Strickland estate and guardian of his three orphaned children: Patricia (Gigi Perreau), Nicky (Richard Miles) and Roy (Dennis Joel).

Goldie relinquishes her job and her apartment and moves to the Strickland duplex on Park Avenue to become the children's guardian. Stories follow Goldie's misadventures as

she struggles to run the foundation and care for and secure the affections of the spendthrift Strickland children.

As middle child Roy put it, Goldie was "buttons and bows" when she first arrived. She refined her wardrobe and her style; she is now "wow" according to Roy. Roy, as Goldie says, "is the Adolphe Menjou of the grade school set." He is the intellectual of the family, always dressed in a suit, very well mannered, and he seems more like a distinguished gentleman of 50 rather than a boy of 12. Goldie and Roy are close and, despite their age difference, Goldie turns to Roy for help and advice.

Patricia, who attends the Blair Academy for Girls, is the oldest child (17) and is struggling to become part of the society circle that members of her family are meant to be a part of; Nicky, the youngest, attends an unnamed grammar school.

A second storyline follows Goldie's misadventures with Lorna and Rosemary. Rosemary works at the Pelican Club in Manhattan; Lorna is a beautician at the Mid Manhattan Salon. While the girls are the best of friends, they constantly bicker (as Goldie says, "Why do they keep Indians on reservations and let nuts like you run around loose?"). Rosemary is somewhat flakey and likes to spend money; the problem is, she never has any. Lorna says, "Somewhere there is a light burning in a nuthouse. Rosemary, why don't you go home?" Lorna, on the other hand is cheap—"She is tighter than Jayne Mansfield would look in Gary Cooper's sweater," says Goldie. On Goldie's birthday, Rosemary treats the girls to a night on the town; on Lorna's birthday, Goldie treats; on Rosemary's birthday, Lorna treats—a tradition that causes problems since Lorna always seeks the cheapest way out.

Goldie's catchphrase is "Cu-cu," which she says when something strikes her fancy. In the episode "Jenny," Betty Hutton's real life daughter, Candy Briskin, appeared in a story about Goldie's efforts to unite a girl named Jenny with her mother. The series is also known as "Goldie."

Jerry Fielding composed the theme.

A similar pilot appeared on NBC on 8/7/56. In "Carolyn," Celeste Holm played Carolyn Daniels, an actress who becomes the guardian of three children when her best friend is killed in an accident. Patricia Morrow (as Elizabeth), Susan Hawkins (Candy) and Jimmy Hawkins (Buster) were the children.

54. *The Beverly Hillbillies*

CBS, 9/26/62 to 9/7/71

Cast: Buddy Ebsen *(Jed Clampett)*, Irene Ryan *(Granny)*, Donna Douglas *(Elly Mae Clampett)*, Max Baer, Jr. *(Jethro Bodine)*, Raymond Bailey *(Milburn Drysdale)*, Nancy Kulp *(Jane Hathaway)*.

Facts: In the Ozark community of Sibly stands a rural cabin near Blueberry Ridge. The cabin is owned by Jed Clampett, a widower, who lives there with his daughter,

The Beverly Hillbillies. **Donna Douglas and Buddy Ebsen (front), Irene Ryan and Max Baer, Jr. (back).**

Elly Mae, and his mother-in-law, Daisy ("Granny") Moses. They are eight miles from their nearest neighbor and are overrun with skunks, possums, bobcats and coyotes. They use kerosene lamps for light and cook on a wood-burning stove. They drink homemade moonshine and wash with Granny's homemade lye soap. The bathroom is 50 feet from the house.

One day, while hunting for food, Jed misses his target, and the bullet strikes the ground near their swamp. Oil sprouts from the ground, but Jed sees this as only another headache to contend with. Shortly after, a wildcatter for the O.K. Oil Company spots the oil and notifies his superiors in Tulsa. John Brewster (Frank Wilcox), the company head, purchases the swamp from Jed for $25 million—a situation that doesn't seem to please Jed as he has never heard of a "million" dollars.

When Pearl Bodine, Jed's cousin, hears that Jed sold the swamp, she tells him that he is the richest man in the hills and should live the life of a millionaire. She convinces him that Beverly Hills is the place to be (Jed likes the thought of "hills"). Jed's money is deposited in the Commerce Bank of Beverly Hills, and the bank president, Milburn Drysdale, purchases the mansion next to his for the Clampetts. With help from Jethro, Pearl's son, and a loan of Pearl's 1920 Oldsmobile truck, Jed, Elly Mae, Granny and Jethro head for "the hills of Beverly Hills," and stories relate the misadventures of the family as they struggle to adjust to a world in which they are totally out of place.

Jed, who dresses as he did in the hills, has a bloodhound named Duke and longs for "the life of luxury" he once enjoyed. Through investments Jed also owns the Mammoth Film Studios in Hollywood. Jed's catchphrase is "Well Doggies," which he says when something tickles his fancy.

Elly Mae, who has a fondness for "critters," has a rooster named Earl (who knows only one trick—playing dead) and two monkeys named Skipper and Bessie (sometimes called Beth). When she was age 12 "the boys came a courtin' and Elly Mae whopped the tar out of 'em." She grew up "wild like a cougar" and wrestles, hunt and fights with bobcats ("who go limpin' off"). She also grew into a very beautiful, well-developed woman—so much woman that Granny wishes she would stop wearing men's clothes ("She done popped another button off her shirt") and "act like the female woman she is." She calls Jed "Paw."

The not too bright Jethro, born on December 4, "was educated and graduated from the sixth grade." He is the only one who delights in the excitement of the big city and is forever trying to attract the opposite sex "and find me a sweetheart."

Granny, who won the "Miss Good Sport Award" at the Bugtussle Bathing Beauty Contest at Expo 1897, has an all-around cure for what ails you called Granny's Spring Tonic. She still practices her mountain doctoring, but complains that she can't make her lye soap (the process pollutes the air) or find needed cooking ingredients (such as possum innards) in the local stores. Granny had a still in the hills, and her unseen cousin, Homer Gribble, painted the Burma Shave signs in Bugtussle (a community in Pike County); he also composed the slogans (for example, "When your beard is stiff and bristly, shave every morning and every night").

The 32-room, 14-bathroom Clampett mansion is located at 518 Crestview Drive. It was said that actor John Barrymore built it. (According to *USA Today* on 1/5/87, the actual mansion used in the series belonged to Arnold Kirkeby, who bought it shortly after it was built in 1933. It was sold to television executive Jerry Perenchio in 1987.)

The original, unaired pilot version of the series was called "The Hillbillies of Beverly Hills." The cast was the same, but the music (uncredited) was different (no singing and a

different tune). The storyline differed in that Jed and his family knew about the oil in their swamp (the hunting aspect was not used) and considered it a nuisance. Jed sold the swamp (which they called a slough) just to rid himself of a headache. The only other change was the name of the bank Milburn Drysdale heads; it was called the Beverly Hills Bank. When the Clampetts first saw their new home, they thought it was a prison; they called the swimming pool in the backyard "the cement pond" (they thought the steps leading to the water were for the wildlife to use when they came down from the hills for a drink).

Relatives: Bea Benaderet (Jethro's mother, *Pearl Bodine*), Max Baer, Jr. (Jethro's sister, *Jethrene Bodine*; voice by Linda Kaye Henning), Roy Clark (Jed's cousin, *Roy*), Harriet MacGibbon (Milburn's wife, *Margaret Drysdale*; she has a pampered poodle named Claude—who is "married" to a poodle named Fifi), Louis Nye (Milburn's son, *Sonny Drysdale*, "a professional student"; he has been in college for 19 years), Charlie Ruggles (Margaret's father, *Lowell Reddinggs Farquhar*), Eddy Eccles (Milburn's nephew, *Milby Drysdale*).

Theme: "The Ballad of Jed Clampett," vocal by Jerry Scoggins.

Note: In the television movie *The Return of the Beverly Hillbillies* (CBS, 10/6/81), Jed has moved back to Sibly, Elly Mae has opened Elly's Zoo and Jethro now runs Mammoth Studios in Hollywood.

55. *Beverly Hills, 90210*

Fox, 10/4/90 to the present

Cast: Shannen Doherty *(Brenda Walsh)*, Jason Priestley *(Brandon Walsh)*, Carol Potter *(Cindy Walsh)*, James Eckhouse *(Jim Walsh)*, Jennie Garth *(Kelly Taylor)*, Tori Spelling *(Donna Martin)*, Gabrielle Carteris *(Andrea Zuckerman)*, Luke Perry *(Dylan McKay)*.

Facts: Brenda and Brandon Walsh are 16-year-old fraternal twins who lived with their parents, Cindy and Jim Walsh, at 1408 Walnut Avenue in Minneapolis, Minnesota 55348. They enjoyed a simple life and had few problems. They were both straight *A* students and enjoyed hiking around nearby Gull Lake. Brenda was a member of the drama club and the student council. Brandon, called "Mr. Popularity," was a writer for the school newspaper and a member of the swim team. But that was then. The address 933 Hillcrest Drive, Beverly Hills, California 90210, is now—a total change in lifestyle when Jim, an accountant with the firm of Powell, Gaines and Yellin, is transferred to the West Coast office and the family is forced to relocate. Brenda and Brandon's experiences at West Beverly Hills High School and their efforts to become part of "the in crowd" are the focal point of the series.

Brenda is four minutes older than Brandon. Brenda is beautiful "but not California beautiful," and she desperately wants to be like her girlfriends Kelly and Donna—blondes who are popular and rich and fit her image of "the

California girl." As the series progressed, Brenda learned to accept herself. As for clothes, she "tries to make for free what the trendy stores sell for $150."

"Keep It Together" is Brenda's favorite television show. She has a porcelain doll collection and uses Colgate brand toothpaste. Brenda is scared to death of heights and is totally honest. (For example, when Brenda was a kid, her mother took her to St. Paul to buy toys. When they got home, Brenda realized they had forgotten to pay for a Barbie doll. Brenda made her mother return to the store to pay for the doll.)

As a kid Brenda rode a horse called Sylvester. When she was thrown and was scared to ride again, her father bought her a plush horse she named Mr. Pony (Brenda also had a plush lion she called Mr. Lion). Brenda had four dogs: Ruby (who was untrainable), Bruno (who bit the mailman), Mr. Pepper (who froze to death; Brenda was nine years old "and how was I suppose to know about wind chill factors?"), and Wally (a stray she adopted). Brenda played Juliet in her seventh grade production of *Romeo and Juliet.* In the fifteenth annual West Beverly High Mother-Daughter Fashion Show, Brenda and Cindy modeled evening wear designed by Furley.

Brandon has a Godzilla alarm clock, is a member of the school's newspaper staff (he is sports editor in second season episodes) and drives a car with the license plate 258 VUB (he later has a '65 yellow Mustang with the plate 2BR1-645). He works as a waiter in a diner called the Peach Pit and has ambitions of becoming a writer. Even though Brenda yearns to be an actress, Brandon's good looks landed him a role on the television soap "Keep It Together" (when Brenda filled in for him at the Peach Pit, she worked as a waitress she called "Laverne"). Brandon also worked as a cabana boy at the Beverly Hills Beach Club during the summer of 1991 (in Minnesota, he was a lifeguard at the community swimming pool).

Cindy and Jim met in college (University of Minnesota) and married shortly after (they have been married 17 years when the series begins). Jim worked for the *Literary Journal* at school before he became an accountant. Cindy worked "at my mom's store in Minneapolis" (her own words; store name not mentioned). She loves gardening and now works as a freelance landscaper. Her license plate reads 2GEE645. Jim calls Brenda "Beautiful" and Brandon "Big Guy."

Kelly Taylor is beautiful, style-conscious and a sun worshiper. She is a rich, spoiled girl who has been called "The Rich Bitch" by some of the boys she has dated. Max is the name of her dog, and her license plate reads 2ABM 543. At the 1991 Junior Prom Spring Dance, Kelly was voted Spring Queen. She is forced to play parent to her divorced, man-hungry mother, whose questionable moral practices she sometimes finds herself copying. Kelly and Brenda take exercise classes at Bob Silvers World.

Donna Martin is tall, pretty and bright but suffers from a learning disability that makes it extremely difficult for her to score well on written exams under pressure. Her favorite movie is *Pretty Woman,* and her fantasy (from the film) is "to run away, become a hooker and meet Richard Gere on Hollywood Boulevard." Donna was born on 12/25/74 and has an account at the National Bank of the West.

Andrea Zuckerman is the editor of the school newspaper, the *Blaze,* and Brandon's on-and-off girlfriend. She and Brenda are also volunteers for the Rap Line (to help troubled teens) of the local social services center. She is a Woody Allen film buff and from a poor family (she lives in the Valley and outside the school district; she lies about where she lives so she can attend West Beverly High and takes advantage of its programs). Andrea is the classic overachiever; she mentioned her mother's name as being Beverly.

Dylan McKay is Brenda's boyfriend. He has a Porsche Speedster (license plate 200T 458) and is a recovering alcoholic. He is a sensitive and misunderstood surfer who is rejected by his parents (his father is in jail for business fraud; his mother lives in Hawaii).

Other Regulars: Steve Sanders (Ian Ziering) is a student whose mother, Samantha Sanders, stars in the television series "The Hartley House" (where she plays Mary Jo Hartley, the mother of three children). Steve was adopted by Samatha; he was born in Albuquerque, New Mexico, and his natural mother, who is now deceased, was named Karen Brown. Steve was born on 5/15/74, and he drives a car with the license plate 18A 4RE. David Silver (Brian Austin Green) is the school D.J. (station KWBH) and the video yearbook cameraman.

Emily Valentine (Christine Elise) is Brandon's girlfriend in the second season episodes. She attends West Beverly High and caused their relationship to end when she slipped Brandon the drug Euphorium against his wishes.

The local hangout is the Peach Pit, a diner run by Nat (Joe E. Tata). It is located on the corner of Olympic and Larabee streets, and many famous Hollywood stars have been its customers (for example, Marilyn Monroe, Steve McQueen and Montgomery Clift). Nat named a milkshake after Brenda. The series was originally called "Class of Beverly Hills" and is also known as "90210."

Relatives: Ann Gillespie (Kelly's mother, *Jackie Taylor*), Christine Belford (Steve's mother, *Samantha Sanders*), Stephanie Beacham (Dylan's mother, *Iris McKay*), Gordon Currie (Brenda's cousin, *Bobby Walsh*), Matthew Laurance (David's father, *Mel Silver*), Katherine Cannon (Donna's mother, *Felice Martin*). David's father, a dentist at the Reston Medical Center, married Kelly's mother.

Theme: "Beverly Hills, 90210," by John E. Davis.

56. *Bewitched*

ABC, 9/17/64 to 7/1/72

Cast: Elizabeth Montgomery *(Samantha Stephens)*, Dick York and Dick Sargent *(Darrin Stephens)*, Agnes Moorehead *(Endora)*, Maurice Evans *(Maurice)*, David White *(Larry Tate)*.

Facts: A beautiful witch (Samantha) and a mortal (Darrin Stephens) accidentally meet on several occasions by bumping into each other. They feel an attraction to each other and begin dating. Soon they fall in love and marry.

They buy a home from the Hopkins Realty Company and set up housekeeping at 1164 Morning Glory Circle in Westport, Connecticut (their address is also given as 164 Morning Glory Circle); 555-2134 is their phone number. Trash pickups are on Tuesdays and Fridays.

Darrin, whose license plate reads 4R6-558, works as an account executive for the McMann and Tate Advertising Agency in Manhattan (his office phone number is 555-6059).

Samantha, who can have anything she desires by twitching her nose and invoking her powers, has agreed to live by Darrin's rules and not use witchcraft (when Sam, as Darrin calls her, does use her powers, it upsets Darrin; to find comfort, he drowns his sorrows at Joe's Bar and Grill).

This agreement has upset the Witches' Council and Samantha's mother, Endora (who is 118 pounds, five feet six inches tall). Endora is a powerful witch and unable to accept her daughter's reasoning—or understand why she married Darrin (whom she most often calls "Durwood" and "Dum Dum"). When Darrin first met Endora, he asked, "Mrs. . . . ?" Endora responded with the reason why no last name is given: "You'd never be able to pronounce it."

Samantha's father, Maurice, a distinguished warlock, accepts Darrin and often sides with Samantha when Endora puts up a fuss. Maurice is a member of the Warlock Club and a fan of the Bard, forever quoting from Shakespeare. He calls Darrin "Dobbin," "Duspin," "Dustin" and "Duncan." When Samantha has a craving for food, she must have ringtail pheasant to satisfy herself.

Tabitha (Erin and Diane Murphy) and Adam (David and Greg Lawrence) are Samantha and Darrin's children, also a witch and a warlock. When Tabitha was born, 1/13/66, no credit was listed; that episode also marked the first appearance of Samantha's beautiful "Goddess of Love" cousin, the mischievous Serena (Elizabeth Montgomery, who played the role, originally received no credit; she later used the name Pandora Spocks). Serena is a member of the Cosmos Club and entertainment chairwoman of the Cosmos Cotillion. She wrote a song called "I'll Blow Kisses in the Wind" and calls Darrin's gray haired boss, Larry Tate, "Peter Cotton Top."

Abner Kravitz (George Tobias) and his nosy wife, Gladys (Alice Pearce and Sandra Gould) are the Stephens' neighbors. Dr. Bombay (Bernard Fox), the nurse-chasing warlock, is Samantha's somewhat wacky family physician (whom Darrin calls a "witch doctor").

Relatives: Marion Lorne (Samantha's aunt, *Clara*, who is famous for her doorknob collection), Paul Lynde (Sam's uncle, *Arthur*, who loves practical jokes), Ysabel MacCloskey and Reta Shaw (Sam's aunt, *Hagatha*), Estelle Winwood (Sam's aunt, *Enchantra*), Jane Connell (Sam's aunt, *Hepzibah*), Arte Johnson (Sam's cousin, *Edgar*), Steve Franken (Sam's cousin, *Henry*), Robert F. Simon and Roy Roberts (Darrin's father, *Frank Stephens*), Mabel Albertson (Darrin's mother, *Phyllis Stephens*), Louise Glenn (Darrin's cousin, *Helen*), Irene Vernon and Kasey Rogers (Larry's wife, *Louise Tate*), Mitchell Silberman (Larry's son, *John Tate*), Mary Grace Canfield (Abner's sister, *Harriet*), Ricky Powell (Gladys's nephew, *Sidney*). Darrin mentioned he had an Aunt Madge who believes she is a lighthouse.

Theme: "Bewitched," by Howard Greenfield and Jack Keller.

Spinoffs: "Tabitha." On 4/24/76, ABC presented the first pilot, with Liberty Williams as Tabitha Stephens, now a beautiful 24-year-old witch and an editorial assistant at San Francisco's fashionable *Trend* magazine. Bruce Kimmel played her warlock brother, Adam; Barbara Cason was Tabitha's editor, Roberta. The second pilot (ABC, 5/7/77), which sold the series (9/10/77 to 1/14/78), featured Lisa Hartman as the beautiful Tabitha, now a production assistant at KXLA-TV in Los Angeles. David Ankrum played her brother, Adam, and Karen Morrow her aunt, Minerva. Lisa Hartman sang the theme, "It's Magic."

57. *The Bickersons*

Syndicated, 1951

Cast: Virginia Grey (*Blanche Bickerson*), Lew Parker (*John Bickerson*), Lois Austin (*Clara Gollup*), Sam Lee (*Barney Gollup*), William Pullem (*Dr. Hersey*).

Facts: "We should have been married by the secretary of war, not a justice of the peace," said John Bickerson after he married Blanche eight years ago. John is a vacuum cleaner salesman for Household Appliances; Blanche is the typical American housewife struggling to make ends meet on what little salary John brings home (to 123 Englewood Drive, Apartment 22). They have a cat named Nature Boy, an unnamed canary and goldfish, and one thing in common: they love to bicker about anything and everything.

John is always in need of money. He is so broke that he picks "fights with Indians because I can't afford a haircut"; I sew "sleeves on Blanche's old drawers and wear[s] them for sweaters"; and cuts "down Blanche's old girdles to make suspenders."

Blanche says, "John doesn't act human until he has his morning coffee and is the only man in town who eats duck eggs and drinks reindeer milk."

When something around the apartment breaks, John refuses to send it to a repair shop—"I'd rather fix it myself than give some crook two bucks to do what I can do." They now have, for example, an electric orange juice squeezer that John hooked up to the vacuum cleaner to replace the burned out motor—"It now sucks up the orange juice and spits the pits in your face."

John is also a chronic snorer (it's so loud that the neighbors often call to complain). "It's like sleeping with a one man band. . . . Now I know what it is like to sleep at Cape Canaveral," Blanche says.

John's pride and joy seems to be the one bedroom slipper he has. Blanche and a friend bought a raffle ticket and won a pair of slippers. They split the prize and John wound up with the right slipper. John keeps the slipper under his pillow—"It's the only slipper I have and I have to protect it with my life."

Blanche gets "dizzy spells every five minutes that last a half hour." John doesn't hate Blanche's cooking, he just doesn't understand it. Possum broth, powdered frog legs, frog omelets, deviled pancakes and two-foot-long rhubarb pies ("I couldn't find a shorter rhubarb") are the norm. Because Blanche has little money to spend, she sometimes borrows from the money John saves for his life insurance payments (she tells the company to pay the premium "by deducting the money they will pay her when John drops dead").

Clara Gollup is Blanche's married sister. She and her husband, Barney Gollup, live at 121 Englewood Drive. Barney is a gambler, "eats like he is condemned" and hangs out at the United Nations Pool Hall. His door bell plays the trumpet song that sounds the start of a horse race.

Dr. Hersey is "the quack," as John calls him, who treats the various "ills" the Bickersons have. His biggest challenge is to cure John of his chronic snoring (he has prescribed two aspirins and a jigger of bourbon every night. John is six months behind on the aspirin and two years ahead on the bourbon).

John and Blanche keep their money in the sugar bowl. The ironing board doubles as the kitchen table and they have a monstrosity of an ice box with six doors in the kitchen. John's favorite hangout is Murphy's Bar and Grill. Prior to Nature Boy, they had a cat named Joy Boy (John said the cat committed suicide after he caught him in the liquor cabinet—"The cat got caught in a ball of string and hung himself").

Mentioned but not seen were Blanche's mother and Blanche's sister, Hortie, who has 12 kids and lives in Idaho. As is common with many early 1950s series, music credits are not given. The program has only the theme music, but the composer is not given. Lew Parker later teamed with Betty Kean and reprised "The Bickersons" via guest shots on various variety series.

58. *Big Eddie*

CBS, 8/23/75 to 11/7/75

Edward ("Eddie") Smith (Sheldon Leonard), a hood-like product of the streets of New York, is a former gambler turned legitimate entrepreneur as owner of the Big E, an East Side Manhattan sports, entertainment and civic center. Stories relate Eddie's experiences with the wide range of people he meets as owner of the Big E.

During World War II, Eddie served in the European theater of war. It was at this time that he met and later married his first wife, a Hungarian countess named Margaret (Eva Gabor). They divorced shortly after. When Eddie returned to New York, he continued his life of gambling. In 1973 Eddie's son and his wife are killed in an automobile accident. In order to gain custody of his six-year-old granddaughter, Ginger Smith (Quinn Cummings), Eddie marries his longtime girlfriend Honey, (Sheree North), a dancer, and establishes the Big E (Ginger is eight years old when the series begins). They live in an apartment at 450 East 56th Street in Manhattan.

Jesse Smith (Alan Oppenheimer) is Eddie's younger brother and assistant. Jesse's attitude toward Eddie is one of ill-concealed resentment (he was the kid in the family, the one with the ambition and drive whom everyone thought would become successful).

Monty ("Bang Bang") Valentine (Billy Sands), an old crony of Eddie's, now serves as his faithful retainer and gourmet cook. Too Late (Lonni Shorr), The Goniff (Milton Parsons) and No Marbles (Cliff Pellow) are Eddie's confederates. In the original pilot version (CBS, 5/2/75), Eddie owns the Big E Rental Business—"Anything You Want for a Price."

Jack Elliott, Allyn Ferguson and Earle Hagen composed the theme.

59. *The Big Valley*

ABC, 9/25/65 to 5/19/69

During the 1830s, Victoria Barkley (Barbara Stanwyck) and her husband, Tom (not seen), established the 30,000 acre Barkley Ranch in the San Joaquin Valley in Stockton, California. When the series begins (set forty years later), Victoria is a widow and the mother of five grown children: Jarrod (Richard Long), Nick (Peter Breck), Audra (Linda Evans), Heath (Lee Majors) and Eugene (Charles Briles). The Barkleys are now a powerful family with ranching and mining interests, but also a family whose name stands for right against wrong, a name that the people of the valley can look up to for wisdom and leadership in troubled times—"We share other people's troubles, it's our duty," says Nick.

THE BARKLEY RANCH, STOCKTON is painted on the sides of the buggies used by the family. Victoria has a horse named Misty Girl. She and Tom were married for 25 years before he was killed by railroad officials attempting to rob him of his land. There is a statue of Tom Barkley, seated on a horse, in the town (the citizens' way of honoring the memory of a man who helped establish the valley). Victoria and Tom were married only a few years when he went to the town of Strawberry to invest in some mines. Strawberry was the beginning; he sold some mines, made a profit and went on from there. But the dream almost never happened. One night, Tom was attacked by two thugs, beaten and left for dead behind the saloon. A girl named Leah Simmons (not seen) found Tom and nursed him back to health. Tom had a brief affair with Leah, but left her before he knew she was pregnant. Tom loved Victoria and his sons, Jarrod and Nick, very much. He was on his way to becoming rich and famous and couldn't afford a scandal if he stayed with Leah. Nine months later, a boy Leah names Heath is born to her. Leah never contacts Tom; she and her friends Rachel (not seen) and Hannah (Beah Richards) raised Heath. The only other family Heath knew were his uncle, Matt Simmons (John Anderson), and his aunt, Martha Simmons (Jeanne Cooper). Sometime after the death of his mother, when he learns that Tom Barkley is his father, Heath decides to find

The Big Valley. Barbara Stanwyck, Peter Breck (left) and Richard Long.

his roots; he eventually attains his birthright—the name of Barkley. Heath is famous for his bullfrog stew on the trail, and he carries a rattlesnake's rattler for good luck.

Jarrod is the first born son. He is a lawyer with offices in Stockton and San Francisco. He handles the family's legal matters and is not as actively involved in the roughness encountered by Nick and Heath. Audra is the only daughter (born about the same time as Heath). She is beautiful, proud and sensuous, "and yet to be tamed by the love of a man." Audra buys her dresses and material at Ida Nell's Seamstress Shop and does volunteer work at the Children's Orphanage (which is located next to the Old Mill). Audra fiercely protects the land her father died for (she often says, "This is Barkley land—and I'm Audra Barkley!" when she encounters trespassers), and has a tendency to fall for men with shady backgrounds (for example, Robert Goulet as Brother Love, a dishonest faith healer).

Nick, the second born son, is the ranch foreman. Nick got his first saddle when he was six years old (he wrote "Nick age 6—keep off" on it). At age 16, Nick fell down an open mine shaft; he fell in love for the first time when he was 18 with a girl named Jeannie Price (not seen), whom he met in a town called Willow Springs (where her family ran the dry goods store). When Nick went back to look her up years later (1877), he found that Jean, born in 1850, had died of typhoid fever in 1870.

Nick is an expert on horses (he rides a cutting horse named Coco) and is responsible for buying horses for the ranch. He doesn't like Audra to ride half-broken stock (he thinks it is too dangerous for her; she thinks she can ride any horse "and break 'em with the best of 'em"). Nick was the only Barkley child to marry—to grant a dying woman's greatest wish. Julia Jenkins (Nancy Olsen) was the unwed mother of a young boy named Tommy (Ron Howard). She had a shady background and wanted her son to have a fresh start with a good last name.

Eugene, called Gene by the family, was the youngest of the children. He was shy and sensitive and was dropped during the first season episodes (he was said to be attending college). Silas (Napoleon Whiting) is the family's servant but is treated more like a member of the family.

George Duning composed the "Big Valley" theme.

60. *Bill and Ted's Excellent Adventures*

Fox, 6/28/92 to 9/20/92

San Demas, California, in the year 2692 is a society based on the philosophy of "The Two Great Ones"—William ("Bill") Preston (Evan Richards) and Theodore ("Ted") Logan (Christopher Kennedy)—and the music of their band, the Wyld Stallyns. It is a "most excellent world" ruled by the Holy Ones. Rufus (Rick Overton) has been assigned by the Holy Ones to protect Bill and Ted and ensure

the future of their excellent society. (Bill and Ted travel throughout time and the lessons they learn—their "excellent adventures"—become the philosophy of San Demas.)

Bill and Ted attend San Demas High School and work for a hardware store called Nail World (Nail World badges must be worn 4¾ inches below the shoulder). "Dude" and "Excellent" are their catchphrases. Bill's home telephone number is 555-1306. Bill and Ted use the Circuits of Time Phone Booth to travel through time (dialing the number 7560 sends the booth on its way). When they land, they put an OUT OF ORDER sign on the booth to protect it.

Mr. Kerlson (Danny Breen) is the manager of Nail World; Detective Chet Logan (Matt Landers) is Ted's father, and Eleanor Logan (Barbara Wood) is Ted's mother. Missy Preston (Lisa Wilcox) is Bill's stepmother and (no first name given) Preston (Don Lake) is Bill's father.

Nathan Wang composed the most excellent theme, "Bill and Ted's Excellent Adventures."

Billy see *Head of the Class*

61. *The Bing Crosby Show*

ABC, 9/14/64 to 6/14/65

Bing Collins (Bing Crosby) is a former singer and musician who gave up his show business career to become an engineer (Bing performed in vaudeville with Barney Jenks [Phil Harris]). After designing a number of buildings he became a respected member of the staff of Colbert University in Los Angeles, where he is a consulting engineer and instructor. (In the 1964 ABC preview special, Bing mentions he is on the staff of Taylor University.)

Bing lives at 168 Valley Tree Lane. He is married to Ellie (Beverly Garland), a former singer he met while on the road, and is the father of two very pretty daughters: 15-year-old Joyce (Carol Faylen) and 10-year-old Janice (Diane Sherry).

Joyce is a freshman at Richmont High School. She is boy-crazy, a member of the school's marching team (she twirls a baton) and has Bing and Ellie worried—she has little interest in schoolwork and it may affect her chances of getting into Colbert University. Janice, on the other hand, is exceptionally bright and a whiz in math—"I'm advanced," she says. She attends Gorman Elementary School and is a very untidy person. Her room is a mess, and she studies in bad light ("I require the sloppy conditions to think"). Janice knows that Bing and Ellie want her "to have a neat and tidy mind for a neat and tidy life." "Right now," she says, "it's not possible." Bing calls her "Champ."

Glenda Farrell appeared as Bing's aunt, Lulu.

Bing Crosby sings the opening theme, "That's Life," and the show's closing signature, "It All Adds Up to Love."

62. *The Bionic Woman*

ABC, 1/14/76 to 5/4/77
NBC, 9/10/77 to 9/2/78

Cast: Lindsay Wagner *(Jaime Sommers)*, Richard Anderson *(Oscar Goldman)*, Martin E. Brooks *(Dr. Rudy Wells)*, Jennifer Darling *(Peggy Callahan)*.

Facts: A spinoff from "The Six Million Dollar Man." As one enters the town of Ojai, California, there is a sign that reads THE HOME OF AMERICAN ASTRONAUT STEVE AUSTIN. Jaime Sommers, a beautiful tennis pro, who is the girlfriend of Colonel Steve Austin (Lee Majors), also lives there. Jaime, a freshman at Ojai High School, first kissed Steve at his senior year New Year's Eve party. (His friends kidded him that "he was robbing the cradle." In another episode, Jaime is not three years younger than Steve; it mentioned that she and Steve met in the third grade "when Jaime dared Steve to eat all that food"; he did and became ill.) The Capri was their "pizza haunt," and when they were troubled, the downed tree near the shore of the lake provided a refuge for sorting things out.

Jaime is one of the top five women's tennis pros. She has the potential to beat Billie Jean King and is set to play her in Barcelona in one week. Days before she is to leave for Spain, Jaime and Steve decide to go sky diving. They jump from a single engine plane (I.D. number N5794A) and are descending to earth. When Jaime's altimeter reads seven, she (and Steve) pull their respective ripcords. Both parachutes open, but Jaime's malfunctions and sends her plunging to the ground. Perhaps it was the fall through tree branches that spared Jaime's life, but the end results were devastating: "Her legs have so many breaks that we can't count them; her right ear is hemorrhaging and her right arm and shoulder are crushed beyond repair."

In 1973 Steve was a U.S. Air Force test pilot. While testing an M3F5, he experienced a blowout that causes the plane to crash and explode. Steve was critically injured. Oscar Goldman of the O.S.I. (Office of Scientific Intelligence) arranged for a special bionic operation to save Steve's life. At a cost of six million dollars, Steve's legs, right arm and left eye were replaced with atomic-powered synthetic parts that endow him with great speed and strength but also make him something that has never before existed—a cyborg (cybernetic organism).

Seeing that a bionic operation is the only way to save Jaime, Steve convinces Oscar to arrange one. Jaime's legs, arm and ear are replaced in a cost-classified operation that saves her life. However, when Jaime awakens and learns what has happened, she is horrified—until Steve reveals that he too had such an operation.

Jaime is taught to use her new limbs (she moves her right foot first) and can soon run the mile in 58 seconds. All seems to be progressing normally until Jaime's body begins to reject her new limbs. Her system begins producing massive amounts of white corpuscles to fight off the bionics and this creates excruciating pain. Dr. Rudy Wells, the bionic surgeon, arranges for an immediate operation. Jaime apparently dies from a massive cerebral hemorrhage, but she is saved with only seconds to spare by Dr. Michael Marchetti (Rick Lenz), a cryogenic surgeon who uses experimental techniques to save her life (Jaime suffers a temporary loss of memory following the surgery).

Jaime, who feels she owes Oscar, Rudy and the government a debt, joins "the team." Oscar is the leader, and Steve (and now Jaime) are his players—special agents "built" to perform hazardous missions that authorities believe can only be accomplished through the use of their bionic powers. (Steve and Jaime's first assignment was to retrieve a computer-generated plate of the American $20 bill.)

Jaime relinquishes her career as a tennis pro to become a schoolteacher (grade levels seven, eight and nine) at the Ventura Air Force Base in California (her cover for the O.S.I.) She then moves into the home of Steve's parents (her "adoptive" parents), Jim and Helen Elgin (Jim is Helen's second husband; Jaime's parents are deceased); Steve lives in the former Marsden Ranch, which he bought to find peace and quiet away from his hectic life. Jaime's phone number was given verbally as 311-555-2368 and seen on camera as 311-555-7306. Steve, who calls Jaime "Babe," drives a car with the license plate 299KKL; he can also run 60 miles per hour. "The Six Million Dollar Man" ran on ABC (10/20/73 to 2/27/78) and featured Alan Oppenheimer as Dr. Rudy Wells from 1973 to 1976. Farrah Fawcett, Lee Majors' wife at the time, appeared in several episodes as both Major Kelly Wood and Victoria Webster, a reporter for KNUZ-TV.

Jaime's Bionic Parts: 1. Bionic Audio Sensor, catalogue number 6314-KAH. Amplification 1400, .081 Distortion, Class BC; 2. Bionic Neuro Link Forearm (Upper Right Arm Assembly), catalogue number 2822/PJI; 3. Neuro Feedback Power Supply: Atomic Type AED-4 (catalogue number 2821 AED-4), 1500 Watt Continuous Duty; 4. Bionic Neuro Link Bi-Pedal Assembly, catalogue number 914-PAH; 5. Neuro Feedback Terminal Power Supply: Atomic Type AED-9A, 4920 Watt Continuous Duty; 6. Overload Follower, 2100 Watt Reserve, Intermittent Duty, Class CC.

Steve's Bionic Parts: 1. Bionic Visual Cortex Terminal, catalogue number 075/KFB. 43mm o.d. (outside dimension), F/095. 200m Ratio: 20.2 to 1. 3135 Line, 60Hz. Extended Chromatic Response: Class JC; 2. Bionic Neuro Link Forearm (Upper Arm Assembly), catalogue number 2921 LV.; 3. Neuro Link Hand, Right, catalogue number 2822/PJI; 4. Power Supply: Atomic Type AED-4 (catalogue number 2031 AED-4); 1550 Watt Continuous Duty Double Gain Overload Follower, Class M2; 5. Bionic Neuro Link, Bi-Pedal Assembly, catalogue number 914 PAM; 6. Power Supply: Atomic Type AED 9A, 4920 Continuous Duty Overload Follower, 2100 Watt Reserve, Intermittent Duty, Class CC.

Other Regulars: Peggy Callahan (a.k.a. Janet Callahan) is Oscar's secretary and Jaime's closest friend; she lives at 22 Land Cliff Drive. Dr. Rudy Wells is the O.S.I. surgeon who is responsible for both Jaime's and Steve's bionic upkeep. Lindsay Wagner also played Jaime's evil twin (through plastic surgery) Lisa Galloway (Lisa sought to learn the secret of Jaime's strength and almost died when she stole Rudy's experimental Hydrazene—a taffy-like substance that produces incredible strength but is fatal when taken in large doses).

In second season episodes, Jaime works with a bionic dog she calls Max. The German shepherd's official name is Maximillion, based on the cost of Rudy's bionic operation to give the canine a new jaw and four legs after he was injured in a fire.

Relatives: Martha Scott (Steve's mother, *Helen Elgin*), Ford Rainey (Steve's father, *Jim Elgin*), Peter Lempert (Oscar's brother, *Sam Goldman*).

Themes: "The Bionic Woman," by Jerry Fielding; "The Six Million Dollar Man," vocal by Dusty Springfield, written by Stewart Phillips and Oliver Nelson.

Note: Two television movies reuniting Jaime and Steve appeared on NBC: *The Return of the Six Million Dollar Man and the Bionic Woman* (5/17/87) and *The Bionic Showdown* (4/30/89).

In the first movie, when the evil organization Fortress begins stealing advanced weapons, Oscar recruits his two former agents (now retired) to help him: Jaime Sommers, who now works for a rehabilitation center, and Steve Austin, who now runs a charter boat service called Summer Babe. The movie also introduces Steve's estranged son Michael (Tom Schanley), who, after a near-fatal accident testing an airplane, is given a bionic operation to save his life (receiving replacements of both legs, his right arm, ten ribs and his right eye). The movie also serves as a pilot for a proposed series (which never materialized) to feature Michael's exploits.

The Bionic Showdown teams Steve, Jaime and a young bionic woman named Kate Mason (Sandra Bullock) to battle a villainous cyborg. Richard Anderson and Martin E. Brooks reprised their original roles in both films.

63. *B.J. and the Bear*

NBC, 2/10/79 to 9/13/80
NBC, 1/13/81 to 8/1/81

Cast: Greg Evigan *(B.J. McKay)*, Sam *(Bear)*.
Facts: Billie Joe ("B.J.") McKay is a former Vietnam chopper pilot turned independent trucker who will haul anything legal anywhere for $1.50 a mile plus expenses. B.J. rides with his simian companion, Bear, and drives a red Kenworth 18-wheeler truck that is registered in Milwaukee (his hometown). License plates seen for the truck are UT-3665, 806-356, 635-608 and 4T-3665. B.J.'s C.B. handle is "The Milwaukee Kid," and his favorite watering hole is the Country Comfort Truckers' Stop in Bowlin County. B.J. named Bear, a chimp, after Paul ("Bear") Bryant, whom B.J. considers to be the greatest football coach (at the University of Alabama). (B.J. befriended Bear when he was a P.O.W. in Vietnam. Bear would bring B.J. food to help him survive.) B.J. sometimes calls Bear "The Kid." B.J. played sax and sang in a band called Ghettoway City.

In 1981 episodes, B.J. establishes Bear Enterprises (formerly Chaffey Enterprises), an independent trucking company in Hollywood at 800 Palmer Street over a bar-restaurant called Phil's Disco (B.J.'s office phone number is 555-7993, and on his desk is a scale model of his truck, which doubles as a lamp). B.J.'s staff members are seven beautiful female truckers: Jeannie Campbell (Judy Landers), Samantha Smith (Barbra Horan), Callie Everett (Linda McCullough), Cynthia ("Cindy") Grant (Sherilyn Wolter), Angela ("Angie") Cartwright (Sheila DeWindt) and twins Teri and Geri Garrison (Candi and Randi Brough).

Jeannie, a blonde bombshell who measures 37C-34-36, has the nickname "Stacks." She is the most feminine of the group, is very sweet and trusting and has an 18-wheeler with the license plate 4JJ-0162. Geri, the hot-headed twin, and Teri, the calm and collected one, work as waitresses in Phil's Disco (they have a truck with the license plate UJJ-4004).

Angie, who works as a radio disc jockey at night, has the air name "The Nightingale" and a truck with the license plate 040-3777. Cindy, the daughter of a corrupt police captain, and Samantha, share a truck (plate XTR-7162). Callie, the toughest of the girls, is the one B.J. counts on for help in desperate situations. Callie prefers to wear jeans, is not as feminine as the other girls ("she has a smart mouth") and believes that "B.J. sees me as only a girl who can drive a rig and fix a flat tire." Her license plate reads 1XT-403. John Dullaghan plays Nick, the bartender at Phil's Disco. B.J. has his trucks serviced at Deke's Truck Repair (Steve Reisch plays Deke).

In 1980 episodes, Snow White (Laurette Spang), a trucker friend of B.J.'s, heads the all-girl Piston Packin' Mamas trucking outfit in Winslow County. The "Mamas" are: Tommy (Janet Louise Johnson), Honey (Angela Aames), Leather (Carlene Watkins), Sal (Julie Gregg), Clancy (Spray Russo), Angel (Darlyn Ann Lindley) and Chattanooga (Sonia Manzano).

B.J. made many friends and enemies throughout the series run. Those out to get B.J. were: Sheriff Elroy P. Lobo (Claude Akins) of Orly County, Georgia, who is after B.J. for breaking up his prostitution ring; Captain John Sebastian Cain (Ed Lauter) of Bishop County; Deputy Beauregard Wiley (Slim Pickens) of Winslow County; J.P. Pierson (M.P. Murphy), the head of the organized High-Ballers Trucking Outfit (which opposes independents' taking their business); Rutherford T. Grant (Murray Hamilton), Cindy's father, the corrupt head of S.C.A.T. (Special Crimes Action Team), Southern Division Headquarters of the L.A.P.D.; and Jason T. Willard (Jock Mahoney), the head of Trans-Cal Trucking. The corrupt Elroy P. Lobo character was spun off into "The Misadventures of Sheriff Lobo" (NBC, 9/18/79 to 9/2/80) and revised as "Lobo" (NBC, 12/30/80 to 8/25/81).

Relatives: Deborah Ryan (B.J.'s sister, *Shauna McKay*), Edward Andrews (Callie's uncle, *Barney*).
Theme: "B.J. and the Bear," vocal by Greg Evigan.

64. *B.L. Stryker*

ABC, 2/13/89 to 5/5/90

Stryker Investigations is a private detective company run by Buddy Lee ("B.L.") Stryker (Burt Reynolds). It is located at 62 Palm Drive in Palm Beach, Florida. He is assisted by Oz Jackson (Ossie Davis), a former world-famous boxer, and Lyynda Lennox (Dana Kaminski), his slightly flighty secretary. B.L. was a former New Orleans police officer who quit the force after he was suspended for being out of control. He returned to his hometown to begin his own company. B.L.'s former wife, Kimberly (Rita Moreno) is now married to the wealthy but elderly Clayton Baskin (Abe Vigoda).

B.L. has a parrot named Gilbert and drives a classic Cadillac (license plate not readable). He lives on a houseboat called the *No Trump,* which is docked at 22 Ocean Park Marina; it was first called Maxie's Marina, then Oliver's Marina. Lyynda has a dog named Fred; Oz's license plate reads OZ II; and Kimberly's Rolls Royce license plate is CIT 86R.

Maureen Stapleton appeared as B.L.'s aunt, Susan Stryker; and Denise Nicholas was Oz's daughter, Darlene Carter.

Mike Post composed the "B.L. Stryker" theme.

Black Jack Savage see *The 100 Lives of Black Jack Savage*

Blacke's Magic see *The Magician*

65. *Blansky's Beauties*

ABC, 2/12/77 to 6/27/77

Bambi Benton (Caren Kaye), Ethel Akalino (Lynda Goodfriend), Arkansas Baits (Rhonda Bates), Jacqueline ("Jackie") Outlaw (Gerri Reddick), Sylvia Silver (Antoinette Yuskis), Hilary Prentiss (Taaffe O'Connell) and Bridget Muldoon (Elaine Bolton) are Blansky's Beauties, showgirls who perform in "The Major Putnam Spectacular—La Plume de la Putnam," a glitzy show at the Oasis Hotel in Las Vegas, Nevada. (Becoming one of "Blansky's Beauties" is the dream of all budding showgirls and an important step on the road to becoming famous.)

Nancy Blansky (Nancy Walker) is the show's producer (most people believe her name is "Nanky Blanky" because the show's announcer says her name so fast that nobody can understand the correct pronunciation). Nancy is the cousin of Howard Cunningham from "Happy Days." She has a dog named Blackjack and lives at 64 Crescent Drive with her assistant, Joey DeLuca (Eddie Mekka) and his younger brother, Anthony DeLuca (Scott Baio). Joey is the cousin of Carmine Ragusa (from "Laverne and Shirley"), and he helps Nancy with the choreography. Anthony has a crush on Bambi and loves peanut butter and bologna sandwiches.

Bambi is from southern California ("I was a showgirl at six hotels and I've been fired six times for having fun; like the time I came down from the ceiling on a trapeze with a seltzer bottle to give the audience a few squirts"). Her mother loved the movie *Bambi* and named her after the main character. Ethel is from Wichita, Kansas ("They call me Sunshine because I smile a lot"); Arkansas is from Arkansas ("I don't sing too good, and I don't dance too good, but I sure do a mean hog call—suuuuuuweeeee!").

Jackie is unmarried and "I'm cool"; Hilary is a stunning blonde who got the job because "I'm a close personal friend of Major Putnam, who owns the hotel, and I wanted to be a chorus girl"; Sylvia is a streetwise but sweet girl from the Bronx; and Bridget is a prim and proper British girl. As the series progressed, three additional girls became "Blansky's Beauties": Lovely Carson (Bond Gideon), Gladys ("Cochise") Littlefeather (Shirley Kirkes) and Misty ("Knight") Karamazov (Jill Owens).

Horace ("Stubs") Wilmington (George Pentecost) is the hotel manager; Pat Morita is Arnold Takahashi, the owner of Arnold's Coffee Shop (the character first appeared on "Happy Days" as the owner of Arnold's Drive-In).

Cyndi Grecco sings the theme, "I Want It All."

66. *Blondie*

NBC, 1/4/57 to 9/27/57
CBS, 9/26/68 to 1/9/69

Blondie Davenport and Dagwood Bumstead met on a blind date. Although they were with different people, Dagwood could see that Blondie didn't care for the fellow she was with. The following night, Dagwood brought Blondie flowers and candy; before long they fell in love and decided to marry. They eloped to a town called Sherman Grove and were married by a justice of the peace. (Dagwood has since lost their marriage license. He accidentally grabbed his marriage license when he went on a hunting trip and lost it—but he bagged three ducks.) In the comics, Blondie was a Depression-era gold digger seeking a rich husband—Dagwood.

Years later Blondie has a home (house number 4224), two kids (Alexander, nicknamed "Baby Dumpling," and Cookie), six dogs (Daisy, a "purebred mongrel," and her "five children"), and a bumbling husband who works as an architect for the J.C. Dithers Construction Company.

"We all adore you Dagwood, even if you are dumb at times," says Blondie. Dagwood is a natural bumbler and becomes a nervous wreck when it comes to his boss, J.C.

Blondie (1968). Left to right: Peter Robbins, Will Hutchins, Patricia Harty and Pamelyn Ferdin.

Dithers. When J.C. says, "Emergency," Dagwood answers like a faithful Saint Bernard: he drops whatever he is doing to rush to the office. (Dagwood is "sort of a vice president—it comes and goes." When he blunders, it goes; when his blundering turns out for the best, he's a v.p. again). On Dagwood's birthday, Blondie gets him something she needs for the house or something the kids want (over the years, Dagwood has gotten a sewing machine, a washing machine, a doll house and a baseball bat and glove). Dagwood and J.C. are members of the Loyal Order of Caribou Lodge; J.C. has an antique gun collection that his wife feels is just a waste of money (he buys his guns at Miller's Sport Shop). Dagwood is famous for his yell—"B-l-o-o-o-n-d-i-e-e-e"—when something goes wrong.

The series is based on the comic strip by Chic Young, and most people readily think of Penny Singleton and Arthur Lake, the stars of the 1930s and 1940s motion picture and radio series, as Blondie and Dagwood.

In 1952 the first attempt was made to bring the comic strip to television. What resulted was an unaired pilot called "Blondie" that staffed Jeff Donnell as Blondie and John Harvey as Dagwood (the film contains no other credits).

The year 1954 saw another unaired pilot called "Blondie" with the following cast: Pamela Britton (*Blondie*), Hal LeRoy (*Dagwood*), Stuffy Singer (*Alexander*), Mimi Gibson (*Cookie*), Robert Burton (*Julius C. Dithers*), Isabel Withers (Julius's wife, *Cora Dithers*), Robin Raymond (Blondie's neighbor, *Tootsie Woodley*), and Lucien Littlefield (*Mr. Beasley*, the mailman). Herb Woodley, Tootsie's husband, was mentioned but not seen.

The first actual series appeared on NBC in 1957 with the following cast: Pamela Britton (*Blondie*), Arthur Lake (*Dagwood*), Stuffy Singer (*Alexander*), Ann Barnes (*Cookie*), Florenz Ames (*J.C. Dithers*), Lela Bliss and Elvia Allman (*Cora Dithers*), Hal Peary (*Herb Woodley*), Lois Collier and Hollis Irving (Herb's wife, *Harriet Woodley*), and Lucien Littlefield (*Mr. Beasley*). Leon Klatzkin composed the theme.

The second and last series appeared in color on CBS in 1968 with the following cast: Patricia Harty (*Blondie*), Will Hutchins (*Dagwood*), Peter Robbins (*Alexander*), Pamelyn Ferdin (*Cookie*), Jim Backus (*J.C. Dithers*), Henny Backus (*Cora Dithers*), Bobbi Jordan (*Tootsie Woodley*), and Bryan O'Byrne (*Mr. Beasley*). Will Hutchins and Patricia Harty performed the theme, "Blondie," written by Bernard Green and Al Brodax.

On 5/10/87, CBS aired the first animated "Blondie" special, "Blondie and Dagwood," with the following voices: Loni Anderson (*Blondie*), Frank Welker (*Dagwood*), Ike Eisenmann (*Alexander*), Ellen Gerstel (*Cookie*), Alan Oppenheimer (*J.C. Dithers*), Russi Taylor (*Cora Dithers*), Laurel Page (*Tootsie Woodley*), Jack Angel (*Herb Woodley* and *Mr. Beasley*), Pat Fraley (*Daisy*).

The same voice cast reprised their roles in "Blondie and Dagwood: Second Wedding Workout" (CBS, 11/1/89), the second animated special based on the comic strip.

67. *Blossom*

NBC, 1/3/91 to the present

Cast: Mayim Bialik (*Blossom Russo*), Ted Wass (*Nick Russo*), Michael Stoyanov (*Anthony Russo*), Joey Lawrence (*Joey Russo*), Jenna Von Oy (*Six LeMeure*).

Facts: "Blossom is the perfect combination of a little sugar and a lot of spice. She's gorgeous, she's popular, she's sophisticated." She's 13 years old and lives with her father, Nick, and brothers Anthony and Joey, at 465 Hampton Drive in southern California. Blossom first attended the Crestridge School for Girls; she transferred to Tyler High School when she discovered they had a better band (she plays the trumpet—"a little bit classical, a little bit jazz"—and hopes to become a musician). Blossom sleeps with her ALF doll, drink's Bailey's Diet Cola and "became a woman" in the first episode (as her friend Six said, "Blossom blossomed"). Blossom earns extra spending money by doing the grocery shopping for Agnes Swanson (Eileen Brennan), an elderly woman who has "a stupid pet bird" named Bill. In one dream sequence, Phylicia Rashad played Blossom's mother; in another, Rhea Perlman played her fairy godmother. Blossom has a scar on her chin from when she fell off the monkey bars as a kid and split her chin open. Joey calls her "a borderline babe" ("You're in the Honor Society, you play the trumpet, but you haven't been visited by the hooter fairy yet"). When Blossom gets upset, she eats ice cream and pound cake. As a kid Blossom had a teddy bear named Dwight.

"I wonder what my husband will look like naked or if I'll laugh the first time I see him. I wonder what it will be like to have a mortgage, a baby or breasts." So says Six, Blossom's best friend. Six also worries that her father "will go into my room and read the lyrics on my album covers" if she stays away from home too long. Every Monday Blossom and Six (who also attends Tyler High School) go the mall after school. They eat lunch together in the school cafeteria and save each other a seat when the other is going to be late. Six considers Blossom "a real decent person with moral values." Six and Blossom also love to dance; Blossom for obvious reasons, Six "to get all sweaty and dizzy and see stars." Six is on the school's debate team, and if detention were a frequent flyer program "I'd have enough miles for a free trip to Hawaii."

The law firm of O'Hara, Schmitt, Rosetti and Bailey handled the divorce between Blossom's parents, Nick and Madelyn (Madelyn, who was married to Nick for 20 years, left the family four years ago to pursue her dream of becoming a singer in Europe). Nick is a musician (he attended Julliard) and plays at various clubs. He played backup for Anita Baker, B.B. King and Chuck Berry; won Cleo Awards for commercials; and played on soundtracks for such movies as *Ghost*, *Fame* and *Dirty Dancing*. As a teenager he was a member of the group Neon Wilderness.

Anthony, the oldest child, was a drug addict for four years but is now clean. He worked as a delivery boy for Fatty's Pizza and as a counter waiter at Dante's Donut Depot. He is also writing a play called "Naked Chick Academy" that he he hopes will make him three million dollars. When Anthony was 12 years old he attended Camp Mountain High (where he smoked his first joint). Peer pressure caused him to continue with drugs and drink "and even wear bicycle pants." In the episode of 10/21/91, Anthony quit the donut shop to become an E.M.T. (emergency medical technician). The first celebrity he helped was Justine Bateman when she fell and injured her elbow.

He believes the sun is on the other side of the moon and his only talent, Blossom says, "is drinking Pepsi through his nose." Joey, Blossom's 16-year-old brother, is not too bright, girl-crazy and obsessed with breasts (which he calls "hooters," "gozangas" and "boobs"). Although Joey attends Tyler High School, he mentions attending Grant High in one episode. Blossom considers Joey to be a dork ("If the dorks had a navy, he'd be their admiral"). "When Blossom and Six talk about their love life," Joey says, "it's like the pope and Mr. Rogers talking about their love life."

The family had a pet cat named Scruffy, and the car license plate reads 629 FZQ. Their living room has flower print wallpaper and flower print slipcovers on the sofa to match.

The original pilot film (NBC, 7/5/90) had the same basic format but a slightly different cast. Mayim Bialik, Jenna Von Oy and Michael Stoyanov played the same roles. Joey Lawrence was Blossom's brother, Donny; and Richard Masur and Barrie Youngfellow were her parents, Terry and Barbara Russo. Terry was an accountant and Barbara worked for an unnamed magazine.

Relatives: Barnard Hughes (Blossom's grandfather, *Francis ["Buzz"] Richman*), Gail Edwards (Six's mother, *Sharon LeMeure*).

Flashbacks: Mayim Bialik *(Blossom age 11)*, Autumn Winters *(younger Blossom)*, Aaron Freeman and Grant Gelt (young Anthony), Matthew Lawrence *(Joey age 11)*, Andrew Lawrence *(Joey age two)*, Paige Pengra and Margaret Reed *(Madelyn in 1986)*, Marissa Rosen *(young Six)*.

Theme: "The Theme from Blossom," vocal by Dr. John.

Note: See also "Molloy" for information on Mayim's first series. On July 4, 1990, ABC presented an unsold pilot called "Beanpole." Like "Blossom," "Beanpole" dealt with the world of a 13-year-old girl, in this case, a five foot eight inch teenager named Lillian Pinkerton (Hayley Brown) and the problems she faces being a pretty but tall girl (she attends Roosevelt Junior High School). Her mother, Wanda (Molly Cheek), is a widow and works as a waitress at an unnamed restaurant. Her shorter kid sister, Katie (Heather Lind), believes she is the most beautiful girl in her school. In the pilot, Lillian and her best friend, Drew Clayton (Leslie Engelberg), try out for the school's cheerleading squad, the Pom Girls.

Falls, Oregon, to begin new lives in a community where the traditional values of family, love and work remain strong.

Annie and her 12-year-old daughter, Zoey (Kim Hauser), and Frank and his children, 12-year-old Sarah (Alyson Croft) and 10-year-old Charley (Danny Gerard), live on a ranch at Old Stone Highway ("Make the first left after Mill Pond"). Frank runs the family business, Cobb's Mill, a lumber operation, with his father, Henry Cobb (Pat Hingle), who lives in a boardinghouse at 831 Overton Road.

Frank and Annie lived in New York for nine years before moving to Oregon. Frank's late wife was named Katherine; Annie is divorced from Alan (Vincent Baggetta). Frank works against the background of classical music; Annie likes to prepare dinner while watching the six o'clock news on television. When Annie is upset, she eats ice cream.

The kids attend the Eagle Falls Grammar School. Zoey calls her new community "Hicksville, U.S.A." (for her, "the nearest beauty parlor is two hours away by plane in San Francisco"). Sarah, who is nicknamed "Scout," has a secret retreat called Scout's Island (a small island across the river from their home) where she goes when she is upset. Dances are held at the Grange Hall; the Cobbs' horse is named Barney.

Myles Goodman composed the theme.

A similar series called "Apple's Way" aired on CBS (2/10/74 to 1/12/75) and dealt with a father's efforts to capture the treasured memories of his childhood for his family by moving to his hometown of Appleton, Iowa. Parents George and Barbara Apple (Ronny Cox, Frances Lee McCain) and their children, Paul (Vincent Van Patten), Cathy (Patti Cohoon), Patricia (Franny Michael, then Kristy McNichol) and Steve (Eric Olson) sought "the wonders of streams and woods, the mystery of growing crops and days filled with adventures in good and comforting things." The family pets were dogs Muffin, Sam and Bijou, and a snake named Ruby.

"Sunday in Paris" (NBC, 7/8/91) is an unsold pilot film that attempted the same theme, but in a comical form. Fed up with life in New York and realizing that her three children are losing sight of their values, television soap star Sunday Chase (Debbie Allen) quits her job and moves back to her hometown of Paris, Texas, so her kids can experience life as she did when she was young. Sunday's children were 15-year-old Taylor (Jennifer Lewis), 10-year-old Brandon (Brandon Adams) and six-year-old Allison (Essence Atkins). The family lives with Sunday's mother, Vernetta Dickson (Diahann Carroll) who is called "Mama Godiva" by the church organization (as a result of Sunday's dropping out of college to appear nude in a production of *Hair*). Sunday played Olivia Decker on the soap "No Faith to Lose"; Taylor believes her mother has "flipped and we'll all be weaving baskets soon." The pilot was originally titled "Fresher Pastures."

68. *Blue Skies*

CBS, 6/13/88 to 8/1/88

Annie Pfeiffer (Season Hubley) and Frank Cobb (Tom Wopat) are newlyweds with children from previous marriages who move from New York City (where they met) to Eagle

69. *Bob*

CBS, 9/18/92 to 5/17/93

Cast: Bob Newhart *(Bob McKay)*, Carlene Watkins *(Kaye McKay)*, Cynthia Stevenson *(Patricia McKay)*, John Cygan *(Harlan Stone)*.

Facts: Dr. Jeffrey Austin is a mild-mannered veterinarian. When a scientific experiment he is conducting backfires, Austin is endowed with the adrenal glands of his Doberman pinscher, Blackie, and given the super powers of a dog. Dr. Austin adopts the alias of Mad Dog, and thus was born "Mad Dog," a comic strip created by Robert ("Bob") McKay and now published by Ace Comics.

Bob, his wife, Kaye, and their daughter, Patricia (nicknamed Trisha), live at 134 Oak Street. Bob created "Mad Dog" in 1964 when he was dating Kaye (he drew the concept on a napkin) and sold the idea to a publisher. But it never caught on and was discontinued shortly after (it sold for 12 cents an issue and was yanked after the twelfth issue; the first issue sold nine copies). Bob then went into the greeting card business. In 1992 Ace Comics showed interest in revising the character and "Mad Dog" was born again.

Mad Dog, "mankind's best friend," wears blue tights with an orange *M* on his chest. He is assisted by two humans: Penny (whom Bob based on Kaye) and Brad. American-Canadian Transcontinental Communications owns Ace Comics. The Zamos Printing Company prints "Mad Dog" (when the first issue hit the newsstands, it did so without the last page, which was missing). A 70 foot balloon of Mad Dog appeared in the 1992 Macy's Thanksgiving Day Parade.

As a kid, Bob had a dog named Freckles; he now has a cat named Otto (who likes to watch the Disney Channel). Bob hates substitute foods (for example, egg substitute "because it's too chewey"). He also dislikes fresh-squeezed orange juice and prefers Tang ("The astronauts drink it"). Issue number one of "Mad Dog" is Bob's most prized possession. Bob still has one of his baby teeth—"It's a medical oddity."

Kaye works at the Museum Shop while Trisha works as Bob's colorist. Trisha previously worked as a "wench waitress" at a pub called the Keg and Cleaver, then as a waitress at Cowboy Tom's Fast Food. Every December Trisha jumps rope for a charity called the Children's Medical Benefit—Jump for Joy for Girls and Boys. As a baby, Trisha slept through the night; she never experienced "the terrible twos"; she was always perky and followed the rules. The one thing she did that was bad "was to let my mind wander one Sunday while attending mass." At the 1992 office Christmas party, Trisha took a dare from a fellow worker to do something bad: she stole a Nabisco brand silver spoon from the office of Mr. TerHorst (which set off an alarm and involved Bob in an underhanded plot to return the spoon).

Harlan Stone is Bob's obnoxious, loud-mouthed co-worker (he draws the graphics for "Mad Dog"). The beautiful but rude and abrasive Shayla (Christine Dunford) is Harlan's girlfriend.

Iris Frankel (Ruth Kobart) is the elderly and nasty letterer who works in the office (she has a sign on her drafting table that reads DON'T TOUCH MY STUFF). Albie Lutz (Andrew Bilgore) is the wimpy office gofer; and the unseen Mr. TerHorst (voice of Michael Cumpsty) runs the company (he is averse to publicity and hates attention; he is heard over speakerphones and has cameras hidden throughout the Ace Comics office building).

Bob enjoys his weekly game of poker with his buddies:

Jerry Fleischer (Tom Poston), creator of the comic "The Silencer"; Don Palermo (Steve Lawrence), creator of the comic "Tales from Beneath the Tomb"; Vic Victor (Bill Daily), creator of the comic "Fizzy"; and Buzz Loudermilk (Dick Martin), creator of the comic "Katy Carter, Army Nurse."

In the original, unaired pilot version, Bob, Kaye and Trisha have the last name Wharten. Here Bob created "Mad Dog" as a kid, and the comic was discontinued because the comic book industry went bad just as "Mad Dog" was catching on.

Theme: "The Super Hero Theme from Bob" by Lee Holdridge.

The Bob Cummings Show see Love That Bob

70. *The Bob Newhart Show*
CBS, 9/16/72 to 9/2/78

Cast: Bob Newhart (*Bob Hartley*), Suzanne Pleshette (*Emily Hartley*), Bill Daily (*Howard Borden*), Peter Bonerz (*Jerry Robinson*), Marcia Wallace (*Carol Kester*).

Facts: Robert ("Bob") Hartley served with the 193rd Combat Support Orchestra during the Korean War. Bob, who played drums in his high school band, was noted as having "the best wrists south of the 38th Parallel." Hoping to become a professional drummer, Bob went to New York after his army hitch and auditioned for the Buddy Rich Orchestra. While Bob thought he did great, Buddy had only three words to say to him: "You stink, man." Bob's dreams fell apart at the seams; he later went to college to study psychology.

When the series begins, Bob is an established psychologist with an office in the Rampo Medical Arts Building in Chicago. His office number varies in each episode: sometimes it's 751, at other times it's 715 (his office phone number is 726-7098). Bob is a Virgo and his Social Security number is 352-22-7439.

Bob lives with his wife, Emily, in Apartment 523 in a building owned by the Skyline Management Corporation. Emily, whose maiden name is Harrison, was born in Seattle, Washington; she and Bob married on April 15, 1970. Emily first taught third grade at Gorman Elementary School; she is later vice principal of Tracy Grammar School.

Bob held a temporary job with the Loggers' Casualty Life Insurance Company (their slogan: "We Gotta Insure These Guys") and appeared on the television show "Psychology in Action" with his therapy group (the announcer called him "Dr. Robert Hartman"). Bob's idea of relaxing around the house in a sloppy manner is to do so in a neatly pressed sweatshirt. On their first wedding anniversary, Emily and Bob received a radio from Bob's parents and a car from Emily's.

The Bob Newhart Show. Bob Newhart and Suzanne Pleshette (front); Marcia Wallace, Peter Bonerz and Bill Daily (back).

Howard Mark Borden, Bob and Emily's neighbor, was originally a 747 navigator for an unnamed airline. After nine years on the job, Howard was replaced by a computer and found the same kind of work with EDS (European Delivery Service) Airline. Howard, who is divorced and the father of a young son (Howard, Jr., who was conceived during the great airplane strike of 1963), has a sister (Debbie) and two brothers: Gordon Borden, the game warden, and Norman Borden, the Mormon doorman.

Jerome ("Jerry") Merle Robinson, Bob's friend, a children's orthodontist, washes his hands an average of 46 times a day and has an office opposite Bob's. Carol Kester is Bob and Jerry's secretary. She was born in Collinsville, Iowa, and lives in Apartment 7 of an unnamed building (she has a tape recording of a barking dog she calls Lobo which is activated when the doorbell rings). Carol later marries Larry Bondurant (Will MacKenzie). Elliott Carlin (Jack Riley), Lillian Bakerman (Florida Friebus), Michele Nardo (Renee Lippin) and Victor Gianelli (Noam Pitlik) are Bob's recurring patients.

Relatives: Pat Finley (Bob's sister, *Ellen Hartley*), Barnard Hughes (Bob's father, *Herb Hartley*), Martha Scott (Bob's mother, *Martha Hartley*), John Randolph (Emily's father, *Cornelius ["Junior"] Harrison*), Ann Rutherford (Emily's mother, *Aggie Harrison*), Heather Menzies (Howard's sister, *Debbie Borden*), William Redfield (Howard's brother, *Gordon Borden*), Moosie Drier (Howard's son, *Howard Borden, Jr.*).

Theme: "Home for Emily," by Lorenzo and Henrietta Music.

71. *Bodies of Evidence*

CBS, 6/18/92 to 8/27/92

Benjamin ("Ben") Carroll (Lee Horsley) is a homicide lieutenant with the Metropolitan Police, Westside Division of the L.A.P.D. Ryan Walker (George Clooney), Nora

Houghton (Kate McNeil) and Walt Stratton (Al Fann) are the detectives in his unit. While the series is virtually a depiction of police work in action, it does present some facts: Ben speaks Chinese ("18 words," which he picked up while he was a beat cop in Chinatown); Nora has a teaching degree and is partners with Walt (their car code is AW-35; Walt's license plate reads 8Z6153; Nora's license plate is 9452LB). Ryan's modus operandi (M.O.) is to identify with a killer in an attempt to guess his every move.

Bonnie Carroll (Jennifer Hetrick) is Ben's ex-wife, and Ethan (Ryan J. O'Neill) is their son (Ethan has a dog named Max). Sergeant Tim Houghton (Francis X. McCarthy) is Nora's father, and Jack Houghton (Jeff Yagher) is Nora's brother.

Christopher Klatman composed the "Bodies of Evidence" theme.

72. *Bold Venture*

Syndicated, 1959 to 1960

Slate Shannon (Dane Clark) is an adventurer who owns Shannon's Place, a hotel in Trinidad, and the *Bold Venture*, a 60-foot sloop that is moored at the Prince George Docks. Slate is also the guardian of Sailor DuVal (Joan Marshall), a beautiful girl who became his responsibility when he promised her dying father that he would look after her. Sailor resides in Room 116 of the hotel ("second floor, left") and is an expert at fishing (when she and Slate go fishing, it is Sailor who makes the catch; Slate attributes it to her "magic touch for spinning reels").

Sailor has romantic inclinations toward Slate. While Slate does call her "Baby" and "Honey" and does kiss her on the hand, he sees her basically as a girl he promised to care for and nothing else. When Slate, who helps people in trouble, needs first aid, he goes to Sailor, but that is not what Sailor really wants—"That's all I am to Slate, a nurse."

Philip Keith-Barker (Mark Dana) is the inspector of police; King Moses (Bernie Gozier) is a guitarist who provides music for Slate's hotel dining room; he also serves as the desk clerk and calls Sailor "Lady Sailor." Mama George (Bella Bruck) is Slate's friend, the owner of a banana plantation; Leta (Lisa Gaye) is one of the dancers at the hotel; Tina (Karen Scott) runs the only dance hall on the island, Tina's Palace of Fun; and Jerri Bender, Narda Onyx, Joyce Taylor and Barbara Wilson are the crew of the *Bold Venture*.

The composer of the theme, "Bold Venture," is not credited; it is seen being performed in the opening and closing segments by three Trinidadians playing drums.

73. *Bonanza*

NBC, 9/12/59 to 1/16/73

Cast: Lorne Greene *(Ben Cartwright)*, Pernell Roberts *(Adam Cartwright)*, Dan Blocker *(Hoss Cartwright)*, Michael Landon *(Little Joe Cartwright)*, Victor Sen Yung *(Hop Sing)*.

Facts: Ben Cartwright is a former first mate who now runs a chandler's store in New England. He is married to Elizabeth Stoddard (Geraldine Brooks), the daughter of his former captain. A year later, a son they name Adam is born to them, but complications from the birth cost Elizabeth her life. Ben possesses a dream of settling in California. Motivated by Elizabeth's desire for him to pursue that dream, Ben sells his business and heads west.

Ben and Adam settle temporarily in St. Joseph, Missouri. Adam (Johnny Stephens) is five years old, and Ben has fallen in love with a Swedish girl named Inger Borgstrom (Inga Swenson). Inger runs the general store (Ben met her when he went to buy food), and she helped Adam over a crisis—breaking his high fever. Ben and Inger marry. Ben is persuaded by Inger to continue his journey west. He organizes a wagon train and takes on the responsibility of bringing settlers to California. During the hazardous trek through Nevada, Inger gives birth to a son they name Eric Hoss. Shortly after, during an Indian attack, Inger is killed. Ben abandons his dream forever and settles in Virginia City, Nevada, where he establishes the Ponderosa Ranch.

The birth of Ben's third son, Joseph Francis ("Little Joe") evolves from a complex story in which Ben journeys to New Orleans to fulfill personally the last request of a ranchhand who died saving Ben's life. Love develops as a result of Ben's meeting with Marie DeMarne (Felicia Farr), the widow of the ranchhand. A marriage ultimately results, and Marie returns to Virginia City with Ben. Shortly after the birth of their son, Marie is thrown by her horse and killed.

Stories are set in the 1880s. The Ponderosa Ranch is a 1,000-square mile timberland ranch in the Comstock lode country (it is located on the outskirts of Virginia City). Ben pays his ranchhands "$30 a month, a bunk and beans." Eric's middle name, Hoss, is a Swedish mountain name for a big, friendly man—something Inger knew the boy would be even though she only lived long enough to see him as an infant. Adam is considered "best at judging horse flesh; better than anyone in the whole territory." Ben's horse is named Buck; Hoss's is named Chuck; and Little Joe's is named Cochise. Michael Landon played Little Joe's evil twin, Angus Borden, in one episode.

The Sierra Freight and Stage Lines deliver mail and freight to Virginia City. The Overland Stage provides passenger service from town to town; the *Enterprise* is the town newspaper.

Relatives: Mitch Vogel (Ben's adopted son, *Jamie*), Guy Madison (Ben's nephew, *Will Cartwright*), Bruce Yarnell (Ben's cousin, *Muley Jones*).

Theme: "Bonanza," by Jay Livingston and Ray Evans; performed by David Rose.

Note: An attempt was made to revive the series in a syndicated television movie pilot, *Bonanza: The Next Generation* (3/16/88). John Ireland is Aaron Cartwright, the late Ben's brother and the new head of the Ponderosa Ranch; Barbara Anderson is Annabelle Cartwright, the wife of Little Joe (who was killed in action while serving with Teddy Roosevelt's Rough Riders). Michael Landon, Jr., is Benji Cartwright, Little Joe's son; and Brian A. Smith is Josh Cartwright, the late Hoss's illegitimate son.

Booker see *21 Jump Street*

74. *Bosom Buddies*
ABC, 11/27/80 to 8/5/82

Cast: Peter Scolari *(Henry Desmond/Hildegard Desmond)*, Tom Hanks *(Kip Wilson/Buffy Wilson)*, Holland Taylor *(Ruth Dunbar)*, Wendie Jo Sperber *(Amy Cassidy)*, Donna Dixon *(Sonny Lumet)*, Telma Hopkins *(Isabelle Hammond)*.

Facts: When their apartment building is torn down to make way for condos, and they find they have no place to live, Kip Wilson and Henry Desmond accept the hospitality of co-worker Amy Cassidy and move into the Susan B. Anthony Hotel, a New York City residence for women only.

In order to live at the hotel, which they see as a bachelor's paradise that costs only $150 a month, Kip and Henry pose as women: Kip becomes his sister, Buffy Wilson, and Henry pretends to be his sister, Hildegarde Desmond—a charade that is known only to Amy (in later episodes, Amy's friends, Sonny Lumet and Isabelle Hammond learn about and keep the deception a secret).

Kip and Henry, who work at the Livingston, Gentry and Mishkin Ad Agency in Manhattan, use clothes that were part of an ad campaign for a client (Blouse City and Dresses for Women). Stories from 11/27/80 to 10/8/81 relate Kip and Henry's misadventures as they attempt to lead double lives.

Hoping to start their own ad agency, Kip, Henry and Amy quit their jobs and invest $2,000 to buy a bankrupt commercial production studio from Henry's Uncle Mort. Later, when they discover that they are $17,000 in the red, Ruth Dunbar, their former boss, becomes their silent partner when she pays off the debt. Ruth acquires 49 percent; Kip and Henry share 49 percent and Amy receives 2 percent. They name the company 60 Seconds Street, and episodes from 10/15/81 to 8/5/82 relate the group's efforts to run the company (Kip and Henry still live at the Susan B. Anthony, but the charade aspect is greatly reduced).

In the pilot episode, when Kip and Henry first pose as women, they are sisters Buffy and Hildy (not related to Kip and Henry), who were working in a logging camp in Canada and had just moved to New York. Amy, who lives in Apartment 313, pretends to know Buffy and Hildy and helps them rent their own apartment (312). An address for the Susan B. Anthony is not given. It has the awning number 3191 and appears to be in midtown Manhattan.

Kip Amos Wilson, a graphic artist at the ad agency, and Henry Desmond, a copywriter, attended Edgar Allan Poe High School (class of '75) in the town of Shaker Heights (near Cleveland). Kip, whose secret desire is to become an artist, had a showing at the Franklin Gallery (he sold one called "Peach Hell"). Henry, a Virgo, longs to be a writer and is penning a book based on his and Kip's experiences (a title was not given). Henry loves Humphrey Bogart movies, is a Cleveland Browns football fan and is called "Winkie" by his mother.

Amy Cassidy, a copyrighter at the agency, has a crush on Henry. At age 15, she "borrowed" a Greyhound bus to impress her friends and become one of them.

Sonny Lumet, a shapely nurse, works at Memorial Hospital in Manhattan and longs to be a dancer. She is from Kalamazoo and her first television commercial was the dancing soda bottle for the Trans-Allied Beverage Company.

Isabelle Hammond, a beautiful model, hopes to become a big name singer. She performs at Budd Shore's Spotlight Club, a Manhattan club that showcases promising talent.

Relatives: Wendy Goldman (Kip's real sister, *Vickie Wilson*), Jana Milo (Henry's mother, *Marjorie Desmond*), John C. Becher (Henry's uncle, *Mort*), Martina Finch (Ruth's niece, *Cecily Dunbar*). Not seen was Ruth's other niece, Gloria Dunbar.

Theme: "My Life," by Billy Joel.

75. *Boston Blackie*
Syndicated, 1951 to 1953

As a figure walks in the shadows of an alleyway, an announcer exclaims: "Danger. Excitement. Adventure. Boston Blackie—enemy to those who make him an enemy; friend to those who have no friends." Boston Blackie (Kent Taylor), called simply Blackie by his friends, is a Los Angeles–based private detective. He lives at the Brownstone Apartments and eats at Andy's luncheonette (also called Andy's Lunch Room). Blackie was a former safecracker and he knows it's not ethical to open a safe—"but who's ethical," he says. He has a gorgeous girlfriend named Mary Wesley (Lois Collier) and is very protective of her. Should anyone make "goo goo eyes" at her, Blackie will give that person a warning before taking action: "Before you get any ideas, Miss Wesley is my girl. Got it?" Mary lives at 712 Walden Avenue and is very independent and gutsy, much in the same manner as Lois Lane on "Superman"; it is not unusual to see Mary get clipped or knocked out as she attempts to help Blackie. Mary is also a bit worried about Blackie's roving eye for beautiful women (Blackie explains to Mary that "if I didn't have a roving eye for beauty, I couldn't appreciate you").

Blackie has a dog named Whitey. If Whitey is around and hears the word *bone* or *stake*, he barks (for example, "I've got a bone to pick with you" or "There's a lot at stake here"). Frank Orth plays Inspector Faraday of the L.A.P.D. Homicide Bureau. As is typical of filmed programs of this era, there are no music or theme credits listed on the screen.

76. *Bourbon Street Beat*
ABC, 10/5/59 to 9/26/60

Cast: Richard Long *(Rex Randolph)*, Andrew Duggan *(Cal Calhoun)*, Arlene Howell *(Melody Lee Mercer)*, Van Williams *(Ken Madison)*, Nita Talbot *(Lusti Weather)*.

Facts: Rex Randolph and Cal Calhoun are private detectives who operate "Randolph and Calhoun—Special Services," an investigative firm located next to the historic Old Absinthe House (a nightclub) on Bourbon Street in the French Quarter of New Orleans. The firm's telephone number is Express 7123.

Rex, born in New Orleans, is an Ivy League man and loves to cook. Cal was raised in the bayou country where his parents worked as sharecroppers. He is untidy and was a lieutenant with the Pelican Point Police Department in Louisiana before joining Rex.

Kenneth ("Kenny") Madison is from an oil-rich Texas family and works part-time for Rex while he attends Tulane University (he is studying to become a lawyer).

Melody Lee Mercer is the firm's receptionist, and she "puts up with Rex and Cal and all the violence" ("I knew when I took the job there would be gunplay and such"). She was born in Shreveport, Louisiana, and was Miss U.S.A. in the 1958 Miss Universe Pageant. Melody Lee (as she wants to be called) was previously the runner-up as "Miss Sazu City" in the Miss Mississippi Pageant (she lost, she says, "because the judges were Northerners"). She longs to become a detective and is thrilled when she does sleuthing for Rex or Cal.

Lusti Weather plays bongo drums, dances and sings at the Racquet Club in the French Quarter. She is tall and beautiful, and says, "The bongos keep my torso from becoming more so." According to Cal, she often gets suspended from gigs and busted by the police—"Too much Lusti, not enough tassles." Lusti talks about such colorful (not seen) friends as "Sunset Strip" and "Midnight Frenzy." Lusti also has a language all her own (for example, "Magnesia" is amnesia, "Hot shot on the rock" is a martini).

Lusti also considers herself a detective and enjoys helping Rex and Cal, despite the fact that Melody Lee becomes extremely jealous ("I'll show that female Sherlock Holmes who does the detective work around here," says Melody Lee—who usually jumps headfirst into a case only to find Lusti coming to her rescue). Rex calls Lusti "Lusti Love."

Eddie Cole plays "The Baron," the leader of a jazz group that plays nightly at the Old Absinthe House; Kelton Garwood plays Beauregard O'Hanlon, a painter who runs a business called Beauregard O'Hanlon's World Renowned Treasure Chest (art objects) next to the Old Absinthe House.

Rex originally ran a company called Randolph and Jelkins—Special Services (his partner, Sam Jelkins, was not seen). When Sam fails to return from a case in Pelican Point, Rex discovers that he has been killed. In Pelican Point, Rex befriends Police Lieutenant Calhoun ("People call me Cal"), who helps him uncover the truth: Sam discovered that Ira Grant (Karl Weber) was blackmailing a wealthy woman. He was killed by Ira when he tried to "muscle in" and blackmail the woman himself. Rex and Cal depart friends. Shortly after, Cal is seen walking into Rex's offices saying, "I kissed Pelican Point goodbye." "Melody," Rex says, "tell Beauregard we'll need a new sign—RANDOLPH AND CALHOUN."

Theme: "Bourbon Street Beat," by Mack David and Jerry Livingston.

77. *The Boys of Twilight*
CBS, 2/29/92 to 4/4/92

Sheriff Cody McPherson (Richard Farnsworth) and his deputy, Bill Huntoon (Wilford Brimley), are two elderly peace officers who uphold the law in Twilight, a small, rural town in Utah. Cody is married to Genelva (Louise Fletcher); Bill is a widower. The sheriff's department 4 × 4 license plate is 56148; Bill has a dog named Bessy. The series was originally titled "Cody and Bill, the Grey Guns."

John McNeely composed "The Boys of Twilight" theme.

78. *The Brady Bunch*
ABC, 9/26/69 to 8/30/74

Cast: Robert Reed *(Mike Brady)*, Florence Henderson *(Carol Brady)*, Maureen McCormick *(Marcia Brady)*, Eve Plumb *(Jan Brady)*, Susan Olsen *(Cindy Brady)*, Barry Williams *(Greg Brady)*, Christopher Knight *(Peter Brady)*, Michael Lookinland *(Bobby Brady)*, Ann B. Davis *(Alice Nelson)*.

Facts: The four-bedroom, two-bathroom home at 4222 Clinton Avenue in Los Angeles, California, is owned by Michael ("Mike") Paul Brady, a widower and the father of three sons (Greg, Peter and Bobby). He shares the house with Carol Ann Tyler Martin, his second wife, a widow and the mother of three daughters (Marcia, Jan and Cindy). They have a dog named Tiger and, in the pilot, a cat named Fluffy. Their telephone number is 762-0799 (later 555-6161), and they have two cars: a sedan (license plate TEL 635) and a station wagon (plate 746 AEH).

Mike is an architect and works for an unnamed company. He was called "the checkers champion of Chestnut Street" as a kid and in 1969 was voted "Father of the Year" by the *Daily Chronicle*. Carol attended West Side High School and had the nickname "Twinkles" as a kid. She wrote an article (unnamed) about her new family for *Tomorrow's Woman* magazine.

Marcia is the oldest of the girls. She was a member of the Sunflower Girls scout troop and first attended Fillmore Junior High School (where she was the senior class president and editor of its paper, the *Fillmore Flier*). Marcia later attends Westdale High School (she yearned to attend Tower High School but was unable to do so because her home is in the Westdale school zone). At Westdale, Marcia was a cheerleader for the Bears football team, and she had an afterschool job as a waitress at Hanson's Ice Cream Parlor.

Jan, described as "pretty, smart and kind," is the middle girl. She attends the same schools as Marcia and also worked with her at Hanson's Ice Cream Parlor. Jan holds the honor of being voted "The Most Popular Girl in Class." Cinnamon spice cookies are her favorites. At age 11, when she felt she was unattractive, Jan pretended to have a boyfriend she called George Glass. In another episode, when Jan wanted

The Brady Bunch. Front: Ann B. Davis, Florence Henderson, Michael Lookinland and Maureen McCormick. Back: Eve Plumb, Barry Williams, Susan Olsen, Robert Reed and Christopher Knight.

to be different from her blonde sisters, she wore a brunette wig to cover her own natural blonde hair.

Cindy, the youngest of the Brady girls, attends Clinton Elementary School. Romeo and Juliet are her pet rabbits, Kitty Carry-All is her favorite doll and Joan of Arc is her heroine.

Greg, the oldest boy, was a Frontier Scout and attends Westdale High School. He had a pet white mouse (Myron), and he attempted to break into the music business as a singer named Johnny Bravo. With his brothers and sisters, he formed the singing group the Brady Six (they performed the song "Time to Change").

Peter, the middle boy, attended both Clinton Elementary and Fillmore Junior High. His hero is George Washington, and he was a member of the Treehouse Club. In one episode, Christopher Knight played his lookalike friend, Arthur Owens.

Bobby, the youngest brother, attends the same school as Cindy. His hero is Jesse James, and he has a pet parakeet he calls Bird. In one episode he tried to make a million dollars by selling Neat and Natural Hair Tonic for two dollars a bottle (the product turned hair orange).

Alice Nelson, their housekeeper, had been working for Mike for seven years when he and Carol married. Her boyfriend is Sam Franklin (Allan Melvin), the owner of Sam's Butcher Shop.

The family appeared together in a television commercial for a laundry detergent called Safe. In the opening theme, the Bradys are seen in a series of squares arranged like a tic-tac-toe board. In the top sequence, from left to right, are Marcia, Carol and Greg. Left to right in the middle sequences are Jan, Alice and Peter. Cindy, Mike and Bobby are in the bottom sequence, left to right.

Relatives: Robbie Rist (Carol's nephew, *Oliver*), J. Pat O'Malley (Carol's father, *Henry Tyler*), Joan Tompkins *(Carol's mother)*, Imogene Coca (Mike's aunt, *Jenny*), Robert Reed (Mike's grandfather, *Hank Brady*), Florence Henderson (Carol's grandmother, *Connie Hutchins*), Ann B. Davis (Alice's cousin, *Emma*).

Theme: "The Brady Bunch," vocal by the Peppermint Trolley Company (first season), then the Brady Kids.

Spinoffs: "The Brady Kids" (ABC, 9/9/72 to 8/31/74). Maureen McCormick (Marcia), Eve Plumb (Jan), Susan Olsen (Cindy), Barry Williams (Greg), Christopher Knight (Peter) and Michael Lookinland (Bobby) reprise their roles in animated stories about the antics of the Brady kids.

"The Brady Bunch Hour" (ABC, 1/23/77 to 5/24/77). Geri Reischl replaced Eve Plumb as Jan Brady in this musical hour, in which the Brady family members entertain from their home in southern California.

"The Brady Girls Get Married" (NBC, 2/6/81 to 2/20/81). Marcia is now a fashion designer for Casual Clothes, and Jan is a college student majoring in architecture. Greg is now a doctor; Peter has joined the Air Force, and Cindy and Bobby are college students. Mike is still an architect, and Carol now works in sales for Willowbrook Realty. The series relates the double wedding of Marcia to Wally Logan (Jerry Houser), a designer for the Tyler Toy Company; and that of Jan to Philip Covington III (Ron

Kuhlman), a chemistry professor. The newlywed couples decide to pool their resources and share a house; their adventures continue in the series "The Brady Brides" (NBC, 3/6/81 to 4/17/81). Jan is now an architect.

A Very Brady Christmas (CBS, 12/18/88) is a television movie that brings together most of the original Brady family for a Christmas reunion. Cindy is now played by Jennifer Runyon; Carol works for Advantage Properties Real Estate; Wally is employed by Prescott Toys. Several additions were also made: Marcia's daughter, Jessica (Jaclyn Bernstein); Marcia's son, Mickey (J.W. Lee); Greg's wife, Nora (Caryn Richman); Greg's son, Kevin (Zachary Bostrom); and Peter's girlfriend, Valerie Thomas (Carol Huston).

"The Bradys" (CBS, 2/9/90 to 3/9/90). An hour series that continues to depict events in the life of the Bradys. Leah Ayres plays Marcia; Michael Malby is Marcia's son, Mickey; Valerie Ick is Jan's adopted daughter, Patty; and Jonathan Weiss is Greg's son, Kevin. New to the cast is Martha Quinn as Bobby's wife, Tracy.

Mike has retired and is now a city councilman for the fourth district (he won the election with 13,119 votes). Carol works as a real estate saleswoman. Marcia and Wally establish their own business—The Party Girls Catering Company—when they are both fired from their jobs. Jan, an architect, has taken over what is now her father's company (name not given). Cindy is a radio disc jockey with station KBLA (she hosts the show "Cindy at Sunrise"; 555-KBLA is the station's phone number).

Greg is still a doctor, and Nora is a nurse at the same unnamed hospital. Bobby is a race car driver, and Peter is his father's assistant. To make the Bradys more contemporary, Marcia was given a drinking problem and Bobby was almost crippled in a racing accident.

79. *Brand New Life*
NBC, 9/18/89 to 4/15/90

Barbara McCray (Barbara Eden) is struggling to get her life back together after her husband walked out on her and left her to raise their three children: Ericka (Jennie Garth), Christy (Alison Sweeney) and Bart (David Thom). Barbara works as a waitress in Order in the Court, a diner located next to the Los Angeles Superior Court Building. She lives at 708 Valley Drive and is pursuing a career as a court stenographer (she attends classes at Pacific Southwest School).

Roger Gibbons (Don Murray) is a widower and the father of three children: Amanda (Shawnee Smith), Laird (Byron Thomas) and Barlow (Eric Foster). Roger is a wealthy lawyer (company not named) and lives at 31304 South Birch Street in fashionable Bel Air.

One day Roger decides to have breakfast at Order in the Court and asks for "an exhibit A with no sausage." Barbara is his waitress, and it is love at first sight. They date and become engaged one month later. They marry shortly after and honeymoon (with the kids) at Lake Helgramite (where

Laird gets a terrible case of poison oak and Ericka injures her back in a water-skiing accident).

The "Blended Family" (the series' original title) establishes housekeeping at Roger's home. Roger, a Yale graduate (class of '59), was a member of the Pi Gamma Sigma fraternity. Barbara, who married young and lost her opportunity to attend college, graduated from Lincoln High School. Amanda and Ericka attended J.F.K. High School; Christy, a talented violinist who hopes one day to perform in an orchestra, attends the Willow Crest School. Bart is enrolled in the Hank E. Woodruff School. Laird has a sports car with the license plate 2AS0043.

Lou Hancock played Barbara's ex-mother-in-law, Grandma Zora (who has a dog named Mombo); Roger's late wife was named Constance.

Jill Colucci performs the theme, "Brand New Life."

80. *Branded*

NBC, 1/24/65 to 9/4/66

Cast: Chuck Connors (*Jason McCord*), Lola Albright (*Ann Williams*), John Carradine (*Joshua McCord*), William Bryant (*Ulysses S. Grant*), Suzanne Cupito [Morgan Brittany] (*Kellie*), Victor French (*Sheriff*).

Facts: When the series begins, the time is 1871. Jason McCord is an ex-army captain who has been branded a coward and dishonorably discharged. He now wanders across the country, using the experience he gained as a geologist in the army to survive. Two years earlier, he served under the command of a general named Reed, a man responsible for many peaceable negotiations with the Indians in southwestern Wyoming. General Reed, however, was aging and becoming incapable of commanding his troops. At the Battle of Bitter Creek, Jason had to relieve him of command. "Something happened after that," Jason said. "I was knocked unconscious (by the attacking Commanche Indians) and when I awoke three days later, I was being treated by a farmer miles from the battle."

Jason, the only survivor of the battle, was then arrested and courtmartialed for deserting his troops. The farmer testified that Jason walked into his place on two good legs and was perfectly rational. "That may be so," Jason said at his trial. "But I can't recall anything for those three days. Maybe I did run."

Jason never testified that he took over the command because it would have blackened the name of General Reed. He blackened the name of McCord, but preserved the good work of a statesman—"I stand by that decision." Jason then pleaded innocent but never said why ("There was nothing to tell that would have done anybody any good," Jason later said). The evidence was overwhelming, and Jason offered no defense.

At the trial, Colonel Snow (Jon Lormer) was the only one of the military brass who believed Jason was innocent. But it was not enough. Jason was dishonorably discharged—stripped of his rank, left with only a broken sword and

branded "The Coward of Bitter Creek." Horace Greeley (Burgess Meredith) wrote about Jason's trial and through his columns, the name *Jason McCord* became a household name to associate with cowardice. Jason is also called "Yellow Tail" and "Yellow Belly." The theme lyric relates Jason's struggles: "What do you do when you're branded and you know you're a man? Wherever you go for the rest of your life you must prove you're a man."

Jason was born in Washington, D.C., and attended West Point, where he graduated at the top of his class. At one time, he was assigned to coach George Armstrong Custer (Robert Lansing), a cadet who was a year behind him, on his entrance exams. Jason fought in the Battle of Shiloh and was a soldier in the Army of the Ohio (stationed at Fort Ohio). He met General Ulysses S. Grant at the Battle of Vicksburg (May 1863) and was a lieutenant with the Union Army during the Civil War. He was later stationed at Fort Lincoln. He voted for Grant when he ran for president.

In the episode "The Mission," Jason is summoned to Washington, D.C., by President Grant. Grant believes the court-martial was the right decision; however: "Whatever the facts, Bitter Creek doesn't nullify all your years as a good soldier... You've already been marked as a coward; how would you like to be branded a traitor as well?"

Grant explains that he needs an undercover agent. Branding Jason a traitor as well would provide the perfect cover for the help Grant needs in dealing with the various problems he has—from people trying to assassinate him to smugglers supplying guns to the Indians. Jason's undercover assignments for Grant are a recurring part of the series.

Jason's jobs as a surveyor took him from Seattle to Alaska. He and his partner, Rufus I. Pitkin (J. Pat O'Malley), surveyed the Alaska Wilderness for William Seward (Ian Wolfe) and the docks of Seattle for the governor. Rufus left Jason to become an undertaker (because his initials spelled *R.I.P.* His horse was named Margaret, and he established business in the town of Cutbank). Jason worked on his own after that, seeking just to leave his past behind him and begin a new life.

In "Cowards Die Many Times," the next to last episode, Jason takes a job surveying for the railroad (which is planning to lay track through the town of Panamint). In town, Jason meets his old flame, Ann Williams, now the editor of the *Banner,* the town's newspaper. Jason's plan to blast through a mountain and build a tunnel earns him the job of engineering supervisor for the project. In the final moments of the episode, Ann approaches Jason and says, "Hey, McCord, are you busy? I'm a newspaper editor. I got a couple of presses and a pretty fair circulation and a piece of land just outside of town that might be right for a small house. Are you interested?" "I'm interested, I'm very interested," Jason says. They kiss and Jason decides to settle down.

In the final episode, "Kellie," Jason and his grandfather, General Joshua McCord, have established an office called McCord and McCord, Survey Engineers." At this same time, Ann takes a pretty orphan girl named Kellie under her wing, and it is assumed that Jason and Ann will marry and raise Kellie. Also introduced as a new regular (had the series continued another season) was the town sheriff (no name given).

Theme: "Branded," by Dominic Frontiere (music) and Alan Alch (lyrics).

81. *Brave Eagle: Chief of the Cheyenne*

CBS, 9/28/55 to 6/6/56

The Black Mountain region of Wyoming (1860s) is the sacred land of the Cheyenne Indians. "We learn to count our wealth in the beauty around us and in the qualities of wisdom and courage that serve us in our way of life," says Brave Eagle (Keith Larsen), the chief of the Cheyenne tribe. Brave Eagle accepts all men as his brothers and has made peace with the white man (specifically, the men of the U.S. Cavalry, which has established Fort Wilson near the reservation). The Peagan tribe are the enemies of the Cheyenne, and the most sacred law of the Cheyenne is the law of hospitality (to offer food and care to their fellow braves). Despite the fact that renegade Indians and "bad guys" use guns, Brave Eagle refuses to use such weapons (he and his tribe use the traditional bow and arrow).

Keena (Keena Numkena) is Brave Eagle's adopted son. (Brave Eagle found Keena, a member of the Lota tribe, as a papoose. Keena was the only survivor of a small band of Lota that was attacked by the Commanche. Brave Eagle took Keena to be his son.) Keena and Brave Eagle hunt on each full moon, and Keena has a pony he calls My Pony.

Morning Star (Kim Winona) and Smokey Joe (Bert Wheeler) are the other featured members of the tribe. Morning Star is a full-blooded Cheyenne; Smokey Joe "was born of the white man's blood" and served with the U.S. Cavalry (he wears a jacket with his sergeant's stripes) before choosing to live with the people on his mother's side of the family.

"Brave Eagle: Chief of the Cheyenne" is the official screen title; the series is commonly known by its *TV Guide* listing of "Brave Eagle." The plight of the American Indian was next explored in a less violent way in the series "Born to the Wind" (NBC, 8/19/82 to 9/5/82). The series, set on the American frontier in 1825, followed the lives of a group of Plains Indians who called themselves The People. Principals of the large cast are Will Sampson (Painted Bear), A Martinez (Low Wolf), Henry Darrow (Lost Robe), Rose Portillo (Star Fire) and Dehl Berti (One Feather).

Bret Maverick see *Maverick*

82. *The Brian Keith Show*

NBC, 9/21/73 to 8/30/74

As the theme plays, an announcer says, "Introducing 'The Brian Keith Show' comedy team: In the title role, Brian Keith (Dr. Sean Jamison); also starring Shelley Fabares as Dr. Anne Jamison; Victoria Young as the vivacious office nurse, Puni; Nancy Kulp as the wealthy landlady (Millar Gruber); and Roger Bowen as the very proper Dr. Austin Chaffey."

Drs. Sean Jamison and his daughter, Anne, both graduates of Harvard Medical School, operate the Jamison Clinic for Children in Kahala, Hawaii. Their phone number is 555-6606, and their staff consists of a beautiful native girl named Puni, who serves as their nurse and receptionist, and a young local boy named Stewart (Sean Tyler Hall) who receives a salary of one dollar a week to sweep, clean and empty trash baskets. Sean also has a parrot named Sam. Puni calls Sean "Dr. Jamie" and Anne "Dr. Anne." Anne also serves as the local vet and runs the local Children's Theater Group. Sean's favorite pastime is fishing.

Millar Gruber, the landlady, charges Sean $450 a month rent and worries about her walls (she owns the building and fears Sean will put holes in them to hang pictures). She attended Audubon University and has been married six times. She lost each husband and says, "Death has been my co-pilot." Puni fears that Mrs. Gruber (as she calls her) will sell the land the clinic stands on for a taco stand.

Dr. Austin Chaffey (referred to as Spencer Chaffey on press releases) is also a graduate of Audubon University (although he and Millar did not know each other until he arrived on the island to open his practice; he rents an office, at $250 a month, in Sean's clinic). Austin is an allergist but isn't fond of children. (When he first met Anne, he told her of his plans to improve the clinic: "Those pictures will have to come down; they are too infantile for my patients. And these tiny tables and chairs should go too; they make the place look like the Seven Dwarves' house. And those monkey bars and swings outside—would like to get rid of them too. They'll just encourage a lot of kids to come around.") Austin's plans for change meets strong opposition from Sean—who is determined to find a loophole in the lease, "even if it takes 50 years."

Austin has a prized collection of frog jumping trophies and keeps his stuffed frog, Big Hopper of Webfoot, on his desk (the frog, Austin says, won him and his grandfather the Frog Jumping Nationals in 1946, '47 and '48).

The series was originally called "The Little People" and aired on NBC from 9/15/72 to 9/7/73.

Themes: "The Little People," by Jerry Fielding; "The Brian Keith Show Theme," by Artie Butler.

83. *Bridget Loves Bernie*

CBS, 9/16/72 to 9/8/73

On an overcast day in New York City, schoolteacher Bridget Theresa Mary Colleen Fitzgerald (Meredith Baxter) hails a cab driven by Bernard ("Bernie") Steinberg (David Birney). Bernie drops Bridget off at her destination (school) and leaves. That rainy afternoon, as Bridget exits the school to return home, she sees Bernie waiting for her. They walk hand in hand through Central Park, kiss and fall in love. Bridget is Irish-Catholic; Bernie is Jewish. Despite the fact that their parents object to a mixed marriage, Bridget and Bernie marry in a civil ceremony (later, to please their parents, in a ceremony presided over by a priest and a rabbi).

Bridget's parents are Walter (David Doyle) and Amy Fitzgerald (Audra Lindley); Sam (Harold J. Stone) and Sophie Steinberg (Bibi Osterwald) are Bernie's parents. Walter and Amy are very rich and live in a luxurious penthouse apartment at 1041 Central Park West. Walter, a staunch Republican, owns a company called Global Investments. Sam and Sophie run Steinberg's Delicatessen on Manhattan's Lower East Side (located next to Goldstein's Bakery); the deli closes at 8:00 P.M. Bridget and Bernie have set up housekeeping in an apartment above the deli. (Feeling that his daughter was meant for the finer things in life, Walter offered Bridget and Bernie a trip around the world and a portfolio of blue chip stocks as a wedding gift. When they refused it, he gave them a one year rent-free twenty-first floor apartment at the Manchester Arms. Bridget and Bernie moved in—but left shortly after; they missed the old neighborhood and its sights and sounds.)

Bridget teaches fourth grade at the Immaculate Heart Academy (the same school she attended as a girl) in mid–Manhattan. When she was a young girl, Bridget fell off her roller skates and broke her wrist; her favorite cartoon was "Mrs. Snuggle Bunny and the Tree Toads." Bernie, who has ambitions of being a theater actor, drives cab 12 (number IC-56); rates are 60 cents for the first mile, ten cents each one-fifth mile. Amy is a member of the Daughters of Isabella Charity League and believes it was a bad day for movies when Loretta Young stopped making them (Sophie believes movies came to a halt when Sylvia Sidney stopped making them).

Moe Plotnic (Ned Glass) is Sophie's brother and runs the catering end of the deli; Father Michael Fitzgerald (Robert Sampson) is Bridget's older brother, a parish priest at the Immaculate Heart Church.

Jerry Fielding and Diane Hilderbrand composed the theme, "Love Is Crazy."

84. *Bringing Up Buddy*

CBS, 10/10/60 to 9/25/61

Bradley Falls is a small town in California. At 1492 Maple Street lives Buddy Flower (Frank Aletter) and his spinster aunts, Violet (Enid Markey) and Iris (Doro Merande). Buddy, an investment broker for Cooper Investments, was raised by Violet and Iris after his parents' death. Buddy has a girlfriend, his secretary, Kathy Donnell (Nancy Rennick), but finds his life complicated by the meddling of his aunts as they try to find him a wife. "Those two can get in and out of trouble without realizing they have ever been in it," says Buddy when he becomes involved in their antics. Violet calls everybody "Love," and in one episode the aunts mention

raising Buddy since he was an infant. Buddy served in the army during the Korean War. The Joe Connelly–Bob Mosher produced series has no credit for the theme music.

85. *Broken Badges*

CBS, 11/24/90 to 12/22/90
CBS, 6/6/91 to 6/20/91

Cast: Miguel Ferrer (*Beau Jack Bowman*), Eileen Davidson (*Judy Tingreedies*), Teresa Donahue (*Eleanor Hardwicke*), Jay Johnson (*Stanley Jones*), Ernie Hudson (*Toby Baker*), Charlotte Lewis (*Priscilla Mathers*).

Facts: When his snitch, Frank Cardenas (Carlos Gomez), is accused of a double murder in California, Beau Jack Bowman, a Cajun sergeant with the Louisiana Police Department, travels to Bay City to clear Frank of the charge.

Bowman immediately encounters hostility from the Bay City Police Department (who did not want to hear that Frank is innocent), but he befriends Eleanor Hardwicke, a lieutenant on the special staff of Chief Sterling (Don Davis).

Eleanor sympathizes with Jack and helps him form his own unit of three cops from the Rubber Gun Squad (officers on psychiatric leave who are "broken and unstable") to help him: Judy Tingreedies, Stanley Jones and Toby Baker.

Jack's somewhat unorthodox team accomplishes their mission to prove land developer Martin Valentine (Tobin Bell) was guilty of the murder. Impressed by Jack and his team of Broken Badges, Chief Sterling offers Jack the opportunity officially to head his previously classified T.A.R.P. (Temporary Assignment of Restricted Personnel Cops). Jack accepts the assignment. He calls his team the Cobra Squad, and they become a nonspecific undercover unit the chief uses when dangerous undercover work is necessary. (Their squad car license plate reads 2ME-A471.)

Beau Jack Bowman is 37 years old and proud of his Cajun heritage. Jack is known for his unorthodox and violent approaches to crime and makes up the rules as he goes along. He prefers his Cajun cuisine but says, "A Cajun will eat anything that won't eat him first." Jack has a large sign posted next to his house that reads CAJUN JACK'S HOSPITALITY HOUSE. His license plate reads N39E467.

Officer Judy Tingreedies, who has the nickname "Bullet," is a punk-pretty, Rambo-style motorcycle cop (she rides a Harley). She loves to wear leather and tops that accentuate her well-developed bosom; however, "I don't like guys staring at my chest—it makes me angry" (and you don't want to get her angry—"I'm a street bitch with an attitude"). Judy is always eager for action and constantly complains: "Are you guys just gonna sit here or are we gonna go out and kick some butt?" Because of her addiction to danger, no other cop would work with her; she was removed from the force due to extreme psychosis.

Sergeant Stanley Jones was a street cop for three years. The pressures of the job forced him to retreat to a ventriloquist's world, and he now communicates through his dummy, "Officer Danny." Stanley believes Danny is real (if the two of them were to engage in a fist fight, Danny would win). Stanley is street-smart; his talent for throwing his voice is a big asset to the team. He has written a book of poems called *The Forest* under the pen name L.S. Jones and has the street name "Whipusual" (while no one can explain what the name means, Jack believes it is a variation of "Whip Us All" because Stanley uses the steel plate in his head like a battering ram and can "whip anybody in a fight"). Stanley is sensitive about his height and gets violently angry when people call him "Little Guy." Officer Danny has a severe attitude problem and is an escort with the All Male Mahogany Escort Service. Stanley lives at 134 Meadow Lark Drive, and his license plate reads 2ME-BOH.

Sergeant Toby Baker is a forensics expert who suffers from fits of depression and deep self-hatred. He is also a kleptomaniac, and when situations becomes stressful, he believes he is an old West Texas Ranger named Cactus Cole Watson.

Eleanor Hardwicke is a lieutenant and apparently the only member of what she calls the chief's Special Staff. She has a Ph.D. from the University of Chicago and did her dissertation on police department procedures. She is now seeking to implement her research in the Bay City Police Department and make it fully operational based on her belief of what a police department should be. While Eleanor does occasionally bend the rules to help Jack, she will not disobey Chief Sterling ("I don't disobey orders; it goes against my operational code"). Eleanor occasionally assists the team in the field, but she is basically their computer expert and department contact.

Dr. Priscilla Mathers is assigned by Chief Sterling to watch over and psychologically help the team. She involves herself with the team and "saves the day" by arriving at crucial moments.

Theme: "Broken Badges," by Mike Post.

86. *Bronco*

ABC, 9/23/58 to 9/20/60

Post office undercover agent, frontier guide, miner, wagon train captain, deputy and army scout are some of the jobs held by Bronco Layne (Ty Hardin), an ex–Confederate Army captain who wanders from town to town fighting injustice in the post–Civil War West.

Bronco was born in Texas ("down around the old Panhandle") and "there ain't a horse that he can't handle, that's how he got his name." His grandfather was a "Yankee," and Bronco continued the proud family tradition by serving with the Texas Confederacy. He has a Colt. 45 with the inscription COURAGE IS THE FREEDOM OF HONOR, a pocket watch that plays the song "Deep in the Heart of Dixie," and a reminder of the Battle of Elmira—a cat he calls Elmira (who dislikes chili). Inside the watch there is a picture of Redemption McNally (Kathleen Crowley), Bronco's one and only love (they grew up together in Texas).

When the war ended, Bronco returned to Texas to become partners with his friend, Enrique ("Rickie") Cortez (Gerald Mohr) in the Layne and Cortez General Store. But Bronco, who has the wanderlust, dislikes staying in one place. He decides to leave town "to go where the grass may be greener." He leaves without Elmira (whom he gives to Enrique) and his gold pocket watch, which he gave to the chief of an Indian war party to save his and Enrique's lives when they were bringing merchandise back to town.

Although he preferred to avoid trouble, Bronco refused to stand by and see others abused ("You've never seen a twister, mister, til someone gets him riled").

In the window of the Layne and Cortez Store, there is one very special item: Bronco's gold watch (which Enrique acquired from a drifter who bought it from an Indian). There is also a sign next to the watch. It reads WILL OWNER PLEASE CLAIM. Bronco never did.

Mack David and Jerry Livingston composed the "Bronco" theme.

87. *Brooklyn Bridge*

CBS, 9/20/91 to 11/14/92

A nostalgic look at life in Brooklyn, New York, in 1956 as seen through the eyes of three generations of a Jewish family: grandparents Sophie and Jules Berger (Marion Ross and Louis Zorich), their married daughter, Phyllis Silver (Amy Aquino), and her husband, George (Peter Friedman), and their children, Alan and Nathaniel Silver (Danny Gerard and Matthew Louis Siegal).

Sophie was born in Poland, Jules in Russia. They met as teenagers in Brooklyn; they now live in Apartment 2A of an unidentified building with the number 1138; Phyllis and her family live upstairs in Apartment 3D. Jules mentioned that he was in the millinery line; his and Sophie's favorite restaurant is the Flower Garden.

George grew up on South 6th Street in Williamsburgh; Phyllis attended Seth Lowell Junior High School and won an award for best speller. George works for the post office as a mail sorter at the main branch at Borough Hall; Phyllis is an office manager for a small insurance agent.

Alan is 14 years old and attends Seth Lowell Junior High School, then Lafayette High School. He was a member of the Royals baseball team (jersey number 8) and hangs out with his friends Benny Belinski (Jake Jundef) and Warren Butcher (Aeryk Egan) at Sid's Candy Store (officially known as Sid Elgart's Fine Confections; David Whol plays Sid). Alan also appeared on the television show "Happy Felton's Knothole Gang" (where kids meet famous baseball players). Nathaniel is nine years old and attends P.S. 205; he is in the fourth grade and is on the Dodgers Little League team (he plays third base; Gil Hodges of the Brooklyn Dodgers is his hero).

Kathleen ("Katie") Monahan (Jenny Lewis) is a very pretty 14-year-old Irish-Catholic girl. She lives in Apartment 2C at 1640 Cortilla Road and attends Saint Matthew's Grammar

School, then Saint Matthew's High School. She is also Alan's girlfriend—and a bit of a problem for Sophie, who disapproves of a Catholic girl dating a Jewish boy.

Constance McCashin and James Naughton play Katie's parents, Rosemary and Patrick Monahan; Yvonne Suhor is Katie's sister, Colleen. Carol Kane is Sophie's daughter, "Aunt" Sylvia.

Art Garfunkel performs the theme, "Just Over the Brooklyn Bridge."

88. *Buck Rogers in the 25th Century*

NBC, 9/27/79 to 9/13/80
NBC, 1/15/81 to 8/20/81

Cast: Gil Gerard *(Buck Rogers)*, Erin Gray *(Wilma Deering)*, Tim O'Connor *(Dr. Elias Huer)*, Pamela Hensley *(Ardella)*.

Facts: The year is 1987. At the John F. Kennedy Space Center, NASA prepares to launch the last of its deep-space probes. Perched in the nose cone of the rocket is the *Ranger III*, a one-man exploration vessel piloted by Captain William ("Buck") Rogers. Shortly after the *Ranger III* is launched, cosmic forces cause a freak accident that freezes Buck's life support system and alters the *Ranger III*'s planned trajectory. The craft is sent into an orbit a thousand times more vast, and a perfect combination of gases (oxygen, ozone and methylene) enters the craft. The gases are instantaneously frozen and preserve Buck.

The craft drifts for 504 years before it is found by the king's flagship, *Draconia*. The Princess Ardella commands the ship; Kane is her aide. The Draconia Empire has conquered three-quarters of the universe and is now en route to Earth on a peace mission (to establish a trade agreement). The *Ranger III* is brought aboard the *Draconia,* and Buck is taken to sick bay. There he is revived but not told about his fate. He believes he is aboard the *Ranger III* and having hallucinations; Ardella and Kane believe Buck is an Earth Directorate spy and allow him to leave (they have repaired and refueled the *Ranger III*).

When Buck's craft comes within Earth Directorate air space, Delta Sector dispatches fighters to intercept it. When Buck fails to comply with orders given by Colonel Wilma Deering, she takes control of his ship and guides him safely through their defense shield (if a ship enters the Earth's atmosphere without clearance, it is immediately incinerated). Buck is still unaware of what has happened to him and now believes he has been captured by the Russians. Wilma takes Buck (whom she calls a barbarian for defying her) to Dr. Elias Huer, the head of the Earth Federation, for interrogation. It is when Buck speaks with Dr. Theopolis, a member of the computer council that runs the Inner City, that he learns it is the year 2491 and that the world as he knew it no longer exists. A holocaust has ravaged the planet. The Earth is now dependent upon trade with other planets

and people live in cone-protected cities (the atmosphere still has traces of radiation from the holocaust). New Chicago is now the capitol of the United States and is the headquarters of the Earth Federation (Wilma is the commander of the Earth Defense Force). Buck is assigned a silver ambuquad named Twiki to help him adjust to life in this new world. Wilma, however, is distrustful of Buck and believes he is a threat to their safety. Wilma's mind is changed when Buck proves the supposedly unarmed Draconia craft that rescued him is armed and foils Princess Ardella's plans to conquer the Earth.

Buck can't go back—the past is gone—but he can help Wilma and Dr. Huer with their future. He becomes a member of the Third Force of the Earth Directorate.

Buck's *Ranger III* code was "Flight 711 to Houston Control." Wilma was called "Dizzy Dee" as a kid. Twiki, voiced by Mel Blanc and played by Felix Silla, has the serial number 2223-T. Buck calls Dr. Theopolis (voice of Eric Server) "Theo." The Capitol Building in New Chicago is the Directorate Building; the national retirement age has risen to 85.

The beautiful Princess Ardella is the daughter of King Draco the Conquerer (Joseph Wiseman), the ruler of the planet Draconia. Ardella is the eldest of Draco's 29 daughters and has her mind set on becoming her own ruler (she wants to defy her father, live her own life "and begin a magnificent new dynasty with Buck"). Ardella measures 34-24-34 and commands the two-mile-wide space ship, the *Draconia*; the series ended before Ardella could accomplish her goal. Henry Silva (pilot) and Michael Ansara (series) played Kane.

The format changed in second season episodes to relate Buck and Wilma's experiences as members of *Searcher,* a spaceship seeking the lost tribes of Earth. Admiral Ephraim Asimov (Jay Garner) is the ship's commander (he is also called Isaac Asimov); Dr. Goodfellow (Wilfred Hyde-White) is the scientific genius; and Hawk (Thom Christopher) is their alien, man-bird ally. While the role of Twiki has been cut back, that of Crichton (voice of Jeff Davis), the robot who refuses to believe that he is manmade, has been added.

Theme: "Theme from Buck Rogers: Suspension," by Glen A. Larson (vocal in the pilot episode by Kipp Lennon).

Note: An earlier version of "Buck Rogers in the 25th Century" ran on ABC from 5/15/50 to 1/3/52 with Kem Dibbs (1950) and Robert Pastine (1951) as Buck; Lou Prentis as Wilma; and Harry Sothern as Dr. Huer. Earl Hammond was Buck Rogers and Eva Marie Saint played Wilma Deering in a 1949 unaired pilot called "Buck Rogers in the 25th Century."

89. *Buffalo Bill, Jr.*

Syndicated, 1955

Following an Indian attack on a wagon train, Judge Ben Wiley (Harry Cheshire) finds two survivors, a young boy and

Buck Rogers in the 25th Century. Erin Gray and Gil Gerard.

his sister, wandering through the desolate Black Hills. The judge takes the children under his wing and brings them to Wileyville, the Texas town he founded.

"I was carrying my sister in a buffalo robe, so the judge named me Buffalo Bill, Jr. He called my mischievous sister Calamity." The time is 1891 when the series begins. Bill (Dick Jones) is the town's deputy marshal. He idolizes the real William ("Buffalo Bill") Cody and dresses like him. He can trick ride and trick shoot and lives by what the judge taught him: "You can't make yourself a big man by standing in the shadow of another man." Bill rides a horse named Chief.

Calamity (Nancy Gilbert), named after Calamity Jane, the tomboyish woman of the Old West who earned a living as a stagecoach driver, works in the Wileyville General Store. She considers herself a preteen law enforcer and strives to help Bill. "I'm goin' with you, Bill," she says when trouble is brewing. "Oh, no, you're not," says Bill. "There might be trouble, besides—" Calamity interrupts: "I know the two reasons—first I'll get in your hair, and girls belong at home." Before Bill rides off, he usually says something like "Go home and bake a cherry pie, Calamity." Calamity's disobedience most often pays off when she saves the day for Bill.

The judge is called Ben ("Fair 'n' Square") Wiley. He charges two dollars for legal advice, runs the barbershop (two bits for a shave), is the owner of the general store (which doubles as his courtroom), is the town doctor, sheriff and blacksmith.

The Dobson Stage Lines services "the One Horse Burg" (what outlaws call Wileyville); Mesquite Canyon is just outside of town; James Best plays Larry, the telegraph operator.

Carl Cotner composed the theme: "...Now with his horse and with his guns, he's not afraid of anyone, 'cause no one's quicker on the draw or quicker to defend the law—he's the son of a son of a gun, Buffalo Bill, Jr."

The Bullwinkle Show see Rocky and His Friends

90. *Burke's Law*

ABC, 9/20/63 to 8/31/65

Amos Burke (Gene Barry) is a millionaire who is also a police captain with the Metropolitan Division of the L.A.P.D. Amos, a ladies' man, resides at 109 North Milbourne and has a limo with the license plate JZG063 (also seen as JE 8495). Henry (Leon Lontoc) is his combination houseboy and chauffeur; Burke's office phone number is Madison 6-7399.

Detectives Tim Tillson (Gary Conway) and Lester Hart (Regis Toomey) assist Burke. Tim's phone number is 676-4882; Lester lives at 106 Essex Drive. Gene Barry played

Amos' uncle, Patrick Harrigan, in the episode "Who Killed the Grand Piano." Each show is a mystery, with celebrities as the suspects in a murder. The original key to solving the crime before Burke was to time the length of questioning each celebrity received; the suspect with the least amount of air time was usually the culprit (with episodes cut by six to eight minutes for syndication, the key is now lost). Herschel Burke Gilbert composed the "Burke's Law" theme.

In the spinoff series "Amos Burke, Secret Agent" (ABC, 9/15/65 to 1/12/66), Burke quits the police force to become a U.S. government secret agent. Carl Benton Reid is his superior, "The Man."

91. *Bus Stop*

ABC, 10/1/61 to 3/25/62

Miller's Hardware on Main Street sells, in addition to nails, hammers and saws, dolls and necklaces. The Cascade Motel offers free television and daily and weekly rates. There is Gahringer's Drug Store, the Freemont Hotel, and the Sherwood Bus Depot (located behind the gas pumps at the bus stop for Arrow-Flite Buslines). Grace Sherwood (Marilyn Maxwell) is the diner owner, and Elma Gahringer (Joan Freeman) is her waitress. Will Mayberry (Rhodes Reason) is the sheriff; Glenn Wagner (Richard Anderson) is the D.A.; and Sally (Dianne Foster) is Glenn's wife. The setting is the small town of Sunrise, Colorado, and stories present character studies of the lost and troubled people who have disembarked for a stopover at the Sherwood Bus Depot.

The series is very loosely based on the 1955 Broadway play by William Inge (most people recall the 1956 feature film version starring Marilyn Monroe as Cherie and Don Murray as Bo). The sixth episode of the series, "Cherie" (11/12/61) is the pilot and the only episode adapted from the play (Tuesday Weld portrayed Cherie, the hopeful singer, and Bo, the cowboy who wants to marry her, was played by Gary Lockwood).

The episode of 12/3/61, "A Lion Walks Among Us," is perhaps the most condemned episode of a series ever broadcast to this date. Although tame by today's standards, in 1961 it was called "an hour of ugliness," "a pure study in evil" and "cheaper than anything yet seen on TV." (Teen idol Fabian Forte played a murderous psychopath with such believability that the episode was cited for excessive violence and sadism).

Theme: "Bus Stop," by Arthur Morton.

92. *Busting Loose*

CBS, 1/17/77 to 11/16/77

Lenny Markowitz (Adam Arkin) is a 24-year-old shoe salesman at the Wear Well Shoe Store. He has moved out of his parents' home and now lives in his own apartment at 36 West 43rd Street in Manhattan. He is a bachelor and hopes one day to become a television sportscaster. Lenny lives by his childhood code always to help a friend in need, and he has one major problem: his mother, Pearl Markowitz (Pat Carroll), who has deemed it her responsibility to find him a girl and a career. While Lenny argues, "When are you going to learn that I am capable of planning my own life and meeting my own girls?" Pearl responds by saying, "I was only trying to help you for your own good; I was only trying to see you happy." Trying to resolve this situation is Lenny's father, Sam Markowitz (Jack Kruschen), who puts it simply to Pearl: "Leonard is a man, you should treat him like a man." Pearl agrees (until the next episode, that is).

Melody Feebeck (Barbara Rhoades) is Lenny's neighbor, a gorgeous redhead who works for Mr. Escort, an escort service that caters to men of all ages. Sometimes Melody has a problem when a date becomes too frisky. When this happens, she gives Lenny the signal (knocks on the wall) to become the enraged husband and burst into her apartment. "The Enraged Husband Bit," as Melody calls it, always works and scares off troublesome dates.

Vinnie Mordabito (Greg Antonacci), a cab driver, and Woody Warshaw (Paul Sylvan) are Lenny's friends. Ralph Cabell (Paul B. Price) is Lenny's employer, the owner of Wear Well Shoes, and Raymond St. Williams (Ralph Wilcox) is Ralph's top-notch salesman.

Louise Williams plays Jacqueline ("Jackie") Gleason, Lenny's steady girlfriend in later episodes; and Dorothy Butts appeared as Raymond's wife, Dorothy St. Williams. The series was originally titled "On Our Own." Mark Rothman composed the "Busting Loose" theme.

93. *Cagney and Lacey*

CBS, 3/25/82 to 9/12/83
CBS, 3/19/84 to 8/25/88

Christine ("Chris") Cagney (Meg Foster and Sharon Gless) and Mary Beth Lacey (Tyne Daly) are detectives with the 14th Precinct of the N.Y.P.D. Chris is single and lives at 11 West 49th Street in Manhattan; Mary Beth lives in Queens (at 7132 46th Street) with her husband, Harvey (John Karlen), and their children, Harvey, Jr. (Tony LaTorre), Michael (Troy Slaten) and Alice (Donna and Paige Bardolph). Harvey is a freelance construction worker; in the fifth grade, Mary Beth was called Mary Number 2 by her teacher (to distinguish her from Mary Number 1—Mary Lazonne). Chris, who never married, has a drinking problem like her father, Charlie Cagney (Dick O'Neill). Chris's car license plate reads 562 BLA (later 801 FEM); her badge number is 763; Mary Beth's badge number is 340. Chris and Mary Beth are partners, and their mobile code is Car 27. Lieutenant Albert Samuels (Al Waxman) is their superior; and detectives Victor Isbecki (Martin Kove) and Mark Petrie (Carl Lumbly) also work at the 14th.

Relatives: Richard Bradford (Mary Beth's father, *Martin Biskey*), Penny Santon (Harvey's mother, *Muriel Lacey*), David Ackroyd (Chris's brother, *Brian Cagney*), Amanda Wyss (Chris's niece, *Bridget Cagney*).

Pilot Episode Roles: Loretta Swit *(Chris Cagney)*, Robert Hunter *(Harvey Lacey)*, Jefferson Maypin *(Victor Isbecki)*, Evan Routbard *(Michael Lacey)*, Jamie Dick *(Harvey Lacey, Jr.)*.

Themes: "Ain't That the Way," vocal by Marie Cain, and "The Theme from Cagney and Lacey," by Bill Conti.

94. *California Dreams*

NBC, 9/12/92 to the present

Jennifer ("Jenny") Garrison (Heidi Noelle Lenhart), her brother, Matthew ("Matt") Garrison (Brent Gore), and their friends, Tiffany Smith (Kelly Packard) and Tony Wicks (William James Jones), are teenagers who compose the music group California Dreams, a soft-rock group managed by Sly Winkle (Michael Cade).

Jenny and Matt live at 128 Ocean Drive in California with their mother, Melody (Gail Ramsey), their father, Darryl (Michael Cutt), and their younger brother, Dennis (Ryan O'Neill).

Jenny, Matt, Tiffany, Tony and Sly attend Pacific Coast High School in California and hang out at a beachside eatery called Sharkey's (where Tony also works as a waiter). Each group member sings and plays a musical instrument: Jenny (keyboard), Tony (drums), Matt and Tiffany (guitar). Matt formed the group and writes their songs (the first one he wrote was "California Dreams"); their first video, "Everybody's Got Someone," aired on a television show called "Video 99." The group plays whatever gigs Sly can get for them, and they still have a long road to walk before they become famous.

Jenny has a collection of stuffed animals she calls "Stuffies," a poster of James Dean on the wall behind her bed and a poster of the film *Giant* on her bedroom door. She is very particular about the guys she dates. When she breaks up with a guy, she locks herself in her room and watches "thirtysomething" reruns.

Jenny and Tiffany have been friends since childhood (they are now 16). As a kid, dreamer Tiffany would pretend to live in a fairy tale forest; realist Jenny would try but fail to convince her it wasn't the real world. When Tiffany, who loves to wear bikinis, is on the beach, she claims, "I can't figure out why the boys stop swimming to watch me."

Sly's real name is Sylvester, but "Sly is the name. Never call me Sylvester." Jenny and Tiffany detest the thought of dating the somewhat sleazy Sly; however, when Tiffany taught Sly how to surf, the unthinkable happened—she fell for him and called him "Splushie" (Jenny awoke her to the fact that it was Sly she was falling for).

Jenny and Matt's parents honeymooned at the Starlight Café; Darryl is a schoolteacher (school name not given).

California Fever. **Jimmy McNichol** (front); then left to right: **Lorenzo Lamas, Michele Tobin** and **Marc McClure.**

Pamela Bowen appeared as Tiffany's mother, Judy Smith; and John Wesley was Tony's father, Darren Wicks.

Steve Tyrell composed the music; the California Dreams sing the theme, "California Dreams."

95. *California Fever*

CBS, 9/25/79 to 12/11/79

Vince Butler (James Vincent McNichol), Laurie (Michele Tobin) and Ross Whitman (Marc McClure) are three 17-year-olds who attend Westside High School and hang out together at Sunset Beach in California. Rick's Place, run by Rick (Lorenzo Lamas), is the local beach hangout, an eatery that also rents and sells bikes, skateboards and surfboards.

Vince lives at 5832 Beachwood Avenue. He drives a sports car with the license plate IM CRUSIN and operates a three watt underground radio station (from the back room in Rick's Place) called K-Fever (Vince is "the Ghost of the Coast at the top of the dial"). His favorite meal at Rick's is alfalfa salad and a protein drink.

Laurie (no last name given), whose favorite singer is Rex Smith, drives a car with the license plate 776 CFE; she lives at 7163 Lincoln Street.

Ross, who frequents an eatery called Junk Burgers, has a mostly inoperable van parked on Beachwood Street with the license plate IF 39016 and "The Grossmobile" (license plate IR 772), a customized dune buggy. Ross also won $500 by dancing 11 hours and 13 minutes in a marathon at the Solar System Disco.

The only relative seen is Vince's mother, Mary Butler (Barbara Tarbuck) who drives a station wagon with the license 872 LWJ.

Theme: "California Fever," vocal by James Vincent McNichol.

96. *The Californians*

NBC, 9/24/57 to 9/6/59

"Now one thing I just can't endure is being broke and being poor . . . so I've come to live where life is best in the golden West, I've come to strike it rich in Cal-i-for-ni-a." The Gold Rush days of old San Francisco are the setting (from 1849 to 1854 for the series). The call of "there's gold in them thar hills" brought both the honest prospectors and pioneers and a group of corrupt Australians who managed to gain control of the city. One such pioneer was Dion Patrick (Adam Kennedy), a crusading newspaper editor (the *California Star*) who established the Vigilante Committee of San Francisco as a means to uphold law and order.

After 22 episodes, Dion Patrick was written out and replaced by Matt Wayne (Richard Coogan), a gentleman from Philaelphia who opens a gambling hall and is later elected marshal by the townspeople. When the second season began (episode 38, "Dishonor for Matt Wayne"), Matt relinquishes his gambling hall to become a full time law enforcer (the idea of a marshal who owned a gambling hall bothered the city fathers). Matt turns over the title of the gambling hall to Wilma Fansler (Carole Mathews), the girl who previously ran the games of chance for Matt.

Jack McGivern (Sean McClory) is the owner of McGivern's General Store; Martha McGivern (Nan Leslie) is Jack's wife; and R. Jeremy Pitt (Arthur Fleming) is a rugged gentleman lawyer with a practice in San Francisco.

The Ken Darby Singers perform the theme, "I've Come to California" (written by Harold Adamson and Harry Warren).

Call Mr. D see Richard Diamond, Private Detective

97. *Camp Runamuck*

NBC, 9/17/65 to 9/2/66

Camp Runamuck is a summer boys' camp "in the middle of the farming country." Wallace ("Wally") Wivenhoe (Arch Johnson) is its owner, a crude, rude and miserable man who is referred to as Commander Wivenhoe. There are 40 boys attending the camp, and state law requires that there be one counselor for every ten campers. "The food is bad," the kids (called Runamuckians) rarely get meat and the camp is, as its name implies, slipshodly run. George Spiffy (David Ketchum) is the senior counselor; Stanley Pruett (Dave Madden) is a counselor; and Malden (Mike Wagner) is the camp's overweight cook. Medical emergencies are handled by Doc Joslyn (Frank DeVol, then Leonard Stone). Doc previously worked for eight years at County General

Hospital; George was a meteorologist in the air force.

Wivenhoe considers his campgrounds a haven and seeks to preserve his "forest paradise" from "the women who have invaded his woods." The "women" Wivenhoe fears are the campers and female counselors at Camp Divine, an all-girls summer camp that is located directly across the lake from Runamuck (it is a 32 mile drive around the lake to Camp Divine). The girls sound assembly (by bugle) at 6:00 A.M. and drive Wivenhoe and his counselors batty with their song "Good Morning to You," which they sing each morning before a day's activities. Wivenhoe is cheap and has few pleasures in life; playing golf relaxes him, eating quinces (fruit) every morning with his breakfast pleases him, but the manipulation of his counselors by the female counselors irritates him. The girls send messages to Wivenhoe via bow and arrow.

Mahala Mae Gruenecker (Alice Nunn) is the head of Camp Divine (she has a crush on Wally). She is assisted by Caprice Yeudleman (Nina Wayne) and Nadine Smith (Beverly Adams). The beautiful and ultrasexy Caprice is a Rhodes scholar (she attended Oxford University) who drives Wivenhoe's men crazy (especially Pruett; when Caprice calls him "Prusey," he gets the shakes, but a slap on the face returns him to normal). Caprice is brighter than she presents herself and loves to walk in the rain; she has a pet rabbit named Bridget. Their camp Jeep has the license plate 405-632.

Hermione Baddeley plays Eulalia Divine, the camp owner; Forrest Lewis appeared as Mahala Mae's uncle, Harvey Apperson. Irving and Virginia are the two unrealistic bears who comment from the woods on the various camp activities.

Howard Greenfield and Jack Keller composed the "Camp Runamuck" theme.

98. *Camp Wilder*

ABC, 9/18/92 to 2/26/93

Cast: Mary Page Keller (*Ricky Wilder*), Jerry O'Connell (*Brody Wilder*), Meghann Haldeman (*Melissa Wilder*), Tina Majorino (*Sophie Wilder*), Hilary Swank (*Danielle*), Margaret Langrick (*Beth*), Jay Mohr (*Dorfman*).

Facts: The house at 1115 Fairlawn Avenue in Los Angeles is the residence of Ricky Wilder, a nurse whose home is affectionately called Camp Wilder by the neighborhood kids who hang out with Ricky's brother, Brody, and her sister, Melissa.

Ricky is 28 years old, divorced and the mother of six-year-old Sophie. Ricky took on the responsibility of raising Brody (16) and Melissa (13) when their parents were killed in a car accident. Beth, Danielle and Dorfman are the other kids of Camp Wilder.

Ricky was married to a man named Dean; she divorced him when she discovered he didn't love her. Ricky has a recurring nightmare "about being back in high school, dressed only in my bra and panties and taking a test, then realizing I haven't been to class all year." In high school, Ricky was insecure about her body and refused to take showers with the other girls (she waited until she was the last one). Sophie, called "Pumpkin" by Ricky, has a hamster named Barney and an invisible friend she calls Morty. When Sophie felt she should be a boy, she started dressing like one and called herself Kurt. Melissa is in junior high school (not named) and has a collection of toy horses. She practices kissing on fruit (peaches) and as a kid wore panties with characters from the cartoon series "Hello Kitty" on them. Brody had the nickname of "Spot" when he was a kid; he also had a part time job with Star View Tours and runs track at high school.

Danielle is partial to the blue mug with the duck on it when she's at the house; Dorfman works for a company called Roses for a Buck and has a pet snake named Ricky. (Dorfman has a crush on Ricky and is obsessed with her shoes—all 12 pairs of them. To be closer to Ricky, Dorfman became a candy striper at the unnamed hospital where Ricky works.) Dorfman also believes, at times, that he is being stalked by a gorilla named Francie.

Outside the house Ricky faces all the pressures of the outside world; "but inside I feel like a teenager with a really good complexion." Beverly Garland appeared as Ricky's "Grandma."

The original, unaired pilot version of the series, titled "Camp Bicknell," has the same format, but a slightly different cast. Ricky Bicknell (Elena Stiteler) was a divorced nurse with two young daughters, Lucy (Ginger Orsi) and Sophie (Tina Majorino). She lived with her 16-year-old brother, Brody Bicknell (Paul Scherrer), in their parents' home. The neighborhood kids were Beth (Margaret Langrick), Danielle (Hilary Swank) and Dorfman (Jay Mohr). Ginger Orsi and the character of Lucy were dropped, and Meghann Haldeman was added as Ricky's sister, Melissa. Mary Page Keller replaced Elena Stiteler as Ricky, and Jerry O'Connell took over the role of Brody.

Theme: "The Camp Wilder Theme," by Jonathan Wolff.

99. *Cannonball*

Syndicated, 1958

"Any kind of weather, any time of day, when the rig is ready, he'll be on his way to carry any cargo anywhere; name the destination and brother, he'll be there..." The theme lyric refers to "Cannonball" Michael ("Mike") Malone (Paul Birch), a seasoned truck driver for the C & A Transport Company in Canada (the company headquarters are in Toronto; Mike and his young partner, Jerry Austin [William Campbell] work out of the North Bay Station).

Before each run, Mike and Jerry (who is called "The Romeo of the Road") have "a cup of java before they shove off" at Gertrude's Diner. They drive various GMC ten ton diesels and are capable of fixing any rig the company owns. They call the cab (where they ride) "The Horse."

There is no credit for the "Cannonball" theme, only music supervision by Raoul Kraushaar.

Prior to "Cannonball," the first series about truckers, an unaired pilot called "The Long Highway," was produced in 1956. J. Pat O'Malley played a dispatcher who introduced tales about truckers.

"Movin' On" (NBC, 9/12/74 to 9/14/76) became the second such series. Veteran trucker Sonny Pruett (Claude Akins) and the rebellious, college educated Will Chandler (Frank Converse) rode an 18 wheeler with the I.D. 78100. Will was unsure about his future and chose the trucker's life to find himself (Sonny paid him two dollars an hour plus 30 percent of a haul). Sonny had a hula doll and fuzzy dice in the cab; Will enjoyed music from his eight-track player. Their license plates: 2-38C5 (Montana), 7-829554 (Oregon). Merle Haggard sang the theme, "Movin' On."

The year 1979 (2/10) saw "Flatbed Annie and Sweetie Pie: Lady Truckers," an unsold CBS pilot about Flatbed Annie (Annie Potts) and Ginny ("Sweetie Pie") La Rosa (Kim Darby), trucking partners who drove a 1978 blue and white Sturdy Built Superliner, license plate 2T1 395. See also "B.J. and the Bear."

100. *Captain David Grief*

Syndicated, 1957 to 1958

David Grief (Maxwell Reed) is captain of the *Rattler*, a two mast, gaff rigged trading schooner "that is not very big but can sail with the best of them." David is based in the West Indies, and he sometimes sets sail to where the wind will take him. Merchandise is his basic cargo, but passengers are also welcome—as long as they pay their way (women have the most difficult time aboard the ship because "the quarters aboard the *Rattler* are not much of a match for a lady").

David is partners with Elihu Snow (Tudor Owen); Boley (Mickey Simpson) is the bosun, and Jackie Jackie (Mel Prestige) is the deck hand. Shipmates are paid $30 a month and repairs to the schooner are made at Papp's Shipyard. The series is based on the stories by Jack London (the series official screen title is "Captain David Grief by Jack London").

Ted Dale composed the theme. In the original, unaired pilot version, David is the captain of a sloop called the *Rattler*. His traveling companion is a beautiful native girl named Anura (Maureen Hingert), and together they roam the West Indies in search of adventure.

101. *Captain Midnight*

CBS, 9/4/54 to 4/28/56

Cast: Richard Webb (*Captain Midnight*), Sid Melton (*Icky Mudd*), Olan Soule (*Tut Jones*).

Facts: In a small bombproof shelter in France during World War II, a general of the Allied Armies is studying a military map. The war has reached a moment of crisis, and the Allies are in danger of terrible destruction. Suddenly a man, whose name the general does not want to know, enters. Only two people in the world know the mission to which he (Captain Jim Albright) has been assigned: the general and the president of the United States. The odds are 100 to 1 against him: "If you fail tonight, it will be the end for all of us... If you succeed tonight, you will have started a long and dangerous task that may require a lifetime to complete." Albright's assignment is to exterminate a man named Ivan Shark, the most dangerous criminal in the world (a traitor who has cost the lives of thousands of Americans). Before the captain leaves, the general tells him, "Henceforth, until you complete your final task, you will not be known by your true name. What name you will be known by rests in the hands of fate." "Sir," the captain says, "if I have not returned by twelve o'clock, you will know I have failed." The captain leaves. The hours slowly pass. It is 15 seconds to midnight, and it appears as though Albright has failed. Suddenly, the faint sounds of an airplane are heard. "Listen to that," the general tells his aide. "We're saved—and it's just twelve o'clock. To me he will always be Captain Midnight."

After the war, Captain Midnight formed the Secret Squadron to battle the enemies of the free world. Ichabod ("Icky") Mudd is his mechanic, and Aristotle ("Tut") Jones, the captain's scientific adviser. Captain Midnight's plane is called the *Silver Dart*. Members of the Secret Squadron are assigned and referred to by a number (for example, S.Q. 7, S.Q. 10). Icky's catchphrase was "Mudd with two d's." Viewers could become members of the Secret Squadron by mailing in a coupon found inside the lid of Ovaltine (chocolate milk–flavoring crystals), the show's sponsor. Secret Squadron members received a decal and a patch identifying them as members of the Secret Squadron, plus a special pin for decoding the secret messsages given at the end of each episode.

Ovaltine canceled the highly rated series in 1956 after 39 episodes were filmed because of a lack of sales (kids were removing the coupons from jars but not buying the product). Ovaltine refused to sponsor the show in syndication and reserved its right to the name *Captain Midnight* (which it created for radio in the 1940s). The title was changed to "Jet Jackson, Flying Commando" and through voiceover dubbing, Richard Webb's character became Jet Jackson.

Theme: "Captain Midnight," by Don Ferris.

102. *Captain Nice*

NBC, 1/9/67 to 9/14/67

Big Town, U.S.A., population 112,000, is situated "somewhere in the Midwestern part of North America." Like all cities, Big Town is crime ridden, and its citizens fear to walk the streets. In an attempt to battle crime,

Carter Nash (William Daniels), a mild mannered police chemist for the Big Town Police Department, invents a liquid power source called Super Juice. When Carter drinks the liquid, he is transformed into Captain Nice, a heroic crime fighter who protects the citizens of Big Town.

Carter works in the City Hall Building (number 1908) and has a basement lab. He was hired by the police department for two reasons: one, he is a good chemist; and two, his uncle, Fred Finney (Liam Dunn), is the mayor of Big Town (Carter's mother's brother). Carter is shy, timid and helpless. His father has trouble remembering his name and calls him "Spot." When Carter tried to join the army, they burned his draft card; when he enrolled in a self-defense class "they said I should carry an axe." Carter believes he is ordinary and doesn't stand out. He is afraid of girls and tends to "think of girls as round men."

Carter lives at home with his bossy mother, Esther Nash (Alice Ghostley), and his father, Harvey Nash (Byron Foulger). Harvey is never fully seen and his main purpose in life seems to be reading the newspaper (his face is constantly obstructed by the Big Town *Chronicle*). At work, the beautiful and sensuous police sergeant, Candice ("Candy") Cane (Ann Prentiss), has a crush on Carter. Carter, however, hasn't the courage to ask her for a date; he does say that she "is quite attractive and a credit to her uniform."

When Candy Cane was threatened by evildoers and a thug tried to steal Carter's briefcase (which contained his secret formula), Carter first tested his experiment. He hiccupped, was struck by lightning and was transformed into Captain Nice (a name Carter made up by using the initials on his belt buckle—C.N.). He saved Candy, then vanished when the job was done. Carter returned home and was planning to destroy his formula. When he told his mother that he was Captain Nice, she convinced him to use his invention to battle evil. She made for him his red, white and blue costume, mask and cape (CAPTAIN NICE is printed on the chest portion of his costume).

As Captain Nice, Carter has incredible speed and strength, the ability to fly and an immunity to harm. The seemingly foul-tasting Super Juice has effects that last about one hour. Citizens describe Captain Nice as "the man who flies like an eagle," "the man with muscles of lead" and "the masked enemy of all evil." "From now on," Carter says, "the forces of evil will have to watch out for Captain Nice!"

Vic Mizzy composed the "Captain Nice" theme.

103. *Captain Scarlet and the Mysterons*

Syndicated, 1967

Voice Cast: Francis Matthews (*Captain Scarlet*), Donald Gray (*Colonel White*), Paul Maxwell (*Captain Grey*), Ed Bishop (*Captain Blue*), Jeremy Wilkins (*Captain Ochre*),

Gary Files *(Captain Magenta)*, Cy Grant *(Lieutenant Green)*, Jana Hill *(Symphony Angel)*, Sylvia Anderson *(Melody Angel)*, Liz Morgan *(Destiny Angel* and *Rhapsody Angel)*, Shin-Lian *(Harmony Angel)*, Charles Tingwell *(Dr. Fawn)*.

Facts: Spectrum is a futuristic organization, headquartered on Cloudbase, which has been established to safeguard the world. It is secretly battling the never-seen Mysterons, the inhabitants of the planet Mars, who have declared a war of revenge against Earth (the Mysterons mistook Spectrum's exploration of the planet as an unprovoked attack).

The Mysterons possess the ability to recreate any person or object once it has been destroyed. They contrive a car accident that claims the life of Captain Scarlet, Spectrum's top agent. Captain Scarlet, however, fails to become a Mysteron once his life is restored; instead, he becomes their indestructible enemy. Characters are marionettes and are named after the colors of the spectrum.

Spectrum Agents: Captain Scarlet was born in England in the year 2036 to a family of distinguished soldiers. He possesses degrees in history, math and technology; he has also been trained in field combat.

Colonel White is the commander-in-chief of Spectrum. He was born in England and is highly educated in computer science, navigation and technology. He served with the World Navy and the Universal Secret Service and enjoys playing war games with Captain Scarlet.

Captain Grey was born in Chicago. He served with the World Aquanaut Security Patrol and was in charge of the submarine *Stingray*. His pastime is swimming, and he spends much time developing new strokes.

Captain Blue is the oldest son of a wealthy Boston financier. He has degrees in economics, technology, computer control, applied math and aerodynamics. He applied this knowledge to become a top test pilot with the World Aeronautic Society before joining Spectrum.

Captain Ochre acquired his pilot's license at age 16 and served with the World Government Police Corps. Before joining Spectrum, he broke up one of the toughest crime syndicates in the United States.

Captain Magenta was born in Ireland. After his parents emigrated to America, he was brought up in a poor New York suburb in an environment of poverty and crime. He worked hard at school, won a scholarship to Yale and graduated with degrees in physics, electrical engineering and technology. He yearned for a life of high adventure and big money and turned to crime. He became a big-time operator and controlled two-thirds of New York's crime organization. When Spectrum leaders realized that they would need such a man—respected and trusted in the underworld—they offered him a job and he accepted.

Lieutenant Green was born at Port of Spain in Trinidad; he is Colonel White's right-hand man. He holds degrees in music, telecommunications and technology, and served with the World Aquanaut Security Patrol, Submarine Corps division. He then became sole commander of communications at the Marineville Control Tower before joining Spectrum.

Dr. Fawn was born in Australia and serves as Spectrum's supreme medical commander. Before joining Spectrum, he developed robot doctors for the World Medical Organization.

The Angels (Pilots): Destiny Angel was born in Paris. She joined the World Army Air Force and was transferred to the Intelligence Corps before heading the women's Flight Squadron. Three years later, she started her own firm of flight contractors. Her intelligence, leadership ability and talent in flying led to Spectrum's naming her leader of the Angels.

Symphony Angel was born in Cedar Rapids, Iowa, and holds degrees in math and technology. She first served with the Universal Secret Service. When Symphony began training as a pilot for a special mission, she fell in love with flying and joined Spectrum as a pilot. She enjoys creating new hairstyles for herself and the other Angels.

Melody Angel was born on a cotton farm in Atlanta, Georgia. She was a tomboy as a child and later took up professional motor racing. It was during her stay at a Swiss finishing school that she developed an interest in flying. Expelled for unruly behavior, she joined the World Army Air Force where she displayed amazing courage and nerves of iron, which led to Spectrum's hiring her as a pilot.

Rhapsody Angel was born in Chelsea, England, to aristocratic parents. She studied law and sociology at London University. She joined the Federal Agents Bureau and later took over its command. Rhapsody next became chief security officer for an airline before starting her own airline company. She joined Spectrum when they asked her to become an Angel; her pastime is playing chess.

Harmony Angel was born in Tokyo, Japan. She is the daughter of a wealthy flying taxi owner. She grew up in a world of high speeds and became a member of the Tokyo Flying Club. When she flew around the world nonstop (breaking all records) she was asked to join Spectrum. Harmony loves sports and spends her spare time teaching the Angels karate and judo.

Theme: "Captain Scarlet and the Mysterons," by Barry Gray.

104. *Captain Video and His Video Rangers*

DuMont, 6/27/49 to 8/16/57

A desolate mountain range is seen as the announcer speaks: "Master of Space! Hero of Science! Captain of the Video Rangers! Operating from his secret mountain headquarters on the planet Earth, Captain Video rallies men of good will everywhere. As he rockets from planet to planet, let us follow the champion of truth, justice and freedom throughout the universe. Stand by for Captain Video and His Video Rangers!"

The series is set in the twenty-second century. Captain Video (Richard Coogan and Al Hodge) is "the Guardian of the Safety of the World." He is the head of the Video Rangers, an organization that battles evil throughout the universe. His teenage assistant is the Video Ranger (Don Hastings), and his rocket ships are the *X-9*, the *Galaxy*, and the *Galaxy II*.

Commissioner Bell (Jack Orsen) and Commissioner Carey (Ben Lackland) are the captain's superiors. They are based on the 144th floor of the Public Safety Building in Planet City. The evil Dr. Pauli (Bram Nossen, Hal Conklin and Stephen Elliott) is the captain's enemy (Pauli is president of the Asteroidal Society and inventor of the Cloak of Invisibility). Bob Hastings played the Video Ranger's brother, Hal, and Dave Ballard was Tobor the Robot (*Tobor* is *robot* spelled backwards). Captain Video's code to his base is 398; copter cabs escort people through space; prisoners are sent to the moon, which has been turned into a penal colony.

During the 1949-50 season, when Richard Coogan played the captain and the program was broadcast live, scenes from old theatrical films were inserted to allow costume and scene changes. The stars of these old films were called Video Rangers, and the action scenes were said to be adventures of other Video Rangers fighting for justice (their code was KRG-L6, and they were said to be seen via Remote Carrier Delayed-Circuit TV Screens). On episodes broadcast without commercials, viewers saw a "Video Ranger Message," a public service announcement geared to kids. Fred Scott, who later played Video Ranger Rogers, announced and narrated.

105. *Captain Z-Ro*

Syndicated, 1952 to 1953 (15 min.)
Syndicated, 1954 to 1955 (30 min.)

Cast: Roy Steffens *(Captain Z-Ro)*, Bobby Trumbull (1952), Jeff Silvers (1953), Bruce Haynes (1954–55) *(Jet)*, H.M. Chamberlain *(Micro)*.

Facts: "Somewhere on an uncharted portion of the planet Earth [a desolate mountainous area that is misty and alive with active volcanoes] stands the laboratory of Captain Z-Ro. In this secret location, known only to a few in the outside world, Captain Z-Ro and his associates experiment in time and space to learn from the past to learn for the future."

The mysterious Captain Z-Ro is the inventor of a time machine that enables him and his assisant, Jet (a young boy) to view the past via the machine's telescreens. When a decision is made to view the past (usually the Captain's way to prove to Jet that something he read about actually happened), the following procedure occurs: 1. The chosen era is divided into latitude and longitude and programed into the time machine's computer; 2. the voltage is set (for example, 8.4); 3. the Electro Generator is set (for example, 8.993); 4. the Isotron output is programed (for example, 4.712); the Trillatron is set (for example, 12.1195); the Lectric Chamber is then readied. Jet hands the Captain the Cycle Reactor which "cracks the fourth dimension and ejects us back into time." The Lectric Chamber is now active; 7. Beeps are heard, and the machine searches all the coordinates that have been programed into it. When the search has been completed, the special television screens allow the Captain and Jet to see an event from the past.

If the Captain feels a figure from the past is in danger, he can go back to that period by standing in the Lectric Chamber. When Jet activates the Spector Wave Length, the Captain begins to dematerialize and disappears from view. Symmetrical impulses are then transmitted over time, and the Captain reappears in the programed era. The Captain helps people in trouble with his Pararay Gun (which paralyzes a subject for 60 seconds). When he has accomplished his mission, he says, "All right, Jet, take me back." Jet then reverses the Symmetrical Impulses, and the Captain returns to the present.

The Captain, a research explorer in space and time, has a rocket ship called ZX-99. The Video Plate aboard the ship is a round picture-like tube that allows the Captain to view outer space. The Gravity Generator regulates the gravity inside the ship (on their first flight, the Captain, Jet and Micro were halfway to the ceiling before they realized they needed to activate it). The ZX-99 travels at the rate of five miles per second, and when one of the team is about to embark on a mission, the Captain says, "Spaceman's luck." A Z is worn slightly off-center on the Captain's uniform and on his helmet. A Z in a circle is worn on each cuff.

"Be sure to be standing by when we again transmit you to this remote location on the planet Earth when Captain Z-Ro and his associates will conduct another experiment in time and space."

106. *Car 54, Where Are You?*

NBC, 9/17/61 to 9/8/63

Gunther Toody (Joe E. Ross) and Francis Muldoon (Fred Gwynne) are police officers with the N.Y.P.D.'s 53rd Precinct on Tremont Avenue in the Bronx. They ride in patrol car 54 and are members of the Brotherhood Club.

Toody and Muldoon were teamed on August 16, 1952, and it has been clear ever since that they can ride only with each other (Toody constantly talks and drives other partners batty; Muldoon rarely speaks and makes other officers uneasy).

Gunther and his wife, Lucille (Beatrice Pons), have been married for 15 years. They live in a five room, rent controlled apartment in the Bronx and pay $45 a month rent. Gunther is five feet eight inches tall. He was born on August 15, and his badge number is 453. His catchphrase is "Oooh, oooh, jumpin' Jehoshaphat," which he says every time something excites him. Lucille's maiden name is Hasselwhite, and she graduated from Hunter College in the Bronx. Toody's unseen parents live on East 160th Street in the Bronx. Gunther is the only member of the Toody family who was not blessed with a singing voice.

Francis is single and was named after his mother's idol, Francis X. Bushman. He lives with his mother (Ruth

Masters) and his sister, Peggy (Helen Parker), at 807 East 175th Street in the Bronx. Francis, badge number 723, was born in July; he weighs 183¾ pounds and is six feet seven inches tall. He collects stamps and belongs to the Bronx Stamp Club. His father, Patrick Muldoon (not seen), made captain in 1919, when, at the age of 25, he captured the Baby Face Gordon Gang. Peggy, an aspiring actress, auditioned for a part in a play called *Waiting for Wednesday* (later retitled *Copper's Capers*).

Officer Leo Schnauser (Al Lewis), badge number 1062, was born on Friday the thirteenth and has been on the force for 20 years. He married the former Sylvia Schwarzcock (Charlotte Rae) 15 years earlier on August 18. He has six sisters, yet Leo is considered the pretty one in the family. The suspicious Sylvia believes that every time Leo goes out with the boys he is having a secret affair with Marilyn Monroe.

Martin Block (Paul Reed) is the stern police captain; other officers at the 53rd are Ed Nicholson (Hank Garrett), Sol Abrams (Nathaniel Frey), and Anderson (Nipsey Russell).

Louise Kirtland and Patricia Bright played Martin's wife, Claire Block; Paul O'Keefe was Toody's nephew, Marvin; and George S. Irving was Gunther's uncle, Igor.

John Strauss and Nat Hiken wrote the theme, "Car 54, Where Are You?"

107. *The Cara Williams Show*

CBS, 9/23/64 to 9/10/65

Cara Wilton (Cara Williams) is a file clerk at Fenwick Diversified Industries, Inc., at 9601 West Beverly Boulevard in Los Angeles (the conglomerate is also known as Fenwick Industries). Cara is a pretty redhead who lives in an apartment at 6758 Riverdale Lane. Her phone number is 736-8876, and she drives a car with the license plate T1204. Cara is also slightly scatterbrained and fears for her job (she has a filing system that only she can understand to protect that job). Cara is also defying company rules. She is married to Frank Bridges (Frank Aletter), Fenwick's top efficiency expert. The company prohibits employee marriages, and their efforts to conceal that fact are the focal point of the series. (The format changed in midseason when Cara approached the company president, Mr. Fenwick [Edward Everett Horton], and convinced him to change the rule.)

Damon Burkhardt (Paul Reed) is Cara's no-nonsense boss. He lives at 790 Parker Way and is strict at work but a pussycat at home with his stern wife, Martha (Hermione Baddeley and Reta Shaw). Fletcher Kincaid (Jack Sheldon) is Cara's next-door neighbor. He is a jazz musician, and his favorite television shows are "Mightyman from Mars," "Charlie Chipmunk" and "Space Mouse."

Kenyon Hopkins composed "Cara's Theme."

108. *The Case of the Dangerous Robin*

Syndicated, 10/60 to 9/61

Robin Scott (Rick Jason) is young and handsome and takes many chances to get his job done as a worldwide investigator for the Gotham Insurance Company. His romantic interest is Phyllis Collier (Jean Blake). She is young and beautiful and worries about Robin—about the dangers he faces and about the beautiful women he meets (she and Robin met a year earlier [1959] in Central Park when each sought shelter from a rainstorm under a tree). Robin, who lives in an apartment at 101 East 86th Street in Manhattan, receives 10 percent of the face value of the items he recovers.

David Rose composed "Robin's Theme."

A similar syndicated series called "The Cheaters" appeared at the same time (1960–61). John Ireland played John Hunter, an investigator for the London-based Eastern Insurance Company, who sought to expose "the cheaters"—people who attempt to defraud insurance companies with false claims.

109. *The Cases of Eddie Drake*

DuMont, 3/6/52 to 5/29/52

Edward ("Eddie") Drake (Don Haggerty) operates the Drake Detective Agency at 130 West 45th Street in Manhattan; Dr. Karen Gayle (Patricia Morison; later Lynn Roberts) is a beautiful private practice psychiatrist with offices at 64 Park Avenue.

Eddie has a remarkable affinity for crimes of violence; he is a specialist in cases that involve murder. He is also personable, intelligent and honest. Karen considers herself a student of "all the abnormal behavior of the human mind." She is writing a book on criminal behavior and wants her material to be fresh and stimulating. "I want to retain you to talk to me," she says when she first meets Eddie. "I want to know all about the criminals you meet, what they say, how they act, why they do the things they do." Eddie takes the assignment.

When Eddie tells Karen about his latest case ("The Brass Key"), we see it via flashbacks. As Eddie concludes his story, Karen remarks, "You know, if you could guarantee a minimum of shooting, I think I'd like to get my material firsthand." "I'll see what I can line up," responds Eddie, and stories follow their case investigations.

Eddie's car license plate reads 3C-26-53; he sometimes gets cases from a bail bond agency called Jenny's Bail Bonds. Karen's office phone number is 346-7112; Eddie's office phone number is 346-1622. Theodore Von Eltz plays Detective Lieutenant Walsh of the Homicide Bureau of the N.Y.P.D.

The Cara Williams Show. Frank Aletter with Cara Williams.

The two stars appear at the end to tell viewers the cast and credits (a credit for the theme is not given). They conclude with Eddie saying, "We hope you'll be with us next week, same time, same station, for another episode in [Karen]: 'The Cases of Eddie Drake.'"

Casey, Crime Photographer
see *Crime Photographer*

Cassie and Company see Police Woman

110. *The Cavanaughs*

CBS, 12/1/86 to 3/9/87
CBS, 8/8/88 to 10/3/88
CBS, 6/29/89 to 7/27/89

This show follows events in the lives of the Cavanaughs, an Irish-Catholic family who resides at 36 Brookhaven Street in Boston. Aged 71½ years old, Francis Cavanaugh (Barnard Hughes) is the head of the family and the oldest living Cavanaugh (the family curse is that no Cavanaugh lives to see age 72; Francis broke the curse when he turned 72 in 1989). He is a staunch Democrat and owns the Cavanaugh Construction Company. He is a widower (his late wife was named Bridget) and is constantly at odds with his brother James (Art Carney), a Republican he calls "The Weasel."

Katherine ("Kit") Cavanaugh (Christine Ebersole) is Francis's oldest child. She is divorced and retains her maiden name (her ex-husband is Tom Elgin, played by John Getz). Kit is an actress and her claim to fame is that she appeared nude in the movie *Wild Women of Malibu*. Mary Margaret Cavanaugh (Mary Tanner) is Francis's sweet granddaughter. She calls him "Poppi" and attends Our Lady of Perpetual Sorrow High School (as did Kit).

Francis's second-born son (and Mary Margaret's father), Charles ("Chuck") Cavanaugh (Peter Michael Goetz), now runs Cavanaugh Construction and is constantly in conflict with his father over how the company should be run. Chuck, a widower, is also the father of three sons: John (Scott Curtis and Parker Jacobs), Kevin (Matt Shakman and Danny Cooksey) and the eldest, Charles Cavanaugh, Jr. (John Short), a parish priest at Our Lady of Perpetual Sorrow Church.

Flashbacks: Matt Shakman (*Francis as a boy* in 1928), Danny Cooksey (*James as a boy* in 1928), Lauren Taylor (*Bridget as a girl* in 1928), Christine Ebersole (*Bridget as a woman*).

Theme: "The Cavanaughs," by Paul Pilger.

111. *Charles in Charge*

CBS, 10/30/84 to 7/24/85

Cast: Scott Baio (*Charles*), Willie Aames (*Buddy Lembeck*), Julie Cobb (*Jill Pembroke*), James Widdoes (*Stan Pembroke*), April Lerman (*Lila Pembroke*), Jonathan Ward (*Douglas Pembroke*), Michael Pearlman (*Jason Pembroke*), Jennifer Runyon (*Gwendolyn Pierce*).

Facts: Jill and Stan Pembroke are a busy working couple who reside at 10 Barrington Court in New Brunswick, New Jersey. When they require help in caring for their children (Lila, Douglas and Jason), they hire a college student named Charles as a live-in helper.

Charles is best friends with Buddence ("Buddy") Lembeck. They attend Copeland College, and the Lamplight (a hamburger joint) is their favorite hangout. "Charles Are Us" was their misguided effort to make money by marketing clones of Charles as live-in housekeepers. The Grotto is Charles's favorite seafood restaurant, and Darby Peterson (Dawn Merrick) is his favorite movie star. In high school in Philadelphia (Scranton), Charles was in a band called the Charles Tones; he also helped Stan's mother, Irene (Rue McClanahan), start a pizza business called Mama Garabaldi's Pizza. For unknown reasons (other than the show's gimmick), Charles has no last name. His girlfriend is Gwendolyn Pierce, a stunning blonde who also attends Copeland College. Buddy, a Leo, was born in California; he will only take courses with five or fewer books to read (any more and it will cause him to cheat).

Jillian ("Jill") Ann Pembroke is a theater critic for the New Jersey *Register*. Her favorite eatery is Willie Wong's Chinese Palace. In high school, Jill was called "Pixie"; Jill's father, Harry Gardner (Dick O'Neill), calls her "Jillybean." Stanley ("Stan") Albert Pembroke is one of 49 vice presidents in an unnamed company.

Lila Beth is "sweet and lovely and dots her *i*'s with little hearts." She first attends Lincoln Elementary School then Northside High School. Lila reads *Co-ed* magazine and is a member of the Circle of Friendship Club. She is a member of Stan's company softball team (she is so bad that she plays deep deep roving right field). She calls Buddy "Goon Machine" and longs to wear makeup and high heels.

Douglas and Jason attend Lincoln Elementary School. Jason is mischievous; Douglas is smart (the only *F* he received was for a book report he did on *TV Guide*; his teacher didn't consider it classic literature). The kids have a never-seen feline named Putty Cat and eat Kellogg's Bran Flakes for breakfast. See the following title also.

Theme: "Charles in Charge," by Michael Jacobs, Al Burton and David Kurtz.

112. *Charles in Charge*

Syndicated, 1/3/87 to 11/12/90

Cast: Scott Baio (*Charles*), Willie Aames (*Buddy Lembeck*), Sandra Kerns (*Ellen Powell*), Nicole Eggert (*Jamie Powell*), Josie Davis (*Sarah Powell*), Alexander Polinsky (*Adam Powell*), James Callahan (*Walter Powell*), Ellen Travolta (*Lillian*).

Facts: A revised version of the previous title. When Charles returns from a two week vacation (mountain climbing in Great Gorge), he learns that the Pembrokes have moved to Seattle and sublet their home to the Powell family: Ellen, her children (Sarah, Jamie and Adam) and Ellen's father-in-law, Walter. Since Ellen's husband, Robert, is a naval commander stationed in the South Seas, Charles finds employment as their live-in helper.

The Cavanaughs. Barnard Hughes and Christine Ebersole.

The Powells' address is 10 Barrington Court in New Brunswick, New Jersey. Before hiring Charles, the Powells' live-in helper was Julie Mercer (played by Liz Keifer).

Charles, still with no last name, was born in Scranton, Pennsylvania. He attends Copeland College and is majoring in education (his first experience was as a teacher's aide to Mr. Mirkin [Jerry Van Dyke] in Central High School). His mother, Lillian (no last name given) calls him "Doodlebug." At age 11 Charles won a spelling bee with the word *quixotic*; in the fifth grade he had a ventriloquist's act with a dummy named Muggsy. When Charles bumps his head, he becomes Chazz Lambergini, a motorcycle hood (Tiffany, played by Denise Miller, appears in these episodes as Chazz's beautiful bimbo girlfriend). In the last first-run episode (11/12/90), Charles leaves the Powells to attend Princeton to get his teaching degree. Lillian first owned Sid's Pizza Parlor, then the Yesterday Cafe—both of which were hangouts for Charles and his friends.

Buddy, whose real name is Buddence, attends Copeland College (his major is political science; aptitude test results rated Buddy as a Jack of no trades and best suited for jury duty). Buddy, born in California, had a dog named Kitty and a hand puppet called Handie as a kid. He now lives in the campus dorm (where he is banned from performing chemistry experiments and bringing livestock into the room). Living with him is a pet lizard named Lloyd and an ant named Arlo (who lives in a plastic ant farm). Buddy says he receives mind transmissions from the planet Zargon and believes that Barbara Mandrell is in love with him (she sent him an autographed picture signed "Love, Barbara"). He once smashed 57 cans of beer against his forehead before passing out ("I could have done more if the cans were empty"). "The Buddy Lembeck Show" was the radio program Buddy briefly held on station WFNZ. The first thing Buddy does after getting up in the morning is take a nap.

In high school, Buddy was voted the class flake. He has an autographed Mickey Mantle baseball that he signed for Mickey (Mickey wasn't around when Buddy bought the ball, so he signed it for him). Of all the troublesome situations in the world, the question that most bothers Buddy is why the park ranger won't let Yogi Bear have a picnic basket. If Buddy had three wishes, he'd wish for "X-ray vision, a portable water bed and a date with Connie Chung." Kelly Ann Cann played Buddy's often talked about (but rarely seen) girlfriend, Nurse Bennett. Buddy is afraid of clowns (he was scared by one as a child); at school he is a member of the scuba club.

Jamie, the oldest of the Powell children, attends Central High School and yearns to be a model. She starred with her sister, Sarah, in a television commercial for Banana Cream Shampoo and Hair Lotion and wears a size five shoe. Jamie, who is growing into a beautiful young woman, is a cheerleader at school but is considered a child by her father (who calls her "Little Scooter"). Jamie won the "Yesterday Café Beauty Pageant" and, under the sponsorship of Jeannie's Boutique, entered the "Miss New Brunswick Beauty Pageant." Jamie had a part time job as a waitress at Sid's Pizza and in one episode, became one of the Followers of Light, a phony religious sect. She also took classes at the Better Image School of Modeling.

Sarah, the middle child, attends Central High School and longs to be a writer. Sarah does freelance reporting for the New Brunswick *Herald* and had her first story, "What It Is Like to Be a Teenager," published in *Teen* magazine. The sensitive child, Sarah has a pet turtle named Ross and a favorite doll named Rebecca. She is a member of the Shakespeare Club at school, and if she had three wishes she'd ask for "world peace, a cleaner environment and an end to world hunger." In the first episode, Sarah claimed Elizabeth Barrett Browning was her favorite poet; later, she says it is Emily Dickinson. Sarah, who is taller than Jamie but just as pretty, won first runner-up title in the "Yesterday Café Beauty Pageant."

Adam, the youngest child, attends an unnamed grammar school. Walter, who was a naval career man, belongs to the John Paul Jones Society for Retired Naval Men. Mr. Hobbs the goat is Copeland College's mascot.

Relatives: James O'Sullivan (Ellen's husband, *Robert Powell*), Kay Lenz (Ellen's cousin, *Joan Robinson*), David Braf (Ellen's uncle, *Steve Colfax*), Nicole Eggert (Ellen's cousin, *Amanda Colfax*), Olivia Burnette (Ellen's cousin, *Melanie Colfax*), Michael Manasseri (Ellen's cousin, *Michael Colfax*), Justin Whalen (Charles's cousin, *Anthony*), John Astin (Charles's uncle, *Joe*, the "Pickle King of Brooklyn"), Ellen Travolta (Charles's aunt, *Sally*), Mindy Cohn (Buddy's sister, *Bunny Lembeck*), Lewis Arquette (Buddy's father, *Clarence Lembeck*), Ruta Lee (Buddy's grandmother, *Gloria*), Willie Aames (Buddy's cousin, *Dudley Krantz*), Dabbs Greer (Walter's father, *Ben ["Buzz"] Powell*). Buddy mentioned that his mother's name was Florence.

Theme: "Charles in Charge," by Michael Jacobs, Al Burton and David Kurtz.

113. *Charlie Hoover*

Fox, 11/9/91 to 2/9/92

Charles ("Charlie") Hoover (Tim Matheson) is a vice president in accounting for Colberton Industries (his office number is 1503). He is married to Helen (Lucy Webb) and is the father of two children, Emily (Leslie Engel) and Paul (Michael Manassari). He is also 40 years old and facing a midlife crisis. When he feels he is being neglected, his alter ego, Hugh (Sam Kinison), appears to him (and only to him) to help guide his life. Hugh is loud-mouthed and obnoxious and the height of a number two pencil; Charlie's secretary, Doris (Julie Hayden), has a parakeet named Binkie.

Chip Taylor composed the theme, "Wild Thing."

114. *Charlie's Angels*

ABC, 9/22/76 to 8/19/81

Cast: Kate Jackson (*Sabrina Duncan*), Farrah Fawcett (*Jill Munroe*), Jaclyn Smith (*Kelly Garrett*), Cheryl Ladd (*Kris*

Charlie's Angels. Jaclyn Smith, Shelley Hack and Cheryl Ladd.

Munroe), Shelley Hack (*Tiffany Welles*), Tanya Roberts (*Julie Rogers*), David Doyle (*John Bosley*), John Forsythe (*Charlie's voice*).

Facts: Private detectives Sabrina Duncan, Jill Munroe and Kelly Garrett are three beautiful ex–Los Angeles Police Department officers who now work for Charles Townsend, the never-seen owner of the Los Angeles–based Townsend Investigations (a.k.a. the Townsend Detective Agency, and Charles Townsend, Private Investigations). The detectives are "pretty, bright and gutsy" and use their former training as police officers to apprehend criminals.

When Jill left to pursue her race car career in Europe (she hopes to become the first woman to win at Le Mans), her gorgeous sister, Kris Munroe, became an Angel when Charlie recruited her from the San Francisco Police Force. (Jill was paying for Kris's education and believed she was attending San Francisco State College to become a teacher. Unknown to Jill, Kris was secretly attending the San Francisco Police Academy.) Boston police officer Tiffany Welles, the stunning daughter of the lieutenant of detectives (and a friend of Charlie's), replaced Sabrina when she left to marry for a second time and raise a family. When Tiffany leaves the agency to pursue a modeling career in New York City, Charlie hires Julie Rogers, a beautiful Los Angeles police officer, to replace her.

Before Kelly and Kris have the opportunity to meet Tiffany, Charlie prepares them to meet the daughter of a friend who graduated with top honors from the police academy. When there is a knock at the door, a stunning, well developed but dim witted blonde in tight jeans and a clinging T-shirt enters and asks, "Is this the Townsend Agency? I got lost three times." A stunned Kelly and Kris are relieved when the real Tiffany enters and the blonde turns out to be from the agency's linen service. (The unnamed blonde, played by Judy Landers, wore a low-cut V-neck T-shirt that read SUPER STAR. Tiffany mentioned that her mother teaches Latin).

Charlie Townsend remained a man of mystery throughout the series' run. He was in the service during World War II and has many important connections throughout the world. He appears to be wealthy, although he does complain at times about the way the Angels have a knack for damaging the company cars. It was revealed that "Charlie loves figures—girls' figures," and he is often seen in plush settings—with a beautiful girl or two at his side. The Angels never see Charlie; they hear him through a speakerphone in the office of John Bosley, Charlie's lawyer and representative (the Angels believed at one point that Charlie didn't exist and Bosley just made him up). The Angels have come close to seeing Charlie, but he always manages to vanish a split second before he can be seen. The Angels have also seen photographs of Charlie, but they don't satisfy their curiosity (for example, Charlie as a baby; Charlie as a boy with Tiffany's father; Charlie in bad light or from the back of the head). The agency phone number is 213-555-0267 (Bosley's direct, untraceable line to Charlie is 555-9626). The building in which the agency is housed has the number 193 (an address is not given). Charlie's favorite folk-rock singer is Amy Waters (Bess Gatewood).

While "Charlie's Angels" is famous for its "jiggle TV" (the actresses not wearing bras and "plots that cause the Angels to trot"), the episode of 10/20/76 ("Angels in Chains") is even more famous because of an "accidental" bit of nudity. While escaping from prison and running through a swamp, Jill (who measures 33½B-23-34) exposed part of her right breast and nipple when she bent over, and her mostly unbuttoned blouse opened to reveal more than it should have. Whether this was intentional or not, the episode scored a huge 56 share rating that night and a 52 share on the rerun.

Relatives: Michael Bell (Sabrina's ex-husband, *Bill Duncan*).

Theme: "Charlie's Angels," by Jack Elliott and Allyn Ferguson.

Note: The episode of 4/2/80, "The Male Angel Affair," was a pilot for the unsold "Toni's Boys." Barbara Stanwyck was Antonia ("Toni") Blake, who runs a detective agency at 612 Essex Road. Her male operatives: Bob Sorenson (played by Bob Seagren), Cotton Harper (Stephen Shortridge) and Matt Parrish (Bruce Bauer).

115. *The Charmings*

ABC, 3/20/87 to 4/24/87
ABC, 8/6/87 to 2/11/88

Once upon a time in an ancient fairy tale land, a vain queen named Lillian (Judy Parfitt) was told by her magic mirror (Paul Winfield) that her stepdaughter, the beautiful Snow White (Caitlin O'Heaney and Carol Huston), is the fairest of all. Unable to accept this fact, Lillian casts an evil spell that backfires and puts her, Snow White, Snow's husband, Prince Eric Charming (Christopher Rich) and their children, Thomas (Brandon Call) and Cory (Garette Ratliff), to sleep. The spell wears off 1,000 years later in 1987. When the series begins, the Charmings have awakened and are attempting to adjust to life in modern times.

The Charmings now live at 427 Van Oakland Boulevard in Burbank, California, in a house that resembles a castle (555-SNOW is their phone number; details are not given about how the family got the house). Snow White, whose favorite color is peach, is a fashion designer for an unnamed company; Eric, who has a horse named Gendel, is a children's storybook writer (his first book was *The Four Billy Goats Gruff*). Lillian White, whose maiden name is Lipschitz, suffers from PMS (post magic syndrome) once every 28 years. She has a pet thing (an unknown creature called Muffin) and a crow named Quoth (from Edgar Allan Poe's poem, "The Raven").

Sally and Don Miller (Dori Brenner and Paul Eiding), their neighbors, live at 425 Oakland Boulevard. Don owns Don's Carpet Kingdom Store, and he and Eric are members of Don's Carpet Baggers baseball team; his license plate reads CRPT KING. Sally has a dog named Friskie, and Thomas and Cory have a pet lizard named Spike. Jacob Kenner plays Sally and Don's son, Donny Miller.

Jonathan Wolff composed the theme.

116. *Chase*

NBC, 9/11/73 to 9/4/74

Captain Chase Reddick (Mitchell Ryan) is the head of Chase, a special unit of undercover police agents who tackle the cases left unsolved by the homicide, burglary and robbery divisions of the Los Angeles Police Department. His code is "Chase Control."

Members of the team are: Sergeant Sam MacCray (Wayne Maunder); 628 DVE is his license plate, and "Chase One" is his car code. Officer Fred Sing (Brian Fong) has the mobile code "Chase 17." "Chase 43" is the mobile code for Officer Tom Wilson (Craig Gardner), and Officer Ed Rice (Gary Crosby), whose license plate reads QVZ 725, has the car code "Chase 2." Fred and Tom also co-pilot the unit's helicopter, "Chase 3" (also its air code). Ed feels he gets the worst assignments (such as janitor, gas station attendant) because he looks the part. The team's German shepherd, who rides with Sam, is Fuzz (a narc dog). The actual energy crises at the time plagues the team. The lights are dimmed at headquarters, and car chases are curtailed due to the gasoline shortage.

Oliver Nelson composed the theme.

The Cheaters see *The Case of the Dangerous Robin*

117. *Cheers*

NBC, 9/30/82 to 5/20/93

Cast: Ted Danson *(Sam Malone)*, Shelley Long *(Diane Chambers)*, Kirstie Alley *(Rebecca Howe)*, Rhea Perlman *(Carla Tortelli)*, Nicholas Colasanto *(Ernie Pantusso)*, George Wendt *(Norm Peterson)*, John Ratzenberger *(Cliff Claven)*, Woody Harrelson *(Woody Boyd)*, Kelsey Grammer *(Dr. Frasier Crane)*, Bebe Neuwirth *(Dr. Lilith Sternin)*.

Facts: A bordello called Mom's was established in 1889 at 112½ Beacon Street in Boston. Six years later it became the bar Cheers (beer was five cents a glass; in 1984, it was a dollar a glass). Cheers has a legal capacity of 75 people; Tecumseh is the wooden Indian that stands to the right side of the front door; and Melville's Fine Sea Food is the restaurant above Cheers. Gary's Old Towne Tavern is Cheers's competition.

Sam Malone is the current owner. He was a relief pitcher for the Boston Red Sox (jersey number 16) before he bought the bar. His good luck charm is a bottlecap he found when he was a ballplayer; he did a television commercial for Fields Beer. He has a moosehead in the bar named Sam, and a wood carving of a whale hangs over his office door. Sam, a ladies' man, sold the bar to a large, unnamed corporation when he became bored with it. He used the

money to buy a ketch and to sail around the world. The ketch sank in the Caribbean, and he founded an uncharted atoll he named "No Brains Atoll" (for selling the bar). When he found he missed the bar, he returned to find that the corporation had already replaced him with Rebecca Howe as the bar's new manager. After hearing Sam's pathetic story, she took pity on him and hired him as a bartender (at six dollars an hour). (Prior to his job as a bartender, Sam had planned to buy a waterfront dive and turn it into a bar called Sam's Place.)

Rebecca Howe was born in San Diego, is gorgeous and always fashionably dressed. She became the bar manager in 1987 and often wonders why she took the job (she is easily exasperated and finds the job frustrating). In 1990 Rebecca began dating Robin Colcord (Roger Rees), a tycoon whom she thought she loved (she planned to marry him but didn't when she realized she loved him only for his money). When Robin used Rebecca's computer code ("Sweet Baby") to access information from her corporation, he was exposed by Sam and arrested for insider trading. The corporation fired Rebecca and sold Sam back the bar for one dollar (Sam was short of cash and could raise only 85 cents—which got him the deed; he put up the sign UNDER OLD MANAGEMENT). With no source of income, Rebecca took a job at the auto show as the Miracle Buff Girl (a wax that preserves a car's shine). She made six dollars an hour (Miracle Buff sold for $9.99). When she became disgusted she quit. Sam then hired her as his bar manager. In the episode of 2/21/91, Rebecca and Sam became partners in Cheers when Rebecca bought the pool room and bathroom from John Allen Hill (Keene Curtis), who owns Melville's Fine Sea Food Restaurant and these two rooms in Cheers (Rebecca put up $25,000; Sam, $5,000). Rebecca's favorite television show is "Spenser: For Hire."

Diane Chambers, the prim and proper barmaid, is an art student and substitute teacher at Boston University (she also held a job as a salesclerk at the Third Eye Bookstore and as a checkout clerk at Hurley's Market). Diane is interested in rare first-edition books and had an on-and-off love affair with ballet since she was seven years old (she abandoned that dream to become a novelist). Diane also had a rocky romance with Sam. As they were about to marry, Diane received word that her book was going to be published (by Houghton Mifflin). Sam backed down and gave Diane the opportunity to finish her novel. She agreed to call off the wedding and return in six months. The book deal eventually fell through and Diane never returned to Sam; she moved to Hollywood to write for television. (When Sam and Diane were dating and thinking about marriage, she wanted to call their first son Emile.)

Diane is a dreamer, "and I have a habit of making those dreams come true." As a kid she was called "Muffin" by her father. She has a cat named Elizabeth Barrett Browning (after her favorite poet) and gets a facial tick when she gets nervous. Diane entered the forty-fifth annual Miss Boston Barmaid competition and won based on her beauty, perkiness and congeniality. She used the pen name Jessica Simpson Bordais to help Sam write his memoirs for a book that never materialized.

Ernie Pantusso, affectionately called "Coach," was the Boston Red Sox pitching coach and was given the job as bartender by Sam when he retired (and became somewhat senile). Ernie holds the record for being hit by a pitch more times than any other coach in minor league history. Ernie also has the nickname "Red" (not because he had red hair, but because he once read a book). *Thunder Road,* starring Robert Mitchum, is his favorite movie, and 1:37 in the morning is his favorite time of day ("I don't know why, I just like it"). Ernie considers the blackouts he has to be a nice break in the day. When he gets angry, Ernie bangs his head on the bar's serving area next to the beer dispensers. Ernie was also coach of a Little League team called the Titans; his late wife (not seen) was named Angela. (After Coach's death, a picture of Geronimo that Colasanto kept in his dressing room was placed on the Cheers set [upper stage wall] to remind them of Ernie.)

Carla Maria Victoria Angelina Teresa Apollonia Lozupone Tortelli LeBec is the three-times married, nasty waitress who previously worked at a bar called the Broken Spoke before acquiring the job at Cheers. Carla attended the Saint Clete's School for Wayward Girls, and at the age of 16 danced on the television show "The Boston Boppers." She entered the 1991 Miss Boston Barmaid Contest. Carla "became nice for the duration" and won the Miss Congeniality Award.

Carla's humor is always at someone else's expense ("It makes me laugh"); she was named after her grandmother's stubborn mule; from her wealthy grandfather, Tony Lozupone, she inherited his lucky quarter. Carla calls Diane "Fish Face"; as a kid Carla was called "Muffin" by her brothers (who stuffed her ears with yeast and tried to bake her face).

Carla, whose phone number is 555-7834, has eight children and used "the Le Mans" method of childbirth ("I screamed like a Ferrari"). The Lozupone family tradition calls for a woman's first male child to be named after her father's first name and her mother's maiden name. Carla broke tradition when she refused to name her son (Anthony) Benito Mussolini. Carla's unpredictable kids, who are known to roll drunks, are: Anthony (Timothy Williams), Sarafina (Leah Remini), Lucinda (Sabrina Wiener), Gino (Josh Lozoff), Anne Marie (Risa Littman), Ludlow (Jarrett Lennon), and twins Elvis (Danny Kramer) and Jesse (Thomas Tulak). The first five listed are by Nick Tortelli (Dan Hedaya), Ludlow by Dr. Bennett Ludlow (John Karlen) and the twins by Eddie LeBec (Jay Thomas), a goalie for the Boston Bruins hockey team, who was also a bigamist (he was also married to Gloria [Anne DeSalvo]). Nick is now married to the beautiful but dim witted Loretta (Jean Kasem); Anthony is married to Annie (Mandy Ingber); and young Ludlow has an eight-foot boa constrictor named Mr. Tibbington.

Clifford ("Cliff") Claven, a bar regular, is a mailman assigned to the South Central Branch of the U.S. Post Office (he previously had the Meadow View Acres route near the airport). He fears the day the Sears catalogue comes out (it puts an extra strain on him) and the Flannigans' dog, which is on his route. Cliff is a member of a lodge called the Knights of the Semitar and has opinions on everything and everybody (he also believes he knows everything about everything). Twinkies are his favorite snack, and each night he watches the Weather Channel for its weather bunnies ("You sort of develop a fatherly feeling after a while"). Cliff believes he is "the wingnut that holds Western civilization together." His car trunk contains an inflatable raft and several cans of tuna fish (he is prepared for the East Coast flooding that will occur when the polar ice caps melt due to global warming). Cliff is also an amateur inventor (he has invented such things as attack submarines) and lost $22,000 on the television show "Jeopardy" (in Final Jeopardy, Cliff was unable to give the real names of Cary Grant, Tony Curtis and Joan Crawford).

Hilary ("Norm") Peterson is a bar regular who loves to eat and drink (Ho-Ho's are his favorite snack, and he eats at the Hungry Heifer Restaurant). Norm held several jobs before beginning his own house painting and decorating service (K & P Painting, Inc.; it was originally called AAAA Painting): accountant for H.W. Sawyer and Associates; "Corporate Killer" (the guy who fires people) for Talbot International Accounting; and an accountant with a two-by-four room (2511) on the twenty-second floor of the Boston Tower for the C.P.A. firm of Masters, Holly and Dickson. Norm's license plate reads CR 4585; in high school Norm was nicknamed "Moonglow."

Norm is married to the never-seen Vera—"I joke about her, but she's all I got. I don't know what I'd do without her." At their wedding, her father said, "Thank God I'm not paying for this." Norm is loyal to the bar first, his wife somewhere down the line (Wendt's real-life wife, Bernadette Birkett, is heard as Vera's voice). Norm, Cliff and Sam pooled their resources and bought a business called "Tan 'n' Wash" (a tanning salon and coin-operated laundry).

Woodrow ("Woody") Tiberias Boyd assists Sam in tending the bar. Woody was born in Hanover, Indiana, and wanted to be a bartender. He wrote to all the bars in the big cities; one was Cheers. The Coach was the only person who ever wrote back to him, and they became pen pals. When Woody came to Boston to look up Coach, he learned that he recently died. Because of Ernie's kindness, Sam gave Woody the job.

Woody attended Hanover High School and invented the game Hide Bob's Pants. When he goes duck hunting he uses an empty Good & Plenty box as a duck caller. Woody is also a hopeful actor and starred in a television commercial for a vegetable drink called Veggie Boy (a mix of broccoli, cauliflower and kale juice). Beth Curtis (Amanda Wyss) was his hometown girlfriend; Truman was his dog; and smallpox was his first childhood disease. Kelly Susan Gaines (Jackie Swanson) is his big-city girlfriend (they married on May 15, 1992). Kelly is rich and spoiled and has over 1,000 Barbie dolls in her collection. Her first job (for a school sociology project) was as a waitress at Cheers. Woody wrote her a song called "The Kelly Song."

Bar regular Frasier Crane is a psychiatrist. He collects first-edition books and considers himself "the solver of all problems personal." Charles Dickens is his favorite author; he has a dog named Pavlov and a spider collection. Frasier is married to Lilith Sternin, a somber-looking woman he says "rides the roost in her bra and panties." Lilith is a psychiatrist and on call at Boston Memorial Hospital. Whitey and Whiskers are her favorite lab rats. Lilith wrote a book called *Good Girls/Bad Boys* and believes that she had the most productive time of her life at Cheers, more so than at any other place (when Lilith enters the bar, Cliff says, "Frost warning"). Frasier and Lilith's son, Frederick (Kevin and Christopher Graves) was born in the back of a cab ("The driver was nice enough to let me bite down on his foam dice," says Lilith of the incident). Frederick now attends the Magic Hours Learning Center Preschool.

In the episode of 11/5/92, Frasier discovers that Lilith has been having a torrid affair with her research partner, Dr. Louis Pascal (Peter Vogt). Pascal, whom Lilith calls "Googie," invented a subterranean environmental bubble called an Eco-Pod. Lilith asks for—and Frasier agrees to Lilith's request—a year-long separation so she can live with Pascal in his bubble.

Frasier was first married to Nanette Goodsmith (Emma Thompson), who is now a famous children's singer called Nancy Gee. Frasier conducts traveling self-help seminars called "The Crane Train to Mental Well-Being"; cost is $350. Before Frasier and Lilith married, Frasier dated Diane, but his rude, snobbish and selfish mother objected (she felt her son would ruin his life if he married a "pseudo intellectual barmaid"). When Diane and Frasier tried living together, Diane got an allergic reaction and the courtship ended.

Relatives: George Bell (Sam's brother, *Derek Malone*), Glynis Johns (Diane's mother, *Helen Chambers*), Marcia Cross (Rebecca's sister, *Susan Howe*), Allyce Beasley (Ernie's daughter, *Lisa Pantusso*), Cady McClain (Ernie's niece, *Joyce Pantusso*), Rhea Perlman (Carla's sister, *Annette Lozupone*), Sada Thompson (Carla's *Mama Lozupone*), Carol Ann Susi (Carla's sister, *Angela Lozupone*), Randy Pelish (Carla's brother, *Sal Lozupone*), Oceana Marr (Carla's sister, *Zia Lozupone*), Ernie Sabella (Carla's cousin, *Santo Carbone*), Anthony Addabbo (Carla's cousin, *Frankie*), Frances Sternhagen (Cliff's mother, *Esther Claven*), Nancy Marchand (Frasier's mother, *Dr. Hester Crane*), Melendy Britt (Kelly's mother, *Roxanne Gaines*), Richard Doyle (Kelly's father, *Elliott Gaines*), Celeste Holm (Kelly's *Grandmother Gaines*).

Theme: "Where Everybody Knows Your Name," vocal by Gary Portnoy.

Note: See also "The Tortellis" for information on the spinoff series.

118. *Cheyenne*

ABC, 9/13/55 to 8/30/63

Cast: Clint Walker (*Cheyenne Bodie*).

Facts: On the third day of the ninth moon of the Indian calendar (September 12; this calendar has 13 moons each year with 28 days in each month), a wagon train traveling through Wyoming territory is attacked by the Cheyenne Indians. Chief White Cloud (Richard Hale) spares the life of a

baby boy and raises him as his son. The boy, whom White Cloud said "was so quiet and solemn that he must have the brain of a wise grey fox," was given the name Grey Fox. At age 12, Grey Fox chose to go the way of the white man and took the name Cheyenne Bodie. He left his home, "south, where the river winds at the foot of the hills," and set out on his own.

A ranchhand, cavalry scout, army undercover agent, deputy, trail boss and wagon train guide were but a handful of the jobs held by Cheyenne Bodie as he drifted across the American frontier of the 1860s.

Cheyenne is a strong, quiet man who fights for the rights of others. He is proud of his heritage and is dedicated to helping the army build up the land and establish a peace treaty with his blood brothers (he can read smoke signals and is trusted by the Indian chiefs). He carries a hunting knife on the left side of his holster (his gun is on the right side) and is looking for a place to settle down and call home (he hopes one day to buy a ranch and raise horses).

The first woman Cheyenne saw who dressed like a man (in pants) was Fay Kirby (Jean Byron), a female reporter doing a story on frontier life (in the episode "The Broken Pledge"). In the episode "Legacy of the Lost," Sloane and Sloane detective Dennis Carter (William Windom) convinces Cheyenne that he is John Abbott, the long lost son of wealthy rancher Lionel Abbott (Peter Whitney). Cheyenne now has a younger brother, James Abbott (Peter Breck), and a sister-in-law, Lorna (Jolene Brand); he is also heir to the vast Abbott wealth. (Cheyenne discovers that James hired Carter to find someone who could be John Abbott and then kill him so James could become the sole heir. By coincidence, Lionel's wife and infant son were on the same wagon train as the infant Cheyenne. Lionel believed that his son was taken by the Cheyenne and would one day return to claim what is rightfully his.)

Theme: "Cheyenne," by William Lava and Stan Jones.

Note: L.Q. Jones as Smitty, a government mapmaker, was Cheyenne's sidekick during the 1955–56 season when "Cheyenne" alternated with "Kings Row" and "Casablanca" on "Warner Bros. Presents."

119. *Chicken Soup*

ABC, 9/12/89 to 11/7/89

Jackie Fisher (Jackie Mason) and Madelyn ("Maddie") Peerce (Lynn Redgrave) are neighbors who are also lovers. Jackie is a 52-year-old single Jewish man who quit his job after 22 years "to enjoy life and help other people enjoy theirs." Maddie is a widowed Catholic woman with three children: Molly (Alisan Porter), Patty (Kathryn Erbe) and Donny (Johnny Pinto).

Jackie worked as a pajama salesman for Sleep Soft, Inc.; Maddie is the supervisor of the Henry Street Settlement House in New York City. Jackie lives in the attached house (number 3266) next to Maddie (number 3268); an exact address is not given.

Bea Fisher (Rita Karin) is Jackie's mother; Mike (Brandon Maggart) is Maddie's brother.

Gordon Lust composed the "Chicken Soup" theme.

120. *China Beach*

ABC, 4/26/88 to 4/30/90
ABC, 9/29/90 to 12/8/90
ABC, 6/4/91 to 7/22/91

Cast: Dana Delany (*Colleen McMurphy*), Marg Helgenberger (*K.C.*), Nan Woods (*Cherry White*), Chloe Webb (*Laurette Barber*), Megan Gallagher (*Wayloo Marie Holmes*), Jeff Kober (*Dodger*), Concetta Tomei (*Lila Garreau*), Brian Wimmer (*Boonie*).

Facts: A harsh look at the Vietnam War as seen through the eyes of a group of people stationed at China Beach, the U.S. Armed Forces R & R facility in Da Nang, Republic of Vietnam. The medical personnel are attached to the 510th Evac Hospital, 63rd Division. The unit has 180 hospital beds and 33 surgical units but is unable to handle critical neurological surgery.

Colleen McMurphy began a career as a nurse in 1966, at age 18, and was inspired by John F. Kennedy to believe that she can make a difference. She joined the army, trained in Houston and volunteered for service in Vietnam. Colleen is representative of the 50,000 women who actually served in Nam. She is a triage nurse, mentioned her bra size to be 34C and has the serial number N91574. Colleen was called "F.N.G." (Fairly New Guy) when she first arrived on China Beach, and is desperately trying to do her job while at the same time struggling to overcome her feelings of frustration and to make sense out of an unjustified war and senseless killing.

Colleen, an Irish Catholic, was born in Lawrence, Kansas, in 1948. She served as a lieutenant in Nam for two years (1967–69) and feels she made a difference—"I couldn't save them all, but I saved some. I mattered. We all did."

In 1967 Colleen had one wish—"a day without choppers" (the helicopters brought the wounded). It never came true. By 1970 Colleen had returned to her home and taken a job as a nurse at the local hospital. Two years later she was "a wild at heart free spirit who took to the open road via a motorcycle."

The year 1975 saw Colleen taking to the road again, this time in a car (license plate CN3 679), to escape the memories of her past. She drifted for a few years and finally settled in Portland, Oregon, where she acquired a job as a hospital administrator. In 1985 she married Joe Arenberry (Adam Arkin), an architect. By 1988 (the last we know of her character) she is the mother of a three-year-old girl named Maggie (uncredited role).

Karen Colosky, who prefers to be called K.C. (after her hometown of Kansas City, she says), is the only civilian on the base. She is a prostitute and charges $100 an hour for her services. She has type O blood and mentioned her middle name as being Charlene. As a kid, Karen loved the rain—

China Beach. **Marg Helgenberger, Dana Delany (back) and Nan Woods.**

it made her feel safe (she would snuggle under the bedcovers and gain a sense of safety). On China Beach, the rains provide Karen with the only sense of safety and security she can feel amid the devastation that surrounds her.

K.C. is an expert at telling pathetic stories about herself and having people believe her. She and Colleen first met on China Beach in 1967 in the women's shower. (K.C. noticed Colleen staring at her navel and said, "Never seen an outie before?" They joked and became close friends.) It was in 1967 that K.C. became pregnant by General A.M. ("Mac") Miller (Wings Hauser). Later that year, while in Saigon for R & R, Colleen helps K.C. deliver her baby—a girl she names Karen. K.C., however, is unable to care for Karen and hires Trieu Au (Kieu Chinh), a Vietnamese woman, to take the child "until I get my life together."

K.C. left China Beach in 1969 without Karen (now age two and played by twins Kelsey and Kirsten Dohring). She moved to Bangkok where she first had an export/import business and by 1975 a nightclub called K.C.'s. It is at this time that K.C. seeks Karen—but it is also a time of great concern as it is the Fall of Saigon. K.C. has only a short time to spend with Karen before she realizes she must get her to safety. At an American military base, K.C. manages to get Karen (Shay Aster), now eight, on a helicopter. With only seconds remaining, K.C. tells Karen to look up Boonie Lanier (a soldier from China Beach who loved her), "who'll take care of you."

In Santa Cruz, California, 1976, K.C. and Colleen meet. K.C. sees that Karen is safe, attending school and with Boonie. She leaves without letting Karen see her.

A Christmas card sent to Colleen from Karen reveals that in 1977 K.C. owned a diner called The Answer. By 1988 K.C. is a high powered businesswoman, and she sees Karen for the first time in 12 years. Karen Lanier (Christine Elise), as she is now called, is attending college. (While it is not mentioned how, Trieu Au also escaped from war-torn Saigon and, in 1985, is working in a beauty parlor in the United States. Boonewell G. ["Boonie"] Lanier was with the First Marine Division, Icor, on China Beach. Karen, who has been living with Boonie and his family for 12 years, considers him to be her father and uses his last name. Boonie always called K.C. "K.C. from K.C.")

Laurette Barber was the sweet U.S.O. entertainer (singer and dancer) who became an active participant in helping the wounded. She was an orphan and raised at the Lady of Perpetual Hope Orphanage. When the tour moved to another base, Laurette was written out (it is assumed that she found a career in show business after the war).

Cherry White was an A.R.C. (American Red Cross) nurse who volunteered for duty in Vietnam. Like Colleen, she was dedicated to helping the victims of a war she felt was unjust. Cherry's greatest hope was to find her brother, Rick, who was reported as missing in action. Cherry was killed by an enemy bomb during the Tet offensive in one of the series' most emotional episodes.

Wayloo Marie Holmes was the U.S. Air Force television reporter who covered the misery of China Beach in the hope that it would lead to bigger and better things. It did; she left the job to become a reporter for ABC-TV in New York. In 1988 Wayloo was the host of a network television series called "This Morning."

Major Lila Garreau was the hospital commander whose life was the army. She had the nickname "Scooter" and most often found herself pushing herself and her nurses far beyond the call of duty. She married Sergeant Bartholomew Pepper (Troy Evans) and later moved with him to Alabama to run a gas station.

Evan ("Dodger") Winslow was the seldom talking, tough on the outside but sensitive on the inside combat soldier. Dodger thought he was meant to die in Vietnam. He stayed behind when the China Beach personnel left in 1975. Shortly after, he befriended a lost Vietnamese girl named Cam Noi (Page Leong); we last see them walking through a stream to safety. When we next see Dodger he is in Red Lodge, Montana, and the father of a son named Archie (Tyronne Tan). Dodger owns a bar called Archie's and is also deeply religious (he is building a church for Vietnam vets out of an old school bus).

Other Regulars: Dr. Dick Richard (Robert Picardo), Nurse Holly Pelligrino (Ricki Lake), Beckett (Michael Boatman). Dick remained in the medical profession and works in a hospital; Beckett worked at the G.R.U. (Graves Registration Unit) on China Beach; he became a teacher after the war (Tony T. Johnson played Beckett at age seven in a flashback sequence).

Relatives: Penny Fuller (Colleen's mother, *Margaret Mary McMurphy*), Donald Moffat (Colleen's father, *Brian McMurphy*), John Laughlin (Colleen's brother, *Brenden McMurphy*), Harold Russell (Colleen's uncle, *Conal*), Kevin McCarthy (Wayloo's father, *Congressman Holmes*), Penelope Windust (Dodger's mother, *Jean Winslow*), Tom Bower and Richard Jaeckel (Dodger's father, *Archie Winslow*), Arlene Taylor (Dodger's sister, *Annie Winslow*), Frederic Lehne (Cherry's brother, *Rick White*), Finn Carter (Boonie's wife, *Linda Lanier*), Sean Ryan (Boonie's son, *Adam Lanier*), Shannon Farrara (Boonie's daughter, *Gillian Lanier*), Conni Marie Brazelton (Boonie's daughter, *Angela Lanier*), Colleen Flynn (Dick's wife, *Coleen Richard*), Troy Searcy (Beckett's son, *Malcolm Beckett*).

Themes: "Reflections" (opening), by the Supremes; "China Beach" (closing), by John Rubinstein.

121. *Chips*

NBC, 9/15/77 to 7/18/83

The exploits of Chips, the California Highway Patrol. The Central Division officers are: Francis ("Ponch") Poncherello (Erik Estrada), Jonathan ("Jon") Baker (Larry Wilcox), Bonnie Clark (Randi Oakes) and Robert "Bobby" Nelson (Tom Reilly). With the exception of Bonnie, who drives a patrol car, the officers ride Kawasaki motorcycles.

Ponch, badge number 2140 (also given as B-600), has the mobile codes 7-Mary-3, LA 15-Mary-2 and LA 15-Mary-6. He was born in the barrio, and his car license plate reads 8003IF. Marinino's is his favorite eatery.

Jon, Ponch's first partner, was born in Wyoming and has the mobile codes 7-Mary-4 and LA 15-Mary-3. His badge number is 5712, and his cycle license plate reads 16A60. Bruce, Ponch's second partner (after Wilcox left the series) has the mobile code LA 15-Mary-7.

Bonnie, a highway patrol car officer, has the code 7-Charles and the license plate 999001. Bonnie took sign communications at Cal State and is now part of the C.H.P. Deaf Liaison Program. Ponch calls her "Bon Bon."

Other members of the C.H.P.: Officer Sindy Cahill (Brianne Leary)—her bike code is LA 15-Mary-11; Officer Bariczu (Brodie Greer)—his bike code is LA 15-Mary-23; Officer Kathy Linehan (Tina Gayle)—she is the C.H.P. headquarters computer operator. Kathy works in the Report Room and lives in a beachhouse at 153½ Malibu Beach Road. Her mobile code is LA-15-Mary-10. Sergeant Joseph ("Joe") Getraer (Robert Pine), badge number 5712, is the superior officer. The phone number for C.H.P. headquarters is 555-7374.

Emily Daniels (Melody Anderson) and Sylvia (Debbie Evans) are the "Highway Angels," two beautiful motorcycle-riding girls who help C.H.P. by spotting lawbreakers and calling in the crime. "They are our streets," says Emily. "We don't want to see them turn into a battlefield . . . If just one driver slows down because of the Highway Angels, then we're accomplishing something."

MERV (Maximum Efficiency Robotization, Vector Series 1)

was the department's attempt to introduce efficiency into C.H.P. via a robotics program (it failed when MERV shorted and became a danger). The motorcycles are equipped with Motorola radios, and the precinct's favorite charity is the Children's Liver Foundation.

Officers Melanie Mitchell (Trisha Townsend) and Paula Wood (Barbara Stock) became the first C.H.P. female unit in the episode of 2/28 and 3/1/81 ("Ponch's Angels"). The episode, produced as a pilot, failed to sell a female version of "Chips." The series is also known as "Chips Patrol."

Theme: "Chips," by John Parker.

122. *City*

CBS, 1/29/90 to 4/16/90

Elizabeth ("Liz") Gianni (Valerie Harper) is a widow, the mother of a 19-year-old daughter named Penny (LuAnne Ponce) and the manager of a large metropolis referred to only as "The City." The series has very little trivia information: Liz, whose office number is 503, grew up in the Belmont Flats section; she now lives with Penelope ("Penny"), who attends City College, at 5741 North Jefferson Drive. Alan Young played Liz's estranged father, Donald Dugan, and Vincent Baggetta played Liz's husband, Michael Gianni, in a ghost sequence.

Roger Barnett (Todd Susman) is the assistant city manager; Anna Maria Batista (Liz Torres), who played Maria in the Havana, Cuba, production of *West Side Story,* is a clerk in Liz's office; Wanda Jenkins (Tyra Ferrell) is Liz's secretary; Ken Resnick (Stephen Lee) is the deputy mayor; and Gloria Elgis (Mary Jo Keenen) is the city's social coordinator.

Carol Levin and Chris Maney composed the theme.

123. *Civil Wars*

ABC, 11/20/91 to 3/2/93

Guilford, Levinson and Howell, Attorneys-at-Law, is a legal office located in Room 712 of an unidentified building in Manhattan. Sydney Guilford (Mariel Hemingway), Charles ("Charlie") Howell (Peter Onorati) and Eli Levinson (Alan Rosenberg) are the lawyers who are also partners in a firm that handles divorce cases. "If it weren't for the misery of others, we'd be out of a job," says Charlie.

Sydney, a matrimonial lawyer, was born in Minnesota (where she lived at 213 Minnetaka Trail; she now lives in an apartment on East 74th Street in New York City). Sydney is beautiful and single, and constantly being hit upon (something she wishes would stop; she is divorced and not ready for another relationship). She carries a gun for protection; orders mineral water before each meal; and posed nude for a photo layout in *New Yorker* magazine.

Denise Iannello (Debi Mazar), the office receptionist, was born in Ozone Park, New Jersey. She went to P.S. 147 (elementary school) then Sacred Heart High School. She has a degree from the Katherine Gibbs Secretarial School and married Jeffrey Lissick (David Marciano), the office messenger, in 1992 (they live at 509 Central Park West). Jeffrey was born in Manhattan and went to Cooper Union High School; he is a poet and writer in his spare time.

Charlie was born in Howard Beach; his father was a police officer. Eli, a lawyer for 15 years, takes the downtown number 104 bus to work (he lives on 85th Street). Constance Towers played Sydney's glamorous mother, Harriet Guilford; Eddie Barth was Charlie's father, Charlie Howell, Sr.; Florence Stanley was Eli's mother; and Ken Lerner played Eli's cousin, Barry Snyder.

Donald Markowitz composed the "Civil Wars" theme.

124. *Clarissa Explains It All*

NIK, 3/24/91 to the present

Cast: Melissa Joan Hart *(Clarissa Darling)*, Elizabeth Hess *(Janet Darling)*, Joe O'Connor *(Marshall Darling)*, Jason Zimbler *(Ferguson Darling)*, Sean O'Neill *(Sam)*.

Facts: "Hi, I'm Clarissa Darling. I didn't choose the name. I wanted Jade, but by that time it was too late already. Anything without a last name would have been better . . . 'Madonna' would have been great, but no one asked me." These are the first words we hear from Clarissa Marie Darling, a very pretty 13-year-old girl who speaks directly to the audience "to explain all the things that go on around here."

Clarissa lives at 464 Shadow Lane in Baxter Beach and attends Thomas Tupper Jr. High School. She receives an allowance of three dollars a week and shops at the Willow Mall. Clarissa has "a security alligator" she calls Elvis (he lives in the "Heartbreak Hotel," a small plastic pool in her room; in the first episode of the second season, Clarissa mentions that she sent Elvis back to Florida when he got too big). She dreams about driving: "I was born to drive. Even before I could walk I knew I was meant to drive. Everyone thinks I'm too young to drive, but I feel you have to start early if you really want to do something right." Her dream is to own a 1976 apple red Gremlin ("The car, not the creature"). She has a collection of hubcaps hanging on her bedroom wall, along with two license plates (EX5-6233 and 514-097; in second season episodes G-85-Q and 217 CWF) and a 28-foot gum chain made from chewed gum ("recycled gum, please"). Clarissa also wears fish earrings and likes junk food (especially Twizzlers licorice and jawbreakers). "I hate the kind of pixie haircuts your mom gives you at home, and I hate germs everywhere."

Clarissa earns extra spending money by walking the neighbor's collie, Sarge, and lost only $12.50 trying to sell Christmas cards by the Yuletide Greeting Company in May. Her favorite cult movie is *Revenge of the Nerds,* and she eats Tasty Taters Potato Chips ("sour cream and garlic flavor").

Clarissa's most embarrassing moment occurred when her obnoxious brother, Ferguson, brought her bra to school for "Show and Tell." Her most harrowing experience occurred on her seventh birthday when she stuck her head in the sour cream dip and almost drowned. The first thing Clarissa does when she gets home from school is head for the fridge. Her real first job was the kiddie attendant (dressed as Little Bo Peep) at the Baxter Beach Carnival. As a kid, Clarissa had a rocking horse named Trigger, and she "starred" in several school plays: the tail of a Tyrannosaurus rex in *The Prehistoric Pageant*, a wise man in *The Christmas Pageant*, and a pillar in *The Greek Day Pageant*. *The Little Mermaid* is Clarissa's favorite Disney movie; peanut butter swirl is her favorite ice cream; and "21 Jump Street" is her favorite television show (she has a crush on star Johnny Depp).

Clarissa is a computer whiz and says, "I'm the abnormal child of two normal parents—unless, of course, you count Ferguson, my brother. That dork boy has been a burn on my butt since he was born. He was a normal, ugly baby. Sometimes I think he was just envious of my natural grace and good looks. Sometimes I think he's related to Freddy" (Freddy Krueger of the *Nightmare on Elm Street* movies).

"Bugs Bunny and Friends" is Ferguson's favorite television show. Clarissa calls him "Ferg-Face" and lives for the day to get even with him for the previously mentioned "Show and Tell" incident. He also attends Tupper Junior High. "Living with my brother," Clarissa says, "is like having your hair set on fire, than having it put out with a sledgehammer." One of Clarissa's favorite pastimes is devising ways to get rid of Ferguson. Ferguson is a Republican and vice president of the Dan Quayle Fan Club (there is no president—"You can't have an office higher than your idol"); he also risks punishment by sneaking down to the living room late at night to watch "Spine Tingley Theater" on television. Ferguson attended Camp Can Do as a kid and appeared with Clarissa on the television game show "Brain" (they lost when Ferguson went about explaining what a pie is when the host meant the algebraic term *pi*).

Marshall and Janet Darling, Clarissa's parents, have been married for 15 years. Marshall, who calls Clarissa "Sport," is an architect; Janet is head of the Children's Museum of Baxter Beach. Marshall's favorite television show is "This Old House"; he reads *Architect World* magazine and a daily newspaper called the *Dispatch*.

Casablanca is Janet's favorite movie. She was in the Modern Ballet Dance Troupe in college and starred in Martha Graham's classical modern ballet, *The Red Rabbits of Dawn*. Janet is a vitamin freak and a health food nut (zucchini lentil surprise is her favorite dinner; carob pudding cake with whipped tofu topping is her favorite dessert). When Janet gets upset, she watches videocassettes of *The Red Shoes* and *The Turning Point*.

Sam, the neglected son of a sportswriter, is Clarissa's "best bud." Sam, who enters Clarissa's second floor bedroom by ladder, is her cohort in crime and shares most of her misadventures. He has three fish (Willie, Mookie and Babe) and a never-seen dog named Ohio. His father writes for the *Dispatch*.

"Clarissa Updates" alert viewers to what has happened; visual aids (special effects) help Clarissa illustrate her points as she reports to the audience. She fancies herself as a network newscaster and has only two words for Jane Pauley—"Watch out."

"This is Clarissa Darling again. Pretty hectic this time, huh? Who knows what'll happen next. See you then."

Relatives: Heather MacRae (Janet's older sister, *Mafalda*. She lives in Canada and is a member of the Ladies' Moose Club, where she is called "Posey").

Theme: "Way Cool," vocal by Rachel Sweet.

125. *Coach*

ABC, 2/28/89 to the present

Cast: Craig T. Nelson *(Hayden Fox)*, Shelley Fabares *(Christine Armstrong)*, Jerry Van Dyke *(Luther Van Dam)*, Bill Fagerbakke *(Michael Dybinski)*.

Facts: Hayden Fox is the coach of the Minnesota State University Screaming Eagles football team. He is assisted by Luther Van Dam (the defense coordinator) and Michael Fabian Dybinski. Hayden, who appeared on the covers of *Sports Illustrated* and *Collegiate Sports Digest* magazines, has a weekly sports show on KCCY-TV, Channel 6, called "The Hayden Fox Show." He lives in an unspecified cabin in the woods. He has a wooden Indian on his front porch, a basketball hoop, rubber tire on a rope (for football tossing) and a treehouse in the backyard. Hayden has his truck cleaned at Helen's Car Wash, and at the weekly poker game (a two dollar bet limit), Hayden is famous for his "five alarm chili." After 21 years of his coaching, Hayden's team won a chance at a bowl game by competing in the twenty-seventh Pineapple Bowl in Hawaii. They won 16–13 against the Texas Wranglers.

Christine Armstrong, a sportscaster for Channel 6, is Hayden's romantic interest. (They met in 1986 at the United Charity Ball. Hayden spotted her, thought she was the most beautiful girl he had ever seen and forced himself upon her.) She and Hayden dine most often at the Touchdown Club. Christine attended Saint Mary's High School and anchored a pilot called "Magazine America." She and Hayden married in the episode of 11/25/92 ("Vows").

Luther has been an assistant coach for 38 years (22 years with Hayden). The day he fears most is the day he has to coach. He is from Danville, Illinois, and has a pet parrot named Sunshine. Luther, now 52, received the parrot (who eats Acme Bird Seeds) from his father when he was ten years old. He also has a dog named Quincy and earns $32,000 a year.

Michael was a student at Minnesota State for eight years and Hayden's star player before he became a full time coach (staff advisor to incoming freshmen), even though he majored in forestry. Hayden nicknamed him "Dauber" because his moves on the field reminded him of the Dauber wasp. Dauber, Luther and Hayden drink beer and watch "Monday Night Football" together at the Touchdown Club. Dauber wears a size 14EEE shoe.

Coach. Craig T. Nelson (center): then left to right: Jerry Van Dyke, Clare Carey, Bill Fagerbakke and Shelley Fabares.

Judy Watkins (Pam Stone), whom Dauber calls "Sweet Stuff," is Dauber's girlfriend. She is coach of the women's basketball team and Hayden's nemesis (the two simply cannot get along with each other). She calls Dauber "Honey."

Kelly Fox (Clare Carey) is Hayden's daughter and a student at the university. She married fellow student Stuart

Rosebrock (Kris Kamm) in her sophomore year and later worked as a bartender at the Touchdown Club. When Stuart left Kelly to become the host of a kid's television show called "The Buzzy the Beaver Show," their marriage also broke up, and they divorced a year later. When Kelly became a senior (1992), she decided to pursue her dream and become an actress (she has posters from the films *Wonderful Town*, *Come Back, Little Sheba*, *Othello* and *Medea* on her dorm room wall).

Relatives: Lenore Kasdorf (Hayden's ex-wife, *Beth Fox*), Nanette Fabray (Christine's mother, *Mildred Armstrong*), James Karen (Christine's father, *Dr. James Armstrong*), Charlotte Stewart (Stuart's mother, *Peg Rosebrock*), James Staley (Stuart's father, *Wilson Rosebrock*), Paul Dooley (Luther's father), Nancy Marchand (Judy's mother, *Merlene Watkins*), John McMartin (Judy's father, *Judge R.J. Watkins*). Judy's parents live in her hometown of Atlanta; Merlene has a pampered poodle named Pepper.

Theme: "The Coach Theme," by John Morris.

126. *Code Name: Foxfire*

NBC, 2/8/85 to 3/22/85
NBC, 4/26/85 (1 episode)
NBC, 7/12/85 (1 episode)

Cast: Joanna Cassidy (*Elizabeth Towne*), Robin Johnson (*Danni O'Toole*), Sheryl Lee Ralph (*Maggie Bryan*), John McCook (*Larry Hutchins*), Henry Jones (*Phillips*).

Facts: In 1981 Elizabeth ("Liz") Towne, a beautiful CIA agent (code name, Foxfire), and a man named Sam Rawlings (David Rasche) had planned on marriage, a house, and kids. Unknown to Liz, Sam was using her to smuggle counterfeit pesos into Mexico. When Liz found out, Sam shot her (in the shoulder) and left her in a hotel room with five million counterfeit pesos. The government knew Liz was innocent—but clearing her would mean the lives of a dozen people. They let her take the fall (Liz knew before she took the job that "if you are ever caught or captured, the government will disavow any knowledge of your existence"). Liz, file number 48412, is forcibly retired from the CIA and sentenced to Cell Block D of the Women's Federal Prison in Blue Lake, New York.

On January 27, 1985, Liz is freed. She takes a cheap apartment in the Flatbush section of Brooklyn, New York, and is surprised by a visit from Lawrence ("Larry") Hutchins, a CIA agent who is the brother of the president of the United States. "Liz," Larry says, "the president has been thinking about you. We want you to come back to work for us." Larry explains that Sam has stolen a guided missile to destroy a Russian satellite and start a global star war.

Liz is intrigued: "1,560 days in prison and I had only one thing on my mind—and that was to get Sam Rawlings."

Liz is first given a place to live—Larry's luxurious Park Avenue penthouse; Larry now stays with his eccentric mother, "who lives in the 80s [somewhere on East 80th Street in Manhattan] with lots of cats." Liz is also given Phillips, the Hutchins' ever-faithful butler, to care for her ("He's been with the family for 200 years," Larry says).

In mid–Manhattan, Liz seeks an old friend named "Crazy" Jack O'Toole. She finds his cab (number 1022) but learns from its new operator, his pretty daughter, Danni

O'Toole, that Jack has died. Liz tells Danni that she needs a driver and that Jack was the best. Intrigued by Liz, Danni drives her from midtown to lower Manhattan and back within four minutes (because of traffic, the trip usually takes 30 minutes). "You're as crazy as your old man," Liz says. "Cloak and dagger is my life," responds Danni—and she gets the job.

Maggie Bryan, a gorgeous con artist and thief, was born in Detroit, and when Liz last saw her, she was doing three to six for grand larceny. Fate brings them together at a gambling club. "I want you to come in with me. I need someone with your skills," Liz tells her. "I've run too long in the gutter," responds Maggie. "I don't know if I can walk on the sidewalk . . . Baby, you're asking for trouble."

The unique team is formed, and they successfully complete their first assignment together (stopping Sam). At the end of the assignment, Larry approaches Liz and gives her a pardon: "It's on the same stationery Ford used for Nixon."

Danni has a car with the license plate 503L KAZ, and her cab station is at East 59th Street. Larry's white Rolls Royce license plate is PBF ZBRO. He gambles at the Gammon Club. Larry's brother, Franklin B. Hutchins (not seen), is the president and hates for Larry to call him on the red phone (it makes him nervous); Larry attends all the social functions his brother hates (for example, the National Truck Stoppers Association) and is publicly thought of as a fool (his cover is "a national bozo," as Franklin calls it). Larry and Liz's security level is G-36; in prison, Liz had a plant she called Sid. Danni calls Phillips "Jeeves," and Phillips hasn't eaten eggs since the Republican Convention of 1972 (when his doctor told him he had high cholesterol).

Theme: "Foxfire," by Joe Sample.

127. *Code R*

CBS, 1/21/77 to 6/10/77

Channel Island is a small coastal community in southern California. On a typical day, the community has about 17,000 tourists, and 500–700 boats abound in the marina. In order to deal with potential problems, Emergency Services (E.S.) has been formed—a specialized organization that combines police, fire and ocean rescue services into the Code R rescue force.

Walt Robinson (Tom Simcox) is the police chief (his code is "Police One"); Rick Wilson (James Houghton), the fire chief, has the code "Fire One"; George Baker (Martin Kove) is the chief lifeguard and captain of the boat *Lifeguard I* (also his radio code); Suzy (Suzanne Reed) coordinates operations from Island Dispatch, their base on Channel Island. When everything is coordinated, Suzy uses the code "Approach Code R." Their hangout is the Lighthouse Bar, which is owned by Harry (W.T. Zacha).

Barbara Robinson (Joan Freeman) is Walt's wife, and Bobby Robinson (Robbie Rundle) is Walt's son, the head of Firehouse Two—a kid fire department.

Lee Holdridge composed the theme.

Code R. Back: Tom Simcox, Martin Kove; front: James Houghton, Suzanne Reed.

128. *Code Red*

ABC, 11/1/81 to 3/28/82

Joseph ("Joe") Rorchek (Lorne Greene) is captain of Battalion number 6, Station Number 1, of the Los Angeles Fire Department (L.A.F.D.). His sons, Ted (Andrew Stevens) and Chris (Sam J. Jones), are also with Battalion number 6—they are firefighters; Ted's code is "Charlie 10," and Chris, who pilots a helicopter, is "Fire Chopper 5" (I.D. Number N405A6). Joe's young, adopted son, Danny Blake (Adam Rich), is a Junior Fire Explorer.

Haley Green (Martina Deignan) is the city's first female firefighter (she works with Joe's battalion). Ann (Julie Adams) is Joe's wife; she and Joe live at 9876 Temple Lane, and their phone number is 555-2364. Danny has a dog named Sophie. In the pilot episode (9/20/81), Joe is an arson investigator with Task Force 5, Station number 9 of the L.A.F.D.

Morton Stevens composed the "Code Red" theme.

129. *Colonel March of Scotland Yard*

Syndicated, 1957

Perceval Clovis Adelbart March (Boris Karloff) is a British police colonel who heads Department D-3 (the Office of Queen's Complaints) of the New Scotland Yard. Colonel March, an expert swordsman, uses deductive reasoning (never violence) to solve crimes. He served with the British Royal Army during World War II and wears a black patch over his left eye (a war injury). He became a police inspector after his discharge and is interested in interplanetary flight. He lives in an apartment at 611 Stable Mews.

Colonel March often works with Inspector Gordon (Eric Pohlmann) of the French Surete. March says of his good friend, "Gordon spends two-thirds of his life at the gambling table and one-third in bed."

Philip Green composed the "Colonel March" theme.

130. *Colt .45*

ABC, 10/18/57 to 9/27/60

Christopher ("Chris") Colt (Wayde Preston) likes a "kick" now and then—but he'd rather get it from gunpowder, not liquor. People say Chris is "just a peddler." Chris says, "I'm the best peddler the company has, and I'm selling the fastest gun in the world."

The gun is "The Peacemaker," a single action army revolver, caliber .45. The company is the Colt Patent Firearms Company of Hartford, Connecticut. Chris, the nephew of Sam Colt (the inventor of the Colt revolver in 1873), is a former army captain who is now an undercover agent for the U.S. government. He poses as a gun salesman to carry out dangerous assignments for his superiors.

"The six shooter," as some people call it, has a high hammer spur that makes for lightning cocking and a finely milled butt "that seems to jump in the hand." The Colt sells for $20, but there is a six month wait once it is ordered (Chris won't sell his demonstrators—"I'd be out of business if I did that"). Chris carries a U.S. Marshal's badge under his shirtsleeve (he has the authority to deputize in the field) and wears the company's symbol, a bucking colt (in a silver circle), on his black gunbelt.

In episode 45 ("Alias Mr. Howard," 12/6/59), Donald May was brought on as Sam Colt, Jr., Chris's cousin, to replace Wayde Preston when he walked off the set over a dispute with the producers. (No reason was given in the stories as to why Sam, an undercover agent also, was brought on or what happened to Chris.) They appeared together in episode 54, "Phantom Trail" (3/13/60).

In the opening theme, Chris approaches the camera and fires six shots—three from each of the .45's he wears—to spell the show's title (Sam does the same thing, but he first rides in on a horse; when he dismounts, he fires his guns).

Bert Shefter and Paul Sawtell (music) and Hal Hopper and Douglas Heyes (lyrics) wrote "The Colt .45 Theme."

131. *Columbo*

NBC, 9/15/71 to 9/1/78
ABC, 2/6/89 to 12/15/91

Philip Columbo (Peter Falk) is a lieutenant with the Central Division of the L.A.P.D. He wears a rumpled raincoat and claims to have a bad memory. He worries, is nervous when he is not driving and smokes cigars (his wife prefers pipes, "but that's too much for me to carry around"). Columbo rarely carries a gun and is a master of deductive reasoning. He slouches, is always early for appointments and studies people's faces for their reactions to situations. He is persistent and is always trying to tie up loose ends (little insignificant details bother him). Columbo feels there is something wrong with him because "I seem to bother people and make them nervous" (especially when he utters his famous catchphrase "Oh, one more thing").

Columbo taught a criminology course at Freemont College on the perfect crime and likes his coffee hot, strong and black ("No decaf for me"). He is married to the never-seen Kate (for 25 years in 1991) and has a basset hound named Fang (NBC) and Dog (ABC; "He's a dog so we call him Dog"). Kate, whom Columbo said wore Maidenform brand of panties, was spun off into her own series with Kate Mulgrew in the title role (see "Kate Loves a Mystery"). Columbo was first attached to the Hollenbeck Division of the L.A.P.D. His badge number is 436, and he drives a 1952 Peugeot with the license plate 448 DBZ. Columbo's original raincoat became very fragile and was retired in 1990. He wore a duplicate raincoat for the first time in "Columbo Goes to College" (ABC, 12/9/90). The Columbo character was first played by Bert Freed on the "Enough Rope" episode of "The Chevy Mystery Show" (NBC, 7/31/60). Peter Falk first played Columbo in two NBC television movies: *Prescription Murder* (2/20/68) and *Ransom for a Dead Man* (3/1/71).

Dave Grusin, Billy Goldenberg and Henry Mancini (NBC) and Mike Post (ABC) composed the various "Columbo" themes.

132. *Coming of Age*

CBS, 3/15/88 to 3/29/88
CBS, 10/24/88 to 11/21/88
CBS, 6/29/89 to 7/27/89

Dr. Edward ("Ed") Pepper (Alan Young), a retired chiropractor, his wife, Trudie (Glynis Johns), and retired airline pilot Richard ("Dick") Hale (Paul Dooley) and his wife, Ginny (Phyllis Newman), reside at the Dunes Retirement Resort in Arizona. Also living at the resort is Pauline Spencer (Ruta Lee), a gorgeous seductress who is nicknamed "The Black Widow" (for her knack of marrying and losing husbands).

Ed and Trudie live in Condo 7-C, Dick and Ginny in Condo 9-C. Ed is president of the community's Duffer's Club, Lapidary Club and the Floating Tanner's Club; Dick heads the Residents' Association. Trudie and Ginny are members of the Theater Club. Because of limited backdrops at the Dunes (owned by the Walnut Corporation), only the plays *Oklahoma* and *Paint Your Wagon* can be staged.

Cindy Krainik (Nada Despotovich) is Dick and Ginny's married daughter; Tom Krainik (Jim Doughan) is Cindy's husband; and Nancy and Scott (Taylor Fry and Jarrett Lennon) are their children. Red Pepper (Van Johnson) is Ed's brother.

Doc Severinsen and his orchestra perform the theme, "Coming of Age."

133. *Commando Cody, Sky Marshal of the Universe*

NBC, 7/16/55 to 10/8/55

Commando Cody (Judd Holdren) is a U.S. government scientist who battles the enemies of the universe. He has perfected a rocket flying suit and has come to be known as "The Sky Marshal of the Universe." Commando Cody works for an unknown government organization, and his real name is never revealed. The government insists that he wear a black mask (like the Lone Ranger's) at all times to protect his identity; not even his superior, Mr. Henderson (Craig

Coming of Age. Alan Young and Glynis Johns.

Kelly), or his assistants, Joan Albright (Aline Towne) and Ted Richards (William Schallert), know his real identity. (The "good guys" refer to him as Commando Cody; the "bad guys" simply say Cody: "We gotta stop Cody," or "It's Cody; run.")

Under a veil of deep secrecy in a ghost town called Graphite, Cody, Joan and Ted built a rocketship to enable them to battle the enemies of Earth on other planets or in space. Commando Cody, Joan and Ted communicate with each other via their identification patches, which contain miniature two-way radios and operate on a frequency assigned only to Commando Cody. Cody's rocket flying suit has a silver helmet, a backpack with two rockets for power and a front panel with these controls: On/Off, Up/Down, Slow/Fast. Cody needs to take a running start, and then jump to be able to fly.

Only 12 episodes were produced, and very little is done to explain things. When the series begins, Commando Cody has perfected the cosmic dust blanket to protect the Earth from a missile attack by Retik, the Ruler (Gregory Gay), an evil extraterrestrial who must conquer the Earth to use it as a staging platform for his conquest of other planets. Stories follow Commando Cody's efforts to stop the Ruler's conquest of the universe.

Dr. Varney (Peter Brocco) was the Ruler's first Earth assistant; he was replaced in episode four by Baylor (Lyle Talbot). Gloria Pall plays the Ruler's home base assistant.

How the Ruler came to invade the Earth or how he acquired his aides is not shown; and, other than that they are scientists, nothing else is known about Joan, Ted or Ted's replacement, Dick Preston (Richard Crane; Dick appeared in episode four, "Nightmare Typhoon," and explained simply that "Ted was transferred"). Joan and Ted originally joined Commando Cody to adapt atomic power for rocketship propulsion. Cody's ship is equipped with a ray gun that can be used in two ways: normal firing, or as a steady, heat-destroying ray when a target is out of firing range.

Hydrogen hurricanes, the magno force ray, radioactive gas, the magnetic drag ray and the refraction force field were some of the weapons our heroes had to overcome as they battled to stop the Ruler on such planets as Mercury, Mars and Venus (the Ruler's original home base was the moon).

The series is based on two Republic theatrical serials: *King of the Rocket Men* (1949) and *Radar Men from the Moon* (1952). In these serials, Cody did not wear a mask and had a real name: Jeff King (1949), and Larry Martin (1952). The television Cody is based on both Jeff and Larry, and the mask is perhaps a way of distinguishing the television and movie Commando Codys.

134. *The Commish*

ABC, 9/28/91 to the present

Anthony ("Tony") Scali (Michael Chiklis) is chief of the Eastbridge (suburban New York) Police Department. Tony, affectionately called "The Commish" by his fellow officers, is hard on criminals but is a softie at heart. He lives at 1209 Beach Street ("a couple of blocks from the drive-in") with his wife, Rachel (Theresa Saldana), and his son, David (Kaj-Eric Erikson). Tony is a Catholic; Rachel, a schoolteacher for the Eastbridge Grammar School, is Jewish; they are raising David in the Jewish faith.

Born in Brooklyn, New York, Tony attended Saint Mary's High School and has a law degree from Fordham University in the Bronx. He was a street cop for ten years and dreams of becoming the police commissioner of New York City. Tony, who reads people's faces, came to Eastbridge in 1988; he is based in the Eastbridge Municipal Building. C-1 and X-Ray-4 are his car codes, and "The Great Pretender" is his favorite song. Rachel drives a car with the license plate LLQ 118; in the opening theme, Tony is seen reading the book *Tissue Decomposition: A Homicide Primer*. As a kid, Yogi Berra was Tony's hero.

David Paymer plays Rachel's brother, Arnie Metzger; Mike Post composed the theme.

135. *Corky and White Shadow*

ABC, 1/30/56 to 2/24/56

Corky Brady (Darlene Gillespie), a pretty teenage girl, and her German shepherd dog, White Shadow (Chinook),

live in the town of Beaumont. Her widowed father, Matt Brady (Buddy Ebsen), is the sheriff; Dolly Porter (Veda Ann Borg), the owner of the Shamrock Café (also called Dolly Porter's), is his romantic interest; and "Uncle" Dan (Lloyd Corrigan) is Corky's friend, a hermit-like character who lives in a cabin in the woods.

Being the daughter of the sheriff, Corky fancies herself as his assistant ("Me and Shadow got a nose for ferreting out lawbreakers"); Matt sees her in a different light and wishes she would just "do girl things" ("Remember, I'm the law around here; you just stick to housekeeping, let me do the sheriffing"). While she is a good housekeeper and can cook ("Pa says there ain't nobody in this whole dern county can make better hush puppies than me—not even Dolly Porter"), she also helps Matt "catch those low down rotten scoundrels." In this "Mickey Mouse Club" serial, Corky and White Shadow attempt to capture the Durango Dude (Rayford Barnes), an outlaw who has robbed the Bank of Glen Forkes, was captured and later escaped from the jail in the town of Waterford.

Uncle Dan calls Corky, who attends the Beaumont School, "The Little Deputy Sheriff." Dan's pets are: Dutchess (a tame coyote), Gabby (a blue jay), Snitch (a bear cub), Cicero (an owl), Lightning (the burro), Minerva (a goat), Cologne (a skunk) and Mr. Frisbee (a squirrel). When Corky gets upset with her dog, she says things like, "White Shadow Brady, what do you mean by walking out on me," or "White Shadow Brady, you come back here." The Durango Dude, whose trademark is a white Stetson, rides a horse called Apache.

Darlene sings "Uncle Dan," "My Pa" and "Little One." Buddy performs "Buckwheat Cakes." The serial is composed of 17 episodes plus an introduction.

William Lava composed "The Theme from Corky and White Shadow."

136. *The Cosby Show*

NBC, 9/20/84 to 9/17/92

Cast: Bill Cosby *(Cliff Huxtable)*, Phylicia Rashad *(Clair Huxtable)*, Lisa Bonet *(Denise Huxtable)*, Sabrina LeBeauf *(Sondra Huxtable)*, Malcolm-Jamal Warner *(Theo Huxtable)*, Tempestt Bledsoe *(Vanessa Huxtable)*, Keshia Knight Pulliam *(Rudy Huxtable)*, Geoffrey Owens *(Elvin Tibideaux)*, Joseph C. Phillips *(Martin Kendall)*, Raven-Symone *(Olivia Kendall)*.

Facts: At 10 Stigwood Avenue in Brooklyn, New York, resides the Huxtable family: parents Cliff and Clair, and their children, Sondra, Denise, Theo, Vanessa and Rudy. Cliff, whose real name is Heathcliff, is an obstetrician/gynecologist who works out of his home and at both Corinthian Hospital and Children's Hospital in Brooklyn. He is a fan of jazz music and calls himself "Mr. Jazz." Cliff's favorite Western movie is *Six Guns for Glory* starring Colt Kirby; as a kid, Cliff accidentally sat on (and killed) his pet bird, Charlie. Cliff had a bike he called "Bob," and in his youth he wanted to become a drummer. Cliff's favorite hangout is Jake's Appliance Store (where, Clair says, he has no sales resistance).

Cliff is a graduate of Hillman College in Georgia. It is here that he met and fell in love with Clair Hanks (he called Clair "Lum Lum"; she called him "Baby Cakes"). They married on 2/14/64 and honeymooned at the Caralu Hotel in the Caribbean.

Clair is a lawyer with the firm of Greentree, Bradley and Dexter. She was also a panelist on "Retrospective," a television show on Channel 37 that explores history. When Clair graduated from law school, she and Cliff celebrated by having dinner at Michael and Ennio's Restaurant. Clair wears a size eight dress, won't let Cliff eat the snacks he likes (for example, chocolate doughnuts with chocolate milk) and restricts him to carrot juice, celery and sprouts.

Sondra, the oldest child, attended Princeton University and was the first of the Huxtable kids to marry (it cost Cliff and Clair $79,648.72 to send her to Princeton). She and her husband, Elvin Tibideaux, later became the parents of twins they named Winnie and Nelson (she was in labor for 8½ hours with them). Elvin calls Sondra "Muffin," and together they ran a business called the Wilderness Store. (Elvin was a pre-med student at Princeton when he first met Sondra, a law student. When they married, they put everything on hold to open their store.) They first lived in Apartment 5B (address not given; the *K* from the Valley Fair Milk sign is against the window). Elvin gave up the medical profession for psychological reasons: he has a problem charging people for medical help. With Cliff's help, Elvin returned to medical school. He later held a job working for Benrix Industries (as Inspector number 36; he would inspect the pill bottles when they came to the end of the line to make sure they had safety seals). He lost this job when the efficiency expert said they didn't need 36 inspectors. When Elvin became a doctor in 1990, Sondra enrolled in an unnamed law school to continue her education. A year later, Sondra is a lawyer and she, Elvin and the twins move in with Cliff and Clair as a temporary measure until they can find their own home. In the episode of 2/6/92, Sondra and her family move to their own home in New Jersey.

Denise, the second born and most troublesome child, attended Central High School and spent three semesters at Hillman College (where she received five *D*s, one *C* and seven incompletes; see "A Different World" for further information). With no interest in college, she quit (much to her parents' regret), returned home and held jobs at the Wilderness Store and at Blue Wave Records (where she earned $25 a week as the assistant to the executive assistant). She later went to Africa for one year as a photographer's assistant and returned one year later married to a navy lieutenant (Martin Kendall) and as the stepmother of his young daughter, Olivia. Denise, who had a dream of teaching disabled children, enrolled in the Medgar Evers College of the City University of New York and began taking education courses. Martin is a graduate of Annapolis. He calls Olivia, whose favorite song is "Pop Goes the Weasel," "Sparky." Dwayne the dog and Howard the parrot are Olivia's invisible pets.

Theodore ("Theo") Aloysius Huxtable, the only son, attended Central High School and later N.Y.U. (where he lives in Apartment 10B of an unidentified building in Greenwich Village). In high school, Theo was called "Monster Man Huxtable" when he was a member of the wrestling team. In 1991 Theo majored in psychology and became a junior counselor at the Seton Hall Communications Center (the Rosa Parks Group). Shortly after, he was accepted into N.Y.U.'s grad school (Department of Psychology).

Vanessa, the fourth born child, first attended Central High School, then Lincoln University in Philadelphia. She is a fan of old movies and in the fall of 1991 announced her engagement to Dabnis Brickley (William Thomas, Jr.), a man 12 years her senior (Vanessa is 18). Dabnis works as a maintenance man at the college, and they later broke off the engagement, but remained friends. In high school, Vanessa was a member of the rock group The Lipsticks.

Rudith ("Rudy") Lillian Huxtable is the youngest of the children. She attends an unnamed grammar school, and has a teddy bear named Bobo and a goldfish she calls Lamont. Vanilla is her favorite flavor of ice cream, and when she joined the Pee Wee League football team (jersey number 32) and proved to be a sensation, Cliff nicknamed her "The Gray Ghost."

In the last first-run episode, "The Graduate" (4/30/92), Denise announces that she is pregnant and Theo, a student with atrocious grades in high school, graduates from N.Y.U. with a bachelor of science degree (Cliff and Clair spent nearly $100,000 on his education).

Relatives: Earle Hyman (Cliff's father, *Russell Huxtable*), Clarice Taylor (Cliff's mother, *Anna Huxtable*), Minnie Gentry (Cliff's great-aunt, *Gramtee*), Joe Williams (Clair's father, *Al Hanks*), Ethel Ayler (Clair's mother, *Carrie Hanks*), Yvette Erwin (Clair's sister, *Sara*), Erika Alexander (Clair's cousin, *Pam Turner*), Marcella Lowery (Elvin's mother, *Francine Tibideaux*), Deon Richmond (Elvin's father, *Lester Tibideaux*), Victoria Rowell (Martin's ex-wife, *Paula*), Nancy Wilson (Martin's mother, *Lorraine Kendall*), Moses Gunn (Martin's father, *Joel Kendall*). Twins Donovan and Darrian Bryant played Sondra's son, Nelson, as an infant; Jalese and Jenelle Grays played Winnie as an infant. Jessica Vaughn (Winnie) and Gary Gray (Nelson) were the twins later.

Theme: "The Cosby Show Theme," by Bill Cosby and Stu Gardner.

137. *The Courtship of Eddie's Father*

ABC, 9/17/69 to 6/14/72

Thomas ("Tom") Corbett (Bill Bixby) and his six-year-old son, Edward ("Eddie") Corbett (Brandon Cruz), live in Apartment C at 146 South Beverly Boulevard in Los Angeles, California. Tom, a recent widower, is the editor of *Tomorrow Magazine*, a newspaper magazine supplement (its

The Courtship of Eddie's Father. **Bill Bixby, Brandon Cruz and Miyoshi Umeki.**

slogan: "Today's Magazine Supplement"; its offices are at number 201 in an unnamed building). Eddie, who attends the Selmer Grammar School, is determined to find his father a new wife. He lives by the last words his mother told him (to watch out for Tom) and plays matchmaker. Although Tom says, "Stop trying to find girls for me," Eddie persists and invites "strays" home to meet "his kind, generous and handsome father."

"Most kids have a father father," says Eddie, "but I have a father who's my best friend." And the special friendship the two share is depicted more often than the matchmaking aspects as the series progressed.

Mrs. Livingston (Miyoshi Umeki) is their housekeeper. She is Japanese, calls Tom "Mr. Eddie's Father" and is attending night classes to improve her English. Norman Tinker (James Komack) is Eddie's adoptive uncle. He is Tom's friend, the magazine's art director; he is also irresponsible and a ladies' man.

"They threw the mold away and they made you," says Tom about his pretty, sometimes dizzy, sometimes brilliant secretary, Tina Rickles (Kristina Holland), whom he confides in when he has a problem with Eddie. Joanna Margaret Jacqueline Kelly (Jodie Foster), better known as Joey, is Eddie's friend (she was originally the school bully, giving Eddie a black eye and knocking a baby tooth out, before Mrs. Livingston refined her). Cissy Drummond (Tippi Hedren) is the magazine's editor-in-chief; and Etta (Karen Wolfe) was Tom's secretary before Tina.

Eddie eats Crunchy Flakes cereal for breakfast, and each morning Mrs. Livingston allows him to bring Tom his coffee (Eddie's biggest challenge is not to spill any). "Eddie," says

Tom, "eats an awful lot of cookies before he goes to bed"; he calls Eddie "Sport." When Eddie is not up to par, he wears his "sick pajamas" (the ones with the dive bombers on them) and refers to women's makeup as "gloop and glup." The first woman Tom seriously dated after his wife's death was model Lynn Bardman (Diana Muldaur); the relationship ended when Lynn found she was not ready to become a housewife and mother.

Relatives: Will Geer (Tom's father, *Harry Corbett*), Francine York (Tom's sister-in-law, *Kate Landis*).

Theme: "Best Friend," vocal by Harry Nilsson.

138. *Cover Up*

CBS, 9/22/84 to 7/6/85

Danielle ("Dani") Reynolds (Jennifer O'Neill) is a beautiful high fashion photographer who owns Reynolds Photography, a studio located at 36 North Dutton Drive in Los Angeles. Mac Harper (Jon-Erik Hexum) is a much decorated former Green Beret who poses as Dani's top model—his guise as a U.S. government undercover agent. Henry Towler (Richard Anderson) is the American ambassador-at-large to whom they report for assignments (to rescue Americans in trouble anywhere in the world).

Rick (Mykel T. Williamson) is Dani's assistant; and Dani's gorgeous models are Gretchen (Ingrid Anderson), Ashley (Dana Sparks), Rachel (Rosemarie Thomas and Sheree J. Wilson), Terri (Terri Wynn) and Billie (Candice Daly and Irena Ferris). Dani, who is reckless and likes to get her own way, drives a car with the license plate 800-QLM-77. She knows all the famous fashion designers of the world and calls in favors when she needs them (for example, clothes for a false front fashion show).

When agent Jack Stryker (Antony Hamilton) blows a case and fails to retrieve a kidnapped writer named Elliott Dawson (Efrem Zimbalist, Jr.), Henry teams him with Dani in an attempt to complete the mission (Henry explains that Mac is on another assignment). Jack is a former Green Beret. Although born in Kansas, he spent most of his life in Australia, where he was sent to live after his parents' death. He is opinionated, self-centered and stubborn. When they successfully rescue Dawson, Dani learns that Mac was killed during his assignment (reflecting the real-life death of Hexum, who accidentally shot himself in October 1984). Dani believes that she sets all the rules; Jack believes that he is "the boss" (letting both believe what they do was the only way Henry could get Dani and Jack to work together). Jack also poses as a top male fashion model.

Peter Brown played Dani's husband, Mark Reynolds, in the first episode. A government agent, Mark was killed when he became involved in a plot to sell high tech American weapons to a foreign agent. Henry first teamed Dani and Mac to go undercover and find Mark's killer.

Jim Pitchford and Dean Steinman composed the theme, "Holding Out for a Hero."

139. *Cowboy in Africa*

ABC, 9/11/67 to 9/16/68

After retiring from Her Majesty's Royal Air Force, Commander Howard Hayes (Ronald Howard) starts up a cattle ranch in Kenya. One day, a wild zebra (whom he later named Pajama Tops) wandered onto the ranch "and sort of adopted us." The animal was so domesticated that it gave Hayes the idea of domesticating wild animals and starting game ranching. It appears that if overgrazing by domestic cattle continues, Africa will turn into a desert. "Domestic cattle move like sardines, eat the grass and pound the ground into volcanic dust. Wild animals travel to water faster and are in great shape off the same land."

The Hayes Ranch becomes a game ranch, and Hayes begins his job of making wild animals part of the economy by hiring James ("Jim") Sinclair (Chuck Connors), a world champion rodeo rider, and his American Indian partner, John Henry (Tom Nardini), his "hazer and team tying buddy," to rope and herd the animals (which include the zebra, wildebeest, buffalo and antelope). Stories relate their struggles and the opposition they face from the diehard cattle ranchers who think Hayes's plan is foolish (they also fear that wild animal diseases will affect their cattle).

Jim previously worked on an unnamed ranch in Texas (which was turned into a highway) and won the "World Champion Cowboy" award (as depicted on his belt buckle) two years in a row at the Calgary Stampede Rodeo in Canada. Howard's plane I.D. number is 5YKSL; other ranch animals are two dogs named Get Off the Couch and You Two, and a monkey called Peeli Peeli.

Malcolm Arnold composed the "Cowboy in Africa" theme.

140. *Crime Photographer*

CBS, 9/26/45 to 12/28/45
CBS, 4/19/51 to 6/5/52

The *Morning Express* is a crusading New York City newspaper. John ("Jack") Casey is the paper's "ace cameraman who covers the crime news of a great city." Casey, as he is called, lives in an apartment at 110 Mulberry Street and works like a detective to uncover the headline making stories. He is assisted most often by Ann Williams, the paper's gutsy crime reporter; she mentioned living in an apartment on 56th Street. Casey's hangout is the Blue Note Café, a mid–Manhattan club where Casey finds relaxation, listens to the Blue Note Café Musicians and gains information from Ethelbert, the bartender. Assisting both Casey and Ann is Bill Logan, a police captain with the Homicide Division of the Police Department of New York City.

The series, also known as "Casey, Crime Photographer" and "Casey, Press Photographer," made its debut on CBS radio in 1943. In 1945 CBS adapted the radio series to television as "Diary of Death," with Oliver Thorndike as Casey, Ruth Ford as Ann and John Gibson as Ethelbert.

In 1951 CBS again attempted a series. Richard Carlyle (1951) and Darren McGavin (1952) played Casey. Jan Miner was Ann; John Gibson again played Ethelbert; and Bernard Lenrow was Captain Logan. Archie Smith was added to the cast as Jack Lipman, the troublesome cub reporter for the *Morning Express*.

The Tony Mottola Trio played the Blue Note Café Musicians (1951–52), and Morton Gould composed and performed the "Crime Photographer" theme (1951–52).

Crimetime After Primetime

The overall title for a series of CBS late-night crime-dramas; *see* "Dangerous Curves," "Dark Justice," "The Exile," "Fly by Night," "Forever Knight," "Silk Stalkings" and "Sweating Bullets."

141. *Crunch and Des*

Syndicated, 1956

Caribe Key is a small island in Florida and the base of operations for Crunch Adams (Forrest Tucker) and Des Smith (Sandy Kenyon), two roughneck friends who operate the *Poseidon,* used in charter boat service that caters to people eager to explore the Bahamas and Florida Keys. Sari Adams (Joanne Bayes) is Crunch's wife; and Stillwell (John Doorman) owns the local tackle shop. The series, also syndicated as "Deep Sea Adventures" and "Charter Boat," is based on the *Saturday Evening Post* stories by Philip Wylie.

142. *Dangerous Curves*

CBS, 2/26/92 to the present

Gina McKay (Lise Cutter) and Holly Williams (Michael Michele) are two beautiful security guards for Personal Touch, a Dallas, Texas–based security firm that is 90 percent female and caters to individuals, P.R. firms, insurance companies and European royalty. Marina Bonelle (Diane Bellego) is the owner of Personal Touch, and Oscar ("Ozzie") Bird (Gregory McKinney), a lieutenant with the Dallas Police Department, is Holly's boyfriend.

Holly was an officer with the N.Y.P.D. She quit the force when she got tired of spinning her wheels (arresting suspects only to have them out before a conviction). Gina was an officer with the San Remo (Arizona) Police Department, who quit the force after she was reprimanded by her captain for stopping fellow officers from beating up a suspect (Bobby Williams). When Holly, who now works for Personal

Touch, sees a videotape of the incident that involved her cousin, Bobby, she travels to Arizona to thank Gina and recruit her for Personal Touch.

Most people believe Personal Touch is a hooker service. Gina hates "macho man" assignments (men who need baby-sitting and hire women so no one will know they need protection). Gina will tackle dangerous undercover assignments and joke about them, "but I'm not going to be an obit in anybody's newspaper." INB 68A is Gina's license plate; 555-0213 is Holly's telephone number; the Blue Cat Blues Bar is their favorite watering hole.

In the episode of 3/1/92, Holly and Gina team with Alexander D'Orleac (François Gendron) of the Paris Personal Touch Bureau to nail the designer of a new drug called Ink. When D'Orleac discovers that Holly and Gina are both ex-cops who like it better when they can make something happen (as opposed to being reactive and waiting for something to happen), he reveals that he is an undercover agent for Interpol and offers them a job: "You're attractive, you're well trained and you're women. There always seems to be a shortage of women." Gina and Holly remain at Personal Touch as a cover and D'Orleac becomes their control (Marina was dropped from the series).

Larry Weir, Michael Parnall and Tom Weiss composed the "Dangerous Curves" theme.

The Danny Thomas Show see *Make Room for Daddy*

143. *Dante's Inferno*

CBS, 10/9/52; 10/1/53; 11/19/53; 4/28/55; 1/26/56; 2/16/56; 5/3/56; 6/28/56

Willie Dante (Dick Powell) is a former gambler turned owner of a San Francisco restaurant called Dante's Inferno. He was a lieutenant during World War II and has two types of customers: the normal dinner guest, and the select people who frequent the establishment's back room—a secret gambling hall. Stories relate Dante's attempts to run a legitimate gambling hall despite the fact that his past reputation attracts unscrupulous characters.

Monte (Herb Vigran) is Willie's friend and the restaurant's bartender. He is one of the best safecrackers in the country and learned to cook while he was in Sing Sing prison. Lieutenant Waldo (Regis Toomey) and Willie "go back a long time." He is with the Homicide Division of the S.F.P.D.'s 27th Precinct; his office is Room 120.

Two other regulars appear but do not receive credit: Mary, the restaurant hatcheck girl; and Barney, the gambling hall's teller. There is also no credit for music (background or theme). The eight episodes aired on Dick Powell–hosted segments of "Four Star Playhouse" (9/25/52 to 9/27/56).

Four years later (10/3/60 to 4/10/61) NBC attempted another series called "Dante's Inferno" with Howard Duff as Willie Dante; Alan Mowbray as Stewart Styles (the club maitre d'); Tom D'Andrea as Biff (Willie's assistant); and Mort Mills as Police Lieutenant Bob Malone.

144. *Dark Justice*

CBS, 4/5/91 to the present

Nicholas ("Nick") Marshall (Ramy Zada; later Bruce Abbott) is a superior court judge in an unnamed U.S. city. As a police officer, Nick lost his collars to legal loopholes. When he became the district attorney, he lost cases to crooked lawyers. As a judge, Nick finds his hands tied as a result of strict interpretation of the law. But he still believes in the system. However, when Nick's wife and daughter are killed (in a car explosion) by Thomas Sacani (Stephen Burleigh), the brother of a mobster Nick killed when he was a cop, Nick stops believing in the system and decides to bring to justice those who are guilty but beat the system. He recruits three people to help him: Catalana ("Cat") Duran (Begona Plaza), Arnold ("Moon") Willis (Dick O'Neill) and Jericho ("Gibs") Gibson (Clayton Prince).

Cat was tired of being mistreated by the system. Nick helped her turn her life around and gave her a new start, a new identity and "a new bra size. I'm half the size I used to be; they got in the way before." She now runs Cat's Liberal Child Care Center. When Cat, who was born in 1963, is killed during an assignment (shot in the back twice in an attempt to save Nick's life), she is replaced by Maria (Viviane Vives), who was born in Barcelona, Spain, and who, like Cat, met a tragic end (shot saving the life of a girl the team was protecting). In the episode "Bump in the Night," Bruce Abbott becomes the judge, and private investigator Kelly Cochran (Janet Gunn) becomes the new member of the team. (After flagging down a police car for help, Kelly is raped by the officers. Due to a lack of evidence, Nick is forced to dismiss the case. He believes they are guilty and sets out to prove it. During his investigation he meets Kelly, who has begun her own investigation. She joins his team and together they dispense justice.)

Moon says only, "I owe the judge 5,000 hours of community service. That's all there is to it." Moon was a minor league baseball player and spent time in prison for gambling and forgery; he now runs Moon's Gym. Gibs is a special effects expert Nick cleared of a false murder charge; to repay the judge, he puts his talents to use for him.

Nick first researches a case "to see how the scuzz got off" then determines what action should be taken to bring the criminal back to justice. The team then sets up an elaborate scam to put the criminal behind bars. "I can't balance the scales all the time, not even half the time," Nick says. "I do what I can and hope I get a break once in a while." The newspapers dubbed Nick's team "Secret Vigilante Force" and "The Night Watchmen" (which they adopt as their name). Nick rides a motorcycle (when avenging crimes) with the license plate IHD 469 (850 COMMANDO is printed on the side). "Justice may be blind, but it can see in the dark" is what Nick says when he decides to go undercover to bring a culprit to justice.

Caitlin Dulany played Nick's late wife, Sandy, in flashbacks. Mark Snow and Jeff Freilich composed the "Dark Justice" theme.

145. *Dark Shadows*

NBC, 1/13/91 to 3/22/91

Cast: Ben Cross (*Barnabas Collins*), Jean Simmons (*Elizabeth/Naomi*), Joanna Going (*Victoria/Josette*), Roy Thinnes (*Roger/Reverend Trask*), Barbara Blackburn (*Carolyn/Millicent*), Joseph Gordon-Levitt (*David/Daniel*), Ely Pouget (*Maggie Evans*), Lysette Anthony (*Angelique*), Barbara Steele (*Julia/Natalie*), Jim Fyfe (*Willie/Ben*), Veronica Lauren (*Sarah Collins*), Stefan Gierasch (*Joshua Collins*), Julianna McCarthy (*Abigail Collins*), Michael Cavanaugh (*Andre DuPres*).

Facts: An Amtrak passenger train is seen heading toward Maine. One of the passengers is Victoria Winters, a young woman who hopes to unlock her mysterious past in Collinsport, a small fishing village. (Victoria was born in 1966 and orphaned. She was raised in a New York City foundling home and has recently been hired as the governess to nine-year-old David Collins. Victoria feels that she is somehow connected to the Collins family.)

Met at the station by Willie Loomis, Victoria is brought to the Great House. There, she meets Elizabeth Collins Stoddard, the family matriarch; Roger Collins, her brother; Carolyn Stoddard, her rebellious 18-year-old daughter; and David Collins, Roger's son.

The horrors at Collinwood Estate begin when Willie learns that the Collins family jewels are buried with an ancestor from the seventeenth century named Barnabas Collins. In a crypt at Eagle Hill Cemetery, Willie finds the coffin and opens it. Barnabas, a 200-year-old vampire, is revived; Willie becomes his slave after being bitten by Barnabas. When Barnabas discovers that the Old House (from his time) is still standing, he pretends to be a descendant of the original Barnabas Collins. He meets with the Collins family and receives permission to stay in the Old House on the pretense that he will be restoring it.

Victoria's first supernatural encounter in 1991 comes when she learns that David has befriended a ghost named Sarah Collins (Barnabas's nine-year-old sister, who died in 1790). It is during a séance to discover what Sarah's spirit wants that Victoria is whisked into the past—1790—before Barnabas was a vampire.

Victoria first meets Daniel (David's ancestor) and a live Sarah Collins. When Victoria meets Barnabas, she is mistaken for the girl hired to be Daniel's governess. Victoria is accepted as the governess (she gets room and board and $30 a year) and is said to resemble Josette DuPres, Barnabas's fiancée. Unknown to Victoria, Phyllis Wick (Laurel Wiley), who was to be Daniel's governess, has been transported to 1991 and is now very ill. Dr. Julia Hoffman, who is seeking to cure Barnabas of his affliction, fears that if Phyllis dies, Victoria will be trapped in the past forever. She is in a desperate battle to return Phyllis to her time to save both young women.

In 1790 the Collinses are shipbuilders, and they live on the Collinwood Estate. They are Barnabas's parents, Joshua and Naomi Collins; his brother, Jeremiah Collins; his aunt, Abigail Collins; and his cousin, Millicent Collins. It is Abigail who believes that Victoria is a witch when she sees that Victoria's dress has no buttons, but a zipper—"Mechanical stitching of the Devil." She brings this to the attention of the Reverend Trask, a witchhunter.

Josette DuPres, her father, Andre DuPres, and her aunt, Natalie DuPres, arrive shortly after. The resemblance between Josette and Victoria is uncanny; apart from Josette's French accent, the two are identical. It is also at this time that we meet Josette's maid, Angelique, the beautiful but evil witch who is in love with Barnabas (when Barnabas rejects Angelique's love, she vows to destroy him).

Angelique begins by casting a love spell over Josette and Jeremiah. When Barnabas discovers that Jeremiah seduced Josette, he challenges him to a duel with pistols. Another spell by Angelique places a live round in Barnabas's pistol when she learns that the brothers agreed to use blanks. Jeremiah is killed in the duel; Abigail suspects Victoria of casting a murder spell. At Jeremiah's funeral, Trask has Victoria arrested as a witch; Peter Bradford (Michael T. Weiss) is assigned to be her lawyer.

Meanwhile, Barnabas has become suspicious of Angelique and searches her room. He finds the figures she created to cast the love spell. Angelique refuses to remove the spell and is angered when Barnabas says he will never love her. In a fit of rage, Angelique grabs a knife and attempts to stab Barnabas. In the ensuing struggle, Angelique is herself stabbed when she falls on the knife. Before she dies, she cries, "I curse you, Barnabas. For all eternity, I curse you."

With the help of Ben Loomis (Willie's ancestor; the blacksmith), Barnabas places Angelique's body in an unmarked grave on a desolate hillside. Believing that the spell has been broken, Barnabas rushes to Josette's room—where he is bitten by a vampire cast in the image of Josette by Angelique's evil spirit. "Your hell shall take whatever shape I choose," cries Angelique; Barnabas dies shortly after.

The Collins family history states that Barnabas left Maine and sailed to England to attend to business after Jeremiah's death. Josette killed herself five days later by jumping off Widow's Hill, and Sarah died two days after that. The first part of the history becomes fact when Joshua covers Barnabas's death by letting it be known he has departed for England (Joshua has placed Barnabas in a secret room in the crypt at Eagle Hill Cemetery; Barnabas, however, is not dead—he has become a vampire).

The following day, Josette meets with Victoria in her jail cell. Victoria tells Josette that she is from the future and that she is Josette reborn in 200 years. She believes that she has been sent back in time to help Josette to save herself. Josette believes her and decides to return to Paris.

That night, Josette encounters Barnabas and is bitten. She comes under his spell. The following night, as Josette is drawn to Barnabas, Angelique breaks the spell and shows Josette her future destiny. When Josette sees that she will become a vampire, she takes her life by jumping onto the rocks below Widow's Hill. Two days later, the third chapter of the Collins history becomes fact when Sarah dies from a very high fever.

In the meantime, Victoria's trial has begun. Peter's defense is hopeless as both Trask and Abigail have overwhelming evidence against her. The judge finds Victoria guilty of witchcraft and sentences her to be hanged in three days—on May 5, 1790. That night Victoria tells Peter that she is the reincarnation of Josette in the 1990s and the reason why Angelique is trying to kill her is so that she can have Barnabas's love in the future.

In the present, Julia has begun another séance. Sarah's spirit appears to warn them of a great evil. But before Sarah can tell them, Angelique's spirit crosses the barrier of time and emerges in 1991.

Back in the past, Barnabas appears to his father and tells him what he has become. He asks Joshua to drive a stake into his heart and end his suffering. Joshua, who cannot bring himself to kill Barnabas, seals Barnabas in his coffin with heavy chains—where he remained until Willie released him in 1991.

It is May 5, 1790. Victoria is removed from her cell and led to the gallows. In the present, a desperate Angelique enters Maggie's body and compels her to turn off Phyllis's life support system. A rope is placed around Victoria's neck, then a hood over her head. Julia enters Phyllis's room and sees that she is not breathing. She injects Phyllis with a substance. The hangman releases the trap door on the gallows. A woman's body falls as the door opens. Victoria appears on the bed in 1991, her hands around her neck and struggling for breath. In 1790, the hangman removes the hood from the hanged woman—it is Phyllis. Victoria, grateful to be back, is surrounded by her "family"—but fear enters her face when she looks at Barnabas. The camera moves in for a closeup on Barnabas as he realizes that Victoria's experience in the past could mean his destruction in the present. The screen fades to black. The series was not renewed and an ending was never filmed.

Theme: "Dark Shadows," by Bob Cobert.

Note: The series is based on the 1966–71 ABC serial of the same title. Victoria Winters (Alexandra Moltke, Betsy Durkin and Carolyn Groves) is a young woman who has come to Collinwood to care for nine-year-old David Collins (David Henesy), the troublesome son of Roger Collins (Louis Edmonds). Roger lives on the great estate of Collinwood with his sister, Elizabeth Collins Stoddard (Joan Bennett) and Elizabeth's rebellious 18-year-old daughter, Carolyn Stoddard (Nancy Barrett).

Victoria was abandoned as a young girl and raised in a foundling home in New York City. She feels that she will find the answers to her unknown past at Collinwood. The Barnabas Collins character was not a part of the series at first. Stories focused on Victoria's involvement in the supernatural existences of the Collins family. The actual horror aspect began when a drifter named Willie Loomis (John Karlen) arrives in Collinsport. When he becomes intrigued by the legend of the Collins jewels, especially those worn by an ancestor named Barnabas Collins, he formulates a plan to rob the Collins crypt at Eagle Hill Cemetery. There, he finds the coffin of Barnabas—hidden behind a wall and bound by heavy chains. He breaks the chains, opens the coffin and restores the life of Barnabas Collins (Jonathan Frid), a 175-year-old vampire.

The first continuing storyline involving Barnabas dealt with his attempts to recreate the image of Josette DuPres (his love from the nineteenth century) through waitress Maggie Evans (Kathryn Leigh Scott)—not Victoria Winters as in the new series. When Barnabas first sees Maggie, he is taken aback by her uncanny resemblance to Josette. It is when Maggie is bitten by Barnabas that the rumors of a vampire begin to spread. Later, when Maggie's body is found in Eagle Hill Cemetery and she is thought to be dead, Barnabas gains control over her. For several months viewers were held in suspense as Barnabas tried (but failed) to accomplish his goal.

Other characters in this version are: Angelique (Lara Parker), the beautiful but evil witch who cursed Barnabas (when he refused to marry her); Julia Hoffman (Grayson Hall), the doctor who is seeking to cure Barnabas of his vampirism; Joe Haskell (Joel Crothers), Maggie's boyfriend; Peter Bradford (Roger Davis), Victoria's love interest when she is transported to the past; Adam (Robert Rodan), the Frankenstein-like man created by Julia; the Reverend Trask (Jerry Lacy), the man out to destroy Angelique; Quentin Collins (David Selby), the spirit of a Collins family member from the past; and Sarah Collins (Sharon Smyth), the spirit of Barnabas's nine-year-old sister, who died from a high fever in the 1890s (she is a friendly ghost who helps Victoria and David).

See also "Strange Paradise," the first attempt to copy "Dark Shadows." On July 31, 1981, CBS attempted a similar series called "Castle Rock," but only a pilot was produced. In it, Cyndi Girling played Celena McKenna, an Irish girl who becomes the governess of 10-year-old Annabel Stratton (Tangie Beaudin) on a mysterious island called Castle Rock. Her involvement with the supernatural activities of the Stratton family was to be the focal point of the series.

146. *A Date with Judy*

ABC, 6/2/51 to 2/23/52
ABC, 7/15/52 to 12/2/52
ABC, 1/7/53 to 9/30/53

Cast: Patricia Crowley and Mary Linn Beller (*Judy Foster*), Frank Albertson, Judson Rees and John Gibson (*Melvyn Foster*), Anna Lee and Flora Campbell (*Dora Foster*), Gene O'Donnell and Peter Avramo (*Randolph Foster*), Jimmy Sommers (*Oogie Pringle*).

Facts: The *Gazette* is the town's newspaper; the Bijou is the local movie theater; and Judith ("Judy") Foster, who lives at 123 State Street, "is the cutest date in town."

Sixteen-year-old Judy Foster is a pretty high school sophomore with a knack for finding misadventure. She receives an allowance of two dollars a week, says things like "Oh, caterpillars" and "Oh, butterflies" when something goes wrong; and believes that her family doesn't understand her: "I think the people who are related to me are unsympathetic and full of a lack of understanding. Every time I offer something constructive and valuable in the way of something concrete, I get stepped on before the germ of my idea ever gets a chance to bud into blossom." While the name of her high school is not given, the afterschool hangout is the Coke Parlor (later, Pop Scully's Soda Fountain).

Two yearly events in town are Boys Day and Girls Day (in which high school students take over city offices for one day). In one episode, Judy becomes the mayor and causes a scandal when she has the police raid a local bingo game—thinking it was a bigtime gambling ring.

Oogie Pringle is Judy's boyfriend and the object of her endless efforts to improve him and make him the man of her dreams. Oogie has a band called the High School Hot Licks (they play school dances three times a year), and Oogie once wrote a song for Judy called "I've Got a Date with Judy" ("I've got a date with Judy, a big date with Judy, oh jeepers and gee. I've got a date with Judy and Judy's got one with me"). Judy and Oogie first met when she ran him over with her tricycle. Melvyn and Dora Foster are Judy's parents. On the day Judy was born, they said, "Our house would always be open to anyone she wants to bring into it. Her friends will be our friends. Her dates will be our dates." What they hadn't counted on were "the kooks" Judy would have for friends (Oogie is the most irritating to Melvyn). Melvyn owns the Foster Canning Company and met Dora while he was in college. He was in a fraternity and belonged to a band. To impress Dora, he and "the boys" would stand beneath Dora's dorm window and sing a song he wrote especially for her: "A Rendezvous with Dora" ("I've got a rendezvous with Dora, not Jenny Belle or Flora; digga-digga-do, 23 skiddoo, I've got a rendezvous with Dora"). Melvyn's favorite movie star is Hedy Lamarr.

Randolph Foster is Judy's 12-year-old brother. He has an allowance of 75 cents a week and loves Humphrey Bogart and Boris Karloff films. He is not as mischievous as Judy (he's more wise-cracking) and tries to help Judy out of a jam when he can—for her allowance. In some episodes the locale is called "the town"; in others, "the city" or "our city." In one episode, Cincinnati was mentioned as the nearest big city. A composer for the theme is not given.

147. *Davis Rules*

ABC, 1/27/91 to 4/9/91
CBS, 12/30/91 to 7/1/92

Dwight Ulysses Davis (Randy Quaid) "is a penny-pinching, coupon-snipping miser." He is a widower and lives at 631 Evergreen with his children, Robbie (Trevor Bullock), Charlie (Luke Edwards) and Ben (Nathan Watt), his father, William ("Gunny") Davis (Jonathan Winters), and his effervescent sister, Gwen Davis (Bonnie Hunt).

Dwight, who teaches math, science and history, is also the principal of the Pomahac Elementary School in the town of Pomahac (an island across from Seattle). He is a big fan of Western movies. As a kid (age 15), he broke his nose while playing football; in high school he drove a red Corvair; before his current job, he was a minor league pitcher in Lodi, California (his career was washed up when he fell in the dugout and injured himself). Dwight loves golf but plays only three times a year; he hangs out at a store called Par for the Course (where he is called a "browse-aholic"). Dwight uses a cologne called Sweaty Lad, and he and his sons fish at Bee's Lake. Dwight's girlfriend is Erika (Kelly Rutherford), a cheerleader for the Seattle Seahawks baseball team.

William received the nickname "Gunny" during his hitch with the Marines during World War II. He calls the U.S.M.C. "Uncle Sam's Miserable Children" and is fascinated by women—especially the unseen Miss Kelly, their apparently gorgeous next-door neighbor (Gunny constantly talks about her). Gunny worked for Falcon Aerospace, has a drinking mug with NO. 1 GRANDPA printed on it, and "can make great stew out of roadkill." Dwight claims that "Gunny is 65 years old, but emotionally he's just approaching puberty." Gunny serves the family Oat Bran Flakes for breakfast.

Gwen Davis first lived in Florida (ABC episodes) and appeared twice. She became a regular on CBS (no reason given why she left Florida) and first worked as a business manager, then selling commercial time for radio station KPLG. When they were kids, Dwight would leave Gwen at the bowling alley counter as a deposit for his shoes.

Robbie, Dwight's oldest son, is the equipment manager of the school's baseball team, the Panthers. When the series returned on CBS, Robbie was dropped (no reason given why Dwight now has two sons); he was replaced by Vonni Ribisi as 16-year-old Skinner Buckley, a teenager Dwight cares for while his parents are in South America to study primitive tribes. Skinner is a fan of blues music and frequents Nick's Blues Club.

Charlie, a gourmet cook at ten years of age, and Ben, the youngest child, also attend Pomahac Elementary School. Charlie is a member of the school band.

Cosmo Louis Yeargen (Patricia Clarkson) was first introduced as Robbie's tutor (she charges $15 an hour); she later becomes a teacher at the school. She was dropped from CBS episodes. (She and Dwight dated for six months. Cosmo left to think about her relationship with Dwight. She later decided to go back and take her vows as a nun).

Elaine Yamagami (Tamayo Otsuki) is the assistant principal; she has a daughter named Nikki (Kristi Murakami). Audrey Meadows appeared as Gunny's ex-wife, Margaret ("Meg") Davis.

Mark Mothersbaugh is the composer of the "Davis Rules" theme.

148. *Dear John*

NBC, 1/6/88 to 4/15/92

John Lacey (Judd Hirsch) is a happily married New York City schoolteacher (institution not named)—or at least he thought so. One day, after ten years of marriage, John returns home from work to find a "Dear John" letter from his wife, Wendy, telling him that she has gone to live with his best friend. Suddenly, John is thrust back into the single life; one day he reluctantly attends a meeting of a singles support group at the One-on-One Club in Manhattan. There he meets an odd assortment of divorced, widowed, lonely and separated pepole, who need help, as he does, in adjusting to the single life.

The club holds its meetings on Friday nights at the Rego Park Community Center. Louise Mercer (Jane Carr) runs the class, and members of the group are Kate McCarron (Isabella Hofmann), Mary Beth Sutton (Susan Walters), Kirk Morris (Jere Burns) and Ralph Drang (Harry Groener). The members frequent Clancy's Bar after each session.

John was born in Binghamton, New York, and now lives in Apartment 42 on Woodhaven Boulevard. He also cares for Snuffy, Fluffy and Snowball, the cats of his unseen 92-year-old neighbor. At age 45 John fulfilled a lifelong dream: he took clarinet lessons at the Charles Moreloft Music School. Pineapple strudel is his favorite dessert, and as a kid he had the nickname "Moochie."

Kate, who had a dog named Skipper as a child, is divorced; Mary Beth is the daughter of the owner of the Sunshine Baby Food Company. She has been a homecoming queen and beauty pageant winner, and is always expecting the best to happen. Her biggest problem is how to act surprised when something good happens. She worked as a writer on the TV soap "The Divided Heart" and as a writer for the airline magazine *Above the Clouds*. She lives in Apartment 3A of an unnamed building.

Schemer and con artist Kirk Morris was born in Scranton, Pennsylvania. He is divorced (his ex-wife, Carol, left him for another woman—Donna [Elizabeth Morehead]); he lives in Apartment 306 with Annie Morono (Marietta DePrima), an actress who joined the group in 1991. Kirk seems to live by scams; in one episode, he and his friend Denise (Olivia Brown) began a catering company called Cuisine by Kirk.

Ralph Drang is the always worried toll-taker in the Lincoln Tunnel in Manhattan. He can tell how much money people throw in the booth collection bin by the sound of the coins. He lives in Apartment 3C and has "Star Trek" wallpaper in his bedroom. His love interest is Molly (Megan Mullally) who works three tollbooths from him in the tunnel.

Louise, who lives in Apartment 5G, is from Cheshire, England. Mrs. Philbert (Billie Bird) is an elderly group member; and Ben (William O'Leary) is the transplanted Montanan who works as the Rego Park maintenance man.

Relatives: Carlene Watkins and Deborah Harmon (John's ex-wife, *Wendy Lacey*), Ben Savage and Billy Cohan (John's son, *Matthew Lacey*), Stephen Elliott (John's father, *Phil Lacey*), Nina Foch (John's mother, *Charlotte Lacey*),

Elizabeth Franz (John's aunt, *Emma*), Wayne Tippett (Mary Beth's father, *Everett Sutton*), Corbin Bernsen (Kate's ex-husband, *Blake McCarron*), Wendy Schaal (Kate's sister, *Lisa*), Judd Trichter (Kate's nephew, *Danny*), Helen Page Camp (Kate's aunt, *Trudy*), Kevin Dunn (Kirk's brother, *Bob Morris*), Kate McNeil (Kirk's ex-wife, *Carol*), Pat Crawford Brown and Alice Hirson (Kirk's mother, *"Mumsey" Morris*), Jenny Agutter (Louise's sister, *Sarah*), Lila Kaye (Louise's mother, *Audrey Mercer*), Clive Revill (Louise's father, *Nigel Mercer*).

Flashbacks: Joshua Smith (*John age 13*), Peter Smith (*John age 17*).

Theme: "Dear John," vocal by Wendy Talbot.

149. *Dear Phoebe*

NBC, 9/10/54 to 9/2/55

"Dear Phoebe" is the advice-to-the-lovelorn column of a Los Angeles newspaper called the *Daily Star*. It is written by Phoebe Goodheart, a "woman" who is actually a man—Bill Hastings (Peter Lawford), a former journalism professor at UCLA. Believing that psychology and science play an important part in determining the outcome of a story, he decides to put his theory to the test by becoming a reporter on the paper where his girlfriend, Michelle ("Mickey") Riley (Marcia Henderson) works as the sportswriter. Bill's theory is put on hold when he finds that the only available position is that of the advice columnist. He takes the position as a temporary measure, hoping for his big break as a reporter. In the meantime, he applies his knowledge to sports to help Mickey investigate and write her stories (Mickey is unsure about Bill's theories and is often reluctant to use them; when she does give in to Bill's pleading, he often proves he is right; Mickey, however, can't be convinced to change her "Lois Lane" style of reporting).

Clyde Fosdick (Charles Lane) is the managing editor of the paper. Humphrey Winston Humpsteader (Josef Corey) is the copyboy. He hangs out at Ye Olde Malt Shoppe ("Teenage Spoken Here"), is tough (can rip phonebooks in half) and constantly gets into fights; fortunately, he has a glass jaw and is easily put out of commission by a slight slap on the face.

Bill lives in an apartment at 165 La Paloma Drive; Mickey resides at 34 West Sunset; the paper is located on Wilshire Blvd. The name of the paper is said to be the *Blade* in printed sources.

Theme: "Dear Phoebe," by Raoul Kraushaar.

150. *December Bride*

CBS, 10/4/54 to 9/24/59

Cast: Spring Byington (*Lily Ruskin*), Frances Rafferty (*Ruth Henshaw*), Dean Miller (*Matt Henshaw*), Harry Morgan (*Peter Porter*).

Facts: Lily Ruskin is a charming, attractive, sixty-years-young widow who lives with her married daughter, Ruth Henshaw, and her husband, Matt Henshaw, at 728 Elm Street in Westwood, California. ("The street is lined with palm trees," Matt says. "One block over is Palm Street which is lined with elm trees." In later episodes, the house is located at 728 North Palm Drive.)

Lily writes an advice-to-the-reader column for the Los Angeles *Gazette* called "Tips for Housewives"; she also had a second column for a short time called "Let Yourself Go" (about doing only what you want to do). Matt, an architect for Coricon Company and Associates (later the Gordon Architectural Firm) designed the house they live in (he also received honorable mention for a project in *Architect's Journal,* August 1955 issue).

Lily was born in Philadelphia. She involves herself with reader problems and says that "if Romeo and Juliet had written to her, they would be alive today." Her best friend is Hilda Crocker (Verna Felton).

Matt and Ruth met in Philadelphia (where Matt would have dinner every night at Lily's home). When Ruth and Matt wed, they had $60 to their names; they have been married five years when the series begins. Matt loves to smoke cigars, but Ruth won't let him: "Some men can look distinguished smoking cigars. You look like a walrus with one tusk." Ruth shops at a grocery store called Harry's Market (she nicknamed it "Old Grouchy's"). Her passion is to squeeze fruit, but store policy forbids squeezing the fruits and vegetables. "Ordinarily I don't mind," Ruth says, "but when I buy tomtaoes, I like to squeeze tomatoes." One day Ruth's dream came true. "For three years I wanted to reach out and say I'll take this one and this one. Well, today I got even with Harry. When I finished shopping I gave him a $20 bill. When he turned his back to put it in the cash register, I squeezed ten tomatoes as fast as I could, but only bought one. I feel wonderful!"

Ruth is also very civic minded, "and when Ruth involves herself with a project, she throws herself into it," says Matt. When Ruth took on more projects than she could handle and began to neglect her family, problem solver Lily hired an absolutely gorgeous model named Linda (Joi Lansing) as a housekeeper. Ruth didn't mind the idea of a housekeeper at first—until she saw Linda. Suddenly cooking and cleaning became more important to Ruth than community service.

Much of the comedy evolves from Peter Porter, the Henshaw's next-door neighbor. Pete is married to the never-seen Gladys, "a tyrant and total boss over Pete." "I'm not henpecked, I'm buzzardpecked. I wear the pants in my family. Even though Gladys makes them, I still wear them." Pete is an insurance salesman and says he is an expert magician (but his tricks never work). He continually insults Gladys, and his excuses are the reason why Gladys never appears (for example, "Gladys will be over later. She glued one of her eyelids closed. She was putting on her false eyelashes, sneezed and glued"). Despite the insults, Pete loves Gladys: "Gladys is a very attractive woman, but not in the morning with the mudpack on her face and those blinkers on her eyes. She looks like Citation on a muddy track." "A

padlock, chains and a straitjacket are the symbols of my marriage," says Pete. Pete also admires the way Ruth throws herself into a project: "My Gladys is the same way. I wish she'd get involved with some river project." Pete mentioned that he and Gladys have a daughter (never seen) named Linda (this character was dropped and Cara Williams added as Gladys when "Pete and Gladys" [see entry] was spun off from "December Bride").

Relatives: Arnold Stang (Pete's brother-in-law, *Marvin*), Isabel Randolph (Hilda's aunt, *Emily*), Sandra Gould (Hilda's niece, *Frieda Manhaim*), Sandor Szabo (Frieda's husband, *Carl Manheim,* a singing wrestler called "The Singing Sheik")

Theme: "December Bride," by Eliot Daniel.

Decoy see Police Woman

151. *Degrassi Junior High*

Syndicated, 10/87

Cast: Nicole Stoffman (*Stephanie*), Stacie Mistysyn (*Caitlin*), Sarah Ballingall (*Melanie*), Rebecca Haines (*Kathleen*), Pat Mastroianni (*Joey*), Duncan Waugh (*Arthur*), Anais Granofsky (*Lucy*), Amanda Stepto (*Spike*), Angela Deiseach (*Erica*), Maureen Deiseach (*Heather*), Amanda Cook (*Lorraine*), Cathy Keenan (*Liz*), Maureen McKay (*Michelle*), Irene Courakos (*Alexa*).

Facts: Events in the day-to-day lives of a group of students attending Degrassi Junior High (1987–89) and later Degrassi High (1989–91). The schools are set in the mythical town of Degrassi, Canada; the local hamburger hangout is a place called 13 Busy Street.

Stephanie Kaye, the 14-year-old school bombshell, is the eighth grade class president (she won the election by trading kisses for votes). She displays her stunning figure in low cut, tight blouses and short skirts. "Steph," as she is called, leaves home dressed as a typical teenage girl; at school she changes into her sexy attire ("My mother would kill me if she knew"). Although she means no harm by her school wardrobe (only as a means by which to attract attention), she acquired a reputation as the school sleeze. Her "dual life" was exposed in the episode "What a Night" when Stephanie's mother caught her preparing for a date, saw what she was wearing and said, "You look like a tramp." She was grounded for a month, temporarily gave up her wardrobe and was dropped from the series when her mother won the lottery and sent her to a private school (Nicole Stoffman left the series to star in "Learning the Ropes").

Caitlin Ryan, the seventh grade class beauty, writes for the school newspaper (the Degrassi *Digest*; articles have to be 200 words; the paper sells for 15 cents) and is the school's crusader (she will back any cause she believes in, from animal rights to fighting pollution). She is a promising actress and journalist and has epilepsy (although it is under control with medication). Caitlin is a member of the Degrassi swim team and played Elizabeth in the school's production of "Love's Fresh Face." She also appeared on the TV quiz show "Quest for the Best."

Melanie Brody, a 12-year-old seventh grader, is a boy-shy girl who has an opinion about everything. She was the first girl in her class to develop her figure and apparently, by the episode "The Great Race," the first girl in that class to wear a bra (which she bought with her friend L.D. when L.D. got fed up with Melanie's complaining that she needs one, but her mother won't get her one). Melanie is a member of the swim team, hates reptiles, and in the play "Love's Fresh Face" she played a wench. She and her friend Kathleen won honorable mention with a project on air pollution in the Degrassi Science Fair.

Kathleen Mead is a seventh grader and one of the smartest girls at Degrassi. She appeared on the quiz show "Quest for the Best" and played Isabel in the school play "Love's Fresh Face." She is desperately struggling to do her best and make her mother proud of her (her mother, an alcoholic, takes little interest in what Kathleen does). She wants to be an actress and won the drama award at Degrassi. Kathleen, who founded the Environmental Action Committee at school, fears she will gain weight and become unattractive (she developed a case of bulimia and overcame it with Melanie's help).

Joey Jeremiah, an eighth grader, is the school wiseguy and forever getting into trouble. The detention room and the principal's office are his second home. He formed a band called the Zit Remedy with his friends Wheels (Neil Hope) and Snake (Stefan Brogen). He keeps pictures of bikini clad "Sunshine Girls" in his locker and held a job as a janitor at radio station CRAZ (91.3 FM). The first song the band recorded was "Everybody Wants Something."

Arthur Kobalewscuy is a seventh grader and Stephanie's brother (their parents are divorced; Stephanie uses her mother's maiden name). He lives with his father (Stephanie lives with her mother) and has a dog named Phil. His best friend is Yick Yu (Siluck Sayanasy), and together they received second place honors in the science fair with a project on robots. They call each other "Broomhead" when something goes wrong, and both got caught attempting to watch an X-rated movie called *Swamp Sex Robots*.

Lucy Fernandez, a pretty black girl who seems to take care of herself (her parents are never seen and are seldom at home) is an eighth grader and has an arrest record for shoplifting. She wants to become a dancer but also has aspirations of being a filmmaker. In the episode "It Creeps," Lucy filmed a female slasher film called *It Creeps* in which Caitlin played the slasher. She also made the Zit Remedy video for Joey. Lucy also became a victim of child molestation in the episode "A Helping Hand" when a substitute teacher named Mr. Colby (Marcus Bruce) became attracted to her. In a later episode ("He's Back"), Susie Rivera (Sarah Charlesworth), the editor of the school yearbook, became Colby's next victim when he was called back

to sub (Lucy never reported the earlier incident); this time, however, the incident is reported. Lucy is famous for giving wild parties.

Christine Nelson, called "Spike" by her friends (because of the spiked hairstyle she wears), became pregnant at age 14. Though she contemplated having an abortion, she chose to keep and raise the baby (whom she named Emma). During counseling, Spike received an egg to care for as if it were a real baby; she named it Egghead. Fellow student Shane (Bill Parrott), Emma's father, attempted to help by providing Spike with half his allowance (Shane became the first student to experiment with drugs; he jumped off a bridge and suffered severe brain damage).

Teenage twins Erica and Heather Farrell (birthsign Gemini) are eighth graders and identical in almost every way. As the series progressed they changed: Heather remained the conservative one while Erica chose "to live on the wild side." Erica was the first one to date—and the first one to become pregnant (at age 16). Erica's pregnancy drove her and Heather even further apart—until Erica chose to have an abortion and found Heather's support a lifesaver in getting through the ordeal. At the science fair, they won first place honors with a report on eating disorders.

Seventh grader Lorraine Delacorte, called "L.D." by her friends, is captain of the girls' swim team and a member of the girls' soccer team. She is a staunch supporter of girls' sports and lives with her widowed father, who owns a gas station. At age 15, L.D. developed leukemia and missed much of her freshman year at Degrassi High. During chemotherapy, L.D. allowed only her dearest friend, Lucy Fernandez, to see her (for her sixteenth birthday, Lucy made L.D. a videotape of her friends wishing her a happy birthday).

Michelle Arsepi, originally a very shy eighth grader, grew out of that shell when she was 16. She began dating a black student named Bryant Thomas (Dayo Ade) and eventually moved into her own apartment when she could no longer get along with her father; she supported herself by working as a waitress at the Donut Express.

Alexa, a popular eighth grader, was the only girl who became a threat to Stephanie. While Stephanie considered herself the most beautiful girl at Degrassi and strove to gain the boys' attention, Alexa was simply herself and got the boy Stephanie wanted—Simon (Michael Carry).

Liz O'Rourke, "the girl with the weird hair" (crew cut in back, long on the sides, bangs in front) is an animal rights activist who possesses a tough exterior but is actually very sensitive. When she first arrived at Degrassi, she had a reputation of being easy.

Relatives (characters who have no verbal or screen names): Pat Beaven *(Stephanie's mother)*, Donna Hird *(Caitlin's mother)*, Steve Behal and Martin Brown *(Caitlin's father)*, Vanessa Dylyn *(Melanie's mother)*, Sheila Brogran *(Kathleen's mother)*, Ross Churchill *(Kathleen's father)*, Laine Williams *(Liz's mother)*, Gretchen Helberg *(Joey's mother)*, Rhonda Kristi *(Spike's mother)*, Frank Quinlan *(Michelle's father)*, Kenneth Taylor *(L.D.'s father)*.

Theme: "The Degrassi Theme," by Lewis Manne and Wendy Watson.

152. *The Delphi Bureau*

ABC, 10/5/72 to 9/1/73

The first episode began simply with these words: "From the Capitol came a young man..." At the end of the first commercial break another line was added: "To uncover some worms in a can..." The man is Glenn Garth Gregory (Laurence Luckinbill), the only operative of the Delphi Bureau, a small, Washington, D.C.–based intelligence agency that is responsible only to the president of the United States. His superior is Sybil Van Loween (Anne Jeffreys), a mysterious society woman who is his only contact for assignments. The can of worms is what results from his investigations: "Sybil, my job is to do research when the president needs to know the facts. But when the shooting starts, that's a whole different department."

Although Glenn Garth (as Sybil calls him) is employed as a researcher, he complains but accepts the dangerous aspects of the job. He has a photographic memory "and remembers everything he has ever seen." He resides in Washington, D.C., in "a fabulous apartment that was given to him by the government." The government has also provided him with an expensive sports convertible (license plate 753-321) and credit cards that have no limit. And, asked what he does for a living, Glenn responds simply, "Research of sorts."

Celeste Holm played Sybil in the two-hour pilot film (ABC, 3/6/72). Harper McKay composed "The Delphi Bureau Theme."

153. *Delta*

ABC, 9/15/92 to 12/17/92

Delta Bishop (Delta Burke) was born in the town of Goose Neck, which is on the Mississippi Delta ("I was named Delta because Mississippi was not the right name for me"). Ever since she was a little girl, Delta wanted to write and sing country music but never had the opportunity to pursue her dream. She became a hairstylist and worked at Mona's House of Hair. She married Charlie Bishop (Kevin Scannell) and thought she had found happiness ("Ode to Billy Jo" was the song Delta heard when she first kissed Charlie; "Love Me Tender" was their wedding song). As the years passed Delta became restless; she was eager to follow in the footsteps of her idol, Patsy Cline, and become a country music star. Charlie encouraged Delta, but every time they saved enough money for Delta to begin her dream, he would spend it on something else. Finally, after eight years of marriage, Delta decided to take charge of her own life. She quit her job, walked out on Charlie and headed for Nashville (she took with her only two items: her wedding ring and the car).

In Nashville, Delta finds an apartment over the garage of a home owned by her cousin, Lavonne Overton (Gigi Rice), and Lavonne's husband, Buck (Bill Engvall).

The Green Lantern is a nightclub located at 211 East Grange; it is reported that Patsy Cline once sang there. The club also has an amateur night, and Delta believes that if she could sing her songs there, it could start her career.

Delta meets with club owner Darden Towe (Earl Holliman) and acquires a job as a waitress. Stories follow Delta's struggle to make her dream a reality.

Delta drives a blue convertible with the license plate BBG 477. Delta was in beauty school when she first met Charlie, who worked in a lumberyard. He bought her a ring at the Shop and Save, and they married shortly after. They signed divorce papers in the episode of 12/3/92; Delta and Charlie previously lived at 1438 Linear Road.

Darden is a former stockbroker whose marriage of 12 years (to Patty) broke up when he began devoting time to his work and not her. He bought the Green Lantern as an investment and took it over to get away from his hectic lifestyle (Darden had a bad time after his marriage broke up; he drank and wrote "an awful gladiator novel called *I, Dardenius*").

Lavonne works as a beautician in a shop caled Thelma's Hair Dressers (Beth Grant plays Thelma Wainwright, the shop owner). Buck works for a garage called Jack's Automotive; he calls Lavonne "Vonnie." Friday is amateur night at the Green Lantern; Delta is off on Tuesdays and Sundays and is frequently late on the mornings she does work.

Tracy Kolis appeared as Darden's daughter, Talia Towe. Reba McEntire sings the theme, "Climb That Mountain High."

154. *Delta House*

ABC, 1/18/79 to 4/28/79

In 1904 Emil Faber founded the town of Faber. Eventually Faber College was established, and Emil's philosophy, "Knowledge Is Good," was inscribed on the base of the statue of him that stands on the campus grounds. Many fraternity and sorority houses surround the college. Omega House, composed of the rich and spoiled, is considered the best fraternity on campus; they live by Emil's creed. Moving right along, we find Delta House, which has the proud reputation of being the worst fraternity on campus. Its legacy is "to hang out with a bunch of animals and get drunk every weekend"; the proud Halloween tradition is to hang lingerie, "borrowed" from sorority houses, from tree branches. To the "Animals" (as they are called) of Delta House, Emil's creed means little, as the house has students with the lowest grade point averages. Another proud Delta tradition is "Don't get mad, get even"; Delta's "secret weapon" is a stunning blonde they call "Bombshell" (Michelle Pfeiffer).

Members of Delta House are Jim Blutarski (Josh Mostel), Robert Hoover (James Widdoes), Eric Stratton (Peter Fox), Kent Dorfman (Stephen Furst), Daniel Simpson Day (Bruce

McGill) and Larry Kruger (Richard Seer). Robert is the chapter president; Eric, whose nickname is "Otter," holds the honor of being the rush chairman; Kent, whose nickname is "Flounder," is from Harrisburg and was inducted only because his brother, Fred, was a member. Daniel, who rides a motorcycle and resembles a hood, has the nickname "D-Day"; Jim, who can eat his weight in food and beer each day, is nicknamed "Blotto"; Larry has the nickname "Pinto."

Seeking to revoke the Delta House charter and close down the campus disgrace is Vernon Wormer (John Vernon), the harsh dean of Faber College. His "cohort in crime" (who does his dirty work against Delta House) is Doug Niedermeyer (Gary Cookson), an Omega House member who is also seeking a way to close Delta House. Doug's pride and joy is his white horse, Trooper.

Other Roles: Muffy Jones (Wendy Goldman), Pinto's girlfriend; Greg Marmalaide (Brian Patrick Clarke), the president of Omega House; Mandy Pepridge (Susanna Dalton), a student. The series is based on the feature film *Animal House*.

Relatives: Gloria DeHaven (Vernon's wife, *Marian Wormer*), Charles Macaulay (Doug's father, *Buster Niedermeyer*), Sue Casey (Doug's mother, *Bootsie Niedermeyer*), Peter Schrum (*Jim's father*), Warren Munson (*Hoover's father*), Carol Worthington (*Hoover's mother*), Lewis Arquette (*Kruger's father*), Ted Chapman (*Kent's father*).

Theme: "Delta House," vocal by Michael Simmons.

155. *Dennis the Menace*

CBS, 10/24/59 to 9/22/63

Dennis Mitchell (Jay North) is a mischievous young boy who lives with his parents, Henry and Alice Mitchell (Herbert Anderson and Gloria Henry), at 627 Elm Street in the town of Hilldale. Henry is an engineer for Trask Engineering; Alice's maiden name is Perkins. Their elderly neighbors are George and Martha Wilson (Joseph Kearns and Sylvia Field). George has a dog named Freemont, and his hobbies include coin collecting and bird watching (he is a member of the National Bird Watchers Society and the Lookout Mountain Bird Sanctuary). His brother, John Wilson (Gale Gordon), is a writer for the *National Journal*.

Tommy Anderson (Billy Booth) is Dennis's friend, and Margaret Moore (Jeannie Russell) is "that dumb old girl" who has a crush on Dennis and just won't leave him alone. Margaret has a rag doll named Pamela and a baby doll named Gwendolyn.

Lawrence Finch (Charles Lane) is the 60-year-old owner of Finch's Drug Store; Mr. Merivale (Will Wright) owns Merivale's Florist Shop; and Mr. Quigley (Willard Waterman) owns Quigley's Supermarket. Esther Cathcart (Mary Wickes) is the "old maid" desperately seeking a husband.

Relatives: Sara Seegar (John's wife, *Eloise Wilson*), Nancy Evans (George's sister, *June Wilson*), Edward Everett Horton (George's uncle, *Ned Matthews*), Elinor Donahue (George's niece, *Georgianna Ballinger*), Kathleen Mulqueen (*Henry's mother*), James Bell (Alice's father, *"Grandpa" Perkins*), Verna Felton (John's aunt, *Emma*).

Theme: "Dennis the Menace," by Irving Friedman.

156. *Department S*

Syndicated, 1971 to 1972

Department S is a special branch of the International Police Force (Interpol) that investigates the unsolved cases of any police organization in the world. It is based at 1703 DeMarne Street in Paris, France. Jason King (Peter Wyngarde), Annabelle Hurst (Rosemary Nicols) and Stewart Sullivan (Joel Fabiani) are its top operatives; Sir Curtis Sereste (Dennis Alaba Peters) is their superior, the director of Department S.

Jason is the successful writer of Mark Cain mystery novels (titles include *High Fashion Murder* and *Two Plus One Equals Murder*). He drives a car with the license plate BE2083E and lives at 43 Puchard Street. Jason attempts to solve each case as if it were one of the plots in his books; he also acquires story ideas from his cases.

Annabelle is a pretty, scientific minded young woman. She lives at 86 Le Parses Avenue and drives a white sedan with the license plate 874Y3L. She possesses the ability to spot a phony American $20 bill simply by its color. Annabelle can also unravel the most complex of codes and often goes undercover in situations where a beautiful woman is needed to infiltrate a crime ring.

Stewart, the American member of the British team, provides muscle when needed; he drives a car with the license plate YYM297. Sir Curtis has a chauffeur driven limo with the license plate 6939PE.

A not widely seen spinoff series, "Jason King," appeared in syndication in 1972, with Peter Wyngarde solving crimes on his own as Jason King.

Edwin Astley composed the "Department S" theme.

157. *Designing Women*

CBS, 9/29/86 to 5/24/93

Cast: Dixie Carter (*Julia Sugarbaker*), Delta Burke (*Suzanne Sugarbaker*), Annie Potts (*Mary Jo Shively*), Jean Smart (*Charlene Frazier*), Meshach Taylor (*Anthony Bouvier*), Julia Duffy (*Allison Sugarbaker*), Jan Hooks (*Carlene Dobber*), Judith Ivey (*B.J. Poteet*), Sheryl Lee Ralph (*Etienne Toussant*).

Facts: Julia and Suzanne Sugarbaker are sisters who own the Sugarbakers Design Firm (later Sugarbaker and Associates—Interior Design) at 1521 Sycamore Street in Atlanta, Georgia (404-555-8600; later 404-555-6787 is the company phone number); they buy their goods from Fabric

Department S. Left to right: Peter Wyngarde, Joel Fabiani and Rosemary Nicols.

World. They are assisted by Mary Jo Shively, Charlene Frazier-Stillfield, Anthony Bouvier, Allison Sugarbaker, Carlene Frazier-Dobber and B.J. Poteet.

In describing Julia and Suzanne, Mary Jo states simply, "Julia got the brains and Suzanne got the boobs"—the sisters are as different as night and day. Julia is fashion conscious, well educated, outspoken and totally dedicated to women's equality. She attended Chapel High School and Southern State University (both in Georgia); she also studied art in Paris. The Gallery Pouzett exhibited a series of fruit bowl paintings Julia once did. "To get a vacation from being myself" (to find her spiritual self), Julia became Giselle and sang at the Blue Note Night Club.

Julia lives above the firm and wears a size seven shoe. She

began the firm (something she always wanted to do) after her husband, Hayden, died. She and Suzanne sponsored a Little League team called the Sugarbaker Giants (Mary Jo was the coach). A gift to Julia and Suzanne from their mother was a birth certificate with no year on it. Julia was also the guardian of Randa Oliver (Lexi Randall), a very pretty, lively and precocious girl, for a short time (Randa, jersey number 3, pitched for the Giants).

Suzanne, the firm's saleswoman, is not as intellectual as Julia. She also attended Chapel High and Southern State, but doesn't like art or art shows ("I'm sick of seeing small busted women with big butts"). Suzanne exercises with a baton to the tune of "St. Louis Blues," is extremely feminine and flaunts her sexuality. She was crowned "Miss

Georgia World of 1976"; her talent was twirling the baton, and Julia speaks proudly of the event:

> She was the only woman in pageant history to sweep every category except congeniality—something women of her family don't aspire to. When she walked down the runway in her swimsuit, five contestants quit on the spot. She did not just twirl a baton, that baton was on fire. And when she threw that baton in the air, it flew higher, further and faster than any baton had flown before, hitting a transformer and showering the darkened arena with sparks. And when that baton came down, my sister caught it and 12,000 people jumped to their feet for 16½ minutes of uninterrupted, thundering ovation as flames illuminated her tear-stained face. And that is the night the lights went out in Georgia!

"Sensational Breakthroughs" (a 30-minute commercial for new products) is Suzanne's favorite TV show. Noel is her pet pig, and Suzanne wears a size 6½ shoe. Suzanne is also fashion conscious—but unlike Julia, Suzanne will show cleavage to get what she wants. Her ex-husband, Dash Goff (Gerald McRaney), wrote the book *Being Belled*. Suzanne has a never-seen "maid to end all maids" named Consuella (she throws hatchets at the Good humor man, makes necklaces out of chicken necks and howls at the moon; she is, as Julia says, "totally psychotic").

Charlene, the most sensitive of the girls, was born in Little Rock, Arkansas, but grew up in Poplar Bluffs (the town's only eatery was Bob's Quick Bite). She attended Three Rivers Secretarial School in Missouri and Claraton University in Atlanta (where she studied psychology). Charlene admires Julia (her heroine) and is always caught in the middle of a dispute between Julia and Suzanne (she most often sides with Julia). "I'll Be Seeing You" is Charlene's favorite song, and she wears a size eight shoe. Charlene, a Baptist, was the office manager and held a part time job as a salesgirl for Kemper Cosmetics. She and Mary Jo wrote a children's book called *Billy Bunny*. Charlene married Bill Stillfield (Douglas Barr), a U.S. Air Force colonel, at the rooftop garden of the Dunwoodie Hotel, in 1989 ("Ave Maria" was her wedding song). In the episode "The First Day of the Last Decade of the Entire 20th Century" (1/1/90), Charlene had a dream in which her "guardian movie star," Dolly Parton, appeared to help her through the birth of her daughter, Olivia. On 10/29/90 Charlene bought the Grand Ghostly Mansion of Atlanta, a supposedly haunted house. Charlene's pride and joy is her autographed picture of Elvis Presley.

Mary Jo is divorced and the mother of two children: Claudia Marie (Priscilla Weems) and Quentin (Brian Lando). Mary Jo is small busted and envious of women with "big bosoms." She has a fixation about breasts and wishes she were as buxom as Suzanne. She feels a big bust means "power and respect"—not only from men, but also from women. She contemplated implants (she wants to be a 36C) but decided against it. Mary Jo attended Franklin Elementary School, wears a size six shoe and says that "the best time of my life was raising my two children." She is a Baptist, works as the firm's decorator/buyer and was voted parent volunteer of the year by the PTA in 1991. Mary Jo's ex-husband, Ted (Scott Bakula), is a gynecologist and recently married a girl named Tammy (Eileen Seeley). Claudia was a contestant in the Miss Pre-Teen Atlanta Beauty Pageant; Mary Jo has a dog named Brownie.

Allison Sugarbaker (Julia's cousin) and Carlene Frazier-Dobber (Charlene's divorced sister) joined the cast with the sixth season (9/16/91). When Suzanne moves to Japan to take advantage of its economy, Allison purchases her house and her share of the company. "Allison looks like Tinker Bell but acts like Leona Helmsley." She worked previously as a seeing-eye person to a Mrs. Digby in New York (who was allergic to dogs; Allison was fired for dying her blonde hair brown), then as a secretary at the Binsford and Walker Investment Agency. Allison sobs at everything and suffers from O.P.D. (obnoxious personality disorder). She is the office manager and also a member of a self-help group called Common Sense.

Carlene joined the firm as the new receptionist when Charlene moved to England to join Bill (now stationed overseas). Carlene worked previously for Ray Flat's Flatbed Furniture Store and is now attending evening classes at college. She was born in Poplar Bluffs, Arkansas, and is a Girl Scout troop leader (Troop 6523). She liked "Chip and Dale" cartoons as a kid "because they had manners."

At the start of the seventh season (9/25/92), Bonnie Jean Poteet becomes the new partner in Sugarbakers when Allison pulls her money out of the firm to open a Victoria's Secret lingerie catalogue franchise. Bonnie Jean prefers to be called B.J. She is a recovering alcoholic and a former court reporter. B.J. was married to James Poteet, a litigant she met and fell in love with at a trial she was covering. They married shortly after, but the marriage was short lived: while dancing in a conga line (to the song "Proud Mary") James died of a heart attack. James was the millionaire owner of a contracting firm, and B.J. inherited his money. B.J. has time and money on her hands and joined the firm when she called Sugarbakers to redecorate her home and learned that Julia was in financial trouble. B.J. loves to shop and enjoys buying things for other people.

Anthony first worked for Sugarbakers as a delivery man, then, in 1990, became a partner (L-3303 is his contracting license number). He is an ex-con who was arrested for participating in a convenience store robbery (later called a liquor store). (Anthony was with a group of friends who decided to rob a liquor store but did not tell him. Anthony was caught in the getaway car and arrested. He served time in Cell Block D of Atlanta State Prison before a judge overturned his conviction.) Anthony is now attending law school and does volunteer work at the Home for Wayward Boys. He is also the director of the Atlanta Community Theater (where Julia starred in a production of "Mame"). Savannah Simington (Bever-Leigh Banfield) was Anthony's first girlfriend. He later fell for Vanessa Chamberlain, a sexy, dim witted girl first played by Olivia Brown, then Jackee Harry (they met when she rear-ended his car). Anthony and Vanessa planned to marry. Two weeks before the wedding, Anthony received a phone call from Vanessa calling off the event. In an attempt to help Anthony forget Vanessa, B.J. takes him and the others to Las Vegas for a good time (they stayed at the Tropicana Resort and Casino). While the women are gambling, Anthony attends the ten o'clock performance of the Folies-Bergère. Heading the show is a beautiful showgirl named Etienne Toussant. During a refrain in the song "Get My Boggie Down," she looks over at Anthony and says, "Hello, handsome." At the end of the number, she singles out Anthony and says, "I hope to see you later." They meet for drinks and polish off several bottles of champagne. When Anthony wakes up the following morning, he finds that he and Etienne are married (by a justice of the peace, who moonlights as a female impersonator, at the Isle of Capri Wedding Chapel).

Etienne likes to be called "E.T.," and she calls Anthony "Tony" because he's my tiger." Etienne believes she is one of the most beautiful women in the world and calls herself "The Ebony Princess." She has to be perfect at everything she does; if she is not, she won't do it. When Etienne first joined the Folies Bergère, she forgot the words to the songs and sang, "Blah, blah, blah, blah."

Etienne's mother was one of 14 children; Etienne is one of nine, and she wants four children with Anthony ("after four, you can't get your figure back"). Despite Etienne's bossiness and Anthony's objections to some of her wants, Anthony is determined to see that the marriage works.

Alice Ghostley appeared semiregularly as Bernice Clifton, a somewhat senile family friend of the Sugarbakers who now lives in Atlanta at the Hillcrest Leisure Condominium. She also hosts "Senior Citizens Roundup" on public access cable TV.

Relatives: Louise Latham (Julia's mother, *Perky Sugarbaker*), George Newburn (Julia's son, *Payne*), Jocelyn Seagrave (Payne's wife, *Sylvia*), Lewis Grizzard (Julia and Suzanne's brother, *Clayton Sugarbaker*), Ginna Carter (Julia's niece, *Camilla*), Mary Dixie Carter (Julia's niece, *Jennifer*), James Ray (Charlene's father, *Bud Frazier*), Ronnie Claire Edwards (Charlene's mother, *Ione Frazier*), Kim Zimmer (Charlene's cousin, *Mavis Malding*), George Wurster (Charlene's brother, *Odell Frazier*), Phyllis Cowan (Charlene's sister, *Darleen Frazier*), Beany Venuta (Charlene's mother-in-law, *Eileen Stillfield*), Geoffrey Lewis (Mary Jo's father, *Dr. Davis Jackson*), Blake Clark (Mary Jo's brother, *Skip Jackson*), Bill Cobbs (Anthony's father, *Charles Bouvier*), Frances E. Williams (Anthony's *Grandma Bouvier*), Marilyn Coleman (Anthony's aunt, *Louise*), Gilbert Lewis (Anthony's uncle, *Cleavon*), Ray McKinnon (Carlene's ex-husband, *Dwayne Dobber*).

Theme: "Georgia on My Mind," performed by Louis Armstrong (first season), Doc Severinsen (second and third seasons), Bruce Miller (fourth, fifth and seventh seasons), Ray Charles (sixth season).

158. *Destry*

ABC, 2/14/64 to 5/9/64

He is six feet four inches tall, rugged and handsome and possesses a great sense of humor. He's not fast on the draw, but he's tough with his fists when he has to be. His philosophy is peace ("I'm the most peaceful man there is"). Money interests him ("I'll do most anything for it"), women find him irresistible and "nothing can stop me from coming to the aid of a beautiful damsel in distress."

This unlikely TV Western hero is Harrison Destry (John Gavin), the son of a rugged gunfighter (Tom Destry) who now roams the West seeking the man who framed him for a robbery. (Destry was arrested, tried, found guilty and served time in the Texas State Penitentiary. He was released early for good behavior.) Destry's 13 episode search to find the man who framed him is depicted. The series, which is based on the 1939 feature film *Destry Rides Again*, was filmed in color but broadcast in black and white.

Randy Sparks composed the "Destry" theme, which was sung by a group called The Ledbetters.

159. *The Devlin Connection*

NBC, 10/2/82 to 12/25/82

Brian Devlin (Rock Hudson) is a Korean War officer turned private detective, turned director of the Performing Arts Center in Los Angeles. He resides at 11632 Ocean River Drive, and his car license plate reads 647 BAJ. His son, Nick Corsella (Jack Scalia), is a private detective (Nick Corsella Investigations) and a racquet ball pro at the Health Club. (Nick was born during the Korean War after Brian's brief affair with a French woman named Nicole Corsella. Brian was transferred to Berlin before he knew of Nicole's pregnancy. In 1981 Nick learned of his father's existence and looked him up.)

Lauren Dane (Leigh Taylor-Young) is Brian's secretary; and Otis Barnes (Herb Jefferson, Jr.) is Brian's friend, the owner of a nightclub called The Home Bass.

Patrick Williams composed "The Devlin Connection" theme.

160. *Diana*

NBC, 9/10/73 to 1/7/74

Diana Smythe (Diana Rigg) is a fashion illustrator for Buckley's Department Store at 37 West 34th Street in Manhattan. Diana is British and previously lived in London. She is 30 years old and came to New York after her divorce to begin a new life. Diana lives at 4 Sutton Place in Manhattan in the apartment (11B) of her brother, Roger. Roger is an anthropologist who is currently on assignment in Ecuador. Diana's phone number is 555-7755, and she cares for Roger's Great Dane (Gulliver). She also has a rather large problem: retrieving all the housekeys Roger gave to his friends and drinking companions.

Norman Brodnik (David Sheiner) is president of the department store; Norma (Barbara Barrie) is his wife and holds the position of head of merchandising; Howard Tolbrook (Richard B. Schull) is the copywriter; and Marshall Tyler (Robert Moore) is the window dresser.

In the original, unaired pilot version, "The Diana Rigg Show" (produced by NBC in 1973), Diana Rigg played Diana Smythe as a 30-year-old divorcée who comes to New York from London to become the assistant to Mr. Vincent (Philip Proctor), head dress designer at a Manhattan store called Sue Ellen Frocks. David Sheiner played Rodney Brodnik, the store owner, and Nanette Fabray was his wife, Norma.

The episode of 11/12/73 ("You Can't Go Back") reunited Diana Rigg and her former "Avengers" co-star Patrick Macnee.

Jerry Fielding composed the "Diana" theme.

Diary of Death see *Crime Photographer*

161. *Dick Tracy*

ABC, 9/11/50 to 2/12/51

Cast: Ralph Byrd *(Dick Tracy)*, Joe Devlin *(Sam Catchem)*, Angela Greene *(Tess Trueheart Tracy)*.

Facts: Richard ("Dick") Tracy is a master police detective. He works in a large, unidentified metropolis for an unnamed precinct (that is only called Headquarters). His badge number is not given, and his squad car license plate (inserted stock footage) cannot be read; his home address and telephone number are also not given. He is married to the lovely Tess Trueheart, and he works with Sam Catchem.

Tracy is fair and honest; when he fires his gun, he never wastes a bullet ("I always hit what I aim at"). While he enjoys the homemade meals Tess prepares, he eats hot dogs and hamburgers and drinks coffee while on the job. Dick and Sam use special two-way wrist radios that allow voice communication when they are on assignment.

Patrick ("Pat") Patton (Pierre Watkin) is the police chief; J. Blackstone Springem (John Harmon) is the crooked criminal lawyer; and Officer Murphy (Dick Elliott) is the overweight, jovial stationhouse cop. The series is based on the comic strip by Chester Gould.

Dick Tracy next appeared in 1961 in the animated "Dick Tracy Show." Everett Sloane provided the voice of Dick Tracy, who rarely participated in crime solving; he acted more like a dispatcher assigning various cops (such as Joe Jitsu, Hemlock Holmes, Speedy Gonzales, Heap O'Calorie) to apprehend the criminals (for instance, Flattop and Bee Bee Eyes, the Brow and Oodles, Stooge Villa and Mumbles, and Prune Face and Itchy). Other voices were provided by Mel Blanc, Paul Frees and Benny Rubin.

In 1967, William Dozier produced a pilot (which never aired) called "Dick Tracy" with the following cast: Ray Mac-

Donnell (Dick Tracy), Davey Davison (Tess Trueheart Tracy), Eve Plumb (Bonny Braids, Tracy's adopted daughter), Jay Blood (Junior Tracy, Dick's son), Ken Mayer (Chief Pat Patton), Monroe Arnole (Sam Catchem) and Liz Shutan (Detective Liz).

In this version, Tracy lives at 3904 Orchid Drive, and his phone number is 555-7268. Tracy has a secret lab in his home (located behind a firing-range target figure) and a two-way wrist TV. In the pilot episode, "The Plot to Kill NATO," Mr. Memory (Victor Buono) plans to destroy a NATO peace conference by kidnapping its ambassadors. The group The Ventures performed the theme, "Dick Tracy."

162. *The Dick Van Dyke Show*

CBS, 10/3/61 to 9/7/66

Cast: Dick Van Dyke *(Rob Petrie)*, Mary Tyler Moore *(Laura Petrie)*, Larry Matthews *(Ritchie Petrie)*, Morey Amsterdam *(Buddy Sorrell)*, Rose Marie *(Sally Rogers)*, Richard Deacon *(Mel Cooley)*, Carl Reiner *(Alan Brady)*, Jerry Paris *(Jerry Helper)*, Ann Morgan Guilbert *(Millie Helper)*.

Facts: Robert ("Rob") Petrie is the head writer of the mythical TV variety series "The Alan Brady Show." He lives at 148 Bonnie Meadow Road in New Rochelle, New York, with his wife, Laura, and their son, Ritchie (their address is also given as 485 Bonnie Meadow Road).

Rob and Laura met at the Camp Crowder army base in Joplin, Missouri. Rob was a sergeant in Company A and first saw Laura (then Laura Meeker) when she came to entertain the troops as part of a U.S.O. show. (Rob is with Company E in some flashbacks; Laura's maiden name was also given as Meehan.) Rob's initial attempts to impress Laura failed and she soon despised him. But Rob, who is known "to make a rotten first impression," is determined to have Laura. He arranges to dance with her in one of the show's production numbers. While singing and dancing to the song "You Wonderful You," Rob, who is wearing combat boots, steps on Laura's foot and breaks her toes. Rob visits Laura at the hospital (bringing her flowers and recipes) and soon her hatred turns to love. Rob and Laura marry shortly after (unknown to Rob, Laura is only 17 years old, not 19, as she told him; they are later remarried when Laura confesses).

Rob and Laura first live in the Camp Crowder housing development. After his discharge, they move to Ohio where Rob becomes a radio disc jockey at station WOFF (the number two station in a two station town; WDDX is number one). It is at this time that Rob has an interview with television star Alan Brady and secures the job as his head writer in New York City.

Rob's first meeting with his staff, seasoned writers Buddy Sorrell and Sally Rogers, begins on a friendly note—until they learn that Rob is inexperienced and is their boss. Rob is ignored the entire day while Buddy and Sally work on an important sketch for the show. Late that day, Rob is approached by the show's producer, Melvin ("Mel") Cooley and given the sketch—crumpled by Alan. Rob covers for Buddy and Sally (who have since gone home) and rewrites the sketch. The following day, Mel congratulates Rob, Buddy and Sally for handing in such a wonderful sketch. Buddy picks up the sketch and realizes it is not the one he and Sally wrote—but sees his and Sally's name on it. Rob explains what happened and shows Buddy the original sketch. "Yup, that's Alan's crumple," exclaims Buddy, and he and Sally welcome Rob as their head writer.

"The Alan Brady Show" airs at 8:30 P.M. (network not named). It airs opposite "Yancy Derringer" (which was on CBS), is number 17 in America and number one in Liberia. Alan Brady, who lives in the Temple Towers on East 61st Street in Manhattan, has several business ventures that pay the bills. The Ishomoro Company, which produces motorcycles, pays Rob's salary. Buddy and Sally were originally paid by Tam-o-Shanter, Ltd., which made Dean Martin and Jerry Lewis coloring books. When it folded, Alan's mother-in-law's company, Barracuda, Ltd., paid them. The show's band is paid by Alan's wife's company, Brady Lady. Alan's wife's name is Margaret; the show's most important sponsor is Henry Burmont (Roy Roberts). The writers' office is on the twenty-eighth floor.

Rob was born in Danville, Ohio, and attended Danville High School. He played Romeo and his high school sweetheart, Janie Layton (Joan O'Brien), played Juliet in their school production of *Romeo and Juliet.* During his army hitch, Rob wrote the song "Bumkis" and was nicknamed "Bones." Rob's mentor is Happy Spangler (Jay C. Flippen). He taught Rob how to write and calls him "Stringbean" (Happy now owns a tie store). Rob, whose middle name is Simpson, has freckles on his back, which, when connected, form a picture of the Liberty Bell. His favorite meals are franks, beans and kraut (dinner), and cold spaghetti and meatballs (breakfast). Rob, who is allergic to chicken feathers and cats, ran for the position of Ninth District Councilman (he lost 3694 to 3619) to Lincoln Goodheart (Wally Cox). Rob wears a size 10D shoe; his tailor is Vito Schneider. The wallet Rob carries came with a photo of actress Paula Marshall inside, which he never removed (a calendar is on the back of the photo).

Laura, who won the title "Bivouac Baby" at Camp Crowder, used the pen name Samantha Q. Wiggins when she attempted to write a children's book. Her favorite TV soap opera is "Town of Passion," and she hides her old love sonnets from high school boyfriend Joe Coogan (Michael Forrest) behind some loose bricks behind the furnace in the basement. Laura, whose favorite food is moo goo gai pan, weighs 112 pounds. "Oh Rob" is Laura's sobbing catchphrase when something goes wrong. Rob once embarrassed Laura by telling the host of "The Ray Murdoch X-Ray Show" how the scatterbrained things Laura does sometimes end up as sketch material for "The Alan Brady Show."

Ritchie, whose favorite TV show is "The Uncle Spunky Show," has the middle name of Rosebud—Robert-Oscar-Sam-Edward-Benjamin-Ulysses-David—one letter for each name various family members wanted for Rob and Laura's

newborn baby. Ritchie, who had two pet ducks (Stanley and Oliver), was born after Rob and Laura were trapped in an elevator with Lyle Delp (Don Rickles), the crook with a heart of gold. When Laura was expecting, everyone had suggestions for what to name the baby: Laura (Robert or Roberta), Rob (Laura or Laurence), Mel (Allen, Alan or Allan), Sally (Valentino—"I was saving it for a parakeet, but you can have it"), and Buddy (Exit—"If the kid is an actor, it'll be in every theater in the country").

Rob and Laura paid $27,990 for their home, which has a huge rock in the basement. (The rock provides Rob with protection from flooding when it rains. He pays his neighbor, Jerry Helper, $37.50 a year to tar his back wall because the rock causes Jerry's basement to flood if the outside is not waterproofed.) Government agent Harry Bond (Godfrey Cambridge) once used the Petrie's home to stake out a house across the street (Harry was disguised as a TV repairman).

The Petries' doorbell rings in the keys of E and G-flat minor, and there are 382½ roses on the wallpaper in Rob and Laura's bedroom. Rob's most unusual gift to Laura was the grotesque Princess (also known as Empress) Carlotta necklace, and the Petrie family heirloom is a cumbersome brooch made in the shape of the United States (jewels mark the birthplace of each member of the family). The Petries' cemetery plots are at Rock Meadows Rest, located on the fifteenth hole of a golf course.

Buddy and Sally, who perform as the comedy team Gilbert and Solomon at Herbie's Hawaiian Lodge, have past TV experiences. Buddy, whose real name is Maurice, worked for "The Billy Barrows Show" and had his own series called "Buddy's Bag." Sally, who attended Herbert Hoover High School, was a staff writer on "The Milton Berle Show" before joining Alan's staff.

Buddy, famous for his "baldy" jokes about Mel, is married to a former showgirl named Pickles (her real name is Fiona, but all girls named Fiona in her hometown are nicknamed Pickles). Buddy has a German shepherd named Larry, and once (after an argument with Pickles) overdosed on Dozy Doodles sleeping pills. Pickles, whose favorite ice cream is Strawberry Sundae-on-a-Stick, was previously married to a forger named Barton Nelson (a.k.a. Floyd B. Bariscale, played by Sheldon Leonard). Buddy plays the cello at every opportunity, and his favorite drink is tomato juice.

Sally is single and looking desperately for a husband. She has two cats (Mr. Henderson and Mr. Diefenthaler) and a mother-dominated boyfriend named Herman Glimshire (Bill Idelson; in some episodes he is called Woodrow Glimshire). Sally wears a size 6½B shoe. At a bowling alley Sally discovered Randy Eisenbauer, a singer-dancer who went by the name Randy Twizzle and who invented a dance called "The Twizzle" (a cross between the Twist and the Sizzle, done while wearing bowling shoes).

Jerry and Millie Helper are Rob and Laura's neighbors. Jerry is a dentist (operates out of his home), and they have an iron jockey on their front lawn. Rob and Jerry bought a boat called the *Betty Lynn.* Rob wanted to change the name to *Shangri-La*; Jerry wanted to call it *The Challenger.* Millie has a pet mynah bird named Herschel and keeps a statue of a bull on the mantel; her father was a clothes presser. For protection, Millie carries a siren pen, which screeches when activated.

Relatives: Jerry Van Dyke (Rob's brother, *Stacey Petrie*), Carol Veazie and Isabel Randolph (Rob's mother, *Clara Petrie*), Will Wright, Tom Tully and J. Pat O'Malley (Rob's father, *Sam Petrie*), Denver Pyle (Rob's uncle, *George*), Cyril Delevanti (Rob's grandfather, *Edward Petrie*), Dick Van Dyke (Rob's great-uncle, *Hezekiah Petrie*), Carl Benton Reid (Laura's father, *Ben Meehan*), Geraldine Wall (*Laura's mother;* first name not mentioned), Eddie Firestone (Laura's cousin, *Thomas Edson*), Joan Shawlee (Buddy's wife, *Pickles Sorrell*), Phil Leeds (Buddy's brother, *Blackie Sorrell*), Peter Oliphant and David Fresco (Millie and Jerry's son, *Freddie Helper*), Willard Waterman (Laura's uncle, *Harold*), Herb Vigran (Hezekiah's half brother, *Alfred Reinbeck*).

Theme: "Theme from the Dick Van Dyke Show," by Earle Hagen.

Note: In the original pilot film, "Head of the Family" (CBS, 7/19/60), Carl Reiner was Rob Petrie; Barbara Britton was Laura; Gary Morgan was Ritchie; Morty Gunty was Buddy Sorrell; Sylvia Miles was Sally Rogers; and Jack Wakefield played Alan Sturdy, the story's television star.

163. *A Different World*

NBC, 9/24/87 to 5/8/93

Cast: Lisa Bonet (*Denise Huxtable*), Jasmine Guy (*Whitley Gilbert*), Dawnn Lewis (*Jaleesa Vinson*), Kadeem Hardison (*Dwayne Wayne*), Marisa Tomei (*Maggie Laughton*).

Facts: A spinoff from "The Cosby Show." Hillman College in Georgia, built by Joshua Hillman in 1880, "is not just a tough school, it's a butt breaker." Denise Huxtable lives at 10 Stigwood Avenue in Brooklyn, New York. She is a recent graduate of Central High School and decides to continue her education at Hillman (as did her parents, Cliff and Clair). Denise is an average student and enters Hillman with an undecided major. She shares Room 20Y in the Gilbert Hall dorm with Jaleesa Vinson and Margaret ("Maggie") Laughton. Denise brought a deer lamp (lights on the antlers) with her to "cheer up the room" and has a problem with money (she doesn't keep track of the checks she writes—"I try but I can't always do it. I'm in college now, I'm busy, I have responsibilities").

Denise is a third generation Hillman student (her grandfather also attended Hillman). She is a member of the track team and is called "The Little Engine" (when her father was on the track team, he was called "Combustible Huxtable"). Denise (top) and Maggie (bottom) have bunk beds; Jaleesa has her own bed on the opposite side of the room. In first season episodes, Denise and Jaleesa work in the school cafeteria; Jaleesa later works in the school library. Denise's grades, however, are not suitable for college. She has a 1.7 average and can't seem to achieve the *A*s and *B*s she got in

high school. She decides to quit after three semesters (see "The Cosby Show" for additional information about Denise).

Maggie is an army brat and is majoring in journalism. Her father is stationed in Minnesota, and she left at the same time as Denise when her father was transferred overseas. Maggie says, "I can talk a lot; I was the captain of my high school debate team."

Jaleesa is from Camden, New Jersey, and grew up with eight brothers and sisters. She is 26 years old and now divorced (she was married for two years; her husband, Lamar, had an affair and the marriage broke up). Jaleesa and Maggie are organized; Denise is very untidy. The number seen on the desk in Denise's room is 807 BNC 75. In 1991 Jaleesa began her own employment agency, Jaleesa Vinson May Temps. During the summer of 1991, Jaleesa married Colonel Bradford Taylor (Glynn Turman), the calculus teacher who is called "Dr. War."

Whitley Gilbert is rich, beautiful and spoiled; her passion is art and shopping. Her grandparents donated the money for Gilbert Hall (built in 1925), and she lives in Room 20S. Whitley is from Richmond, Virginia (her father is a judge), and considers herself "The Ebony Fashion Queen" (she despises anyone touching or wearing her clothes). Whitley sleeps with a tape recorder playing the sounds either of crickets chirping in the forest or of the sea and seagulls. She uses a bar of soap only once, won't eat cheese or let anyone else eat cheese in her presence. Whitley locks her phone and is proud of the fact that her beauty allows her to steal men from other girls. She has taken dance lessons (jazz, ballet and tap) since she was a little girl; she was also crowned "Miss Magnolia" as a child.

Whitley is a sophomore when the series begins and an art major. Four years later, she is an art buyer "with my own office" at E.H. Wright Investments, an insurance company (she now lives in the Dorothy Height Hall, which was donated by her parents).

Dwayne Creofus Wayne is a math major "and wears those funny-looking flip down sunglasses that drive you crazy." Dwayne is from Michigan and hits on almost every woman he sees—"over 12 billion bothered," Jaleesa says. Dwayne has a music and talk show on the school's radio station (WHZU) where he calls himself Darryl Walker. Dwayne graduated in 1990 and remained at Hillman to pursue his Ph.D. in math. Dwayne and Whitley became engaged in the fall of 1991 and married on May 14, 1992 (they honeymooned in Hawaii). Dwayne, whom Whitley calls "Pookie Bear," became a professor in 1992 (he teaches math at Hillman). He and Whitley live in Apartment 1, and a plush rabbit ("Bunny") was the first Christmas present Dwayne gave to Whitley.

Other students are Lena James (Jada Pinkett), a streetwise girl from Nebraska who is at Hillman on an engineering scholarship (she attended Lincoln High School); Kim Reese (Charnele Brown) is a pre-med student from Columbus, Ohio; Winifred ("Freddie") Brooks (Cree Summer) is from New Mexico and studying to become an archaeologist; Charmaine Brown (Karen Malina White) is a freshman (1992) and works as a waitress at The Pit, the campus eatery (she previously worked at the Burger Barn in Brooklyn, New York).

Stevie Rallen (Loretta Devine) was the original Gilbert Hall dorm director. When she married (and left the series), she was replaced by Lettie Bostic (Mary Alice), a Hillman alumna. (Vernee Watson was first cast to play the replacement dorm director, Carla Myers. The episode "My Dinner with Theo," was taped and introduced Vernee in the role. For unknown reasons, Vernee was dropped—but the episode did air. It was quietly presented on July 7, 1988, during the height of reruns). Jaleesa next became the dorm director (until May 1992). When Dawnn Lewis left the series, Kim and Freddie became the co–dorm directors.

The school's mascot is the Hillman Falcon, and the hangout is a diner called The Pit, which is owned by Vernon Gaines (Lou Myers). KHV 426, EM2 549, and 5TB 80N6 are the license plates seen on the wall in The Pit.

Relatives: Diahann Carroll (Whitley's mother, *Marion Gilbert*), Harold Sylvester (Dwayne's father, *Woodson Wayne*), Patti LaBelle *(Dwayne's mother)*, Cory Tyler (Bradford's son, *Terence Taylor*).

Flashbacks: Brandi Royale Petway *(Whitley as a girl)*.

Theme: "It's a Different World," vocal by Aretha Franklin; later Boyz II Men.

164. *Diff'rent Strokes*

NBC, 11/13/78 to 8/31/85
ABC, 9/27/85 to 3/21/86

Cast: Conrad Bain *(Phillip Drummond)*, Dana Plato *(Kimberly Drummond)*, Gary Coleman *(Arnold Jackson)*, Todd Bridges *(Willis Jackson)*, Dixie Carter *(Maggie McKinney*, NBC), Mary Ann Mobley *(Maggie McKinney*, ABC).

Facts: Phillip Drummond is a millionaire and the father of a daughter named Kimberly. They are cared for by Lucy Jackson (not seen), a black woman Phillip hired after the death of his wife. Lucy is a widow and lives in Harlem (Apartment 12 at 259 East 135th Street) with her sons, Willis and Arnold. When Lucy dies, Phillip keeps a promise he made to her: to care for her sons if anything happened to her. Willis and Arnold move into Phillip's thirtieth floor penthouse apartment (A; in some episodes, penthouse B) at 679 Park Avenue in Manhattan. Stories relate events in the lives of the two families as they attempt to live together. Edna Garrett (Charlotte Rae), Pearl Gallagher (Mary Jo Catlett) and Adelaide Brubaker (Nedra Volz) were Phillip's housekeepers during the series run.

Phillip, who owns Drummond Industries (also given as Trans-Allied, Inc.), attended the Digby Prep School as a boy. His original last name is Van Drummond (which was changed when his Dutch ancestors first came to America). In one episode, Conrad Bain played his Dutch cousin, Anna. Phillip is a member of the Riverside Athletic Club (where he is called "L & M"—"Lean and Mean"). In 1984,

Phillip married Maggie McKinney, a divorcée with a young son named Sam. Kimberly, Willis and Arnold each have ten shares of stock in Phillip's company.

Kimberly, Phillips' pretty and perky daughter, first attended the Eastlake Academy in Peekskill, New York, then Garfield High School in Manhattan (where she is a member of the swim team). She receives an allowance of ten dollars a week and held a job as a waitress at the Hula Hut, a fast food diner in Manhattan. Kimberly is a prima ballerina and played the lead in the Eastlake school's production of "Swan Lake." She received ice skating lessons from Dorothy Hamill (when she attempted to become a world class skater; Kimberly faked a pulled hamstring when she felt she couldn't handle the daily routine). Kimberly's good looks enabled her to get a job as a teenage fashion model at Baun's department store, but also caused her to develop bulimia several years later when she felt she was losing her slender figure. When Kimberly turned 18, she took a job as a nanny to Anna and Rudy Valente, a couple who required help in caring for their son in Italy; she later attended school in Paris.

When Kimberly's blonde hair turned green (her all-natural Mother Brady's Shampoo reacted with rainwater affected by acid), Kimberly spoke out for a cleaner environment. "Pumpkin" was the name Phillip called Kimberly as a child; in one episode, Dana Plato played her Dutch cousin, Hans.

Arnold, the younger brother, attended the following schools: P.S. 89, P.S. 406, Roosevelt Junior High, Edison Junior High and Garfield High. Arnold, whose favorite expression is "What you talkin' about...," loves model railroading (he had both "HO" and "O" scale pikes); he had a ratty old doll (first season) named Homer, a goldfish (Abraham) and a cricket (Lucky). As a baby, he had a plush cow named Fuzzy Wuzzy Moo Moo. Arnold's favorite afterschool hangout is Hamburger Heaven (later called The Hamburger Hanger) and he was video champ at the arcade game "Space Sucker" (where he scored one million points). Arnold was a reporter for his P.S. 89 newspaper, *The Weekly Woodpecker* and editor of the Edison Junior High paper, *The Beacon*.

Arnold was a member of the Super Dudes Gang and formed a band called Frozen Heads. Arnold considers himself a magician and calls himself "Arnoldo." The never-seen Gooch is the bully who picks on Arnold; Lisa (Nikki Swasey) is the girl who annoys Arnold at school. Arnold played Lincoln in his high school play, "Abe Lincoln in Illinois," and had a first job handing out circulars for Guido's Pizza Palace on 63rd Street.

Willis, the older brother, attended Roosevelt Junior High, Garfield High and an unnamed college. As a kid, he had a doll named Wendy Wetems. Willis, whose favorite expression is "Say what?," formed a rock band called The Afro Desiacs; Kimberly and Willis's girlfriend, Charlene DuPres (Janet Jackson) were its singers. Willis was a member of the Tarantulas Gang and held a job at Kruger's Garage.

Maggie has a daily TV show called "Exercise with Maggie," owns her own mid–Manhattan health club (not named) and teaches aerobics at the Manhattan Health Club.

She mentioned that her first paycheck amounted to $37. (Phillip mentioned that his first paycheck was for $1.8 million. Before acquiring the role of Maggie, Mary Ann Mobley played Arnold's teacher, Miss Osborne, in 1979.)

Sam (Danny Cooksey) has a pet goldfish named Montgomery, is a member of Scout Troop 14 and is on the Hawks baseball team. His favorite sandwich is peanut butter and tuna fish.

Relatives: Dody Goodman (Phillip's sister, *Sophia*), Irene Tedrow *(Phillip's mother)*, LaWanda Page (Arnold's cousin, *Muriel Waters*), Hoyt Axton (Maggie's ex-husband, *Wes McKinney*). Not seen were Arnold's mother and father, Lucy and Henry.

Theme: "Diff'rent Strokes," by Alan Thicke, Gloria Loring and Al Burton.

Note: See also "The Facts of Life," the spinoff series.

165. *Ding Howe and the Flying Tigers*

Syndicated, 1950

During the Second World War, Ding Howe (Richard Denning), an ace U.S. Air Force fighter pilot, organized the Flying Tigers, a small group of American volunteers who flew daring missions against the enemy. The Flying Tigers were based in the south of China near the town of Kunsang and carried out an almost single-handed air war against the forces that threatened liberty. When the war ended, the small base used as the Flying Tigers' headquarters was abandoned. Shortly after, Hu Fang (Richard Loo), the evil leader of the Hill Bandits, joins with a group of renegade pilots called the Flame Dragons and sets out to conquer Kunsang. When Ding Howe learns about this, he returns to China and reorganizes the Flying Tigers in an effort to stop Hu Fang.

Ding Howe was born in China, and his name means "Good Friend." His squad includes Speed Darrow (Bill Lester), Sergeant Burdy (Bob Bratt) and Wing Lee (Rob Lee), his Chinese mechanic. Bombay Fay (Evelyn Ankers) is the beautiful American newspaper reporter for the *Bombay News* who helps Ding Howe in an effort to get stories. General Ching (Victor Sen Yung) is the leader of the Chinese forces that are battling Hu Fang.

Ding Howe reestablishes the previously abandoned airfield, and three P-40 fighter planes, hidden by the local Chinese after the war, become his air force. Ding Howe's air code is "Grey Hawk"; the Tigers' code for headquarters is "Home Town." Dutchess (Dorothy Vaughan) runs Kunsang's watering hole, the Gentle Dragon; she is assisted by Lum Chow (Spencer Chan).

Music credits are not listed; James Wallington does the narrating. See also "Major Del Conway of the Flying Tigers."

166. *Dinosaurs*

ABC, 4/26/91 to the present

Voice Cast: Stuart Pankin *(Earl Sinclair)*, Jessica Walter *(Fran Sinclair)*, Sally Struthers *(Charlene Sinclair)*, Jason Willinger *(Robbie Sinclair)*, Kevin Clash *(Baby Sinclair)*.

Facts: The series is set in the year 60,000,003 B.C. One million years prior to this, dinosaurs lived in the forests and in a world where they ate their children. They came out of the forests to marry and raise a family. They live in houses, work, pay taxes and complain just like modern-day people. Human beings of this era, however, are portrayed as cavemen and as a less-intelligent lifeform.

A view of this reversed society is seen through the activities of the Sinclairs, a family of six who live in a city called Pangaea. They had a pet cavegirl named Sparky (Hanna Cutrona), whom they later set free.

Earl Sneed Sinclair, the father, is a Megalasaurus and works as a tree pusher (knocks down trees by pushing them) for the Wesayso Development Corporation. (The company has little respect for the environment. Earl is working on a project to destroy a redwood forest for condos.) Earl is 43 years old, earns four dollars an hour and has been working for Wesayso for 20 years. He is a chronic complainer and dreams of reverting to the wilderness life of his barbaric grandfather. Earl has a caveman alarm clock and is a member of the YMCA (Young Men's Carnivore Association, an organization that places male dinosaurs in the food cycle as meateaters; the food chain is what they live by—the biggest eat the smallest—and it gives order to their world). The Meteor Tiki Lounge is Earl's watering hole, and 000-00-0018 is his Social Security number. Earl eats Sugar Frosted Boo Boo Bears cereal for breakfast.

Frances ("Fran") Sinclair is Earl's wife. She is an Allosaurus, 38 years old and the typical dinosaur housewife. She cooks, cleans, cares for the kids and watches the Dinosaur Shopping Network on TV. She and Earl have been married for 19 years (Earl keeps the marriage license under the TV to balance it). Fran buys food at the Swamp Basket and prepares waffle meat pancakes for breakfast. She is a Pisces, and roses are her favorite flower. Fran makes refrigerator mold pie as a special treat and shops at the Kave Mart Department Store. She also held a job as a TV advice show host on "Just Advice with Fran."

Robert ("Robbie") Mark Sinclair is Earl and Fran's 14-year-old son. He is a precocious visionary (he believes, for example, that the caveman might have a bright future) and attends Bob LaBrea High School. He has locker number 38 and a poster of the film *Teenage Mutant Ninja Cavemen* on his bedroom wall. When Robbie turned 15 he had to observe the Ceremony of the Howling. The *Book of Dinosaurs*—the rules by which they live—states that when a male dinosaur becomes of age he must go to the top of a mountain and howl at the moon. "Only by howling do we defeat the dark spirit which turns dinosaur against dinosaur and brings an end to our days on Earth.") Robbie, an herbivore, studies "prehistory" in school, and RAMPAGING

TRILOBITES is printed on the back of his school jacket. He was also a member of the Scavangers Gang for a short time.

Charlene Sinclair is Fran and Earl's 12-year-old daughter. She is a material girl, attends Bob LaBrea High and purchases her cosmetics at Fifth Avenue Scales in the mall. She is an average student (*C* grades) and strives to remain so—so she can be average. Charlene is not the brightest kid in school, and her grandmother says, "The only way Charlene will get into college is in a cake at a frat house."

Baby Sinclair (Junior) was hatched in the first episode. The baby seems to know who everyone is except Earl. When Earl cares for him, Baby says, "Not the Mama," and hits him on the head with a pot. Baby Sinclair is a TV addict and watches such shows as "Mr. Ugh" (a "Mister Ed" takeoff about a talking caveman), "Raptile" (a Phil Donahue type of show) and "Ask Mr. Lizard" (a science show). Whenever he does something wrong Baby remarks, "I'm the baby, gotta love me." Infant dinosaurs must be brought to the chief elder for a name. As Baby was about to be named, the chief elder had a heart attack and said to his assistant, "Aaah, aaah, I'm dying, you idiot." The assistant recorded that quote as Baby's official name (the newly elected chief elder renamed him Baby Sinclair).

Ethyl Phillips (Florence Stanley) is Fran's 72-year-old mother. She is wheelchair bound and now lives with the family. A million years ago, Bob LaBrea (Harold Gould) created Hurling Day. When dinosaurs reach the age of 72 (when they become old and useless), they must be hurled into the tar pits (thus was created the LaBrea Tar Pits). The one pleasure Earl looked forward to was hurling his mother-in-law off the mountain and into the tar pits. He had a special blue silk Hurling Day tie for the occasion—but he also had a son named Robbie. Robbie questioned the practice and talked Earl out of hurling Ethyl. She now lives with Earl and calls him "Fat Boy." Ethyl's late husband was named Louie (voiced by Buddy Hackett in a vision sequence).

Roy Hess (Sam McMurray) is a T-Rex and has been Earl's friend for 27 years. He is Earl's co-worker "and eats like a pig and dresses like a slob." B.P. Richfield (Sherman Hemsley) is Earl's boss, a vicious three-horned Triceratops.

Calendars begin with the last day of the month and end with the first day; Earl reads a paper called the Pangaea *Tribune*. All characters are named after oil companies. The elders rule from the Cave of Destiny, and the Job Wizard decrees what job dinosaurs will hold. Their Christmas is Refrigerator Day—"A celebration of the invention of cold storage" (it ended migrating to find food so dinosaurs could remain in one place). The elder-in-charge is the head of the country. Pistachio nuts are the dinosaurs' favorite snack.

Theme: "Dinosaurs," by Bruce Broughton.

167. *Diver Dan*

Syndicated, 1960

Diver Dan (Frank Freda) is a fearless ocean explorer who risks his life to protect the good fish of the Sargasso Sea

from the evil Baron Barracuda and his dim witted assistant, Trigger Fish, as they plot to control the ocean floor.

Dan assists the beautiful Miss Minerva (Suzanne Turner), a mermaid to whom the good fish look for guidance. Miss Minerva lives in an area called Minerva's Palace (which is opposite the Bottomless Pit, the home of the Glowfish). She contacts the creatures of the sea with her magic Shell-o-Phone. The Baron and Trigger have a hideout in a cave near the treacherous Teetering Rock.

Dan and Miss Minerva are the only live characters. The fish are marionettes and voiced by Allen Swift. The fish are Gabby the Clam, Sawfish Sam, Sea Biscuit the Seahorse, the Glowfish, Finley Haddock, Skipper Kipper, Scout Fish (complete with tomahawk and feathers), Goldie the Goldfish, the Hammer-Head Shark and Gill-Espie, the beatnik fish (who plays the bongo drums).

There are no music or theme song credits listed on the screen (or in any other source).

168. *Dobie Gillis*

CBS, 9/29/59 to 9/18/63

Cast: Dwayne Hickman *(Dobie Gillis)*, Bob Denver *(Maynard G. Krebs)*, Frank Faylen *(Herbert T. Gillis)*, Florida Friebus *(Winnie Gillis)*, Sheila James *(Zelda Gilroy)*, Tuesday Weld *(Thalia Menninger)*, Steve Franken *(Chatsworth Osborne, Jr.)*.

Facts: Dobie Gillis and his friend, Maynard G. Krebs, are teenagers who live in a mythical community called Central City. Dobie lives with his father, Herbert T. Gillis, and his mother, Winifrid ("Winnie") Gillis, at 285 Norwood Street; Maynard lives with his parents at 1343 South Elm Street.

At 285 Norwood (also given as 285 Elm Street, 9th and Main and 3rd and Elm), one will also find the Gillis Grocery Store, which is run by Herbert, a hard working, always complaining businessman (he and the family live above the store). Herbert is a member of the Benevolent Order of the Bison Lodge and always claims he is 46 years old. He is known as a cheapskate and was voted the "citizen most likely to hang onto his last dollar." Herbert first mentions that he fell in love with Winnie when they danced the Kangaroo Hop; he later recalls falling in love with her when they met at a high school beauty pageant (Winnie finished 27 out of 29 contestants). He and Winnie honeymooned in Tijuana, Mexico. Herbert's favorite expression (when affected by Dobie's antics) is "I gotta kill that boy, I just gotta." Herbert frequents the Scarpitta Barber Shop (named after the show's producer, Guy Scarpitta).

Dobie and Maynard first attend Central City High School, then S. Peter Pryor Junior College. Their favorite afterschool hangout is Charlie Wong's Ice Cream Parlor, and in 1961 they both served a hitch in the army (in some episodes they are in Company A; in others Company C and Company Q). In college Dobie was the second assistant editor of the school's newspaper, the *Pryor Crier*. The college radio station was KSPP. While in the service, Dobie gained 14 pounds eating army food.

Dobie is the girl chasing, all–American teenage boy; unfortunately, he "picks girls with caviar tastes for his peanut butter wallet." While schoolmate Zelda Gilroy has a never-ending crush on him and has set her sights on marrying him, Dobie has eyes for beautiful girls who seem to cause him only misery. Dobie is most famous for his infatuation with the stunning Thalia Menninger, the girl who knows Dobie is dirt poor and the son of a cheap father, but who has high hopes of his making "oodles and oodles of money"—not for her but for her family, "a 60-year-old father with a kidney condition, a mother who isn't getting any younger, a sister who married a loafer and a brother who is becoming a public charge."

Dobie's rival for Thalia is Milton Armitage (Warren Beatty), the rich, spoiled schoolmate who nicknamed her "Mouse" for her inability to choose between him and Dobie. While Dobie can't afford to buy Thalia even one ounce of her favorite perfume (MMMM, which costs $18 an ounce), she always returns to him with the hope of improving him.

Although the Thalia character was dropped when Tuesday Weld left the series, a new beauty—Linda Sue Faversham (Yvonne Craig)—was brought on to tempt Dobie in 1961.

Like Thalia, Linda Sue seeks only to marry money and has high hopes of turning Dobie into a success so they can marry and support her unemployable family. Linda Sue considers herself blessed with a "stunning body, perfect teeth, beautiful hair and a fabulous face"—her "equipment," as she calls it—for only one purpose: "to marry money and support her dismal relatives."

Following in Linda Sue's footsteps is her gorgeous sister, Amanda Jean (Annette Gorman), who had "the same fabulous face, perfect teeth, beautiful hair and stunning body," and who is being groomed by Linda Sue to marry money. Following in Dobie's footsteps is his younger, dirt poor cousin, Duncan Gillis (Bobby Diamond), who fell for Amanda Jean and found, like Dobie, that girls like Linda Sue (and Amanda Jean) "are not for poor slobs like us."

Maynard, a beatnik who loves to play the bongo drums, is also a fan of jazz and hangs out at Riff Ryan's Music Store (where he plays records so much that he wears out the grooves). He has a stuffed armadillo named Herman and claims that the *G* in his name stands for Walter. He has a weekly allowance of 35 cents and was turned down 46 times in six years for a driver's license. He has the world's largest collection of tin foil and three cousins named Flopsy, Mopsy and Cottontail.

While the longest word that he can pronounce is *delicatessen*, Maynard's idea of great Americans include General MacArthur, Admiral Dewey and Captain Kangaroo. Maynard's favorite activities are watching the old Endicott Building being knocked down and watching workmen paint a new white line down Elm Street. Maynard's favorite movie is *The Monster That Devoured Cleveland* (apparently the only movie that ever plays at the Bijou). Maynard always responds with "You rang?" when his name is mentioned and panics when he hears the word *work*.

Zelda Gilroy, the girl who taught Dobie how to play the guitar, is very intelligent (one of the reasons why she thinks that Dobie is not attracted to her). She is pretty but not as attractive as the girls Dobie falls for; she is always there for Dobie when he is dumped by his latest heartthrob. Zelda is from a large family and has six sisters (played by Sherry Alberoni, Jeri Lou James, Larraine Gillespie, Judy Hackett, Marlene Willis and Anna Marie Nanassi).

Chatsworth Osborne, Jr., is the rich and spoiled son of Clarissa Osborne and is a friend of Dobie and Maynard's. He has type "R" (for royal) blood and is heir to the fabulous Osborne National Bank fortune. He lives in a 47-room Louis XIV home (with broken glass embedded in the wall that surrounds it), belongs to the Downshifters Club, is president of the Silver Spoon Club (for snobs) at S. Peter Pryor Junior College and dreams of getting into Yale University. His favorite expression is "mice and rats." He calls Dobie "Dobie Do" and his mother "Mumsey" (she calls him "you nasty boy").

Professor Leander Pomfritt (Herbert Anderson; later William Schallert) teaches English at the high school and later at the college. He refers to his students as "young barbarians." He wrote nine novels (destroying eight of them) and wishes, at times, that he had gone into the aluminum siding business (also the air conditioning business, in some episodes).

Dr. Imogene Burkhart (Jean Byron) teaches psychology 1-B and biology at the high school. In early episodes, Jean Byron appeared as Ruth Adams, the math teacher at Central High. The character of Imogene Burkhart was originally played by Jody Warner—not as a teacher, but as a classmate on whom Dobie had a crush.

Relatives: Darryl Hickman (Dobie's brother, *Davey Gillis*), Roy Hemphill (Dobie's cousin, *Virgil T. Gillis*), Gordon Jones (Winnie's brother, *Wilfrid*), Jeane Wood (Winnie's sister, *Gladys*), Esther Dale *(Winnie's mother)*, Michael J. Pollard (Maynard's cousin, *Jerome Krebs*), Kay Stewart (Maynard's mother, *Alice Krebs*; a.k.a. Ethel Krebs), Willis Bouchey *(Maynard's father)*, Dabbs Greer (Zelda's father, *Walter Gilroy*), Joan Banks (Zelda's mother, *Edna Gilroy*), Doris Packer (Chatsworth's mother, *Clarissa Osborne*), Lynn Loring (Chatsworth's third cousin twice removed, *Edwina Kagel*), Iris Mann (Chatsworth's cousin, *Sabrina Osborne*), Barbara Babcock (Chatsworth's cousin, *Pamela Osborne*), Joyce Van Patten (Leander's wife, *Maude Pomfritt*). Not seen were Herbert's brother (Duncan's father), Tim; and Winnie's sister, Margaret (who lives in Cleveland).

Theme: "Dobie," by Lionel Newman and Max Shulman.

Note: The series is also known as "The Many Loves of Dobie Gillis." In the pilot, "Whatever Happened to Dobie Gillis?" (CBS, 5/10/77), Dobie (Dwayne Hickman) is married to Zelda (Sheila James) and is the father of a teenage son, Georgie (Stephen Paul). Maynard (Bob Denver) is an entrepreneur, and Dobie and his father, Herbert (Frank Faylen) have an expanded Gillis Grocery Store.

In the TV movie *Bring Me the Head of Dobie Gillis* (CBS, 2/21/88), Dobie and Zelda are still married, the parents of Georgie (Scott Grimes) and owners of the Gillis Market and Pharmacy. Recreating their original roles were

Dwayne Hickman, Sheila James, Bob Denver, Steve Franken and William Schallert. Connie Stevens played Thalia Menninger and, Tricia Leigh Fisher was Chatsworth Osborn III, Chassie for short.

169. *Doctor, Doctor*

CBS, 6/12/89 to 7/24/89
CBS, 11/13/89 to 2/26/90
CBS, 8/20/90 to 1/3/91

The antics of Dr. Mike Stratford (Matt Frewer), an eccentric general practitioner who uses unusual but effective techniques to deal with patients. Mike and his fellow doctors, Dierdre Bennett (Maureen Mueller), Abraham Butterfield (Julius Carry III) and Grant Linowitz (Beau Gravitte), are partners in the Rhode Island–based Northeast Medical Partners (on 10/3/90, Grant's sister, Dr. Leona Linowitz [Anne Elizabeth Ramsey], a psychiatrist, joins the practice).

Mike, who has written the medical books *Panacea: A Medical Love Story* and *The Practice*, is also the advice doctor on "Wake Up Providence," a local morning news show on WNTV-TV that is hosted by Pia Bismark (Sarah Abrell). Mike attended Harvard Medical School (as did Dierdre, Abraham and Grant) and eats at Johnny's Bar and Grill; the New York Mets are his favorite baseball team. Dierdre, whose maiden name is Murtagh, reads *Rhode Island Monthly* magazine; Abraham's license plate reads BIG DOC. Leona is divorced from her unseen husband, Philip, who called her "The Domineering Bitch." The building number of the clinic is 808.

Relatives: Inga Swenson (Mike's mother, *Connie Stratford*), Dakin Matthews (Mike's father, *Harold Stratford*), Tony Carreiro (Mike's gay brother, *Richard Stratford*), Candy Ann Brown (Abraham's wife, *Gail Butterfield*), Marlon Taylor (Abraham's son, *Justin Butterfield*), Dion Anderson (Dierdre's father, *Bill Murtagh*), Anna Slotky (Leona's daughter, *Emily Linowitz*).

Theme: "Good Lovin'," adapted by Artie Butler.

170. *Dr. Quinn, Medicine Woman*

CBS, 1/1/93 to the present

Cast: Jane Seymour *(Dr. Michaela Quinn)*, Joe Lando *(Byron Sully)*, Erika Flores *(Colleen Cooper)*, Chad Allen *(Matthew Cooper)*, Shawn Toovey *(Brian Cooper)*.

Facts: Michaela ("Mike") Quinn is a doctor. She was born on February 15, 1833, in Boston. "I was the last of five children; all those before me were girls. My father, being a man of science, firmly believed that the odds would finally dictate the birth of a long-awaited son. He would be named

Michael. I was named Michaela. I was determined to attend medical school, but none would admit a woman. I finally received my medical degree from the Women's Medical College of Pennsylvania. To my mother's dismay, my father made me his partner." Michaela and her father worked side by side for seven years. "When he died, I lost my mentor, my advocate, my best friend. He spoiled me but gave me the freedom to discover myself. With my father gone, our practice virtually disappeared. I was afraid my life as a doctor was over, but I promised him to carry on."

While reading the local newspaper, the *Globe,* Michaela finds an ad for a doctor in the Colorado Territory. She sent the Reverend Timothy Johnson a telegram detailing her experiences. A week later, she received a reply offering her the position. Despite the objections of her mother (who wants her to settle down and raise a family), Michaela leaves Boston and heads for Colorado Springs. "It was the frontier, a place where people make new beginnings; a place where my services would be needed, my skills appreciated; where I would finally be appreciated as a doctor."

It is circa 1865 when Michaela arrives in Colorado Springs. She meets with the Reverend Johnson (Geoffrey Lower) and introduces herself as the doctor he hired. Johnson fears she is mistaken, as he hired a man named Dr. Michael Quinn. When Michaela insists that it is she who sent the telegram, Johnson checks with Horace (Frank Collison), the telegraph operator and finds that he left the *a* off her given name thinking it was just her middle initial. "Folks in these parts don't trust doctors, don't trust women and don't trust people from the East." Michaela is a woman of determination and sets her mind to stay and establish a practice.

Michaela is a woman—and single—in a town where there are 20 men for every woman. She finds lodging at Mrs. Cooper's Rooms and Meals and befriends the owner, Charlotte Cooper (Diane Ladd), who has three children (Colleen, Matthew and Brian). Charlotte is called "Widow Cooper," although she is not a widow. Charlotte and her husband had a farm in Topeka, Kansas. One day her husband sold the farm and told her they were going to mine gold at Pikes Peak. When the mine went bust, he left her. The townspeople call her "Widow Cooper" out of respect.

Shortly after, Michaela advertises for permanent lodgings. Byron Sully answers the ad and offers her his former log cabin for one dollar a month rent. Charlotte and the kids help Michaela, whom they fondly call "Dr. Mike," settle in. (Sully was a miner who built the cabin when he married. When his wife died, he abandoned it and became a mountain man. He is compassionate toward the Cheyenne Indians and has one true friend, a wolf, whom he calls "Boy" or just snaps his fingers at to get his attention.) Sully is afraid of horses, uses a tomahawk as a weapon and risks his life to protect Michaela.

Although Charlotte is not a doctor, she does perform midwife duties. When a young mother named Emily (Heidi Kozak) comes to Charlotte for help and Charlotte finds that she is losing Emily, she sends for Dr. Mike. Michaela performs a cesarean and saves the life of Emily and her child; still, people are reluctant to trust a woman doctor.

Several weeks later, Charlotte is bitten by a rattlesnake;

but by the time Dr. Mike is summoned, the poison has already spread and there is nothing she can do for her. On her deathbed, Charlotte begs Dr. Mike to care for her kids. Suddenly, Michaela is the guardian of three children. Charlotte also left behind bills; when the Bank of Denver forecloses on the boardinghouse, the children move in with Michaela (Colleen and Matthew call her "Dr. Mike"; Brian, the youngest, calls her "Maw").

The Indians think Michaela is "a crazy white woman" because "only white men make medicine." When Michaela helps the chief of the Cheyenne (who has a bullet wound), he gives her the Indian name "Medicine Woman." Sully later makes a shingle for Michaela to hang on her cabin; it reads DR. MICHAELA QUINN, M.D.—MEDICINE WOMAN.

While Dr. Mike has much to overcome before she can win the confidence of the townspeople, her biggest test came in the second episode, "Epidemic," when influenza hits the town. Michaela saved many people, receiving help from Sully and Colleen, but she gave up her own dosage of quinine to help others. When Michaela becomes ill and there is no medicine for her, Sully takes her to an Indian medicine man whose herbs cure her. Michaela's dedication to helping people made her feel she is really needed, especially when Colleen told her, "Dr. Mike, I wanna be a doctor like you when I grow up."

Dr. Mike has a horse named Belle; Loren Bray (Guy Boyd, then Orson Bean) owns Bray's General Mercantile; Jake (Jim Knobeloch) is the owner of the town saloon; Myra (Helene Udy) is the saloon girl (and Dr. Mike's friend); Olive (Gail Strickland) is Loren's sister.

Theme: "Dr. Quinn, Medicine Woman," by William Olvis.

171. *Doctor Who*

Syndicated, 1973

Cast (The Doctors): William Hartnell (*Doctor number 1*), Patrick Troughton (*Doctor number 2*), Jon Pertwee (*Doctor number 3*), Tom Baker (*Doctor number 4*), Peter Davison (*Doctor number 5*), Colin Baker (*Doctor number 6*), Sylvester McCoy (*Doctor number 7*).

Facts: Susan Foreman is a pretty 15-year-old girl who attends the Coal Hill School in London, England. She is exceptionally brilliant in science and history but terribly incompetent in other subjects. Susan resides with her grandfather, who is known as the Doctor but is very evasive about where she lives.

Barbara Wright and Ian Chesterton are two of Susan's teachers. When they become concerned about her (why her grades are slipping in all subjects but science and history), they decide to visit her at home. At 76 Trotters Lane, the address Susan has given as her home, Barbara and Ian find a junkyard. As they investigate, they discover a British police call box (which resembles an old-fashioned American public telephone booth)—the home of Susan and her grandfather. They are invited in and are amazed to find themselves

standing in the middle of a vast control room—an impossibility, Ian believes, because the police box is just not that big. Susan explains that the police box is actually a time machine called the TARDIS and can go anywhere in time and space. "I made up the name from the initials—Time and Relative Dimensions in Space. I thought you would understand when you saw different dimensions inside from those outside."

The Doctor tells them that he and Susan are wanderers in the fourth dimension and have been exiled from their home planet (Gallifrey). He then becomes concerned about Ian and Barbara; they have seen the TARDIS and may tell others about it. As Ian tries to find the control to open the door, a scuffle ensues and the TARDIS is accidentally sent into time. It resurfaces in the year zero (according to the Year-o-Meter), and the very first story ("An Unearthly Child") dealt with the group's witnessing the birth of humanity. (Susan's grandfather has no name; but when Barbara called him Dr. Foreman, Ian said, "That's not his name—but Dr. Who" and thus the name was born.)

"Doctor Who" is TV's longest running science fiction series. It began in Britain on 11/23/63 and ceased first-run production in 1990. In that time over 600 half-hour episodes were produced; unfortunately, over 130 of these segments are thought to be lost forever (one story, for example, "Invasion of the Dinosaurs," has an announcement telling viewers that what they are about to see is all that exists and segments that tell the complete story are believed to have been destroyed). Virtually all the episodes that could be syndicated have been (beginning in the United States in 1973). At the time only a few stations were willing to run the half-hour episodes. When the multipart stories were combined into feature length films, PBS stations picked them up and the series became an instant cult favorite.

The basic premise deals with the adventures of a Time Lord and a companion who travel through time and space to battle evil—and have a good time while doing it.

A Time Lord is a being from Gallifrey, a planet in the constellation Casterborus. The planet appears to be covered with vast wastelands as the citizens live in domed cities (Capitol City is the most important) that are governed by the Cardinals; the High Council is concerned with the aspect of time. Each Time Lord has the ability to regenerate himself 12 times. He or she possesses two hearts, two pulses, a body temperature of 60 degrees and a bypass respiratory system (our Doctor has regenerated himself seven times by 1990 and is said to be over 750 years old; however, nothing is revealed about his family or his youth).

Our Doctor has built-in resistance to any form of violence—except for self-defense. At college ("The University"), the Doctor had the nickname "Feta Sigma"; his specialty was thermodynamics. He thrives on challenge, and his favorite drink is carrot juice. "Street blowing jazz" is his favorite type of music. Doctor number 4 was fond of a candy called Jelly Babies and was lost without his sonic screwdriver. The Doctor claims to have the directional instincts of a homing pigeon. Doctor number 2 thinks best when he is playing his flute (which he calls his "recorder").

The Time Lords of Gallifrey have a goal of possessing all

knowledge and achieving eternal life. Their source of power is the Eye of Harmony, a large black stone through which awesome forces make time travel a reality. The Time Lords originally designed the TARDIS as a research and study lab. It was mentioned that our Doctor stole a TARDIS to pursue his desire for knowledge; due to a defect in the instruments, he cannot be sure of where his landings may take place. His unit is also malfunctioning and has become stuck in the guise of a 1960s police call box (the TARDIS can take on any appearance and is supposed to disguise itself wherever it goes. Its original shape resembles a metal cabinet with a sliding door). The Doctor's enemies were many (anything that threatened to destroy life), but he was most famous for his battles against the Master, the Daleks and the Cybermen.

The Master (Roger Delgado, Peter Pratt, Anthony Ainley) was a renegade Time Lord who was dedicated to corrupting good and destroying all that is beautiful (he fled Gallifrey to pursue power and conquest).

"Ex-ter-min-ate, ex-ter-min-ate" are the words (spoken in metallic tone) used by the deadly cone-like robots, the Daleks, before they disposed of an enemy (via a ray). Any lifeform was their enemy. Their exact origin is unknown. In one episode they inhabited Dalek City on the planet Skaro; in another they evolved from a race of blue-skinned intellectuals; in still another, they were mutations produced by a race of genetically crippled warriors called Kaled. The Doctor lost one companion to their death rays: Katarina.

The Cybermen were deadly robots who lived in the city of Cybermen on the planet Telos. They too were seeking control but could easily be destroyed by gold dust. The Doctor's companion, Adric, sacrificed his life to save the Earth from a Cybermen bombing.

The Companions: Susan Foreman (Carole Ann Ford) was the Doctor's teenage niece; how she came to be with him was never explained. She left her grandfather to help rebuild a world devastated by the evil Dalek robots.

Barbara Wright (Jacqueline Hill) and Ian Chesterton (William Russell) were Susan's teachers. Barbara, who taught history, and Ian (science) became the unwitting companions until they were returned to their own time in 1965.

Vicki (Maureen O'Brien), a pretty but naive and clumsy girl, was a castaway on the planet Dido and became a companion when the Doctor rescued her. Shortly after, she changed her name to Cressida and left the Doctor to be with Prince Troilus, the Trojan youth with whom she fell in love.

Steven Taylor (Peter Purves) was an astronaut the Doctor rescued from a killer robot on the planet Mechanus. He left the Doctor to become the leader of a primitive tribe called the Savagen.

Katarina (Adrienne Hill) was a slave girl to the prophetess Cassandra in ancient Troy. She saved Steven's life during the Battle of Troy and joined the Doctor in the hope she would be transported to the Palace of Perfection.

Sara Kingdom (Jean Marsh) appeared in only one story, the 12-part "Dalek Master Plan." Sara was a forty-first century secret agent who sided with the Doctor to defeat the Dalek robots.

Dodo Chaplet (Jackie Lane) was a mischievous teenage girl who became a companion when she stepped into the TARDIS thinking it was a real police call box. Her cockney slang drove the Doctor batty.

Polly (Anneke Willis) worked in the Post Office Tower as the assistant to Professor Brent, creator of the supercomputer Woton. She met the Doctor and Dodo when they came to assist Brent. When Woton became all-powerful and threatened to destroy humans, Polly and Ben Jackson (Michael Craze), a merchant seaman Polly met at the Inferno Bar, helped the Doctor defeat Woton. Dodo, whose mind was taken over by Woton, remained in 1966 England to recoup. Polly and Ben, seeing the Doctor enter the TARDIS, followed him in and became his companions. Polly was a bit scatterbrained; Ben possessed technical knowledge that helped the Doctor defeat his enemies.

Jamie McCrimmon (Frazer Hines) was a Scotsman who joined the Doctor in 1745 when the Time Lord arrived in Culloden Moor following the slaughter of the Jacobite Sympathizers.

Victoria Waterfield (Deborah Watling) was the daughter of a scientist whom the Doctor took under his wing when the scientist gave his life to save the Time Lord. She was a screamer (everything frightened her) and left the Doctor to settle down.

Wendy Padbury (Zoe Herriett) was a computer scientist on a drifting space station called the Wheel. When she helped the Doctor defeat the Cybermen robots, she became a companion.

Liz Shaw (Caroline John) was a research scientist (specializing in meteorites) at Cambridge University and possessed degrees in medicine and physics. She was recruited by UNIT (United Nations Intelligence Task Force) to assist the Doctor during his exile on Earth. (She first joined the Doctor to battle an invasion from space in the episode "Spearhead from Space." In this same episode, the Doctor mentions his name to be "Dr. John Smith.")

Jo Grant (Katy Manning) was a UNIT member and skilled in espionage techniques; she was a bit accident prone when it came to everything else. She was the only companion to witness the Doctor seeing his former and future selves. (The First Law of Time prohibits this. The High Council needed to unite Doctors 1, 2 and 3 to battle Omega, the Time Lord who developed the concept of time travel many thousands of years ago. He now threatened to destroy the universe with antigravity creatures from a black hole—a force too powerful for the High Council to battle alone.)

Sarah Jane Smith (Elisabeth Sladen) was a freelance journalist (for *Metropolitan* magazine) who met the Doctor while covering a story about a missing scientist. Sarah was totally liberated and was inclined to take action rather than scream for help. She was returned to her own time when the Doctor was summoned to Gallifrey.

Harry Sullivan (Ian Marter) was a former Royal Navy lieutenant and member of UNIT who was assigned to assist Doctor number 4. Harry disbelieved the Doctor's tales about the TARDIS—until he was invited to join him and Sarah Jane.

Leela (Louise Jameson) was the most savage of the companions. She was a beautiful warrior in the fierce Sevateen tribe. When the Doctor ended the war her people had been fighting all their lives, Leela forced herself on the Doctor;

she craved action and knew she could get it with the Time Lord. She left to marry and live on Gallifrey.

Romana (Mary Tramm). Lady Romanavoratrelunder, Romana for short, was a female Time Lord assigned to help the Doctor find the Key to Time, a powerful device the White Guardian of Light and Time requires to prevent the evil Black Guardian from taking over the universe. She was intelligent and considered herself far superior to the Doctor.

Romana (Lalla Ward.) When Romana realized that her academic learning was no substitute for the Doctor's practical knowledge, she regenerated herself into a more effervescent girl who took on the features of Princess Astra of the planet Atrois (where they found the sixth part of the key). She was still highly intelligent but not as bossy.

Adric (Matthew Waterhouse) was a young boy from a group known as the Outlers on the planet Alzarius who stowed away on the TARDIS to join the Doctor in adventure.

Tegan Jovanka (Janet Fielding) was an airline stewardess who accidentally walked into the TARDIS when it was grounded in England (Doctor number 5 was trying to repair the chameleon unit at the time). She was aggressive and had a score to settle: the evil Master killed her aunt.

Nyssa (Sarah Sutton) was the daughter of the peace-loving Consul Tremas. When the Master needed to regenerate himself, he killed Nyssa's stepmother and took over Tremas's body and will. Nyssa joined the Doctor hoping that their travels would bring her in contact with the Master so she could return her father to his normal self.

Perpugilliam ("Peri") Brown (Nicola Bryant) was a companion to the cricket-loving Doctor number 6. She was totally liberated, and her name, which has its origins in Persian mythology, means "a good and beautiful fairy."

Melanie Bush (Bonnie Langford) was born in Sussex, England, and assisted Doctor number 7. She was a computer programmer and partially understood the TARDIS. "Mel" was also independent, enthusiastic and prone to jumping to conclusions (which often led her into dangerous situations).

Ace (Sophie Aldred), whose real name is Dorothy, was a 16-year-old Earth girl who was an expert with explosives, especially nitro ("I don't feel quite dressed without a couple of cans of nitro"). Ace was caught in a time storm and transported to a planet called Ice World. It was here, while working as a waitress in a fast food store, that she met the Doctor and Mel. Together they joined forces to find the treasure beneath the planet. Mel leaves the Doctor, whom she called "The Professor," for adventure elsewhere with a man named Glitz (Tony Selby). Mel suggests that the Professor take Ace on as a companion because she has no one on Earth (born in Parivalle).

Other Roles: Brigadier Alastair Lethbridge-Stewart (Nicholas Courtney) was the head of UNIT (where the Doctor is its scientific adviser; UNIT investigates the odd and unexplained). Sergeant John Beaton (John Levine) and Captain Mike Yates (Richard Franklin) were also members of UNIT. An additional companion to Doctors 4 and 5 was the mechanical dog K-9 (voice of John Leeson; later David Brierly). K-9 was introduced in the episode "Invisible Enemy." It was created by Professor Marius as a companion (real pets were not permitted in the lab). K-9 possessed advanced weaponry, speaking ability and sensors. Doctor number 4 and Leela inherited it when the professor returned to Earth (due to weight restrictions on the spacecraft, he was not able to take K-9 with him).

An attempt was made to team the dog with Sarah Jane Smith in a series called "K-9 and Company." Only a pilot episode resulted. In it, Sarah Jane (Elisabeth Sladen) has returned to work as a reporter. When she visits her Aunt Lavinia (Mary Wimbush), she learns that a large crate has been waiting for her. When she opens it, she discovers its contents to be K-9, a gift from the Doctor. While the proposed series was to relate Sarah's efforts to solve crimes with the help of K-9, only one case evolved: her investigation of witchcraft in England. Sarah Jane drove a car with the license plate OKR 5190; John Leeson was K-9's voice and Fiachra Trench and Ian Levine composed the theme.

Theme: "Doctor Who," by Ron Grainer.

172. *Dog and Cat*
ABC, 3/5/77 to 5/14/77

"Dog and Cat" is precinct slang for male and female police teams. Sergeant Jack Ramsey (Lou Antonio), the "dog," and Officer J.Z. Kane (Kim Basinger), the "cat," compose one such team. Their superior, Lieutenant Art Kipling (Matt Clark), teamed J.Z. with Ramsey when Jack's original partner, Earl Seagram, was killed during a stakeout at the Welcome House Café in Venice, California. Jack and J.Z. (full name not revealed) are with the 42nd Division of the L.A.P.D.

Jack is a "hothead" (as Art calls him). He has been with the force for 14 years and drives a sedan (license plate 751 FTR) with a number of problems (for example, the driver's side door will not open, the starter needs replacing). Jack is not too fond of animals (J.Z. is) and calls J.Z. "Farm Girl": You're from the sticks, I'm from the pavement. I go to the zoo once a year—that's as close to nature as I want to get." Despite his feelings that a dog and cat team will not work, Jack feels obligated to stick with it—"Who knows, maybe after a while we can work together."

J.Z. is a beautiful blonde from Georgia. She lives at 2317 Englewood Road, loves country and western music and TV dinners (she hates cooking). J.Z. drives a Volkswagen with a Porsche 912 engine that she installed herself (the car is now capable of high speeds). She says she does things by female intuition and held a job as a cashier at the Greenwich Theater (a porno house) while "working my way through the police academy." Prior to being teamed with Jack, J.Z. worked as an undercover cop amid the hookers, sleazy producers and pornographic filmmakers of Venice. J.Z., who is an expert shot, attributes her various skills to "my uncle back in Georgia" (an unseen man who apparently taught her everything she knows, including how to be streetwise).

Barry DeVorzon composed the theme.

173. *Dolphin Cove*

CBS, 1/21/89 to 3/11/89

Michael Larson (Frank Converse) is a research scientist based in Los Angeles. When an opportunity arises for him to study dolphins in Australia, he moves his family to Queensland and begins the project on behalf of Baron Trent (Nick Tate), the owner of Trent Enterprises, who has a research lab on the shore of the ocean he calls Dolphin Cove.

Michael is a widower and the father of two teenage children: Katie (Karron Graves) and David (Trey Ames).

Katie, who suffered a traumatic shock in a car accident that killed her mother, is unable to speak and attends the all-girl Southberry School; she receives special instruction at home from one of its teachers, Allison Mitchell (Virginia Hey). Katie's birthday is given as April 24, 1976, and her disability gives her a special affinity with the dolphins Michael is studying—a situation that he cannot explain. David attends the all-boy Saint Crispin's School. Michael's research dolphins are named Slim and Delbert. Michael, who drives a truck with the license plate 471 PZU, is assisted by James ("Didge") Desmonde (Ernie Dingo), a local aborigine.

Relatives: Teresa Wright (Michael's mother-in-law, *Nina Rothman*), Stephen Elliott (Michael's father-in-law, *Jeff Rothman*), Anthony Richards (Allison's son, *Kevin Mitchell*), Richard Moir (Allison's ex-husband, *Scott Mitchell*), Bill Sandy (Didge's grandfather, *Vince*).

Theme: "Dolphin Cove," by Bill Conti.

174. *Domestic Life*

CBS, 1/4/84 to 9/11/84

"The Domestic Life Report" is a commentary delivered each day by Martin Crane (Martin Mull) for "The Active 8 News" program on KMRT-TV, Channel 8, in Seattle, Washington. Martin's commentary reflects the world of bliss he would like to live, not the actual problems he faces at work and at home.

Martin lives at 106 Liberty Lane (telephone number 555-5551) with his wife, Candy Crane (Judith-Marie Bergan), and his children, Didi (Megan Follows) and Harold (Christian Brackett-Zika). Didi is a very pretty, fashion conscious 14-year-old girl who attends Lincoln High School. She is smart, but not as bright as her ten-year-old brother, Harold, an apparent genius who reads the *Wall Street Journal* and dabbles in the stock market. (He has already made a killing and opened up an IRA account; all of Martin's money, on the other hand, is "tied up in bills." When Martin is in need of money, he borrows it from Harold.) Harold attends the Conklin Street Grammar School and is a member of the Sox Little League team. The afterschool hangout is the Burger Corral, and Didi and Harold see movies at the Rialto Theater.

Harold's possessive girlfriend is Sally Dwyer (Tina Yothers), a fellow ten-year-old who is "wildly attracted" to him. She calls him "Dough Boy"; he calls her "Sookie." On his way home from school, Harold stops by E.F. Hutton to read the ticker; Sally makes gourmet meals in her Patty Playpal Oven.

Cliff Hamilton (Robert Ridgely) is the "Active 8" news anchor; Jane Funakubo (Mie Hunt) is the co-anchor. Allyn Ann McLerie plays Cliff's wife, Enid, and Sandra Alexander is their daughter, Amy Hamilton.

Martin Mull performs the theme, "God Bless the Domestic Life."

175. *The Donna Reed Show*

ABC, 9/24/58 to 9/3/66

Cast: Donna Reed (*Donna Stone*), Carl Betz (*Alex Stone*), Shelley Fabares (*Mary Stone*), Paul Petersen (*Jeff Stone*), Patty Petersen (*Trisha Stone*), Bob Crane (*Dave Kelsey*), Ann McCrea (*Midge Kelsey*), Candy Moore (*Bebe Barnes*), Darryl Richard (*Morton ["Smitty"] Smith*).

Facts: The setting is the small town of Hilldale. In the fifth district is a house with a carob tree growing on the front lawn. Alexander ("Alex") Stone, his wife, Donna, and their children, Mary and Jeff, are its residents. Their phone number is first Hilldale 4-3926, then Hilldale 7281. Amanda Featherstone Bullock (Sarah Marshall) owned the house prior to the Stones.

Donna and Alex, a pediatrician, have been married for 15 years when the series begins. Alex was an intern when his friend Dr. Matthews (not seen) introduced him to a nurse named Donna Mullinger. Donna was wearing a flower print dress on the night Alex proposed to her. They went to an unnamed restaurant where they were seated next to the kitchen and ignored by waiters. To make matters worse, Alex's plans for a romantic evening soured when the check came and he didn't have enough money to pay for the meal. Donna and Alex held their wedding reception at an unnamed club where Tony Bennett was performing. In another episode, Donna mentions that she and Alex were watching *Strange Cargo* (with Joan Crawford) at the Loewe's Orpheum theater when Alex proposed.

Donna, who was born in Denison, Iowa (as was Donna Reed; her real name was Mullenger), is the dedicated wife, loving mother and all-around problem solver. She is said to have a younger brother, but no name was given. Alex, who works out of an office in his home (next to the kitchen), is mentioned as having "a couple of brothers" (not named); lamb curry is his favorite meal. Donna once chaired the "Have a Heart, Hilldale" charity campaign, and she and Alex carved their initials in a tree at a summer house called Evans' Heaven, where they vacationed with a couple of friends. The home was located on Echo Lane, and the initial carving process took 42 minutes. During their honeymoon, Alex heard the song "Melancholy Baby" over and over again and came to hate it; as an early birthday gift, Donna gave

Alex a musical apothecary jar that played the song. Alex was stationed at Fort Dix, New Jersey, during World War II. He and Donna read a daily paper called the *Sentinel*.

Mary is three years older than Jeff. She first attended Hilldale High School (also given as Central High School), then an unnamed college that is 4 2/10 miles from her home. Mary, who wears a size eight dress, frequents the Blue Lantern, a burger and soft drink place. After dances, she and her friends hang out at Kelzey's Malt Shop; her favorite place for dancing is the Round Robin. In one episode, Mary sings the song "Johnny Angel," which became a hit for Shelley Fabares. In high school, Mary ran against Betsy Cartwright (Melinda Byron) for the office of class president.

Jeff, who weighed 10½ pounds at birth, has perfect pitch but no other discernible musical talent. As a kid, he put on puppet shows for his friends with a marionette named Bongo. Jeff has a pet mouse named Herman, was a member of the Bobcats football team (their uniforms were blue and gold) and attended Hilldale High School. He wanted to be a counselor at Camp Win-a-Pal, and his favorite TV Western is "Gunbutt" (sponsored by Happy Gum, "the all-purpose chewing gum"). His hangouts are Kelzey's and Hotenmeyer's (a hamburger joint); his favorite club for dancing is the Round Robin. At age 16, Jeff was 5 feet, 8½ inches tall. His girlfriend Bebe, who lives at 1650 Maple Street, dreams of wearing her Aunt Martha's wedding dress at her wedding.

Trisha, a young girl whose parents died two years before her appearance on the show, was being raised by her uncle, Fred Hawley, who had hired a woman to care for her. One day, while the Stones were playing touch football in a nearby park, Trisha, longing for a family, attaches herself to them. When Donna and Alex meet Fred and Fred learns that Trisha is not happy with him, he allows the Stones to adopt her. Trisha's favorite TV show is "Jingo the Clown."

The most expensive restaurant in Hilldale is Pierre's. Code 34592 bars eviction from one's home. The local college custom a couple observes to make it clear that they are "serious" was called "walking the lion." The couple walks behind a huge lion statue in town and shares a kiss. The city commissioner is Timothy ("Tiger") Trimmitt (Paul Reed).

The Stones' neighbors are Dave and Midge Kelsey. When Bob Crane first appeared, he was called Dave Blevins (his last name was changed when he and Midge bought the house next door to the Corbetts). Before buying this house, they lived with Midge's parents; they were said to have been married for nine years. During the last season, when Bob Crane left to do "Hogan's Heroes," Midge still appeared but Dave is only mentioned. Midge is an only child, and her mother's name is Helen. The Kelseys' phone number is 538-4192.

Jimmy Hawkins played a series of Jeff's friends: George Haskell, Jerry Hager, Jerry Scott and Scotty Simpson.

Relatives: Gladys Hurlbut (Alex's aunt, *Belle*), Rhys Williams (Donna's uncle, *Frederick Jonathan Sutton*), Charles Carlson (Trisha's uncle, *Fred Hawley*), Marlo Thomas (Dave's goddaughter, *Louise Bissell*), John

Stephenson (Bebe's father, *Ben Barnes*), Hollis Irving (Bebe's mother, *Harriet Barnes*), Ray Montgomery (*Smitty's father*). Not seen were Alex's aunts, Lettie and Rhoda, and Donna's uncle, Ralph.

Theme: "Happy Days," by William Loose and John Seely.

176. *Doogie Howser, M.D.*

ABC, 9/19/89 to the present

Cast: Neal Patrick Harris (*Doogie Howser*), James B. Sikking (*David Howser*), Belinda J. Montgomery (*Katherine Howser*), Max Casella (*Vinnie Del Pino*).

Facts: Douglas ("Doogie") Howser is a 16-year-old whiz kid who completed high school in nine weeks, graduated from Princeton at age 14 and is now a second year resident physician at the Eastman Medical Center (in second season episodes, Doogie is a third year resident and is made the supervisor of interns). His birthday is 9/21/73, and he lives at home (Brentwood, California) with his father, Dr. David Howser, and his mother, Katherine. (David is 15 years older than Katherine; they married when she was 20. In college, Katherine was a member of the rock group Mother Earth and the Penguins.)

Doogie's phone number is 555-9980, and he appeared on TV twice: on the quiz show "High I.Q." and in public service announcements called "Ask Dr. Doogie." Doogie, a Humphrey Bogart fan, has a poster of his idol on the wall behind his bed and summarizes the day's events in his computer diary, "The Personal Journal of Doogie Howser, M.D." Doogie's girlfriend, Wanda Plenn (Lisa Dean Ryan), whom Doogie calls "Wanda Bear," was the first person he let see his computer diary. In the opening theme, the following newspaper stories are seen: SIX YEAR OLD SCORES PERFECT S.A.T.'S; WHIZ KID BREEZED THROUGH HIGH SCHOOL IN 9 WEEKS (by Cory Tick); PRINCETON GRADUATES 14 YEAR OLD PRODIGY; KID DOCTOR CAN'T BUY BEER; CAN PRESCRIBE DRUGS; KID DOCTOR DELIVERS BABY IN SHOPPING MALL (by Dan Staffin).

Doogie's best friend is Vincent ("Vinnie") Del Pino, a Catholic who has "committed all the major sins in thought, word and deed and is looking forward to committing the big one." He has delicate sinuses, and his good luck charm is an enchanted rabbit's foot he got from a Madame Sonia. Vinnie, who has a dog named Mitzi, "the psychotic cocker spaniel," is hoping to become a filmmaker (he plans to major in film at California's Institute of the Arts). When Doogie was six years old, he had leukemia; Vinnie stole Doogie's Matchbox ambulance when they were nine; and when they had a fight, Doogie called Vinnie "booger," and Vinnie called Doogie "snot nose." When they made up, Doogie's mother would make them grilled cheese sandwiches. Vinnie's girlfriend is Janine Stewart (Lucy Boryer); she plans to attend L.A. State College (Wanda, an artist, plans to attend the Art Institute of Chicago).

Other regulars are Nurse Curly Spaulding (Kathryn

Layng), Dr. Jake McGuire (Mitchell Anderson) and the hospital administrator, Dr. Canfield (Lawrence Pressman).

Relatives: Tim O'Connor (Katherine's father, *Don O'Brien*), Gloria Henry (Katherine's mother, *Irene O'Brien*), Don Calfa (Vinnie's father, *Carmine Del Pino*), Sherry Rooney (Wanda's mother, *Mrs. Plenn*), Lesley Boone (Wanda's cousin, *Yvette*), Noel Conlon *(Janine's father)*.

Theme: "Doogie Howser, M.D.," by Mike Post.

177. *The Doris Day Show*

CBS, 9/24/68 to 9/3/73

Doris Martin (Doris Day) is a widow who relinquishes her career as a singer in San Francisco to return to the ranch of her father, Buck Webb (Denver Pyle), to raise her two sons, Billy (Philip Brown) and Toby (Todd Starke). The following year (1969) Doris secures a job as the executive secretary to Michael Nicholson (McLean Stevenson), the editor of *Today's World*, "The Now Magazine." In 1970 Doris leaves 32 Mill Valley Road and moves to San Francisco where she, her children and a large sheepdog named Lord Nelson move into Apartment 207 over Palucci's Italian Restaurant at 965 North Parkway. Her rent is $140 a month, and her landlords are restaurant owners Angie (Kaye Ballard) and her husband, Louie Palucci (Bernie Kopell); her neighbor is Willard Jarvis (Billy DeWolfe), a set-in-his-ways bachelor who feels that his life is plagued by the Martin gang. Cyril Bennett (John Dehner) becomes Doris's new boss.

Doris, who in 1971 becomes a reporter for *Today's World*, has a car with the license plate 225 NOZ; Cyril's license plate reads 495 CCF. Doris's own words describe her favorite dessert: "One scoop of strawberry, chocolate and vanilla ice cream. On the strawberry goes chocolate topping; on the chocolate goes strawberry topping. But on the vanilla goes pineapple topping. Cover it all with hot marshmallow sauce and whipped cream—and heavy on the whipped cream."

Doris Day sings the theme, "Que Sera, Sera" (scoring by Bob Mersey; written by Jay Livingston and Ray Evans for the film *The Man Who Knew Too Much*).

178. *Double Trouble*

NBC, 4/4/84 to 5/30/84
NBC, 12/1/84 to 4/20/85

Allison and Kate Foster (Jean and Liz Sagal) are identical 18-year-old twins. Allison and Kate have brown hair and brown eyes and are each five feet three inches tall (Kate weighs 95 pounds, and her driver's license expires on October 9, 1987). Allison is quiet and serious; Kate is a bit wild and mischievous. The girls live at 1555 North Ridge Drive in Des Moines, Iowa, with their widowed father, Art Foster (Donnelly Rhodes). The girls, recent graduates of Des Moines High School, work as aerobic instructors in Art's

Gym, which is owned by Art and his partner, Beth McConnell (Patricia Richardson).

In later episodes (second date listing), Allison and Kate move to New York City to pursue their career ambitions: Allison wants to be a fashion designer, and Kate an actress. They move in with their aunt, Margo Foster (Barbara Barrie), the famous author of the "Bongo the Bear" children's stories. Margo lives at 49 West 74th Street (later given as 51 West 74th Street), and her phone number is 555-7767. Allison attends the Manhattan Fashion Institute; Kate, who most often works as a dancer for the Wacko Wiener Works Company (promoting their product), attends audition after audition, hoping for her big break.

Ray Colcord composed the "Double Trouble" theme.

179. *Down Home*

NBC, 4/12/90 to 5/12/90
NBC, 2/28/91 to 8/3/91

Cast: Judith Ivey *(Kate McCrorey)*, Dakin Matthews *(Walt McCrorey)*, Eric Allan Kramer *(Drew McCrorey)*, Ray Baker *(Wade Prescott)*.

Facts: Fifteen years after leaving her small coastal fishing town (Hadley Cove), Kate McCrorey, a successful New York designing firm executive, returns for a vacation. When she discovers that the town is going to be torn down and made into a minimall, she decides to stay and fight Wade Prescott, her old boyfriend, who now represents the company (Python Development) that is planning to build the mall. Stories also focus on Kate as she helps her father, Walt, and brother, Drew, run McCrorey's Landing, a combination café, mooring dock, bait, fish, tackle and gas store. Walt has run the business for 40 years (McCrorey's Landing is Sector G-12 on Wade's development plan and will become the amusement area—"The Roaring McCrorey Water Slide").

Hadley Cove has a phone book called "The Yellow Page." In one episode, it was mentioned that the town was founded by 100-year-old Jeremiah Hadley (Roy Dotrice), "the meanest man in town" (he loves to torment the citizens). In another episode, the town is much older—the big tourist attraction is a recreation of a Civil War battle called the Battle of Hadley Cove (it was said that Phineas T. Hadley founded the town). In honor of the town's reliance on its catch of shrimp to sustain itself, a big celebration called "Shrimp Day" is held each year at the start of the shrimp season.

At McCrorey's Landing, clam chowder sells for a dollar a bowl and the special of the day is fresh catfish. Its phone number is 824-9333.

In New York, Kate was famous for engineering the takeover of a Fortune 500 Company; in Hadley Cove, she won an award for playing Golda in her high school production of "Fiddler on the Roof." On the back porch of the café, where Walt enjoys fishing, is a life preserver with the name Diamond River, Panama. Every year, when the carnival comes to town, Drew gets into shape to tackle "Battling Bob, the Wrestling Bear." Drew's shrimp boat is named *The Sea Tramp*.

Tran Van Din (Gedde Watanabe), a Vietnam refugee, is Walt's cook; Grover (Tim Scott), the town's mayor, has a pig named Buddy; and Trini Van Din (Kimiko Gelman) is Tran's beautiful sister, who is attending an unnamed convent school in Connecticut. For many years Tran thought Trini worked as a prostitute (when she first came to America she told Tran that she worked in a warehouse; with her accent, Tran thought she said "whorehouse").

In the opening theme, the following fishing boats are seen: *Miss Pauline*, *Miss Gladys* and *C. Lorraine*.

Theme: "Down Home," by Stewart Levin.

180. *Down the Shore*

Fox, 6/21/92 to 9/20/92
Fox, 12/3/92 to the present

The Victorian-style summer house at 738 Surf Avenue in Belmar, New Jersey (off Exit 11 on the Garden State Parkway), is shared by six young people searching for fun and sun on the Jersey shore. The house costs $8,000 for the summer. Three guys are seeking to rent it but find they can't afford it. Three girls are also seeking to rent it, but they too can't afford it. They decide to split the rent and share the house.

Miranda Halpern (Pamela Segall), Arden (Anna Gunn) and Donna Chipkow (Cathryn de Prume) are the girls; Zack Singer (Lew Schneider), Eddie Cheever (Tom McGowan) and Aldo Carbone (Lou Mandylor) are the guys.

The girls all work at Dow and Hummel ad agency in New York City. Arden is their superior and drives a car with the license plate 491C WLD; she attended Cornell University and got her M.B.A. at Columbia University. Miranda works in the merchandising department as a receptionist and longs to become an artist; Donna works in the merchandising department also. She attended Teaneck High School (class of '85) and previously held a job as a salesclerk at K-Mart. Although Donna is extremely attractive, she feels she is just a dumb blonde and is apprehensive about meeting men she thinks are smart; she has no self-confidence: "I know I'll never be smart; I just have to accept it."

The guys have been friends since childhood. Zack is an inner-city junior high school teacher (seventh grade social studies); Eddie is a computer game designer; and Aldo, a ladies' man, works as a clothing salesman for Clingware Fabrics. Aldo's pride and joy is a 1973 Nicks-Celtics basketball from their final game.

When the series returned (second date listing), it was mentioned that Miranda is no longer a part of the group; she became an artist, got a gallery opening and decided to remain in New York to devote her time to painting (there were too many distractions at the beach house). The group now needs a new roommate to help with the rent. While on the beach, Arden meets a childhood friend (they have

known each other since the fourth grade) named Sammy (Nancy Sorel). Arden invites Sammy over to see the house; she falls in love with it and decides to move in. Sammy spent one semester at Brown University (she was expelled for having an affair with a professor). She now designs jewelry exclusively for Bloomingdale's and the Guggenheim Museum.

When the girls go to the beach, Sammy sleeps, Arden reads and Donna stares for hours at the water. The Tidal Wave is the singles' club frequented by the group (at the end of the night, Aldo and Sammy compare notes to see who got the most phone numbers slipped to them).

Kim Walker appeared as Arden's younger sister, Hillary. In the original, unaired pilot film, Heidi Swedberg played Miranda, Marjorie Monaghan was Arden, and Jeff Yagher played Aldo.

Southside Johnny and the Asbury Jukes sing the theme, "I Don't Wanna Go Home."

181. *Downtown*

CBS, 9/27/86 to 12/27/86

At 339½ East First Street stands the Los Angeles Parole Department Special Projects Field Office. There, Inspector John Forney (Michael Nouri), a 14-year detective with the Metro Division of the L.A.P.D., is made special parole officer to a mixed bag of parolees: Jesse Smith (Mariska Hargitay), file number 372-237A; Terry Corsaro (Blair Underwood), file number 504-632A; Dennis Shothoffer (Robert Englund), file number 845-231A; and Harriet Conover (Millicent Martin), file number 238-718A.

Jesse is a beautiful and rebellious girl who grew up in Oakland with six brothers: "Three were Hell's Angels; three joined the Marines." This "apparently affected her personality," as she was arrested for assault and battery; she is also a karate expert. Terry, a streetwise black youth, was arrested for car theft. Dennis feels he is a nobody; when he pretends he is someone else, he feels important. He was arrested for impersonating a doctor and performing three operations. Harriet is a genteel British socialite who is also a con artist; she was arrested for selling beachfront properties that were actually under water.

The city jails are overcrowded, and releasing less dangerous criminals early is one way of easing the burden. John has an impressive record (two life-saving medals, a citation for rescuing hostages from an embassy, and a heroism award for pulling a man from a burning car on Harbor Freeway), Delia Bonner (Virginia Capers), the head of the program, believes John is the right man for the job. Although John's philosophy is "if the jails are overcrowded, just build more jails," he reluctantly agrees to the assignment.

John calls his charges "losers": "All eight balls who are like children. Once the nursery door is opened they run loose and get busted for the same thing they were put away for in the first place." John is "very good at putting criminals away." Now he has to keep four criminals out of trouble (any arrest will mean immediate incarceration). To help accomplish this, John uses Harriet's large home at 145 Mara Linda Lane as his base of operations. The four will live together, with Harriet acting as a den mother to the other three. (Jesse, Harriet, Dennis and Terry often assist John with his undercover work—one additional way he can keep an eye on them.)

Unit 6 Alpha is John's car code; ILNN 506 is his car license plate; and he has a dog named Bob. Tom Reilly appeared as Jesse's brother, Jack Smith, in one episode.

Johnny Harris and Barry Goldberg composed the theme, "That's What I Want."

182. *Dracula: The Series*

Syndicated, 9/29/90 to 9/21/91

Cast: Geordie Johnson *(Alexander Lucard)*, Bernard Behrens *(Gustav Von Helsing)*, Mia Kirshner *(Sophie Martineck)*, Jacob Tierney *(Max Townsend)*, Joe Roncetti *(Chris Townsend)*, Lynne Cormack *(Eileen Townsend)*, Geraint Wyn Davies *(Klaus Von Helsing)*.

Facts: When Eileen Townsend, a Philadelphia banking executive, receives an assignment in Europe, she brings her sons, Maximillian (Max) and Chris, with her. While Eileen attends to business, Max and Chris are to stay with their uncle, Gustav Von Helsing, a vampire hunter, and Sophie Martineck, a teenage girl who lives with Gustav while she is attending school. Soon after, Sophie, Max and Chris learn that the ruthless tycoon Alexander Lucard is actually the infamous Count Dracula and is now in a position to take over the world via his corporate connections (he owns Lucard Industries). They also discover that Gustav is a descendant of the famous Helsing family of vampire hunters and is seeking to destroy Lucard before he can spread his evil. Stories relate the group's various encounters with Lucard as they seek to end his reign of terror.

The Cross of Magarus, which hangs over the staircase in Gustav's home, protects the premises from Lucard (who can't enter the house). In the 1950s, Gustav was in a band called the Five Flying Dutchmen and a Dutch Girl; he is now a member of the Far Travelers Explorers Club. Gustav has seen the movie *The Vampire's Tomb* 27 times.

Lucard is the most sophisticated vampire of his breed. He can live in the daylight (but has no vampire powers); hence, a stake through the heart is the only way to destroy him. His car license plate reads JC 456. In the episode of 1/19/91, when Sophie is bitten by a vampire with strange blood antibodies, Gustav learns that purified water from the Podgotts Springs contains an antigen that can cure her—and kill Lucard who has pure vampire blood. Lucard's deepest secret is located behind a secret wall in the fireplace of his castle. It is another dimension—"a hole in the fabric of time"—which gives Lucard his strength.

Sophie is young, beautiful and sensuous and has type AB-negative blood—Dracula's favorite. She hopes to become a musician and is studying the viola. Schools for Sophie, Chris and Max are not mentioned; Max considers himself a vampire expert and carries his "bag of weapons" with him at all times (holy water, stakes, crosses and garlic).

Eileen, who drives a car with the license plate 3N 101, works for the Pennsylvania Industrial Bank. Klaus is Gustav's son—bitten by Lucard and now a vampire. He is seeking to destroy Lucard and become "the greatest vampire of all."

Theme: "Dracula," by Christopher Dedrick.

Note: An earlier serial, "The Curse of Dracula," aired as ten segments of the series "Cliffhangers" (NBC, 2/27/79 to 5/1/79). In it, Kurt Von Helsing (Stephen Johnson) and Mary Gibbons (Carol Baxter) seek to destroy the 512-year-old Count Dracula (Michael Nouri), whom they believe is posing as a professor of Eastern European history at Southbay College in San Francisco.

183. *Drexell's Class*

Fox, 9/19/91 to 7/9/92

Otis Drexell (Dabney Coleman) is a maverick corporation executive who told the bosses to shove it. He was branded "the crookedest man in town" (Cleveland) and owes the IRS $153,000 in back taxes. He is also divorced (from Mona), behind in alimony payments and the father of two very pretty teenage girls: 16-year-old Melissa (A.J. Langer) and 14-year-old Brenda (Brittany Murphy). In college, Drexell had the nickname "Skippy."

The Grantwood Avenue Elementary School at 2402 Grantwood Avenue in Iowa was founded by Isaac Grantwood, who invented the manure spreader for farmers. Its fifth grade teacher is Otis—"A drifter who failed in business and somehow crawled out of a sewer grate into my school to preach his amoral poison to 20 impressionable children," says principal Francine Itkin (Randy Graff). The school is part of the Cedar Rapids School District.

Otis is a cantankerous teacher who treats his kids like adults and Francine like an ogre. He believes smoking is the answer to a long life, and that if a $10 bill is attached to a test or homework assignment, it guarantees an *A* grade. Otis fails to comply with the school rules, is tardy and discourteous to fellow staff members and enjoys pinching the student teachers ("but only the female ones").

A rather untidy apartment at 603 Essex Drive is home to Otis. He has a picture of the *Titanic* sinking on his living room wall. His dinnerware comes from White Castle ("Do you know how many hamburger dinners I had to eat to make a complete service for eight?"). His pride and joy is his autographed 1947 Dodgers baseball.

Melissa believes she is a very sexy and desirable girl and wears clothes that prove her point. Miniskirts, tight, low cut blouses and Madonna-like bra outerwear is the wardrobe that Otis thinks needs more clothes to cover up. Otis was playing cards on the night Melissa was born. When he heard the news, he jumped up from the poker table and walked away from a straight flush. In the episode of 1/23/92, Melissa entered the Miss Cedar Bluffs Beauty Pageant, with her only apparent talent of pitching a softball Otis calls "the 75 mile-an-hour curveball that breaks about two feet." Although her curveball won her many trophies, she lost the pageant to a girl who sang opera. Melissa's boyfriend is Harold ("Slash") Hudson (Phil Buckman), a sleazy musician Otis despises (Slash and Melissa are members of the band The Resentments).

Brenda shows potential for becoming another Melissa, but for the moment Otis has few problems with her (she is a homebody and while she and Melissa share the housework and cooking, Brenda does the lion's share of the work). Melissa is a sophomore and Brenda a freshman at Cedar Bluffs High School.

Otis's principal students are Nicole Finnegan (Heidi Zeigler), Willie Trancus (Jason Biggs) and Kenny Sanders (Damian Cagnolatti). Roscoe P. Davis (Dakin Matthews) is the only featured teacher (he was a clinical psychologist before becoming a teacher; he uses a puppet called Grandma Grammar to teach English). Elsie Engelhoff (Florence Stanley) became the acting principal when Francine left; she was replaced by Marilyn Ridge (Edie McClurg), who became the principal on 11/14/91.

Joanna Cassidy appeared as Otis's ex-wife, Mona (she receives $900 a month in alimony), and Lu Leonard was Otis's mother-in-law, "Grandma" Kodiak. In the original, unaired pilot version ("Shut Up, Kids"), Suzie Plakson played principal Francine Itkin.

Scott Gale and Rick Eames composed the theme.

184. *The Duck Factory*

NBC, 4/12/84 to 7/11/84

Sherry Jurwalski (Teresa Ganzel) is blonde, beautiful and a bit dizzy. She was a topless Las Vegas ice skater when Buddy Winkler (not seen) spotted her. He introduced himself, they fell in love and married. Three weeks later, Buddy was gone. Sherry Winkler inherited everything: Buddy's house (Casa Contento), his money and his business holdings, including his chain of adult motels, his religious radio station, Buddy Winkler Realty and Buddy Winkler Productions, a TV studio that produces a network Saturday morning cartoon series called "The Dippy Duck Show."

Although Buddy Winkler Productions is a losing business and is located in "The Duck Factory," a rundown building at 1579 Bruckner, Sherry decides to keep the company going to save the jobs of her employees: Skip Tarkenton (James Carrey), the producer and animator; Brooks Carmichael (Jack Gilford), the animation director; Agatha ("Aggie") Aylesworth (Julie Payne), the business manager; Andrea Levin (Nancy Lane), the film editor; Wally Wooster (Don Messick), the voice of Dippy Duck; Marty Fenneman (Jay Tarses), the writer; and Roland Culp (Clarence Gilyard, Jr.), an animator.

Pancho's is the local coffeehouse hangout; Brooks has been an animator for 40 years; Aggie calls Sherry "the Widow Winkler"; the unnamed network only airs "The Dippy Duck Show" because it can get it real cheap; Irving the Terrible and Rotten Renaldo are two of Dippy's enemies.

Relatives: Maureen Arthur (Sherry's mother, *Debbie Jurwalski*), Jo Ann Harris (Wally's daughter, *Wendy Wooster*), Walter Olkewicz (Brooks's son, *Bumps Carmichael*), William Schallert (*Skip's father*), Allyn Ann McLerie (*Skip's mother*), John Hancock (*Roland's father*).

Theme: "Sure Beats Working for a Living," by Mark Vieha.

185. *Dudley Do-Right of the Mounties*

ABC, 4/27/69 to 9/6/70

Voice Cast: Bill Scott (*Dudley Do-Right*), Paul Frees (*Ray K. Fenwick*), June Foray (*Nell Fenwick*), Hans Conried (*Snidley Whiplash*), William Conrad (*Narrator*).

Facts: One day, in the early twentieth century, Dudley Do-Right, a simple-minded and naive young man, leaves his home to see a movie. Three miserable hours later, while waiting for the movie to begin, Dudley realizes that he has fallen through an open manhole and is sitting in a sewer. Believing that he is guilty of trespassing, and with a proud family tradition (a Do-Right must always do right), Dudley decides to turn himself in to the police—at the North Alberta Mountie Camp in Canada, which is 500 miles from his home.

When Dudley tells Inspector Ray K. Fenwick about his foul deed, the shocked inspector reprimands him ("How could you..."), then asks Dudley if he would like to become a Mountie. Dudley is undecided at first—until he sees the string that attaches Ray's gun to his holster. Now hooked, Dudley signs up and 90 minutes later completes his training. His assignment: to maintain the peace and apprehend Snidley Whiplash, "that scandalous, nefarious, odious, obnoxious, villainous villain of the Northwest."

Constable Dudley Do-Right has a horse named Horse and is in love with the inspector's daughter, Nell Fenwick, "the apple of Dudley's eye." Unfortunately for Dudley, "the fair and lovely Nell" is in love with his horse and will never marry Dudley ("Why, Nell?" "Because you are too good, Dudley"). In one episode, however, Dudley, "the man who can do no wrong," became a disgrace to the Mounties when he ate his peas with a knife at dinner—"something a Mountie would never do."

At times the narrator would run out of words to describe "that meaner than mean, downright villainous, no-good Snidley Whiplash." Snidley, who usually thanks the narrator for his kind words, owns a sawmill and "has this thing about tying ladies to railroad tracks" (especially Nell, whom he kidnaps on a regular basis). As the narrator puts it, "Each day Dudley brings Snidley in to the post and places him under lock and key. And each morning he escapes."

In some episodes, when the opening theme plays, the characters are credited as follows: Dudley Do-Right (played by Sid Gould, Jr.), Snidley Whiplash (played by Sid Gould XVIII), Dudley Do-Right's Horse (played by Sid Gould, Sr.), Nell Fenwick (played by Sid Gould's wife), and Inspector Fenwick (played by Sid Gould's mother-in-law). Other episodes credit only Dudley (played by Proctor Proone) and Snidley (played by Lester Flem).

Theme: "Dudley Do-Right of the Mounties," by Sheldon Allman and Stan Worth.

Note: The series originally appeared as a segment of "Rocky and His Friends" (see entry).

186. *Duet*

Fox, 4/19/87 to 8/20/89

Laura Kelly (Mary Page Keller) and Ben Coleman (Matthew Laurance) are recent newlyweds; they live in an apartment at 981 Fairfax Street. Marrieds Richard and Linda Phillips (Chris Lemmon and Alison LaPlaca) live at 10 West Florist Street and have a four-year-old daughter named Amanda (Ginger Orsi). Stories relate events in their lives.

Laura is a caterer and runs Laura's Cornucopia with her younger, unmarried sister, Jane Kelly (Jodi Thelen). Ben is a mystery writer and penned the novel *Death in the Fast Lane*; he also writes the column "True Stories" for the Los Angeles *Daily Banner*. Ben has a dog named Reuben, and his fictional detective is Zack Murdock.

Linda, originally a high-powered executive for an unnamed movie studio, joins Laura's company (now called Cornucopia Caterers) when she is fired. In the last episode, she and Laura secure jobs with the Juan Verde Real Estate Company (see "Open House"). Richard was originally a patio furniture salesman at the House of Patio before becoming a piano player (his true calling) at Jasper's Bar and Restaurant. Geneva (Arleen Sorkin) is the Phillipses' sexy maid and baby-sitter for their young daughter, Amanda. Linda's father called her "Cookie Nose" when she was a child.

Relatives: K Callan (Laura's mother, *Rose Kelly*), Reid Shelton (Laura's father, *Frank Kelly*), Jane Persky (Laura's older sister, *Mary Margaret Kelly*), Nick Segal (Laura's brother, *Michael Kelly*), Summer Phoenix and Mary Tanner (Laura's younger sister, *Molly Kelly*), Allan Arbus (Ben's father, *Nate Coleman*), Bette Ford (Ben's mother, *Barbara Coleman*), Pat Harrington, Jr. (Linda's father, *George Hartley*), Christopher Templeton (Linda's sister, *Diana Hartley*), Robert Reed (Richard's father, *Jim Phillips*).

Flashbacks: Maia Brewton (*Linda as a girl*).

Theme: "Duet," vocal by Ursula Walker and Tony Franklin.

187. *Duffy's Tavern*

NBC, 4/5/54 to 9/3/54

Cast: Ed Gardner (*Archie*), Alan Reed (*Clifton Finnegan*), Pattee Chapman (*Miss Duffy*), Veda Ann Borg (*Peaches La Tour*).

Facts: Located in a shabby section of New York City on Third Avenue is Duffy's Tavern, a friendly neighborhood bar where "the elite meet to eat" and where, with a beer, the free lunch costs 15 cents. Duffy's Tavern is not difficult to find, espcially if you are on Park Avenue: "Go into the street. You'll see a lot of them dames with the new look— long dresses. Well, just keep going east till you see knees." The Feinschmecker Brewery of Greater Staten Island services the tavern (Duffy orders the Weehawken Lager Beer Nectar). On rainy nights the tavern loses business—"Who wants to go out and lay in the gutter?" The tavern also has a caring attitude about its customers: "At Duffy's we have ethics. We don't roll customers until they're drunk." The safe is a hole in the wall, and "the books are a little unbalanced." A large three-leaf clover is painted on the window above the door to the tavern.

Archie (no last name) is the manager of the tavern for the never-seen Mr. Duffy (although Archie does talk to him on the phone). When the phone rings, Archie answers with, "Hello, Duffy's Tavern ... Archie the manager speaking, Duffy ain't here." Archie attended P.S. 4 grammar school and has known Duffy for 15 years (they despise each other). Archie is a con artist and out to make a buck any way he can. He is also an expert in medicine ("For four years I watched *Dr. Kildare* movies") and a crack lawyer ("For ten years I worked for Muelbacker, Bushwacker, Millstone and Briggs painting the ipsos on the factos").

His girlfriend (whom he takes to the Stork Club when he has the money—"which ain't often") is Peaches La Tour, a gorgeous stripper at the Burlesque Palace (later called the Bijou Burlesque).

Clifton Finnegan is Archie's childhood friend, "a subnormal chowderhead; a dope; a low grade moron." But, as Archie says, "You have to forgive him. When he was born, the baby doctor was a little nearsighted and Finnegan got slapped on the head." Although he is simpleminded, beware when Finnegan gets riled: "He'd throw a termite on a lame man's cane." Finnegan mentioned that he would never marry because of what happened to his parents— "They became a mother and father." Archie never married "because I wanted my wife to have everything—money, a mansion, a big car, a yacht. But I ain't found the right dame yet." Finnegan mentioned that collecting cigar bands was his hobby.

Miss Duffy is Duffy's daughter, whom Archie calls "Mother Nature's revenge on peeping toms." She works as the cashier at the tavern and is seeking a husband. She freely gives out her home phone number (Murray Hill 3-8000) to anyone she has the opportunity to meet. "Unfortunately," Archie says, "her phone ain't never rung." Miss Duffy, like Archie, has only one name. When she calls her father she says, "Poppa, this is your daughter, Miss Duffy"; she introduces herself to people as Miss Duffy.

Charley (Jimmy Conlin) is Archie's elderly friend, a waiter at the tavern; Second Story Jackson (Herb Vigran) is Archie's old schoolmate (they both flunked out of kindergarten together) who now leads a somewhat shady life.

Theme: "Duffy's Tavern," by Peter Van Steeden.

188. *The Dukes of Hazzard*

CBS, 1/26/79 to 2/8/85

The setting is Hazzard County, a small community in Georgia. There is a movie theater (the Hazzard Picture Palace), a bowling alley (Dawn Till Dusk Bowling), a watering hole (the Boar's Nest Bar), the Hazzard County Bank and the Hazzard County Garage. There is also "J.D." Jefferson Davis ("Boss") Hogg (Sorrell Booke), a corrupt politician (the commissioner of Hazzard County) who runs the community and seeks only to fatten his wallet through his crooked business dealings (for example, he owns or sells Hogg Alarm Systems, Hoggoco Motor Oil, J.D. Shocks, Hogg's Happy Burgers ["The only burgers that make you straighten up and fly right"]; the Hoggo Car Charger Kit and Hoggamufflers).

The good in this community of evil is represented by the Dukes, a family whose goal is to ferret out corruption in accordance with the law—"The law is the law, and us Dukes gotta obey it no matter what." Those wise words were spoken by the head of the Duke clan, Uncle Jesse Duke (Denver Pyle), a former moonshiner who once ran stills; he now runs the Duke Farm on the Old Mill Road. Living with Jesse are his nephews, Bo Duke (John Schneider) and Luke Duke (Tom Wopat), and his gorgeous niece, Daisy Duke (Catherine Bach). Jesse has a goat named Bonnie; Daisy works as a waitress at the Boar's Nest; and cousins Bo and Luke have the *General Lee,* a souped-up 1969 Dodge Charger. Bo and Luke built the orange car from the ground up (it is patterned after a racing car, with the doors welded shut; they enter the car through the side windows). The *General Lee* has a Confederate flag painted on the roof and the racing number 1. Boss believes the *General Lee* is half human and that Bo and Luke were born with silver gas pedals in their mouths (as they use the car to foil Boss's schemes). The Dukes also have C.B. codes when on the road; Jesse is "Shepherd"; Bo and Luke are "Lost Sheep"; and Daisy, who has a Jeep named *Dixie,* is "Country Cousin." The Dukes also have a rule about fighting each other: "Dukes don't fight Dukes to settle differences" (they use bows and arrows and shoot at a target).

When John Schneider and Tom Wopat left the series (9/24/82 to 2/25/83) over a dispute with Warner Brothers regarding income from merchandise tie-ins, Bo and Luke's cousins Vance Duke (Christopher Mayer) and Coy Duke (Byron Cherry) were brought on to replace them. While Vance and Coy returned to Hazzard County to help Jesse run the farm, Bo and Luke left to pursue a racing car career on the NASCAR circuit. After 18 episodes, Bo and Luke returned to Hazzard County after a triumphant tour on the circuit (Coy and Vance were dropped).

Other Regulars: Sheriff Roscoe P. Coltraine (James Best) is Boss's corrupt right-hand man. He has a bloodhound named Flash and office 101 in the Hazzard County Police Department. His squad car license plate reads 835-22; the license plate on his office wall reads 442-629; Cooter Davenport (Ben Jones) runs the garage; his tow truck license plate is SU0265. Enos Strate (Sonny Shroyer) is Roscoe's naive deputy; and Boss's nephew, Cletus Hogg (Rick Hurst), is the reserve deputy.

Relatives: Miriam Byrd Nethery (Jesse's cousin, *Holly Comfort*), Lori Lethin (Holly's daughter, *Laurie Comfort*), Edward Edwards (Holly's son, *John Henry Comfort*), Peggy Rea (Boss's wife, *Lulu Hogg*), Les Tremayne (Boss's father, *Big Daddy Hogg*), Jeff Altman (Boss's nephew, *Hughie Hogg*), Jonathan Frakes (Boss's nephew, *Jamie Lee Hogg*), Mickey Jones (Cooter's cousin, *B.B. Davenport*).

Theme: "Good Ol' Boys," vocal by Waylon Jennings.

Spinoffs: "Enos" (CBS, 11/20/80 to 9/19/81). When Deputy Enos Strate (Sonny Shroyer) captures two of America's most wanted felons, he is recruited by the L.A.P.D. and teamed with Turk Adams (Samuel E. Wright), a tough black cop (both are with the Metro Squad, Division 8). Stories follow their comical attempts to uphold the law.

"The Dukes" (CBS, 2/5/83 to 11/5/83) is an animated series that uses the voices of the series stars to relate an auto race in which Bo, Luke and Daisy Duke are competing against Boss Hogg for a large cash prize—money needed by the Dukes to pay off their mortgage to Boss, and sought by Boss "'cause it's money."

189. *Dusty's Trail*

Syndicated, 1973

"Let's follow the path of Dusty's Trail ... a stage and a wagon headin' West, part of a wagon train lost from the rest." Hoping to begin a new life in California, a group of pioneers organizes a wagon train in St. Louis. The group hires a wagon master named Mr. Callahan (Forrest Tucker) and a trail scout named Dusty (Bob Denver). Among the pioneers are Lulu McQueen (Jeannine Riley), Betsy McGuire (Lori Saunders), marrieds Carter and Daphne Brookhaven (Ivor Francis and Lynn Wood) and Andy Boone (Bill Cort).

Shortly after, a "Gilligan's Island" out West is born. Through the efforts of the dim-witted Dusty, one wagon and the Brookhavens' fancy coach are separated from the main body and lost. Hostile Indians, deserts, mountains and outlaws are part of the trek as "the wagon master's hand keeps 'em a rollin' to the promised land."

Mr. Callahan (no first name given) and Dusty (no other name given) have been friends for a number of years despite the fact that they are as different as night and day. Callahan, an ex–army officer, is competent and dedicated to his job; he has a horse named Barney. Dusty, on the other hand, is a bumbling klutz whose foulups always seem to work out for the best; he has a horse named Freckles.

Lulu is a gorgeous dance-hall girl who is traveling to California to open her own saloon ("Lulu's"). She wears a sexy, bosom revealing dress and carries a gun in her garter on her right leg ("Men say I'm a woman; this little baby [the gun] helps keep the odds even"). Lulu, like Ginger on "Gilligan's Island," is the group's secret weapon for getting out of a scrape when a beautiful girl is needed.

Betsy is a pretty, shy and demure schoolteacher who is seeking to begin her own school in California. Although she is just as gorgeous as Lulu, she hides her sexuality under ankle-length dresses and buttoned-up-to-the-neck blouses.

Carter and Daphne Brookhaven are a wealthy Boston couple who are journeying West to cash in on the recent gold rush and open a bank. The firm of Jones, Bean, Bean and Stringfellow is Carter's stockbroker in New York; he cries when he hears that someone else is making money. Daphne is totally devoted to Carter and is amazed "that everything out West is so Western." Like the Howells of "Gilligan's Island," they seem to have an endless supply of everything.

Andy is the resourceful pioneer whose genius for taking nothing and making something helps the group endure the long trek. He studied the Indians, the rivers and the mountains, and his knowledge of the area helps Mr. Callahan as he seeks the road to California.

Theme: "Dusty's Trail," vocal by Bill Street.

190. *E.A.R.T.H. Force*

CBS, 9/16/90 to 9/29/90

Cast: Gil Gerard (*John Harding*), Tiffany Lamb (*Catherine Romano*), Clayton Rohner (*Carl Dana*), Robert Knepper (*Peter Roland*), Joanna Pacula (*Diana Randall*), Stewart Finlay-McLennan (*Charles Dillon*).

Facts: At 8:47 A.M. on an unspecified day, an accident occurs at the Rideway Nuclear Plant. Fearful of calling in the government and having it botch the situation, billionaire industrialist Frederick Winter (Robert Coleby) organizes a special team of highly professional people to prevent a meltdown. When the team accomplishes its goal, they form E.A.R.T.H. (Earth Alert Research Tactical Headquarters) Alert Foundation. Their job: battle the enemies of the planet—polluters.

The Team: Dr. John Harding: Previously the head of the City Hospital Medical Center, he is the only American on the team (the others are Australian). He is an expert in trauma emergencies and was made head of the team by Winter. His Korean War experience and heroism make him a natural team leader.

Catherine Romano: A gorgeous marine biologist, Catherine grew up in a scientific atmosphere and spent much of her childhood on her father's research ship, *Life Saver*. She is nicknamed "The Dolphin Lady" (for her amazing break-

throughs in dolphin research) and is an expert on containing oil spills. Catherine is extremely fond of animals, and it is through her eyes that stories of animal mistreatment or poaching are seen. Because of her marine studies, she will not eat fish.

Carl Dana is a top-notch nuclear physicist who quit his job to become an environmental activist (he worked for Greenpeace but was dismissed for being too radical). A year before joining the team, Dana threw sheep's blood on Winter's car in New York during a demonstration.

Peter Roland is a brilliant zoologist and anthropologist who is famous for his wildlife speeches. His is a recluse but finds himself at home with the native tribes and animals he studies. Peter is opposed to eating meat.

Charles Dillon is a mercenary who is an expert in surveillance and tracking and is only part of the team for the money Winter offers (the others receive unlimited research grants).

Diana Randall is Winter's beautiful aide, his "right-hand man," so to speak. While she does not actively participate in team missions, she is their "boss" and gets the team what they need for the job that has to be done.

The team incorporates a cargo plane (strangely, with no identification numbers), a helicopter called the *Big Zebra* (it has zebra stripes) and a Jeep with the license plate 147 GKG; Diana has a Mercedes with the license plate KZ9-267. The team's lab hamster is called "Harvey, the Hamster from Hell," and the foundation deer (which they rescued) is named Mr. Keegan. "Green Machine" was the series' original title.

Theme: "The E.A.R.T.H. Force Theme," by Bill Conti.

191. *Easy Street*

NBC, 9/13/86 to 5/27/87

"Easy Street" refers to life at a luxurious Beverly Hills mansion located at 4163 Hillcrest Drive. L.K. McGuire (Loni Anderson), a glamorous ex–Las Vegas blackjack dealer, inherited the mansion following the accidental death of her husband, Ned, in a plane crash. To maintain controlling interest in the estate, L.K. (name never revealed) must share it with her snobbish sister-in-law, Eleanor (Dana Ivey), and her wimpy husband, Quentin Standard (James Cromwell).

Shortly after, when L.K. learns that her impoverished uncle, Alvin ("Bully") Stevenson (Jack Elam), is living in Los Angeles at the Shady Grove Retirement Home, she invites him and his equally impoverished roommate, Ricardo Williams (Lee Weaver), to spend the weekend at the mansion. Suddenly, the dreary mansion becomes what L.K. considers a home, and she extends an invitation for Bully and Ricardo to live with her (over Eleanor's objections). Stories relate the problems that occur as an unlikely "family" struggles to live together in a 17 room, four bathroom mansion.

L.K., who loves parties and wearing stunning gowns, is a "blonde bombshell" who enjoys her new life-style but worries that Eleanor's dreary outlook on life may one day rub off on her. Her biggest challenge is to change the conservative, always businesslike Eleanor's outlook on life. Quentin, who has been married to Eleanor for four years, is an investment broker who is hopelessly henpecked. The mansion's phone number is 555-4926.

Bobby (Arthur Malet) is the mansion butler; Angelica (Amy Aquino) is the maid; and Ravenskeep (Richard Sanders) is the rather strange gardener (there is a horror film–like air about him).

Loni Anderson sings the "Easy Street" theme.

192. *The Eddie Capra Mysteries*

NBC, 9/22/78 to 1/12/79

Cast: Vincent Baggetta (*Eddie Capra*), Wendy Phillips (*Lacey Brown*), Ken Swofford (*J.J. Devlin*), Seven Ann McDonald (*Jennie Brown*), Michael Horton (*Harvey Mitchell*).

Facts: Eddie Capra, an attorney with the mind of a detective, was born in Brooklyn, New York, and attended Brooklyn Polytech High School. After graduating from the New York University School of Law, he acquired a job in Los Angeles with the prestigious law firm of Devlin, Linkman and O'Brien. Unlike the three-piece-suit attorney, Eddie is unconventional; he dresses casually, takes a real interest in his clients' problems, and will go to any lengths to prove them innocent—even if it means breaking all the rules (which causes friction between Eddie and his employer, J.J. Devlin, the only one of the three partners who is seen).

Eddie, who lives at 64 Holland Drive in Los Angeles, drives a car with the license plate 836 PCE; his phone number is 656-1656.

Lacey Brown, who lives at 10360 La Paloma, is Eddie's romantic interest; she works as the receptionist at the law firm and drives a station wagon with the license plate XJQ 492.

Jennie Brown, Lacey's pretty 11-year-old daughter, attends Franklin Elementary School and longs to be a professional singer-guitarist like her adult friend, Julie Heller (Tricia O'Neil).

Harvey Mitchell, Eddie's legman, is studying to become a lawyer. He strives to be like Eddie but falls short when push comes to shove.

In the busy opening theme, the following actions occur: 1. Eddie breaks into Apartment number 4; 2. a stopwatch reads 13 seconds; 3. a broken clock is stopped at 11:25; 4. fingerprints of the right thumb, index finger and middle finger are seen; 5. a bullet hole is seen in the left lens of a pair of eyeglasses; 6. Eddie hands Lacey a gun and the stopwatch; 7. the right rear hubcap of a car flies off as it makes a sharp turn; 8. an HO-scale Southern Pacific 0-4-0 tank locomotive (engine number 14) derails (the tower signal seen just before the engine derails has the number 122 on its mast).

Relatives: Renata Vanni (Eddie's aunt, *Teresa*).

Theme: "Theme from the Eddie Capra Mysteries," by John Addison.

193. *Eddie Dodd*

ABC, 3/12/91 to 6/5/91

A TV adaptation of the feature film *True Believer,* which chronicles the exploits of Edward ("Eddie") J. Dodd (Treat Williams), a tough defense attorney who tackles the cases nobody else wants. The series offers very little trivia: Eddie, who attended the Columbia School of Law, is a private practice attorney who claims that breaking the Stuyvesant case (government corruption in a nuclear power plant) "put him on the map." The street taught Eddie how to fight, but law school taught him how to win. Eddie lives on Sheridan Square in Manhattan and has an office above the Grove Pharmacy in New York City. In the pilot episode it was mentioned that Eddie has been practicing law for 20 years; the second episode placed Eddie at 39 years of age and about to celebrate his fortieth birthday (TV's Eddie Dodd was made ten years younger than his film counterpart; a script error was apparently overlooked, as no mention was made that Eddie was evidently a child genius who graduated from law school at age 19).

Roger Baron (Corey Parker) is Eddie's associate; Eddie is short-tempered and "Roger keeps me from blowing my cool; he makes me see the light." Kitty Greer (Sydney Walsh) is Eddie's legman; Billie (Anabelle Gurwitch) is Eddie's 24-year-old secretary-receptionist (she answers the phone with "Law offices, may I help you?"). Jessica Tilden (Mary Cadorette) is Eddie's love interest, a tough prosecuting attorney for the Manhattan D.A.'s office.

Robert King appeared as Roger's father, Mr. Baron, in one episode. In the original unaired pilot version, titled "True Believer," Mary Mara played Kitty Greer.

Dennis McCarthy composed the theme.

194. *Eerie, Indiana*

NBC, 9/15/91 to 4/12/92

The population of Eerie, Indiana, is 16,601. Daylight Savings Time does not exist here because the lost hour that occurs exists only in Eerie (if you set your clock back you upset the time-space continuum and live in a non–time zone). The town newspaper is the Eerie *Examiner;* the Eerie Dairy provides the town with Eerie Milk ("An utter delight") and the only department store is the World o' Stuff; WERD is its only TV station; and the Eerie Bank offers a free toaster with every new account. The area's only motorcycle gang is the Lost Ones. Beneath the town lives Mr. Large Poole (Henry Gibson), the proprietor of the Bureau of the Lost (he is a certified reappropriation engineer, a man who takes items from people so they will replace them and keep the economy going). The citizens celebrate Tornado Day (once a year a tornado named Bob strikes the town), and Eerie's sister city is Normal, Illinois.

Statistically speaking, Eerie appears to be the most normal place in the entire country. But one boy, Marshall Teller (Omri Katz), believes Eerie is the center of weirdness for the entire planet: "Ever since moving here I've been convinced that there is something wrong with Eerie, Indiana." Marshall, his sister, Syndi (Julie Condra), and their parents, Edgar (Francis Guinan) and Marilyn (Mary-Margaret Humes), moved to Eerie (from New Jersey) to find a wholesome life. Bigfoot eats out of their garbage can, and Elvis (Steven Peri) is on Marshall's paper route. People preserve themselves in giant plastic kitchen containers called "Forever Wear," and women care more about vacuum-fresh food than they do about their husbands. Edgar, whose license plate reads SIE 63K (later 28R 86K4), is a scientist for Things, Inc. He did his internship at the Smithsonian and undergraduate work at Syracuse University, and he received a NASA scholarship to MIT. Marilyn runs the Teller Party Planning Service in the Eerie Mall (her station wagon license plate reads 45L 738C), and Syndi attends Eerie High School.

Marshall is in seventh grade at Eerie Grammar School. He has two lizards named Godzilla and Mothra. He also has a friend named Simon Holmes (Justin Shenkarow): "I let him hang around because his parents don't seem to want him around. He's also the only one who believes me about Eerie." Marshall and Simon have a secret evidence locker where they store all the evidence they have found (for example, a petrified bologna sandwich, a watch set on Daylight Savings Time). Stories follow Marshall's adventures as he gathers the evidence he needs to prove that Eerie "is the weirdest place on Earth."

John Astin appeared as Bartholomew J. Radford (Social Security number 951-96-1235), the owner of the World o' Stuff; Christian Cousins played Simon's brother, Harley Holmes.

Gary Chang composed the theme.

195. *The Egg and I*

CBS, 9/3/51 to 8/1/52

Allagain County is a small farming community in upstate New York. Betty Blake (Patricia Kirkland and Betty Lynn) and her husband, Jim Blake (John Craven), are "city slickers" who sell their Manhattan home for the pleasures of country living as the owners of a chicken farm. Betty takes care of the planting; Jim and handyman Jed Simmons (Grady Sutton) tackle the other chores.

Ma and Pa Kettle (Doris Rich and Frank Tweddell) are the Blakes' neighbors. Ma and Pa (no other names given) married in 1912; Pa is lazy and, according to Ma, "He could be the best worker in all of Allagain County." "I could," Pa says, "But I don't want to." They have a pig named Penny. Goods are purchased at Ed Peabody's General Store. The

series is based on the book by Betty MacDonald. Alan Edwards is the announcer (there are no music credits).

196. *Eight Is Enough*

ABC, 3/15/77 to 8/29/81

Cast: Dick Van Patten (*Tom Bradford*), Diana Hyland (*Joan Bradford*), Betty Buckley (*Abby Bradford*), Lani O'Grady (*Mary Bradford*), Laurie Walters (*Joanie Bradford*), Dianne Kay (*Nancy Bradford*), Connie Needham (*Elizabeth Bradford*), Susan Richardson (*Susan Bradford*), Grant Goodeve (*David Bradford*), Willie Aames (*Tommy Bradford*), Adam Rich (*Nicholas Bradford*), Joan Prather (*Janet McCarther*), Brian Patrick Clarke (*Merle Stockwell*), Michael Thoma (*Dr. Craig Maxwell*).

Facts: Thomas ("Tom") Bradford is a columnist for the *Sacramento Register*. He lives at 1436 Oak Street in Sacramento, California, with his current wife, Abby, and his eight children (from a previous marriage to Joan Wells. Joanie, as Tom called her, was married to Tom for 25 years and loved photography. Joanie "died" when Diana Hyland lost her life to cancer in 1977).

Sandra Sue ("Abby") Mitchell became Tom's second wife. She is a guidance counselor at Memorial High School and lived at 1412 Compton Place prior to her marriage (Frank, her first husband, died as a P.O.W. in Vietnam).

David, the oldest Bradford child, is a contractor (license number 789 3382). He originally worked for the Mann Construction Company before forming Bradford Construction with his father. David dated and later married Janet McCarther, a lawyer with the firm of Goodman, Saxon and Tweedy. Janet lived at 2475 DeVanna Place and later worked for the firm of Ted O'Hara and Associates. Mark Hamill played David in the pilot episode.

Mary is the most studious of the Bradford children. She is in medical school and struggling to become a doctor. She interns at Saint Mary's Hospital where her inspiration, Dr. Craig Maxwell, also practices. Craig, who is a family friend and called Dr. Max, was also associated with Sacramento General and Sacramento Memorial Hospital.

Joanie, named after her mother, has her mother's eyes, smile and sensitivity. She works as a researcher, then reporter for KTNS-TV, Channel 8, in Sacramento. While all the Bradford children found it difficult to adjust to Abby at first, it was Joanie who felt the most out of place (Joanie believed that because she bore her mother's name and looked like her, Abby resented her).

Nancy, the prettiest of the Bradford girls, attended Sacramento High School, but dropped out of State College when she felt incapable of doing the required work. Before acquiring a job at the Bates, Callahan and Chester brokerage house (later called the Fenwick, Hargrove and Elliott brokerage house), Nancy worked as a model and appeared on the cover of *Epitome* magazine; she was also the "Sunshine Soda Girl" in TV commercials. Kimberly Beck played Nancy in the pilot episode.

Eight Is Enough. Front: Willie Aames, Adam Rich; center: Laurie Walters, Dick Van Patten, Betty Buckley, Lani O'Grady; back: Susan Richardson, Grant Goodeve, Dianne Kay and Connie Needham.

Susan, the most sensitive of the Bradford children, attended Sacramento Central High School and, while undecided about her future, attempted to become a police officer (but failed the physical endurance test). Her fondness for children, and a disastrous attempt by Nancy to start a day care center, led Susan to find her true calling in an unnamed day care center. Susan later married Merle ("The Pearl") Stockwell, a minor league pitcher for the Cyclones baseball team who later became a pitcher for the New York Mets. In 1981, after an arm injury ended his career, he became a coach at Central High School.

Tommy, the most troublesome of the Bradford children, attends Sacramento High and formed his own band, Tommy and the Actions. Tommy constantly rebels against parental authority and longs to quit school and become a rock musician. Chris English played Tommy in the pilot episode.

Elizabeth, who attends Sacramento High, and Nicholas, who attends the Goodwin-Knight Elementary School, are the youngest of the Bradford children. Elizabeth, who is studying dance, hopes to become a professional dancer. She was one of several students who was not permitted to attend her senior graduation ceremonies for pulling a prank that caused a teacher to be injured. The Bradfords' telephone number is 555-0263 (later 555-6023); Tom's license plate reads 460 EKA (station wagon) and 842 CU1 (sedan). Abby's British M6 car (which she calls Gwendolyn) has the license plate YNH 872. David's van license plate reads HIR 312; Tommy's license plate is 553 VFZ.

Tommy's hangouts are the Cluck 'n' Chuck (fast food chicken) and Bennie's Burger Bin. Nicholas, who has two pet hamsters (Ron and Marsha), also won a racehorse named Royal in a contest (as a kid, Abby had a horse named Blaze).

On 10/18/87, NBC aired the television movie *Eight Is Enough: A Family Reunion.* Tom is now editor of the *Sacramento Register,* and Abby (played by Mary Frann) owns her own restaurant (the Delta Supper Club). Mary, now a doctor, is married to Chuck (Jonathan Perpich); Susan and Merle have a daughter named Sandy (Amy Gibson).

Elizabeth and her husband, Mark (Peter Nelson), own a car restoration business; Tommy is a struggling lounge singer. Joanie, an actress, married film director Jean Pierre (Paul Rosilli); David, an architect, is divorced from Janet. Nancy is married to Jeb (Christopher McDonald) and is now a sheep rancher; Nicholas is in college.

In a second television movie, *An Eight Is Enough Wedding* (NBC, 10/5/89), David marries his second wife, Marilyn ("Mike") Fulbright (Nancy Everhard). The role of Abby is now played by Sandy Faison.

Relatives: Janis Paige (Tom's sister, *Vivian ["Auntie V"] Bradford*), David Wayne (Tom's father, *Matt Bradford*), Dennis Patrick and Robert Rockwell (Abby's father, *Harry Mitchell*), Louise Latham (Abby's mother, *Katherine Mitchell*), Ralph Macchio (Abby's nephew, *Jeremy Andretti*), Sylvia Sidney (Abby's aunt, *Felicity*), Joan Tompkins (Joan's mother, *Gertie Wells*), Robert F. Simon (Joan's father, *Paul Wells*), Richard Herd (Janet's father, *George McCarther*),

Fay de Wit and Emmaline Henry (Janet's mother, *Sylvia McCarther*), Sondra West (Merle's sister, *Linda Mae Stockwell*).

Theme: "Eight Is Enough," vocal by Grant Goodeve.

197. *Electra Woman and Dyna Girl*
ABC, 9/11/76 to 9/3/77

Laurie (Deidre Hall) and Judy (Judy Strangis) are reporters for *Newsmaker* magazine and are secretly the gorgeous Electra Woman and her stunning partner, Dyna Girl, crimefighters whose secret identity is known only to Frank Heflin (Norman Alden), the commander of Crime Scope—an ultramodern computer complex designed to battle evil.

Electra Base is Crime Scope's headquarters. Laurie and Judy use the power of electricity to its full potential. Devices used by Laurie and Judy are the Electra Strobe (a wrist-worn device that allows Electra Woman and Dyna Girl to perform anything at 10,000 times normal speed); the Electra G (a device that adds gravity to Electra Woman's and Dyna Girl's bodies when it is activated); the Electra Comp (Laurie and Judy's portable computerized link to Electra Base); and Electra Power (when activated by Electra Beams, it gives Electra Woman and Dyna Girl a sudden burst of power to help in difficult situations).

Cleopatra (Jane Elliot), the Pharaoh (Peter Mark Richman), the Spider Lady (Tiffany Bolling), the Empress of Evil (Claudette Nevins) and the Sorcerer (Michael Constantine) are the villains who met defeat at the hands of Electra Woman and Dyna Girl.

Jimmie Haskell composed the "Electra Woman and Dyna Girl" theme.

198. *Ellery Queen*
NBC, 9/11/75 to 9/19/76

The series is set in New York City in 1947. Ellery Queen (Jim Hutton) is a gentleman detective and writer who intervenes in baffling police matters to solve the case and get story material. He lives at 212-A West 87th Street in Manhattan with his widowed father, Richard Queen (David Wayne), an inspector with the Third Division of the N.Y.P.D.'s Center Precinct. Simon Brimmer (John Hillerman) is a criminologist and host of a radio program called "The Case Book of Simon Brimmer" (in which he tries to solve a crime over the air before Ellery does). Frank Flannigan (Ken Swofford) is the investigative reporter for the New York *Gazette*; Sergeant Velie (Tom Reese) is Richard's assistant; and Vera (Maggie Nelson) is Frank's secretary. The program's gimmick was to allow viewers to solve crimes before Ellery. (Every clue was given to the viewer; nothing extra was given to Ellery. Keeping an eye out for the small, inconspicuous things was the key to solving the crime.)

Elmer Bernstein composed the "Ellery Queen" theme.

199. *Empire*

NBC, 9/25/62 to 9/17/63

James ("Jim") Howard Redigo (Richard Egan) is the foreman of the half-million-acre Garret Ranch in Santa Fe, New Mexico. Jim was named after two uncles (both engineers), and he supervises operations for Lucia Garret (Anne Seymour), the ranch owner (her husband, Dave Garret, was born in 1924 and lost his life in 1954 during a bad storm; he drowned in a flash flood). Lucia has two grown children: Connie (Terry Moore) and Tal (Ryan O'Neal). Constance ("Connie") Garret runs a guest ranch called the Lazy G Guest Ranch. Milo Dahlbeck (Victor Jory) was Dave Garret's best man at his wedding; he is Connie and Tal's godfather. Jim's late father was named Walt. Charles Bronson played ranchhand Paul Moreno.

The series returned for its second season as "Redigo" (NBC, 9/24/63 to 12/31/63); Jim had become the owner of his own cattle ranch in Mesa, New Mexico. Elena Verdugo was Gerry, the assistant manager of the Gold Hotel, and Linda Franks was the ranch cook, Mina Martinez.

Jack Keller and Gerry Goffin composed the theme, "Redigo."

200. *Empty Nest*

NBC, 10/8/88 to the present

Cast: Richard Mulligan (*Harry Weston*), Kristy McNichol (*Barbara Weston*), Dinah Manoff (*Carol Weston*), Lisa Rieffel (*Emily Weston*), Park Overall (*Laverne Todd*), David Leisure (*Charlie Deitz*).

Facts: Harry Weston is a widowed pediatrician who lives with his daughters, Carol, Barbara and, later (1993), Emily, at 1755 Fairview Road in Miami Beach, Florida. They have a lazy dog named Dreyfuss, and 555-3630 is their phone number.

Harry graduated from the Bedford Medical School in 1959 and now has an office on the tenth floor of the Community Medical Center in Miami Beach (he later has a second-floor office when the Greykirk Corporation purchases the building). Harry uses Starbright Bandages for his patients and buys his supplies from the Radacine Medical Supplies Company. Harry's mentor was Dr. Leo Brewster (Danny Thomas); Leo took Harry under his wing and inspired him to become a doctor. Harry's late wife was named Libby; the first girl Harry ever loved was Jean McDowall (Shirley Jones), whom he met in the sixth grade (Robin Lynn Heath played Jean in a flashback sequence). Gerard's and Berna-

dette's are Harry's favorite restaurants; his parking space at the medical center is J-25 and DR. HARRY is printed on his coffee mug. "Ask Dr. Weston" was the name of the call-in radio program Harry hosted on station WWEN (990 AM), and "The Sword of Weston" is the family crest.

Carol Olivia Weston is Harry's oldest daughter (mid-thirties). She had a bad marriage (divorced after five years), a nervous breakdown and was in therapy. She laughs too loud, can't sew and has a dream of opening a self-help bookshop. Carol is good with money but had ten jobs before the series began (she quit the last one because the air conditioning was too cold). Her first regular series job was that of assistant director of the University of Miami Rare Books Library (which she quit on 10/12/91 to open her own catering business, Elegant Epicure). Carol has fat attacks each spring and is a member of a support group called Adult Children of Perfectly Fine Parents. Carol has a difficult time finding boyfriends and tends to drop them abruptly (for example, "because he ordered veal. It's one step from clubbing baby seals, which is one step from forgetting my birthday"). By 1993, Carol had 37 bad relationships but is hopeful that the one with Patrick Arcola (Paul Provenza) will be a lasting one. Paul is an avant-garde sculptor who is broke and living in Harry's garage.

Barbara, the middle child, is perky, upbeat and carefree. She is terrible with money and plunges into the unknown. Barbara is first a police officer, then a sergeant, with the Miami Police Department (with the force since 1983). She and Harry co-wrote a book for children called *Jumpy Goes to the Hospital,* and her favorite comic strip is "Beetle Bailey." Barbara collects backscratchers and uses Zesty, "the official antiperspirant of the Miss Junior Teen U.S.A. Pageant." As kids Carol and Barbara attended Camp Weemawalk; Carol was called "Stay in Tent"; Barbara was "Swim Like a Fish." Carol calls Barbara "Barbie Barb."

Due to manic depression, Kristy McNichol was forced to leave the series (she last appeared in the episode of 10/17/92, although she still receives credit in the opening theme). Barbara's absence was explained by characters' saying that she was on vacation or on various undercover assignments for the police department. Emily is Harry's youngest daughter (23 in 1992). She was previously unseen and first said to be living in New York, then "attending college up North." Emily appears for the first time in the episode of 1/2/93 when she returns home to work out her boyfriend problems (she was pursued by an unwanted Italian admirer). Harry thought Emily was in college (the Hollyoak Girls' School), but she was in reality a globe-trotter. At school Emily heard about a program offering work in a clinic in Vietnam, and she put school on hold to pursue it. After that she took a moped over the Himalayan Mountains. She next went to Japan (where she worked as a karaoke waitress) and finally to Italy where she was a hand model. Although Emily had planned to stay only for a week, Harry convinced her that family is what she needs and asked her to stay. Emily calls her father "Harry"; Carol calls him "Daddy" (as did Barbara).

Laverne Todd, Harry's nurse-receptionist, is from Hickory, Arkansas, and is married to the rarely seen Nick Todd (her memento of their first date is a hot dog wrapper from a ballgame at the Hickory Municipal Stadium). To get to Hickory, Laverne takes a plane to Little Rock, then Dwayne's plane to Hickory. Laverne, whose maiden name is Higbee, reads the *National Inquisitor,* wears the lipstick shade Passion Pink, and her license plate reads BGF 5N7. To protect her job, Laverne has a secret decoder to unscramble her filing system. Laverne lost Nick, a baseball player, when he joined the Osaka Hens, moved to Japan and fell for a Japanese girl. Winifred McConnell (Barbara Billingsley) was Harry's nurse for 20 years before Laverne took over in 1981.

Charlie Deitz is Harry's obnoxious, food pilfering neighbor. He is the fifth assistant purser on a luxury liner called the *Ocean Queen* (the ship docks at Fort Lauderdale, and Charlie has been with the company for ten years). He is a ladies' man (although Carol and Barbara despise him) and a member of the Stallion Club, and his favorite eatery is the Weiner Shack. When Harry and his daughters took a four day cruise on the *Ocean Queen,* Barbara entered the ship's talent show. She performed the song "Fever" in a sexy gown and won first prize.

Relatives: Harold Gould (Harry's father, *Dr. Stanfield Weston,* a surgeon at Boston Community Hospital), Lee Grant (Harry's sister-in-law, *Susan*), Cynthia Stevenson (Harry's niece, *Amy*), Christopher McDonald (Laverne's husband, *Nick Todd*), Ami Foster (Laverne's cousin, *Wanda Sue*), Doris Roberts (Laverne's aunt, *Rheta*), Erika Flores (Laverne's niece, *Louella*), Marian Mercer (Charlie's mother, *Ursula Deitz*), Richard Stahl (Charlie's father, *Fred Deitz*), Richard Mulligan (Harry's British cousins, *Basil* and *Baroness Daphne Weston*). Not seen were Carol's ex-husband, Gary; Harry's cousin, Russell; and Harry's aunt, Rosalie (who lives with 20 cats).

Flashbacks: Christopher Pettiet (*Harry as a boy*).

Theme: "Life Goes On," vocal by Billy Vera and the Beaters.

Note: "Empty Nest" was a spinoff from "The Golden Girls." The original pilot (NBC, 5/16/87) focused on the lives of Renee (Rita Moreno) and George (Paul Dooley), a middle-aged couple whose children have left home and who now seek a new meaning in life.

201. *The Equalizer*

CBS, 9/18/85 to 9/7/89

Robert McCall (Edward Woodward) is a former operative for a government organization called the Agency. He now helps people facing insurmountable odds. To find Robert, one simply looks in the personals column of the daily newspaper: "Got a Problem? Odds Against You? Call The Equalizer. 212-555-4200." Robert lives on West 74th Street in Manhattan. He is divorced from Kay (Sandy Dennis) and is the father of a son named Scott (William Zabka). Robert's license plate reads 5809 AUJ. Control (Robert Lansing) is his former superior, and Mickey Kostmeyer (Keith Szarabajka) is his legman. Robert's police department con-

tacts are Inspector Isadore Smalls (Ron O'Neal) of the 74th Precinct of the N.Y.P.D. and Lieutenant Jefferson Burnett (Steven Williams) of the 83rd Precinct.

Melissa Sue Anderson played Control's goddaughter, Yvette; Tim Woodward appeared as Robert's father in a flashback sequence.

Stewart Copeland composed "The Equalizer Theme."

202. *Evening Shade*

CBS, 9/21/90 to the present

Cast: Burt Reynolds (*Wood Newton*), Marilu Henner (*Ava Newton*), Melissa Martin and Candace Hutson (*Molly Newton*), Jacob Parker (*Will Newton*), Jay R. Ferguson (*Taylor Newton*), Elizabeth Ashley (*Frieda Evans*), Hal Holbrook (*Evan Evans*), Ossie Davis (*Ponder Blue*), Michael Jeter (*Herman Styles*), Charles Durning (*Harlan Eldridge*), Ann Wedgeworth (*Merleen Eldridge*), Charlie Dell (*Nub Oliver*).

Facts: In the small town of Evening Shade, Arkansas, in a house with the number 2102, live Woodrow ("Wood") Newton, his wife, Ava, their children, Molly, Will and Taylor, and a dog named Brownie.

Wood, nicknamed "Thumper," played football for Evening Shade High School (jersey number 37). He attended the University of Arkansas and became a quarterback for the Pittsburgh Steelers (he was called "Clutch" and 22 was his jersey number). He was Honorable Mention, All-American one year, All-American the next. Wood next became the Southwest Conference most valuable player, runner-up for the Heisman Trophy and rookie quarterback of the year in the NFL. He still holds the record as fourth ever in completed passes in NFL record books. He single-handedly won the Eastern Division playoff game, completing six passes with a minute and 53 seconds left on the clock, and with ten seconds left and no time-outs, he scored the winning touchdown with a broken collarbone. (On a sad note, years later, when Wood had films of that state championship game transferred to videotape, he sees that the greatest moment of his life never happened—his winning catch was out of bounds.) Wood is now the P.E. teacher and football coach of the Mules, a team that can't play football, at Evening Shade High School (the team hasn't won a game in 2½ years); the school's mascot is Carl the mule. Wood's favorite song is "Blueberry Hill" (selection B-5 on the jukebox at Blue's Barbecue Villa, the local diner run by Ponder Blue). Wood's good luck charm is the towel he dyed black when he was with the Steelers 15 years ago; he recalled that his first sexual experience was with a girl named Big Ruthie Ralston at the Purple Dawn whorehouse in Hot Springs, Arkansas. When Hollywood came to Evening Shade to shoot the miniseries "The Blue and the Gray II," Wood was chosen to play Colonel Rodney Stone. Although Wood had a marvelous football career, he also holds records for most fumbles and most yardage lost.

Ava, now 33 years old, has been married to Wood for 15 years. She is the town's first female prosecuting attorney (she graduated second in her law class). When Ava was 12, she was overweight and was called "Chubby Evans" (Evans is her maiden name); it took her two years to lose the weight. On Wood's thirteenth wedding anniversary, a stripper named Fontana Beausoleil (Linda Gehringer) ran naked across the field during a football game (causing the Mules to do what they do best—lose). Ava gave Wood a jukebox that plays "Blueberry Hill" and announced she was pregnant (a girl they named Emily Frieda was born to them on 5/6/91; she was played by Caroline Rhymer). Ava's most cherished possession in her house is her antique bathroom window.

Taylor, Wood's oldest child (15) is a sophomore at Evening Shade High School and is a member of the Mules—but would prefer not to play the game (he wants to be a movie star "and doesn't want to get his face hurt").

Molly, who wears a size 5½ shoe, attends the Evening Shade Grammar School. She is 11 years old, but Wood and Ava think of her as nine (so she can always be their little girl; Molly wishes they would stop treating her like a baby). Molly entered the Little Miss Evening Shade Contest (but lost when she attempted to walk in high heels and fell). Her favorite movie is *The Wizard of Oz*.

Evan Evans, Ava's father, is the publisher of the town's newspaper, the Evening Shade *Argus*. He feels Wood ruined his life—"He married my daughter when she was only 18 and ruined my life." Evan married Fontana in the episode of 3/2/92.

Harlan Eldridge, the town doctor, works at City Hospital (a.k.a. Evening Shade Hospital). He and his gorgeous wife, Merleen, live on an estate they call Tara. Merleen is most proud of three pictures that hang on the wall: an American Indian, Billy Graham and a poster of Tom Selleck that she bought for a dollar. Harlan's pride and joy is his trophy room, where he has stuffed fish of all kinds on the walls. Merleen believes that she exudes sexuality and is thus a magnet to perverts. For Christmas 1990 Merleen prepared a pamphlet called "A Styrofoam Christmas" (how to make a reindeer out of styrofoam). *Tara of the Sea* is Harlan's boat.

Herman Styles, the math teacher at Evening Shade High, earns an extra $400 a year as the assistant football coach. Nub Oliver, the newspaper delivery boy, calls his paper wagon the Chariot of Fire. He claims to have seen every movie that was ever made.

Relatives: Florence Schauffler (Wood's mother, *Pauline Newton*), Brian Keith (Herman's father, *Brick Styles*), Melissa Renee Martin (Ponder's sister, *Frances Blue*), Billy Bob Thornton (Wood's ex-con cousin, *Alvin*).

Theme: "Evening Shade," vocal by Hans Olson (first season); second season theme is an instrumental version by Snuff Garrett.

203. *The Exile*

CBS, 4/2/91 to 10/15/91

John Phillips (Jeffrey Meek) was an undercover agent for U.S. intelligence in East Germany where he was framed for a murder and made to look like a traitor. The only two people he could trust—Charles Cabot (Christian Burgess), an American intelligence officer, and Danny Montrose (Patrick Floersheim), a French cop—staged his death, gave him a new name (John Stone) and the opportunity to clear himself by finding those responsible for framing him. (The *New York Times* reported John was killed when he went undercover as a double agent during the Cold War.) Jacquie (Nadria Fares) is the beautiful French woman who assists John; Morley Parker (Rebecca Pauly) is John's ex-wife.

John's passport I.D. number is 2889209, and his license plate reads 64TJ92. Danny is a colonel with the Special Action Directorate of the French Police Department, and his car license plate reads 723-MTK-75.

Michel Rubini composed the theme.

204. *Eye to Eye*

ABC, 3/21/85 to 5/2/85

Tracy Doyle (Stephanie Faracy) is "a pretty, slightly wacky Jill of all trades." When she was five, her father, Howard Doyle, walked out on her and her mother. Twenty years later, Howard (not seen) attempts to re-establish ties with Tracy but is killed before he can do so. Oscar Poole (Charles Durning), an aging private detective who was partners with Howard (Doyle & Poole—Private Investigators), finds himself teaming with Tracy to help her solve Howard's murder. Oscar finds the case routine and boring; Tracy feels needed and wanted and convinces Oscar to let her remain his partner. Stories follow their efforts to solve crimes.

Tracy, who drives a convertible with the license plate IGH 0568, lives in a loft over a factory at 120 Waverly Boulevard. Tracy sells real estate and star maps, does interior decorating, caters parties, is a Smoke Enders counselor and "the personal manager of a famous singer." She has a dog named Pal, and her telephone answering machine message says, "Hi, this is Tracy. I'm not in right now. Wait a second, I think I hear myself coming up the elevator. No, it wasn't me, better leave a message."

When rough characters are encountered, it is Oscar who takes the beating—"I didn't think he'd beat us up," says Tracy. Oscar clarifies it—"He didn't beat us up. He beat me up." Oscar calls Tracy "Doll" and "Pussycat." They eat lunch at a fast food place called Tail of the Pup and dine at Sardi's. Oscar's lady love is Diane (Rita Taggart), a waitress at Sardi's (Oscar's favorite pastime is buying Diane lingerie at Frederick's of Hollywood).

Jimmie Haskell composed the theme.

205. *F Troop*

ABC, 9/14/65 to 9/7/67

Cast: Forrest Tucker *(Morgan O'Rourke)*, Larry Storch *(Randolph Agarn)*, Ken Berry *(Wilton Parmenter)*, Melody

Patterson *(Wrangler Jane)*, Frank DeKova *(Chief Wild Eagle)*, Don Diamond *(Crazy Cat)*.

Facts: The series is set in 1866. Fort Courage is an army fort situated in the midst of the Apache, Chiricahua and Hekawi Indian tribes. It was named after the much decorated Colonel Sam Courage (Cliff Arquette) and is now run by Wilton Parmenter, a captain from a military family (with such relatives as General Thor X. Parmenter and Colonel Jupiter Parmenter). Despite the fact that Fort Courage houses F Troop, a collection of the army's worst misfits, Wilton believes he has a fighting troop and is proud to be their captain.

Wilton is called "The Scourge of the West" but became a hero by accident. During the closing months of the Civil War, Wilton was a private with the Union Quartermaster Corps and was put in charge of officers' laundry. One day, while doing the laundry, he encounters an excess of pollen and sneezes, blurting out what sounds like "Charge!" Troopers on stand-by were prompted into an action that foiled a Confederate plan and brought victory to the Union. Wilton was promoted to captain and assigned to Fort Courage in Kansas to replace the former commander, "Cannonball" Bill McCormick (Willard Waterman), who had retired.

Wilton was born in June and believes that his reputation is responsible for keeping the "ferocious" Hekawis in line. Unknown to him, the Hekawis are a friendly tribe and partners with Sergeant Morgan O'Rourke in the illegal O'Rourke Enterprises.

Morgan Sylvester O'Rourke, a 25-year career army officer, and nine-year veteran Corporal Randolph Agarn (no middle name), run O'Rourke Enterprises from the barracks of Fort Courage (Morgan is the president and Agarn his vice president). The company, which owns the Fort Courage Saloon and the International Trading Company, deals in souvenirs, whisky and anything else that will make money. Their goods supplier is Wild Eagle, chief of the Hekawis. Wild Eagle is a money-hungry Indian who has brought his tribe to a point where they are completely dependent on money and rapidly forgetting the hard life they once lived.

While O'Rourke seeks new ways of increasing business, Agarn is forever seeking ways to make money on his own (for example, buying his way out of the army to manage a British rock group called the Bedbugs). Like Chief Wild Eagle, who has problems with Crazy Cat (the assistant chief who is seeking his job), O'Rourke must contend with Agarn's endless antics (for example, getting carried away by the beat of the tom-toms at the Hekawi Festival of the Succotash and yelling, "Kill the Paleface") and his array of weird relatives (including his Mexican cousin, El Diablo; his French cousin, Lucky Pierre; and his Russian cousin, Dimitri Agarnoff—all played by Larry Storch). O'Rourke and Agarn are also members of the Hekawi Playbrave Club (an 1860s Playboy type of club). Agarn's horse is named Barney; O'Rourke is the only trooper who can read smoke signals.

Wilton is totally unaware of O'Rourke's illegal business operations. He does, however, have problems of another kind—trying to avoid the matrimonial plans of his girl-friend, the beautiful Jane Angelica Thrift. Jane, who has the nickname of "Wrangler Jane," owns Wrangler Jane's (the general store, post office and hay/feed store). Jane fell in love with Wilton at first sight and has made it her goal to marry him (although Wilton has no intentions of marrying her or any other girl).

Jane was born in November and wears a size ten dress. She has a horse named Pecos and was the lead singer in the Termites, a rock group formed by O'Rourke and Wilton (Jane sang the songs "Lemon Tree" and "Mr. Tambourine Man").

Other Troopers: Private Hannibal Shirley Dobbs (James Hampton) is the troop's inept bugler; Private Vanderbilt (Joe Brooks) is the nearly blind lookout; Private Duffy (Bob Steele) is a survivor of the Alamo and rambles endlessly about his and Davy Crockett's exploits; and Private Hoffen-muller (John Mitchum) is the German recruit who is unable to speak English.

Relatives: Patty Regan (Wilton's sister, *Daphne Parmenter*), Jeanette Nolan *(Wilton's mother)*, Allyn Joslyn (Wilton's uncle, *Colonel Jupiter Parmenter*), Forrest Tucker (Morgan's father, *Morgan O'Rourke, Sr.*), George Gobel (Jane's cousin, *Henry Turkel*), Nydia Westman (Hannibal's mother, *Mama Dobbs*), Mike Mazurki (Wild Eagle's cousin, *Geronimo*), Don Rickles (Wild Eagle's son, *Bald Eagle*), Laurie Sibbald (Wild Eagle's daughter, *Silver Dove*), Cathy Lewis (Wild Eagle's sister, *Whispering Dove*), Paul Petersen (Wild Eagle's nephew, *Johnny Eagle Eye*). In one episode, Ken Berry played Wilton's outlaw double, Kid Vicious.

Theme: "F Troop," by William Lava and Irving Taylor.

206. *The Facts of Life*

NBC, 8/24/79 to 9/10/88

Cast: Lisa Whelchel *(Blair Warner)*, Nancy McKeon *(Jo Polniaszek)*, Kim Fields *(Tootie Ramsey)*, Mindy Cohn *(Natalie Greene)*, Charlotte Rae *(Edna Garrett)*, Cloris Leachman *(Beverly Ann Stickle)*.

Facts: A "Diff'rent Strokes" spinoff that follows the lives of Blair, Jo, Tootie and Natalie, four girls who attend the Eastland School (originally called the Eastlake School for Girls) in Peekskill, New York.

Blair Warner is the most beautiful girl at Eastland. She is rich (heir to Warner Textile Industries), conceited and something of a snob. She was voted "Eastland Harvest Queen" three years in a row and won a blue ribbon for being "Most Naturally Blonde." Blair also won the Small Businesswomen's Association Award for inventing contour top sheets. After graduating from Eastland, Blair enrolled in nearby Langley College and joined the Gamma Gamma Sorority. Blair, who had a horse at Eastland named Chestnut, is studying to become a lawyer. With her stunning good looks, almost perfect figure (she tends to gain "a little") and always fashionable wardrobe, Blair is simply a picture of beauty; however, when Blair sustained a black eye in an accident, fellow student Tootie summed it all up: "It's like defacing a national treasure."

Jo Ann ("Jo") Polniaszek is Blair's complete opposite. She was born in the Bronx and attends Eastland on a scholarship. Jo comes from poor parents (her father is in jail and her mother is a waitress) and appears tough. She rides a motorcycle, cares little about fashion or makeup and prefers dressing in jeans and sweatshirts. Though very pretty, Jo hides her beauty, has an attitude problem, and is constantly a source of irritation for Blair (she and Blair share the same room and have little in common). Jo mellowed over the years, and she and Blair became close friends. Like Blair, Jo also attends Langley College (where she is a disc jockey for the college radio station, WLG, 90.8 FM). Jo later worked as a counselor at the Hudson Valley Community Center. In one episode, Jo started her own business: Mama Rosa's Original Bronx Pizza, Inc.

Dorothy ("Tootie") Ramsey and Natalie Greene were roommates before moving in with Blair and Jo in later episodes. Tootie, who lived on roller skates during her first year at Eastland, is the youngest of the girls. With ambitions of becoming an actress, she became the first black girl in the history of Eastland to play Juliet in *Romeo and Juliet*. She is the most darling of the girls, has two rabbits (Romeo and Juliet) and a cat named Jeffrey. Natalie, who yearns to become a journalist, worked as a reporter for the *Peekskill Press,* where her first article, "An Eighth Grader Gets Angry," was published. She is the peacemaker of the group and constantly tries to resolve the differences between Jo and Blair.

Other Students: Molly Parker (Molly Ringwald) is a pretty, free spirited freshman (she had a ham radio with the call letters WGAIO); Nancy Olson (Felice Schachter) is a beautiful, boy-crazy girl who yearns to become a model. Sue Anne Weaver (Julie Piekarski) is the school's star track runner. Like Nancy, she strove for the model's figure but was hampered by a tendency to gain weight. Cindy Webster (Julie Anne Haddock) is a very pretty teenage tomboy and the toughest of the girls before Jo's arrival (she shed her tomboyish ways and became a lovely young woman as the series progressed).

In the episode "The Reunion," Nancy, Cindy and Sue Anne returned for a visit. Cindy (last name now Brady) is a world-famous model; Nancy, three months pregnant and about to marry, is a successful businesswoman; Sue Anne, a gofer, lies about her job and pretends to be the vice president of a major company.

Edna Garrett, the school dietician, cared for the girls as if they were her own children. She is divorced (from Robert) and is the mother of a boy (Raymond), and she left her housekeeping duties with the Drummonds to work at Eastland.

When Edna learns that her pension fund has been lost and she can't get a raise, she leaves Eastland to begin her own business: Edna's Edibles, a gourmet food shop at 320 Main Street in Peekskill (she took over a store called "Ara's Deli"). Blair, Jo, Tootie and Natalie work here and at the novelty store, Over Our Heads (which replaces Edna's

Edibles when it burns down). Edna, whose license plate reads 845 DUD, was born in Appleton, Wisconsin.

Following Edna's marriage in 1987, her sister, Beverly Ann Stickle, is brought on to care for the girls (who now live above the store). Beverly Ann is divorced and adopts an orphan named Andy (MacKenzie Astin); he attends South Junior High School. Beverly Ann later takes in Pippa McKenna (Sherrie Krenn), a foreign exchange student from Eastland's sister school, Colunga, in Sydney, Australia.

The headmasters at Eastland were Harold J. Crocker (Jack Riley), Mr. Harris (Ken Mars), Stephen Bradley (John Lawlor) and Charles Parker (Roger Perry).

In the series' last episode, "The Beginning of the End," Blair learns that Eastland has gone bankrupt and will soon close. She uses the money she had been saving to open her own law offices to buy the school. Blair becomes the headmistress and changes the enrollment policy to allow boys. This pilot for the unsold "Lisa Whelchel Show" was also set to star Juliette Lewis and Mayim Bialik as students Terry Rankin and Jennifer Cole.

Tootie leaves to pursue her acting classes at the Royal Academy of Dramatic Arts in London; Natalie moves to New York's Soho district to pursue her writing career; and Jo marries her boyfriend, Rick Bonner (Scott Bryce).

Relatives: Pam Huntington and Marj Dusay (Blair's mother, *Monica Warner*), Nicolas Coster (Blair's father, *Steve Warner*), Geri Jewell (Blair's cousin, *Geri Warner*), Eve Plumb (Blair's sister, *Meg Warner*), Ashleigh Sterling (Blair's sister, *Bailey Warner*), Robert Alda (Edna's ex-husband, *Robert Garrett*), Joel Brooks (Edna's son, *Raymond Garrett*), Mitzi Hoag (Natalie's mother, *Evie Greene*), Chip Fields (Tootie's mother, *Diane Ramsey*), Duane LePage and Robert Hooks (Tootie's father, *Jason Ramsey*), Kevin Sullivan (Tootie's brother, *Marshall Ramsey*), Peter Parros (Tootie's cousin, *Michael*), Claire Malis (Jo's mother, *Rose Polniaszek*), Alex Rocco (Jo's father, *Charlie Polniaszek*), Sheldon Leonard (Jo's grandfather, *Joseph Polniaszek*), Megan Follows (Jo's cousin, *Terry Largo*), Donnelly Rhodes (Jo's cousin, *Sal Largo*), Rhoda Gemignani (Jo's aunt, *Evelyn*), William Bogert (Molly's father, *Jeff Parker*), Dick Van Patten (Beverly Ann's ex-husband, *Frank Stickle*), Mike Preston (Pippa's father, *Kevin McKenna*), Billie Bird (Andy's *Grandma Polly*).

Theme: "The Facts of Life," vocal by Charlotte Rae (first season) and Gloria Loring.

Note: Two TV movies also appeared: *The Facts of Life Goes to Paris* (NBC, 9/25/82), in which the regulars vacation in France; and *The Facts of Life Down Under* (NBC, 2/15/87), in which the regulars visit their sister school, Colunga, in Australia.

207. *The Fall Guy*

ABC, 11/4/81 to 5/2/86

Cast: Lee Majors (*Colt Seavers*), Heather Thomas (*Jody Banks*), Douglas Barr (*Howie Munson*).

Facts: Colt Seavers is a Hollywood stuntman for the Fall Guy Stunt Association and a bounty hunter for the Los Angeles Criminal Courts System. He considers himself the best tracker in the world and charges $500 a day plus expenses to track down bail jumpers. His license plate reads FALL GUY, and his favorite watering hole is the Palomino Club. Colt uses a movie stunt gun with three-quarter load blanks—"to impress people." He lives in what people call "a shed in the woods." Despite the fact that it is off the beaten path and always in need of repair, Colt calls it home (his favorite pastime is soaking in his outdoor tub). "Wild" Dan Wilde (Jock Mahoney) taught Colt how to become a stuntman.

Jody Banks, a voluptuous stuntwoman who measures 36-24-36, is Colt's associate. She lives at 146 Del Mar Vista (in the Marina), and drives a car with the license plate 1GS-1267.

Howard ("Howie") Munson is Colt's cousin (a budding stuntman and his business manager). He spent seven years in college. Howie attended Iowa State and specialized in Latin American culture. He was the boxing champion at Yale University for a year, took accounting for a year at Oklahoma State, and spent a year at Harvard majoring in business. He also attended Cornell University, Cal State (majoring in archaeology) and Fresno State College. Colt calls him "Kid."

Throughout the series run, Colt worked for three bail bondswomen with Bond Street Bail (telephone 555-5000): Samantha Jack (Jo Ann Pflug), nicknamed "Big Jack" and "Soapie" (because her life is like a soap opera); Teri Michaels (Markie Post), also known as Teri Shannon; and Pearl Sperling (Nedra Volz). Colt also worked for a bail bondsman named Edmond Trent (Robert Donner).

Complicating Colt's life were Kim Donnelly (Kay Lenz), the beautiful but greedy insurance investigator; Kay Faulkner (Judith Chapman), the rival bounty hunter; Charlene ("Charlie") Heferton (Tricia O'Neil), "the world's most beautiful stuntwoman"; and Cassie Farraday (Dana Hill), "the rowdy little stuntwoman."

Relatives: Jennifer Holmes (Colt's sister, *Tracy Seavers*), Lee Majors II (Colt's son, *Dustin Seavers*), Cameron Mitchell (Howie's father, *Bronco Munson*).

Flashbacks: Michael Hartung (*Colt as a young boy*).

Theme: "The Unknown Stuntman," vocal by Lee Majors.

208. *Family*

ABC, 3/9/76 to 6/25/80

Events in the day-to-day lives of the Lawrences, a middle-income family of six: Doug (James Broderick), a private practice attorney; his wife, Kate (Sada Thompson); their divorced daughter, Nancy Maitland (Elayne Heilveil and Meredith Baxter Birney); their younger daughter, Buddy (Kristy McNichol); their son, Willie (Gary Frank); and their adopted daughter, Annie Cooper (Quinn Cummings). Annie became a part of the family in the episode of 9/21/76

("Starting Over"). When Annie's parents, Grace and Ralph, are killed, Annie's only living relative, Mrs. Sullivan (K Callan), asks Kate and Doug to honor a promise they made years ago: to raise Annie should anything ever happen to Annie's parents. Annie is a highly advanced and coldly courteous 11-year-old girl who mistook the family's warmth as pity and patronization when she first moved in with them.

The Lawrences live at 1230 Holland Street in Pasadena, California, and their phone number is 555-2789. Nancy attends the Matthew Hamblin School of Law; Buddy and Annie attend Quinton Junior High School (later Quinton High); Willie works for the mythical TV show "The Dame Game" (a takeoff on "The Dating Game"). Buddy's real name is Letitia; Kate's maiden name is Skinner; the family's station wagon has the license plate number 268 CNP.

Relatives include Nancy's ex-husband, Jeff Maitland (John Rubinstein), Doug's father, James Lawrence (David Wayne and Henry Fonda), and Nancy's son, Timmy Maitland (David and Michael Shackelford).

John Rubinstein composed the "Family" theme.

209. *Family Affair*

CBS, 9/12/66 to 9/9/71

When his brother and sister-in-law are killed in a car accident, William ("Bill") Davis (Brian Keith) takes on the responsibility of raising their three orphaned children: Catherine (Kathy Garver), and twins Buffy and Jody (Anissa Jones and Johnnie Whitaker). The children were first sent to relatives—who didn't want them. When Bill realizes that he is the last hope the children have of remaining together, he takes pity on them and decides to raise them.

A swinging bachelor who is president of the Davis and Gaynor Construction Company in New York City, Bill resides at 600 East 62nd Street, Apartment 27A, in Manhattan. Bill is a world-famous engineer, and his picture appeared on the cover of *World* magazine for completing an almost impossible construction job in India. Bill is often on the road and is assisted in rearing the children by his very proper gentleman's gentleman, Mr. French (Sebastian Cabot), an English valet who has the seldom used first name of Giles.

Catherine, whose nickname is "Cissy," is 15 years old and attends Lexy High School on Lexington Avenue in Manhattan. Bill had originally planned to send her to the Briarfield School in Connecticut, but changed his mind when he saw how much Buffy and Jody missed her. Buffy has a doll named Mrs. Beasley; Jody is a quarterback for the neighborhood Spartans football team (his jersey number is 24). Mr. French put his culinary skills to good use by opening a restaurant called Our Mr. French's.

John Williams appeared as Giles's brother, Nigel French; Nancy Walker played Bill's maid, Emily Turner. Frank DeVol composed the "Family Affair" theme.

Family. Front: Jame Broderick, Kristy McNichol; back: **Meredith Baxter Birney, Gary Frank and Sada Thompson.**

A Family for Joe see The Mac-Kenzies of Paradise Cove

210. *The Family Man*

CBS, 9/11/90 to 12/1/90
CBS, 6/10/91 to 7/17/91

Cast: Gregory Harrison *(Jack Taylor)*, Ashleigh Blair Sterling *(Allison Taylor)*, Matthew Brooks *(Brian Taylor),*

Scott Weinger *(Steve Taylor)*, John Buchanan *(Jeff Taylor)*, Al Molinaro *(Joe Alberghetti)*.

Facts: John ("Jack") Taylor is the family man of the title. He is a widower (his late wife was named Terry) and is the father of four children: Allison, age six; Brian, age 11; Steve, age 14; and 16-year-old Jeff. Also living with them is Joe Alberghetti, Jack's father-in-law, who serves as the family's housekeeper.

Jack and his family live in Eagle Ridge, California, at 6521 Oak Valley Lane. Jack is the captain of the E.R.F.D. (Eagle Ridge Fire Department), Truck Company number 27 and Ladder Company number 3. Jack's badge number is the same number as the one truck they have—27. Jack drives a sedan with the license plate BEX 257.

Allison was born in Rose Memorial Hospital (fifth floor private room) and is a member of the Buttercups, a Girl Scout troop. She has two teddy bears named Mama and Papa Bear, and three dolls: Ken, Barbie and Surfside Susie. At her unnamed school, she has two pets: Fred the mouse and Turtle the turtle; at home she has a pet mouse named Mr. Whiskers. When Allison eats dinner, she gets very upset if any of the foods touch each other (she fears her plate will explode); she and Jack drink Swiss Miss hot cocoa mix.

Jeff and Steve attend Ulysses S. Grant High School (Jeff is a sophomore; Steve a freshman); a school for Brian is not given. Brian is a member of his school's soccer team and is also a member of the Youth League Wild Cats basketball team (jersey number 21). He also has a bad habit of giving Jack phone messages when it is too late — "Oh yeah, I forgot." Jeff is the neat child; Steve, the sloppiest one.

Joe has been living with the Taylors since Terry's death four years ago. His favorite meal is pasta and squid, and he enjoys playing checkers with Allison (he calls her "Little Darling" and is determined to beat at checkers at least once). Joe's love interest is Lillian (Magda Harout), the crossing guard at Allison's school.

In the episode of 11/17/90, guest star Kim Ulrich played Pat Jenkins, who became the first female firefighter at the station. The other firemen — Gus Harbrook (Ed Winter), Eddie (Peter Parros) and Ted (Adam Biesk) — called her "Firebabe" and "Hose Honey." The model plane seen flying in the opening theme has the I.D. number NC16850.

Jill Nichols (Nancy Everhard), a reporter for the Satellite News Network, was Jack's romantic interest in several episodes; Patrick Kozak (Josh Byrne) was Allison's friend. Peg Taylor (Doris Roberts) was Jack's mother; and Hillary Kozak (Gail Edwards) was Patrick's mother. "Four Alarm Family" was the series' original title.

Theme: "The Family Man," by Jesse Frederick and Bennett Salvay.

Note: On 7/31/89, CBS aired "The Gregory Harrison Show," an unsold pilot about Sean Evans (Gregory Harrison), a widowed photographer struggling to raise two sons: Sam (Kurt-Christopher Kinder) and Matthew (Billy O'Sullivan). Sean ran the Evans Studios, and Doris Roberts appeared as his mother, Cecile. Patrick Williams composed the theme.

211. *Family Matters*

ABC, 9/22/89 to the present

Cast: Reginald VelJohnson (*Carl Winslow*), Jo Marie Payton France (*Harriette Winslow*), Kellie Shanygne Williams (*Laura Winslow*), Darius McCrary (*Eddie Winslow*), Jaimee Foxworth (*Judy Winslow*), Telma Hopkins (*Rachel*), Rosetta LeNoire (*Mama*), Jaleel White (*Steve Urkel*).

Facts: At 263 Pinehurst Street in Chicago lives the Winslow family: parents Carl and Harriette; their children,

Edward, Laura and Judy; Harriette's sister, Rachel; Rachel's son, Richie; and Carl's mother, Estelle. Their phone number is 555-6278, and L9S 541 is their station wagon's license plate number. The series, a "Perfect Strangers" spinoff, relates events in their lives.

Carl, whose middle name is Otis, graduated from Kennedy High School in 1969 (in later episodes he mentions Vanderbilt High School). He is an officer (later sergeant) with the Chicago Police Department, Metro Division of the 8th Precinct (2-Adam-12 is his car code). His worst day as a cop came when he ran out of gas in the middle of a high speed car chase. In his youth, Carl played pool at the Corner Pocket and was known as "Rack and Roll Winslow." He was also a member of the singing group the Darnells in high school (he is now a member of the department's Strike Force bowling team). Carl has an account at the Investors Bank of Chicago, and every time he sees a slasher movie, he sleeps with the light on — "the one with the 200-watt bulb." Carl also held a job as the WNTW-TV, Channel 13, traffic reporter on the 4:00 P.M. news.

Harriette was originally the elevator operator at the Chicago *Chronicle*; she now works as the paper's security director and has keys to 300 offices. Chocolate chip cookies are her favorite snack, and she has a scar on her left knee from when she fell off her tricycle as a kid. Her and Carl's favorite restaurant is Chez Josephine. She also attended Vanderbilt High School, where she and Carl first met.

Edward James Arthur Winslow is the oldest child (born 1/28/74), and he attends Vanderbilt High School. He is not too bright when it comes to school and takes after Carl when it comes to pool (he is known as "Fast Eddie Winslow"). Eddie is on the Muskrats basketball team (jersey number 33); he believes that when it comes to looks "God smiled on the men in his family."

Laura, the middle child, is a freshman at Vanderbilt High in third season episodes; she previously attended an unnamed junior high school. She is very pretty, fashion conscious and bright. Rainbow Cloud is the scent of her favorite perfume, and she attempted a business venture called the Winslow Babysitting Service (it failed because there were too many kids and no sitters). Laura is a cheerleader for the Muskrats basketball team.

Judy, the youngest child, attends an unnamed grammar school. She is bright, pretty and holds the record for selling 232 boxes of Girl Scout cookies.

Rachel is a gorgeous 34-year-old, freelance writer and the widowed mother of a young son named Richie. In first season episodes, Rachel's last name is Cochran and Richie is an infant (played by twins Joseph and Julius Wright). When the second season began, Richie was advanced to three years of age (now played by Bryton McClure), and Rachel's last name became Crawford (no reason given). When LeRoy's, the afterschool hangout where Laura worked, burns down, Rachel buys the property and rebuilds it as Rachel's Place, a diner that then became the new hangout. Rachel and Harriette, who is three years older than Rachel, were born at Regis Memorial Hospital.

Steven ("Steve") Quincy Urkel is the "nerd" with an unrelenting crush on Laura (who he believes is the the most beautiful girl in the world). He and Laura first met in kindergarten—when Laura made him eat Play-doh—and it has been love at first sight for him ever since. He attends the same schools as Laura, has a Laura placemat for lunch at school, a picture of Laura on his desk and pictures of her in his locker. Laura, however, does not "love" Steve and feels her life is plagued by Steve's unwanted affections. At school Steve must walk 20 feet behind Laura (by mutual agreement). Steve has a term of endearment for Laura for every occasion (for example, on the school cafeteria line—"My little Jell-O mold"; when she stands up for a cause—"My little crusader"; or just plain "Laura, my love"). Steve is equipment manager of the golf club at school and says he is "98 percent brain, 2 percent brawn."

Steve has a stay-away fund (his relatives send him money so he will not come to visit). After people see Steve, they remark, "I thank God I never had children." Steve, who plays the accordion, was said to have eaten a mouse, and his favorite snack is anchovy paste on a dog biscuit. His catchphrase is "Did I do that?" Steve created the Urkelbot, a robot made in his own image, for the National Robotics Contest (he later made one in Laura's image which he called the Laurabot). Steve has always been a straight–*A* student. He got his first *C* (and fainted) in a home economics class (he tried to make bread, but the dough didn't rise). He is also a stringer for the school newspaper, the *Muskrat Times*.

Relatives: Paul Winfield (Rachel and Harriette's estranged father, *Jimmy Baines*), Jaleel White (Steve's cousin, *Myrtle Urkel*), Shaun Baker (Harriette's cousin, *Clarence Baines*). Sam was Carl's late father; Darlene was Rachel's late mother; and Robert was Rachel's late husband.

Themes: "What a Wonderful World," vocal by Louis Armstrong; "As Days Go By," vocal by Jesse Frederick.

212. *Family Ties*

NBC, 9/22/82 to 5/14/89

Cast: Meredith Baxter Birney (*Elyse Keaton*), Michael Gross (*Steven Keaton*), Michael J. Fox (*Alex P. Keaton*), Justine Bateman (*Mallory Keaton*), Tina Yothers (*Jennifer Keaton*), Brian Bonsall (*Andrew Keaton*).

Facts: Steven Richard Keaton and Elyse Catherine O'Donnell met at Berkeley in the late 1960s. They were flower children, attended Woodstock, and married shortly after. They lived in a commune when their first child, Alex, was born (they had contemplated naming him Moon Muffin). The family then lived in an apartment on Rosewood Avenue in Columbus, Ohio, before moving into their series home (address not given) in Leland Heights. In college, Steven wrote a play called "A Draft Card for Burning" and was president of the south campus aluminum can recycling program. He is now the manager of public TV station WKS, Channel 3. Elyse is a freelance architect who has a lifelong dream of becoming a folk singer. She worked briefly for the firm of Norvacks, Jenkins and St. Clair; the

Cavanaugh Building in Columbus was the first structure Elyse designed.

Alex P. Keaton worships money. He is a staunch Republican and prides himself on being different. Alex, who always wears a shirt and tie, first attended Harding High School, then the prestigious Leland College (where he majored in economics). He was president of the college's Young Businessmen's Association and the Young Entrepreneurs Club (he is also a member of the Young Republicans). Alex won the Matthews, Wilson, Harris and Burke scholarships, reads the *Wall Street Journal* and had a radio show on WLEL (Leland College radio) called "Syncopated Money" (blues music and business news). Alex carries his résumé with him at all times and held jobs at the Harding Trust Company and the American Mercantile Bank (Melinda Culea played his boss, Rebecca Ryan). In the last episode, Alex accepts a job offer from the Wall Street firm of O'Brien, Mathers and Clark. The first day of school is Alex's favorite day of the year; he has a collection of his report cards from nursery school through college.

Mallory, the second born child, is very pretty, bright in her own way and always fashionably dressed. She first attended Harding High, then Grant College. (She majored in fashion design, and was a member of the Gamma Delta Gamma sorority. WGRW is the school's radio station, and "Grant is conveniently located near all the major highways.") Mallory wrote the advice column, "Dear Mallory," for the Columbus Shoppers Guide (a throwaway newspaper).

Mallory finds schoolwork difficult (her teachers report that she doesn't apply herself). She is not as smart as Alex or her younger sister, Jennifer, but finds solace in her dream of becoming a fashion designer. She has a gift for being able to tell fabrics apart blindfolded, and she deplores polyester. In one episode, Alex mentioned that he tried to teach Mallory long division once but got a concussion from banging his head against the wall. Mallory also dreams of marrying her hood-like artist boyfriend, Nick Moore (Scott Valentine). (Nick's greeting is "Heyyy." He has a dog named Scrapper, and his father, Joe, owns a used car lot called Joe Moore's Motors. Nick later opened an art school for children. "Woman with a Half-eaten Hamburger" was the first painting Nick sold.)

Jennifer, the baby of the family before the birth of Andrew, was a member of the Sunshine Girls Club (Troop 247, patch number 27) and first attended Thomas Dewey Junior High School. She later attends Harding High, then Leland College. Jennifer admires Mallory's beauty and taste in clothes and had an afterschool job as an order taker at the Chicken Heaven fast food restaurant.

Andrew, the youngest Keaton, is an Alex clone and attends Harper Preschool. Irwin ("Skippy") Handelman (Marc Price) is Alex's best friend; he is adopted and has a crush on Mallory. Ellen Reed (Tracy Pollan) was Alex's first college girlfriend. Lauren Miller (Courteney Cox) was Alex's girlfriend after Ellen. She is a psychology major at Leland and met Alex when he volunteered to participate in her experiment on overachievers.

Relatives: Priscilla Morrill (Elyse's mother, *Kate O'Don-*

nell), Karen Landry (Elyse's sister, *Michelle*), Stuart Pankin (Michelle's husband, *Marv*), Dana Anderson (Michelle's daughter, *Monica*), Jeffrey B. Cohen (Michelle's son, *Marv, Jr.*), Barbara Barrie (Elyse's aunt, *Rosemary*), Tom Hanks (Elyse's brother, *Ned O'Donnell*), John Randolph (Steven's father, *Jake Keaton*), Norman Parker (Steven's brother, *Robert Keaton*), Tammy Lauren (Robert's daughter, *Marilyn Keaton*), Edith Atwater (Steven's aunt, *Trudy*), Tanya Fenmore (Skippy's sister, *Arlene*), Lois DeBanzie (Skippy's mother, *Rose*), Raleigh Bond (Skippy's father, *Harry*), Dan Hedaya (Nick's father, *Joe Moore*), Kaylan Romero (Nick's nephew, *Rocco*), Ronny Cox (Ellen's father, *Franklin Reed*).

Flashbacks: Chris Hebert (*Alex as a boy*), Kaleena Kiff (*Mallory as a girl*), Adam Carl (*Steven as a boy*), Margaret Marx (*Elyse as a girl*), Maryedith Burrell (*Steven's mother, May, when young*), Anne Seymour (*Steven's mother, May, when old*), Michael Alldredge (*Steven's father, Jake, when young*).

Theme: "Without Us," vocal by Mindy Sterling and Dennis Tufano (first ten episodes only), then by Johnny Mathis and Deniece Williams.

Note: On 9/23/85, NBC presented the TV movie *Family Ties Vacation,* in which the Keatons spend the summer vacationing in England.

213. *The Fanelli Boys*

NBC, 9/8/90 to 2/16/91

Cast: Ann Guilbert (*Theresa Fanelli*), Joe Pantoliano (*Dominic Fanelli*), Ned Eisenberg (*Anthony Fanelli*), Christopher Meloni (*Frankie Fanelli*), Andy Hirsch (*Ronnie Fanelli*), Richard Libertini (*Father Angelo Lombardi*).

Facts: Following the death of her husband, Carmine, 62-year-old Theresa Fanelli decides to sell her home and move to Florida. Just as she is about to leave, the unexpected happens: her son Anthony, an undertaker, declares that the family buisness is $25,000 in debt; her son Dominic, the wheeler-dealer, has a run of bad luck; her son Frankie gets dumped by his latest heartthrob (Joanna); and Ronnie, the youngest son, drops out of college and announces his engagement to a middle-aged woman named Beverly Goldblume (Melanie Chartoff). Seeing that her family is falling apart, Theresa changes her mind about moving, orders her sons to move back home, and now struggles to guide their lives.

The Fanelli boys are all members of a neighborhood club called the Knights of Sicily. Anthony, who is compassionate and generous, took over the Fanelli Funeral Home when his father passed away; Dominic, a bit of a hustler and con man, is in hot water with loan sharks (especially Jimmy the Needle)—"when the chips are down, however, Dom always comes through." He has been married three times.

Frankie, the handsome playboy, works as a bartender at Caggiano's Bar (all the brothers are members of Caggiano's softball team). Ronnie, whom Frankie calls "Kid," has a habit of falling in love with women more than twice his

age; he and Frankie eat Lucky Charms cereal for breakfast.

Father Angelo Lombardi, Theresa's brother, is a priest at Saint Helen's. He hosts a local television show called "Voice of the People," and is also the founder of the Saint Helen's Halfway House for Teens. Angelo was in law school and drove a cab before deciding to become a priest. He says that every couple he counsels gets a divorce and every idea he has the archbishop knocks down.

In the last episode, Theresa married a 65-year-old man named Ernie (William Windom). He is a restaurant owner, and they honeymooned in Mexico. The series was originally called "The Boys Are Back."

Relatives: Bruce Kirby (Theresa's brother-in-law, *"Uncle" Dominic Fanelli*), Jessica Lundy (Ernie's daughter, *Lauren*, a lawyer), Randee Heller (Dom's ex-wife, *Viva Fontaine*). Randee is the actress who played the role. All print sources list Leslie Easterbrook as Viva.

Flashbacks: Jacob Kenner (*young Frankie*), Raffi Di Blasio (*young Dominic*), Benny Grant (*young Anthony*).

Theme: "Why Should I Worry," by Dan Hartman and Charlie Midnight.

214. *Fantasy Island*

ABC, 1/28/78 to 7/21/84

Cast: Ricardo Montalban (*Mr. Roarke*), Herve Villechaize (*Tattoo*).

Facts: Fantasy Island is a mysterious tropical resort where, for an unspecified price, dreams are granted. Stories begin with guests arriving on the island (via a seaplane), followed by their meeting with Mr. Roarke, the man who arranges for people to act out their wildest fantasies. The individual's fantasy is then dramatized, with the program showing how that person's life changes as a result of the experience. (The mysterious white room behind Mr. Roarke's office has the power to send people into the past or future—to fulfill their fantasies.)

Tattoo, Mr. Roarke's assistant (1978–83), is famous for ringing the tower bell and proclaiming, "Da plane, da plane," as the seaplane approaches the island. Christopher Hewett played Lawrence, Mr. Roarke's assistant, for the remainder of the series.

Tattoo calls Mr. Roarke "Boss." "Smiles, everyone, smiles" (which Mr. Roarke says to his greeters before his guests arrive) and "My dear guests, I'm Mr. Roarke, your host. Welcome to Fantasy Island" are the series' catchphrases.

Very little is known about Mr. Roarke. On January 12, 1980, Marge Corday (Tina Louise) comes to the island to end a recurring nightmare about a castle and an evil spirit named Elizabeth. When Mr. Roarke allows Marge to face her nightmare, we learn that the spirit has possessed Marge and brought her to the island so she can live again to kill Mr. Roarke—whom she loved more than 300 years ago (but Roarke refused to marry her at the time). And, through Roddy McDowall's recurring role as the Devil, who is seeking Mr. Roarke's immortal soul, it is possible to assume that

Mr. Roarke is a messenger of God who has been given a mission to help people who are in trouble. (Roarke always defeats Satan. "Oh, well," Satan says, "we'll play again. We have all eternity before us. Sooner or later I vow to win.")

Wendy Schaal appeared in several episodes as Julie, Mr. Roarke's goddaughter and assistant. Kimberly Beck as Cindy also played Mr. Roarke's assistant in 1983. Princess Nyah (Michelle Phillips) is the beautiful mermaid who lives in the waters surrounding the island; and Harilla (Ingrid Wong), Lola (Phileca Sempler) and Lana (Barbra Horan) are the native girls (who are credited) who frequent the island.

In 1979 episodes, Samantha Eggar had the recurring role of Helena Marsh, a fashion designer who fell in love with and married Mr. Roarke (in the episode of 11/3/79). In the emotional episode, it is learned that Helena has an inoperable brain tumor and "dies" shortly after. Paul John Balson played her son, Jamie Marsh.

Theme: "Fantasy Island," by Laurence Rosenthal.

Note: Prior to the series, two ABC TV movie pilots aired: *Fantasy Island* (1/14/77) and *Return to Fantasy Island* (1/20/78). In the first pilot, $50,000 was mentioned as the cost of a fantasy, and guests included Carol Lynley, Eleanor Parker, Victoria Principal and Sandra Dee. Second pilot guests included Adrienne Barbeau, Nancy McKeon, Karen Valentine and Patricia Crowley.

215. *Fast Times*

CBS, 3/5/86 to 4/23/86

Linda Barrett (Claudia Wells) and Stacy Hamilton (Courtney Thorne-Smith) are students at Ridgemont High, the "in" school in Ridgemont, California. Linda and Stacy are friends and work together as waitresses at the Cattle Burger, a fast food store in the Ridgemont Mall. Stacy, who has been called "Spacey Stacy," likes classical music and mocha almond crunch ice cream; she lives at 100 Ellen Drive. Her brother, Brad Hamilton (James Nardini), is the "big shot" high school senior (his license plate reads 783-XNS). Linda, who likes contemporary music, lives at 97 Wrightson Place.

Jeff Spicoli (Dean Cameron) is the "skateboard dude," a student who has a hard time accepting rules and regulations. Mike Damone (Patrick Dempsey) is the hustler (he sells event tickets for three times what they are worth and has been banned from Disneyland).

Arnold Hand (Ray Walston) is the stern history teacher. He locks the door when the third bells rings and gives a 20 question quiz every Friday (his grades are based on all the quizzes and a midterm and final exam). He never laughs in class; when he feels like a laugh, he goes home and reads his students' test papers. Hector Vargas (Vincent Schiavelli) is the rather weird and somewhat unorthodox biology teacher.

The series is based on the feature film *Fast Times at Ridgemont High*. (In the film, Linda and Stacy work for Perry's Pizza. The series' Cattle Burger was the Bronco Burger in the film; Brad worked for the competition, All-American Burger.)

The group Oingo Boingo performs the theme, "Fast Times" (written by Danny Elfman).

216. *The Father Dowling Mysteries*

NBC, 1/20/89 to 3/17/89
ABC, 1/4/90 to 9/5/91

Cast: Tom Bosley (*Father Frank Dowling*), Tracy Nelson (*Sister Steve*), Mary Wickes (*Marie*), James Stephens (*Father Phil Prestwick*), Regina Krueger (*Sergeant Clancy*).

Facts: Father Frank Dowling, pastor of Saint Michael's Catholic Church in Chicago, and Sister Steve, of the Saint Michael's Convent, are also amateur detectives who strive to solve crimes. Frank, who is a Cubs fan, has been pastor at Saint Michael's for nine years. (He has been a priest since 1958. Prior to entering the seminary, Frank worked as a counselor for a parish youth group. It was at this time that he fell in love with a girl named Mary Ellen Connell. Frank asked her to marry him and gave up his plans to become a priest. After a brief romance, Mary Ellen felt that Frank was destined to become a priest and convinced him to return to the seminary—"I later knew she was right." In 1990 Frank discovered that he had a grown son named Tim Connell—a secret Mary Ellen had kept from him.)

Sherlock Holmes is Frank's mentor. When a case stumped Frank and he stopped believing in his hero, Sherlock Holmes (Rupert Frazer) appeared in ghostly form to restore Frank's faith. Frank reads *Armchair Sleuth* magazine, and when he is really upset he twists his ear.

Steve, whose real name is Stephanie Oskowski (she is also called Sister Stephanie), teaches at Saint Michael's Elementary School. Her Christian name (taken at confirmation) is Sivle (*Elvis* spelled backward). Steve and Frank first met at F.W. Woolworth—she was a juvenile delinquent and he caught her stealing. Frank's guidance helped Steve to make the right decision and become a nun (she stayed at the Holy Mother Convent before her assignment to Saint Michael's). Steve has quick reflexes ("It's what you get from playing stickball in a rough neighborhood") and street knowledge, which helps her to go undercover to help Frank solve a case. In the episode, "A Royal Mystery" (9/20/90), Tracy Nelson played her lookalike, Lady Cara, a princess. Steve's favorite Chicago Zoo animal is Diogenes, a monkey she has known since she was a kid.

Father Philip ("Phil") Prestwick is the harassed archdiocese liaison. His favorite stop is Saint Michael's (for Marie's cooking), and he has a fear about traveling (when he was eight years old, his parents lost him at O'Hare Airport); he also has a fear of elephants (when he was seven years old, an elephant stole his snowcone at the zoo).

Marie is the rectory cook at Saint Michael's. She came to work at the church 22 years ago when Father Hunnicker was the pastor. Her favorite dessert is strawberry and rhubarb strudel. Her license plate reads CGR-438, and she was given two last names—Brody and, later, Gillispie. She has two unseen sisters: Mildred (who lives in Cleveland) and Rose (who lives in Florida).

The church funds are kept at the First National Bank of Chicago, and R3H-698 is the parish's station wagon license plate number. A television pilot called "Father Flaherty Investigates" was filmed at Saint Michael's. In the pilot episode, "Fatal Confession: A Father Dowling Mystery" (NBC, 11/30/87), the church car is a sedan (license plate AA 101), and Frank's nephew, Phil Keegan (Robert Prescott), was a sergeant with the Metro Police Squad (for the series, Sergeant Clancy was Frank's Chicago Police Department contact).

Relatives: Tom Bosley (Frank's con artist twin brother, *Blaine Dowling*), Stephen Dorff (Steve's brother, *Mark Oskowski*), John Rubinstein (Frank's son, *Tim Connell*).

Theme: "The Father Dowling Theme," by Dick DeBenedictis.

217. *Father Knows Best*

CBS, 10/3/54 to 3/27/55
NBC, 8/31/55 to 9/17/58
CBS, 9/22/58 to 9/17/62

Jim and Margaret Anderson (Robert Young and Jane Wyatt), and their children, Betty (Elinor Donahue), Bud (Billy Gray) and Kathy (Lauren Chapin), live at 607 South Main Street in the town of Springfield. Jim, the manager of the General Insurance Company, married the former Margaret Merrick and is known for his ability to solve virtually any problem his family may encounter (Jim says, however, "I'm just an ordinary guy who sells insurance"). Jim reads the Springfield *Star News*, and each year he and Margaret donate $25 to the Children's Home Society. Margaret is a member of the Women's Club of Springfield.

Betty, the eldest child, is nicknamed "Princess" and attends Springfield High School, then Springfield College; her hangout is the Malt Shop. A typical 1950s girl, Betty is the smartest of the children and the most sensitive. When she is unable to solve a problem on her own or tell her parents about it, Betty retreats to the shore of a babbling brook in Sycamore Grove Park. In this, her "secret thinking place," Betty often finds a solution to what has been bothering her. In one episode, Betty won *Photo Screen* magazine's "Donna Stewart Twin Contest" and flew to Hollywood to meet the famous movie star (Elinor Donahue in a dual role).

James Anderson, Jr., nicknamed "Bud," is the middle child. He has a fascination with cars, attends Springfield High (later Springfield College) and has set his goal as that of becoming an engineer.

Kathy, the youngest, is nicknamed "Kitten." She has a teddy bear named Bear and attends Springfield Grammar School. She is a member of the Maple Street Tigers baseball team; Bud's nicknames for Kathy are "Shrimp," "Squirt" and "Shrimp Boat."

In the original NBC pilot film, "Keep It in the Family" (which aired 5/27/54 on "Ford Theater"), Robert Young was Tom; Ellen Drew, his wife, Grace; Sally Fraser, their daughter, Peggy; Gordon Gebert, their son, Jeff; and Tina Russell, their daughter, Patty.

On 5/15/77, NBC aired *The Father Knows Best Reunion*, in which the original cast reunites to celebrate Jim and Margaret's thirty-fifth wedding anniversary. Betty is now a widow and the mother of two girls: Jenny (Cari Anne Warder) and Ellen (Kyle Richards); Bud is married to Jean (Susan Adams) and is the father of a young boy, Robby (Christopher Gardner); Kathy is engaged to Dr. Jason Harper (Hal England). A second television movie, *Father Knows Best: Home for Christmas*, aired on NBC on December 18, 1977; the cast remained the same.

Relatives: Sylvia Field (Margaret's mother, *Martha Merrick*), Ernest Truex (Margaret's father, *Emmett Merrick*), Lynn Guild (Margaret's cousin, *Louise Decker*), Katherine Warren (Jim's sister, *Neva Anderson*), Parker Fennelly (Jim's uncle, *Everett*).

Theme: "Father Knows Best," by Irving Friedman.

218. *Fay*

NBC, 9/4/75 to 10/23/75
NBC, 5/19/76 to 6/2/76

Fay Stewart (Lee Grant), described as "classy, sophisticated and very attractive," is a middle-aged divorcée who works as a legal secretary to Daniel ("Danny") Messina (Bill Gerber), the senior partner in the San Francisco law firm of Messina and Cassidy. Fay, who lives at 73416 Langley Avenue, is divorced from the womanizing Jack Stewart (Joe Silver) and is the mother of a married daughter named Linda Baines (Margaret Willock). Valentino's is Fay's favorite restaurant, and her phone number is 555-6355.

Linda is married to Dr. Elliott Baines (Stewart Moss); Danny's partner is Al Cassidy (Norman Alden); Letty Gilmore (Lillian Lehman) is Al's secretary; and Lillian (Audra Lindley) is Fay's neighbor.

Jaye P. Morgan sings the theme, "Coming into My Own" (music by George Aliceson Tipton, lyrics by Elayne Heilveil and Stuart Margolin).

219. *Ferris Bueller*

NBC, 8/23/90 to 12/16/90

Cast: Charles Schlatter (*Ferris Bueller*), Jennifer Aniston (*Jeannie Bueller*), Cristine Rose (*Barbara Bueller*), Sam Freed (*Bill Bueller*), Ami Dolenz (*Sloane Peterson*), Richard Riehle (*Edward Rooney*), Judith Kahan (*Grace*).

Facts: A television adaptation of the film *Ferris Bueller's Day Off*. This program tells the story of Ferris Bueller, a carefree, outgoing high school student "who gets away with

Father Knows Best. Back: Jane Wyatt and Robert Young; front: Billy Gray, Lauren Chapin and Elinor Donahue.

murder and everywhere he goes fun happens." He has the soul of a con man and is a genius at manipulating his parents and teachers.

Ferris, whose birthstone is the opal, is 17 years old and lives at 164 North Dutton Place with his parents (Bill and Barbara) and his sister, Jeannie. He is a junior at Ocean Park High School in Santa Monica, California, and drives a 1962 Corvette with the license plate ASB 589. Ferris claims, "High school is the best way to keep track of friends," and his only vice is vanilla malteds. He hangs out with his friends at Danny's Pizza Palace.

Jeannie Bueller is 18 years old and a senior at Ocean Park High. She is beautiful, vicious and nasty—and proud of it. She has a body "other women would kill for" and loves to wear bikinis to the beach—but her mother refuses to let her; she tries but always gets caught ("What is the point of having a great body if I can't show it off," she sobs). While her mother is concerned about what Jeannie wears to the beach, she doesn't seem to mind the tight, short skirts and

low cut blouses Jeannie wears to school (Jeannie calls these her "dress to kill clothes"). When Jeannie needs a new look to attract a boy, she dresses as Pippi Longstocking (with long dress and pigtails); she calls this "my innocent look."

Jeannie's greatest fear is that her friends will discover she had her nose fixed and that she is not perfect. When Jeannie gets upset or breaks up with a boy, she goes on an ice cream and chocolate sauce eating binge ("Boys bad, ice cream good," she says). Jeannie, who is called "Princess" by her father, despises Ferris, refuses to associate with him and doesn't want anyone to know she is related to him. She believes Ferris "is a scrawny, immature pile of dog do. My life was perfect until he was born. At least I had one good year." She lives for the day Ferris will get caught and be punished by her parents. Jeannie's license plate reads 2PEK635 (later 2RNT-672).

Sloane Peterson, the junior class beauty, is Ferris's girlfriend. She attended Saint Catherine's school for girls as a kid and hopes to become a ballet dancer. Edward Rooney is the stern principal of Ocean Park High. He had high hopes of becoming a pilot—but he has a fear of high places and tight spaces, "and a fear of throwing up at mach two." Rooney has been principal for nine years and eats a fruit cocktail every day at 2:15 P.M. No matter what he does, the newspapers never get his name right (for instance, Ted Rooney, Ned Nooney, Red Fooney). Grace is Rooney's ever faithful secretary. She loves Ed despite the fact that he has nothing positive to say about her ("I hate your hair, your clothes and your teeth. Your dresses ride up in the back, and you floss too much").

Ocean Park High, which is part of the unified school district, was called Palisades High in the pilot episode. On Thursday, the school serves macaroni and cheese for lunch. Bill Bueller reads a magazine called *Outlook*.

Relatives: Cloris Leachman (Barbara's mother, *Margaret Whitman*).

Theme: "Ferris Bueller," by Glen Jordan.

220. *Fibber McGee and Molly*

NBC, 9/15/59 to 1/26/60

"Can I watch the fight, Mister, can I?" This catchphrase is spoken by an adorable nine-year-old girl named Teeny (Barbara Beaird) to her adult neighbor, Fibber McGee (Bob Sweeney), when she realizes that Fibber and his wife, Molly (Cathy Lewis), are about to engage in one of their famous verbal battles.

Fibber is an amateur inventor and "the world's greatest liar"; Molly is totally honest and devoted to him. Fibber believes that he is a man of stone (until he meets a man with a chisel), can tackle any job (until he tries) and can resolve any problem (if he puts his mind to it). Fibber finds that stretching the truth seems to work best for him—until he gets in so deep that additional lies cause additional problems, and the famous verbal battles when Molly has come to his rescue.

Fibber McGee and Molly live at 79 Wistful Vista in the town of Wistful Vista. "The McGees may not be in the blue book," Fibber says, "but we're in the phone book." Fibber is a member of the Wistful Vista Men's Club and the president of the Chamber of Commerce, and at one time he performed in vaudeville with Fred Nitney (Jack Kirkwood) as the act "Nitney and McGee, the Two Likable Lads." Fibber's favorite meal is a buffet supper ("He goes around the table like Seabiscuit on a fast track"), and lemon meringue pie with spumoni ice cream is his favorite dessert. Everyone, including Molly, calls Fibber "McGee" ("Fibber" is rarely mentioned). Molly buys her dresses at Polly's Department Store.

John Gamble (Addison Richards) is the town physician. Doc Gamble, as he is called, says (about Fibber), "I took an oath to tend the sick and I have never known anyone sicker." Charles La Trivia (Harold Peary), whom Fibber calls "La Triv," is the town's mayor. Teeny, the McGees' neighbor, lives at 81 Wistful Vista. The series is based on the radio program of the same title.

Relatives: Reta Shaw (Molly's mother, *Mrs. Driscoll*), Harry Cheshire (Fibber's cousin, *Oliver*), Gladys Hurlbut (Fibber's cousin, *Florence*), Dorothy Neumann (*Charles's wife*).

Theme: "Fibber McGee and Molly," by Raoul Kraushaar.

221. *First Impressions*

CBS, 8/27/88 to 10/1/88

Frank Dutton (Brad Garrett) is a celebrity voice impressionist who owns Media of Omaha, an ad agency in Nebraska that caters to clients who want celebrities to endorse their products (but do not want to pay for the actual celebrity). Frank, who is divorced, lives at 1130 Eckland Place with his nine-year-old daughter, Lindsay (Brandy Gold). Their phone number is 555-1222, and Lindsay attends the Martin Grammar School.

Raymond Voss (James Noble) is the agency's sound man, and Donna Patterson (Sarah Abrell) is the receptionist. The series was originally titled "You and Me."

Harry Nilsson sings the theme, "First Impressions."

222. *Fish*

ABC, 2/5/77 to 6/8/78

The house, owned by the city of New York, is located at 316 Chambers Street in Brooklyn (it is called the Group Home). The solid oak furniture that adorns the dining room is from the cafeteria at Ellis Island. Phil Fish (Abe Vigoda), a retired police sergeant, and his wife, Bernice (Florence Stanley), are part of a social services department project designed to help troubled kids (abandoned or orphaned) find a decent home life. Despite the fact that Phil hates kids ("They make me nervous"), Bernice convinces him to take the job ("Living with these children will make us young again").

As part of the program, Phil and Bernice are assigned five wise-cracking kids from the Children's Center: Jilly (Denise Miller), Diane Palanski (Sarah Natoli), Mike Feroni (Lenny Bari), Victor Croiton (John Cassisi) and Loomis (Todd Bridges). They are also assigned an associate host parent named Charlie Harrison (Barry Gordon) to help care for the kids.

"Phil's digestion is not so good," so he eats cottage cheese; he finds caring for the kids a royal pain—but he made a commitment "and will stick by it." Phil and Bernice have been married for 40 years. They have kids (who are not seen but are mentioned in the pilot), and they previously lived in an apartment at 46 Fulton Street in Brooklyn. Phil, with the N.Y.P.D. for 38 years, was with the 12th Precinct in Manhattan before he retired (at age 62). Charlie, who is 27 years old, is studying for his doctorate in child psychology at N.Y.U. In later episodes, a sixth delinquent kid named Manuel (David Yanez) is brought on to try Phil's patience.

In his first of many speeches to the kids, Phil stated: "You're all here on probation to see if you can act like human beings. Why I'm here is none of your business; whether I stay is anybody's guess. If you want my opinion, I think our chance of making this thing work are about as good as Fred's down in the basement [Fred is a dead cat the kids found in the cellar]. Meanwhile, no yelling and no fighting. We'll give it a try, and if it doesn't work, we'll try a little harder."

Bernice calls Phil "Fish" and looks upon the kids as her own children. Before Phil was able to get back on the force (the retirement age was raised to 70), he held jobs as a vacuum cleaner salesman and as a night watchman in an unnamed factory (jobs acquired for him from the Police Employment Center). Jilly, whose mother is a prostitute, had a short career as a model for the Yarnell Model Agency at 652 Prospect Drive ("second floor, rear"). She was making $20 an hour and quit when she was asked to pose nude for a magazine—"I got too much breedin' to pose nude. Besides, I catch cold too easily." (Phil stepped in, discovered it was child pornography, "and the guy got from one to three years.")

The series is a spinoff from "Barney Miller." Jack Elliott and Allyn Ferguson composed the theme.

223. Fish Police

CBS, 2/28/92 to 3/19/92

An animated adult series about the comical exploits of Inspector Gil (voice of John Ritter), a good cop in a bad town ("I'm a cop who's a carp"). Fish City is Gil's beat—"a crime-ridden, polluted underwater city and a lousy place to live." The city's newspaper is the *Ancient Mariner*; Fort Lox is the treasury; Haddica is its prison; and Weenie King Hot Dogs is the fast food establishment.

Gil's favorite color is red, but he wears nothing but beige. His favorite eatery is Pearl's Diner, and The Shell Shack is his watering hole. Gil takes his coffee black, with a side order of cream and sugar.

Angel Jones (JoBeth Williams) is the voluptuous singer at The Shell Shack. Angel, called "Chick of the Sea," once worked for Gil "as a sort of a fish Friday." She speaks 18 languages and wears Maidenform bras. She won the thirty-third annual "Miss Fish City Pageant."

Pearl (Megan Mullally) is the owner of Pearl's Diner. She has a crush on Gil and calls Angel's breasts "those babies." Pearl named a special after Gil: The Inspector Gil (corn flakes and coffee).

Chief Abalone (Edward Asner), badge number 5, is Gil's boss; Detective Crabby (Buddy Hackett) is Gil's partner; Detective Catfish (Robert Guillaume) is the undercover cop; and Calamara (Hector Elizondo) is the evil owner of The Shell Shack.

James Horner composed the "Fish Police" theme.

224. Five Fingers

NBC, 10/3/59 to 1/6/60

Wembley and Sebastian Ltd., office number 2318 (of an unidentified building) is a European-based theatrical agency that handles clients in Paris, New York and London. It is also the front for a U.S. government counterintelligence agency. Victor Sebastian (David Hedison) is a U.S. government secret agent who operates under the code name "Five Fingers" and poses as a theatrical agent. Simone Genet (Luciana Paluzzi) is his assistant; she poses as his client, a nightclub singer (she was born in France and loves roses). "Robbie" Robertson (Paul Burke) is their American contact; and Wembley (Charles Napier) is their superior (he tends to the agency while Victor and Simone are out on assignments).

David Raksin composed the "Five Fingers" theme.

225. The Flash

CBS, 9/20/90 to 11/19/91

Cast: John Wesley Shipp (*Barry Allen*), Amanda Pays (*Tina McGee*).

Facts: Barry Allen, a chemist for the Central City Police Department, is working in the lab when a bolt of lightning from a fierce electrical storm strikes a shelf of chemicals. Barry is doused with various highly volatile chemicals (such as aluminum sulfate, potassium nitrate, phosphorus glycerin, hydrochloric acid) and taken to Central City Hospital. Tests are done and the data sent to Star Labs, a government research unit. There, scientist Tina McGee becomes intrigued by the results.

Barry learns from Tina that all his systems have been accelerated and that his muscle and bone tissue is changing to keep the pace. Further tests reveal that Barry is capable of fantastic speeds (he broke the treadmill at 347 mph); Tina estimates that he is capable of speeds up to 620 mph and of causing sonic booms. However, because of the fantastic amount of energy he uses, Barry needs to consume enormous amounts of food to sustain himself.

With a growing crime problem in Central City, Barry decides to use his power of speed to battle evil. Tina, who fears the government will want to study Barry, decides to keep his secret and help him. To control and regulate Barry's body temperature, Tina adapts a prototype red friction Soviet-made deep sea suit as a costume for him. She builds sensors into the suit (to monitor him), makes a red hood (to conceal his identity), gloves (so he can't leave fingerprints) and a symbol: a bolt of lightning (so villains will have something to fear). Stories relate Barry's efforts to battle crime as the Flash.

The corn dog was invented in Central City. The Central City Cab Company charges 25 cents for the first mile; five cents for each one-fifth of a mile. The *Daily Star* is the city's newspaper, and WCCN-TV, Channel 6, is its television station. Barry lives in Apartment 34 in an area called North Park. He attended Central High School and was a member of the science and Latin clubs. He has a dog named Earl, a car with the license plate PRC 358, and Burger World and Lucky Dogs are his favorite eateries. Barry's car is hidden behind a wall in his building. The billboard on that wall reads OUR WORLD IN YOUR HANDS—LOVE IT OR LOSE IT.

Tina lives at 1530 South Street. She is a widow (her late husband was named David), and she follows Barry (as the Flash) in a Star Labs 05 Field Truck. In the episode of 2/14/91, a lab accident turned Tina into a criminal when a brain wave experiment altered her sense of good and evil. She became a member of the all-girl Black Rose Gang. Star Labs uses Panasonic and Sony television monitors.

The only other people who know the Flash's true identity are: Megan Lockhart (Joyce Hyser), a private detective who uncovered his identity and promised to keep it a secret; Reggie (Robert Shayne), the blind newsstand operator who recognized Barry's voice as that of the Flash; and Desmond Powell (Jason Bernard), a doctor at Central City Hospital (a.k.a. County Hospital). In 1955, Desmond was Central City's first masked crime fighter—the Night Shade. He rode in a black car, wore a black costume and used "tranq bullets" (tranquilizer darts) as his weapon. Because of his age, he had to put Night Shade to rest; he is now chief of staff at the hospital.

Relatives: M. Emmet Walsh (Barry's father, *Henry Allen*; he was a cop for 41 years), Patrie Allen (Barry's mother, *Eve Allen*), Tim Thomerson (Barry's brother, *Jay Allen*), Justin Burnette (Barry's nephew, *Shawn Allen*), Carolyn Seymour (Tina's mother, *Jocelyn Weller*).

Theme: "The Flash," by Danny Elfman.

226. *Flesh 'n' Blood*

NBC, 9/19/91 to 11/21/91

Rachel Brennan (Lisa Darr) is a young grade two prosecutor with the Baltimore D.A.'s office. She is the yuppie type and lives in a fashionable home at 3611 Tenner Street. Arlo Weed (David Keith) is a brash con artist with two children: Beauty Weed (Meghan Andrews) and King Hollis Weed (Chris Stacy). Arlo is Rachel's long-lost older brother; he moves in with Rachel when he discovers she is looking for him. (The Weeds were a poor Florida family. Their mother put Rachel up for adoption to give her a better life. The mother abandoned Arlo "when she went gator hunting with Billy Moses and never came back." Arlo survived through cons and later married, but his wife deserted him after the birth of Beauty: "She is now living with a gravedigger in Florida.")

Rachel and Arlo are as different as night and day. While Rachel struggles to make ends meet as an assistant D.A., Arlo devises various cons to make money (such as selling Bibles personally autographed by Moses). Arlo's dream is to open his own business—Weed Tours International. (Prior to

moving in with Rachel, the Weeds resided in Sarasota, where they were evading a public nuisance charge in Daytona Beach. When they first came to Baltimore, they stayed in the King Crab Motor Lodge. Before Rachel's mother put her up for adoption, she grew the biggest squash in Florida. She hollowed it out and made it into a cradle for Rachel; Rachel lived in it for two years.)

Beauty is 12 years old and very pretty. She got her name, Arlo says "when she popped out of the missus and I said what a beauty. The nurse took me seriously and wrote it down." Beauty says that sometimes she believes her father wishes she were a boy: "Last Christmas he bought me a bat. I had to kill it when it bit me." Arlo calls her "Baby"; she has a snake named Stinky.

King is a 16-year-old "hulking dimwit" who says, "Sometimes I'm as dumb as a post." ("Son," Arlo says, "if you were half as useful as a post, I'd be proud of you.") King has a dent in his head (he was hit by the windmill when playing miniature golf) and seems to have only two talents: playing the violin (he can play any song once he hears it) and shooting milk through his nose. "King got his name," Arlo says, "when me and the wife were playing strip checkers and she said, 'King me.' I did, and nine months later our son was born."

David Keith and Leon Russell composed the theme.

227. *The Flintstones*

ABC, 9/30/60 to 9/2/66

Voice Cast: Alan Reed *(Fred Flintstone)*, Jean VanderPyl *(Wilma and Pebbles Flintstone)*, Mel Blanc *(Barney Rubble)*, Bea Benaderet and Gerry Johnson *(Betty Rubble)*, Don Messick *(Dino and Bamm Bamm)*.

Facts: The series is set in the year 1,000,040 B.C. Sixteen years prior to this (1,000,056), Fred Flintstone and his friend Barney Rubble worked as bellboys at the Honeyrock Hotel. There they met Wilma Slaghoople and Betty Jean McBricker, two hotel waitresses. It was love at first sight, and soon after, Fred and Wilma and Barney and Betty married.

Fred and Wilma set up housekeeping at 345 Stone Cave Road (also given as Cobblestone Lane) in the town of Bedrock; Barney and Betty purchased the cavelike home next to them. Fred and Barney are members of the Royal Order of the Water Buffalo Lodge (originally the Loyal Order of Dinosaurs). As kids, they were Boy Scouts in the Saber-toothed Tiger Troop; they are now members of the Bedrock Quarry baseball team. Their favorite television show is "Jay Bondrock" (a takeoff on James Bond), and they bowl at the Bedrock Bowling Alley.

Fred works as a dino operator for Howard Slate (a.k.a. George Slate), the owner of the Slaterock Gravel Company (but also seen as the Rockhead Quarry Construction Company, the Bedrock Quarry Gravel Company, the Bedrock Gravel Company and the Rockhead and Quarry Cove Construction Company). The Bedrock Boulders are Fred's favorite baseball team (in Rockville Center High School, Fred played football [jersey 22] and was called "Fireball Freddy" when he pitched for the school's baseball team). Fred's favorite food is bronto burgers, and pterodactyl pie is his favorite dessert. His catchphrase is "Yabba dabba do."

Wilma is a Capricorn (born in November) and "fixes the best roast dodo bird in Bedrock." To make extra money, Wilma took a job as a singer on "The Rockinspiel Happy Housewives Show" for the Bedrock Radio and TV Company. Wilma became animated television's first pregnant woman; she gave birth to a girl she and Fred named Pebbles. Fred and Wilma also have a six-foot tall pet Snarkasaurus named Dino, who is purple with black spots on his back.

Barney originally worked for the Pebble Rock and Gravel Company (when he was laid off, Fred got him a job with his company). In Bedrock High School, Barney was a member of the Betta Slatta Gamma fraternity. He now coaches the Giants Little League baseball team and eats Rock Toasties cereal for breakfast. One night Barney and Betty see a falling star and wish they could have a baby like Fred and Wilma. The following morning they find an orphaned baby on their doorstep (there is a note attached asking them to care for little Bamm Bamm; they later adopt the baby, who has incredible strength, as their own). Barney's hometown was mentioned as Granite Town, where he lived at 142 Boulder Avenue. He and Betty have a pet Hoparoo called Hoppy.

In the opening theme, the film seen on the marquee is *The Monster*. The population of Bedrock is 2,500. Arnold (voice of Don Messick) is the newspaper boy (he delivers the *Bugle*); John Stephenson provides the voice of Mr. Slate. "The Flintstones" is television's first adult cartoon and is actually a stone age version of "The Honeymooners."

Theme: "The Flintstones Theme: Rise and Shine," by William Hanna and Joseph Barbera.

228. *Fly by Night*

CBS, 4/4/91 to 10/17/91

Cast: Shannon Tweed (*Sally Monroe*), David James Elliott (*Mack Sheppard*), François Guetary (*Jean Philippe Pasteur*).

Facts: As a kid, Sally ("Slick") Monroe dreamed about flying. One day, while she was working at the Fancy Lady Beauty Salon, a Lear jet made an emergency landing just outside the front window. Sally was green with envy. With only $64 to her name, Sally quit her job and acquired a position as a stewardess with Air Canada. Three years later, when an opportunity allows her to buy a used plane (which transported zoo animals), Sally cons investors into helping her start Slick Air, a one plane airline that is based at the Ellis Airport in Canada. Her struggles to maintain Slick Air are the focal point of the series.

Sally was born in Alberta, Canada, and now lives in a warehouse loft (number 283) at 1755 Vasser Road in Vancouver, British Columbia (she hides her spare key above the

doorjamb). SLICK-1 is her car license plate; her plane, I.D. number 485 GKFT, is a B-27 that can handle 30 passengers. Sally earned her nickname by pulling off wild schemes that turned her failures into successes. The Federal Trade Development Bank holds the mortgage on the plane, and Sally's hangout is the Bomber's Bar.

Mack Sheppard is Sally's pilot, a Vietnam vet with a checkered past. (He lost ten jobs in four weeks. Mack was a major with the air force who was set up—accused of gun smuggling while he was actually delivering food "down south.") Mack had a dog named Clipper and worked for a crop dusting/sky writing firm called Silver Lining before Sally found him.

Jean Philippe Pasteur ("no relation to Louis") is Mack's co-pilot. He worked previously in Brazil, "flying gold miners in and out."

Sally's advertising flyers read: "Slick Air. Non-stop daily service from Vancouver, Canada, and connecting you to the world. Private luxury charters. Highly trained security specialists. Discover world vacations. First in personal service. Call toll free from anywhere. 1-604-555-4567. Telex: 346-SLIC."

Theme: "Fly by Night," by Bob Buckley and David Sinclair.

229. *Flying Blind*

Fox, 9/13/92 to the present

Cast: Tea Leoni (*Alicia Smith*), Corey Parker (*Neil Barash*), Clea Lewis (*Megan*), Robert Bauer (*Jordan*), Michael Tucci (*Jeremy Barash*).

Facts: Alicia Smith is beautiful, wild and unpredictable. She lives for the moment and seems to have a magic aura that attracts men. One day, while attempting to avoid a man, Alicia enters a restaurant (the Madison Bistro) and sees mild mannered Neil Barash sitting at a table. Alicia approaches Neil, grabs him and kisses him, discouraging the unwanted admirer. Alicia becomes attracted to Neil and vice versa, and stories follow the ups and downs of the two mismatched lovers.

Alicia lives in a loft at 386 Bleeker Street in New York's Greenwich Village with two roommates: Megan and Jordan. Alicia's friends say she is "sexy, funny and free spirited and should be committed." She is an artist and fashion model and works for various artists and photographers. When she first began modeling, she called herself "Kero"; when she was tired of her real name, she called herself "Chloe" for several months. Alicia has an uneasy relationship with her somewhat psychotic father (Peter Boyle), a man of mystery who claims that "if I tell you what I do for a living I'll have to kill you." He has no name and appears to be working for some secret government agency.

Alicia loves to wear sexy, bra-revealing dresses and claims that the most embarrassing moment of her life happened when she was dating a UN dignitary "who stole a pair of my panties and sold them to a Third World country as their flag." Alicia discovered she possessed extreme sex appeal when she was 14 years old. (She would run through the sprinklers in a see-through sundress and drive her neighbor, an elderly doctor, crazy. He begged for just 15 minutes of her time. Alicia's repeated refusals led him to invent the artificial aorta.)

Neil was born in Hartsdale and works with his father, Jeremy Barash, in the advertising department of a snack food company called Hockman Foods (Jeremy got Neil the job after he graduated from college and couldn't find work elsewhere). Neil attended Camp Tomahawk as a kid and won the "Most Improved Camper" award. As a kid, Neil had a parakeet named Mickey.

Megan is an artist's model who falls for men she thinks hate women. She is not as glamorous or sexy as Alicia and was the inspiration for a now famous painting called "Depression Ascending a Staircase." She also posed topless for two lithographs of her nipples: "One is on tour in Paris; the other is on display at Milt DeLeon's Steak House in Oceanside."

Relatives: Cristine Rose (Neil's mother, *Ellen Barash*), Greg Grunberg (Neil's brother, *Barry Barash*), Jessica Tuck (Barry's wife, *Diandra Barash*), Jason Bennett (Barry's son, *Max Barash*), Meredith Scott Lynn (Neil's cousin, *Leslie Barash*).

Theme: "A Million Miles Away," vocal by David Byrne.

230. *Flying High*

CBS, 9/29/78 to 1/23/79

Only one applicant in 20 is accepted by Sun West Airlines to train as a stewardess. Of 20 selected applications, only 15 will actually survive the training course. Pamela ("Pam") Bellagio (Kathryn Witt), Lisa Benton (Connie Sellecca) and Marcy Ann Bower (Patricia Klous) are three hopeful flight attendants who meet and become best friends at stew school. "The Three Bs" (Bellagio, Benton and Bower), as Lisa calls them, pass the course and request Los Angeles as their home base. Stories relate their experiences as stewardesses for Sun West Airlines.

Pam is 21 years old, five feet seven inches tall and weighs 104 pounds. She was born in Trenton, New Jersey, and comes from a large family (she has seven brothers and sisters). Pam is a little nervous about flying and pretends to be riding on a bus when she flies.

Lisa is 21 years old, five feet nine inches tall and weighs 115 pounds. She lives in Greenwich, Connecticut, and is the daughter of rich parents. Lisa was tired of being pampered and belonging to the idle rich. She wanted to do something with her life. She likes flying (she has her own pilot's license), travel and people, and so applied for the job at Sun West.

Marcy is 19 years old, five feet nine inches tall and weighs 118 pounds. She was born in Sweetwater, Texas, and helped

in the daily operations of her family farm. (A weight of 125 pounds is the maximum for a stewardess; every six months each stewardess must attend a two week refresher course.)

Carmen Zapata appeared as Pam's mother; Louis Zito was her father, Tony; and Brion James played Marcy's brother, Clyde. David Shire was the composer of the theme, "Flying High."

In 1971 (3/19 to 8/16), NBC presented "From a Bird's Eye View," the first series about flight attendants. Millicent Martin was Millie Grover, and Pat Finley was Maggie Ralston; they worked for the London-based International Airlines.

231. *The Flying Nun*

ABC, 9/7/67 to 9/18/70

When Elsie Ethrington (Sally Field) hears her aunt talking about her work as a missionary, she decides to devote her life to helping the less fortunate. She joins a convent and is given the new name of Sister Bertrille. She is assigned to the order of the Sisters of San Tanco and assigned to the Convent San Tanco in San Juan, Puerto Rico. After beginning her duties, Sister Bertrille discovers she has the ability to fly. Her coronets (headgear) have sides that resemble wings. Sister Bertrille weighs only 90 pounds, and San Juan is an area affected by trade winds. When she is caught by strong gales, she is able to soar above the ground. By manipulating her coronets she acquires some control over flight, but landings remain difficult. She now attempts to use her gift of flight to help the people of her poor community.

To the children of working mothers, the Convent San Tanco is a day care center. The convent was built in 1572 on land given to the sisters by King Philip of Spain. Their rent is one dollar a year. San Tanco is a small town with a population of 3,956. In high school, Elsie was voted "Most Far-Out of 1965," and during the summer of 1966 she worked as a counselor at Camp Laughing Water. In one episode Sister Bertrille mentioned that in high school she played with a rock band called the Gorries (which refers to Sally Field's earlier series, "Gidget," in which she belonged to a group of that name).

Carlos Ramirez (Alejandro Rey) is a playboy who owns a discotheque in San Juan called Casino Carlos. His niece, Linda Shapiro (Pamelyn Ferdin), is a young girl who yearns to be a sister and is called "The Little Nun."

Other characters include: Reverend Mother Plaseato (Madeleine Sherwood), Sister Jacqueline (Marge Redmond), Sister Ana (Linda Dangcil) and Sister Sixto (Shelley Morrison). Elinor Donahue appears as Elsie's sister, Jennifer; June Whitley and Laurence Haddon played Linda's mother and father. Henry Corden was Carlos's uncle Antonio, and Frank Silvera was Carlos's uncle Thomas. Rich Little had a recurring role as Brother Paul Bernardi, whom the sisters considered a jinx.

Warren Barker composed "The Flying Nun Theme."

Flying High. Kathryn Witt (left), George Gobel (guest) and Connie Sellecca.

The Flying Tigers see Ding Howe and the Flying Tigers and Major Del Conway of the Flying Tigers

232. *FM*
NBC, 8/17/89 to 9/14/89
NBC, 3/28/90 to 6/28/90

Cast: Robert Hays (*Ted Costas*), Patricia Richardson (*Leann Plunkett*), Nicole Huntington (*Maude Costas*), Rainbow Harvest (*Daryl*), Fred Applegate (*Harrison Green*), James Avery (*Quenton Lamereaux*).

Facts: WGEO, 91.6 FM, is a public radio station in Washington, D.C. Its phone number is 555-4367, and "Radio Free D.C." is its slogan. Ted Costas is the program director. He was born in St. Louis and now lives in Apartment B (address not given). Ted has a daily radio program called "Long Day's Journey into Lunch."

Leann Plunkett is Ted's ex-wife. She attended Georgetown University and co-hosts a talk show called "Toe to Toe" with Harrison Green (Harrison is also the theater critic for the *D.C. Press*). Maude Costas is Ted and Leann's daughter, a freshman at Georgetown University.

Daryl, the beautiful station volunteer, attends Georgetown University, models nude for art classes, worked as a decorative icer in an erotic bakery, and is now a barmaid at the Ta Ta Room. Daryl drinks only hot Dr. Pepper soda, and the only meats she will eat are yak and warthog. She was conceived at Woodstock and plays strip Pictionary.

Quenton Lamereaux hosts "The Classical Show," and Don Baumgartner (John Kassir) is the host of a satire show called "Capitol Punishment."

From a Bird's Eye View. Millicent Martin (left) and Pat Finley.

Gretchen Schreck (DeLane Matthews) is Ted's secretary (in the original unaired pilot, she had the name Gretchen Schmidt). Naomi Sayers (Lynne Thigpen), the station manager, was called Naomi Miller in the pilot. Jack Bannon played Leann's new husband, Jonathan Plunkett.

Ted and Leann's wedding anniversary is on April Fool's Day, and the gang's favorite watering hole is a bar called P.J.'s.

Theme: "FM," by Patrick Williams.

233. *Forever Knight*

CBS, 5/5/92 to the present

Nicholas ("Nick") Knight (Geraint Wyn Davies) is a detective with the 37th Precinct of the Toronto Metro Police Department. He is single, lives at 7 Curity Avenue and is 800 years old!

In Paris in 1228 a man named Nicholas wished for immortality. A master vampire named LaCroix (Nigel Bennett) arranged for Nicholas to have his wish. But Nicholas was unable to kill anyone and turned his back on vampirism; he used his powers to help good defeat evil.

When the series begins, Nick is already established as a detective. He drives a 1962 Cadillac (license plate 358 VY5) and works the night shift with an obnoxious partner named Don Scanke (Gary Farmer). Nick told his captain, Joe Stonetree (John Kapelos), that he was allergic to sunlight and could work only at night. Nick doesn't kill for blood; he has a supply of cow blood in his refrigerator, which sustains him (although Nick is tempted to bite necks—especially those of beautiful women).

For Nick to become mortal he must face his mortal fears (for example, looking at a cross, which makes him weak, or facing the light of day, which can destroy him). LaCroix still stalks Nick, seeking to keep him a vampire. LaCroix possesses the one item Nick needs to become mortal—the jade glass of the Mayan Indians tribe (European legend states that if the blood of a sacrificial victim is drunk from the glass, it will cure vampirism). Assisting Nick is Natalie Lambert (Catherine Disher), the police department's medical examiner. She is aware that Nick is a vampire and is seeking a way to help him become mortal without the jade glass (Nick came to her and begged her to help him see the sunrise and regain his mortality).

Nick's favorite hangout is the nightclub The Raven, which is run by Janette (Deborah Duchene), a beautiful vampire Nick met in 1228 and who now warns him when LaCroix appears. Scanke's license plate is 123-05A.

Fred Mollin composed the theme, "Forever Knight."

The series is based on a failed pilot called "Nick Knight," which aired on CBS on 8/20/89. Rick Springfield was Nick Knight, a modern-day vampire who works as a detective with the L.A.P.D. He is assisted by the obnoxious Don Scanke (John Kapelos); their superior was Captain Brunetti (Richard Fancy). LaCroix was played by Michael Nader, and Dr. Jack Barrington (Jack Harper) was the medical examiner

(not Natalie Lambert). Cec Verrell played Janette, the beautiful female vampire in this version.

234. *Free Spirit*

ABC, 9/22/89 to 1/21/90

Winnie Goodwin (Corinne Bohrer) is a very pretty and kind but slightly dizzy witch. She was born in Salem, Massachusetts, in 1665, and Halloween is her least favorite holiday ("It strains my powers"). Winnie is one of several witches who help needy earthlings through a public service duty program.

Thomas J. Harper (Franc Luz) is a divorced private practice attorney and the father of three children: Jessica (Alyson Hannigan), Robb (Paul Scherrer) and Gene (Edan Gross). They live in a comfortable home at 33 Essex Drive in Connecticut, but Gene, the youngest, feels insecure and wishes he had someone to take care of him, Jessica and Robb. Gene's wish is granted when Winnie appears (Gene made his wish at the exact same moment Winnie's turn for duty came up). Gene convinces his father that they need help, and Tom hires Winnie as their housekeeper (her true identity is known only to the children). Stories relate Winnie's efforts to provide a stable influence for three children whose father has little time to spend with them.

Schools for the children are not given. Jessica is a member of "the cool club" at her school, the "Debs"; Gene is a member of the Pizza House Little League team. Josie Davis played Winnie's beautiful younger sister, Cassandra Goodwin, and Michael Constantine was their father (no name given).

In the original, unaired pilot film (taped in May 1989), Christopher Rich played Thomas and Shonda Whipple was Jessica. Steve Dorff and John Betts composed the theme, "She's a Free Spirit."

235. *The Fresh Prince of Bel Air*

NBC, 9/10/90 to the present

Cast: Will Smith *(Will Smith)*, James Avery *(Philip Banks)*, Janet Hubert-Whitten *(Vivian Banks)*, Tatyana M. Ali *(Ashley Banks)*, Karyn Parsons *(Hilary Banks)*, Alfonso Ribeiro *(Carlton Banks)*, Joseph Marcell *(Geoffrey)*.

Facts: When Viola Smith feels that her son, Will Smith, a West Philadelphia youth, is hanging out with the wrong crowd and headed for trouble, she sends him to Bel Air to live with his rich relatives, Philip and Vivian Banks, in the hope that they will straighten him out, teach him values and give him an education. Will's efforts to fit into a ritzy new life-style is the focal point of the series.

Will, born 7/3/73, now attends the prestigious Bel Air

Free Spirit. Rare photo from the unaired pilot version. Back: Shonda Whipple (left) and Corinne Bohrer. Front (left to right): Paul Scherrer, Edan Gross and Christopher Rich.

Academy (in Philadelphia, Will attended West Philly High and would carry his books in a pizza box so no one would know he was studying; he felt sorry for the kids who tried to steal his pizza). When Will joined the poetry club at Bel Air, he invented a poet he called Raphael De La Ghetto to impress a girl with his nonsense poetry. Will held a job as a waiter at the Brawney Deep (where he dressed as a pirate).

Will's Uncle Philip and Aunt Vivian live two houses from Ron and Nancy Reagan ("We even share the same pool man"). Philip is now a lawyer with the firm of Furth and

Meyer. As a kid, Philip Zeke Banks grew up on a farm in Yamacrow, Nebraska, and had a pet pig named Melvin. He won the Young Farmers of America Pig Passing Contest four years in a row; he was also the first black president of the Young Farmers of America. Philip attended Princeton University and Harvard Law School. He is famous for winning a discrimination case called *Winston v. Jones.* He is a Capricorn (born January 30) and has a pool stick he calls "Lucille." Philip was also awarded the Urban Spirit Award for work in his community.

Vivian is a professor who does substitute teaching at the Bel Air Academy, USC and UCLA. Vanilla Swiss almond is her favorite flavor of ice cream.

Hilary Banks is Philip and Vivian's oldest child (21). She is beautiful, extremely feminine and very conceited. She attended UCLA but quit when she found the work too difficult. She dreams of having a glamorous job so when people ask what she does she can see them turn green with envy. She first worked in the Bel Air Mall, then for a short time as the personal assistant to a has-been movie star named Marissa Redmond (Queen Latifah). When Philip took Hilary's credit cards away ("You spend more money on clothes than some small nations spend on grain") Hilary found a job with a catering company called Delectable Eats.

At age nine, Hilary took up the violin but gave it up when it irritated her chin. She later took up ballet—but gave that up when "I thought I would get feet like Fred Flintstone." In high school Hilary was a cheerleader, but had to give that up also ("They wanted me to cheer at away games and travel by bus").

Hilary reads *17* and *SHE* magazines and will never wear the same clothes twice. Although she is a bit dense, she will involve herself in good causes (those that include handsome young men). Hilary has a knack for losing her housekeys. She has 30 copies made each month and hopes someone will return the ones she lost (her name and address is on each key).

Carlton Banks, the middle child (born 8/4/74), is an honor student at the Bel Air Academy. He is majoring in prelaw and hopes to follow in his father's footsteps (he has a 3.9½ grade point average and is hoping to get into Harvard Law School). Carlton is also a member of the school's poetry and glee clubs. He had his first crush on Tootie ("The Facts of Life") and still hopes to meet her.

Ashley Banks, Philip and Vivian's youngest daughter (born in 1979), attends the Hollywood Preparatory Institute. Hilary is proud of the fact that Ashley is dating right and becoming a beautiful young lady. For her thirteenth birthday, Hilary gave her a dream: a date with teen idol Little T (Tevin Campbell). She plays the violin, and her favorite video game is Tetris. Ashley's most embarrassing moment occurred at an honor awards ceremony. She was sitting with her legs crossed. When her name was called for an English award, she got up, her leg fell asleep and she fell flat on her face.

Geoffrey is the Bankses' prim and proper English butler. He got his start as a butler for Lord Fowler (William Glover) and calls Will "Master William." Jazz (Jeff Towers) is Will's friend; he lives on Cobb Street and works as a D.J. at the Flyers' Club in Los Angeles.

Relatives: Vernee Watson (Will's mother, *Viola ["Vi"] Smith*), Jenifer Lewis (Vivian's sister, *Helen Lewis*), Charlayne Woodard (Vivian's sister, *Janice Smith*), Gilbert Lewis (Philip's father, *Joe Banks*), Virginia Capers (Philip's mother, *Hattie Banks*), Vivica A. Fox (Jazz's sister, *Jenny*).

Theme: "The Fresh Prince of Bel Air," vocal by Will Smith.

236. *Friday the 13th: The Series*
Syndicated, 10/87 to 9/90

Lewis Vendredi (R.G. Armstrong) runs a curious goods shop called Vendredi Antiques. For his own sinister purposes, Lewis makes a pact with the Devil to sell cursed antiques—items that compel their owners to kill. Following Lewis's mysterious death by demonic forces, his estranged cousins Micki Foster (Louise Robey) and Ryan Dallion (John D. LeMay) inherit the shop. Micki and Ryan decide not to keep the shop and are about to sell off the inventory, when they meet Jack Marshak (Chris Wiggins), an antique dealer who was friends with Lewis. Jack tells them about Lewis and convinces them they must retrieve the cursed antiques. They become a team and reopen the shop as Curious Goods. (They store the cursed antiques they retrieve in a secret vault in the basement; they are helped greatly by Lewis's journals of the objects sold and to whom. Unfortunately, the items have changed hands since the original sale and much detective work is required to track down the new owners. The cursed objects appear to be harmless—until they come into someone's possession.)

Michael Constantine played Ryan's father, Ray Dallion, and Zachary Bennett was Micki's nephew, J.B.

Fred Mollin composed the "Friday the 13th" theme.

From a Bird's Eye View see *Flying High*

237. *The Fugitive*
ABC, 9/17/63 to 8/29/67

Cast: David Janssen (*Richard Kimble*), Barry Morse (*Philip Gerard*), Bill Raisch (*Fred Johnson*), William Conrad (*Narrator*).

Facts: Richard Kimble is a fugitive. He is wanted for the murder of his wife, but he insists he is innocent. Richard is seeking the real killer, a mysterious one-armed man named Fred Johnson, whom Richard saw running from his house on the night of the murder, a night Richard Kimble will never forget—September 19, 1961.

Richard Kimble was born on March 27, 1927, in Stafford, Indiana, to parents John and Elizabeth. With ambitions of becoming a doctor, he attended Cornell University in New York and interned at the Fairgreen, Indiana, County Hospital. He did his residency at Memorial Hospital in Chicago and specialized in pediatrics and obstetrics. Richard began his practice in Stafford and married Helen Waverly. On that fateful night, Richard and Helen began to discuss the prospect of adopting a child. Helen is unable to have children, a result of the stillbirth of their first child. She refuses to adopt any, feeling it would be living with a lie. Richard feels just the opposite but can't convince her otherwise. After a heated argument, Richard storms out of the house. As he drives off, Helen invites her neighbor, Lloyd Chandler (J.D. Cannon) over to talk about adoption. While upstairs, they hear a noise coming from downstairs. Helen, believing it is Richard, goes down to welcome him home. She startles a burglar, who hits her with the base of a lamp and kills her. As the burglar, a one-armed man named Fred Johnson, looks up the stairs, he sees Chandler cowering in fear, and leaves the house. Chandler, a former war hero who did nothing to help Helen, now fears that if word gets out, he will be ruined. He decides to keep quiet about having been present.

Meanwhile, as Richard contemplates his actions, he decides to return home and apologize. When Richard enters the driveway, his car headlights catch the figure of a one-armed man running from the house. Richard rushes into the house and finds Helen. Because he cannot prove his alibi, Richard is arrested and charged with murder.

Kimble is booked (number KB 7608163), fingerprinted (classification: 19M 9400013) and sent to jail. When he is tried (case number 33972), he is unable to prove his innocence and is sentenced to death. Although Kimble insists that a mysterious one-armed man killed Helen, an exhaustive police search fails to uncover any suspects.

While being escorted to the death house by Indiana detective Lieutenant Philip Gerard, Kimble escapes when the train on which they are riding derails. Now Kimble is wanted for murder and interstate flight, and a reward is offered for information leading to his capture. Kimble, who weighs 175 pounds and is six feet tall, dyes his salt-and-pepper hair black and begins a crosscountry search to clear his name—by finding the one-armed man. His mission is jeopardized, however, by Gerard, who has sworn to apprehend his escaped prisoner.

Kimble's search ended four years later in the concluding segment of the two part episode "The Judgment." Johnson has returned to Stafford to blackmail Chandler for cowardice. Kimble has been captured by Gerard in Los Angeles and the two are returning to Stafford. When Kimble and Gerard learn that Chandler is planning to kill Johnson, they rush to a closed amusement park where Johnson has set up a meeting. At the park, Gerard orders Chandler to drop his rifle. Just then, Johnson fires his gun and hits Gerard in the leg. Gerard gives Kimble his gun, and Richard takes off in pursuit. On top of a water tower, when Kimble has Johnson pinned against the railing, he hears what he has been longing to hear since 1961: Johnson's confession to Helen's

murder. Another fight ensues and Johnson manages to get Richard's gun. Just as it looked like curtains for Richard, Gerard appears and kills Johnson with Chandler's rifle.

A relieved Kimble tells Gerard that Johnson confessed—but the confession is worthless since Richard is the only one who heard it. Just then Chandler steps forward and tells Gerard that Kimble is innocent and that he will testify for him in court.

Outisde the courthouse, Richard Kimble stands a free man. Gerard makes the first move, and he and Richard shake hands for the first time. "Tuesday, August 29th, 1967. The day the running stopped."

Relatives: Robert Keith (Richard's father, *Dr. John Kimble*), Jacqueline Scott (Richard's sister, *Donna Taft*), Andrew Prine (Richard's brother, *Ray Kimble*), James B. Sikking and Richard Anderson (Donna's husband, *Leonard Taft*), Barbara Rush (Philip's wife, *Marie Gerard*; name also given as *Ann Gerard* and played by Rachel Ames), Bill Mumy (Donna's son, *David Taft*), Clint Howard and Johnny Jensen (Donna's son, *Billy Taft*).

Flashbacks: Diane Brewster (Richard's wife, *Helen Kimble*).

Theme: "The Fugitive," by Pete Rugolo.

238. *Full House*

ABC, 9/22/87 to the present

Cast: Bob Saget (*Danny Tanner*), Candace Cameron (*D.J. Tanner*), Jodie Sweetin (*Stephanie Tanner*), John Stamos (*Jesse*), David Coulier (*Joey Gladstone*), Lori Loughlin (*Rebecca Donaldson*), Andrea Barber (*Kimmy Gibler*), Mary Kate and Ashley Olsen (*Michelle Tanner*).

Facts: Danny Tanner, his wife, Pamela, and their daughters, D.J., Stephanie and Michelle, live at 1882 Gerard Street in San Francisco, California. Shortly after the birth of Michelle, Pam is killed in a car accident. Danny then asks his brother-in-law, Jesse, and his best friend, Joey, to move in with him and help him raise the girls. The unlikely situation proves successful when the six become a family.

Danny is the co-host (with Rebecca Donaldson) of "Wake Up, San Francisco," a daily half-hour early morning information show on KTMB, Channel 8. (Danny originally did the sportscasts on Channel's 8's "Newsbeat." In college, Danny had a television show called "College Pop.") Danny is a neat freak, buys his special low sodium pickles (gerkins) at Pickle Town, and as a kid had a "friend" named Terry, the talking washcloth. When D.J. was a little girl, Danny would sing the song "My Girl" to her. In first season episodes, Danny has a car he calls Bullet. He later has a sedan (license plate 4E11449). He attributes his excessive neatness to his fifth birthday, when his mother gave him a set of vacuum cleaner attachments; she called him her "special helper."

D.J. (Donna Jo) is the oldest and prettiest of the Tanner girls. She attended the Fraser Street Elementary School,

Beaumont Junior High, Van Allen Junior High and Van Allen High School. She loves to shop at the mall, is editor of the school newspaper (not named) and has her own phone (number 555-8722). As a kid, D.J. had a favorite pillow she called Pillow Person; "she loves to spend hours in the bathroom." She wears Passion Plum eyeshadow and had a job as "The Happy Helper" at Tot Shots (a mall photographer). D.J.'s dream is to own a horse; when she was in the sixth grade, she briefly had one called Rocket.

Stephanie Judith, the middle child, was also given the middle name Julie in one episode. She attends the Fraser Street Elementary School and carries a Jetsons lunchbox to school. Mr. Bear is her favorite plush toy, and Emily is her favorite doll. When the kids at school made fun of her name and called her "Step on Me," she temporarily changed her name to Dawn. During the taking of the class picture, Stephanie sneezed and was called "Sneeze Burger" by her friends. Stephanie (jersey number 8) was a member of the Giants Little League team (coached by Danny) "and throws a curveball like no other girl." She called the throw the "Tanner Twister." Stephanie is a Capricorn, and her catchphrase is "How rude." When she was five, Stephanie thought D.J. was born so she could have someone to play with. Stephanie, who was a member of the Honeybees Scout troop, did a television commercial for Oat Boats Cereal. *Charlotte's Web* is Stephanie's favorite book, and pizza and frozen strawberry yogurt are her favorite foods.

Michelle Elizabeth is the baby of the family. She first attended Meadowcrest Preschool, then Fraser Street Elementary. On her first day in preschool, she let the class bird, Dave, out of his cage and he flew away. Michelle's first punishment (for setting up her swimming pool in the kitchen) was sitting in the corner and staring at the wall. She had an "invisible friend" named Glen and eats Honey Coated Fiber Bears breakfast cereal. She also served as Officer Michelle of the Polite Police in school. Martin and Frankie are the names of her goldfish, and her catchphrase is "You got it, dude." Her favorite movie is *The Little Mermaid.*

Jesse, whose heritage is Greek, has the real first name of Hermes (he was teased so much in school that he begged his mother to change it to Jesse; Hermes was Jesse's great-grandfather's name). He also has two last names—Cochran (when the series began) and Katsopolis (from the second season). Jesse is partners with Joey in a commercial jingle writing company called J.J. Creative Services (later changed to Double J. Creative Services). Jesse, whose music idol is Elvis Presley, has a band called Jesse and the Rippers (who play at the Smash Club). In high school (Golden Bay Union High, class of '80), he was part of a band called Disciplinary Action. He was later with a band called Feedback. He also rode a motorcycle and was known as Dr. Dare (he would take on any dare). The high school band was called Discipline Problem in another episode.

On his first day in preschool, Jesse was goldfish monitor and killed the fish when he took it home without the bowl. He was called "Zorba the Geek" by kids, and his first love was Carrie Fowler (Erika Eleniak), whom he met at the dentist's office and whom he dated through high school; their

song was "Muskrat Love." He later fell in love with and married Rebecca Donaldson. Bubba is Jesse's pet turtle, and his favorite expression is "Have mercy." Prior to becoming partners with Joey, Jesse worked with his father in the bug exterminating business (he calls himself a "pest control specialist"). He buys Elvis Peanut Butter (Hunka Hunka Chunka type). Jesse calls his Mustang convertible (license plate RDV 913) Sally.

Joey is a talented standup comic and cartoon voice impersonator who's hoping for his big break. He appeared on "Star Search" and did a pilot called "Surf's Up" with Annette Funicello and Frankie Avalon (Joey was Flip, the surfer-dude mailman; Frankie and Annette owned the beachside restaurant). The live action format was dropped for a cartoon version with Joey as Flip, the surfing kangaroo, and Frankie and Annette as dolphins. Joey then made a pilot called "The Mr. Egghead Show," with Jesse as the music professor. In the episode of 10/22/91, Joey became the host of "The Ranger Joe Show" on Channel 8 (he had a hand puppet named Mr. Woodchuck and entertained kids from the Enchanted Forest; Jesse became a regular as Lumberjack Jesse). Joey and Jesse were members of the Chi Sigma Sigma fraternity in college (their mascot was a seal). Joey has a 1963 Rambler he calls Rosie (license plate JJE 805), and his favorite expression is "Cut it out."

Rebecca was born on a farm in Valentine, Nebraska (where she had a pet cow named Janice). Rebecca married Jesse in the episode of 2/15/91, and they honeymooned in Bora Bora. They first moved into Rebecca's apartment (a ten minute walk from Danny's house); however, when Jesse began to miss the family, he and Rebecca moved into a converted attic apartment at Danny's house. Rebecca's engagement ring is inscribed with the words LOVE ME TENDER, and the last "crazy thing" Jesse did before marrying Rebecca was to go skydiving. Jesse wanted to get married at Graceland; Rebecca wanted the ceremony to be held in Montana; they married in San Francisco. Twins named Nicholas and Alexander (Kevin and David Renteria) were born to Rebecca in the episode of 11/12/91. Vickie Lawson (Gail Edwards) replaced Rebecca during her maternity leave as Danny's co-host.

Kimberly ("Kimmy") Louise Gibler is D.J.'s best friend (she attended the same schools). She is very pretty and tends to get D.J. into trouble with her antics. Kimmy calls Danny "Mr. T" and has a French poodle named Cocoa. She and D.J. frequent the Food Court at the mall and Kimmy writes the column "Madame Kimmy's Horoscope" for the school newspaper. Kimmy's favorite movie is *Dirty Dancing* (which she fast-forwards to the kissing scenes). In the second grade Kimmy faked the mumps by stuffing two Hostess Sno-Balls (snack cakes) into her cheeks. Kimmy says, "People say I look like Julia Roberts. I wish I was Madonna. She's rich." Kimmy cuts economics class because "I'm going to marry a doctor and hire a maid"; she later mentions that she has a dog named Sinbad.

The Tanners have a dog named Comet; Friday is "mop the floors till you drop day" at the Tanner house; Hill Top Cable provides cable TV service to the area; Danny hosted the "We Love Our Children Telethon" on Channel 8.

Relatives: Alice Hirson and Doris Roberts (Danny's mother, *Claire Tanner*), Kirk Cameron (Danny's nephew, *Steve Tanner*), Darlene Vogel (Danny's sister, *Wendy Tanner*), Mary Kate Olsen (Michelle's cousin, *Melina Tanner*; while Ashley played Michelle), Rhoda Gemignani and Yvonne Wilder (Jesse's mother, *Irene Katsopolis*), John Aprea (Jesse's father, *Nick Katsopolis*), Beverly Sanders (Joey's mother, *Mindy Gladstone*), Arlen Dean Snyder (Joey's father, *Colonel Gladstone*), Debbie Gregory (Rebecca's sister, *Connie*), Michael John Nunes (Connie's son, *Howie*), Lois Nettleton (Rebecca's mother, *Nedra Donaldson*), Don Hood (Rebecca's father, *Kenneth Donaldson*), Dee Marcus (Rebecca's aunt, *Ida*), Jack Kruschen (Jesse's grandfather, *Iorgos*), Vera Lockwood (Jesse's grandmother, *Gina*), Jennifer Gatti (Jesse's cousin, *Elena*), Josh Blake (Jesse's cousin, *Sylvia*).

Flashbacks: Philip Glasser (*young Danny*), Kristopher Kent Hall (*young Joey*), Adam Harris (*young Jesse*), Christine Houser (Danny's wife, *Pamela*).

Flash Forwards: Melanie Nincz (*adult D.J.*), Julia Montgomery (*adult Stephanie*), Jayne Modean (*adult Michelle*), Rhoda Shear (*adult Kimmy*).

Theme: "Everywhere You Look," vocal by Jesse Frederick.

Funny Face see The Sandy Duncan Show

239. Gabriel's Fire

ABC, 9/12/90 to 5/1/91

Cast: James Earl Jones (*Gabriel Bird*), Laila Robins (*Victoria Heller*), Madge Sinclair (*Josephine Austin*), Dylan Walsh (*Louis Klein*).

Facts: Gabriel ("Gabe") Bird served in Korea during the war and was decorated four times. He came home to Chicago, attended junior college and enrolled in the police academy in 1959. For nine years he was a beat cop and dedicated to the force. He was determined to advance the cause of the black man within the system. Neighborhood people felt safe and looked up to him. In 1969 Bird was assigned to the new State's Attorney Prosecuting Team. He was the only black man in the unit.

At 4:45 A.M. on December 21, 1969, the unit raided an apartment on Hampton Street, an address believed to be the armed headquarters of the Black Liberation Army. It was a witch hunt—but Bird didn't know it. Inside the apartment was the family of John C. Elner. Elner and his two brothers were killed by Bird's partner. Just as his partner was about to kill a woman and her child, Gabe killed him. The police department disowned Bird and considered him a Black Liberation supporter. He was convicted of murder one; because of his war record, he was not sentenced to death but received life. Two years into his sentence, his wife divorced him and disappeared. Seven thousand two hundred forty-three days later, an inmate named Ted Duke (Lincoln Kilpatrick) is killed for protesting. While investigating Ted's death, his lawyer, Victoria Heller, meets Gabriel Bird (prison number D-72721). When Victoria discovers what has happened to him, she files a writ of habeas corpus, and case number 2266 is reopened. On day 7,271, Gabe is released.

Josephine Austin owns a restaurant called Empress Josephine's Soul Food Kitchen on Emerald Street. Gabe was the cop on the beat when Josephine's husband died. He came by with candy for the kids and groceries when they needed them. He took the kids to the park and became a substitute father to them.

After having two hot dogs with everything on them (the first thing he does when he is released), Gabe returns to his old neighborhood on Emerald Street. When Josephine sees "a ghost from her past," she repays a favor she never forgot and gives Gabe free room and board in the attic above her restaurant.

Although Gabe is bitter, he helps Victoria find Ted's killer (a recently released ex-con). Gabe then accepts Victoria's offer to work for her as an investigator. Stories relate their case investigations.

Gabe goes to extremes to get his man and keeps a diary of everything he does. He says, "It's a big world out there and I'm having a great time getting to know it again."

Victoria is a tough, dedicated attorney who will fight for any cause she believes in. Her offices are located at 14301 North La Salle Street; 555-4748 is her phone number, and K87-463 is her license plate number. Louis Klein is her partner (Heller & Klein, Attorneys-at-Law).

The series returned for its second season (ABC, 9/26/91 to 1/2/92) as "Pros and Cons." When Victoria leaves her practice to become a judge, Gabe opens his own agency (Gabriel Bird Investigations). Shortly after, he is hired by a woman to follow her husband, who she believes is having an affair. Gabe follows the suspect (a hit man) to Los Angeles, where he sees the man about to shoot private detective Mitch O'Hannon (Richard Crenna). Gabe saves Mitch's life—but loses the suspect when he runs and is killed by a garbage truck. Gabe teams with Mitch to discover that Mitch's secretary, Teri (Randy Graff), used information in a file to blackmail a client (the client thought Mitch was a blackmailer and hired a hit man).

Mitch was previously partners with a man named Pryor (deceased). When Gabe asks Mitch if the vacant chair in his office (605) is available, the firm of Bird and O'Hannon, Private Investigators, is born (their office phone number is 555-6464).

Gabe, who is fond of gardening, buys a house with a backyard at 808 Magnolia Drive. He then asks his love interest, Josephine, to marry him. She accepts and moves to Los Angeles to becomes Mrs. Gabriel Bird on 10/10/91 (Josephine acquires a job as the manager of a restaurant called the Angel City Grill). The Bird and O'Hannon Agency is located at 1122 North Plaza; Gabe's license plate reads 2PEK 674.

Mitch, who lives in apartment 705 at 455 Lane Street,

served in Korea with the 40th Sunburst Unit (Gabe was with the 24th Infantry). His car license plate reads 2NR 1853 (later 2GAT 123).

Relatives: Janet MacLachlan (Gabe's ex-wife, *Ellie Bird*), Michele Richards and Irene Cara (Gabe's daughter, *Celene Bird*; a physician with the World Health Organization in Nigeria), Len Cariou (Victoria's father, *Judge Norton Heller*), Mary Carver (Victoria's grandmother, *Wallis Heller*), Michael Beach (Josephine's son, *Michael Austin*), Maureen O'Sullivan (Mitch's mother, *Barbara O'Hannon*), Don Ameche (Mitch's father, *Mitchell ["Mitch"] O'Hannon, Sr.*; he calls his son "Little Mitch"). Cecelia Hart (James Earl Jones's wife), appeared as Mitch's ex-wife, Lauren.

Flashbacks: Todd Davy *(young Gabe)*, Yvonne Farrow *(young Ellie)*.

Themes: "Gabriel's Fire" and "Pros and Cons," by William Olvis.

Note: The original spinoff for "Gabriel's Fire" was titled "Bird and Katt." In this unaired version, Gabe becomes partners with Peter Katt (Richard Crenna), a retired Chicago police officer.

Galactica 1980 see *Battlestar Galactica*

240. *The Gale Storm Show: Oh! Susanna*

CBS, 9/29/56 to 4/11/59
ABC, 10/1/59 to 3/24/60

The SS *Ocean Queen* is a luxury liner owned by the Reardon Steamship Lines which sets sail from the port of Southampton in England and docks at New York Harbor. Susanna Pomeroy (Gale Storm) is the ship's beautiful social director; Simon Huxley (Roy Roberts) is the captain; and Elvira ("Nugey") Nugent (ZaSu Pitts) is first a manicurist in the beauty salon, then a salesgirl in the souvenir shop.

Susanna teaches dance lessons and deck tennis; she also arranges shuffleboard and bridge matches and does whatever is necessary to keep passengers occupied and happy. Susanna and Nugey look forward to each cruise as a means of meeting men; they also involve themselves in passengers' problems and inevitably cause problems by trying to solve them (the basic format of the series). Once a year, Susanna treats herself to a bottle of perfume that costs $50 an ounce.

Nugey shares a cabin with Susanna. She is rather timid and shy and innocently becomes involved in Susanna's misadventures. As the captain says to her, "I know your aim is not to go through life destroying me; it just works out that way."

The captain, who joined the navy after college, objects to bonuses (he believes it destroys the morale of the other

members of the crew). Simon was awarded a bust of John Paul Jones for his work by the Anglo Globetrotters. Cedric (James Fairfax), the British steward, hides the captain's favorite caviar in his footlocker ("the emergency supply"). The ship's physician is Dr. Eugene Reynolds (Rolfe Sedan); J. Pat O'Malley appeared as Mr. Reardon, the gruff president of the steamship lines. The purser's office was said to be located on C-deck opposite the grand staircase. In the opening theme, the ship sounds its horn once; the ship's bell rings four times; and THE GALE STORM SHOW: OH! SUSANNA is spelled out by the ship's flags.

Leon Klatzkin composed the theme.

In some printed sources, ZaSu Pitts is referred to as Esmerelda Nugent. The series, commonly referred to by *TV Guide* as the "Gale Storm Show" or as "Oh! Susanna" in its listings, has the official screen title as used for this entry.

While Gale Storm had the first series to be set aboard an ocean liner, Larry Storch had the second one: "The Queen and I" ("The Love Boat" was still eight years away). In "The Queen and I" (CBS, 1/16/69 to 5/1/69), Larry Storch was Charles Duffy, a master schemer who was the first mate on the *Amsterdam Queen*, a once famous luxury liner that has fallen on hard times and is now headed for the scrap heap. The ship, which docks at New York Harbor, is a floating paradise to Duffy, and his efforts to save the ship were the focal point of the series. Oliver Nelson (Billy DeWolfe) was the spit-and-polish first officer; Wilma Winslow (Barbara Stuart) was Duffy's love interest; and Captain Washburn (Liam Dunn) was the skipper.

241. *The Gemini Man*

NBC, 9/23/76 to 10/28/76

Cast: Ben Murphy *(Sam Casey)*, Katherine Crawford *(Abby Lawrence)*, Richard Dysart *(Leonard Driscoll)*.

Facts: Federal agent Samuel ("Sam") Casey, born April 16, 1948, in New York City, is a special operative for Intersect, a U.S. government research organization. Sam, who received a juris doctor's degree from Harvard Law School in 1973, has clearance level A-6. When an unidentified satellite falls from the sky and sinks to the ocean floor, Sam is assigned to retrieve it. While attempting to recover the satellite in what is called "Operation Royce Explorer," the satellite explodes and renders Sam invisible when the heavy radiation affects his DNA structure. Intersect doctor Abigail ("Abby") Lawrence saves Sam's life by fitting him with a DNA stabilizer. Sam is later removed from the stabilizer and hooked up to a computer to control his visibility. Shortly after, Abby develops a sophisticated subminiature DNA stabilizer in an atomic battery–powered digital wristband (top secret file 487384). The stabilizer, which looks like a wristwatch, has three gold contacts on its base. When these contacts touch Sam's skin, he remains visible. By pressing on the stem of the watch, Sam can change the frequency and become invisible—but for only 15 minutes a day; any longer and he will disintegrate. Stories relate

Sam's exploits as he uses his invisibility to solve cases for Intersect (International Security Technics).

Leonard Driscoll (played by William Sylvester in the pilot) is Sam's superior (his office phone number is 555-4431). See also "The Invisible Man" (two titles).

Theme: "The Gemini Man," by Lee Holdridge.

242. *Gentle Ben*

CBS, 9/10/67 to 8/31/69

Tom Wedloe (Dennis Weaver) is a game warden in the Florida Everglades. He is married to Ellen (Beth Brickell) and is the father of a young boy named Mark (Clint Howard). Mark attends the Ocheechokee School; they have a pet goat named Charlie and a flamingo they call Pinky. Old Joe is the 12-foot bull alligator who lives in the swamp near their home. Tom patrols the Everglades in an air boat (he has a Jeep for land patrol, but its license plate is either missing or too caked with mud to read). There is one other member of the family: Mark's pet, Ben, a 600-pound black bear. (Several months earlier, Mark was exploring the Bear River Game Reserve when he stumbled upon a bear cub. He was suddenly confronted by its angry mother and climbed to the safety of a tree. Seconds later, a hunter named Fog Hanson shot the bear. Unaware of Mark's presence, Fog took the cub. When Mark discovered that Fog was keeping the cub in a waterfront shack, he befriended it by sneaking in to feed it. He named the cub Ben. Later, when Ben was grown, Mark overheard Fog talking about killing the bear, so he asked his father to buy Ben for him. Tom did when he accepted the position of game warden in the Everglades.)

Vera Miles played Ellen in the pilot, and Ralph Meeker was Fog Hanson. Harry Sukman composed the "Gentle Ben" theme.

243. *The George Burns and Gracie Allen Show*

CBS, 9/12/50 to 9/22/58

Cast: George Burns, Gracie Allen, Ronnie Burns and Harry Von Zell (themselves), Bea Benaderet *(Blanche Morton)*, Larry Keating *(Harry Morton)*.

Facts: "I'm George Burns, Gracie Allen's husband. I'm a straightman"—these were the first words George spoke to introduce his first television series to viewers. Gracie is a comedienne and scatterbrained. She has a knack for confusing people and complicating the simplest situations. George is level-headed and knows that if it weren't for Gracie's antics, "I'd still be selling ties."

George and Gracie live at 312 Maple Street in Beverly Hills, California, with their son, Ronnie. (In New York–based episodes, George and Gracie lived in Suite 2216 of the St. Moritz Hotel.) Gracie planted a hedge in the front windowbox when they first moved into their home (she trims it with George's electric razor).

George and Gracie met while performing in vaudeville in the 1920s. When George first dated Gracie, he gave her flowers (which Gracie pressed between the pages of the book *A Report on the Sheep Herding Industry*). They married, according to Gracie, due to the meat shortage. (Gracie had invited George over for dinner one night in 1927. When Gracie's mother had only enough steaks to feed four of the six people waiting for dinner, she told Gracie to elope—and so she and George did.) They were married in Cleveland, and George's friend, Jack Benny, was the witness. Gracie mentions in another episode that her mother was also at the wedding and cried all through the ceremony. Gracie's mother dislikes George and was actually crying because she had to miss the premiere of *The Sheik*, with Rudolph Valentino. George and Gracie first lived at the Edison Hotel in New York City for three years before buying their home in California.

Gracie wrote her first article, "My Life with George Burns," for *Look* magazine in 1952. (She had to type two copies; she tried using carbon paper, "but it's black and you can't see what you type on it." She also has a theory about misspelled words: she won't use that word again, "so I won't make the same mistake twice.")

According to George, Gracie inherited her writing ability from her uncle, Harvey. He was the first one in the family to write an article ("Famous Forgers and How They Work") but didn't get paid for it: "By force of habit he signed someone else's name." The never-seen Uncle Harvey is a frequent resident of the San Quentin Prison (every time Gracie mentions him, he is in jail). Gracie's never-seen mother, who lives in San Francisco, has the phone number Market 1-0048.

George is a member of the Friars' Club and is famous for "The Pause" that he developed after Gracie's response to one of his questions. George tries to discourage salesmen from coming to the house: "You heard of the play *Death of a Salesman*? Well, trying to sell Gracie something is what killed him." Gracie believes she is well versed on worldly matters and even knows what's in yesterday's newspaper ("I should, I wrapped the garbage in it myself"). Gracie, who sews up the buttonholes on George's shirts so that no one will know the buttons are missing, believes that her father is younger than her husband ("I met my husband when he was 30; I first saw my father when he was 24"). When George and Gracie go to the movies, they sometimes have to sit through the film twice ("Gracie wants the movie and her popcorn to end at the same time").

George and Gracie's neighbors, Blanche and Harry Morton, live at 314 Maple Street; they have been neighbors for 12 years. Blanche grew up on Elm Street in Seattle; Harry, a CPA, went to Dartmouth and will drink only one alcoholic beverage—blackberry cordial. In 1953 it was mentioned that the Mortons were married for 13 years; a 1952 episode mentions that George and Gracie were married for 25 years.

Before Larry Keating played Harry, Hal March, John Brown, Bob Sweeney and Fred Clark played the role. Harry was first an insurance salesman, then a real estate salesman and finally an accountant.

Bill Goodwin (himself), a ladies' man, was George's first announcer; he was replaced by Harry Von Zell, who frequently found himself the pawn in George's efforts to resolve problems arising from Gracie's antics. Ronnie attends UCLA in later episodes; Bonnie Sue McAfee (Judi Meredith) is his girlfriend; and Ralph Grainger (Robert Ellis) is his best friend. Many of the episodes in syndication include references to the show's longtime sponsor, Carnation Milk (cans can be seen in kitchen shots, and Gracie was confused by the product—"How do they get milk from carnations?"). When Gracie retired from show business in 1958, the series continued on NBC as "The George Burns Show" (10/21/58 to 4/14/59), with George playing himself as a theatrical producer. Ronnie Burns, Bea Benaderet, Larry Keating and Harry Von Zell continued their roles from the earlier series.

Relatives: Sarah Selby (Gracie's married sister, *Mamie Kelly*), Jeri James (Mamie's daughter, *Jeri*), Jill Oppenheim (Mamie's daughter, *Jill*), Linda Plowman (Mamie's daughter, *Linda*), Russell Hicks (Harry's father, *Harry Morton, Sr.*), King Donovan (Blanche's brother, *Roger*), Ann Steffins (Blanche's niece, *Linda*).

Theme: "Love Nest," played first by Leith Stevens, then Mahlon Merrick.

244. *Get a Life*

Fox, 9/23/90 to 5/31/92

Cast: Chris Elliott (*Chris Peterson*), Bob Elliott (*Fred Peterson*), Elinor Donahue (*Gladys Peterson*), Sam Robards (*Larry T. Potter III*), Robin Riker (*Sharon Potter*).

Facts: The locale is Greenville, a small town in Minnesota. Our "hero" is Chris Peterson, a 30-year-old who never forgot what it is like to be a kid. Chris is a newspaper delivery boy for the *Pioneer Press*. His parents, Fred and Gladys, believe "he is like a diamond in the rough that needs polishing" (in other words, Fred says, "an idiot"). Larry Potter, his friend and neighbor, believes "Chris is a gas-headed idiot who gets on everyone's nerves"; Larry's wife, Sharon, knows "Chris is an idiot and has disgusting Chris microbes." Chris believes and says, "I have a happy-go-lucky outlook on life. I'm happy being an idiot."

Our tale of an idiot began in 1971 when Chris wanted to buy a Neptune 2000 submarine from an ad at the back of a comic book. To pay for it, he got a job as a paperboy. Twenty years later, Chris is still a paperboy—and the sub finally arrived in the mail (it runs on 54 "D" batteries). Chris is a failure at everything, but he is the last one to realize it. He watches the show "Fraggle Rock" every morning, believes Daryl Hannah is the greatest actress since Lillian Gish and worries that the local video store will be discontinuing the X-rated section ("I can't tell you how many nights I lost sleep over that").

Chris has a ventriloquist doll he calls Mr. Poppy, and he has been "psychotically obsessed" with a girl named Stacey (Katherine Kahmi) since the sixth grade. His male ancestors dressed as women to get off the *Titanic*, he likes turkey—"but the dark meat"—and his proudest moment occurred when he had his picture taken with Adam West at an auto show.

Chris believes that he was meant to be many things but was dealt a cruel hand by fate. He attempted to become a male model by enrolling in the Handsome Boy Modeling School. He took the name "Sparkles" Peterson, crashed the model show at Dresler's Department Store and, while attempting to live his dream of being a male model, achieved another failure. Thinking he was meant to be an actor, Chris landed the role of the lead (a wildebeest) in "Zoo Animals on Wheels" at the Greenville Musical Theater.

Our "aging Dennis the Menace" (as Larry calls him) lives in a room above the garage at his parents' home at 1341 Meadow Brooke Lane. Peach is his favorite color; "The Family Circus" is his favorite comic strip; his favorite television show is "Sandy's Laff and Song Jackpot" (hosted by Martin Mull as Sandy Connors); and his favorite Bugs Bunny cartoon is "the one where Daffy tries to get Bugs killed by the hunters."

Chris has been a paperboy for 20 years. He was almost replaced by the Paperboy 2000, an automatic robot that delivers papers. The paper sought to save four dollars a week by firing the boys and using the robot (the machine proved defective and became a killer when its tires were kicked). Chris's phone number is 555-9034.

In the opening theme, Chris is seen riding his bicycle and delivering papers. When he spies his ultrasexy neighbor, Patti (Lee Garlington), he throws the paper on the ground in front of her. Patti, wearing a short black negligee, bends over to pick up the paper. Chris crashes his bike into a parked car as he watches her.

Fred, who was born in Chicago, and Gladys, an army brat, are Chris's parents. Their wardrobe mainly consists of bathrobes, which they wear virtually everywhere. They eat breakfast off presidential commemorative plates and use Mrs. Butterworth's pancake syrup. Chris and Fred enter the newsboy father and son gladiator competition every year. They won the 1990 event by breaking all the rules. Fred's license plate reads IRC 522.

When Chris turned 31 (11/19/91), he moved into the garage of Gus Borden (Brian Doyle-Murray), an embittered ex-cop with a drinking problem. Gus, who reads the girlie magazine *Thigh World*, lives at 1804 York Avenue; Chris pays him $150 a month rent.

Chris's neighbors, Larry and Sharon Potter, live at 1343 Meadow Brooke Lane and have two children, Amy (Taylor Fry) and Bobby (Bradley Bluhm, then Zachary Benjamin). Larry works as an accountant for the firm of Bushman and Simon. He also hems Sharon's dresses and makes homemade taffy with the kids. Sharon considers Chris to be her worst enemy in life. She has "idiot proofed" the house to keep Chris out. Each year, Sharon bakes chocolate divinity squares and distributes them to the neighbors.

Chris's Relatives: James Keane (*Uncle Milt Peterson*), Jackie Earle Haley (*Cousin Donald Peterson*), Bill Cort

Uncle Sid Peterson), David Wiley *(Uncle Brad Peterson)*, Pat Crawford Brown *(Aunt Molly Peterson)*, Bibi Osterwald *(Aunt Jilly Peterson)*, Marte Boyle Slout *(Aunt Kathy Peterson)*.

Flashbacks: Brandon Crane *(Chris age 12)*.

Themes: "Stand" (opening), by R.E.M.; "Get a Life" (close), by Stewart Levin.

245. *Get Christie Love*

ABC, 9/11/74 to 7/18/75

"You're under arrest, Sugah" and "Drop that gun, Sugah" are two of the catchphrases used by Christine ("Christie") Love (Teresa Graves), a gorgeous undercover policewoman with the Homicide Division, Metro Bureau of the L.A.P.D.

Christie considers her beauty, charm, wit and understanding of human nature as her "weapons." Her badge number is 7332, and she lives at 3600 La Paloma Drive. Her phone number is 462-4699, and her license plate reads 343 MCI (later 089 LIR). Christie's favorite eatery is Papa Caruso's Restaurant. She keeps her shooting skills sharp by practicing at a range called Hogan's Alley. She never shoots to kill— "Just enough to stop 'em."

Lieutenant Joseph ("Joe") Caruso (Andy Romano) is Christie's partner (their car code is 5-Baker-5). Although Joe says, "My partner here is a mean lady," Christie tends to panic when she gets in a tight situation and scream.

Arthur P. Ryan (Jack Kelly) is Christie's superior (his car code is 10-William-10). In the pilot episode (ABC, 1/22/74), Andy Romano played Sergeant Seymour Greenberg, and Harry Guardino was the captain, Casey Reardon. Titos Vandis played Joe's father, "Papa" Luigi Caruso, the restaurant owner.

Luchi DeJesus composed the theme.

246. *Get Smart*

NBC, 9/18/65 to 9/13/69
CBS, 9/26/69 to 9/11/70

Cast: Don Adams *(Maxwell Smart)*, Barbara Feldon *(Agent 99)*, Edward Platt *(Chief)*, Bernie Kopell *(Conrad Siegfried)*.

Facts: When an evil organization called KAOS threatens to destroy all that is good in the world, the U.S. government establishes CONTROL, a secret organization designed to stop KAOS. Admiral Harold Harmon Hargrade (William Schallert) is appointed to head CONTROL. When the series begins, Hargrade has retired, and a man identified only as Thaddeus is the head of CONTROL (he is most often called "Chief"). Maxwell Smart, Agent 86, and Agent 99 (real name never revealed) are CONTROL's top operatives. Max is a bumbling klutz; 99 is an agent with beauty as well as brains who uses various aliases to protect her true identity

(even after 99 and Max marry, Max continues to call her 99 and her mother, "99's mother" or "Mrs. 99"). Max uses the cover of Maxwell Smart, a salesman for the Pontiac Greeting Card Company; the Chief poses as his boss, Howard Clark.

Max and 99 were voted "Spy Couple of the Year" in 1968. Max believes that his constant vigilance and razor-sharp instincts are the "weapons" he possesses to defeat KAOS. Max wears a size 40 regular jacket and has a standard issue shoe phone (the Chief's means of contacting Max in the field). Max has a midnight snack before he goes to bed and uses the password *Bismark* for entry into his booby-trapped apartment. Max drives a red sports car with the license plate 6A7-379 and became famous for the catchphrases "Sorry about that, Chief," "Would you believe..." and "I asked you not to tell me that."

CONTROL is located at 123 Main Street in Washington, D.C.; 555-3734 is its phone number. The seldom-working Cone of Silence is the agency's antibugging device; and CONTROL's top "male" agent is the beautiful Charlie Watkins. As played by Angelique Pettyjohn, Charlie is supposedly a man in drag. (Max didn't believe it either. After a short career in television, Pettyjohn, who appeared on such shows as "The Felony Squad," "Star Trek" and "Bracken's World," turned to X-rated films and appeared in such movies as *Body Talk* and *Titillation*).

Other featured CONTROL agents are Larrabee (Robert Karvelas), the Chief's dim-witted aide; Agent 13 (Dave Ketchum); Agent 44 (Victor French); Hymie the Robot (Dick Gautier); and Fang (the dog agent). Hymie is a former KAOS robot that has been programed for good by CONTROL. He is assigned most often to Max, and his only fault is that he takes everything he is told to do literally. Agent 13 goes undercover wherever he can find a place to hide (for example, in a mailbox, a desk drawer, a grandfather clock).

Conrad Siegfried is the dastardly head of KAOS (whose symbol is a vulture standing on top of the world). Siegfried is assisted by the bumbling Schtarker (King Moody) and has set his goal to "get Schmart."

In 1974 the government closes CONTROL, and stores its records in a warehouse at 96427 43rd Street in Washington. Fifteen years later, KAOS again creates havoc when it steals a weather machine from the U.S. government and threatens to destroy the world. Thus was born the television movie *Get Smart, Again* (ABC, 2/26/89). Commander Drury (Ken Mars), the head of U.S. Intelligence, decides to reactivate CONTROL to stop KAOS. Max is now a protocol officer for the State Department; 99 is writing her memoirs in a book called *Out of Control*; Hymie has been working as a crash dummy for the National Car Testing Institute; and Agent 13 has been doing various undercover assignments for the government. Drury's phone number is 555-3931; Hover Cover (a meeting on the roof over the noise of three helicopters) and the Hall of Hush (where one's words can be seen as one speaks) replaced the Cone of Silence as the antibugging devices.

Relatives: Jane Dulo *(99's mother)*, Charles Lane (Max's uncle, *Albert*), Maudie Prickett (Max's aunt, *Bertha*).

Theme: "Get Smart," by Irving Szathmary.

247. *The Ghost and Mrs. Muir*

NBC, 9/21/68 to 9/6/69
ABC, 9/18/69 to 9/18/70

Cast: Hope Lange *(Carolyn Muir)*, Edward Mulhare *(Daniel Gregg)*, Kellie Flanagan *(Candy Muir)*, Harlen Carraher *(Jonathan Muir)*, Charles Nelson Reilly *(Claymore Gregg)*, Reta Shaw *(Martha Grant)*.

Facts: In the 1800s, a sea captain named Daniel Gregg settled in a small New England town called Schooner Bay. He built a house he called Gull Cottage and planned to turn it into a home for retired sailors. One night as a southwest gale approached town, the Captain closed his bedroom window. While sleeping, Daniel "kicked the blasted gas heater with my blasted foot" and was killed by the escaping fumes. The coroner's jury brought in a verdict of suicide because "my confounded cleaning woman testified that I always slept with my windows open."

As the years passed, Gull Cottage remained intact—believed to be haunted by Captain Gregg's ghost and unrentable. The cottage eventually fell into the hands of Claymore Gregg, the Captain's wimpy descendent, who runs Claymore Gregg Real Estate Sales and Services (he is also the justice of the peace and the town's notary public). In a last-ditch attempt to save Gull Cottage (the state is threatening to seize the property for nonpayment of taxes), Claymore leases it to Carolyn Muir, an attractive widow with two children (Candy and Jonathan) and a housekeeper (Martha). Carolyn, a freelance magazine writer, previously lived in Philadelphia and has come to New England to begin a new life. Despite its reputation, Carolyn sees the cottage as charming: "It's exactly what I had in mind, a dear, gentle, lovely little house."

As Carolyn and her family settle into the house, the rumblings of Captain Gregg can be heard. When Carolyn decides to make Daniel's old room ("The Captain's Cabin") her bedroom, she has her first confrontation with the Captain.

"Now that we're moved in," Carolyn explains, "I hope you'll be kind enough to do your haunting elsewhere." "You do your living elsewhere," the Captain responds. "I spent my life's savings on this house." "We can't," explains Carolyn. "We spent all our savings to move here" (she begins to cry). "Don't cry," Daniel says. "I could never stand to see a woman cry." As Carolyn composes herself, she explains that "the minute I saw this house I seemed to belong here. It's as though it was welcoming me, asking me to rescue it from being empty." "You love this house," the Captain says; "that counts for you. And you have spunk; that counts for you too. You can stay." An appreciative Carolyn responds simply, "Thank you."

That night, as Carolyn sleeps, the Captain appears in her bedroom. As he looks at her, we learn of a love that can never be. "I never once allowed a woman aboard my ship. If I had met you a hundred years ago, I would have carried you off to sea and shown you how beautiful the world can be. I've met my match in you. Lord knows, I've waited for

you and hunted for you. How was I to know you were not even born yet? No, you won't remember any of this when you wake up, Madame . . . How sad that you were not born in my time, nor I in yours."

In his time, the Captain was a ladies' man and had a girl in every port. He was also a scoundrel, as he calls himself, and was "never tied to an apron string." (In the episode "Vanessa," it is learned that the Captain did have one true love in the 1840s, an enchanting girl named Vanessa, who had "hair like a storm at midnight, eyes like black pearls from the ocean depths, and a voice like an angel-soft wind"—a memory that came to life for him when Vanessa Peekskill [Shelley Fabares] came to Gull Cottage. She had letters written by Captain Gregg to her great-great-grandmother and sought to do research on the Captain.) The Captain now wishes only for peace and quiet, but seldom finds it. He calls Carolyn "Madame," and his favorite expressions are "Blast" and "Blasted." The porch above Carolyn's bedroom is his bridge (he stands watch on it each night); his treasured telescope remains in Carolyn's bedroom; and the wheel house (attic) is the last retreat the Captain has. A monkey puzzle tree, which the Captain planted 100 years ago, stands on the lawn in front of the house.

When it comes to Claymore, the Captain is seldom composed, especially when Claymore impersonates him (for example, when Carolyn's parents visit; they believe she is in love with a sea captain). The Captain doesn't believe Claymore is related to him: "I'm the only son of an only son. I never met Claymore's grandmother. I've been trying to tell him that for years, but every time he sees me, he faints." Claymore calls the Captain his great-uncle (in some episodes, the Captain calls Claymore his nephew).

Candy (Candice) and Jonathan attend the Schooner Bay School and have a dog named Scruffy. Martha calls the Captain "The Old Barnacle."

Norrie Coolidge (Dabbs Greer) owns the Lobster House Restaurant; Ed Peevey (Guy Raymond) is the town's handyman (he charges $1.75 an hour).

Relatives: Jane Wyatt (Carolyn's mother, *Emily*), Leon Ames (Carolyn's father, *Brad*), Jack Gilford (Carolyn's uncle, *Arnold*).

Theme: "The Ghost and Mrs. Muir," by Dave Grusin.

248. *The Ghost Busters*

CBS, 9/6/75 to 9/4/76

Cast: Forrest Tucker *(Kong)*, Larry Storch *(Eddie Spenser)*, Bob Burns *(Tracy)*.

Facts: "Spenser, Tracy and Kong: Ghost Busters" is the name of the company. Kong (no other name given), Eddie Spenser and Tracy (a trained gorilla) are its operatives. They have offices in a somewhat rundown building, drive a 1920 Ford touring car with the license plate GB (ghost busters) and enjoy seeing movies at the Bijou Theater.

Their superior is the never-seen Mr. Zero, a tape-recorded

The Ghost and Mrs. Muir. Left side: Kellie Flanagan and Charles Nelson Reilly; right side: Harlan Carraher, Hope Lange and Edward Mulhare.

voice that gives them their assignment (as on "Mission: Impossible"). Spenser and Tracy (the driver) pick up their assignments at a hardware store called LeChler's. The tape is hidden in the most unlikely places (such as a rubber fish, a bouquet of flowers, a bicycle wheel). After the assignment is given, it concludes with "This tape will self-destruct in five seconds." In each episode, a disbelieving Tracy tempts fate by counting off the seconds; whether it is three seconds or eight seconds, the message always blows up in his face.

With an assignment in hand, the trio attempts to de-energize ghosts with their unique Ghost Dematerializer (a ray gun type of weapon). The Old House, the Castle, or the

Graveyard are the haunts of the series' ghostly manifestations (such as the cowardly Simon de Canterville [Ted Knight], the ghost of the Werewolf [Lennie Weinrib] and Big Al Caesar [Larry Storch in a dual role], the spirit of a gangster).

With the exception of Tracy (who has a wardrobe of hats), the characters appear in the same outfits in each episode. Kong wears a vest over a sweatshirt (with the number five on it); Spenser wears a 1940s style zoot suit. Spenser attended Camp Gitchagoomie as a kid, has a never-seen girlfriend named Mabel and his favorite movie is *Wings Over Hoboken*. The cowardly Tracy is an excellent bowler (can bowl 300 with a golfball), ball player (even though he can't hit, he scores home runs—"You gonna tell him he can't hit?") and artist (his pictures are so lifelike that they actually come to life). In one episode, Tracy fell in love with a client, the beautiful Carla Canterville (Kathy Garver), when she hired the team to rid her castle of the ghost of Simon de Canterville.

In the opening theme, Larry Storch is credited as Spen*c*er; on their office door, the name reads Spen*s*er.

Theme: "The Ghost Busters," vocal by Forrest Tucker and Larry Storch (written by Diane Hildebrand and Jackie Mills).

249. *Ghostwriter*

PBS, 10/4/92 to the present

Lenni Frazier (Blaze Berdahl), Jamal Jenkins (Sheldon Turnipseed), Alejandro ("Alex") Fernandez (David Lopez), Gabriella ("Gaby") Fernandez, Alex's sister, (Mayteana Morales), and Tina Nuen (Tram-Ahn Tran) are friends who live in Brooklyn, New York. Lenni, Jamal and Alex attend the Zora Neale Hurston Middle School; Gaby and Tina attend Washington Elementary School.

One day, while moving a very old trunk in the basement of his home, Jamal unknowingly knocks over a book. Seconds later, a mysterious light emerges from the book. The light, unnoticed by Jamal, travels throughout the house and takes refuge in Jamal's computer. Later, when Jamal attempts to use his computer, he finds that he is receiving messages from an unknown source. Through questions typed into the computer, Jamal learns that the spirit can speak to him only through written or printed words and is dedicated to helping children. The spirit appears to be very old (it is not familiar with modern technology); it is also unsure of what it is (male or female) and has no recollection of a past life. Jamal contacts his friend Lenni and shows her what he has discovered. They name the spirit Ghostwriter.

When Gaby becomes a victim of THABTO, a mysterious gang of kids who wear double-faced masks, and her lunch money and schoolbag are stolen, Lenni and Jamal decide to investigate. With Ghostwriter's help, they recruit Alex, Gaby and Tina and expose the gang (THABTO stood for Two Heads Are Better Than One). Members of the Ghostwriter Team, as they call themselves, now work as amateur detectives to solve crimes.

Ghostwriter is not bound to a computer; it can rearrange any word that it sees and communicate with team members in this manner (team members can ask Ghostwriter a question by writing it out on a piece of paper; Ghostwriter will rearrange the words to answer them). Each team member carries a felt-tip pen necklace and uses the word *Rally* with an initial (for example, Rally L—L for Lenni) to arrange a meeting (Ghostwriter picks up on this and alerts the other team members).

Lenni, a talented young musician and songwriter, composed a song called "Friends Forever." She lives at 361 East 46th Street with her widowed father, Max (Richard Cox), and her late mother was named Colleen. Alex and Gaby share a bedroom in a small house at 1102 East 33rd Street; when they lived in El Salvador, Alex had a pet chicken named Naomi (Alex was three years old at the time). Gaby and Tina are also reporters for their school newspaper (Gaby is the reporter and Tina the videographer; Tina carries a camcorder with her at all times). Jamal lives with his Grandma Jenkins (Marcella Lowery), a post office worker, at 11 East 39th Street.

Each program is 60 minutes long but is composed of two 30-minute episodes—a repeat and a first-run episode (the repeat is the previous week's first-run episode; if, for example, chapters 2 and 3 aired this week, chapter 3 would be repeated next week, with chapter 4 as the first-run episode).

Peter Wetzler composed the "Ghostwriter" theme.

250. *Gidget*

ABC, 9/15/65 to 9/1/66

Cast: Sally Field *(Gidget Lawrence)*, Don Porter *(Russell Lawrence)*, Peter Deuel *(John Cooper)*, Betty Conner *(Anne Cooper)*, Lynette Winter *(Larue)*.

Facts: "For 15½ years my life was a complete and total ick. But then on the twenty-third of June two things happened. I fell in love with two things: Jeff, my Moondoggie, and surfing." These are the first words we hear from Frances Lawrence, a pretty teenage girl who is nicknamed Gidget ("a girl who is neither tall or a midget—a Gidget").

Gidget resides at 803 North Dutton Drive in Santa Monica, California, with her widowed father, Russell, an English professor at UCLA; their phone number is Granite 5-5099, later 477-0599. Gidget attends Westside High School, and her best friend is Larue. At school Gidget is president of the Civics Club and author of the "Helpful Hannah" advice column for the newspaper, the *Westside Jester*. The hamburger/soda shops, The Shack, The Shaggy Dog and Pop's are Gidget and Larue's afterschool hangouts. Gidget performed with a rock group called The Young People (later changed to Gidget and the Gorries), and she sees movies at the Spring Street Theater. Her slang for goodbye is "Tootles." Gidget is the only one who is aware of a viewing audience, and she speaks directly to it. Gidget and Larue like to eat snacks right before dinner, and Larue, whose number one passion is horseback riding, has an old

The Ghost Busters. Forrest Tucker, Larry Storch and Tracy the Gorilla.

gelding named Snowball. Gidget's father calls her "Gidge" and "Francie."

Gidget's first love is surfing, which she enjoys doing at Malibu Beach. Larue, on the other hand, is allergic to the sun and rarely wears a bathing suit (she protects herself with large hats and lightweight clothes; Gidget loves to wear two piece bathing suits that cover a bit more than a bikini).

Jeffrey ("Jeff") Matthews (Stephen Mines), who is nicknamed "Moondoggie," is Gidget's second love. He is two years older than Gidget and attends Princeton University. Other friends of Gidget are the well-endowed Eleanor Chest (Beverly Adams), who is called "Treasure Chest" by the boys; Janie Carmichael (Bonnie Franklin), Shirley Marshall (Beverly Washburn) and Peter ("Siddo") Stone (Mike Nader).

Anne ("Annie") Cooper is Gidget's older sister. She is married to John, and they live in Apartment 417 (address not given). Anne considers Gidget to be "my little sister" and takes on the role of a mother figure ("I know Annie means well," Gidget says, "but I wish she would stop being my mother"). John is a graduate student pursuing his master's degree in psychology (he finds Gidget and her friends to be the perfect research material). Gidget thinks John is a bit "whacko and it is going to be a contest to see whether they'll let him practice or put him away."

The world's greatest surfer, the Great Kahuna (whose real name is Cassius Cobb), is a friend of Gidget's and was played by Martin Milner. When Gidget is on the phone and her father or sister enters the room, she stops what she is saying and warns her friend by saying "Parentville" or "Sisterville."

Relatives: Hazel Court (Jeff's mother, *Laura Matthews*), Hal March (Jeff's father, *Jim Matthews*), Jan Crawford (Larue's cousin, *Roger Haimes*), Paul Lynde (Shirley's father, *Herman Marshall*), Jeff Donnell (Shirley's mother, *Hannah Marshall*).

Theme: "Gidget," vocal by Johnny Tillotson.

Note: See also "The New Gidget." Two pilots were made prior to "The New Gidget": "Gidget Grows Up" (ABC, 12/30/69), with Karen Valentine as Gidget, Paul Petersen as Jeff and Bob Cummings as Lawrence Russell; and "Gidget Gets Married" (ABC, 1/4/72), with Monie Ellis as Gidget, Michael Burns as Jeff and Macdonald Carey as Russell Lawrence.

251. *Gilligan's Island*

CBS, 9/26/64 to 9/3/67

Cast: Alan Hale, Jr. *(the Skipper)*, Bob Denver *(Gilligan)*, Tina Louise *(Ginger)*, Jim Backus *(Thurston Howell III)*, Natalie Schafer *(Lovey Howell)*, Dawn Wells *(Mary Ann)*, Russell Johnson *(the Professor)*.

Facts: The SS *Minnow* is a small sightseeing boat based in Hawaii. Jonas Grumby is its Skipper, and Gilligan is his first mate. On September 26, 1964, a movie star (Ginger Grant), a millionaire and his wife (Thurston and Lovey Howell), a girl from Kansas (Mary Ann Summers) and a professor (Roy Hinkley) charter the *Minnow* for a tour of the islands. Unknown to the Skipper and Gilligan, the Coast Guard has given them an inaccurate forecast for clear sailing. Shortly after leaving the Honolulu Harbor for its three-hour tour, the *Minnow* is hit by a fierce storm at heading 062.

The Skipper's quick thinking saves the lives of his passengers, but Gilligan's bumbling helps to shipwreck the *Minnow* on an uncharted island about 300 miles southeast of Hawaii. The island, once inhabited by a tribe of headhunters called the Kubikai, soon becomes the home of the Shipwrecked Seven when all attempts at rescue fail. Stories relate their efforts to find a way off the island.

The Skipper is a navy man in love with the sea. He lost everything when the *Minnow* was beached but has high hopes of buying a new boat and beginning a new business when rescued. He calls Gilligan his "Little Buddy" (he hits him on the head with his captain's hat when Gilligan annoys him).

Gilligan (first name never revealed) was born in Pennsylvania. His favorite dessert is coconut, papaya and tuna fish pie. He has a pet duck named Gretchen, a lucky rabbit's foot that seems to be anything but lucky and a solid steel four-leaf clover. Gilligan's image, carved in wood, graces the top of a Kubikai totem pole (the natives believe that he is their once noble chief who has come back to life). Gilligan's best friend stateside was Skinny Mulligan.

Thurston Howell III, called the "Wolf of Wall Street," and his wife, Lovey (the former Lovey Wentworth), are multimillionaires who packed a fabulous wardrobe and several hundred thousand dollars in cash for their three-hour tour (Ginger, by contrast, had virtually nothing and had to make a dress from the sail of the *Minnow*). Thurston, the head of Howell Industries, has a teddy bear named Teddy (his security blanket), a favorite stock called Amalgamated and a practice polo pony the Professor made for him named Bruce. The New York Stock Exchange is his favorite club, and the Social Register is his favorite reading matter. Thurston is very particular about his bath, which must occur at 8:05 P.M. with a water temperature a consistent 79 degrees. He attended SMU (Super Millionaires University), and if he were given a choice of giving up his money or his wife, he'd give up his wife. He and Lovey are also members of the Newport Country Club. In one episode, Thurston included the castaways in his will. He gave the Skipper 40 acres of land in downtown Denver, Colorado; Gilligan, an oil well; Ginger, a diamond mine; Mary Ann, a plantation; and the Professor, the Transcontinental Railroad. Lovey was once voted "Queen of the Pitted Prune Bowl Parade."

Ginger is a gorgeous movie actress who measures 38-27-35 (36-25-36) in another episode. She broke into show business in a mind-reading act with Merlin the Mind Reader. Ginger was voted "Miss Hour Glass" ("They said I had all the sand in the right places") and appeared in the following movies: *San Quentin Blues, Sing a Song of Sing Sing, Belly Dancers from Bali Bali, The Rain Dancers of Rango Rango* and *Mohawk Over the Moon* (the last picture she made before the shipwreck). Tina Louise played Eva Grubb, Ginger's double in one episode.

Mary Ann was born on a farm in Horners Corners, Kansas (also given as Winfield, Kansas). She is a pretty clerk whose knowledge of planting and crops helped greatly in adding vegetables to the castaways' diet of fish and fruit. In one episode, Mary Ann, Ginger and Lovey formed a singing group called the Honeybees as a ploy to get island visitors the Mosquitos to take them to the mainland. (The band the Wellingtons played Mosquitos Bingo, Bango and Bongo; Les Brown was their leader, Irving.)

The Professor is a well-known and respected high school science teacher whose knowledge and ingenuity made life on the island as modern as possible. He discovered five different mutations of ragweed in his first week on the island; halibut with kumquat sauce is his favorite dessert. On the mainland, he was also a Scout troop leader.

First season episodes also feature Wrong Way Feldman (Hans Conried), a famed World War I flier who has no sense of direction (his plane is *The Spirit of the Bronx*); and Dr. Boris Balinkoff (Vito Scotti), a mad scientist from a nearby island who sought to experiment on the castaways.

There are apparently several pilot versions of the series. Jayne Mansfield was originally chosen to play the Tina Louise role, but it is doubtful that a pilot was ever filmed. It was next reported that a pilot was filmed with nine castaways (the Skipper, Gilligan and seven passengers). When this failed, two reworked pilots were made to feature seven castaways—one as we know them today, one with a slightly different cast: Alan Hale, Jr. (the Skipper), Bob Denver (Gilligan), Jim Backus (Thurston Howell III), Natalie Schafer (Lovey Howell), Kit Smythe (Ginger), Nancy McCarthy (Bunny) and John Gabriel (the Professor). In this version, Ginger and Bunny (later to become Mary Ann) are both secretaries. Ginger is a brunette and bright; Bunny is somewhat dim-witted and blonde. Thurston mentioned that he and Lovey are members of the Sunnybrook Yacht Club, and it is learned that the Skipper and Gilligan served in the navy together. The SS *Minnow*, I.D. Number GG12001, set sail for "a six-hour ride" here. Cable station TBS aired this 1964 pilot for the first time on 10/16/92. Producer Sherwood Schwartz mentioned that if Gilligan had a first name, it would have been Willie.

Three television movies were also produced; with the exception of Ginger, the cast remained the same. In *Rescue from Gilligan's Island* (NBC, 10/14 and 10/21/78), the castaways lash their huts together and form an odd-looking raft when a tidal wave hits the island. They are rescued by the Coast Guard and brought to Hawaii. Several months later, they reunite for a cruise on the Skipper's new boat, the *Minnow II*. During the cruise, the ship is caught in a tropical storm, and the seven castaways are again shipwrecked on the same island. Judith Baldwin plays Ginger. *The Castaways on Gilligan's Island* (NBC, 5/3/79) finds the Professor salvaging the parts from two World War II airplanes to make one operable plane. They leave the island, and Mr. Howell later turns it into a tropical resort called the Castaways. Judith Baldwin plays Ginger.

In *The Harlem Globetrotters on Gilligan's Island* (NBC,

5/15/81), the castaways are all partners in the island resort. The story follows their efforts to protect the island from J.J. Pierson (Martin Landau), a madman who wants to control the world with Supermium, a rare mineral he found on the island. Constance Forslund plays Ginger.

Theme: "The Ballad of Gilligan's Isle," vocal by the Wellingtons.

252. *Gimme a Break*

NBC, 10/29/81 to 5/5/87

Cast: Nell Carter (*Nell Harper*), Dolph Sweet (*Carl Kanisky*), Kari Michaelsen (*Katie Kanisky*), Lauri Hendler (*Julie Kanisky*), Lara Jill Miller (*Samantha Kanisky*).

Facts: Margaret Kennedy and Nell Ruth Harper are friends who have not seen each other for many years. By coincidence, they meet at Mr. Funky's Night Club in Glenlawn, California, where Nell is performing (as a singer) and where Margaret and her husband, police officer Carl Kanisky, have come for dinner. The reunion ends on a sour note when Nell is fired for refusing to sleep with the club owner. Margaret extends an invitation for Nell to stay with her and her family. There, Nell quickly wins the affections of Margaret's daughters, Katie, Julie and Samantha.

Five weeks later, when Nell is about to leave for a gig in Bakersfield, Margaret tells her a secret that she has kept from the family: she is dying. Margaret then asks Nell to raise her girls (knowing all too well that Carl could never manage alone). After much thought, Nell agrees to do this one last favor for her dearest friend. The series is set some years later (when Carl is the police chief) and follows Nell's efforts to raise three mischievous girls.

The Kaniskys live at 2938 Maple Lane in Glenlawn, California. Their phone number is 555-8162 (later 555-2932), and they have a goldfish named Gertrude. Also living with them is Carl's father, "Grandpa" Stanley Kanisky (John Hoyt), and Joey Donovan (Joey Lawrence), an orphan Nell later adopts. Grandpa came to America from Poland in 1924 via the ship *Karkov*.

Katie, the oldest daughter, is also the prettiest. She attended Glenlawn High School (also given as Lincoln High School) and was a member of the Silver Slippers sorority. Katie was part of a rock group called the Hot Muffins. She also had her own business, Katie's, a clothing store in the Glenlawn Mall. In 1986 Katie moved to San Francisco to become a buyer for the Chadwick Department Store.

Julie, the middle child, has an IQ of 160 and attends Lincoln High. She is pretty, awkward and not sure of herself. She needs to wear glasses and feels comfortable with being plain and simple. Julie was the only one of the girls to marry (Jonathan Silverman, played by Jonathan Maxwell), a delivery boy for Luigi's Pizza Parlor; they later move to San Diego to set up housekeeping. Julie gave birth to a girl she names Little Nell.

Samantha, the youngest of the girls, is also the closest to Nell. She is a tomboy and loves horror movies—but not for the obvious reasons (for example, she roots for the shark in *Jaws*). Sam, as she is affectionately called, attended Glenlawn Elementary, Lincoln High and finally Littlefield College in New Jersey. As a kid, Sam had an imaginary friend named Debbie Jo.

When Samantha leaves for college, Nell, who was born in Alabama and had been taking child psychology classes at Glenlawn Junior College, decides to move to New York (where she acquires a job as an editor at the McDutton and Leod publishing house).

Nell's friend, Addie Wilson (Telma Hopkins), is Phi Beta Kappa and taught at Glenlawn Junior College (later at Littlefield when she too moves to the East Coast). Joey was a member of the fourth grade Dodgers baseball team. The police station house dog (a German shepherd) was named Rex.

Relatives: Lili Valenty, Elvia Allman, Elizabeth Kerr and Jane Dulo (Stanley's wife, *Mildred Kanisky*), Ed Shrum (Carl's brother, *Ed Kanisky*), Ben Powers (Nell's ex-husband, *Tony Tremaine*), Lynne Thigpen (Nell's sister, *Loretta Harper*), Hilda Haynes and Rosetta LeNoire (Nell's mother, *Maybelle Harper*), Matthew Lawrence (Joey's brother, *Matthew Donovan*), Fred McCarren and Patrick Collins (Joey's father, *Tim Donovan*).

Flashbacks: Sharon Spelman (Carl's wife, *Margaret*), Nicole Roselle (*Katie age eight*), Keri Houlihan (*Julie age six*), Jeann Barron (*Samantha age four*).

Theme: "Gimme a Break," vocal by Nell Carter.

253. *The Girl with Something Extra*

NBC, 9/14/73 to 5/24/74

Sally (Sally Field) is a one of a kind young woman. Not only is she pretty and effervescent, but she possesses a form of E.S.P. that gives her the ability to pick up on things. She can't read everybody's mind—"Some people some of the time, some people most of the time and a very few people all the time." Sally can't always be specific; sometimes she can only get a general feeling.

Sally is married to John Burton (John Davidson), a handsome young lawyer who is a very private person. They met at an art show—"I should have realized there was something different about Sally the first time we met" (she turned him down for a date before he even asked). Since she was free the following night, she and John went bowling; later, while on a beach, Sally accepted John's proposal—without his asking. On their wedding night Sally reveals her special powers to John—"I married you because I know exactly who you are; no illusions, just the man I fell in love with." "It's not going to be easy getting used to having you inside my head ... with my thoughts hanging out," John says, "but we'll try."

Sally and John live at 10 Havilland Drive. Yellow is Sally's favorite color, and she is partners with Annie (Zohra Lam-

pert) in a variety shop called The Store. John is a lawyer with the firm of Metcalf, Klein and Associates in Los Angeles. When John was a baby, Lawrence Welk music was the only thing that would put him to sleep. John was asked to pose as the centerfold for *A Woman's Place* magazine but was rejected for being "too wooden."

Jerry Burton (Jack Sheldon) is John's brother, a gambler (he plays pool at a hall called Family Billiards); Angela (Stephanie Edwards) is John's secretary; and Owen Metcalf (Henry Jones) is John's boss.

Dave Grusin composed the theme.

Gloria see *All in the Family*

254. *Going Places*

ABC, 9/21/90 to 3/8/91

Cast: Heather Locklear (*Alex Burton*), Hallie Todd (*Kate Griffin*), Jerry Levine (*Jack Davis*), Alan Ruck (*Charlie Davis*), Holland Taylor (*Dawn St. Claire*), Staci Keanan (*Lindsay Bowen*).

Facts: "Here's Looking at You" is "a 'Candid Camera' type of show without the bald guy [Allen Funt]." It is produced in Los Angeles by Dawn St. Claire for National Studios. The writers are Alexandra ("Alex") Burton, Kate Griffin and brothers Jack and Charlie Davis. ("They couldn't afford the guy they wanted so they hired a team for less money," says Dawn). Dawn allows her writers to share her three bedroom house at 1800 Beach Road (one of two she got in a divorce settlement) for a very simple reason: "If I have to fire you, I only have to make one call."

The team's job is simple: devise situations that involve ordinary people in unsuspecting situations. They celebrated getting the job by having a pizza, and the first segment they wrote involved a staged 1 millionth customer contest at the West Pavillion Mall.

Alex, "a sexy blonde bombshell," was born in Denver and loves to cook (as Kate says, "She looks like that and loves to cook? What is she, the product of some genetic experiment?"). Alex keeps the argumentative group together and has a rich fantasy life—she has an impressive answer for everything (for example, "I was Miss Colorado of 1985" or "I lived with Arnold Schwarzenegger")—and always fools people; "I'm only kidding," she says when they start to believe her. Although Alex did not reveal her weight, she "blew up to 103 pounds" when she stopped smoking. Alex produced the show "Wake Up Denver" for two years before joining "Here's Looking at You." She has a plush rabbit named Mr. Fluffy.

Kate is from New York City and is the sharp tongued one of the group (she is also their self-proclaimed boss). Kate had been teamed by Dawn with three previous groups of writers (but it never worked out). Her favorite ice cream is rocky road, and prior to working for Dawn, she wrote for standup comics in New York. She wears a nail polish called Colonial Red.

Jack and Charlie Davis are from Chicago. They had the impression they were the only writers. When Dawn mentioned they would be working with Alex Burton, they balked—until they saw Alex, bent over a desk in a short, tight skirt: "No problem." Charlie is the creative one but has to be pushed; he has a 32 inch waist and wears a 40 regular; Jack wears a 38 regular suit.

Lindsay Bowen is a very pretty teenage girl who lives next door to the team. She loves horror movies, attends Hollywood High School and is most friendly with Alex (from whom she seeks advice about boys and dating). Lindsay's parents are always traveling and are rarely home for her. "You're not just my friends," she tells the team, "you're my family."

In the opening theme, the regulars are seen on the Hollywood Walk of Fame. Alex places her hands in the imprints of Betty Grable; Kate places her hands in the impression of Bette Davis's hands; Charlie places his foot in the footprints of Jack Benny; and Jack places his hands in the imprints of Al Jolson.

"In Your Face" is the "Here's Looking at You" competition; National Studios is owned by the Mitsuoka Company; and in the original, unaired pilot version, Holland Taylor played the producer, Joyce Strickland.

On January 11, 1991, the format changed. "Here's Looking at You" is canceled and replaced by a reality show called "American's Funniest Most Wanted." Alex, Kate, Jack and Charlie acquire jobs as writers on "The Dick Roberts Show," a daily talk show patterned after "Oprah" and "Phil Donahue." The program airs five days a week, and they are hired to produce the first season (260 episodes).

Holland Taylor appeared in the first new episode to establish the premise (she is then dropped); Staci Keanan is still a regular (her role has been drastically cut back).

New to the series is Dick Roberts (Steve Vinovich), the star of the talk show. He is an egomaniac, difficult, arrogant, pompous and abrasive. Arnie Ross (Philip Charles MacKenzie) is the ulcer-ridden executive producer who lives on Maalox and Pepto Bismol. He and Dick have been together for ten years.

Nick (J.D. Daniels) is Kate's nephew, who comes to live with her while her brother, an anthropologist, is away on assignment. Sam (Christopher Castile) is Dick's delicate son (he suffers from allergies and has been babied all his life; his most "horrifying" experience in life occurred one summer night when the pollen count was high and he had no tissues). Sam and Nick are members of the Junior Campers.

Relatives: Dena Dietrich (Kate's mother, *Claire Griffin*), Ralph Bruneau (Kate's brother, *Michael Griffin*), Jonathan Ward (Jack and Charlie's brother, *Jay Davis*).

Unseen Relatives: Jack and Charlie's parents, Howard and Noreen Davis.

Theme: "Going Places," vocal by Mark Lennon.

255. *The Golden Girls*

NBC, 9/14/85 to 9/12/92

Cast: Rue McClanahan *(Blanche Devereaux)*, Betty White *(Rose Nylund)*, Bea Arthur *(Dorothy Zbornak)*, Estelle Getty *(Sophia Petrillo)*.

Facts: Blanche Devereaux owns a home at 6151 Richmond Street in Miami Beach, Florida. When "the two old biddies from Minnesota" she had been living with suddenly leave, Blanche places a notice on a supermarket bulletin board for two new roommates. At the supermarket, Blanche meets her first new roommate, Rose Nylund, who was evicted from her apartment when a new landlord would not allow her to keep her cat, Mr. Peepers.

Later that day, Dorothy Zbornak became Blanche's second roommate when she answers the ad. Shortly after, Dorothy's mother, Sophia Petrillo, moves in with them when her residence, the Shady Pines Retirement Home, burns down.

Blanche Elizabeth Devereaux, who proudly boasts that her initials spell *BED,* is totally liberated and the most attractive of the women (all of whom are over 50 years old; Blanche insists that she is 42—"Living with women who look older than me makes it look possible"). Blanche flaunts her sexuality, shows cleavage and is known to have had many affairs. She was born in Atlanta, Georgia, is a Baptist, and her house is financed by Miami Federal at 7 percent interest. Blanche works in an unnamed museum, and her favorite dessert is chocolate cheesecake. In 1989 Blanche was chosen the Citrus Festival Queen; a year later she became a model (her picture appeared on the cover of the Greater Miami Penny Saver for Ponce de Leon Itching Cream). Each year on her wedding anniversary Blanche tries on her wedding gown. If she gained weight, she drastically diets to keep her figure. Blanche's maiden name is Hollingsworth. At age 18 she ran off to Copenhagen with "a tortured house painter"; in college, she was a member of Alpha Gams sorority. The Rusty Anchor is Blanche's favorite bar.

Dorothy, the most outspoken of the women, was born in Brooklyn, New York, and is now a substitute English teacher in the Florida public school system. She was married to Stan Zbornak (her maiden name is Petrillo) for 38 years before they divorced. In the episode of 2/9/91, Dorothy contemplated remarrying Stan, but refused when he wanted her to sign a marital agreement saying that what's his is his and what's hers is his (Debbie Reynolds as Trudy was a guest star in the episode as the new Golden Girl ready to move in if Dorothy remarried). Dorothy's favorite television show is "Jeopardy"; she was the first in her family to go to college (she majored in U.S. history). In the last first-run episode (5/9/92), Dorothy marries Blanche's uncle, Lucas Hollingsworth (Leslie Nielsen) and moves to Atlanta, Georgia, to begin a new life.

Dorothy's mother, Sophia, was born in Sicily and has a part-time job at the Pecos Pete Chow Wagon Diner (later, she works for Meals on Wheels, then as activities director for the Cypress Grove Retirement Home). Sophia calls Dorothy "Pussycat" and "Big Foot." Sophia, who is over age 80, became somewhat senile as the series progressed; she has a never-seen uncle named Nunzio who lives with a goat. She plays bingo at Saint Dominic's Church; she and Dorothy are Catholic; Sophia buys her shoes at Shim Shacks.

Rose, the most naive of the women, was born in the strange little farming town of St. Olaf, Minnesota, the "broken hip capital of the Midwest" ("We revere our old people and put them on pedestals—but they fall off and break bones"). Rose's natural father was Brother Martin, a monk. Her mother was Ingrid, a cook in the monastery kitchen. They had an affair, but it ended when Ingrid discovered she was pregnant. She quit her job and later died giving birth to Rose. The baby was placed in a basket with hickory-smoked cheese, beefsteaks and crackers and left on the doorstep of the Lindstrom family, who raised Rose. (In another episode, Rose mentions it was the Gierkleckibiken family.) Raised as a Lutheran, Rose heard rumors that her father was a clown in the Ringling Brothers and Barnum & Bailey Circus.

Rose attended St. Olaf's Grammar School and the St. Olaf High School (the school system forbade girls to wear their hair in braids, which didn't matter to Rose, who continually wore a paper duncecap). As a girl Rose had a pet mouse named Larry (whom she would walk to school; she made the leash out of kite string). She then attended Rockport Community College (where she was a member of the farmers' sorority, the Alpha Yams) and finally the St. Paul Business School. Her hobbies are making cheese, studying Viking history and collecting stamps. Rose also had dogs named Rusty and Jake and another cat named Scruffy.

Rose married Charlie Nylund (not seen), the owner of a tile grouting business, at St. Olaf's Shepherd's Church (the St. Olaf Wedding March, "The Cuckoo Song," became very famous when Laurel and Hardy used it as their theme song). Following the ceremony, Rose and Charlie followed the St. Olaf wedding tradition: "You tie a dead fish to the back of the wedding car. You drive until you can't stand the smell anymore and that is where you live." When Charlie died, Rose moved to Florida.

Rose listens to all-talk radio WXBC, and she works as the production assistant at WSF-TV, Channel 8, for the consumer affairs program, "The Enrique Ross Show." She is later associate producer of "Wake Up, Miami" (Rose first worked as a waitress at the Fountain Rock Coffee Shop; prior to the series, she was a counselor in an unnamed grief center). Rose is also a Sunshine Volunteer at the Community Medical Center.

Rose was struck by lightning ("but only once") and "put these hands into a chicken for a breech birth." People say Rose looks like Wilma Flintstone, and Rose is known to do outrageous things (for example, eating raw cookie dough and running through the sprinklers without a bathing cap). "Twinkle Toes" was what her mother called her; Rose has a teddy bear she calls Fernando (later, Mr. Longfellow). Rose is a volunteer leader for the Sunshine Girls Cadets, and she always tells the truth ("I lied only once—to get out of class to see a movie. I'm sorry I did it because it must have been the day they taught everything—which may explain why I am so dense").

Rose's favorite number is 12. She wrote the St. Olaf High School fight song ("Onward St. Olaf") but lost the "Little Miss Olaf Beauty Pageant" 23 years in a row (her talent was rat smelling). Her biggest disappointment was losing the title "Miss Butter Queen of St. Olaf" (her parents groomed her for 16 years; when the big day came, she was a finalist but lost when her churn jammed). On her farm in St. Olaf, Rose had a pet pig named Lester who could predict the Oscar Award winners by wagging his tail. In the episode "The Inheritance," Rose acquired custody of Bob, a 29-year-old pig from a rich uncle.

Blanche's Relatives: Sheree North (her sister, *Virginia*), Billy Jacoby (her grandson, *David*), Hallie Todd (her niece, *Lucy*), Murray Hamilton (her father, *Curtis ["Big Daddy"] Hollingsworth*), Shwan Scheeps and Debra Engle (her married daughter, *Rebecca*), Monte Markham (her brother, *Clayton Hollingsworth*), Barbara Babcock (her estranged daughter, *Charmayne*), George Grizzard (her brother-in-law, *Jamie Devereaux*; later, her ex-husband, *George Devereaux*), Alisan Porter (her granddaughter, *Melissa*).

Dorothy's Relatives: Herb Edelman (her ex-husband, *Stan Zbornak*), Doris Belack (her sister, *Gloria*), Scott Jacoby (her son, *Michael Zbornak*), Deena Freeman and Lisa Jane Persky (her daughter, *Kate Zbornak*), Marian Mercer (Stan's cousin, *Magda*).

Rose's Relatives: Polly Holliday (her daughter, *Lily*), Christina Belford and Lee Garlington (her daughter, *Kirsten*), Marilyn Jones (her daughter, *Bridget*), Jeanette Nolan (her mother, *Alma Lindstrom*), Casey Snander (her cousin, *Sven*), Bridgette Andersen (her granddaughter, *Charley*), Don Ameche (her natural father, *Brother Martin*).

Sophia's Relatives: Bill Dana (her brother, *Angelo*), Nancy Walker (her sister, *Angela*).

Flashbacks: Estelle Getty (*Sophia at age 50*), Lyn Greene (*young Dorothy*), Sid Melton (Sophia's husband, *Salvatore Petrillo*), Kyle Heffner (*young Salvatore*), Bea Arthur (*Sophia's mother*), Rue McClanahan (*Blanche's mother*), Richard Tanner (*young Stan*).

Theme: "Thank You for Being a Friend," vocal by Cindy Fee.

Note: The series returned to TV (CBS) as "The Golden Palace" (9/18/92 to the present). Following Dorothy's marriage, Blanche sells her home and becomes partners with Rose and Sophia when they pool their resources and purchase the 42 room Miami hotel called the Golden Palace. Their plan is to make money and provide for their golden years. The hotel, however, is anything but profitable, and their attempts to make a go of it are the focal point of the program.

Blanche becomes the manager; Rose, the housekeeper; and Sophia, the kitchen manager. New to the cast are Chuy Castillos (Cheech Marin), a Mexican chef, and Roland Wilson (Don Cheadle), Blanche's assistant. Chuy attended the Fashion Institute of Technology. He wanted to make a statement in men's fashion, but he drew number seven in the 1969 lottery draft and went into the army—where he learned how to cook. Roland previously worked at Disney World as one of the Seven Dwarfs—Sneezy. Andrew Gold composed the theme, "Thank You for Being a Friend." See also "Empty Nest."

The Golden Palace see *The Golden Girls*

256. *Gomer Pyle, U.S.M.C.*

CBS, 9/25/64 to 9/19/69

Cast: Jim Nabors (*Gomer Pyle*), Frank Sutton (*Vince Carter*).

Facts: Gomer Pyle is a naive gas station attendant at Wally's Filling Station in Mayberry, North Carolina. When he learns from his draft board that he is expected to serve a term of military duty, he joins the U.S. Marine Corps.

Gomer first reported to Camp Wilson at the Wilmington Base in North Carolina. Here he first meets his superior, Vincent ("Vince") Carter, the hot-headed gunnery sergeant—"It will do you well to remember that name because it is the only name that is going to matter from now on." (Gomer was given four weeks K.P. for being late on his first day, and two additional weeks of kitchen patrol for trying to explain why he was late—a leaky air valve on the car's tire. Gomer is most proud of the fact that he knows all the words to "The Marine's Hymn" ["From the Halls of Montezuma to the shores of Tripoli"], which he learned from the back of a calendar put out by Nelson's Funeral Parlor.)

After basic training, Private Gomer Pyle is transferred to Camp Henderson in Los Angeles, where he becomes a member of the Second Platoon, B Company; his superior again becomes Sergeant Carter, who is also transferred to head B Company. Stories focus on the problems Gomer causes when he unconsciously breaks from the rules of the system and complicates matters; and on Carter's relentless efforts to resolve the chaos that results from Gomer's antics.

"I can't hear you!" is the catchphrase Carter uses when he asks his squad something and they fail to reply in a loud enough voice. "Shazam" and "Golly" are Gomer's remarks when something fascinates him; his greeting is "Hey" (for example, "Tell the captain Gomer says hey"). Gomer buys his suits from Friendly Freddy, the Gentleman's Tailor (Sid Melton played Freddy, the shady one-man discount store). Gomer had an old horse named Polly (whom he bought to save her from the glue factory). When Gomer, who runs like greased lightning, competed in the platoon's foot race, he was called "Crazy Legs Gomer." When Gomer and Vince appeared on the television show "Win a Date," Gomer won a free trip to Hawaii with starlet Wendy Sparks (Jeannine Riley). Carter starred in a documentary called "A Day in the Life of a Sergeant"; the local dance club is the Way Out a Go-Go; the platoon's booby prize is the Lead Combat Boot. Gomer was promoted to Pfc (private, first class) before the series, a spinoff from "The Andy Griffith Show," ended.

Lou Ann Poovie (Elizabeth MacRae) is Gomer's girlfriend, a nightclub singer at the Blue Bird Café. Bunny Olsen (Barbara Stuart) is Vince's patient girlfriend; other members of B Company are privates Duke Slater (Ronnie Schell) and Frankie Lombardi (Ted Bessell). Corporal Charles Boyle (Roy Stuart) is Carter's aide; Colonel Edward Gray (Forrest Compton) is the commanding officer; Lou Ann's former boyfriend was Monroe Efird (Med Flory).

Relatives: George Lindsey (Gomer's cousin, *Goober Pyle*), Norris Goff (*Grandpa Pyle*), Enid Markey (*Grandma Pyle*), Kathleen Freeman (Vince's mother, *Mrs. Carter*), Marlyn Mason (Vince's sister, *Bebe Carter*), Reva Rose (Vince's sister, *Muriel Carter*), Tol Avery (Lou Ann's father, *"Pop" Poovie*), Suzanne Benoit (the colonel's daughter, *Janice Gray*), Bobby Rhea (the colonel's nephew, *Danny Gray*).

Theme: "Gomer Pyle, U.S.M.C.," by Earle Hagen.

257. *Good and Evil*

ABC, 9/25/91 to 10/30/91

Charlotte Sandler Cosmetics is a large, Washington, D.C.–based company owned by cosmetics queen Charlotte Sandler (Marian Seldes) and run by her two opposite-in-personality daughters, Denise Sandler (Teri Garr) and Genvieve ("Genny") Sandler (Margaret Whitton).

Denise is a schemer and, as Charlotte calls her, "a bitch." Denise believes her mother favors Genny. ("She was cuter," Charlotte tells Denise. "You had this oozing skin condition. We just didn't want to touch you.") Denise was sent to a boarding school in Peru, and the only thing she was good at was being bad.) She is now plotting to take control of the company from her mother—who is 65 years old but won't retire until she looks 65. Denise is the mother of David (Seth Green), who attends the Pudget Academy for Boys. Denise was married to Ronald Ethan (Marius Weyers), "who died in a suspicious plunge off Mount Everest four years ago" (Denise pushed him). He was found at the bottom of the mountain, thawed out and returned to "his loving wife" (who now seeks to finish him off for good).

Genny is a brilliant biochemist and dedicated to her job. She won't experiment on animals; she tests her experiments on herself (which produce various side effects, like delusions and personality changes). Genny is the mother of a beautiful teenage girl named Caroline (Brooke Theiss). Two years ago, Genny's husband, Jonathan, died; Caroline suffered a traumatic shock as a result and is now unable to speak.

George Aliceson Tipton composed "The Good and Evil Theme."

258. *Good Grief*

Fox, 9/30/90 to 2/3/91

Sincerity Mortuary in the town of Dacron, the sixty-third largest city in Ohio, is owned by the Pepper family: Debbie (Wendy Schaal) and her brother, Warren (Joel Brooks).

Assisting the conservative Warren in running the business is Ernie Lapidus (Howie Mandel), Debbie's vile, despicable and simply dishonest husband. Sincerity Mortuary has been in business for 60 years; it has fallen on hard times, and Ernie's underhanded attempts to make the business profitable again are the focal point of the series.

Debbie and Warren eat Honey Nut Pops cereal for breakfast. Warren is a member of the Daughters of the American Revolution and lives in a room that is an exact duplicate of Ralph and Alice's apartment on "The Honeymooners." His hobby is macaroni art.

Ernie calls Debbie "my little orange blossom," and their favorite restaurant is Swordfish, Swordfish, Swordfish; their favorite fast food takeout is chicken from Mr. Cluck. Ernie has a past—and it is a matter of public record in a number of other states (for instance, he was Ernie Love, the Evangelist, in Chicago).

Ringo Prowley (Tom Poston) is a jack of all trades who raised Ernie after his father's death (he also taught Ernie the tricks of the trade); Raoul (Sheldon Feldner) is Ernie's nonspeaking flunky; he does anything Ernie requests at a moment's notice.

There is a tissue dispenser vending machine in Ernie's office; Meditation Pond is where mourners toss coins; and Slumber Hills is where plots are available.

Steve Nelson sings the theme, "Celebrate Life."

259. *The Good Guys*

CBS, 9/25/68 to 1/23/70

Cast: Bob Denver (*Rufus Butterworth*), Herb Edelman (*Bert Gramus*), Joyce Van Patten (*Claudia Gramus*).

Facts: "We're the Good Guys who never let a friend down. Friends forever, ask anyone in this town. When you're in a hustle and need some muscle, I'll be there at your side..." The theme is referring to Rufus Butterworth and Bert Gramus, friends since they were infants, who did everything together. When Bert (jersey number 20) who is tall, joined the high school basketball team, Rufus (jersey number 6), who is much shorter, was there at his side. When Rufus (jersey number 21) joined the school football team, Bert (jersey number 12) was there for him. When the series begins, Bert is married to the former Claudia Arsdale, and together they run Bert's Place, a Los Angeles diner; Rufus is a bachelor and owner of a taxi cab. In second season episodes, Rufus sells his cab and joins Bert as his partner when Bert moves the diner to the beach. Since childhood, through school and the army, Bert and Rufus have only one dream: to make it big. Right now they have only one thing going for them: failure.

"Hear no Rufus, speak no Rufus and see no Rufus" is the credo Bert tries to live by when he feels Rufus is about to approach him with a harebrained scheme to make money. Together they invested in and lost money on paper socks, low-cal aspirin, quick drying paint, George Hamilton buttons, and managing a deadbeat songwriter. Claudia adds

that Bert and Rufus "are like the local chapter of the Salvation Army. When a stranger comes along for money and clothes you give it to him." Bert and Claudia have been married for ten years. Claudia is studying to become a teacher at UCLA; when Claudia agrees with him on a matter, Bert calls her "a good guy." Arnold Schreck (William Daniels), now a wealthy used-car salesman, was the man Claudia had been dating before Bert came along.

Bert and Claudia have been the owners of Bert's Place for five and one-half years when the series began. The daily dinner menus are: meatballs and spaghetti (Monday), Southern fried chicken (Tuesday), German pot roast (Wednesday), beef Stroganoff (Thursday), international goulash (Friday; a combination of leftovers from the four previous days). In first season episodes, Bert's competition was D.W. Watson (Liam Dunn), the owner of the Mother Watson diner chain. Alan Hale, Jr., played Rufus's friend, Big Tom, the truck driver, in several episodes.

Relatives: Jim Backus (Claudia's father, *Henry Arsdale*).

Theme: "Two Good Guys," by Jay Livingston, Ray Evans and Jerry Fielding.

260. *The Good Life*

NBC, 9/18/71 to 1/8/72

"In the beginning, God created the Earth. Then God created man and woman. So far so good. Then man got into the act, and he created trouble. He created houses and cars and TV sets and waffle irons, washing machines, etc., etc., etc. And the Lord said unto man, 'Dummy, you better create a loan company because you can't pay for all this stuff.' But one man found a better way." The man is Albert ("Al") Miller (Larry Hagman), a stockbroker plagued by life's endless problems—from a house in need of repair to numerous unpaid bills. He gets an idea about how to better life for himself and his wife, Jane (Donna Mills), when their car breaks down and they are befriended by a butler. After seeing the mansion and the style in which the butler lives, Al thinks, "Maybe there is a better way."

Al places an ad in the newspaper that reads "Couple for hire. Experienced husband and wife seek position with a pleasant family in country setting. P.O. Box 444."

Many requests are received, but Jane is still reluctant: "Honey, I don't even like to do my own housework; now I'm going to do someone else's?" Al assures Jane that she can fake it; he poses at a butler, while Jane pretends to be a cook. At 332 Ridgeway Drive, Al and Jane find employment with Charles Dutton (David Wayne), the wealthy head of Dutton Industries. Charles, who is "totally committed to a life of decadence," is impressed by Jane's legs (she is wearing a miniskirt) and hires them based on that. Al quits his job and sells their house ("Honey," he says, "we lost only $3,000"). They now struggle to maintain their cover, attend household duties, and live the good life. "I love it," Al says, "because we don't own it. This good life is going to take some getting used to."

Kate Reid (pilot) and Hermione Baddeley played Charles's sister, Grace Dutton; and Danny Goldman was Charles's son, Nick Dutton ("Offspring from my third marriage; good breeding, bad marriage").

Sacha Distel performs the theme, "The Good Life."

Good Morning, Miss Bliss see Saved by the Bell

261. *Good Morning, World*

CBS, 9/3/67 to 9/17/68

Cast: Joby Baker *(Dave Lewis)*, Ronnie Schell *(Larry Clark)*, Julie Parrish *(Linda Lewis)*, Billy DeWolfe *(Rolland B. Hutton, Jr.)*, Goldie Hawn *(Sandy Kramer)*.

Facts: "The Lewis and Clark Show" is an early morning (6:00–10:00 A.M.) comedy, music and news program on an unidentified radio station in Los Angeles (there are no call letters, no AM or FM designation and no dial frequencies given). David ("Dave") Lewis, who is married (to Linda), and Lawrence ("Larry") Clark, who is single and a ladies' man, are the hosts, longtime friends who have been working together for years (another episode relates a story in which Dave was a nightclub comedian and partners with Jerry Carroll [Jerry Van Dyke], a now successful star with his own series). Based on the first premise, the longtime friends were working for radio station KOUA in Honolulu, Hawaii, when two events occurred: Dave fell in love with Linda (no last name given), the receptionist/switchboard operator; and Rolland B. Hutton, Jr., the owner of that unidentified L.A. station, hired them to do their show for him (he was vacationing and just happened to hear "The Lewis and Clark Show"). Two days before they were to depart, Dave and Linda were married at the Prince Kali Hiki Tiki Lodge; Larry was the best man and maid of honor.

Linda, who was born in San Francisco, set up housekeeping with Dave at 63 Court Plaza, Apartment 1-B; Larry at his "swinging singles pad" at 3126 Orion Place. Dave and Linda have been married one year when the series begins. Dave's hobby is building model airplanes ("The wings always fall off," Linda says), and his dream was to fly one day (he took lessons at the Speed Gonzalez Flying School and learned that he could never fly—an inner ear "malfunction"). Dave calls Linda "Pumpkin," and his favorite lunch is clams oreganta and garlic bread. Linda wears a flannel nightgown, which Dave hates, and his cousin "Bibian" always thanks Linda for being so beautiful ("It's a pleasure just to look at you," she says). Linda also says that Dave has frequent attacks of clumsiness.

Crestview 6-7399 is the radio station's phone number. Dave and Larry broadcast from Studio B and take turns buying their morning doughnuts at Mrs. Jelly Donuts (Tuesday is cinnamon jelly doughnut day). Larry's favorite record is "Pipati Papa," by Billy and the Bing Bongs. It is also a record he has had to replace many times because Rolland hates it, Larry, and all rock and roll music. Despite Rolland's warnings not to play "that awful music," Larry spins such "classic" groups as The Tijuana Symphony Orchestra, the Daydreamers, and the Four Dropouts and Murray.

Dave and Larry hosted a telethon for the Camp Wanderlust Children's Fund; Dave's General Electric alarm clock rings at 4:30 A.M.; he drives to work, enters the station and says, "Good morning, world," over the microphone. When Larry has to take a plane, he buys $60,000 worth of life insurance at the airport and sends it to the latest girl he is dating (his way of getting devotion and home cooked meals). His favorite comedians are Laurel and Hardy.

Rolland B. Hutton, Jr., is mentioned as the general manager of the station in some episodes. He hopes to be a legend in his own time and once performed in vaudeville as Billy Jones in 1932. He met his wife that year. She was wealthy and her family disapproved of actors, so he married her and gave up show business.

Rolland can't stand for anything to be broken in his Beverly Hills home (address not given). The house was featured in *Home and Terrace* magazine (pages 9–16), and there is so much crystal in the house that he lives in fear of sonic booms. Rolland has a bust of himself in the master bedroom and many house rules (for example, number 4: No shoes on the white carpets; number 6: No strangers allowed; number 7: No yelling).

Sandy Kramer is Dave and Linda's pretty, energetic upstairs neighbor. She is Larry's girlfriend and a professional dancer ("She has the craziest legs in town," Larry says). Each year Sandy enters (and hopes to win) the Pillsbury Bake-Off. She has a very slender waist, is "not too busty or hippy" and can eat a nine course meal without gaining an ounce. She is very dedicated to Larry despite the fact that he has eyes for other girls.

Captain Eddie is the unseen station traffic reporter; and "Big" Jack Jackson (Gene Klavan) is the always intoxicated newscaster ("When you're tuned to Jack Jackson, you're tuned to the truth") and host of "The 5 O'Clock Platter Party" (a show Dave and Larry sometimes host when Jack can't be sobered up). Vinnie (Burt Taylor) is the engineer seen in the control booth for "The Lewis and Clark Show."

Relatives: Byron Morrow *(Linda's father)*, Jackie Joseph (Dave's cousin, *"Bibian"*; her real name is Vivian, but when she was young she couldn't pronounce *V*s so it came out "Bibian"; she calls David "Dabid").

Other Relatives: Linda's mother (no name given), and Linda's aunt, Rose (both seen but not credited).

Theme: "Good Morning, World," by Dave Grusin.

262. *Good Sports*

CBS, 1/10/91 to 7/13/91

Cast: Farrah Fawcett *(Gayle Roberts)*, Ryan O'Neal *(Bobby Tannen)*, Lane Smith *(R.J. Rappaport)*, Christine

Dunford (*Missy Van Johnson*), Brian Doyle-Murray (*John McKinney*).

Facts: Gayle Roberts and "Downtown" Bobby Tannen are the co-anchors of "Sports Central," an information program for the Rappaport Broadcasting System's ASCN (All Sports Cable Network).

Gayle, a supermodel, appeared on the cover of *Sports Illustrated* magazine. She had a dream of becoming a sports journalist; R.J. Rappaport, the owner of the network, gave her a chance. Gayle, whose birth name is Gayle Gordon (which she changed to avoid confusion with Lucille Ball's longtime sidekick, Gale Gordon) is called the "Doris Day of the Sports World." She has a goldfish named Frankie (Bobby has one named Valley), is 40 years old and her favorite poet is Carl Sandburg ("Fog" is her favorite poem).

Gayle has a poster on the front of her office wall that reads PROVIDENCE FRIARS; she can't stand hearing the word *bitch*, is allergic to goat cheese and can't eat baby back ribs. Her favorite charity is the Los Angeles Mission.

Bobby, now 42 years old, was the number one draft pick from the University of Miami (jersey number 12). He became a recording star ("Downtown" Bobby Tannen) and released his own album ("Downtown Sings 'Downtown' and Other Chart Busters—Including the Hit Single, 'Wichita Lineman'").

Two years later he quit football to manage the career of his new wife, singer-stripper Yvonne Pomplona (Sherie Rose). Three weeks later, Bobby, saddened by his divorce, made a comeback with the L.A. Rams (jersey number 13). His new career was cut short when he punched a reporter; he was imprisoned shortly after when he disagreed with a judge about his tax bill. Bobby then joined the Oakland Raiders (jersey number 49) and wrote the tell-all book *Panty Raiders*. When Lyle Alzado read the book, "he broke Bobby's body and tore his face off." Bobby next appeared in bandages on the cover of *Look* magazine with the headline BYE BYE BOBBY. He then worked as a delivery boy for the Friends of Pizza before R.J. hired him.

Gayle considers Bobby "a self-destructive punk who never grew up." She and Bobby met 20 years earlier: he was with the Jets and in Michigan to play the Lions. Bobby crashed a party at Gayle's sorority. Her girlfriend Robin Blankman introduced them. Bobby told Gayle she had pretty eyes. She believed him, and they went to a nightclub called the Shangri-La. They danced and later went to her apartment in Ann Arbor (where they stayed for the next 48 hours). Bobby was fired for missing the plane back to New York and two days of practice. At this time Gayle Roberts was Gayle Gordon (Bobby's mother feared that he slept with "the guy who played Mr. Mooney on the 'Here's Lucy' show").

Bobby's affairs have included such "bimbos" as Monique Kowanga, Mami Van Hyland and Dr. C.C. Doucette. When Bobby scored a touchdown, the organist at Shea Stadium would play the song "Downtown." Bobby got the job as sports anchor after the former anchor, Stu Ramsey (Arthur Burghardt), had a heart attack on the air. Gayle and Bobby are also hosts of the interview show "Sports Chat" and of "Sports Brief" (updates) for "Sports Central."

Gayle and Bobby live in separate apartments at the Landmark Building. Bobby collects beer cans (he doesn't drink it; he has 147 brands from 98 countries), and his third wife left him for his second wife. In the opening theme, the credits read "Farrah Fawcett vs. Ryan O'Neal."

R.J. Rappaport runs the station like a military general (he attended Culver Military Academy and Amherst College). R.J. also runs Rap-Ha-Port (the 24 hour comedy channel). He calls John McKinney his "yes man" ("I need my Mac"); he and R.J. had a morning radio show called "Mac and Rap in the Morning."

R.J.'s hobby is taking TV sets apart—even though they are not broken (he throws the "innards" in a box and gives them to Mac so his kids can put them back together again). Rappaport Airlines sponsors "Sports Brief" ("The airline with fewer fatalities than any bicoastal airline").

Missy Van Johnson is a field reporter for Sports Central. She is a former Women's Pro Am golf champion and always miserable ("I'm a skinny ex-golfer whose goal in life is to be abused by men"). Her favorite classical music piece is Brahms's Waltz.

Local 107 handles the electrical work at the station. In the episode of 6/3/91 ("Electricity") Ryan O'Neal is seen reading the book *Love Story* while Farrah Fawcett reads *The Burning Bed* (both starred in film adaptations of the books they were reading). Michael Cole appeared in the episode of 6/8/91 ("Moody Blues Swings") as Dr. M'odsquad (pronounced "Mod Squad," from his series of the same title), a vet Bobby and Gayle sought for Bobby's sick fish.

Relatives: Lois Smith (*Bobby's mother*), Howard Keel (Gayle's father, *Sonny Gordon*; he calls Gayle "Angel"). Unseen was R.J.'s son, Antoine.

Theme: "Good Sports," vocal by Al Green.

263. *Good Times*

CBS, 2/8/74 to 8/1/79

Cast: John Amos (*James Evans*), Esther Rolle (*Florida Evans*), Jimmie Walker (*J.J. Evans*), BernNadette Stanis (*Thelma Evans*), Ralph Carter (*Michael Evans*), Ja'net DuBois (*Willona Woods*), Janet Jackson (*Penny Gordon*), Ben Powers (*Keith Anderson*), Johnny Brown (*Nathan Bookman*).

Facts: The Evanses (parents James and Florida, and their children, J.J., Thelma and Michael) are a poor black family struggling for survival during the bad times of the 1970s. Their rent is $104.50 a month, and they live in Apartment 17C of the Cabrini Housing Project at 963 North Gilbert in Chicago (their phone number is 555-8264, and their address is also given as 763 North Gilbert).

James, the father, is a totally dedicated husband to Florida and a loving but stern father to his children. He takes what work he can get and usually holds down several jobs at a time. James later enrolls in trade school and graduates on 9/9/75.

Florida, nicknamed "Pookie Poo" as a child, becomes a

schoolbus driver (for the Roadway Bus Company) to support the family when James is killed in a car accident in Mississippi (in the episode of 9/22/76).

J.J. (James Jr.) is a ladies' man who considers himself the "Ebony Prince." He is a hopeful artist who later works as an art director for the Dynomite Greeting Card Company (in first season episodes, J.J. was a delivery boy for the Chicken Shack fast food store). At age 12, J.J. painted a naked lady eating grits on an elevator wall (he didn't know how to draw clothes then). When he needs money, J.J. borrows it from "Sweet Daddy" (Teddy Wilson), a loan shark who charges 25 percent a week interest. J.J.'s catchphrase is "Dyn-O-Mite," and he hides his money "in that sock" in his dresser drawer. In one episode, Dennis Howard played a white version of J.J. in a dream sequence; artist Ernie Barnes produces the pictures J.J. paints.

Thelma, the middle child, was born on June 15, 1957, and like J.J. attends an unnamed high school. While J.J. sees Thelma as having "a face whose mold could make gorilla cookies" (Thelma sees J.J. as a "Beanpole"), Thelma is actually a very attractive girl with aspirations of becoming an actress. She attends classes at the Community Workshop and marries her boyfriend, Keith Anderson (a former football player who now drives a cab for the Windy City Cab Company).

Michael, the smartest of the children, attends Harding Elementary School, and is dedicated to the Black Movement. While his high school is not named, he was a member of the Junior War Lords Gang for a short time.

Willona, the family friend, worked in a beauty parlor, a department store, and finally George's Fashion Boutique. She adopted Penny Gordon, a battered child, in later episodes. Nathan Bookman, the overweight building super, is called "Buffalo Butt" by J.J. and Willona, and is a member of the "Jolly Janitors Club." His middle name is Millhouse. Gary Coleman played Gary Daniels, the obnoxious kid who lived in the building, in several episodes; Saundra Sharp played his mother, Joyce. Willona calls Michael "Gramps."

Relatives: Richard Ward (James's father, *Henry Evans*), Percy Rodrigues (Florida's cousin, *Edgar Edwards*), Calvin Lockhart (Florida's cousin, *Raymond*), Kim Hamilton (Raymond's wife, *Betty*), Carl Lee (Willona's ex-husband, *Ray*), Chip Fields (Penny's natural mother, *Mrs. Gordon*), Marilyn Coleman (Nathan's wife, *Violet Bookman*).

Theme: "Good Times," by Dave Grusin, Alan Bergman and Marilyn Bergman.

Note: "Good Times" is a spinoff from "Maude."

264. *Goodnight, Beantown*

CBS, 4/3/83 to 1/15/84

WYN-TV, Channel 11, in Boston is the number three news station in a three station market. In an attempt to improve the ratings of "WYN's 6 O'Clock Report," manage- ment hires Jennifer Barnes (Mariette Hartley) as the co-anchor for Matt Cassidy (Bill Bixby), the station's lone newscaster. Matt, who signs off his broadcast with "That's the news. I'm Matt Cassidy. Goodnight, Beantown," has been the anchor since the mid-1960s (apparently his only television job since graduating from Boston University, as no other background information is given). Jennifer was born in California and worked as a special features reporter for KRF-TV. With little chance for advancement, she left the station when the opportunity arose at WYN to become a co-anchor. "They have their differences," management says, "but they work well together."

Matt, a bachelor, lives at 321 Waverly Place (Apartment 1). Jennifer wanted a place near the station, so management found her an apartment—Number 2 at 321 Waverly Place, right across the hall from Matt. Jennifer is divorced and the mother of Susan Barnes (Tracey Gold), a very pretty 13-year-old girl who cooks and cares for herself and the apartment while her mother is working. Susan attends Ridgefield Junior High School.

Matt reads the Boston *Tribune*; the local watering hole is Kelly's Bar and Grill; and 555-NEWS is the station's news hotline phone number. Dick Novack (George Coe) and, later, Albert Adelson (G.W. Bailey) were the news directors, and Frank Fletcher (Jim Staahl) was the sportscaster.

Dennis McCarthy composed the theme.

265. *The Goodtime Girls*

ABC, 1/22/80 to 8/29/80

"We all had an uncle and his name was Sam; we had to go in and get him out of a jam; the job wasn't easy, but the burden was shared; back in the forties when everyone cared." The theme is referring to World War II. The series is set in Washington, D.C., in 1942. There is rationing, housing problems and a man shortage. Camille Rittenhouse (Francine Tacker), Betty Crandall (Lorna Patterson), Edith Beatlemeyer (Annie Potts) and Loretta Smoot (Georgia Engel) are four working girls who are enduring the homefront hardships and struggling to live together in a small, converted attic in a boardinghouse at 1115 Sycamore Street South, better known as Coolidge House.

Camille is a pretty freelance magazine photographer who uses her feminine wiles to get what she wants. She was born in Washington, has a difficult time handling money and connived her way into Coolidge House after having been evicted from the Shoreham Apartments for nonpayment of rent.

Betty was born in Sioux City, Iowa. She is direct, firm and honest and works in a defense plant (Office of Price Administration). "But I can't tell you any more than that. Loose lips sink ships."

Edith is from California and works as a USO (United Servicemen's Organization) showgirl. She has a heart of gold and feels sorry for the soldiers she meets who have been sta-

The Goodtime Girls. **Left to right:** Georgia Engel, Annie Potts, Adrian Zmed, Lorna Patterson, Francine Tacker.

tioned overseas (she has a bad habit of getting herself engaged to them to make them feel better).

Loretta is sweet, kind and very trusting. She works for a general at the War Department and is the only one of the girls who is married. She and Bill Smoot (Russ Thacker) were married only one hour when he was called to active duty. The girls may bicker, but they care for each other— "It's like having a whole new wonderful family."

Also living at Coolidge House, which is owned by George and Irma Coolidge (Merwin Goldsmith and Marcia Lewis), are Frankie Molardo (Adrian Zmed), a cab driver (license plate 856 973), and his friend and roommate, Benny Lohman (Peter Scolari). Frankie claims that flat feet kept him from the service. Sparky Marcus plays George and Irma's son, Skeeter.

The Charles Fox Singers perform the theme, "When Everyone Cared" (written by Charles Fox and Norman Gimbel).

266. *Grand*

NBC, 1/18/90 to 12/27/90

Life in the small town of Grand, Pennsylvania. The *Daily Bugle* is the town's newspaper, the Grand Movie Theater seems to show only one film, *Grand Illusion,* and the main industry appears to be the Grand Piano Works, a company owned by the elderly and wealthy Harris Weldon (John Randolph). The company is located on Weldon Boulevard, and it takes one year to make a Weldon Grand Piano.

Janice Pasetti (Pamela Reed) is a pretty divorcée who lives in a mobile home and earns a living by cleaning the Weldon mansion (as well as other homes in town). Janice is the mother of a teenage girl named Edda (Sara Rue) and later lives in the Weldon mansion after a tornado destroys her home (she is now the mansion maid and despises the sexy black cocktail waitress uniform Harris forces her to wear). Janice, who attended Grand High School (as Edda does now), takes three sugars in her coffee.

Carol Ann Smithson (Bonnie Hunt) is Harris's niece. She is married to Tom (Michael McKean), and together they own the Smithson Group (a realty company). Tom calls her "Hamster," and in second season episodes Carol Ann writes a daily column "Ask Carol Ann" for the *Bugle* after she loses Tom (who is swept away in a tornado).

Norris Weldon (Joel Murray) is Harris's indecisive son. He has a dog named Fallon and first took on the personality of comedian Jack E. Leonard (believing it was his goal in life to be a standup comic); he next had a cable access television show called "Let's Not Think, with Norris Weldon" on Channel 128; and finally he believed that his calling in life was to be a mime. He co-owns the town's only watering hole, the Beethoven Bar, with Desmond (John Neville), Harris's ever faithful butler.

Wayne Kazmersky (Andrew Lauer) is the local motorcycle cop (Grand Police Department) who has a crush on Janice.

Relatives: Britt Ekland (Harris's ex-wife, *Viveca*), Ed Marinaro (Janice's ex-husband, *Eddie Pasetti*), Jacky Vinson (Tom's son, *Dylan Smithson*; from a previous marriage), Shawn Phelan (Carol Ann's estranged son, *Timmy*), Jane Hoffman (Wayne's mother, *Dot Kazmersky*).

Theme: "Play It Grand," by Michael Leeson and Tom Snow.

267. *Grand Slam*

CBS, 1/28/90 to 3/14/90

Dennis Bakelenekoff (John Schneider) is a bounty hunter and works for the Blue Bird Bail Bonds Company. Pedro Gomez (Paul Rodriquez) is also a bounty hunter, but he works for Aztec Bail Bonds. Tired of always going after the same bail jumpers—but for different reasons—Dennis and Pedro decide to form their own company and cut out the middleman. The old adage "Friends should never work together" is put to the test when the two bickering friends team up to catch bail jumpers.

Dennis was a cop with the San Diego Police Department who was fired after a bad shooting. He was also a professional baseball player; he was nicknamed "Hardball" and signed a contract for $175,000 a year. Two months later he was out of work again (he was famous for giving up the only home run hit in the Jack Murphy Stadium). Dennis has a dog named Grace and a van with the license plate 92LT07.

Pedro drives a car with the license plate VATO UNO. He and Dennis named the company Associate and Associate as it was the only title they both could agree upon (it was originally called Hardball and Associates).

Irv Schlosser (Larry Gelman) was Dennis's boss at Blue Bird; Al Ramirez (Abel Franco) was the owner of Aztec Bail Bonds. Lupe Ontiveros played Pedro's Grandma Gomez in two episodes.

Joseph Conlan composed the "Grand Slam" theme.

268. *The Great Gildersleeve*

Syndicated, 1954 to 1955

Cast: Willard Waterman (*Throckmorton P. Gildersleeve*), Stephanie Griffin (*Marjorie Forrester*), Ronald Keith (*Leroy Forrester*).

Facts: The Gildersleeve Girdle Works is a company owned by Throckmorton P. ("Gildy") Gildersleeve in the town of Wistful Vista (the company motto is "If you want the best of corsets, of course it's Gildersleeve's"). When his sister and her husband are killed in a car accident, Gildy travels to nearby Sommerfield to take over the administration of his brother-in-law's estate (an automobile agency that hasn't been doing well) and to find a home for their children, Marjorie and Leroy Forrester. When Gildy is unable to find a home for the children, he petitions the court to adopt them.

During Gildy's hasty attempts to resolve the situation and return to Wistful Vista, he encounters the objections of Henry J. Hooker (Harry Antrim), a judge who thinks that Gildy, a carefree, womanizing bachelor, needs some discipline himself if he is to take care of his niece and nephew. Hooker grants Gildy custody of the children provided he posts a $100,000 bond and resides in Sommerfield for six months. Although reluctant, Gildy agrees.

The six month trial becomes a permanent stay for Gildersleeve. He sells his girdle company and takes up residence in the Forrester home at 217 Elm Street. He is later appointed the water commissioner by the mayor.

On spring mornings, Gildy likes to putter around in the backyard. He contemplates the flowers, admires the butterflies, inspects the blossoms on his apple tree, marvels at the green grass and stays away from the back of the garage (where everything the family doesn't want gets tossed). Gildy is president of the Jolly Boys Club ("All for One and One for All"; the weekly meeting is called "Jolly Boys Night"); he also has an enormous appetite.

As previously mentioned, Gildy is a ladies' man. He compares his luck with women to that with streetcars: "If one streetcar goes by without me, another will be along in a few minutes. The tracks are loaded." He also says, "When you want women, you can't have 'em; when you don't want 'em, you can't get rid of 'em." While Gildy has an eye for the ladies, they also have an eye for him: the Southern belle Leila Ransom (Shirley Mitchell); Kathryn Milford (Carole Mathews), a nurse at Sommerfield Hospital's maternity ward; Amy Miller (Marian Carr), a member of the Sommerfield Ladies' Poetry Club; and Lois Kimball (Doris Singleton), the librarian (who lives at 181 Oak Street).

Birdie Lee Coggins (Lillian Randolph) is Gildy's housekeeper; Floyd Munson (Hal Smith) is the town barber; Mr. Peavy (Forrest Lewis) owns Peavy's Pharmacy; and Bessie (Barbara Stuart) is Gildy's secretary.

Marjorie, who attends Sommerfield High School, calls Gildy "Unkie"; Leroy, who attends Sommerfield Elementary School, calls Gildy "Unk."

Theme: "The Great Gildersleeve," by Jack Meakin.

269. *The Greatest American Hero*

ABC, 3/18/81 to 2/3/83

Cast: William Katt (*Ralph Hinkley*), Robert Culp (*Bill Maxwell*), Connie Sellecca (*Pamela Davidson*), Mary Ellen Stuart (*Holly Hathaway*).

Facts: Aliens from an unknown planet feel that crime on Earth must be stopped to save the planet Earth from destroying itself. They choose two earthlings for the job: Ralph Hinkley, a special education teacher at Whitney High School, and William ("Bill") Maxwell, an FBI agent with the Los Angeles bureau.

The aliens think Ralph has integrity, a strong moral character and a healthy idealism. They give him a special costume (red tights with a black cape and silver belt) that endows him with superhuman powers and an instruction manual on how to use the costume (which Ralph calls "the Suit"). Complications set in when Ralph and Bill lose the instruction book and Ralph has to play being the Greatest American Hero by ear.

Ralph, who married his girlfriend, Pamela Davidson, on January 6, 1983, attended Union High School, and his telephone number is 555-4365 (later given as 555-0463). When Ralph wears the Suit, which Bill calls "the jammies," he acquires a number of superpowers, including incredible speed and the abilities to fly, to appear and disappear at will, to deflect bullets and to tune in to people's whereabouts via a mental image he gets by touching something that that person touched. The *Daily Galaxy* was the first newspaper to publish a picture of Ralph flying.

Bill, who calls the aliens "the little green guys," is a hotheaded FBI agent who snacks on Milkbone dog biscuits; his license plate numbers are 508 SAT and 293XUJ.

Pamela, a lawyer with the firm of Carter, Bailey and Smith, is their unwitting assistant in most cases that involve Ralph and the Suit. Pam is later with the firm of Selquist, Allen and Minor, and has a car with the license plate 733 LBL (later 793 LAF).

Two of Ralph's students, Rhonda Harris (Faye Grant) and Tony Villacona (Michael Pare) are with the musical group L.A. Freeway.

In May 1986 Bill's "worst case scenario" happens: Ralph's true identity as the "Greatest American Hero" is revealed (exactly how is not shown). Ralph becomes a celebrity—but Pam objects to all the publicity and wants her old Ralph back.

As Ralph takes great pride in his new life-style, "the little green guys" are very upset. They summon Ralph and Pam to Palmdale. There, they meet with the alien leader (John Zee), who tells Ralph that they are displeased with his new celebrity status. Now that he and the Suit are known to the world, the situation will not work; the Suit must be given to someone else so that crime can be battled in secret. Ralph learns that once the Suit is given to someone else, the world will forget that Ralph was a superhero. He

and Pam, however, will be allowed to keep their memories.

Ralph suggests giving the Suit to Bill—but the aliens refuse: "He is not the right type. Mr. Maxwell was always meant to serve as an associate. You will find someone and when you do, you will know it." The aliens thank Ralph and Pam for all they have done, and Ralph begins a quest to find his replacement.

Holly Hathaway is a very pretty young woman who is devoted to helping others. She is the foster parent of a seven-year-old girl named Sarah (Mya Akerling), runs a day care center and is the founder of the Freedom Life Foundation and an animal shelter called Anything's Pawsable. She cares. She is honest, has a strong moral character and a healthy idealism. She is the girl Ralph chooses to become the "Greatest American Heroine."

"You did it to me again, Ralph. You picked a skirt . . . you paired me with Nancy Drew"—this is Bill's reaction when he sees that Holly is to be his new partner. Thus is the beginning of the "Greatest American Heroine," a failed attempt to continue the series with a female lead.

Holly faces the same problems Ralph did: an inability to understand the powers of the Suit without the instruction book (Ralph tried but couldn't convince the aliens to give him another book). Holly is never in a bad mood—something she is sure Bill will like about her. Holly tells only Sarah about her secret identity "because you are the most important thing in my life." Holly and Bill's first (and only) assignment was in Newfoundland, where they investigated the illegal killing of whales. Holly's license plate reads 5Q8 HPO.

Bill ended this nonnetwork pilot episode (seen only in syndication) with the words "As I always said, we're gonna make a terrific team."

Relatives: Simone Griffeth (Ralph's ex-wife, *Alicia Hinkley*), Brandon Williams (Ralph's son, *Kevin Hinkley*), E.J. Peaker (Rhonda's mother, *Rose Harris*), June Lockhart (Pam's mother, *Alice Davidson*), Norman Alden (Pam's father, *Harry Davidson*).

Theme: "Believe It or Not," vocal by Joey Scarbury.

270. *Green Acres*

CBS, 9/15/65 to 9/7/71

Cast: Eddie Albert (*Oliver Douglas*), Eva Gabor (*Lisa Douglas*), Tom Lester (*Eb Dawson*), Pat Buttram (*Eustace Haney*), Frank Cady (*Sam Drucker*), Alvy Moore (*Hank Kimball*).

Facts: Oliver Wendell Douglas is a New York lawyer with a lifelong dream of becoming a farmer. He grows corn on his Park Avenue patio and vegetables in his office desk drawer. But it is not enough. When he sees an ad for a farm for sale in the small town of Hooterville, he purchases it (the 160 acre Haney farm) sight unseen.

Oliver is married to a glamorous and sophisticated Hungarian woman named Lisa. Lisa is reluctant to leave her life of luxury but agrees to try "farm living" for six months. If she feels she cannot become a farmer's wife, Oliver will move back to Park Avenue.

When Oliver and Lisa arrive at their farm (Green Acres), which is located four miles outside the town of Hooterville, Oliver sees his dream about to come true; Lisa sees it as it really is: a shabby, broken-down nightmare. Despite the farm's appearance, Oliver is determined to make a go of it and become part of "the backbone of the American economy."

Oliver attended Harvard Law School and was a fighter pilot during World War II (his biggest regret was having to bomb farmlands). He does his farming in a suit and tie and plows using an ancient, rundown Hoyt-Clagwell tractor. He and Lisa live in a historic Hooterville landmark—the home and birthplace of Rutherford B. Skrug, "the founder of the great state of Hooterville." Oliver is a member of the Hooterville Fire Department Band and has his mind made up to be a farmer. (He constantly makes his farmer's speech: "It is the dream of my life to buy a farm, move away from the city, plow my own fields, get my hands dirty, sweat and strain to make things grow. To join hands with other farmers, the backbone of the American economy...")

Lisa is the only person who hears a fife playing when Oliver gives his patriotic speech. She calls the town "Hootersville" and has a cow named Eleanor and a group of chickens she calls "the girls." (She originally had only one chicken named Alice. Eleanor gives just the amount of milk Lisa requires; she merely places a glass under Eleanor and says, "One cup, please." "The girls" also oblige Lisa by giving her the eggs she needs.)

Eb Dawson, Oliver's farmhand, has a poster of his hero, Hoot Gibson, on his bedroom wall, and he calls Oliver "Dad." Eb has a second job—standing in for Stuffy, Oliver's scarecrow, when he goes to the neighboring town of Pixley for lunch.

Sam Drucker, the owner of the town's general store, publishes the community's only newspaper, the *Hooterville World Guardian,* and is its postmaster (their zip code is 40516½), as well.

Farmers Fred (Hank Patterson) and Doris Ziffel (Fran Ryan and Barbara Pepper) are the "parents" of Arnold the pig, the most colorful resident of Hooterville. Unable to have children, the Ziffels raised Arnold as their son (his official name is Arnold Ziffel). Arnold is in the third grade, drinks lime soda, has tea with Lisa, predicts the weather with his tail, gets "the shys" in front of beautiful women, plays cricket (he has his own cricket bat), looks forward to watching "The CBS Evening News, with Walter Cronkite" and is allowed to paint his own room (he is partial to orange walls).

Mr. Haney, the valley's con artist (who sold Oliver Green Acres), is a member of the Hooterville Chamber of Commerce and the chairman of the Bringing Outside Money into Hooterville Committee. Haney, who works out of his truck—and will sell anything to make a dollar—has a wooden Indian named Irving Two Smokes.

Hank Kimball is the forgetful state agricultural represen-

tative; Alf (Sid Melton) and Ralph Monroe (Mary Grace Canfield) are the inept brother and sister carpenters Oliver hired to repair Green Acres.

Oliver likes his coffee black with sugar; Lisa prefers cream; Eb, cream with no sugar. Oliver's telephone is located at the top of a nearby telephone pole (the phone company ran out of wire); Fred Ziffel has no phone receiver (he uses a hammer to represent one and can only talk to people, not hear them). Hooterville, according to a sign at the train station, has an elevation of 1,427 feet. An 1890s steam engine, coal car and mail/baggage/passenger coach called the Cannonball Express services the area.

On May 18, 1990, CBS presented the television movie, *Return to Green Acres.* After years of frustration, Oliver sells Green Acres back to Mr. Haney, and he and Lisa return to their penthouse at 255 Park Avenue in New York City. However, when Oliver learns that the Armstrong Development Company is planning to turn Hooterville into a modern development, he and Lisa return to the town to represent the people. When Oliver wins the case and realizes he still loves Hooterville, he buys back Green Acres.

The original cast recreated their roles, with the exception of Fred and Doris Ziffel (who had passed away). Their lovely niece, Daisy Ziffel (Mary Tanner), inherited the farm and Arnold (Frank Welker was credited as "Arnold's voice"). Mr. Haney, still a con artist, runs a hotel called Haney's House of Hospitality. Sam has a new sign in his store that reads CREDIT CARDS NOT ACCEPTED. Eb is now married to Flo (Lucy Lee Flippin) and the father of a teenage son named Jeb (Mark Ballou).

Relatives: Eleanor Audley (Oliver's mother, *Eunice Douglas*), Lilia Skala *(Lisa's mother).*

Flashbacks: Jackie J. Jones *(Oliver as a boy).*

Theme: "Green Acres," vocal by Eddie Albert and Eva Gabor (written by Vic Mizzy).

271. *The Green Hornet*

ABC, 9/9/66 to 7/14/67

Cast: Van Williams *(Britt Reid/The Green Hornet),* Bruce Lee *(Kato),* Wende Wagner *(Lenore Case),* Walter Brooke *(Frank Scanlon),* Lloyd Gough *(Mike Axford).*

Facts: Dan Reid (not seen) is the publisher of the *Daily Sentinel,* America's greatest newspaper. Hoping to mature his playboy son, Britt, Dan makes him the editor of the paper. He then secretly asks his good friend, ex-cop turned reporter Mike Axford to watch over Britt's activities.

Britt is reluctant to take the job at first—until he begins reading about his great-grand-uncle, John Reid ("The Lone Ranger"). He decides to follow in his footsteps and protect the rights and lives of decent citizens (the job as editor gives him the perfect cover). Britt adopts the disguise of the Green Hornet (the insect that is most deadly when aroused) and establishes a base in an abandoned building. He reveals his secret identity to only three people: Kato, his Asian houseboy (who also serves as the Green Hornet's assistant),

Lenore ("Casey") Case, his secretary, and Frank Scanlon, the district attorney.

Because they are considered criminals and wanted by the police, the Green Hornet and Kato avenge crimes as semifugitives rather than as a law enforcement organization, always disappearing before the police arrive.

Britt, as the Green Hornet, drives the Black Beauty (license plate V 194), a 1966 Chrysler Imperial. Its features include rockets front and rear, knock-out gas in the front and smoke in the rear for a smoke screen. The *Sentinel* is housed in the Daily Sentinel Building (the paper is "put to bed at 10:30 P.M."). The back of the building, which conceals the Black Beauty, has a large billboard that reads CANDY MINTS (left side; a girl and boy kissing are in the middle) and HOW SWEET THEY ARE (on the right). The secret elevator that gives access to the Green Hornet's secret headquarters beneath Britt's home is located behind the fireplace. The Black Beauty stands on a revolving floor section. When it is not in use, Britt's normal street car is seen. When the Black Beauty is needed, Kato pushes a button on the wall, and clamps grip Britt's car. The floor revolves to reveal the Hornet's car. The district attorney's phone number is 555-6789.

Theme: "Flight of the Bumble Bee," performed by Al Hirt.

272. *Griff*

ABC, 9/29/73 to 1/4/74

Wade ("Griff") Griffin (Lorne Greene), a former police captain (with the Parker Center Division of the L.A.P.D.), is now a private detective who operates Wade Griffin Investigations at 19734 Mays Street in Westwood, California. Griff's office number is 1103½, and he shares the floor with the following businesses: J.M. Bachman, D.D.S. (office 1103), and D.E. Mitner, Real Estate (office 1105). One other business is also listed on the building directory (1105½), but camera angles prevent the viewer from reading it. Griff's office phone number is 555-6696, and he drives a sedan with the license plate 795 DCH (in another episode, his license plate reads A1121). His favorite restaurant is Farino's; Griff also does volunteer work for the Boys' Club. He carried badge number 26 when he was a police officer.

Michael ("Mike") Murdock (Ben Murphy) is Griff's legman and drives a car with the license plate 634 QTV. Grace Newcombe (Patricia Stich) is Griff's secretary (she lives in Apartment 5C at 43 Ridgedale Lane; her phone number is 555-5515). Barney Martin (Vic Tayback) replaced Wade as the new police captain; his favorite lunch is pastrami on rye with mustard. The Parker Center Building (number 150) is dedicated to William H. Parker, 1950–66 (as stated on the plaque in front of the building).

Mike Post and Pete Carpenter composed the "Griff" theme.

273. *Growing Pains*

ABC, 9/24/85 to 8/26/92

Cast: Alan Thicke (*Jason Seaver*), Joanna Kerns (*Maggie Seaver*), Kirk Cameron (*Mike Seaver*), Tracey Gold (*Carol Seaver*), Jeremy Miller (*Ben Seaver*), Ashley Johnson (*Chrissy Seaver*).

Facts: At 15 Robin Hood Lane in Huntington, Long Island, New York, lives the Seaver family: parents Jason and Maggie, and their children, Mike, Carol, Ben and Chrissy. The family's station wagon license plate reads FEM 412 (later KMQC 487); the Municipal Removal Service picks up garbage on Tuesdays and Fridays.

Jason Roland Seaver and Margaret ("Maggie") Malone, who is 13 months older than Jason, first met at Boston College (where Jason was a member of the rock group the Wild Hots). Jason, a psychology major, and Maggie, a journalism major, married shortly after graduation. When the series begins, Jason is just leaving his position as a doctor of psychology at Long Island General Hospital to open a private practice from his home. Maggie worked as a researcher for *Newsweek* magazine for two years before giving up her career to raise a family; she is now returning to work as a reporter for the Long Island *Daily Herald*. Maggie later becomes a reporter for Channel 19's "Action News" (she works here as Maggie Malone) and a columnist for the Long Island *Sentinel* (she writes the column "Maggie Malone, Consumer Watchdog"). Maggie originally studied child psychology in college. When she got a taste of journalism, she switched majors in her junior year. In later episodes, Jason also does volunteer work for the Free Clinic to help the people of his community. As a kid, Jason's imaginary friend was 1950s television game show host Bud Collyer ("who would come over to my house to play games"). Maggie won the 1989 "Working Mother of the Year" award.

Michael ("Mike") Aaron Seaver, the oldest child, first attended Dewey High School, then Alf Landon Junior College and finally Boynton State College. Mike had aspirations of becoming an actor. He starred in the Dewey High production of "Our Town" and had his first professional acting job on the television series "New York Heat" as Officer Bukarski (who was killed off; Mike's name was misspelled in the credits as Michael Weaver). Mike was also a member of the Alf Landon Drama Club and starred with his girlfriend, Kate McDonald (Chelsea Noble), in the play *The Passion* (Kate, who lives in Apartment 144, later became a model and appeared in the 1992 *Sporting Man*'s swimsuit edition). Mike next landed a role on the TV soap opera "Big City Secrets" before he found an interest in teaching. Although Mike hated high school and was the number one problem student, he acquired a job as a teacher of remedial studies at the learning annex of the Community Health Center (at $100 a week). Mike's previous jobs: paperboy for the Long Island *Herald* (200 customers on his route), waiter at World of Burgers, salesman at Stereo Village, carwash attendant, nightman at the Stop and Shop convenience store and sing-

Growing Pains. Cast from the unaired pilot version: Kirk Cameron (back; then left to right): Joanna Kerns, Jeremy Miller, Alan Thicke and Elizabeth Ward (as Carol).

ing waiter at Sullivan's Tavern. Mike's license plate reads BLA 592 (later 236R DKS).

Carol Ann Seaver is the second-born child. She is sensitive, very smart and very pretty, but wishes she could shed her brainy image and be thought of as "dangerous, provocative and sexy. Not the kind of girl who is voted recording secretary, left in charge of the class when the teacher leaves and immaculate." Carol first attended Dewey High School, then Columbia University in Manhattan. She dropped out of Columbia in 1990 to take a job as a computer page breaker at GSM Publishing. The following year, she returned to Columbia to study law. She takes the number 1 IRT subway train to school and works with Jason at the Health Clinic. Carol originally lived in the school dorm (room 436) before she decided to commute.

At age seven Carol was a member of the Happy Campers; she was voted the 1988 Dewey Homecoming Queen and was president of the Future Nuclear Physicists in high school. Posters of W.C. Fields, Laurel and Hardy and the Marx

Brothers adorn the walls of Carol's bedroom. In late 1991 to early 1992 episodes, Carol is said to be in London attending school. In real life, Tracey Gold had been suffering from anorexia nervosa, an eating disorder (she took a break from the series on doctor's orders). The episode of 2/29/92 was dedicated to Tracey and ended with the words "We miss you, Tracey." (Tracey rejoined the cast when Carol returned from England in the episode of 4/11/92.) Elizabeth Ward played Carol in the original, unaired pilot version of the series.

Benjamin ("Ben") Hubert Humphrey Seaver is the third-born child. He had an imaginary friend named Pirate Sam as a kid. He first attended Wendell Willkie Elementary School, then Dewey High—where he had the potential to surpass Mike as the worst problem student ever. A very pretty but bossy girl named Laura Lynn (Jodi Peterson) was Ben's girlfriend during the 1989-90 season.

Christine, affectionately called Chrissy, is the youngest member of the Seaver family. She is an adorable six-year-

Growing Pains. Back: Joanna Kerns, Alan Thicke; front: Kirk Cameron, Jeremy Miller and Tracey Gold (as Carol).

old, who, despite the bad influence of Mike and Ben, appears to be following in Carol's footsteps. She was born at 12:30 A.M. and weighed eight pounds four ounces. It was Ben who gave the baby her name (after a dying man named Chris [Dick O'Neill] he met and befriended at the hospital). Chrissy attends the Parkway Preschool (then Greenway Elementary School), and her favorite bedtime story is "Mr. Mouse." In one episode, Chrissy had an invisible six foot mouse "friend" she named Ike (who liked to drink beer). Kirk Cameron played Ike in mouse makeup (Mike is Chrissy's hero, and she envisioned Ike looking like Mike). Chrissy's stuffed animals are Bertha Big Jeans (a bear), Papa Pig and Mr. Blow Hole (a whale). Chrissy was originally an infant (played by twins Kristen and Kelsey Dohring); in the episode of 9/19/90, the character of Chrissy was advanced to the age of six and played by Ashley Johnson.

In the series' last first-run episode (4/25/92), Maggie accepts a job in Washington, D.C., as the executive director of media relations for an unseen senator. Jason, Maggie, Ben and Chrissy relocate; Carol moves into the dorm at Columbia University; and Mike remains in his apartment over the Seavers' garage (he mentions that he "has to break in new landlords").

Other Regulars: Julie Costello (Julie McCullough), a sophomore at Columbia University (majoring in child psychology), was the Seavers' nanny (for Chrissy) and Mike's first steady girlfriend. In 1987, when they break up, Julie apparently quit school to become a waitress at the La Village Restaurant. Richard ("Boner") Stabone (Josh A. Koenig) is Mike's best friend and comrade in misadventure. He was replaced in 1990 by Edward ("Eddie") Cornelius Zeff (K.C. Martel). Tina Louise (played by Melissa Young) is Eddie's flaky girlfriend, a hatcheck girl. Luke Brower (Leonardo DiCaprio) is the homeless teenager befriended by Mike.

Relatives: Jane Powell (Jason's mother, *Irma Seaver*), Gordon Jump (Maggie's father, *Ed Malone*), Betty McGuire (Maggie's mother, *Kate Malone*), James Callahan (Jason's uncle, *Bob*), Ruth Silveira (*Boner's mother*), Richard Marion (*Boner's father*), Gary Grubbs (Luke's father, *George Brower*; he deserted the family years ago).

Flashbacks: Judith Barsi (*Carol age four*), Victor DiMattia (*Mike age five*).

Flash Forwards: Khrystyne Haje (*Chrissy age 18*).

Theme: "We've Got Each Other," vocal by B.J. Thomas and Jennifer Warnes (later by B.J. Thomas and Dusty Springfield).

Note: See also the spinoff series "Just the 10 of Us."

Guestward Ho. (left to right): Mark Miller, J. Carrol Naish, Joanne Dru and Earle Hodgins.

274. *Guestward Ho!*

ABC, 9/20/60 to 9/21/61

William ("Bill") Hooten (Mark Miller), an advertising executive who is fed up with the rat race of New York City, purchases Guestward Ho, a dude ranch in New Mexico, from a scheming Indian chief named Hawkeye (J. Carrol Naish). Hawkeye runs the local trading post and a souvenir stand opposite the reservations desk at Guestward Ho. Bill, his wife, Barbara ("Babs") (Joanne Dru), and their son, Brook (Flip Mark), relinquish their life in the city for what they believe will be an easier life out West, "under a sun so bad it can rattle your brains" (so says the theme).

Brook and Bill adjust quickly. Babs, who was reluctant from the beginning, is not an outdoors woman; Bill is afraid that if she hears a coyote she'll pack her bags and move back to Manhattan.

Rates are $25 a day, and Guestward Ho lacks a number of things, including paying guests. The Hootens' struggle to make their dude ranch profitable is the focal point of the series.

Santa Fe is the nearest town, and the Flying Horse Dude Ranch is their nearest competition. Babs wants a dude ranch where she can get a rest from all the work that has to be done at Guestward Ho. "When the spirits delivered the Hootens to me," says Hawkeye, "they said, 'Hawkeye, there are no more where these came from.'" Hawkeye reads the *Wall Street Journal,* orders his "genuine Indian bows and arrows" souvenirs from Hong Kong and struggles to keep the Hootens, his only chance of ever unloading Guestward Ho, happy. Pink Cloud (Jolene Brand) is Hawkeye's gorgeous assistant, and Lonesome (Earle Hodgins) is Bill's wrangler.

In the original, unaired pilot film (produced for CBS in 1959), Leif Erickson played Bill Hooten and Vivian Vance was Barbara Hooten.

Arthur Hamilton wrote the "Guestward Ho" theme.

275. *Guns of Paradise*

CBS, 10/26/88 to 9/1/90
CBS, 1/4/91 to 6/14/91

The series is set in the 1890s. When Lucy Carroll (Kathryn Leigh Scott), a St. Louis entertainer, is no longer able to care for her four children (due to a serious illness that later claims her life), she sends them to live with her brother, Ethan Allen Cord (Lee Horsley), whom she believes is a hardware store owner in the town of Paradise. Unknown to Lucy, Ethan is a wanted gunfighter, and Paradise is a ruthless mining town.

When Lucy's children, Claire (Jenny Beck), Joseph (Matthew Newmark), Ben (Brian Lando) and George Carroll (Michael Patrick Carter), arrive, Ethan relinquishes his career as a hired gun to become a rancher and provide a decent life for the children. The children quickly adjust to the fact that their uncle is a gunfighter when they see that the whole town turns to him for help and that he sides with right against wrong.

Amelia Lawson (Sigrid Thornton) is the owner of the Paradise Bank and Ethan's romantic interest (she also helps Ethan care for his kids). John Taylor (Dehl Berti) is Ethan's friend, an Indian who is learned in the ways of both the white man and his own people. He appears to be the only person with medical knowledge (he saved Ethan and the kids on several occasions) and helps Ethan in rearing the children. Charlie (James Crittenden) is the deputy sheriff; Tiny (John Bloom) is the blacksmith; and P.J. Brackenhouse (Nicholas Surovy) was the marshal for one season.

Episodes broadcast under the title "Paradise" (first date listing) are a harsh portrayal of life in the Old West. There are very few women and children there. Claire, at age 13, is the oldest girl in town. She is very close to Amelia and had no friends her age until she met a girl named Katie Hamilton (Milla Jovovich). Katie, a strikingly beautiful young girl (age 13), was raised by her mother, Sarah (Irene Miracle), the owner of Zack's Traveling Social Club, to become a high-priced prostitute (an idea borrowed from the Brooke Shields film *Pretty Baby*). It was Claire's friendship that allowed Katie to experience the childhood she was denied by her mother. Claire has two dolls, Juliet and Rapunzel.

As "Guns of Paradise" (second date listing), the town became more civilized. Women and children are now prominent, and when a copper mine opens near town, Claire remarks, "Paradise is becoming a real city." Claire now works as a teller at Amelia's bank; Joseph (age 12), works at the Paradise Hotel; Ben (age eight), who collects wanted posters, and George, the youngest (age six), attend the Paradise School. Ethan is building a new home for his family in an area called the Meadow. The town also has the Paradise Theater, Paradise Hardware, and the Paradise Barber Shop (a shave is 25 cents).

In the episode of 1/4/91, the corrupt marshal, Blake (Robert Fuller), plots to kill Cord and take over the town. Ethan opposes Blake. In the ensuing gunfight, Blake is killed. Claire removes the badge from Blake's vest and pins it on Ethan's vest. He never wanted kids, he never wanted to be a rancher, and he never wanted to be marshal—"But it looks like I got all three."

Relatives: Ted Shackelford and Charles Frank (Amelia's ex-husband, *Pierce Lawson*), Edward Albert (Lucy's husband, *Robert Carroll*. He was a drifter and gambler who deserted his family when Lucy became pregnant with George. To shield her children, Lucy told them that their father died a hero's death).

Themes: "The Theme from Paradise" and "Guns of Paradise," by Jerrold Immel.

276. *The Guns of Will Sonnett*
ABC, 9/8/67 to 9/15/69

Cast: Walter Brennan *(Will Sonnett)*, Dack Rambo *(Jeff Sonnett)*, Jason Evers *(James Sonnett)*.

Facts: Will Sonnett and his 20-year-old grandson, Jeff Sonnett, are seen riding together as the theme plays. Over the music Will is heard saying, "We search for a man named Jim Sonnett and the legend folks tell may be true. Most call him gunman and killer—he's my son, whom I hardly knew. I raised Jim's boy from the cradle, till the day he said to me, 'I have to go find my father'; and I reckoned that's how it should be—so we ride, Jim's boy and me."

Jeff has never seen his "paw"; Will aims to see that he does. Twenty years earlier in Bensfort, Wyoming (1852), Jeff was born; his mother died during childbirth. Unable to face the prospect of life without his wife, Jim abandoned his family. Will, Jim's father, raised Jeff as if he were his own son.

Jim carries a gold watch, given to him by Will, with the inscription TO JAMES FROM HIS LOVING FATHER. He is a wanted gunman and killer and has a difficult road to travel—a road with no turning back. Will and Jeff begin their search in 1872 and are hampered by the fact that Jim is unaware he is being sought by kin. As they travel from town to town, Will and Jeff learn that Jim may be thought of as a killer but he is kind to people he finds in trouble and will kill only in self-defense. Each mile brings new hope that soon the Sonnetts will be a family again: "I thought our search was over, Lord; now with your help we'll start again. Please guide the path we take."

Will was an army scout and stationed at Fort Levenworth. It was said that as a boy, Jim would hang out at the fort trading post (run by Sam Cochran, played by Denver Pyle). At this time, Will saved the life of Red Leaf (Anthony Caruso), a Sioux Indian chief who called him "Sharp Eyes" (Will persuaded Red Leaf to surrender to General Bill Harney rather than face the army in battle). Will was later stationed at Fort Kerney.

Will is fast on the draw, and James showed promise—"Trouble is, he left before I taught him half what I know. No brag, just fact." Jim was born in 1833. The Sonnetts' strategy when facing a gunfighter: "Keep 'em waitin'—it makes 'em edgy." When an opponent faces Will, he says, "They say Jim is fast. Well, he ain't; I am. No brag, just fact." When Will and Jeff have lost their way, Will says, "Look at the sun, check the wind and ride north till we find him." Will taught Jeff the art of gunplay, how to fight and "to be respectful to women no matter what or where."

In the last episode, Will and Jeff find Jim and convince him to give up his life of running. With a hope of beginning new lives, the Sonnetts settle down in the town of Sampson. Will becomes the sheriff and Jim and Jeff his deputies. Had the series been renewed, it would have focused on the Sonnetts' attempts to maintain law and order in Sampson.

Theme: "The Guns of Will Sonnett," by Earle Hagen and Hugo Friedhofer.

277. *Gunsmoke*

CBS, 9/10/55 to 9/1/75

The Atcheson, Topeka and Santa Fe Railroad services the area in and around Dodge City, Kansas, during the 1860s. Boot Hill is the graveyard; the Dodge House, the hotel; and the Longbranch Saloon, the local watering hole. There is also Ma Smalley's Boarding House and the Marshal's Office on Front Street. Matthew ("Matt") Dillon (James Arness) occupies that office—a tough but honest U.S. Marshal who earns $100 a month. Matt has a horse named Marshall (with two *l*'s) and pays $35 for a saddle; the office wall has six rifles chained together in a rack.

Chester Goode (Dennis Weaver) first served as Matt's deputy; he was replaced by the unsophisticated Festus Hagen (Ken Curtis). Chester walks with a limp (his right leg) and calls Matt "Mr. Dillon." Chester carries a shotgun and enjoys eating lunch with Mr. Dillon at Delmonico's Café.

Kitty Russell (Amanda Blake), called "Miss Kitty" by Chester, owns the Longbranch Saloon and is Matt's romantic interest, although they never kissed. Matt's first kiss occurred in the episode "Matt's Love Story" (9/24/73) in which widow "Mike" Yardner (Michael Learned) finds Matt wounded and suffering from amnesia after being ambushed by a murder suspect named Les Dean (Victor French). Mike and Matt fall in love during his recuperation; unknown to Matt, Les has been hired to kill Mike so a land baron can acquire her property. Matt, of course, saves Mike and her ranch. Shortly after this episode, "Kitty's Love Affair" aired on 10/22/73. Here Kitty falls for Will Stambridge (Richard Kiley), a reluctant gunfighter, when he risks his life to save hers.

Galen Adams (Milburn Stone), affectionately called "Doc," is the town's lone physician (he drives a horse and buggy). Newly O'Brien (Buck Taylor) is the gunsmith, and Sam (Glenn Strange) is the Longbranch bartender. Other citizens are Quint Asper (Burt Reynolds), the blacksmith; Nathan Burke (Ted Jordan), the freight agent; Mr. Jones (Dabbs Greer), the general store owner; Percy Crump (John Harper), the undertaker; and Louie Pheeters (James Nusser), the town drunk. In the opening theme, when Matt faces his opponent in the famous showdown, the opponent fires first. John Wayne introduced the series at the beginning of the first episode. The series is also known as "Marshal Dillon."

Rex Koury and George Spencer composed the theme, "Gunsmoke."

Three TV movies also aired: *Gunsmoke: Return to Dodge*

(CBS, 9/26/87), in which Matt faces an outlaw with a score to settle.

Gunsmoke: The Last Apache (CBS, 3/18/90) finds Matt reunited with Mike Yardner (Michael Learned), who is now the owner of the Yardner Cattle Company in Arizona. Matt also learns that he has a daughter named Beth (Amy Stock) from the affair he had with Mike 20 years ago (Matt had amnesia and Mike never told him when he regained his memory). The story follows Matt's efforts to save Beth when she is kidnapped by renegade Indians.

Gunsmoke: To the Last Man (CBS, 1/10/92) finds Matt and Beth involved in the notorious Arizona blood feud of the 1880s (it was revealed that Mike "died" from a high fever).

278. *The Halls of Ivy*

CBS, 10/19/54 to 10/13/55

"Oh, we love the halls of Ivy that surround us here today, and we shall not forget though we be far, far away..." Life at Ivy College, located in the town of Ivy, U.S.A., as seen through the eyes of Dr. William Todhunter Hall (Ronald Colman), the college president, and his wife, Vickie (Benita Hume), a former London stage star.

William was originally a student at Ivy. When he graduated and became an instructor, he lived in the boardinghouse across the street from Faculty Row. He had a top floor apartment and kitchen privileges; female visitors were permitted only as far as the front parlor, and "please turn off the lights before leaving the room" was a rule. When he was appointed an assistant professor, he moved to the opposite side of Faculty Row. He had a sitting room, bedroom and bath and hot plate privileges; but no wild parties ("which in those days consisted of more than two people laughing at the same time").

It was when William became a full professor that his life changed. During a summer vacation in England, William met, fell in love with and married Victoria ("Vickie") Cromwell, a celebrated stage star. He brought her back to America with him, and they shared what William called "a Charles Addams mansion," a rented house that William had found lonely and empty until Vickie arrived; Vickie found it a home no matter what William thought ("I never had a home of my own. It was hotel rooms and flats or living out of the backs of dressing rooms").

Their new residence is One Faculty Row, a house reserved for the president of Ivy College. The mailbox reads PROF. WILLIAM TODHUNTER HALL AND MRS. VICTORIA CROMWELL HALL; their phone number is Ivy 4-0042. Vickie sometimes calls William "Toddie," and William's pride and joy is coming out ahead with the finances ("One seldom sees an annual report as superb as the one I just prepared. I call it out of the red and over the hump with Hall").

Professor Warren (Arthur Q. Bryan) is one of the dedicated instructors at Ivy. "Teaching hardly ever pays off in money," he says. "And it hardly ever pays off in glory. I myself can name ten baseball players or ten burlesque queens, bless 'em, for every teacher you can bring to mind... It's pride in the job that makes us stick with it." It is also a good bet to avoid accepting an invitation for coffee from Professor Warren: "In all the world no one concocts as nauseating a cup of coffee as I do."

Alice (Mary Wickes) is the Halls' housekeeper, and Clarence Wellman (Herb Butterfield) is the chairman of the board of Ivy College (Sarah Selby appears as his wife, Mrs. Wellman).

Ivy is a small school and always has been. The personalities of the faculty play a much bigger part at Ivy than they do at those giant "diploma factories." It's a school rich in tradition and dedicated to giving its students the best education that is possible. It also has a century-old Christmas tradition: at this time of year, if a reasonable amount of snow has fallen, students build a snowman in front of the home of each faculty member. The more affection the students have for a professor, the larger the snowman they build. Of all the faculty ever at Ivy, only Professor Bessemer (the president in 1900), who was nicknamed "Old Pinch Face Bessemer," never got a snowman (he resigned "due to illness" shortly after).

Theme Adaptation: "The Halls of Ivy," by Les Baxter.

279. *Hangin' with Mr. Cooper*

ABC, 9/22/92 to the present

The spacious house at 15 Robin Hood Lane in Huntington, Long Island, New York, belonged to television's Seaver family ("Growing Pains"). The house was "magically" transported to Oakland, California, and became the new residence for three friends who are also roommates: Mark Cooper (Mark Curry), Vanessa Russell (Holly Robinson) and Robin Dumars (Dawnn Lewis). By the second episode, the roomies of a black version of "Three's Company" were seen in a new house at 653 Hamilton Street.

Mark is a former Oakridge High School basketball star (jersey number 15) who failed to make the N.B.A. He is now looking for his first coaching job and earns a living as a substitute teacher. He drives a 1967 Dodge Dart and often finds work at his alma mater—from teacher to cheerleader coach (of the Penguinettes). Mark's dream came true when he received a chance to try out for the Golden State Warriors (a basketball team). He wore jersey number 7, made the team, but was cut when a regular player came back after an injury.

Vanessa is an executive assistant (secretary) at an investment firm called Toplin and Toplin. She is ambitious and working her way up the corporate ladder (she wants to be a stockbroker). Her car license plate reads 011 JJE; salmon mousse garnished with mandarin orange is her favorite meal to cook. Vanessa was born in Washington, D.C.; for Christmas she would make Russellnog (eggnog with cinnamon).

"Vanessa," Robin says, "is thin, beautiful and never lifts a finger; she eats like a horse and never gains an ounce." Robin diets, exercises two hours each day and would kill for Vanessa's body. Robin and Vanessa were college roommates (they belonged to the Alpha Delta Rho sorority) and moved in with Mark to save on expenses. Robin is the music teacher at Oakridge High School and believes that she is mechanically inclined—but isn't (like the time she fixed the toaster and Vanessa's hair caught fire; or the time she fixed Vanessa's car and had three parts left over).

Holly Robinson and Dawnn Lewis sing the theme, "Hangin' with Mr. Cooper."

Happy see *Baby Talk*

280. *Happy Days*

ABC, 1/15/74 to 7/19/84

Cast: Tom Bosley (*Howard Cunningham*), Marion Ross (*Marion Cunningham*), Ron Howard (*Richie Cunningham*), Erin Moran (*Joanie Cunningham*), Henry Winkler (*Arthur Fonzarelli*), Anson Williams (*Potsie Weber*), Donny Most (*Ralph Malph*), Cathy Silvers (*Jenny Piccolo*), Scott Baio (*Chachi*).

Facts: A nostalgic look at life during the 1950s (and later 1960s) as seen through the experiences of the Cunninghams, a family of five living in Milwaukee, Wisconsin: parents Howard and Marion, and their children, Richie, Joanie and Chuck.

Howard and Marion married in 1936 (based on first season episodes being set in 1956) and set up housekeeping at 618 Bridge Street. Howard, called "Cookie" during his hitch in the army during World War II, owns the Cunningham Hardware Store and is a member of the Leopard Lodge (local 462). His favorite color is blue and omelets are his favorite breakfast. A Republican, Howard drives a black DeSoto with the license plate F-3680. He gets a headache if he doesn't have dinner by 7:00 P.M., and when he has an irritating day at work, his back goes out.

Howard won a free trip to New York for selling the most Mr. Happy Plungers. In college, he was on the shot put team, and with Fonzie he created the Garbage Gulper, a trash compactor (they called the company Fonz-How, Inc.). Howard was a young man when he found his goal in life. It all started when the toilet overflowed and he went to the hardware store to get a plunger. He saw the shelves lined with hardware and was hooked. He began work in that store as a stockboy, and by 1946 he owned it. He still has the plunger that began it all. He buys his supplies from Ernie's Hardware Supplies. In 1933, when Howard was 18, he ran away from home and journeyed to New York (by hitching on boxcars). He sustained himself by working as a hot dog vendor at Yankee Stadium. The saddest day in Howard's life was that on which he could no longer hold his daughter, Joanie, in his arms ("It was the day I knew she

Happy Days. **Left to right: Donny Most, Henry Winkler, Anson Williams and Ron Howard.**

was no longer my little girl"). The Cunningham Hardware Store is located on 8th Street and offers free paint color mixing.

Marion, a secretary for an unnamed company before she married Howard, has a favorite drinking glass with a picture of Rudolph Valentino on it. Her mother ("Mother Kelp") calls Howard "Fatso." Marion is a member of the Milwaukee Women's Club and Howard's bowling team, the Ten Pins (she bowls a 119). Marion and Howard dine at Kelly's House of Beef. They honeymooned at the Holiday Shore Lodge in Lake Geneva (55 miles from their current home). They stayed in Suite 325. Marion called Howard "Snookems"; he called her "Baby Cakes." They danced to the song "Moonlight in Vermont" on their wedding night. Marion's favorite television shows are the actual soap operas of the day: "As the World Turns," "The Edge of Night" and "The Secret Storm." Marion is allergic to spices, especially cayenne pepper. With Fonzie as her partner, Marion entered the WZAZ-TV "Harvest Moon Dance Contest."

Richie weighs 135 pounds, is five feet nine inches tall, has blue eyes and red hair. He had the nickname "Freckles" at age nine and was said to resemble Howdy Doody. He first attended Jefferson High School (where he wore jersey number 17 on the basketball team), then the University of Wisconsin. (In first season episodes, Richie is a junior; the theme of his junior prom was "Teen Angel.") Richie's trademark became the song "Blueberry Hill" (he would frequently sing the first line, "I found my thrill on Blueberry Hill").

Blueberry pancakes and fresh-squeezed orange juice constitute Richie's favorite breakfast (meatloaf is his favorite dinner), and in the family photo album a full page is devoted to Richie as a baby attempting to eat his first bowl of oatmeal. In grammar school, Richie received a medal for reading comprehension.

"The Love Bandit," license plate F-7193, is what Richie called his 1952 Ford. In high school, Richie was a member of the French Club, his ROTC 3rd Squad leader, and a reporter for the school newspaper, the Jefferson *Bugle*. Richie first had aspirations of being a lawyer, then a journalist. He was also a disc jockey at radio station WOW (where he earned $25 a week) and appeared as a contestant on the WZAZ-TV quiz show "Big Money" (his category was baseball). "Cheap Work" ("Any job for money") was the short-lived company Richie formed with friends Potsie and Ralph to earn extra money. Richie was later a cub reporter for the Milwaukee *Journal*.

Arlene (Tannis G. Montgomery), Gloria (Linda Purl) and Lori Beth Allen (Lynda Goodfriend) were Richie's girlfriends. He married Lori Beth (who called him "Sizzle Lips"), and they had a son named Richie Jr. Richie left the series when he joined the army and was transferred to Greenland. Lynda Goodfriend originally played Kim, a friend of Richie's.

Richie's older brother, Chuck (see "Relatives"), who appeared to do nothing but bounce a basketball, left the series during the second season (he was written out) and was said to be attending college.

Joanie Louise, Richie's younger sister, is a member of the Junior Chipmunks Scout troop and later attends Jefferson High (where she is a cheerleader; her grammar school is not named). She has the nicknames "Shortcake" and "Pumpkin," and her first word as a baby was *hardware*. Joanie's favorite meal is baked macaroni and applesauce. When she had a crush on Richie's friend Potsie, she would play "Secret Love" (selection H-14) on the Seebring 100 Selecto-Matic jukebox at Arnold's Drive-In. Her first nighttime date was with Fonzie's nephew, Spike. Joanie has a pet hamster named Gertrude.

Joanie was a member of the singing group, the Suedes. She and Suedes Milly and Lilly (Jan and Jill Bunker) provided the backup vocals for Leather Tuscadero (Suzy Quatro). Fonzie's cousin, Charles ("Chachi") Arcola, became Joanie's romantic interest in Jefferson High School. Chachi was a member of the Lords gang and part of the Velvet Clouds band (playing drums). Joanie and Chachi married in the last episode, but before doing so were spun off into the series "Joanie Loves Chachi" (3/23/82 to 8/13/83). Chachi's mother, Louisa (Ellen Travolta), marries Al Delvecchio (Al Molinaro), and the family moves to Chicago where they open Delvecchio's Family Restaurant at 1632 Palmer Street. Chachi joins a motley band as a singer and asks his girlfriend, Joanie, to join him. Joanie receives permission and moves to Chicago. Stories followed their efforts to make a name for themselves in the music world. When the series failed, Joanie returned home and married Chachi shortly after.

Arthur Herbert Fonzarelli, better known as "The Fonz" and "Fonzie," is the cool high school dropout who once rode with a motorcycle gang called the Falcons. After quitting the Falcons, he worked as a mechanic at Otto's Auto Orphanage (then at Herb's Auto Repairs and finally Bronco's Auto Repairs). Fonzie later returned to Jefferson High to get his diploma. He first taught auto shop at Jefferson High, then became the dean of boys at the rowdy George S. Patton High School. Fonzie was also a member of the Demons gang, and his "offices" at Arnold's Drive-In are the "Guys' Room" and the four-for-a-quarter photo booth outside the drive-in. Fonzie portrayed Hamlet in the local church production of *Hamlet* and first lived in Apartment 154 (no address given) before moving into the room above the garage at Cunninghams' (his rent is $50 a month).

Fonzie appeared on the television show "You Wanted to See It" (where he attempted to jump over 14 garbage cans with his motorcycle in the parking lot of Arnold's Drive-In; he was called "Fearless Fonzarelli" and failed to complete the jump—he crashed into Arnold's Milwaukee Fried Chicken Stand).

The Lone Ranger is Fonzie's hero (he has a Lone Ranger toothbrush), Spunky is his dog, and he uses Mr. Musk aftershave lotion. In one episode, Fonzie mentions that his father deserted him and his family when he was three years old; in another he says his father split when he was two. His mother split two years later, and he was raised by his grandmother (who called him "Skippy").

Fonzie has a bathrobe and a toolbox that says "Sweetums" ("Hey, it's a gift from a girl"), and he has an autograph from Annette Funicello ("She gave me hers and I gave her mine"). He is plagued by the "Fonzarelli Curse" (when Fonzie is asked to be the best man at a wedding, disaster happens). Girls flock to Fonzie like bees to honey. He commands attention by snapping his fingers and his catchphrases are "Aaayh" and "Whoooa." While Fonzie could have any girl he wanted, he became serious about two women: Pinky Tuscadero (Roz Kelly), a biker who dressed in pink, and Ashley Pfister (Linda Purl), a widow with a young daughter named Heather (Heather O'Rourke). In 1984 episodes, Fonzie adopted an orphan boy named Danny (Danny Ponce).

As a boy Warren Weber would make things out of clay; his mother nicknamed him "Potsie." He is Richie's best friend, weighs 145 pounds, is five feet ten inches tall, and has blue eyes and black hair. He attended the same schools as Richie, and together they shared many misadventures (such as using fake I.D.'s to see Bubbles the Stripper [Barbara Rhoades] at Eddie's Pink Palace; attempting to join the Demons gang to become "cool"; and pooling their resources to pay $175 for a car whose best feature was the chrome eagle ornament on the hood). When Potsie visits the Cunninghams, he wears a white shirt with blue stripes. His parents (who own a garage) have a car with the license plate BFJ 380. Potsie (lead vocal), Richie (sax) and Ralph (keyboard) formed the Happy Days band (later called the Velvet Clouds). In one episode, Potsie performed professionally at the Vogue Terrace Club, and he, Richie and Ralph were members of the Alpha Tau Omega fraternity in college (also given as the Pi Kappa Nu fraternity).

Jennifer ("Jenny") Piccolo is Joanie's best friend. She is boy crazy and calls herself "the object of mad desire." She is very sexy, reads *Passionate Romance* magazine and calls Joanie "Joans." Jenny memorized the entire Milwaukee phone book to join the Rondells, a girls' club at Jefferson High. Jenny ordered (under Joanie's name) the "Ajax Bust Developer" (for $12.99) "to become more of a sexpot than I already am." Jenny's phone number was given as 555-4242.

The afterschool hangout is Arnold's Drive-In, a hamburger joint located at 2815 Lake Avenue. It was originally owned by Arnold Takahashi (Pat Morita), then by Al

Delvecchio (Al Molinaro). In the first episode, the hangout is called Arthur's Drive-In. When Arnold's burns down, Fonzie becomes Al's silent partner in the new Arnold's Drive-In (rebuilt by Trans Allied Construction). Fonzie wanted to call it "Fonzie's"; "Big Al's" was the name Al wanted. They settled for "Arnold's—Fonzie and Big Al, Proprietors." Al's delivery truck (Arnold's Catering) license plate reads B9362, and his favorite television show is "Dreams Can Come True." The vending machine at Arnold's dispenses a soda called Spring Time Cola; the local haven for making out is Inspiration Point. College banners on the walls of Arnold's represent Iona, State, Purdue, Yale and Indiana.

During the opening theme, the record seen being played on the jukebox has a label that reads "Happy Days." Lyrics by Norman Gimble. Music composed by Charles Fox." While this song is heard in the closing theme (later the opening theme), the song "Rock Around the Clock," by Bill Haley and the Comets, is actually heard as the record is played. In the original pilot, "New Family in Town," Harold Gould played Howard and Susan Neher was Joanie. Fonzie did not appear, and the roles of Marion, Richie and Potsie were played by the same performers as in the series. The pilot, retitled "Love and the Happy Days," aired on "Love, American Style" on 2/25/72.

Relatives: Ric Carrott, Gavan O'Herlihy and Randolph Roberts (Richie's brother, *Chuck Cunningham*), Danny Thomas (Howard's father, *Shawn Cunningham*), Nancy Walker (Howard's cousin, *Nancy Blansky*), Crystal Bernard (Howard's niece, *K.C. Cunningham*), Richard Paul (Howard's brother, *Dick Cunningham*), Pat O'Brien (Howard's uncle, *Joe Cunningham*), Jackie Coogan (Richie's uncle, *Harold*), Peggy Rea (Richie's aunt, *Bessie*), Bo Sharron (Richie's son, *Richie Jr.*), Ted McGinley (Marion's nephew, *Roger Phillips*, the basketball coach at Jefferson High), Eddie Fontaine (Fonzie's father, *Vito Fonzarelli*), Danny Butch (Fonzie's nephew, *Spike*), Frances Bay (Fonzie's *Grandma Nussbaum*), Charles Galioto (Fonzie's cousin, *Angie*), Phil Silvers (Jenny's father, *Roscoe Piccolo*), Al Molinaro (Al's brother, *Father Anthony Delvecchio*), Alice Nunn (Al's *Mama Delvecchio*), Alan Oppenheimer and Jack Dodson (Ralph's father, *Mickey Malph*), Craig Stevens (Ashley's father, *George Pfister*), Marla Adams (Ashley's mother, *Millicent Pfister*), J.J. Barry (Chachi's uncle, *Gonzo*). Not seen were Fonzie's mother, Angela, and Marion's uncle, Ben (the owner of a dude ranch in Colorado).

Theme: "Happy Days," by Charles Fox and Norman Gimble.

Note: See also "Laverne and Shirley," the spinoff series.

281. *Hardball*

NBC, 9/21/89 to 6/29/90

Charles ("Charlie") Battles (John Ashton) and Joseph ("Joe") Kaczierowski (Richard Tyson), called "Kaz" for short, are officers with the Metro Division of the Los Angeles Police Department. Charlie, the veteran cop, was with the Fighting 52nd Unit of the U.S. Army Corps in Korea. He weighs 205 pounds, eats Oaties breakfast cereal, and has a car with the license plate 2LYN 596; his badge number is 6483.

Kaz, the streetwise cop, weighs 192 pounds and uses various disguises to apprehend criminals. He was formerly a vice squad detective with the San Diego Police Department; he now wears badge number 696. Charlie and Kaz are members of the Slammers Baseball Team, and their car code is 1-K-9.

Kaz rides a motorcycle with the license plate 25862L; Charlie's favorite meal to cook is chili; and Kaz listens to radio station KRTW (where his favorite D.J. is the sexy-sounding Jamie Steele, played by Lydia Cornell).

Yvette Nipar played Charlie's daughter, Cindy Battles; Patricia Harty appeared as Kaz's mother, Beverly Kaczierowski. Eddie Money sings the theme, "Roll It Over."

282. *The Hardy Boys and the Mystery of the Applegate Treasure*

ABC, 1/7/57 to 2/1/57

Cast: Tim Considine (*Frank Hardy*), Tommy Kirk (*Joe Hardy*), Russ Conway (*Fenton Hardy*), Carole Ann Campbell (*Iola Morton*), Sarah Selby (*Gertrude Hardy*), Florenz Ames (*Silas Applegate*).

Facts: The setting is the small town of Bayport, Massachusetts. At 8966 Elm Street live Frank and Joe Hardy, the sons of private detective Fenton Hardy. Fenton, a widower, and his sons are cared for by Fenton's sister, Gertrude Hardy. (Fenton's license plate reads 16-943.)

Frank and Joe idolize their father and hope to become private detectives also. Fenton spends much time working in the city and is rarely home. Thus, the opportunity for the boys to work on a case never arises. Frank and Joe think it is just going to be another dull summer until Joe's girlfriend, Iola Morton, stumbles upon a real mystery and involves the three in a dangerous quest to solve "The Mystery of the Applegate Treasure."

Iola is young and very pretty and yearns for a life of excitement like Frank and Joe ("My father's only a doctor," she says. "But your father is a detective. Can't I be a Hardy boy too?"). The mystery begins when Iola and a new boy in town, Perry Robinson (uncredited role) bump into each other. They are both knocked to the ground and the contents of Iola's purse are scattered about. Iola gathers her belongings and leaves. As Perry picks himself up, he realizes that something of his is missing, and he believes Iola accidentally took it.

Moments after she leaves Joe and Frank, someone throws a canvas bag over Iola and steals her purse. Her screams for help bring Joe to her side; Frank follows shortly after with her purse (which he found lying on the sidewalk). When Iola checks her purse and finds nothing is missing, they begin to wonder why someone would steal Iola's purse and not take anything.

Their investigation begins with Perry, whom they find working for Silas Applegate, the old man who lives in a rundown mansion. Perry tells them that he mugged Iola in order to get back a gold coin he found while digging up weeds on the estate. Joe and Frank discover that the 1803 coin is a doubloon (pirates' gold) and is linked to stories about the mysterious Applegate treasure.

From Silas they learn that the legend began during the War of 1812 when Silas's great-grandfather, Colonel Nathaniel Applegate, received 3,000 gold coins from the pirate Jean Laffite in payment for unspecified damages. The gold was placed in a treasure chest and passed down as the Applegate legacy. But ten years ago it was stolen. By whom is the question and the mystery Frank, Joe and Iola set out to solve.

Their investigation leads them to Jackley (Robert Foulk), a plumber Silas hired to make repairs, and Boles (uncredited role), a man who worked for Silas ten years ago. A search of Boles's residence in a roominghouse near the railroad tracks uncovers a letter that reads, "I hid it in the wall—old Applegate's treasure in the old tower wall." However, a search of the tower on the Applegate estate fails to uncover any gold. Despite the disappointment, Frank and Joe are still determined to find it and feel that Boles is the key to solving the mystery. They begin to follow him. It is late evening when Boles finally returns to his home. Joe notices an old abandoned steam engine water tower and wonders if that might be the tower referred to in the letter. Frank and Joe search the tower and find the gold (which is then returned to Silas). The thief is revealed as a man named Jenkins, who worked for Silas ten years ago. After stealing the gold, he hid it in the water tower but was arrested on other charges before he could claim it. Jenkins wrote the note to his friend Jackley, asking him to retrieve the gold. Before Jackley could find it, Boles stole the note. "Oh, I think the Hardy boys are the most wonderful detectives in the whole wide world," says Iola, who then kisses Joe. The End.

Theme: "Gold Doubloons and Pieces of Eight," by George Bruns and Jackson Gillis.

Note: The same regular cast (Frank, Joe, Iola, Fenton and Gertrude) returned for a second adventure, "The Hardy Boys and the Mystery of Ghost Farm" (ABC, 9/30/57 to 10/15/57). Frank, Joe and Iola attempt to solve the mystery of a farm that is supposedly haunted by a ghost. Both serials were broadcast as segments of "The Mickey Mouse Club." See also "The Nancy Drew Mysteries" for information on "The Hardy Boys Mysteries."

The Franklin W. Dixon stories were later adapted to television in an unsold NBC pilot called "The Hardy Boys" (9/8/67), with Tim Matheson as Joe Hardy, Rick Gates as Frank Hardy, Richard Anderson as Fenton Hardy and Portia Nelson as Gertrude Hardy (the story followed their efforts to locate a stolen jade collection). A short-lived animated ver-

sion called "The Hardy Boys" appeared on ABC (9/6/69 to 9/4/71; 17 episodes that were repeated many times). Byron Kane was the voice of Frank and Dallas McKennon provided Joe's voice.

283. *Harper Valley*

NBC, 1/16/81 to 8/28/81
NBC, 10/29/81 to 8/14/82

Cast: Barbara Eden *(Stella Johnson)*, Jenn Thompson *(Dee Johnson)*, George Gobel *(Otis Harper)*, Fannie Flagg *(Cassie Bowman)*.

Facts: The house at 769 Oakwood Street in Harper Valley, Ohio, is owned by Stella Johnson, a beautiful, flamboyant woman who hopes to begin a new life in what she believes is a warm, friendly town. Stella is a widow and the mother of a girl named Dee. Stella is also independent and outspoken and finds Harper Valley to be a hotbed of hypocrisy when a group of prudes who call themselves the P.T.A. claim she is a bad influence and want her to leave town. Stella's efforts to remain in Harper Valley by "teaching my neighbors some lessons and showing them up for the hypocrites they are" are the focal point of first season episodes.

Stella sells Angel Glow Cosmetics; Dee attends Harper Valley Junior High School. During second season episodes, when the P.T.A. aspect is dropped, Stella becomes the executive assistant to Otis Harper, the often intoxicated mayor whose ancestors founded the town. Stella's maiden name is Smith.

Cassie Bowman is Stella's friend. She is a beautician at the LaModerne Beauty Shop (first season episodes) and later the publisher of the Harper Valley *Sentinel*. Cassie lives at 675 Pine Valley Lane, and her car license plate reads TNT 456.

William Homer ("Uncle Buster") Smith (Mills Watson) is Stella's mischievous uncle, a would-be inventor who has yet to invent something that works. Flora Simpson Reilly (Anne Francine) is the woman who most despises Stella's beauty and flamboyant style. She is the owner of the Harper Valley Bank and president of the P.T.A. Her limo license plate reads NNT 552.

Wanda Taylor (Bridget Hanley) is Flora's married daughter. She is rich, spoiled and married to the womanizing Bobby Taylor (Rod McCary), who works as the city attorney. Wanda and Bobby have a rich and "spoiled rotten" daughter named Scarlett Taylor (Suzi Dean), who also attends Harper Valley Junior High. The Taylors live with Flora at 699 Tremont Street.

Tom Meechum (Christopher Stone) is the editor of the town's second newspaper, the Harper Valley *Sun*; and Doug Peterson (Fred Holliday) is the news reporter for WHV-TV, Channel 29. Barbara Eden also played Stella's sister, Della Smith, in one episode. The Tri-Star Bus Line services Harper Valley and neighboring Columbus, Ohio. The series is based on both the song and movie *Harper Valley P.T.A.* (also its series title during first season episodes).

Theme: "Harper Valley P.T.A." (first season theme vocal by Jeannie C. Riley), and "Harper Valley, U.S.A." (second season theme by Carol Chase).

284. *Harry and the Hendersons*

Syndicated, 1/12/91 to the present

Cast: Bruce Davison (*George Henderson*), Molly Cheek (*Nancy Henderson*), Carol-Ann Plante (*Sarah Henderson*), Zachary Bostrom (*Ernie Henderson*), Noah Blake (*Brett Douglas*).

Facts: George Henderson, his wife, Nancy, and their children, Sarah and Ernie, are returning from vacation and traveling on Interstate 5 in Seattle. Without warning, a creature (the legendary Bigfoot) steps onto the road and is hit by the Hendersons' van. Believing that they killed the creature, they somehow manage to tie it to the van's roof and bring it home. The creature, however, is not dead, just stunned, and it shows signs of sociability—so much so that he adopts the Hendersons and becomes a member of the family (whom they must conceal, fearing authorities will claim him for experiments; he lives in the Hendersons' loft).

Shortly after, Tiffany ("Tiffy") Glick (Cassie Cole), the young daughter of their neighbor, Samantha Glick (Gigi Rice), sees Bigfoot (Kevin Peter Hall, then Dawan Scott and Brian Steele) and tells her mother about "a big hairy guy in the Hendersons' backyard." Samantha dismisses it as just Tiffany's imagination, but Tiffany's description, "hairy guy," prompts the Hendersons to name their houseguest Harry.

The Hendersons live at 410 Forest Drive in Seattle. George was first a marketing executive for the People's Sporting Goods Company, then the publisher of a magazine called *A Better Life* (he is assisted by Nancy's brother, Brett Douglas). George's childhood dream was to go to Hollywood, meet Annette Funicello and sing on "The Mickey Mouse Club." When George gave Nancy her engagement ring (on 6/26/72), he wrapped it in a piece of paper with a note saying, "Dear Nancy, will you murry me" (*murry* was a typo). George's 4 × 4 van license plate reads 608 GHR. Brett calls George "G-Man," Nancy "Nance," Ernie "E-Man" and Harry "Hair Monger." Club 700 is Brett's favorite hangout.

Nancy, whose middle name is Gwen, works with the Student Council Exchange of Seattle. When she gets upset, she eats a half gallon of Breyer's Rocky Road ice cream. She first played triangle in her high school marching band. The most risqué thing Nancy ever did, she says, "was not to wear a bra between 1972 and 1975." She was later arrested (civil disobedience) for protesting without clothes on a nude beach. When Nancy gets mad at Harry, she calls him "Mister" (for example, "Now you cut that out, Mister!"). As a kid, Nancy had a pet frog she called Slimey.

Sarah is 15 years old and attends Madison High School. She runs track (long distance), wrote the song "Somewhere Out There" for the Homecoming Dance and hopes to one day write a book about her family and Harry—"But I'm

going to use a pen name. I don't want anyone to think I'm nuts." Sarah, whose middle name is Nicole, had a pet hamster named Melissa and worked as a countergirl at Photo Quickie. She calls her white lace bra "my lucky bra."

Samantha works for Channel 10 and reports on "The News at 5." She has a prime-time series called "Crime Time, with Samantha Glick." Her most famous story is "Housewives by Day, Strippers by Night," and she also hosts an interview series called "Seattle Celebrities." Samantha, who learns of Harry's existence in later episodes, wishes the Hendersons "would get a pet duck like a normal family." Tiffany, called "Tiffy" by Samantha, calls Harry "Hairy Man." For unexplained reasons, Samantha and Tiffany were dropped when the second season began. New to the cast was Darcy Farg (Courtney Peldon), a pretty, feminine and rich young girl whose unseen parents purchased the home next door to the Hendersons. Although Ernie disliked girls, he befriended Darcy (who had a crush on him). Ernie and Darcy were members of the Padres Pee Wee League baseball team; Darcy has a cat named Damian ("the bird killer") and in one episode started a sidewalk mineral water stand called Chez Darcy. (When she was first introduced, Darcy's last name was given as Payne.)

Harry is eight feet one inch tall and weighs 680 pounds. The first word he spoke was *Ernie* (whom he admires the most). When Sarah became involved in a class project to raise money to help an injured sea lion (Milton), a charity wrestling match was staged. Harry, disguised with a mask, wrestled as Bigfoot Man. Harry has a Barry Manilow tape collection and loves granola bars (he calls them "Num Num" and "Numie Numie"). Patrick Pinney provides Harry's voice.

Relatives: Marian Mercer (Nancy's mother, *Monica Douglas*), Diane Stilwell (Nancy's sister, *Emily Graham*), Julie McCullough (Darcy's Swedish cousin, *Uma Farg*), Angela Vesser (Darcy's cousin, *Ema Farg*), Mark L. Taylor (George's cousin, *Melvin Henderson*). Not seen were Nancy's aunt, Jane, and Samantha's ex-husband, Victor Glick.

Theme: "Your Feets Too Big," vocal by Leon Redbone.

285. *Harry O*

ABC, 9/12/74 to 8/12/76

At 1:20 A.M. on the night of January 18, 1969 (a Friday), police detective Harry Orwell and his partner reported to a burglary in progress at a drugstore. A shootout ensued. Harry was shot in the back and his partner was killed.

When the series begins, Harry Orwell (David Janssen) is living on a policeman's disability pension and supplementing his income by moonlighting as a private detective. He now has a bullet lodged in his spine and is working on a boat called the *Answer*—"which I'll have as soon as I put it back together. I'm going out on the ocean where they have no telephones; telephones bug me."

Harry does a lot of walking (he has a car, but it needs a

new transmission—"I don't have the $300 needed to fix it"); will spring for a cab when it's needed ("It's tax deductible") and does his grocery shopping at the Agryz Market.

Harry never discusses politics, nor the shooting that injured him. He has some romantic interests, but wishes he were 17 again ("Because when I was 17 I once said, 'A woman is like a bus. There'll be another one along in a few minutes.' Now that was a long time ago").

First season episodes are set in San Diego (where Harry could be reached at 101 Coast Road). The remainder of the series is set in Los Angeles (Harry's phone number is 555-4617).

Living at the beach provided Harry with a gorgeous view of the ocean—and four stunning neighbors: Mildred (Barbara Leigh), Betsy (Kathrine Baumann), Sue Ingram (Farrah Fawcett) and Lindsay (Loni Anderson—as a brunette). Lindsay, an airline stewardess, shared a home with Sue.

Manuel ("Manny") Quinn (Henry Darrow) of the San Diego Police Department and K.C. Trench (Anthony Zerbe) of the Los Angeles P.D. were the lieutenants involved with Harry and his cases. Recurring roles were played by Keye Luke as Dr. Fong, a criminologist, and Les Lannom as Lester Hodges, Fong's assistant, a wealthy chap who liked to dabble in detective work (the characters were part of a failed pilot called "Lester Hodges and Dr. Fong," which aired 3/18/76).

Relatives: Kathleen Lloyd (Manny's niece, *Marilyn Quinn*).

Theme: "Harry O," by Billy Goldenberg.

Note: Two pilots were made: "Harry O" (ABC, 3/11/73), which had the subtitle "Such Dust as Dreams Are Made On"), and "Smile, Jenny, You're Dead" (ABC, 2/3/74).

286. *Hart to Hart*

ABC, 9/22/79 to 7/3/84

Jonathan Hart (Robert Wagner), the wealthy head of Hart Industries (a.k.a. Jonathan Hart Enterprises), and his wife, Jennifer (Stefanie Powers), live at 3100 Willow Pond Road in Bel Air. Max (Lionel Stander) is their man Friday; Freeway is their dog; and 555-1654 (later 555-3223) is their phone number.

Jonathan started Hart Industries, located at 112 North Las Palmas in Los Angeles, when he issued its first shares of stock in March 1969. The Hart Shipping Lines and Chem-O-Cal are two of the many divisions of Hart Industries, the phone number of which is 555-1271.

Jennifer, whose maiden name is Edwards, was born in Hillhaven, Maryland. She had a horse named Sweet Sue, attended Gresham Hall Prep School, and majored in journalism at an unnamed college. After graduation, Jennifer moved to New York City to become a freelance journalist. While on assignment in England for the *London Herald,* Jennifer learns that Jonathan Hart has come to the city to close a big deal (to prevent Kingsford Motors from going bankrupt). Her efforts to get an interview with the press-shy Jonathan fail—until they meet by chance at the bar of the

Hotel Ritz and find an instant attraction to each other. After a brief courtship, they marry and honeymoon at the O'Berge Inn (Room 7) in San Francisco's Napa Valley.

Jennifer gets a little tipsy from champagne, lunches at La Scala's and has her hair done at Salvatore's on Wilshire Boulevard. She also appeared in a bit part (a party hostess) on her favorite daytime television soap opera, "Doctors' Hospital." Stefanie Powers also played her double, Dominique Bitten, a mobster's wife (Jennifer was mistaken for her and kidnapped), in one episode. Nikki Stefunos (Christina Belford) was Jonathan's girlfriend before Jennifer. Jonathan has pancakes for breakfast on Monday mornings.

HART I, HART II (also seen as 2 HARTS) and HART III are Jonathan and Jennifer's license plates. Max, who likes a good cigar and is addicted to gambling, did a commercial with Freeway for Dog Gone It dog food.

Relatives: Ray Milland (Jennifer's father, *Steve Edwards*), Eva Gabor (Jennifer's aunt, *Renie*), Marilyn Kagan (Jennifer's cousin, *Betsy Bach*), Craig Wasson (Jennifer's cousin, *Steve Thomas*), Allyn Ann McLeries (Max's ex-wife, *Pearl*).

Theme: "Hart to Hart," by Roger Nichols.

287. *The Hat Squad*

CBS, 9/16/92 to 1/23/93

In Los Angeles during the 1940s there was a special unit of police officers who wore black fedoras and dusters. They were called the Hat Squad. Their hats made them different, and criminals feared them because they had no respect for the law; they did whatever it took "to get their man." Fifty years later, Michael ("Mike") Ragland (James Tolkan), a captain with the 77th Precinct of the L.A.P.D., organizes a four-man unit he calls the Hat Squad. Like the original unit, the new squad has little respect for the law. They wear black fedoras and dusters and specialize in solving violent crimes. But unlike the original unit, the new Hat Squad is made up of Mike's three sons: Raphael Martinez (Nestor Servano), Buddy Capatosa (Don Michael Paul) and Matt Matheson (Billy Warlock)—three orphans of crime who were adopted by Mike and his wife, Kitty (Shirley Douglas, then Janet Carroll), and raised to be cops.

Buddy is the eldest son; his car code is BH-2 and his car license plate reads THE BEAST. Raphael, a ladies' man, went to Jefferson High School. BH-1 is his car code; BVN 891 is his car license plate number. Raphael carries a special jack of spades playing card that is a certified weapon (it has razor-sharp edges—"It's my calling card"). Raphael saw his parents gunned down; to this day he won't use firearms. Matt, the youngest, attended Hoover High School and is now taking classes in pre-law; BH-3 is his car code.

The squad wears Second Chance bullet-proof vests. Mike's car code is 1-0-30 (later X-Ray-6), and MXN 701 is his car license plate number. Mike and Kitty also have a younger, adopted son named Darnell Johnson (Bruce Robbins), who is being groomed as a future Hat Squad member.

Mike Post composed "The Hat Squad Theme."

Hart to Hart. Stefanie Powers, Robert Wagner and Lionel Stander.

288. *The Hathaways*

ABC, 10/6/61 to 8/31/62

Walter Hathaway (Jack Weston) and his wife, Elinor (Peggy Cass), are a happily married couple who live in a modest home at 148 Magnolia Drive in Los Angeles. They have a car (license plate 0846249); a housekeeper, Amanda Allison (Mary Grace Canfield); and two sources of income: the Hathaway Realty Company, which Walter runs; and the Hathaway Chimps, Charlie, Enoch and Candy (The Marquis Chimps), three theatrical chimpanzees Elinor adopted, trained and now manages.

"The Kids," as Elinor calls them (Walter calls them "the children"), are a sought-after act for TV shows and films. Enoch is easily impressed and copies Walter's mannerisms and gestures. Charlie, the oldest, is the mischievous one. He has a mind of his own and costs the "family" jobs (he gives the "raspberry" to producers he doesn't like). Candy is the baby of the family and clings to Enoch for comfort.

Amanda earns $1.25 an hour; the Hathaway Chimps

appeared on such shows as "Ed Sullivan," "Jack Benny" and the mythical "Al Jolson Show"; they also had their own segment (in which they clowned around) on "Barney Holt's Merchandise Showcase." Walter had a development called Desert Charm Estates ("Home Sites for People with Foresight") that he could never seem to unload.

Herbert W. Spencer composed the theme.

289. *Have Gun—Will Travel*

CBS, 9/14/57 to 9/21/63

HAVE GUN—WILL TRAVEL. WIRE PALADIN, SAN FRANCISCO read the calling card of a man known only as Paladin, a fast gun for hire who operates out of the Hotel Carlton in San Francisco. Paladin is a connoisseur of the arts. He has box seats at the opera house, enjoys fine food (he even has his own recipes) and has an eye for the ladies. He smokes expensive cigars (he carries a spare in his boot), collects chessmen (especially the knight) and is lucky at gambling. He also has one rule: never to go anyplace without his gun. Paladin, a right-handed gunman, carries a Colt .45 revolver ("The balance is excellent; the trigger responds to the pressure of one ounce. It was handcrafted to my specifications." He rarely draws it—"But when I do I aim to use it").

Paladin's work clothes are a black outfit with a chess knight—the Paladin—embossed on his black holster. He also wears a black hat and carries a small derringer under his gunbelt. Paladin is a graduate of West Point, and his experiences with the Union army have given him a knowledge of war tactics that he uses to help people. He has a talent with a gun, a devotion to duty and relaxes in luxury at the hotel, genuinely enjoying life between assignments. (He reads the newspapers from various states and sometimes sends his calling card to people he thinks may need his help; his fee is $1,000.)

The theme from the unaired pilot version of "Have Gun—Will Travel" exclaims, "There are campfire legends that the plainsmen spin, telling of the man with the gun, of the man called Paladin." Little is known about Paladin. His legend began when an unnamed ex–army officer lost a large sum of money to a wealthy land baron (William Conrad) in a poker game. To repay the debt, the army officer agreed to help the land baron by killing Smoke, an outlaw who has been plaguing him. In a duel to the death, the officer kills Smoke. The officer then adopts Smoke's black outfit and the symbol of the Paladin as his own. He calls himself Paladin and begins a policy of hiring out his guns and experience to those who are unable to protect themselves. (In this particular episode, "Genesis," Richard Boone played three roles: the older and younger Paladin and Smoke.)

Hey Boy (Kam Tong) and Hey Girl (Lisa Lu) are Paladin's servants at the Hotel Carlton; Mr. McGunnis (Olan Soule) is its manager; and W. Beal Wong played Hey Boy's uncle, Sing Wo, owner of Sing Wo's Chinese Laundry, in one episode.

Johnny Western sings the theme, "The Ballad of Paladin."

290. *Hawaii Five-O*

CBS, 9/26/68 to 4/5/80

Hawaii Five-O is a special investigative branch of the Hawaiian Police Department which is based in the Iolani Palace ("The only palace on American soil"). Its regular phone number is 732-5577; 277-2977 is its special emergency number.

Steve McGarrett (Jack Lord) is the head of Five-O and works in conjunction with the governor of Hawaii (Richard Denning). Daniel ("Danny") Williams (James MacArthur), Chin Ho Kelly (Kam Fong) and Kono (Zulu) are the main detectives who work with Steve.

Steve, a Capricorn, was born in San Francisco. He is a commander in the Navy Reserve and has an account at the National Bank of Oahu. His car license plate is 163958, and he has his hair cut every Tuesday. Danny, whom Steve calls "Dan-O," was said to have been born in both Honolulu and the Midwest. He majored in philosophy at the University of Hawaii for one year, then transferred to the University of California to major in police science. CBS affiliate station KGMB-TV, Channel 9, is seen frequently as the station that covers Steve's cases.

In last season episodes, when the series was also known as "McGarrett," Steve was assisted by a new team of investigators: detectives Lori Wilson (Sharon Farrell) and James ("Kimo") Carew (William Smith), and Officer Moe ("Truck") Kealoha (Moe Keale). Wo Fat (Khigh Dhiegh) was Steve's principal nemesis from the pilot to the series' last episode, "Woe to Wo Fat." "Book 'em, Dan-O" and "Patch me through to McGarrett" became the series' well-known catchphrases.

Tim O'Kelly played Danny in the pilot film; Helen Hayes appeared as Danny's aunt, Clara, in one episode.

Morton Stevens composed the theme, "Hawaii Five-O."

291. *Hawaiian Eye*

ABC, 10/7/59 to 9/10/63

Cast: Connie Stevens (*Cricket Blake*), Anthony Eisley (*Tracy Steele*), Robert Conrad (*Tom Lopaka*), Grant Williams (*Gregg MacKenzie*), Troy Donahue (*Philip Barton*), Poncie Ponce (*Kim*), Tina Cole (*Sunny Day*), Mel Prestidge (*Lieutenant Danny Quon*).

Facts: Tracy Steele, Thomas Jefferson ("Tom") Lopaka and Gregg MacKenzie are the operatives of "Hawaiian Eye—Investigation-Protection," a security firm located in the lobby of the Hawaiian Village (later the Hilton Hawaiian Village) Hotel in Honolulu, Hawaii. The "Eyes" as they are called, provide the hotel security and hire out their investigative services to people in trouble.

Chryseis ("Cricket") Blake is their friend, a gorgeous singer who runs Cricket's Corner, the hotel's gift shop. Cricket also sings nightly in the hotel's Shell Bar (also seen as the Shell Lounge). She is 20 years old, five feet two inches tall and measures 37-20-36. Cricket was born in San Francisco and is a fan of jazz music. As a teenager, she hung out at a club on Fisherman's Wharf to hear a trumpet player named Joey Vito. She now frequents the Blue Grotto on Kalakalu Street in Honolulu, where Joey now performs. Cricket is also an amateur photographer and hopes to make it big by selling her pictures to newspapers.

Philip ("Phil") Barton is the director of special events at the hotel. He and Cricket were "sweethearts" in last season episodes (when Phil joined the cast). Phil calls Cricket "the original do-gooder" (as she will help anybody she believes is in trouble).

Sunny Day is a hopeful singer who works at the Hawaiian Village Hotel's information booth. Kim Kasano, who does occasional work for Tracy and Tom, runs a taxi cab service called Kim's Kab. Danny Quon is a lieutenant with the Honolulu Police Department.

Moke (Doug Mossman) works as a security guard for Hawaiian Eye; Maila (Karyn Kupcinet) is Tom's receptionist; Daro (Mikio Kato) is Tracy's receptionist; and Bert (Clayton Naluai) is the parking lot attendant at the hotel.

Cricket's Jeep license plate reads M3L 071; 643-421 is Tom's sedan's license plate. Gregg's license plate is LPQ 401; and JK3-961 is Tracy's license plate. Phil's license plate reads 15-652; and 7T403 is the license plate of Kim's Kab.

The regulars dine at the Café House; hotel benefits are held in the Dome Room; Tracy and Tom call Cricket "Lover"; an ad for United Airlines is seen on the window next to Cricket's Corner. When Tracy needs Kim to follow a suspect, he says, "Control to Kim" (via a radio link). In the episode "The Comics," in which Cricket does not appear, Tom performs the song "I Love You Pretty Baby" in the Shell Bar.

Relatives: George Montgomery (Phil's uncle, *Miles Maitland*), Peggy McCay (Phil's cousin, *Lucy McDowell*).

Theme: "Hawaiian Eye," by Mack David and Jerry Livingston.

292. *Hawaiian Heat*

ABC, 9/14/84 to 11/23/84

With little chance for promotion and fed up with the conditions that exist in Chicago, Metro Department police officers Mac Riley (Robert Ginty) and Andy Senkowski (Jeff McCracken) decide to reconstruct their lives and move to Hawaii. There, after helping Major Taro Oshira (Mako) of the Oahu Police Department, solve a complex case, they become detectives with the Criminal Investigation Division. Mac (badge number 6314) and Andy (badge number 316) originally worked on file duty. When they bought a car (a 1965 Cadillac convertible, license plate DEW 592), they became undercover officers for major Oshira.

Irene Gorley (Tracy Scoggins) is their friend and neighbor, a beautiful young woman who runs a helicopter sight-seeing service called Cupid Eyes Tours. Detective

Harker (Branscombe Richmond) is Taro's aide; and Dr. Robin Barnett (Diane Civita) is the police psychologist who assists Mac and Andy.

Shelley Winters played Andy's mother, Florence Senkowski, and Moana Anderson appeared as Harker's niece, Keiki. Tina (Tina Marie Machado), Leila (Leila Hee Olson) and Julie (Julie Marie Olson) were the gorgeous native girls who shared an apartment with Irene at 187 La Lanola Place in Oahu.

Tom Scott and Candy Patterson composed the theme, "Goodbye Blues."

293. *Hazel*

NBC, 9/28/61 to 9/6/65
CBS, 9/10/65 to 9/5/66

Cast: Shirley Booth (*Hazel Burke*), Don DeFore (*George Baxter*), Whitney Blake (*Dorothy Baxter*), Bobby Buntrock (*Harold Baxter*), Ray Fulmer (*Steve Baxter*), Lynn Borden (*Barbara Baxter*), Julia Benjamin (*Susie Baxter*).

Facts: At 123 Marshall Road in an unspecified city (possibly in New Jersey, as New York and Philadelphia are mentioned as neighboring cities) reside attorney George Baxter, his wife, Dorothy, their son, Harold, and their live-in maid, Hazel. The Baxters' phone number is Klondike 5-8372 (later 555-8372). In the episode "Sweepstakes Ticket," George receives a Western Union telegram addressed as follows: GEORGE BAXTER, 123 MARSHALL ROAD, CITY. YOU ARE THE HOLDER OF A TICKET ON BONNIE BOY IN THE NATIONAL SWEEPSTAKES. THE GREAT NATIONAL SWEEPSTAKES CORP.

Hazel has an insurance policy to cover her back when she bowls, and she is famous for her fudge brownies. She owns 11 shares of stock in the Davidson Vacuum Cleaner Company and was the television spokesperson for Aunt Nora's Instant Cake Mix. Hazel has been working for the Baxters for 14 years, according to 1964 episodes. She is a member of the Sunshine Girls (a society of local neighborhood maids) and was voted "Maid of the Month" by *American Elegance* magazine. Hazel owned a 1920 Model-T Ford (license plate 306-579); she paid $25 and sold it to a collector for $1,250. Hazel calls George "Mr. B," Dorothy "Missy" and Harold "Sport." In one episode Hazel inherited six tarnished sterling silver spoons from her great-grandmother, Countess Patricia Burke (who lived in England in 1882); in another episode, Hazel mentions that her only true love was Gus Jenkins (Patrick McVey), whom she first met in the Empire State Building's observation tower (he was throwing paper airplanes). He called her "Brown Eyes," and she would have married him if he had asked her. He was a merchant sailor, and things just never worked out.

Hazel, George says, will never tell a lie; she has "George Washington heroics." George also says that Hazel is the only person who knows the true meaning of Christmas ("She makes her own presents"). Hazel says, "Just dustin' these cobwebs off Mr. B's law books makes me feel smart."

Hazel. Front: Whitney Blake, Bobby Buntrock; back: Don DeFore, Shirley Booth.

Hazel's catchphrase when George asks, "Is everything all right, Hazel?" is "Everything is just peachy keen, Mr. B." She keeps her government bonds in her footlocker. Thursday is Hazel's day off, and she takes time off on Sunday to attend mass. Hazel serves breakfast at 7:00 A.M., lunch at 12:15 P.M. and dinner at 6:30 P.M. She has an account at the Commerce Trust Bank.

George, who began practicing law in 1949, is a corporate lawyer with the firm of Butterworth, Hatch, Noll and Baxter. He attended Dartmouth and is a member of the board of regents of the University Law School (he delivers the Oliver Wendell Holmes Memorial Lectures). George drives a convertible (license plate 49-753) and a red sedan (license plate J2R 8255; later 53-859); he calls Hazel's brownies "Hazel's peachy keen pecan brownies." He is constantly nagged by Hazel to stay on his diet and gets additional annoyance from Harvey ("Call me Harve") Griffin (Howard Smith), his firm's biggest client (the owner of Griffin Enterprises). George is also an attorney for the Symphony Association.

George often regrets telling Hazel anything associated with his work—she tries to help him with it. "It's remarkable," George says, "Two years of pre-law training, four years of law school and 12 years of successful practice and I still haven't learned to keep my mouth shut around Hazel." George reads the *Daily Chronicle,* and chocolate fudge cake is his favorite dessert. For his birthday, Hazel gives George handkerchiefs (with the exception of his 1963 birthday, when Hazel gave him a sweepstakes ticket—at the same time he became a member of the antigambling committee).

Dorothy is a freelance interior decorator (no business name given) and a member of the I.D.S. (Interior Decorator's Society). She is also a member of the local women's club and buys her dresses at Montague's Boutique; she buys her lingerie at Blackstone's Department Store (second floor; she wears a size eight negligé).

Harold attends an unnamed grammar school and has a dog named Smiley. His favorite breakfast is pancakes, and he calls Hazel's brownies "the good stuff." His first crush was on a girl named Zelda Warren (Vickie Cos). The infatuation was short-lived, for she wanted him to join her ballet class, wear tights and be a fairy in "Sleeping Beauty."

George's offices are in the Arcade Building. His most frequently seen partner is Harry Noll (Lauren Gilbert), a man who believes he is irresistible to women; he married Rita Linda (Karen Steele), a famous singer who is 20 years his junior; they purchased a house next door to the Baxters at 121 Marshall Road. Linda (Linda Marshall) was George's original secretary ("The best secretary I ever had"); she was replaced by (no reason given) Miss Scott (Molly Dodd). Rosie Hamicker (Maudie Prickett) is Hazel's best friend, a maid also; Mr. Griffin uses a fortune teller named Madame Farina (Rowena Buracke) to help him make business decisions (he also believes Hazel's opinions are more valuable than the money he pays George). Barney Hatfield (Robert B. Williams) is the mailman; and Herbert Johnson (Donald Foster) and his wife, Harriet (Norma Varden), are the Baxters' elderly neighbors (Herbert, an investor, cornered the market on whale bones—427 tons of it).

In the episode of 9/10/65, Hazel and Harold move in with George's younger brother, Steve Baxter, when George is transferred to the Middle East to handle a big oil deal for Mr. Griffin. (George and Dorothy decided to leave Harold in Steve's care to avoid having him miss a semester at school. They were only suposed to be away for a few months; they are in Baghdad when the episode begins.)

Steve, his wife, Barbara, and their daughter, Susie, live at 325 Sycamore Street in the same unnamed city (an hour's drive from George's home). Steve owns the Baxter Realty Company and is called "Mr. Steve" by Hazel. Hazel plays poker with Steve and his friends on Friday nights; with Barbara, she attempted to make money by marketing "Aunt Hazel's Chili Sauce" for Richie's Supermarket (they made it for 15 cents a bottle and sold it for 98 cents). Susie and Harold both attend an unnamed school; Steve and Barbara go to bed at 10:00 P.M.

Other Roles: (1965-66): Millie Ballard (Ann Jillian) is Steve's secretary (she reads *Teenager* magazine and works after school and on Saturdays); Fred Williams (Charles Bateman) is Steve's neighbor; Mona Williams (Mala Powers) is Fred's wife; and Jeff Williams (Pat Cardi) is Fred's son.

Relatives: Cathy Lewis (George's sister, *Deirdre Thompson*), Robert P. Lieb (Deirdre's husband, *Harry Thompson*, a salesman for the Sawyer Computer Company), Davey Davison (Deirdre's daughter, *Nancy Thompson*), Nina Wilcox *(George's mother),* Linda Watkins (George's cousin, *Grace Baxter*), Frederic Downs (George's cousin, *Fred Baxter*; later George's cousin *Charlie Parkins*), Michael Callan (George's nephew, *Kevin Burkett*), Margaret Bly (Kevin's wife, *Helen Burkett*), Johnny Washbrook (Hazel's nephew, *Eddie Burke*), Frank Aletter (Hazel's nephew, *Walter Burke*), Rosemary DeCamp (Hazel's cousin *Susie*; a.k.a. Lady Sybil), Lois Roberts (Rosie's cousin, *Marge Logan*), William Cort (Marge's husband, *Jim Logan*).

Relatives Not Seen: Hazel's brother, Steve Burke (who lives in California and sends her candied fruit for Christmas), Hazel's cousin Alfred, the wrestler; Hazel's cousin Myrtle Mae Burke; Dorothy's aunt, Grace.

Themes: "Hazel" (theme with lyrics), by Helen Miller and Howard Greenfield; "Hazel" (musical version), by Sammy Cahn and Jimmy Van Heusen.

Note: The series is based on the *Saturday Evening Post* character created by Ted Key.

294. *He and She*

CBS, 9/8/67 to 9/18/68

Richard Hollister (Richard Benjamin) is a cartoonist and the creator of the comic strip turned television series "Jetman." Paula Hollister (Paula Prentiss) is Richard's beautiful wife, an employee of the Manhattan Tourist Aid Society (she has a heart of gold and can't resist helping people in trouble). Paula met Richard in 1962, and they had their first date in the Adirondacks. Richard parked his car in a falling rocks zone, and, as he attempted to kiss Paula, a rock (an upstate New York grey stone) fell and hit him on the head. Paula kept the rock as a memento of their first kiss.

The Hollisters live in an apartment at 365 East 84th Street in Manhattan. When Richard becomes upset, he goes to Hammond's Bar; Paula has their clothes cleaned at the Fiore Brothers Cleaners. Their side living room window faces the side of the local firehouse (station number 26). Fireman Harry Zarakardos (Kenneth Mars) has placed a plank from their window to the firestation window to provide easy access to both buildings.

Oscar North (Jack Cassidy) is the egotistical star of "Jet-man" (a superhero with a jet-shaped helmet and two jets on the back of his vest for flying). Oscar is a connoisseur of the arts (he has, for example, a $65,000 Picasso painting) and has a large picture of himself in his dressing room with devotional candles at each side. Oscar arrives at the studio at 5:30 A.M. for makeup; 4½ hours later, the makeup is completed. "Jetman" is filmed on Stage 2. Andrew Humble (Hamilton Camp) is the not-so-handy apartment house handyman (Andrew's first present from his wife 25 years ago was a blue shirt—which he still wears).

Jerry Fielding composed the "He and She" theme.

295. *Head of the Class*

ABC, 9/17/86 to 6/25/91

Cast: Howard Hesseman (*Charlie Moore*), Billy Connolly (*Billy MacGregor*), Jeannetta Arnette (*Bernadette Meara*), William G. Schilling (*Harold Samuels*).

Facts: Life at New York's Fillmore High School as seen through the eyes of I.H.P. (Individual Honors Program) history teachers Charles ("Charlie") Moore (1986–90) and William ("Billy") MacGregor (1990-91).

Charlie was born in Idaho and attended Weesur High School and Idaho State College. The afterschool hangout was a place called George's, and he wrote and directed a high school musical called *Goodbye Weesur, Hello Broadway*. His dream girl at the time was Patricia Van Arsdale. Before becoming a teacher, Charlie came to New York to direct Broadway, but it never happened. He staged the off-Broadway play *Hamlet* at the Playhouse Theater in Newark, New Jersey (where he now runs a small group of players). He began his acting career in 1969, and his most embarrassing moment occurred when he appeared in the play *Hair* (he did the nude scene in the wrong act). Charlie, who cannot abide the taste of anchovies, also appeared in plays by Chekhov and Ibsen and directed the off-Broadway play *Little Shop of Horrors*.

Charlie began as a substitute teacher at Fillmore and became a faculty member when the previous I.H.P. teacher, Vernon Thomas (Roscoe Lee Browne), left. Charlie lives next door to the Plant Store and appeared in television commercials as "The King of Discount Appliances" for Veemer Appliances. He left Fillmore to become an actor when he accepted the lead in the road company production of *Death of a Salesman*. In the opening theme, Charlie is seen going to work, ready to enter the uptown 8th Avenue subway line at 50th Street. The school (in real life, the Washington Irving High School—the exterior shots for Fillmore) is downtown at 16th Street and Irving Place. Charlie wears a 16½-34 shirt.

Billy is from Glasgow, Scotland, and attended Oxford University in England (he was the spelling champion of Glasgow three years in a row). Billy, who claims he was raised in the slums of Glasgow, has a second job at the Mother Hubbard Day Care Center. He has a comical approach to teaching and interweaves his life experiences with his lessons.

Bernadette Meara is the attractive vice principal. She is from North Carolina and came to New York on 8/9/74 to take the job she now has. The saddest Christmas she ever experienced happened when she was seven years old and didn't get a Susie Q Easy Bake Oven.

Dr. Harold Samuels is the principal. He proposed the I.H.P. to the school board as a means of letting students monitor their own studies. He relaxes by taking folk dance lessons on Wednesday nights. Harold attended Canarsie High School in Brooklyn and has a brother-in-law who owns a restaurant called Mr. Stanton's.

The Students: Simone Foster (Khrystyne Haje) is the prettiest girl in the Honors Program. She is sweet, shy and very sensitive and has been a straight–A student all her life. Her greatest gift is her romantic vision of life. Simone's specialty is English, and her spare time is occupied by charity work. Her father works in the bookbinding department of a publisher, and her favorite poet is Robert T. Lasker (mythical). As a member of the chess club, Simone loses her femininity; the teacher calls her "Mister."

Darlene Merriman (Robin Givens) is from a wealthy family and lives on Park Avenue. For a school project, she traced her family history and found that she was a descendant of Sally Hemmings, the black woman by whom Thomas Jefferson had children. Her specialty is speech and debate, and she believes she is extremely attractive to men: "I represent the physical and intellectual ideals men want." She tends to put herself on a pedestal. Darlene is editor of the school newspaper, the Fillmore *Spartan*.

Sarah Nevins (Kimberly Russell) is president of the Student Council and works after school at City General Hospital.

Maria Borges (Leslie Bega) is dedicated to learning. If she gets a *B*, she grounds herself ("It's the only way I can learn"). Her greatest gift is her understanding of the human condition. She left after three years to further her singing career at the High School of the Performing Arts.

Arvid Engen (Dan Frischman) is a math major and has a perfect attendance record (2,252 days with the episode of 10/2/90). He has not missed one day of school since he first started—nothing has stopped him—"not subway strikes, blizzards, hurricanes or illness." Arvid is a member of the glee club, the school orchestra (he plays triangle) and runs the school radio station. On his first day at Fillmore, he wore a leisure suit. He plays the accordion and his favorite writer is Carl Sagan. He wears a size nine shoe (usually brown) and had the nickname "Badges" (he has a 4.0 grade

He and She. Left to right: Richard Benjamin, Paula Prentiss and Jack Cassidy.

point average and won many awards). Arvid was a Boy Scout (Troop 645) and is also the lunchroom monitor. When he gets upset, he speaks to a picture of Albert Einstein he carries with him.

Dennis Clarence Blunden (Dan Schneider) is the practical joker of the group. He is skilled in chemistry and physics and has been sent to the principal's office more times than any other student (in the office, he stares at the picture of George Washington on the wall). He has borrowed $326.92 and a John Travolta lunchbox from Darlene since the first grade. Dennis loves to eat, but not the cafeteria food (he sends out for lunch at Izzy's, a fast food store). Dennis also held a part-time job as a waiter at Charlie's favorite eatery, Casa Falafel. His locker combination is 27-14-5.

Eric Mardian (Brian Robbins) has a father who is an alcoholic. When he was four, his father read *Treasure Island* aloud to him; one year later, Eric read it back to him. When the I.H.P. challenges other schools in a competition, Eric calls the meets "Nerd Bowls."

Janice Lazarotto (Tannis Vallely) is gifted in all areas of study and has a photographic memory. She is a child genius and entered the I.H.P. program at age ten—"She knows everything; she's spooky." She plays the cello (second chair) in the school orchestra and "dreams of colonizing another planet entirely out of Legos." She left the I.H.P. after three years to attend Harvard.

Alan Pinkard (Tony O'Dell) is a member of the Young Americans for Freedom and has set his goal as that of becoming president of the United States. He is gifted in the natural sciences, and his favorite movie is *Cattle Queen of Montana.*

Viki Amory (Lara Piper) is adopted and has a knack for falling in love with her teachers: "It's something I can't control. It comes, poof; it goes, poof." She is from Florida and her family is always on the move.

Jawaharlal Choudhury (Jory Husain) is gifted in the political sciences (he left after three years when his family moved to California to take advantage of a business opportunity). T.J. Jones (Rain Pryor) calls Billy "Mr. Bill" and has a beautiful singing voice. Jasper Quincy (Jonathan Ke Quan)

Head of the Class. Khrystyne Haje and Brian Robbins.

speaks five languages. Aristotle MacKenzie (De'Voreaux White) and Alex Torres (Michael DeLorenzo) are the remaining students.

I.H.P. classes are held in Room 19. Dr. Samuels calls his honors class "a well oiled machine," as they know the answers to everything. The class starred in a school production of *Grease*, directed by Charlie. Bernadette reads the *Post*; Charlie reads the *Times*. The I.H.P. class computers are called Fred and Wilma. Classes begin at 8:50 A.M.; Fillmore is sometimes mentioned as being on the Upper West Side of Manhattan. The school's radio station is WFHS (410 on the AM dial); the basketball team is the Fillmore Spartans; Billy has a Rand McNally world map (number 429) on the wall in his classroom.

In the last episode, graduation is held at the same time the school is to be demolished. The students chose the following colleges: Cal Tech (Arvid), Stanford (Darlene), Columbia (Sarah), Vassar (Alex), MIT (Viki), Sarah Lawrence (Simone), University of Iowa (Eric), MIT (Dennis), Harvard (Alan).

Relatives: Patricia McCormack (Eric's mother, *Madeline Mardian*), Dan Lauria (Eric's father, *Frank Mardian*), Gloria Hayes (Maria's mother, *Francesca Borges*), Susan Krebs (*Dennis's mother*), John DiSanti (*Dennis's father*), Marlene Clark (*Darlene's mother*), David Downing (*Darlene's father*), Enid Kent (Simone's mother, *Maureen Foster*), J. Patrick McNamara (Simone's father, *Robert Foster*), Bruce Gray (Arvid's father, *Dr. Euric Engen*), Nancy Fish (*Arvid's mother*), William Edward Lewis (*Janice's father*), Cinda Jackson (*Janice's mother*), Robert Hooks (*Sarah's father*), June Gable (Vicki's adoptive mother, *Greta Amory*), Cynthia Mace (Vicki's birth mother, *Rose Gibson*), Denice Kumagai (*Jasper's mother*), Tzi Ma (*Jasper's father*), Liz Torres (*Alex's mother*), Adrienne Barbeau (Harold's sister, *Gilda Minnetta*), Claudette Nevins (Harold's wife, *Lois Samuels*), Ken Mars (Charlie's *Uncle Charles*).

Flashbacks: Ryan Rushton (*Charlie as a boy*).

Theme: "Head of the Class" by Ed Alton.

Note: Billy Connolly next played Billy MacGregor on "Billy" (ABC, 1/31/92 to 7/4/92). Following his departure from Fillmore High School, Billy moves to California to teach night school at Berkeley Community College. Billy came from Scotland to teach in the United States. Mary Springer (Marie Marshall) is one of his students. She is separated from her husband, struggling to raise three kids and pay off a large mortgage. She has converted the basement into an apartment but can't find anyone to rent it. On 9/30/91 Billy's work permit expires. Billy and Mary decide to help each other: they wed so he can stay in the United States and she can find a tenant and keep the house. Stories relate their attempts to maintain a platonic relationship. Natanya Ross, Johnny Galecki and Clara Bryant play Mary's kids, Laura, David and Annie. Mary is a dental hygienist; Billy's passport number is K0618468, and he has a plant named Robert. Laura plays the violin and attends the Debbie Daniels Tap Dance School; David is a freshman at Berkeley High School and has a job at the Chicken Pit restaurant. Annie, the youngest, has a security blanket ("Blankey") and a plush bear (Marty). The series was originally called "Immediate Family."

296. *Heart of the City*

ABC, 9/21/86 to 1/10/87

Wesley ("Wes") Kennedy (Robert Desiderio) is a street cop with an impressive record who was chosen and trained to head a S.W.A.T. (Special Weapons and Tactics) team for the Los Angeles Police Department. He is married to Susan (Irena Ferris) and is the father of two children: Robin (Christina Applegate) and Kevin (Jonathan Ward). One day, while Susan is exercising along with a television aerobics show, a news bulletin informs the public of a shooting involving a police S.W.A.T. team. Fearing that Wes was shot, Susan ignores Wes's warnings that she is never to go to a crime scene and rushes out of the house. Susan's mind is eased when she sees that Wes is fine—but then she is killed when she is caught in the crossfire between the cops and the criminals. Eighteen months later (when the series begins), Wes is still haunted by the memories of that afternoon. Sixteen-year-old Robin, who was sweet, innocent and the image of the pretty girl next door, became bitter and holds Wes responsible for her mother's death. Robin suddenly changed her image. She shortened her hair, changed her attitude and started dressing in clothes that make her look like a high priced call girl ("I may look like a tramp, but boys are not getting near me—no way, no chance. I dress to please myself, not some boy" [as the series progressed, Robin mellowed; she became less bitter when she forgave her father for what happened]).

Robin attends West Hollywood High School and takes dance lessons (she starred as Beauty in a "Beauty and the Beast" theme rock video for singer Radical Conrad [Corey Feldman]). Robin claims that "dance is a celebration to make people feel good." Although she is very attractive, she says, "I don't think I'm as beautiful as other people see me."

Wes solves 24 percent of his case load (which is 10 percent

higher than the rate of other cops in the precinct) and is now a detective with the D.H.D. Division of the L.A.P.D. (He resigned as S.W.A.T. commander to become a detective after Susan was killed. He remains a cop "to get the animals off the streets. It's what I do, it's what has to be done.") Wes has a photographic memory and an impressive arrest record, but "too many shootings." His car license plate reads ICYD 198, and he lives at 5503 Pacific Way (house number 4607 in the pilot). He is currently dating Kathy Priester (Kay Lenz), a pretty waitress at a diner called Trio's Grill.

Kevin, who is 15, also attends West Hollywood High. He is confused by girls and doesn't know what to make of them. He is bright and wears glasses, but thinks girls want muscles, not brains (Wes mentioned that Kevin gets *A*'s and *B*'s from his male teachers and *C*'s from his female teachers, but can't explain why).

Dick Anthony Williams played Wes's superior, Ed Van Duzer, the watch commander, and Branscombe Richmond was Sergeant Halui, a Hawaiian by birth who calls everyone "Brother."

Patrick Williams composed the theme.

297. *Heartland*

CBS, 3/20/89 to 7/31/89

The McCutcheon Ranch is a 350-acre farm in Pritchard, Nebraska. B.L. McCutcheon (Brian Keith) owns the ranch and runs it with his son, Tom (Richard Gilliland), Tom's wife, Cassandra (Kathleen Layman), and their children, Kim (Daisy Keith), Johnny (Jason Kristopher) and Gus (Devin Ratray). B.L. is "a cantankerous old coot" who is set in his ways and has an opinion about everything. He is a widower and had three dogs: Chester, General Patton and Silky. His favorite recording artist is Elmo Tanner, the World's Greatest Whistler; he enjoys relaxing in the chair on the front porch of his home.

Tom and Cassandra, whom Tom calls "Casey," have been married for 15 years. Johnny and Gus are their biological children; Kim is adopted. The kids attend Pritchard High School; Kim is a talented violinist who hopes one day to play with the New York Philharmonic Orchestra; Johnny longs for a life away from the farm in a big city; Gus is content with farm life and has a pet pig named Dolly.

Dion sings the theme, "Heartland."

298. *Hearts Afire*

CBS, 9/14/92 to 4/5/93

Cast: John Ritter (*John Hartman*), Markie Post (*Georgie Ann Lahti*), George Gaynes (*Strobe Smithers*), Wendie Jo Sperber (*Mavis Davis*), Beth Broderick (*Dee Dee Star*), Ed Asner (*George Lahti*).

Facts: Strobe Smithers is a somewhat senile, conservative Southern senator. He is married but having a secret affair with the office receptionist, Dee Dee Star. John Hartman is Strobe's senatorial aide; he is divorced and the father of two children, Ben (Justin Burnette) and Eliot (Clark Duke), and lives in a spacious home at 1184 Arlington Drive in Georgetown. (Ben is in the fifth grade and Eliot in second grade at the Overland Elementary School. Eliot's first word as a baby was *moon,* and he has a pet snake named Sam.)

Georgie Ann Lahti is a liberal journalist who now works as Strobe's speechwriter. She previously lived at the Fairprice Hotel and was flat broke when she applied for the job. When John hired her and learned that she had been evicted, he offered to let her stay at his house; the temporary stay became a seemingly permanent one when they began romancing each other.

Miss Lula (Beah Richards) has cared for Georgie since she was three years old (Georgie's mother died shortly after her birth). Georgie's father, George Lahti, is a disbarred attorney (he spent two years in prison and was the former president of the American Trial Lawyers Association). George took up ceramics in prison and is an excellent cook (he is staying with John and works as the housekeeper). John's ex-wife, Diandra (Julie Cobb), is an interior decorator. She left John for another woman (Ruth, played by Conchata Ferrell). John calls Georgie "Miss Lahti"; Georgie calls John "Hartman." John and the senator have a monthly meeting at Harry's Bar.

Georgie Ann is a liberal feminist. She began her career by writing questions for "Jeopardy" (she created the category "Potent Potables"). She next wrote an episode of "Rhoda." Georgie then worked for the *Chicago Tribune* and finally for the *Chicago Post*. She was with the *Tribune* for eight years and left the *Post* to write a book called *My Year with Fidel* (she had an affair with Castro and thought it should be told). When that failed, she went to work as "a cultural liaison in Paris" ("I worked at Euro Disney helping people on and off the teacup ride"). Georgie is a Pulitzer Prize nominee and has done outrageous things (for example, "I ran around the Trevi Fountain in Rome in my bra and panties"). Georgie is trying to quit smoking but can't ("I smoke when I get upset, and I get upset a lot"). Georgie also says, "My credit line is not enough to buy a Vivien Leigh commemorative plate, and I have a problem being taken seriously because of my good looks."

As a kid Georgie had a snow cone ice stand and wanted to wear her Halloween costume (a devil) to school every day. When she took her SAT test, she was singled out for writing the longest answers ever given on a multiple choice test ("I wasn't satisfied with E—none of the above"). Georgie plays the trumpet; John changes her motor oil and buys her pantyhose.

Dee Dee was born in Amarillo, Texas, and worked as a beautician at the Beauty Pit salon. Before becoming the office receptionist, she worked at the Foto Mat. Dee Dee is having an affair with Strobe because she is motivated by patriotism and love of country—or, as Georgie puts it, "Apparently Miss Star feels that anytime a man plays an important role in world events, she feels it is her patriotic duty to throw her skirt over her head." Mavis Davis, the office secretary, calls Dee Dee "the last bimbo on the hill." Despite what others think about her, Dee Dee is also making money with her own business: "Mail Order Bikini Bra and Panties." She started the business to show people that she has brains as well as beauty (she thinks that other women are threatened by her looks and that becoming a businesswoman will show them she is intelligent).

Strobe plays the piano and had his own band during the 1940s. He is also aging and married to a beautiful younger woman named Mary Fran (Mary Ann Mobley). Mary Fran was born in Sparta, Georgia, and took the beauty pageant route to get out of town. (She was crowned Miss Tennessee, then Miss U.S.A. Strobe met Mary Fran when he was a judge in a beauty contest. She sang "As Time Goes By," and he could see no one but her.) Mary Fran has been married to Strobe for 30 years. She wants him to retire so she can take his seat in the Senate ("It's now my turn after putting up with him for 30 years"). If Strobe doesn't quit, Mary Fran is threatening to air their dirty laundry in public. Strobe goes to bed at 8:30 P.M.

Billy Bob Davis (Billy Bob Thornton) is Mavis's husband and John's assistant; Carson Lee Davis (Doreen Fein) is Billy Bob and Mavis's daughter; Adam Carlson (Adam Carl) is the office gofer.

Theme: "Hearts Afire," by Bruce Miller.

299. *Hearts Are Wild*

CBS, 1/10/92 to 3/13/92

Jack Thorpe (David Beecroft) is 36 years old. He is a graduate of Harvard and now owns Caesar's Palace Hotel and Casino in Las Vegas (he inherited the business from his late father, Hank Thorpe). Kyle Hubbard (Catherine Mary Stewart), who lived on Boston's Beacon Hill, is in charge of guest relations; and Leon ("Pepe") Pepperman (Jon Polito) is Jack's right-hand man. Jack's father ran the hotel for 20 years; rooms at the hotel start at $90 a day; businesses in the complex pay $7,000 a month rent. Barbara Rush appeared as Jack's mother, Caroline Thorpe. The song "Viva Las Vegas" is used as the theme.

300. *Heaven for Betsy*

CBS, 9/30/52 to 12/25/52

"Being married to Peter is heaven for Betsy" says an unidentified announcer after an episode's opening teaser. Betsy (Cynthia Stone) is a former secretary who is now married to Peter Bell (Jack Lemmon), "an underpaid, underappreciated, overworked cog in the Willmot Department Store." Peter is timid and shy and easily taken advantage of; Betsy is strong and forceful and gives Peter the courage he needs to face obstacles.

Peter and Betsy are newlyweds and reside at 136 Oak Tree Lane in New York. Peter earns $42.50 a week as an apprentice executive to Mr. Willmot, but "do you realize the services I've been performing that are not even part of my job? I'm a combination salesman, floor walker, buyer, accountant, working store detective, complaint bureau and errand boy." Peter's haphazard attempts to make his boss, Alonzo Willmot (Cliff Hall), realize his worth paid off in one episode when Peter received a ten dollar raise.

The series is 15 minutes in length (including two commercials and an uncredited opening and closing theme song). It depicts the struggles that make up a marriage via short skits. The end credits read: "Starring Jack Lemmon and Cynthia Stone. They're also Mr. and Mrs. Lemmon."

301. *Hello, Larry*

NBC, 1/26/79 to 4/26/81

Lawrence ("Larry") Alder (McLean Stevenson) and his daughters, Ruthie (Kim Richards) and Diane (Donna Wilkes and Krista Errickson), live at 46 Lafayette Street in Los Angeles; their phone number is 555-7778. Larry is divorced from Marian (Shelley Fabares) and works for radio station KTCS as the host of a call-in talk show called "The Larry Alder Show." When the opportunity arises for Larry to begin a new life for himself and his daughters, he accepts a job at radio station KLOW-AM in Portland, Oregon. There he hosts a call-in show called first "Hello, Larry," then "The Larry Alder Show." The station is owned by Trans-Allied, Inc., and its phone number is 555-3567. Larry, Ruthie and Diane now live in Apartment 2B of an unnamed building (555-4521 is their phone number). Ruthie and Diane attend Portland High School; in Los Angeles, Ruthie had a dog named Rusty; she now longs for her father to buy a house.

Morgan Winslow (Joanna Gleason) is Larry's attractive producer; she lives at 67543 Baker Avenue, and her phone number is 555-0098; Henry Alder (Fred Stuthman) is Larry's father (who resides with them in second season episodes). Wendell the Drunk (Will Hunt) is the president of the Larry Alder Fan Club. When the series first began, the main characters had the last name of Adler.

John LaSalle and Tom Smith composed the theme, "Hello, Larry."

302. *Here We Go Again*

ABC, 1/20/73 to 6/23/73

Cast: Larry Hagman (*Richard Evans*), Diane Baker (*Susan Evans*), Nita Talbot (*Judy Evans*), Dick Gautier (*Jerry Standish*).

Facts: Living at 1450 North Valley Lane in Encino, California, are Richard Evans, an architect (owner of Evans

Architecture, Inc.), and his new wife, Susan. One block away, at 1490 North Valley Lane, lives Jerry Standish, Susan's ex-husband, a former Los Angeles Rams quarterback, who now owns the Polynesia Paradise Café. Half a mile away is 361 Oak Tree Drive, the address of Richard's ex-wife, Judy Evans, the editor of *Screen World* magazine.

Jan (Kim Richards) and Cindy (Leslie Graves), Jerry and Susan's preteen children, now reside with Susan and Richard (Jerry maintains a bachelor pad), and Richard and Judy's son, Jeff (Chris Beaumont), now lives with his father (Richard) and stepmother, Susan.

Richard and Susan's struggles to find serenity in a neighborhood where they are plagued by the constant intrusion of their former spouses constitute the focal point of the series.

Richard and Judy were married for 17 years before their marriage ended. Richard, who thought that "my first marriage had an Edgar Allan Poe quality to it," just couldn't take Judy's bossiness and left. Jerry and Susan met in college, fell in love, married and hoped for a storybook life together. What they found was a divorce after ten years of marriage.

While Judy is bossy, formidable and efficient, Susan is sweet, tender and very trusting. While Richard is easygoing and trusting, Jerry is a playboy and unfaithful. Jerry's philandering cost him his marriage ("I was a kid from nowhere. Suddenly, when I became a Ram, all these gorgeous girls began throwing themselves at me. What was I supposed to do?").

Shortly after divorcing Jerry, Susan, a representative of the Better Boys Foundation (an organization that provides facilities for underprivileged boys), meets Richard when she hires him to design a new center ("We're replacing a recreation center we built a few years ago and would like you to design it"). Richard takes Susan to dinner that night to discuss matters. They fall in love, marry and, "even though we share one life with your ex-husband and my ex-wife, here we go again."

Theme: "Here We Go Again," vocal by Carol Sager and Peter Allen.

303. *Herman's Head*

Fox, 9/8/91 to the present

Cast: William Ragsdale (*Herman Brooks*), Jane Sibbett (*Heddy Newman*), Yeardley Smith (*Louise Fitzer*), Jason Bernard (*Paul Bracken*), Hank Azaria (*Jay Nichols*).

Facts: Herman Brooks is a magazine fact checker and researcher for the Waterton Publishing Company in Manhattan. He lives at 564 West 58th Street, Apartment 3C, and hopes one day to become a writer. Viewers see not only this side of Herman but also "inside" Herman's head as characters representing his sensitivity, intellect, lust and anxiety battle over his actions.

Angel (Molly Hagan) is Herman's sensitivity ("Without me he wouldn't feel tenderness, honesty or love—the good things in life"). Animal (Ken Hudson Campbell) represents Herman's lust ("Without me he'd miss out on all the good stuff—you know, fun, food, babes"). Wimp (Rick Lawless) is Herman's anxiety ("I keep him out of trouble. And believe me, there is trouble everywhere"). Genius (Peter MacKenzie) is Herman's intellect ("Without me he couldn't hold a job, pay his rent or tie his shoes").

Herman earns $22,500 a year. He was born in Milbury, Ohio, and attended Milbury High School and Ohio State College; Herman's father is a tire salesman. Herman had a parakeet named Pookie as a kid. His favorite watering hole is McAnally's Pub-Restaurant. Herman had a brief romantic affair with Elizabeth (Julia Campbell), a writer for *Manhattan Weekly* magazine. Elizabeth had an apartment at Washington Square Park and set her bedroom alarm clock one hour behind to give herself extra time to get ready in the morning.

Paul Bracken is Herman's boss. He is an editor and "knows facts about everything." He suffers from "Bozo phobia" (when he was a kid his parents hired a clown for his birthday party; the clown scared him, and now even people with too much makeup on make him nervous).

Heddy Newman is a researcher and Herman's beautiful colleague. She was born in Baltimore on November 28 and believes she is a "ten." She posed nude for a magazine and let it slip that she once made love to another woman. Heddy uses Herman's desk phone to make long distance calls and wants to marry a man of wealth—"But all I meet are men who are married or gay."

Louise Fitzer was born in Pennsylvania and is the office assistant. She is very sweet and trusting and looking to find a husband (she is saving herself for that special man and is a member of the Virgin Support Group and the Women Who Cry Too Much Support Group). Louise has a pet iguana named Kitty. Jay Nichols is Herman's lecherous, womanizing friend; he works for the same company and lives in Apartment 925 (address not given). Jim Crawford (Edward Winter) is the senior editor (he calls Herman "Sherman"). The series was originally called "It's All in Your Head."

Waterton Publishing is on the twenty-sixth floor; Animal wears an Ohio State jersey; Jay attended Jefferson High School.

Relatives: Jennifer Aniston (Herman's 19-year-old sister, *Suzie Brooks*), John Scott Clough (Herman's brother, *Stan Brooks*), Alaina Reed Hall (Paul's wife, *Margaret Bracken*), Victoria Powell (Paul's daughter, *Susan Bracken*), Gigi Rice (Jim's wife, *Mrs. Crawford*), Elinor Donahue (*Louise's mother*), Richard Paul (*Louise's father*), Christine Cavanaugh (Louise's sister, *Martha Fitzer*). Louise also has a crazy cousin the family calls "Crazy Phil" (seen but not credited).

Flashbacks: Edan Gross (*Herman as a boy*), Taylor Fry (*Suzie as a girl*), Joey Wright (*Stan as a boy*).

Theme: "Inside Herman's Head," by Bill Bodine.

304. *Hey Landlord!*

NBC, 9/11/66 to 5/14/67

Cast: Will Hutchins (*Woody Banner*), Sandy Baron (*Chuck Hookstratten*), Michael Constantine (*Jack Ellenhorn*).

Facts: At 140 West 41st Street in Manhattan stands an old brownstone that has been converted into a ten room apartment house by its youthful owner, Woodrow ("Woody") Banner, an aspiring writer who inherited the building from his late uncle. Woody shares his ground-floor apartment with his friend Charles ("Chuck") Hookstratten, a brash city boy who aspires to be a comedian. Pursuing girls is uppermost in their minds, and they take whatever jobs they can find while waiting for their big breaks.

Woody grew up on a farm in Ohio. He was a Boy Scout (a member of the Skunk Troop) and attended Fillmore High School in Toledo (the school colors were scarlet and maroon). He was on the school's football team (he quit after the tackling dummy broke and he substituted for it one day); he then joined the swim team.

Chuck was born and raised in New York City. He was, as he says, "a rotten kid." He wrote on the school walls, stuck chewing gum under the seats in the auditorium and once tried to burn down the school. He somehow managed to graduate and attended Ohio State University—where he met Woody. The two became quick friends. After graduation, they decided to pursue their career goals in New York City.

The boys sleep in bunk beds (Woody on top, Chuck in the bottom bed) and have a rather cluttered apartment. An old door over an old-fashioned free-standing bathtub serves as the kitchen table. Piles of books are stored in the space on the right side of the front door. A suit of armor and a wooden Indian also occupy floor space. The walls are cluttered with posters (for example, of the 1933 Chicago World's Fair), stereo speakers and a dartboard. Chuck reads books like *Great Moments in Baseball* ("The one with the blonde in the bikini and a guy sneaking up on her with a bat on the cover"); Chuck also takes shredded coconut in his hot tamales.

"Why did I move into this building? They said the rent would be lower. But what about my medical bills—who else buys pills by the gross?" Such is one of the many complaints from upstairs tenant Jack Ellenhorn, an ulcer-ridden, easily exasperated commercial photographer who feels that the antics of "the Boy Landlord" (this is how he refers to Woody) and "Chuckula" (Chuck) are tied with the aggravation of his job to see who can kill him first. Although Jack shouldn't drink, he does (it's the only pleasure he gets from life) at the Elegant Palace (which is a three minute walk from the apartment house). Jack's favorite model is Gayle (Jayne Massey), and Chuck did an ad for Jack's client—Sedgewick Socks.

Other tenants are Timmie Morgan (Pamela Rodgers) and Kyoko Mitsui (Miko Mayama), two gorgeous girls who share an upstairs apartment; and Mrs. Henderson (Ann Morgan Guilbert), another complaining tenant. In the opening theme, a tie, a pair of socks, a bathtub with a dripping pipe and a poster of Marilyn Monroe (highlighting her lips) are seen.

Relatives: Sally Field (Woody's sister, *Bonnie Banner*), Tom Tully (Woody's father, *Lloyd Banner*), Ann Doran (Woody's mother, *Marcy Banner*), Jack Albertson (Woody's uncle, *Dwight*), Joseph Leon (Chuck's father, *Leon Hookstratten*), Naomi Stevens (Chuck's mother, *Fanny Hookstratten*).

Theme: "Hey Landlord," by Quincy Jones.

305. *Hey, Mulligan*

NBC, 8/28/54 to 6/4/55

"The Trials and Tribulations of Auntie Julia," "Macaroni and His Enchanted Piano," "True to Life Tim," "The Saturday Night Super Dooper Special" and "Breakout" are some of the television series (all mythical) broadcast over I.B.C., the fictitious International Broadcasting Company. Michael ("Mickey") Mulligan (Mickey Rooney) is a page (official title: Guest Relations Staff) at the Los Angeles Bureau of the New York–based network. Mickey earns $47.62 a week take-home pay and believes he is meant for bigger and better things; his only problem is, what are those bigger and better things?

Mickey, who considers himself "the tallest short man you'll ever meet," feels that his five-foot height is preventing him from going places at the network. He has enrolled in the Academy of Dramatic Arts (figuring acting may be his goal), but he also seizes upon every opportunity to find his actual goal in life (for instance, opening a war surplus store at 232 South Main Street, applying for an executive position with the Hercules Manufacturing Company). He has a blue suit that he calls his "sincere suit," which he wears to make him feel like an aggressive young businessman.

Patricia ("Pat") Harding (Carla Balenda) is Mickey's romantic interest, the secretary to Mr. Brown (John Hubbard), the program director at I.B.C. Freddie Devlin (Joey Forman) is Mickey's friend, a page also (they eat lunch at the Hamburger Hut). J.L. Patterson (John Hoyt) is the head of the network.

Mickey's father, Joseph ("Joe") Mulligan (Regis Toomey) is a retired police officer (with the 23rd Precinct of the L.A.P.D.), and his mother, Nell Mulligan (Claire Carleton), is a former vaudeville actress. In the episode "Mickey the Novelist," Mickey Rooney played a dual role: Mickey Mulligan and Jacques DeVaronne, the author of a book called *Forbidden Journey,* which inspired Mickey to write a book and become a famous author. Mickey, who never titled his novel, had two ideas: an adventurer lost in the Amazon jungle, and a story about a boy and his dog. Neither went past a first typewritten page.

The series is also known as "The Mickey Rooney Show." Van Alexander composed the theme.

306. *Hi Honey, I'm Home*

ABC, 7/19/91 to 8/23/91
NIK, 7/21/91 to 8/25/91

Cast: Charlotte Booker *(Honey Nielsen)*, Stephen Bradbury *(Lloyd Nielsen)*, Julie Benz *(Babs Nielsen)*, Danny Gura *(Chuckie Nielsen)*, Susan Cella *(Elaine Duff)*, Peter Benson *(Mike Duff)*, Eric Kushnick *(Sidney Duff)*.

Facts: In September 1952, "Hi Honey, I'm Home" premiered at 8:00 P.M., following "Dragnet." It was a typical sitcom about the Nielsens, a squeaky clean American family: parents Honey and Lloyd and their children, Babs and Chuckie. They lived in the town of Springfield. Honey was the problem-solving housewife, and Lloyd, "the idiot father"; he was a businessman, "but darned if I know what kind." Babs was the high school beauty queen, and Chuckie, the youngest, a Boy Scout. Then it happened — their show was canceled; but it was picked up for syndication and ran for many more years in reruns. As the years passed, stations began to drop the series. When the last station on which the series was running decided to pull the plug, the S.R.P. (Sitcom Relocation Program) stepped in and relocated the black and white characters to 178 Morgan Road in New Jersey (all characters from canceled television shows are sent to different cities across the country. When their shows are picked up for another run, they return to TV land).

The Nielsens live in a black and white world. The "Turnerizer" allows them to switch to color to live in the modern world, or to black and white to feel secure. They are also given a book, *A Modern Life User's Manual,* to help them adjust to life in 1991. The S.R.P. places them next door to the Duffs, a single mother (Elaine) and her two children (Mike and Sidney), who are the direct opposite of the Nielsens.

The Nielsens live in a 1950s style spick-and-span home (the Duffs' home is rather disorganized and very untidy; their "junk" is inside and out). Honey and Lloyd sleep in double beds; at dinner every night, they have "Family Tell Time" (in which they tell each other what happened that day); their doorbell plays the notes "Hi Honey, I'm Home." Lloyd doesn't like the 1990s Honey — she has ideas and thinks; Honey considers leftovers "reruns of last night's dinner."

Honey Nielsen looks like a Barbie doll. She is starched and ironed and cheerfully goes about her wifely household duties. Honey has a naturally sunny disposition; when something goes wrong she says, "Oh pooh." She is the only one who can grasp the reality of life in the 1990s, and "Snicker Doodles" is her own cookie recipe.

Lloyd Ralph Nielsen is impervious to what is going on. He is a wimp — but a hero in Honey's eyes. He first worked for Mr. Mooney (Gale Gordon) in an unnamed position; then as a salesman for the Bijou Furniture Company, as a broker for a savings and loan company, and finally as a golfball salesman at Mr. G's World-o-Golf.

Barbara ("Babs") is rather well developed and loves to

Hey Landlord. **Will Hutchins (left) and Sandy Baron.**

wear tight, cleavage-revealing sweaters. Elaine has a tendency to call her "Boobs" (the 1950s Babs doesn't realize what Elaine means and just smiles). Babs says, "I'm not only beautiful on the outside, I'm beautiful on the inside too." She is the most popular girl in high school (not named) and dates only the most handsome boys. In some episodes, she seems to have adjusted to her new life; in others she is bewildered. Babs mentioned that on her old show (fourth episode) she was voted "perkiest sophomore girl" — and she was only a freshman.

Charles ("Chuckie") Nielsen is a Boy Scout (Nest 14). In many sitcoms of the 1950s and 1960s, parents were given kids — even if they didn't know what to do with them. If Chuckie, who has virtually no scenes, is not needed, he is simply ignored (as is Sidney Duff).

Elaine Duff is a hard working single mother struggling to raise two kids. While she never mentioned a job, she was seen wearing a phone company tool belt, and she seems to be either a line "man" or an in-home installer. Elaine attends night classes three times a week and is involved in various projects to save the planet. When Elaine needs to make dinner in a hurry, she uses the "Elaine Duff Emergency Dinner Kit — Instant Everything." Elaine can't believe a woman like Honey exists and is determined to make a 1990s woman out of her. Elaine mentioned that her husband, Ted, deserted her and the family.

Michael ("Mike") Duff is Elaine's oldest son. He uses television to escape from reality and "Hi Honey, I'm Home" is his favorite daily TV show (when it was replaced by "Joanie Loves Chachi," the Nielsens appeared next door). The show made Mike laugh and feel happy. When he visits his new neighbors, he realizes they are the TV Nielsens, and he agrees to help them and keep their secret (if the truth were known about the Nielsens, they would never get picked up for reruns again and would have to remain in the real world forever).

Sidney Duff is Elaine's youngest son. He is a punk dresser and goes by the name of "Skunk." Mike refers to him as "the crime of the neighborhood"; he calls Mike "Coma Boy."

"Hi Honey, I'm Home" is the first series to be broadcast on both network TV and cable.

Theme: "Hi Honey, I'm Home," vocal by Rupert Holmes.

307. *High Mountain Rangers*

CBS, 1/2/88 to 7/9/88

High Mountain Rangers is a rescue organization based in the Sierra Nevadas near Lake Tahoe. It was founded by Jesse Hawkes (Robert Conrad) as an attempt to rescue people who become trapped in perilous situations while in the mountains. His sons, Matt Hawkes (Christian Conrad) and Cody Hawkes (Shane Conrad), assist him. "Frostbite" is headquarters code for the rangers; Yamaha snowmobiles are used. Jesse's sled is *Top Gun*; Cody's is *White Eagle*; Ranger T.J. Cousins (Toni Towles) rides a sled called *Black Magic*; and *Snow Babe* is the sled of Ranger Robin Carstairs (P.A. Christian). Jesse has a dog named Ding, and a girl named Jackie (Robyn Peterson) appears to be Jesse's romantic interest (it is not made clear whether Jesse is a widower or divorced).

Lee Greenwood performed the "High Mountain Rangers" theme.

A revised version of the series appeared the following year as "Jesse Hawkes" (CBS, 4/22/89 to 5/27/89). When drug smugglers invade the High Sierras and Matt is injured, Jesse travels to San Francisco to track them down. There, with the help of Matt and Cody, Jesse accomplishes his mission. Rather than return to the mountains, Jesse, Matt and Cody decide to become modern day bounty hunters and help people who have nowhere else to turn.

David Cummings sings the new theme, "Edge of the Sky."

308. *Highlander*

Syndicated, 10/1/92 to the present

Duncan MacLeod (Adrian Paul) looks 35 years old but is in actuality 400. He was born in the Scottish Highlands and is an immortal. He represents the clan MacLeod and is seeking to become the last immortal and acquire the power of all immortals to rule the world. All knowledge is contained by the immortals. When one immortal encounters another, the Gathering is held (combat by sword, called the Quickening, follows to acquire additional strength. An immortal can only be killed by beheading; when this happens, the surviving mortal acquires the other's knowledge and strength). When Duncan was a young man he was mortally wounded in battle with a rival clan. In death Duncan's father praised him as a brave warrior. However, when Duncan returned to life (his wounds healed), his father condemned him, saying he was in league with the devil. Duncan was cast out by his parents. He knows only that he was brought to his father as an infant by a midwife when the baby that was born to his mother died at birth. MacLeod was the only name Duncan ever knew, and he kept it through the centuries.

When the series begins, Duncan owns an antique store called simply Antiques, in the Heights section of an unidentified city. He co-owns the store with Tessa Noel (Alexandra Vandernoot), a rich sculptress who is also his lover (but a mortal). They live in a loft over the store (which says ANTIQUES, APPRAISALS in the window). Tess drives a car with the license plate RC8 737; Duncan drives a Thunderbird with the license plate 827 KEG and uses a Japanese ornamental sword in combat. Tessa and Richie Ryan (Stan Kirsch), a young hood Duncan reformed, are the only mortals who know Duncan's secret.

Randi McFarland (Amanda Wyss) is the beautiful television reporter (for KLCA, Channel 8 news) who covers incidents that just happen to involve Duncan (he seeks to prevent the evil immortals from harming innocent people and thus becomes a vigilante of sorts). Tessa dislikes Randi because she believes that Randi is only out for airtime and does not care about the victims of crime. The program is based on the feature film of the same title.

Queen performs the theme, "I Am Immortal."

309. *Highway to Heaven*

NBC, 9/19/84 to 8/4/89

Arthur Morton (Michael Landon) was born in 1917 and worked as an honest lawyer all his life. He died in 1948. He was married to Jane (Dorothy McGuire) and was the father of a daughter named Mandy (Joan Welles). Sometime after his death, Arthur became an apprentice angel and was given an assignment in order to gain his wings: to help people on earth. He was given the new name of Jonathan Smith and worked alone until he met Mark Gordon (Victor French), a cynical ex-cop. When Jonathan restored Mark's faith in his fellow man and revealed himself to be an angel, Mark asked to let him help. Mark attended Lathrop High School and had the nickname of "Stick." He was with the Oakland Police Department for 15 years. Mark wears a

California A's baseball cap and drives a Ford sedan with the California license plate 1DT0458. Jonathan calls God "The Boss" (Mark blames "The Boss" for all the little misadventures he encounters). In one episode, Mark purchased a hamburger that turned out to be the five billionth burger sold by Munchie Burger; he won five million dollars and donated the money to the South Side Boys Club for a new gym.

Bob Hope made a rare dramatic appearance as Symcopop, the Assignment Angel. David Rose composed the theme, "Highway to Heaven."

310. *The Highwayman*

NBC, 3/4/88 to 5/6/88

Narrator William Conrad states, "Most crimes in our society begin and end on some stretch of road where laws often terminate at county lines. Combating these legal blackouts is a new breed of lawman working in secret and alone and known simply as Highwaymen."

Our hero is the Highwayman (Sam J. Jones), a mysterious U.S. government agent who uses a high tech 12-ton black Mack truck and an awesome handgun (capable of firing grenade-like bullets) to battle crime. The agent, also called "Highway," works on behalf of the Justice Department for a test program called the Stealth Project. His field code is "Highway One"; his code to the base of operations is "Master Key." His partner is Jetto (Jacko), an Australian-bred Highwayman.

Highway's original contact was Dawn (Claudia Christian), a government agent who posed as a disc jockey (host of "The Dawn Patrol" on an unnamed 50,000 watt clear channel station—"The Mighty 690 from New Orleans"). She was replaced by Tanya Winthrop (Jane Badler), an agent who met with Highway in the field (as opposed to over the airwaves). Their superior is Admiral Conte (Jack Ging) who supervises operations for the Control Center as Master Key.

IF YOU LOVE SOMETHING, SET IT FREE is printed on the back of Highway's truck. The following license plates are also posted there: 29-3588, PC-6045, 13-8R41, PC-2986, 76R-8E2, T-28032 and 7GR-8E2. THE HIGHWAYMAN is written in script on the cab doors (the cab is actually the cockpit of a helicopter, and it can operate independently of the truck). The truck can also be made invisible when Full Stealth Power is ordered.

Highway has no other name. If someone asks, "Who are you?" he responds, "Someone who may be able to help." The narrator also tells us, "They say his mother was born of fire and his father was born of the wind . . . You hear a lot of legends told when you ride the long hard slab—some who say the man is good and some who say he is bad; but all agree who try to play a cheatin' hand, you only get one chance to draw against the Highwayman."

Stu Phillips and Glen A. Larson composed the theme.

The Highwayman. Sam Jones (center), Claudia Christian and Stanford Egi.

311. *His and Hers*

CBS, 3/5/90 to 8/22/90

Douglas ("Doug") Lambert (Martin Mull) is divorced and the father of two children, Mandy (Lisa Picotte) and Noah (Blake Soper). Regina ("Reggie") Hewitt (Stephanie Faracy) is a divorcée with no children. They are also marriage counselors—and married to each other (they honeymooned at Lake Tahoe). They live at 960 North Eagle Lane in Los Angeles and have a pet cat named Fluffy.

Doug and Reggie share adjoining offices in an unnamed high-rise building in downtown Los Angeles. They also co-host "Marriage Talk," a call-in radio program on station KRTM.

Doug was born in Muncie, Indiana. He is a Capricorn, and banana pancakes are his favorite breakfast. He collects Civil War cigar bands as a hobby and estimates that he saved 84 marriages. Reggie is a Taurus and was born in Los Angeles. She was voted "the psychologist you'd most like to share a couch with" in grad school. Her mentor (not seen) is Dr. Emile Ludwig.

William Windom and Barbara Barrie were Doug's parents, Bill and Belle Lambert; Peggy McCay was Reggie's mother, Marian Hewitt; and Randee Heller was Doug's ex-wife, Lynn.

James Beasley composed the theme, "Love Crazy."

312. *The Hogan Family*

NBC, 3/1/86 to 9/14/87
NBC, 9/21/87 to 6/18/90
CBS, 9/15/90 to 12/1/90
CBS, 7/10/91 to 7/20/91

Cast: Valerie Harper (*Valerie Hogan*), Sandy Duncan (*Sandy Hogan*), Josh Taylor (*Michael Hogan*), Jason Bateman (*David Hogan*), Danny Ponce (*Willie Hogan*), Jeremy Licht (*Mark Hogan*), Edie McClurg (*Patty Poole*), John Hillerman (*Lloyd Hogan*).

Facts: Valerie Angela Hogan, the manager of Forman-Lydell Antiques (a.k.a. the Forman-Lydell Auction House), is married to Michael, an airline pilot, and the mother of three sons (David, Willie and Mark). The Hogans live on Crescent Drive in Oak Park, Illinois (house numbers were given as 840, 46 and 540). Their phone number is 555-4656, and the family dog is named Murray. Valerie and Michael have been married for 17 years when the series begins. Because Mike is a pilot (airline not named) and cannot always be home for their anniversary, Valerie waits for "The Anniversary Call" from Michael on their special day. Valerie's maiden name is Varone; Mike is based at Chicago's O'Hare International Airport.

When a contract dispute between Valerie Harper and the show's producers could not be resolved, Valerie Hogan was written out (killed in a car crash). Michael, who is unable to raise his sons alone, asks his sister, Sandy, to come and live with him and help in their upbringing. Sandy was first a guidance counselor, then the vice principal of Colfax High School. She majored in psychology in college and eats lunch at the Soup and Such.

David, the eldest son, first attended Colfax, then Northwestern University. He was a member of the Bulls basketball team in high school and had a job as a waiter at the Four Corners Café; for a college project, he produced "Mrs. Poole's Kitchen," a cooking show for WZIN-TV, Channel 29. He buys his shirts at Shirt World.

Twins Willie and Mark attended Lincoln Junior High, Oak Park Junior High and finally Colfax High. Mark won the good citizenship award at school (Colfax) for being a perfect gentleman. He has a lizard (Chuck) and two fish (Socrates and Plato) and is a member of the Chess Club. He and Willie held jobs at Bossy Burger and at a shoe store called Hi Tops. When they were 14, they rented an X-rated movie called *Bimbo Mania* starring Desiree DeJour.

"Hi-dee-ho" is the shrill cry the Hogans and viewers hear when next door neighbor Patricia ("Patty") Poole drops by for a visit. Mrs. Poole (as she is called) won the 1973 Iowa Casserole Contest with her tuna casserole. She is a member of the sewing club and happily married to Peter Poole, whom she calls "The Mister." Patty has a dog named Casey and a parrot she calls Tweeters.

Lloyd Hogan is Sandy and Michael's father. He has a yacht called the *Bounty*, can't read paperback books ("It makes the story seem so disturbing") and says Sergio's is his favorite restaurant. He is rather bossy, set in his ways and came to live with his children in last season episodes (he previously lived in California). The series was originally called "Valerie" (first date listing).

Other Regulars: Cara Eisenberg (played by Josie Bissett) is Mark's girlfriend; Brenda (Angela Lee) is Willie's girlfriend; and Burt Weems (Steve Witting) is David's friend. Annie (Judith Kahan) is Valerie's neighbor (before Mrs. Poole).

Relatives: Nan Martin (Valerie's aunt, *Josephine*), Francine Tacker (Mike's sister, *Caroline Hogan*), Gretchen Wyler (*Mike's mother*), Robert Rockwell (*Mike's father* in "Valerie" episodes), Anne Haney (Mike's aunt, *Mildred*; she calls Mike "Butterfingers"), Steve Vinovich (Sandy's ex-husband, *Richard*), Willard Scott (Patty's husband, *Peter Poole*), Kathleen Freeman (*Patty's mother-in-law Poole*), Jodie Sweetin (Patty's niece, *Pamela Poole*), Dylan Shane (Patty's nephew, *Paulie Poole*), Paula Hoffman (Annie's daughter, *Rebecca*).

Theme: "Together Through the Years," vocal by Roberta Flack.

313. *Hollywood Off Beat*

Syndicated, 1952 to 1953

STEVE RANDALL, INVESTIGATOR is the sign on the door at 6103 Gentry Avenue in Hollywood, California. "Trouble is his business," and he charges $25 a day for his services. Steve Randall (Melvyn Douglas) has one weakness: "insatiable curiosity." He is "allergic to being detained when a lady is screaming for help," and bitter—determined to regain his right to practice law by finding those who are responsible for a frame that got him disbarred. He became a private detective to gain the legal authority to find those who framed him.

"This is Hollywood," Melvyn Douglas would say over a scene of Steve driving his car.

It is a town like any other town . . . There may be a few more pretty girls because of the pull of the motion picture studios, but otherwise just another American town . . . And there is Steve Randall, who knows Hollywood like the palm of his hand. Steve Randall is in his own way a composite of Hollywood. He's seen everything a man can see anywhere and has been disillusioned by most of it. And he belongs in Hollywood, for its fame and so-called glamour are magnets for the money-hungry riffraff of the outside world . . . They bring their greed to Steve Randall's town, and greed's companion is trouble. And that's fine for Steve Randall because trouble is his business.

There are no music or theme credits listed. The series was filmed, despite its Hollywood locale, at the Parsonnet Studios on Long Island.

314. *Home Fires*
NBC, 6/24/92 to 7/18/92

Ted and Anne Kramer (Michael Brandon and Kate Burton) have been married for 21 years. They are the parents of two children, Libby (Nicole Eggert) and Jesse (Jarrad Paul), and are in good shape. "We have enough money, the roof stopped leaking and the kids are healthy," says Ted. "I don't think our family has one large problem, just a lot of little pieces that need fine tuning. The problem is, I thought we'd have time to fix everything. I didn't expect Libby and Jesse to grow up so fast." Helping the family "fine tune" those little pieces is Dr. Frederic Marcus (Norman Lloyd), a therapist who appears to be having a difficult time understanding and helping the family—each member of which has his or her own unique outlook on life.

Ted is old-fashioned and has traditional values. Anne also claims "he is opinionated and should have his own albeit page. It's amazing what I put up with—that sexy, slightly dangerous diamond-in-the-rough style, it's real old." Despite the complaints, Anne loves Ted: "I do, it's just that we grew up in very different homes. In his, the more flawed, the more flawed the reason, the louder the volume. In mine, a little decorum went a long way."

Libby is a beautiful 18-year-old girl whom Ted would like to see remain a little girl ("Life was a lot easier before children were given their rights," says Ted). "The idea that I am a product of them is terrifying," says Libby. "My father thinks he is clever and insightful. He's not; he's annoying and irrational. My mother sees the world in an angle undiscovered in any geometry textbook. This dimension of Dad's for me to change is another thing. I swear there must be some correlation between breast development and parental psychic degeneration. I always wished I was in another family."

Jesse is 14 years old and is obsessed with driving. He wants a Saab—"The only trouble is, my parents want me to get a driver's license for it." He would also like to race in the Daytona 500 and generally accepts his family members for what they are. Libby, however, believes "Jesse's pubescence makes it impossible for him to participate in family discussions." In another episode Jesse wants a Ferrari and claims that his favorite car is a 1966 Shelby Cobra.

Anne believes her incompatible family is about to go the way of the elephant and the crocodile—endangered species on the brink of extinction. Ted fights with Libby; Libby argues with Jesse; and Anne is constantly at odds with her mother, Nana (Alice Hirson). Nana is a widow (her late husband was named Herbert) and goes through everything. She has no concept of privacy and says whatever is on her mind without taking into consideration Anne's feelings (one of the reasons why Anne feels Nana embarrasses her). Nana has a roadster and hates snapdragons. Libby belives that Nana is the only cultured member of the family.

Also living with the family are two dogs named Nick and Nora. Jobs, schools, addresses and phone numbers are not given.

J.A.C. Redford composed the theme, "Home Fires."

315. *Home Improvement*
ABC, 9/17/91 to the present

"Tool Time" is a comical Detroit cable TV home improvement show, with host Tim Taylor (Tim Allen), a master of any project on television but a klutz at home when it comes to fixing things ("It needs more power" is his remedy; he has, for example, a blender that can puree a brick).

Tim is married to Jill (Patricia Richardson) and is the father of three boys: Randy (Jonathan Taylor Thomas), Mark (Taran Noah Smith) and Brad (Zachery Ty Bryan). Jill and Tim have been married for 12 years. They first danced a slow dance at the Glitter Ballroom to the song "Without You." Jill is a song title expert and considers herself the "High Priestess of Pop Songs." She had a temporary job as a researcher for *Inside Detroit Magazine*. As a kid Jill wore Tinker Bell perfume and had a dog named Puddles. She never had a haircut she liked.

Tim wears 32-inch waist/length pants and shops at Kelly's Hardware Store. His sacred "no women allowed" area at home is the garage, where he has his workshop. The Sears catalogue home improvement sale is something that Tim can't resist. Tim is also a sports addict, and trout almondine is his favorite dinner. When Jill gets angry at Tim she slams the door to his workshop; the vibration knocks his Binford tools off their pegboard hooks. Binford Power Tools sponsors "Tool Time" (the address of which is P.O. Box 32732, Minneapolis, Minn. 48252). Maureen Binford (Vicki Lewis), the daughter of Mr. Binford, produces the show; she is a bit clumsy and tends to bump into the set's walls.

Al Borland (Richard Karn) is Tim's competent assistant on "Tool Time" (he manages to cover Tim's mistakes); he lives in Apartment 505 and has his own fan club. Al is taking a correspondence course called "Getting in Touch with the Square Dancer in You." His and Tim's favorite eatery is Big Mike's.

Lisa (Pamela Denise Anderson) is the gorgeous "Tool Time Girl" (assistant), and Wilson (Earl Hindman) is Tim's knowledgeable neighbor. Wilson's face is never fully seen (it is obstructed by a high wooden fence); he has a scarecrow called Oliver in his yard and constantly gives Tim advice on how to handle his problems. He calls Tim "Good Neighbor."

Dan Foliart composed the "Home Improvement" theme.

316. *Honey West*
ABC, 9/17/65 to 9/2/66

The apartment at 6033 Del Mar Vista in Los Angeles is the home of Honey West (Anne Francis), a beautiful and shapely blonde (36-24-34), who is also a cunning private investigator and owner of H. West and Company, a private detective agency she inherited from her late father. She is assisted by Sam Bolt (John Ericson), her father's original partner.

Honey possesses a black belt in karate and uses the latest in scientific deduction equipment. She has a mobile base (disguised as a television repair truck; license plate 1406 122; later 1ET 974) and a secret office in her apartment (hidden behind the living room wall). Honey's pet ocelot is named Bruce.

Irene Hervey plays Honey's sophisticated aunt, Meg West. The pilot episode, "Who Killed the Jackpot?" (ABC, 4/21/65), aired on "Burke's Law."

"Wild Honey" (opening theme) and "Sweet Honey" (closing theme) were composed by Joseph Mullendore.

317. *The Honeymooners*

CBS, 10/1/55 to 9/22/56

Cast: Jackie Gleason *(Ralph Kramden)*, Audrey Meadows *(Alice Kramden)*, Art Carney *(Ed Norton)*, Joyce Randolph *(Trixie Norton)*.

Facts: Ralph Kramden was born in Brooklyn, New York. He attended P.S. 73 grammar school but had to quit school at age 14 to help support his family. He had high hopes of playing the cornet in a band but could never take lessons. He first worked as a newspaper delivery boy. During the Great Depression, he managed to find work with the WPA. He later met and fell in love with a girl named Alice Gibson, but three versions are given. In an early episode, Ralph first notices Alice in a diner when she yells to the waiter, "Hey Mac, a hot frank and a small orange drink." In a later episode, it is a cold, snowy afternoon, and Ralph is standing in line for a snow shovel; Alice is a WPA employee who is handing them out. In a 1970 episode, Ralph mentions that he and Alice first met in a restaurant called Angie's (they had spaghetti and meatballs). Ralph took Alice dancing at the Hotel New Yorker on their first date.

In 1941 the courtship ended; Ralph and Alice married and moved in with Alice's mother (whom he calls "Blabbermouth"). When Ralph secured employment with the Gotham Bus Company, they rented their first (and only) apartment at 728 Chauncey Street in Bensonhurst, Brooklyn, New York (the address is also given as 328 and 358 Chauncey Street). Although Ralph and Alice wanted children, they were apparently unable to have any. Their desire for a child led them to adopt a baby girl Ralph named Ralphfina. The joy was short-lived; a week later the natural mother decided not to give her baby up for adoption. Although Ralph balked, he felt that giving the baby back was the right thing to do.

Edward L. Norton and his wife, Trixie, are the Kramdens' upstairs neighbors. When Ed came down to invite Ralph and Alice to dinner, he and Ralph became instant friends, and, despite numerous trials and tribulations, their friendship has endured (Ralph often says "Norton, you're a mental case," when Ed upsets him).

Ralph and Alice's phone number is Bensonhurst 0-7741

and their typical gas bill is 39 cents a month (Ralph is also "too cheap" to buy Alice a television set; he claims he is waiting for them to perfect 3-D television). Ralph's salary was $42.50 a week in early episodes and $60 a week in 1955. To supplement Ralph's income, Alice took two part-time jobs: stuffing jelly into doughnuts at Krausmeyer's Bakery (she was later promoted to jelly doughnut taster), and as a secretary to a man named Tony Amico. Alice was also chosen "Cleaning Lady of the Month" by Glow Worm Cleanser. Ralph and Alice dine out most often at the Hong Kong Gardens.

Ralph's astrological sign is Taurus and Alice's is Aquarius (her birthday is February 8). Ralph, who owns two suits (one black, one blue), drives bus number 247 (also given as number 2969) along Madison Avenue in Manhattan. Over the course of his 14 years with the Gotham Bus Company (located at 225 River Street in Manhattan), he has been robbed six times. Five times the robbers got nothing; the sixth time they got the bus and $45 (J.J. Marshall is the company president and was played in one episode by Robert Middleton).

When talking to Alice, Ralph's favorite expressions are "Pow! One of these days—right in the kisser" (waving his fist at her), "You're going to the moon, Alice" and "Baby, you're the greatest."

Ed, who majored in arithmetic at vocational school, mentioned that the *L* in his name stood for "Lilywhite" (his mother's maiden name). As a kid he had a dog named Lulu. He was in the navy and took up typing under the G.I. bill. He couldn't stand being cooped up in an office, so he took a job in the sewer (he has been working there for 17 years in 1955 episodes). Ed's astrological sign was given as both Pisces and Capricorn. His favorite televisison show is "Captain Video" (where he is a Ranger Third Class in the Captain Video Fan Club), and his hero is Pierre François de la Brioski (whom Ed thought designed the sewers of Paris; in reality, he condemned them). Ed calls Ralph "Ralphie boy." Ed and his wife, Trixie, have the phone number Bensonhurst 6-0098.

Ralph and Ed belong to the Raccoon Lodge (also referred to as the International Order of the Friendly Sons of Raccoons and the International Loyal Order of Friendly Raccoons). Ralph is the treasurer and Alice and Trixie are members of the Ladies' Auxiliary of the Raccoon Lodge. The cost of a lodge uniform is $35, and to become a member an applicant must comply with section two of the lodge rules: 1. Applicant must have earned a public school diploma. 2. Applicant must have resided in the United States for at least six months. 3. Applicant must pay $1.50 initiation fee.

Ralph and Ed are also members of the Hurricanes bowling team (they bowl at the Acme bowling alley on 8th and Montgomery).

With a dream of making it big, Ralph ventured into many moneymaking schemes that all eventually failed. He is most famous for investing in the uranium mine in Asbury Park, low calorie pizza and glow in the dark wallpaper (to save on electric bills). His joint failure with Ed was the Handy Housewife Helper (where Ralph appeared on television as the "Chef of the Future"). "Kran-Mars Delicious Mystery Appetizer" and the Ralph Kramden Corporation

The Honeymooners. Jackie Gleason, Audrey Meadows, Art Carney and Joyce Randolph.

also failed. Together, Ralph and Ed wrote a hit song called "Love on a Bus" (dedicated to Alice) that was later made into a movie, and won a radio contest with the song "Friendship." Ralph also appeared on the television shows "Beat the Clock" and "The $99,000 Answer" (his category was popular songs but he failed to answer the first question correctly: "Who wrote 'Swanee River'?" He responded with "Ed Norton"). Ralph also did a TV commercial for Chewsey Chews candy bars (for "The Chewsey Chews Musical Hour" program).

Relatives: Ethel Owens played Alice's mother, Mrs. Gibson. Ralph's mother appeared in one episode, but credit was not given. Ralph mentioned his father's name as both Ed and Ralph Sr. He also has an Aunt Fanny who once wrote asking for six dollars he supposedly owed her. Alice has a brother named Frank and a sister named Peggy (not credited).

Theme: "You're My Greatest Love," by Jackie Gleason and Bill Templeton.

Note: "The Honeymooners" first appeared in 1951 on DuMont's "Cavalcade of Stars." Pert Kelton played Alice on the Jackie Gleason–hosted episodes of the series. On "The Jackie Gleason Show" (CBS, 9/17/66 to 9/12/70), Sheila MacRae played Alice, and Jane Kean, Trixie, in "Honeymooners" segments. Additional segments of the original series (and the original cast) appeared on "The Jackie Gleason Show" from 9/29/56 to 1/2/61. On "Jackie Gleason and His American Scene Magazine" (CBS, 9/29/62 to 6/4/66) Sue Ane Langdon was Alice and Patricia Wilson was Trixie.

"The Honeymooners" with Jackie Gleason (Ralph), Art Carney (Ed), Sheila MacRae (Alice) and Jane Kean (Trixie) were also part of Jackie's only two television specials, both called "The Jackie Gleason Special" (CBS, 12/20/70 and 11/11/73). Four ABC specials also aired: "The Honeymooners' Second Honeymoon" (2/2/76), "The Honeymooners' Christmas" (11/28/77), "The Honeymooners' Valentine Special (2/13/78) and "The Honeymooners' Christmas Special (12/10/78).

Live segments from Jackie's 1950 series have been syndicated as "The Lost Honeymooners," and hour-long segments produced in 1970 have been syndicated as "The Honeymooners' European Vacation."

318. *Hong Kong*

ABC, 9/28/60 to 9/20/61

Glen Evans (Rod Taylor) is a foreign correspondent based in Hong Kong. He works for the World Wide News Service and lives at 24 Peak Road. Ahting (Harold Fong) is his houseboy. Glen drives a car with the license plate AB1651, and his home phone number is 004-79.

Neil Campbell (Lloyd Bochner) is the police chief; Tully (Jack Kruschen) is the owner of Glen's favorite watering hole, Tully's Bar; and Ching Mei (Mai Tai Sing) is a waitress at the Golden Dragon Café.

Lionel Newman composed the "Hong Kong" theme.

Hot Off the Wire see *The Jim Backus Show—Hot Off the Wire*

319. *Hotel De Paree*

CBS, 10/2/59 to 9/23/60

"There is no law in Georgetown, Colorado [1870s]—only what a man makes for himself," says a man known only as Sundance (Earl Holliman), an ex-gunfighter turned law enforcer. Sundance was born in Tombstone, Arizona, and is now half owner of Georgetown's Hotel De Paree, "One of the West's most colorful gathering places." Sundance is partners with a French woman named Annette Devereaux (Jeanette Nolan) and her niece, Monique Devereaux (Judi Meredith). Sundance, also called "The Sundance Kid," has a very special trademark: a black Stetson with a hatband of ten small mirrors. He has a dog named Useless and carries a Colt .45—which he will only use (or wear) when there is a need. Sundance also has a knack for whittling. While the Hotel De Paree has a bar and gambling hall, there is another watering hole in town called simply "The Saloon."

Aaron Donager (Strother Martin) runs Donager's General Store and is sweet on "Miss Annette" (who enjoys playing checkers with him).

Dimitri Tiomkin composed the theme, "Sundance."

320. *How to Marry a Millionaire*

Syndicated, 1958 to 1960

Cast: Barbara Eden *(Loco Jones)*, Merry Anders *(Mike McCall)*, Lori Nelson *(Greta Hanson)*, Lisa Gaye *(Gwen Kirby)*.

Facts: Michele ("Mike") McCall, Loco Jones and Greta Hanson are three beautiful girls who are seeking to marry millionaires. The girls met in an apartment house on Amsterdam Avenue in New York City. Each was renting a small apartment and each had the same goal. Figuring it takes money to attract money, they pool their resources and rent Penthouse G (on the twenty-second floor) of the Tower Apartment House on Park Avenue in Manhattan (Plaza 3-5099 is their phone number). Their rent is due on the tenth of each month; they have a perfect record—they haven't paid it on time yet. With their front established, the girls struggle to find men with money and help each other marry the man of her dreams (their pledge is "On my honor I promise to do my best to help one of us marry a millionaire. So help me, Fort Knox").

At the start of the second season (fall 1959), Greta left the series (she was said to have married a man who owns a gas station and moved to California; she simply fell in love and money no longer mattered. Mike caught the bridal bouquet). Requiring a third girl to share the rent, Loco and Mike advertise in the *Journal News* for a new roommate. Gwen Kirby answers the ad and becomes the new girl on the team.

"The neckline is a little too low, the hem is too short, the waist is too tight, the back is too low—she looks beautiful!" That is how Mike and Greta describe Loco in a dress. Loco (her given name) was born in North Platte, Nebraska, on February 25 (Loco wouldn't reveal the year). She attended North Platte High School and was voted "the one most likely to go further with less than anyone else." She is a bit dense and naive when it comes to world affairs—but she is a whiz at useless information (for example, she has encyclopedic-class knowledge of the comic strips, which she keeps current by reading *Super Comics* magazine). Loco, who is somewhat vain, needs to wear glasses, but won't when she has to (she fears a man will see her and fail to be impressed). She faints standing up with her eyes open and has been called "a fabulous blonde with an hourglass figure."

Loco is a fashion model with the Travis Modeling Agency (later the Talbot Agency) and has her photos taken at Marachi's Photography Studio. She reads *Fashion Preview* magazine and was voted "Queen of the Madison Square Garden Rodeo" in 1958. Loco has a bad habit of falling for "strays" who are anything but rich; she also enjoys feeding the pigeons in Central Park.

"She borrows our nylons and gets runs in them; she doesn't make her bed; she hogs the bathroom to soak in a bubble bath"—using Loco's bubble bath. She is Greta, hostess on a television game show called "Go for Broke" (a takeoff on "The $64,000 Question"), which airs at 9:00 P.M.

(station not given). Greta reads *Who's Who in America* (her research source) and has a Marilyn Monroe quality that she uses to lure men.

"The only way for a girl to be smart is to be dumb," says Mike, the schemer of the group. She reads *Dun and Bradstreet* (her research matter) and works as an analyst on Wall Street. Gwen, who is from Illinois, works for *Manhattan* magazine ("Our Business Is Publicity"). She is almost a clone of Greta: she has a Marilyn Monroe figure, is a borrower (Loco and Mike's nylons) and a bathroom-hogger (loves to take bubble baths using Loco's bubble bath).

The girls shop at Burke's Department Store; they eat at Nate's Deli; they take turns making dinner (when it's Loco's turn, she buys it at Savo's Drugstore); and they each seek men with two qualifications: "Have money, will marry." In one episode, Loco appeared on "Go for Broke" as an expert on comic strip characters (but she lost everything she had won up to $2,000 because she wouldn't wear her glasses on television and couldn't identify the picture of a comic strip character).

Joseph Kearns, as Augustus P. Tobey, and Dabbs Greer, as Mr. Blandish, play the apartment-house managers. Jimmy Cross plays Jessie, the elevator operator. The series is based on the feature film of the same title.

In the original, unaired 1957 pilot film, Greta Lindquist (Lori Nelson), Loco Jones (Charlotte Austin) and Mike Page (Doe Avedon) share a thirtieth floor Manhattan penthouse apartment—something they really can't afford, but Mike says, "Millionaires will only go to millionaires' apartments." "So, here we are," says Loco. The girls buy their food at Magillicuddy's Delicatessen.

Loco is a brunette in this version, but is just as nearsighted and vain about wearing her glasses as Barbara Eden's blonde portrayal of Loco. Loco mentioned here that her real name was Rita Marlene Gloria Claudette Jones; Loco is her nickname. She is a model, but no agency is given.

Greta, a blonde who majored in psychology in college, works as a hostess on a television program called "The Dunlap Quiz Show." Mike is a stockbroker and works for the firm of Hammersmith, Cavanaugh and Hammersmith on Wall Street (Joseph Kearns played her co-worker, Maurice Kincaid, not the landlord as in the series).

Theme: "How to Marry a Millionaire," by Leon Klatzkin.

321. *Hull High*

NBC, 8/20/90 to 10/14/90
NBC, 12/13/90 to 12/30/90

"Be True to Your School" was the original title for this musical comedy-drama about life at Cordell Hull High, a large, full service middle-class suburban school to which many of the minority kids are bused (by the Whitmarsh Bus Lines).

Camilla Croft (Cheryl Pollak) is the new student on campus. She originally lived in Philadelphia, where she attended Rush High School. She now lives in a mobile home in King's Trailer Park at 34 Cove Road. Camilla is older than the other girls in her sophomore class (she started

school late), and rumors began to spread that she was a narc.

Student D.J. Cameron (Kristin Dattilo) is a gorgeous redhead who knows she is very sexy, and she strives to drive the boys wild. She lives at 27461 Havenhurst Drive; 555-3165 is her phone number. D.J. also has a reputation for doing the outrageous (for example, inciting a riot "to protest the revolting cafeteria food," joining the men's wrestling team to prove that a woman is equal to a man).

Cody Rome (Harold Pruett) is another new student and has a mysterious past; and 16-year-old Mark Fuller (Mark Ballou) is a lovesick student with a crush on Camilla. Although she wants nothing to do with him, he takes desperate measures to impress her.

Only two teachers are given full names: Donna Breedlove (Nancy Valen) and John Deerborn (Will Lyman). Donna is 23 years old and lives in an apartment at Farrington Place. She is considered so beautiful that the students in her English class tend to watch her rather than listen to what she is saying. She dresses in short skirts and tight blouses, and moves in such sexy ways that her students are mesmerized. Donna drives a sedan with the license plate 3UM-411; her phone number is 555-4134.

John Deerborn, who drives a car with the license plate 2GR-1682, is a history teacher who taught previously at All City High School.

Jennifer Blang and April Dawn are billed as the "Hull High Bulletin Announcers," and Trey Parker, Philip DeMarks, Carl Anthony Payne and Lawrence Edwards are credited as the "Hull High Rappers" (also called "Hull High Devils"). In the original pilot, Mark Ballou played Mark Pastorelli.

Kenny Ortega is the choreographer, and Stanley Clarke composed the theme and musical score.

322. *The Human Target*

ABC, 7/20/92 to 8/29/92

During the Vietnam War, Christopher ("Chris") Chance (Rick Springfield) was with a special unit that went into villages to destroy them. During one such raid, Chris was captured by the Vietcong and placed in a tiger cage. A lieutenant at the time, Chris spent ten days in the cage before he was rescued (he now has a fear of small places). When he was discharged from the service, he realized what he had done and it all came crashing in on him—so much so that he was sent to the Walter Reed Hospital, psychiatric ward, for 19 months. When he was released he knew that the only way to keep sane was somehow to balance it all out and right wrongs through his unique abilities.

While it is not made clear, Chris is apparently wealthy. He commissions the building of a huge, highly technical mobile base of operations he calls the Wing—a black plane that resembles the wings of an airliner. He then hires three highly skilled people to assist him: Libby Page (Signy Coleman), Philo Marsden (Kirk Baltz) and Jeff Carlyle (Sami Chester). With his unique ability to impersonate voices and highly advanced computer makeup (masks), Chris steps into the lives of people who are marked for murder and becomes a human target until he restores his client's safety.

Chris's fee varies, depending on the client's job: the fee is 10 percent of his yearly salary. The client remains in safety on the Wing until Chris solves the case. The Wing has worldwide television reception and an advanced audio and visual communications system (Chris can communicate with the Wing from any part of the world via a special disk that he carries); he uses the RX 7000 ("The Squirrel") to scramble calls.

Chris saw the movie *Zombies on Holiday* and was impressed by the computer-generated masks makeup artist Philo Marsden used in the film. Philo now uses his computer skills to make the target masks for Chris (which combine Chris's general features with the specific features of a target's face).

Elizabeth ("Libby") Page has known Chris for several years. She previously worked for the Company, a U.S. government organization, in a top level Security position. When a project she was working on fell apart, she went to work for Chris, who needed someone to operate his high tech communications equipment.

Jeff Carlyle served with Chris in Vietnam; he now flies the Wing for Chris. The team also assists Chris in the field if necessary. When a woman is in danger, Chris goes undercover as a male who is close to her.

Kevin McCarthy appeared as Chris's father, Harry Chance. In the original, unaired pilot version (filmed in March 1991), Frances Fisher played Libby and Clarence Clemmons was Jeff. The series is based on the D.C. comic book character.

Anthony Marinelli composed the "Human Target" theme.

323. *Hunter*

NBC, 9/18/84 to 8/30/91

Detective Sergeants Rick Hunter (Fred Dryer) and Dee Dee McCall (Stepfanie Kramer) are with Division 122 of the Los Angeles Police Department (also called the Central Division and the Parker Center Police Station). Rick is the son of a mobster who became a tough but honest cop. His car codes are 1-William-56, 1-William-156 and L-56; his license plate reads 1ADT-849 (later IADT 89 and 2IQ 1584).

Dee Dee, nicknamed "The Brass Cupcake," resides at 8534 Mezdon Drive. Her car codes are 1-Adam-43 and Charles Albert 420; her license plate reads IG045 48.

Dee Dee left the force to marry an old boyfriend, Alex Turnan (Robert Conner Newman) in the episode "Street Wise" (5/7/90). She was replaced by Officer Joann Molenski (Darlanne Fluegel), badge number 1836 (car code R-21-Charles; license plate 2GEE 645). Joann, who lived at 4535 North Sheridan, was killed off (shot three times by a psychopathic woman named Loreen Arness [Ellen Wheeler]) in the episode "Fatal Obsession" (1/9/91). She was replaced by Christine ("Chris") Novak (Lauren Lane), a sergeant with a young daughter named Allison ("Allie") Novak (Courtney Barilla). Chris lives at 6341 West Beverly Drive, and eight-year-old Allie attends the Worster Avenue Grammar School.

She and Chris shop at a store called One Life; Chris's mobile code is R-30 Charles.

Sporty James (Garrett Morris) is Hunter's snitch, the owner of Sporty James Enterprises.

Relatives: Gene Dynarski (Joann's father, *Mike Molenski*), Robin Thomas (Chris's ex-husband, *Al Novak*), Mitchell Ryan (Chris's estranged father, *Tom*).

Flashbacks: Franc Luz (Dee Dee's husband, *Sergeant Steve McCall*; killed in the line of duty).

Theme: "Hunter," by Mike Post and Pete Carpenter.

324. *I Dream of Jeannie*

NBC, 9/18/65 to 9/8/70

Cast: Barbara Eden *(Jeannie)*, Larry Hagman *(Tony Nelson)*, Bill Daily *(Roger Healey)*, Hayden Rorke *(Dr. Alfred Bellows)*, Emmaline Henry *(Amanda Bellows)*.

Facts: On April 1, 64 B.C., a young girl is born to a peasant couple. When the girl comes of age, the Blue Djin (Michael Ansara), the most powerful and feared of all genies, asks for her hand in marriage. When the girl refuses him, he turns her into a genie, places her in a bottle and sentences her to a life of loneliness on a deserted island. The centuries passed and the girl remained unchanged.

During the test flight of a NASA rocket in 1965, a third stage misfires and the craft crash-lands on a deserted island in the South Pacific. As its pilot, astronaut Tony Nelson, looks for items to make an S.O.S. signal, he finds a strange looking green bottle and opens it. A pink smoke emerges that materializes into a beautiful girl dressed as a harem dancer—a genie. "Thou may ask anything of thy slave, Master," she informs him. With her hands crossed over her chest and a blink of her eyes, she grants his first wish and produces a rescue helicopter for him. Although Tony sets the girl, whom he calls Jeannie, free, he finds that he cannot get rid of her and finally allows her to remain with him—provided she refrains from using her powers and grants him no special treasures. A reluctant Jeannie agrees, but Tony finds his life turned upside down when he attempts to keep Jeannie's presence a secret.

Jeannie, who was born when the planet Neptune was in Scorpio, weighs 109 pounds (later mentioned as 127 pounds). Jeannie wears a pink harem costume that is designed to cover her navel (showing a girl's navel on television at that time was considered indecent). Her mischievous sister, Jeannie II (Barbara Eden), has been married 47 times, has had many masters and would like to make Tony husband number 48 (Jeannie II's efforts to discourage a relationship between Jeannie and Tony is a recurring feature of the series). In 1969, when Jeannie and Tony marry, Jeannie becomes a member of the National Wives Association at NASA. Although it was said in later episodes that a genie cannot be photographed, she was photographed in earlier ones (for example, when she was declared Rodeo Queen and her picture appeared in the newspaper). Gin Gin is Jeannie's mischievous genie dog (she hates uniforms, and therefore wreaks havoc at NASA, because the palace guards used to mistreat her). Pip Chicks is the name of Jeannie's homemade candy, which brings out people's hidden fantasies. Jeannie also wrote a book, *How to Be a Fantastic Mother* (published by Woodhouse Publishers in New York), and used Tony's name as her nom de plume.

Tony, who lives at 1020 Palm Drive in Cocoa Beach, Florida, is first a captain, then a major, as is his playboy friend, Roger Healey—the only other person who knows that Jeannie is a genie. Tony's address was also given as 1137 Oak Grove Street and as 811 Pine Street. Tony, who was born in Fowler's Corners, was called "Bunky" Nelson in his youth, and his girlfriend in high school was Bonnie Crenshaw (Damian Brodie). July 15 is Tony's birthday, and he weighs 181¼ pounds (Roger weighs 175 pounds). In one episode, Tony, Roger and fellow astronaut Captain Larkin (Richard Mulligan) flew an Apollo 15 mission.

Dr. Alfred Bellows, the base's psychiatrist, has two goals in life after he meets Tony: to prove to someone else that something strange really is going on, and to figure out what it is. (Dr. Bellows usually just happens to be the only person around when Jeannie has used her powers and he experiences the results). Alfred's wife is Amanda, and the base's commanders are General Martin Peterson (Barton MacLane) and General Winfield Schaefer (Vinton Hayworth). Schaefer has a dog named Jupiter.

Relatives: Barbara Eden (*Jeannie's mother*), Henry Corden (*Jeannie's father*), Jackie Coogan (Jeannie's great-uncle, *Sule of Bensengi*), Ronald Long (Jeannie's uncle, *Asmir*), Arthur Malet (Jeannie's uncle, *Vasmir*), Hal Taggart (*Tony's father*), Spring Byington and June Jocelyn (*Tony's mother*), Gabriel Dell (Tony's cousin, *Arvid*), Michael Barbera (Amanda's nephew, *Melvin*), Bob Hastings (Amanda's cousin, *Homer Banks*), Butch Patrick (Alfred's nephew, *Richard*), Janice Hanson (Winfield's niece, *Patricia*), Hilary Thompson (Winfield's daughter, *Susie Schaefer*), Kimberly Beck (Martin's granddaughter, *Gina*).

Theme: "I Dream of Jeannie," by Hugo Montenegro, Buddy Kaye and Richard Weiss.

Note: Julie McWhirter provided the voice for Jeannie in an animated version of the series called "Jeannie" (CBS, 9/8/73 to 8/30/75), and Barbara Eden reprised her character in the NBC television movie *I Dream of Jeannie: 15 Years Later* (10/20/85). Wayne Rogers played Tony Nelson (now a colonel), and he and Jeannie were the parents of a teenager named T.J. Nelson (MacKenzie Astin). See also "I Still Dream of Jeannie."

325. *I Had Three Wives*

CBS, 8/14/85 to 9/11/85

Elizabeth ("Liz") Bailey (Shanna Reed) is a reporter for the Los Angeles *Chronicle*; Samantha ("Sam") Collins (Teri Copley) is an aspiring actress (she starred in the film *Hatchet Honeymoon*); and Mary Parker (Maggie Cooper) is a lawyer with the firm of Maxwell, Cooper and Associates.

These women have something in common with Jack Beaudine (Victor Garber), the owner of Jackson Beaudine Investigations: each was once his wife. Humor, mystery and crime detection are combined to relate the ex-wives' efforts to help Jackson solve crimes.

"Just about every client I ever had wants to kill me" are Jack's own words and the best description of why he needs all the help he can get. He drives a car with the license plate TUB 285 and lives in an apartment near the waterfront (address not given). Jack married three career women; the marriage failed because "they got in the way of each other's career and stopped each other's personal growth." Sam lives in an apartment at the Roxbury Apartment Complex; Mary lives in a house at 12718 Kenmore Road in Brentwood.

Andrew ("Drew") Beaudine (David Faustino) is Jack's son (by Mary; he now lives with her); and Lucy Baines (Keri Houlihan) is Andrew's cousin.

Bill Conti composed the theme.

On 8/1/79, NBC aired a similar series idea via an unsold pilot called "The Three Wives of David Wheeler." David Wheeler (Art Hindle), the owner of a company called Wheeler Graphic Arts, is a man with three wives: Ginger (Cathy Lee Crosby), his first ex-wife, who is still his business partner; Bibi (Sherilynn Katzman), his second ex-wife, a model he still employs; and Julia (Nancy Grigor), his current wife, who understands—usually.

326. *I Love Lucy*

CBS, 10/15/51 to 6/24/57

Cast: Lucille Ball (*Lucy Ricardo*), Desi Arnaz (*Ricky Ricardo*), William Frawley (*Fred Mertz*), Vivian Vance (*Ethel Mertz*).

Facts: Lucille ("Lucy") Esmerelda McGillicuddy is a small town girl newly arrived in New York City. It is 1941 when her friend, Marian Strong (not seen), arranges a blind date for her with Ricky Ricardo Alberto Fernando Acha (a.k.a. Ricky Alberto Ricardo IV), a Cuban drummer. The unlikely couple fall in love and marry shortly after. They set up housekeeping in an apartment at 623 East 68th Street in Manhattan in a converted brownstone owned by Fred and Ethel Mertz (the building is in Ethel's name). Their later apartment is 3B, and their rent is $125 a month (their phone number is first Murray Hill 5-9975, then Murray Hill 5-9099). Mrs. Benson (Norma Varden) was the prior tenant.

Lucy was born on August 6 (she has been juggling her age for so many years that "I kinda lost track of how old I am") in Jamestown, New York. In grade school, she was called "Bird Legs" and played Juliet in her Jamestown High School production of *Romeo and Juliet*. Lucy also played the saxophone in the high school band, and "Glow Worm" was the only song she ever learned to play. Lucy is always overdrawn at the bank. She tried to win $1,000 to pay off her debts by appearing on the radio stunt show "Females Are Fabulous" ("Any woman is idiotic enough to win a prize"). She attempted to market her Aunt Martha's recipe for salad dressing as "Aunt Martha's Old Fashioned Salad Dressing" (she and Ethel appeared on television and sold it for 40 cents a quart). Lucy also did a television commercial for Vitameatavegamin, a vitamin product, on "Your Saturday Night Variety Show." (The product has meat, vegetables, vitamins, minerals and 23 percent alcohol; Lucy became intoxicated during rehearsals). Lucy married Ricky when she was 22 years old (she weighed 110 pounds at the time; she now claims to weigh 132 pounds).

Ricky has a rumba band and performs at the Tropicana Club in Manhattan. He later bought part interest in the club and renamed it the Ricky Ricardo Babalu Club (also called the Club Babalu and the Babalu Club; Bob Hope was the opening night guest). Plaza 3-2099 is the club's phone number; Ricky plays the conga drums and "Babalu" is his favorite song. Roast pig is his favorite meal, and he and Lucy were the hosts of a television show called "Breakfast with Ricky and Lucy" (sponsored by Phipps Drug Store).

In 1953 Lucy and Ricky became parents, with the birth of Ricky Ricardo, Jr., better known as Little Ricky. Little Ricky's pets are: Tommy and Jimmy (turtles), Hopalong (frog), Mildred and Charles (fish), Alice and Phil (parakeets) and Fred (dog). In his first school play, "The Enchanted Forest," Little Ricky played the lead; Lucy was the witch; Ricky, the hollow tree; Fred, a frog; and Ethel, the Fairy Princess.

Ethel Louise Mertz was born Ethel Potter in Albuquerque, New Mexico (she is called "Little Ethel" by her unseen Aunt Martha and Uncle Elmo). She met "cheapskate" Fred while they were performing in vaudeville. Fred was born in Steubenville, Ohio, and is a member (with Ricky) of the Recreation Club. Fred says that "the only way for Ethel to keep a secret is if she doesn't hear it." "Fred," Ethel says, "tried to come up with an idea to make a million dollars, but he is mad at Edison for coming up with the idea of the light bulb before him and at Ford for inventing the horseless carriage before he did." When Ethel gets upset, Fred slips her a sedative.

Ricky's most annoying habit, according to Lucy, is tapping. Lucy stirring her coffee (hitting the spoon against the cup) most bothers Ricky. Fred's most annoying habit to Ethel is jingling his keys. Ethel's "chewing like a cow" most bothers Fred.

In California-based episodes, the Ricardos and the Mertzes stayed at the Beverly Palms Hotel (Ricky went to Hollywood to make the movie *Don Juan*, which premiered at Radio City Music Hall on Februray 29). In Europe-based episodes, the group books passage on the oceanliner SS *Constitution*. After living at the Mertzes' for 15 years, the Ricardos move to their own home in Westport, Connecticut. Fred and Ethel become their boarders shortly after, and Lucy and Ethel begin their own egg business.

In the original pilot (produced in 1951 and aired March 30, 1990), Ricky and Lucy are already married and live in a seventh floor apartment in Manhattan (Fred and Ethel are not part of the program). Despite published reports to the contrary, Desi Arnaz played Ricky Ricardo (not Larry Lopez), a bandleader; and Lucille Ball, his wife, Lucy Ricardo (not Lucy Lopez). The pilot has most of the elements of the actual series, including Lucy's desperate attempts to break into show business.

Relatives: James John Gauzer, Richard Lee Simmons, the Mayer twins and Richard Keith (Lucy and Ricky's son, *Little Ricky*), Kathryn Card (Lucy's mother, *Mrs. McGillicuddy*).

Theme: "I Love Lucy," by Eliot Daniel.

327. *I Married Dora*

ABC, 9/28/87 to 1/8/88

Cast: Daniel Hugh-Kelly (*Peter Farrell*), Elizabeth Pena (*Dora Calderon*), Juliette Lewis (*Kate Farrell*), Jason Horst (*Will Farrell*).

Facts: Dora Calderon, from El Salvador, works as the housekeeper to Peter Farrell, a recent widower and the father of two children, Kate and Will. When Dora's visa expires and she faces deportation, Peter marries her to keep her in the country and with his family.

An architect with the firm of Hughes, Whitney and Lennox, Peter lives at 46 LaPaloma Drive in Los Angeles (telephone number 555-3636). In high school, Peter was the star football player; he holds the record for making the most touchdowns in a single season.

Dora, who calls Peter "Mr. Peter," is actually in love with him (as he is with her), but each refuses to admit it. (Dora's jealous streak is evident, though, when Peter is with other women.) While Dora seems to be the perfect wife for Peter and mother for his children, she respects their marriage of convenience and functions only as his live-in housekeeper. Her pride and joy—and Peter's nightmare—is her kitchen junk drawer where she stores, and can find, "all the stuff you don't know what to do with, but you don't want to throw away, because one day you are going to need that thing you don't know what to do with right now."

Kate, Peter's 13-year-old daughter, is somewhat dim-witted, and plays miniature golf with Peter at Putter World. As a child, she was a member of a Brownie troop; she now plays saxophone in her high school band. While Kate is growing up into a beautiful young woman, Peter continues to see her as his little girl, with posters of Strawberry Shortcake on her bedroom walls (later replaced by Bon Jovi). Kate is also a member of her unnamed high school's cheerleading squad (for the Badgers football team)—she possesses the three required *P*s: positive, pretty and perky. When Kate, who wears a perfume called Sensual, and her friend Lorie (Mandy Ingber) "dress hot" (in short skirts and tight blouses) and "feel sexy," they go to the local mall "to drive shoe salesmen crazy."

Will, the smarter of the two Farrell children, attends an unnamed junior high school. Buck, Peter's brother, works for the Big Ball Wrecking Company.

Relatives: Peggy McCay (Peter's mother, *Lucille Farrell*), Alley Mills (Peter's sister-in-law, *Janine Desmond*), Frederick Coffin (Peter's brother, *Buck Farrell*), Evelyn Guerrero (Dora's sister, *Marisol*), James Victor (*Dora's father*), Lupe Ontiveros (*Dora's mother*).

I Married Dora. Daniel Hugh Kelly, Juliette Lewis, Jason Horst and Elizabeth Pena.

Flashbacks: Wendel Meldrum (Peter's wife, *Janet Farrell*).
Theme: "I Married Dora," by Glenn Jordan.

328. *I Married Joan*

NBC, 10/15/52 to 4/6/55

Cast: Joan Davis (*Joan Stevens*), Jim Backus (*Bradley Stevens*).

Facts: Pretending she is an item on an auction block, Joan Stevens, the wife of Judge Bradley ("Brad") Stevens, says, "Folks, I have here item 45—a wife. Due to circumstances beyond her control, this wife is losing its owner. Now, what am I bid for this wife? This is not an ordinary wife. This one's a real goof. This wife is unconditionally guaranteed to louse things up."

Joan means well, but all her good intentions inevitably backfire (even her fortune cookie fortunes are against her—"When you opened this cookie, you read the fortune we put in it. But when you opened your mouth, you just stuck your foot in it"). She is president of the local Women's Club (she and her friends get together every other Monday to play bridge) and a member of the Women's Welfare League. Joan considers herself to be very popular ("When you have a wife as popular as I am, you have to make a date five weeks in advance") and can't resist a bargain (salesmen call her "one of those yo-yo dames").

Joan is also a whiz at maneuvering the household funds "to balance the books." She loves to buy clothes; when she doesn't have the money to pay for something at the moment, she has it sent C.O.D. To get Brad to pay for the item, she does one of two things: "the crying bit" (although she doesn't like to send Brad to work with a wet handkerchief), or making Brad his favorite breakfast (hotcakes with melted butter and coffee).

Brad, on the other hand, is level-headed, patient, understanding and deeply in love with Joan. He is a domestic relations judge for the county of Los Angeles. Brad loves hunting and golf. Pot roast is his favorite dinner, and he calls Joan "Lover" (she calls him "Honey"). Brad's hobby is stamp collecting.

The Stevens live at 133 Stone Drive (also given as 345 Laurel Drive), and their phone number is Dunbar 3-1232. Joan's favorite television soap opera is "Two Hearts Against the World," and she is a fan of Guy Lombardo. What Brad likes to hear most, according to Joan, is "Dinner is ready." When Brad and Joan married, they checked into a resort hotel (Room 203) and had only 12 hours for a honeymoon (due to a trial Brad had to preside over the next day). As an incentive to get Joan on a schedule and do housework, Brad promised her a diamond bracelet if, after six months, the house was running properly (the inscription read FOR THE MOST WONDERFUL HOUSEKEEPER IN THE WHOLE WORLD). When Brad runs for re-election, his campaign posters read RE-ELECT JUDGE BRADLEY STEVENS. HONEST BRAD, ALWAYS KEEPS HIS PROMISES. The series' official screen title is "The Joan Davis Show: I Married Joan."

Relatives: Beverly Wills (Joan's sister, *Beverly Grossman*; her favorite meal is spare ribs), Alan Grossman (Beverly's husband, *Alan Grossman*, an army lieutenant stationed at Fort Williams), Elvia Allman (Joan's aunt, *Vera*), Norma Varden (Brad's mother, *Florry Stevens*).

Theme: "I Married Joan," vocal by the Roger Wagner Chorale.

329. *I Still Dream of Jeannie*

NBC, 10/20/91

Cast: Barbara Eden (*Jeannie/Jeannie II*), Bill Daily (*Roger Healey*), Christopher Bolton (*Tony Nelson, Jr.*).

Facts: A telefilm update of the 1965–70 series "I Dream of Jeannie." In the series, Jeannie was born in Baghdad 2,000 years ago. She was a normal girl who was transformed into a genie as punishment when she refused the marriage proposal of the Blue Djin, the most powerful and most feared of all genies. The Blue Djin placed her in a bottle and sentenced her to a life of loneliness on a deserted island. It was on that South Pacific island in 1965 that astronaut Tony Nelson found the genie (whom he called Jeannie) when his space capsule crash-landed. Tony became Jeannie's master, and they married in 1969.

In the television movie, Jeannie is still a genie, still married to Tony Nelson (now a colonel, but not seen) and the mother of a 16-year-old boy named Tony Nelson, Jr. The locale of the series moved from NASA in Cocoa Beach, Florida, to the Lyndon B. Johnson Space Center in Houston, Texas. Jeannie's past was also quite different: Jeannie is now 4,233 years old (although she claims "I'm only 4,229"). She was born a genie in Mesopotamia and attended genie school to learn her craft. She was said to have had many masters over the centuries.

Jeannie II, Jeannie's older sister, was also brought back.

In the series, Jeannie II had many masters, but none pleased her, so she sought to steal Tony away from Jeannie. The television movie depicts Jeannie II as the same devious girl and still seeking Tony as her master. It is said that Jeannie II never had a master; because of this, she is now bound to remain in Mesopotamia forever (she can leave, but only for periods of 24 hours at a time; she must return to maintain her youth, beauty and powers). Tony's friend, Roger Healey, now a colonel, was also brought back. He is married to the never-seen Tanya and has also been transferred to the Johnson Space Center. General Westcott (Al Waxman) is the base commanding officer; and Shamir (Peter Breck) is the chief of the genies (in the series it was Michael Ansara as the Blue Djin). Jeannie's genie dog, Gin Gin, was also brought back.

The movie begins with Tony being launched into space on a top secret mission—a mission so secret that not even Jeannie can know his whereabouts. The situation doesn't seem to bother Jeannie until her sister brings one of the laws of the Sacred Scroll of Rismock to Shamir's attention: "A genie without a master for more than three months must return to Mesopotamia forever" (a genie cannot remain in a plain of reality without a master; by leaving the planet, Tony forfeited his right as a master). The story relates Jeannie's desperate efforts to find a temporary master until Tony (who has been gone three months) can return to claim her as his genie. (Jeannie chose Bob Simpson [Ken Kercheval], the local high school guidance counselor, as her temporary master. She could not choose Roger because he was married ["a master must be single"] or her son ["a master must be over 21"].) The movie ended with Tony still in unknown space and a rather dim-witted Bob trying to comprehend his decision to become Jeannie's temporary master.

Theme: "The New I Dream of Jeannie Theme," by Ken Harrison.

330. *Ichabod and Me*

CBS, 9/26/61 to 9/18/62

Bob Major (Robert Sterling), a widower with a young son named Benjie (Jimmy Mathers), quits his job as an editor for the *New York Times* and moves to Phippsboro, a small town in New Hampshire. There, he purchases the Phippsboro *Bulletin*, the town newspaper, from its owner, Ichabod Adams (George Chandler). Ichabod, who has a beautiful daughter named Abigail ("Abby") Adams (Christine White), is the town's mayor, traffic commissioner and overall problem solver. Abby is a member of the Garden Club; Ichabod grows petunias as a hobby.

Bob lived at 720 Madison Avenue in New York City; he now resides at 432 Maple Lane (Ichabod and Abby [Bob's romantic interest] live at R.F.D. number 6). It is an eight hour drive from Manhattan to Phippsboro. Bob eats lunch at Bailey's Drug Store (Tim Graham plays Mr. Bailey).

When Bob sets his mind to get a story, he doesn't give up until he gets it (he uses "the famous Major charm" to get what he wants). The biggest story Ichabod ever covered as editor was "the day Dustin Farnum got lost in the blizzard of '22." Bob's first major story was interviewing Eugene Hollenfield (Rod Serling), a famous writer (author of "Life with Louie") when he came to live in Phippsboro. Bob's housekeeper, Ichabod's aunt, Lavinia Perkins (Reta Shaw), receives $35 a month and room and board (she has dinner ready at 6:00 P.M.). Jonathan (Jimmy Hawkins) assists Bob at the paper. In the closing theme, the clock in the town square reads 12:00 noon.

Pete Rugolo composed the theme.

In the original pilot ("Adams Apples"), which was broadcast on "G.E. Theater" (4/24/60), Fred Beir played Terry Major, an advertising executive (company not named), who gives up his job "to emancipate himself and become a gentleman farmer." Ichabod (George Chandler) and his daughter Abby (Christine White) own an unnamed lodge (where, a year before, Terry vacationed; when Terry returned to New York and found he missed the peaceful life of Phippsboro, he arranged to rent an apple farm from Ichabod for $125 a month). Dorothy Neuman played Terry's housekeeper, Aunt Lavinia; Terry had a dog named Fownes (after his former boss, Herbert Fownes [Leon Ames]) and was never married (Abby became his romantic interest). Conrad Salinger composed the original theme.

331. *I'm Dickens ... He's Fenster*

ABC, 9/28/62 to 9/13/63

Harold ("Harry") Dickens (six feet tall, 187 pounds) and Archibald ("Arch") Fenster (six feet one inch tall, 193 pounds) have been friends for ten years. They are carpenters and work together at the Bannister Construction Company in Los Angeles. Harry is married and henpecked; Arch is a swinging young bachelor with more girls than he can handle.

Harry (John Astin) married Katherine ("Kate") Conway (Emmaline Henry) in 1953. They live at 285 South Lakehurst, their phone number is 555-3438 and they eat Diet Krisp breakfast cereal. Harry, the shop foreman at Bannister, is a bit of a klutz and not very handy when it comes to making repairs around the house (for example, he has "this thing about magnets" and always uses ones that are too powerful for the job at hand). Kate, a stunning blonde, dyed her hair black when she and Harry were dating; she became a natural blonde after she married. Harry's most embarrassing moment occurred when he took a break from hunting to go for a swim. He hung his clothes on what he thought was a tree branch; he later had to chase his clothes three miles up a mountain — the tree branches were the horns of a moose.

Ichabod and Me. Robert Sterling and Christine White.

Arch (Marty Ingels), who is famous for "his little black book" (a 300-page, six-by-nine-inch softcover), lives in an apartment (no door number) at 366 Brockhurst Avenue and dines most often at Fontano's Restaurant. He is more competent than Harry and can usually repair the damage Harry's bungling has caused.

Arch has a unique talent with bread (he makes dolls out of it) and loses his confidence around brainy girls (he is not used to "the intellectual breed" and goes to pieces around them). Before Arch enters Harry's home, he knocks to the beat of the song "Shave and a Haircut, Two Bits" ("dum-de-de dum-dum, dum-dum").

Melvin ("Mel") Warshaw (Dave Ketchum), a fellow carpenter, has 11 kids, two dogs and three cats; his never-seen wife is named Isabel. Robert ("Bob") Mulligan (Henry Beckman), who lives at 317 South Lakehurst (eight blocks from Harry), is also a carpenter and constantly teases Harry about his foul-ups. Bob calls Arch "Lover Boy" and has a never-seen wife named Eloise. Joe Bentley (Noam Pitlik) is a fellow carpenter; Myron Bannister (Frank DeVol) is the owner of the company.

Harry and Arch are members of the Carpenter's Four singing group; and, strange as it may seem, the carpenters do not use power tools.

Roger Mobley appeared as Mel's son, Ralph Warshaw, and Karla Most played Bob's cousin, Arlene.

Irving Szathmary composed the theme, "The Dickens and Fenster March."

332. *In the Heat of the Night*

NBC, 3/6/88 to 7/5/92
CBS, 10/28/92 to the present

Law enforcement procedures in a small Southern town as seen through the experiences of William O. ("Bill") Gillespie (Carroll O'Connor), the white police chief of Sparta, Mississippi, and Virgil Tibbs (Howard Rollins), his Philadelphia-bred black chief of detectives.

Bill has a hunting dog named Roscoe and drives a squad car with the license plate M-7246 (later, M-7555). Bill first mentions he was married to a woman named Anna Caterina but never had any children ("I lost him when I lost her"). In a later episode, Bill mentions he was married to a woman named Georgia Farren, who deserted him shortly after the birth of their daughter (Christine Elise played Bill's estranged daughter, Lana Farren). In 1988 Bill dated JoAnn St. John (Lois Nettleton), a cashier at the Magnolia Café. Ten years earlier, JoAnn was a $100 a night call girl known as Kelly Kaye. In 1991 Bill began romancing Harriet DeLong (Denise Nicholas), a black city councilwoman. When Carroll O'Connor suffered a heart attack in 1988, Joe Don Baker replaced him for four episodes as Tom Dugan, the former police chief (Bill was said to be away at a police convention).

Virgil is married to Althea Peterson (Anne-Marie Johnson), a teacher at Sparta Community High School. They live at 4602 Cherry Lane, and 555-2002 is their phone number. In 1990 Althea gave birth to a son they named William Calvin Tibbs. M-1320 is Virgil's license plate number.

Officer Parker Williams (David Hart) has three cats (Fuzz Face, Old Man and Wrencher); the Big T Truck Stop is his favorite watering hole. Other officers are Bubba Skinner (Alan Autry), Wilson Sweet (Geoffrey Thorne) and Chris Rankin (Sheryl Lynn Piland).

Relatives: Traci Wolfe (Althea's niece, *Nicole Sands*), J.A. Preston and Mel Stewart (Althea's father, *Calvin Peterson*), Ellen Holly (Althea's mother, *Ruth Peterson*), Mitchell Anderson (Bubba's nephew, *Bobby Skinner*).

Theme: "In the Heat of the Night," vocal by Bill Champlin.

333. *The Insiders*

ABC, 9/25/85 to 1/8/86

Nicholas ("Nick") Fox (Nicholas Campbell) is an investigative reporter for the Los Angeles–based *Newspoint* magazine. He and his partner, James Mackey (Stoney Jackson), an ex-con, acquire stories by becoming a part of them. Alice West (Gail Strickland) is Nick's editor, and Melissa (Kelly Ann Conn) is Alice's secretary. Nick has a pet cat named Dillon and lives at 34 Brewster Avenue.

Jeannie Elias played Nick's cousin, Roxanne, and Jane Greer appeared as Alice's mother, Louise West.

Peter Robinson composed the "Insiders Theme."

334. *The Invaders*

ABC, 1/10/67 to 9/17/68

Cast: Roy Thinnes *(David Vincent)*.

Facts: Landers and Vincent is an architectural firm at 3006 Willow Street in Santa Barbara, California (telephone number 555-5235). David Vincent, a graduate of State College, is the eager, young partner; Alan Landers (James Daly), the senior partner, has been an architect for 30 years.

David is returning home (36 Heming Drive) from a business trip one night when he decides to take a shortcut. He exits Highway 166 and soon finds himself on a dark and desolate country road. He passes a closed and deserted café (Bud's Diner) and decides to stop. The time is 4:20 A.M. and David has been driving (car plate 812-249) for 20 hours. David is suddenly startled by a loud, strange noise. He sees a bright light and witnesses the landing of a spacecraft from another galaxy.

David reports the incident later that morning, but an investigation by the sheriff's department fails to uncover any evidence of what David saw. Unable to accept the explanation that he had gone too long without sleep and just imagined what he saw, David begins an investigation on his own. In the town of Kinney, he uncovers proof of what he saw: in an abandoned hydroelectric plant, aliens from a dying planet (unnamed) have established a base of operations as the beginning of an invasion to make the Earth their home. Before he is able to show others his proof, the Invaders vanish (a series problem for David). Stories relate David's efforts "to convince a disbelieving world that the nightmare has already begun."

The Invaders take human form, and their plan is to assimilate into society. David knows their one flaw—"Some of them have mutated hands: a crooked fourth finger"—and he knows that where an invasion has begun, there must also be a recharging base for them (to maintain their human forms, the aliens must use their glass tube–like regeneration chambers. These tubes are also a device by which the aliens kill humans—by producing an untraceable heart attack or cerebral hemorrhage). Failure to rejuvenate in time causes an alien's death (disintegration in a glowing light).

The Invaders are emotionless. Aliens who develop emotions are mutants, and alien leaders are called Leaders. The Invaders have no pulse and do not bleed if they are cut. They use hypnotic interrogation on captured humans and can gain control over humans with a disk made of a metal that is unknown on Earth (by placing the disk, which is warm to the touch and vibrates, on the back of the neck, amnesia or a cerebral hemorrhage can be induced). The aliens appear to be horrifying and indistinguishable in their natural form; on Earth, they reproduce themselves by passing electricity through seawater. Their spaceships are cup-and-saucer shaped, with a large center light and two smaller lights (to each side of the center).

Police departments have David listed as "a kook who believes aliens are trying to take over the Earth." As David gathers evidence to prove his story, he makes contact with several powerful people who have seen what David has seen and who know the aliens must be stopped. The group becomes known as the Believers. (Corporate head Edgar Scoville, played by Kent Smith, is the only Believer with a recurring role. Guests Carol Lynley, as Elyse Reynolds, and Anthony Eisley, as Bob Talman, were two of the group of seven Believers.)

"You can't stop it, it's going to happen. Don't fight us," the aliens tell David. But for as long as it takes, David will fight, "for they must be stopped, they must be exposed. If David Vincent doesn't do it, who will?"

Theme: "The Invaders," by Dominic Frontiere.

335. *The Invisible Man*

Syndicated, 1958 to 1960

Cast: Lisa Daniely *(Diane Wilson),* Deborah Watling *(Sally Wilson),* ? *(The Invisible Man).*

Facts: The series concept (that made it to the air) began innocently enough with scientist Peter Brady's own words:

My name is Peter Brady. For some time now I have been engaged in a highly secret experiment designed to bring about a giant step forward in the conquest of space and matter. Here in my lab, working day and night, I've been prying into the mysteries of the future. Only a few hours ago I felt that there were secrets that would never be known to us here on earth. And then suddenly in the midst of a routine experiment, a strange and unpredictable event took place. Whether a mistake or the natural conclusion of the experiment, I cannot say. I can say that what happened is one of the most fantastic experiences in our modern day.

The experiment Peter is referring to is one he is conducting on the problems of optical density (the refraction of light) at the Castle Hill Research Lab in England. During a test, reactor number three springs a leak and sprays Peter with a gas. His body absorbs the gas and it renders him invisible.

Brady, however, lacks the knowledge to become visible. (He wears facial bandages, sunglasses and gloves to be seen. In one episode, Peter mentions that his clothes will become invisible if they are made of animal fibers, such as wool.) Before Peter can do anything, he is put under lock and key by the Ministry (they fear panic will result if it is known an invisible man exists). Peter escapes and retreats to the home of his sister, Diane Wilson. There he explains to Diane and her daughter, Sally, what has happened. He concludes with, "It's quite simple. Take a jellyfish, put it in water and you can't see it. That's happened to me. My reflective index has been lowered to that of theirs."

The situation changes drastically when a rival experimenter learns what has happened and attempts to steal Brady's formula for invisibility. The Ministry reverses its decision about Peter and allows him to continue his research: to find the key to becoming visible again. In the meantime, Peter uses his great advantage of invisibility to assist the British government in its battle against crime. (Peter first made a guinea pig invisible, then a white rabbit before he himself became invisible. In later episodes, Peter's invisibility is known to the general public.)

The identity of the actor portraying the lead (Peter Brady) had been (and still is) a closely guarded secret. (The cast for each episode, including the regulars, is listed only during the end credits. While the lead is listed first, he is credited only as "The Invisible Man"; the remainder of the cast follows, each with a character name.) It has been rumored that series producer Ralph Smart played Brady (Smart did the same anonymous casting for "The Iron Mask"; see note), or that actor Tim Turner, who appeared in the episode "Man in Disguise," was actually the uncredited actor behind the bandages. The actor's identity was concealed not only from the public, but also from the cast and crew. (The actor wore bandages on the set; his voice was dubbed in after the episodes were shot. In some episodes he sounds American; in others there is a slight British accent.)

A dramatically different version of the H.G. Wells story was produced in early 1958 but was scrapped and never aired. In it, Peter Brady is conducting an experiment in optical density on a guinea pig (which disappears, then reappears) when a reactor begins leaking. Peter's system absorbs too much of the gas, and he is rendered invisible; his clothes, however, do not become invisible. Peter is free to leave the lab; in fact, it is known that Peter Brady has become invisible (as television and newspaper reporters constantly annoy him). In this version he lives with his widowed sister Jane Wilson (Lisa Daniely) and her daughter Sally (Deborah Watling).

It is difficult to predict how this version of the series would have progressed, since there was only one episode. Based on the storyline—Brady using his invisibility to rescue Sally from kidnappers—it appeared that he would either become a detective and use his invisibility to help solve crimes; or would follow the aired format and work with the British government—which would give him the greatest chance of discovering the formula for visibility. There is no real ending explaining what Brady would do next.

Peter lives with Diane (a widow) and her daughter, Sally, at 21 Hugo Drive in London. Peter works for Sir Charles (Ernest Clark; later Ewen MacDuff), the British cabinet minister (his telephone number is Whitehall 7402, and his license plate reads 234-A). Sir Charles's superior is the prime minister (Basil Dignam). (Sir Charles and the prime minister did not appear in the unaired pilot version.) Diane's license plate is 2490PC; Peter's license plate reads VON 495. When "Dee" (as Peter calls Diane) goes to the Continent, she spends most of her time at the gambling tables.

Theme: "The Invisible Man Theme," by Sydney John Kay (both versions of the show).

Note: See the following title also. "The Iron Mask," Ralph Smart's earlier series using an anonymous lead, was syndicated in 1957. It was set in the seventeenth century and related the adventures of Philippe (the Iron Mask), an escaped political prisoner who helps people in their battle against the soldiers of Louis XIV.

336. *The Invisible Man*

NBC, 9/8/75 to 1/9/76

Cast: David McCallum *(Daniel Westin)*, Melinda Fee *(Kate Westin)*, Craig Stevens *(Walter Carlson)*.

Facts: Believing that it is possible to transfer objects from one place to another with laser beams, Daniel Wilson, a scientist for the Los Angeles–based KLAE Corporation, receives the authority to prove his theory via his Tele-Transportation Project. Eight months later, and after having spent $1.5 million in research money, Daniel reaches the point where he believes he can make a man invisible. Although the project is still experimental, Daniel is able to make himself invisible (by standing between two laser beams) and bring himself back to visibility (by injecting himself with a special serum he developed).

Although excited about his discovery, Daniel is soon dismayed when he learns from his superior, Walter Carlson, that his invention can be used as the ultimate military weapon. Opposed to a military use of his weapon, Daniel takes matters into his own hands and decides to destroy the Tele-Transporter. In order to escape from the building, Daniel makes himself invisible, then destroys the machine. Later, when Daniel injects himself with the visibility serum, it fails to work; he discovers that he is permanently invisible.

Daniel seeks help from his friend, Nick Maggio (Henry Darrow), a brilliant plastic surgeon who has been experimenting with a plastic lifelike substance he calls Derma Pleque (which can reconstruct a patient's face). To help Daniel, Nick modifies the process to what he calls Derma Plex, a rubbery liquid plastic that he uses to reconstruct Daniel's face and hands (for his eyes, Nick develops a special set of contact lenses; caps are used for his teeth; a wig becomes his hair—hence Daniel appears as he did before).

Daniel, however, must take his new face (the mask) off every six to eight hours to allow his invisible skin to breathe. When Daniel realizes that KLAE Corporation's research center is his only way of finding the means to become visible, he becomes their chief investigator, using his invisibility to tackle very dangerous national and international assignments.

Daniel and his wife, Kate, live at 40137 Hazelton Road in Los Angeles; their car license plate reads 758 CKP. The KLAE Corporation is a highly specialized research center that undertakes government contracts. Daniel's lab rabbit is named Harvey, and Kate calls Daniel "Danny." In the 90 minute NBC pilot film (5/6/75), Jackie Cooper played Walter Carlson. And, as strange as it may seem, Daniel wears visible clothes over his invisible clothes. (Articles of clothing that are made of animal fibers are invisible also—but take longer to reappear. Modesty demands that he put on something, as he will reappear before his clothes do.)

Theme: "The Invisible Man," by Richard Clements.

Note: NBC tried to revive the series as "The Gemini Man" (see entry) and in a variation called "The Invisible Woman," a two hour pilot that failed to generate a series. While visiting with her uncle, Dudley Plunkett (Bob Denver), a biochemist, Sandy Martinson (Alexa Hamilton), a cub reporter for the Washington, D.C., *Daily Express,* touches a spilled chemical solution (mixed and knocked over by Dudley's lab chimp, Chuck) that renders her invisible. When Sandy learns that Dudley is unable to replicate the formula to make her visible again, she makes the best of the situation by using her misfortune to investigate crimes (by using makeup, contact lenses, a wig and clothes, Sandy appears a normal woman). David Frank sings the theme, "She Must Be Around Here Someplace."

See also the preceding title for information on the British version of "The Invisible Man." The series is also known as "H.G. Wells' The Invisible Man."

The Invisible Woman see *The Invisible Man* (second title)

337. *Isis*

CBS, 9/6/75 to 9/2/78

Andrea Thomas (JoAnna Cameron) is a science teacher at Larkspur High School in California. One summer, during an expedition in Egypt, Andrea found a magic amulet that endowed her with the powers of Isis, a champion of truth and justice. (The amulet was given to the queen of Egypt by the royal sorcerer. It holds the power of Isis [the goddess of fertility] and bestows upon any woman who possesses it the ability to soar, power over animals, and control over the elements of the earth, sea and sky.) When Andrea holds the amulet and says, "O mighty Isis," she becomes Isis (the clouds darken, the symbol of Isis is seen, and Andrea is magically transformed into the goddess). She wears a white, miniskirted Egyptian costume and a tiara that allows her to see beyond her normal vision. Her hair also increases in length—from Andrea's midback length to hip length for Isis. Little effort is made to hide JoAnna Cameron's beauty as Andrea. Conservative dress, glasses and a ponytail are the "disguises" Andrea uses to conceal her secret identity.

Andrea, who lives at 21306 Baker Place (Apartment 4A) in the town of Larkspur, drives a red sedan (later yellow, after it is stolen and repainted) with the license plate 69 CBE; her phone number is 555-3638. Andrea's teaching assistant (first season) is Cindy Lee (Joanna Pang), and later, Renee Carroll (Ronalda Douglas). Rick Mason (Brian Cutler), Andrea's friend, a teacher, has a boat called the *Star Tracker.*

Andrea has a pet crow named Tut, and when she needs help, she calls on the services of Captain Marvel (John Davey; see "Shazam!" for additional information). To perform any feat, Isis must recite special rhymes related to the task at hand; the rhyme most often heard is "O zephyr winds which blow on high, lift me now so I may fly." The series is also known as "The Secrets of Isis."

Yvette Blais and Jeff Michael composed the "Isis" theme.

338. *The Islanders*

ABC, 10/2/60 to 3/26/61

Latitude 4° south, longitude 128° east in the East Indies is the location of Ambowina, a small island off the coast of Sumatra, whose "chief natural resources are beautiful native girls." The tropical paradise is also the base for Lato Airlines, a Grumman Goose seaplane that is owned by Sandor ("Sandy") Wade (William Reynolds) and Zachary ("Zack") Malloy (James Philbrook), two argumentative partners who share billing as president of the company on alternate months. They paid $35,000 for the plane and have another partner, a beautiful but scheming woman named Wilhelmina ("Willie") Vandeveer (Diane Brewster), who manages the business ("I'll be your treasurer") for 15 percent of the profits. (Sandy and Zack were once friends who flew for the same airline. Both left after a dispute. Sandy drifted up and down the islands for five years; Zack ventured into the business world. Willie, a mutual friend, thought they were both going nowhere and needed a business of their own. She conned each into investing $17,500 in the Goose. Neither knew about the other's investment until they went to claim the plane. The bickering started but was put aside long enough to save Willie's life when she became the target of a killer and drug smugglers. The adventure united the trio, and Willie convinced them to run the airline.)

Jim ("Shipwreck") Callahan (Gordon Jones) runs Shipwreck Callahan's American Bar on Ambowina. He served on the destroyer USS *Houston* during World War II, and his favorite drink to serve is a Bamboo Bomb. The Bank of Jakarta holds the mortage on the bar. Willie lives in Room 32 of the small hotel that is part of the bar.

Naja (Daria Massey) is a gorgeous 20-year-old Balinese girl who works in the American Bar as a dancer. She previously worked as a switchboard operator at Macaser Imports in Singapore. Naja looks more European than Balinese ("My father was Portuguese but more of an Islander than my mother") and loves to dance. At age ten she was a La Gona dancer with the Bedalu Group on Bali (the La Gona is danced by children and is based on the ancient story of Malotz, which tells of a beautiful princess who is stolen by the arrogant king, Lofson).

Sandy was born in Cincinnati, and he and Zack served in Korea together during the war. Willie was born in Holland, and the Vandeveer family was one of the biggest plantation owners in the Dutch East Indies. When the war broke out, they fled to the States. Her father managed to get back to Holland but died before Willie could join him. She is now fighting back and trying to salvage what was stolen from her—"That's why I sail a little close to the wind." Islanders also call her "Steamboat Willie" because after a con "she always catches the next steamboat out."

The Goose has the I.D. and radio code PK-DPB. Before deciding on the name Lato Airways (for "latitude zero"), the trio planned to call the company Malloy and Company (but Sandy objected—"Get a load of him"). Willie suggested Southern Cross ("It's too much like double cross," said Zack). Sandy suggested, and all liked, Lato Airways.

Theme: "The Islanders," by William Lava.

339. *It Takes Two*

ABC, 10/14/82 to 4/28/83

Molly and Sam Quinn (Patty Duke and Richard Crenna) are a busy professional couple with two children, Lisa (Helen Hunt) and Andy (Anthony Edwards). Molly is an assistant district attorney with the Manhattan D.A.'s office; Sam is the chief of surgery at the Rush-Thornton Medical Center.

Apartment 1110 (address not given) is home to the Quinns (555-6060 is their phone number). In addition to her and Sam's joint checking account (blue checks), Molly has her own personal checking account (pink checks). Sam and Molly's favorite restaurant is Chez Paolo's and Sam's fondest memory of their first date together is that of the pink sweater that Molly wore "that just wouldn't quit." Lisa's high school is not named. She works as a waitress at the Pizza Palace and is dedicated to helping save the environment (she does volunteer work for No Nukes). Her favorite hangout is Brandy's Café. Also living with the Quinns is Molly's elderly mother, Anna (Billie Bird), who is called "Mama."

Crystal Gayle and Paul Williams sing the theme, "Where Love Spends the Night."

340. *It's a Living*

ABC, 10/30/80 to 1/29/81
ABC, 10/24/81 to 1/9/82
ABC, 2/12/82 to 9/10/82
Syndicated, 9/85 to 3/89

Lois (Susan Sullivan), Jan (Barrie Youngfellow), Cassie (Ann Jillian), Dot (Gail Edwards), Vickie (Wendy Schaal), Maggie (Louise Lasser), Amy (Crystal Bernard) and Ginger (Sheryl Lee Ralph) are waitresses who work at Above the Top, a posh thirtieth floor Los Angeles restaurant that features "Sky High Dining" (Above the Top is owned by Pacific Continental Properties). Nancy (Marian Mercer) is the hostess; Sonny (Paul Kreppel) is the lounge singer; and Howard (Richard Stahl) is the chef.

Lois Adams is the most sophisticated of the waitresses. She is married to the never-seen Bill and is struggling to raise two children (Amy and Joey). She lives at 8713 Mercer Street.

Maggie McBirney is a widow and lives at 1417 Brooke Avenue. She has become shy and unsure of herself since the death of her husband, Joseph (who was a salesman for Kitchen Help dishwashers).

Katie Lou ("Cassie") Cranston is the sexiest and most beautiful of the group. She was born in Kansas and now lives in a condo at the Sun Palace. Cassie is man-crazy and looking to marry money. On her night off, she reads to senior citizens at the Willow Glen Rest Home.

Jan Hoffmeyer is divorced and the mother of a young girl named Ellen. Jan's maiden name is Frankel, and she attended Templar High School (class of '66). During the late 1960s she was arrested during a college demonstration for mooning a cop. Jan has a cat named Ralph and is attending night classes at North Los Angeles Law School. Jan married Richard Grey (Richard Kline) on November 24, 1985.

Dorothy ("Dot") Higgins, who was born in Detroit, majored in theater at Baxter College. Dot is a hopeful actress and appeared in the following productions *Bye Bye Birdie* (as Kim), *The Garden of Countess Natasha* (as Natasha) and *Esmerelda* (a play about the history of the Philippine Islands). On television, Dot played three roles (a nun; the nun's sister, Esmerelda; and Esmerelda's sickly triplet, Juanita) on the soap opera, "All My Sorrows." She made her television debut in a commercial for Autumn Years dog food. She also appeared in the Le Stiff hair spray commercial on TV and on the "Adopt a Pet Telethon" (where she sang "My Buddy" to a dog). Dot's character appeared as "Betty Spaghetti, the waitress" in the comic strip "Billy Bonkers." Dot has several pets: Mr. Puss, the cat; Pardon, the dog; and Mouse, the mouse. Her mother (not seen) has a dog named Scrappy.

Victoria ("Vickie") Allen, born in Pocatello, Idaho, is best friends with Dot and the most sensitive of the women. She has a pet parakeet named Squeaky and lives at 102 North Brewster Place, Apartment 304.

Amy Tompkins was born in Snyder, Texas, and now lives in the Carrie Nation Hotel for Women in Los Angeles. She has fish named Oscar and Cletus and is a member of A.G.O.A. (American Gun Owners Association). Amy owns a chrome-plated .357 Magnum with a six inch barrel that her father gave her (with these words: "Keep you chin up and your skirt down"). Amy hides her gun in her "pink Jammy Bunny with a zipper in its tummy." She also has a plush rabbit named Snuggle Bunny and shares the apartment with Ginger in later episodes.

Virginia ("Ginger") St. James was born in Buffalo, New York, and has a flair for fashion designing. She is the only black waitress employed by Above the Top. She has many boyfriends (one of whom named his boat after her—*Ginger Snaps*) and in high school was called "booby soxer" (for stuffing her bra with socks).

Nancy Beebee, the snobbish hostess, was a ballerina for 15 years, then a waitress at Above the Top before acquiring her current position; she was born in South Philadelphia and married Howard Miller, the restaurant's chef. Howard was born in Trenton, New Jersey, has a dog named Bluto and two fish (Ike and Mamie). His favorite pastime is fishing on the Rogue River in Oregon.

Sonny Mann, the restaurant's one-man entertainment center, was born in Reno, Nevada (his real last name is Manischewitz). Sonny has aspirations of becoming a singer. His idol is Jack Jones, and he has a Franklin Mint All Nations doll collection. He is a charter member of the Bullwinkle the Moose fan club and had his first gig at a club called Vinnie's Romper Room (his second gig was at the Play Pen Lounge at Chuck's Game Room in Las Vegas). As a kid, Sonny had a dog named Buster, and when he couldn't get a publisher to print his book, *Man to Man* (a guide for picking up girls), he had 750 copies printed himself.

Relatives: Tricia Cast (Lois's daughter, *Amy Adams*), Keith Mitchell (Lois's son, *Joey Adams*), Sandy Simpson (Maggie's brother, *Bobby*), Lili Haydn and Virginia Keehne (Jan's daughter, *Ellen Hoffmeyer*), Dennis Dugan (Jan's ex-husband, *Lloyd Hoffmeyer*), Georgann Johnson (Jan's mother, *Phyllis Frankel*), Richard McKenzie (Jan's father, *Will Frankel*), Richard Schaal (Vickie's father, *Emmett Allen*), K Callan (Dot's mother, *Harriet Higgins*), Edye Byrde *(Ginger's grandmother)*, Kelly Britt (Nancy's cousin, *Grace Beebee*), Linda G. Miller (Nancy's sister, *Gloria Beebee*), Arlen Dean Snyder *(Amy's father)*, Nita Talbot (Sonny's mother, *Rose*), Donnelly Rhodes (Sonny's brother, *Buddy*), Paul Kreppel (Sonny's father, *Irv Manischewitz*), Sue Ball (Howard's daughter, *Lori Miller*), Kathleen Freeman (Howard's mother, *Mae Miller*), Mary Betten (Richard's mother, *Beth Grey*), Maura Soden (Richard's ex-wife, *Cindy*), Andre Gower (Richard's son, *Charlie Grey*).

Theme: "It's a Living," vocal by Leslie Bricusse.

341. *It's a Man's World*

NBC, 9/17/62 to 1/28/63

Moored at Stott's Landing in the Ohio River town of Cordella is the *Elephant*, a houseboat owned by Wesley ("Wes") Macauley (Glenn Corbett), Thomas A. ("Tom Tom") DeWitt (Ted Bessell) and Vernon ("Vern") Hodges (Randy Boone), three friends who are also students at Cordella College. Also residing with them is Howard ("Howie") Macauley (Michael Burns), Wes's younger (14-year-old) brother (Wes, 22, became Howie's guardian after their parents were killed in an automobile accident).

Wes, who drives a Jeep with the license plate 899-11, pumps gas for Houghton Stott (Harry Harvey, Sr.), the owner of Stott's Landing and Stott's Service Station. PH 3-047 is the six digit phone number of the station, and 3 Star Top Grade gasoline is sold. Houghton's "bucket of rusted nuts and bolts" pickup truck has the license plate 818P. Houghton is a former river barge pilot; he constantly yells at the younger captains as they pass his station. Houghton was forced to retire after 50 years and is bitter about losing his job; he never had the time to raise a family and looks upon Howie as the son he never had. His favorite pastime is playing checkers with Howie.

Tom Tom is the lazy one of the group—"he'll sleep his

The Islanders. Back, left to right: Daria Massey and Diane Brewster. Front, left to right: James Philbrook and Williams Reynolds.

life away if he could," says Wes. He is a kid at heart and is fascinated by everything. Tom Tom enjoys every moment of life, but is in a dither most of the time and unreliable. He plays games with kids, helps the local sanitation men clear the trash (for which he gets a free ride to school on the truck) and hangs out at the Windmill, the local coffee house. He is sometimes called "Dimwit DeWitt."

Vern is from the South, is quiet, and loves to play the guitar. He works at Dobson's Market. Howie, who attends Cordella High School, has a paper route for the Cordella *Gazette* and works part time at Stott's Service Station.

Irene Hoff (Jan Norris) is Wes's girlfriend and is also a student at Cordella College. Nora Fitzgerald (Ann Schuyler) is Tom's friend, a kindred free spirit and aspiring artist. She attends Cordella College, rarely wears shoes or socks (even in the winter), dresses in jeans and sweatshirts and, as Tom says, "Can't even tell you're a girl." She was born in Westchester County and does her studying in the cemetery near the headstone of Priscilla Butler, who died in 1802.

Wes has an account at the Cordella Trust Company; he, Tom and Vern are members of the Delphi fraternity. They each take turns shopping, cleaning and cooking; rule two of the *Elephant*'s house rules states, "No girls below decks without an acceptable chaperone." The college library has 120,000 volumes.

Theme: "It's a Man's World," by Jack Marshall.

342. *It's About Time*

CBS, 9/11/66 to 9/3/67

Cast: Frank Aletter (*Mac MacKenzie*), Jack Mullaney (*Hector Canfield*), Joe E. Ross (*Gronk*), Imogene Coca (*Shad*), Mary Grace (*Mlor*), Pat Cardi (*Breer*), Cliff Norton (*Cave Boss*), Mike Mazurki (*Clon*).

Facts: As the series begins, the U.S. spaceship *Scorpio* is completing a NASA mission and about to land. The capsule sets down in a remote jungle area that its astronauts, Captain Mac MacKenzie and Lieutenant Hector ("Hec") Canfield find has the same gravity as Earth, but no electron field or radiation. Believing they are on another planet, they begin to explore their surroundings. When they spot a cave family and then a dinosaur (a Tyrannosaurus rex), Mac theorizes that when they blacked out at 60,000 miles a second, they broke the time barrier and are now in the year 1 million B.C.

Just then, Mac and Hec hear a cry for help. They rush to a cliff and see a young caveboy (Breer) clinging to a branch. Breer, who grabbed the branch to escape from the rex, is rescued by Mac and Hec. Breer, beginning his test of manhood (to survive one day in the jungle) runs away. As Mac and Hec head back to their capsule, they are surrounded by a group of cavemen. Because of their dress, the Cave Boss believes they are evil spirits and orders Clon, his dim-witted aide, to kill them. Just then, Breer appears and saves the astronauts by telling the Cave Boss that they saved his life. Later, Mac and Hec befriend Breer's family—his father, Gronk; mother, Shad; and teenage sister Mlor.

Later, after a thorough examination of the *Scorpio*, the astronauts discover that the condenser points have been damaged, and without crystal and carbon it is impossible to fix and they cannot return to their time (in another episode, Mac mentions that they need copper to replace the filament of the solenoid transistor block, which controls liftoff). Stories relate Mac and Hec's efforts to survive and find the minerals they need to repair their craft and return home.

The *Scorpio*, identification number E-X-1, took 184 men (50 of whom were scientists) 39 months to build. Mac, who was born in Los Angeles, and Hec, born in 1938 and raised in Columbus, Ohio (he later mentions Riverview, Ohio), earn $12.50 an hour. The astronauts are believed to be evil spirits by the other cavepeople and to have come from a forbidden area called "The Other Side of the Hill." Shad calls Gronk "Gronkie." Mlor, a teenage beauty, is a fabulous cook and famous for her mastodon stew. The Cave Boss wears a necklace of cooper to signify that he is the chief. The size of one's cave determines importance in the tribe.

Several months later, Gronk realizes what minerals Mac and Hec are seeking and takes a diamond from the eye of his tribal idol. Hec is able to repair the condenser points; Mac reverses the flight information from their last trip and programs it into the computer. Just as they are about to blast off, Gronk, Shad, Mlor and Breer run to Mac and Hec for help (the Cave Boss now considers Gronk and his family traitors for helping evil spirits). Mac and Hec take the cave family aboard the capsule and blast off. Soon it is traveling faster than the speed of light—"Past the Roman senator, past an armored knight, past the fighting Minute Man to this modern site." The *Scorpio* touches down on the front lawn of a home about 50 miles outside Los Angeles.

Realizing that the cave family would become like animals in a zoo if the government knew about them, Mac and Hec decide to conceal their presence; they hide them in the three room apartment they share. Stories relate Mac and Hec's efforts to educate the cave family and keep not only the government but also their apartment house manager, Howard Tyler (Alan DeWitt), from finding out who the cave family really are.

The first "monster" the cave family sees in Los Angeles is a Volkswagen driven by an elderly lady (Gronk "kills the car animal" when he hits it with his club). The cave family believes that Los Angeles is "The Other Side of the Hill." Hec's favorite singers are Morris the Missionary and Dick the Dentist and His Four Cavities. In the episode "Cave Family Swingers," Rick Stewart (Jack Albertson) of the Stewart Travel Agency heard the cave family singing the song "Dinosaur Stew," signed them up with Big Beat Records and got them an appearance on "The Fred Gulliver Show" on television.

Relatives: Imogene Coca (Shad's mother, *Krek*), Kathleen Freeman (Cave Boss's wife, *Mrs. Boss*), Edson Stroll (Cave Boss's son, *Brak*).

Relatives Not Seen: Shad's father ("He was lost in jungle and never came home"), Gronk's mother ("She live on other side of tar pits"). Shad's mother lives on the other side of the volcano.

Theme: "It's About Time," (original and revised versions) by Sherwood Schwartz, Gerald Fried and George Wyle.

343. *It's Always Jan*

CBS, 9/10/55 to 6/30/56

The Harry Cooper Talent Agency represents Janis ("Jan") Stewart (Janis Paige), a talented but relatively unknown singer who is hoping to make the big time. Jan is a widow and the mother of ten-year-old Josie (Jeri Lou James). Jan and Josie share an apartment at 46 East 50th Street in Manhattan with Valerie Marlowe (Merry Anders), a shapely blonde model, and Patricia Murphy (Patricia Bright), a secretary with a heart of gold.

Jan currently works as a nightclub entertainer who performs regularly at Tony's Cellar, a small supper club in New York's Greenwich Village. She dreams of starring on Broadway and singing at the prestigious Sky Room of the Sherry-Waldorf Hotel. Sid Melton plays Jan's agent, Harry Cooper.

Earle Hagen and Herbert Spencer composed the theme, "It's Always Jan."

344. *It's Your Move*

NBC, 9/26/84 to 1/10/85

Eileen Burton (Caren Kaye) is a beautiful legal secretary for a never-seen private practice lawyer named Mr. Clayburn. She is a widow and lives with her two teenage children, Julie (Tricia Cast) and Matt (Jason Bateman), at 46 Wilshire Boulevard (Apartment 407) in Van Nuys, California. Sixteen-year-old Julie, and Matt, who is 14, attend Van Buren High School.

Julie is a cheerleader and captain of the Pom Pom Team. She "practices kissing on her stuffed Snoopy toy" and, according to Matt, "stuffs her bra with Kleenex." "Hell Hound" is but one of the many terms Julie uses to describe Matt, a juvenile wheeler-dealer. Matt enjoys "torturing" Julie at every opportunity (for instance recording her telephone conversations for blackmail purposes), and he has a scam for any occasion to make money (such as holding annual term paper sales). When Matt does use a scam to acquire money, his intentions are good—to supplement Eileen's income (Eileen appears to be a bit confused when it comes to money; Matt sneaks the money into her purse; and Eileen is always amazed to find extra money—but she has no idea where it came from).

Dialing the telephone number "Zoo Life" will get you Mort Stumplerutt, the rich but boring owner of the Stumplerutt Lumber Mills. This is the man Matt believes is right for his mother, the man who can give her the life of luxury she deserves. Matt's efforts to spark a romance between the two is hampered when Norman Lamb (David Garrison), a former insurance salesman from Chicago turned freelance writer, moves into the apartment (406) across the hall. Norman is always in need of money and is not the man Matt wants for Eileen. Fate brings Eileen and Norman together (a chance meeting in the hallway); Mort becomes a

thing of the past. (Matt believes that if his mother went to a millionaires' convention, she'd wind up with the bellboy. He is concerned about her future and feels it is his obligation to find her the right man.) Matt's antics were curtailed halfway through the series when Eileen caught him red-handed in a scam. He was put on probation, and the original series concept was lost. Norman, who became an English teacher at Van Buren, and Eileen were now the focal point (the series declined and soon went off the air).

Eli (Adam Sadowsky) is Matt's "cohort in crime" (English is his worst subject—"I couldn't even spell my first name until I was seven"); Lou Donatelli (Ernie Sabella) is the apartment building super; and Dwight Ellis (Garrett Morris) is the principal of Van Buren (brought on when the format changed).

Rik Howard and Bob Wirth composed the theme.

345. *The Jack Benny Program*

CBS, 10/29/50 to 9/15/64
NBC, 9/25/64 to 9/10/65

In a dungeon beneath the home at 366 North Camden Drive in Beverly Hills, California, is a large, banklike vault. A mine field, poison gas, rickety bridge, alligator pool and flame throwers are the obstacles one must overcome to reach the vault. The one man who is able to accomplish this is Jack Benny, the man who owns the home.

Jack, who stands five feet 11 inches tall and weighs 158 pounds, is 39 years old (he has been 39 for so long that he has forgotten how old he really is). Jack was born in Waukegan and served in the navy during World War I. Jack had show business in his blood, and when he was discharged from the service he broke into vaudeville. He did badly by himself and even worse when he met George Burns in Philadelphia and they formed their own comedy team (with George as the straight man). The act bombed, and when it broke up both men became famous—George when he teamed with a girl named Gracie Allen and Jack when he went into radio.

Jack's television show is a glimpse of his life at the studio and at home, where he lives with his ever faithful valet, Rochester (Eddie Anderson), who calls him "Boss" and "Mr. Benny." Jack claims that his writers are responsible for the image that people have of him as being cheap. Besides the vault in his dungeon, Jack also has an account at the California Bank. He rarely withdraws money (when he does, he causes a run on the bank), and he goes for only two reasons: to deposit money and to visit it. Jack has a laundry business on the side and loves to attend parties (he's listed in the Yellow Pages as "Available for Parties"). He once wrote a song called "When You Say I Beg Your Pardon, Then I'll Come Back to You"; if a crook were to come up to Jack and say, "Your money or your life," he would pause long enough for the thief to repeat what he said; Jack would then respond, "I'm thinking, I'm thinking."

Jack is most proud of his "ability" to play the violin

It's Always Jan. Left to right: Merry Anders, Janis Paige and Patricia Bright.

(which everyone hears off-key except him). Professor Pierre LeBlanc (Mel Blanc) is Jack's long-suffering violin teacher. Don Wilson (himself) is Jack's longtime overweight announcer; and Mary Livingston (herself) is Jack's girlfriend, who works as a salesgirl for the May Company. Jack's idea of taking Mary to the movies is going over to her house "because the TV screen is bigger than mine." Jack buys his suits at Fenchel and Gordon; he also mentioned living at 904 Santa Monica and that he was in vaudeville in an act with Bing Crosby and George Burns.

Jack's singer is Dennis Day (himself), whom Jack found during his years on radio. Jack wanted "a nice, cheap Morton Downey–like singer for $35 a week who also had comedy potential." Jack's agent, Steve Burke (Jesse White) recommended an unknown singer named Dennis Day who was working at the Lotus Blossom Inn slinging hash. When Jack heard him sing—and agree to the $35 a week—he hired him. Dennis is later a member of the Elks Club. Lois Corbett played Don's wife, Lois Wilson; and Dale White was Don's overweight son, Harlow (whom Don was grooming to become a television announcer). Mel Blanc also played Si, the Mexican who confuses Jack.

Mahlon Merrick performed the theme.

346. *The Jackie Thomas Show*

ABC, 12/1/92 to 3/30/93

Cast: Tom Arnold *(Jackie Thomas)*, Alison LaPlaca *(Laura Miller)*, Dennis Boutsikaris *(Jerry Harper)*, Maryedith Burrell *(Nancy Mincher)*.

Facts: The mythical "Jackie Thomas Show" is America's top-rated comedy series. It is about a wacky father (Jackie), his wife, Helen, and their teenage son, Timmy. Its star, Jackie Thomas, is conceited, demanding, obnoxious and overbearing; his mere presence strikes fear in the hearts of his writing staff, co-stars and network executives. The series presents a behind-the-scenes look at the making of a weekly television show as Jackie attempts the impossible—to deliver a funny show without bloodshed.

Jackie is from Iowa and previously worked in a slaughterhouse. He wants the show to himself and gets very upset when a co-star gets too popular, too much fan mail or too much airtime. Jackie can't act and think at the same time, and he is quite naive when it comes to world affairs. Jackie's favorite song is the theme from "Green Acres" (also his favorite television show), and he enjoys owl hunting ("in Iowa, where it's legal"). Jackie also likes to get even with people (for example, when Oprah Winfrey didn't invite him to a party, Jackie threw a bigger bash and didn't invite her). Jackie has his own zoo (he hates llamas) and started his own charity—Jackie Thomas Save Our Universe. Jackie knows a lot of celebrities and lives in a house on the beach—but nobody knows where ("And I'd like to keep it that way," he says). Franks and beans in a casserole is his favorite meal. Tom's real-life wife, Roseanne Arnold, appeared in one episode as Regina, a crazed fan Laura called "The Psycho Lady."

Jerry Harper is the new head writer (he has office number 26). When Jerry arrived for work, he was greeted by a bonfire—made from the scripts of the previous head writer (staff members have a policy of not making friends with each other because "it's really sad when they get fired"). Jerry previously wrote for "Barney Miller," "Cheers" and "Taxi"; he has a picture of his idol, Dick Van Dyke, on his desk.

Laura Miller is Jerry's assistant; she says simply, "Jackie is insane. I'm not talking wacky, funny insane; I'm talking clinical, dangerously insane." Laura longs to be a writer, and though she works for an egomaniac, Dustin Hoffman is her favorite performer. Laura is the only one "who can unjam the copy machine," and she received a temporary promotion to Senior Vice President of Charities and Stuff when Jackie went on a charity kick; she also worked for UNICEF for a year.

Nancy Mincher is a staff writer and previously wrote for "The Brady Bunch" and "Who's the Boss?" She was fired from "The Brady Bunch" for trying to seduce Greg and claims, "I'm the one responsible for giving Marcia her depth."

Grant Watson (Michael Boatman) and Bobby Wynn (Paul Feig) are the remaining members of Jerry's writing team. Bobby is Jackie's drinking buddy from Iowa. He performs standup comedy at various clubs, and Jackie keeps him around as the writers' joke man.

Doug Talbot (Martin Mull) is the network's flunkie. He was a vice president at NBC and worked there at the same time as Jerry (when he wrote for "Cheers"). Doug was fired for trying to cancel "Cheers."

The co-stars of "The Jackie Thomas Show" are Sophia Ford (Jeannetta Arnette), who plays Jackie's television wife, Helen, and Chas Walker (Breckin Meyer), who plays their son, Timmy. Jackie plays a butcher; Sophia dreads the thought of having to kiss Jackie on the show and does so only to keep her job.

Chris Farley appeared as Jackie's brother, Chris Thomas.

Theme: "The Jackie Thomas Show Theme," by W.G. Snuffy Walden.

347. *Jack's Place*

ABC, 5/26/92 to 7/7/92

Jack's Place is actually Jack's Bar and Restaurant. It is world famous for its chocolate fudge cake, and customers are not obligated to pay for a meal if they do not like it. Jack Evans (Hal Linden) is the charming proprietor, a former jazz musician during the 1960s. The only information revealed about Jack is that he was on the road a lot as a musician and felt it would be best for his wife and daughter if he left them to lead his own life. Chelsea Duffy (Finola Hughes) is the waitress and Greg Toback (John Dye) is the bartender. Michele Greene appeared as Jack's estranged daughter, Susan Sullivan.

David Schwartz and Bill Elliott composed the theme, "Jack's Place."

348. *Jackson and Jill*

Syndicated, 1949

"Jackson and Jill," one of television's earliest domestic comedies, relates the misadventures of Jackson Jones (Todd Karns) and his beautiful wife, Jill Jones (Helen Chapman), newlyweds struggling to survive the difficult first years of marriage.

Jackson and Jill live in Apartment 1A at 167 Oak Street in Manhattan. Their phone number is Main 6421, and Jackson has a shortwave radio set with the call letters W10GEC (his shortwave "radio buddy" is Gladys Harvey [Jan Kayne], whom Jill calls "the glamour gal of the airwaves"; her call letters are W10GAL).

Jackson works as an accountant for the Gimmling Company, and his office phone number is Main 6244. Jill has a jealous streak, and much of the comedy stems from Jill's assumption that Jackson is having affairs with other women.

William Vedder plays Mr. Winks, the building's snoopy, hard of hearing janitor; Russell Hicks is Jackson's boss, Mr. Gimmling; Norma Varden is Gimmling's secretary, Miss Debney; and Almira Sessions is Jill's neighbor, Mrs. McBeedle.

Each episode opens with Jill jotting an entry in her diary. The audience hears her via voiceover narration, and the episode itself explains the entry. The show closes with Jill completing her diary entry. The arranger of the show's theme, a parody of the song "Home, Sweet, Home," is not credited.

349. *Jake and the Fatman*

CBS, 9/26/87 to 8/22/92

J.L. McCabe (William Conrad) is the district attorney of an unnamed southern California city (1987-88), then prosecuting attorney for the Honolulu Police Department (1988–90) and finally the D.A. of Costa Del Mar, a small city in California. He is assisted in all cases by Jake Styles (Joe Penny), a stylish investigator; and in 1991 by Neely Capshaw (Melody Anderson), "the new kid on the block" (an investigator for the Costa Del Mar D.A.'s office).

Besides the nickname "Fatman," J.L. (Jason Lochinvar) is also called "Buster." McCabe has a dog named Max and works out of building 310 of the Costa Del Mar Municipal Court House. His favorite watering hole (first season) is Dixie's Bar (owned by Dixie, played by Anne Francis).

As a kid, Jake had the nickname "Butchie," and his childhood hero was Tom Cody (star of the mythical series "Sky Hawk"; Ernest Borgnine played Cody in one episode). 2VAK087 is Jake's license plate number, and 555-4796 is his phone number. Neely lives at 5440 Canyon Drive with her daughter, Sarah (Taylor Fry). Sarah has a teddy bear named Georgie Bear and attends the Folger Park Grammar School. Neely's station wagon license plate reads 2VT MOV3.

Each episode is titled after a song (for example, "The Tender Trap," "It Had to Be You"), and this song is played over that episode's particular after-theme credits.

Relatives: Tom Isbell (J.L.'s son, *Danny McCabe*), Cassandra Byram (Jake's sister, *Angela Styles*), Rhoda Gemignani (Jake's mother, *Carla Styles*).

Theme: "Jake and the Fatman," by Dick DeBenedictis.

350. *Jane*

Syndicated, 7/89

The series is set during World War II. A gorgeous young woman, known only as Jane (Glynis Barber) works as an undercover agent for the British government. She has a dog named Fritz and an assignment: perform hazardous missions behind enemy lines. Jane also has one major problem: keeping her clothes on. Jane wears only dresses. If she attempts to climb over a wall, the dress manages to catch on something and get ripped off; if Jane finds it is too hot to sleep (for instance, when she checked in to the Inn of the Seven Veils in Egypt), off comes the dress; if she is stranded at sea and needs a sail for her raft, her dress becomes the sail. Jane is seen most often in her sexy lingerie; finding outerwear is her number one priority. To add further spice, Jane often manages to lose her bra (she is seen from the side or back or in silhouette) and, once per story, everything (seen only from the back and in dim light). When she does manage to stay fully clothed, it is typical to hear "By golly, Jane, I didn't recognize you with your frock on."

In addition to Jane's lack of wardrobe, the program is unique in its presentation. The series is based on the World War II *Daily Mirror* British comic strip, *Jane*. To capture that feeling, stories are presented like a comic strip come to life. Each scene is in a panel; all props (such as cars, trucks, boats) are drawings. Through special effects the live actors are placed in comic book situations. The series was produced by the BBC in 1984.

Georgie (John Bird) is Jane's boyfriend, a British army agent; the Colonel (Robin Bailey) is Jane's superior; Tombs (Max Wall) is the Colonel's butler (he longs for "the rationing, blitzes and blackouts of England"). Lola and Pola Pagola (Suzanne Danielle in a dual role) are the evil sisters who seek to kill Jane.

Neil Innes performs the title song, "Jane."

351. *The Jean Arthur Show*

CBS, 9/12/66 to 12/12/66

Marshall and Marshall, Attorneys at Law, is a prestigious law firm located at 100 West Beverly Boulevard in Beverly Hills, California. Patricia Marshall (Jean Arthur) is an attractive widow (in her fifties) who founded the firm with her late husband. She is now partners with her 30-year-old son, Paul Marshall (Ron Harper).

Patricia, who attended Harvard Law School, lives at 367 South Oak Street. She has a brilliant record of corporate litigation wins, but is known for helping the underdog and taking cases that no other high-class firm would handle (for example, defending a boy's pet rooster, who is accused of crowing and disturbing a neighborhood; or defending a two-bit hood). Her favorite pastime is going to the beach and hunting for sea shells.

Paul, who also attended Harvard, lives in an apartment at 360 Etchfield Road. Unlike his mother (who will go to extremes), Paul is a by-the-books, laid-back attorney who will never tackle the cases she does (he seems to represent only corporate clients). Paul is a young man with spunk, Patricia makes things happen, and together they form a team that clients seem to want.

Leonard J. Stone plays Patricia's chauffeur, Morton, and Sue Taylor is the Marshalls' receptionist, Sally.

Johnny Keating, Richard Quine and Richard Kennedy composed the theme, "Merry-Go-Round."

352. *The Jeffersons*

CBS, 1/17/75 to 7/23/85

Cast: Sherman Hemsley *(George Jefferson)*, Isabel Sanford *(Louise Jefferson)*, Mike Evans and Damon Evans *(Lionel Jefferson)*, Franklin Cover *(Tom Willis)*, Roxie Roker *(Helen Willis)*, Berlinda Tolbert *(Jenny Willis)*.

Facts: A spinoff from "All in the Family" in which Archie Bunker's neighbors George, Louise and Lionel Jefferson have moved to Manhattan to begin new lives. George is wealthy and snobbish and owns the successful Jefferson Cleaners (with stores in Manhattan, the Bronx, Brooklyn, Harlem and Queens). He and Louise, his long-suffering wife, have been married 25 years—and the reason the marriage lasts—according to George, is that "I put up with all her faults."

Prior to moving to their luxurious New York apartment (12D), George and Louise lived in Harlem, then on Houser Street in Queens (where George opened his first dry cleaning shop). Before marrying George, Louise lived on 13th Street and Amsterdam Avenue. Louise, whom George calls "Weezie" and "Weez," has type O blood; her maiden name is Mills and she is den mother to the Red Robins, a Girl Scout troop. George, who was born in Georgia, served on a navy aircraft carrier (in the galley). While George is always thought of as cheap, he does do something very special. There were always bad Christmases when George was growing up in poverty (in apartment 5C at 984 West 125th Street). He made a promise that if he ever made it big, he would do something for the people who moved into that same apartment, and so each month he anonymously sends them $100. George's competition is Feldway Cleaners.

Tom and Helen Willis, their upstairs neighbors (on the fourteenth floor), are television's first interracial couple. Tom (who is white) is an editor for the Pelham Publishing Company. He has been married to Helen (who is black) for

23 years. They have a beautiful daughter, Jenny, who is engaged to George and Louise's son, Lionel. Lionel, who had the street name "Diver" when they lived in Harlem, calls Jenny "Honey Babes." Helen's maiden name is Douglas. Lionel and Jenny marry and become the parents of a girl they name Jessica (Ebonie Smith).

Harry Bentley (Paul Benedict) is George's across-the-hall neighbor (Apartment 12E). He was born in England, attended Oxford University and now works as an interpreter at the UN. Florence Johnston (Marla Gibbs) is George's sassy maid. The character was spun off into a series called "Checking In" (4/9/81 to 4/30/81), in which Florence took a leave of absence to work as the executive housekeeper for Lyle Block (Larry Linville), the manager of the St. Frederick Hotel in Manhattan.

Relatives: Zara Cully (George's mother, *Olivia Jefferson*), Leonard Jackson (Louise's father, *Howard Mills*), Josephine Premice (Louise's sister, *Maxine Mills*), Lillian Randolph (Olivia's sister, *Emma*), Leon Ames (Tom's father, *Henry Willis*), Victor Kilian (Tom's uncle, *Bertram*), Fred Pinkard (Helen's father, *"Grandpa" Douglas*).

Theme: "Movin' on Up," by Jeff Barry and Ja'net DuBois.

353. *Jeff's Collie*

CBS, 9/12/54 to 12/1/57

"To Jeff Miller I leave the best thing I've got, my dog, Lassie." With these words, read at the will of his neighbor, Homer Carey, ten-year-old Jeffrey ("Jeff") Miller (Tommy Rettig) inherits a beautiful and intelligent collie named Lassie. Jeff lives with his widowed mother, Ellen Miller (Jan Clayton), and his grandfather, George Miller (George Cleveland), on a farm on Route 4 in Calverton, a small town about 30 miles from Capital City.

George, affectionately called "Gramps," owns the farm—"I was born on the land, married on the land and raised a family on the land." Ellen was married to George's son, Johnny. (In episode nine, Gramps tells Jeff that he got Johnny a rifle when he was 12 years old and put that "gun away ten years ago when we heard about your father." In episode 81, it is mentioned that Johnny lost his life attempting to save 20 men in his squadron, in 1944, during World War II.)

Ellen took French in college. She refers to herself as "George Miller's daughter" (although she is actually his daughter-in-law). She makes ice cream every Saturday, and the family has it with pie on Sunday. Ellen's sedan license plate number is 98916 (later 5J9773).

Gramps, who was born on the 22nd (month not given) is a volunteer fireman and head of the school board. His pickup truck license plate is 9881304, and he likes to call anyone who irritates him a "pusillanimous polecat." Gramps had a cousin named Alf (unseen) who ran away from the farm and went to Paris (where he married a French girl and became an artist).

Jeff attends Calverton Elementary School and is planning to become a veterinarian. He was valedictorian at graduation (episode 113) and gave a speech on responsibility. Jeff's best friend is Sylvester ("Porky") Brockway (Donald Keeler), who has a dog named Pokey (the dog is a basset hound and has the official name of Pokerman III). They are blood brothers, and their signal to each other is "Eee-ock-eee." Jeff also had a horse (a yearling) named Domino, a cow (Daisy; later Bessie) and a burro (Lucky).

Florence Lake plays the rarely seen but often needed telephone operator, Jenny. Paul Maxey is Porky's father, Matt Brockway, and Marjorie Bennett is Porky's mother, Berdie Brockway.

Dr. Peter Wilson (Frank Ferguson) was the original vet; he was replaced by Dr. Frank Weaver (Arthur Space), who is also the game warden. Clay Horton (Richard Garland) was the original sheriff; he was replaced by Sheriff Jim Billings (House Peters, Jr.); Clay now runs a garage. Raoul Kraushaar composed the theme.

The spinoff series, "Timmy and Lassie" (CBS, 9/8/57 to 8/30/64) begins with episode 103. Lassie finds a seven-year-old orphan named Timmy Martin (Jon Provost) hiding in the barn. When Timmy's parents were killed in "the accident," he was sent to live with his elderly Uncle Jed (George Selk) and Aunt Abby Clawson (Hallene Hall) in Olive Ridge. Timmy ran away when he felt he wasn't wanted. (Jed and Abby feel they are too old to care for Timmy, and they allow him to stay with the Millers.) Timmy calls Ellen "Aunt Ellen."

Shortly after, Gramps dies (episode 114). When Ellen learns that a young couple named Paul and Ruth Martin are seeking to adopt Timmy and are looking for a place in which to settle down, she sells them the farm. Ellen and Jeff move to 311 Cedar Street in Capital City (where Ellen will give music lessons and Jeff will attend the science high school). Before Ellen and Jeff depart, Jeff gives Lassie to Timmy (feeling she would be better off on the farm). "Eee-ock-eee" are Jeff and Porky's parting words.

Cloris Leachman and Jon Shepodd first played Ruth and Paul Martin (to episode 141; they were replaced by June Lockhart and Hugh Reilly). George Chandler plays Paul's brother, Petrie J. Martin; Todd Ferrell is Timmy's friend, Boomer Bates; and Andy Clyde is Timmy's elderly friend, Cully Wilson. Paul's truck license plate is 3B 2675; Boomer's dog is named Mike; and Silky (a.k.a. Sam) is Cully's dog. "Uncle Petrie," as Timmy calls him, lived previously in Millvale, Pennsylvania. Paul went on 22 missions during World War II. See also "The New Lassie."

354. *Jennifer Slept Here*

NBC, 10/21/83 to 12/16/83

Cast: Ann Jillian (*Jennifer Farrell*), Georgia Engel (*Susan Elliot*), Brandon Maggart (*George Elliot*), John P. Navin, Jr. (*Joey Elliot*), Mya Akerling (*Marilyn Elliot*).

Facts: Jennifer Farrell is a young girl with a dream of becoming a movie star. At age 17 she defies her mother (who wants her to become a beautician) and leaves her home in Illinois to pursue her dream in Hollywood. She made her television debut as a banana in the audience of "Let's Make a Deal," and several months later, in 1966, when Jennifer was 18 years old, hungry and flat broke, she posed nude for a calendar (the calendar was never actually released; Jennifer acquired a job shortly after and bought up all the copies). Jennifer landed a small role in the movie *Desire,* but it was her outstanding singing and dancing performance in her next film, *Stairway to Paradise,* that brought her overnight stardom. Jennifer soon became one of America's most glamorous and beloved stars.

Jennifer's untimely death in 1978 saddened the world. Five years later, New York lawyer George Elliot, his wife, Susan, and their children, Joey and Marilyn, move into Jennifer's fabulous mansion at 32 Rexford Drive in Beverly Hills. (While it is not made clear, the mansion was apparently seized by the state for nonpayment of taxes. It is also apparent that the Elliots are not wealthy, and it is assumed they bought the mansion on the condition that they pay off Jennifer's debts; George complains about these debts in several episodes.)

Shortly after, while settling into his room, Joey is startled to see the ghost of Jennifer Farrell—who appears and speaks only to him (she feels he needs help and has decided to guide his life). Joey attends Beverly Hills High School. A school for Marilyn is not given, nor is a company name for George.

When she was six years old, Jennifer was a tomboy and made a neighborhood kid eat dirt—literally. Jennifer attended the Pinehurst Elementary School and three years of Lanford High School in Illinois (she dropped out in her senior year to pursue her dream). Her first paying job in Hollywood was as a waitress in a grease pit called Danny's Diner.

Relatives: Debbie Reynolds (Jennifer's mother, *Alice Farrell,* also a ghost).

Theme: "Jennifer Slept Here," vocal by Joey Scarbury.

Jesse Hawkes see *High Mountain Rangers*

355. *Jessica Novak*

CBS, 11/5/81 to 12/3/81

Jessica Novak (Helen Shaver) is the on-the-air reporter for "Closeup News" on KLA-TV, Channel 6, in Los Angeles. She lives at 318 Briarwood Avenue; 555-6676 is her phone number, and her license plate reads 327 WED. Phil Bonelli (Andrew Rubin) is her field cameraman, and Ricky Duran (Eric Kilpatrick) is her field soundman.

Fred Karlin composed "The Theme from Jessica Novak."

356. *Jessie*

ABC, 9/18/84 to 11/13/84

Dr. Jessica ("Jessie") Hayden (Lindsay Wagner) is a beautiful police psychiatrist with the Behavioral Science Department of the Metro Division of the San Francisco Police Department. She rejected a job with "big bucks" at a hospital and even nixed the idea of her own private practice to do what she wants to do: be a part of the action and help the police solve crimes through her psychological profiles and work with suspects. Jessie refuses to carry a gun ("I wouldn't know what to do with it. A doctor's duty is to preserve human life, not destroy it").

Jessie doesn't drink coffee, likes Mexican food and "lives in a little shack in the hills." When she sets her mind on something, "trying to talk her out of it is a waste of time." Jessie rarely complains, except when she is in her office: "People are always walking off with my pens." Jessie grew up on Winterhaven Street, where her widowed mother, Molly Hayden (Celeste Holm), still lives.

Alexander ("Alex") Ascoli (Tony Lo Bianco) is a lieutenant with the Metro Division who has been taken off street duty and assigned as Jessie's liaison—"to interface her with the department." Alex's car code is 17-Abel-33, and his license plate reads IDH Z834. The pilot episode had Alex constantly complaining about the change (he is and wants to be a street cop). In the series, Alex was both Jessie's liaison and a street cop; unfortunately, storylines were slow-moving psychological profiles and not action-oriented; not even the talents and beauty of Lindsay Wagner (looking much as she did as Jaime Sommers on "The Bionic Woman") could save the series, and it was canceled after seven episodes.

William Lucking played the captain, "Mac" McClellan; Tom Nolan was Officer "Hub" Hubbell; and Renee Jones was Mac's secretary, Ellie.

John Cacavas composed "Jessie's Theme."

357. *The Jetsons*

ABC, 9/23/62 to 9/8/63

Voice Cast: George O'Hanlon (*George Jetson*), Penny Singleton (*Jane Jetson*), Janet Waldo (*Judy Jetson*), Daws Butler (*Elroy Jetson*).

Facts: A futuristic view of life in the twenty-first century as seen through the experiences of the animated Jetson family: George and Jane and their children, Judy and Elroy.

George is employed by Cosmo G. Spacely (voice of Mel Blanc), the owner of Spacely Space Sprockets. George is also in the Army Reserve (U.S. Space Guards Division at Camp Nebula). Gina Lolajupiter is his favorite movie star, and "Dr. Ken Stacey" (a takeoff on "Ben Casey") and "The Stuntley-Hinkley Report" (a parody of "The Huntley-Brinkley Report") are his favorite television shows.

Jane is 33 years old, wears a size eight dress and measures 36-26-36. She buys her dresses at Satellite City and has her hair done at the Constellation Beauty Salon. Jane entered the "Miss Solar System Beauty Pageant" and was crowned "Miss Western Hemisphere." She and George live at the Sky Pad Apartments, and their favorite song is "Saturn Doll," by Count Spacey and His Orchestra (which they danced to while dating).

Fifteen-year-old Judy attends Orbit High School. She measures 32-22-32, has a jalopy with the license plate 738, and a talking diary she calls Di Di (voice of Selma Diamond). Elroy is their eight-year-old son, and he attends the Little Dipper School. He has a pet dog named Astro (voice of Don Messick) and is a member of the Little Dipper League baseball team. His favorite television show is "Spies in Space."

Rosie (voice of Jean VanderPyl), the Jetsons' robot maid, is a model XB-500 service robot they acquired from "U-Rent-a-Maid." Henry Orbit (voice of Howard Morris) is the apartment house janitor. Mr. Spacely and his wife, Stella, reside at 175 Snerdville Drive. Spacely's competition is Cogswell Cogs, a company owned by Mr. Cogswell (voice of Daws Butler). Spacely Space Sprockets produces three million sprockets a day.

Theme: "The Jetsons," by William Hanna and Joseph Barbera.

358. *Jigsaw John*

NBC, 2/2/76 to 9/13/76

John St. John (Jack Warden) is a detective with the Robbery-Homicide Division of the L.A.P.D. His talent for figuring out people and solving complex crimes has earned him the nickname "Jigsaw John." He has a record of crime solution and criminal conviction that is the highest in the nation. John likes Chinese food for breakfast but has to take pills for his stomach—"worries related to the job." His license plate reads 182 FYN, and his mobile car code is 4-King-90.

Maggie Hearn (Pippa Scott) is his girlfriend, and Detective Sam Donner (Alan Feinstein) is his partner. In the television movie pilot, *They Only Come Out at Night* (NBC, 4/29/75), John was married to a woman named Helen (Madeleine Sherwood) and was said to "take bits and scraps, find patterns and solve cases"—hence the name "Jigsaw John."

Pete Rugolo composed the "Jigsaw John" theme.

359. *The Jim Backus Show— Hot Off the Wire*

Syndicated, 1960 to 1961

The Headline Press Service is a New York City–based news gathering organization that is run by John Michael

("Mike") O'Toole (Jim Backus), a publisher who was banned in his hometown of Boston and now seeks to turn a faltering service into a profitable one. While O'Toole fancies himself an editor, he finds that he must resort to his former skills as a reporter to get the stories he wants ("If you want a story done right, you have to do it yourself. I can't trust my reporters to do anything right").

Dora Miles (Nita Talbot), Mike's glamorous secretary, is also his reporting assistant. She constantly complains about the money Mike owes her, claims she has only two outfits for work (one dress and one tight skirt) and will not date loafers—burglars are okay, "as long as they are working."

Sidney (Bobs Watson) is Mike's combination office boy, photographer and reporter. He believes he has a nose for news—but rarely has a chance to put it to the test.

Fingers Larkin (Lewis Charles), Mike's information man, has a business card that reads FINGERS LARKIN, THIEF EXTRAORDINAIRE. HOLDUPS, SECOND STORY JOBS, MUGGINGS AND SAFES CRACKED WHILE YOU WAIT. 24 HOUR SERVICE; DAY WORK DOUBLE TIME. He lives at 123⅔ Hope Street and is a member of Ex-Cons Anonymous (when an ex-con gets the urge to go straight, another ex-con comes over to talk him out of it).

Bob's Alterations and Tailoring is the office across the hall from the paper (no numbers are on the doors); Mike uses the services of the New York *Globe* for research material and publication of stories; his car license plate reads RXV 451. Dora, who concludes episodes by saying, "My boss, he's so clever" (when Mike solves a case), lives at 146 West 57th Street.

David Rose composed the theme, "Hot Off the Wire."

360. *J.J. Starbuck*

NBC, 9/26/87 to 2/27/88
NBC, 4/19/88 (1 episode), 6/28/88 (1 episode)

J.J. Starbuck (Dale Robertson) is an eccentric Texas billionaire who meddles in other people's business in the name of justice.

J.J. (Jerome Jeremiah) lives on the Starbuck Ranch in San Antonio. He owns a Beverly Hills company called Marklee Industries and drives a 1964 Lincoln Continental with the license plate TX BRONCO. Shawn Weatherly plays his niece, Jill Starbuck.

Ronnie Milsap performs the theme.

Joanie Loves Chachi see *Happy Days*

361. *Joe and Mabel*

CBS, 9/10/55 to 9/17/55
CBS, 6/26/56 to 9/25/56

A blind date brought Mabel Spooner (Nita Talbot) and Joe Sparton (Larry Blyden) together. Mabel is beautiful, stubborn, a bit wacky and ready for marriage. Joe is hard working, level headed and "chicken" (not ready to tie the knot); he is a long range planner and looks ahead. Joe feels Mabel is the prettiest girl in his crowd—"She loves me no matter how stupid I am; she laughs at all my old jokes and knows how to fix my eggs. I say every guy ought to have a girl like Mabel, even if she sometimes inspires you to do crazy things." Mabel is dead set on convincing Joe that she is the perfect wife for him. She does her best to impress him (although her plans most often backfire) and has already planned on a house and three kids (Joe Jr., Adele and Stanley).

Mabel lives with her mother, Adele Spooner (Luella Gear), and her brother, Sherman Spooner (Michael Mann), at 2314 Bushwick Avenue (Apartment 3H) in Brooklyn, New York. Mabel works as a manicurist at the Westside Beauty Shop (telephone number 934-3114) in Manhattan. Mabel mentioned that five years ago (1950) she worked at the Beverly Hills Hotel, and in high school, as a member of the glee club, she performed solo in a production of *The Bells of St. Mary's*. Sherman is 14 years old and attends an unnamed public school; when he was five years old, he thought girls were boys with long hair. Fourteen years ago (1941) Adele invested $50 in a company called Miracle Mines and Metals for Mabel's future; the stock is now worth $250.

Joe, who lives at 764 Chauncey Street in Brooklyn (no apartment number on his door), is an independent cab driver (license plate T124T; rates are 25 cents for the first fifth of a mile; five cents for each additional fifth of a mile). Joe has a picture of Mabel above his rearview mirror. (Each episode begins with Joe driving his cab and relating an incident about himself and Mabel. A flashback is used to relate the tale. Joe returns right before the closing theme to give a final remark and tell the audience about next week's episode.)

Joe's hangout is Mac's Coffee Shop ("the Waldorf Astoria of the coffee shops"). While MAC'S COFFEE SHOP is seen on the front door, it is called Harry's Coffee Shop in dialogue.

Norman Fell played Mike, Joe's friend, a cabbie also. Mabel mentioned that she had an uncle named George; Joe said he had an uncle named Harry.

Wilbur Hatch composed the theme.

362. *The Joey Bishop Show*

NBC, 9/20/61 to 6/20/62

Joey Barnes (Joey Bishop) is a public relations man for the Los Angeles firm of Wellington, Willoughby and Jones (originally called the J.P. Willoughby Company). The sign on his desk reads KEEP SMILING; 257-7734 is his home phone number, and he owns a house on Wilshire Boulevard. Joey is also a bachelor and the sole support of his family: his widowed mother, Mrs. Barnes (Madge Blake), his sister, Stella Barnes (Marlo Thomas) and his young brother, Larry Barnes (Warren Berlinger). He also finds himself supporting his married sister, Betty Grafton (Virginia Vincent), and her adverse-to-work husband, Frank Grafton (Joe Flynn).

Joey, whose catchphrase is "son of a gun," was a Boy Scout (with a merit badge) and a sergeant in the army (82nd Airborne Division, Abel Company), and he gives his mother $300 a month to run the house.

Stella is studying to become an actress (Joey pays for her acting lessons), and Larry is attending medical school (he has a "used skeleton" called "Mr. Bones" that he paid $60 for—it's their "skeleton in the closet"). Mrs. Barnes looks as if she is in her sixties, claims she is 55, but is actually 57.

Frank impresses people by telling them he doesn't need a job (Joey says he should impress people by telling people he needs a job). He looks for work every day and is willing to take anything (he worked, for example, as a potato-peeler salesman, process server and used car salesman). Betty says, "Frank is just waiting for his ship to come in." "Yeah," Joey remarks. "It'll be secondhand and cost me $620." But "it's not that Frank doesn't want to work. If there were a job for him, he'd take it," says Betty.

Frank and Betty have been married for ten years in 1961 (they live in Apartment 236; no address given). Frank borrowed five dollars from Joey for the marriage license and still hasn't paid him back. Frank's favorite pastime is entering contests. In 1956 he won the Aunt Martha Bird Seed Contest. He was awarded a year's supply of bird seed; he had to borrow money from Joey to buy the birds. In 1961 he entered the Sweetheart Biscuit Company Contest with this rhyme: "When it comes to biscuits, let's not be wishy-washy; be sure they're Sweetheart Biscuits because they're never squishy-squashy." He won $10,000 for it.

Nancy Hadley played Joey's girlfriend (and secretary), Barbara Simpson, and John Griggs was Joey's employer, J.P. Willoughby.

The original pilot version of the series aired on "The Danny Thomas Show" (CBS, 3/27/61) as "Everything Happens to Me." In it, Joey Bishop played Joey Mason, a Hollywood press agent. Billy Gilbert and Madge Blake played his parents, "Pop" and "Mom" Mason. See also the following title.

Herbert W. Spencer composed "Joey's Theme."

363. *The Joey Bishop Show*

NBC, 9/15/62 to 9/20/64
CBS, 9/27/64 to 9/7/65

A revised version of the preceding title. "You couldn't call him pretty, but you'd have to say he's kind of witty.

Joey, Joey, Joey"—this is the new theme to introduce a new Joey Barnes (Joey Bishop), now a former nightclub comedian who gave up the circuit in 1960 to host "The Joey Barnes Show," a daily 60 minute talk-variety series. Joey, who is from Tenth Street in South Philadelphia, is now married to Ellie (Abby Dalton) and, a year later, becomes the father of a young son, Joey Barnes, Jr. (Matthew David Smith). Ellie was born in Texas, and she and Joey live in the Carlton Arms Apartments in New York City.

Larry Corbett (Corbett Monica) is Joey's writer. (He was voted the 1963 "Writer of the Year" by the TV Critics Association. The critics also awarded Joey twelfth place in the comedy category; he came in just ahead of Bullwinkle the Moose. Joey is full of acceptance speeches but never has a chance to use them.) Joey first met Larry in 1953 when he was a struggling young writer. (Prior to his role as Larry, Corbett Monica played Johnny Edwards, a comedian at the Purple Pussycat Club, who substituted for Joey when he went on vacation.)

Freddie (Guy Marks) is Joey's agent; they have known each other since childhood. Jillson (Joe Besser) is the building's overweight superintendent. He has a wife who watches the eleven o'clock news for laughs, and the one word he can't pronounce is *aluminum* ("I'd give anything to say that word right"). Hilda (Mary Treen) is the baby's nurse.

Joey's catchphrase is "son of a gun," which he says when something stuns him. If Joey has an argument with Ellie, he comes to the studio irritated. The first thing Joey did when he got his show was an impression of a midget sneezing. Ellie attempted to write a song called "The One I Love Most," which Joey thought was the worst song ever written. ("...I love Lillian, she's one in a mill-i-on, but the one I love most is my mother. I love Gracie, she reads me Dick Tracy ... and I love Jewel, she lets me beat her at pool ... but the one I love most is my mother"). Bobby Rydell thought differently and recorded it for Ellie.

Sammy Cahn and James Van Heusen composed "Joey's Theme."

364. *Johnny Jupiter*

DuMont, 3/21/53 to 6/13/53
ABC/Syndicated, 9/5/53 to 5/29/54

In the mythical town of Clayville, U.S.A., lives Ernest P. Duckweather (Wright King), a mild mannered clerk at the Frisby General Store. Horatio Frisby (Cliff Hall), who attended Hyldeberg University, owns the store; and Katherine Frisby (Patricia Peardon), Horatio's daughter, is Ernest's girlfriend.

Ernest, who earns $15 a week, is a jack-of-all-trades. He accidentally discovered interplanetary television when he fooled around with a television set and contacted the inhabitants of Jupiter. The planet is 600 million miles from Earth, and the Jupiterians we see are puppets Johnny

Jupiter, Major Domo (the head robot) and Reject, "the factory rejected robot" (all voiced by Gilbert Mack).

Stories relate Ernest's misadventures as he seeks the Jupiterians' help in solving his earthly problems. When Ernest contacts Johnny, he turns several dials on a large television and says, "Duckweather on Earth, calling the planet Jupiter." Through some primitive but effective special effects, Jupiter comes into view. Ernest can see and speak to Johnny and vice versa.

If Ernest requires extraordinary help, Johnny sends Reject the Robot to Earth. To accomplish this, Johnny touches the puppet Reject and says, "Super Jelly Bean Power." Reject is sent through space and appears to Ernest (the only one who can see him). During the trip from Jupiter to Earth, the puppet becomes life-sized (the actor playing the robot is not credited). Reject's favorite television show is "The Robot Club" (Jupiterian television programs are all educational and instructive). On Jupiter, robots were built to service the humanoid inhabitants (for example, Johnny) and are excellent repairmen. Johnny calls Ernest "Mr. Duckweather."

Reta Shaw (as Mrs. Clandish, a townsperson) and Florenz Ames (as Mr. Latham, Horatio's nemesis) were semiregulars in this version of the series (ABC owned and operated stations; syndicated elsewhere).

An earlier version aired on DuMont, but acquiring actual episodes of DuMont series is extremely difficult, and is sometimes impossible, as it proved to be in this case (the following information is compiled from other sources).

In the original format of the show, Ernest P. Duckweather (Vaughn Taylor) is a television station janitor who dreams of becoming a producer. One night he sneaks into the control room and begins playing producer. While fiddling with the various controls, he accidentally discovers interplanetary television when he contacts the people of Jupiter (puppets Johnny Jupiter; Major Domo, "the head robot"; Reject, "the factory rejected robot"; and Johnny's pal, B-12). Due to limited available information, it is difficult to compare both versions. *TV Guide* first listed the series as "Fantasy," but changed the category to "Puppets" and later "Comedy." *TV Guide*'s listings for the DuMont version (and even ABC) are of little help as the following will attest: "Mr. Duckweather tries to get the Jupiterians on television. Vaughn Taylor" (6/6/53); "Vaughn Taylor tunes his TV set to a far off spot and introduces another adventure (6/13/53); "Adventures of Mr. Duckweather" (10/17/53); "Comedy starring Wright King with Pat Peardon and Cliff Hall" (11/7/53).

It appears that the DuMont version, which was broadcast live, had only two actors: Vaughn Taylor as Ernest and Gilbert Mack doubling as Ernest's boss at the television station and as the puppet voices. Stories revolved around Johnny and Ernest assessing the values of their respective planets (which differed greatly; what was commonplace on Earth was usually just the opposite on Jupiter).

There are no credits listed for theme or even musical background.

365. *Johnny Midnight*

Syndicated, 1960

"Broadway is the world of make-believe, but I found out that the curtain never comes down on the real things that happen on the Street of Dreams. That's why I gave up acting to become a private investigator." Johnny Midnight (Edmond O'Brien) is that former actor turned private detective. Johnny lives in a penthouse on West 41st Street and Broadway ("My favorite street in my favorite town—New York City").

Johnny owns his own theater (The Midnight Theater) and still frequents Lindy's, where he likes to eat and keep in touch with his show business friends. Cost doesn't matter much when it comes to clients. If he sees that a person is in real trouble, the money becomes secondary. Johnny also works on behalf of the Mutual Insurance Company and uses his skills as a former actor to help him solve cases (his favorite disguise is Gearhart Houtman, the Old German).

Aki (Yuki Shimoda), who calls Johnny "Mr. Johnny Midnight," is Johnny's houseboy; Lupo Olivera (Arthur Batanides) is Johnny's police department contact, a sergeant with the Homicide Division of the N.Y.P.D.

A jazz adaptation of "The Lullaby of Broadway," played by Joe Bushkin, is the show's theme song.

366. *Johnny Ringo*

CBS, 10/1/59 to 9/29/60

Cast: Don Durant (*Johnny Ringo*), Mark Goddard (*Cully*), Karen Sharpe (*Laura Thomas*), Terence deMarney (*Cason Thomas*).

Facts: "Ringo, Johnny Ringo, his fears were never shown, fastest gun in all the West, the quickest ever known." Velardi, Arizona, is a growing town in the 1870s; there is a lot of traffic. The railroad has started laying track going east and there is also a lot of trouble—from outlaws who find the town an easy mark. To stop the growing crime rate, Mayor Hartford (Willis Bouchey) hires Johnny Ringo, an ex-gunfighter, as the town's sheriff. Johnny, a right-handed gunfighter, receives $200 a month and has to prove he is as fast as his reputation—"Velardi didn't hire me, they hired my guns. I know that and got to live with it. Maybe someday it will be different."

Johnny doesn't know much about the law—he puts things on a personal basis. He philosophizes, and people say he sounds more like a preacher than a gunfighter. He sometimes poses as a wanted man and calls on his reputation as a gunfighter to apprehend criminals. Johnny never killed a man for money. He relinquished his gunfighting career to become a lawman and recalled that he didn't know how he came to be a gunfighter: "I don't know, it just grew ... All of a sudden you're a big man and you find yourself like a turkey in a shoot. Everybody wants to try their luck.

You can't stop it, you wanna but you can't. You run, but they catch you; you hide, but they find you. Perhaps the badge will make up for some of the things I did."

Johnny's gun is a variation on the French firearm, the Le Met Special. It was designed by Cason ("Case") Thomas, Johnny's original deputy, "to even up the odds." Cason calls it "a seven shooter." It looks like a regular Colt .45 and fires the normal six bullets. But there is a separate barrel for an extra shell—a .410 shotgun shell (the seventh barrel, located under the standard one, is activated by setting the gun's hammer in the firing position). It was said that Johnny's reputation was known from the Gulf to the Pacific Ocean.

William Charles, Jr., better known as Cully, is Johnny's young deputy. Cully's father was a trick shot and taught him how to use a gun when he was five years old. Four years later Cully's father was killed, and Cully went to work as a roustabout in a carnival. He practiced shooting every day and eventually became a traveling show attraction called "Kid Adonis, the Fastest Gun in the World." When the show came to Velardi and the Kid found Johnny was a split second faster than he was, he decided to settle down and lead a normal life. When Cason tells Cully that he is getting too old for the job, Cully steps into his shoes and becomes Johnny's deputy. Cason buys the general store (which he runs with his daughter—Johnny's romantic interest—Laura Thomas). The town saloon is the Golden Wheel.

The original pilot film for the series, titled "Man Alone," aired on "Dick Powell's Zane Grey Theater" (CBS) on 3/5/59. Don Durant played Johnny Ringo, Thomas Mitchell was Cason Thomas and Marilyn Erskine was Laura Thomas (Cully did not appear; the reworked pilot, titled "Arrival" for "Johnny Ringo," is a word-for-word remake of "Man Alone." The proposed series title at the time was "The Loner").

Theme: "Johnny Ringo," vocal by Don Durant.

367. *Johnny Staccato*

NBC, 9/10/59 to 3/24/60

Johnny Staccato (John Cassavetes) is a former jazz musician (the Staccato Combo) turned private detective who operates out of New York City. Johnny, who was born in Manhattan (he now lives at 860 West 40th Street), says, "I'm a native, but I still ask questions, especially of pretty girls, to get around." He also knows a lot—"It's all from odd bits of information I picked up here and there." Johnny's hangout is Waldo's, a mid–Manhattan bar owned by his friend Waldo (Eduardo Ciannelli), an Old World Italian who likes opera but puts up with jazz. It's here where Johnny seems to find his only means of relaxation when he plays piano in the jazz band that supplies the bar's music. The series is also known as "Staccato."

Elmer Bernstein composed "Staccato's Theme."

368. *Judge Roy Bean*

Syndicated, 1955 to 1956

During the 1870s, as the railroads pushed their way west, they attracted the most vicious characters in the country. Soon, the desolate region west of the Pecos River became known as the wildest spot in the United States. It was said that civilization and law stopped at the east bank of the Pecos. "It took the courage of one man, a lone storekeeper who was sick of the lawlessness, to change all this. His name was Judge Roy Bean."

Roy Bean (Edgar Buchanan), the self-appointed judge of Langtry, Texas, is also the town's sheriff and owner of Roy Bean's General Store. He is a bit on the heavy side, near-sighted without his glasses, older than the typical Wild West lawman and fond of apple pie. He is not quick on the draw, nor does he carry a fancy gun. He does possess a genius for figuring out the criminal mind and conning the con man. The judge does take an active part in apprehending outlaws; the rough work falls on the shoulders of his deputy, Jeff Taggard (Jack Beutel), a young man who is fast on the draw and quick with his fists.

Assisting Roy in the store is his niece, Letty Bean (Jackie Loughery), who came to live with him after the death of her parents. She is beautiful, extremely feminine and dynamite with a gun (her dress conceals a gun strapped to her ankle). While Jeff does court her, he calls her "a big tomboy" and admires her ability to handle a gun—"You shoot just like a man." Letty is forever getting angry when Jeff thinks of her as a man and remarks, "Can't you think of me as a woman just once?" He tries—at least for the remainder of that particular episode.

Carson City is the neighboring town; Salt Lake City is the community north of Langtry; and the Southern Pacific Railroad services the area. There is no credit given for the music or the theme song, "The Land of the Pecos."

369. *Julie*

ABC, 5/30/92 to 7/4/92

"The Julie Carlisle Show" is a top rated variety series produced in Hollywood. When star Julie Carlisle (Julie Andrews) decides to marry Dr. Sam McGuire (James Farentino), a veterinarian with a practice in Sioux City, she also decides to move her show to Iowa—to make her marriage work (Julie's first marriage ended in divorce when "my career got in the way. I'm not going to let it happen again"). The series is now taped at KCDM-TV, Channel 10, in Sioux City.

Julie sings in the key of C, and her first job was that of understudy to an actress named Minerva Philbert. Sam calls Julie "Jules," and she hates the song "Feelings."

Sam is a widower and the father of two children: 14-year-old Allie (Hayley Tyrie) and 12-year-old Adam (Rider

Strong). Sam runs the animal clinic and teaches at Iowa State University. Allie takes singing and dancing lessons and has a dog named Dog; Sam coaches the Tigers Little League team.

I.F. ("Wooley") Wollstein (Eugene Roche) is Julie's always complaining, easily upset producer; and Clem (Alicia Brandt) is Sam's gorgeous assistant (a situation that seems not to upset Julie). The series was originally titled "Millie" and starred Julie Andrews as Millie Cramer (storyline and supporting characters are the same).

Henry Mancini composed the theme, "Julie" (which, surprisingly, has no vocal by Julie Andrews).

370. *Julie Farr, M.D.*

ABC, 3/7/78 to 4/18/78
ABC, 6/12/79 to 6/26/79

Julie Farr (Susan Sullivan), an obstetrician with a private practice at 13471 East La Brea, also works for City Memorial Hospital in Los Angeles. Julie's license plate is 183 HYE; L.A. Mobile 4788 is her car phone number; and 213-555-3255 is her office phone number.

Julie originally worked at Riverside Hospital and is proud of her work. It has taken her a long time to build her practice. She has put off marrying and raising a family of her own to help women she feels are dependent upon her.

Dr. Blake Simmons (Mitchell Ryan) works with Julie at City Memorial Hospital, and Kelly Williams (Beverly Todd) is Julie's receptionist (Alice Hirson, as Mimi, was Julie's original receptionist).

Martha Cooper (Lee Meriwether) is Julie's married older sister, and Jenny Cooper (Tracy Marshak) is Julie's 14-year-old niece (Martha's daughter).

The series, which deals with the joys and traumas of childbirth, was originally titled "Having Babies" (the title under which the first three episodes aired). Marilyn McCoo sings the theme, "There Will Be Love."

Three ABC television movies preceded the series: *Having Babies* (10/17/76), *Having Babies II* (10/28/77), and *Having Babies III* (3/3/78). The second and third movies feature the Julie Farr character, and in *Having Babies II*, the actual birth of twins (a girl and boy) is graphically depicted through Paula Plotkin (Cassie Yates).

371. *Just in Time*

ABC, 4/6/88 to 5/18/88

The *West Coast Review*, "California's Monthly Magazine," was established in 1967 and is based in a skyscraper at 133 Wilshire Boulevard. When its rival, *California Magazine*, begins to show an increase in circulation (to 350,000 copies) and *Review*'s numbers begin to fall drastically, management hires Harry Stadlin (Tim Mathe-

son), the editor of *Chicago Magazine,* to turn their publication around. His assignment (which he has six months to accomplish): make the revamped *West Coast*, "California's Weekly Magazine," a success. Stories follow his efforts and his romantic relationship with Joanna Gail Farrell (Patricia Kalember), the magazine's beautiful, vibrant and free spirited columnist-reporter.

Isabel Miller (Nada Despotovich) is the art department director, and Carlie Hightower (Ronnie Claire Edwards) is the magazine's gossip columnist. The La Crosse is the local bar-restaurant hangout.

Lee Holdridge composed the theme.

In the original 1987 unaired pilot version, "It Had to Be You," Joanna Farrell (Annette Bening) and Harry Stadlin (Tim Matheson) were editors for Metropol Press, a publisher of literary books that has not had a successful book in 30 years (they are seeking to lure Carlie Hightower [Ronnie Claire Edwards], an author of three successful novels). In this version, Isabel Miller (Nada Despotovich) was the flaky girl Friday.

372. *Just the Ten of Us*

ABC, 4/26/88 to 7/27/90

Cast: Bill Kirchenbauer (*Graham Lubbock*), Deborah Harmon (*Elizabeth Lubbock*), Heather Langenkamp (*Marie Lubbock*), Jamie Luner (*Cindy Lubbock*), Brooke Theiss (*Wendy Lubbock*), Jo Ann Willette (*Connie Lubbock*), Heidi Zeigler (*Sherry Lubbock*), Matt Shakman (*J.R. Lubbock*).

Facts: A spinoff from "Growing Pains." Graham Lubbock, the former coach at Dewey High School on Long Island (New York), is now the athletic director and coach of the Hippos football team at Saint Augustine's, a Catholic high school for boys in Eureka, California. Graham is married to Elizabeth and is the father of eight children (Marie, Cindy, Wendy, Connie, Sherry, J.R. and twins Harvey and Michelle). They have a dog named Hooter and a milk cow named Diane. Their phone number is 555-3273.

Elizabeth, a deeply religious Catholic, met Graham at a C.Y.O. (Catholic Youth Organization) mixer, and they fell in love at first sight. They married in 1970. Marie, Wendy, Cindy and Connie formed a sexy singing group called the Lubbock Babes (who perform regularly at Danny's Pizza Parlor). Wendy and Cindy say "Hi-eee" and "Bye-eee" for hello and goodbye. Graham is overweight and constantly nagged by Elizabeth to go on a diet. His favorite bedtime snack is Ovaltine and Ho-Ho's. Elizabeth does volunteer work at the food bank, and, for a short time, Graham held a second job as a counter boy at Burger Barn.

Marie is 18 years old and very religious (she is hoping to become a nun). She is also very attractive and boy-shy and hides her obvious beauty behind glasses and loose fitting clothes. Marie mentioned she wears a size five dress and (proudly) a 34C bra. Her first job was cooking and serving food at the Eureka Mission. In one episode, Marie began

Just the Ten of Us. **Left to right:** JoAnn Willette, Heather Langenkamp, Bill Kirchenbauer, Jamie Luner and Brooke Theiss.

her career as a nun by taking a two-week seminar at Saint Bartholomew's Convent.

Wendy, 17, the most beautiful of the Lubbock girls, is boy-crazy and appears totally self-absorbed (although she'll secretly help one of her sisters in a crisis). Wendy wears a size five dress, a 34B bra, a size 7½ shoe, and the lipstick shades Midnight Passion and Dawn at His Place. Although she acts like a bimbo—her ploy to attract the opposite sex—she is deeply hurt when called one. In a dream sequence, Wendy was the star of a comedy series called "Wendy and the Butler" (Wendy was a princess and her father played the butler).

Cindy, 16, the beautiful but not too bright Lubbock Babe, is as boy-crazy as Wendy—but is also constantly in a dither about everything else. Cindy, who wears a size eight dress and a 36C bra, has a slight weight problem and is a member of the Diet Control Clinic. She had her own radio show (over KHPO, "The Voice of Saint Augie's") called "What's Happening, Saint Augie's" and her first job was as the receptionist at the Eureka Fitness Center (where she earned eight dollars an hour). Cindy's middle name is Anne, but for years she thought it was Diane.

Fifteen-year-old Constance, nicknamed Connie, is pretty, very intelligent and the most sensitive of the girls. She wears a size five dress and a 34A bra. While not as boy-shy as Marie, she is quite intimidated by Wendy and Cindy, feels she is flat chested and will never attract "hunks" as do Cindy and Wendy. Connie, who hopes to become a journal-ist, is a writer for the school newspaper, Saint Augie's *Herald-Gazette*; her first job was sweeping animal entrails at the MacGregor slaughterhouse (where she earned four dollars an hour).

Sherry, the youngest of the girls before Michelle's birth, is 11 years old and the most intelligent of the girls. She strives for excellent grades, and although she should be in grammar school she is seen attending Saint Augustine's (an exception to the all-boy rule was made to allow the Lubbock girls to attend). Sherry is constantly amazed by the antics of her sisters and has trouble believing Cindy and Wendy are related to her. In later episodes, Sherry wants to be like Wendy "and live on the wild side" (she smokes cigarettes and brags about wearing a training bra to get attention).

J.R. (Graham Lubbock, Jr.) is the older male child. He attends Saint Augustine's, loves horror movies, peanut butter and playing practical jokes on his sisters. There is no information on the infants, Harvey and Michelle, except that only Harvey is credited (Jason Korstjens).

Father Robert Hargis (Frank Bonner) is the priest in charge of Saint Augustine's, and Sid Haig plays Janitor Bob, the strange ex-con custodian at school.

Relatives: Manfred Melcher (Robert's nephew, *Damien*).

Flashbacks: Taylor Fry *(young Marie)*, Robyn Faye Book-land *(young Wendy)*, Hartley Haverty *(young Cindy)*.

Theme: "Doin' It the Best I Can," vocal by Bill Medley.

373. *Karen's Song*

Fox, 7/18/87 to 9/12/87

Karen Matthews (Patty Duke) is 40 years old and has finally come into her own. She is liberated, independent and ready for anything, even the possibility of marrying a much younger man—28-year-old Steven Foreman (Lewis Smith). Stories follow Karen as she re-examines her traditional values and learns to sing a different tune to make the relationship work. A newly promoted executive with the Dexter Publishing Company in Los Angeles, Karen lives at 31 Evergreen Place. Steven, the ambitious owner of a catering company called A Tasteful Affair, lives on Pinewood Lane. Karen is a graduate of the New York University School of Journalism and previously held a job as a proofreader-editor for Masterson Publishers. Karen lives with her 18-year-old daughter, Laura (Teri Hatcher), a freshman at UCLA (Laura is opposed to her mother's romance with a younger man and is trying to change her mind). Granville Van Dusen appeared as Karen's ex-husband, Zach.

Suzanne Pleshette was originally cast in the role of Karen when CBS had the project. When Fox bought the series, Steven was first made 18 years old. Douglas Timm composed the theme.

374. *Kate and Allie*

CBS, 3/19/84 to 9/11/89

Cast: Susan Saint James (*Kate McArdle*), Jane Curtin (*Allie Lowell*), Ari Meyers (*Emma McArdle*), Allison Smith (*Jennie Lowell*), Frederick Koehler (*Chip Lowell*), Sam Freed (*Bob Barsky*).

Facts: Katherine ("Kate") Elizabeth Ann McArdle is the divorced mother of a girl named Emma. Kate was married to Max, an actor who now lives in California. Before Emma's birth, Kate and Max had contemplated calling her Angela (if a girl) or Chey (if a boy).

Allison ("Allie") Julie Charlotte Adams Lowell is the divorced mother of two children, Jennie and Chip. Allie was married to Charles, a doctor who now resides in Connecticut with his second wife, Claire. They were planning to call their first born child Tiffany (if a girl) or Brooks (if a boy).

Kate and Allie are longtime friends (they met as kids at the orthodontist's office) who now share an apartment in New York's Greenwich Village to save on expenses. Kate has an account (number 375-70-60-572) at the Holland Savings Bank and works as a travel agent for the Sloane Travel Agency. Kate was a radical during the later 1960s (she attended Woodstock, burned her bra, protested the bomb and participated in sit-ins and college demonstrations). Kate took cooking lessons from Julia Peterson (Lindsay Wagner) and always gives Allie a purse as a gift.

Allie loves to cook and cares for the kids while Kate works. She attends night classes at Washington Square College and held several part time jobs: bookstore salesclerk, box office cashier at the 9th Street Cinema and volunteer at Channel G, a Manhattan cable station run by a woman named Eddie Gordon (Andrea Martin). In 1986 Kate and Allie formed their own company, Kate and Allie Caterers, which they operate from their home. Allie always gives Kate a sweater as a gift.

In the episode of 12/11/87, Allie marries former football player Robert ("Bob") Barsky, a sportscaster for WNTD-TV, Channel 10, in Washington, D.C. (He commutes between New York and Washington and does the 11 O'Clock Sports Update.) Allie and Chip move to a new apartment (21C) on West 55th Street; Kate remains for a short time at their old apartment and later moves in with Allie.

Jennie, Allie's daughter, wears a size five dress and had an afterschool waitressing job at Le Bon Croissant, a French diner. Jennie yearns to dress like Madonna, but Allie won't let her. While a high school for Jennie is not given, she attends Columbia University in 1987 and lives in dorm room 512.

Emma, Kate's daughter, who also wears a size five dress, attended the same unnamed high school as Jennie and moved to California in 1987 to attend UCLA.

Chip, Allie's son, attends an unnamed grammar school. He has two cats (Iggie and Tristan) and a Sunday morning job delivering bagels to the neighbors; he later opened a pet cemetery in the backyard. Chip considers Alan Thicke to be America's greatest actor.

In "The Monkey's Paw" episode, Kate inherits a supposedly magic monkey's paw that can grant a secret desire. Kate wished to win the lottery; Allie asked that the national debt be reduced; Emma wanted a new stereo; Jennie wished for breasts (she had a boyish figure at the time); Chip wanted a pony. When he was eight years old, Bob had the nickname "Mickey Pants" (when he was playing ball, a mouse ran up the little left-fielder's pants. The only thing he could do to rid himself of the rodent was to drop his pants in front of everyone).

Relatives: John Heard (Kate's ex-husband, *Max McArdle*), Paul Hecht (Allie's ex-husband, *Dr. Charles Lowell*), Marian Seldes (Kate's mother, *Marian*), Wendie Malick (Charles's second wife, *Claire Lowell*), Robert Cornthwaite (Allie's father, *Dr. Ed Adams*), Elizabeth Parrish (Bob's mother, *Eileen Barsky*), Rosemary Murphy and Scotty Bloch (Allie's mother, *Joan Adams*).

Flash Forwards: Brad Davidson (*adult Chip*).

Theme: "Along Comes a Friend," vocal by John Leffler.

375. *Kate Loves a Mystery/Mrs. Columbo*

NBC, 2/26/79 to 3/24/79
NBC, 10/18/79 to 12/6/79

Cast: Kate Mulgrew (*Kate Columbo/Kate Callahan*), Lili Haydn (*Jenny Columbo/Jenny Callahan*), Henry Jones (*Josh Alden*), Don Stroud (*Sergeant Mike Varrick*).

Kate and Allie. Back: Ari Meyers and Susan Saint James; front: Allison Smith, Frederick Koehler and Jane Curtin.

Facts: Kate Columbo is the previously unseen wife of television's famed Lieutenant Philip Columbo (see "Columbo"). She is (in "Mrs. Columbo," first date listing) a housewife, mother and writer for the *Weekly Advertiser*, a "throwaway" newspaper that is published by Josh Alden. Kate lives at 728 Valley Lane in San Fernando, California (her phone number is 555-9861; later 555-9867). Her daughter, Jennifer ("Jenny"), attends the Valley Elementary School, and Kate drives a sedan with the license plate 859KTL. While Phil's absence is explained in various ways (for example, he is said to be away at a police convention or on a case), Kate keeps his badly in need of repair 1952 Peugeot (license plate 044APD) in tune by driving it on occasion. The family also has a lazy basset hound named White Fang. Kate studied journalism in college, worked at it for a time, but gave it up when she married Philip. Six

months ago she woke up and asked herself where she was. She then found herself a job at the newspaper. The paper goes to press at 2:00 P.M. on Tuesdays; Kate takes the dog to the Parker Street Pet Hospital; and Southwest Telephone services the area. Josh has an unseen wife named Charlotte.

In "Kate Loves a Mystery" (second date listing), Kate is divorced from Phil and uses her maiden name, Kate Callahan. She now works for the *Valley Advocate* in the San Fernando Valley (published by Josh Alden) and her daughter, Jenny, attends Valley Elementary School. Kate lives in the same house, has the same dog, but drives a car with the license plate 304 MGD. Her friend, Mike Varrick, is a sergeant with the Valley Municipal Police Department.

Themes: "Mrs. Columbo" and "Kate Loves a Mystery," by John Cacavas.

376. *King of Diamonds*

Syndicated, 9/61 to 9/62

Continental Diamond Industries is a New York based company that is responsible for protecting gems and industrial diamonds from the time they come out of the ground until they reach their final destination. John King (Broderick Crawford) is the company's security chief. Along with his partner, Casey "Case" O'Brien (Ray Hamilton), John investigates crimes associated with the diamond district. Continental Diamond Industries is located on West 47th Street in Manhattan in the heart of the diamond industry. John, who wears a white trench coat (making him look more like a shady character than the hero) lives at 146 East 36th Street; he refers to diamonds as "ice."

Frank Ortega composed the theme.

377. *Klondike*

NBC, 10/10/60 to 2/13/61

The muddy gold mining camps of Skagway, Alaska, in 1898 are the setting for a series that follows events in the lives of four people: Michael ("Mike") Halliday (Ralph Taeger), an adventurer who has come to Skagway to find his fortune; Katherine ("Kathy") O'Hara (Mari Blanchard), the daughter of a sea captain, who is struggling to operate the Golden Nugget Hotel and maintain an honest operation in a lawless territory; and Jeff Durain (James Coburn) and Goldie (Joi Lansing), an ingenious con artist and his beautiful assistant, who seek to become rich on the fortunes of others.

Mike resides in Room 2 of the hotel; the town saloon is the Monte Carlo Gambling Hall; and the *Circuit Queen* is the riverboat that services the area. J. Pat O'Malley appeared as Kathy's uncle, Jonah.

The "Klondike" theme was written and performed by Vic Mizzy.

On another show, the theme said it all: "Got the fever, got the fever, gold fever." The series was "The Alaskans" (ABC, 10/4/59 to 9/25/60), and Silky Harris (Roger Moore), Rocky Shaw (Dorothy Provine) and Reno McKee (Jeff York) were the adventurers seeking to get rich quick in the Klondike region of Alaska in 1898.

Silky was a slick con artist who lived by his wits and refused to dig for gold if there was a better way to get it; Rocky was the beautiful "café thrush," a singer and dancer who performed most often at the Palace Bar in Dawson (episodes were set in various towns, but in Dawson most often); Reno was a rugged cowpoke who thought like Silky and assisted him. Mack David and Jerry Livingston composed the "Alaskans" theme (which is also kown as "Gold Fever").

378. *Knight and Daye*

NBC, 7/8/89 to 8/14/89

"Knight and Daye" is a 6:00 A.M. to 10:00 A.M. morning radio show on station KLOP in San Diego, California. Longtime friends Henry ("Hank") Knight (Jack Warden) and Everett Daye (Mason Adams) are the hosts. Hank and Everett first teamed in the 1940s when they began "Knight and Daye" on New York radio station WLMM. KLOP, 580 on the AM dial, is the number 16 station in a 17 station market. It is managed by Janet Glickman (Julia Campbell), a very pretty but easily upset young woman. Janet attended San Diego State College and now lives at 11 Waverly Place. Hank is a ladies' man and his claim to fame is his book *Mr. Fabulous: My 50 Years As the King of Show Business.*

Hank lives with his wife, Gloria (Hope Lange), at 3465 Gentry Avenue with their married daughter, Eleanor ("Ellie") Escobar (Lela Ivey), her husband, Cito Escobar (Joe Lala), a cab driver, and Ellie's children, Chris, Amy and Laurie (Emily Schulman, Shiri Appleby and Brittany Thornton).

David Michael Frank composed "The Knight and Daye Theme."

379. *Knight Rider*

NBC, 9/26/82 to 8/8/86

Cast: David Hasselhoff *(Michael Knight)*, Edward Mulhare *(Devon Miles)*, William Daniels *(Voice of KITT)*, Patricia McPherson *(Bonnie Barstow)*, Rebecca Holden *(April Curtis)*.

Facts: Michael Long is an undercover cop who is shot in the face during a bust that went wrong and left for dead. He is saved by Wilton Knight (Richard Basehart), a dying billionaire (the owner of Knight Industries), who provides life saving surgery, a new face (patterned after his own when he was young), a new identity (Michael Knight) and a mission: to apprehend criminals who are above the law.

Knight Industries is part of the Foundation for Law and Government. Devon Miles is its head, and Bonnie Barstow (first and third seasons) and April Curtis (second season) are the mechanics who are responsible for the delicate maintenance of KITT, the Knight Industries Two Thousand, an indestructible black Trans-Am car (license plate KNIGHT) that is given to Michael to help him battle injustice.

KITT, as the car is called, is made of a molecular bonded shell and has the serial number Alpha Delta 227529. The car is able to talk via its ultrasophisticated and elaborate microcircuitry. Microprocessors make it the world's safest car; it has also been programed with a chip to protect human life. KITT has long-range tracking scopes, turbo boost, normal and auto driving and a pursuit mode (that gives it extra speed). KITT is also programed to avoid collisions and is equipped with a minilab and a third stage aquatic synthesizer that allows it to ride on water (system developed by April). Bonnie, a computer whiz and electronics expert, developed SID (Satellite Infiltration Drone), a bugging device that can go where KITT cannot.

The Roving Knight Industries portable lab is a black with gold trim 18-wheel truck (license plate 1U1 3265); a chess knight is painted on each side of the trailer.

KITT's prototype is KARR (Knight Automated Roving Robot), an evil car voiced by Peter Cullen. When designing KARR (the car of the future), Wilton neglected to program it with a respect for life. Now KARR is self-servicing with no respect for life. KITT's enemy is Goliath, an indestructible truck owned by Wilton's evil son, Garthe (David Hasselhoff). Garthe seeks to kill Michael because he feels he is a living and breathing insult to his likeness.

Michael calls KITT "Buddy." As Michael Long, Michael was with the 11th Precinct of the L.A.P.D. and lived at 1834 Shore Road; his badge number was 8043. See also the following title.

Relatives: Mary Kate McGeehan (Wilton's daughter, *Jennifer Knight*), Lynne Marta (April's sister, *Laura Phillips*).

Theme: "Knight Rider," by Glen A. Larson and Michael Sloan.

380. *Knight Rider 2000*

NBC, 5/19/91

Cast: David Hasselhoff *(Michael Knight)*, Susan Norman *(Shawn McCormick)*, Carmen Argenziano *(Russ Maddock)*, Edward Mulhare *(Devon Miles)*, William Daniels *(Voice of KITT)*.

Facts: A two-hour pilot film for an updated version of "Knight Rider" (see preceding title). The motion picture *Star Trek 10* has just been released. Dan Quayle, the vice president under George Bush, is now the president of the United States. Handguns have been outlawed (cops use ultra stun guns), and the Foundation for Law and Government and Knight Industries have been combined to form the Knight Foundation, an independent corporation that is concerned with law enforcement and seeks to help various police departments enforce the law. The time is the year 2000, and the foundation's ultimate weapon against crime is the Knight Rider 4000 car, a highly upgraded model of the Knight Industries 2000 (KITT) from the series "Knight Rider."

Although the red Knight Rider 4000 is still in the experimental stage, Devon Miles, the head of the foundation, decides to recruit Michael Knight, KITT's former driver, to come back to the foundation and help them launch the new car. Michael left the foundation in 1990 to open a bass charter service. He now lives in a house by the lake and drives a classic 1957 Chevrolet.

Michael is reluctant at first and becomes bitter when he learns that KITT has been dismantled and his parts sold off. Devon orders the repurchase of KITT's parts; all but one

memory chip is recovered. The recycled KITT is first incorporated in the Chevrolet; it is later placed in the Knight 4000.

Meanwhile, Officer Shawn McCormick of the Metropolitan Police Department (car code Adam 20-20) is shot in the head at point blank range during a case investigation. To save her life, Shawn is given a memory chip transplant to replace the part of her brain that was lost. The chip used is KITT's missing chip, which was sold to a trauma hospital. When Shawn finds that she has lost all memory of what happened to her and will be assigned to desk duty, she quits. She applies for a position at the Knight Foundation—and is hired when Russell ("Russ") Maddock, Devon's assistant and the designer of the Knight 4000, discovers that she carries KITT's memory chip in her brain. She is teamed with Michael, and together they solve their first crime via the Knight 4000 (breaking up a ring of illegal handgun smugglers).

The only other information about Shawn is that she wears a perfume called Desire; nothing else is said about Michael.

The Knight 4000 is a ten million dollar, three-liter, 300 horsepower red car that can go from zero to 300 mph in a matter of seconds. It runs on nonpolluting hydrogen fuel that is refined from gases emitted by algae fields. KITT now has an aromanator to detect odors, and sonic beams to immobilize evildoers. A collision factor analyzer tells Michael when it is safe to run a red light or speed through traffic. Virtual reality allows Michael to look through the windshield to see an enhanced simulation of the road's topography and vehicles in pursuit. Digital sampling allows KITT to analyze voice patterns and duplicate them exactly. The thermal expander heats the air in the tires of fleeing cars and explodes them.

Theme: "The New Knight Rider Theme," by Jan Hammer.

381. *Kojak*

CBS, 10/24/73 to 4/1/78
ABC, 11/4/89 to 4/7/90

Cast: Telly Savalas *(Theo Kojak)*, Kevin Dobson *(Robert ["Bobby"] Crocker)*, Dan Frazer *(Frank McNeil)*, George Savalas *(Detective Stavros)*, Vince Conti *(Detective Rizzo)*, Mark Russell *(Detective Saperstein)*.

Facts: The hours are long, and working past quitting time is part of the job. Headquarters is cold in the winter and hot in the summer, "the coffee is one step ahead of suicide," and the squad room detectives joke all the time— "They have to. These guys don't know what they'll find out there. It could be a killer with a .357 Magnum or a body chopped up into pieces. They gotta get their laughs when they can." The cases are the things nightmares are made of; one man is dedicated to ending those nightmares: Lieutenant Theo Kojak, a homicide detective with the Manhattan South Precinct in New York City (eight years earlier, Theo was an officer with the 26th Precinct).

Kojak works on hunches (which often pay off), and when he becomes personally involved in a case (such as investigating the murder of Azure Dee [Denyce Liston], a beautiful girl he once helped and cared for), he doesn't care what it takes—"I don't care about you [the suspect] or what you are. I don't care about my badge; I don't care about my pension. But somebody's gonna take a hard fall for what they did to Azure." (In this particular episode, "Elegy in an Asphalt Graveyard," Telly Savalas sings "Azure Dee," the song heard over the episode's credits.)

Kojak drives a sedan with the license plate 394 AFL (later 383 JDZ) and lives at 215 River Street. He smokes pencil-thin cigars, but is famous for being the only cop on the force who loves lollipops (the round Tootsie Roll Pops). In the episode "Lady in the Squad Room" (3/18/77), Theo is teamed with Detective Jo Long (Joan Van Ark) in a department experiment to introduce female cops into the homicide division. (Because of the nature of the cases, it was believed that a female detective couldn't handle assignments. Despite the gory cases and Theo's abrasive attitude, Jo proved that a woman could handle the job.) Kojak's favorite restaurant is Stella's (owned by Marie Stella, played by Carole Cook), and Diane Baker appeared as Theo's romantic interest, Irene Van Patten. "Who loves ya, baby" is Theo's catchphrase.

Frank McNeil is the chief of detectives, and Theo most often works with detectives Crocker, Stavros, Rizzo and Saperstein. While Kojak is forever yelling "Crocker!" "Saperstein!" and "Rizzo!" he calls only Crocker by a first name. The Greek-born Theo refers to his men as "yo-yo's" (when they get into arguments), and he calls Crocker and Saperstein "Laurel and Hardy" or "Abbott and Costello" when they work together. George Savalas, Telly's brother, originally worked under the name Demosthenes.

In the ABC version, Kojak is now a police inspector with the 74th Precinct in Manhattan. He drives a sedan with the license plate NRV 171, and his new assistant is Detective Warren Blake (Andre Braugher). Kevin Dobson reprised his role as Bobby Crocker in the episode of 2/3/90 ("It's Always Something"). This time, however, he is an assistant D.A. Kojak's lollipops have also changed—from Tootie Roll Pops to an unknown sugar-free brand (the pops are wrapped in clear cellophane).

Relatives: Penny Santon (Theo's sister, *Sophie*), Janice Heiden (Sophie's daughter, *Alexandra*), Gigi Semone (Theo's niece, *Ellena*), Michael Mullins (Theo's nephew, *Johnny*), Eunice Christopher (Johnny's mother, *Mary*), Shelley Winters (Frank's sister-in-law, *Evelyn McNeil*).

Themes: "Kojak," by Billy Goldenberg (CBS); "The New Kojak Theme," by Mike Post (ABC).

Note: Telly Savalas also played Kojak in three TV movies: *The Marcus-Nelson Murders* (CBS, 3/8/73), the actual pilot for the series, in which Theo helps a teenager who is being wrongly convicted for the murder of two men.

Kojak: The Belarus File (CBS, 2/16/85). Kojak teams with FBI agent Dana Sutton (Suzanne Pleshette) to find the killer of elderly Russian immigrants. Dan Frazer, George Savalas, Mark Russell and Vince Conti reprised their roles.

Kojak: The Price of Justice (CBS, 2/21/87). Theo, now

an inspector at the precinct ("they let me join the club") investigates a case in which Kitty Keeler (Kate Nelligan) is accused of murdering her two children. Previous regulars were dropped; new were Detective Catalano (Tony De Benedetto), Chief Briscoe (Stephen Joyce) and Chief Barnes (Lee Wallace).

382. *Kung Fu*
ABC, 10/14/72 to 6/27/75

Cast: David Carradine *(Kwai Chang Caine)*, Keye Luke *(Master Po)*, Philip Ahn *(Master Kan)*, John Leoning *(Master Teh)*.

Facts: In China during the 1850s, a young orphan boy named Kwai Chang Caine (born of a Chinese mother and an American father) is accepted into the Temple at Whonon. There, he begins his studies of Kung Fu, the medieval Chinese science of disciplined combat developed by Taoist and Buddhist monks. While learning the knowledge of inner strength, a disciplining of the mind and body to remove conflict from within one's self and to "discover a harmony of body and mind in accord with the flow of the universe," Caine befriends Master Po, the blind Shaolin priest who becomes his mentor. One day, while in the garden, Master Po speaks to Caine: "What do you hear?" "I hear the water, I hear the birds," responds Caine. "Do you hear the grasshopper at your feet?" asks Master Po. "Old man," remarks Caine, "how is it that you hear these things?" "How is it that you do not?" responds Master Po, and from that moment on, Master Po would always call Caine, his favorite student, "Grasshopper." It is at this time that Caine learns of Master Po's great ambition: to make a pilgrimage to the Forbidden City.

"Learn this, Grasshopper: the mind of every creature, great or small, is the master of his own body—but only if the mind flows with nature ... There is no limit to the wondrous powers of the body, nor is there a limit to the ways one may harness those powers to the mastery of the harmonious mind. It may take half a lifetime to master one system." Caine masters them all.

As Caine, now a young man, completes his training, he approaches a cauldron of burning coals. On the sides of the cauldron are the embossed symbols of a tiger and a dragon. Caine places his arms around the cauldron and brands himself—the final step to becoming a Shaolin priest. Caine leaves the temple with the final words of Master Teh in his ears: "Remember. The wise man walks always with his head bowed, humble like the dust."

Recalling Master Po's dream and desiring to help him celebrate it, Caine meets the old man on the road to the Temple of Heaven. As they journey, they encounter the bodyguards of the royal nephew. When one of the guards yells, "Get out of the way," to Master Po, Po trips him. "You dare to touch an escort of the Imperial House?" "Humble apologies," responds Po to the guard. Just then the royal nephew signals his escort to slap Master Po. A ruckus ensues, and a guard shoots Master Po. At the request of his mentor, Caine takes a spear away from a guard and kills the royal nephew. Before he dies, Master Po warns Caine to leave China and begin a new life elsewhere.

The emperor dispatches men to find Caine; the Chinese legation circulates posters: WANTED FOR MURDER. KWAI CHANG CAINE. $10,000 ALIVE. $5,000 DEAD.

Caine's adventures begin on the American frontier of the 1870s, where he has fled and where he begins a search for an unknown brother. Stories also depict his battle against injustice and his memories of his days of training (via flashbacks) while a student in China. Situations he encounters parallel those of the past. Through flashbacks, the viewer learns of Caine's strict training and of the wisdom of his masters as he disciplines himself to face circumstances as a respected Shaolin priest. (Although Caine is seen taking a life in the pilot film, the series depicts him as humble, just and wise, with a profound respect for human life.)

Relatives: Tim McIntire (Caine's half brother, *Danny Caine*), Season Hubley (Caine's cousin, *Margit McLean*).

Flashbacks: Stephen Manley *(Caine age 6)*, Radames Pera *(Caine, older)*.

Theme: "Kung Fu," by Jim Helms.

Note: David Carradine reprised his role as Caine in the television movie *Kung Fu: The Movie* (CBS, 2/1/86). The story, set in the 1880s, pits Caine against the Manchu (Mako), an evil warlord who is seeking to kill him. On 6/19/87, CBS presented a 60-minute pilot called "Kung Fu: The Next Generation," a modern adaptation of the series. After years of wandering, Kwai Chang Caine (David Carradine) marries and begins a family. Caine passes his wisdom as a Shaolin priest on to his son, who in turn passes it on to his son, Kwai Chang Caine (David Darlow), a 1980s father with a son named Johnny Caine (Brandon Lee). This would-be series was to relate their efforts to battle crime.

Six years later, David Carradine again appeared as Caine in "Kung Fu: The Legend Continues," a first-run syndicated series that appeared in January 1993. Kwai Chang Caine is now the grandson of the original Caine and the father of Peter Caine (Chris Potter), a police officer with the Metro Division of the 101st Precinct. Peter attended the temple with his father and learned the ways of the Shaolin priests. However, he felt the ideals of the priests were all empty and opted for a different life; he eventually became a cop (he grew up watching "The Rockford Files" and "Hill Street Blues" and wanted to be one of the good guys). Peter and Kwai Chang are reunited after a 15-year separation and team up to battle injustice—Peter as a law enforcement officer; Kwai Chang as his unofficial martial arts assistant. Jeff Danna composed the new "Kung Fu" theme.

383. *Ladies' Man*

CBS, 10/27/80 to 2/21/81

"How do I fit in, in a room full of women, when they don't even know I exist? Daily I rehearse—"Ladies first,"

"Up with women"—still I'm at the bottom of the list..." The theme lyric refers to Alan Thackeray (Lawrence Pressman), the token male writer for *Women's Life,* a New York–based monthly magazine that is staffed by a bevy of gorgeous women.

Elaine S. Holstein (Louise Sorel) is the managing editor; Andrea Gibbons (Betty Kennedy), Gretchen (Simone Griffeth) and Susan Watson (Allison Argo) are the featured writers.

"The publisher," says Elaine, "wants a man's point of view. I don't," and hence, Alan got the job. Alan, who lives in Apartment 306 at 461 West 46th Street in Manhattan, is 38 years old, divorced and the father of a pretty 10-year-old girl named Amy Thackeray (Natasha Ryan); she is in the fourth grade at P.S. 108. Betty Brill (Karen Morrow), who lives across the hall from Alan, has a never-seen husband named Harry and believes she is the world's best problem solver (she has a master's degree in clinical psychology).

At the office (Room 212), Alan first worked on an article called "Sexual Harassment and the Working Woman." When he has to use "the powder room," he has to remove the WO from the WOMEN sign on the door. Elaine, who says, "I don't do anything to keep in shape," has men saying, "If you were in any better shape, you'd need a full time bodyguard." She lives in an apartment on East 56th Street in Manhattan, is highly fashion conscious and once spent a night in the drunk tank.

Gretchen has a dry wit, lousy moods and once posed as a centerfold for the girlie magazine *Body* ("I was a senior in college and it was a political statement"). The sign on her desk reads RESEARCHER. Susan was on the varsity swim team in high school and ran track in college. Andrea, who is from Kansas, is the most naive of the group. She has a degree in journalism from Kansas State College and hopes one day to become a top notch reporter.

Julie Cobb appeared as Alan's ex-wife, Sheila Thackeray, in one episode.

Jack Elliott and Brian Neary composed the "Ladies' Man" theme.

384. *Land of the Giants*

ABC, 9/22/68 to 9/6/70

Cast: Gary Conway *(Steve Burton)*, Don Marshall *(Dan Erickson)*, Heather Young *(Betty Hamilton)*, Deanna Lund *(Valerie Scott)*, Don Matheson *(Mark Wilson)*, Kurt Kasznar *(Alexander Fitzhugh)*, Stefan Arngrim *(Barry Lockridge)*.

Facts: On June 12, 1983, as the *Spinthrift,* suborbital flight 612, approaches London (departure was from New York), Captain Steve Burton and his co-pilot, Dan Erickson, find they have lost all communication with the London control tower. Suddenly, the ship hits an area of solar turbulence and is pulled into a large glowing green cloud. All control of the ship is lost until they exit the cloud. With only partial reserve power remaining, Burton, who is still unable to contact the control tower, spots what he believes are airport

Ladies' Man. Front: Allison Argo and Simone Griffeth. Center: Betty Kennedy, Natasha Ryan and Lawrence Pressman. Back: Karen Morrow and Louise Sorel.

lights and lands the craft. A thick fog makes visibility zero. Steve and Dan venture outside the craft to investigate. They are walking on a paved road when an enormous car passes over them. They then hear footsteps and rush back to the ship. Betty Hamilton, the stewardess, prepares the passengers for an emergency takeoff. As Steve fires up the engines, they are picked up by "a giant boy." As the giant looks at the ship, Steve manages to escape his grasp. At 5,000 feet they are still passing buildings. With the reserve power virtually exhausted, Steve makes an emergency landing in a dense forest. In addition to crew members Steve, Don and Betty, the passengers are Valerie Scott, a beautiful but rich and spoiled heiress; Mark Wilson, an engineer who is also a wealthy business tycoon (he has to be in London at the start of business to close a $50 million deal); Commander Alexander Fitzhugh, a master thief who is being pursued by authorities for stealing one million dollars (which he is carrying with him in a briefcase); and Barry Lockridge, an orphan with a dog (Clipper), who is to live with cousins in England.

Shortly after, when they realize they have crashed on a strange planet, the *Spinthrift* is attacked by a giant cat. The ship is damaged and the seven earthlings are now marooned. Stories follow their adventures as they struggle for survival and seek the material they need to repair the craft and find a way to reverse the time warp.

The Land of the Giants, as this world is called, appears to be parallel to Earth. English is spoken, the alphabet is the same and all devices used by these people are identical to what is used on Earth—only bigger. A broken razor blade and a giant safety pin are the two weapons the earthlings first devise. Steve and Valerie are also the first two to be captured (by a giant scientist) when they wander into one of his traps (they are rescued by Dan and Mark).

As their presence becomes known, they are branded "The Little People" (they are only about six inches tall in this world), and a reward has been offered for their capture; death is the penalty for assisting them. The giant Kobic (Kevin Hagen) is the inspector seeking them.

Theme: "Land of the Giants," by John Williams.

385. *Land of the Lost*

NBC, 9/7/74 to 9/3/77

Forest ranger Rick Marshall (Spencer Milligan) and his children, Holly (Kathy Coleman) and Will (Wesley Eure), are exploring the Colorado River on a raft when they are caught in a time vortex and transported to a closed universe they call the Land of the Lost, a prehistoric world from which there is no escape. They make a home in a cave they call High Bluff and discover that two other races inhabit the land: the simple, simian Palcus, and the saurian Sleestak. Through Enik (Walker Edmiston), an intelligent Sleestak who fell through a time doorway and is now in his future, the Marshalls learn that their world is controlled by a series of pyramid-shaped triangles called Pylons. Each Pylon con-

tains a series of colored crystals; escape can only be made by finding the right series of crystals that will open a time doorway. However, the crystals control the delicate balance of life; it is extremely dangerous to disturb them.

It is also learned that, although Enik is friendly, the other Sleestak (who hunt with bow and arrow) are not; they pose a constant threat to the Marshalls' survival. Enik's mission is to find the doorway and return to his time, and prevent his people from becoming savages.

Ron Harper joined the cast in 1976 as Rick's brother, Jack. (While experimenting with the crystals, Rick finds the time doorway, but he is swept away before he can get Holly and Will. Since this is a closed universe, for each being that leaves it, one must take his place or her place to maintain the harmony. As Rick is freed, Jack becomes his replacement.)

Dinosaurs co-exist with the inhabitants. Holly has befriended a baby brontosaurus she calls Dopey. Grumpy, a Tyrannosaurus rex, and Big Alice (Dopey's mother) are the creatures that most often plague the Marshalls. Philip Paley plays the Palcus boy, Chaka, and Sharon Baird, the Palcus girl Sa. See also the preceding title for information on the revised version.

Linda Laurie and Michael Lloyd composed the theme.

386. *Land of the Lost*

ABC, 9/7/91 to the present

A revised version of the previous title. While riding in their camper, Tom Porter (Timothy Bottoms) and his children, Annie (Jennifer Drugan) and Kevin (Robert Gavin), "fall into a time warp" when an earthquake opens a time doorway and transports them to a world of prehistoric creatures called the Land of the Lost. The Porters, who were on a camping trip at the time, quickly adjust to their new home when they feel there is no escape. They establish a new home in a large tree ("The Compound") and quickly make friends with Christa (Shannon Day), a beautiful but mysterious jungle girl, and her companion, Stink (Bobby Porter), a simian creature who is a member of the Palcu tribe. Their enemies are the Sleestak, intelligent saurian creatures led by Shung (Tom Allard). Shung and his bungling assistants, Nim (R.C. Tass) and Keeg (Brian Williams), are based in an old temple in a cave. (The Sleestak were forced underground by pollution; Shung, Nim and Keeg are criminals who were banished to the surface. Shung uses a power crystal as his main weapon and believes everything in the Land of the Lost is his—including the humans.)

SAN FRANCISCO—TWO JILLION MILES is the sign the Porters have posted on the grounds next to their home. Tom is convinced that there is a tunnel or a canyon concealing a time doorway that will take them back to their world. He believes that the camper (license plate IMQH438) is their ticket home (he rarely uses it in order to preserve a now precious liquid—gasoline).

Tom calls Annie, his youngest child, "Sweet Face." Annie, who cares for the family garden, wears the nail polish shades Flaming Pink and Rosey Red Siren. While the main dinosaur threat to the Porters is a Tyrannosaurus rex they call Scarface, Annie has a baby Parasausolophus she calls Tasha (after her late mother, Natasha). Annie found a dinosaur egg, brought it home and kept it warm. When it hatched, the lizard first saw Kevin and believed he was her mother. Kevin uses his camcorder to record his surroundings (he is hoping to make the epic dinosaur picture with the footage he has when he gets back).

Christa first made herself known to the Porters when she saved Tom's life after he had been bitten by a poisonous lizard. Christa, whom Shung calls "Long Hair," is apparently an American who was engulfed by the Land of the Lost at an early age. She understands English, but cannot speak it well. She has a language all her own and has control over the dinosaurs via a Tarzan-like yell; she rides a tricieratops with a broken left horn she calls Princess. Christa lives in a cave and has a Giants baseball cap and a picture of herself as a child—but she doesn't remember who she is or where she came from. Stink is intelligent and can understand and speak English once he grasps it.

Kevin Kiner composed the theme.

387. *Lanigan's Rabbi*

NBC, 1/30/77 to 7/3/77

The partially clothed body of a young girl named Arlette is found on the grounds of the Temple Beth Hallel Synagogue in Cameron, California. While investigating the case, Paul Lanigan (Art Carney), the Irish police chief, meets David Small (Bruce Solomon), a rabbi with the mind of a detective, who has begun his own investigation. The two form an unlikely alliance and solve the homicide (proving it was the least thought-of suspect—the cop on the beat). They remain a team and stories relate their efforts to solve crimes.

Paul has been a cop for 22 years and lives with his wife, Kate (Janis Paige), at 3601 Sycamore Lane. His car license plate reads WQW 898, and his office is in Room 121 of the Cameron Police Department. Paul doesn't make arrests that don't stick, he doesn't speculate about murder cases, and he strives not to let innocent people get hurt; he also drinks a special blend of coffee he calls Turkish coffee.

David and his wife, Miriam (Janet Margolin), live at 171 Circle Drive; his telephone number is 555-1211, and his license plate reads 886 LYN.

In the pilot film, "The Rabbi Slept Late" (NBC, 6/17/76), Stuart Margolin played Rabbi David Small.

Leonard Rosenman composed the theme.

Lassie see *Jeff's Collie* and *The New Lassie*

388. *Laurie Hill*

ABC, 9/30/92 to 11/4/92

Laurie Hill (DeLane Matthews) is a midthirties woman struggling to balance her roles as housewife, mother and doctor. She is married to Jeff (Rob Clohessy), a freelance journalist and eternal kid at heart, and is the mother of five-year-old Leo (Eric Lloyd). Leo attends the Davis Preschool and has a plush dog named Floppy Dog.

Laurie has a B.A. from Cornell University, an M.D. from the University of Michigan and ten years of clinical experience. She now works at (and is partners in) the Weisman, Kramer and Hill Family Medical Clinic. Laurie listens to radio station KOLD (91.3 FM) and is on emergency call at Saint John's Hospital.

Laurie's business partners are Dr. Walter Weisman (Joseph Maher), a grandfatherly physician with one eye on retirement; and Dr. Spencer Kramer (Kurt Fuller), a family practitioner with an aversion to people—he attended the Crittendon Academy for Boys. Nancy MacIntire (Ellen DeGeneres) is an office doctor, and Beverly Fiedler (Doris Belack) is the office receptionist.

W.G. Snuffy Walden composed the "Laurie Hill Theme."

389. *Laverne and Shirley*

ABC, 1/27/76 to 5/10/83

Cast: Penny Marshall (*Laverne DeFazio*), Cindy Williams (*Shirley Feeney*), David L. Lander (*Squiggy Squigman*), Michael McKean (*Lenny Kosnoski*), Eddie Mekka (*Carmine Ragusa*), Phil Foster (*Frank DeFazio*), Betty Garrett (*Edna Babish*), Leslie Easterbrook (*Rhonda Lee*).

Facts: A spinoff from "Happy Days." Laverne DeFazio and Shirley Feeney are friends who live in Milwaukee, Wisconsin, during the 1960s. They first lived at 730 Knapp Street, Apartment A (also given as 730 Hampton Street). The girls work in the beer bottle–capping division of the Shotz Brewery. They shop at Slotnick's Supermarket and served a hitch in the army. (They did their basic training at Camp McClellan. Shirley wrote of their experiences under the pen name S. Wilhelmina Feeney. They played hookers in the army training film *This Can Happen to You.*) Laverne and Shirley are graduates of Fillmore High School.

The series changed locales beginning with the episode of 10/31/81 when Laverne and Shirley moved to California to begin new lives. They acquire an apartment at 113½ Laurel Vista Drive in Los Angeles and find employment in the gift wrapping department of Bardwell's Department Store. One year later, Shirley marries her fiancé, Dr. Walter Meeney; Laverne now works for the Ajax Aerospace Company.

Laverne, an Italian Catholic, suffers from a fear of small places. She loves milk and Pepsi (her favorite drink), Scooter Pies (favorite snack), and peanut butter and sauerkraut on raisin bread is her favorite sandwich. She

Laverne and Shirley. **Front:** Michael McKean and David L. Lander. **Center:** Penny Marshall and Cindy Williams. **Back:** Carol Ita White, Phil Foster, Eddie Mekka and Betty Garrett.

wears a large capital *L* on all her clothes, including her lingerie.

Shirley, an Irish Protestant, is famous for the Shirley Feeney scarf dance, has a plush cat named Boo Boo Kitty, and uses the Feeney family traditional greetings "Hi-Yooo" (for hello) and "Bye-Yooo" (for goodbye). Shirley's favorite novel is *Black Beauty* (she read it eight times), and she has

"The Ringo Dream," which drives Laverne nuts (Shirley constantly dreams that her idol, Ringo Starr, is in love with her). Shirley never orders chicken with extra barbecue sauce ("It's too messy and gets under my nails"). On her first day in kindergarten, Candy Zarvarkes made Shirley eat a box of Crayola crayons.

Andrew ("Squiggy") Squigman and Leonard ("Lenny")

Kosnoski are friends of Laverne and Shirley and work as beer truck drivers for the Shotz Brewery. In California episodes, they are co-owners of the Squignoski Talent Agency of Burbank, and ice cream vendors with a truck called Squignoski's Ice Cream. As talent agents, they wrote a movie called *Blood Orgy of the Amazon* and searched for young starlets to star in it. Their favorite food is Bosco (which they put on everything).

Lenny, whose home away from home is the gutter, likes horror movies and sports; his only toy when he was a kid was sauerkraut. He also had a pet turtle, but it killed itself trying to scratch Lenny's name off its back.

Squiggy, whose prized possession is his moth collection, is "blessed" with the Squigman birthmark (a big red blotch shaped like Abraham Lincoln), and he has two favorite things: old sandwiches and toenail clippings.

In one episode, Lenny inherited his late Uncle Lazlo's restaurant. He and Squiggy reopened the place (naming it Dead Lazlo's Place) and hired Laverne and Shirley. Shirley worked as Betty the waitress, while Laverne did the cooking.

Frank DeFazio, Laverne's father, first owns the Pizza Bowl (a pizzeria and bowling alley); then, after he and Edna Babish marry and move to Burbank, Cowboy Bill's Western Grub (a fast food chain with the slogan "Stuff your face Western style"). Frank's nickname for Laverne is "Muffin."

Carmine Ragusa, Shirley's boyfriend (who calls her "Angel Face"), is nicknamed "The Big Ragu," and works as a singing messenger.

Rhonda Lee, Laverne and Shirley's beautiful Hollywood actress neighbor in Burbank, mentioned that she starred in the stage play *Bono Mania* (the life of Sonny and Cher).

Relatives: Ed Begley, Jr. (Shirley's brother, *Bobby Feeney*), Wynn Irwin (Squiggy's father, *Helmut Squigman*), David L. Lander (Squiggy's sister, *Squendelyn Squigman*), Linda Gillin (Edna's daughter, *Amy*).

Theme: "Making Our Dreams Come True," vocal by Cyndi Grecco.

390. *Law of the Plainsman*

NBC, 10/1/59 to 9/22/60

With his right hand raised and his left hand on the Bible, a Harvard educated Apache Indian (Michael Ansara) takes the oath to become a U.S. Marshal: "Do you swear to uphold the Constitution of the United States and the territory of New Mexico, to do your duty as a deputy U.S. Marshal without favor or prejudice, so help you God?" The Apache, named Sam Buckhart, responds, "I do." While Sam covers a great deal of New Mexico (1880s), he is based in Santa Fe and must overcome many obstacles to perform his job—especially the prejudices that existed at the time between Indians and whites. But it was a white man who changed the course of Sam's life.

During a battle between the cavalry and the Apache Indians, a 14-year-old brave encounters a wounded army captain. Instead of killing the captain, the brave befriends him and gets help. The captain and the brave, whom the captain names Sam Burkhart, soon become blood brothers. Two years later, after the captain is killed in an Indian ambush, Sam inherits a great deal of money, which enables him to attend Harvard University, as once did the captain. Wishing to help his people, Sam decides to become a law enforcement officer upon graduation.

Tess Logan (Gina Gillespie) is Sam's ward, a pretty seven-year-old he rescued from a wagon train massacre; Martha Cominter (Nora Marlowe) runs the Santa Fe Boarding House and helps care for Tess; Billy Lordan (Robert Harland) is Sam's assistant, the marshal of the nearby town of Glorieta; A.L. Morrison (Dayton Lummis) is the sheriff of Santa Fe. The town saloon is the Red Bar Saloon and the bank is the Territorial Bank of New Mexico. The pilot episode, "The Indian," aired on "The Rifleman" (2/17/59).

Leonard Rosenman composed the "Plainsman Theme."

391. *Lawman*

ABC, 10/5/58 to 10/9/62

When a girl, "someone special" to Dan Troop (John Russell), is killed by a stray bullet in a pointless gunfight, Dan decides to devote his life to upholding the law. As the years pass, Dan becomes a legend—"The Famous Gun from Texas." It is 1879 when Dan, the marshal of Abilene, receives a telegram from the town council in Laramie, Wyoming, asking him to rid the town of three outlaw brothers, one of whom killed the previous marshal ("The town is tough on lawmen and horse thieves").

Dan is fast with his guns and tough with his fists. He is also high priced and likes his gratitude once a month—waiting for him at the bank. The town council members want a city where their wives and children can walk down the street without being afraid. Dan realizes that he can't do the job alone and advertises for a deputy (a job that pays $50 a month). A young man named Johnny McKay (Peter Brown) applies for the position—but is turned down because Dan thinks Johnny is too inexperienced. However, when Dan arrests one of the three brothers and the other two trap him in a crossfire, Johnny comes to his defense—and is hired by Dan. Stories follow their efforts to uphold the law.

As a kid Dan worked in a hash house. He believes that a man has to wear a gun because of the way things are now; he also thinks there will be a time when it is not necessary.

Lily Merrill (Peggie Castle) owns the town's watering hole, the Birdcage Saloon; Dru Lemp (Bek Nelson) runs the Blue Bonnet Café (where Johnny worked prior to becoming a deputy; it was then called Good Eats); and Julie Tate (Barbara Lang) is the editor of the town newspaper, the *Laramie Weekly* (originally called the *Laramie Free Press*). The Hotel Laramie, the Bank of Laramie and the Laramie Trading Post are other businesses in town.

Mack David and Jerry Livingston composed the "Lawman" theme.

392. *Learning the Ropes*

Syndicated, 10/88 to 10/89

Cast: Lyle Alzado *(Robert Randall)*, Nicole Stoffman *(Ellen Randall)*, Yannick Bisson *(Mark Randall)*.

Facts: Robert Randall is a single father (separated from his wife, Anne) who cares for his two teenage children, Ellen and Mark. Robert has a daytime job as a history teacher and vice principal at the Ridgedale Valley Preparatory School, and a second, nighttime job as a wrestler called "The Masked Maniac."

Home to the Randalls is 34 Hampton Street (phone number 555-6613). Even though Ellen and Mark are not wealthy, they attend Ridgedale Prep, "a private school for rich kids," became their father teaches there. Robert's main concern is to see that Ellen and Mark get a college education. (His mind was eased one day when his health club manager asked him to become the Masked Maniac, "the animal of the wrestling ring." Robert originally did it for laughs; but when the character caught on and the money started rolling in, he kept the job to provide for Ellen and Mark's future. Robert must now keep his wrestling job a secret because school regulations prohibit teachers from moonlighting.)

When Mark discovered his father was a wrestler (he was looking for his tennis racket and found the mask in the closet), he was thrilled ("It's like finding out your father is Freddy from *Nightmare on Elm Street*"). Ellen's reaction was just the opposite when Mark told her. She was stunned and unable to accept it ("It's not every day you get to see your father maiming people").

Ellen is the smarter of the two children. She does the cooking (and is very proud of her ability to prepare meals) but does not want to be a housewife and mother—"I want to be a career woman." Even though Robert tells Ellen that she is "naturally beautiful" and doesn't "need to wear makeup," Ellen says that she does have to wear makeup—"I look more like Madonna when I do." Mark, the mischievous one (he enjoys, for example, throwing water balloons at cheerleaders), wants "the big bucks job."

The Burger Palace is Ellen and Mark's afterschool hangout; fellow wrestlers call Robert "The Professor"; Robert's black mask has a skull and crossbones in the center of the forehead area and an *M* on each side of the eyeholes (Dr. Death and Gary Sabaugh performed the Masked Maniac stunts). Anne, who is never seen, is in England studying to become a lawyer. Beth (Jacqueline Mason) is Ellen's boy-crazy girlfriend; and Carol Dickson (Sheryl Wilson) is the school's French teacher.

In the original, unaired pilot version, Anne was said to have walked out on her family and Robert was romantically involved with Carol (this episode and two previously taped episodes were re-edited to delete the romantic aspect, which was not a part of the actual series).

Theme: "Learning the Ropes," vocal by David Roberts.

393. *Leave It to Beaver*

CBS, 10/11/57 to 9/26/58
ABC, 10/3/58 to 9/12/63

Cast: Hugh Beaumont *(Ward Cleaver)*, Barbara Billingsley *(June Cleaver)*, Tony Dow *(Wally Cleaver)*, Jerry Mathers *(Beaver Cleaver)*, Ken Osmond *(Eddie Haskell)*, Frank Bank *(Lumpy Rutherford)*.

Facts: Life in a small American town (Mayfield) as seen through the experiences of the Cleaver family: parents Ward and June and their children, Wally and Beaver. The Cleavers first live at 211 Pine Street (also given as 211 Maple Drive and 211 Pine Avenue); they sell this house to a Mr. Benner and move to a new home at 211 Lakewood Avenue (KL5-4763 is their phone number).

Ward grew up on Shannon Avenue in the Shaker Heights section of town. He was on the shot put team in high school and a member of the 4H Club (he entered a hog in a fair and won first prize). Ward, who studied engineering in college, was an engineer with the Seabees during World War II. He now works as a businessman (his exact profession is never revealed), and he drives a sedan with the license plate WJG 865 (later KJG 865). Ward enjoys fishing at Crystal Lake and reads the *Mayfield Press*. June's maiden name is Bronson. She loves to wear jewelry, is an excellent cook and housewife and received a letter in basketball at boarding school.

Wallace, nicknamed "Wally," is their firstborn son. He attended the Grant Avenue Grammar School and later Mayfield High School. He is a three letter man in high school, and 53.2 seconds is his best time on the Mayfield swimming team. Wally is captain of the varsity football team and wears Arabian Knights aftershave lotion. Wally is in the eighth grade and Beaver in the second grade when the series begins (they buy an alligator for $2.50 from an ad in the comic book *Robot Man of Mars* in the first episode). Wally has locker number 221 (its combination is 10-30-11); JHJ 335 is the license plate of his green convertible. Wally attends State College in last season episodes. His first dinner date was with Julie Foster; they dined at the White Fox Restaurant.

Theodore, Ward and June's second child, is named after June's Aunt Martha's brother. Theodore acquired the name "Beaver" from Wally. Wally couldn't pronounce Theodore and said "Tweder." Ward and June thought "Beaver" sounded better. Beaver, who attends the Grant Avenue School, wears a green baseball cap, hates "mushy stuff," likes to "mess around with junk" and would rather smell a skunk than see a girl. His favorite "fishin' hole" is Miller's Pond. The biggest thing Beaver does is walk in the gutter on his way home from school. He played a tree in his kindergarten play and the lead (Hans) in his fifth grade play, *The Little Dutch Boy*. Mary Margaret Matthews (Lori Martin), who called Beaver "Teddy," was the first girl Beaver found pretty and not "icky." He took up the clarinet for the school orchestra in the second grade; as a kid he had a teddy bear named Billy; he is also called "Beave."

Edward ("Eddie") W. Haskell is Wally's wisecracking friend. He is extremely polite to adults but mean to everybody else (in another episode, Eddie mentions that his middle name is Clark). Eddie attends the same schools as Wally and lives at 175 Grant Avenue. He was the first one to get a credit card (from the Universal Gas and Oil Company; card number 06212312), and he is allergic to mayonnaise. He calls Wally "Sam," "Gertrude" and "Ellwood," and Beaver "Squirt." Woody Woodpecker is Eddie's favorite cartoon character and television show.

Clarence Rutherford, who is nicknamed "Lumpy," is Wally and Eddie's friend. He attends the same schools as Wally and Eddie and has "a sickly green" car with the license plate PZR 342. Lumpy takes tuba lessons, and 433-6733 is his phone number.

Fred Rutherford (Richard Deacon) is Lumpy's father and Ward's boss (he calls Ward "Lord of the Manor"). Fred originally talked about having three children: a girl, Violet (Wendy Winkelman), and two boys who were offered football scholarships. Later he had only two children: Lumpy and Violet (Veronica Cartwright). Helen Parrish, Majel Barrett and Margaret Stewart played Fred's wife, Gwen (originally called Geraldine), throughout the series run.

Larry Mondello (Rusty Stevens), Gilbert Grover (Stephen Talbot) and Hubert ("Whitey") Whitney (Stanley Fafara) are Beaver's friends (Larry was first credited as Robert Stevens; Gilbert was first introduced as Gilbert Harrison, then Gilbert Gates and finally Gilbert Bates). Judy Hessler (Jeri Weil) is the obnoxious girl who kisses up to teachers and annoys Beaver and his friends; she was replaced by Karen Sue Trent as Penny Woods (same type of character in last season episodes).

Julie Foster (Cheryl Holdridge) is Wally's girlfriend (Cheryl originally played the role of Gloria Kusig, a classmate of Wally's). Cornelia Raeburn (Doris Packer) is the principal of the Grant Avenue School; and Alice Landers (Sue Randall) is Beaver's teacher. Gus (Burt Mustin) is the old fire chief Beaver visits at Fire Station Number 5.

Madison is mentioned as being the neighboring town. June's aunt, Martha, who sends umbrellas as gifts at Christmas, first appeared when June's unseen sister, Peggy, had a baby and Martha came to stay with them. In the original pilot film, "It's a Small World" (syndicated in 1957 on "Studio '57"), Casey Adams played Ward, Paul Sullivan was Wally and Harry Shearer was Freddie (the character would later become Eddie). See also "The New Leave It to Beaver."

Relatives: Edgar Buchanan (Ward's uncle, *Billy*), Madge Kennedy (June's aunt, *Martha*), Karl Swenson and George O. Petrie (Eddie's father, *George Haskell*), Ann Doran and Ann Barton (Eddie's mother, *Agnes Haskell*), Ross Elliott and Bill Baldwin (*Julie's father*), Madge Blake (*Larry's mother*), Carleton G. Young and Alan Ray (Gilbert's father, *John Bates*); Claudia Bryar (*Gilbert's mother*).

Theme: "The Toy Parade," by Michael Johnson and Melvyn Lenard.

394. *Leg Work*

CBS, 10/3/87 to 11/7/87

Cast: Margaret Colin (*Claire McCarron*), Frances McDormand (*Willie Pipal*), Patrick James Clarke (*Fred McCarron*).

Facts: Claire McCarron is an assistant district attorney who quits her job to become her own boss. McCarron Investigations is the business she begins to make ends meet. Claire charges $500 a day plus expenses and lives at 365 East 65th Street in New York City. She has a dog named Clyde and drives a silver Porsche (license plate DEX 627; mobile phone number 555-4365). When a case bothers her and she has to think, Claire makes oatmeal raisin cookies — one of two foods she can prepare (the other is coq au vin — chicken in wine sauce). Claire also has a collection of rare Lionel "O" gauge electric trains that she inherited from her father. The title refers to all the walking Claire must do because her car is always in need of repair (it also refers to Claire's shapely legs, which she prominently displays by wearing miniskirts).

Fred McCarron is Claire's brother, a lieutenant with the Office of Public Relations at One Police Plaza in Manhattan; and Wilhelmina ("Willie") Pipal is Claire's friend, the Manhattan assistant district attorney. The series' alternative title was "Eye Shadow" (Margaret had the choice of using either title. While she preferred neither, she chose "Leg Work").

Michael Omartian composed the "Leg Work" theme.

The original concept began as a pilot called "Adams Apple" (CBS, 8/23/86) in which Sydney Walsh played Toni Adams, a private detective working out of Manhattan. (The title refers to Toni, who works the Big Apple — New York.) Carolyn Seymour is Tricia Hammond, the D.A.; and Cherry Jones is Janice Eaton, Toni's contact at the Manhattan D.A.'s office. Toni has a dog named Mary Jo. Both "Leg Work" and "Adams Apple" were produced by Frank Abatemarco.

In "Leg Work," Claire is a former assistant D.A. This refers to the series "Foley Square" (CBS, 12/11/85 to 4/8/86), in which Margaret Colin played Alex Harrigan, an assistant D.A. working out of the Criminal Courts Building at Foley Square in Manhattan. Clearly, aspects of "Foley Square" and "Adams Apple" were combined to create "Leg Work."

395. *Lenny*

CBS, 9/10/90 to 11/23/90
CBS, 12/15/90 to 3/9/91

Cast: Lenny Clarke (*Lenny Callahan*), Lee Garlington (*Shelly Callahan*), Jenna Von Oy (*Kelly Callahan*), Alexis Caldwell (*Tracy Callahan*), Peter Dobson (*Eddie Callahan*).

Facts: When Leonard ("Lenny") Joseph Callahan met Shelly Morrison, he had to borrow ten dollars for their first date. When Lenny brought Shelly home to meet the family, his younger brother, Eddie, remarked, "What great torpedoes—and what a tush!" Lenny and Shelly eventually married and set up housekeeping in Boston. Lenny works at two jobs: gasman for Boston Utility, and doorman at an un-named hotel at night. Shelly is kept busy caring for their three daughters, Kelly, Tracy and baby Elizabeth (played by the Hall twins).

Lenny was born in 1953, and as a kid had a teddy bear named Buzzer. Shelly calls Lenny an easy touch ("A friend in need is a friend of Lenny's"). The Boston Celtics are Lenny's favorite baseball team, and Fielding Insurance handles his life insurance. Lenny enjoys cold pizza in the morning and can belch the song "White Christmas." His favorite robe is a terrycloth one he stole from their honey-moon hotel; he calls Shelly "Shell" and "Love Muffin."

Kelly, their 13-year-old daughter, receives an allowance of three dollars a week. She is a complainer, like her father, and has a negative view of everything. She desperately wants "cleavage like my other girlfriends" and feels she is overweight, unattractive and going to be flat chested. Kelly had her ears pierced at Hadley's Jewelry Store and attends Saint Theodore's Catholic Grammar School.

Tracy, their 10-year-old daughter, receives an allowance of two dollars a week. She has a doll named Wendy and a hamster she calls Fuzzball. Tracy is very bright and very knowledgeable for a girl her age (for instance, she watches a lot of television, especially the medical channel, and is thus an expert on all types of diseases). Tracy also attends Saint Theodore's, and both she and Kelly hide their money in a box under their beds. Tracy is addicted to peanut butter (a habit Shelly is trying to break) and eats Nutri Grain cereal for breakfast (as does Kelly). Tracy is a member of the In-dian Braves (a Scout troop). She belongs to the Muttinhead tribe; her name is Little Fawn. Lenny is the troop leader and is called Fat Bear; Lenny's father, Pat, is also a member and is called Chief Aching Back. Lenny remarks that for a ten-year-old girl, Tracy is somewhat unusual. He did ask her, "When you look out into space at night, do you feel homesick?" Tracy performed her first dance recital as a daffodil in "The Flower Dance."

Edward ("Eddie") Callahan is Lenny's uncouth brother (he has no respect for anyone and, in the presence of Kelly and Tracy, refers to breasts as "ta ta's," "hooters" and "honkers"). Eddie is on the run from the cops, has 1,500 unpaid parking tickets, writes bad checks, and is wanted for mail fraud and petty theft. Although he should be in jail, he's just smart enough to stay one step ahead of the police. For income, Eddie receives a disability payment (he goes under the name Louie Lonzo and pretends to have a glass eye). His favorite hangout is Snooky's Copa Cabana Club.

Relatives: Eugene Roche (Lenny's father, *Patrick ["Pat"] Callahan*), Alice Drummond (Lenny's mother, *Mary Callahan*), Judith Hoag (Lenny's sister, *Megan Callahan*). Pat and Mary hide their vacation money in a tin can under the sink; Mary believes that Michael J. Fox got his name because he was raised by wolves. In the episode of 1/5/91, Megan married Richard Johnson (Scott Lawrence), a black

lawyer. Henry Harris played Richard's father, Tom Johnson, and Ann Weldon was Richard's mother, Sarah Johnson.

Relatives Not Seen: Pat's brother, Shawn Callahan (who sends Pat a gift of whiskey once a year; the whiskey is made in Shawn's basement in Ireland and can remove paint); Lenny's uncle, Chick.

Theme: "Lenny's Theme," vocal by Dion.

Note: In the original, unaired pilot film, Alyson Croft played 13-year-old Trisha Callahan (who became Kelly), and America Martin was 10-year-old Kelly Callahan (who became Tracy for the series).

396. *Leo and Liz in Beverly Hills*

CBS, 4/25/86 to 6/6/86

When the Lovely Lady Bra Manufacturing Company sud-denly begins to show a tremendous profit, its owners, Leo Green (Harvey Korman) and his wife, Liz (Valerie Perrine), leave New Jersey to begin new lives in Beverly Hills. They suddenly become an affluent couple and will go to any lengths to impress people with their idea of class. Stories relate their attempts to fit in among the rich and famous.

Leo, Liz and their daughter, Mitzie Green (Sue Ball), live in a mansion at 105 North Bevon Drive; their phone number is 555-6636; Leo drives a car with the license plate 392 EGC.

Lucille Trumbly (Julie Payne) is their housekeeper; Leonard (Michael J. Pollard) is their handyman; and Diane and Jerry Fedderson (Deborah Harmon, Ken Kimmons) are their neighbors (at 103 North Bevon; Jerry is a private prac-tice accountant). Peter Ackroyd played Diane's son, Bunky Fedderson.

Carrie Fisher played Mitzie Greene in the pilot episode, which aired as "The Couch" (10/16/85) on "George Burns Comedy Week."

David Frank composed the music; the theme is the original recording of "Mr. Sandman."

397. *Life Goes On*

ABC, 9/12/89 to 5/23/93

Cast: Patti LuPone (*Libby Thatcher*), Bill Smitrovich (*Drew Thatcher*), Kellie Martin (*Becca Thatcher*), Monique Lanier and Tracey Needham (*Paige Thatcher*), Chris Burke (*Corky Thatcher*), Mary Page Keller (*Gina Giordano*).

Facts: Glen Brook, Illinois, is the setting for a dramatic look at the lives of the Thatchers, a Catholic family of five: parents Libby and Drew, and their children, Paige, Becca and Corky. They have a dog named Arnold ("the semi–wonder dog") and live at 305 Woodridge Road; 555-1967 is their phone number, and JNE 734 (later RAH

Life Goes On. **Left to right: Monique Lanier, Kellie Martin, Bill Smitrovich, Christopher Burke, Patti LuPone and Arnold.**

207) is their car license plate number. The automatic coffeemaker seen in the opening theme activates at 6:55 A.M. (later, 6:40 A.M.); Drew and Libby's alarm clock rings at 7:00 A.M. (later, 6:45 A.M.). Libby buys mostly No Frills products at the supermarket.

On their first date together, Andrew ("Drew") Thatcher, a divorced construction worker with a young daughter (Paige), and Elizabeth ("Libby") Giordano, a singer and dancer, saw the movies *Curse of the Swamp Creature* and *Curse of the Stone Hand* at the Glen Brook Drive-In (in Drew's old

Plymouth). They later married. Drew acquired work with the Quentico Construction Company, and Libby gave up her career to raise a family—Paige and their natural children, Becca and Corky. Drew later quits his job and purchases a diner called the Glen Brook Grill. Libby, now working as an account executive at the Berkson and Berkson ad agency, temporarily gives up her job to help Drew run the new business. Drew and Libby became parents of a baby boy (Nicholas James Thatcher) in the episode of 5/5/91 ("Proms and Prams").

Libby worked under the stage name Libby Dean and starred in a production of *West Side Story*. Her favorite television soap opera is "Forever and a Day"; Libby's boss, Jerry Berkson (Ray Buktenica), calls her "Libs." Drew's dream car is an Austin Healey 3000; Martin Sporting Goods was the first account for Berkson and Berkson.

Paige, whose natural mother is Katherine Henning (Lisa Banes), is the oldest child and is called "Button" by Drew. She loves to paint and has two rabbits named Sammy and Matilda. She first worked as a receptionist at the Matthews Animal Hospital. The original Paige (Monique Lanier) left home at the end of the first season. When Paige (Tracey Needham) returned in November 1990, she moved back home but seemed to lack direction. She worked at several temporary jobs, then enrolled in acting classes at Glen Brook Community College. Paige next worked as a waitress at the family diner, then as a cross worker (doing what is necessary, from picking up metal scraps to stacking pipes) at Stollmark Industries. Shortly after, Paige meets and falls in love with a roustabout sculptor named Michael Romanov (Lance Guest). They marry and run off to Europe, but the marriage is short-lived. In the episode "Portrait of a Scandal" (9/27/92), Paige leaves Michael ten weeks later and returns home when he chooses his work over her (he left her stranded in Bulgaria). Paige also loses her job at Stollmark but begins the Darlin Construction Company with a former co-worker named Artie (Troy Evans). Michael called Paige "Gus."

Rebecca, nicknamed "Becca," is 15 years old, weighs 85 pounds and attends Marshall High School. She is a bright student and a member of both the debating club and the gymnastics team. Becca is also a talented ballerina and hopeful writer who fears that her figure will never develop (in the opening theme, Becca looks sideways into a mirror and, referring to her small bust, remarks, "Come on, where are you guys already?"). When Becca turned 16 (10/20/91), Paige called her "a major babe"; the compliment helped Becca to shed "the ugly duckling" image she held of herself. Becca's favorite breakfast is French toast with whipped cream. She wrote for the *Underground Marshall*, the school's forbidden tabloid and took ballet lessons from Lillian Doubsha (Viveca Lindfors), a world-famous prima ballerina.

Becca's relationship with Jesse McKenna (Chad Lowe), a boy who is HIV positive, is the focal point of many 1992 episodes. Jesse is a budding artist, and he painted a picture of Becca in the nude—it was displayed at the Bookstore. Prior to Jesse, Becca dated Tyler Benchfield (Tommy Puett); his license plate read DLW 352 (later GOK 720).

Maxene ("Maxie") Maxwell (Tanya Fenmore) is Becca's best friend. She is physically more developed than Becca, but not as bright (she is somewhat flaky and boy-crazy). Just the opposite is Rona Lieberman (Michele Matheson), a blonde bombshell who is the most beautiful girl at school—and the envy of both Becca and Maxie. Rona is an average student who seems to shun the friendship of other girls. She uses her beauty to become the best at everything. Becca, under the sponsorship of the Salcedo Bagel Company, and Rona, backed by the Glen Brook Savings Bank, entered the Tri-State Teenage Miss Pageant. Becca was crowned third runner-up and received a $5,000 scholarship; Rona, who has been entering beauty pageants since she was a child (pushed by her mother), received first runner-up honors and a $10,000 scholarship.

Charles, nicknamed "Corky" and "The Cork," has Down syndrome. He first attended the Fowler Institution, then Marshall High School. Though older than other freshmen, Corky became "one of the guys," proving that despite a handicap, he can become a part of society and do what other kids can do—from playing drums to running for class president. He first worked at the family diner, then as an usher at the Glen Brook Theater (he earns $165 every two weeks). He originally had a paper route and competed in the Glen Brook 50K Bike Race (he was number 277). Although he came in last, it was a victory for Corky as he was able to accomplish something. His favorite sandwiches are ham and cheese on whole wheat, and sliced turkey on raisin bread.

Like Paige, Corky impulsively married, but he is determined to make his marriage work. Amanda Swanson (Andrea Friedman), a girl with Down syndrome, is Corky's wife. She is attending college, and they live on what Corky makes as an usher.

Angela ("Gina") Giordano, Libby's younger sister, was brought on to help Libby care for the family during her pregnancy (11/25/90 to 5/5/91). Gina is the mother of a pretty nine-year-old girl named Zoe (Leigh Ann Orsi) and is separated from Zoey's father, Dennis Rydell (Drew Pillsbury), who deserted Gina when he learned she was pregnant. Gina is impressed by people who can cook; she ran an unnamed cheesecake business. After the birth of Libby's child, Gina moved out and returned to school.

Relatives: Al Ruscio (Libby's father, *Sal Giordano*), Penny Santon (Libby's mother, *Teresa Giordano*), Gina Hecht (Libby's cousin, *Angela Giordano*), Patti LuPone (Libby's cousin, *Gabrielle ["Gaby"] Giordano*), Pat Hingle (Drew's father, *Jack Thatcher*), Rick Rosenthal (Drew's brother, *Richard Thatcher*), Claire Berger (Drew's cousin, *Frances*), Jennifer Warren (*Rona's mother*), Julie Cobb (Maxie's mother, *Marina Maxwell*), Sandy Baron (Jerry's father, *Sam Berkson*), Drew Snyder (Amanda's father, *Bill Swanson*), Charlotte Stewart (Amanda's mother, *Collette Swanson*).

Flashbacks: Jenna Pangburn (*Paige as a girl*), Heather Lind (*Becca as a girl*), Bert Remsen (*Drew's grandfather;* ghost sequence).

Theme: "Ob-La-Di, Ob-La-Da" (opening theme), by John Lennon and Paul McCartney; and "Life Goes On," (closing theme) by Craig Safan.

398. *The Life of Riley*

On April 13, 1948, NBC presented "The Life of Riley," a test film (the term *pilot* had not yet come into use) for a television version of the radio series of the same title. Herb Vigran was Chester A. Riley, a riveter for the Cunningham Aircraft Company in Los Angeles; Alice Drake was his wife, Margaret ("Peg") Riley; and Lou Krugman and Jo Gilbert played their neighbors, Jim and Honeybee Gillis. When this failed to generate a series, NBC tried again and cast Lon Chaney, Jr., in the role of Chester A. Riley (information based on the actual print; no record of an air date could be found). This too failed to generate a series for NBC.

The following year, the DuMont Network presented the first "Life of Riley" series (10/4/49 to 3/28/50; also aired on NBC stations where DuMont had no affiliates) with the following cast: Jackie Gleason and Rosemary DeCamp as parents Chester and Peg Riley, and Gloria Winters and Lanny Rees as their children, Barbara ("Babs") and Chester ("Junior") Riley.

Chester, who lives at 1313 Blue View Terrace, and his neighbor, James ("Jim") Madison Gillis (Sid Tomack), who resides at 1311 Blue View Terrace, earn $59 a week as riveters for Stevenson Aircraft and Associates in Los Angeles. Chester and Peg, and Jim and his wife, Olive ("Honeybee") Gillis (Maxine Semon), were married in a double wedding ceremony in Brooklyn, New York, in 1932; they moved to California together to begin new lives. Junior and Jim's son, Egbert Gillis (George McDonald), attend John J. Boskowitz Junior High School; Babs attends North Hollywood High; Peg calls Chester "Riley."

Bill Green (and later Emory Parnell) played Riley's boss, Carl Stevenson; Bob Jellison was Riley's friend, Waldo Binny; and John Brown played Digby ("Digger") O'Dell, "the friendly undertaker." (When Riley gets into a jam and mutters something like "I'll wind up diggin' ditches," Digby appears—"And what is wrong with digging ditches? It is I, Digby O'Dell, the friendly undertaker." The conversation that follows always helps Riley overcome his troubles.)

A second series appeared on NBC from 1/2/53 to 8/22/58 which continued to depict the misadventures of Chester A. Riley (William Bendix), his wife, Peg (Marjorie Reynolds), their daughter, Babs (Lugene Sanders), and their son, Junior (Wesley Morgan). The Rileys first lived at 1313 Blue View Terrace in Los Angeles, then at 5412 Grove Street (this same house is later given the address 3412 Del Mar Vista). Chester, who is called "Riley" by Peg, works as a riveter for Cunningham Aircraft in Los Angeles; his catchphrase is "What a revoltin' development this is." Babs married Don Marshall (Martin Milner) and set up housekeeping at 1451 Blue View Terrace, Apartment number 3.

In a flashback episode, Peg recounted her and Chester's early years together. When Chester married Peggy Barker, they were broke and moved in with her parents in Brooklyn. Shortly after, when Chester learned that Peg was pregnant, he told her to quit her job ("I want you to be with the baby when it's born") and found a job as a milkman for the Sunbeam Dairy. (He had a horse-drawn wagon, a route

with mostly "the beer drinking crowd" and a basic pay of four dollars a day. His horse was named Daisy, the milk cost 13 cents a quart and he made a commission on every quart he sold.)

With their newfound prosperity, Chester and Peg moved into their own apartment—a $15 a month "walk down" (basement) apartment located under a bowling alley near the East River and next to the subway. It was after the birth of the baby (Babs) that they moved to Los Angeles.

Other Roles: Tom D'Andrea (Riley's neighbor, *Jim Gillis*), Veda Ann Borg, Marie Brown and Gloria Blondell (Jim's wife, *Olive ["Honeybee"] Gillis*), Gregory Mitchell (Jim's son, *Egbert Gillis*), Sterling Holloway (Riley's friend, *Waldo Binny*), Henry Kulky (Riley's friend, *Otto Schmidlap*).

Relatives: Larraine Bendix (Chester's niece, *Annie Riley*), Mary Jane Croft (Chester's sister, *Cissy Riley*), James Gleason and James Gavin (Chester's father, *Pa Riley*), Sarah Padden (Chester's mother, *Ma Riley*), Jack Kirkwood (Peg's uncle, *Bixby*), Bea Benaderet (*Honeybee's mother*).

Theme: "The Life of Riley," by Lou Kosloff (1949) and Jerry Fielding (1953).

399. *Life with Luigi*

CBS, 9/25/52 to 12/25/52
CBS, 4/9/53 to 6/4/53

Cast: J. Carrol Naish (*Luigi Basco*, 1952), Vito Scotti (*Luigi Basco*, 1953), Alan Reed (*Pasquale*, 1952), Thomas Gomez (*Pasquale*, 1953), Jody Gilbert (*Rosa*, 1952), Muriel Landers (*Rosa*, 1953).

Facts: With a devious plan to get his overweight daughter, Rosa, married, a man named Pasquale arranges for his friend, Luigi Basco, to join him in Chicago's Little Italy.

Luigi arrives in the United States (at Ellis Island) from Italy on 9/27/47 with three dollars to his name. Pasquale sets Luigi up in an antique business, and the struggles of an immigrant to adjust to the American way of life—and escape Pasquale's endless matchmaking attempts—are the focal point of the series. In these early episodes, stories begin and end with Luigi reading a letter he wrote to his "Mama Basco" in Italy.

Pasquale, who calls Luigi "Cabbage Puss" and "Little Banana Nose," runs Pasquale's Spaghetti Palace at 19 North Halsted Street. Luigi, who was born in the town of Cantaloma, runs a shop called Luigi Basco, Antiques at 21 North Halsted Street (he lives in the back of the store, and his phone number is Circle 2-0742). His most cherished possession is a bust of George Washington that was made in 1833. Luigi does his banking at the Chase National Bank (he opened an account with $50; Pasquale charges him $40 a month rent). Pasquale has been running his café for 26 years. Luigi patterned his store after the Marshall Field Department Store; on his second day in the United States, Luigi was conned into buying Union Station for five dollars (the writers forgot he had only three dollars).

While Luigi is grateful to Pasquale for bringing him to Chicago, he refuses to marry the 250 pound Rosa ("I would rather finda my owna girl"). Despite Luigi's attitude toward Rosa, Pasquale still looks after Luigi ("like Mama tiger help little baby deer") and hopes one day to change Luigi's mind ("What if a girl is beautiful," says Pasquale, "and she gotta nice shape, pretty hair and all that. That's nothing. My Rosa's got some-a-thing none of those girls is got—character. When you see my Rosa in a bathing suit there is so much to pinch you gonna go crazy with power"). Luigi wears a size 38 suit; Pasquale a size 54 suit; and Rosa a size 50 dress.

Other Regulars: Miss Spaulding (Mary Shipp), Luigi's nightschool English teacher; Schultz (Sig Ruman), the owner of Schultz's Delicatessen; Olson (Ken Peters) and Horowitz (Joe Forte) are Luigi's classmates. Joe (Ben Welden) is Pasquale's deadbeat customer.

In 1953 the series returned with a new cast and a slightly revised format. Luigi Basco is now working for Pasquale as a waiter in Pasquale's Spaghetti Palace. Luigi still lives at 21 North Halsted Street, but his phone number is now Hollycort 9937. Pasquale's efforts to marry Rosa are still featured. Mary Shipp reprised her role as Miss Spaulding. Based on the radio series of the same title.

Theme: "Oh, Marie," by Lud Gluskin.

400. *Lightning Force*

Syndicated, 10/1/91 to 9/12/92

An abandoned shipping yard in the Canadian Northwest is the secret headquarters for an elite intelligence unit called the Lightning Force. It was organized by Mike Rodney (Michael A. Jackson) for the International Organization for Anti-Terrorism. Mike assembled the best of the collective strike forces to help the FBI and CIA battle the growing problem of terrorism. (Mike was killed during the first assignment; the strike force used Mike's nickname of "Lightning" as their official name.)

Matthew ("Matt") Coltrane (Wings Hauser) is a lieutenant in the U.S. Army and now heads the team. He is nicknamed "Trane" and is a very private person (nothing is known about him, other than that he was in the Intelligence Division).

Jo Marie Jacquard (Guylaine St. Onge) was an agent with the French Security Service. She is a combat pilot, computer expert and selective terminator. She is a genius at unscrambling codes and is known to get even with anyone who crosses her (for example, she killed the man who betrayed her father).

Winston Churchill Staples (David Stratton) was a lieutenant with the Canadian Forces, Seventh Field Regiment. He is a trained engineer and an expert in demolition. He is the youngest member of the group and the most impetuous.

Sieb Abdul Rahmad (Marc Gomes) is a colonel in the Egyptian Army. He is an expert in operations and intelligence and is also a language specialist.

Schaur Tozer composed the "Lightning Force" theme.

401. *Little House on the Prairie*

NBC, 9/11/74 to 9/21/82

Cast: Michael Landon (*Charles Ingalls*), Karen Grassle (*Caroline Ingalls*), Melissa Gilbert (*Laura Ingalls*), Melissa Sue Anderson (*Mary Ingalls*), Lindsay and Sidney Green Bush (*Carrie Ingalls*), Wendi and Brenda Turnbeaugh (*Grace Ingalls*).

Facts: Under the Homestead Act, the Ingalls family receives 160 acres of land in Kansas. Parents Charles and Caroline and their daughters, Mary, Laura and Carrie, leave their home in Wisconsin's Big Woods and journey west to begin new lives. After battling the elements—the weather, wolves and Indians—Charles manages to build a home, barn and stable—only to learn that the government has moved their boundaries and they must pack up and start all over again.

Their journey next takes them to Walnut Grove in Plum Creek, Minnesota (1878), where Charles, called "Pa" by Laura, builds his "Little House on the Prairie" for his family. The family's experiences are viewed through the sentimental eyes of Laura, the second-born daughter, who hopes one day to become a writer. Mary is the oldest daughter, and Carrie the youngest, until the birth of Grace later in the series.

Charles ran a lumber mill but found it necessary to take whatever jobs he could find to make money. Mary, who later lost her sight through disease, married Adam Kendall (Linwood Boomer) in the episode of 11/6/78 ("The Wedding"). Adam is a blind teacher Mary met when she attended the Sleepy Eye School for the Blind. (Adam's sight was restored in the episode "To See the Light," 12/1/80.) Laura, who later taught at the Plum Creek School, married Almanzo Wilder (Dean Butler) in the episode of 9/29/80 ("Laura Ingalls Wilder"). Almanzo is the brother of the school's second teacher, Eliza Jane Wilder (Lucy Lee Flippin). (Eliza replaced the original schoolteacher, Grace Beadle [Charlotte Stewart], who left when she married. In 1886 Eliza Jane married Harve Miller [James Cromwell] and left town; Laura then became the schoolmarm.)

Laura's dogs were named Jack and Bandit; Charles called her "Half Pint."

Isaiah Edwards (Victor French), commonly called Mr. Edwards, was Charles's best friend and, in later episodes, his partner in the lumber mill. Isaiah was married to Grace (Bonnie Bartlett and Corinne Michaels); they were the parents of three adopted children: Aliscia (Kyle Richards), John (Radames Pera) and Carl (Brian Part).

Nels (Richard Bull) and his bossy wife, Harriet Oleson (Katherine MacGregor), ran Oleson's Mercantile, Plum Creek's only general store. They have a rather nasty (spoiled) daughter named Nellie (Alison Arngrim) and a mischievous son named Willie (Jonathan Gilbert). When Harriet started a restaurant, she first gave Nellie the responsibility of running it (Nellie's Restaurant); it eventually became Harriet's Restaurant when Nellie, a Protestant, married Percival Dalton (Steve Tracy), a Jewish accountant, in the episode of 5/5/80 ("He Loves Me, He Loves Me Not"). They moved to New York to help Percival's mother after his father's death. Without Nellie, Harriet went into a state of deep depression. Her spirits were lifted when she and Nels adopted an orphan girl named Nancy (Allison Balson), a Nellie lookalike who was twice as obnoxious. Willie also married. In the episode of 3/14/83 ("May I Have This Dance") he and Rachel Brown (Sherri Stoner) were wed.

Charles too adopted three children after Mary left to live in Sleepy Eye: Albert (Matthew Laborteaux), Cassandra (Missy Francis) and James (Jason Bateman). The characters of James and Cassandra were introduced in the episode "The Lost Ones" (5/4/81). Their last name was Cooper and they were the offspring of Alvin (George McDaniel) and Sarah Cooper (M.E. Loree). When their parents were killed, they are adopted by Charles (in the episode of 10/19/81, "Growing Pains").

Jonathan Garvey (Merlin Olsen) purchased a farm in Walnut Grove and became friends with the Ingallses. He was married to Alice (Hersha Parady) and had a son named Andy (Patrick Laborteaux).

In the spinoff series "Little House: A New Beginning" (NBC, 9/27/82 to 3/21/83), Charles, who is unable to make a living in Plum Creek, sells his "Little House" to John (Stan Ivar) and Sarah Carter (Pamela Roylance), a young couple with two children: Jeb (Lindsay Kennedy) and Jason (David Friedman). Charles, Caroline, Carrie and Grace move to Fir Oak, Iowa; Laura and Almanzo remain behind to continue the lumber mill Charles started and ran with Mr. Edwards. The time is 1887. Shortly after, when Almanzo's brother, Royal Wilder (Nicholas Pryor), dies of a heart attack, Laura gives up her job as a teacher to care for Royal's daughter, Jenny (Shannen Doherty), as well as her own infant daughter, Rose. Etta Plum (Leslie Landon) becomes the new schoolmarm.

Other Regulars: Dabbs Greer (*the Reverend Robert Alden*), Ted Gehring (*Ebenezer Sprague*, the banker), Ketty Lester (*Hester Sue*, Harriet's restaurant cook), Karl Swenson (*Lars Hanson*, the lumber mill owner), Kevin Hagen (*Dr. Baker*).

The series is based on the *Little House* books by Laura Ingalls Wilder (Laura was born in a log cabin on the edge of the Big Woods in 1867. She based her stories on her travels with her family by covered wagon through Kansas, Minnesota and finally the Dakota Territory, where she met and married Almanzo Wilder. The books were first published in 1935, when Laura was 68 years old).

Relatives: Barry Sullivan (Caroline's father, *Frederick Holbrook*), Anne Archer (Harriet's niece, *Kate Thorvald*), Rossie Harris (Almanzo's nephew, *Rupert Wilder*), Ham Larson (Almanzo's nephew, *Myron Wilder*), John McLiam (Sarah's father, *Mr. Carter*).

Theme: "Little House on the Prairie," by David Rose.

Note: Three NBC TV movies aired: *Little House: Look Back to Yesterday* (12/12/83). Charles, now a purchasing agent for J.R. Bennett and Company in Iowa, and Albert (who hopes to become a doctor) return to Walnut Grove for a visit—an event that turns tragic when Albert is found to have an incurable blood disease.

Little House: The Last Farewell (2/6/84). The citizens of Walnut Grove unite to protect their homes from Nathan Lassiter (James Karen), an unscrupulous mining entrepreneur who has purchased their land and now wants them to leave.

Little House: Bless All the Dear Children (12/17/84). The story, set in Walnut Grove during the Christmas of 1896, relates Laura's efforts to find her infant daughter, Rose, who has disappeared and whom Laura fears has been kidnapped.

402. *Live-in*

CBS, 3/20/89 to 6/5/89

Sarah Mathews (Kimberly Farr) is manager of the clothing department of Macy's Department Store in Manhattan. Her husband, Ed Mathews (Hugh Maguire), owns the Mathews Sporting Goods store in New Jersey. They are the parents of two teenage boys, Danny (Chris Young) and Peter (David Moscow), and an infant daughter named Melissa (Allison and Melissa Lindsay). When Sarah decides it is time to return to work after her maternity leave, she applies for a live-in housekeeper at the Broder Domestic Agency.

The agency finds Lisa Wells (Lisa Patrick), a beautiful Australian girl, and the Mathewses pay the cost of flying her to the States (it is not explained why the agency had to go to Australia to find a live-in housekeeper). Lisa grew up in the Australian Outback and lived in a small house with seven brothers and sisters. She now has her own room at the Mathewses' home (30 Hogan Place in New Jersey; telephone number 555-0012) and the responsibility of caring for Melissa and watching over Danny and Peter.

Danny and Peter attend Whitney High School. Peter, a freshman, has yet to become overly concerned about girls, and he and Lisa get along fine together. Danny, a sophomore, is just the opposite, a girl-crazy teenager who can't believe a girl like Lisa is living in his house. He has set his goal as seeing her naked—despite the fact that fate seems determined not to let that happen (for example, Lisa caught him making a peephole in the bathroom wall). Lisa's experiences in America are depicted as she cares for the Mathews children.

Muriel Spiegleman (Jenny O'Hara) is Sarah's neighbor and commuting partner to Manhattan; she has a dog named Corkey. Ray Walston appeared as Sarah's father, Jack Hanson.

Ray Colcord composed the theme, "Happy Together."

403. *Living Dolls*

ABC, 9/26/89 to 12/30/89

The theme lyric "Pretty baby, you've got the look" refers to Charlene ("Charlie") Briscoe (Leah Remini), Caroline Weldon (Deborah Tucker), Emily Franklin (Halle Berry) and Martha Lambert (Alison Elliott), four beautiful 16-year-old models who live with Trish Carlin (Michael Learned), a gorgeous former high fashion model turned agent (owner of the Carlin Modeling Agency, which she operates from her home at 68th Street and Madison Avenue in New York City).

The girls attend Lexy High School and share two rooms in Trish's home. Charlie is from Brooklyn and first appeared on the "Life's a Ditch" episode of "Who's the Boss?" (as Sam's [Alyssa Milano] friend). She is streetwise and doesn't believe she is as beautiful as people tell her she is. Martha, whose nickname is "Pooch," is from (and constantly talks about) Idaho. Caroline enjoys shopping at Bloomingdale's, and her biggest challenge is to decide what to wear each day. She is a C student and a bit dense. She hates to read and joined the Book on Tape Club (her initial selections were *Moby Dick,* as read by Sandy Duncan, *The Grapes of Wrath,* read by Ernest and Julio Gallo, Arnold Schwarzenegger reading *Little Women* and Engelbert Humperdinck reading *Tom Jones*). Emily is a straight–A student and wants to become a doctor ("Being a doctor is all I ever dream about"); she gets extremely upset if she scores badly on a test. Caroline calls her "M." Despite the fact that the girls strive to do their best, their teachers consider them "Human Hangers" ("Girls who are so pretty that they can't be smart"). The girls did their first music video for rock star Nick Austin (Robert Bauer). Trish, who appeared on the covers of such magazines as *Vogue, Vanity Fair, Redbook* and *Ladies' Home Journal,* has a houseplant she calls Amadeus.

David Moscow plays Trish's son, Rick (whom Charlie calls "Twerp"); Marion Ross appeared in two episodes as Trish's sister, Marion; and Edward Winter was Trish's ex-husband, Todd Carlin.

In the original, unaired pilot film, the cast was: Michael Learned (Trish Curtis), Leah Remini (Charlie), Melissa Willis (Caroline), Vivica Fox (Emily), Alison Elliott (Martha) and Jonathan Ward (Rick Curtis).

John Beasley and John Vester composed the theme.

404. *Logan's Run*

CBS, 9/16/77 to 1/16/78

Cast: Gregory Harrison *(Logan 5),* Heather Menzies *(Jessica 6),* Randy Powell *(Francis 7),* Donald Moffat *(Rem).*

Facts: In the year A.D. 2319, an atomic holocaust ravages the world. The remaining segment of civilization establishes itself in the City of Domes, a programed society wherein no one over the age of 30 is permitted to live. At precisely that age, everyone goes willingly into the Carousel for the Ceremony of the Great Sleep, where they are led to believe that their lives will be renewed; in reality, they are exterminated. Those who try to circumvent this tradition are called Runners and become the prey of the Sandmen, whose duty is to pursue and destroy them. Runners are seeking Sanctuary, a supposed haven where all are free to live beyond the age of 30.

Logan 5, a Sandman, begins to question the Carousel. Never having seen a reborn citizen, Logan becomes curious. He follows a male Runner to Quadrant 4. There he meets Jessica 6, a girl runner who helps those seeking Sanctuary. Jessica confirms Logan's doubts and tells him that the Carousel means death; she also convinces him that beyond the city there is a Sanctuary. Before Logan is able to do anything, Francis 7, a Sandman, appears and orders Logan to destroy the runners. Logan's hesitation prompts Francis to kill the male; as he is about to kill Jessica, Logan knocks him unconscious. Now, a traitor, Logan becomes a Runner and joins forces with Jessica in an attempt to find Sanctuary.

Concerned about Logan's escape, the Council of Elders, who run the City of Domes (a.k.a. Dome City), assign Francis the task of returning Logan and Jessica so they can be used as an example and testify that there is no Sanctuary. Francis is then told the Carousel is a myth—but necessary because the city can support only a limited number of people. He is promised a seat on the council when he completes his mission. Stories follow Logan and Jessica's adventures with Rem, the android with humanlike qualities who abandoned his robot-run society, as they search for Sanctuary—before Francis finds and captures them.

As Logan, Jessica and Rem proceed in their search, they encounter a world of unknown dangers never before faced in the City of Domes. Logan's most dangerous adventure: being imprisoned by Dr. Rowan (Ed Nelson), a scientist bent on creating a master race based on Hitler's concept of society. Rowan's tests have produced only cowards; he seeks to implant the missing trait of courage by extracting it from Logan, who shows no signs of fear.

Jessica's most perilous encounter was that with the Patron (William Smith) and his wife, Rama II (Kim Cattrall), who have developed a process for splitting human beings into two separate people. When Jessica is forced into the processing chamber, she emerges as Jessica Positive (Good) and Jesssica Negative (Evil). Logan and Rem are confronted with a dilemma: how to convince the two Jessicas to become one again when Negative has sided against them and Positive wants to remain in what she considers an idyllic state.

Rem's electromagnetic attraction to Ariana (Mariette Hartley), a beautiful female robot, brought forth his human emotions and nearly cost Logan and Jessica their lives when they were placed in a dream analysis station. Rem and Ariana put their mechanical genius to work and released Logan and Jessica from jeopardy.

Lance LeGault as Matthew 12, was the first Runner to make his escape from the Carousel. He is now the Provider of his own dictatorial society in a life that parallels the one from which he escaped. (The sole function of the personnel around him is to protect him from invaders. They are rewarded with an hour of joy provided by a computer's memory bank before being exterminated.)

Morgan Woodward (Morgan), Wright King (Jonathan) and E.J. Andre (Martin) were the leaders with speaking roles in the City of Domes. The series is based on the feature film of the same title.

Theme: "Logan's Run," by Jerrold Immel.

405. *The Lone Ranger*

ABC, 9/15/49 to 9/12/57

Cast: Clayton Moore (*The Lone Ranger*; 1949–51, 1954–57), John Hart (*The Lone Ranger*; 1952–53), Jay Silverheels *(Tonto)*, Chuck Courtney *(Dan Reid)*.

Facts: "A fiery horse with the speed of light, a cloud of dust and a hearty Hi-yo Silver! The Lone Ranger! With his faithful Indian companion Tonto, the daring and resourceful masked man of the plains led the fight for law and order in the early West. Return with us now to those thrilling days of yesteryear; the Lone Ranger rides again!"

While the Lone Ranger and Tonto "cut a trail of law and order across seven states, forcing the powers of darkness into the blinding light of justice," it was a tragic event that led to the Lone Ranger's evolution. As a Texas Ranger, John Reid and five other Rangers (Captain Dan Reid [John's brother], Jim Bates, Jack Stacey, Joe Brent and Ben Cooper) were assigned to capture the notorious Butch Cavendish and his Hole in the Wall Gang. At Bryant's Gap, a canyon about 50 yards wide and bound by cliffs, the Rangers are attacked by the Cavendish Gang. Butch, believing that all the Rangers have been killed, rides off.

Later that day, Tonto, a Potawatomi Indian riding through the valley hunting for animals, discovers a lone survivor of the attack, John Reid.

Tonto takes Reid into the shelter of a cave and begins to nurse him back to health. When Reid regains consciousness and first sees Tonto, he remembers him as the Indian he befriended as a child. When Tonto was a young brave, his village was raided by renegade Indians. His parents were killed and he was left for dead. A young John Reid found Tonto and nursed him back to health. It was at this time that Tonto called Reid "Kemo Sabe"—translated as both "Trusted Scout" and "Faithful Friend."

Amid the rocks broken by countless years of wind and storm, there lies a small patch of grassland—and six graves, each marked by a crudely constructed cross. One cross bears the name of John Reid, placed there by Tonto to convince Cavendish that all the Rangers had been killed; to conceal the fact that one Texas Ranger had lived to avenge the others—the Lone Ranger.

To conceal his true identity, Reid fashions a mask from the cloth of his brother's black vest. At first, Reid and Tonto posed as outlaws to enable them to apprehend the Cavendish Gang—some of which were hanged, others imprisoned.

Having accomplished this goal, Reid and Tonto became fighters for justice and strove to maintain law and order in a restless territory.

Reid's trademark is the silver bullet—a precious metal that constantly reminds him to shoot sparingly and to remember always the high cost of human life. The silver comes from a mine Reid inherited. Jim Blaine (played by Ralph Littlefield) is the oldtimer who works the Ranger's secret silver mine; George Wilson (Lyle Talbot) is the Ranger's secret banker in Border City who exchanges silver for money for him.

To help people in a capacity other than that of the Lone Ranger, Reid uses various disguises to assist without arousing suspicion (for instance, the Old Timer, Professor Horatio Tucker, the smooth-talking Medicine Man, Don Pedro O'Sullivan, the Swede, and Juan Ringo, the Mexican bandit).

Reid's horse is named Silver; Tonto's horse is Scout; Dan (John's nephew, who assisted them in later episodes) has a horse named Victor. Tris Coffin played John's brother, Dan Reid; Glenn Strange appeared as Butch Cavendish; and David Leonard played Father Paul, Reid's friend, the padre of the San Brado Mission. The series is based on the radio program of the same title (created by George W. Trendle).

As the Lone Ranger and Tonto completed a mission and rode off into the sunset, someone would say, "Who was that Masked Man?" "Why, don't you know? That was ... the Lone Ranger!"

Theme: "The William Tell Overture," by Rossini ("Les Preludes," by Liszt, is the show's bridge music).

406. *Lost in Space*

CBS, 9/15/65 to 9/11/68

Cast: Guy Williams *(John Robinson)*, June Lockhart *(Maureen Robinson)*, Marta Kristen *(Judy Robinson)*, Angela Cartwright *(Penny Robinson)*, Billy Mumy *(Will Robinson)*, Mark Goddard *(Donald West)*, Jonathan Harris *(Zachary Smith)*, Bob May *(The Robot)*, Dick Tufeld *(Robot's Voice)*.

Facts: The time: October 16, 1997. The place: Alpha Control Center. The mission: Explore the planet Alpha Centauri in the hope that it will provide homes for ten million families a year and reduce the desperate overcrowding on the planet Earth.

A series of deep thrust telescopic probes into neighboring galaxies have established that Alpha Centauri is the only planet within the range of current technology with the ideal conditions for supporting human life.

Two million families volunteer for the mission. But only one family, the Robinsons, possess the unique balance of scientific achievement, emotional stability and pioneer resourcefulness that make them the perfect candidates to begin the colonization of deep space. The Robinsons will spend the 98 years of their voyage frozen in a state of suspended animation. They will be traveling at the speed of light in the *Gemini 12*, "the culmination of 40 years of intensive research and the most sophisticated hardware yet devised by the mind of man."

Heading the expedition is Dr. John Robinson, a professor of astrophysics, his wife, Maureen Robinson, a distinguished biochemist, and their children, "Judith ("Judy") Robinson, age 19; Penelope ("Penny") Robinson, age 11; and William ("Will") Robinson, age nine. Their assistant is Dr. Donald West, a world famous radio astronomer.

The Robinsons and Dr. West are placed in a state of suspended animation. The *Gemini 12* is launched. All is

Lost in Space. **Left to right:** Angela Cartwright, Mark Goddard, Marta Kristen, Jonathan Harris, June Lockhart, Guy Williams, Billy Mumy.

progressing smoothly until the ship encounters a fierce meteor shower and is thrown off course. The ship is traveling at 18,400 mph and cannot be shifted by Alpha Control to escape the meteors. "The ship's fantastic ability to regenerate its own damage control is now the last hope of the safety of the Robinson family and the success of the flight. Alpha Control's final analysis of the *Gemini 12* might indicate that, unhappily, the spaceship has been either damaged or it must be presumed Lost in Space."

We see a page in a diary and hear the voice of John Robinson: "December 3rd in the year 2001. None of us knows for sure how long we were in suspended animation. Our atomic clock indicates three and one-half years, but we're not positive. We do know for a fact that it is six months since our landing on this unknown planet. Thank

heavens we survived that terrible crash, which completely disabled the spaceship. We are hopeful of its eventual repair and our ability to use it again. Meanwhile all goes reasonably well. We've established a base camp, domesticated some wildlife and cultivated a small farm." (Penny has a simian pet she calls Debbie.)

Their new world changes drastically when Dr. West discovers that the seasons are changing and they will not be able to survive this planet's extreme cold. They abandon their saucer shaped craft and head for the tropics and warmth. After several frightening experiences (a giant creature, a cave of lightning bolts, a turbulent sea), they find the tropics.

"December 8th, 2001. Our great adventure in the wild sea is happily behind us. At last we reached the tropics . . .

So much has happened in our short stay on this strange planet that we take nothing for granted. We have experienced dangers unknown by Earth-bound man. We breathe easily now—but only for the moment. Our every instinct tells us there are wonderful adventures ahead."

This was the original filmed concept of "Lost in Space." It has never aired and is quite different from the concept that finally materialized. The unaired version is not campy; it is a frightening look at what life might be like for a family lost in space. The situaions are tense and scary; Bernard Herrmann's musical score is chilling and adds the final ingredient to make one feel the tension as the Robinsons struggle for survival. With a much toned down musical score by Johnny Williams, comic relief from Jonathan Harris, and not so intense situations, a different format emerged.

In the year 1967, scientists become concerned with the problem of overpopulation. After ten years of preparation and study, construction is begun on the *Jupiter II,* a ship that will initiate humanity's move into space. It will be programed to land on a planet (unnamed) orbiting the planet Alpha Centauri; scientists believe this planet is the only one within the range of contemporary technology that can support human life.

In 1997 the *Jupiter II* is completed at a cost of $30 billion. The ship stands two stories high and contains the most sophisticated scientific equipment imaginable. The upper level contains the guidance control system, and an electronic elevator connects both floors. Both levels are operationally self-contained. The lower deck houses the pulsating atomic motors "that will propel the ship to new worlds." Living quarters, staterooms and galleys complete the lower deck. There is also an environmental control robot (called Robot) whose key function is to perform the final analysis of the physical environment of the new planet. The *Jupiter II* has also been shrouded by vigorous security precautions, as other nations, even more desperate for breathing room, may resort to sabotage to beat the United States to the new planet.

A geologist, Major Donald West, is chosen to pilot the *Jupiter II,* and the Robinsons, one of two million families who volunteered for the project, are selected to colonize the new planet. West and the Robinsons (John and Maureen and their children, Judy, Penny and Will) are to spend the five and a half years of their voyage frozen in a state of suspended animation that will terminate automatically as the spaceship enters the atmosphere of the new planet.

As countdown preparations continue, an enemy agent named Colonel Zachary Smith sneaks aboard the *Jupiter II* and reprograms the robot to destroy the radio transmitter and the cabin pressure control system eight hours after takeoff.

At minus two minutes and counting, the Robinsons enter the freezing tubes. Will and Penny enter first, followed by Maureen, Judy, Donald and John. At zero minus 45 seconds, the freezing units are activated. All hatches are secured and Smith is trapped aboard the craft.

The ship is launched and is proceeding normally until Smith's unaccounted-for extra weight (200 pounds) alters the ship's flight path. Suddenly the ship encounters a massive meteor shower. Unable to steer the ship, Smith awakens West in the hope of saving the ship. "Who the devil are you?" West asks. "I was trapped just before takeoff," Smith explains. "You helium nitrogen ratio; I neglected to adjust the balance valve. The hatch closed before I could get off." West accepts Smith's explanation and manages to steer the ship clear of the shower; but they are off course.

West revives the Robinsons. Smith insists that they reprogram the ship and return to Earth; John thinks it would be best to continue with the mission. Just then Smith notices the departure time clock: 7:57 and counting. He attempts but fails to reprogram the robot. The robot's rampage starts as scheduled and seriously damages the ship before West immobilizes it by disconnecting its power pack.

The *Jupiter II* is now beyond the range of Alpha Control's tracking. West assumes they are lost two million miles in space. "There is not one constellation you can recognize," he says (during its rampage, the robot sent the ship into hyper drive; it traveled into space until West regained use of the controls). The ship crash-lands on an unknown planet that becomes their temporary home. First season episodes relate their adventures on the planet (which Will believes to be Cerberus); second and third season stories find the Robinsons back in space when the *Jupiter II* is repaired and they decide to continue with the mission—despite Smith's persistent efforts to get them to return to Earth.

John was a professor of astrophysics at the University of Stellar Dynamics. Maureen, a biochemist with the New Mexico College of State Medicine, is the first woman in history to pass the International Space Administration's grueling physical and emotional screenings for intergalactic flight. Judy, it was said, "heroically postponed all hopes for a career in the musical comedy field"; D-12 is her room on the ship. Penny, who has an I.Q. of 147, is interested in zoology; she had an invisible friend she discovered in a grotto and called Mr. Nobody. Will, who graduated from the Campbell Canyon School of Science at the age of nine, held the highest average in the school's history; his field is electronics.

Donald, a graduate student from the Center for Radio Astronomy, "rocketed the scientific world with his theory of other planets' fitness for human habitation." Don was also an officer in the U.S. Space Corps. Colonel Zachary Smith, champion of the Oxford Chess Club three years in a row, operated under the code Aeolus-14 Umbre for his unidentified superiors.

The relationship between Smith and the Robot provides much of the comic relief. Smith sees the Robot as a slave and calls it such names as "Potbellied Pumpkin," "Bucket of Bolts," "Disreputable Thunderhead," and "Tin Plated Tattletale." His favorite name for it is "Booby" ("Press the button, Booby," "Move it, Booby," "Silence, Booby"). The Robot most often obeys Smith, but does object at times: "A robot does not live by programing alone. Some culture is required to keep my tapes in balance. My computer tapes are not programed for day and night work. I need eight hours rest like other robots." The Robot defends itself with electrical discharges.

Smith, who eats peanut butter and salami sandwiches before bed, is most often responsible for a setback. He is a coward and greedy; if an opportunity comes up to make money, he will take advantage of it (for example, he turns the *Jupiter II* into a hotel called Smith's Happy Acres Hotel to accommodate [and fleece] visiting aliens). He calls Will "William." In the opening, right before the theme plays, a countdown is seen, beginning with 7 (followed by 6, 5, 4, 3, 2, 1).

Other Roles: Sue England (various female computer voices), Vitina Marcus *(Athena, the Green Alien Lady)*, Dee Hartford *(Nancy Pi Squared,* the space beauty), Fritz Feld *(Mr. Zumdish,* the space entrepreneur. He was originally the keeper of the Intergalactic Department Store, then owner of a tourist business called Outermost Fundish Ltd. ["Let Fun Be Your Guide"], and finally owner of the Zumdish Insurance Company), Leonard J. Stone *(Farnum the Great),* Dawson Palmer (various alien roles).

Relatives: Henry Jones (Zachary's cousin, *Jeremiah Smith*).

Theme: "Lost in Space," by Johnny Williams.

Note: On 9/8/73, ABC aired "Lost in Space," an animated special in which Craig Robinson (voice of Michael Bell) is the pilot of the *Jupiter II,* now a space shuttle. Other voices: Jonathan Harris (Professor Smith), Sherry Alberoni (Dodi Carmichael), Vincent Van Patten (Linc Robinson). The story finds the crew battling the Tyranos, metallic creatures on a strange planet, when the *Jupiter II* is shot down.

407. *Love and Curses*

Syndicated, 3/4/91 to 4/8/91

Cast: Kate Hodge *(Randi Wallace),* Neil Dickson *(Ian Matheson).*

Facts: A revised version of "She-Wolf of London" (see entry). Randi Wallace is a pretty Los Angeles student attending the University (as it is called) in London and preparing her thesis on disproving the supernatural. She was attacked and bitten by a werewolf while doing research on the Moors, and now through a curse, she becomes a beast when the moon is full. Ian Matheson is Kate's love interest, a professor of mythology who teaches at the University.

When the new version begins, it is learned that the University has decided to phase out Ian's classes. He is not upset because his experiences with Randi (encountering supernatural creatures in the "She-Wolf" version) prove that everything he has been teaching is wrong ("I don't know if I can go on teaching if I don't know the truth. Perhaps I'll join the ranks of the idle rich.").

In Los Angeles, Randi's friend, Ellen Cravitz (Mary-Ellen Dunbar) believes space aliens have invaded her neighborhood in Northridge, and she calls Randi in London. Randi becomes curious and decides to investigate. Ian decides to go with her and check on the progress of one of his books, which is being made into a movie at Monumental Pictures. They fly to Los Angeles via Pan Am.

In Northridge, Randi and Ian discover that trolls are living beneath the town and have made their way from the Earth's center to the surface "to eat all the Big Macs we can and get crystal clear TV reception." When all seemed lost, the Grand Wizard of the Golden Oracle (Milton Selzer) appears to help. He originally banished the trolls to the center of the Earth and disposed of them by turning them into frogs.

With their first adventure behind them, Randi and Ian decide to stay in Los Angeles and, they hope, find someone who can cure Randi of her curse. Ian acquires a job as the host of "How Strange, with Dr. Matheson," on Channel 89, when his movie deal falls through and his former contact, now the station owner, Skip Seville (Dan Gilvezan) needs a show to replace "Count Phil's Creature Theater." Ian sees the show as interviewing "scholars, researchers and academics of the highest order"; Skip sees it as "hype, horror and hooters." By the second episode, Randi is working with Ian as his producer. They now live in a luxurious apartment. Behind the bookcase is a secret room that contains a cell—to keep Randi from killing when she becomes a werewolf. The six-episode series follows Randi and Ian's adventures as they investigate supernatural occurrences in the hope of finding a cure for Randi (they never did).

The only other show mentioned on Channel 89 was "Bikini Baking with Bambi" (Skip hired Bambi [Heather Haase] "because she's a 36D cup").

Theme: "Love and Curses," by Steve Levine.

408. *Love and War*

CBS, 9/21/92 to the present

Cast: Susan Dey *(Wally Porter),* Jay Thomas *(Jack Stein),* Suzie Plakson *(Mary Margaret),* Michael Nouri *(Kip Zakaris),* Joel Murray *(Ray Litvak),* Joanna Gleason *(Nadine Berkus).*

Facts: The Blue Shamrock is a quaint 1940s-like bar in Manhattan. It is slow on Monday nights and closes daily at 12:30 A.M. It is located between a bail bondsman and a credit dentist. Ike Johnson (John Hancock) owns the establishment, and bar regulars are newspaper columnists Jack Stein and Mary Margaret ("Meg") Tynan and sanitation worker Ray Litvak.

Wallis ("Wally") Porter is a beautiful 35-year-old businesswoman and famous chef who owns the trendy Chez Wally Restaurant on 72nd Street. She is married to a conceited actor named Kip Zakaris. After five and a half years, the marriage breaks up. When Wally loses the restaurant in the divorce settlement, she walks out of the courtroom and wanders into the shabby Blue Shamrock. She becomes intoxicated (too many double vodkas) and buys the bar from Ike for $70,000. Stories focus on Wally's efforts to turn the Blue Shamrock into a thriving business, and on her romantic ups and downs with Jack.

Wally lives in Apartment C at 1016 East 74th Street. She attended the Cordon Bleu School in Paris after college and can debone a chicken in 20 seconds. She can serve 12 dinners in 21 minutes and once received a letter from Julia Child telling her that her *coq au vin* was the best she ever tasted. Wally was born in Connecticut.

Wally first saw Kip in an off–Broadway production of *West Side Story* (where he played Jet number 2). Other credits for Kip are *The Front Page* (off–Broadway), the deranged typesetter on "Lou Grant"; Ozzie the Terrorist in the television movie *Victory at Entebbe*; a vampire in the film *Vampire Hotel II*; the insane crossing guard in an episode of "Sweating Bullets"; the star of a pilot film called "Turf and Surf" (about a meat inspector who drives a Ferrari); Stone, the bartender, on the television serial "The Bold and the Beautiful"; and Mr. York, the psychopathic math tutor in an episode of "Jake and the Fatman." When Kip appeared in *Richard III,* the newspapers called him "a nightmare in tights."

Jack writes the opinion column "The Steinway" for the *New York Register.* He is 42 years old and lives in Apartment 4C (address not given). Jack won the Algonquin Award for his story on illiteracy, and he frequents Maurice's House of Steaks and Waffles. For a charity event, he and columnist Jimmy Breslin ran naked across the Brooklyn Bridge. Jack and Wally exchanged gifts to celebrate their two month anniversary: they unknowingly gave each other the same item: red satin boxer shorts.

Ray works as a "sanitation engineer" (garbage man) for the New York City Department of Sanitation. He calls the bar's lone pinball machine "Line Drive." Mary Margaret, who is nicknamed Meg, is a sportswriter for the *Register.* Nadine is the Shamrock's waitress. She drives a minivan with the license plate SUPER MOM. She lives in Westchester; her kids are in college, and her husband, Charles, is in prison for stock fraud.

Ike drove a 1970 Buick (license plate XUJ 345) and worked as the Shamrock's bartender after selling the bar to Wally. Ike passed away one night while watching television (reflecting the real life death of John Hancock). Several weeks later, Ike's brother, Abe Johnson (Charlie Robinson), approaches Wally and tells her that Ike left him 20 percent of the bar in his will. When Abe learns that Wally can't pay him the 20 percent, as the bar has not yet turned a profit, Abe offers himself a job—as the new bartender. Abe is an unemployed auto worker ("I worked on all the losers—the Corvair, the Pinto, the Gremlin and the Pacer. I then went to Ireland and worked on the DeLorean").

In the original, unaired pilot version, titled "Love Is Hell," Jay Thomas was columnist Jack Simon and Joel Murray was Joe, the garbage man. In some preproduction sources, Susan Dey is mistakenly listed as playing Meg.

Theme: "Love and War," by Jonathan Tunick.

409. *The Love Boat*
ABC, 9/29/77 to 9/5/86

Merrill Stubing (Gavin MacLeod) is captain of the *Pacific Princess,* a luxury cruise ship that has been nicknamed "The Love Boat" by her crew: cruise director Julie McCoy (Lauren Tewes), purser Burl ("Gopher") Smith (Fred Grandy), Dr. Adam Bricker (Bernie Kopell) and bartender Isaac Washington (Ted Lange). Merrill's daughter, Vicki Stubing (Jill Whelan) became the assistant cruise director (1979), and Julie's sister, Judy McCoy (Patricia Klous), replaced Julie as the cruise director in 1985. Merrill married Emily Haywood (Marion Ross), a wealthy widow, in the episode of 5/24/86 (Emily became the special events director). Ashley ("Ace") Covington-Evans (Ted McGinley) became the ship's photographer in 1984 (later the purser, when Gopher left). To spice up the cruises, the gorgeous "Love Boat Mermaids" were added in 1985: Susie (Deborah Bartlett), Maria (Tori Brenno), Jane (Nancy Lynn Hammond), Amy (Teri Hatcher), Patti (Deobrah Johnson), Starlight (Andrea Moen), Mary Beth (Beth Myatt), and Sheila (Maccarena). On May 4, 1985, the *Pacific Princess,* which is owned by the Pacific Cruise Lines in Los Angeles, became the *Royal Princess* in honor of its one-thousandth guest star, Lana Turner.

There are nine decks on the ship. Guests stay on such decks as the Fiesta Deck, the Promenade Deck and the Aloha Deck. Pirate's Cove is the barroom (the restrooms are called "Pirates" and "Damsels"); dinner is served in the Coral Room at eight bells (eight o'clock); and entertainment can be found in the Acapulco Lounge and the Terrace Room. The ship docks at the Port of Los Angeles.

Crews Quarters Cabin C-125 is Julie's room and C-130 is Isaac's cabin. Merrill, who wears a size 16 collar, has only a name plate on his door—CAPTAIN MERRILL STUBING. Julie's clock radio rings at 7:30 A.M.; in high school, Julie was called "Monkey McCoy." To change what she thought was a drab image, Julie dyed her hair platinum blonde; when she tried to dye it back to strawberry blonde, it turned green.

Isaac is from Oakland, California. He attempted to write a science fiction book called *Invasion from a Forgotten Galaxy*; when this failed, he penned a novel called *Pacific Passions* (about the people who board the ship). His nickname in junior high school was "Freight Train."

Vicki calls her father "Captain Merrill" and has a cabin that adjoins his; she has a pet frog she calls Frog and looks up to Julie for guidance in becoming a woman (when she first "signed on," Vicki felt unattractive and feared she would be flat chested). Adam, the much married and divorced ship's physician, wanted to be a radio sports writer when he was 14 years old.

The actual concept for "The Love Boat" began as the "Luxury Liner" episode of "The Dick Powell Show" (NBC, 2/12/63), wherein Rory Calhoun played Victor Kihlgren, the captain of a cruise ship. James Stewart was slated to be the host and the series was to chronicle dramatic incidents in the lives of the passengers. A second pilot, "The Love Boat" (ABC, 9/17/76), featured the crew of the *Sun Princess*: Captain Thomas Allenford (Ted Hamilton), Dr. Adam O'Neill (Dick Van Patten), cruise director Jeri Landers (Terri O'Mara), yeoman purser "Gopher" (Sandy Helberg), and Isaac the bartender (Theodore Wilson). "The Love Boat II" pilot (ABC, 1/21/77) featured Captain Thomas Madison (Quinn Redeker), cruise director Sandy Summers (Diane Stilwell), purser Burl ("Gopher") Smith

(Fred Grandy), bartender Isaac Washington (Ted Lange) and Dr. Adam Bricker (Bernie Kopell). "The Love Boat III" pilot, a.k.a. "The New Love Boat (ABC, 5/5/77), actually sold the series and featured the series cast (Gavin MacLeod, Lauren Tewes, Bernie Kopell, Fred Grandy and Ted Lange).

On 2/12/90 "The Love Boat: A Valentine Cruise" aired on CBS and reunited most of the original cast for a cruise to the Caribbean via the *Sky Princess*. Kim Ulrich signed on as Kelly Donaldson, the cruise director. Repeating their roles: Gavin MacLeod (Captain Merrill Stubing), Bernie Kopell (Dr. Adam Bricker) and Ted Lange (Isaac Washington, now the chief purser). Vicki Stubing (Jill Whelan) is now a travel agent (she is aboard the "Love Boat" as part of her vacation); Kelly is a former English literature major; Emily, Merrill's wife, was said to have passed away. CBS repeated the episode as "The Love Boat: A Summer Cruise" (even though Valentine's Day was mentioned on the show) on 7/20/91.

Relatives: Red Buttons (Merrill's uncle, *Cyrus Foster*), Olivia de Havilland (Merrill's aunt, *Hilly*), Phil Silvers (Merrill's father, *Merrill Stubing, Sr.*). Gavin MacLeod (Merrill's brothers, *Milo* and *Marshall Stubing*), Bonnie Franklin (Merrill's ex-wife, *Stacy Stubing Scoggstaad*), Norman Fell (*Julie's father*), Betty Garrett (*Julie's mother*), Carol Channing (Julie's aunt, *Sylvia*), Richard Dean Anderson (Julie's cousin, *Carter Randall*), Linda Blair (Carter's wife, *Muffy Randall*), Ellen Bry (Judy's cousin, *Gretchen*), Ethel Merman (Burl's mother, *Rosie Smith*), Bob Cummings (Burl's father, *Elliott Smith*), Melissa Sue Anderson (Burl's sister, *Jennifer ["Chubs"] Smith*), Pearl Bailey (Isaac's mother, *Millie Washington*), Isabel Sanford (Isaac's aunt, *Tanya*), Mel Stuart (Isaac's uncle, *Charles*), Juliet Prowse (Doc's ex-wife, *Samantha Bricker*), Elizabeth Ashley (Doc's ex-wife, *Nancy Bricker*), Stephanie Beacham (Doc's ex-wife, *Elaine Riskin*), Heidi Bohay (Doc's new wife, 11/21/86, *Cheri Sullivan Bricker*), Cyd Charisse (Doc's ex-mother-in-law, *Connie Carruthers*).

Theme: "The Love Boat," vocal by Jack Jones (1977–85), Dionne Warwick (1985–87).

410. *Love on a Rooftop*

ABC, 9/6/66 to 1/6/67

Cast: Judy Carne (*Julie Willis*), Peter Deuel (*Dave Willis*), Rich Little (*Stan Parker*), Barbara Bostock (*Carol Parker*).

Facts: The boy is Dave Willis, an apprentice architect with the firm of Bennington and Associates, who earns $85.37 a week. The girl is Julie Hammond, the beautiful 22-year-old pampered daughter of a rich car salesman, who is studying to become an artist. They meet one day when Dave, preparing to eat lunch at a construction site, drops his liverwurst on rye sandwich. The sandwich falls several stories and lands in Julie's open handbag as she is walking past the site. Dave chases after his sandwich and when he and Julie meet, it's love at first sight. They marry and set

up housekeeping in a rooftop apartment at 1400 McDoogal Street in San Francisco.

"You're rich, go ahead and admit it, you're rich" is Dave's reaction when he learns that Julie is wealthy (her reaction: "You make it sound like some sort of disease"). Dave, being the independent type, insists that they live on his income. Julie agrees and relinquishes her world of luxury—a situation that angers her father, Fred Hammond (Herbert Voland), who was in Europe when she and Dave married. "You may as well know right now," Fred says when he first meets Dave. "If I had been here I would have stopped this marriage." A dumbfounded Dave responds simply, "Nice to meet you too, Mr. Hammond."

While Julie's mother, Phyllis Hammond (Edith Atwater), is hoping only the best for Julie and Dave, Fred firmly believes that Dave will never be able to support her. "We may have some rough times," Dave tells Fred, "but we're going to be all right . . . because we love each other . . . and we're gonna do it on our own with no help from you or anyone."

When Fred and Phyllis were first married, they had an apartment that was smaller than "the pillbox," as he calls Dave and Julie's apartment. Fred says he didn't mind it: "I didn't know the difference then. I thought everybody lived that way." They were also so broke that they lived on beans and rice for weeks. It was only when Fred hit it big that he realized life could be better. He wants only the good life for Julie and strives to convince Dave to accept his help (which Dave constantly refuses).

Julie considers the roof a patio; Dave considers it a roof ("Honey, where I come from, anything with TV antennas and pigeons is a roof"). Julie is emotional and sensitive, and tends to give inanimate objects human characteristics. She feels, for example, that a bed should be a friend of the family and purchased with love, and that when a telephone rings, "it cries to be picked up when nobody does."

Dave and Julie keep their spare key in the lamp next to the door (there are no numbers on the doors). Julie is also studying to be a fashion artist and Dave's favorite dinner is beef Stroganoff. Dave's former girlfriend was Barbara Ames (Gayle Hunnicutt), an airline stewardess. For a wedding gift, Fred gave Julie and Dave a window (the apartment was windowless; Julie had painted one on a wall to represent one).

Dave and Julie's friends and downstairs neighbors are Stan and Carol Parker. Like the Willises, they too are struggling to make ends meet on a small income. Stan is an idea man who hopes one day to make it big by inventing something that everyone needs (the problem is, "I can't figure out what it is because it is so obvious"). While Stan often says, "Sometimes I amaze myself," one of his "crazy" ideas that doesn't sound so crazy 25 years later was opening an agency called "Drive a Drunk" ("Somebody gets drunk at a party and they phone me to drive them home"). Other ideas were "The Stan Instant Alert System" (a cowbell hooked up to a door to alert a person inside an apartment that the door has been opened; and the "L.L.L.Y." (Let's Lose Leap Year): "When I'm through, February wil have 30 days just like every other month. All I need is 59¼ seconds for four years and no more leap year." He figured to do this with the "Parker Time Concept" — "A clock that gains two minutes and 43 seconds a day, 365 days a year and uses up February 29th. Everyone will have to have my clock."

Charles Lane appeared as Dave's boss, Bert Bennington and Hope Summers played his wife, Bertha Bennington.

Theme: "Love on a Rooftop," by Howard Greenfield and Jack Keller.

411. *Love, Sidney*

NBC, 10/28/81 to 12/25/82
NBC, 3/28/83 to 8/29/83

Cast: Tony Randall (*Sidney Shorr*), Swoosie Kurtz (*Laurie Morgan*), Kaleena Kiff (*Patti Morgan*), Chip Zien (*Jason Stoller*).

Facts: Apartment 405 at 136 East 46th Street in Manhattan is the home of Sidney Shorr, a lonely, middle-aged commercial artist. Sidney, who is a homosexual, has been depressed since the death of his lover, Martin (seen only in a photograph on the fireplace); he now has no social life and little or no fun.

One of the few joys in Sidney's life is seeing Greta Garbo films. At the Thalia Theater, where the cost of a ticket is two dollars, Sidney is seated midway in the theater watching *Camille* (with Greta and Robert Taylor). A pretty, spirited young actress named Laurie Morgan is sitting directly behind him. While she is slurping soda through a straw and munching on popcorn, Sidney is becoming very emotional over the film. When the movie ends, Sidney is crying into his handkerchief. "Hey, sir, are you all right?" asks Laurie. "It's wonderful, it's wonderful," replies a teary eyed Sidney. When Laurie remarks that *Camille* is one of her least favorite Garbo films, she and Sidney get into a discussion about Greta. In an attempt to convince Laurie that Greta is a great actress, Sidney takes her to his apartment to show her his Garbo photo collection.

Sidney's discussion with Laurie seems to make a new man out of him — he is happy. When Laurie is about to leave, a thunderstorm begins. Laurie convinces a reluctant Sidney to let her spend the night. "One thing," she says. "Don't get any ideas." "Me?" responds Sidney. "You don't have to worry about me." "Oh, I get it, that's good," says Laurie. "I'll see you in the morning then." (This exchange of dialogue is virtually the only indication that Sidney is gay. NBC bowed to Moral Majority objections about a gay character and changed Sidney's sexual preference to a point where he could be either straight or gay.)

The following day, Sidney is changed; he is cheerful and looking forward to the day ahead. He prepares breakfast for Laurie (she has bagels and lox for the first time) but is saddened again when she leaves. That night, as he is sitting down to dinner, the doorbell rings. It is Laurie. Sidney's eyes light up as she enters and says, "We'll split the rent." Sidney responds by saying he never lived with a woman. "I'll be the best thing that ever happened to you, exclaims

Laurie. She immediately begins by redecorating the dreary eight room apartment. That night Laurie prepares her first meal for Sidney — Goulash Joe E. Brown (regular goulash spiced with "lots of tabasco sauce").

Three months later the apartment is cheery and Sidney is a changed man. Sidney also begins to get jealous when Laurie starts daring, and he becomes what he believes is a father figure to her.

On Christmas Eve, 1981, Sidney and Laurie begin a tradition: eggnog and the exchange of one gift. He gives her a book called *The Life of Eleonora Dale*. Laurie begins to cry and tells Sidney she is seeing a married man (not named) and that she is pregnant. She also tells Sidney that the man has given her the money to have an abortion. Sidney, who strongly opposes this, talks Laurie out of having an abortion: "I'll take care of the baby . . . Let this be your Christmas gift to me." They agree (Sidney is to become the baby's uncle).

Six and a half months later, at Flower Hospital, Laurie gives birth to a girl. Laurie names her Patti (after her favorite song as a kid, "Patty Cake"); Laurie also gives the baby a middle name — Greta — as a reference to how they met. As Laurie finds work on a television soap opera, Sidney becomes more and more of a father to Patti.

Five years later, Laurie falls for a man named Jimmy (Graham Beckel) and decides to marry him. The big blow comes when Laurie tells Sidney she is moving to California. Although it breaks Sidney's heart, he agrees to let Laurie take Patti with her.

The pilot ended with Sidney writing a letter: "Dearest Patti: Your latest drawing arrived tonight . . . I can hardly wait until I see you next July. I've got 643 wonderful things we'll do together. I just hope you don't grow up so much I don't recognize you. Give your mommy a hug for me — and your daddy. And tell them if they don't treat you nicely, they'll have to answer to your best friend, who loves you higher than anyone can count. Sidney."

One year later, Laurie returns to New York for a visit and eventually decides to stay when she acquires a role on a television soap opera. When Laurie and Jimmy split up, Sidney convinces Laurie to share his apartment once again. Stories follow events in the lives of Sidney Shorr and his adopted family, Laurie and Patti Morgan.

Sidney, who was born in New York City, was originally a freelance commercial artist; he is later employed by Jason Stoller at the Graham and Ludwig Advertising Agency in mid–Manhattan. His favorite dessert is pineapple cheesecake. His unseen mother (deceased) was named Yetta.

Laurie, who was born in the small town of Smote, Wisconsin, first appeared in a television commercial for Amore Soap. She then appeared in four episodes of the TV soap "Another World" and later on the fictional soap "A Time for Loving" (where she played a homewrecker who was in love with the wife). She finally landed the permanent role of Gloria Trenell on the mythical soap "As Thus We Are."

Other Regulars: Alan North (Sidney's neighbor, *Mort Harris*), Barbara Bryne (Sidney's landlady, *Mrs. Gaffney*), Lynne Thigpen (Jason's secretary, *Nancy*).

Love, Sidney. Tony Randall, Lorna Patterson and Kaleena Kiff.

Relatives: Lenka Peterson (Laurie's mother, *Eve Morgan*), Hansford Rowe (Laurie's father, *Dan Morgan*).

Theme: "Friends Forever," vocal by Tony Randall, Swoosie Kurtz and Kaleena Kiff; later by Gladys and Bubba Knight.

Note: In the NBC pilot film, "Sidney Shorr" (10/5/81), Lorna Patterson played Laurie and David Huffman, Jimmy (no last name given).

412. *Love That Bob*

NBC, 1/2/55 to 9/25/55
CBS, 10/5/55 to 9/19/57
NBC, 9/22/57 to 9/15/59

Cast: Bob Cummings (*Bob Collins*), Rosemary DeCamp (*Margaret MacDonald*), Dwayne Hickman (*Chuck Mac-*

Donald), Ann B. Davis (*Schultzy*), Joi Lansing (*Shirley Swanson*).

Facts: The name on the office door reads BOB COLLINS— PHOTOGRAPHY. Robert ("Bob") Collins, a swinging young bachelor, is owner of the downtown Hollywood studio (Western Pictures Productions is the office opposite Bob's). Bob lives with his widowed sister, Margaret MacDonald, and her teenage son, Charles ("Chuck") MacDonald, at 804 Grummond Road.

Bob was born in Joplin, Missouri, and is descended from Scottish ancestors. He served in the air force during World War II. His hobby is flying, and he owns a twin engine Beechcraft that is rarely seen. Bob is simply a suave and sophisticated ladies' man whose job is to photograph the world's most beautiful women. He considers his models "lumps of clay. I mold them into bright, shimmering butterflies. I give them grace, style and charm." Bob shoots fashion layouts for various magazines and stipulates that his swimsuit models cannot have a waist larger than 23 inches.

He can make girls swoon, and he desperately seeks to avoid the path to matrimony. His worst month is June—when girls are the most marriage-minded and he finds it extremely difficult to remain a bachelor.

Bob says he is married—to his camera: "Any other type of marriage is a serious commitment and I need my time before settling down. I need to find the right person—no matter how many girls I have to date to find her."

Bob's fascination with girls began at the age of four, when he first started playing post office ("Bob is now the Post Office General," says Margaret).

"The Casanova of the Camera," as Margaret calls Bob, simply cannot resist a beautiful woman and insists that he is a confirmed bachelor. "All the Collins men are confirmed bachelors," Margaret says, "until something snaps and they suddenly get married." Bob wears a cologne called Moustache that "drives the girls crazy."

"Margaret is young and attractive," Bob says. "I keep telling her she should get married again, but does she listen to me? No." Margaret takes care of the house, cooks, cleans, does the shopping and manages to find a little romance—but despite what Bob thinks is best for her, she is not ready to settle down again. (Her longest romance was with Paul Fonda [Lyle Talbot], Bob's World War II air force buddy. Paul is now an airline pilot [a captain] and married one of his stewardesses, Betty Havilland [Dorothy Johnson].)

Margaret considers Bob a father for Chuck: "He's a kind man. He lets us share his house and is putting Chuck through school." But Margaret also says, "Chuck has been raised in an atmosphere of girls, girls, girls." This has been a delight for Chuck, who hopes that whatever his Uncle Bob has, it can be inherited by a nephew. It is this kind of thinking that has Margaret worried about Chuck. Bob just shrugs it off because "Margaret worries a lot about Chuck. It all started when Chuck was an infant. She put him in a high chair and he cried. She called the pediatrician to see if he had the colic, then a child psychologist to see if he had acrophobia. She finally called the upholsterer to pad the high chair. Altogether it cost $150 to find out the kid needed changing."

Chuck first attended Hollywood High School (where he was on the R.O.T.C. drill team). He joined the National Guard after graduation and in last season episodes enrolled in Gridley College (majoring in premed). Francine Williams (Diane Jergens) was Chuck's original girlfriend; Carol Henning (Olive Sturgess) replaced her in last season episodes (she enrolled in nearby Beaumont College).

"When Bob decides to get married, there is someone waiting for him—me," says Charmaine Schultz, better known as Schultzy, Bob's plain-looking girl Friday. Schultzy is totally dedicated to Bob and in love with him—"I can't compete with the models on the sofa, but give me the kitchen and food and I'll land him." Bob has found the perfect assistant in Schultzy (who calls him "Boss"); if, for example, Bob needs a gorilla for the shoot, the ever faithful Schultzy is there for him in costume. "I feel comfortable with her," Bob says. "Before Schultzy, I would train girls only to lose them to marriage."

The hours may be long at times, but Bob rarely complains when it comes to photographing his beautiful models. The voluptuous blonde bombshell, Shirley Swanson, is the model dead set on marrying Bob. Shirley, who measures 38-26-36, is very jealous and called the "Wild Flower" by Bob (Schultzy calls her "Blondie"). Shirley has some talent in the kitchen (she can make ham and eggs) and, despite the fact that she does not have a 23 inch waist, Bob does let her model swimsuits ("I may be strict, but I'm not crazy"). (Neither were the producers who cast Joi Lansing in the role of Shirley. Joi, one of the sexiest women on television at the time, is best remembered as Sergeant O'Hara—the girl who "married" Superman.) Shirley mentioned she lived in downtown Hollywood opposite Bob's studio in a large white building with a red tile roof. She wears a perfume called Bachelor's Doom.

Other recurring models included Collette DuBois (Lisa Gaye), a French knockout Bob called his "Sly Little Thief" (for example, "No matter how many girls there are, I can only see you. You steal my heart, you sly little thief"); her culinary expertise is pancakes. Marie DiPaolo (Donna Martell) is an Italian model Bob calls "My Little Venutian Ambassador of Loveliness." She calls him "Roberto" and her kitchen specialty is meatballs and spaghetti. Mary Beth Hall (Gloria Marshall) and Ingrid (Ingrid Goude) are two additional models who worked for and drove Bob crazy.

Bob, like his father, is a photographer; but before them there was and still is "Josh Collins—Photography," a business run by Bob's elderly but young at heart grandfather, Joshua ("Josh") Collins, in Joplin, Missouri. Grandpa Collins (Bob Cummings in a dual role) lives in a drafty old house his father built (and died in from pneumonia). His favorite song is "Some Enchanted Evening," and like his grandson, Bob, he can eye a girl and guess her measurements. Josh, a member of the Joplin Globetrotters Basketball Team, has a girlfriend named Dixie Yates (Lurene Tuttle). He calls Bob "Young Rooster," Chuck "Chuckie Boy" and Margaret "Mag Pie."

Other Roles: Harvey Helm (King Donovan) is Bob's friend, a henpecked wholesale furniture salesman for the Gravener Furniture Company. He calls Bob "Bobby Boy" and was his co-pilot during the war. "Harvey brings home the bacon, but his wife decides how to slice it," says Bob. Harvey is married to Ruthie (Mary Lawrence), a former swimsuit model of Bob's. Carol, Chuck's girlfriend, is Ruthie's niece.

Pamela Livingston (Nancy Kulp) is Bob's friend, a member of the Bird Watchers' Society. Frank Crenshaw (Dick Wesson) is the sailor with a crush on Schultzy. Kay Michael (Lola Albright) is the actress Bob dated. Martha Randolph (Rose Marie) is Schultzy's husband-hunting friend.

Relatives: Tammy Marihugh (Bob's niece, *Tammy Johnson*), Bonita Granville (Schultzy's cousin, *Bertha*), Charlie Herbert (Harvey and Ruth's son, *Tommy Helm*).

Theme: "Theme from the Bob Cummings Show," by Mahlon Merrick.

Note: "Love That Bob" is the now established title for a series that was originally called "The Bob Cummings Show." In both versions, the music is the same (as is Bob's opening line—"Hold it, I think you're gonna like this picture"). The only change is the title.

Bob Cummings continued his role of a suave and sophisticated ladies' man in "The New Bob Cummings Show" (CBS, 10/5/61 to 3/1/62). Bob plays Bob Carson, a Palm Springs, California–based freelance pilot who sticks his neck out to help people (usually beautiful women) who are in trouble. Bob, who keeps his money in the Bank of Palm Springs, owns the never marketed Aero Car (a car that could be converted into a plane in ten minutes. Its inventor could never get it mass produced and Bob flew the prototype model; it was slated to sell for $13,000). Bob is also a gourmet (he orders exotic foods from Cleauseau's Famous Specialties for the Discriminating Palate (for example, salted filet of buffalo tongue, kangaroo tail soup and marinated rattlesnake).

Murvyn Vye is Bob's sidekick, Lionel, and Roberta Shore is Bob's neighbor, Henrietta ("Hank") Gregory. Juan Esquivel composed the theme.

413. *Love That Jill*

ABC, 1/20/58 to 4/28/58

"They ought to marry so they can argue legally," say friends of Jill Johnson (Anne Jeffreys) and Jack Gibson (Robert Sterling), the rival heads of all-female modeling agencies in New York City. Jill, who owns Model Girls, Inc., and Jack, the head of the Gibson Girls Agency, are friendly enemies who snare each other's accounts, publicity and models in an attempt to become the number one modeling agency in Manhattan (both cater to television, film and print ads that require gorgeous girls). Their constant attempts at skullduggery and their continual bickering over accounts has led to an unforeseen love that neither one is willing to admit to under normal circumstances.

To merge agencies or for one even to ask the other out on a date is impossible; hence, each devises elaborate schemes to acquire the other's company—even if it means mixing business with pleasure and snaring the other's account at the same time.

Models Girls, Inc., is located at 670 Madison Avenue; Jill lives in apartment 14A at 1064 Park Avenue; her phone number is Plaza 6-7017. She buys her clothes at Abercrombie and Fitch, and her favorite ploy to get Jack's attention is to make him jealous by pretending to fall for handsome men.

Jack lives in an apartment at 1360 West 63rd Street, and the Gibson Girls Agency is located at 540 Madison Avenue. The special cigars for Jack's clients are kept in the lefthand drawer of his office desk. In *TV Guide* and other printed sources, Jack's agency is called the House That Jacques Built (the name Gibson Girls Agency is seen on screen).

Ginger (Barbara Nichols) and Peaches (Kay Elhardt) are Jill's top models (Ginger is the buxon, dumb blonde type; Peaches is the girl with the hourglass figure). Richard (Jimmy Lydon) is Jill's secretary (a former crewman at Harvard).

Pearl (Betty Lynn) is Jack's secretary; and Brooklyn-born Monty Callahan (Henry Kulky), a former glass-jawed boxer who was called "One Round Callahan" (he never lasted more than one round) is Jack's masseur.

Lud Gluskin composed the "Love That Jill" theme.

414. *Love Thy Neighbor*

ABC, 6/15/73 to 9/19/73

At 327 North Robin Hood Road in the Sherwood Forest Estates in San Fernando, California, live Charlie Wilson (Ron Masak) and his wife, Peggy (Joyce Bulifant), a middle class white couple. Charlie, a Democrat, is the shop steward at Turner Electronics. Living next door, at 325 North Robin Hood Road, is Ferguson Bruce (Harrison Page) and his wife, Jackie (Janet MacLachlan), a black couple from Passaic, New Jersey, who are the first to move into an all white neighborhood. Ferguson, a Republican, is the efficiency expert at Turner. Peggy and Jackie quickly become friends; Charlie and Ferguson, on the other hand, are friendly but distrustful of each other. Racial prejudices are satirized as the couples attempt to live side by side and "follow the golden rule, love thy neighbor, you'll find out that it's really cool."

The local bar hangout is Lenny's Tap Room, and the Sherwood Forest Estates were named after the developer: he thought of himself as Robin Hood, only he stole from the poor and made himself rich.

Solomon Burke sings the theme, "Love Thy Neighbor."

415. *Lucan*

ABC, 9/12/77 to 3/2/78
ABC, 11/13/78 to 12/4/78

Cast: Kevin Brophy *(Lucan),* John Randolph *(Don Hoagland),* Don Gordon *(Prentiss).*

Facts: In 1957 an infant is abandoned by his parents and left to die in the forests of northern Minnesota. The infant survives, however, and is raised by a pack of gray wolves. Ten years later, in summer 1967, a hunting party stumbles upon a strange creature: a humanlike child who eats, sleeps, hunts and howls like a wolf. Authorities are informed and an expedition is organized to find the wolf child.

October 10, 1967: The wolf boy is captured and brought to the University Research Center in California to begin his journey from the forest to civilization. He is watched over and taught by Dr. Donald ("Don") Hoagland. Progress is slow, but on January 17, 1969, the first breakthrough occurs: the boy learns to eat at the table with utensils.

September 5, 1970: The day the boy got his name. When the boy is having difficulty placing geometric shapes in their appropriate places on a board, Don tells him, "You can, you can." When the boy does do it, he says "Lu can, lu can."

1977: Lucan is now 20. His is the first known case in which a human raised in the wild has been successfully treated and restored to human behavior. His senses are remarkably acute, especially his sense of smell. In his ten years of captivity, his sleeping patterns have not changed: his time of greatest activity is still night, and he wanders about restlessly, which reflects the hunting habits of his early childhood—"No amount of training can erase the early struggle for survival. Metabolically, he is more wolf than man."

Lucan is always tired if he doesn't get a good day's sleep. He mostly needs food at night; in the day he has mostly milk. His retreat is a small hill overlooking the university. Here he thinks and makes up stories about his parents: "Don, I wish they weren't stories. I wish I knew."

Shortly after, the school's board of directors tells Don that Lucan is still too wolflike and should be placed in a state sanitarium. Don protests, and all changes when he is injured in a car accident. He speaks to Lucan: "You must leave this place. I've felt for some time you must go . . . to find your parents . . . Even if you never find them, you promised yourself some day you would search . . . I can't protect you anymore."

Lucan leaves the university and begins his search, taking what jobs he can (his first was as a carpenter for the McElwaine Construction Company) and helping people along the way.

In the two month interval between telecasts of the first and second episodes, a dramatic change occurred: instead of Lucan's leaving on his own to search for his parents, the revised storyline finds him escaping from the authorities who tried to keep him captive, fearing he would revert back to being a wolf. The university then hires a bounty hunter named Prentiss to capture him. After another short absence, the series returned with a new storyline: Lucan's adventures as a fugitive from justice. (When two thieves break into the university lab seeking drugs, they encounter Lucan. A fight ensues and one of the thieves is killed. When Lucan is unjustly accused of murder, he escapes to find the only man who can clear him—the other thief. Hindering Lucan's efforts is Prentiss, now a police lieutenant relentlessly pursuing him.) The series ended before Lucan could find his parents or clear his name.

Flashbacks: Todd Olsen *(Lucan, age ten)*.

Theme: "Lucan," by Fred Karlin; later version theme by J.J. Johnson.

416. *The Lucie Arnaz Show*

CBS, 4/2/85 to 6/11/85

WPLE-AM is a radio station nicknamed "Advice Radio 88" (88 KHz is its location on the dial). It is located in Manhattan at 1700 Broadway (at 53rd Street), and 555-WPLE is its advice line phone number. While the station apparently has many programs, we know of only one: "The Love and Lucas Show," an afternoon comedy and advice program that combines the psychological advice of Dr. Jane Lucas (Lucie Arnaz) with the comic talents of Larry Love (Todd Waring) and his invisible dog, Tippy.

Jane lives in Apartment 4A on East 70th Street. She graduated from New York University and also has a daily advice column, "Dear Jane," in the *Daily Mirror*. While Jane seems capable of helping other people resolve their difficulties, she can't seem to work out her own problems—hence the situation for stories.

Thirty-one-year-old Jane plays shortstop on the station's unnamed softball team; the slogan for "The Love and Lucas Show" is "Your spot for music and mental health in the afternoon."

Jim Gordon (Tony Roberts) is the station manager; Jill (Lee Bryant) is Jane's sister (she lives in New Jersey) and Sarah (Melissa Hart) and Billy (Sandy Schwartz) are Jill's children. Gwyn Gillis appeared as Jim's wife, Peggy Gordon. The series is based on the British series, "Agony" (with Maureen Lipman as Jane Lucas, an advice columnist who can help people with their problems but is unable to solve her own).

Jack Elliott composed the theme.

417. *MacGruder and Loud*

ABC, 1/20/85 to 9/3/85

Malcolm MacGruder (John Getz) and Jennifer ("Jenny") Loud (Kathryn Harrold) are patrol car officers with the L.A.P.D. Malcolm (badge number 459) and Jenny (badge number 449) are secretly married (department regulations prohibit married couples from working together). They live at 165 North Veranda—Malcolm in Apartment 2A; Jenny in Apartment 2B (the bookcase in Malcolm's apartment has been secretly converted into a revolving door to allow access to both apartments).

Jenny hates Code 3s ("They're too dangerous") and drives a car with the license plate IC 21501 (Malcolm's license plate reads 698917). Their mobile code is 8-Z-11, and their patrol car license plate reads 275816. Malcolm's badge number was also given as 445 and Jenny's as 458.

Paul Chihara composed the theme.

418. *MacGyver*

ABC, 9/29/85 to 12/30/91

Angus ("Mac") MacGyver (Richard Dean Anderson) is opposed to firearms and relies heavily on his imagination and duct tape. He is a survival expert and scientific genius who tackles seemingly impossible missions for the government (Mac first worked for Western Tech, then U.S. Intelligence, the Company and finally the Phoenix Foundation). Mac was born in Mission City. His high school sweetheart was Ellen

Stewart (Mary Ann Pascal), and during his college summer vacations, he worked as an usher at Met baseball stadium. Mac is a vegetarian and lived on a houseboat. When the boat was destroyed by a fire (1991), Mac moved to a loft in Los Angeles owned by a sculptor named Melvin Krasney (Adrian Sparks); Mac's phone number is 555-8990.

Mac's favorite sport is ice hockey and he first drove a Jeep (license plate IRQ 104) then a sedan (license plate 2ASB 795). The second half of the two part episode "Goodnight, MacGyver" (11/18/91) revealed Mac's first name to be Angus. He previously had no first name; he was called "Stace" MacGyver on a preproduction press release; "Mac" by his friends; and "Bud" by his grandfather.

Peter ("Pete") Thornton (Dana Elcar) is Mac's superior; Nikki Carpenter (Elyssa Davalos) is Mac's friend and occasional assistant (she was born on 3/5/59, resides at 2723 Foster Lane and can be reached by phone at 555-3082). Jack Dalton (Bruce McGill) is Mac's misadventure-prone friend, a pilot who runs the Dalton Air Service. Maria Romburg (Brigitta Stenberg) appeared as Mac's romantic interest for a short time in 1990.

The series' last episode, "The Stringer," was broadcast as a special on 4/25/92. In it MacGyver meets Shawn A. Molloy (Dalton James), the son he never knew he had. Shawn, who uses the nickname Sam, is the son of Kate Molloy (Lisa Savage), Mac's college sweetheart. Kate, a photo-journalist, was killed by the Chinese while investigating the democratic movement in China. Her son, nine years old at the time (played by Nicholas Matus), survived and later became a photo-journalist. While investigating a case involving smuggled goods from China, Mac and Sam meet. The *A* in Sam's name stands for Angus and in a locket he carries a picture of his mother and a man who was unknown to him, until now, MacGyver. After completing the assignment, Mac leaves the Phoenix Foundation to spend time with his son.

Relatives: John Anderson (Mac's grandfather, *Harry Jackson*), Michele B. Chan (Mac's foster daughter, *Sue Ling*), Penelope Windust and Linda Darlow (Pete's ex-wife, *Connie Thornton*), Scott Coffey (Pete's son, *Michael Thornton*).

Flashbacks: Sean Wohland and Shawn Donahue *(Mac as a boy)*, Phil Redrow and Martin Milner (Mac's father, *James MacGyver*), Sheila Moore (Mac's mother, *Ellen MacGyver*), Jan Jorden *(Harry's wife)*.

Theme: "MacGyver," by Randy Edelman.

Note: Although the above episode was promoted as "The Last MacGyver," another first-run episode ("The Mountain of Youth") aired on ABC on 5/21/92.

419. *McHale's Navy*

ABC, 10/11/62 to 8/30/66

The series is set on the island of Taratupa in the South Pacific during World War II. The navy has established a base and has put Wallace B. Binghamton (Joe Flynn) in

MacGruder and Loud. John Getz and Kathryn Harrold.

charge. Binghamton was born in New York and was head of the Long Island Yacht Club before the war; he is somewhat inadequate at being a captain. He is assisted by Lieutenant Elroy Carpenter (Bob Hastings), who commands PT Boat 16.

Quinton McHale (Ernest Borgnine) was born in Michigan and was the captain of a tramp steamer in the South Pacific when Admiral Reynolds commissioned him as a lieutenant and assigned him to Taratupa as the commander of Squadron 19 and PT Boat 73.

McHale and "his crew of pirates" (as Binghamton calls them) live on the far side of the island in what is called "McHale's Island." The crew, who wheel and deal, have turned Taratupa into "The Las Vegas of the Pacific" and have ruined what Binghamton considers a paradise. His attempts to get the goods on McHale are the focal point of the series. McHale's crew calls Binghamton "Old Lead Bottom," and they have an unreported prisoner of war named Fuji Kobiaji (Yoshio Yoda); Fuji is a Japanese soldier who went over the hill and now serves as McHale's cook. McHale's "pirates" are Lester Gruber (Carl Ballantine), Harrison ("Tinker") Bell (Billy Sands), Willy Moss (John Wright), Happy Haines (Gavin MacLeod), Virgil Edwards (Edson Stroll) and Quartermaster ("Christy") Christopher (Gary Vinson).

Last season episodes are set in Voltafiore, Italy—McHale, his crew and Binghamton have been transferred to the European theater of war.

Axel Stordahl composed the "McHale's Navy" theme.

420. *The MacKenzies of Paradise Cove*

ABC, 3/27/79 to 5/18/79

Each Sunday before dinner, Frank and Laura MacKenzie would go sailing. One Sunday afternoon in 1978, a tragic accident claims their lives and leaves their five children, Bridget (Lory Walsh), Kevin (Shawn Stevens), Celia (Randi Kiger), Michael (Sean Marshall) and Timothy (Keith Mitchell), orphans.

When authorities threaten to break up the family by sending the children to orphanages, the MacKenzie children convince local fisherman Cuda Weber (Clu Gulager) to pretend to be their uncle, William ("Willie") MacKenzie, so the Child Welfare Department will allow them to live together. Stories, set in Hawaii, follow the adventures of the five MacKenzie children as they struggle to remain together as a family.

Cuda owns the boat, the *Viking*. He held jobs as "dishwasher, grease monkey, bartender, outhouse builder and fish cleaner." He now lives in a cabin by the sea in Oahu and balks when Bridget and Celia clean it: "The house looks too clean; it loses all its character." Cuda buys his supplies at the Chantler, and his favorite hangout is Flora's Pool Hall (Ethel Azama plays Flora).

The children live in a house on Paradise Cove and buy their food at Chang's Groceries. Bridget, called "Missy" by Cuda, is the oldest daughter (17). She had a job as a model for Pippa's Fashions, but quit when she was asked to wear a string bikini "and didn't want to let it all hang out." She later held a job as a cocktail waitress at O'Toole's (assigned to station one) but was let go when it was discovered she was underage.

Celia and Michael started a fruit punch business but were busted by the police when it was discovered that they had spiked the punch with liquor (unaware of whta liquor was, nine-year-old Celia used it to give the punch some flavor; they were fined $150). Timothy, whom Cuda calls "Champ," is the youngest MacKenzie (age six) and believes that Cuda really is his Uncle Willie. In the episode "Crate Expectations," the MacKenzie children acquire a crate their father never had a chance to pick up; it contained an antique piano he had bought for his wife on the occasion of their twentieth anniversary. In the original pilot film, "Stickin' Together" (ABC, 4/14/78), Sean Thomas Roche played Kevin MacKenzie, the oldest boy.

Theme: "The MacKenzies of Paradise Cove," by John Rubinstein.

Note: The series "A Family for Joe" (NBC, 3/24/90 to 5/6/90) used the identical concept. Joe Whitaker (Robert Mitchum), a maverick, homeless man, becomes the adoptive grandfather of Holly (Juliette Lewis), Mary (Jessica Player), Nick (David Lascher) and Chris (Ben Savage) Bankston—four orphaned children (their parents were killed in a plane crash)—when they convince him to become their guardian and keep the family together.

Joe was a merchant marine and, as a vagrant, would get his meals from Saint Anthony's soup kitchen. The Bankston's dog is named Leon (he only eats cat food); Nick has a pet snake named Hugo; Mary's plush monkeys are named Judy and Jingles. In the pilot episode (2/25/90), Maia Brewton played Holly, Chris Furrh was Nick and Jarrad Paul was Chris. Charles Fox composed the theme.

421. *Mad About You*

NBC, 9/23/92 to the present

One Sunday evening in December of 1989, Paul Buchman (Paul Reiser) stops at a newsstand to buy the *New York Times*. There is only one copy left, and he is about to pay for it when a girl named Jamie Stemple (Helen Hunt) appears, seeking the *Times* also. She tells Paul that she needs the paper because it contains her parents' obituary ("Beams fell on them during an earthquake"). Jamie is very pretty, has a very sexy voice and Paul halfheartedly believes her story; he gives her the paper. As Jamie leaves, she drops a dry cleaning receipt with her name on it. That night, while with a friend, Paul checks the obit page of the *Times* and sees no Stemple—"I knew she was lying." The following day, Paul picks up Jamie's dry cleaning (he told the cleaner he was Jamie's houseboy, Coco, to find out where she works) and tracks her down. Jamie is a bit distrustful of Paul (having just broken up with a guy), but Paul knows this is the girl for him.

After talking, Jamie feels Paul may be the man she is seeking and invites him to the office Christmas party. They learn they are literally neighbors. Paul resides at 129 West 81st Street (Apartment 5B) and Jamie across the street at 142 West 81st Street (Apartment 11C). The strangers brought together by a newspaper begin dating and marry in 1992 (they are married five months when the series begins).

The newlyweds take up residence in Jamie's apartment; Paul sublets his to Kramer (Michael Richards from the series "Seinfeld"). Jamie is 30 years old and works as regional vice president at a public relations firm called Ferrah-Gantz on Madison Avenue. She was born in New Haven, Connecticut, and attended Yale University; her father calls her "Peanut." Jamie likes to be liked by other people; she gets extremely upset if people don't like her and goes out of her way to impress them so they will like her (in high school, Jamie was known as "the Stemple sister who showed a boy her boobs to be liked").

Paul is a documentary filmmaker and owns his own company (Buchman Films) in Manhattan. He was born in New York City and attended NYU Film School. Paul hates the opera ("I feel like I'm being scolded") and has a dog named Murray. "Color Our World" was Paul and Jamie's wedding song, and Riff's Bar is their favorite watering hole.

Dr. Mark Devanow (Richard Kind) and his wife, Fran (Leila Kenzle), are Paul and Jamie's friends (they live downtown on 2nd Avenue). Mark is a gynecologist and called "Snookie" by Fran. Lila Stemple (Anne Ramsay) is

Jamie's sister; and Gus and Theresa Stemple (Paul Dooley and Nancy Dussault) are Jamie's parents. Al Ruscio appeared as Paul's Uncle Julius.

In the pilot episode, Paul and Jamie's last name is Cooper. Don Was and Paul Reiser composed the theme, "Final Frontier."

422. *Madame's Place*

Syndicated, 9/82 to 9/83

Cast: Wayland Flowers (*Voice of Madame*), Judy Landers (*Sara Joy Pitts*), Johnny Haymer (*Pinkerton*), Susan Tolsky (*Bernadette Van Gilder*), Corey Feldman (*Buzzy St. James*), Barbara Cason (*Lynn LaVecque*).

Facts: Madame is a puppet (controlled by Wayland Flowers) who hosts "Madame's Place," a late-night talk show, from her mansion in Hollywood (she insists on doing the show from her home because it is titled "Madame's Place"). Madame was a struggling comedian who worked the dingy nightclub circuit before she made it "big" in the movies. She was the star of such films as *A Woman Named Hey You* (with Clint Eastwood) and *Trampoline Honeymoon*. Madame was also set to star in *Ride the Wild Surf* with Tab Hunter but lost the role to Barbara Eden (who looked stunning in a bikini). In an attempt to win back the role, Madame accused Barbara of painting stretchmarks on her bikini.

Madame, who has an antique Rolls Royce (license plate MADAME), enjoys reading the *Enquiring Star*, is a member of the Fetish-of-the-Month Club, and uses Me Tarzan—You Jane Body Rub (which she orders from the House of Pleasure catalogue). She orders her groceries from Tony's Market, was married six times (seven times in the pilot) and had 200 boyfriends; her third husband was a fan who sent her a picture of himself playing polo in the nude. Like many stars, Madame has had her harrowing moments: she was kidnapped by Egbert Tegley, a famous criminal known as "Sweet Tooth" Tegley, who held her hostage at an Atlantic City saltwater taffy stand. Her butler, Walter ("Pinky") Pinkerton, broke down the door and rescued her. Madame was also the target of a crazed fan (played by Archie Hahn) who believed she was the most beautiful woman in the world (he also believed that when the moon is full he turns into a parakeet).

Sara Joy Pitts is Madame's ultrasexy blonde niece. She is the daughter of Madame's sister, Marmalina, and has come to Hollywood (from Georgia, where Madame was born) to become an actress—"just like my Auntie Madame." Sara Joy measures 37-24-36 and is described by Madame as "a sexpot who doesn't realize she is a sexpot." (When Sara Joy first arrived, Madame thought she was getting "a boob-o-gram" and said her name sounded as if it should be in a limerick: "There once was a girl named Sara Joy Pitts who had . . ."). Sara Joy, who wears very low cut and off-the-shoulder blouses, as well as short shorts, watches her favorite soap opera, "The Young and the Stupid," with the sound off ("It's so sad, it makes me cry").

Bernadette Van Gilder, whom Madame calls "Bernie," is her shy, mousy secretary. Buzzy St. James is the 11-year-old kid who lives next door. Lynn LaVecque, a former "two bit band singer," is Madame's competition, the host of "Naked All-Star Bowling."

Other Characters: Lawrence ("Larry") Lunch (John Moschitta, Jr.), the owner of the Lunch Agency, is Madame's exasperating, superfast talking agent ("Lunch has cut more throats than a cross-eyed barber," says Madame). Rollin Espinoza (Hector Elias) is the leader of the Madame's Place All-Divorced Orchestra. R. Ray Randall (voice of Chandler Garrison) is the never-seen (heard over a speaker phone) head of the unnamed network on which "Madame's Place" airs. Madame calls him "No Face" because "he has no face." Eric Honest (a.k.a. Mr. Honest; played by Don Sparks) is Madame's most frequent and most exasperating guest.

The network has established the Madame Scholarship for male freshmen students at the University of Georgia; she also has a line of designer jeans ("They're hard to get out of, but easy to get into").

Relatives: E.J. Peaker (Buzzy's mother, *Carla St. James*), John Reilly (Buzzy's father, *Max St. James*). Madame mentioned that she had an aunt named Glow Worm (who was born with radioactive skin).

Theme: "Here at Madame's Place," vocal by Denise DeCaro.

423. *The Magician*

NBC, 10/2/73 to 5/20/74

Cast: Bill Bixby (*Anthony Blake*), Keene Curtis (*Max Pomeroy*), Jim Watkins (*Jerry Anderson*).

Facts: While performing in South America, illusionist Anthony Blake is arrested on a trumped up espionage charge and later imprisoned. Ten years later, he escapes from prison and takes his cellmate, a dying old man, with him. The old man, grateful for the few months of freedom Tony provided for him, leaves Tony a considerable fortune—money he uses, in part, to help people who are unable to turn to the police for help.

Tony now performs regularly at the Magic Castle Club in Los Angeles. He drives a white Corvette with the license plate SPIRIT, and he originally lived on his plane, a Boeing 737 called the *Spirit* (he later lives in a home at 315 Vinewood in Los Angeles). Tony's wrists bear the scars of the prison shackles; he can read people (their faces, eyes and hands) and knows when they need help. Tony, however, doesn't interfere; he enlists in a cause and uses the wizardry of his craft to foil evil. The plane's I.D. number is N1355, and it is piloted by Tony's assistant, Jerry Anderson.

Max Pomeroy is an internationally known magazine and newspaper columnist who is also Tony's best friend and a vital source for information. He lives in San Francisco (at 36 Beverly Drive) in a private residence that also serves as his headquarters. Max is continually in battles with his editors for daring to touch what he writes and he has unconventional views on "money, sex, marriage, religion, soccer and cheese." Max keeps a microfilm record of all photos taken of him during his world travels and has a handicapped, wheelchair-bound son named Dennis (Todd Crespi). While Max is not married, he does live with a charming woman named Lulu (Joan Caulfield). "I'm everything to Max except a wife," she says. By this line of dialogue, it is learned that Lulu is Dennis's mother: (Max to Lulu) "Lulu, whatever else you do in this life, the simple act of giving birth to a son like Dennis has made your stay on earth a complete success." When Max relates the story of Tony's prison experiences, he compares it to a book: "Have you ever read the book *The Count of Monte Cristo*? In a sense, Tony lived it..."

In the 90 minute pilot episode (NBC, 3/17/73), Bill Bixby played Anthony Dorian and Jim Watkins was Jerry Wallace.

Theme: "The Magician," by Patrick Williams.

Note: Three earlier projects also dealt with the exploits of magicians who use their abilities to help people in trouble: "Mandrake the Magician" (Syndicated, 1954), "Mandrake" (NBC, 1/24/79) and "Blacke's Magic" (NBC, 1/8/86 to 6/11/86).

The story of "Mandrake the Magician" begins in the twelfth century when the hordes of Genghis Khan swept the Eastern world and virtually destroyed the wizards who practiced the secrets of ancient Egypt and the magic of ancient China. The few wizards who escaped established the College of Magic in a secret Tibetan valley where the lore was preserved. Once a decade, one youth was selected and taught the ancient secrets.

In the twentieth century, a young boy is brought to the college by his father, a former graduate who has only a few months to live. The boy is taught the ancient secrets by Theron, the Master of Magic.

Ten years later, the boy becomes greater than his masters. Upon his release from the college, that boy, named Mandrake (Coe Norton) teams with his servant, Lothar (Woody Strode), and together they set out to foil evil.

NBC's two hour pilot "Mandrake" dealt with the exploits of Mandrake (Anthony Herrera), a magician who uses the secrets of the twelfth century Chinese and Egyptians to battle crime. Ji-Tu Cumbuka played Lothar.

"Blacke's Magic": After a near fatal accident while performing a trick for the television show "Danger Darers," famed illusionist Alexander Blacke (Hal Linden) decides to retire. Shortly after, at a magician's convention in Los Angeles, Blacke witnesses the death of Nick Gasparini (Cesare Danova), who dies from a gunshot wound while submerged in ten feet of water. Determined to solve the murder, Alexander enlists the aid of his father, Leonard Blacke (Harry Morgan), a retired con artist. Together they solve the crime and decide to use their unique skills to help the police solve baffling crimes.

Claudia Christian played Alexander's daughter, Claudia Blacke, and Stephen Macht was Lieutenant Hank Wallenstein of the N.Y.P.D. 18th Precinct.

424. *Magnum, P.I.*

CBS, 12/11/80 to 9/12/88

Cast: Tom Selleck (*Thomas Magnum*), John Hillerman (*Jonathan Higgins*), Larry Manetti (*Rick Wright*), Roger E. Mosley (*T.C. Calvin*), Kathleen Lloyd (*Carol Baldwin*).

Facts: Thomas Sullivan Magnum is a private detective who operates out of Hawaii and charges $200 a day plus expenses for his services. He is a former naval intelligence officer and lives on the estate of pulp writer Robin Masters in return for providing its security. Magnum attended Annapolis and resigned because "when I woke up one morning I realized I was 33 and never was 23." Magnum served with the VM02 unit in Da Nang during the Vietnam War. He was born in the town of Tidewater, Virginia, and his first paying job was delivering newspapers for the *Daily Sentinel* (he earned $12 a week plus one penny for each paper he sold). Magnum, who is writing a book called *How to Be a World-Class Private Investigator*, drives a red Ferrari with the license plate 308TTS (also seen as 56E 478 and ROBIN I); his phone number is 555-2131. The King Kamehameha Club is one of his hangouts, and Magnum hates to be called "Tommy." He calls Robin's estate "Robin's Nest."

Jonathan Quayle Higgins is the estate's major domo. He served with both MI5 and MI6 (Military Intelligence) during World War II and has a ham radio with the call letters NR6DBZ. His hobbies are building model bridges and painting. He has two guard dogs named Apollo and Zeus (whom he calls "The Lads"). Higgins created his own blend of tea called Lady Ashley tea, and he is the chairman of the board of directors of the King Kamehameha Club. He is also chairman of the Honolulu branch of the Britonic Seaman's Fund charity. Higgins, a survival expert with endless tales of heroic deeds, is writing his memoirs of the war in a diary he calls "Crises at Suez." Magnum is 99 percent sure that Higgins is Robin Masters, "But it is that 1 percent that could mean disaster." Higgins's mobile car code is N6DBZ.

Tom's friend, Rick Orville Wright, first worked as the bartender at the King Kamehameha Club, then as the owner of his own club (Rick's Place). Theodore ("T.C.") Calvin, who served with Magnum and Rick in Nam, is a former Golden Gloves boxer who owns the Island Hoppers Helicopter Service (rates are $100 an hour; Bravo 516 is T.C.'s air code). Carol Baldwin, who has a dog named Chelsea, is Tom's friend, the assistant district attorney. Francis Hoffstetler (Elisha Cook, Jr.), better known as Ice Pick, is the underworld boss who assists Magnum. Robin Masters, who is seen from the back only (Bruce Atkinson) is voiced by Orson Welles. Robin's Ferraris have the license plates ROBIN I and ROBIN II, and his favorite charity is the Home for Wayward Boys. Tom (number 14), Rick (number 17) and T.C. (number 32) are members of Robin's softball team, the Paddlers. Robin's first published story was "The Last Days of Babylon."

Relatives: Gwen Verdon (Tom's mother, *Katherine Peterson*), David Huddleston (Tom's stepfather, *Frank Peterson*),

Robert Selleck, Sr. *(Tom's grandfather)*, Julie Cobb (Tom's cousin, *Karyn*), Brandon Call (Tom's cousin, *Billy*), Barbara Rush (Tom's aunt, *Phoebe Sullivan*), Sally Pontig (Higgins's niece, *Jilly Mack*), John Hillerman (Higgins's half brothers, *Father Paddy MacGuinness* and *Don Luis Monqueo*), Alice Cadogan (Rick's sister, *Wendy*), Fay Hauser (T.C.'s ex-wife, *Tina*), Shavar Ross (T.C.'s son, *Bryant*), Celeste Holm (Carol's mother, *Abigail*), Linda Grovenor (Carol's niece, *Becky Damon*), Matt Clark (Carol's uncle, *Jack Damon*), Tate Donovan (Robin's nephew, *R.J. Masters*).

Flashbacks: R.J. Williams *(Tom as a boy)*, Susan Blanchard *(Tom's mother)*, Robert Pine *(Tom's father)*, Marta DuBois (Tom's wife, *Michele*), Robert Mederros III *(Higgins as a boy)*.

Themes: "Magnum, P.I.," (first season theme) by Ian Freebarin-Smith; "Magnum's Theme," by Mike Post and Pete Carpenter.

425. *Major Dad*

CBS, 9/17/89 to 5/17/93

Cast: Gerald McRaney *(Major John MacGillis)*, Shanna Reed *(Polly Cooper)*, Marisa Ryan *(Elizabeth Cooper)*, Nicole Dubuc *(Robin Cooper)*, Chelsea Hertford *(Casey Cooper)*.

Facts: The story of a tough marine (John D. ["Mac"] MacGillis) who marries a pretty widow (Polly Cooper) with three children (Elizabeth, Robin and Casey) and the misadventures that occur when they set up housekeeping together (first in Oceanside, California, then in Farlough, Virginia).

John was born in Snake River, Mississippi, where his parents owned a farm on Decatur Road. His grandfather taught him to whittle at age 11; the biggest mistake of his life occurred when he was seven years old: he stole a Zorro watch that cost $7.95 from Peavey's Five and Dime. He wound it up, but instead of going "tick, tick, tick, it went thief, thief, thief." Thirty-three years later, John called Mr. Peavey and confessed.

John, a history major at Vanderbilt College, joined the marines in 1967 (in another episode, he mentions being in the marines for 20 years; he joined in 1969). His basic training was done on Parris Island, and he served three tours of duty as a corporal in Vietnam. When the series began, John was stationed at Camp Singleton in Oceanside (he was assigned to building 52419, and his favorite eatery was Zaff's Hamburgers). When a typo on his retirement papers forced John to retire, he held a job as vice president of product relations for Teleteck Defense. When the typo was discovered, he re-enlisted in the marines.

On 9/17/90, John and his family move to Virginia when John is transferred to Camp Hollister (which Polly calls "a military hellhole"). They now live on the base (house number 485) and John becomes "a staff weenie" (the nickname for the job he holds as staff secretary to General Marcus Craig). John enjoys sitting on the front porch and listening to crickets chirp. In the episode of 5/13/91, John adopts Polly's girls (whose last name changes to MacGillis).

Polly was originally a reporter for the Oceanside *Chronicle*; at Camp Hollister she becomes the managing editor of the camp newspaper, the *Bulldog*, when she is turned down for a reporter's job on the family owned town newspaper, the Farlough *Free Press*. Polly also writes the column "The Suggestion Box" and is in charge of the "At Ease" section of the paper. Polly is a Democrat and a member of the Officers' Wives Club (where once a year she has to participate in Jane Wayne Day, when the wives become marines for a day). Polly once worked for a radical magazine called *What's Left*, with her former love, Evan Charters (Jameson Parker), whom she met two years after her husband, Sandy, died (the episode reunited McRaney with his former "Simon and Simon" costar). Polly and the girls have a family birthday tradition: the birthday girl gets breakfast in bed, is waited on hand and foot and receives a special "birthday surprise." Polly and John met on September 11; they married on October 11 and honeymooned in Hawaii. Every month on the eleventh, John gives Polly flowers.

Elizabeth, the oldest daughter, attends Keefer High School (Oceanside episodes). She is the prettiest of the girls; when she looks through the family photo album, she worries about how her hair looked at the time. Purple is her favorite color; R.E.M. is her favorite group; and her little toes are double jointed. In Virginia, she attends Hollister Base High School.

Robin, the middle girl, attends Martin Elementary School (Oceanside), where she is a member of the Condors basketball team. In Virginia, where she attends the base school, Robin is a member of the girls' softball league, the Hollister Hornets. She and Elizabeth enjoy Minute Maid orange juice and Welch's grape juice.

Casey, the youngest of the girls, attends Martin Elementary School (Oceanside) and the base school (Virginia). Ruby and Henrietta are her dolls; Mr. Smithers is her teddy bear; and Whoobie is her plush toy. Casey played the only squash with a solo in the school "Harvest" play, and Ocean Spray cranberry juice (brick pack) is her favorite drink.

The family has a pet bird named Lemon; the station wagon license plate reads 638 574 (Oceanside), and 2RW 308 (Virginia). Their phone number is 555-6703, and the Major (as the girls call him) objects to three things about living with four females: a bedroom with pink walls, a Strawberry Shortcake shower curtain and hair clogging the sink drains. When the girls found a rare Rock Island turtle under the front porch, the general turned the major's home into the Rock Island Turtle Preserve until the eggs hatched (the girls named the turtle Claudette).

General Marcus Craig (Jon Cypher) is the commanding officer of Camp Hollister. He attended Cornell University, and when he gets upset he goes to the firing range to shoot off several hundred rounds. His unseen wife is named Mimsey. Alva Lou ("Gunny") Bricker (Beverly Archer) is the administrative chief of the general's office (she replaced Whitney Kershaw as Merilee Gunderson, John's secretary at Camp Singleton). Gunny has instituted a daily morning snack pastry schedule: bran muffins (Monday), jelly doughnuts (Tuesday), bear claws (Wednesday), bagels (Thursday) and assorted cookies (Friday). Gunny calls Casey "Little Cooper," and she has a dog named Elmo. Lieutenant Eugene ("Gene") Holowachuk (Matt Mulhern) is John's second in command. He is from Idaho and also has a job as the manager of the Fuel-R-Up service station.

Relatives: Chance Michael Corbitt (Marcus's nephew, *Jeffrey Craig,* a mischievous brat who is called "the beast of the base").

Theme: "Major Dad," by Roger Steinman.

426. *Major Del Conway of the Flying Tigers*

Syndicated, 1953

The Flying Tigers is a U.S. fighter squadron based in China during World War II. Major Del Conway (Art Fleming) is the head of the Third Pursuit Squadron, one of three such units that are part of General Chennault's Gallant Fighters (in Chinese, "Foo-hoo"; in English, "Flying Tigers").

While the Flying Tigers is a military outfit that fights the forces that oppose liberty, it is made up of volunteers who are only out to make money. Discipline is easy, and their mission is to help the Chinese overcome the invading Japanese. Pilots get $500 for each Japanese Zero they shoot down (when a Japanese squadron is spotted, it is typical to hear "Money, money, the joint's jumpin' with Zeros").

Members of Del's squadron are Cashbox Potter (Sandy Kenyon), Dick Rossi (Carl Shanzer), Joe Suie (Warren Nsien) and Catfish (Eddie Luke). The squad's planes (P-40s) are called "Sharks" (the face of a shark is painted on the nose). Their base is called "Firehouse"; Del's air code is "Fire Chief"; Rossi's is "Arson One"; Cashbox's is "Arson Two." The backs of the pilots' jackets are marked with the Chinese flag.

Al Evans composed the theme.

The DuMont Network also presented a series called "Major Del Conway of the Flying Tigers," with both Eric Fleming (4/14/51 to 5/26/51) and Ed Peck (7/29/51 to 3/2/52) as Major Del Conway. This version, however, was set in the time it was filmed and dealt with the exploits of Major Del Conway, a former World War II air force pilot, who was now the chief pilot for the Los Angeles–based Flying Tigers Airline. He and his partner, Caribou Jones (Luis Van Rooten, then Bern Hoffman), were also investigators for G-2, American military intelligence. See also "Ding Howe and the Flying Tigers."

427. *Make Room for Daddy*

ABC, 9/29/53 to 7/17/57
CBS, 10/7/57 to 9/14/64

Cast: Danny Thomas *(Danny Williams),* Jean Hagen *(Margaret Williams),* Marjorie Lord *(Kathy Williams),* Sherry Jackson and Penney Parker *(Terry Williams),* Rusty Hamer *(Rusty Williams),* Angela Cartwright *(Linda Williams),* Louise Beavers and Amanda Randolph *(Louise),* Sid Melton *(Charlie Halper).*

Facts: Daniel ("Danny") Williams is a nightclub entertainer who performs regularly at the Copa Club in New York City. He is first married to Margaret and the father of two children, Terry and Rusty. They live in Apartment 1204 at the Parkside Apartments in Manhattan. They have a dog named Laddie. In 1957, a year after Margaret's "death," Danny marries Kathleen ("Kathy") Daly (a.k.a. Kathy O'Hara), a widowed nurse with a young daughter named Linda. Danny, Kathy, Terry, Rusty and Linda now live in Apartment 542 (also given as Apartment 781) at 505 East 56th Street; their phone number is Plaza 3-1098 (later Plaza 3-0198). Danny calls Kathy "Clancey."

Danny was born in Toledo, Ohio, and attended Ursuline Academy (a school run by nuns of the Ursuline Order). Danny dropped out of school after one year to go to work. (In another episode, Danny mentions he was born in Deerfield, Michigan, and raised in Toledo. His school was said to be Woodward High, which later awarded him an honorary diploma.)

Margaret Summers, Danny's first wife, was born in Baraboo, Wisconsin, and met Danny when she was 17 years old (she was a part-time waitress and piano player; Danny was a 24-year-old comedian). In another episode, it is mentioned that Danny has known Margaret since she was a young girl. As a child, Margaret was cared for by Mom and Pop Finch (Kathryn Card and Will Wright) while her mother and father were on the road in vaudeville.

Kathy was born in Peoria, Illinois. She and Danny honeymooned in Las Vegas (they stayed in Room 504 of the Sands Hotel). When Kathy was first introduced (to care for Rusty when he became ill), she had a daughter named Patty (Lelani Sorenson). Patty became Linda when the series switched to CBS.

Terry (Teresa), Danny's oldest child, attended West Side High School, then an unnamed college where she was a member of the Alpha Beta Chi sorority. She left the series in 1960 when she married Pat Hannigan (Pat Harrington, Jr.).

Rusty (Russell), Danny's son, was born on February 15, 1947. He first attended P.S. 54, then Claremont Junior High, and finally West Side High School. He is also a member of Scout Troop 44. In a 1956 episode, Rusty, who has a fascination with Elvis Presley and television's "Wyatt Earp," called himself Elvis Earp, ran away from home and began a career as an orphan at Miss Martin's Children's Home. Rusty thought the best parts of school were recess, lunch and holidays, and he had his first crush on a girl named Sylvia Watkins (Pamela Beaird).

Linda, Kathy's daughter, attends P.S. 54, believes in Santa Claus and the Tooth Fairy, and has an "imaginary friend," who nobody believes exists, called Mr. Jumbo (he is ten feet tall and wears a red coat. He did actually exist—as the doorman at the Drake Hotel).

Other Characters: Louise is Danny's maid; Charlie Halper is Danny's boss, the owner of the Copa Club; he is married to Bunny (Pat Carroll).

Gina Minelli (Annette Funicello) is the Italian exchange student who comes to stay with the Williams family. She attends West Side High School and tutors the school's star football players, Buck Weaver and Bronco Lewis (Mr. Inside and Mr. Outside on the team). Her favorite singer is Frankie Laine, and she had a dream become a reality when Danny arranged for Frankie to sing at Gina's beside when she was stricken with the measles and couldn't attend his performance at the school.

Danny's Uncle Tonoose (Hans Conried) is the head of the family. He is nicknamed "Hashush-al-Kabaar" (Lebanese for "The Man Who Made a Monkey Out of a Camel") and loves goat cheese and grape leaves. He claims the family ancestors include King Achmed the Unwashed. Prior to his role as Uncle Tonoose (from spring 1956 on), Hans Conried played Margaret's cousin, Carl, who drank a lot and traveled with jugs of wine.

Harvey Lembeck (as Chip Collins), Jesse White (Jesse Leeds) and Horace McMahon and Sheldon Leonard (Phil Arnold) played Danny's agents over the years. In several episodes, Steven Geray played the Williamses' family physician, Dr. Verhagen (which is Jean Hagen's real last name).

The lives of the Williams family members were updated in the special "The Danny Thomas TV Family Reunion" (NBC, 2/14/65). Two years later, on "The Danny Thomas Hour," the cast reunited for "Make More Room for Daddy" (NBC, 11/6/67) in a story that found Rusty in the army and preparing to marry Susan McAdams (Jana Taylor).

In 1969 (9/14), CBS aired the one hour pilot "Make Room for Granddaddy." In the ensuing series (ABC, 9/23/70 to 9/2/71), Rusty and Susan are struggling newlyweds, Linda is attending a boarding school in Connecticut, and Terry (Sherry Jackson) is married to Bill Johnson (not seen), a serviceman stationed in Japan. Terry is the mother of six-year-old Michael (Michael Hughes); as Terry leaves to join Bill, Michael is left with Danny and Kathy—and hence the title.

Relatives: Tony Bennett (Danny's cousin, *Steven*), Nana Bryant (Margaret's mother, *Julie Summers*), William Demarest (Kathy's father, *Mr. Daly*), Louise Lorimer (Margaret's aunt, *Faye*). Margaret mentioned that her father's name was Harry.

Theme: "Danny Boy," by Herbert Spencer and Earle Hagen.

428. *Makin' It*

ABC, 2/1/79 to 3/16/79

Billy Manucci (David Naughton) is an easygoing young man who lives at home (232 King Street, Passaic, New Jersey) with his parents, Joseph (Lou Antonio) and Dorothy (Ellen Travolta), his sister, Tina (Denise Miller), and in the shadow of his swinging older brother, Tony (Greg Antonacci), "a great dancer who just drifts."

Billy, who takes the number 4 bus to college (Passaic University), is studying to become a teacher. He works for Ivy Papastegios (Jennifer Perito) at an ice cream parlor called Tasty Treats and hangs out at a disco called the Inferno. Thirteen-year-old Tina attends Saint Bernadette's Elementary School, and when Billy seeks advice from Tony, he gets the "Manucci Prediction" ("I don't give advice, I predict").

Corky Crandall (Rebecca Balding), an agent for the William Morris Agency in Manhattan, is Billy's girlfriend; and Al ("Kingfish") Sorrentino (Ralph Seymour) and Bernard Fusco (Gary Prendergast) are Billy's friends.

David Naughton sings the theme, "Makin' It."

429. *Mama's Family*

NBC, 1/22/83 to 9/15/84
Syndicated, 9/86

Cast: Vicki Lawrence (*Thelma Harper*), Ken Berry (*Vinton Harper*), Dorothy Lyman (*Naomi Harper*), Karin Argoud (*Sonia Harper*), Eric Brown (*Buzz Harper*), Allan Kayser (*Bubba Higgins*), Beverly Archer (*Iola Boylen*).

Facts: Residing at 1542 Ray Lane (in some episodes, 1542 Ray Way) in Raytown, U.S.A., are the Harpers, a not so typical American family.

Thelma ("Mama") Harper is the cantankerous head of the family. She was married to a man named Carl (deceased) who called her "Snooky Ookems." Mama, who wears a perfume called Obsession and cleans her oven with Easy-Off, is a member of the Raytown Community Church League. She can extract truth from people with her gift—the look (a stare that forces people to be honest)—and she marketed Mother Harper's Miracle Tonic to make money (a supposed cold remedy that contained Mama's secret ingredient—pure vanilla extract. With its 35 percent alcohol content, the tonic made users forget why they took it in the first place).

Mama made all her children take tap dancing lessons: "There ain't a Harper who can't sing or dance," Mama says, "except Eunice" (Mama's third-born daughter). Mama held a job as a receptionist for the Raytown Travel Agency. Her most treasured recipe is for Million Dollar Fudge, and her home was originally 10 Decatur Road (at which time it was a brothel called Ma Beaudine's). As a child, Thelma was jump rope champion of the second grade.

Vinton Harper is Mama's second-born child (born April 23, at 8 pounds 2 ounces, and 22 inches long). He is a locksmith and works for Kwick Keys, a company that is owned by the Bernice Corporation. He collects *TV Guides* (he has a collection dating back 25 years, to 1958). His favorite hangout is the Bigger Jigger Bar, and he is a member of the Mystic Order of the Cobra Club. Vint has an insurance policy with Mutual of Raytown and as a kid had a pet rabbit named Fluffy. His favorite breakfast cereal is Dino Puffs (not for the high fiber count but for the surprise toy dinosaur that comes in each box).

Naomi Oates, "the sexiest woman in Raytown," and the Harpers' next door neighbor, married Vint in 1983. (Vinton's former wife, Mitzi, ran out on him. Naomi had four previous marriages, to Tom, Bill, Leonard and George.) Naomi is a checker at the local supermarket, Food Circus, and is called "Skeeter" by Vinton (Mama believes Naomi is the kind of girl mothers fear their sons will marry). As a kid, Naomi had a dog named Marlon, and her favorite candy is red licorice whips. Naomi also became a wrestler (a "Queen Bee") to help her friend, Didi Mason (Spice Williams), in the Women's Wrestling Championships (Vint was the ringside attendant, the Bee Keeper, and Naomi battled the Masked Mabels).

Sonia and Vinton Harper, Jr. ("Buzz") are Vint's children from his first marriage. Sonia has a midnight curfew; Buzz must be in by 1:00 A.M. Both attended Raytown High School, and both were dropped from the syndicated version of the series. Sonia is named after her cousin, Sonia, "a schoolteacher for 35 years who one day went berserk and set the gym on fire."

Bubba Higgins is Mama's grandson (Eunice's son). He attends Raytown Junior College and entered Mama in the Lovely Be Lady Grandma U.S.A. Pageant (she won first runner-up).

Iola Boylen is Mama's longtime friend and neighbor, a spinster who lives with her never-seen domineering mother. She is a member of the Peppermint Playhouse Theater Company and loves to sew and do arts and crafts.

NBC episodes feature Mama's other children: Ellen Jackson (Betty White), Thelma's first-born daughter, now a widow and a society woman; and Eunice Higgins (Carol Burnett), Mama's third-born, neurotic daughter. Fran Crawley (Rue McClanahan), Thelma's sister, writes a column "for the local paper that is thrown on the porch."

When Mama found a girlie magazine under Bubba's bed, she formed M.O.P. (Mothers Opposing Pornography). Mama's "Crazy" Uncle Oscar thought he was a pirate and owned a boat rental business. When he passed on, Mama inherited Captain Petey, Oscar's parrot. Vinton won a talent contest at the Bigger Jigger by imitating Fred Astaire. The success went to his head, and he called himself Vinnie Vegas.

James Ray founded the town. The major tourist attraction is the tomb of the unknown Raytonian; the makeout spot is Ray Point. The program is based on a series of skits originally performed on "The Carol Burnett Show."

Relatives: Harvey Korman (Eunice's husband, *Ed Higgins*), Vicki Lawrence (Thelma's cousin, *Lydia,* and *Thelma's mother* in a ghost sequence), Dorothy Van (Thelma's sister, *Effie*), Imogene Coca (Thelma's aunt, *Gert*), Jerry Reed (Naomi's ex-husband, *Leonard Oates*), Penelope Sudrow (Iola's niece, *Vernette*).

Flashbacks: Vicki Lawrence *(Thelma as a young woman),* Tanya Fenmore and Heather Kerr *(Eunice as a girl),* Amy O'Neill *(Ellen as a girl),* David Friedman *(Vinton as a boy),* Nikki Cox *(Iola as a girl).*

Theme: "Bless My Happy Home," by Peter Matz.

430. *A Man Called Shenandoah*

ABC, 9/13/65 to 9/5/66

"O, Shenandoah, you're doomed to wander; so roam in search of home, 'cross this land so lonely." As this theme played, the figure of a man (Robert Horton) is seen riding through the deep snow. The blistering winds and bitter cold have become part of his life as he wanders from town to town seeking to discover his past—an identity that was lost to him when he was shot in the head for unknown reasons and left to die on the prairie. He was found by two bounty hunters and brought to a nearby town. There he was nursed back to health by a saloon girl named Kate (Beverly Garland). But upon awakening, he found himself a man without a memory and unaware of who or what he was. Now, as Shenandoah (the Indian name for an amnesiac), he searches for his past throughout the turbulent West of the 1860s ("You can't build a future unless you know the past," he says).

Shenandoah never uncovered his true identity. He learned only that he was a U.S. Army lieutenant assigned to the Western Division of the Second Regiment at Fort Smith and that Fort Todd was the only place he could remember ever having lived.

Robert Horton sings the theme, "Shenandoah."

431. *A Man Called Sloane*

NBC, 9/22/79 to 12/22/79

Thomas Remington Sloane III (Robert Conrad) is a Priority One Agent for UNIT, a secret U.S. government counterespionage team. Torgue (Ji-Tu Cumbuka) is his assistant, and Mr. Director (Dan O'Herlihy) is the head of UNIT. The front for UNIT is a Los Angeles toy store called the Toy Boutique; the brains behind UNIT is Effie, an E.F.I. series 3000 computer (Michele Carey provides the offscreen, sexy voice for Effie). The enemy of UNIT is KARTEL, an organization that is bent on destroying the world. Patrick Williams composed the theme, "A Man Called Sloane."

In the original 1979 pilot film, "Death Ray 2000," which was broadcast by NBC on 3/5/81, Robert Logan was Thomas R. Sloane, an agent for UNIT and the owner of an antique business called Sloane and Sons in Carmel, California (Penelope Windust played Sloane's business associate, Emma Blessing). Dan O'Herlihy played Mr. Director, but Ji-Tu Cumbuka was a villain named Torgue, who sought to kill Sloane. UNIT was located in Kentucky, where Mr. Director posed as a rural farmer (UNIT's offices were in the back of a barn). John Elizalde composed the original theme.

432. *The Man from Atlantis*

NBC, 9/22/77 to 5/2/78

Cast: Patrick Duffy *(Mark Harris)*, Belinda J. Montgomery *(Dr. Elizabeth Merrill)*, Victor Buono *(Mr. Schubert)*.

Facts: A storm deep within the Pacific Ocean unearths the sole survivor of the fabled lost kingdom of Atlantis and washes him ashore. A father and son, walking on a beach in California, find the unconscious Atlantian and call an ambulance.

The Atlantian, who has webbed hands, is brought to a hospital, where doctors are unable to determine what is wrong with him (other than desiccated lungs and the fact that "he has forgotten how to breathe").

Elizabeth Merrill, a naval doctor, takes an interest in the case and examines the victim. "I know how to save him," she exclaims. With the help of paramedics, she returns Mark to the sea. The water revives and saves the Atlantian's life. The Atlantian, whom Elizabeth names Mark Harris, is brought to the Naval Undersea Center. Through Elizabeth's examination of Mark, we learn the following:

After two weeks he was able to leave the pool for short periods ... Evidence shows a humanoid being only marginally equipped for life on land ... His eyes are sensitive; we have prepared a pair of dark glasses for him. He tires easily and physical exertion will exhaust him ... After 12 hours out of water, actual physical deterioration begins—the first signs of which are the prompt discolorization of the extremities ... More than 16 hours ... will cause death. However, in water a different picture emerges. He is perfectly adapted to aquatic life. He has great strength and agility. The chest cavity has gill-like membranes in place of lung tissue. His skin appears humanoid with dolphinlike characteristics. His eyes are catlike and he can see in almost total darkness ... He is becoming as curious about us as we are about him ... He hasn't spoken yet, but he is teachable and has vocal equipment ... His diet is kelp and plankton. As for his origins, we have very little to go on.

All the information Elizabeth has is fed to the WRW 1200 computer in Washington, D.C. The computer responds with "Last Citizen of Atlantis?????"

Mark is then put through a series of additional tests. He can swim faster than a dolphin and can go to depths of over 36,000 feet. As Mark begins to learn about humans, he is asked to help the navy find a missing research submarine called the *Sea Quest* (which went off scope at 36,000 feet and is believed to be at the bottom of the Marianas Trench). Mark speaks for the first time, saying, "I say yes, Admiral" (referring to Admiral Dewey Pierce, played by Art Lund). Pierce appoints Elizabeth as Mark's supervisor.

While exploring the Marianas Trench, Mark spies a mysterious black submarine. He follows it through unexplored waters to a hidden passageway that leads to a sea mountain habitat owned by Mr. Schubert, "an ocean junkman who wised up, became rich and now gets whatever he wants." Schubert has created what he believes is a perfect world and is seeking to destroy the diseased world above, then make it good once again. Mark is captured, but he escapes and foils Schubert's plan (by flooding the habitat and stopping a signal beam from detonating the world's missiles, those that each power has aimed at the other in the event of war).

Although the government allows Mark to return to the sea, he elects to remain and help further humanity's knowledge of the sea and increase his own knowledge of human beings. Stories detail Mark and Elizabeth's work on behalf of the O.R.F. (Oceanic Research Foundation).

C.W. Crawford (Alan Fudge) is the head of the foundation, and Jane (Jean Marie Hon), Jimmy (J. Victor Lopez) and Juno (Anson Downes) are crew members of the foundation submarine, the *Citation*. Brent (Robert Lussier) is Mr. Schubert's fumbling assistant (Schubert's goal is to capture Mark for his own sinister purposes).

Mark calls himself a citizen of the ocean. He can't talk to fish, but he can understand dolphins and whales. Elizabeth, who gets withdrawal symptoms if she is away from the water too long, calls Mark "The Project Atlantis Affair."

Theme: "The Man from Atlantis," by Fred Karlin.

433. *The Man in the Family*

ABC, 6/19/91 to 7/31/91

When Sal Bavasso (Ray Sharkey) learns that his father, Carmine (Al Ruscio), is dying, he leaves Las Vegas and returns to his home in Brooklyn, New York. Sal, the black sheep of the family (Carmine disapproved of his playboy life-style, his friends and his spending habits), promises his father that he will care for the family and run the family business. Carmine's Deli is the business, and the family consists of Sal's mother, Angie Bavasso (Julie Bovasso), his divorced sister, Annie Bavasso (Annie DeSalvo), his teenage sister, Tina Bavasso (Leah Remini), Annie's son, Robby (Billy L. Sullivan), and his uncle, Bennie Bavasso (Louis Guss).

Carmine's Deli is located at 38 Benson Drive (its phone number is 718-642-1361). Sal and the family live in Apartment 4 on the first floor above the deli; they attend Sunday mass at Saint Vincent's Church. The family was profiled on the television show "Real Americans" for saving the life of an elderly homeless man who broke into the store and had a heart attack.

Sal is a wheeler-dealer and has a shady quality about him (possibly mob connections). He has been knocking around from one job to another since high school. He drives a car with the license plate 324 ZYH and frequents Ed's Lounge (his favorite night is Tuesday—Lingerie Night). When the womanizing Sal feels lucky, he takes his dates to the sleazy Honeymoon Inn Hotel. Sal came close to marriage only once—but he left his bride-to-be, Christina Minetti (Catherine Parks), at the altar for a rendezvous with her bridesmaid.

Annie, who is 33 years old, has been divorced for seven years and now works as a salesclerk at Macy's on 34th Street in Manhattan.

Tina, who is 17 years old, attends Saint Vincent's High School. She is very pretty, but sometimes doubts her beauty and ability to attract the opposite sex (if Sal feels a date is not right for Tina, a simple line like "Don't lay a finger on Tina" gets the message across). While Tina confesses that if a boy even tried to kiss her on a first date she would "knock his face off," Sal just can't trust them ("I was once their age"). On such occasions, Tina retreats to sloppy dress, uncombed hair, moping around and eating potato chips, ice cream and a very large bowl of chocolate pudding (Sal was right about one thing — "It's not a pretty sight").

Robby attends an unnamed grammar school (possibly Saint Vincent's Elementary School); Uncle Bennie shops at Vito's, Sal's competition, "because their prices are lower"; Angie mentioned a sister named Katie.

Cha Cha (Don Stark) is Sal's not too bright friend. He runs a dry cleaning shop and has a crush on Annie (his idea of impressing her is getting her tickets; he buys whatever he can at Ticketron and hopes she'll be impressed and go with him).

In the original, unaired pilot, "Honor Bound," Camille Saviola played Sal's mother, Angie Bavasso.

Louis Prima sings the theme, "When You're Smilin'."

434. *Man of the People*

NBC, 9/15/91 to 12/6/91

James ("Jim") Doyle (James Garner) is a city councilman who has to pull off scams to survive — "I can't survive on what they pay me in this burg." The "burg" is an unidentified town in the 7th District. Jim is a bookmaker and gambler. When his ex-wife, Margie Patterson, dies, the mayor, Lisbeth Chardin (Kate Mulgrew), appoints Jim to replace her for she believes the public wants the appointment to be that of someone close to the deceased councilwoman. It is also Lisbeth's plan to manipulate Jim for her own benefit. Unknown to Lisbeth, Jim is aware of her intentions but doesn't let on; he wheels and deals for his benefit, which includes winning the upcoming mayor's race and becoming the man of the people.

Jim drives a car with the license plate 20CE 465; Kelly's Pool Hall is his favorite hangout; as a kid, Jim worked as a shill for an evangelist. Lisbeth has a horse named Jack Hammer, and the Barham Realty Company supplements Lisbeth's income in return for favors.

Constance LeRoy (Corinne Bohrer) is Jim's former sister-in-law; she now works as his office assistant (she is determined not to let him run scams from the office). Her goal is to keep Jim on the straight and narrow; in her mind she is right and everybody else is wrong. Rita (Romy Walthall) is Jim's ditsy receptionist, an ex-hooker who was arrested twice for prostitution. Kathleen Quinlan played the part of Constance in the unaired pilot version.

J.D. Hart, Steve Tyrrell and Darnell Brown composed the theme, "I'm the Man."

435. *Mancuso, FBI*

NBC, 10/13/89 to 5/18/90

Nick Mancuso (Robert Loggia) is a no-nonsense FBI agent with the Metropolitan Bureau Field Office in Washington, D.C. Nick grew up on the Lower East Side of New York City and was married to a woman named Mary Louise (who died in 1964). He now lives at 311 Delaware Street, and 555-1121 is his phone number. Gertie's Bar is his favorite watering hole, and 8E9-356 is his license plate number. Lee Garlington plays Gertie, the bar owner.

Jean St. John (Randi Brazen; a.k.a. Randi Brooks) is Nick's secretary; she lives at 1032 Fairgreen Place. Kristen Carter (Lindsay Frost) is an FBI agent who assists Nick; she resides at 1136 Arlington Place, Apartment 7.

Lorraine Kovacs (Janet Carroll) is Nick's married daughter; Andy Kovacs (Michael Bell) is Lorraine's husband; Lee Ann Kovacs (Leigh Hughes) is Lorraine's daughter.

Susan Hamilton and Doug Katsaros composed the theme, "Mancuso, FBI."

Mandrake the Magician see *The Magician*

436. *Mann and Machine*

NBC, 4/5/92 to 7/14/92

The series is set in "the near future in Los Angeles," in a time where manmade robots assist live police officers in upholding the law. (Laser fences protect crime scenes; the San Francisco Giants are now the Tokyo Giants.) After a year and a half "with a bucket of bolts" lab-created partner named Warner, Detective Bobby Mann (David Andrews) is teamed with Sergeant Eve Edison (Yancy Butler), a highly sophisticated and beautiful female robot, when his partner is put out of commission by a bullet. Stories relate their case investigations.

Eve was created through the Artificial Intelligence Program by Dr. Anna Kepler (Samantha Eggar). Eve's body is basically a combination of plastic compounds and alloy metals. Her brain is like the human brain, and Eve is the first creation that is capable of assimilating artificial material. Eve can learn to be human — "She just needs the opportunity." She is the prototype for the Protector, the future partner of every police officer. Eve is highly advanced in technical terms, but emotionally she is very young (the age of a seven year old girl). She has the deductive reasoning of Sherlock Holmes and a genuine sense of humor (she will react if somebody says something she thinks is funny). She eats, sleeps and daydreams. Her eyes are capable of emitting laser beams; her tears are a lubricant; and she can speak 40 languages.

The only way that Eve can grow is to experience life— "the good, the bad and the ugly of it." Eve watches a lot of television to learn things she doesn't think she would normally learn on the job ("The Three Stooges" and "The Mod Squad" are her favorite shows). Her brain downloads directly to the computer in her apartment (the Advanced A.I. Work Station Computer). She can access any computer through a special earplug adapter.

Eve believes she was built for only one purpose: to enforce the law. She is a retrieval expert, "an information specialist. There isn't a mainframe in the country that I can't access." Eve was transferred to the San Francisco Bay area (she was created in Danville in the Silicon Valley) and scored the highest marks ever recorded on the sergeant's exam. She has a worm collection, and her lucky number is the algebraic term "pi." Eve lives in Apartment 1407 at the Metropolitan Hotel.

Bobby has to fill out a special report on Eve after each case. He is divorced and the father of a young girl (not seen). He is a Catholic and was an altar boy when he attended grammar school. Bobby has a dog named Rose and A-positive blood. He and Eve are with the Metropolitan Police Department; Captain Margaret Claghorn (S. Epatha Merkerson) is their superior.

Mark Mothersbaugh composed the "Mann and Machine" theme.

437. *Many Happy Returns*

CBS, 9/21/64 to 4/12/65

"Every customer is a satisfied customer" is the policy of Krockmeyer's Department Store in Los Angeles. The store's object is "not to accept returns. Talk customers into actually believing the object they are returning is what they actually need."

Walter Burnley (John McGiver) is the man hired by Owen Sharp (Russell Collins), the store owner, to manage the Adjustments and Refunds Department and follow his rule. Walter is a man who talked a cop out of giving him a ticket for driving the wrong way on a one way street, going through a red light and driving on the sidewalk. He's good, but when it comes to managing his department, he finds it one of the biggest challenges of his life. Lynn Hall (Elena Verdugo), Joseph ("Joe") Foley (Mickey Manners) and Wilma Fritter (Jesslyn Fax) are his annoying staff. Lynn is very pretty, but something of a dizzy blonde. She can handle the job, but irritates Walter by using her telephone extension (402) for more personal calls than business calls. Joe is not too bright, has trouble spelling, is forgetful and can't handle a customer with a complaint. He calls Walter "Boss." Wilma is "the old biddie" who is a combination of both Lynn and Joe and seems to have been working at the store since before it was even built.

The bad way to start a day is with a return. Items can be held for only ten days, then become nonreturnable. Items that are accepted for return are marked "Return to Stock."

Many Happy Returns. Elena Verdugo and John McGiver.

Walter, who has an account at the Friendly First National Bank, is a widower who lives in an apartment at 50 Chestnut Street. His daughter, Joan Randall (Elinor Donahue), her husband, Bob Randall (Mark Goddard), and their daughter, Laurie Randall (Andrea Sacino), live at 609 North Elm Street—just a short distance from his nephew, Ralph Conway (Martin Braddock), his wife, Ellen Braddock (Ina Victor), and their son, Jimmy (Bobby Buntrock), who live at 629 North Elm Street. Walter's involvement with their problems is also depicted. Don Beddoe appeared as Mr. Krockmeyer and Elvia Allman as Mrs. Sharp.

David Rose and Parke Levy composed the theme.

The Many Loves of Dobie Gillis see *Dobie Gillis*

438. *Marblehead Manor*

Syndicated, 9/87 to 9/88

The luxurious mansion located at 14 Sunflower Lane (city not identified) is called Marblehead Manor. It is owned by the eccentric millionaire Randolph Stonehill (Bob Fraser) and his gorgeous, level-headed wife, Hilary (Linda Thorson). Randolph is the owner of a company called Stonehill, Inc. (exactly what they do is not said). Hilary is over 40 years old and her fabulous figure still turns men's heads (she wears a 38C bra). She has a dog named Albert. Hilary named Albert after their ever faithful butler, Albert Dudley

(Paxton Whitehead). Albert is a third generation butler to a third generation of Stonehills.

Lupe Lopez (Dyana Ortelli) is the manor's sexy cook and maid. She is the mother of Elvis (Humberto Ortiz), who weighed 11 pounds, five ounces at birth. Rick (Michael Richards) is the inept, misadventure-prone estate gardener.

Carol Bruce appeared as Randolph's mother, Margaret Stonehill, and Natalie Core was Randolph's aunt, Charlotte. In the original pilot episode (shown as the last episode of the series), Charo played Cookie, the ultrasexy maid. Dan Foliart and Howard Pearl composed the theme, "It's a Grand Life."

439. *Margie*

ABC, 10/12/61 to 8/31/62

The comic adventures of Marjorie ("Margie") Clayton (Cynthia Pepper), a pretty teenage girl who lives in the small town of Madison during the 1920s. Central 4734 is her phone number, and she lives with her parents, Harvey and Nora Clayton (Dave Willock and Wesley Marie Tackitt), and her younger brother, Cornell (Johnny Bangert); an address is not given.

Margie attends Madison High School with her friends, the stunning Maybelle Jackson (Penney Parker) and the awkward Heywood Botts (Tommy Ivo). Maybelle lives at 63 Oak Tree Lane and fancies herself as a flapper; Heywood has a crush on Margie. The afterschool hangout is Crawford's Ice Cream Parlor.

Margie is the editor of the school newspaper, the *Madison Bugle,* and writes the gossip column, "Through the Keyhole." In the episode of 1/4/62 ("Fly the Coop"), Margie and Maybelle test their independence and leave home to become roommates in a cheap apartment at 211 Clark Street. Harvey is a loan officer at the Great Eastern Savings Bank; he and Nora also attended Madison High School.

Hollis Irving appeared as Margie's aunt, Phoebe; and Maxine Stuart and Herb Ellis played Maybelle's parents. Lionel Newman composed the theme adaptation of the song "Margie."

440. *Married People*

ABC, 9/18/90 to 1/30/91
ABC, 3/16/91 (1 episode)

Cast: Bess Armstrong *(Elizabeth Meyers)*, Jay Thomas *(Russell Meyers)*, Barbara Montgomery *(Olivia Williams)*, Ray Aranha *(Nick Williams)*, Megan Gallivan *(Cindy Campbell)*, Chris Young *(Allen Campbell)*.

Facts: A domestic comedy about incidents in the lives of three married couples who live in a three-family home at 862 Central Park North (at 73rd Street) in New York City. The rent is $500 a month, and the house is a brownstone that is actually located in Harlem—but the tenants prefer to call it "Central Park North" after the street sign on the corner.

Nick and Olivia Williams, a black couple in their fifties, own the building (they live in Apartment 1) and have been married for 32 years (they wed on 7/16/58 at 9:45 A.M.). Nick's Fruits and Vegetables is the name of the store Nick operates and has owned for 23 years (his delivery truck's license plate is 586M066). Nick's hangout is Morry's Pool Hall ("where for the first 15 years of his life he got his brains beat out"; he was called "Nick the Stick"). They have five children.

Occupying Apartment 2 are Elizabeth and Russell Meyers, a thirtyish white couple who met in college and married after graduation. Elizabeth is 36 years old, attended Yale University and now works as an attorney for the Wall Street law firm of Michaelson and Michaelson; in the episode of 12/5/90, Elizabeth adds her name to the firm when she becomes a partner. Elizabeth "lived on coffee and cheese doodles" while attending law school and did her clerking for a judge who called her "Toots."

Russell is a freelance writer who has penned articles for *TV Guide* and the *New Yorker* magazine. He later acquires a monthly column for *Manhattan Life* magazine called "The Worst of New York" (wherein he reviews ten worst things each month; for example, worst landlords, worst diners). He attended the Columbia School of Journalism and hates to be called "Russie" (his mother, Evelyn, was in labor for 52 hours with him). Elizabeth says she is "36 but looks 32; Russell is 37 but looks 42." When the series began, Elizabeth was already pregnant; in the episode of 11/14/90, she gave birth to a son she and Russell name Max (8 pounds, 5 ounces). Elizabeth buys her groceries at the 85th Street Market and baby items at Bob's World of Babies. Their phone number is 555-8274. Russell attended Woodstock in 1969 and claims the gray spot on the album cover is his tent.

Apartment 3 is rented by Cynthia ("Cindy") Campbell and her husband, Allen, a young white couple (18 years old) from Mineral Wells, Indiana, who moved to New York so Allen could attend Columbia University. Cindy, a cheerleader in high school who has aspirations of being a dancer, works as a waitress at the East Side Diner. Her first professional dancing job was with the Exotic Porthole Dancers, and in the last episode she auditioned for and got the part of a dancer (Girl number 2) in the Broadway play "The Phantom of the Opera" (which, according to the marquee, was playing at the Majestic Theater in Manhattan). At home in Mineral Wells, Cindy had a cat named Simone. She is famous for her "Sticky Treats" (a gooey Rice Krispies and marshmallow snack). Allen works after classes in the school's lab; Cindy is extremely jealous of Izzy (Elizabeth Berkley), Allen's gorgeous lab partner at school (her real name is Isabel). Cindy's favorite meal to cook is three-bean and marshmallow casserole (which was her final project in

Margie. **Front: Cynthia Pepper and Richard Gering; back: Tommy Ivo and Penney Parker.**

home economics). In Indiana, Allen was allergic to walnuts; in New York, he is allergic to hazelnuts. Cindy's co-worker at the diner is Madeline (Andrea Elson).

Relatives: Florence Stanley (Russell's mother, *Evelyn Meyers*), Paul Gleason (Cindy's father, *Paul Graham*; owns a farm in Indiana), Christopher Rich (Elizabeth's brother, *Ned*), Lela Ivey (Ned's wife, *Jane*), Thora (Ned's daughter, *Emily*), Brian Bonsall (Ned's son, *Brian*), J.J. Jones (Nick and Olivia's son, *Joey Williams*).

Theme: "Married People," by Bob Boykin.

441. *Married . . . with Children*

Fox, 4/5/87 to the present

Cast: Ed O'Neill *(Al Bundy)*, Katey Sagal *(Peggy Bundy)*, Christina Applegate *(Kelly Bundy)*, David Faustino *(Bud Bundy)*, Amanda Bearse *(Marcy Rhoades)*, David Garrison *(Steve Rhoades)*, Ted McGinley *(Jefferson D'Arcy)*.

Facts: At 9674 (also given as 9764) Jeopardy Lane in

Chicago, Illinois, live the Bundy family: a husband (Al) who has a pathetic life; a wife (Peggy) who doesn't cook or clean but loves to spend Al's hard-earned money; their beautiful but dense daughter (Kelly); and their girl-crazy son (Bud) who can't get a date.

The family members rarely speak to each other; Al can't remember his kids' names; and Peggy is always in a romantic mood (much to Al's regret). The Bundy philosophy is "If you're gonna lose, lose big." The Bundy credo is "When one Bundy is embarrassed, the rest of us feel good about ourselves." The dream of the male Bundys is to build their own room and live apart from their wives; the Bundy legacy states that "what a Bundy doesn't finish in 30 seconds they will never finish." No judge will believe a Bundy in court (because of a case in which Al sued the Girl Scouts for choking on a bone in a butter cookie).

For Thanksgiving, they have the "Bundy Turkey" (a pizza) and on Labor Day, the Bundy Barbecue and Bundy Burgers (last year's grease and ashes for this year's burgers). The dreaded annual event is the family vacation, and the family stores all their junk at Chico's Storage Bin. The Bundys don't have a VCR; Al borrows neighbor Marcy's to watch his only form of entertainment—"Hooter Classics" (for example, *Breast Monsters from Venus* and *Planet of the D Cups*).

Al and Peggy's checks read "Mrs. Peggy Bundy and the Nameless Shoe Salesman." Their wedding song was "We've Only Just Begun"; for their wedding gift, Al's parents gave them a bag of Jiffy Pop Popcorn. When Kelly and Bud were very young they thought Al was the dim-witted handyman. The Bundys have a gun, but Peggy is afraid the kids will find it and shoot themselves (she hides the bullets in Al's bowling ball). In the entire history of the Bundy family, no Bundy wife has ever worked inside or outside of the house. The Bundys also have a dog named Buck, whom they don't like to pet ("He might expect it from us").

Al works as a shoe salesman for Garry's Shoes and Accessories for the Beautiful Woman in the New Market Mall (he did a television commercial for Zeus Athletic Shoes). He attended James K. Polk High School (where he was voted Most Valuable Player of 1966. He wore jersey number 33, made four touchdowns in one game and was offered a college scholarship; he turned it down to marry Peggy). Al believes his life was ruined when he met a fellow student named Margaret ("Peggy") Wanker at a hamburger joint named Johnny B. Goods (where Al holds the record for eating ten bags of fries at one sitting). She was a sex kitten; Al was a guy. He let his hormones do his thinking for him, and he has been sorry ever since. They married in 1972. Al loves women, except "my red-headed plague," and often has dreams about "gorgeous big-busted babes" (his dreams are always interrupted when something good is about to happen). After 20 years on the job, the unbelievable happened: Al got a "shoe groupie," a beautiful girl named Rickie (Jessica Hahn) who was turned on by shoes and shoe talk. Reluctantly, Al gave her up to remain faithful to Peggy. Why? Al doesn't know either.

Al's pride and joy is his collection of *Playboy* magazines, which his father started him on when he was 12 years old

(he took Al into the garage; behind the toolbox were the magazines and the beginnings of the Bundy legacy). Jim's Fish and Chips and Insurance is Al's insurance company; "Psycho Dad" and "Tube Top Wrestling" are Al's favorite television shows.

In one episode Peggy mentions that Al makes $3.20 an hour; in another, $3.25 an hour. Al's only raise occurred in 1972 when he was given an extra ten cents a week. Al's brainstorm to make money was a telephone call-in service called Dr. Shoe (555-SHOE; as could be expected, no one called and Al lost $50,000). When Al was laid off, he took a job as a security guard at Polk High. In 1957 Al checked out *The Little Engine That Could* from the library and never returned it (30 years later, when he found the book, the fine was $2,163). When Al has a craving for cheesecake, he must have cherry cheesecake from Chuck's Cheese Bowl in Wisconsin (baked by Hans).

IF YOU CAN READ THIS, YOU'RE ALREADY DEAD says the sign on the shore of Lake Chicamocomico, a toxic waste dump Al bought as his retirement land (Lot 31; he has an "Andy Griffith Show" dream of retiring to a small community). Al's Dodge license plate reads F3B-359; the shoe store is sometimes called Garry's Shoes and Accessories for Today's Woman; Al has nightmares about feet and was a judge in "The Ugly Feet Contest of 1990."

Peggy was born in Wanker County, Wisconsin (mentioned as being in Milwaukee in another episode), a community that was founded by her ancestors. Peggy knows what will make Al happy, but she will never leave him. Although Peggy is a housewife, she never shops for food, cooks or cleans (she calls the oven "the big hot thing"). Her days are spent watching television and eating Bon-Bons. Finding food has become the family's number one priority. Al's favorite food is turkey (but he never gets it), and he has resorted to begging for leftovers at the local pizza parlor. On the rare occasion when Al has food to take to work, he carries a Charlie's Angels lunchbox. Because of the lack of plates in the house, Al has to share Buck's bowl (both their names are on it). Peggy makes her own garbage (which she borrows from Marcy) to show Al she does housework.

When the TV stations placed "Donahue" and "Oprah" opposite each other, Peggy asked Al to buy her a VCR. When he refused, she got a job in Muldin's Department Store in the clock department ("I hate working. That's why I got married"). In the episode of 2/17/91 Peggy took interior decorating classes at Cook County School of Design and ruined Al's one place of refuge—the bathroom he built for himself in the garage (she turned it into a "frilly pink nightmare." Al considered his "cold, white and soothing restroom" his "oasis away from pantyhose and women").

Peggy, a 36C cup, wears the Perfect Figure Model 327 bra. She has a stuffed parrot named Winky. On their wedding anniversary, Al gives Peggy shoes; she gives him a tie. While Al's favorite sport is bowling, Peggy holds the record at Jim's Bowlarama for bowling a perfect 300 game. Peggy's "chalkboard screech" annoys Al the most.

When Peggy became pregnant (sixth season), she held weekly "baby meetings" (the family had to say, "Hail baby," at each meeting). Al considered her a "Pregasaurus" ("Pregzilla" to be exact). Peggy's cravings included cream cheese and coffee grind sandwiches, bologna and Miracle Whip sandwiches and Super Whoopie Cookies. In October 1991 Katey Sagal, who was seven months pregnant, had a miscarriage. It was decided not to continue the pregnancy storyline on the series. In the episode of 11/24/91, Al wakes up from a dream and finds that Peggy is not pregnant.

Kelly, a blonde bombshell (typically dressed in tight jeans or tight miniskirt and low cut blouses) is, as Peggy calls her, "a hussy. She became a hussy when she learned to cut her diapers up the side." When Kelly was five years old, Peggy had her earning money by selling kisses. Kelly attends Polk High School (not for an education—but to pick up messages, supply the family with pens and get a hot meal). Kelly was born in February ("I'm an aquarium") and originally bleached her blonde hair (she was called "the white-haired girl" in some early episodes).

Kelly, whose sexy dress makes her very popular with the boys, calls herself "The Beatles of the 1980s." Kelly says, "Working is a bummer; I'm glad I'm a pretty girl so I don't have to work," but she actually held several jobs. She started as the Weather Bunny Girl on Channel 83's "Action News" program. What began as an intern project for school became a $1,000 a week job when management discovered that Kelly's stunning good looks were boosting ratings. Despite the fact that she didn't know where "East" Dakota was, she ws given a raise to $250,000 a year. She lost the job when she couldn't read the teleprompter. She was next a roller skating waitress at Bill's Hilltop Drive-In, then Miss Weenie Tots, a model who represented Weiner Tots (hot dogs wrapped in bread and fried in lard) at supermarkets.

In the episode of 9/23/90 Kelly graduates from Polk High. After seeing an ad in a newspaper for a modeling school, she decided that being a model would be her career. She got the $400 tuition money from Al when she pouted (Al can't resist her pouting). Although Kelly got tension headaches from smiling, she was told she was a natural leg crosser ("I can do it at will"). Her first job was as the Allanti Girl (the Allanti is a foreign car; she got the job by inventing the "Bundy Bounce," a modeling move where she jiggles her bosom). When Al finally got cable (at $60 a month), Kelly learned she could get her own show on public access television for $35. She got the money, and Channel 99 ran "Vital Social Issues 'n' Stuff with Kelly." With topics like "Slut of the Week," "Hunks" and "Bad Perms," the mythical NBS Network picked up the show (it was canceled when the vital issues became milk and books). When her modeling school closed, Kelly acquired a job at Chicago's TV World Theme Park. She was first the exit gate hostess, then the Verminator Girl (representing the environmentally safe insect killer; Bud worked as King Roach in the Verminator TV commercial exhibit). Kelly was later said to be born on November 27, and she writes her name on her palm so she can look at it to remember who she is. She knows she is very beautiful and that no other girl can measure up to her—that is, until Al hit on an idea to make $500 a month by hosting a foreign exchange student. A French bombshell named Yvette (Milla Jovovich) became

Kelly's only threat (the Bundys lost Yvette, whom Kelly called Y-vette, when she followed in Kelly's footsteps, cut classes and failed all her subjects, including French). Kelly appeared as the "Rock Slut" in the Gutter Cats music video and often eats at friends' houses "because they make homemade things." Kelly's favorite meal is veal, and Al calls her "Pumpkin" (Al can recall doing only two things for Kelly: carrying her home from the hospital—although he left her on the car roof—and buying her ice cream when she was ten years old).

Although Kelly had several jobs, as previously described, the episode of 11/8/92 exclaimed, "The unthinkable! The unbelievable!—Kelly gets a job!" The job was that of waitress in an unnamed diner (Kelly knew what a plate looked like, what a table looked like and that a waitress has to bring the plate to the table—not vice versa—and she got the job).

Bud, whose real name is Budrick, first attended Polk High School, then Jermaine College. He is called "Rat Boy" and "Toad Boy" by Kelly and has a crush on his next door neighbor, Marcy Rhoades. Bud wears Open Sesame aftershave lotion and watches "Dateless Dude Late Night Theater" when he can't get a date. Kelly claims Bud watches "Star Trek" reruns "to get a glimpse of Klingon cleavage." Bud is a member of the Polk High soccer team, the Reepers (jersey number 5). In 1991 Bud pretended to be the street rapper Grand Master B to impress girls. In the opening theme, Bud is seen reading a girlie magazine *Boudoir* and he calls his cowboy pajamas his "love clothes." Bud (jersey 00), Kelly (jersey 10), Peggy (jersey 11) and Al (jersey 14) were members of the New Market Mallers softball team. When Bud turned 18 (2/9/92), Al took him to the Nudie Bar (a tradition for male Bundys "when they become a man").

In the episode of 9/13/92, Peggy's gorgeous cousin, Ida Mae (Linda Blair), her strange husband, Zemus (Bobcat Goldthwait), and their five-year-old son, Seven (Shane Sweet), pay the Bundys a visit. Shortly after, Ida Mae and Zemus run off and leave Seven with Al and Peggy. "Oh no, another kid!" is Al's reaction; Peggy finds him adorable and shows signs that she can be a mother; Kelly and Bud feel cheated, as Peggy was never a mother to them.

Marcy Rhoades, the Bundys' neighbor, is a loan officer at the Kyoto National Bank. She was first married to Steve Bartholomew Rhoades, a loan officer at the Leading Bank of Chicago. She and Steve were married on Valentine's Day and are both vegetarians. When Steve lost his job for loaning Al the $50,000 to start Dr. Shoe, he became a cage cleaner at Slither's Pet Emporium, then a ranger at Yosemite National Park (at which time he left Marcy and the series). In the episode of 1/6/91, we learn that Marcy was a wild party animal at a banking seminar and woke up in bed with Jefferson D'Arcy—a man she married at Clyde's No Blood Test Needed Chapel. When Al discovered they did not have a proper wedding, he threw them one (for $2,000). The Bundy back yard was the wedding chapel; a Twinkie was the cake; Buck the maid of honor; Bud the wedding artist; Peggy, on accordion, the orchestra; and Al, the shortwave operator to the preacher—Captain Hank of the garbage scow *Toxia*. As a kid, Marcy had a dog named Winkems. She buys her lingerie at Hempley's Department Store.

Jefferson is a con artist and is now on parole (he was caught stealing money from investors). He calls Marcy "Bon Bon Bottom" (she calls him "Cinnamon Buns"). Steve, who was a member of his high school band (the Tuxedos), called Marcy "Angel Cups" (she called him "Sugar Tush"; Al calls Marcy as he sees it—"Chicken Legs"). When a house number is needed for Marcy, 9674 or 9476 is seen. Steve and Marcy had a yearly tradition: "On the first sunny day in May, we go to the beach to shake hands with Mr. Sunshine." Steve returned in the episode of 2/16/92 to reclaim Marcy (she rejected Steve, still a forest ranger, for Jefferson). There is an X-rated version of the series, titled *Married . . . with Hormones,* that appeared on home video in 1992 (featuring Hal, Meg, Nellie and Dud Undy).

Relatives: Ed O'Neill (*Al's father*), Charlie Brill (Al's uncle, *Eugene Bundy*), Joey Adams (Peggy's gorgeous cousin, *Effie Wanker*), William Sanderson (Peggy's uncouth cousin, *Eb Wanker*), James Haake (Peggy's cousin, *Otto Wanker*), King Kong Bundy (Peggy's cousin, *Irwin Wanker*), Milly, Elena and Eadie Del Rubio (Peggy's triplet cousins, *Milly, Elena* and *Eadie Wanker*), Karen Lynn Scott (Al's aunt, *Heather Bundy*). Not seen were Peggy's father, Pa Wanker; Peggy's grossly overweight mother (who needs to be transported by flatbed truck); and Peggy's cousin, Hootie Wanker (half man, half owl).

Theme: "Love and Marriage," vocal by Frank Sinatra.
Note: See also "Top of the Heap," the spinoff series.

442. *The Marshall Chronicles*

ABC, 4/4/90 to 5/2/90
ABC, 7/22/90 (1 episode)

High school student Marshall Brightman (Joshua Rifkind) lives with his parents Michael and Cynthia (Steve Anderson and Jennifer Salt) at 64 Gramercy Place in Manhattan. Michael is a private practice doctor, and Cynthia is a children's storybook editor for Fawn Publishing. Marshall attended P.S. 84 Grammar School and now takes the number 6 IRT subway train to his unidentified high school. He scored 1100 on his S.A.T. tests: 570 points in verbal, 530 in math. Stories relate Marshall's activities at school, where he is intelligent but constantly put down.

Marshall's friends are Melissa Sandler (Nile Lanning) and Sean Bickoff (Bradley Gregg). Melissa is a member of the school's Quiz Bowl team; Sean reads the girlie magazine *Big Babes in Water*. Other students are Leslie Barash (Meredith Scott Lynn), Vincent (Todd Graff) and Johnny Parmetko (Gabriel Bologna). The school is called "our school" or just "the school."

Karen Medak played Johnny's sister, Donna; and Jack Wohl appeared as Leslie's father, Jack Barash.

Randy Newman sings the theme, "Falling in Love."

443. *Martin Kane, Private Eye*

NBC, 9/11/49 to 8/20/53

Doll Face and *Sweetheart* are two of the terms he uses when speaking to female suspects; determination and force of character are two methods he uses to achieve results. He'll go where the work is and charges fees that he believes are appropriate to the case at hand (as much as $500). He's Martin Kane, a rugged private detective who operates out of New York City.

MARTIN KANE—PRIVATE INVESTIGATOR appears on his office door in the Wood Building in Manhattan (identified only by its zone—New York 20—zip codes did not yet exist). McMann's Tobacco Shop, telephone number El Dorado 5-4098, is his hangout. Kane smokes a pipe and uses Old Briar pipe tobacco mixture (15 cents a pouch). The shop is a vital part of the live series, as the sponsor's products are prominently displayed. In addition to Old Briar, other products of the United States Tobacco Company that are sold are Dill's Best pipe tobacco, Encore filter tip cigarettes and Sano cigarettes (no filter tips). When Kane discusses a case with shop owner Tucker ("Hap") McMann, customers appear to purchase a product. Hap excuses himself and pitches the sponsor's product while Kane (or someone else involved with the case) waits patiently on the side. The sale concluded, the show picks up from where the customer entered. (When Kane places tobacco in his pipe, the camera zooms in for a closeup of the product. Interestingly, announcer Fred Uttal said during the closing theme, "And now a few seconds, friends, to remind you that your annual federal and state cigarette taxes provide almost ten times as much as it costs to operate the United States Coast Guard. So remember, in buying cigarettes, over half your packs go to tax").

William Gargan (1949–51), Lloyd Nolan (1951–52) and Lee Tracy (1952–53) played Martin Kane; Walter Kinsella was Tucker ("Hap") McMann; Frank M. Thomas was Police Captain Burke; and King Calder was Lieutenant Grey Redfield (both of the N.Y.P.D. Homcide Squad).

Charles Paul composed and performed the organ theme, "Martin Kane, Private Eye."

A revised version of the series, "The New Adventures of Martin Kane," appeared on NBC from 8/27/53 to 6/17/54. Martin Kane (Mark Stevens, then William Gargan) was now a former U.S. Air Force colonel turned private detective who operates out of London (it is a 40 minute trip from the airport to his flat). While he still works with the police, he is not the hardboiled character depicted in the earlier series: "I don't speak in a fancy jargon, and I don't go around beating up beautiful women—an impression people get from seeing detectives in movies and reading about them in books." (The most the "old" Martin Kane ever did to a beautiful woman was slug her if he felt she deserved it or if needed to do so to save his life.) Women were often referred to by the slang of the day—"Skirt," "Doll," and "Tomato."

Brian Reece played Scotland Yard Inspector Headley; his

mobile car code was 19-C. There are no music credits, which is typical of series of this era.

444. *Mary*

CBS, 12/11/85 to 4/8/86

Mary Brenner (Mary Tyler Moore) is an attractive, middle aged magazine writer. She lives at 103 South Coast Road in Chicago and writes for a magazine called *Women's Digest*. When her magazine folds, Mary takes a job as the Consumer Helpline columnist for a newspaper called the *Chicago Eagle* (originally called the *Chicago Post*). Mary feels the job is beneath her, but she wants to remain in Chicago, and the Helpline Columnist job is the only one she could find.

Edward ("Ed") LaSalle (John Astin), the theater critic, writes the column "Stepping Out with Ed LaSalle," and Josephine ("Jo") Tucker (Katey Sagal) pens the column "The Mainline Reporter." Jo is a chainsmoker and lives in rather untidy surroundings in an apartment at 704 Holland Street. The fast food service used by the staff is Mr. Yummy.

Dennis Patrick and Doris Belack appeared as Jo's parents, Charles and Norma Tucker. Dan Foliart and Howard Pearl composed "Mary's Theme."

445. *Mary Hartman, Mary Hartman*

Syndicated, 1/6/76 to 7/3/77

The setting is the mythical town of Fernwood, Ohio, a peaceful little community until the mass murderer of Fernwood claimed the lives of the Lombardi family, their two goats and eight chickens, and put the town on the map.

The murders occurred on Mary June Street. A short distance from this street is Bratner Avenue in the Woodland Heights section of town. At 343 Bratner live Mary Hartman (Louise Lasser), a pretty housewife who constantly worries about the waxy yellow buildup on her kitchen floor, her husband, Tom (Greg Mullavey), an auto plant assembly line worker, and their daughter, Heather (Claudia Lamb), who attends the Woodland Heights Elementary School (Heather witnessed the killings and was kidnapped by the mass murderer, Davy Jessup, played by Will Seltzer).

Mary, who is 31 years old (born 4/8/45), and Tom, who is 35 (born 10/4/41), met at Fernwood High School (Tom and Mary have been married 14 years when the series begins; Mary married Tom when she was 17).

While Tom often cheats on mary (who often suspects he is unfaithful), Mary has only one extramarital affair—with the Fernwood Police Department's Sergeant Dennis Foley (Bruce Solomon). Mary, whose middle name is Penny and whose maiden name is Shumway, was once held hostage by a killer in the Chinese laundry at 414½ Miller Road.

Mary's parents, George (Phil Bruns) and Martha Shumway (Dody Goodman), her sister, Cathy Shumway (Debralee Scott), and her grandfather, Raymond Larkin (Victor Kilian), live at 4309 Bratner Avenue. George works with Tom at the Fernwood Auto Plant and has been married to Martha for 36 years. Grandpa Larkin, now 83, was born in Macon, Georgia, and has been arrested for being the Fernwood Flasher. He is somewhat senile and is always asking, "Where's the peanut butter?" Cathy, who is ten years younger than Mary, is a pretty, man-crazy free spirit.

Mary's next door neighbors are Charlie and Loretta Haggers (Graham Jarvis and Mary Kay Place), who live at 345 Bratner Avenue. Loretta, age 22, is a sweet and trusting country girl who is hoping to make it big as a recording artist. Charlie, her husband and manager, is 43 years old and works with Tom at the auto plant. Loretta, who calls Charlie "Baby Boy" (also the title of her first hit record), has two fish named Conway and Twitty, and performs at the local Fernwood watering hole, the Capri Lounge.

With the exception of Louise Lasser (whose character Mary ran off with Sergeant Foley), the series continued under the title "Forever Fernwood" (syndicated, 1977–78).

Earle Hagen composed the theme, "Mary Hartman, Mary Hartman" (Dody Goodman calls the name as the music plays).

446. *The Mary Tyler Moore Show*

CBS, 9/19/70 to 9/3/77

Cast: Mary Tyler Moore (*Mary Richards*), Ed Asner (*Lou Grant*), Gavin MacLeod (*Murray Slaughter*), Ted Knight (*Ted Baxter*), Valerie Harper (*Rhoda Morgenstern*), Cloris Leachman (*Phyllis Lindstrom*), Lisa Gerritsen (*Bess Lindstrom*), Betty White (*Sue Ann Nivens*).

Facts: Following a breakup with her boyfriend, Bill (Angus Duncan), Mary Richards leaves New York and heads for Minneapolis to begin a new life. There she takes Apartment D at 119 North Weatherly in a building owned by her friend, Phyllis Lindstrom. Shortly afterward, she secures a job as the assistant producer of the WJM-TV, Channel 12, "Six O'Clock News" program. Mary, who has a large *M* on her living room wall, is over 30, single and female—and the first such character to be portrayed on a weekly situation comedy.

Mary, a Presbyterian, originally applied for the job as a secretary at WJM. The job had been filled, but Lou Grant, the news show producer, hired her as the associate producer instead. Mary has spunk (which Lou hates) and "a nice caboose" (which Lou likes), and the job pays $10 a week less than the secretarial job (which is agreeable to both). Mary, who types 65 words a minute, was later promoted to producer when Lou decided to make himself executive producer. Mary is known for her terrible parties ("You give rotten parties. I've had some of the worst times of my life at your parties," says Lou, who broke up with his wife, Edie, at one such party). Mary tries to give good parties, but fate is against her (for example, she runs short of food when unexpected guests arrive, or has Johnny Carson as a guest on the same night there is a blackout).

Lou Grant is the exasperated producer of the news program. His favorite watering hole is the Happy Hour Bar ("Happy Hour" is from 5:00 to 6:00 P.M.), and his bar bill comes to the station on the fifteenth of every month. Lou has a bottle of booze in the bottom right drawer of his desk and a picture of himself as a college football player on his office wall. Lou, whose favorite actor is John Wayne, is a distinguished newsman who realizes that his news show will never become a ratings winner.

Though technically not a spinoff, a series called "Lou Grant" (CBS, 9/20/77 to 9/13/82) evolved following cancellation of "The Mary Tyler Moore Show." In it, Ed Asner played Lou Grant in a dramatic role as the city editor of the Los Angeles *Tribune,* the second largest newspaper in the city.

Ted Baxter, the station's incompetent newscaster, earns $31,000 a year, has trouble pronouncing words (for example, "Arkansas" becomes "Are-Kansas") and has a fake newspaper headline in his office that reads TED BAXTER WINS 3 EMMYS. He longs for an anchor job in New York with his hero, Walter Cronkite. Ted takes six sugars in his coffee and pays a high school senior five dollars a year to do his taxes. *Snow White* is his favorite Disney movie, and when he had a nonexclusive contract, he did television commercials (of all the ads he did—for a tomato slicer, a woman's product and a dog food product—only one was given a name: Ma and Pa's Country Sausage, where Ted was Farmer Ted, the spokesman). Ted also opened the Ted Baxter's Famous Broadcasting School, and Antonio's is his favorite place to eat. Ted hates to part with money, and he calls the station's control room "the Technical Place." Ted married Georgette Franklin (Georgia Engel), a shy windowdresser at Hempell's Department Store. Ted's closing is "Good night and good news."

Murray Slaughter, the only newswriter on the show, calls Ted's cue cards "idiot cards," and has been married to his wife, Marie (Joyce Bulifant), since 1955; their home phone number is 555-3727. Sue Ann Nivens, the host of WJM's "Happy Homemaker Show," has advice for everybody and has made it her goal to catch Lou (who wants nothing to do with her).

Mary's upstairs neighbor is Rhoda Morgenstern, a New Yorker who moved to Minneapolis when she couldn't find a job or an apartment in Manhattan. Although she and Mary did not hit it off at first (she wanted Mary's apartment), they became the best of friends. Rhoda was born in the Bronx in December 1941. In the third grade she won the science fair prize with a model of the human brain; as a teenager she was an usherette at Loew's State Theater. In high school she was a member of a gang called the Sharkettes. Rhoda now works as a windowdresser at Hempell's Department Store. She is Jewish, has a goldfish named Goldfish and once got a $40 fine at the Minneapolis Zoo for feeding yogurt to a buffalo.

When Rhoda returns to New York for a two week vacation, the spinoff series "Rhoda" (9/9/74 to 12/9/78) begins. Shortly after she arrives, her mother arranges a blind date for her with Joe Gerard (David Groh), the owner of the New York Wrecking Company. Joe is divorced from Marian (Joan Van Ark) and the father of ten-year-old Donny (Todd Turquand and Shane Sinutko). After a short courtship, Rhoda and Joe marry. They set up housekeeping in Apartment 9B at 332 West 46th Street in Manhattan, and Rhoda begins her own business, Windows by Rhoda.

Two years later, Rhoda and Joe divorce. Rhoda now lives in Apartment 6G (also seen as 4G) and works for the Doyle Costume Company. Her sister, Brenda Morgenstern (Julie Kavner), lives in Apartment 2D and works as a teller at the midtown branch of the First Security Bank in Manhattan. Rhoda's parents, Ida and Martin Morgenstern (Nancy Walker and Harold Gould), live in the Bronx near Fordham Road at 3517 Grand Concourse.

Phyllis Lindstrom is the owner of Mary's apartment building in the series, but only a tenant in the pilot. She has a never-seen husband named Lars (a dermatologist) and a very pretty daughter named Bess. According to Phyllis, "wearing makeup and putting on her mother's wigs" is what Bess does best. Bess is very close to Mary and calls her "Aunt Mary." Following the death of Lars, Phyllis and Bess move to San Francisco to live with Lars's parents in the spinoff series "Phyllis" (CBS, 9/8/75 to 8/30/77). Phyllis and Bess live at 4482 Bayview Drive, and Phyllis first works for Julie Erskine (Barbara Colby and Liz Torres) at Erskine's Commercial Photography Studio; she is then the administrative assistant to Dan Valenti (Carmine Caridi) of the San Francisco Board of Administration.

The clocks seen in the newsroom (behind Mary and Murray's desks) do not operate (the hands do not move). The most tragic event to hit WJM was the death of its star performer, Chuckles the Clown (whose real name was given only as George). Chuckles was the Grand Marshal of a parade and dressed as Peter Peanut. He was crushed to death when a rogue elephant tried to shell him. Chuckles was played at various times by Mark Gordon and Richard Schaal. In the last episode, the new station manager (Vincent Gardenia) fires everyone but Ted.

Relatives: Nanette Fabray (Mary's mother, *Dotty Richards*; Mary originally referred to her as Marge), Bill Quinn (Mary's father, *Dr. Walter Reed Richards*), Eileen Heckart (Mary's aunt, *Flo Meredith*), Sherry Hursey (Murray's daughter, *Bonnie Slaughter*), Tammi Bula (Murray's daughter, *Ellen Slaughter*), Helen Hunt (Murray's daughter, *Laurie Slaughter*), Lew Ayres (Murray's father, *Doug Slaughter*), Priscilla Morrill (Lou's ex-wife, *Edie Grant*), Nora Heflin (Lou's daughter, *Janie Grant*), Liberty Williams (Rhoda's sister, *Debbie Morgenstern*), Brett Somers (Rhoda's aunt, *Rose*), Robbie Rist (Ted's adopted son, *David Baxter*), Liam Dunn (Ted's father, *Robert Baxter*), Jack Cassidy (Ted's brother, *Hal Baxter*), Pat Priest (Sue Anne's sister, *Lila,* who hosts a cooking show in Augusta, Georgia), Robert Moore (Phyllis's gay brother, *Ben Lindstrom*).

Theme: "Love Is All Around," vocal by Sonny Curtis.

447. M*A*S*H

CBS, 9/17/72 to 9/19/83

A bittersweet look at the Korean War as seen through the eyes of a group of doctors and nurses assigned to the 4077th M*A*S*H (Mobile Army Surgical Hospital) unit.

Colonel Henry Blake (McLean Stevenson) was the unit's first commanding officer. He was born in Bloomington, Illinois, and loves fishing. He ordered adult films for his officers from the Tabasco Film Company in Havana, Cuba. Henry was killed in a helicopter crash on the day he was to return home (his copter went down over the China Sea).

Colonel Sherman Potter (Harry Morgan) replaced Blake. He was born in Riverbend, Missouri, and loved horses (he has one named Sophie). Potter has made the army his career, and his wife calls him "Puddin' Head." He began practicing medicine in 1932 and mentions he is from Hannibal, Missouri, in another episode. Harry Morgan originally played General Bartford Hamilton Steele, a West Point graduate, spit-and-polish military man in the episode "The General Flipped at Dawn" (9/10/74). (Kurtis Sanders played a young Colonel Potter in a dream sequence.)

Captain Benjamin Franklin Pierce (Alan Alda), Captain John McIntire (Wayne Rogers) and later Captain B.J. Hunnicutt (Mike Farrell) are dedicated doctors who are opposed to the war and are constantly defying authority—as their way of fighting back at the system. The nurse-chasing Pierce, who is nicknamed "Hawkeye," was born in Crabapple Cove, Maine, and has the dog tag number 19095607. He was drafted and will not carry a gun. He calls the unit "a cesspool" and has a still (for making martinis) in his tent (which he calls "The Wellspring of Life"). Hawkeye earns $413.50 a month and enjoys reading the magazine *The Joys of Nudity*. He starred in the army documentary "Yankee Doodle Doctor."

McIntire, his first tentmate, is nicknamed "Trapper John" and shares Hawkeye's love of playing practical jokes. His favorite magazines are *Field and Stream* and *Popular Mechanics*. When the locals need medical help, they turn to Trapper John. When Trapper John leaves (transferred stateside two hours before Hawkeye, badly hung over from a leave in Tokyo, returns to the 4077th), B.J. Hunnicutt replaces him. B.J. (name never revealed) was born in Mill Valley, California. He is a surgeon fresh from civilian residency (he attended Stanford Medical School). He is married to Peggy (played in a dream sequence by Catherine Bergstrom), and his wedding anniversary is May 23.

Major Margaret Houlihan (Loretta Swit), nicknamed "Hot Lips," is head of the unit's nurses and earns $400 a month. Margaret "is a woman of passion but a stickler for rules." She tries to be alluring and beautiful despite the deplorable conditions that surround her. For reasons that no one can understand, Margaret is attracted to Frank Burns (Larry Linville), a wimpy major who is married and fears his wife will discover he is having an affair. Frank, who is nicknamed "Ferret Face," uses the brokerage house of Snaders, Landers, and Flynn in New York City. When Frank left in 1977,

Margaret married Major Donald Penobscott (Beeson Carroll, then Mike Henry).

Harvard-educated Major Charles Emerson Winchester III (David Ogden Stiers) replaced Frank and resides in the same tent with Hawkeye and B.J. Before joining the 4077, Charles was assigned to Tokyo General Hospital. Gustav Mahler is Charles's favorite composer, and he has a sister, Honoria, send him his favorite newspaper, the *Boston Globe*.

Maxwell Klinger (Jamie Farr) was born in Toledo, Ohio, and was first a corporal, then a sergeant. He is the unit's resident loon. Totally against the war and desperate to get out, he dresses as a woman and pretends to be insane to qualify for a Section 8 discharge. He started a camp newspaper called *M*A*S*H Notes*.

Corporal Walter Eugene O'Reilly (Gary Burghoff), serial number 3911880, was born in Iowa and has the nickname "Radar" (for his ability to perceive what others think). He drinks only Grape Nehi and mailed a Jeep home piece by piece. Radar is the company clerk and has a number of pets: Daisy (a mouse), Mannie, Moe, Jack, Babette and Margo (guinea pigs), Fluffy and Bingo (rabbits). When Radar left, Klinger became the company clerk.

First Lieutenant Father Francis Mulcahy (George Morgan, then William Christopher) is the unit's chaplain (he raises money for the Saint Theresa Orphanage).

The signpost on the unit's grounds has arrows pointing to Coney Island, San Francisco, Tokyo and Burbank. Rosie's Bar is the local watering hole; the nearest airfield is Kimpo Airport in Seoul; "The Swamp" is the nickname for Hawkeye's tent.

Relatives: Robert Alda (Hawkeye's father, *Daniel Pierce*), Andrew Duggan (Margaret's father, *Colonel Alvin Houlihan*), Gary Burghoff (Radar's mother, *Edna O'Reilly*), Dennis Dugan (Potter's son-in-law, *Bobby*).

Unseen Relatives: Henry's wife, Lorraine; Henry's daughter, Molly; Henry's Grandma Mavis; B.J.'s daughter Erin; Potter's wife, Mildred, and his grandson, Cory; Frank's wife, Louise; Father Mulcahy's sister, Sister Maria Angelica; Trapper's daughter, Becky.

Theme: "Suicide Is Painless," by Johnny Mandel.

448. Matlock

NBC, 9/23/86 to 9/4/92
ABC, 11/5/92 to the present

Cast: Andy Griffith *(Ben Matlock)*, Linda Purl *(Charlene Matlock)*, Julie Sommars *(Julie March)*, Nancy Stafford *(Michelle Thomas)*, Kari Lizer *(Cassie Phillips)*, Don Knotts *(Les Calhoun)*.

Facts: Benjamin ("Ben") Layton Matlock and Charlene Matlock are a father and daughter team of private practice attorneys who operate out of Atlanta, Georgia (the firm was originally called Matlock and Matlock; it changed to Ben Matlock, Attorney at Law, when Charlene left to begin her own practice in Philadelphia in 1987).

Ben is known "for his high prices [$100,000 a case] and

and his high rate of successfully defending clients." Ben was born in the town of Mount Harlan, Georgia, and attended Harvard Law School. He was a public prosecutor in Atlanta before beginning his own practice. He lives in a house with the number 618 (street not given) and drives a sedan with the license plate RAF 285; his office phone number is 555-9930. Ben snacks on hot dogs at every opportunity and prefers "to wash it down" with grape soda. He doesn't trust police labs ("They're not working to help my clients") and prefers to do his own investigating. Ben doesn't make unsubstantiated charges and will occasionally take on a case for free. He was voted Man of the Year by the Atlanta Chamber of Commerce in 1991, and his wardrobe apparently consists of white suits (he is always seen wearing one; a camera shot of his closet showed a number of wrinkled white suits). Ben rises at 5:00 A.M. ("It's the best time for thinking") and won't allow anyone to smoke in his office — "Not even my best-paying clients."

Paying taxes is one of Ben's biggest complaints ("I owe thousands and thousands of dollars"). He does fudge when he can (for example, declaring a birthday dinner for Julie March as a business expense). Ben collects old coins (his oldest is an 1804 silver dollar), and he most often defends clients at the Fulton County Courthouse. The mailing address for the firm reads simply "Matlock and Matlock, Atlanta, Georgia, 30303." When a female voice is heard answering the office phone, it says, "Ben Matlock's office." Ben did lose one case — his own, in small claims court (he bought a used 1962 refrigerator for $68.42 from a woman and sued her when it broke down).

Julie March is the prosecuting attorney with the Atlanta D.A.'s office. She is from Nebraska and is an expert on jewelry. She considers herself one of the best legal minds in the South; Ben calls her "the wildest, most ruthless prosecutor they [the state] have."

Michelle Thomas is the attorney who joined Ben when Charlene left. Her name appears in small letters (MICHELLE THOMAS—ATTORNEY AT LAW) below Ben's—B.L. MATLOCK—ATTORNEY AT LAW (in large letters)—on the office door.

Cassie Phillips is Ben's law clerk. She was attending the University of Chicago when she heard a speech by guest lecturer Ben Matlock. Cassie interviewed Ben for the school newspaper and was so impressed by him that she decided to become an attorney. After graduation, Cassie enrolled in the Baxter Law School in Atlanta and asked Ben for a job. When Ben discovered that Cassie had said she was Ben's law clerk in order to get into Baxter, he refused to hire her; he later changed his mind and decided to give her a chance.

"Les Calhoun, your new neighbor; just call me Ace" is what Ben first heard when his new neighbor introduced himself. Les is retired; he made plastic eyelets for sneakers, "ate chop suey ever day and wore lizard skin shoes every day." He calls Ben "Benje" and "Benjie."

Tyler Hudson (Kene Holliday) was Ben's first investigator. He was a stock market investor who was named Young Atlanta Businessman of the year. Tyler was replaced by Conrad McMasters (Clarence Gilyard, Jr.), a police deputy who doubled as Ben's investigator.

Lori Lethan played Charlene Matlock in the pilot episode, "Diary of a Perfect Murder" (NBC, 3/3/86). Betty Lynn was Ben's receptionist, Sarah, in first season episodes (Alice Hirson played the role as Hazel in the pilot). In the last first-run NBC episode, "The Assassination" (5/8/92), Brynn Thayer appeared as Ben's daughter, Lee Ann McIntyre (no mention was made of Charlene). Lee Ann is a prosecutor in Philadelphia who comes to Atlanta to visit her father following a legal separation from her husband, Peter. She helps her father defend a client and decides to remain in Atlanta.

"Tonight, look who's coming to ABC"—these were the words that preceded the ABC premiere of "Matlock" on 11/5/92 with a two-hour episode called "The Vacation."

Ben and Lee Ann have formed a partnership and operate a firm called Matlock and McIntyre in Atlanta. Lee Ann is still separated from her husband (whom Ben calls "the jerk") and still uses his last name (although Ben is trying to convince her to use her maiden name).

While on vacation in Wilmington, Ben meets Cliff Lewis (Daniel Roebuck), a recent law school graduate, at the Food Lion supermarket. Cliff is the son of Billy Lewis (Warren Frost), Ben's old nemesis from Mount Harlan (Billy blames Ben for breaking the heart of his sister, Lucy; he claims Ben dated her for eight years, then dumped her; Ben claims they mutually agreed to separate). When Cliff, who is a member of the Mount Harlan Volunteer Fire Department, is set up on a murder charge, Ben hires Cliff as his legman (to assist Conrad) when he clears him.

Relatives: Bill Mumy (Ben's nephew, *Irwin Bruckner*, a genius who works at the Mansbridge Institute), Anne Haney (Ben's aunt, *Elsie*), Christina Pickles (Ben's cousin, *Diana Huntington*), Kay E. Kuter (Ben's uncle, *Bink*).

Flashbacks: Steve Witting *(Ben in 1956)*, Andy Griffith (Ben's father, *Charlie Matlock*, the owner of a gas station).

Theme: "Matlock," by Dick DeBenedictis.

449. *Matt Helm*

ABC, 9/20/75 to 1/3/76

The McGuire Beach House at 2001 Postal Road in Malibu Beach, California, is the residence of Matthew ("Matt") Helm (Anthony Franciosa), a former U.S. government intelligence agent for the Company, who has turned private detective, and his live-in girlfriend, Claire Kronski (Laraine Stephens), a beautiful private practice attorney. Their telephone number is 555-2040, and Matt drives a red Thunderbird convertible with the license plate 258-8PP. When he was an agent with the Company, Matt was teamed with a girl named Karen Ashley (Marlyn Mason). Matt calls Claire "Kronski" (her first name is rarely mentioned) and says she is "the most honest lawyer who ever lived—but one of the sneakiest people I have ever known." Claire was born in Texas; her office address is 36 Primrose Lane; and her phone number is 555-1333.

Ethel (Jeff Donnell), who calls Matt "Matthew," runs

Ethel's Answering Service; and Lieutenant Hanrahan (Gene Evans), Matt's friend, is with the Homicide Division of the Parker Center of the L.A.P.D.

Morton Stevens composed the theme.

450. *Matt Houston*

ABC, 9/26/82 to 3/29/85

Houston, Inc., is a conglomerate at 200 West Temple Street, Los Angeles, California 90012 (the address is later given as 100 Century Plaza South in Los Angeles). It is owned by Matlock ("Matt") Houston (Lee Horsley), a millionaire oil baron, cattle rancher and playboy who helps people who are in deep trouble. Matt also owns Houston Investigations in Los Angeles (telephone number 555-3141) and the Houston Cattle Ranch in Texas (he purchased the ranch from movie star Ramona Landers [Janet Leigh]).

Matt also has a Rolls Royce (license plate COWBOY 1) and a car he calls the Excalibur (license plate 21 VE 124). Matt calls his computer Baby, and N1090Z is the identification number of the Houston Industries helicopter.

C.J. Parsons (Pamela Hensley) is Matt's beautiful cohort; she lives at 8766 West Beverly, Apartment 3C; Roy Houston (Buddy Ebsen) is Matt's uncle (and assistant in last season episodes); Vince Novelli (John Aprea) is a lieutenant with the S.C.P.D. (Southern California Police Department); Vince's mother, Rosa (Penny Santon), owns the Mama Novelli Restaurant; Michael Hoyt (Lincoln Kilpatrick) is a lieutenant with the L.A.P.D.; and Murray Chase (George Wyner) is Matt's harried business manager.

Relatives: Lloyd Bridges (Matt's natural father, *Virgil Wade*), David Wayne (Matt's adoptive father, *Bill Houston*), Michael Goodwin (Matt's cousin, *Will*), Christina Hart (Michael's daughter, *Kathy Hoyt*), John Moschitta, Jr. (Murray's brother, *Myron Chase*).

Theme: "Matt Houston," by Dominic Frontiere.

451. *Maverick*

ABC, 9/22/57 to 7/8/62

Cast: James Garner *(Bret Maverick)*, Jack Kelly *(Bart Maverick)*, Roger Moore *(Beau Maverick)*, Robert Colbert *(Brent Maverick)*.

Facts: Bret and Bartram (Bart) Maverick are brothers. They are gentlemen gamblers who roam the Old West in search of rich prey. They are also cowards at heart, but more often than not they find themselves helping people in trouble. They are unconventional, self-centered and untrustworthy, and they possess a genius for conning the con man.

Although they served with the Confederacy during the Civil War, they became Union soldiers when they were captured and figured it would be better to help the enemy than spend time in a Union prison camp. As "Galvanized

Matt Houston. Pamela Hensley, Lee Horsley and Lincoln Kilpatrick.

Yankees" (as Bart puts it), they were assigned to keep the Indians under control out West. At this same time, it is mentioned that another Maverick, Cousin Beauregard (Beau), became a family disgrace when he was honored as a war hero. Beauregard ("Pappy") Maverick (James Garner in a dual role), the head of the family, instilled in his sons his cowardice and con-artist genius. When Pappy, as he is called, learned that his nephew, Beau, did something to bring honor to the Maverick name, he branded him "the white sheep of the family" and banished him to England. (Actually, Beau had been captured. While he was playing poker with a Union general, the Confederates attacked the camp. Just as the general lost a game and exclaimed, "Son, I give up," Confederate troops entered the tent. Beau was credited with the capture.) To make up for this family disgrace, Beau spent five years tarnishing his "good" name and was actually brought on (1960–61) to replace James Garner (who left the series in 1960). The following year, and until 1962, another brother, Brent, appeared when Roger Moore left at the end of the 1961 season.

It is against a Maverick's principles to drink alone, and they have one serious vice—curiosity. The Mavericks are from Little Bent, Texas, and a sheriff is not their best friend. A Maverick is not fast on the draw (if there is a way to get out of a gunfight, they will find it). Bret promised his Pappy that on his thirty-eighth birthday he would find himself a wife and raise 12 Mavericks. Bart, who enjoys smoking cigars, often says, "Sometimes it frightens me what I'll do for money." Bret contends that he is a cautious man—"It's the other faults that bother me." Bret calls Bart "Brother Bart," and Beau has a horse named Gumlegs.

Although Beauregard ("Pappy") Maverick appeared only once (in the episode, "Pappy"), his proverbs became an established part of the series. One of the Mavericks would exclaim, "As my old Pappy would say," followed by the saying (for example, "No use crying over spilled milk, it could have been whiskey," or "You can tell more about a town by looking at its gambling emporium than any other building";

most people would remark, "Maverick, I'm sick of hearing what your Pappy would say"). Pappy left each of his sons a $1,000 bill (which is pinned to their shirt pocket) and these profound words of wisdom: "Never hold a kicker and never draw to an inside straight." Pappy is a ladies' man and a gambler like his sons—but women call him "an old coot" and "a lecherous old goat." On screen, Pappy is credited as "Pappy . . .?" Jack Kelly also played Pappy's brother, Bentley Maverick, in "Pappy."

Besides the Indians, the outlaws and the sheriff, another threat to Bret and Bart was Samantha ("Sam") Crawford (Diane Brewster), a beautiful con artist who was just as cunning and clever as the Mavericks. A Northern girl at heart, Sam faked a Southern accent and used, besides her genius at the con, her feminine wiles to acquire easy money.

Richard Long (as Gentleman Jack Darby) and Efrem Zimbalist, Jr. (as Dandy Jim Buckley), had recurring roles as gamblers who also sought easy money and easy prey. In the episode "Hadley's Hunters," the stars of the various Warner Brothers Western series had cameos: John Russell and Peter Brown ("Lawman"), Clint Walker ("Cheyenne"), Will Hutchins ("Sugarfoot"), Ty Hardin ("Bronco") and Edd Byrnes (as Cookie, a horse groomer at the stables of "77 Cherokee Strip").

Theme: "Maverick," by David Buttolph and Paul Francis Webster.

Spinoffs: On 9/3/78, CBS aired *The New Maverick*, a television movie pilot (for "Young Maverick") that reunited Bret (James Garner), Bart (Jack Kelly) and Beau (Roger Moore) in a story that introduced the newest Maverick—Ben (Charles Frank), Beau's young and inexperienced son who is eager to become a professional gambler like his father.

Ben's exploits as a gambler continued in the series "Young Maverick" (CBS, 11/28/79 to 1/16/80). Susan Blanchard plays his lady friend, Nell McGarrahan, and John Dehner is Marshal Edge Troy.

Although "Young Maverick" lasted only 13 episodes, NBC brought back James Garner as Bret in the series "Bret Maverick" (12/1/81 to 8/24/82). Said to be "20 years older and 40 years wiser," Bret finally decides to end his life of wandering and settles down in the town of Sweetwater, Arizona (where he runs the Red Ox Saloon and the Lazy Ace Ranch—both of which he won in a poker game). Mary Lou Springer (Darleen Carr) is a photographer for the town newspaper, the *Territorian*; Kate Hanrahan (Marj Dusay) owns the Klondike Room Gambling Hall; and Philo Sandine (Stuart Margolin) is a con man called Standing Bear by the Comanche Indians. Ed Bruce sings the theme, "Maverick Didn't Come Here to Lose."

452. *Max Headroom*

ABC, 3/31/87 to 5/7/87
ABC, 8/14/87 to 10/16/87

Cast: Matt Frewer *(Edison Carter/Max Headroom)*, Amanda Pays *(Theora Jones)*, Morgan Sheppard *(Blank Reg)*, Hilary Tindall and Concetta Tomei *(Dominique)*, Paul Spurrier *(Bryce Lynch)*.

Facts: The time is "20 minutes into the future." Television cannot be turned off and ratings are all that matter. With an average low rating of 11.5 million and an average high of 23.6 million viewers a day, Network 23 has become the number one broadcast signal. But it has stiff competition from the other networks: TKO-TV, Channel 28, Prime Time, PornoVision, Channel 42, Global TV, BBC 126, Planet Wide, Channel 1111, Flicks, Big Time TV (a pirate station), Fantasma, Horrovitz, Rubbish TV and BBC DIY-TV.

In addition to the competition, channel switching during commercials has become a major problem (it causes a dip in Network 23's ratings). To resolve the problem, Bryce Lynch, the head of Network 23's research and development, creates Blipverts, a system that compresses 30 seconds of commercials into only three seconds. The Blipverts work fine at first, until the unexpected happens—viewers begin to explode (spontaneously combust). The human body has millions of nerve endings, each of which contains a small electrical charge. Individually they are harmless and active people burn them off. However, in overweight or inactive people, the electrical charges build up. When a Blipvert is seen, the impulses violently stimulate these nerve endings. They cause a short circuit in inactive people who then explode. Authorities have not yet been able to associate Blipverts with these deaths. Bryce does have, however, a videotape (called a Rebus) of a Blipvert-caused explosion—a tape that can destroy Network 23 if it should fall into the wrong hands.

Edison Carter is a world famous journalist who hosts "The What I Want to Know Show" (a news program that goes after stories) on Network 23. His control (newsroom director) is Theora Jones, a beautiful computer genius who worked previously for the defunct World One Network. Edison decides to investigate the mysterious viewer explosions. When he gets too close, hitmen are hired to stop him. Carter finds the Rebus tape at the same time he realizes he is being followed. The hitmen's initial attempt to kill Carter fails when he escapes on a motorcycle. Carter is caught, however, when he misjudges a parking lot crossing gate (which reads MAX HEADROOM 2.3 FEET) and crashes into it. He is then brought to Bryce's lab. Carter, however, can't be killed; he is too famous and will be missed. Bryce devises a way to resolve this: he computes the physical characteristics of Carter's head into his computer, then he "prints the synpatic circuits of his mind." A computer generated image of Carter can then be seen and programed to do what Bryce wants. Before the theory is tested, Carter, still unconscious, is given to the hitmen for disposal (they sell him for body parts at the Nightingale Body Parts Clinic). When Bryce activates his Edison Carter, he finds that it is not Carter but an image that calls itself Max Headroom (the last image Carter saw before the accident). The image is wisecracking and a joker and only faintly resembles Carter. When Bryce finds that he cannot erase the image, he tells the hitmen to dispose of the computer unit that houses it. The hitmen sell it to Blank Reg, the operator of Big Time TV. Blank Reg activates Max Headroom and Max soon becomes a top Big Time TV personality. Meanwhile, Edison has regained consciousness and escapes from the body parts clinic. With Theora's help, he exposes Network 23 and its deadly Blipverts. Stories follow Edison's adventures as a reporter for Network 23 and those of his alter ego, Max Headroom.

Network 23, "The Network That Means Business," broadcasts via the Comstat 2058 Satellite. Its major sponsor is the Zik Zak Corporation. Network 23 begins its broadcast day with "Dr. Duncan's Video Symptom Show." "Making Tomorrow Seem Like Yesterday" is the slogan of Big Time TV, which broadcasts to the Blank Generation. Dominique assists Blank Reg in its operations. Bryce's office is on the 105th floor of the Network 23 Building (his door code is IJ2FI).

Theme: "Max Headroom," by Midge Ure and Chris Cross.

453. *Max Monroe: Loose Cannon*

CBS, 1/5/90 to 1/26/90
CBS, 4/5/90 to 4/19/90

Maximilian ("Max") Monroe (Shadoe Stevens) is an unorthodox police detective with Precinct 157 of the Los Angeles Police Department. He is assisted by Charles ("Charlie") Evers (Bruce A. Young), a by-the-books detective who often fears for his job when Max decides to take the law into his own hands. Max plays chess at the Westside Chess Club and lives at 4320 Melrose Avenue in Bel Air. His (and Charlie's) car code is 3-Henry-18; "Charlie Blue Dog" is Max's police code name, and he drives a car with the license plate PEK 560 (later IYXQ 753). Arnetia Walker plays Charlie's wife, Loretta.

The theme, "Tied Up," is performed by Yello.

454. *Me and Maxx*

NBC, 3/22/80 to 9/12/80

When a daughter (Maxx) is born to Elaine and Norman Davis, Norman deserts his wife and child, for he feels he cannot handle the responsibility. Eleven years later, Elaine (not seen) decides that it is time to even up the score.

Believing that she is only going to stay with her father for two weeks while her mother is on vacation, Maxx Davis (Melissa Michaelsen) packs a suitcase and crosses the Brooklyn Bridge to Norman's apartment in Manhattan. Norman (Joe Santos) is surprised by Maxx's visit and shocked when the letter Elaine gave to Maxx for Norman reveals that Elaine is abandoning Maxx and it is now his turn to care for her.

Me and Maxx. Joe Santos and Melissa Michaelsen.

Norman has only seen Maxx four times in 11 years. He lives in a small, one bedroom apartment and leads a swinging life-style. When Maxx learns about the letter, she feels unwanted and decides to leave. Norman prevents her from going to New Jersey to live with her elderly grandmother and tells her that she can stay with him. Maxx's attempts to become close to a father she rarely saw and hardly knows are the focal point of the series.

Norman lives in Apartment 738 at 86 East 65th Street in Manhattan and runs Empire Tickets from his apartment. Norman's assistant is Barbara (Jenny Sullivan), and 212-555-TIXX is the agency's phone number (which supplies tickets for sporting, cultural and theatrical events). Norman believes everyone is created equal—although Maxx says he looks at women more than men.

Maxx, whose real name is Maxine, receives an allowance of five dollars a week. She attends Public School 135, and says she spells her name with two *x*'s "because my mother says I was double-crossed."

Leonore O'Malley sings the theme, "Is It Because of Love?"

In 1979 a similar series idea was rejected by ABC. "Maxx" is an unaired pilot about a womanizing New York bachelor named Norman (Tim Thomerson) and the complications that set in when he is suddenly made the guardian of his ten-year-old daughter, Maxx (Melissa Michaelsen), whom he deserted at birth.

Me and Mom. Holland Taylor, Lisa Eilbacher and James Earl Jones.

455. *Me and Mom*

ABC, 4/5/85 to 5/17/85

Kate Morgan (Lisa Eilbacher), a beautiful young criminologist, her wealthy and glamorous mother, Zena Hunnicutt (Holland Taylor), and Lou Garfield (James Earl Jones), a tough ex-cop, are all partners in the Los Angeles–based Morgan, Garfield and Hunnicutt Detective Agency.

The agency is located at 2936 Hampton Boulevard and can be reached by phone at 213-555-5631. Kate lives in an apartment at 137 Stepford Place; her mother resides in a luxurious home at 51 Chevia Street. Lou was formerly a detective with the Homicide Division of the L.A.P.D.

Amy Holland sings the theme, "Me and Mom."

456. *Me and Mrs. C*

NBC, 6/21/86 to 7/26/86
NBC, 4/11/87 to 7/4/87

Rather than spend her golden years with her son and his family, Ethel Conklin (Peg Murray), an indepedent 60-year-old widow, decides to remain in her home at 2709 Webb Street (city not identified). When she finds that her Social Security income is not sufficient, she decides to take in a boarder to help with the expenses. Gerri Kilgore (Misha McK), a gorgeous black girl with a prison record, responds to Ethel's newspaper ad. Despite the fact that Gerri is an ex-convict (arrested for armed robbery), Ethel feels Gerri deserves a chance and allows her to become her boarder.

Gerri works for the Martin, Barton and Fargo computer company and pays Ethel $100 a month plus expenses (she paid $62.50 a month when the series first began). Ethel's first phone number is 555-1311, then 555-3313.

Ethan Conklin (Gary Bayer) is Ethel's son, a private practice certified public accountant. He is married to Kathleen (Ellen Regan), and they have a young son named Jamie (Jeremy Brown). Ethan is opposed to his mother's living arrangements and tries to convince Ethel to live with him and his family at 4330 South Beverly Drive.

Scoey Mitchlll appeared as Gerri's father, the Reverend Kilgore.

LaVonne Rucker sings the theme, "Side By Side."

The original pilot, titled "Me and Mrs. C," aired on NBC on 3/18/84. Doris Roberts was Ethel Connelly, the widow; and Deborah Malone played her boarder, Jeri Monroe. Terrence McGovern played Ethel's son, Ethan Connelly, and Mary Armstrong was Ethan's wife, Kathleen. Deborah Malone performed the theme, "Me and Mrs. C."

457. *Meet Corliss Archer*

CBS, 7/12/51 to 8/10/51
CBS, 1/26/52 to 3/29/52
Syndicated, 1954 to 1955

Cast: Lugene Sanders (1951–52) and Ann Baker (1954–55) (*Corliss Archer*), Fred Shields (1951–52) and John Eldredge (1954–55) (*Harry Archer*), Frieda Inescort (1951), Irene Tedrow (1952) and Mary Brian (1954–55) (*Janet Archer*), Bobby Ellis (1951–54) (*Dexter Franklin*).

Facts: "And now we invite you to meet Corliss Archer, America's teenage sweetheart." Sixteen-year-old Corliss Archer, the daughter of Harry and Janet Archer, lives at 32 Oak Street in what appears to be a small American town (acquired episodes do not mention a locale).

Corliss is a pretty high school sophomore with a penchant for getting herself into trouble. She has a weekly allowance of one dollar ("Gee, I wish I could get my father to increase my allowance; a dollar doesn't go far these days") and is a fan of Gregory Peck ("He's so dreamy. I just love going to his movies"—which cost 25 cents). Corliss is jealous of Betty Campbell, a mentioned (but not seen) girl whom she feels will steal her boyfriend, Dexter ("Ooh, I just know that scatterbrain is putting on an act to woo the boys," she says). For breakfast, Corliss has two eggs, toast and orange juice. Her favorite dinner is lasagna, and she has a tendency to drop the toothpaste tube cap down the sink drain. She tried out for the school glee club, but "they said if I sang with the glee club, there would be no glee in the glee club." When Dexter first heard Corliss singing ("I Dream of Jeannie with the Light Brown Hair"), he remarked, "Who's beating that poor horse to death?"

Dexter Franklin is Corliss's boyfriend and the man she plans to marry some day. He drives a hot rod with a sign that reads TAXI, LADY? RIDE IN STYLE. RATES ARE LOW.

A KISS A MILE. Dexter also receives an allowance of one dollar a week ("I have an allowance that rattles. I wish I could get one that rustles"). He is a steak and potatoes man and loves Marilyn Monroe movies—although Corliss can't see what he sees in her ("What has Marilyn Monroe got that Gregory Peck hasn't got?" says Corliss. "Holy cow, Corliss," remarks Dexter. "If you don't know, I'm not gonna tell you"). Dexter can also drink a whole soda with one in-breath through a straw.

Dexter is the innocent victim of Corliss's endless attempts to improve him (she feels he needs to be more mature). More often than not, Corliss's attempts backfire. "Golly," says Corliss. "How do I manage to mess things up?" "I'll admit it takes talent," says her father, who often resolves the problems at the end of each episode. Despite Harry's help, Dexter still feels, as he says, "lower than a midget with flat feet." Dexter wants to keep on the good side of Harry because if he and Corliss marry, "we may want to live here one day."

Harry Archer is a private practice lawyer (Harold Archer, Attorney at Law) who has been married to Janet for 18 years. His most annoying client is Mrs. Luella Grummond (Doris Packer), who pays him a healthy retainer but drives him up the wall with her eccentric ways (for example, not investing in a stock until she consults a fortune-teller). Janet, who was a secretary before marrying Harry, is, as Harry says, "a remarkable woman. She is not only attractive and intelligent, but she's also a wonderful housekeeper and an extremely talented cook."

Relatives: Ken Christy (Dexter's father, *Bill Franklin*; 1954–55), Vera Marshe (Dexter's mother, *Mary Franklin*; 1954–55).

Note: On 8/5/56, NBC broadcast a rare color special called "Meet Corliss Archer" with the following cast: Robin Morgan (*Corliss*), Jerome Cowan (*Harry*), Polly Rowles (*Janet*) and Warren Berlinger (*Dexter*).

458. *Meet Millie*

CBS, 10/25/52 to 3/6/56

"A gay new comedy about the life and loves of a secretary in Manhattan" was the introduction viewers heard for this series. The secretary is Millie Bronson (Elena Verdugo), a beautiful 21-year-old single girl who lives with her mother, Bertha Bronson (Florence Halop) at 137 West 41st Street (Apartment 3B) in New York City. Millie attended Public School 98 and Central High School and now works as a secretary to Johnny Boone, Jr. (Ross Ford). Johnny's father, John Boone, Sr. (Earle Ross, then Roland Winters), is the owner of the company (it is impossible to tell what kind of company Boone owns from acquired episodes, for there is no name on the door or office walls, and office conversation revolves around Millie and Johnny; printed sources describe it as both an ad agency and an investment company). Stories focus on the relationship between Millie and Johnny—a romance that Millie originally only dreamed

Meet Millie. Florence Halop (left) and Elena Verdugo.

about until one of Bertha's endless attempts to spark a romance between the two finally worked.

Bertha, called "Mama," is a widow who is 48 years old but tells everyone she is 37; in some episodes she says she is "48 minus ten minus five." If Mama had had the opportunity to have a second daughter, she would have named her Gwendolyn. She and Millie vacation yearly at the Live Right Lodge. In last season episodes, Millie and Mama spent time as ranchhands on the Weems Cattle Ranch in Texas (Harry Cheshire played ranch owner E.K. Weems).

"It all started the day I was born. My father said he wanted a girl and my mother said she wanted a boy. I was born and they were both disappointed," says Alfred E. Printzmetal (Marvin Kaplan), Mama and Millie's "life is depressing" seemingly permanently unemployed friend (Bertha says, "Alfred's job is standing in line at the unemployment office"). Alfred can't get along with his parents, especially his father, has a parrot named Irving and likes his socks starched so they can stand up in his dresser drawer. He eats "like there is no tomorrow" and hopes one day to build up the courage to leave home and find his own apartment. "I'll never understand women," he says. "They're too complicated. I'll wait until there is something else to marry."

"Pop," John Boone, Sr. (Earl Ross, then Roland Winters) believes that when P.T. Barnum said, "There is a sucker born every minute," he was referring to women. He is henpecked, calls his wife many things behind her back but is a pussycat when he is with her (Isabel Randolph). Based on the radio series of the same title (in which Audrey Totter played Millie).

Irving Miller composed the theme.

Meet Mr. McNutley see The Ray Milland Show

459. *Melba*

CBS, 1/28/86 (1 episode)
CBS, 8/2/86 to 9/13/86

Melba Patterson (Melba Moore) is a divorced black mother who is the director of the Manhattan Visitors Center in New York City. She lives with her daughter, Tracy (Jamila Perry), at 623 Bleeker Street, and her phone number is 555-3748. Tracy attends P.S. 89 in Manhattan.

Susan Slater (Gracie Harrison) is Melba's "white sister," a carefree single girl who works at the Furth and Preston Ad Agency. She is looking for a husband and hoping to begin a family; she was raised by Melba's mother, Mama Rose (Barbara Meek), when she was orphaned as a young girl.

The theme, "We're Sisters," is sung by Melba Moore.

460. *Michael Shayne*

NBC, 9/30/60 to 9/22/61

Michael ("Mike") Shayne (Richard Denning) is a private detective "who is practical and realistic and will never get rich at what he is doing." Despite what his clients say, Mike enjoys his work. He is relaxed, and easygoing, and tries not to fly off the handle. He'll avoid violence if possible, offers a cigarette to clients (and suspects) to relax them, and manages to sneak in a kiss when the client is a gorgeous female. Mike gathers the evidence, sorts through the clues and "uses every trick in the book" to get the truth from both clients and suspects. He uses Brazer's Chemical Lab to do his analyses, and he is a member of the Private Investigators of America.

Mike has an office (number 322) at 483 Adams Street in the city of Miami, Florida (Mike often complains that his mail occasionally gets rerouted to Miami Beach by mistake). His phone number is 236-6236, and he never sees a client before ten in the morning.

"Angel" is the affectionate name Mike uses for Lucy Hamilton (Patricia Donahue; then Margie Regan), his ever faithful secretary and sometimes "legman." Lucy, who can type 90 words a minute, never lets a client get away. She lives "in a respectable apartment" at 8 Gower Street and her phone number is 976-6616.

Timothy ("Tim") Rourke (Jerry Paris) is Mike's friend, a reporter-photographer for the Miami *Tribune*; Will Gentry (Herbert Rudley) is the homicide police chief (based in the Municipal Justice Building), who Mike says is "one of the most cooperative police officers I've ever worked with." Gary Clarke appeared as Lucy's brother, Dick Hamilton, in several episodes. Leith Stevens composed "The Theme from Michael Shayne."

The Brett Halliday–created character first appeared on television on 9/28/58 in an unsold pilot called "Man on a Raft" (broadcast on NBC's pilot series, "Decision"). Mark Stevens played Michael Shayne, Merry Anders was Lucy Hamilton and Robert Brubaker portrayed Tim Rourke. In the story, Mike is hired by Ann Conway (Diane Brewster) to find her husband's killer. Had the pilot sold, the series would have been called "Michael Shayne, Detective."

461. *The Mickey Mouse Club*

ABC, 10/3/55 to 9/25/59

For an hour (later half an hour) each weekday afternoon, children of all ages were entertained by a group of talented children (called "Mouseketeers") who were members of the Mickey Mouse Club. There were no rules and there were no fees; the only requirement was to have fun—to sit back, "put on your Mouseke-ears" and join the Mouseketeers in songs, dances and sketches.

"Who's the leader of the club that's made for you and

me" meant the start of the show and fun with club leader Mickey Mouse and his friends. While Mickey Mouse (voice of Jim MacDonald) appeared in animated form to introduce each episode, it was Jimmie Dodd and co-host Roy Williams who actually conducted the club. The stage was the official Mouse Club House and the Mouseketeers were introduced in many ways via song, but perhaps most fondly remembered was this one: "We're the Mouseketeers, we wanna say hello and give three cheers for all of you who see us everyday ... We'd like to introduce ourselves to you ... it's time to meet the Mouseketeers." Jimmie would then say, "Mouseketeers' roll call, count off now," and viewers would meet the (principal) Mouseketeers: Annette (Annette Funicello), Darlene (Darlene Gillespie), Cheryl (Cheryl Holdridge), Karen (Karen Pendleton), Cubby (Carl O'Brien), Bobby (Bobby Burgess), Doreen (Doreen Tracy), Sharon (Sharon Baird), Lonny (Lonny Burr), Tommy (Tommy Cole), Jay Jay (Jay Jay Solari), Dennis (Dennis Day).

The sight of Mickey, seated at a piano meant it was Monday and "Fun with Music Day." Tuesday found Mickey in a tuxedo and preparing for "Guest Star Day." A flying carpet, carrying Mickey in a sorcerer's suit, meant Wednesday's "Anything Can Happen Day." Thursday's "Circus Day" found Mickey dressed as a ringmaster. And "Talent Round Up Day" was the Friday show, with Mickey outfitted in cowboy duds.

Each show was geared to a specific theme, and each had its own song (for example, "Today is Tuesday, you know what that means: we're gonna have a special guest, so get out the brooms, sweep the place clean ... 'cause Tuesday is Guest Star Day." Wednesday, first called "Stunt Day," had this song: "Today is the day that is full of surprises, nobody knows what is going to happen 'cause Wednesday is Anything Can Happen Day").

Guest Star Day featured groups (such as the Firehouse Five Plus Two), up and coming stars (like Carol Lynley) and established performers (for instance, Judy Canova). "Anything Can Happen Day" featured the Mouseketeers in specific outfits during the lengthy day song: Bobby (man riding a unicycle), Sharon (Indian maiden), Dennis (pneumatic drill operator), Cheryl (bird in a gilded cage), Lonny (cowboy), Doreen (ballerina), Tommy (fireman), Darlene (dancer), Jay Jay (Keystone Kop), Annette (Flapper), Cubby (a rabbit who pulls a magician out of his hat), Karen (pretty marionette), Roy (marionette master), Jimmie (astronaut).

"Time to twist our Mousekedial to the right and left with a great big smile; this is the way we get to see a mouse cartoon for you and me. Meeska, Mooseka, Mouseketeer, Mouse Cartoon Time is now here" (a door to the Mickey Mouse Treasure Mine would then open and a Disney cartoon would be seen).

"From the far corners of the Earth; from across the Seven Seas, the stories of today for the leaders of tomorrow" signaled the beginning of "The Mickey Mouse Club Newsreel" (reported by Hal Gibney). "Fun with a Camera" was a segment with photographer Earl Kyser teaching the Mouseketeers aspects of photography.

Other segments included the animated Jiminy Cricket (voice of Cliff Edwards) in safety segments for children, and "Sooty and His Friend Harry Corbett" (Harry is the straightman for his nonspeaking hand puppet, Sooty, who plays songs on his electric organ).

Jimmie Dodd, who played the Mouseguitar (especially made by the Mattel Toy Company), concluded each show with a Words of Wisdom segment. (For example, Jimmie, holding a rubber band, would say, "You know, Mouseketeers, this rubber band is a lot like truth. You can twist it but it will always come back the way it was. It is strong, but you can stretch it. The more you stretch it, the thinner it gets. Finally you can't stretch it any further and it's so thin you can't hold it—and that's the time it's going to snap back. And when it does, you're the one that's been hurt. The truth is just the same as it was. You haven't changed it; but by twisting and stretching, you've hurt yourself.")

"Now it's time to say goodbye to all our company. M-I-C (see you real soon), K-E-Y (why? Because we like you). M-O-U-S-E-Eeeeee."

Theme: "The Mickey Mouse Club March," by Jimmie Dodd.

Note: See also "The Mickey Mouse Club Serials."

462. *The Mickey Mouse Club Serials*

ABC, 10/3/55 to 9/25/59

Perhaps the best remembered part of "The Mickey Mouse Club" was the comedy and adventure serials that were presented over the years (first on a daily basis in the hour series, then twice weekly—Tuesday and Thursday—when the series switched to a half hour on 9/29/57). Twelve major serials were presented. It was impossible to acquire all 390 episodes of "The Mickey Mouse Club" for this entry. Titles not listed here, but referred to elsewhere in this book, were those on which all the segments were acquired; others, listed in this entry, are based on several segments of those serials.

1. **Adventures in Dairyland.** Annette Funicello and Sammy Ogg, as themselves and representing "The Mickey Mouse Club," learn about the operation of a dairy farm by visiting the Sunny Acres Dairy Farm in Wisconsin. The antics of Moochie McCandless (Kevin Corcoran), the young son of the farm owners (played by Herb Newcombe and Mary Lu Delmonte), adds to the fun of their stay.

2. **The Adventures of Clint and Mac.** A mystery in which Clint Rogers (Neil Wolfe), an American boy living in England, and his friend, Alistair MacIntosh (Jonathan Bailey), attempt to solve a crime—the theft of the original manuscript of *Treasure Island*.

3. **Annette.** See entry.

4. **Bordie Collie.** The story, set in Hamilton County, a small town in southern Illinois, relates young Rod Brown's

(Bobby Evans) efforts to train a Scottish Border collie named Scamp for competition in a local dog show.

5. **The Boys of the Western Sea.** The story of a teenage boy named Paul and his struggle to support his family, as a fisherman, after his father's untimely death. This particular serial was a Russian film that was edited into a serial and dubbed into English. There is no cast listed on the screen or in *TV Guide*.

6. **Corky and White Shadow.** See entry.

7. **The Hardy Boys and the Mystery of the Applegate Treasure.** See entry.

8. **The Hardy Boys and the Mystery of Ghost Farm.** See above entry.

9. **The Secret of Mystery Lake.** Naturalist Bill Richards (George Fenneman) and his pretty guide, Lanie Thorne (Gloria Marshall), explore the wonders of Real Foot Lake in Tennessee.

10. **Spin and Marty.** The first serial to appear on the club. The story is set at the Triple R Ranch (a summer boy's camp) in North Fork and revolves around the adventures of campers Spin Evans (Tim Considine) and Marty Markham (David Stollery). Jim Logan (Roy Barcroft) is the ranch head, and Bill Burnett (Harry Carey, Jr.) is the counselor. Other campers: Ambitious (B.G. Norman), Joe (Sammy Ogg), George (Joe Wong) and Speckle (Tim Hartnagel). The plot itself followed Spin and Marty as they prepared for competition in a local rodeo.

11. **The Further Adventures of Spin and Marty.** Continued events in the lives of Spin Evans and Marty Markham—this time in a rivalry over the affections of Annette, a pretty camper at the Circle H girls' camp (which is across the lake from the Triple R). Exactly the same cast as in "Spin and Marty," with these additions: Circle H campers Annette (Annette Funicello) and Darlene (Darlene Gillespie) and Circle H camp head Helen Adams (Joyce Holden).

12. **The New Adventures of Spin and Marty.** A second spinoff that uses the casts of the preceding titles. In the final story, Spin and Marty stage a variety show to pay for damages caused by Marty's jalopy when it ran into the ranch house.

Note: See also "The Mickey Mouse Club."

The Mickey Rooney Show
see Hey, Mulligan

463. Midnight Caller

NBC, 10/25/88 to 8/2/91

Cast: Gary Cole (*Jack Killian*), Wendy Kilbourne (*Devon King*), Lisa Eilbacher (*Nicky Molloy*).
Facts: Jack Killian is a police inspector who accidentally

shoots and kills his partner while pursuing a felon. Jack is exonerated but quits the force. Devon King owns a radio station and is seeking a host for a late night call-in show to help people who are worried about street crime. She hires Jack, and stories relate his exploits as he strives to solve crimes that result from listeners' calls.

Jack hosts "Midnight Caller" (12:00 midnight to 3:00 A.M.) on KCJM (93.3 FM; telephone 555-TALK) in San Francisco (located at 9009 Howard Street, thirty-eighth floor). Jack, who calls himself "The Nighthawk," lives at 928 Fargo Street (Apartment 3C) and drives a car with the license plate 2HN 267. Carmen's Bar is his favorite watering hole, and when "Blotto" hit $46 million, Jack appeared on Channel 3 to pick the six winning numbers (6, 42, 14, 1, 4, 34).

Devon, whose Mercedes license plate reads 2RA 0834, lives at 3546 North Weatherly, and her phone number is 555-6023. At the beginning of the 1990-91 season (9/28), Devon is seen pregnant. Stockbroker Richard Clark (Christopher Lawford) was revealed to be the father in the episode of 10/19/90. It had been rumored that Jack was "the lucky father" by Jack's nemesis, Becca Nicholson (Eugenie Ross-Leming), a gossip columnist for the San Francisco *Dispatch*. The following week (10/26) Devon and Richard marry. Before moving to Tahiti, Devon sells the radio station to Foster Castleman (Don Meredith) of Aradella, Inc. Nicky Molloy, Foster's "talent lady" (who programs radio stations) is given the responsibility of running KCJM. She previously worked for KSPN (as a tape loader), KLTX (promo copy writer) and KSCO (general manager). When Devon has her baby (at Saint Francis Memorial Hospital), she and Richard name him Jack.

Other Regulars: Deacon Bridges (played by Mykel T. Williamson) is a reporter for the San Francisco *Dispatch*; Carl Zymak (Arthur Taxier) is a lieutenant with the Homicide Division of the S.F.P.D.; and Billy Po (Dennis Dun) is Jack's engineer.

Relatives: Peter Boyle (Jack's father, *J.J. Killian*), Terri Garber (Jack's sister, *Katie*), Scott Valentine (Jack's brother, *Frankie Killian*), Bonnie Bartlett (Devon's mother, *Hilary King*), Richard Bradford (Devon's father, *Mel King*).

Flashbacks: Chad Harden (*Jack as a boy*), Thomas Drayden (Devon's father, *Mel, as a young man*).

Theme: "Midnight Caller," by Brad Fiedel.

464. Mike Hammer

Syndicated, 1957 to 1958
CBS, 1/26/84 to 1/12/85
CBS, 9/27/86 to 9/9/87

The Syndicated Series: Mickey Spillane's fictional Mike Hammer (Darren McGavin) is a two-fisted private detective working out of New York City. He has an eye for the girls ("Watch it, Mike, your fangs are showing"), and if there is a beautiful "doll" or "dish" in trouble, he is there to help. He uses force to get results and considers a social call roughing up a suspect. Mike seems to take the law into his own hands and dish out his own brand of justice—violence (and get away with it). He has an office (812) in mid–Manhattan and lives in a hotel on West 47th Street. For research, Mike uses the newspaper morgues of both the *Daily News* (at 220 East 42nd Street) and the mythical *Chronicle* (Raymond Bailey plays Marty Collins, the *Chronicle*'s editor). Patrick ("Pat") Chambers (Bart Burns) is Mike's friend, a captain with the Homicide Division of the 19th Precinct of the N.Y.P.D.

Brian Keith was originally selected to play the role of Mike Hammer. Dave Kahn and Melvyn Lenard composed the theme, "Riff Blues."

The CBS Series: Hard-boiled New York private detective Mike Hammer (Stacy Keach) was once a cop—"But I knew all the rules, that's why I'm not a cop now." He now operates the Mike Hammer Agency at 304 West 16th Street in Manhattan. He has an eye for the ladies, but is not as violent as his predecessor. Mike lives at 4100 Tenth Avenue, and his office phone number is 212-555-6974. He drives a blue 1966 Mustang and has a gun named Betsy. As a kid Mike had a dog named Ike (they were called "Mike and Ike"); his hangout is Marty's Bar.

Velda (Lindsay Bloom) is Mike's gorgeous secretary; Patrick ("Pat") Chambers (Don Stroud) is the N.Y.P.D. homicide captain; Lawrence Barrington (Kent Williams) is the Manhattan D.A.; and Ozzie the Answer (Danny Goldman) is Mike's information man. (Velda, Barrington and Ozzie did not appear in the earlier series.)

The series gimmick was "The Face" (Donna Denton), a beautiful but mysterious girl who was seen briefly in every episode (she appeared to be following Mike). In the final episode, Mike discovered her to be a writer named Laura who wrote Nick Steele mystery novels under the pen name Frederick Flynn (she had been following Mike for three years to get story material; prior to this last episode, the girl playing the role had only been identified as "D.D.").

Emma Samms played Mike's daughter, Jamie, a singer (known as Jamie Jinx) with the group Green Lipstick. The series is also known as "The New Mike Hammer" (third date listing). Earle Hagen composed the theme, "Harlem Nocturne."

Prior to the 1984 CBS series, three CBS television movies appeared: *Mickey Spillane's Mike Hammer: Margin for Murder* (10/15/81), with Kevin Dobson (*Mike Hammer*), Cindy Pickett (*Velda*) and Charles Hallahan (*Pat Chambers*); *Mickey Spillane's Mike Hammer: More Than Murder* (1/26/83; series cast); and *Mickey Spillane's Mike Hammer: Murder Me, Murder You* (4/9/83; series cast with the exception of Velda, here played by Tanya Roberts). Before the series returned in 1986, the CBS television movie *The Return of Mickey Spillane's Mike Hammer* aired (9/18/86). Two years after the series left the air, CBS aired *Mickey Spillane's Mike Hammer: Murder Takes All* (5/21/89); both movies featured the series cast.

465. *The Millionaire*

CBS, 1/19/55 to 9/28/60

Cast: Marvin Miller (*Michael Anthony*), Paul Frees (*Voice of John Beresford Tipton*).

Facts: A man, seated behind a desk, speaks: "My name is Michael Anthony. For many years, I was executive secretary to the late multibillionaire, John Beresford Tipton. He was one of the very few men who ever earned, by the use of his phenomenal brain, a fortune that ran into the billions of dollars. Among my duties was the unique job of delivering one million dollars which Mr. Tipton frequently gave away tax free, to a total stranger."

Of the 2.5 billion people populating the world in 1955, only 19 were worth $500 million or more. One such man was John Beresford Tipton (never fully seen). Mr. Tipton lived a life of treasured seclusion and conducted his business activities from Silverstone, his 60,000 acre estate. Here, he indulged in many hobbies, the most unusual of which began when his doctor told him that he must find a means of relaxation.

Mr. Tipton, seated in his study, is toying with one of his ivory chess figures, when he sends for his executive secretary, Michael Anthony. "You sent for me, sir?" "You know, Mike," Tipton says, "these chessmen were the first luxury I ever allowed myself . . . I decided to make my hobby a chess game with human beings . . . I'm going to choose a number of people for my chessmen and give them each a million dollars. The bank will issue the check . . . No one is to ever know that I'm the donor. I want a complete report on what happens to each person's life in writing."

After Mr. Tipton's death, the will instructed Michael Anthony to reveal the files of people, selected by a means known only to Mr. Tipton, who were mysteriously presented with a tax free cashier's check for one million dollars. Via flashback sequences, John Beresford Tipton's intrusion on fate is revealed as stories disclose how the money helped or hindered lives.

John Beresford Tipton issued 188 checks for one million dollars (drawn on the Gotham City Trust and Savings Bank). His unique hobby was related to the subject of human nature. "Every subject in his vast store of knowledge was close analysis and was always related to the behavior and destiny of man." Each check recipient must sign a document agreeing never to reveal the exact nature of the gift or its amount. Spouses can be told, but telling anyone else results in a forfeiture of any remaining monies. The series' catchphrases were: (Mike) "You sent for me, sir," and (Tipton, handing Mike a check) "Mike, our next millionaire." The series is also known as "If You Had a Million."

Note: On 12/19/78, CBS presented "The Millionaire" (a.k.a. "The New Millionaire"), an unsold pilot that attempted to update the earlier series. Robert Quarry played Michael Anthony, the man who distributes the checks.

Prior to this, NBC aired an unsold pilot called "If I Had a Million" (12/31/73), which was based on the 1932 feature film of the same title. In the movie, an elderly man, not wanting his greedy relatives to have his money, decides to give his money to total strangers by selecting names from a phone book. For television, Peter Kastner played a wealthy man who decides to give million dollar checks to people he doesn't know. (At the local library he would randomly choose a name from a phone book and deliver to that person a check for one million dollars.)

466. *The Misfits of Science*

NBC, 10/4/85 to 2/21/86

"Weird 'R' Us" and the "Misfits of Science" are the nicknames for H.I.T. (the Human Investigative Team) of Humanidyne ("Science to help the human condition"), the largest defense contractor in the United States. Dr. William ("Billy") Hayes (Dean Paul Martin) and Dr. Elvin ("El") Lincoln (Kevin Peter Hall) are the research scientists who head H.I.T.; Dick Stetmeyer (Max Wright) is their easily exasperated supervisor. Billy and El are assisted by Gloria Dinallo (Courteney Cox), Johnny Bukowski (Mark Thomas Miller) and Jane Miller (Jennifer Holmes). They are extraordinary people who happen to be different—but who use their unique powers to help people in trouble.

Billy possesses no special powers; he looks out for the other members of the group (he drives a '65 Dodge Dart with the license plate 6LNK 534). El complains constantly about the poor working conditions, the broken equipment and "a salary that would make a paperboy cry." He is also very tall (seven feet four inches) and self-conscious about his height. He was born in Watts, "but I can't play basketball." El has been working on glandular research and developed what Billy calls the "shrinking stuff" (El injected himself with it; now when he touches the back of his neck, he can reduce himself to the size of a Ken doll; the condition lasts for 14 minutes, but he can only reduce his height once an hour. In his reduced size, El wears Ken's jogging outfit).

Gloria Dinallo is a very pretty 17-year-old girl who possesses amazing telekinetic powers. She is also a juvenile delinquent and cared for by her probation officer, Jane Miller (Gloria's father deserted her some months ago). "Glo," as Billy calls her, works as a waitress at the Burger Barn.

Johnny Bukowski, a former rock star known as Johnny B, was "fried" by 20,000 volts of electricity at his last concert and is now a human dynamo. "B Man," as Billy calls him, attracts electricity and discharges lightning bolts. His fingers spark, water can kill him and his eyes glow (he wears sunglasses to cover them).

Miss Nance (Diane Civita) is the agency's pretty receptionist. She loves Snickers bars, and "The Days of Our Lives" is her favorite television soap opera. She is oblivious to what is happening around her and considers it her duty to give recipients their telephone messages—no matter what the circumstances (there is usually a crisis in progress).

The Misfits of Science appeared on the covers of the following magazines: *Timely* (the group), *Miz* (Gloria and Jane—"Women as Heroes"), *America's Youth Weekly* (group), *Roving Stone* (Johnny), *Party Boys* (group) and *Shapely* (group).

Kathleen O'Malley appeared as Billy's mother, Mrs. Hayes. Basil Poledouris composed the theme, "The Misfits of Science."

467. *Mr. and Mrs. North*

CBS, 10/3/52 to 9/25/53
NBC, 1/26/54 to 7/20/54

TO JERRY, WITH LOVE, PAM is the inscription on the pocket watch Pamela North (Barbara Britton) gave to her husband, Gerald ("Jerry") North (Richard Denning), on the occasion of their first wedding anniversary. (They have been married five years when the series begins. Pam and Jerry married on a Friday afternoon during Pam's lunch hour and honeymooned in Paris.) Jerry, a lieutenant in the navy during World War II, is a former private detective who relinquished the rough life for a peaceful existence as a publisher (for an unidentified house; his office number is 901). Pamela is young, beautiful and fashion conscious, and she believes she possesses the mind of a detective (when she sees something that is wrong, she immediately associates it with foul play). Much to Jerry's regret, Pam is most often right and he finds himself playing detective again to solve a crime. It is unfair to give Jerry all the credit. Pam does solve crimes on her own. She is so unassuming that the culprit is unaware of her brilliance and is caught by surprise. Pam is extremely proud of herself at these moments and tells Jerry, "If I hadn't used my brains, I'd be dead. You'd have a corpse for a wife." (Unfortunately, Pam tells Jerry this when he is trying to sleep or is involved with a manuscript; the remark falls virtually on deaf ears—"Yes, honey, that's nice, dear." Occasionally, Jerry's subconscious hears what Pam is saying. When he realizes what she said, he shows great concern and tells her not to do it again. She agrees—until the next episode.)

Jerry and Pam live at 24 Sainte Anne's Place, Apartment 6A, in New York's Greenwich Village. (Their address is also given as 23 Sainte Anne's Place, Apartment 408—even though Apartment 6A is seen in the opening theme.) NN 1139 is their car license plate (the car is parked in the Sainte Anne's Garage), and their phone number was given as Gramercy 3-4098, Gramercy 3-8099, and Granwell 3-4370. Their closest friend is Bill Weigand (Francis DeSales), a lieutenant with the Homicide Division of the Police Department of New York City (he was best man at their wedding; his phone number is PE 6-0599).

The series is based on the novel by Frances and Richard Lockridge. On 5/19/46, NBC presented a test film (the term *pilot* had not yet come into use) called "Mr. and Mrs. North," with John McQuade as Jerry North and Maxine Stuart as Pamela North. NBC presented a second "Mr. and Mrs. North" test film on 7/4/49, with Joseph Allen as Jerry

North and Mary Lou Taylor as Pamela North. While neither of these versions produced a series, "Mr. and Mrs. North" is the only series at the time to have had three pilots, one of which dates back to the experimental days of television (the third pilot, produced with Richard Denning and Barbara Britton is 1952, is called "Weekend Murder" and aired as the first episode of the series).

468. *Mr. Belvedere*

ABC, 3/15/85 to 12/30/89
ABC, 7/1/90 to 7/8/90

Cast: Christopher Hewett (*Lynn Belvedere*), Bob Uecker (*George Owens*), Ilene Graff (*Marsha Owens*), Tracy Wells (*Heather Owens*), Rob Stone (*Kevin Owens*), Brice Beckham (*Wesley Owens*), Michele Matheson (*Angela*).

Facts: Lynn Aloysius Belvedere appeared on the cover of *World Focus* magazine ("Housekeeper of the Year"). He possesses medals for climbing Mount Everest and winning the Pillsbury Bake-off. He worked for English nobility (valet to Winston Churchill and housekeeper to Queen Elizabeth II). Lynn now resides at 200 Spring Valley Road in Beaver Falls, Pittsburgh, with his new employers, the chaotic Owens family: parents George and Marsha, and their children, Kevin, Heather and Wesley.

Mr. Belvedere was born in England. He lived on Higby Road and attended the Pennington School. Once every seven years, Lynn is affected by the Stonehedge Curse—a force that strikes the people of his hometown of Stonehedge (it makes him bounce back and forth between himself and someone else; the cure is to wait it out or return home and dance around the statue of Stonehedge, the founder of the town). Lynn possesses a $750,000 Fabergé egg (given to him by a sheik for saving his life); he also served as a housekeeper to Gandhi. Lynn wrote a book on his experiences with the Owens family called *An American Journal: The Suburban Years*. Ding Dongs and Scooter Pies are Lynn's favorite junk foods, and Donut World is his favorite store.

In the last episode, Lynn marries Louise Gilbert (Rosemary Forsyth), an animal behaviorist he met at a laundromat. Lynn leaves the family to join Louise in Africa when she is asked to return to the University of Boutari to take a gorilla census. In the final minutes of the show, Lynn remarks that he left his weekly journals (the diaries that he was seen writing at the end of each episode) at the Owens home, with a possibility that he may one day return for them.

George Owens, who attended Cleveland High School, originally hosted "Sports Page" (later "Sports Rap"), a radio program on WBK-AM (phone number 555-2222). Later, he is the sports anchor of WBN-TV, Channel 8's "Metro News," and writer of the "Sports Beat" column for the Pittsburgh *Bulletin*. George calls Lynn "Big Guy"; his favorite dinner is meatloaf, potato logs and creamed corn; pork rinds and Spam dip are his favorite snacks. Shopping at

LumberRama is George's favorite pastime. As a kid, George would play pinball machines at the arcade on First Avenue, stay out till midnight, then sneak into his room. To overcome his fear of flying, George closes he eyes and pretends to be on a bus. George and Lynn were members of the "Happy Guys," a neighborhood crime watch.

Marsha Owens, originally a law student, passed the bar exam in July 1987 and joined the firm of Dawson, Metcalfe and Bach. The following year, she became an attorney for the Legal Hut. Marsha dreamed of helping the underdog; when she couldn't find it at the Legal Hut, she quit and became "Babs," a waitress at the Beaver Falls Diner.

Marsha's favorite dinner is lobster thermidor; she has a never-seen Porsche she calls Wolfgang, and her maiden name was given as both Cameron and McClellan. Marsha spent $30,000 on law school (University of Pittsburgh, where she ranked 76 out of 278 students). In one episode, Ilene Graff played Marsha's double, Sharon Witt, a dangerous criminal.

McSwarley's is Marsha and George's favorite restaurant. In early episodes, George and Marsha's wedding date is mentioned as both 9/2/67 and 9/17/67; in a later episode, 1968 is mentioned, as is George and Marsha's honeymoon at the Altoona Motor Lodge, room 14.

Kevin Owens, their oldest child, attends Van Buren High School. George and Marsha contemplated calling him either Moon Shadow (if a girl) or Moondoggie (if a boy). But when the baby was born, it looked more like a Kevin. Kevin worked part time at Mr. Clucks's Fried Chicken and as a salesman for Phil's Friendly Motors (a used car lot). He was born in 1967 and was an Eagle Scout. In later episodes, Kevin has his own apartment (number 5), which is next to a sewage treatment plant ("I'm a student [University of Pittsburgh] and the rent is cheap"). Kevin is allergic to raisins, and he was a member of a band called The Young Savages (he played drums).

Heather Owens, the middle child, attends Van Buren High School and is called "Kitten" by George. She eats Kellogg's Corn Flakes for breakfast, has her hair done at Snyder's Beauty Salon and had an afterschool job at Traeger's Record Store. When Heather gets depressed over losing a boyfriend, she eats Rocky Road ice cream then goes shopping at the mall. At age 16, Heather felt she needed a more sophisticated name and called herself Bianca.

Heather's best friend is Angela, a very pretty but kooky girl who has a hanger collection and calls Lynn everything but Mr. Belvedere (for example, "Mr. Bumper Sticker," "Mr. Beaver Dam," "Mr. Beer Belly," "Mr. Bell Ringer"). She and Heather were cheerleaders at school (for the Beavers football team) and members of the Iron Maidens, a community group that reads to old people. Angela and Heather entered the Miss Beaver Falls Beauty Pageant. Heather did a patriotic tap dance; Angela, who won, performed a ventriloquist's act with a dummy patterned after Mr. Belvedere.

Thinking blondes get everything, Heather dyed her tawny brown hair blonde. She suddenly got whistled at, had doors opened for her and got free food from "the guy in the cafeteria." She went back to what Angela called her "muddy color hair" ("Well, I don't know what color it is") when

Mr. Belvedere. **Front: Tracy Wells (left) and Brice Beckham; back, left to right: Ilene Graff, Christopher Hewett, Bob Uecker, Rob Stone.**

Heather's new popularity threatened to destroy her friendship with Angela ("Being blonde and pretty are about the only assets Angela has," says Heather).

In one episode, Angela set herself up as a psychic counselor to win back Heather after she befriended a more intellectual girl. Angela became the life form of a Swedish dairy farmer named Lars Fredrickson, the healer of mankind (she practiced at the mall's psychic fair). Angela was rarely called by a last name; but when she needed one, she was given three—Shostakovich, Gilbert and Jostakovich.

Wesley Owens, the youngest and most mischievous of the Owens children, attended Conklin Elementary School, Allegheney Junior High and finally Beaver Falls Junior High. He has a dog named Spot, a snake called Captain Nemo and a hamster named Inky. Wesley is a member of the Colts Little League team (coached by George) and the Junior Pioneers (Group 12), and his favorite sandwiches are tuna fish and marshmallow spread and bologna and marshmallow spread on raisin bread. Wesley, who is called "Wesman" by George, made a home movie about Mr.

Belvedere called "The Housekeeper from Hell." Wesley delights in playing practical jokes on his never-seen, but always complaining neighbors, the Hufnagels (in the next to last episode, Teresa Ganzel played the only Hufnagel to be seen, the gorgeous Giselle). To make money, Wesley sold Heather's lingerie, claiming it belonged to Madonna. He attended Camp Chippewa and wore jersey number 31 when he was on the school football team.

Relatives: David Rappaport (Lynn's cousin, *Galen Belvedere*), Sylvia Kauders (Lynn's mother, *"Mumsey" Margaret Belvedere*).

Flashbacks: Trevor Thiegen *(young Lynn)*.

Theme: "Theme from Mr. Belvedere," vocal by Leon Redbone.

Note: While not as outrageous as "Mr. Belvedere," a similar series called "Our Man Higgins" aired on ABC (10/3/62 to 9/11/63). The MacRobertses are a typical American family. There is the father, Duncan (Frank Maxwell), his wife, Alice (Audrey Totter), and their children, Joanne (Regina Groves), Tommy (Ricky Kelman) and

Dinghy (K.C. Butts). When Sir Dougall MacRoberts, a distant relative in England, passes away, the MacRobertses inherit a 127 piece, 250 year old silver service (the MacRoberts silver) and Higgins (Stanley Holloway), a high tone English butler who delivers the inheritance and whom they must retain to keep the service.

Linda Talbot (Frances Robinson) is their neighbor. She resides at the Kimberly Terrace Apartments, is attracted to Higgins and is determined to acquire his services, despite the fact that Higgins has no intention of giving up employment with the MacRobertses.

Alan Carney appeared as Duncan's cousin, Ernie MacRoberts. Based on the radio series "It's Higgins, Sir." Frank DeVol composed the theme.

469. *Mister Ed*

Syndicated, 1960 to 1961
CBS, 10/1/61 to 9/4/66

Cast: Alan Young *(Wilbur Post)*, Connie Hines *(Carol Post)*, Allan ("Rocky") Lane *(Voice of Mister Ed)*.

Facts: Newlyweds Wilbur and Carol Post purchase a home at 17230 Valley Spring Lane in Los Angeles from Golden Acres Real Estate. Shortly after, Wilbur discovers an unusual resident in the barn: a talking horse, named Mister Ed, who was left by the previous owners. Because Wilbur is the only human Ed (as Wilbur calls him) likes well enough to talk to, he will only talk to him (thus begin Wilbur's problems as the owner of a talking horse).

"It's been a long time since I was a pony," were the first words Ed, "the playboy horse of Los Angeles," spoke to Wilbur. Ed weighed 96 pounds at birth. He was an incubator baby, and his birthsign is Taurus. Ed's favorite word is *filly* (he considers it the prettiest word in the English language), and he inherited the family curse—a fear of heights (begun when his grandfather fell off a cliff while chasing a filly). Ed, who is seven years old when the series begins, loves carrots and wrote the hit song "Pretty Little Filly."

Wilbur, an independent architect, operates his office from the barn (which doubles as Ed's home); he was originally slated to be a lawyer (as depicted in sales pitches for the show in early 1960). Wilbur's office phone number is Poplar 9-1769, and his home address was also given as 17340 Valley Boulevard, 17290 Valley Spring Lane and 1720 Valley Road in Los Angeles. Wilbur, whose birthsign is also Taurus, is a member of the Lawndale Men's Club and drives a Studebaker with the license plate FIM 921.

Carol, a former dancer, measures 36-22-36, and had a job as a dance instructor at Miss Irene's in Hollywood. Her maiden name is Higgins (also given as Carlyle).

Roger and Kay Addison (Larry Keating and Edna Skinner) are the Posts' original neighbors (replaced later by Gordon and Winnie Kirkwood [Leon Ames and Florence MacMichael]). Roger and Kay have been married 19 years; their phone number is DLO-2599; and Roger was a member of Sigma Nu Delta fraternity in college.

In the original, unaired pilot version, "The Wonderful World of Wilbur Pope," Scott McKay played Wilbur Pope, Mister Ed's owner, and Sandra White was his wife, Carlotta Pope. Allan ("Rocky") Lane was the voice of Mister Ed, and Peggy Converse and Ray Walker were their neighbors, Florence and John Reese.

Relatives: Barry Kelley (Carol's father, *Mr. Carlyle*), Eleanor Audley (Wilbur's aunt, *Martha*), Jack Albertson (Kay's brother, *Paul Fenton*). Mentioned but not seen was Kay's niece, Peggy.

Theme: "Mister Ed," by Jay Livingston and Ray Evans.

470. *Mr. Lucky*

CBS, 10/24/59 to 9/10/60

Cast: John Vivyan *(Mr. Lucky)*, Ross Martin *(Andamo)*, Pippa Scott *(Maggie Shank Rutherford)*.

Facts: When first introduced (in the episode "The Magnificent Bribe," 10/24/59), a man known only as Mr. Lucky and his partner, Andamo (no other name given), are seen entertaining the corrupt president (Nehemiah Persoff) of an unnamed Latin American country. At this time it is made clear that Mr. Lucky owns a gambling club called Joba Lobo and a pleasure yacht called the *Fortuna*. (The exact locale of the club is not given; it is assumed to be a foreign country, possibly in Latin America, by street signs and the accents of the club gamblers. In the second episode, the club is mentioned as being on "The Island.")

During El Presidente's stay at the Joba Lobo, Lucky becomes involved with revolutionaries (who are planning to assassinate the president), when Andamo, a supporter of free government, uses the *Fortuna* to smuggle in guns.

Realizing that their lives are now at risk, Lucky and Andamo attempt to flee—but before they can, El Presidente is killed by a beautiful assassin named Elena (Ziva Rodann). With Elena's help, Lucky and Andamo escape from the club. At the dock, they learn from an old fisherman (Francis J. MacDonald) that the *Fortuna* has been sunk. With the only money they have left to them, the $3,000 Andamo managed to stash, they buy the fisherman's motorboat and escape. The episode ends with Andamo betting Lucky the boat won't make it to the nearest island, which he predicts is 200 miles away. In the second episode ("They Shall Not Pass," 10/31/59), Lucky and Andamo are seen walking on a dock in Los Angeles (they are dressed as sailors and carrying duffle bags). Andamo mentions that he was glad to "get off that freighter" and has only ten cents to his name. Lucky counters with having only a dollar. Just then, they see a beautiful girl, dressed as a harem dancer, heading for a costume party on a yacht. Because of their dress, Lucky and Andamo are believed to be guests and invited aboard. There Lucky meets Maggie Shank Rutherford, an old friend, whose father owns the yacht. During the party Lucky learns that Maggie's father, Julius Shank, a con man who is known as Chicago Julius, is in debt to a gambler named 12th Street (Lou Krugman) for $85,000.

Lucky devises a plan to help himself and Julius. At 12th Street's gambling casino, Lucky parlays a $5,000 loan from 12th Street into a large but unspecified amount at the dice table. Lucky buys the yacht from Julius (possibly for $100,000, based on Julius's statement of the value of the yacht) and turns it into a gambling yacht called Lucky's. To be his own law and free of syndicate interference (including 12th Street's revenge), Lucky anchors the yacht, which he names the *Fortuna,* three miles off shore in international waters. Episodes 1–15 depict Lucky and Andamo's efforts to maintain an honest operation; episodes 16–34 focus on Lucky and Andamo's adventures as the owners of a floating nightclub (Lucky's) when they convert the *Fortuna* into a supperclub (Lucky applied for a private club license when he felt it was time for a change and to avoid the hassle of the police trying to arrest him and shut down the club).

In the opening theme, two dice are rolled which stop at seven (six and one). Eight playing cards are also seen, which reverse to spell the series' title, "Mr. Lucky" (ace of spades, three of diamonds, two of hearts, five of clubs, ace of diamonds, six of hearts, four of spades, and eight of diamonds). An artist's depiction of a one-eyed black cat is seen over the credits (the right eye winks). The *Fortuna's* I.D. number is 27533, and the two large, illuminated dice that blink on the yacht show the various combinations of seven (six and one, four and three, five and two). Lucky's car (license plate: LUCKY) has a plaque over the glove compartment that reads MADE ESPECIALLY FOR MR. LUCKY. Life preservers on the yacht read FORTUNA II.

Lucky, who gets his name because he is lucky at gambling, is two-fisted and a master of the con (which he will only use to help good defeat evil). He carries a pocket watch that plays the first four notes, when opened, of the song "Mr. Lucky" ("They say I'm lucky").

Andamo, who manages the *Fortuna,* is a Latin and has an eye for the ladies. He is a genius at the con also and calls Mr. Lucky "Lucky" and "Compadre." According to Lucky, "Andamo fights with the police instead of cooperating with them." Lucky and Andamo are not on the best of terms with the police, especially with Lieutenant Rovacs (Tom Brown) of the L.A.P.D., who, like many other officers of the law, would like to see Lucky and Andamo put away for 20 years.

Other Regulars: Joe Scott (the Fortuna's croupier, then maitre d'), Della Sharm (Doris, the *Fortuna* cashier).

Relatives: Conrad Nagel (Maggie's father, *Julius Shank*), Lillian Bronson (Maggie's mother, *Mrs. Shank Rutherford*; no first name given).

Theme: "Mr. Lucky," by Henry Mancini.

471. *Mr. Merlin*

CBS, 10/7/81 to 3/22/82

Cast: Barnard Hughes *(Max Merlin)*, Elaine Joyce *(Alexandra)*, Clark Brandon *(Zack Rogers)*.

Facts: King Arthur was a student of his; he taught Attila the Hun to brush his teeth; he was born in Wales in A.D. 381 as Merlin Silvestra; his father was an incubus and his mother a Welsh princess. He didn't part the Red Sea ("I'm good, but not that good"), but he did become a sorcerer, a magician of the highest order who was known as Merlin the Magician.

When the series begins, in modern times, Merlin is seen as the owner of a garage in San Francisco. Max Merlin (as he is now known), is 1,600 years old and has fallen behind on the performance of his good deeds. One day, Max receives a visit from Alexandra (whom he calls "Alex"), a gorgeous courier from above, who informs him that he must find an apprentice and teach him the art of sorcery. Max balks: "I've never needed an apprentice before, why now?" "You're overworked and falling behind," says Alex, "and if you refuse you will give up your immortality and your powers."

Though reluctant, Max places a "help wanted" sign at his garage (which has no visible name; it is called Mr. Merlin's). It has also been decided by celestial powers that whoever is able to remove a crowbar from a block of cement (like King Arthur and his sword, Excalibur), will become the Sorcerer's apprentice.

One day while riding his skateboard, young Zachary ("Zack") Rogers, a girl-crazy, awkward teenager, crashes into Max's supply of oil cans and knocks a car off the hydraulic ramp. Looking for something to help Max lift the car, Zack spots the crowbar and pulls it from the cement. The crowbar glows (and briefly changes to Excalibur), and Max finds his apprentice.

Even though Max hasn't instructed anyone since King Arthur, Zack becomes his new student (Zack works part time at the garage and spends 14 hours a week learning from Mr. Merlin). Stories relate Zack's attempts to learn the art of sorcery, and his and Max's efforts to help people in distress.

Max's garage is located at 61 Hope Street in the High Park section of San Francisco (it is open from 1:00 P.M. to 1:00 A.M.). Max drives an antique car with the license plate 927 LYN, and he lives in a home at 573 Arlington Drive. Max does 30 pushups a day and avoids fried foods to stay fit. The first illness he ever got was tonsillitis (in 1981; he had his tonsils removed at Memorial Hospital). Max has an owl named Luther and a secret room called "The Crystal Room" (which contains Max's sorcerer's equipment. To enter this room, he taps on a wall in the living room. The wall vanishes and reveals a staircase that leads to the Crystal Door—which, when opened, leads to the Crystal Room). When Max needs eggs for cooking, he conjures up a chicken named Dorothy. In another episode, Max's birthdate was given as September 29, A.D. 856.

Zack and his cohort in misadventure, Leo Samuels (Jonathan Prince), attend Mumford High School. Zack lives with his mother, Elizabeth Rogers (Betty Garrett), at 13761 Havenhurst Road, and his phone number is 555-5515. Leo reads *Punk Junk* magazine, and he and Zack formed a rock singing duo called Hot Pink Heads (they dressed in shocking pink and sang the song "I'll Never Stop Loving You").

Theme: "Mr. Merlin," by Ken Harrison.

472. *Mister Peepers*

NBC, 7/3/52 to 9/25/52
NBC, 10/26/52 to 6/12/55

Jefferson City is a small American town rather than a city. There is the local newspaper, the Jefferson City *Press and Collector*, City High School, City College, Jefferson General Hospital and, most important, Jefferson City Junior High School, the focal point of the first series to spoof the public schoolteacher.

The hero of our saga is Robinson J. Peepers (Wally Cox), an army corporal who returns to teaching (general science) after an honorable discharge (poor eyesight). Robinson is gentle and kind, and his students are all his fans. He is also timid and shy and easily taken advantage of. Robinson was born in the neighboring town of Williamsport where his mother, "Ma Peepers" (Ruth McDevitt), and his sister, Agnes Peepers (Jenny Egan), still live (Agnes is a teacher at the Jefferson Observatory; Mrs. F.R. Peepers is the name on the mailbox). Robinson talks directly to the audience when he feels the need. To open his locker at school, he goes through the following ritual: he first bangs on the radiator on top of the lockers three times; he then pushes up and down on the handle of the locker next to his. At the end of the lockers (left side) he measures three feet up from the floor and kicks the first locker door. His locker door (second from the right) then opens.

Royala Dean (Norma Crane), the school's music teacher, was Robinson's first love interest (first date listing). When the series, intended only to be a summer replacement for "The James Melton Show," achieved high ratings, it was quickly brought back to replace the Eddie Mayehoff series, "Doc Corkle," which was canceled after three episodes. Robinson's new love interest was Nancy Remington (Patricia Benoit), the school nurse. They became engaged in the episode of 4/25/54 and married on 5/23/54 (Sylvia Field and Ernest Truex appeared as Nancy's parents. For this particular episode, 50 couples, honeymooning in New York City, occupied the studio audience).

Harvey Weskit (Tony Randall) is the history teacher. He is married to Marge (Georgann Johnson) and is best friends with Robinson (whom he calls "Ace" and "Rob"; Marge calls him "Robbie"). Marge and Harvey became parents of a baby boy (1954) they named Harrison Brookfield Weskit. Marge was born in Chicago, and Robinson calls Harvey, who was best man at his wedding, "Wes."

Mrs. Gurney (Marion Lorne) is the wife of school principal Gabriel Gurney (Joseph Foley) and is an English teacher. She fusses, mutters to herself, sentimentalizes and forgets what she is about to say (she is almost identical to "Aunt Clara," the character she played on "Bewitched"). Gage Clark as Mr. Bascomb, became the principal in 1954.

Jack Warden played the school's coach, Frank T. Whipp III; in 1953, Carol Lynley played one of Robinson's students, Madeline Schreiber.

Bernie Green composed the theme.

473. *Mr. Terrific*

CBS, 1/9/67 to 8/28/67

A U.S. government scientist named Dr. Reynolds (Ned Glass) begins an experiment to find a cure for the common cold. After much experimentation, he accidentally invents a pill that produces incredible strength in animals "but makes the strongest of men quite ill." The Power Pill, as it is called, is brought to the attention of Barton J. Reed (John McGiver), the head of the Bureau of Special Projects. His assignment is to find a human on whom the pill will work. His search ends with Stanley Beemish (Stephen Strimpell), "a weak and droopy daffodil," who is partners with Hal Waters (Dick Gautier) in Hal and Stanley's Service Station. When Stanley takes the pill, it endows him with amazing abilities (the power to fly, incredible strength and an immunity to harm). Reed decides to use Stanley as Mr. Terrific, "the government's secret weapon against crime." Stanley must now lead a double life: ordinary citizen and the mysterious Mr. Terrific.

Stanley's Mr. Terrific costume is a jacket with wing-like sleeves (which he flaps in order to fly), a pair of goggles and a scarf—all of which he stores in a locker at the gas station. When Mr. Terrific is needed, Reed sounds the Purple Alert. Before each assignment, Reed gives Stanley a box with three pills (one base pill that lasts one hour and gives Stanley the strength of 1,000 men, and two booster pills that last ten minutes each). Three pills is the maximum Stanley can take in one day. The pills are specially candy coated so Stanley will take them (even then, they appear to be foul tasting). Stanley is a bit trouble-prone and has difficulty with his landings.

Hal and Stanley's Service Station is located at Northeastern and Wyoming streets in Washington, D.C.; the phone number of the bureau is National 8-0397. Hal, a ladies' man, introduces himself to women by saying, "Hi, I'm Hal, gas station attendant, snappy dresser and lady killer." Ellen Corby appeared as Hal's meddling mother, Mrs. Waters.

The original, unaired version of the series is a bit different. Stanley Beemish (Alan Young) works as a shoe clerk for Mr. Finney (Jesse White) and was recruited by the chief of the Office of Special Assignments (Edward Andrews) to test a power pill that transforms him into Mr. Terrific, a daring but misadventure-prone crime fighter. A girlfriend for Stanley was not incorporated in the actual series, but in this pilot version, Sheila Wells played his romantic interest, Gloria Dickinson.

Gerald Fried composed the theme, "Mr. Terrific."

474. *Mobile One*

ABC, 9/12/75 to 12/29/75

Pete Campbell (Jackie Cooper), a top notch reporter for ABC-TV, is fired for excessive drinking. After drying out and getting his life back together, Pete acquires a job as a sportscaster for WQPR radio (103.1 FM) in Crown City, Georgia.

When Maggie Spencer (Julie Gregg), the producer of "The 11 O'Clock News" on KONE-TV, Channel 1, in southern California, thinks she needs the hard hitting news stories of the past in order to improve ratings, she hires Pete as a reporter. Doug McKnight (Mark Wheeler) is assigned as his cameraman, and stories follow Pete as he uses his ingenuity as a seasoned reporter to go where the news is to get the stories.

Pete and Doug ride in a station wagon with the license plate 27-704-Q. Their radio code to the television station base (K-One Base) is Mobile One. Sony television monitors are used in the newsroom, and the Channel 1 news helicopter I.D. number is N30DB. In the pilot episode ("Mobile Two," ABC, 9/2/75), Pete works for KITE, Channel 10. His and Doug's radio code for the station wagon is 646-Mobile Two. They also wear badges on their jackets that read "10 News." KLIX-TV, Channel 8, is their main competition.

Nelson Riddle composed the theme.

475. *Molloy*

Fox, 7/25/90 to 8/15/90

Cast: Mayim Bialik *(Molloy Martin)*, Pamela Brull *(Lynn Martin)*, Kevin Scannell *(Paul Martin)*, Jennifer Aniston *(Courtney Martin)*, Luke Edwards *(Jason Martin)*.

Facts: Molloy Martin is a professional 13-year-old actress who attends Beverly Hills Junior High School and works after school on the live KQET-TV children's show, "Wonderland."

Molloy recently moved to Beverly Hills, following the death of her mother, to live with her father, Paul Martin, her stepmother, Lynn Martin, her half sister, Courtney, and half brother, Jason. (Molloy's parents were divorced when she was three years old; her mother's name was not mentioned, nor was a reason why they divorced; Molloy's previous address was also not given.)

Molloy now lives at 6113 Fullerton Drive and struggles to contend with a family she finds it hard to adjust to. Paul, who calls her "Mo," works as the program director at KNAP radio in Beverly Hills. Unlike Molloy, who questions everything and tries to understand what is going on, Paul seems to accept everything that happens and considers it all just part of life.

Lynn, who was born in Nashville and is a Republican (Paul is a Democrat), owns a business called Martin Interior Decorating. Like Paul, she is a carefree individual who has a lighthearted approach to life.

Courtney, called by students (including girls) "the most beautiful girl at Beverly Hills Private School," is deserving of the title. Molloy says, "But beneath all that beauty she is just an airhead." Courtney is totally devoted to herself; her number one priority is looking gorgeous. She is easily distracted from whatever she is doing, is upset by the simplest things (such as a chip in her fingernail polish or a strand of hair out of place), and she blames Molloy for something she does that goes wrong. (Molloy takes the blame to keep peace in the family. "Courtney," Molloy says, "is a crybaby and puts up a fuss when she gets blamed for something or doesn't get her way.") Despite Courtney's childish behavior, Molloy desperately wants to look like her "and become a woman, but without the dullard interior."

Jason, Courtney's younger brother, attends an unnamed school and has a pet turtle named Lance (it is also mentioned that he has a dog named Sparky).

I.M. Hobson plays Simon Lansburg (who plays Joey the Squirrel, the host of "Wonderland"). Ashley Maw is Sara Peters, Molloy's friend and co-star on the show.

Theme: "Molloy's Theme," by Ed Alton.

Note: A year before the series premiered, Fox produced a pilot called "Molloy," with Mayim Bialik, in a story that differed somewhat from the aired format. In the unaired pilot, Mayim played Maude Molloy, an independent 12-year-old New York girl who is sent to live with her father, Malcolm Molloy (Robert Desiderio) in California after her mother's death. Maude finds life somewhat different, and her attempts to adjust to her new surroundings were to be the focal point of the series, had it sold. Ashley Maw played Maude's friend, Tripper.

476. *The Monkees*

NBC, 9/12/66 to 8/19/68

Micky Dolenz, Davy Jones, Mike Nesmith and Peter Tork are the Monkees, an out-of-work rock group looking for a job anywhere. They live together in an apartment at 1438 North Beachwood Street in Los Angeles (on their living room wall is a sign that reads MONEY IS THE ROOT OF ALL EVIL). They have a car with the license plate NPH 623 and use the incompetent Urgent Answering Service. *Sheik* magazine selected them as "Typical Young Men of the Year."

Davy was born in England and is the most sensible one of the group (although he often gets carried away by the antics of the others). Peter is the most passive one. He cries at card tricks, gets the hiccups when he auditions for big producers, has hay fever and is prone to seasickness. Mike was born in Texas and was an Eagle Scout as a kid. He collects fortune cookies to feed to a dog they don't have (but Mike thinks they have). Micky was born in Burbank and was called "Goo Goo Eyes" as a kid by his mother. In one episode, Micky Dolenz played Micky's vicious double, a killer named Baby Face Morales, "the Most Wanted Man in America." Micky Dolenz was originally known as Mickey Braddock and starred in the series "Circus Boy."

In the opening theme, when the Monkees are credited, Peter's name is seen four times: once for his own credit and once each for the other three Monkees. Jacqueline DeWit played Mike's Aunt Kate, and Ben Wright was Davy's grandfather.

The Monkees sing the theme, "Hey, Hey, We're the Monkees."

477. *The Monroes*

ABC, 9/7/66 to 8/30/67

Cast: Michael Anderson, Jr. *(Clayt Monroe)*, Barbara Hershey *(Kathleen Monroe)*, Tammy Locke *(Amy Monroe)*, Keith Schultz *(Jefferson Monroe)*, Kevin Schultz *(Fennimore Monroe)*.

Facts: The year is 1875. With a hope of beginning a new life in Wyoming, Albert and Mary Monroe (Russ Conway, Marilyn Moe) and their children, Clayt (age 18), Kathleen (16), twins Jefferson and Fennimore (12) and Amy (six), leave their farm in Illinois and head west—to find an unknown valley that Albert laid claim to in 1866.

After a hazardous trek through treacherous country, the Monroes reach the banks of the Snake River, the last crossing before the valley is within reach. Although all precautions are taken, including using float logs for the wagon, a rope becomes loose and pulls Mary into the perilous water. Albert dives in after her, and in a tragic moment both are lost. "Now we were orphans. I was the oldest . . . I'm Clayt . . . I kept wondering what Pa would do. We couldn't stay here (banks of the river) and we didn't have a farm anymore to go back to. And up ahead there was nothing but wilderness—and one valley Pa had marked with a pile of rocks. But I was the Pa now and I had no choice. I had to find that valley for him . . . We moved out into strange new country. All I had to guide me was a map Pa had made ten years before." After several days, landscape features begin to appear (square top mountains) that fit the map. Soon, they are in "Pa's Valley." "Where are we?" asks Amy. "We're home," a tearful Kathleen responds.

"The rocks were just where Pa said." As Clayt lifts them, he finds Albert's U.S. Army belt buckle and his claim to the land: "Now it was ours to root down, to hold if we could."

That night Clayt's narration reveals some doubts: "I tried to keep the happiness we shared in the afternoon but I couldn't help but worry. How could a farm family from Illinois survive in this wild country they call Wyoming?"

That next day, as the Monroes begin to establish their home, they meet Major Mapoy (Liam Sullivan), an Englishman who heads the Mapoy Cattle Company. He tells them they have settled on cattle grazing land and must move on. But Clayt refuses—"If it means fighting, we'll fight. We've come too far to turn back now." The Major, being a reasonable man, listens to Clayt's story and believes him. He allows the Monroes to stay (hoping the harsh life will discourage them), but tells them that although they have won him over, the Wales family is another battle that may not be as easily won.

Shortly after Clayt files a claim for the land in Greenwood City, he meets Barney Wales (Robert Middleton), a roughneck horse rancher who claims the valley is his.

(Because of the Monroes' claim, his land now borders on "the dry creek"; he needs the Monroe's land, which is on "the new creek," for its water. The Waleses run horses, not cattle, and are even the enemy of Mapoy). Again Clayt refuses to move out—"Being a Monroe is the only thing we've got." While the Monroes win the initial battle, they find the Waleses a constant threat to their safety. "It's just as Pa said. If it were easy it wouldn't be worth having."

The Monroes are called "nesters" by Wales and Mapoy. Clayt wanted to become a sailor and had planned on journeying to San Francisco once his family was settled in Wyoming. Clayt calls Kathleen "Kath"; Amy calls Kathleen "Sister." Jefferson is nicknamed "Big Twin" and Fennimore, who is slightly shorter, "Little Twin." The family has a white dog named Snow, and the valley they have settled in is called Bear Valley. Albert and Mary were married for 20 years; Paradox is the nearest town.

Other Regulars: Jim (Ron Soble) is the renegade Sioux Indian the Monroes befriended ("Big Twin gave him the name"). Jim, called "a lariat Red who drifted in from the north," was wanted by the Major for butchering his cattle in the benchland. Jim was blamed because he is an Indian; the Major believes he may be innocent and places him in Clayt's custody—"Any more cattle missing and he'll be hung." (The Monroes first encountered Jim on a stormy night when he sought shelter in their camp.)

Ruel Jaxon (James Westmoreland), Sleeve (Ben Johnson) and John Bradford (Buck Taylor) are employees of Major Mapoy. Sleeve and Ruel, who calls Kathleen "Miss Kathleen," are friends of the Monroes, despite some initial scrapes.

Dalton Wales (James Brolin) and Billy Dan Wales (Tim O'Kelly) are Barney's rowdy sons; Lorna Wales (Lisa Jak) is Barney's beautiful, mute daughter, who, despite her father's attitude, is sympathetic to the Monroes.

Theme: "The Monroes," by David Rose.

478. *Moonlighting*

ABC, 3/3/85 to 5/14/89

Cast: Cybill Shepherd *(Maddie Hayes)*, Bruce Willis *(David Addison)*, Allyce Beasley *(Agnes DiPesto)*, Curtis Armstrong *(Herbert Viola)*.

Facts: When her business manager embezzles her funds and leaves Madeline ("Maddie") Hayes, a beautiful and sophisticated model, penniless, she decides to recoup some of her losses by selling one of her business holdings, a Los Angeles detective agency called City of Angels Investigations. Her mind is changed, however, when David Addison, the fast talking agency manager who is fearful of losing his job, persuades Maddie to save the agency by becoming a partner. The agency name is changed to Blue Moon Investigations (a.k.a. the Blue Moon Detective Agency), and stories relate the adventures of Maddie and David, detectives who are also lovers.

Office 206 is home to Blue Moon Investigations (which

The Monroes. Back: Barbara Hershey, Michael Anderson, Jr. Front, left to right: Kevin Schultz, Tammy Locke, Keith Schultz.

closes at 6:00 P.M.). Maddie and David bicker about everything but especially about how to run an agency that is losing Maddie money—"Addison, we need a client, a client we can depend on, a bread and butter client who can help us pay our light bill." As Maddie complains about the lack of clients, David always seems to come through: "Maddie, we have to create our own opportunities . . . We are sitting on a money machine; we only have to figure out how to turn it on." Despite David's optimism, Maddie believes, "We are standing on the decks of the *Titanic*; no one calls, no one comes in, and it is bankrupting me. Why am I living this life? I don't deserve this!" (In the episode "Portrait of Maddie," Maddie was delighted when the agency showed its first profit of $2,035.76.)

Despite the first profit, Maddie believes she is right (by the second season, she has only her home left); David believes that they only have to "work out the kinks and we're in." The clients or jobs David finds are not to Maddie's liking (for example, as collectors for a company called Ak Yak Insurance; or as investigators of infidelity cases, which Maddie says "are too full of deception and dirt"). When a client walks in off the street, Maddie also complains: "I should have known when a client walks in off the street she'd be nuts" (for instance, a girl claiming to be a leprechaun who hires them to protect her pot of gold).

Maddie and David have nothing in common. David jokes all the time, makes lewd sexual remarks and sings whenever the opportunity permits (even when it doesn't). Maddie is serious about everything and is trying to mature David. "Do bears bear? Do bees bee?" is David's catchphrase. David says, "I'm a capitalist—I take my capital wherever I can get it." He called Maddie "Blondie blonde" and drives a car with the license plate 2900LB. Dana Delany played Jillian Armstrong, David's former girlfriend.

Maddie, said to be the world's most photographed model, was born on October 11 in Chicago (David was born November 27). As a kid, Maddie had a sheepdog named Sport, and she has a perfect driving record. Her license plate reads 280018.

Maddie graced the covers of such magazines as *Vogue*, *Glamour*, *Vanity Fair* and *Fashion*. She appeared in television commercials as the Blue Moon Shampoo Girl.

"Blue Moon Detective Agency. If persons are missing, if objects are lost, we'll find them for you at a reasonable cost," or "Blue Moon Investigations. Get in some trouble, we'll be there on the double. Wife a philanderer, don't worry, we'll handle her . . ."—these are but two of the many ways Agnes DiPesto, the agency's receptionist, answers the phone. Agnes, who talks in rhyme, lives at 633 Hope Street, Apartment 723. Herbert Viola is Agnes's romantic interest and the agency's bookkeeper.

In the black and white episode, "The Dream Sequence Always Rings Twice," Maddie dreams she is a 1940s singer named Rita Adams at the Flamingo Cove nightclub (she sings the song "Blue Moon"); she envisioned David as a cornet player named Chance McCoy. The episode "Atomic Shakespeare" was a parody of *The Taming of the Shrew*, with Cybill as Katrina, Allyce as her sister, Bianca, and Bruce as the gentleman of Verona, Petruchio, who sets his

goal as that of taming the shrewish Katrina (Bruce sang the song "Good Lovin'").

"Moonlighting" is a series that comes along once in a blue moon. It was unique, imaginative, romantic and daring. But production problems abounded and eventually killed it (when a new episode could be had, it was heavily promoted by ABC). David and Maddie were finally brought together in the final four episodes of the 1986-87 season.

The following season, Maddie returned to her parents' home in Chicago to sort out her relationship with David; she discovered she was pregnant (to reflect Cybill's real life pregnancy with twins). Maddie wasn't sure who the father was: David or her friend Sam Crawford (Mark Harmon). In the episode of 2/9/88, Maddie married Walter Bishop (Dennis Dugan), a man she meets on a train. In the episode "A Womb with a View," Bruce Willis appeared in diapers and played Maddie's unborn child who commented on his relationship with Maddie. As the season progressed, the show simply lost its spark.

Relatives: Robert Webber (Maddie's father, *Alexander Hayes*), Eva Marie Saint (Maddie's mother, *Virginia Hayes*), Virginia Madsen (Maddie's cousin, *Annie*), Paul Sorvino (David's father, *David Addison, Sr.*), Charles Rocket (David's brother, *Richard Addison*), Imogene Coca (Agnes's mother, *Clara DiPesto*), James Stephens (Annie's husband, *Mark*).

Theme: "Moonlighting," vocal by Al Jarreau.

Note: On 5/4/92, ABC presented "Stormy Weathers," a television movie pilot with Cybill Shepherd as Stormy Weathers, a Los Angeles–based private detective. Stormy charges $300 a day plus expenses and lives by three rules: "I never take money I haven't earned; I never turn my back on a killer; and I never fall for a guy who isn't just a cab fare away." Stormy's real first name is Samantha; she received the nickname "Stormy" from the nuns at Saint Ursula's, her Catholic grammar school. Ten years ago Samantha and her father ran a detective agency called Weathers and Weathers, Confidential Investigations. After his death, Samantha took over the company and now runs it on her own. She is assisted by Squirrel (Charlie Schlatter), a computer expert who works out of her office. Also slated to be a regular was Bogey (Diane Salinger), Stormy's childhood friend. Bogey is a lesbian and anxious to change Stormy's mind about sleeping with her. David Bell composed the theme.

479. *Mork and Mindy*

ABC, 9/14/78 to 8/5/82

Cast: Robin Williams *(Mork)*, Pam Dawber *(Mindy McConnell)*, Conrad Janis *(Fred McConnell)*, Jonathan Winters *(Mearth)*, Tom Poston *(Frank Bickley)*, Robert Donner *(Exidor)*, Ralph James *(Orson's Voice)*.

Facts: Ork is a planet about 200 million miles from Earth. It has three moons, and its inhabitants, who resemble humans, evolved from the chicken (their spaceships resemble eggs). Orson is a leader on the planet. He assigns

Mork, a former dinner diver in a lobster tank turned explorer who charted 16 galaxies, the job of Earth Observer. Mork is assigned to study life on Earth and to relate his observations to Ork via his Scorpio Reports (which he transmits to Orson via mind transference).

Mork lands on Earth in Boulder, Colorado, and befriends Mindy McConnell, a pretty student who takes him to her apartment at 1619 Pine Street. When she learns about his mission, she agrees to help him. Stories depict their adventures as Mork attempts to learn about life on Earth.

Mork was born in a test tube (there are no parents on Ork) and comes with a guarantee that covers rusted skin and ankle blowouts. Mork attended Ork Prep School and travels through time via his red sequined Time Traveling Shoes (size eight). Mork has a pet Orkan Nauger Chump named Beebo and an Earth caterpillar he calls Bob. The enemies of Orkans are the Necotons (Raquel Welch played Captain Nevana of the Necoton Black Army who sought Mork; she considered Mindy a pretty pet and kept her in a large bird cage). On Earth, Mork works as a counselor at the Pine Tree Day Care Center and celebrates the Orkan holiday, National Backwards Day.

Mindy, the first girl to play Little League baseball in Boulder, attended Boulder High School (her locker combination was 33-17-3), then the University of Colorado, where she majored in journalism. She first worked in her father's store (McConnell's Music Store), then as a newscaster at KTNS-TV, Channel 31, and finally as the host of "Wake Up, Boulder." Her Jeep license plate reads ML29HJ. On Earth, Mindy was the first human to eat Fleck, an Orkan food that brings out strange behavioral qualities; on Ork, Mindy is known as "the Soft-Lapped One."

When Mork and Mindy marry (10/5/81), they honeymoon on Ork (Mindy won fourth place title in a pet show; Orkans consider Earthlings to be pets). Shortly after they are married, Mork becomes pregnant and lays an egg. The egg hatches and Mork and Mindy become the parents of an elderly "baby" they name Mearth (Orkan children are born old and become young with time). Mearth is a combination of Mork, Mindy and Earth. Mearth has a teddy bear he calls Teddy and attends Ork Prep School one day a month via the Orkan Schoolbus—the 828 Transport Beam.

Fred McConnell, Mindy's father, was originally the owner of McConnell's Music Store and later was the conductor of the Boulder City Orchestra. Cathy (Shelley Fabares) is Fred's new wife and Mindy's young stepmother (Mindy's natural mother, Beth, is deceased); she plays flute in the orchestra.

Exidor, the local loon (and Mork's friend), has an invisible dog named Brutus (a Doberman) and an invisible aide named Pepe. He wrote an autobiographical book called *Lauren Bacall: By Myself* ("If it worked for her...") and had a business called Exidor T-Shirts which failed.

Frank Bickley, Mindy's downstairs neighbor, is a greeting card writer and has a dog named Bickley. Remo (Jay Thomas) and Jeanie DaVinci (Gina Hecht) are a brother and sister who own DaVinci's Restaurant (later called the New York Delicatessen). Mork's greeting is "Na-nu, Na-nu."

Relatives: Elizabeth Kerr (Mindy's grandmother, *Cora*

Mork and Mindy. Pam Dawber and Robin Williams.

Hudson; she calls Fred a "weiner"), Jim Staahl (Mindy's cousin, *Nelson Flavor*), Jonathan Winters (Mindy's uncle, *Dave McConnell*), Beverly Sanders (Mindy's aunt, *Caroline McConnell*).

Flashbacks: Missy Francis *(Mindy as a girl)*.
Theme: "Mork and Mindy," by Perry Botkin.

480. *Morton and Hayes*

CBS, 7/24/91 to 8/28/91

"Everybody remembers great comedy teams like Laurel and Hardy and Abbott and Costello. But who remembers Morton and Hayes—nobody!" The reason why nobody remembers Morton and Hayes, says host Rob Reiner, is "because their films were thought lost forever in a tragic fire. But recently in Los Angeles, while workers were either in the process of tearing down a Burger King to make way for a Sizzlers, or vice versa, a rusty, battered old vault was discovered." Inside that vault more than 100 black and white "Morton and Hayes" classic comedy shorts of the 1930s and 1940s were found. The prints were restored and presented for the first time on television by Rob Reiner in a weekly series (which aired only six "Morton and Hayes" classics).

Chick Morton (Kevin Pollak) and Eddie Hayes (Bob Amaral) began their career in vaudeville with a mind reading act called the Great Vincenzo (Chick) and Al (Eddie). Chick, who is thin, was the straightman; Eddie, who is overweight, was the foil. They were discovered by Max King, a filmmaker, who produced the comedy shorts. Their earliest known film is "The Vase Shop"; their last film, "Sheeps," made $19 on opening day. But between the good and the bad, Morton and Hayes had a string of hits, including "Society Saps," "The Bride of Mummula" and "Pardon My Puss." They were most famous for their series of detective films, which include "The Case of the Cranky Corpse," "Mr. and Mrs. Murderer," "Dial 'N' for Nincompoops," "Morton and Hayes Meet Sherlock Holmes at Charlie Chan's" and "Daffy Dicks" (the first film shown on television).

The success of Morton and Hayes comedies spawned fan clubs. People just couldn't get enough of them. By 1939 virtually every child had in his possession Morton and Hayes hand puppets. For adults there were Morton and Hayes coffee mugs, and "for a more comfortable walking experience, you could purchase a pair of Morton and Hayes foot pads." In 1948 Max released the boys from their contracts. They last appeared together on "The Glen Campbell Goodtime Hour" on CBS in 1968. Eddie became rich through investments. Chick gambled, drank and was slapped with four paternity suits. He did a guest shot on "Hawaii Five-O" and some television commercials before he retired to the Old Actors' Home in San Fernando. Morton and Hayes were reunited for the first time in 23 years by Rob Reiner in the final two episodes of the series.

Hummie Mann composed the theme.

In the original CBS pilot, "Partners in Life" (8/31/90), Rob Reiner played Max King III, the grandson of Max King, the producer of the classic "Morton and Hayes" comedy films of the 1930s and 1940s. A total of 144 films, thought to be lost forever, was found by workers when they were tearing down the Max King film studios. Each week, one of these lost films was to be seen, hosted by Max King III. Kevin Pollak played Chick Morton and Joe Guzaldo was Eddie Hayes. Marc Sharman composed the theme.

481. *The Mothers-in-Law*

NBC, 9/10/67 to 9/7/69

Cast: Eve Arden (*Eve Hubbard*), Herbert Rudley (*Herb Hubbard*), Deborah Walley (*Suzie Hubbard*), Kaye Ballard (*Kaye Buell*), Roger C. Carmel and Richard Deacon (*Roger Buell*), Jerry Fogel (*Jerry Hubbard*).

Facts: Herbert ("Herb") Hubbard is a private practice lawyer who resides at 1805 Ridgeway Drive in Los Angeles with his wife, Eve, and their daughter, Suzie. Living next door, at 1803 Ridgeway, are Roger Buell, a television script writer, his wife, Kaye, and their son, Jerry.

Roger and Kaye had been married three months and two days and previously lived in Encino when they moved next door to the Hubbards. To welcome her new neighbors, Eve brought them a bouquet of roses from her garden, a pot of

hot coffee and some homemade breakfast rolls. Roger and Kaye were forced to move out of their old apartment because, Kaye says, "they moved our furniture out and we decided to go along with it. Can you imagine, 33 neighbors not liking my singing?" The four quickly became friends, despite some early squabbles (for example, over the Buells' borrowing everything when they first moved in). Kaye and Eve became pregnant at about the same time. Their children grew up together, played together and eventually fell in love with each other. After graduating from high school, they eloped and moved into the Hubbards' garage, which they converted into an apartment (Suzie and Jerry planned on a church wedding, but their meddling mothers-in-law forced them to elope).

Suzie and Jerry are now in college (UCLA); they live next door to their parents and they have a difficult time finding any privacy or peace as Eve and Kaye constantly interfere in their lives. On occasion, Herb and Roger meddle in an attempt to help Suzie and Jerry, but not on a daily, 24 hour basis like their wives (who say, "We only go to the kids' place to advise and suggest." Herb has forbidden Eve to do Suzie's term papers; Roger has put his foot down about Kaye's doing the kids' laundry).

In an attempt to lessen their meddling time, Eve and Kaye worked up a show business singing act called "The Marvies" and performed at the Café Cabaret. To find a life of peace away from their mothers, Suzie and Jerry attempted to rent an apartment at Sunset Manor. The apartment was rundown and dingy, and Suzie and Jerry's hoped-for peace was short lived when Eve and Kaye found excuses to visit. Suzie and Jerry missed the conveniences they had and moved back to "their lovely little garage apartment" despite the fact they will never be free of their interfering parents.

Kaye brings spaghetti and meatballs to the kids at every opportunity. If anything is plugged into the right side of the kids' apartment, the garage door opens automatically. Had Suzie and Jerry married in a church, Eve and Kaye planned to sing "Because." In the 1940s, Roger was a radio writer and scripted such shows as "The First Nighter," "The Lone Ranger" and "Miss Primrose of Feathertop Hill" (he gets into costume or wears hats to get in the mood when he is writing). He now writes freelance for television. Roger hardly understands Kaye—"It's probably the one thing that holds our marriage together." Roger calls Kaye "Creampuff"; Kaye calls Roger "Cupcake." Kaye, whose maiden name is Bellota, had her teeth straightened when she was 16 years old. Kaye was in show business before she married Roger and sang (as Angelina DiVina, "The Little Girl with the Big Voice") in the Ozzie Snick Orchestra and with Charlie Banks and His Ten Tellers. She also plays flute, impersonates Bette Davis and sings "La Dona Mobalay" when ironing clothes. Eve, who can impersonate Marlene Dietrich, wrote poetry in college and was scenic designer for the drama club. Their favorite television serial is "Brave New Day."

In the original, unaired pilot film for the series (produced for CBS), Kay Cole played the role of Suzie Hubbard.

Theme: "The Mothers-in-Law," by Wilbur Hatch.

Mr. Ed see *Mister Ed*

Mr. Peepers see *Mister Peepers*

Mrs. Columbo see *Kate Loves a Mystery*

482. *Mulligan's Stew*

NBC, 10/25/77 to 12/13/77

International Airlines flight 237 from Hawaii lands in Birchfield, California. Aboard the plane are Polarus ("Polly") Friedman (Lory Kochheim; a.k.a. Lory Walsh), Star Shine ("Stevie") Friedman (Suzanne Crough), Adam Friedman (Chris Ciampa) and Kimmy Friedman (Sunshine Lee), five orphaned children who have come to live with their uncle, Michael ("Mike") Mulligan (Lawrence Pressman), his wife, Jane (Elinor Donahue), and their children, Melinda (Julie Anne Haddock), Jimmy (K.C. Martel) and Mark (Johnny Doran), following the death of their parents, Kathy (Mike's sister) and Steve Friedman, who perished in a charter plane crash.

The Mulligans live in a three bedroom, two bathroom house at 1202 Circle Drive. Melinda, Stevie and Kimmy share a room; Mark, Adam and Jimmy also share a room; the den has been converted into a bedroom for Polly; and Mike and Jane have the master bedroom. "We're crowded, but we take it day by day," says Mike, the football coach at Birchfield High School. Jane is the school's consulting nurse, and Polly (age 17), Stevie (14½), and Mark (16) also attend the school. Jimmy (age nine) and Adam (age eight) attend Birchfield Elementary School.

Mike and Jane were childhood sweethearts; Mark plays the guitar and is part of a group that plays at school dances. Stevie "knows guy things" (like fixing cars) and is the mechanical genius of the family. Melinda "knows girl things" like cooking and cleaning and is struggling to shed her tomboyish ways for her newfound interest in makeup, clothes, boys and dating. Polly, the oldest girl, is approaching her eighteenth birthday and longs for privacy; Kimmy, who is five years old, is a Vietnamese orphan Kathy and Steve, a civil rights lawyer, adopted six months before their death. She calls Jane "Mommy Jane"; won't say "no" to anybody; and is violently allergic to strawberries. Adam, who is nicknamed "Moose" for his stocky build, is well versed in the martial arts. The license plate for the family station wagon is 261MVP2, and 555-1631 is the Mulligans' telephone number. Johnny Whitaker played the role of Mark Mulligan in the pilot film (NBC, 6/20/77).

Theme: "We've Gotta Stick Together," by Michael Price and Daniel Walsh.

483. *The Munsters*

CBS, 9/24/64 to 9/8/66

Cast: Fred Gwynne *(Herman Munster)*, Yvonne DeCarlo *(Lily Munster)*, Al Lewis *(Grandpa)*, Beverley Owen and Pat Priest *(Marilyn Munster)*, Butch Patrick *(Eddie Munster)*.

Facts: Herman and Lily Munster, their son Eddie, niece Marilyn and Lily's father, Count Vladimir ("Grandpa") Dracula, live in a spooky, rundown house at 1313 Mockingbird Lane in the town of Mockingbird Heights. The family members look like movie monsters of the 1930s but believe they are normal and that the rest of the world is strange.

Herman, who resembles Frankenstein, is 150 years old and now works as a gravedigger for the Gateman, Goodbury and Graves Funeral Parlor. He was at the Heidelberg School of Medicine—in several jars—for six years. His body temperature is 62.8 degrees; his pulse is 15; blood pressure, minus three; and his heartbeat, none. Herman is seven feet three inches tall and weights three spins on the bathroom scale. His favorite fairy tale is "Goldilocks and the Three Bears" (he can't wait for it to be made into a movie with Doris Day), and his ham radio call letters are W6XRL4. Herman writes poetry for *Mortician's Monthly* magazine; his first poem was "Going Out to Pasture." In the episode "Follow That Munster," Herman became a private detective for the Kempner Detective Agency and called himself Agent 702. His hot rod license plate number is HAJ 302. "Darn, darn, darn" is his catchphrase (which he says when something goes wrong).

Lily, Herman's wife, is a vampire whose maiden name is Dracula. She is 304 years old and married Herman in 1865. Her favorite charity is Bundles for Transylvania; her and Herman's favorite food is Bat Milk Yogurt.

Count Vladimir Dracula, called Grandpa, is a 378-year-old vampire and mad scientist. His hometown is in Transylvania, and he has been married 167 times. Grandpa's favorite television show is "My Three Sons," and his pet bat is Igor ("a mouse with wings who joined the Transylvanian Air Force"). His newly transistorized divining rod picks up reruns of "My Little Margie."

Marilyn, their normal-looking (to the viewer) niece, is the black sheep of the family; she attends State University, where she is studying art. Edward ("Eddie") Wolfgang, Herman and Lily's son, is a werewolf and attends Mockingbird Heights Elementary School. He has a werewolf doll named Woof Woof and a pet snake called Elmer (who lives under the garbage pail in the backyard). Eddie's mechanical brother (created by Grandpa) was Boris the Robot (Rory Stevens).

The family pets are Spot, a fire breathing dragon Grandpa found while digging in the back yard (he eats Doggie's Din Din brand of pet food and lives under the living room staircase); Kitty Kat, a cat who roars like a lion; and an unnamed raven who says "Never more." John Carradine plays Herman's employer, Mr. Gateman.

In the original, unaired color pilot (the series is in black

Mulligan's Stew. Suzanne Crough (front). Middle, left to right: Sunshine Lee, Elinor Donahue, Lawrence Pressman, K.C. Martel. Back, left to right: Chris Ciampa, Lory Kochheim, Julie Ann Haddock, Johnny Doran.

and white), titled "My Fair Munster," Fred Gwynne played Herman; Joan Marshall was his wife, Phoebe; Al Lewis was Grandpa; Beverley Owen was Marilyn; and Happy Derman was Eddie.

Relatives: Fred Gwynne (Herman's twin brother, *Charlie Munster*; and Herman's prototype, *Johan*), Richard Hale (Lily's uncle, *Gilbert,* the Creature from the Black Lagoon), Irwin Charone (Lily's brother, *Lester Dracula*).

Theme: "At the Munsters'," by Jack Marshall.

Note: In the 1966 theatrical film, *Munster Go Home,* Debbie Watson played Marilyn. In the 1981 NBC television movie, *The Munsters' Revenge,* Jo McDonnell was Marilyn and K.C. Martel was Eddie. (Fred Gwynne, Yvonne DeCarlo and Al Lewis recreated their roles in both films.) See also "The Munsters Today."

484. *The Munsters Today*

Syndicated, 10/8/88 to 9/29/91

Cast: John Schuck *(Herman Munster),* Lee Meriwether *(Lily Munster),* Howard Morton *(Grandpa),* Hilary Van Dyke *(Marilyn Munster),* Jason Marsden *(Eddie Munster).*

Facts: An update of the 1964–66 series "The Munsters" (see preceding title). Parents Herman and Lily Munster, their son Eddie, niece Marilyn, and Lily's father, Count Vladimir Dracula, better known as Grandpa, resemble 1930s movie monsters and consider themselves normal people living in a strange world. In 1966 Grandpa conducts an experiment that backfires and places the family in a state of suspended animation. Twenty-two years later, the family awakens to the new world of the 1980s. Their attempts to adjust to society are depicted. The family still lives at 1313 Mockingbird Lane in the town of Mockingbird Heights, and the phone number is 555-1313.

Herman, who stands six feet eight inches tall, was "born" in Dr. Frankenstein's lab in Transylvania over 300 years ago. He was made from many parts, including the muscles of Count Schwarzenegger, the nose of Gregory Fabrock (the village idiot) and the right arm of Igor Johnson (a pickpocket). His teeth squeak when he gets thirsty; his eyes are brown, blue and undetermined; and his neck bolts (for the electricity that supplied life) itch when he gets an idea. He is a gravedigger and works for Mr. Graves (Stanley Ralph Ross) of the Gateman, Goodbury and Graves funeral parlor (telephone 1-800-Forever). When Herman felt he was able to start his own business, he opened a funeral parlor called The House of Herman; the business folded and he returned to his regular job.

For a bedtime snack, Herman enjoys refried armadillo bladders (which give him nightmares) and weasel burgers; his favorite breakfast is legs benedict; rack of lamb is his favorite dinner. Herman was the first person in Mockingbird Heights to eat sushi, and he possesses the Golden Shovel Award for being the best gravedigger. Judge Wapner ("The People's Court") is Herman's television hero; he is also a member of the Christina Applegate ("Married . . . with Children") fan club and owns stock in Amalgamated Crematorium.

Herman worships the ground his wife, the former Lily Ann Dracula, was buried under. Lily is 324 years old and married Herman 299 years ago in Transylvania. Before Lily met Herman, she worked as a singer in Club Dead in Transylvania. She won the beauty pageant title, "Miss Transylvania of 1655" and the Silver Shroud Award for Fashion Design. Lily's lifelong dream was to dance "Swan Lake." Her normal body temperature is 25.8 degrees, and her favorite song is "Transylvania the Beautiful." She gave birth to Eddie within 24 hours of becoming pregnant (a tradition in her family); Herman calls her "Lillikins." Herman mentioned that he first met Lily when he was walking along the moor in Transylvania and saw a girl stretched out on the ground. She saw him and it was love at first sight.

Grandpa, the original Count Dracula, is a mad scientist who enjoys conducting experiments in the lab beneath the Munsters home. He was married to a woman named Katja (who left him when she got tired of ironing capes and mopping dungeons). They first met at the Joan of Arc roast, and the first home they purchased became the Bates Motel (they sold it to "a nice young fellow and his mother"). Grandpa's first love, however, was a woman named Shirley Zlebnick, and Joan of Arc also had a crush on him (she wrote him love letters saying, "Vlad, you enflame me").

Grandpa attended the University of Transylvania and majored in philosophy. He was a member of the Sigma Alpha Aorta fraternity, and after college he and Genghis Khan operated the first blood bank in Transylvania. Grandpa is a member of the A.V.A. (American Vampire Association), and Dracu-Cola is his favorite soft drink. Leeches and cream is his favorite food; he prefers poison oak pancakes for breakfast, and stuffed piranhas are his favorite dinner. Igor is his pet bat, Stanley his lab rat, and Leonard is the skeleton he befriended in his college days who now lives in the dungeon. Grandpa also has a computer named Sam and once had a business in Transylvania sharpening fangs (workers were paid 2,000 sloskies an hour—about eight cents). His last job was guillotine janitor.

Marilyn is blonde, beautiful and the black sheep of the family. She is 17 years old and attends Mockingbird Heights High School. She is a neat freak, reads *Teen Scene* magazine and desperately wants a bigger bosom ("I wanna be a 36D") to attract boys. She first wanted to be an actress, then a magazine writer-editor. She has a porcelain bunny collection and mentioned she was studying art in school. She appeared in the school's production of *To Kill a Mockingbird.* Herman mentioned that he was not sure how Marilyn is related to them (in one episode she is Herman's niece; in another she is Lily's niece). Marilyn also possesses an award—Bronx Pom Poms—for cheerleading.

Edward ("Eddie") Wolfgang Munster, Lily and Herman's son, attends Mockingbird Heights High School and wants to become a rock video producer. He buys his clothes at Kiddie Casuals and is a member of the Dukes Little League baseball team. His favorite ice cream is rocky toad, and he has a pet Tasmanian devil named Irving.

The Munsters also own Munster Moor, a swamp at 13

13th Avenue; their insurance company is Grave Diggers Mutual—"The Good Hands People." Spot, the fire breathing dragon, lives under the staircase in the living room; Maxine is the sea serpent who lives in the moat that surrounds their home; and Boris is the name of the boar's head mounted on the living room wall. In one episode, Daniel Wilson played Herman as a kid and Whitby Hertford was Grandpa as a child.

Relatives: Jo deWinter (Lily's mother, *Katja Dracula*), Angelina Fiordessisi (Lily's cousin, *Bella*), Christopher Fielder (Lily's cousin, *Damien*), Jerry Houser (Lily's cousin, *Wolfgang Dracula*), Camilla Ashland (Lily's aunt, *Lucretia Dracula*), Peter Isacksen (Herman's cousin, *Gill*), Peter Schuck (Herman's brother, *Frank Munstser*), Foster Brooks (Herman's cousin, *Igor*), Ruth Buzzi *(Grandpa's mother)*, Sandy Baron (Grandpa's brother, *Yorga Dracula*).

Theme: "At the Munsters'," (an updated but uncredited version based on the original theme by Jack Marshall).

485. *Murder, She Wrote*

CBS, 9/30/84 to the present

Cabot Cove, Maine, population 3,560, is home to Jessica Fletcher (Angela Lansbury), a best-selling murder mystery author, who resides at 698 Candlewood Road. Her first book was *The Corpse Danced at Midnight,* which was said to be published by Sutton Place Publishers in New York City (in the pilot episode, her first book was published by Covington House). Jessica's books revolve around Damian Sinclair, her fictional thief (a "Saint"-like character). Jessica rides a bicycle around town, and her favorite pastime is fishing with her friend, Dr. Seth Hazlitt (William Windom) off his boat, *Cavalier.* "Doc" has been practicing medicine for 37 years and lives in a 120-year-old house. Jessica was a former English teacher, and her late husband was named Frank. Other books by Jessica include *The Killer Called Collect, Yours Truly, Damian Sinclair, Ashes, Ashes, All Fall Down Dead, The Messenger of Midnight* and *The Corpse Wasn't There.*

Amos Tupper (Tom Bosley) was the original sheriff; he was replaced by Sheriff Mort Metzger (Ron Masak). Mort calls Jessica "Mrs. F" and rides in patrol car 103, with the license plate 0170702. He was formerly with the N.Y.P.D. but quit the force because he couldn't handle the politics. Seth drives a car with the license plate 60062, and his favorite Boston restaurant is Clams 'n' Claws.

The Cabot Cove Bus Lines (later seen as the Tri-County Bus Lines) services the area. The Cabot Cove cemetery was established in 1710, and the town newspaper, the *Globe Gazette* (also seen as the *Cabot Cove Gazette*), was established in 1822. Bennett Devlin (Joe Dorsey) is the editor-publisher. Other businesses are the Light House Motel, the Cabot Cove Boat Works and the Cabot Cove Depot (the local eatery).

In episodes not featuring Jessica, Keith Michell as Dennis Stanton takes over. Dennis, a former jewel thief (and an old flame of Jessica's), is now a suave and sophisticated investigator for the Consolidated Casualty Insurance Company in San Francisco. Hallie Todd is Rhoda, his secretary, and Ken Swofford is Lieutenant Perry Catalano. Dennis's license plate is 2NBA 750.

Beginning with the episode of 9/15/91, Jessica took an apartment in Manhattan to be near her publisher and to teach criminology at Manhattan University. She resides in Apartment 4B at the Penfield House Apartments.

Relatives: Genie Francis (Jessica's niece, *Victoria ["Vicki"] Brandon-Griffin*; she works as a real estate broker for Precious Premises, Inc.), Belinda J. Montgomery (Jessica's niece, *Pamela Crane*), Alice Krige (Jessica's niece, *Nita Cochran*), Courteney Cox (Jessica's niece, *Carol Fletcher*), Linda Grovenor (Jessica's niece, *Tracy Macgill*), Kristy McNichol (Jessica's niece, *Jill Morton*), Michael Horton (Jessica's nephew, *Grady Fletcher*), Angela Lansbury (Jessica's cousin, *Emma Fletcher*), Peter Bonerz (Jessica's cousin, *Calhoun Fletcher*), Penny Singleton (Jessica's aunt, *Mildred*), Shirley Jones (Jessica's cousin, *Ann Owens*), Robert Walker (Jessica's cousin, *George Owens*), Debbie Zipp (Grady's wife, *Donna Fletcher*), Eugene Roche (Donna's father, *Franklin Mayberry*), Gale Storm (Donna's mother, *Maisie Mayberry*), Dean Butler (Vicki's husband, *Howard Griffin*), Anne Meara (Amos's sister, *Winnie Banner*), Guy Stockwell (Winnie's husband, *Elmo Banner*), Bruce Abbott (Mort's brother, *Wayne Metzger*).

Theme: "Murder, She Wrote," by John Addison.

486. *Murphy Brown*

CBS, 11/14/88 to the present

Cast: Candice Bergen *(Murphy Brown)*, Faith Ford *(Corky Sherwood)*, Joe Regalbuto *(Frank Fontana)*, Charles Kimbrough *(Jim Dial)*, Grant Shaud *(Myles Silverberg)*, Robert Pastorelli *(Eldin Bernecky)*, Pat Corley *(Phil)*.

Facts: Murphy Brown is a beautiful, hard hitting investigative reporter for "F.Y.I." ("For Your Information"), a CBS-TV, Washington, D.C.–based newsmagazine series. Murphy was born in May 1948 and as a kid was called "Stinky." Her inspiration for becoming a journalist was Ken Hamilton (William Schallert), her eleventh grade journalism professor ("The best educator I ever had"). Murphy became editor of her high school newspaper, and years later Ken opened the Murphy Brown School of Broadcasting.

In college Murphy majored in journalism and after graduating set out to become the best broadcast journalist of her day. Newsman Howard K. Smith was her hero. She made a video audition tape and had a friend submit it to Smith. After six weeks, she got a response from Smith: "You stink, but you've got a nice tush." At some point after this (not specified) Murphy became a foreign correspondent. She auditioned for "F.Y.I." on 8/16/77 and beat out newswoman Linda Ellerbee for the role. Since then she has won the Robert F. Kennedy Journalism Award (for her piece "No Place to Call Home"), an Emmy Award and eight Humboldt News Story Awards.

MURPHY BROWN HAVING BIGFOOT'S BABY was the cover story the *National Enquirer* told; "Mouthy Brown" was how the daily comics lampooned her. *Time, TV Guide, Newsweek, Esquire* and *Harper's Bazaar* are but a few of the magazines that have honored Murphy with a cover shot and story.

Murphy has a reputation for getting even with anyone who crosses her. She is easily exasperated, has a tendency to yell a lot and "watch out when she doesn't get her way." But she does have a caring side—"I once fed the cat next door." People say Murphy Brown could never take care of a pet—'But I got a Chia Pet to grow." She has only one television ("and it's under 27 inches"), Sterling Roses are her favorite flowers and she has a white Porsche (license plate 189 347). She goes through number 2 pencils quickly, and after Ollie North was interviewed by Murphy he said, "It was like sticking my face in a buzzsaw." Murphy is banned from the White House (she ran over President Bush with her bicycle; now, every time Bush hears Murphy's name, he screams and runs for his life). Murphy's favorite singer is Aretha Franklin ("Respect" is Murphy's favorite song).

Murphy met Jake Lowenstein (Robin Thomas) at the Democratic National Convention in 1968. They demonstrated together, were maced together and were arrested together. It was love at first sight, and they were married by the judge who heard their case (on August 28). The wedding dinner was two corn dogs and a candied apple; five days later they were divorced. When Jake re-entered Murphy's life in 1990, they had a brief affair, and Murphy became pregnant (beginning 9/16/91). She chose to raise the baby alone. On 5/18/92, at 5:32 A.M., Murphy gave birth to a nine pound seven ounce boy she first called "Baby Brown" (she was in labor for 39 hours). Prior to naming the baby Avery Brown (after her late mother), Murphy called him such names as Winston Churchill Brown, Woodward and Bernstein Brown, Jacques Cousteau Brown and Adlai Stevenson Brown. Kate Mulgrew as Hillary Wheaton replaced Murphy on "F.Y.I." during her maternity leave.

On her forty-second birthday (11/26/90; although previously mentioned as being in May), Corky, Myles and Jim gave Murphy a home blood pressure kit, and Frank gave her something she had always wondered about but never had: a sister (he hired actress Christine Ebersole to play Murphy's sister, Maddie Brown, for a day).

Corky Lynn Sherwood is an "F.Y.I." news team reporter who can recite all the books of the Bible by heart. She was born on a farm in Louisiana and was crowned Miss America at age 19. She was seen in a flashback as a model prior to working for "F.Y.I." (she was "The Check Girl" for the First Bank of New Orleans). Corky won the 1989 Humboldt News Award for her story "A Woman's Touch at West Point" (she broke Murphy's eight year winning streak). "Woody Woodpecker's 50th Birthday," an interview with the San Diego Chicken and getting Nancy Reagan to perform stomach exercises on television—these are typical of the kinds of stories Corky reports for the show.

Corky has a First Lady doll collection, a pet cat named Mr. Puffy and is the cheerleader for the Bulletins, the F.Y.I. football team. Her first special for the network was "Corky's Place" (wherein she interviewed Gary Collins, Mary Ann Mobley, cookie queen Mrs. Fields and Murphy Brown). Corky's phone number is 555-7261. At the end of the first season Corky married Will Forrest (Scott Bryce), thus becoming Corky Sherwood-Forrest (Will proposed to her in the Air and Space Museum and gave her a moonrock landing ring as their engagement ring). Will is a struggling writer and authored a book called *The Dutch Boy*.

Frank Fontana joined the F.Y.I. team as an investigative reporter in 1977 (he previously worked as a reporter for the *New York Times*). He was babied as a kid and attended the Bishop Fallon High School for Boys. *The Maltese Falcon* is his favorite movie, and he is afraid to sleep with his closet door open as a result of watching the film *Poltergeist*. In 1991 Frank won the Humboldt News Award for his story "A Death in Dade County." Frank mentioned that he has been in therapy "for 13 or 14 years"; *TV Guide* has a tendency to list Frank as "Fred Fontana." Frank and Murphy cohosted the premiere of the network's early morning newscast, "Overnight News."

James ("Jim") Dial, the senior anchor, has been with CBS News for 25 years. In 1956 he was the only news correspondent to get an interview with John F. Kennedy when he lost the presidential nomination. If Hubert Humphrey had won the presidency in 1968, he would have made Jim Dial his press secretary. A later episode changed Jim's background somewhat: He was a struggling news reporter for Channel 9 in Chicago who doubled as the host of "Poop Deck Pete and Cartoons Ahoy."

Jim wears expensive Italian suits and has been called "America's Most Trusted Anchorman." He has a pink and blue coffee mug shaped like a fish; before each broadcast Jim orders fried rice from Wo Pong's and taps his knee three times for good luck. His proudest moment was interviewing Gandhi, but the show got killed in the ratings—"It was opposite an episode of 'The Facts of Life' in which Tootie got her first bra" (no such episode actually exists). Jim's most humiliating moment occurred during a live, national 20-second spot when he laughed uncontrollably after reporting that the president had been stung by a wasp. Jim's most embarrassing moment was interviewing the Queen of England with his fly open. Jim is famous for the Dial family apple-prune turkey stuffing.

Jim, a Presbyterian, lives at 3134 South Bedford Drive. His favorite dinner is lamb chops, mashed potatoes and mint jelly. Jim has been married to his wife, Doris, for 30 years (they honeymooned at historic Williamsburg; Doris's maiden name is O'Rourke). Jim first mentions he has a dog named Victor; later the dog's name is Trixie and Trixter. Both Jim and Murphy are members of the Dunfriars Club, a club for distinguished news people. Jim mentioned he has never had a dream; in the episode of 3/4/92, he had his first one (about terrible service in Heck's Shoe Store).

Myles Silverberg is the executive producer of "F.Y.I." He attended Harvard (class of '84) and was known as "Myles Silverbrain" in his freshman class. Murphy's antics have driven Myles to the point of hysteria, and he is a good candidate for ulcers and heart attacks—"I'm 27 years old and living on Mylanta." Myles also hears Murphy's voice in his sleep: "They should pipe it into cornfields to scare the crows away." He has a car with the license plate 400 928 (later 452 689J) and gets "the good doughnuts" each morning for the staff at Marino's Bakery.

Eldin Stanislaus Bernecky is Murphy's around-the-clock housepainter. He is struggling to paint what appears to be a rather large house but is having difficulty matching colors with Murphy's moods. He paints murals, uses Murphy's good pantyhose to strain paint and buys his supplies at Ed's Paints. He has an Apostles watch (each of the 12 are represented by an hour), and he hangs out at the House Painter's Bar. Eldin painted a mural of the Iran-Contra hearings on Murphy's bathroom ceiling. After several bad experiences with nannies, Murphy appointed Eldin as Avery's nanny.

Phil (no last name given) is the owner of the local watering hole, Phil's Bar and Grill (established in 1919). The bar is located at 1195 15th Street (although number 406 is seen on the front door). Phil donated the swinging door to the men's room to the Smithsonian Institution (the door has signatures of various presidents). Murphy's favorite meal is a Phil Burger and Fries.

On 9/17/90 "F.Y.I." began its thirteenth season, with show number 390. During the summer hiatus, Murphy went to baseball camp; Frank went on an archaeological dig (he found a Pez dispenser); Jim and Doris spent four weeks in Nantucket with Andy Rooney and his wife; Corky went on her honeymoon. The episode of 1/29/90 featured "F.Y.I. for Kids," with hosts Mayim Bialik (as Natalie Moore, a mini–Murphy), Laura Mooney (as Tracy Knight, a mini–Corky), Mark-Paul Gosselaar (as Wes Jordan, a mini–Jim) and Troy Slaten (as Hank Caldwell, a mini–Frank).

When the network decided to do a comical version of "F.Y.I.," Murphy Brown became the model for "Kelly Green," a series starring Julia St. Martin (guest star Morgan Fairchild played Kelly Green). The episode of 5/13/91 found F.Y.I. competing against Yale University on the television show "Collegiate Q & A" (F.Y.I. lost 110 to 155; consolation prizes were Scuffy Shoe Shine kits, Rice-a-Roni and dinner at the Black Angus Restaurant). In the episode of 2/18/91 the network was purchased by American Industrial, a company that manufactures appliances (for example, talking coffeemakers).

The show's gimmick is to exasperate Murphy even more than she already is by assigning her a different (and rather strange) secretary in virtually every episode (when Murphy felt unappreciated at the network, she contemplated accepting an offer from the rival Wolf network—which offered her an efficient secretary named Barbara [Patti Yasutake]).

Relatives: Darren McGavin (Murphy's father, *Bill Brown*; he publishes the Chicago *Voice* and calls Murphy "Susie Q"), Colleen Dewhurst (Murphy's mother, *Avery Brown*), Susan Wheeler (Bill's second wife, *Karen Brown*), Alice Hirson (Corky's mother, *Bootsie Sherwood*), Courtney Gebhart (Corky's sister, *Cookie Sherwood*), Sarah Abrell (Corky's sister, *Kiki Sherwood*), Bryan Clark (Corky's father, *Edward Sherwood*), Janet Carroll (Jim's wife, *Doris Dial*), Barney Martin (Frank's father, *Dominic Fontana*), Rose Marie (Frank's mother, *Rose Fontana*), Sara Ballantine (Frank's sister, *Mary Fontana*), Gracie Moore (Frank's sister, *Pat Fontana*), Richard Zavaglia (Frank's uncle, *Sal*), Brittany Murphy and Shanelle Workman (Frank's unnamed sisters), Dena Dietrich (Phil's wife, *Phyllis*), Jon Tenney (Myles's brother, *Josh Silverberg*).

Flashbacks: Meghann Haldeman (*Murphy as a girl*), Sean Baca (*Frank as a boy*), Jason Marsden (*Myles as a boy*), Eva Chainey (*Myles's mother*).

Theme: "Murphy's Theme" (normally heard only during the closing credits), by Steve Dorff.

487. *Murphy's Law*
ABC, 11/2/88 to 3/18/89

Daedalus Patrick Murphy (George Segal), a recovering alcoholic, works as an investigator for Wes Hardin (Josh Mostel), the claims manager at the First Fidelity Casualty Insurance Company in San Francisco. Murphy, who originally worked for Triax Insurance, lives in a loft at 3116 Hillside with Kimiko ("Kimi") Fannuchi (Maggie Han), a beautiful Eurasian model who often helps him solve cases. Kimi, born of an Italian father and a Japanese mother, is famous for being the calendar girl for Morgan's Power Tools. She drives an old Saab; Murphy has a sedan with the license plate SPM 162.

Murphy was ten years old when his father walked out on him (his last words to Murphy were "Go to Hell, kid"). "Dangerous Eggs" is what Murphy calls the breakfast his mother made for him out of leftovers. Murphy and his ex-wife, Marissa (Kim Lankford), lived on Baker Street when they were married. She called him "Paddy," and they had a daughter named Kathleen (they divorced when Murphy took up drinking). Marissa is now married to a wealthy lawyer named Charles Danforth (Bruce Gray). Murphy's battle with Marissa to win visitation rights with Kathleen (Sarah Sawatsky), who is now ten years old, is a recurring storyline.

Morgan DeSade (Elizabeth Savage) is Murphy's nemesis, the manager of Triax Insurance. Ronnie Claire Edwards appeared as Murphy's aunt, Cornelia Bingham, a mystery writer in love with the macabre. In a flashback sequence, Will Nipper played Murphy as a young boy and Susan Snowdon played his mother.

Al Jarreau sings the "Murphy's Law" theme.

488. *My Favorite Husband*
CBS, 9/12/53 to 12/27/55

A lovely home, decorated in Chinese modern and located at 1561 Briar Street in Westwood, California, is the residence of George Cooper (Barry Nelson) and his wife, Elizabeth ("Liz") Cooper (Joan Caulfield, then Vanessa

Brown). "George is a husband and banker," says Liz; "Liz is a wife and homemaker," says George. George is level headed and is an executive with the Sunset State Bank. Liz is beautiful but scatterbrained. Before she enters contests, she figures she has won and plans what to do with the prizes; she gets carried away at auctions ("We have a whole attic full of stuff because you thought it was pretty," says George), collects for various charities and involves herself in other people's problems. Elizabeth, as portrayed by Joan Caulfield, was tall and blonde. Her 1955 replacement, Vanessa Brown, was petite and brunette. Despite the obvious difference in wives, "the beguiling combination of wit, femininity and attractive sex which has become a hallmark of the role" remained the same.

Alix Talton first played Myra Cobb (1953–55), then Myra Shepard (1955), Liz's friend. Bob Sweeney was Myra's husband, Gillmore Cobb (1953–55); Dan Tobin became Myra's husband, Oliver Shepard in 1955. George's sister, Janice Cooper (Carolyn Jones) is a commercial artist (she buys her supplies from Dottie Broom's Art Supply; Adele Jergens plays Dottie); and George's Uncle Norman (David Burns) broke into show business with a "talented pet pig" (whom he calls "Pig" or "The Show Biz Pig"). Based on the radio series of the same title with Lucille Ball (Liz) and Richard Denning (George).

Lud Gluskin composed the theme.

489. *My Favorite Martian*
CBS, 9/29/63 to 9/4/66

Cast: Ray Walston *(Uncle Martin)*, Bill Bixby *(Tim O'Hara)*, Pamela Britton *(Lorelei Brown)*, Alan Hewitt *(Bill Brennan)*.

Facts: Tim O'Hara is a reporter for the Los Angeles *Sun*. One morning, while en route to an interview, Tim witnesses the crash-landing of a UFO (unidentified flying object). He investigates and befriends its pilot, Exagitious 12½, a professor of anthropology from Mars whose specialty is the primitive planet Earth. (During the U.S. Air Force's testing of an X-15 plane, the Martian's spacecraft entered the Earth's atmosphere and locked into a head-on collision course with it. To avoid disaster, Exagitious 12½, who was traveling at 9,000 miles per hour, strained his ship to get out of the path of the X-15. The strain caused a malfunction and the saucer crash-landed.)

Tim takes the stranded Martian to his apartment at 21 Elm Street, in a home owned by Lorelei Brown, a very pretty but slightly dizzy widow. To protect his true identity, the Martian adopts the alias of Uncle Martin, a relative who has come to live with his nephew, Tim. (Martin's silver spaceship is hidden in Lorelei's garage.) While Martin seeks a way to repair his craft (the materials he needs are still unknown to Earth), he struggles to adjust to a more primitive world and to keep his true identity a secret. His task is complicated by Bill Brennan, a detective with the 12th Precinct of the L.A.P.D., who is suspicious of both Tim and Martin.

Murphy's Law. **Maggie Han and George Segal.**

Tim drives a car with the license plate JFI 561 and tries to get up for work at 8:00 A.M. (he has three alarm clocks set to ring within seconds of each other). Martin weighs more because of Earth's gravity. He has a superior intellect and claims to be the greatest living authority on the history of Earth. He mentions that he is "in the prime of life" (he has advised people from William Shakespeare to Thomas Jefferson). "Earth is a nice place to visit," he says, "but I wouldn't want to live here." Martin is puzzled by earthly emotions and thinks humans lack intelligence ("We use all of our brain, not just a portion of it").

On Earth, Martin needs an accurate barometer so he can monitor storms. Thunderstorms are a Martian's worst fear on Earth because if struck by lightning and not properly grounded by his antennae, he gets "Popsy," a condition that causes him to appear and disappear uncontrollably. Martin is prone to short circuits, has the ability to project his dreams, can read minds (unless there is a conscious effort to shut him out), speak to and understand animals, levitate (with his right index finger) and appear and disappear at will (by raising the antennae at the back of his head).

When Bill, the human bloodhound who is called "Bulldog Brennan," is around, Martin's antennae quiver. Mrs. Brown, who is famous for her fudge brownies, is the mother of two beautiful daughters: Annabel (Ina Victor) and Angela (Ann Marshall). Lorelei gives bridge lessons, sells Christmas cards and beauty creams, is studying real estate and plays the stock market with a Ouija board. On page 64 of *The Martian Compendium of Home Remedies, or What to Do Until the Zigoblat Comes*, there is a recipe for a love potion called the Irresistible Spray (A Formula A-673-5-K²). The potion brings instant love to anyone who uses it. On Earth, an aspirin neutralizes its effects. (*Zigoblat* is Martian for doctor.)

In the unaired pilot version of the series, Martin did not have the power of levitation (he used a control device from his ship to levitate), and Lorelei had only one daughter, Annabel (Ina Victor), who was Tim's romantic interest.

Relatives: Paul Smith, (Tim's cousin, *Harvey O'Hara*), Sean McClory (Tim's granduncle, *Shamus O'Hara*), Madge Blake *(Martin's mother)*, Wayne Stam (Martin's nephew, *Andrometer*), Marlo Thomas (Lorelei's niece, *Pamela*), Bill Idelson (Lorelei's brother, *Leroy Wanamaker*), Bernie Kopell (Lorelei's nephew, *George*), Gavin MacLeod (Lorelei's brother, *Alvin Wanamaker*), Yvonne White (Lorelie's sister, *Dulcie*), Don Keefer (Dulcie's husband, *Henry*), Rory Stevens (Dulcie's son, *Stanley*).

Theme: "My Favorite Martian," by George Greeley.

490. *My Friend Irma*

CBS, 1/8/52 to 6/26/54

Cast: Marie Wilson *(Irma Peterson)*, Cathy Lewis *(Jane Stacy)*, Mary Shipp *(Kay Foster)*, Sid Tomack *(Al)*, Hal March *(Joe Vance)*, Brooks West *(Richard Rhinelander III)*, Gerald Mohr *(Brad Jackson)*, Donald MacBride *(Milton J. Clyde)*, Sig Arno *(Professor Kropotkin)*, Gloria Gordon *(Mrs. O'Reilly)*.

Facts: Irma Peterson is a beautiful and shapely "dumb blonde" who has a knack for bouncing back and forth across the thin line that separates genius from insanity. She is sweet and very trusting, and will do anything to help someone she believes is in trouble. Irma was born in New York City and now lives in Apartment 3B at Mrs. O'Reilly's boardinghouse at 185 West 73rd Street in Manhattan. She lives simply, enjoys life's little pleasures and works as a secretary for Milton J. Clyde, the owner of the Clyde Real Estate Company at 631 East 41st Street.

Jane Stacy is a girl who has both feet planted firmly on the ground. She lives in Connecticut (at 1362 Post Valley Road) and dreams of marrying a wealthy man. She begins that quest by moving to Manhattan. While looking for an apartment, Jane is bumped into and knocked to the ground by "a dizzy dame" named Irma Peterson (who rarely looks where she is going). In the process of helping Jane to her feet, Irma manages to tear Jane's dress ("Ooops, look what we did ... They're wearing split skirts in New York this year," says Irma). As Jane looks at her dress and tries to cover her slip, she remarks, "Yeah, but not all the way up to the neck!" Irma offers Jane her jacket, and when she learns that Jane is having a difficult time finding a place to live, she offers to let Jane stay with her—"in a one room furnished basement Irma calls home."

After settling in at Irma's, Jane befriends a secretary at the Richard Rhinelander Investment Company at 113 Park Avenue. When the secretary leaves to get married, Jane replaces her and becomes the personal secretary to her dream man, Richard Rhinelander III. Jane secretly loves Richard and desperately tries to impress him, despite the fact that she lives with Irma, who is well below his social status.

After living with Irma a few days, Jane came to the conclusion that "Mother Nature gave some girls brains, intelligence and cleverness. But with Irma, Mother Nature slipped her a mickey." She also believes that Irma's boyfriend, Al, an impoverished and averse-to-work con artist who calls Irma "Chicken," is "a live wire and it is only a matter of time before they hook him up and put a chair under him."

In fall 1953, Jane is transferred to Panama. Irma places an ad in the New York *Globe* for a roommate, and Kay Foster, a bright and beautiful reporter for the *Globe,* answers it and becomes the new audience for Irma's scatterbrained antics. Kay's boyfriend is Brad Jackson, a fellow reporter on the *Globe*. At this same time, Irma also has a new romantic interest named Joe Vance, a much more respectable character who works for the Spic and Span Cleaners.

Irma's neighbor, Professor Kropotkin, plays violin at the Paradise Burlesque Theater (later the Gypsy Tea Room). To avoid the inconvenience of always having to do her nails, Marie Wilson wears gloves in virtually every episode.

Relatives: Richard Eyer (Irma's nephew, *Bobby Peterson*), Margaret DuMont *(Richard's mother)*. Mentioned but not seen was Joe's cousin, Ruthie.

Theme: "My Friend, Irma," by Lud Gluskin.

491. *My Hero*

NBC, 11/8/52 to 9/12/53

The "hero" of the title is Robert S. Beanblossom (Bob Cummings), a handsome salesman for the Thackery Realty Company in Los Angeles, who uses his suave and sophisticated style and "power over women" to sell real estate.

The girl to whom Robert is a hero is Julie Marshall (Julie Bishop), a red haired, brown eyed beauty who works as the office secretary. Julie sees Robert as other women do (a playboy bachelor), but she also sees a side of him that other women do not—his somewhat klutzy approach to selling properties when he becomes desperate. Despite Robert's misadventures, he always manages to come out on top (at which time Julie hugs him and says, "My hero").

Willis Thackery (John Litel), the owner of the company, has been in the real estate game for 27 years. He is a member of the Ancient and Exalted Order of the Araby Club and lives in Apartment 323 (address not given; Robert lives in an unnamed "one room apartment"). When Willis likes what Robert is doing, he calls him "Bob," "Bob-O" and "Robin." When he gets angry at Bob, it's "Beanblossom!" Willis's favorite soup is mock turtle, and the biggest sale Thackery Realty ever made was a mansion

(17 rooms, eight baths, six acres of land and a four car garage) that sold for $150,000.

In the opening theme, the following items are seen: Bungalow—5 Rooms and Bath—$150 down. 4 Flat Building, 2 Bedrooms Each—$1250 Down. For Rent—Furnished Apartments. G.I. Loans. For Sale—Nearly New House, 3 Bedrooms. Wanted: Houses, Farms. Buyers' Biggest Bargains. Don Holmes—See Me for Listings. Although he did not name his college, Bob mentioned the school colors as yellow and purple. Thackery's competition is Yeager's Developments.

Leon Klatzkin composed the "My Hero" theme.

492. *My Life and Times*

ABC, 4/24/91 to 5/30/91

Cast: Tom Irwin *(Ben Miller)*, Helen Hunt *(Rebecca Miller)*.

Facts: "I wouldn't say I've seen it all, but I've seen a lot. I've seen the world change, I've seen myself change. I've watched footsteps on the moon; I've seen myself stumble. I've made a fortune, I've lost a fortune ... I've loved and lost and lived to love again. The one thing I know, life is an adventure. You've got to hold on and let it carry you away. It carried me all the way to the year 2035. And I'm here to tell the tale. I'm Ben Miller and this is my life and times."

From an unidentified retirement home in the year 2035, 85-year-old Benjamin ("Ben") Miller spoke those words (over the theme music), and through flashbacks, as Ben recalled his life, we saw his life and times. Unfortunately, ABC canceled the critically acclaimed adult "Wonder Years" after only six episodes, leaving many stories untold. Ben's life was not presented in any specific order; it is the bits of dialogue scattered throughout the various episodes that tie the information presented here together.

On September 17, 1968, Ben began his journalism studies at Northwestern University. It was here that he met and first fell in love with Rebecca Elizabeth Eastman, a student majoring in psychology (he was going down the library stairs; she was going up the stairs when they first saw each other). After graduation they drifted apart: Ben went to New York to pursue his writing career; she remained in Chicago to attend graduate school; the time is 1972.

We next learn about Ben in 1978. He has written a story about an enchanting girl he met named Jessie (Claudia Christian) for the Illinois *Review*. At age 35 in 1985, Ben returned to Chicago to look up Rebecca, who is 31. Ben is now a reporter for the New York *Globe,* and he and Rebecca find that they still love each other. She accepted his proposal. They married ("Lean on Me" was their wedding song) and returned to New York to live. From this point on, information was not given to link Ben's past.

Ben and Rebecca had two children, Melanie and Daniel. Daniel was born in 1989; Melanie in 1994. At some point between 1989 and 1998, Ben wrote two books: *A Break in the Clouds* and *Come the Redeemer*. Ben also left his job at the *Globe* (possibly in 1986) and began driving a Checker Cab in Manhattan. With only $2,300 in their bank account, Ben bought 900 shares in a company called Lightbridge Systems. He lost virtually everything when the stock market fell 500 points on "Black Monday."

Apparently the times were getting hard for Americans. There was the Crash of 1998, and 50 million people were out of work. It was in 1998 that Ben and his family moved from their home at 323 Sycamore Drive in Seattle to Washington, D.C., where Ben found work as a bookkeeper with Colby-Stern (Unit 23, West 57), a government contracting company.

On Memorial Day, 1999, Ben and his family vacationed at Pearl Lake in Illinois. On Labor Day of that year, Rebecca died of cancer. Ben then moved to St. Louis to take a factory job.

We saw Ben celebrate the millennium with his family, and we know from an early episode that in the year 2000 Ben married Lily Matheson (Lisa Zane). We also know that Rebecca drove a car with the license plate UEA 542 and loved working with kids in a Manhattan Welfare center. And, we learn that Ben's favorite candy in the year 2036 (the series progressed one year in the fourth episode) is Milk Duds.

Relatives (Year 2035): Regina Leeds (Ben's daughter, *Melanie Miller*), Tim Stack (Ben's son, *Daniel Miller*), Harriet Medin (Daniel's wife, *Jessie Miller*), Matt McGrath (Daniel's son, *Robert Miller*), Christopher Pettiet (Daniel's son, *Michael Miller*).

Flashbacks: Emily Ann Lloyd *(Melanie in 1999)*, Sean Baca *(Daniel in 1999)*, Angela Patton (Ben's mother, *Sarah Miller in 1985)*, Priscilla Pointer *(Rebecca's mother in 1985)*, Paul Dooley *(Rebecca's father in 1985)*.

Theme: "My Life and Times," by Lee Holdridge.

493. *My Little Margie*

CBS, 6/16/52 to 9/8/52
CBS, 6/1/53 to 7/10/53
NBC, 9/9/53 to 8/24/55

Cast: Gale Storm *(Margie Albright)*, Charles Farrell *(Vern Albright)*, Don Hayden *(Freddie Wilson)*, Hillary Brooke *(Roberta Townsend)*, Gertrude Hoffman *(Clarissa Odetts)*.

Facts: As the opening theme music is heard, the audience sees the framed pictures of two people: a beautiful 21-year-old girl named Marjorie ("Margie") Albright, and her distinguished father, Vernon ("Vern") Albright. The camera first focuses on the portrait of Vern. The picture comes to life and we learn about his problem—Margie: "I've been both mother and father to her since she was born. She's grown up now ... When she was little I could speak to her and make her mind me. I had control over her ... When she disobeyed, I took her roller skates away for a week. What can you do when a girl reaches this age? She's completely out of hand. I've got a problem, believe me, I've got a problem."

The camera pans to the picture of Margie and we learn of her problem—Vern: "I've raised him from my childhood. He's nearly 50 now and you'd think he'd settle down, wouldn't you? Today, he looks better in shorts on a tennis court than fellows 25. Girls wink at him, and what's worse, he winks back at them. I want a nice old comfortable father. I try to look after him, but he just won't settle down. I've got a problem, believe me, I've got a problem."

Stories relate incidents in Margie and Vern's lives as they attempt to resolve their respective problems.

Margie and Vern live in Apartment 10A of the Carlton Arms Hotel in New York City; their phone number is Carlton 3-8966. Vern is an investment counselor with the Manhattan firm of Honeywell and Todd. Mrs. Clarissa Odetts, their neighbor, lives in Apartment 10C, and Vern's romantic interest, Roberta Townsend, lives in Apartment 10B. The name tag under the Albrights' doorbell reads VERNON ALBRIGHT.

Margie, who is described as "pretty, shapely and attractive," appears to have no job. She attracts men like bees to honey and uses her beauty to get men to do what she wants them to do. Margie loves to meddle in Vern's business (and private) affairs. When Margie does something, Vern finds out. Vern decides to get even and teach her a lesson. However, as Vern tries to teach Margie a lesson, she finds out and turns the tables and tries to teach him a lesson for trying to teach her a lesson (the basic plot of virtually every episode).

Margie, who has Irish blood from her mother, is a talented dancer; since she first learned to dance as a kid, she has dreamed of attending the International Ball—but was never able because it was for bluebloods.

Freddie Wilson is Margie's impoverished boyfriend. He seems permanently suited for unemployment, and, as Vern says, "Freddie is the only man I know who got fired from five different jobs in the same week." Despite the fact that Vern dislikes Freddie and calls him a "droop," Margie loves him. His favorite television show is "Captain Stratosphere," and he once wrote a play called "Girl Against the World" ("The heartwarming story of Gwendolyn Lovequist, a typical American girl with the odds stacked up against her").

Mrs. Odetts is Margie's elderly neighbor and her "cohort in crime." She is an 82-year-old, young at heart widow who had British ancestors at Valley Forge. Her lifelong ambition was to be an actress, and she finds pure delight in helping Margie turn the tables on Vern.

George Honeywell (Clarence Kolb) is Vern's boss at the investment agency, and Charlie (Willie Best) is the building elevator operator.

Relatives: Lela Bliss Hayden *(Freddie's mother)*, Harry Hayden *(Freddie's father)*, Sheila James (Clarissa's granddaughter, *Norma Jean Odetts*), Crystal Reeves (Clarissa' sister, *Amy McKenna*), Fess Parker, (Clarissa's nephew, *Lonny Crunchmeyer*), Gloria Talbott (Clarissa's granddaughter, *Amy McKenna*), Angela Stevens (George's niece, *Nancy Crumbley*), Alvy Moore (George's nephew, *Dillard*

Crumbley III). In one episode, Margie pretended to be her 11-year-old sister, Sally Albright.

Theme: "My Little Margie," by Lud Gluskin.

494. *My Living Doll*

CBS, 9/27/64 to 9/8/65

Cast: Julie Newmar *(Rhoda Miller)*, Bob Cummings *(Bob McDonald)*, Doris Dowling *(Irene Adams)*, Jack Mullavey *(Peter Robinson)*.

Facts: Rhoda Miller is a beautiful female robot that was built by Dr. Carl Miller (Henry Beckman) for a U.S. space project designed to send robots into outer space. His creation, AF 709 (AAF 709 in the pilot), is made of low-modulus polyethylene plastics, miniature computers "and assorted components."

Rhoda, called "the ultimate in feminine composition," stands five feet ten inches tall and measures 37-26-36. On her back are four small birthmarks—each of which acts as an emergency control button. Her main "off" switch is located in her right elbow, and her eyes provide a source of power obtained from light (covering her eyes causes a system relaxation). Her microscopic sensors keep her body temperature at a constant 98.6 degrees, making her immune to cold. Rhoda's memory bank contains 50 million items of information, and her computer brain can compute any piece of programmed information in one second. Carl calls his creation "Living Doll" (the original series title), "It," "709" or "the Robot"—and sees her as just that, not as a beautiful woman.

Carl assigns her to Dr. Robert ("Bob") McDonald, a psychologist at the Cory Psychiatric Clinic, to mold her character. She poses as Rhoda Miller, Carl's niece. At the office, she is Bob's secretary (who types 240 words a minute with no mistakes and no coffee breaks) and at home (an apartment at 5600 Wilshire Boulevard), where Bob lives with his sister, Irene Adams, Rhoda is a patient who requires special attention and is living with them until she can function on her own.

Bob is a ladies' man, and his favorite supperclub is the Galaxy Club in Los Angeles. He is also the chairman of the fund-raising committee for the Cory Clinic, which was founded in 1937 and has 55 beds. Peter Robinson, Bob's neighbor, is like everyone else and is unaware that Rhoda is a robot (Peter has fallen in love with her and desperately wants to date her; Bob is trying to prevent this from happening, fearing Rhoda will learn all the wrong things, as Peter is a playboy).

After the twenty-first episode, Bob Cummings left the series (he and Julie Newmar simply could not get along together). Bob's hasty departure was explained as his being sent to Pakistan on an assignment. Rhoda became Peter's ward for the remaining five episodes.

Theme: "My Living Doll," by George Greeley.

495. *My Mother the Car*

NBC, 9/14/65 to 9/6/66

Cast: Jerry Van Dyke *(Dave Crabtree)*, Maggie Pierce *(Barbara Crabtree)*, Cynthia Eilbacher *(Cindy Crabtree)*, Randy Whipple *(Randy Crabtree)*, Ann Sothern *(Mother's Voice)*, Avery Schreiber *(Bernard Manzini)*.

Facts: On August 23, 1949, Agatha Crabtree, the mother of David Crabtree, passed away. In November 1957, David, now a lawyer, and his high school sweetheart, Barbara Natwick, married. Eight years later, they have two children (Cindy and Randy), a dog (Moon), a comfortable home (at 213 Hampton Street; telephone number Madison 6-4699) and the need for a station wagon.

On September 14, 1965, Dave sets out to buy a station wagon for the family. While in a used car lot, he becomes fascinated with a decrepit looking 1928 Porter with the sign FIXER UPPER on it. Dave gets into the car, touches the radio—and hears a female voice say, "Hello, Davey." Davey responds, "Mother?" and is startled to learn that the voice is emerging from the car's radio. Agatha, who liked automobiles, has been reincarnated as a car to help Davey ("You need help, son") and his family. His mother, however, will speak only to him. Dave pays $200 for the Porter—which still has the original 1928 "Stops on a Dime" brakes and a Stromley-Gaxton carburetor (16 nuts, 14 screws and 3 bolts)—and drives home.

He immediately encounters the objections of Barbara (whom he calls "Barb"), who wants a station wagon. In an attempt to make Mother more presentable, Dave takes her to Doc Benson's Auto Clinic for an overhaul and then to A. Schreib's Auto Painting for a new paint job (red). A proud Dave Crabtree returns home—to encounter Barbara's objections once again; she and the kids want a station wagon.

Just then Captain Bernard Manzini, an easily exasperated and eccentric antique car collector arrives and offers to buy the Porter for his collection (Dave bought it minutes before Manzini had a chance to acquire it). Dave, of course, refuses to sell, and Manzini's continual efforts to acquire the Porter are a recurring theme. Stories relate Mother's attempts to guide Davey's life and Dave's efforts to conceal the fact that his mother is a car.

Complicating Dave's life is his neighbor, Ernie Stewart (Peter Leeds) who believes the Porter is an eyesore and has started a petition drive requesting that Dave get rid of the car.

When Mother needs servicing, Dave brings her to Doc Benson (Harry Holcomb), who runs the auto clinic. Dave places Mother in the garage each night directly following the eleven o'clock news on television (the dew gets the seats wet). He places a blanket on her radiator (so she won't catch cold) and stays with her five minutes before returning to the house. Mother sees through her headlights, and her license plate reads PZR 317. Mother did a commercial for Stops on a Dime Brakes (for the Video Advertising Agency); her favorite television show (she has a ten dollar used set in the garage) is "Jalopy Derby."

Bernard Manzini, who considers the Porter "Our Vehicle" (referring to himself and Dave), desperately wants the car and calls Dave everything but Crabtree (for example, Crabmaster, Kravitz, Crabmeat, Kragle); he always responds with "Whatever" when Dave corrects him.

Relatives: Paula Wilson (Barbara's mother, *Mrs. Natwick*), Bruno VeSota (Manzini's *Uncle Louie*).

Theme: "My Mother the Car," vocal by Paul Hampton.

496. *My Partner the Ghost*

Syndicated, 1973

Jeff Randall (Mike Pratt), who offers free advice, and Marty Hopkirk (Kenneth Cope), who always arrives five minutes ahead of his appointments, co-own Randall and Hopkirk—Private Investigators, at Marshall and Brooks Street in London, England. Marty's wife, Jean Hopkirk (Annette Andre) works as their secretary-receptionist (Jeff is single).

Jeff and Marty are investigating a case involving a woman's philandering husband when the woman dies suddenly from a heart condition. While Jeff writes off the case, Marty believes the woman was murdered and continues his investigation. One Wednesday evening, while walking across the street, Marty is killed by a hit and run driver—a murder arranged by the husband. Because of the circumstances surrounding his death, Marty is allowed to return to Earth as a ghost to solve his own murder. Because he is now a spirit, Marty is unable to function as before and must use a person to perform for him. Marty chooses Jeff and appears only to him ("Jeff, it's all right. Jeannie can't see or hear me, nobody can; only you, Jeff, only you"). With Jeff's help, Marty finds his killer, but he violates an ancient rule and is rejected by his grave: "Before the sun shall rise on you, each ghost unto his grave must go. Cursed be the ghost who dares to stay and face the awful light of day. He shall not to the grave return until a hundred years be gone."

Marty, now forced to remain on Earth, decides to resume his former life as a detective and becomes Jeff's ghostly assistant. The curse also gives Marty the opportunity to watch over his beautiful wife, whom he still worries about. Jean inherited everything from Marty, including trouble from those he convicted who are now seeking revenge: "I've waited eight years to get Hopkirk, now he's dead. But his lovely wife inherited everything, including my revenge. What would have been good enough for him is just as good for her."

Jean lives at 36 Paddington Square, Apartment E; her phone number is Vincent 6-3840. Jeff, who drives a car with the license plate RXD 996F, lives in Apartment 7 at 112 Stable Mews; his phone number is 067-3864. The series is also known as "Randall and Hopkirk (Deceased)."

Edwin Astley composed the theme.

497. *My Secret Identity*

Syndicated, 10/9/88 to 9/15/91

Cast: Jerry O'Connell (*Andrew Clements*), Derek McGrath (*Dr. Benjamin Jeffcoat*), Wanda Cannon (*Stephanie Clements*), Marsha Moreau (*Erin Clements*).

Facts: Fourteen-year-old Andrew Clements wanders into the lab of his neighbor, Dr. Benjamin Jeffcoat, and is hit by blue gamma rays from an experimental machine. The rays endow Andrew with extraordinary powers he uses to foil evil as Ultraman.

Andrew, who attends Briarwood High School, lives with his divorced mother, Stephanie, and sister, Erin, at 43 Meadow Drive (also given as 51 Meadow Drive) in Briarwood, Canada. Andrew based his alter ego on his favorite comic book character, Ultraman (Andrew wears no special costume, however. His powers consist of strength, the ability to fly, speed and an immunity to harm). Andrew's favorite hangout is Jerry's Burger Barn, and he held a job as a parking lot valet for the Le Club Restaurant. His phone number is 555-7175, and he started a pirate radio station (90 on the AM dial) called Gonzo Radio.

Stephanie, a freelance real estate agent, drives a station wagon with the license plate 483 ENX (later CFN 148) and does volunteer work at the York Community Center. Erin, who loves horseback riding, attends Briarwood Elementary School. Her favorite dinner is lamb chops, and her favorite television show is the mythical soap opera "Morning Heat."

Dr. Jeffcoat, the fifth smartest man in the world, lives at 45 Meadow Drive (his lab is maintained at a constant temperature of 75.5 degrees Fahrenheit). He writes scientific articles for the *Quantum Quarterly* magazine, has a boat called the *Kahuna* and drives a 4 × 4 with the license plate 592 BAJ. His answering machine tone is 440 cycles, and when working away from his lab he carries an Albert Einstein lunchbox. "Dr. J," as Andrew calls him, attended Broadhurst University (he played the tree in the school's production of *A Tree Grows in Brooklyn*). In Briarwood High School, Ben was called "Sparky" for blowing up the science lab.

Ruth Shellenbach (Elizabeth Leslie) is Ben's nosy neighbor. She lives at 47 Meadow Drive and is an Elvis fanatic (although in another episode she said that Tony Orlando was her favorite singer). Ruth has a dog named Elvis and is a member of the Women's Helicopter Action Rescue Team. In her youth, she was a member of the Bruise Brothers roller skating team.

Relatives: Susannah Hoffman (Ben's niece, *Rebecca*; she attends the Claridge School for Girls).

Flashbacks: Jaymie Blanchard (*Andrew as a boy*), Wanda Cannon (*Stephanie as a teenager*), Marc Marcutt and Kyle LaBine (*Ben as a boy*), Derek McGrath (*Ben's father*), Rona Polly (*Ben's mother*).

Theme: "My Secret Identity," by Fred Mollin.

498. *My Sister Eileen*

CBS, 10/5/60 to 4/12/61

A basement apartment at the Appopolous Arms at 121 Broadway in New York's Greenwich Village is the residence of Ruth and Eileen Sherwood, sisters from Columbus, Ohio, who moved to the big city to further their career goals.

Ruth (Elaine Stritch) is the older sister, a writer who hopes to turn her hometown experiences into a book. She first works as a manuscript reader for the McMann Publishing House, then as a writer for *Manhattan Magazine*. Ruth writes wholesome short stories (such as "My First Hiking Trip," "My Day at the Zoo") but finds it difficult selling them to magazines.

Eileen (Anne Helm, then Shirley Boone) is the younger, more glamorous sister. She is a hopeful actress and dreams of starring on Broadway. She has an agent named Marty (Stubby Kaye), but few jobs and many struggles as she seeks to achieve her goal. Eileen does have admirers, however—men simply cannot take their eyes off her, and she is constantly wooed by them.

Alan Dahorsameche (Tom Reese, then Hal Baylor), better known as "The Wreck" is the Sherwoods' upstairs neighbor. He is a football player for the New York Giants and extremely jealous. He fears that every "wolf" in New York is after his wife, Helen (Pattee Chapman, then Treva Frazee), whom he calls "Princess."

Chick Adams (Jack Weston) is Ruth's friend, a reporter for the *Daily News*; Bertha Bronsky (Rose Marie) is Ruth's co-worker; and Mr. Appopolous (Leon Belasco) owns the building (in the pilot episode, "You Should Meet My Sister" [NBC, 5/16/60], Henry Corden played the landlord as Mr. Spevak, the owner of the Spevak Arms). Agnes Moorehead appeared as Ruth and Eileen's aunt, Harriet.

The series is based on the book by Ruth McKinney and was first adapted for television on 11/30/58 in a two hour CBS special with Rosalind Russell (Ruth), Jacqueline McKeever (Eileen), Jordan Bentley (The Wreck), Michelle Burke (Helen) and Joseph Buloff (Mr. Appopolous).

499. *My Sister Sam*

CBS, 10/6/86 to 4/13/88

Cast: Pam Dawber (*Samantha Russell*), Rebecca Schaeffer (*Patti Russell*), Jenny O'Hara (*Dixie Randazzo*), Joel Brooks (*J.D.*), David Naughton (*Jack Kincaid*).

Facts: Samantha ("Sam") Russell is a beautiful 29-year-old girl who runs the Russell Scouts Photography Studio from her apartment (5C) at 1345 Benchley Street in San Francisco, California (555-6687 is her phone number). Sam shares the apartment with her pretty 16-year-old sister, Patti. Patti previously lived in Oregon, where her Aunt Elsie and her Uncle Bob had been caring for her since her parents were killed in a car accident. Patti wanted to be with Sam and moved out.

Sam was a straight–*A* student at Bennett High School in Oregon (with the exception of a *C*-minus in Spanish); the theme of her homecoming dance was "Undersea Adventure" and featured the group Sharky and the Fins. Sam's biggest disappointment in life occurred when *Epicure* magazine rejected her "Table Settings" photo for its cover; her dream is to make the cover of a national magazine before she is 30. Sam alphabetizes her fruit juices in the refrigerator and arranges the shoes in her closet so that all the toes point north.

Patti shared a cab with Sunflower Wong Chow, and her fare from San Francisco International Airport to Sam's apartment was eight dollars. Patti is a sophomore at Millard Fillmore High School; her dream is to quit school and become a rock star. In one episode, Patti's teacher, Mrs. Friedman, assigned her a five pound bag of flour to care for as if it were a real baby; she named it Dweezil. Sam and Patti attempted to make money by selling hand decorated sweatshirts at the Serendipity Boutique (the boutique ordered 150 and returned most of them).

Jack Kincaid is Sam's neighbor (Apartment 5D) and a photojournalist who got his first cover story in *Newsweek* magazine when he was 22. He drives a 1955 Buick convertible (not seen), and when he gets depressed he looks into the mirror and sings "Happy Talk" (from *South Pacific*) to himself. Dixie Randazzo, Sam's assistant, is married and the mother of six children (five of whom are not seen). She was a member of the Ink Skulls Club in high school and has a tattoo on her behind that says I LOVE DWAYNE. J.D., Sam's agent, attended the University of Bridgeport and has a never-seen wife named Lorraine.

There are three flights of stairs to climb before one reaches Sam's apartment. Each flight is made up of 26 steps.

Relatives: Nan Martin (Sam's aunt, *Elsie*), Patrick Breen (Jack's nephew, *Scotty Kincaid*), Stuart Fratkin (Dixie's son, *Mickey Randazzo*).

Theme: "Room Enough for Two," vocal by Kim Carnes.

500. *My Three Sons*

ABC, 9/29/60 to 9/9/65
CBS, 9/16/65 to 8/24/72

A house at 837 Mill Street in the town of Bryant Park is home to widower Steven ("Steve") Douglas (Fred MacMurray) and his three sons: Michael ("Mike") Douglas (Tim Considine), Robert ("Robbie") Douglas (Don Grady) and Richard ("Chip") Douglas (Stanley Livingston). Also living with them is Steve's father-in-law, William ("Bill") Michael Francis Aloysius O'Casey (William Frawley), who is affectionately called "Bub." (CBS episodes are set in North Hollywood, California.)

The town was named after Seth Bryant, an itinerant pots and pans salesman who founded the town after his wagon broke down and forced him to stay. Steve, who stands six feet two inches tall, is an aeronautical engineer (structural design) for Universal Research and Development (he began his career as a test pilot). Steve finds wearing a cardigan sweater and smoking a pipe most relaxing.

Steve is a graduate of Midwest University (class of 1938) and married Louise O'Casey when he was 21 years old (Louise died 12 years later on the night before Chip's first birthday); Steve's phone number is Larson 0-6719, and his license plate reads JXN-127. The family dog is named Tramp. In Steve's 1938 graduating class, there was only one female student—Heather Marlowe (Frances Rafferty). In 1969 Steve married a teacher named Barbara Harper (Beverly Garland), a widow with a young daughter named Dodie (Dawn Lyn); Dodie had a doll named Myrtle.

Mike is the eldest of Steve's children (18). He attends an unnamed high school (he is a senior when the series begins). He is on the track team and has a girlfriend named Jean Pearson (Cynthia Pepper). Mike next attends State College (he is a member of the Sigma Gamma Chi fraternity), then joins the air force reserves. Prior to the CBS episodes, Mike marries Sally Ann Morrison (Meredith MacRae), a girl he met in 1963, and moves East to accept a job as a psychology professor.

Robbie (14) first attended Webster Elementary School, then Bryant Park High. He was a member of a club called the Chieftains and wrote a song called "Ugga Bugga." In 1967 episodes he marries a college friend named Katie Miller (Tina Cole) and becomes the father of triplets two years later: Charley, Steve Jr. and Robbie II (Michael, Joseph and Daniel Todd).

Chip, the youngest child (seven) attended Webster Elementary School and was a member of the Moose Patrol scouting troop. In the second grade, a girl named Doreen Peters had a crush on Chip. He called her "Goof Eyes"; Chip's friends teased him by calling him "Hot Lips Douglas." In fall 1970, Chip married Polly Williams (Ronne Troup). They eloped and honeymooned in Mexico (they stayed at the Concha Azul Hotel—the hotel at which Steve and Barbara were married).

Ernie Thompson (Barry Livingston) was Chip's friend (beginning with 1963 episodes). When Ernie is orphaned (his parents are killed, but how is not related), he is sent to the King's County Children's Home. Steve then adopts him; at the time Ernie had a dog named Wilson and attended the Susie B. Dorsey School. He and Chip were later classmates at Buchanan Elementary School.

Bub, who helps care for the family, says, in one episode, that he got his nickname from Mike (when Mike was an infant, he tried to say Grandpa but it came out "Bub"); in another episode it is mentioned that when Chip tried to say Bill it came out "Bub." Bub was a member of the Brotherhood of the Cavaliers and left the series in 1964. Steve tells the kids that Bub has gone "to visit his mother in Ireland" (actually he went to Ireland to help his aunt, Kate, celebrate her 104th birthday). To fill the void left by Bub, Steve hires Fedocia Barrett (Reta Shaw) as a temporary housekeeper until Bub returns from Ireland. Shortly after, Bub's brother, Charles ("Charlie") O'Casey (William Demarest), a former merchant marine, arrives at the Douglas home seeking Bub. When Steve learns that Charlie is en route to the Caribbean, he invites him to stay with the family for a few days. Fedocia refuses to cook for another male and gives Steve her notice. Charlie, who comes to be called "Uncle Charlie," agrees to stay and help look after the boys (Charlie was born in Sandusky, Ohio).

Relatives: Fred MacMurray (Steve's Scottish cousin, *Fergus McBain Douglas*), Joan Tompkins (Katie's mother, *Louise Miller*), Marsha Hunt (Katie's aunt, *Cecile*), Sebastian Cabot (Sally's father, *Thomas Morrison*, an archaeologist), Doris Singleton (Sally's mother, *Helen Morrison*), Norman Alden (Polly's father, *Tom Williams*), Doris Singleton (Polly's mother, *Margaret Williams*), Eleanor Audley (Barbara's mother, *Mrs. Vincent*), Barbara Collentine and Barbara Perry (*Ernie's mother*), Richard Jury (*Ernie's father*), Robert P. Lieb (Jean's father, *Henry Pearson*), Florence MacMichael (Jean's mother, *Florence Pearson*).

Flashbacks: George Spicer (*Steve as a college student*), David Marklin (*Steve as a high school student*), Tom Skerritt (*Steve when he proposed to Louise*), Vera Stough (Steve's fiancée, then wife, *Louise*), Bee Peters (Bub's wife, *Mary O'Casey*).

Theme: "My Three Sons," by Frank DeVol.

501. *My Two Dads*

NBC, 9/20/87 to 6/18/90

Cast: Greg Evigan (*Joey Harris*), Paul Reiser (*Michael Taylor*), Staci Keanan (*Nicole Bradford*), Florence Stanley (*Margaret Wilbur*).

Facts: Joseph ("Joey") Harris and Michael Taylor are two friends who were also the former lovers of the late Marcie Bradford. At the reading of her will, Judge Margaret Wilbur appoints Joey and Michael as the co-guardians of Nicole Bradford, Marcie's pretty 12-year-old daughter, when it cannot be determined who is the actual biological father.

Joey, Michael and Nicole live in Apartment 4B at 627 North Brewster Street in Manhattan in a building owned by Judge Wilbur (who resides in Apartment 3B).

Joey is a Greenwich Village artist (1987–88), art director for *Financial Update* magazine (1988), artist again (1989) and finally art teacher at New York University in 1990. Joey also wrote the children's book *Mr. Biggles* (about a leprechaun).

Michael is first a financial advisor for the Taft-Kelcher Agency (1987–89), then marketing manager for *Financial Update* magazine. As kids, Joey and Michael both attended Camp White Fish.

Nicole, who has a teddy bear named Mr. Beebles, attends an unnamed junior high school, then Kennedy High. With the introduction of her girlfriend Shelby Haskell (Amy Hathaway), the series focused on Nicole's growth into young adulthood—and on the worries faced by her two dads when she discovers boys and dating. Nicole became envious of girls with bigger bosoms and thought that large breasts meant boys and attention. She ordered a $29.95 "Bust-O-Matic" breast developer that failed to give her the

results she wanted (she backed out of using it once it arrived).

Ed Klawicki (Dick Butkus) is a former football player who owns Klawicki's, a diner located on the ground floor of the judge's building. In the third season, Margaret takes over the diner under the name the Judge's Court Café.

Prior to becoming a judge, Margaret was a lawyer and partner with her husband, Louis Fraser, in the law firm of Fraser and Wilbur in 1960.

Relatives: Polly Bergen (Michael's mother, *Evelyn Taylor*), Lisa Sutton (Michael's sister, *Lisa Taylor*), Jan Murray (Michael's uncle, *Raymond*), Kenneth Kimmins (Joey's father, *Lou Harris*), Robert Mandan (Margaret's ex-husband, *Louis Fraser*), Wendy Schaal (Margaret's niece, *Christine*), Kim Ulrich (Ed's sister, *Patty Ann*).

Flashbacks: Emma Samms (Nicole's mother, *Marcie Bradford*).

Theme: "You Can Count on Me," vocal by Greg Evigan.

502. *My World . . . and Welcome to It*

NBC, 9/15/69 to 9/7/70

John Monroe (William Windom) is a cartoonist for *Manhattanite* magazine. He is discontented with his job (his office is next to the freight elevator, and his boss, Hamilton Greeley [Harold J. Stone] constantly complains that "his cartoons talk with their mouths closed"); he is suspicious of smart children and hostile animals; he is intimidated by his loving wife and precocious daughter, and scared to death of life. When life becomes intolerable or when he is troubled, John retreats to the secret world of his imagination. His cartoons become real, life becomes tolerable and he is transformed into a person who is irresistible to women and a tower of strength in the eyes of men.

John's ambition is to write a book ("Wanting to do a book is important; what it is about comes later"). "The trouble with women," he says, "is that when you get to know them and trust them, you realize that you can never get to know them and you can't trust them."

John lives at 130 Post Road in Westport, Connecticut, with his wife, Ellen (Joan Hotchkis), and his daughter, Lydia (Lisa Gerritsen). Ellen is totally dedicated to John and worries that he is much too critical of the world that surrounds him. Lydia is ten years old, very bright, very pretty, and attends Compton Elementary School. She carries a flower decorated lunchbox to school, wears a retainer at night and wants to attend Yale University. Her attitude ("I better start getting all *A*'s now") makes John think he is raising "a girl with the I.Q. of a 55-year-old CPA." Ellen considers Lydia a sensitive child.

The Monroe family dogs are Christabel and Irving; *Manhattanite* magazine is housed in the Manhattanite Building in New York City; the Metropolitan Paper Company of New York supplies the magazine's paper.

My Two Dads. Paul Reiser (left), Staci Keanan and Greg Evigan.

Carole Cook appeared as John's sister, Kate Monroe. The series is based on "drawings, stories, inspirational pieces and things that go bump in the night, by James Thurber."

Warren Barker and Danny Arnold composed the theme.

On June 8, 1959, NBC's "Goodyear Playhouse" presented "Christabel," the pilot episode for an unsold series called "The Secret Life of John Monroe." Arthur O'Connell was John Monroe, the cartoonist whose drawings, based on James Thurber's work, came to life. Georgann Johnson was his wife, Ellen, and Susan Gordon played their daughter, Lydia. The family dogs were Christabel (a poodle) and Muggs (a hound dog).

Another pilot, "The Secret Life of James Thurber," aired on "The June Allyson Show" (CBS, 3/20/61), with Orson Bean as James Thurber, the cartoonist who often slips into the fantasy world of his drawings. Sue Randall played his wife, Ellen.

Although not based on James Thurber's drawings, a similar pilot titled "Pen 'n' Inc." aired on CBS on 8/15/81. In it, Matt McCoy played Alan Ozley, an artist for the Essex, Connecticut, *Register,* who dreams of becoming a political cartoonist. Alan's thoughts and fantasies come to vivid life for him through animation. Peter Hobbs played T.W. Winson, the publisher; Brianne Leary was T.W.'s daughter, Debbie Winson; and Andra Akers was Gretchen Vanderwyck, Alan's landlady.

"The People Next Door" (CBS, 9/18/89 to 10/16/89) was another series that used the same idea. Walter Kellogg (Jeffrey Jones) is a cartoonist with the ability to make things appear just by imagining them. Mary Gross is his wife, Abigail, and Jaclyn Bernstein and Chance Quinn are his children, Aurora and Matthew, from a previous marriage. Walter, who draws the comic strip "The People Next Door," and Abigail, a therapist, live at 607 Sycamore Lane in the town of Covington (555-0098 is their phone number, and the kids attend Covington High School).

503. *Mysteries of Chinatown*

ABC, 12/4/49 to 10/23/50

Yat Fu's is a curio shop at 1302 Golden Avenue in San Francisco's Chinatown. Dr. Yat Fu (Marvin Miller) is its owner, an amateur crime sleuth who helps the police solve crimes. Ah Toy (Gloria Saunders) is his beautiful niece and shop assistant and sometimes partner in crime solving; she lives with her uncle at 0734 Magnolia Street.

Dr. Yat Fu works closely with Lieutenant Hargrove (Bill Eythe) of the S.F.P.D.'s Homicide Bureau. When East Coast commitments forced Eythe to leave the live West Coast–produced series, Hargrove was killed during "a volley of slugs pouring out of a Chinatown alley." He was replaced by Richard Crane as Lieutenant Cummings (when commitments called Crane away from the show, Cummings was not killed off; he was simply contacted by phone and not seen).

"Mysteries of Chinatown" is a unique show for its time,

as no expense was spared to make authentic sets. While shows like "Captain Video" had a weekly props budget of $25 in 1949, "Mysteries" spent more than $10,000 just to furnish the set. Some of the most notable props were a genuine teakwood tabaret valued at $3,000, a real Chinese sacred urn (so ornate it couldn't be replaced; valued at $1,500) and two genuine opium pipes, each over 155 years old. The program also employed four exterior sets and four interior sets (which cost many thousands of dollars and took one thousand man hours to build). Topping it off was $5,000 worth of theatrical lights to illuminate the eight sets.

504. *Naked City*

ABC, 9/30/58 to 9/29/59
ABC, 10/12/60 to 9/11/63

"Ladies and Gentlemen, you are about to see the Naked City ... This story was not photographed in a studio; quite the contrary. The actors played out their roles in the streets and buildings of New York itself."

Producer Herbert B. Leonard spoke these words during first season (half hour) episodes to prepare viewers for a gritty and realistic character study of the people of a large metropolis. It was also the first time a weekly series moved out of the studio to film entirely on location, using the best and worst that a city has to offer. Whether a two character play (such as "A Wood of Thornes") or a shoot 'em up action drama (like "Belvedere Tower"), it was a unique program for its time, and it now gives a nostalgic glimpse of New York's past.

First season regulars (first date listing), attached to the 65th Precinct in Manhattan, were Detective James ("Jimmy") Halloran (James Franciscus), Lieutenant Dan Muldoon (John McIntire), Lieutenant Michael ("Mike") Parker (Horace McMahon), and Sergeant Frank Arcaro (Harry Bellaver). Jim, who was married to Janet (Suzanne Storrs) and was the father of Evie (Dorothy Dollivaire), had badge number 41367. Dan's license plate was seen as 8T5657. George Duning and Ned Washington composed the theme, "This Is the Naked City."

Hour episode regulars (second date listing) were: Detective Adam Flint (Paul Burke), Lieutenant Mike Parker (Horace McMahon), and Sergeant Frank Arcaro (Harry Bellaver). The detectives were attached to the 65th Precinct, which was built in 1938; the precinct phone number is WA2-9970.

Adam was born in the Bronx, lived at 166th Street and McClelland Avenue and attended P.S. 11 (near Yankee Stadium); he now lives at 393 West 48th Street, Apartment E, in Manhattan, and is romantically involved with Libby Kingston (Nancy Malone), an actress who lives in an apartment at 363 East 65th Street; she takes the 8th Avenue IND subway line to work, to an unidentified television studio in Manhattan; her phone number was given as 346-3593. Adam, Libby says, always forgets to clean out his pockets when she takes his suits to the cleaners; his car license plate reads 6N7878.

Like the half-hour version, the hour series is also a character study of people in trouble with the law; hence very little trivia information is given. Frank's license plate is 2G45-45, and Mike's license plate reads 4T893. It takes 28 minutes for a police van to travel from the 65th Precinct to the Tombs Holding Cell in Lower Manhattan. Before it became known by the initials N.Y.P.D., "P.D.N.Y.C." (Police Department of New York City) appears on police vehicles. Mike walked a beat on Fordham Road in the Bronx in 1931; to celebrate his thirtieth anniversary (3/1/61) on the force, Mike was given a trophy that said THE MIKE PARKER FAN CLUB. Libby was listed as the cheerleader.

Each episode ended with one of the most famous lines in television history: "There are eight million stories in the Naked City. This has been one of them."

Billy May composed "The Naked City Theme" (used 1960–62) and Nelson Riddle composed "The New Naked City Theme" (1962–63).

505. *The Nancy Drew Mysteries*

ABC, 2/6/77 to 7/30/78

"The day she began part time investigative work for me was the start of my gray hairs," says Carson Drew (William Schallert), a brilliant criminal attorney, about his beautiful daughter, Nancy Drew (Pamela Sue Martin and Janet Louise Johnson), "a girl with a very inquisitive mind who loves to unravel a mystery." The Municipal Building in the town of River Heights, in New England, houses the offices of Carson Drew. Nancy, who has been out of school for five years when the series begins, works as a part time investigator for her father. Her ambition is to become a private detective, but in the meantime she settles for the mundane—researching legal files and checking license plates. However, when a case turns into a mystery for Carson, Nancy becomes the detective she wants to be and tries to help Carson solve it—despite the fact that she is always taking chances and adding to his gray hairs.

Nancy and her girlfriend, George Fayne (Jean Rasey and Susan Buckner), attended River Heights High School. George is always at Nancy's side, and like her best friend she too wants to become a detective. Nancy feels George is not ready and lets her practice (for example, by going undercover as a maid in a hotel while Nancy poses as a reporter to crack a case). George lives at 16 River Avenue; Nancy and her father at 8606 Bainbridge Street.

The character of Ned Nickerson was first played by George O'Hanlon, Jr., as Carson's assistant, and later by Rick Springfield as an investigator for the Boston D.A.'s office.

In the opening theme, the following book titles are seen: *Mystery of the Whale Tattoo*, *The Clue in the Crossword Cipher*, *The Quest of the Missing Map*, *The Spider Sapphire Mystery*, *The Sign of the Twisted Candle*, *The Criss-*cross Puzzle*, *The Shattered Helmet* and *While the Clock Ticked*. The series is based on the stories by Carolyn Keene. Glen A. Larson composed the theme.

"The Nancy Drew Mysteries" was broadcast on an alternating basis with "The Hardy Boys Mysteries" (ABC, 1/30/77 to 8/26/79), which followed the investigations of juvenile detectives Frank (Parker Stevenson) and Joe Hardy (Shaun Cassidy), the sons of world famous private detective Fenton Hardy (Edmund Gilbert). The Hardys lived in the town of Bayport; Edith Atwater was Fenton's sister, Gertrude Hardy, and Lisa Eilbacher was Fenton's secretary, Callie Shaw.

506. *Nanny and the Professor*

ABC, 1/21/70 to 12/27/71

Phoebe Figalilly (Juliet Mills) is not a witch or a magician, but she possesses the ability to spread love and joy. She drives an antique car she calls Arabella and seems to appear when someone needs help. Professor Harold Everett (Richard Long) is a widowed college professor and the father of three mischievous children: Harold ("Hal") Jr. (David Doremus), Prudence (Kim Richards) and Bentley (Trent Lehman). Professor Everett is having a difficult time caring for his kids (housekeepers are frightened off by the children), until Phoebe, who prefers to be called Nanny, arrives to help him and take charge of his household.

The Everetts live at 10327 Oak Street in Los Angeles. Professor Everett teaches math at Clinton College, and the family pets are Waldo (a dog), Sebastian (a rooster), Mike and Myrtle (guinea pigs) and Geraldine and Jerome (baby goats). Bentley's nickname is Butch.

Elsa Lanchester plays Nanny's mystical Aunt Henrietta. Harry Nilsson sings the theme, "Nanny."

507. *National Velvet*

NBC, 9/18/60 to 9/10/62

Cast: Lori Martin *(Velvet Brown)*, Arthur Space *(Herbert Brown)*, Ann Doran *(Martha Brown)*, Carole Wells *(Edwina Brown)*, Joey Scott *(Donald Brown)*, James McCallion *(Mi Taylor)*.

Facts: Velvet Brown is the pretty 12-year-old daughter of Herbert and Martha Brown, the owners of the Brown Dairy Ranch in a Midwestern community called the Valley (on the outskirts of Birch City; Cornwall and Flintwood are the nearest towns). She has a beautiful 16-year-old sister named Edwina and a curious and mischievous six-year-old brother named Donald. Velvet also has a dream: to own a horse and train it for competition in the Grand National Steeplechase.

Nancy Drew Mysteries. **Left to right: George O'Hanlon, Jr., William Schallert, Pamela Sue Martin and Jean Rasey.**

National Velvet. Lori Martin with King.

One day, while walking home from school, Velvet sees her neighbor's chestnut horse jump a four rail, six foot fence. She theorizes that the chestnut is a natural jumper and can be trained for the steeplechase. (Prior to seeing the horse, Velvet was reading a book called *Thoroughbred Stakes Records*.)

When Velvet learns that the chestnut's owner, Homer Edie (Tim Graham), plans to sell the unmanageable horse for dog meat at 30 cents a pound (about $30), she asks her father to buy it for her. A badly needed water pump takes precedence and makes it impossible for Herbert to buy the horse. Velvet hits on an idea to offer a raffle for

the horse. She receives Mr. Edie's permission to do so and sets about making and selling 100 raffle tickets at 50 cents each.

That Saturday at the local fair, the raffle is held. An excited Velvet listens as the winning ticket is drawn—number 9, a ticket that is not hers. Velvet believes that her hopes and dreams have been shattered until she learns that her father purchased the ten tickets she left at the post office and among them was number 9. A teary eyed Velvet rushes over to the horse. It were as if fate had intended Velvet and the chestnut to be together. Velvet, riding bareback, enters the fair's steeplechase race and wins. "You're mine, all mine," she says to the horse after the race, "forever and ever."

The following week, while Velvet is training the horse, she remarks, "I just decided something. You hold your head so high and you look so proud, I'm going to call you King." Velvet then tells Mi (their ranchhand) that she named the horse King. "That's not much of a racing name," Mi says. "There has to be something ahead of it, like Regal King." Velvet thinks for a moment and says, "How about Blaze King?" That's not bad at all," says Mi, and it becomes the chestnut's official name.

Velvet's most difficult task in training King (as he is most often called) was breaking him to the saddle. She won her first loving cup when she entered King in the junior hurdles at the Valley Hunt Club (six jumps in a figure eight track). Velvet attends the Valley Elementary School. She is a member of the Pioneers Club (a group of local kids who go exploring), is not allowed to ride King bareback and cannot go out after dark.

Edwina, called "Winna," shares a bedroom with Velvet. She was born in August and is very feminine (she almost always wears a dress). Winna is a sophomore at Valley High and a member of the Teen Club. She breeds canaries (she has several in her room but never calls any by name) and reads a magazine called *The Canary Breeders Journal*. Edwina has a 9:00 P.M. curfew and cannot date on school nights (the local makeout point is Honeymoon Lane). She has a lucky doll (name not given), which she has had since she was six years old. Winna had two boyfriends: the more steady Theodore P. Nelson (Carl Crow), an anthropology major at State College; and the occasional Carl Evans (Michael Vandever).

Donald is a realistically typical little boy. He gets hurt (for example, falling down the stairs), he adopts stray animals, has a bug collection (which he keeps in a jar and wears with a string around his neck), fibs, blames his sisters for something he did, and is often confused by "big words" (such as *elopement*). He is the mascot of the Pioneers Club, and his favorite dessert is blueberry pie.

Mi Taylor, a former steeplechase rider in England, was born in Ireland and now works for the Browns. (His career ended when he was thrown from a horse during a race. The fall injured Mi's leg, and he now walks with a limp.) He has been working for the Browns seven years when the series begins (the first horse Mi rode was named Calico King; he received a five pound English note as his fee). His favorite pastime is playing checkers with Velvet, and he uses his "grandmother's sayings" to get a point across (for example, "As me wise grandmother used to say, the wise man laughs at himself and the fool laughs at everything else").

The Browns sell their milk in Flintwood at the Winters Dairies; E3597 is the license plate of Herbert's Dodge pickup truck.

Relatives: Edgar Buchanan (*Velvet's grandfather*), Nora Marlowe (Homer's wife, *Aggie Edie*).

Theme: "National Velvet," by Robert Armbruster.

508. *Neon Rider*

Syndicated, 10/13/90 to 10/7/91

Michael Terry (Winston Rekert) has a Ph.D. in child psychology and taught science and human behavior at the university level for five years. He had an article published in the most highly regarded sociology magazine in the world and is the author of a book called *The Development of Teenage Behavior*. Despite his achievements, Michael feels it's all talk and no action. He decides to put his schooling to work and get firsthand experience working with troubled teens and developing their character.

Michael quits his job and purchases a ranch in Canada's Fraser Valley. There, with the cooperation of the juvenile court, he begins his program of helping troubled teens deal with poverty, parental neglect, gang wars and drug abuse. The court considers the juveniles on the Ranch (as it is called) to be in confinement; if they attempt to leave, it will be considered an escape; if they are caught it means being tried as adults and prison.

Michael drives a car with the license plate YDF 524, and the ranch truck has the plate ITT 483. Michael's former colleagues call the Ranch "Michael's Folly."

Fox Devlin (Antoinette Bower), who has a white horse named Saddles, is the Ranch foreman. Vic (Samuel Sarker) is a Native American who works as a ranchhand; he has a horse named Dundee. C.C. Dechardon (Alex Bruhanski) is the cook; Rachel Woods (Suzanne Errett-Balcom) is the social worker assigned to assist Michael (her license plate reads SNZ 752).

Bill Henderson sings the theme, "Neon Rider."

509. *Nero Wolfe*

NBC, 1/16/81 to 8/25/81

Nero Wolfe (William Conrad) is a gourmet cook, horticulturist, connoisseur and master criminologist who helps the police and the FBI solve complex crimes. He lives in a brownstone at 918 West 35th Street in Manhattan, but seldom leaves his house to solve crimes. Through the legwork of others, namely Archie Goodwin, who collects the pieces of the puzzle for him, Nero solves crimes. When a case is solved in Nero's mind, he gathers all the suspects at his home. He recaps the crime, questions the suspects and reveals the culprit.

Archie Goodwin (Lee Horsley) is a private detective who works for Nero. Besides collecting the puzzle pieces (as he calls them), he "jumps in and grabs something [evidence] before the other guy does." "I do nothing without Archie," Nero says. "He's inquisitive, charming, impetuous, alert and forceful. He gets me what I need to solve crimes." Archie lives at 237 East 46th Street and doesn't take notes when he questions a suspect. Pointing to his head he says, "Virtual computer." His favorite eatery is Rusterman's Restaurant.

Other Regulars: Saul Panzer (George Wyner), Nero's field operative; Fritz Brenner (George Voskovec), Nero's cook (he and Nero constantly argue over the ingredients of exotic dishes); Theodore Horstman (Robert Coote), Nero's horticulturist (Nero is fond of tropical plants, especially orchids, which require constant attention); Inspector Cramer (Allan Miller), Nero's police department contact (N.Y.P.D., 18th Precinct); and Peter Drossos (David Hollander), Archie's friend, a boy who works the wiper racket at 67th Street and Park Avenue (a car stops for a red light; the kid wipes off the windshield for a tip). The series is based on the stories by Rex Stout.

Theme: "Nero Wolfe," by John Addison.

Note: In 1979 (12/18) ABC aired an unsold pilot called "Nero Wolfe" with the following cast: Thayer David *(Nero Wolfe)*, Tom Mason *(Archie Goodwin)*, David Hurst *(Fritz Brenner)*, John O'Leary *(Theodore Horstman)*, Lewis Charles *(Saul Panzer)*, and Biff McGuire *(Inspector Cramer)*.

510. *The New Adventures of Beans Baxter*

Fox, 7/18/87 to 4/2/88

Cast: Jonathan Ward *(Beans Baxter)*, Elinor Donahue *(Susan Baxter)*, Scott Bremner *(Scooter Baxter)*, Karen Mistal *(Cake Lase)*, John Vernon *(Number One)*, Kurtwood Smith *(Mr. Sue)*.

Facts: Benjamin ("Beans") Baxter is a typically normal 17-year-old boy. He lives in the small town of Witches Creek, Kansas, with his mother, Susan, father, Benjamin, Sr., and younger brother, Scooter. Unknown to the family, Ben Sr. is a courier for the Network, a postal service for the secret agencies of the U.S. government, which is headed by Number One.

When the series begins, Ben Sr. is transferred to Washington, D.C. He and his family take up residence at 1341 Maple Street (telephone number 555-6060), and Beans enrolls in Georgetown High School. Shortly after, Beans stumbles into his father's secret life (he believes he is a mailman) when he sees him being kidnapped by U.G.L.I. (Underground Government Liberation Intergroup), an evil organization headed by Mr. Sue. In an attempt to rescue his father, Beans comes in contact with Number One and is recruited by the Network as a spy-courier to help him in his quest to find his missing father (his "new adventures").

Darla (Kristin Cumming) was Beans's original girlfriend (in Witches Creek); in Washington, he is pursued by Cake Lase, "the most gorgeous girl on his high school campus." Beans, however, sees no other girl but Svetlana (Shawn Weatherly), a beautiful Soviet defector, when he learns he is going to be working with her. Scooter, "a pint-sized Albert Einstein," has a pet guinea pig named Alvin.

Relatives: Rick Lenz (Beans's father, *Ben Baxter, Sr.*), Sarah Sawatsky (Cake's sister, *Cupcake Lase*), Lorraine Foreman (Number One's wife, *Mrs. Number One*), Shawn Clements (Number One's son, *Little One*).

Theme: "The New Adventures of Beans Baxter," by Joseph Birtelli.

The New Adventures of Martin Kane see *Martin Kane, Private Eye*

511. *New Attitude*

ABC, 8/8/90 to 9/7/90

Beauticians Vicki St. James (Sheryl Lee Ralph) and her younger sister, Yvonne St. James (Phyllis Yvonne Stickney), own New Attitude, a beauty salon located at 41 South La Brea in Los Angeles. The salon's telephone number is 213-555-7981, and KPYL is the radio station heard in the background during business hours.

Vicki, the prettier sister, is also the smarter one; she is seeking Mr. Right and wants to settle down. Yvonne, who attended Carver High School (as did Vicki), looks to Vicki for guidance. While not exactly a flake, she seems to have a knack for complicating everything she does. Yvonne's favorite television shows are "Mr. Ed" and "The Arsenio Hall Show."

Selena's Hair Affair, located at 44 South La Brea (and run by Jedda Jones as Selena) is New Attitude's main competition. The store located directly across the street from New Attitude is Checks Bakery.

Lamaar (Morris Day) is Vicki's hairstylist and runs the "Hair by Lamaar" corner of New Attitude. Audrey Laker (Karen Bankhead) is the manicurist; Taylor (Larenz Tate) is the assistant who is hoping to pass her beautician's test (which, as of 9/2/90, she had failed 12 times); Leon (Earl Billings) is Vicki's landlord.

Sheryl Lee Ralph sings the theme, "New Attitude."

The New Bob Cummings Show see *Love That Bob*

512. *The New Dick Van Dyke Show*

CBS, 9/18/71 to 9/3/73
CBS, 9/10/73 to 9/2/74

Richard ("Dick") Preston (Dick Van Dyke), his wife, Jennifer ("Jenny") Preston (Hope Lange), and their children,

Annie (Angela Powell) and Lucas (Michael Shea), reside in a ranch-style house on Hayes Creek Road in Carefree, Arizona. Dick is the host of "The Dick Preston Show," a 90 minute talk-variety program that is produced by KXIU-TV, Channel 2, in Phoenix (the station is owned by the Compton Broadcasting Company).

Michelle ("Mike") Preston (Fannie Flagg) is Dick's sister, booking agent and secretary at Channel 2; Bernard ("Bernie") Davis (Marty Brill) is Dick's agent and business manager; and Carol Davis (Nancy Dussault) is Bernie's wife.

Dick collects old 78 rpm records; his most treasured one is that of Jack Sena playing "Bumble Boogie" (it took him 20 years to locate it). Dick and Jenny's dream home is the historic Morgan house. When the owner, old man Morgan, passed away, the house became available. Dick purchased it, but backed out of the deal when he discovered the potential buyers of his current house were planning to make drastic changes to it. When Jenny and Carol hit on an idea to make money by selling clothes made by the local Sioux Indian tribe, they obtained a vacant store in the Phoenix Mall. The store, which cost $200 a month to rent, was the former Moskowitz Butcher Shop. Jenny and Carol called their business Delicatique, and Carol painted the restrooms in her high school colors of purple and green.

Annie Preston is nine years old and attends Camelback Grammar School. She eats Puffed Wheat Flakes cereal for breakfast, has a hand puppet she calls "Nosey" and did a television commercial with Dick for a product called Cicely's Instant Oatmeal. Dick calls Annie "Pumpkin," and Bernie's affectionate name for her is "Sweetness."

Lucas Preston is 16 years old. Like Annie, he appears only in episodes when the children are needed. He attends an unnamed high school, presumably, that is some distance from his home (he lives on campus). He is a young Romeo and seems to have a never-ending supply of girlfriends. The episode of 10/2/71 ("Interracial Dating") was very controversial for its time and showed Lucas dating a black girl named Judy Williams (Ta-Tanisha). The family's acceptance of Judy was made easier when Annie wrote a poem ("Roses are red, violets are blue, so why can't people be colors too?").

Dick and Jenny also have an infant son named Chris (Tiffany Graff). Before the birth of the baby (Jenny became pregnant while she was secretary of the Planned Parenthood Association), their working name for it was Florence Scruffarini. Dick closes his show with "Bye, have a nice rest of the day." His mother hates his show, and Dick buys his clothes at Mr. Mens. The family cat is Mr. Rosenbloom (named after Annie's music teacher).

Mabel Albertson played Dick's mother, Marge Preston; Carl Reiner's voice was heard as that of the studio director; and Dick's real life children, Barry and Stacy Van Dyke, played various roles.

In 1973 (second date listing) the series switched locales (to California) when Dick quit his local talk show to play Dr. Brad Fairmont on the television soap opera "Those Who Care." Hope Lange and Angela Powell continued their roles as Jenny and Annie Preston. They now live in Tarzana at 747 Bonnie Vista Road. New to the cast were Max Mathias (Dick Van Patten), the show's producer; Alex Montez

(Henry Darrow), the director; and Dennis Whitehead (Barry Gordon), the show's writer.

Richard Richardson (Richard Dawson) is Dick's neighbor, an actor who stars in the televison series "Harrigan's Hooligans"; Connie Richardson (Chita Rivera) is Richard's wife; and Margot Brighton (Barbara Rush) is the star of "Those Who Care" (she plays Dr. Susan Allison, Brad's supervisor at Pleasant Valley Hospital).

Theme: "The New Dick Van Dyke Show Theme," by Jack Elliott and Allyn Ferguson.

513. *The New Gidget*

Syndicated, 9/86 to 9/88

Cast: Caryn Richman (*Gidget Griffin*), Dean Butler (*Jeff Griffin*), Sydney Penny (*Danni Collins*), William Schallert (*Russ Lawrence*), Lili Haydn (*Gail Baker*), Jill Jacobson (*Larue Powell*).

Facts: The home at 656 Glendale Avenue in Los Angeles is owned by Frances and Jeff Griffin, a young married couple who met as teenagers on Malibu Beach—when Jeff was a surfer called "Moondoggie" and Frances was nicknamed "Gidget" ("a girl who is not a giant or a midget—a Gidget"). Gidget now owns her own business (Gidget Travel) and Jeff is a city planner. Gidget's license plate reads GIDG TVL (she first had a Dodge van, then a Volkswagen Rabbit); their phone number is 555-1385 (later 555-9099).

Gidget and Jeff attended Westside High School. Jeff was taught to surf by the Great Kahuna (Don Stroud), a legendary surfer. Jeff entered the 1978 Laguna Open and won a surfboard for Gidget (when she first learned to surf, her friends kidded her about needing training wheels). Gidget turned her love for surfing into a home video called "Gidget's Guide to Surfing." Her biggest thrill as a kid was being called "Perky Doo-Bee" by Miss Connie on the television show "Romper Room." As a teenager, Gidget "tracked Frankie Avalon for three weeks just to get his autograph." She also became a fan of Lawrence Welk and has an autographed album from him. Jeff did a commercial with the Great Kahuna for Wipeout Deodorant. Jeff was originally a construction worker for the Bedford Construction Company.

Danielle ("Danni") Collins is Gidget's pretty niece (the daughter of her unseen sister, Anne). Danni is temporarily living with Gidget and Jeff while her parents are away on business. Gidget and Jeff are new to being parents "and we make it up as we go along in raising Danni."

Danni is tall, slender and very attractive, and she inherited Gidget's love for surfing. She and her friend, Gail Baker, attend Westside High School and listen to radio station K-GOLD. Like Gidget, Danni's favorite hangout is Malibu Beach. Danni calls Gidget "Aunt Gidget" and has a 9:00 P.M. curfew on school nights. She carries her Uncle Jeff's credit card "for emergency use only." Gidget and Danni eat Ghost Busters cereal for breakfast.

In 1986 Gidget staged the "Passion for Fashion Show" for

The New Gidget. **Front:** Caryn Richman (left) and Sydney Penny; **Back:** Dean Butler and William Schallert.

the P.T.A. (Danni and Gail were models); Danni was a contestant in the Young Debs Pageant.

Gidget's father, Russell ("Russ") Lawrence, is now retired (he was an English professor at UCLA) and assists Gidget at the travel agency (as does her longtime friend, Larue).

In the original pilot film, "Gidget's Summer Reunion" (syndicated, 6/85), Allison Barron was Gidget's niece, Kim; William Schallert was Gidget's father, Russ Hoover; and

Anne Lockhart played Gidget's friend, Larue. See also "Gidget."

Relatives: J. Michael Flynn (Danni's father, *John Collins*), R.J. Williams (Jeff's nephew, *Dennis*).

Flashbacks: Shiri Appleby *(Gidget as a girl)*, Bridget Hoffman *(Gidget's mother)*.

Theme: "One in a Million," by Jeff Vilinsky, Craig Snyder and Marek Norman.

514. *The New Lassie*

Syndicated, 9/24/89 to 9/15/91

Cast: Dee Wallace Stone (*Dee McCulloch*), Christopher Stone (*Chris McCulloch*), Wendy Cox (*Megan McCulloch*), Will Nipper (*Will McCulloch*), Jon Provost (*Steve McCulloch*).

Facts: Glen Ridge is a small town in California. At 415 Latimor Road live the McCullochs: parents Dee and Chris, their children, Megan and Will, and their dog, Lassie, a descendant of television's original 1954 Lassie, who became a part of the family (1986) when Chris rescued her from a car wreck and named her (a puppy at the time) Lassie.

Chris is self-employed and runs the McCulloch Construction Company. He has Scottish ancestors, and he and the family are members of the Highlands Lodge, a brotherhood of the McCulloch and McPhearson families (who purchased land in California over 100 years ago). Chris's license plates are 999 358 (4 × 4) and 938 IYN (sedan). Dee works at the Willingham Pet Adoption Center and did a television commercial with her family for Williams Flea Free Stay Free pet beds. When the pet agency closed, Dee acquired a job as a placement officer at the Glen Ridge Employment Agency.

Megan, who wears a perfume called Wind Shadow (ten dollars an ounce) attended Glen Ridge Elementary (first season), then Glen Ridge High. She is a cheerleader (for the Gophers football team) and worked after school with her mother at the pet adoption center. Megan is a budding photographer and has a plush stuffed rabbit named Gabby. Her girlfriend (second season) is Tracy Edmonston (played by Jodi Peterson). (In one episode, Megan mentioned attending Madison High School.)

Will, the youngest McCulloch, attends Glen Ridge Elementary School (first season) and the Evergreen School (second season). He has a lucky baseball catcher's mitt he calls "Trapper," and his first crush was on a tomboyish girl named Frankie Warren (Debbie Slaboda). Megan and Will's afterschool hangout is Dominick's Burger Palace.

Steve, a freelance writer and member of the Glen Ridge Hang Gliders Society, is Chris's adopted brother. Steve is actually Timmy Martin, the second owner of Lassie ("Timmy and Lassie," 1957-64). In this series, Timmy was the adopted son of Paul and Ruth Martin and lived on a farm in Calverton). In the episode "Roots" (11/89) it is learned that 25 years ago young Timmy was taken away from his foster parents. Later, Timmy began using his middle name of Steve and was adopted by the McCulloch family. In 1989 Ruth Martin-Chadwick (June Lockhart), Timmy's first adoptive mother (now remarried) tracks Chris down to reclaim her dog—the puppy Chris rescued from the car wreck. Ruth is unaware that Timmy is now Steve or part of a new family. It is a bittersweet reunion—Timmy blames Ruth for abandoning him—until Ruth explains that she fought tooth and nail to get him back but couldn't. When Ruth sees how much Will and Lassie love each other, she allows the McCullochs to keep Lassie.

In the episode of 11/25/90 Tommy Rettig, Lassie's original owner (1954–57), appeared as Professor Jeff Miller and was reunited with Jon Provost when Steve and Will bring Lassie to the university for an experimental project involving dogs and computers.

The episode of 12/16/90 saw Lassie become the owner of a gold credit card (number 562-4309-72112) when the First Monument National Bank issued one to Ms. Lassie McCulloch with a credit line of $15,000.

Roddy McDowall appeared in several episodes as Andrew Leeds, a famous writer and friend of the McCullochs; in first season episodes, a stray cat named Sam frequented the McCullochs' house for food.

Theme: "The New Lassie Theme," by Al Burton and Timothy Thompson; whistle by Les Baxter.

Note: See also "Jeff's Collie."

515. *The New Leave It to Beaver*

TBS, 9/86 to 9/89 (cable)

Cast: Barbara Billingsley (*June Cleaver*), Tony Dow (*Wally Cleaver*), Jerry Mathers (*Beaver Cleaver*), Ken Osmond (*Eddie Haskell*), Janice Kent (*Mary Ellen Cleaver*), Kaleena Kiff (*Kelly Cleaver*), John Snee (*Oliver Cleaver*), Kipp Marcus (*Kip Cleaver*), Ellen Maxted (*Gert Haskell*), Eric Osmond (*Freddie Haskell*), Christian Osmond (*Bomber Haskell*), Frank Bank (*Lumpy Rutherford*), Keri Houlihan (*J.J. Rutherford*).

Facts: An updated version of "Leave It to Beaver" (see entry) that continues to depict events in the lives of the Cleaver family. June is now a widow and a member of the Mayfield City Council. She lives in the original series house at 211 Pine Street with her younger son, Theodore ("Beaver") Cleaver, and his two sons, Kip and Ollie; Beaver is divorced from Kimberly (Joanna Gleason). Kip attends Mayfield High School, and Oliver, the Grant Avenue School. Beaver is now partners with Clarence ("Lumpy") Rutherford in the Cleaver and Rutherford Company (exactly what they do is not revealed). Lumpy is now married and the father of a daughter (J.J.).

Wally, June's older son, is an attorney and lives at 213 Pine Street. He is married to Mary Ellen, and they have a daughter named Kelly. Mary Ellen was Wally's high school sweetheart (played in the original series by Pamela Beaird); Kelly attends the Grant Avenue Grammar School and is a member of the Junior Chipmunks. She is also part of the Mayfield Youth soccer team and the Soda Shop is her favorite afterschool hangout. Oliver, called "Ollie" by Beaver, has a pet dove named Wilma, hangs out with Kelly, and his favorite place to hide is in the clothes hamper. Kip's first job was attendant at Vince's Full Service gas station.

Eddie Haskell is now married to Gert and is the father of two boys, Freddie and Bomber. He is still the same wisecracking character he was in the 1960s. Eddie, who still watches "Woody Woodpecker" cartoons on television, owns the rather slipshodly run Eddie Haskell Construction Company. Beer and pop tarts is Eddie's favorite breakfast, and chocolate pudding is his favorite dessert. Gert's maiden name is Bronson; Freddie (who takes after Eddie), attends Mayfield High School. Bomber (also mischievous) is enrolled at the Vicksburg Military School.

The population of Mayfield is 18,240; June's license plate reads NO. 1 MOM; Beaver's license plate is 6102; Lumpy's Mercedes's license plate is 203056.

Theme: "The Toy Parade" (new adaptation by Cabo Frio).

The New Operation Petticoat see Operation Petticoat

516. The New Phil Silvers Show

CBS, 9/28/63 to 6/27/64

Cast: Phil Silvers (*Harry Grafton*), Stafford Repp (*Fred Brink*), Herbie Faye (*Waluska*), Jim Shane (*Lester*), Pat Renella (*Roxy Klinger*).

Facts: Plant 4 of Osborne Industries in Los Angeles is the location. Office B-116 of Factory D is the base of operations. Harry Grafton, the maintenance department foreman, is the man assigned to that office. There is a picture of Harry on the side wall (behind it is a secret safe), and there is a secret room located behind the back wall. There is an illuminated sign above the door that reads HONESTY IS THE ENEMY OF GREED. While Osborne Industries makes everything from plumbing supplies to machinery parts, Harry has his own business called Grafton Enterprises, which he runs from his office and struggles to keep secret from his superiors. Harry is the only man who can get the assembly line started again when it breaks down; he is also a master manipulator who is totally dedicated to acquiring money (he has a coffee break service called Harry Grafton's Coffee Break Wagon).

Harry's favorite colors are green and gold; his birthday is on the seventeenth (there is no month listed on the calendar); and his 160-year-old turtle (for the annual turtle races) is named Cyclone.

Fred H. Brink (hard hat number 51) is the plant supervisor. When Brink approaches Harry's office, the word *Enemy* in the sign above the door blinks, and the lights around a picture of Fred (next to a picture of George Washington) flash. In the opening theme, Harry is seen in animated form, and he says, "Glad to see ya." When the factory whistle blows smoke for the show's title and star, Phil Silvers's name appears in various combinations (for instance, Slip Hilvers, Shil Pilvers).

Waluska, Roxy and Lester are Harry's assistants and cohorts in crime. Douglas Dumbrille played the company owner, Mr. Osborne. The series is a reworking of the Sergeant Bilko character from "The Phil Silvers Show" (see entry).

Relatives: Elena Verdugo (Harry's sister, *Audrey*), Sandy Descher (Audrey's daughter, *Susan*), Ronnie Dapo (Audrey's son, *Andy*), Evelyn Patrick (Osborne's niece, *Della Osborne*).

Theme: "Theme from The New Phil Silvers Show," by Harry Geller.

517. The New WKRP in Cincinnati

Syndicated, 9/7/91 to the present

Cast: Gordon Jump (*Arthur Carlson*), Richard Sanders (*Les Nessman*), Frank Bonner (*Herb Tarlek*), Tawny Kitaen (*Mona Loveland*).

Facts: A revised version of "WKRP in Cincinnati" (see entry). WKRP, 1530 on the AM dial, is a 5,000 watt rock station in Ohio. The station made its premiere broadcast on December 7, 1941, with the news story "The Japanese have just attacked Pearl Harbor." The station is still located on the fourteenth floor of the Flimm Building and is still very low rated. Its slogan is "The Mighty 1530 AM."

Arthur Carlson manages the station for his mother, Lillian ("Mama") Carlson (Carol Bruce); his late father founded WKRP. Arthur has high hopes that one day the station will crack the top ten. He rarely listens to WKRP and spends most of his day dreaming about fishing, reading magazines (for example, *Ohio Fisherman*) and playing with various toys (from yo-yos to computer games). He has a plaque on his office wall that reads THE FISHERMAN IS FISHING (or sometimes THE FISHERMAN IS HOME). Arthur's wife, Carmen (Allyn Ann McLerie), runs a business called Carmen's Crystal Critter Corner in the Pinedale Mall.

Les Nessman is WKRP's news director. He has been with the station for more than 20 years and won the Buckeye Hawk News Award nine times. He still wears a bandage (to remind him of an injury he received in 1978 on the original series) and still has "invisible walls" that surround his desk in the bull pen office. Les has a bird named Hilda and calls himself "The News Beacon of the Ohio Valley." He leaves for work every day at 6:32 A.M.

Herb Tarlek is still the station's salesman. He is still married to Lucille (Edie McClurg), and he still hits on every beautiful girl he sees. He continues to call Arthur "Big Guy."

Mona Loveland is the late night D.J. (her character replaced Venus Flytrap from the original series). Mona's sexy voice has made her a hot item at the station. Her show, "Mona Till Midnight," begins at 9:00 P.M. with these words: "This is Mona Loveland, I'll be your guide to dreamland. It's just you and me and music till midnight."

Mona, who loves to wear blouses that accentuate her well-developed bosom, says, "I have a hard time finding bikini tops that fit." She is a Leo and was a compulsive gambler who resolved her problem through professional counseling. She lives in a former firehouse.

Dana Burns (Kathleen Garrett) and Jack Allen (Michael Des Barres) are divorced D.J.'s who host a music and talk program called "The Burns and Allen Show" (the replacement for Dr. Johnny Fever). Radical D.J. Razor Dee (French Stewart) replaced "Burns and Allen" in second season episodes. Dee works as "The Razor Man" and was a monks' barber for two years in the Order of Our Lady of the Forgetful.

Ronnie Lee (Wendy Davis) was the first receptionist (Jennifer Marlowe's replacement). Ronnie, a Virgo, was not as glamorous or buxom as Jennifer and was dropped (she was said to be attending night school to get her master's degree). She was replaced by Nancy Brinkwink (Marla Jeanette Rubinoff), a busty blonde who has the hots for "the only man for me—Herb." Nancy has a B.A. in communications from Dennison College and was a former buyer for Studor and James in Cincinnati (she left the job because all the men she worked with were either married or gay). If Nancy thinks another girl is hitting on Herb, she says, "OK, here's the story. You're kinda cute. Herb is a hunk of a man. He oozes charm and he reeks class. You remember one thing—he's mine!"

Claire Hartline (Hope Alexander-Willis) is the traffic manager (she arranges commercial time); her character replaced Bailey Quarters. Donovan Aderhold (Mykel T. Williamson) is the new program director (his character replaced Andy Travis). New to the concept was Arthur's son, Arthur Carlson, Jr. (Lightfield Lewis), the obnoxious junior salesman (Herb calls him "Little Big Guy").

Several series regulars from the old show appeared: Jennifer Marlowe (Loni Anderson) was first a wealthy widow ("My husband, Cesare, died on our honeymoon; he was smiling at the time"); she later announced her engagement to Reynaldo Roberio Ricky Ricardo Goulegant III (Robert Goulet), the prince of a small European country called Rosario Roberto. Venus Flytrap (Tim Reid) now lives in Washington, D.C. After leaving WKRP he acquired a job with BET (Black Entertainment TV), first in marketing, then as chief executive officer.

Dr. Johnny Fever (Howard Hesseman) was first living in New York's Greenwich Village and writing a book about rock and roll music. Hesseman received special guest star billing in second season episodes when Johnny returned to WKRP as the new overnight D.J.—the midnight to 6:00 A.M. shift. (He replaced the unseen Moss Steiger. Moss went up to the roof to smoke a cigarette. He fell off and landed on the theater marquee on the Fourth Street side of the building. An air conditioner came loose, fell on the marquee and tossed Moss into the street where he was hit by a bus. Chuck Blore provided Moss's voice.)

WPIG is still WKRP's main competition. To boost ratings, WKRP's staff staged an old time radio show called "Those Ugly Unspeakable Disgusting Things from Outer Space." The biggest promotion gimmick ever at WKRP was the free mug giveaway (callers got a mug with the call letters "WRKP" on it; the station got the mugs for free because of a printer's error).

Theme: "WKRP in Cincinnati," by Tom Wells and Jim Ellis.

518. *Newhart*

CBS, 10/25/82 to 9/8/90

Cast: Bob Newhart (*Dick Loudon*), Mary Frann (*Joanna Loudon*), Julia Duffy (*Stephanie Vanderkellen*), Tom Poston (*George Utley*), Peter Scolari (*Michael Harris*), William Sanderson (*Larry*), Tony Papenfuss (*Darryl One*), John Volstad (*Darryl Two*).

Facts: Richard ("Dick") Loudon, a history buff and "how-to" book author, and his wife, Joanna, own the 200-year-old Stratford Inn at 28 Westbrook Road in River City, Vermont.

Dick attended Cunningham Elementary School. In college Dick was the drummer in a band called the Jazz Tones (he was nicknamed "Slats" Loudon). His favorite sport is diving, and as a kid he attended Camp Cowapoka; he also had a goldfish named Ethel Merman. Dick has written such books as *Pillow Talk* (how to make pillows), *How to Make Your Dream Bathroom* and *Installation and Care of Your Low Maintenance Lawn Sprinkler*. His first novel was *Murder at the Stratley* (a takeoff on the Stratford Inn). Dick wears a size 8½ DDD shoe and hosts the televison show "Vermont Today" on WPIV, Channel 8. Dick's most devastating act was accidentally burning down the French restaurant Maison Hubert (he carelessly tossed a cigarette in the wastebasket in the men's room).

Joanna was born in Gainsville, Ohio. She and Dick met when they both worked for an ad agency in New York City. Their first date was at a Memorial Day picnic. Joanna's maiden name is McKenna; she loves to wear sweaters but on their anniversary Dick gives her a yellow scarf. Joanna is a real estate broker and hosts a television show called "Your House Is My House" on Channel 8; the show was later called "Hot Houses." Joanna holds the town record for renting the video "60 Days to a Tighter Tummy."

George Utley, Dick's handyman, is a member of the Beaver Lodge (the annual Beaver Bash is on the Memorial Day weekend, and the featured meal is a spaghetti and tomato sauce sit-down dinner). George has a favorite hammer he calls "Old Blue" and invented the board game "Handyman: The Feel Good Game." He does birdwatching at Johnny Kaye Lake, and when he is upset he rents the movie *It's a Mad, Mad, Mad, Mad World*. "The Goldbergs" was his favorite radio program; "Barnaby Jones" and "It's Always Moisha" (a mythical series starring Don Rickles) are his favorite television shows. George keeps a lucky penny in his shoe or sock.

Stephanie Vanderkellen is Dick and Joanna's maid. She is the spoiled daughter of a wealthy family (who live in Newport) and took the job to experience real life. Stephanie replaced her sister, Leslie Vanderkellen (Jennifer Holmes), the original maid, when she left to complete her education at Oxford. In addition to being spoiled, Stephanie is very moody and looks down on people of lower social status. She buys her designer clothes at Peck's Department Store and had a show on WPIV called "Seein' Double" (in which she played twins Jody and Judy Bumpter; Dick Loudon played her father, Henry Bumpter, and the show was produced, written and directed by Stephanie's boyfriend, Michael Harris).

Michael was an executive at WPIV (he produced Dick's show), then a salesman at Circus of Shoes after he was fired for insulting the boss's daughter. He was then a produce clerk at Menke's Market, a mime, and finally a resident of the Pine Valley Psychiatric Hospital. Michael is totally devoted to Stephanie, calls her "Cupcake," "Gumdrop" and "Muffin" and constantly showers her with gifts. He has a special area in his apartment (9B) devoted to photographs of Stephanie which he calls "Cupcake Corner." To give Stephanie even more gifts, Michael created "Cupcake Day," which comes between Valentine's Day and Easter. As a kid, Michael was the singing assistant to Captain Cookie on the television show "Captain Cookie's Clubhouse." He and Stephanie once sought professional relationship counseling under the assumed names Chuck and Dawn. In 1989 Stephanie became pregnant and gave birth to a girl she and Michael named Baby Stephanie (played at age five by Candy Hutson).

Larry and his two nonspeaking brothers, Darryl and Darryl, are rural types who own the local diner, the Minuteman Café. Larry attended the Mount Pilard Technical School; Darryl One was enrolled at Oxford University; and Darryl Two, who majored in royalty, attended Cambridge University under a rowing scholarship. Larry does all the talking for his brothers. When he enters a scene, he starts by saying, "Hello. My name is Larry. This is my brother, Darryl, and this is my other brother, Darryl."

The flounder is the town fish, and the flying squirrel is the town's bird. The key to the city won't open anything, but it will start Willie Frye's tractor.

On May 21, 1990, the final first-run episode aired: "The Last Newhart." Mr. Takadachi (Gedde Watanabe) offers each resident of the town one million dollars for their property with a plan of building the 5,000-room Takadachi Hotel and golf course. All but Dick and Joanna sell. Michael and Stephanie, with plans to build "Stefi Land," move to Switzerland; George, who once bought some land when he was drunk to build "Utley Land" (an amusement park for handymen), sells it; and Larry and the Darryls move to Chicago to live with an uncle.

Five years later, the Stratford Inn is on the fourteenth fairway, and it has a Japanese motif. It is also the site for a reunion of the old gang. With the exception of Larry and the Darryls, all have remained the same. Larry is now married to Ronda (Christie Mellor), Darryl One has wed Sada (Lisa Kudrow) and Darryl Two is married to Zora (Nada Despotovich). The occasion marks the first time the Darryls speak—to yell "Quiet!" at their arguing wives ("They never spoke before," Larry says, "because nothing ever pissed them off before").

As the reunion becomes unruly, Dick decides to leave. He is standing in the doorway when he is hit by a golf ball. He passes out and the screen goes black. A figure is seen in bed. He switches on the light, and we see that it is not Dick Loudon but Dr. Bob Hartley (from "The Bob Newhart Show"). His wife, Emily (Suzanne Pleshette), asks what is wrong, and Bob proceeds to tell her about a horrible nightmare in which he was an innkeeper and married to a beautiful blonde; about an heiress for a maid; about three strange brothers....

Apparently, the eight years of "Newhart" were but the one night's dream of Dr. Bob Hartley.

Relatives: Bob Elliott (Dick's father, *Bill Loudon*), Peggy McCay (Joanna's mother, *Florence McKenna*), Nancy Walker (Joanna's aunt, *Louise*), Richard Roat and José Ferrer (Stephanie's father, *Arthur Vanderkellen*), Priscilla Morrill (Stephanie's mother, *Mary Vanderkellen*), Ann Morgan Guilbert (George's aunt, *Bess*), Derek McGrath (George's cousin, *Eugene Wiley*), Ruth Manning (Michael's mother, *Lily Cassiano*), Henry Gibson (Michael's father, *Ted Harris*).

Flashbacks: Jason Marin *(George as a boy)*, Tom Poston *(George's father)*.

Theme: "The Newhart Theme," by Henry Mancini.

519. *Nichols*

NBC, 9/16/71 to 8/8/72

The series is set in the town of Nichols, Arizona, in 1914. A former cavalry officer called only Nichols (James Garner), returns to his hometown after an 18 year absence. He discovers that the town, which was founded by his parents, no longer belongs to him; it has been taken from his late mother by two mean brothers named Scully One (John Quade) and Scully Two (Jesse Wayne). With no plans to stay in town, Nichols decides to drown his sorrows. At the Salter House Bar, Nichols begins to talk with Ruth (Margot Kidder), the barmaid. When Ketcham (John Beck) thinks Nichols is flirting with Ruth (whom he considers his girlfriend), a fight breaks out. Nichols is arrested and held responsible for $300 in damages. When Sara ("Ma") Ketcham (Neva Patterson), Ketcham's mother and the town's self-appointed law, finds that Nichols cannot pay what he owes, she sentences him to six months' duty as sheriff. Though reluctant, Nichols becomes the sheriff—"But don't let that worry you, it's only a sideline." His real genius, though, is at the con—which he uses to outwit the bad guys and help maintain the peace.

Nichols, who lives in Room 3 of the Salter House Hotel, is assisted by "Mitch" Mitchell (Stuart Margolin), a deputy who reports directly to Sara and obeys her every command. Mitch has a dog named Slump.

Ketcham, who has no first name (Sara calls him "Ketch"), drives a car with the license plate AB1Z. Nichols rides a 1914 model motorcycle. He was with the U.S. Cavalry's 19th Unit and was the division's boxing champion.

Ruth sleeps with a Colt .45 under her pillow, carries a

large hatpin for protection in her purse and hides a tiny derringer in her bosom-revealing dress near her heart. "I have ambitions to be a sheriff," she says. "But since I'm a woman and can't, I'm happy where I am."

The series, which was expected to be renewed, was not, and the last episode introduced a more courageous and forceful hero named Jim Nichols (James Garner)—Nichols's twin brother. When Nichols attempts to break up a bar-room brawl, he is killed. Several days later, Jim arrives in town. After learning what has happened, he apprehends his brother's killer. Sara offers him the job of sheriff, but Jim refuses. In a substituted ending, Jim leaves town, never to return.

Bernard Segall composed the "Nichols" theme.

520. *Night Court*

NBC, 1/4/84 to 5/13/92

Cast: Harry Anderson *(Harry T. Stone)*, Markie Post *(Christine Sullivan)*, Richard Moll *(Bull)*, John Larroquette *(Dan Fielding)*, Charles Robinson *(Mac Robinson)*, Marsha Warfield *(Roz Russell)*, Joleen Lutz *(Lisette Hocheiser)*.

Facts: The Manhattan Criminal Courts Building in New York City is the setting for a comical look at life inside the night court of arraignment judge Harold T. ("Harry") Stone. The building is also called the Municipal Court House, and Harry's sessions are held on the eighteenth floor in Room 808 (1808 in some episodes).

The name *Harold T. Stone* was the last one on a list of prospective judges. It was a Sunday, the mayor's last day in office, and he had to appoint a judge for a spot on the criminal courts bench. Each name on the list was called, but nobody was home—except for Harry ("It was a Sunday, I was home and I got the job"). Harry attended East Chesapeake State College and attempted to break into show business as a magician. His idol is singer Mel Tormé (he owns every record Mel ever made and has decided to marry the first girl who is impressed by that). Harry also has a picture of Jean Harlow behind the desk in his office (a framed picture of Mel Tormé graces his desk). Harry's inability to meet Mel under normal circumstances was a recurring gimmick of the series.

Magic and genetics are Harry's hobbies; he bowls at the Bowl-a-Line alleys. He eats Zipp Bits breakfast cereal and mentioned that cherry Kool-Aid and Fresca soda were his favorite drinks. Harry has a pet rabbit named Cecil; as a kid he had a dog named Oliver and a teddy bear named Jamboree. When he was a teenager, Harry stole a 1964 Cadillac for a joy ride. His foot slipped off the pedal and he knocked over a liquor store with the car. He spent two nights in jail and two weeks in a reformatory as a result.

Harry, voted "Most Fascinating Judge in New York" by the Empire Magicians' Society, processes 12 percent fewer cases than any other judge in his position (the reason: he talks to defendants and lectures them). Harry was also voted "Man of the Month" by the Society of Goodfellows, and he

had a part in a television pilot called "The Littlest Lawyer" (about a kid attorney).

Harry's true love is magic: his hero is Harry Houdini, and his favorite television show as a kid was "Magic Time." Harry's lucky charm is a Mercury-head dime, and he teaches law classes at the Ed Koch Community College (Ed Koch is the former mayor of New York; the school's mascot is a pigeon that got caught in the air conditioning vent). Harry is also faculty advisor for the school's newspaper, the *Harpoon*. He is also famous for his "$55 and time served" sentences.

"My, what a pretty blouse," says Harry when he first meets Christine Sullivan, the legal aid attorney. "Your honor," replies Christine, "I would prefer if the court not think of me as a nervous woman who needs to be placated with compliments about the state of her wardrobe. I don't want to be treated any differently because I have breasts."

Christine was born in the small town of North Tonawanda near Buffalo, New York. As a girl, she had a dog named Puddles and dreamed of becoming an ice skater, competing in the Olympics and winning a gold medal for the United States. The ice stopped her ("It's slippery on that stuff"). At age 19 she was a junior in Buffalo State College and majored in psychology (she is now an expert on depression). Christine measured 37-23-35 and entered the Miss Greater Buffalo Beauty Pageant of 1978; she lost for taking a stand on women's rights.

Christine is very beautiful and always fashionably dressed. She is easily exasperated and often remarks, "I should have worn my underwire" (she has a tendency "to jiggle," as the lecherous Dan Fielding says, when she gets upset). She lived in the following apartments: 1611E, 616 and 7C (addresses not given). She is a member of "Ha Ha" (Happy Alone, Happy Adults; their slogan is "Happy to Be Happy"), has a car (not seen) with Happy Face hubcaps and says, "The most artistic people I get as clients are hookers with makeup skills." Christine mentioned in one episode that in her youth, she gave up the chance to become the Buffalo Starch Queen.

Christine lost the first case she ever had. She broke out in tears, hyperventilated and had to be dragged out of the courtroom (the case involved a man who tried to dismantle a record store with his bare hands). In 1990 Christine had a one night stand with an undercover cop named Tony Juliano (Ray Abruzzo). She became pregnant and married Tony in an Italian restaurant. Tony left the following day to track down a criminal in Colombia. Because of Tony's absence, Christine had her night court friends as her pregnancy coaches (she chose "The Song of the Humpback Whale" as her birthing song). In the episode of 5/2/90, Christine becomes trapped in an elevator and gives birth to a boy (whom she names Charles Otis). In a flash-forward sequence prior to the birth (3/28/90), Christine envisioned her unborn child as both a boy named Tony Jr. (Benny Grant) and as a girl named Toni (Nikki Cox). When Christine returned from maternity leave, she handed out videos called "Charles Otis Juliano—The Movie." She and Tony divorced in the episode of 2/6/91. When a street artist named Ian McKee (Bill Calvert) became inspired by Christine, he painted a large mural of her on a warehouse door called "The Naked Body of Justice." Christine's father calls her "Peaches"; she wrote a children's book called *Mommy's World* under the pen name Mother Sullivan. In the episode of 2/12/92 Christine ran for congresswoman of the 13th District; she was elected to Congress in the final first-run episode (5/13/92) and moved to Washington, D.C., to begin her new career.

Reinhold Fielding Elmore (he assumed the name Dan Fielding when he started school) was born in Paris, Louisiana. His parents were rural, and he lived with pigs in his room. He was six before he realized he wasn't related to them. His parents named all their kids and pigs after characters in books. Dan's hometown was founded by his great-grandfather. As an infant, Dan also thought he had a pet turtle named Scruffy (he was two years old when he found out that his father had pained a potato to look like a turtle). As a teenager Dan worked as a lifeguard at the Lone Star Beach Club in Galveston, Texas (during the summer of 1967).

Dan now lives in an apartment on Hauser Street on Third Avenue in Manhattan. He is the prosecuting attorney and drives a Mercedes with the license plate HOT TO TROT. Dan, a ladies' man, calls his car "The Dan Mobile" and has an Annette Funicello inflatable doll on backorder. Dan has been in the army reserve for the past five years and has stock in a company called the Fletko Corporation (which is famous for tearing down landmarks). He is also the overseer of the Phil Foundation, a charity that supports needy causes (when Dan's flunky, a bum named Phil Alfonce Sanders [Will Utay], was killed by a falling piano, it was discovered that he was rich and had willed Dan eight million dollars to use for charity).

Dan hosted a television show called "In Your Face" (a putdown show) and picks up girls at a club called the Sticky Wickey. When Christine became pregnant, Dan started a "Guess the Size of Her Boobs" contest on television (he referred to Christine's breasts as "puppies" during her pregnancy). Dan dreams of working for the law firm of Taylor, Woods and Johnson. Girls call Dan "The Prince of Passion." Dan left his job in the last episode to pursue the woman of his dreams—Christine—in Washington.

On a judicial system I.Q. test, bailiff Bull Shannon scored 181; despite this, his friends still think he is "dumber than dirt." His real first name is Nostradamus; he got the name Bull from his mother (she said "Bull" when she found out she was pregnant). Bull's favorite television show is "The Smurfs," and he has a pet python named Bertha (he later has one called Harvey). When he gets depressed, Bull retreats to the Museum of Natural History to talk to the early man exhibits; in later episodes he goes to the roof of the courthouse. As a young man Bull worked as an usher at the Majestic Theater. He attempted to write a children's book called *Bully the Dragon* (but it scared kids); he then wrote *The Azzari Sisters: An Adventure in Fun, The Snake Pit of Chuckie's Mind* and *Bull on Bull*. When *Bull on Bull* was rejected by 426 publishers, he had it published by the vanity press Random Author; he bought enough copies to make it a best-seller at $11 a copy.

Bull eats Frosted Neon Nuggets Cereal for breakfast. He entered the "Little Tikes Golly-Gee-O-Rama" cereal contest and won the mystery prize—the Shatner Turbo 2000 Whimberly Wig. Bull's address is given only as Apartment 7 (there is a giant *B* on his front door). He has a concrete sofa ("durable, practical and easy to patch") that he made himself. The apartment is next to a subway line and shakes when a train passes.

Because Christine is so sweet and kind to Bull, he calls her "a lily pad in a pond full of sludge." Bull is very devoted to Harry—"I'd swallow molten lava for that man. Fortunately, he never asked me." He also says people mistake his humor for a rare pituitary disease. Bull still believes in Santa Claus and had a short career as a wrestler (Bull, the Battling Bailiff).

Bull weighs 250 pounds and earns $320 a week. He uses lacquer thinner to remove the shine from his bald head. Bull is also a member of the Volunteer Father Organization. The first child he was assigned was named Andy (Pamela Segall), whom Bull thought was a boy (her real name was Stella and she pretended to be a boy because the organization would not assign fathers to girls). In the episode of 11/20/91, Bull married Wanda (Cathy Appleby) on the roof of the courthouse (Bull wore his mother's wedding dress, which she made into a jacket; Harry performed the ceremony). In the last episode, Bull is taken to the planet Jupiter by two aliens to become somebody—"The man who can reach the items on our top shelves."

Mac Robinson is the court clerk. He is married to a pretty Vietnamese women named Quon Le Dac (Denice Kumagai), who works as a checker at the Vegetable Mart. Mac met Quon Le in Vietnam during the war. She was only 12 years old and fell in love with him when he helped her family overcome the ravages of recent bombings. In 1985 Quon Le left Vietnam when the new regime took over and came to New York to find Mac. Mac married her in an attempt to keep her in the United States. They had planned to annul the marriage, but decided against it when they discovered they loved each other.

In his youth, Mac was a singer with the group the Starlights, "before they became famous." Mac taped 60 hours of Bull's wedding and turned it into a 90 minute movie called *Connubial Fusion*. Mac's love for movie making caused him to quit night classes at City College in law to turn to film classes.

Rosalind ("Roz") Russell is a bailiff and earns $410 a week. She does volunteer work for Toys for Toddlers at the Canal Street Youth Center and hates to have her picture taken (when she was a kid, they said her picture looked like that of famous comedian Slappy White). Before becoming a bailiff, Roz was a stewardess for Paramus Airlines (it was here that she found her goal in life "was to kick butt"; a group of annoying passengers made her "see the light"). She was married to Eugene Westfall (Roger E. Mosley) for six weeks (she met him at the senior prom; he was a member of the band, the Expectations).

Lana Wagner (Karen Austin) was the original court clerk; she was engaged to a never-seen man named Emerson. Lana was on the dean's list at college and edited the school's poetry magazine. She was replaced by D.D. Howard as Charli Tracy; Mac Robinson then replaced Charli.

In the original pilot, Gail Strickland played Sheila Gardner, the public defender. Sheila was replaced by Liz Williams (Paula Kelly). Wilhelmina ("Billie") Young (Ellen Foley) replaced Liz. Mary (Deborah Harmon) replaced Billie and Christine replaced Mary as the legal aid lawyer.

Selma Hacker (Selma Diamond) and Florence Kleiner (Florence Halop) were the female bailiffs before Roz. Selma was a chainsmoker and hadn't missed a day of work in 27 years. Florence had the maiden name of Nightingale and "went through hell in grade school."

Lisette Hocheiser is the pretty, curly haired blonde court stenographer. She is a sweet girl who knits sweaters for birds and gets a kick out of folding socks. Lisette whines to get what she wants, has a goldfish named Orca, a lamp she calls Sparky and a plush giraffe named Too Tall. She takes mosaic classes and sells Cantel Cosmetics in her spare time.

Craven (Terry Kiser) is the sleazy court reporter for the New York *Herald*. Buddy Ryan (John Astin) is Harry's stepfather (he spent much of his time in a mental hospital; 1977, for example, was the year Buddy devoted to figuring out ways to get Gilligan off the island. He thought of 10,000 ways—excluding building a raft out of bamboo). Buddy is now married to Amanda (Karen Morrow). Harry's unnamed mother abandoned him and his father when he was five years old. She spent time in a mental hospital where she met and later married Buddy. Harry's mother died 23 years later. Shortly after, Buddy found Harry to give him something his mother left for him: a Groucho Marx face mask (as Buddy says, Harry inherited his mother's weird sense of humor).

Relatives: Eugene Roche (Christine's father, *Jack Sullivan*), John McIntire (Dan's father, *"Daddy" Bob Elmore*), Jeanette Nolan (Dan's mother, *Musette Elmore*), Susan Diol (Dan's sister, *Donna Elmore*, the vice president of Farmer Frank Meats, Inc.), Paddi Edwards (Bull's mother, *Henrietta ("Hank") Shannon*), Gordon Clapp (Bull's cousin, *Ralph Shannon*, a crooked lawyer), Keye Luke (Quon Le's father, *Ho Dac*), Charles Lampkin (Mac's father, *Clarence Robinson*), Della Reese (Roz's aunt, *Ruth*). Unseen were Harry's uncle, Otto, and Roz's uncle, Lionel.

Theme: "Night Court," by Jack Elliott.

Note: NBC first attempted a comedy series about a night court in "Sirota's Court" (12/1/76 to 4/13/77), wherein Matthew Sirota (Michael Constantine) was the compassionate night court judge. Maureen O'Connor (Cynthia Harris) was the court clerk; Gail Goodman (Kathleen Miller), the public defender; Sawyer Dabney (Ted Ross), the private attorney and H.P. ("Bud") Nugent (Fred Willard), the assistant D.A.

521. *The Night Stalker*

ABC, 9/13/74 to 8/30/75

Cast: Darren McGavin (*Carl Kolchak*), Simon Oakland (*Tony Vincenzo*).

Facts: When first introduced in the television movie *The Night Stalker* (ABC, 1/11/72), Carl Kolchak is a down-on-his-luck reporter for the Las Vegas *Daily News*. He has been a reporter for 22 years, and he apparently first becomes involved with the supernatural when he attempts to prove that Janos Skorzeny (Barry Atwater) is a modern-day vampire and responsible for the deaths of several showgirls. Although he does prove it (and kills Janos by driving a stake through his heart), Carl is prevented by the police from printing his story; he is charged with murder (but not jailed) and ordered to leave town.

Carl, who wears a white suit and hat, next turns up in Seattle as a reporter for the Washington, D.C., *Daily Chronicle* (in the television movie, *The Night Strangler*, ABC, 1/16/73). Here, Carl tries to solve the bizarre murders of young women: beginning in 1889, and every 21 years thereafter (during an 18 day period from March 29 through April 16), six women have been murdered—found with crushed necks and partially drained of blood. Carl discovers that the crimes were committed by Dr. Richard Malcolm (Richard Anderson), a doctor who had found a means of gaining immortality which requires human blood.

When the series begins, Carl is a reporter for the INS (Independent News Service) in Chicago. His easily exasperated editor, Anthony ("Tony") Vincenzo, has assigned him to investigate stories of general interest, not the bizarre (which Carl manages to stumble upon week after week). Episodes relate the constant bickering between the two men as Carl defies Tony and seeks stories involving supernatural creatures.

The telephone number of the INS is 555-8842. Ruth McDevitt plays Emily Cowles, the INS advice columnist ("Dear Emily"); Jack Grinnage is INS reporter Ron Updyke; and John Fiedler is Gordon ("Gordie the Ghoul") Spangler, Carl's contact at the morgue. Simon Oakland also played Carl's editor, Tony Vincenzo, in both television movies; Darren McGavin also narrates each episode.

Theme: "The Night Stalker," by Gil Mille; Robert Cobert composed the television movie version themes.

522. *Nightingales*

NBC, 1/21/89 to 4/26/89

Nightingale House is a dorm for student nurses in Los Angeles. It has 20 rooms and two clothes dryers. Christine Broderick (Suzanne Pleshette), the director of student nursing at Wilshire Memorial Hospital, is the den mother to the featured nurses: Samantha ("Sam") Sullivan (Chelsea Field), Allyson Yates (Kim Ulrich), Bridget Loring (Susan Walters), Becky Grainger (Kristy Swanson) and Yolonda ("Yoyo") Puente (Roxann Biggs).

Christine attended the Wellington School of Nursing in 1968; she took the job as den mother when the previous woman "took a job up north and suddenly left." At Wilshire Memorial, a teaching hospital, Christine has office 728. Samantha, who teaches "Cardio Funk" (aerobics) at the

523. Nightmare Café; 524. 9 to 5

Health Club, was an alcoholic who lost custody of her daughter, Megan (Taylor Fry), to her mother, Effie Gardner (Jennifer Rhodes); Sam is now waging a court battle to regain custody of Megan. Bridget is in the witness protection program (she witnessed a murder); and Becky mentioned she is from a town called Blue Springs. Room 124 is the nurses' lounge at the hospital; Megan's address was given as 2300 Laurel Drive. The series has little trivia but many "lingerie scenes." (Each episode features some or all the student nurses in their underwear. It is the first time lingerie became a "vital" part of an American series. The scenes, which included some in the opening theme, were blasted by critics and eventually caused the show's cancellation when it became "to hot to handle.")

Dr. Paul Petrillo (Gil Gerard) is Christine's ex-husband; Dr. Garrett Braden (Barry Newman) is head of the hospital; and Charlene Chasen (Doran Clark) is the "evil" doctor who opposed Christine. In the original pilot film (6/27/88), Mimi Kuzak played Liz McCarren, the den mother.

Additional Relatives: Scott Curtis (Garrett's son, *Scott Braden*), David Gale (Becky's father, *David Grainger*), Carol Mayo Jenkins (Becky's mother, *Evelyn Grainger*), William Cort *(Allyson's father)*.

Theme: "Nightingales," by John E. Davis.

523. *Nightmare Café*

NBC, 1/29/92 to 4/3/92

The All Night Café is located near the docks in Los Angeles. The café has strange powers: it gives people a second chance at life, the opportunity to go back and relive a crucial moment that can alter their future existence. A mysterious man named Blackie (Robert Englund) operates the café "for a higher authority." Fay Peronovick (Lindsay Frost) is the waitress, and Frank Novak (Jack Coleman) is the cook. (The café needed a new waitress and cook; Fay and Frank's lives ended in the waters overlooking the café; Fay, when she was jilted and committed suicide; Frank, when he stumbled upon toxic waste polluters. Both were given a second chance to right their wrongs—by working at the café and helping other people through personal crises.)

Blackie seems sinister (possibly a messenger of the devil) and appears to delight in the circumstances that cause a person's downfall (he views second chance lives via a special television set in the café; he can also send Fay or Frank into that person's life to help). Blackie calls Fay "Faysie." Fay was born in Tulsa, and her middle name is Petula; she lived at 341 Gateway. Penny Fuller appeared as her mother, Victoria, and Molly Parker was Fay's sister, Ivy.

J. Peter Robinson composed the "Nightmare Café Theme."

90210 see *Beverly Hills, 90210*

524. *9 to 5*

ABC, 3/25/82 to 4/15/82
ABC, 9/28/82 to 10/27/83
Syndicated, 9/86 to 9/88

A television adaptation of the feature film about incidents in the lives of a group of secretaries at a large corporation. When the series first began, it was set at Consolidated Industries in Cleveland, Ohio. American Household Products (AHP) in New York City became the locale in second season episodes. In 1986-87 it was Berkley Foods International, and finally (1987-88) Barkley Foods International—both of which were located at 36 East 46th Street in Manhattan.

The Sexist Bosses: Franklin Hart, Jr. (Jeffrey Tambor), first date listing; Franklin Hart, Jr. (Peter Bonerz), 1982-83; Dag Larson (James Komack), 1983; and William ("Bud") Coleman (Edward Winter), third date listing. Last season syndicated episodes had one additional boss: E. Nelson Felb (Fred Applegate), the vice president of foreign sales.

The Assistants: Roz Keith (Jean Marsh), Hart's assistant, the Budget Department head; Charmin Cunningham (Dorian Lopinto), Bud's girl Friday; Harry Pearlman (Herb Edelman), a salesman, ABC episodes; Mike Henderson (George Deloy), a salesman, 1983 ABC episodes; and Russ Merman (Peter Evans), a salesman in syndicated episodes.

The Secretaries: Violet Newstead (Rita Moreno) was the secretarial supervisor in ABC episodes; Doralee Rhoades (Rachel Dennison) was Hart's secretary in ABC episodes; in syndicated episodes, she is Doralee Brooks, secretary to Bud and married to the never-seen Curtis Brooks.

Judy Burnley (Valerie Curtin) was originally an office secretary (ABC); later she is Russ's secretary. Marsha McMurray (Sally Struthers) was first Charmin's secretary, then Felb's. Third season episodes (9/28/83 to 10/27/83) also feature office secretary Linda Bowman (Leah Ayres).

Violet, who lives at 36 Fallon Avenue in Cleveland, is the mother of a young son (Tommy) and has the maiden name of Fernandez. To make extra money, she sold Loverware (sexy lingerie). Judy, whose maiden name is Zendell, lives in Manhattan on West 48th Street. Doralee, who is sweet and trusting, lives in an apartment at 102 West 72nd Street. Franklin is a Republican and, while he may be a sexist, does go out on a limb for his secretaries—"Didn't I break all the rules to get you Sweet and Low for the coffee room?" The *E* in Nelson's name stands for Excellent, and his nickname is "Spanky." Bud was the vice president of acquisitions. While the president of Berkley Foods is not seen, his daughter, Evelyn Berkley (Robin Dearden) was. In a rare sitcom appearance, Jane Fonda played O'Neal, the security guard, in the episode of 10/12/82; her guard dog was named Nunzio.

Relatives: Lawrence Pressman (Marsha's ex-husband, *Don*), Gail Strickland (Franklin's wife, *Lois Hart*), Tony LaTorre (Violet's son, *Tommy Newstead*), Maylo McCaslin (Felb's niece, *Debbie Felb*), Eileen Heckart *(Judy's mother)*.

Theme: "9 to 5," vocal by Phoebe Snow (first season), then Dolly Parton.

9 to 5. Front, left to right: Rachel Dennison, Rita Moreno, Leah Ayres. Back, left to right: James Komack, Tony LaTorra, Peter Bonerz, George Deloy.

525. *N.O.P.D.*

Syndicated, 1956

Victor Beaujac (Stacy Harris) and John Conroy (Louis J. Sirgo) are detectives with the homicide division of the New Orleans Police Department (N.O.P.D.). Stories, based on official N.O.P.D. files, relate their investigations in a "Dragnet" style presentation that is rather primitive (in terms of the acting and camerawork) and slow-moving (the writing). The series is also filmed on location, and it appears that actual citizens were used in the dramas (acting is not their forte; only the two stars receive credit). Stacy Harris plays his character like Jack Webb's Sergeant Joe Friday on "Dragnet." He narrates and questions the suspects while Conroy, whom Victor calls "John-O," takes notes. Victor resides in an apartment on Bourbon Street, while John was said to have a home on Shady Pine Avenue. "N.O.P.D." is one of the lost series of early television. Virtually nothing was known about the program prior to the information uncovered here; even after the acquisition of episodes, information is still very limited. In addition to the stars' credits, the only other information appearing on the screen is that of the names of the producer (Frank Phares) and the director (John Sledge).

526. *Normal Life*

CBS, 3/21/90 to 7/18/90

Cast: Cindy Williams (*Anne Harlow*), Max Gail (*Max Harlow*), Moon Unit Zappa (*Tess Harlow*), Dweezil Zappa (*Jake Harlow*), Josh Williams (*Simon Harlow*), Bess Myer (*Prima*).

Facts: Incidents in the lives of the Harlows, a "normal" family of five living in Los Angeles. Max Harlow, the father, is a novelist (supposedly famous, but titles of books he has written were not given). Anne, his wife, is seldom content, harassed either by her job or by the antics of her children. Since the series was not broadcast in the order the episodes were made, information on Anne is not consistent. When first seen, Anne apparently worked for a lawyer (based on a conversation with Max). She next worked as a member of the school board. She quit this job when she got fed up with the school board's ignoring her suggestions. Two episodes later, she is now head of the public school board, 5th District. In an episode after this, she is unemployed. When something upsets Anne, she takes a long bath.

Information on Tess, their oldest child, is also conflicting. When first introduced, she is 22 years old and working for New Market Films in Hollywood. Later, she is 21 years old and looking for a job (having just quit her job as a tour guide at the Hollywood Wax Museum). One week she is living at home, the next she has her own apartment "seven blocks away." In one episode, when she is not living at home, Tess has a job in an unnamed art gallery.

At age two, Tess had a favorite blanket she called "Baby Bankey." She has a plush monkey called "Mr. Muggs" and eats Captain Crunch cereal for breakfast. She and her best friend, the seemingly spaced-out Prima (no last name given), have their hair done at a salon called Chez Brad. Bess, who attempted to follow in her father's footsteps, wrote a rather bad short story called "The Pond." Her favorite dinner is lasagna.

Jake, the middle child (19 years old), plays guitar in a professional (but unnamed) band. While it is difficult to tell, it seems that he is attending college (not named). Jake, who makes video movies (with a Magnavox camcorder) featured Tess in two: "Tess Flosses Her Teeth" and "Tess Moves Out."

Simon, the youngest child, attends Valley Junior High School and is a member of the Wildcats basketball team. He was almost expelled from school for charging fellow students one dollar for a peek at Mona the Love Doll—an inflatable doll he kept in his locker.

Dr. Bob Gordon (Jim Staahl) is the Harlows' neighbor (he is seen videotaping the Harlows with a Magnavox camcorder in the opening theme).

Relatives: Bill Morey (Anne's father, *Jesse*). Not seen was Anne's sister, Carol, the ballerina.

Theme: "Normal Life," by Dweezil Zappa.

Note: In the unaired pilot version (produced in 1989), Janet Margolin played Anne Harlow.

527. *Northern Exposure*

CBS, 7/12/90 to 8/30/90
CBS, 4/8/91 to the present

Cast: Rob Morrow (*Joel Fleischman*), Janine Turner (*Maggie O'Connell*), Barry Corbin (*Maurice Minifield*), John Cullum (*Holling Vincoeur*), Cynthia Geary (*Shelley Tambo*), John Corbett (*Chris Stevens*), Darren E. Burrows (*Ed*).

Facts: After 74 rejections for a medical school scholarship, Joel Fleischman finds that the state of Alaska will pick up the $125,000 tab if he will begin his practice (and spend four years) in Alaska. Joel attended Richfield High School, Columbia University Medical School and did his internship at Beth Sinai Hospital in New York City (he also attended Camp Indian Head as a kid). Joel leaves his home in Flushing, New York, and his girlfriend, Elaine Schulman (Jessica Lundy), and heads for Alaska. In Anchorage, Joel finds that he has been assigned to the remote town of Cicely—a growing community in the borough of Arrowhead—which was founded by Maurice Minifield, a former NASA astronaut, who arranged for Joel's scholarship.

Cicely is a small town desperately in need of a doctor. It has a population of 215 (214 until Joel arrived) and an elevation of 6,572 feet. Joel's office is established in the abandoned Northwestern Mining building, and a native woman named Marilyn Whirlwind (Elaine Miles) serves as his nurse. Joel's truck license plate reads 5792-H2; he reads *Golf Digest* and the *New Yorker* magazine. A threat to the town is Jessie, a Great Bear that roams the area (the bear is missing two toes, which were shot off by Holling Vincoeur, the owner of the Brick Bar; Rosalyn's Café is the local eatery). In addition to Jessie, a legendary man-beast named Adam (Adam Arkin) is believed to be living in the great woods that surround the town. The kind mountain man married Eve (Valerie Mahaffey) in the episode of 5/11/92.

Maurice served with the marines and was stationed on Parris Island. He drives a classic Cadillac (license plate 39-759) and likes gourmet cooking and show tunes. As a kid he had a dog named Buddy.

Margaret ("Maggie") Mary O'Connell, a pretty brunette who was born in Michigan, is Joel's landlady and the owner of the one plane (I.D. # N8326; later N41492) O'Connell Air Taxi Service. Her pickup truck license plate reads 8346 MA, and she lives on the south corner of Katunik and Washington.

Shelley Tambo, the beautiful young wife (age 23) of Holling (age 68), is the waitress at the Brick Bar; she won the beauty pageant title "Miss Northwest Passage." She attends the Lady of Our Refuge Church.

Chris Stevens, who was born in West Virginia, is the only D.J. on the town's only radio station—KBHR (57 on the AM dial; "Great Bear Radio," as it is called, is owned by the Minifield Communications Network).

Ed Chigliak is a native Alaskan who assists Joel. He drives a Jeep (license plate JR 38LC) and reads *Teenage Mutant Ninja Turtles* comic books.

The town newspaper is the Cicely *World Telegram*. Cicely is virtually crime free—except when the ice breaks (during the spring thaw); people then go crazy and steal things. At the Brick Bar (telephone number 907-555-7328), the book *The Rainbow*, by D.H. Lawrence, is under the leg of the kitchen table to keep it from wobbling. People say Maggie is cursed when it comes to beaus; she has had five who have died under tragic circumstances: Harry (choked at a picnic on potato salad), Bruce (a fishing accident), Glen (took a wrong turn in his Volvo onto a missile range), Dave (fell asleep on a glacier and froze) and Rick (killed by a falling satellite). The series is filmed in Roslyn, Washington.

Relatives: John McCann (Maggie's father, *Frank O'Connell*), Bibi Besch (*Maggie's mother*), Anthony Curry (Shelley's father, *Gordon Tambo*), Wendy Schaal (Shelley's young stepmother, *Tammy Tambo*), Rob Morrow (Joel's twin brother, *Jules Fleischman*). Not seen was Maurice's brother, Malcolm, who died owing him $8,000.

Theme: "Northern Exposure," by David Schwartz.

Nothing Is Easy see *Together We Stand*

528. *Occasional Wife*

NBC, 9/13/66 to 8/29/67

Cast: Michael Callan (*Peter Christopher*), Patricia Harty (*Greta Patterson*), Jack Collins (*Max Brahms*), Susan Silo (*Vera Frick*), Jack Riley (*Wally Frick*), Chris Noel (*Marilyn Granville*), Stuart Margolin (*Bernie Cramer*), Bryan O'Byrne (*Man in the Middle*).

Facts: Peter Christopher, called "The Company Bachelor" at work, is a ladies' man who is best at romancing women. He has a nice apartment on East 57th Street in Manhattan and a good job with the Brahms Baby Food Company. Each Friday night he has dinner with his mother. On one night in September 1966, his world suddenly changed. It began with his mother—"Peter, a man of your age should be married"—and concluded with his family- and corporate image-minded boss, Max Brahms—"A man should be judged by his ability. The only thing that counts around here is whether you are married or not."

When an executive position becomes available, Peter applies but is refused—"I'm sorry, Peter. I believe in married executives. No marriage, no promotion." Later that day, while drowning his sorrows in an unnamed bar, he begins talking with his friend, Greta Patterson, the hatcheck girl. Greta has problems too, with men hitting on her, and she remarks, "Too bad you can't do what I do to protect myself in this place—pretend you're married."

An idea forms in Peter's mind. "Greta, you've given me the solution to my problem, a fake wife, that's the answer for Brahms." "You must be out of your mind," Greta says. "No, Greta, I mean it. I want you to be my wife, occasionally." Greta refuses until Peter offers to find her an apartment and pay for her rent and art classes (she is studying to be a dress designer). Peter buys her a damaged wedding ring for $15, and she goes on salary as his occasional wife.

Peter, who lives in Apartment 7C, sets Greta up in Apartment 9C in his building. For access to each other's apartments, Peter and Greta use the back fire escapes (they fear getting caught if they use the elevators or their front doors). Apartment 8C is between them—the residence of "The Man in the Middle" (who witnesses their antics and has come to enjoy watching them).

Peter and Greta then devise a story for Mr. Brahms: they met at the Huntington Yacht Club. It was love at first sight, and they married immediately after (Greta pretends to be a dancer turned librarian who lived in Boston).

"How long will the marriage last?" asked Greta. "The marriage is going to last until I get a vice presidency," Peter says. "Then Greta will have a boating accident, then you'll be lost, I'll be a widower and Brahms will love me." Peter's plan begins to work—he is made an advertising executive when Brahms learns of his marriage.

Greta pretends to be Peter's wife whenever the need arises. Peter has a girlfriend named Marilyn Granville. Mr. Brahms believes that she is Peter's sister. Greta has a boyfriend named Bernard ("Bernie") J. Cramer. He believes

Peter is Greta's brother. Peter's mother believes Peter and Greta are really married and that it was love at first sight.

The first major crisis in Greta's unmarried life was a visit from her mother-in-law. To pay for a third day of art school, Greta took a job as a receptionist for the Bellfield General Employment Agency at $65 a week. To break a date with Bernie (when she has to be Peter's wife), Greta pretends to be sick (usually a bad cold). Bernie, nicknamed "Fiddles" as a kid, is wimpy and lets people take advantage of him. The slogan of the Brahms Baby Food Company is "Every Meal a Lullaby."

Wally Frick is Peter's office rival and will stop at nothing to advance his position within the company. He is married to a pretty, power seeking woman named Vera. Vera is unable to make Wally as aggressive as she is; to compensate for this, she stays by Wally's side and coaches him on how to "kiss up" to the boss.

Relatives: Sara Seegar *(Peter's mother)*, Pert Kelton (Greta's mother, *"Mom" Patterson*), Paul Hartman (Greta's father, *"Pop" Patterson*), Herb Edelman (Peter's uncle, *Harry*), Joan Tompkins (Max's wife, *Lydia Brahms*; her maiden name is White and her favorite color is green; she and Max have a summer home in Westport, Connecticut); Eileen Baral (Max's niece, *Amanda*).

Theme: "Occasional Wife," by Ernie Pintoff and Howard Greenfield.

529. *The Odd Couple*

ABC, 9/24/70 to 7/4/75

Cast: Tony Randall *(Felix Unger)*, Jack Klugman *(Oscar Madison)*, Al Molinaro *(Murray Greschner)*, Penny Marshall *(Myrna Turner)*, Elinor Donahue *(Miriam Welby)*, Joan Hotchkis *(Nancy Cunningham)*.

Facts: Felix Unger is an excessively neat perfectionist; Oscar Madison is an irresponsible slob. Both men are divorced and live together at 1049 Park Avenue (at 74th Street and Central Park West in New York) in Apartment 1102. Felix and Oscar first met when they were chosen as jurors for the trial of Leo Garvey, a man accused of driving his roommate crazy (Oscar was a sportswriter for the *New York Times* at the time). Together, they wrote the song "Happy and Peppy and Bursting with Love" for singer Jaye P. Morgan, and appeared on the television show "Let's Make a Deal" as a horse (Felix was the head; Oscar, the rear). Nino's Italian Restaurant is their favorite place to eat.

Felix, who suffers from sinus attacks, was born in Chicago, moved to Oklahoma and grew up on a farm in Glenview, New York (another episode mentions Toledo, Ohio, as his hometown). He is a member of the Radio Actors' Guild (as a kid he appeared on "Let's Pretend"), and in college he had his own radio show called "Felix."

Felix was stationed in England during World War II (he was a member of the 22nd Training Film Platoon, Educational Division of the Special Services). It was at this time that he starred in the army training film *How to Take a* *Shower*; he originated the line, "Men, don't let this happen to you." He also won the Silver Canteen Award for his song about Adolf Hitler called "To a Sour Kraut." Felix, a lieutenant at the time, was later transferred to Greenland (for two years) and retired as a captain.

Felix refuses to let Oscar bring a copy of *Playboy* magazine into the house as it reminds him of a bitter incident from his past. Before Felix established his own photography business ("Portraits a Specialty"), he worked as a photographer for *Playboy* at the same time Oscar worked there as a writer and his fiancée (now ex-wife) Gloria worked as a bunny in the Manhattan Playboy Club. Felix used the name Spencer Benedict ("You don't think I'm going to use my real name to shoot nudies") and threw a fit when he learned Gloria was one of the candidates for the Miss April centerfold. He photographed her in the nude but put up such a fuss about using her picture that Hugh Hefner agreed to pull the photo.

Felix has a parrot named Albert and is a member of the Sophisticates band and the Lexington Avenue Opera Club (he subscribes to *Opera News* magazine). He won the Dink Advertising Award for directing a commercial for Fataway diet pills on television. Before moving in with Oscar, Felix and Gloria lived together in New Rochelle, New York. Their first child, Edna, was born at Mid-Memorial Hospital in Manhattan (from which Felix is now banned because of the fuss he made when Edna was born). His son, Leonard, has a pet frog named Max. Gloria divorced Felix after seven years of marriage because of his excessive neatness (he cooks better than she does, buys her clothes and cleans after she cleans). Felix's boyhood friend was Orville Kruger ("the boy with the odd-shaped head"), and his first girlfriend was "Big Bertha." When they were kids Felix and his brother, Floyd, were called "Spic and Span" (Floyd now makes Unger bubble gum). Floyd calls Felix "Big F"; Felix calls Floyd "Little F."

Oscar, a sportswriter for the *New York Herald*, was born at Our Lady of Angels Hospital in Philadelphia (another episode states that Oscar was born in Chicago—where he and Felix met briefly as kids). As a kid, Oscar attended the Langley Tippy-Toe Dancing School and was enrolled in James K. Polk High School. Oscar's vice is gambling, and he wears a size 11D shoe. He drinks beer for breakfast, and catsup is his favorite dressing for food (lasagna and French fries are his favorite dinner; Boston cream pie is his favorite dessert). Oscar's first job in New York was as a copywriter for *Playboy* magazine; he had a radio show called "The Oscar Madison Sports Talk Show" (later changed to "Oscar Madison's Greatest Moments in Sports"). His favorite song is "Reckless." Oscar divorced Blanche after eight years of marriage because of excessive arguing. He got his current apartment by looking in the obituary column of the newspaper to see who died in the better neighborhoods. The previous tenant was a postman named Irving Cohen. After his divorce, Oscar was so upset that he went on an eating binge and gained 301 pounds. The series is based on the play by Neil Simon.

Other Characters: Murray Greschner is a police officer with the N.Y.P.D. Myrna Turner is Oscar's secretary. She was born in the Bronx, is disorganized, sloppy and lazy—"The best secretary I ever had." Myrna is forever having boyfriend trouble, especially with "Sheldn" ("They forgot the *o* on his birth certificate"). She calls Oscar "Mr. M." Myrna is a Scorpio (born in November) and says, "I talk nasal, I have an unproud bust and I sit like a frog"—her reasons why she'll "never be a lady."

Miriam Welby is Felix's romantic interest; and Dr. Nancy Cunningham is Oscar's lady love.

Relatives: Janis Hansen (Felix's ex-wife, *Gloria*), Pamelyn Ferdin and Doney Oatman (Felix's daughter, *Edna Unger*), Leif Garrett and Willie Aames (Felix's son, *Leonard Unger*), William Redfield (Felix's brother, *Floyd Unger*), Tony Randall (Felix's great-uncle, *Albert Unger*, who lives at Sunshine City), Madge Kennedy *(Felix's grandmother)*, Brett Somers (Oscar's ex-wife, *Blanche*), Hilary Thompson (Oscar's niece, *Martha*), Elvia Allman and Fran Ryan *(Oscar's mother)*, Jane Dulo and Alice Ghostley (Murray's wife, *Mimi Greschner*).

Flashbacks: Adam Klugman *(Oscar as a boy)*, Johnny Scott Lee and Sean Manning *(Felix as a boy)*, Tony Randall (Felix's father, *Morris Unger*, an optometrist), Jack Klugman (Oscar's father, *Blinky Madison*, a bookie and restaurant owner), Tony Randall *(Felix's grandfather)*.

Theme: "The Odd Couple," by Neal Hefti.

Note: In "The New Odd Couple" (ABC, 10/29/82 to 6/9/83), Ron Glass was Felix and Demond Wilson was Oscar in a black version of the series.

530. *Oh, Madeline*

ABC, 9/27/83 to 3/13/84

Madeline Wayne (Madeline Kahn) lives at 217 Faircourt Avenue in the Eastfield section of Chicago. She is a housewife and married to Charles ("Charlie") Wayne (James Sloyan), a romance novelist who writes under the pen name Crystal Love. Charlie has written such books as *Love in the End Zone* and *Love's Burning Blazing Tender Purple Passion*. He also writes romantic short stories for the Sunday magazine section of a newspaper called *The Outlook*. Madeline says that if Charlie ever decides to give up writing, he has a standing invitation from her uncle Percy to work for him in a slaughterhouse.

Madeline and Charlie have been married for ten years. Charlie works at home and Madeline does her best not to disturb him (for example, she bought a Walkman so she can do her housework while listening to music). Madeline, whose maiden name is Vernon, attended the Julia Farraday High School (class of '63) and was a Farraday cheerleader. She believes that singer "Johnny Mathis has such a beautiful voice that it makes brassiere hooks fly open by themselves" and feels that "all the horrible things that happen to me could happen to someone else—but they happen to me in front of someone else" (for instance, giving the band for her high school prom the wrong address: "Three hundred kids had to dance to the one polka record the school owned").

Robert Leone (Louis Giambalvo) is Charlie's friend, a womanizing travel agent Madeline calls "Mr. Gunk Face." Doris Leone (Jesse Welles) is Robert's ex-wife, and Annie McIntyre (Francine Tacker) is Charlie's agent (she lives in Apartment 2 at 34 Bainbridge Avenue).

Reese and Charlotte Vernon (Ray Walston and Geraldine Fitzgerald) are Madeline's parents, and Joyce Vernon (Melanie Chartoff) is Madeline's younger sister. "Oh, Madeline" is based on the British series "Pig in the Middle."

Dan Foliart and Howard Pearl composed the theme.

Oh! Susanna see *The Gale Storm Show: Oh! Susanna*

531. *Oh, Those Bells!*

CBS, 3/8/62 to 5/31/62

Hoping to begin new lives in America, the three Bell brothers leave Germany and head for California. Shortly after, Herbert Bell (Herbert Wiere), Harry Bell (Harry Wiere) and Sylvester Bell (Sylvester Wiere) are flat broke and hungry. It is not stated exactly how the Bell brothers met their future employer, Henry Slocum (Henry Norell), other than "We were broke and hungry and taken in by Mr. Slocum."

The boys, as they are sometimes called, are put to work by Slocum as custodians in Cinema Rents, a motion picture and television show prop rental business located at 4 Ridgeway Drive in Hollywood. They live together in a bungalow at a complex referred to as Mrs. Stanfield's (no address given), and the comedy stems from the antics of the insecure brothers as they attempt to adjust to life in America and do the best job that they can for Mr. Slocum.

Reta Shaw played Mrs. Stanfield, the Bells' landlady; and Carol Byron portrayed Kitty Matthews, Slocum's secretary. The series was originally produced for the 1960-61 season but was pulled by CBS and shown as a spring replacement series that lasted only 13 weeks. Cinema Rents (as seen on the screen) is called the Hollywood Prop Shop in printed sources.

Tutti Camarata composed the theme.

532. *On Our Own*

CBS, 10/9/77 to 8/20/78

J.M. Bedford (Bob Randall) owns the Bedford Advertising Agency (thirty-third floor) at 605 Madison Avenue in New York City. Toni McBain (Gretchen Wyler) is the creative director; Julia Peters (Bess Armstrong) and April Baxter (Dixie Carter) are its copywriters; and Maria Teresa Bonino (Lynnie Greene) is the art director.

Oh, Those Bells! Jesse White (in pin-stripe suit) with the Wiere Brothers.

Julia lives at 345 East 45th Street; April at 61 East 54th Street; and Maria at 62 West 72nd Street. Julia is neat; April is a perfectionist; and Maria, who was born in Brooklyn, sings herself to sleep, forgets to pay her bills, eats enough for three people (yet maintains a slender figure) and is a rather untidy housekeeper.

Craig Boatwright (Dan Resin) is the agency's salesman (he belongs to "Mr. Meat," a monthly freezer plus meat rental plan); Eddie Barnes (John Christopher Jones) is the commercials' producer; and Vanessa Oblensky (Sasha von Scherler) is Julia's "I don't want to hear nothing" landlady.

Relatives: Kay Medford (*Maria's mother*), Larry Haines (*Maria's father*), Louis Criscuolo (Maria's uncle, *Vito*), Mary Denham (Craig's wife, *Corkey Boatwright*).

Bob Israel composed the theme.

533. *On the Air*

ABC, 6/20/92 to 7/4/92

The time is 1957, and television is still relatively new. One New York–based network, the Zoblotnick Broadcasting Corporation (ZBC), decides that the only way to attract viewers (and save their network) is to give movie idols their own shows. They begin by hiring Lester Guy (Ian Buchanan), a fading matinee idol who is hoping to make a comeback via "The Lester Guy Show," an 8:00 P.M. music, comedy and variety show that is plagued by the (overexaggerated) mishaps that actually occurred on live television during its "Golden Years."

Lester was a contract player at Amalgamated Studios and got his start with a bit part in the film *The White Cliffs of Dover*. Betty Hudson (Marla Rubinoff) is Lester's co-star. She is from Westport, Connecticut, and the sister of movie star Sylvia Hudson (Anne Bloom). Betty, however, has no acting experience and is a bit dim witted. To make Guy look good, Betty was chosen to be his co-star.

Buddy Budwaller (Miguel Ferrer) is the tyrannical head of the network and the "yes man" for the never-seen Mr. Zoblotnick. Vladja Gochtch (David L. Lander) is the inexperienced, impossible to understand foreign director who directs Guy's show. Ruth Trueworthy (Nancye Ferguson) is Vladja's assistant (she translates his thick German accent into English for the crew). Dwight McGonigle (Marvin Kaplan) is the often distressed producer of "The Lester Guy Show."

Blinky Watts (Tracey Walter) appears to be blind—"He's not. He suffers from Bozman Symplex; he sees 25.6 times as much as we do." So naturally, Blinky is the sound effects man (he has pre-set levers on his control board and operates from memory rather than sight).

Wembley Snaps dog food sponsors "The Lester Guy Show"; Everett Greenbaum is the show's announcer; and Susan Russell is the announcer's assistant.

Angelo Badalamenti composed the theme.

534. *Once a Hero*

ABC, 9/19/87 to 10/3/87

Cast: Jeff Lester (*Captain Justice*), Robert Forster (*Gumshoe*), Caitlin Clarke (*Emma Greely*), Milo O'Shea (*Abner Bevis*), Dianne Kay (*Rachel Kirk*), Dana Short (*Tippy Kirk*).

Facts: Comic Book World is a world beyond the third dimension, where characters live out the adventures drawn by their creators. Pleasantville is one such world. Good citizens like Rachel Kirk, her sister, Tippy, and her beloved schoolteacher Brad Steele live here. But there are also villains like Max Mayhem (Harris Laskawy). Battling these villains is Captain Justice, the secret alias of Brad Steele. Captain Justice, who is also called "The Crimson Crusader," wears a red costume with blue gloves and a blue triangle on his chest with a gold C.J. in the center. Captain Justice doesn't have a cape; he does, however, possess the ability to fly, an immunity to harm, incredible strength and infrared and X-ray vision. He also has one major problem: his creator, Abner Bevis, has run out of fresh ideas and has begun using plots from earlier adventures (he has been drawing the strip for 30 years). One day, while saving the lovely Rachel Kirk and Tippy from Max Mayhem, Captain Justice begins to fade. Soon, Rachel, Tippy and Max begin to fade. "This is not good," says Captain Justice. "We are dependent upon the affections of people in the real world. As long as we remain in their hearts, we are safe. Should they start to forget us or lose interest, we simply fade away. I've seen this happen before. Remember Andy Hardy? They're now forgetting Captain Justice. I won't let this happen. I'll go to the third dimension and force them to remember." To do this, Captain Justice crosses the Forbidden Zone into the real world.

In Los Angeles, Captain Justice finds Abner and learns that Pizazz Comics is planning to discontinue Captain Justice. "The kids don't go for it like they used to," Abner tells him. But Captain Justice is determined to change that. But before he begins, he learns that he has another problem—no superpowers in the real world "because superpowers do not exist in the real world."

Back in Comic Book World, the Great and Magnificent One summons Gumshoe, a 1940s-style private eye and hires him (at $40 a day plus expenses) to cross through the Forbidden Zone and bring Captain Justice back—"If he stays he will experience a fate more horrific than a superhero can endure. He should spend his remaining days here, with dignity and honor."

Gumshoe drives through the Forbidden Zone (Captain Justice flew through) and finds Captain Justice, whom he calls "Cap." Gumshoe tells Cap about his mission, but Captain Justice refuses to return with him: "I must get people to remember me." With Gumshoe's help, Captain Justice begins his crusade on crime. He soon accomplishes his goal. The *Comic Book News* reports that Pizazz Comics has reinstated Captain Justice; Emma Greely, a reporter for the Los Angeles *Gazette*, writes the stories: CAPTAIN JUSTICE DOES IT AGAIN. BUT WHO IS HE?

Once a Hero. Jeff Lester (left) and Robert Forster.

Captain Justice eats only peanut butter and jelly sandwiches with milk, "except when he sees a ballgame at Pleasantville Stadium. Then he has two hot dogs and lemonade." The Captain always believes in telling the truth, and his moral code prevents him from killing anyone. In Pleasantville, Captain Justice received the key to the city 103 times, and he "has a bad habit" (as criminals say) of showing up in the nick of time to save Rachel and Tippy. IB 429 is Gumshoe's 1940s-style car license plate number. Woody Greely (Josh Blake) is Emma's son (she is divorced), and T.J. North (Adam West) plays the Crimson Crusader on the television show "Captain Justice." When Captain Justice comes to their rescue, Rachel always says (with a sigh of relief), "Captain Justice." A relieved Tippy exclaims, "The Crimson Crusader!"

Jim Turner played Captain Justice in the unaired pilot version of the series.

Theme: "Once a Hero," by Dennis Dreith.

535. *One Big Family*

Syndicated, 9/86 to 9/87

At First and Hastings Street (telephone number 555-6369) in Seattle, Washington, live Jan and Don

Hastings (Kim Gillingham and Anthony Starke), a young married couple who become the guardians of Don's younger brothers and sisters when their parents are killed in a car accident: Marianne (Anastasia Fielding), Kate (Alison McMillan), Brian (Michael DeLuise) and Roger (Gabriel Damon). Helping Jan and Don is Don's uncle, Jake Hatton (Danny Thomas), a retired vaudevillian who oversees the family—"I'm here to give you advice, not mow lawns or do windows."

Jan works at the Seattle Zoo; Don is an officer with the Washington Police Department (he rides in patrol car 309); Marianne attends Seattle State College, and Kate and Brian are students at Fillmore High School. Jan uses the term *Ny-folk* (not in front of the kids) when she and Don are about to have an argument; Brian works in a fish store and sometimes gets paid in salmon. He belches "Born in the U.S.A." to impress girls; Roger has a pet white rat named Maxwell.

George Aliceson Tipton composed the theme.

536. *One Day at a Time*

CBS, 12/6/75 to 9/2/84

Cast: Bonnie Franklin (*Ann Romano*), Valerie Bertinelli (*Barbara Cooper*), Mackenzie Phillips (*Julie Cooper*), Pat

Harrington, Jr. *(Dwayne Schneider)*, Mary Louise Wilson *(Ginny Wrobliki)*, Michael Lembeck *(Max Horvath)*, Shelley Fabares *(Francine Webster)*, Boyd Gaines *(Mark Royer)*.

Facts: Ann Romano is a liberated, 34 year old divorcée (who has resumed her maiden name) who lives with her two daughters, Barbara and Julie Cooper (who carry their father's last name), at 1344 Hartford Drive, Apartment 402, in Indianapolis, Indiana; 555-4142 is their phone number.

Ann was born in Logansport, Indiana, and attended Logansport Hgih School. She was first an account executive at the Connors and Davenport Advertising Agency, then co-owner of the Romano and Handris Ad Agency with Nick Handris (Ron Rifkin); the agency was later called Handris and Associates. When the business folded, Ann and her former co-worker (and rival) at Connors and Davenport, Francine Webster, pooled their resources and opened the Romano and Webster Ad Agency. Ann's biggest account at Connors and Davenport was Rutledge Toys; her first account after leaving was Startime Ice Cream. Ann's first boss, Al Connors (John Hillerman), called her "M.S. Romano" (pronounced *MS* Romano) when Ann insisted that she be called Ms. Romano.

Ann's first season boyfriend was David Kane (Richard Masur), her divorce lawyer (with the firm of McInerney, Wollman, Kollman and Schwartz). She later married architect Sam Royer (Howard Hesseman) on May 16, 1983, and moved to 322 Bedford Street, Apartment 422. Almond mocha is Ann's favorite ice cream flavor.

Julie, Ann's oldest and more troublesome daughter, attended Jefferson High School. She wears a size 32B bra, has a plush bear called TuTu Bear, and her favorite snacks are pickles and bananas, and celery and ice cream.

Julie, who did not attend college, was a receptionist for a veterinarian at the Curran Animal Center, a freelance fashion designer and a counselor at the Free Clinic. She and Ann have bank accounts at the First Security Bank (Julie's account number is 1-222-1220-877-02453). Julie later married Max Horvath, a flight attendant for PMA Airlines, on October 10, 1979. When Max is laid off, he turns to writing. When he is unable to make a go of it, he takes a job as a waiter at Barney's Tavern. Julie attended the Berkum Management Institute in Ohio for training as the manager of a doughnut shop. Max calls Ann (his mother-in-law) "Shortie," and he and Julie became the parents of a daughter they named Annie (played by twins J.C. and R.C. Dilley and Paige and Lauren Maloney).

Barbara, Ann's younger daughter, began the series as a tomboy and evolved into a beautiful young woman. She attended Jefferson High School and later City College (but dropped out), and held the following jobs: cook at Quickie Burger, salesclerk at Olympia Sporting Goods (owned by Erickson Enterprises) and travel agent at the Gonagin Travel Agency. Her favorite snack is a huge banana split, and Rocky Road is her favorite flavor of ice cream.

At Jefferson High, Julie and Barbara were envious of Trish the Dish, a well-endowed (never seen) girl who is the dream of all the boys. While Julie went only so far as to pad her bra with Kleenex to attract boys, Barbara took it one step further and pretended to be on the pill.

Barbara's greatest disappointment occurred shortly after her marriage (on October 3, 1982) to Mark Royer, a dentist. Having always dreamed of raising a family, Barbara learned that she cannot bear children (an inability to conceive that even surgery cannot cure). As a kid Barbara ate a caterpillar when Julie told her it was a fuzzy Tootsie Roll.

Dwayne F. Schneider, the building superintendent, lives in the basement (Apartment 1) and is a member of I.B.M. (Indianapolis Building Maintenance). Dwayne's first job was, at the age of two months, that of a model in diaper ads. Dwayne, who was born in Secaucus, New Jersey, attended Irvington High School. He married in 1957, but the marriage lasted only one week. (His wife got up one morning, hot-wired his truck and just took off. However, in the pilot episode, Dwayne is married; in a later episode, Dwayne was married for five days and got a divorce.) Dwayne, whose C.B. handle is "Super Stud," is a member of the Secret Order of the Beavers Lodge, North Central Chapter (he is activities chairman and entertainment producer for the lodge). His favorite pickup joint is the Boom Boom Room of the Purple Pig Club. In one episode, Dwayne invested $10,000 in one of Ann and Francine's accounts—Georgette Jeans.

Ginny Wrobliki, Ann's sexy neighbor, is a waitress at the Alibi Room bar; Bob Morton (John Putch) is Barbara's friend; Kathryn Romano (Nanette Fabray) is Anne's mother (she calls Barbara "Muffin"). The telephone number of Connors and Davenport is 555-7974.

Relatives: Joseph Campanella (Ann's ex-husband, *Ed Cooper*), Elizabeth Kerr (Ann's grandmother, *Helen Romano*), Jeff Corey (Ann's father, *Michael Romano*), Priscilla Morrill (Ann's mother-in-law, *Estelle Cooper*), Gretchen Corbett (Ann's cousin, *Sophie*), Van Johnson (Francine's father, *Gus Webster*), Dick Van Patten (Ginny's ex-husband, *Frank*), Mark Hamill (Dwayne's nephew, *Harvey*), Darrell Larson (Dwayne's son, *Ronnie Baxter*), Claudette Nevins (Sam's ex-wife, *Marge Royer*), Elinor Donahue (Nick's ex-wife, *Felicia*), Glenn Scarpelli (Nick's son, *Alex Handris*).

Theme: "One Day at a Time," by Nancy and Jeff Barry.

537. *The 100 Lives of Black Jack Savage*

NBC, 3/31/91 to 5/26/91

Cast: Daniel Hugh-Kelly *(Barry Tarberry)*, Stoney Jackson (pilot) and Steven Williams *(Black Jack Savage)*, Steve Hytner *(Logan Murphy)*.

Facts: On the Caribbean island of San Pietro in the 1790s, a pirate named Black Jack Savage is hanged. The ghost of Black Jack remains on the island and haunts his former residence, Blackbird Castle. Three hundred years later in New York City, billionaire Barry Tarberry, the owner of Tarberry Enterprises, is arrested for insider trading (violating federal statute 1678). While he is out on bail,

One Day at a Time. Pat Harrington (left), Bonnie Franklin (center, right), with Valerie Bertinelli (left) and Mackenzie Phillips.

Barry gathers his available assets and goes into exile—on the island of San Pietro. There he pays $300,000 to Herve Abel Vasquez (Bert Rosario), the island's corrupt governor general, for immunity. Abel's niece, Reya Montegro (Roya Megnot), who runs Vasquez Realty for her uncle, sells Barry the haunted Blackbird Castle for $1,500,000. Barry does not believe in the legend of the ghost—until he comes face to face with Black Jack. It is a situation he must learn to accept when he discovers that he is wanted by the FBI and now broke (the government seized all his other assets).

The current owner of Blackbird Castle is the only person who can see and hear Black Jack. Barry also learns that Black Jack killed 100 people as a pirate and is now cursed to remain on Earth until he can save an equal number of lives to make up for those he took. Black Jack is also incapable of affecting physical matter; he can, however, possess lower lifeforms.

Black Jack has a spiritual advisor named Larry. Through Larry, Black Jack learns that Barry is headed all the way down for his past deeds—"Right now they've got you scheduled in the Ivan the Terrible chamber in the southeast corner of hell." Now that both are virtually in the same predicament, they agree to help each other by saving lives. Each life they save they split (51 percent goes to Jack, 49 percent to Barry). It's the only chance Barry has to save his soul, and it's Jack's only chance to find eternal peace. Stories relate their somewhat bumbling efforts to save lives.

Assisting Barry and Jack (but he doesn't know about Jack) is Logan Murphy, a brilliant scientist who once worked for the Pentagon as a defense specialist. He wears a NASA cap and has the nickname "FX." Logan carries a seven ton generator in the back of his car (license plate S-359) to power his various inventions (for example, his ASOP Troop Spotter—a laser gun). Logan also believes that Barry is crazy (he sees Barry talking to air), and he invented the *Blackbird*, a high tech speedboat made from the body of a SR71 spy plane, which Barry uses to battle crime (Barry hides the boat at a secret dock near the castle). Logan's favorite James Bond movie is *Diamonds Are Forever,* and he has a Thermal Imager (which tracks people like radar) he calls Isosceles.

Barry is number 18 on America's 20 most wanted list. His middle name is Danforth, and he has written a book called *Dealing, Not Stealing.* He has appeared on the cover of *Forbes* magazine and on the following television shows: "Hollywood Squares," "The Mike Douglas Show," "Jeopardy," "The $100,000 Pyramid" and "Circus of the Stars." On "Pyramid" he did poorly in the category "Things a Boy Scout says"; on "Jeopardy" he said that a cow falling 4,000 feet was the fastest land animal—"What would you do if you were $2,000 behind in Final Jeopardy?" Barry was also the grand marshal of the 1990 Macy's Thanksgiving Day Parade.

Black Jack was born as Niamu in the Monokanga kingdom of Africa. When he was a young man, Portuguese slave traders abducted him. One night, a drunken sailor forgot to lock Niamu's chains. Niamu freed himself, began a revolt and killed 25 sailors. He set his people free and retreated to the Caribbean. There, the British press dubbed him "Black Jack Savage" for killing the sailors. The *Blackbird* was Black Jack's pirate ship, and he killed 100 people in the years that followed, prior to his execution. Black Jack now fears Snarks — "Little Dirt Bags" that will send him to hell if he leaves the castle. (Snarks are actually ghostly creatures in a different dimension, and they can cause Black Jack harm. If the Snarks catch Jack, they can transport him to hell by bringing him to the roots of the tree where he was hanged; the roots lead to hell.) To combat the Snarks, Barry had Logan create an anti–Snark weapon he calls "The Snark Buster." (It resembles a vacuum cleaner, and Logan's official name for it is the "Proton Ion Positive Negative Field Adjuster.")

Relatives: Mary Kay Adams (Barry's ex-wife, *Marla Lance*).

Theme: "The 100 Lives of Black Jack Savage," by Mike Post.

Note: The series is also known as "Black Jack Savage" (*TV Guide* title) and "Disney Presents the 100 Lives of Black Jack Savage" (which also appears on the screen; "Disney Presents" is in small lettering above "The 100 Lives of Black Jack Savage"). Each episode concluded with the number of lives left to save. At the end of the last episode, "89 Lives Left to Save" appeared.

538. *Open House*

Fox, 8/27/89 to 7/21/90

A "Duet" spinoff in which Laura Kelly (Mary Page Keller) and Linda Phillips (Alison LaPlaca) become brokers with the Juan Verde Real Estate Company in Los Angeles (telephone number 555-1612).

Laura, who had a catering business, gave it up when she and her husband, Ben, divorced. She lives at 13205 Ocean Avenue and has an account at the Happy Valley Bank. Laura is sweet, innocent, a bit naive and troubled by a drinking problem. She has one regret: having had her address tattooed on her left breast (which she had done so she could remember where she lives when on a drinking binge). In the opening theme, Laura is seen reading a book called *Real Estate for Beginners*.

Linda is still married to Richard (Chris Lemmon) when the new series begins. They later separate and divorce. Their daughter, Amanda (Ginger Orsi), appears in the first episode and is then said to be cared for by Geneva (Arleen Sorkin), the Phillipses' housekeeper.

Linda is a high powered sales agent and is constantly engaged in a battle of wits with fellow agent Ted Nichols (Philip Charles MacKenzie) to make the most sales. Richard plays piano at Jasper's Bar and Restaurant. (Richard lives in

an apartment at 549 Palisades Avenue; Linda resides in their former home at 10 West Florist Street.) Margo Van Meter (Ellen DeGeneres), the receptionist, has a cat named Boris and wears a size seven ring. Roger McSwain (Nick Tate) is the agency's owner, and Scott Babylon (Danny Gans) is an agent who uses celebrities' voices to make sales.

Sherrie Krenn appeared as Roger's man-crazy daughter, Phoebe, and Marian Mercer played Ted's mother, Dorothy. In the first few episodes, John Greene (played by Jon Cypher) owned Juan Verde (he was bought out by McSwain).

John Beasley and John Veiter composed the "Open House" theme.

539. *Operation Petticoat*

ABC, 9/17/77 to 8/25/78

Lt. Cmdr. Matthew Sherman (John Astin), the son of an admiral and a man who is longing to see action at sea, receives orders to report to the commander of submarine forces, Adriatic Fleet, Manila, to command the USS *Sea Tiger*. The *Sea Tiger* was christened in 1941. In August 1942, just 45 minutes before Sherman arrives to take command, the *Sea Tiger* is attacked by Japanese planes and sunk.

Figuring that perhaps he will never get another chance to live his dream, Sherman convinces the base admiral (Jackie Cooper) to let him save the *Sea Tiger* and make her seaworthy again. With the help of his crew, the 2,000 ton *Sea Tiger,* identification number 393, is made seaworthy — put back together again with junk, from bathroom fixtures to Jeep steering wheels to six feet of the admiral's office wall.

On the island of Marquis, the *Sea Tiger* (called "The Boat" by Sherman), is brought in for minor repairs and a paint job. Shortly after an undercoat of shocking pink paint is put on the sub, an enemy plane attacks the base and destroys the supply of gray paint. For reasons that are never really explained (other than that the *Sea Tiger* is always on patrol and can't get into a port for repainting), the sub remains pink. Stories relate the crew's adventures as they roam the South Pacific.

Sherman's Crew: Lieutenant Nick Holden (Richard Gilliland) is the supply officer who uses cons to get what he needs. He was previously an admiral's aide and called "The Darling of the High Brass Set" (he and the admiral's wife won the rumba championship two years in a row). Prior to this, he was an idea man for the navy (for example, he coordinated parades) then recreation officer at the navy-occupied Royal Arms Hotel in Honolulu. He was also a member of the fleet swimming team.

Chief Herbert Molumphrey (Wayne Long) is the sub's mechanic; he can work miracles when it comes to jerry-rigging. Alvin Hunkle (Richard Brestoff) is the overeager yeoman; Seaman Broom (Jim Varney) is called "Doom and Gloom Broom" for his negative outlook on everything; Ensign Stovall (Christopher J. Brown) is the navigator; and

Seaman Williams (Richard Marion) is the radio technician.

The Army Nurses: Major Edna Howard (Yvonne Wilder) measures 35-25-36 and can work wonders by substituting clothes for scarce items (for instance, a girdle became a much needed valve spring). She was born in Seattle, and her father was a chief engineer with the local power plant.

Lieutenant Dolores Crandall (Melinda Naud) is the sexiest of the girls and measures 38-24-36. She is a health nut (she is always nagging Sherman to take his vitamins), sweet and a bit clumsy. Dolores means well, tries so hard to do her best, but things just don't work out her way. She has a habit of getting the captain wet—whether it is from a broken shower, a wet towel, or a dunk in the ocean.

Lieutenant Barbara Duran (Jamie Lee Curtis), who measures 36-24-34, was born on a farm in Pocatello, Idaho. She is the most sophisticated of the nurses and is fascinated with Holden (his wheelings and dealings impress her).

Lieutenant Ruth Colfax (Dorrie Thomson), who measures 36-24-35, and Claire Reid (Bond Gideon), who measures 36-24-36, are the remaining bombshells who Sherman believes are distractions to his crew (although when duty calls, the guys seem to forget the girls and become the crew Sherman needs).

The nurses first became a part of the crew when they were stranded on an island and picked up by the *Sea Tiger*. They now seem to be trapped aboard the sub (every time they are supposed to leave, something comes up to prolong their stay; for example, just as they were about to leave, an enemy plane attacked the island and forced the cancellation of their ride out). Despite the fact that their lingerie hangs here and there to dry, and Molumphrey believes substituting bras for springs is indecent "and not navy," and the nurses' complaints about 90 second showers (because of limited fresh water supplies), Sherman is most often content—"Rather this than a desk in Washington." The series is based on the feature film.

The series returned for its second season (9/25/78 to 10/19/78; 6/1/79 to 8/30/79) as "The New Operation Petticoat." Despite its chronic mechanical problems, the *Sea Tiger* is assigned to duty as a lifeguard rescue vessel patrolling the Pacific for downed fliers. Sam Haller (Robert Hogan), the dedicated but compassionate lieutenant, is now the sub's commander, and Michael ("Mike") Bender (Randolph Mantooth) is the unregimented, wheeling-dealing second lieutenant who assists him.

Katherine O'Hara (JoAnn Pflug) is the self-assured head of the Navy Nurse Brigade; Lieutenant Dolores Crandall (Melinda Naud) is the ingenious but naive nurse; and Ensign Betty Wheeler (Hilary Thompson) is the sharp and witty one.

The Crew: Chief Engineer Stanley Dobritch (Warren Berlinger); Yeoman Hunkle (Richard Brestoff), Seaman Broom (Jim Varney), and Seaman Horner (Don Sparks). Before the series was actually filmed, JoAnn Pflug was cast as Lieutenant Dorothy O'Hara and Hilary Thompson as Ensign Betty Miller.

Themes: "Operation Petticoat," by Artie Butler; "The New Operation Petticoat," by Peter Matz.

Note: The pilot film contains a scene in which the nurses are fitted with men's uniforms. The uniform selected for Jamie Lee Curtis had the name tag of the actor who first wore it sewn inside the neckband—Tony Curtis, Jamie's father (who starred in the 1959 movie *Operation Petticoat*, with Cary Grant).

540. *Our Family Honor*
ABC, 9/17/85 to 1/3/86

Vincent Danzig (Eli Wallach) and Patrick ("Pat") McKay (Kenneth McMillan) were childhood friends who grew up in "the old neighborhood" in New York City. Vincent took the criminal path and is now a syndicate boss. Pat followed in a proud family tradition and became a policeman; he is now dedicated to destroying the Danzig criminal empire (he also blames the family for killing his eldest son, Officer Patrick McKay, Jr.). Serial-like episodes relate events within the two rival families.

The Danzigs live in a mansion at 63-1432 Southcrest Lane on Long Island. Vincent is married to Marianne (Barbara Stuart), his second wife (his first wife died two years after the birth of his son, August). His children are August ("Augie") Danzig (Michael Madsen) and Jerry Danzig (Michael Woods). Augie is married to Rita (Sheree J. Wilson) and is the father of a young son named Mark (Scott Sherk). He prefers violence to achieve his goals. Jerry is a lawyer for the First Federated Bank in Manhattan; he uses the name Jerry Cole in order to have his own life away from the Danzig family.

The McKays are a hard working family living in Manhattan. Patrick and his wife, Katherine (Georgann Johnson), reside at 6340 Bridge Street. Patrick began his career as a patrolman and was the chief of operations when first introduced; by the end of the first episode, he was the police commissioner—and a threat to Vincent: "Every time McKay moves up in the police department, it's like a cancer growing inside me."

Frank McKay (Tom Mason) is Pat's son and a detective with the 8th Precinct in Manhattan. The newscasters report that Frank is "the man who is single-handedly cleaning up New York City"; others say he uses "Gestapo tactics" to apprehend criminals.

Elizabeth ("Liz") McKay (Daphne Ashbrook) is Pat's granddaughter. She is a police officer with Unit 41 of the 8th Precinct. Liz, whose badge number is 9514, rides in patrol car 2708 with her partner, Officer Ed Santini (Ray Liotta); Ed's badge number is 3210. Her father was Patrick Jr.; her mother is Rose (Patricia Duff). Liz is romantically involved with Jerry Cole.

Matthew ("Matt") McKay (James O'Sullivan) is Pat's second-born son, a criminal attorney who is seeking to destroy the Danzig family. His wife is Roxanne (Juanin Clay).

Pat's hangout is O'Shaughnessey's Bar; his license plate reads 174L TFH. Vincent's license plate is 9Z3C-JGR;

Frank's plate reads 640N-KAZ; and JNC-4R is Matthew's license plate. Liz and Frank's precinct is referred to as "The O-Eight."

Theme: "Our Family Honor," by Barry DeVorzon and Douglas Timm.

541. *Our House*

NBC, 9/11/86 to 6/26/88

Jessica ("Jessie") Witherspoon (Deidre Hall) is a widow and the mother of three children: Kris (Shannen Doherty), Molly (Keri Houlihan) and David (Chad Allen). They live at 14 Ashton Street in Los Angeles with Jessie's father-in-law, Gus Witherspoon (Wilford Brimley), a widower who extended an invitation to Jessie and her family to live with him after the death of her husband, John. Their phone number is 555-4680 (later 555-4847).

Gus, whose hobby is model railroading ("HO scale"), is a retired engineer (judging by the roadnames of his model equipment, Gus worked for the Santa Fe Railroad). Gus and his friend Joe Kaplan (Gerald S. O'Loughlin) are members of the Monona Service Club; Joe has a never-seen wife named Gladys.

Jessie was originally a models photographer for Cathcart Architects, then a photographer for the Los Angeles *Post-Gazette*. Kris, her oldest daughter, attends James K. Polk High School (in United School District 8). David, her middle child, is enrolled in Naismith Junior High, and Molly, her youngest, attends Naismith Elementary School. Jessie and her family, who have a dog named Arthur, originally lived in Fort Wayne, Indiana.

William Katt appeared as Gus's estranged son, Ben Witherspoon; Rebecca Balding was Ben's wife, Gail; and Laurie Burton played Jessie's sister, Sheila. Gus's late wife was named Mary; Patrick Duffy played Jessie's husband, John Witherspoon, in a flashback sequence.

Billy Goldenberg composed the "Our House" theme.

Our Man Higgins see *Mr. Belvedere*

542. *Our Miss Brooks*

CBS, 10/3/52 to 9/21/56

Cast: Eve Arden *(Connie Brooks)*, Robert Rockwell *(Philip Boynton)*, Gale Gordon *(Osgood Conklin)*, Richard Crenna *(Walter Denton)*, Jane Morgan *(Mrs. Davis)*, Gloria McMillan *(Harriet Conklin)*, Leonard Smith *(Stretch Snodgrass)*.

Facts: Constance ("Connie") Brooks is an English teacher at Madison High School in a small town called Madison. She lives at Mrs. Davis's boardinghouse on Carroll Avenue (Margaret Davis, the owner, has a cat named Minerva). Tomato juice and pancakes is Connie's favorite breakfast. Connie has a tendency to forget her birthday and is soft hearted—she can't turn down anyone with a hard luck story. She shops at Sherry's Department Store and is known to frequent Fisher's Pawn Shop when money becomes a problem. After a hard day at school, Connie has what she calls "Schoolteacher's B & B"—bath and bed. Connie also has frequent dreams about her boyfriend, Philip Boynton, Madison's biology teacher. "As usual," Connie says about her dreams, "nothing happens."

Philip is shy, and Connie wishes he would take "brave shots." Connie started dating Philip in 1948 when he got his pet lab frog, McDougal. She says "that even though Philip is a biology teacher, there is a big difference between teaching it and learning it." Philip is just not romantic. He treats Connie with respect (too much, Connie believes) and tells Connie, "I know I haven't been the most aggressive chap in the world, and I do think of other things than my biological experiments. Things that are more personal; things like a man thinking about a woman whether she is a teacher or not..." As Connie hopes to hear more, Philip either loses confidence and changes the subject or someone interrupts him before he can go any further. Despite the lack of affection (even kisses), Connie loves Philip and hopes to make a man out of him.

Philip is also the school's track team coach and a member of the Elks' Club, and he plays the ukulele. He carries jellybeans with him at all times: "The dextrose contained in them is one of the best sources of quick energy known to science" (Connie likes the purple ones). In 1952 Philip undertook a confidential research project: the fertilization of the long-stem lily. He was born in Seattle, attended Cavendish High School and has a collection of frogs, rabbits and guinea pigs.

Osgood Conklin is Madison's always yelling, easily upset and stern principal. He was a major during World War II and spent four years as commander of Camp Fabrick in Ohio. He is also a member of the Elks' Club.

"He is a lame-brain dunce," says Osgood about Walter Denton, a student at the school. Walter is the manager of the track team, drives a hot rod that cost him $30 (it was missing a right rear tire when purchased) and each morning stops by Mrs. Davis's to drive Connie to school—and have a second breakfast. Walter is crazy in love with Osgood's daughter, Harriet, a student at Madison High. "Harriet is a wonderful girl," Walter says. "Walter's my life, my future, my all," exclaims Harriet; but if someone else should catch her fancy—"Who needs Walter," she says.

Madison's star basketball player is Fabian ("Stretch") Snodgrass, a not too bright student who is the school's hope of winning the state championship. Connie tries, but it is hopeless—"I know I ain't no good in English, Miss Brooks. Ever since the first test you give me, I know that I was gonna improve and get the kind of marks in English that I've stroven for." Stretch has an unseen sister named Rapunzel Snodgrass.

The format changed in last season episodes: Madison High is demolished to make way for a highway. Connie acquires a job as an English teacher at Mrs. Nestor's Elementary School in California's San Fernando Valley. Philip and Connie's relationship is broken off when he secures employment as a biology teacher at an Arizona high school. Osgood acquires the job as principal at Mrs. Nestor's, and Mrs. Davis finds a new boardinghouse on Maple Street (where Connie again resides). Connie's new romantic interest is Gene Talbot (Gene Barry), the school's handsome athletic director (by coincidence, Gene and Philip were both born in Seattle; Gene also attended Cavendish High School). (On their last day at Madison High, Walter gave Connie an apple and the right door of his car to remember him by. When Philip visited Connie five months later, he gave her not flowers or candy she was hoping for but a box of Arizona desert lizards.)

Other Regulars (New Version): Clint Albright (William Ching), the gym instructor; Mrs. Nestor (Nana Bryant), the school's owner; Oliver Muncey (Bob Sweeney), Mrs. Nestor's brother; and Benny Romero (Ricky Vera), the problem student.

Relatives: Virginia Gordon and Paula Winslow (Osgood's wife, *Martha Conklin*), Eddie Ryder (Stretch's brother, *Winston ["Bones"] Snodgrass*), Jesslyn Fax (Mrs. Davis's sister, *Angela*), Hy Averback (*Benny's father*).

Theme: "Our Miss Brooks," by Wilbur Hatch.

543. *Out of the Blue*

ABC, 9/9/79 to 10/21/79
ABC, 12/6/79 (1 episode)

Cast: Dixie Carter (*Marion MacNelmor*), James Brogan (*Random*), Olivia Barash (*Laura Richards*), Tammy Lauren (*Stacey Richards*), Clark Brandon (*Chris Richards*), Jason Keller (*Jason Richards*), Shane Keller (*Shane Richards*), Eileen Heckart (*Boss Angel*).

Facts:

Once upon a time there was a lady [Marion] who came to live with five children. Two of them were twins [Jason and Shane, age eight] and she was forever getting them mixed up. And there was a funny, darling, fresh-faced, laughing little tomboy [Stacey, age ten]; and another little girl [Laura, age 13], so adorable, so like her mother that the lady got chills when she looked at her. And there was the oldest [Chris, age 16], a boy who was growing up to be a fine, decent young man. Oh, but this silly, silly lady got it into her head that none of these children loved her until one day they did something so magical that all of a sudden she knew she was part of this wonderful family.

Marion MacNelmor is the aunt of the five Richards children; she became their guardian after their parents were killed in a plane crash. As Marion said above, she believed the children did not love her until something "magical" happened: the children gave her a surprise birthday party

and a bottle of perfume as a gift—the same gift her sister (the children's mother) had always given her on her birthday. Just as Marion realizes that she has become part of the family, celestial powers believe that Marion cannot handle the job alone.

On orders from her superior, Boss Angel assigns a Class Three Angel named Random to help Marion watch over the kids; but he is prohibited from using any of his heavenly powers to solve their problems.

Shortly after, Random arrives at the Richards house (217 Southampton Street in Chicago), seeking a basement apartment they have for rent. He quickly wins over the family, even Marion, who finds it strange that he has only one name ("I just have one name, Random, like Rambo and Cher"). Although Random is supposed to keep his true identity a secret, he reveals it to the children ("I'm an angel from heaven"), who vow to keep his secret. To be in a better position to help the children, especially Chris (who Boss Angel feels needs the most guidance), Random becomes a science teacher at the local high school (he teaches in Room 203, but the school is not named). Although angels are not permitted to interfere in human destiny (Noninvolvement Act, Subsection B), Random uses magic "to help matters along."

In the opening theme, Marion and Random are seen riding a tandem bicycle; Stacey is playing baseball (running to home plate to score); Laura is roller skating; and Chris is playing football (jersey number 51). Right before the theme ends, the family is seen jogging, roller skating and playing football (the twins are wearing jerseys with the number 10; in the series they wear jerseys with the number 86).

It is mentioned that Stacey attends Clinton Elementary School and loves baseball (she apparently spends much of her allowance, $1.50 a week, on chewing gum—"It helps me with my spitball"—and enjoys watching Chris and his friends in football practice; she likes "the grunts and groans when they get tackled"). Laura, on the other hand, is fast becoming a young woman and developing interests that Stacey finds hard to believe (such as wearing a dress and makeup). Laura attends Clinton Junior High School and is starstruck (she is saving her allowance, three dollars a week, "to travel to Hollywood and see movie stars"). Random walks from heaven through clouds to the front yard of the Richards house (in the opening theme).

Theme: "Out of the Blue," by Ben Lanzarone.

544. *Out of This World*

Syndicated, 9/87 to 9/91

Cast: Donna Pescow (*Donna Garland*), Maureen Flannigan (*Evie Garland*), Doug McClure (*Kyle Applegate*), Joe Alaskey (*Beano Froelich*), Christina Nigra (*Lindsey Selkirk*), Stephen Burton (*Chris Fuller*), Burt Reynolds (*Troy's Voice*).

Facts: In 1972 an Earth girl named Donna Froelich was working as a waitress at Natural Norman's Organic Ice Cream Parlor. At this same time, Troy Ethel Garland, a

Out of This World. **Donna Pescow (left) and Maureen Flannigan.**

being from the planet Anterias, was sent on a mission to get help from the other planets in his galaxy (Anterias is battling the warring Frigians from the planet Frigid). During his mission, Troy's mortal enemy, Krangle the Skull Basher (Richard Moll), shoots at Troy and disables his ship. Troy crash-lands on Earth. Sometime after (not specified), Troy wanders into Natural Norman's and orders a Raspberry Radish Rocket Ship. It was love at first sight when Donna and Troy saw each other. They dated and married on July 27, 1974 (at the Our Lady of the Strip Wedding Chapel in Las Vegas) and blended life forms. Shortly after, Donna gave birth to a girl they named Eve ("Evie") Ethel Garland. Troy repaired his ship, completed his mission and returned to Anterias. Stories, which begin when Evie is 13 years old, relate events in her life.

Evie, half Earthling and half Anterian, possesses several powers: freezing and unfreezing time (by placing her two index fingers together, she freezes time; by placing her palms together she unfreezes it), "gleeping" (the ability to rearrange molecules by concentrating) and teletransportation (by snapping her fingers, she can transport herself to another place). Evie first attended the Marlowe School for Gifted Children, then Marlowe High School (both in Marlowe, California). She has a plush cat named Twinky, and her favorite hangout is a soda shop called the Goodie Goodie. Evie is third string on the school's basketball team, the Fighting Hamsters, and a member of the Marlowe Teenage Bowling Team, and she communicates with her father via a generic-link crystal cube that allows voice transmission (Troy calls her his "Earth Angel"). The Anterian measles (blue dots on the face) was the first alien disease to affect Evie (but it cured itself in eight hours).

Evie's favorite breakfast is orange juice, hotcakes and bacon. Her favorite movie star is Kevin Costner, and she loves to wear earrings ("I'm an earring-holic"). She rents movies at Vic's Video Rentals, and her favorite soap opera is "All My Yesterday's Tomorrows." Evie has a midnight curfew on nonschool nights.

Evie lives with Donna in a spacious house at 17 Medvale Road in Marlowe, California; their phone number is 406-555-4669. She explains her father's absence to her friends by saying that he is in the CIA.

Donna ran the Marlowe School for Gifted Children (1987-88), then became owner of the catering service Donna Delights Planning and Catering (1988–90) and finally was the mayor of Marlowe (1990-91). Her car license plate reads 2XHX-622, and she hosts "Meet the Mayor," a talk show on public access television, Channel 108. Donna attended Marlowe High School (she was a cheerleader), has a fear of Jell-O ("It's just not right, the way it wiggles") and as a kid rode Mr. Trotter, the ten-cent a ride horse at Sherman's Market.

Evie's Uncle Beano (Donna's brother) is the overweight owner of the Waist-a-Weigh Diet Clinic (later changed to Beano's Health Club). He has a plush bear named Sparky and lives next door to Donna.

Kyle X. Applegate, a former Hollywood film and television star, was the original mayor of Marlowe (1987–90). He lost in an election to Donna by one vote (500 to 501) and now serves as the police chief (he calls his patrol car Betsy). In first season episodes, Kyle was the star of two former television series, "The Floridian" and "Mosquito Man." During the second season, Kyle was a movie performer and the star of "Cowboy Kyle" feature films (titles include *The Good, the Bad and the Unattractive* and *Gunfight at the Pretty Good Corral*). Third season episodes find Kyle the star of a former television series called "Cowboy Kyle." (He had a horse named Myron, and Sheldon Moskowitz, the frontier dentist, was his sidekick. Kyle was the marshal of Laramie Heights and wore fancy shirts with ruffles. Off the set he was called "The Ruffleman." Charlie Brill played Sheldon.)

Kyle dropped out of high school the night before his last test in senior year to play a cannibal in the movie *Please Don't Eat the Daileys* in 1962. He then appeared in the film *Gidget Goes to Gettysburg*. In 1976 Kyle crashed the Emmy Awards presentation and pretended to be John Travolta. The biggest villain Marlowe ever had was the Cereal Thief (he broke into 7-11s to steal cereal; Kyle caught him with 200 boxes of Rice Krispies). Kyle has a dog named Buster.

Lindsey Selkirk is Evie's boy-crazy girlfriend. She is a

member of the Movie Mania Video Club and has a dog named Mimi. She and Evie appeared on the television game show "Stump Your Neighbor" (Evie won 900 to 0).

Chris Marian Fuller is Evie's on-and-off boyfriend. Like Lindsey, he too attended Marlowe High School (although he was a year ahead of Evie). He worked as the assistant manager of Chicken in a Basket and attends Marlowe Community College (1990-91). His favorite treat at the Goodie Goodie is a Fudgie Bear sundae.

Troy (who is never seen) is also called Troy of Anterias. Anterians, "who shop Sears," possess two hearts and their children mature at the age of 13. Anterias is three billion miles from Earth ("just left of the moon"), and Anterians resemble humans. Darth Vader appears on the Anterian $100 bill. "Doo-wop" was Troy's favorite type of music when he was on Earth; he was in the Interplanetary Air Force for 14 years. Loni Anderson is his favorite television star, and "Evening Shade" (starring Burt Reynolds) is his favorite television show (which is running on Anterias). When Evie presents Troy with a problem that he cannot solve, he consults Professor Bob. Evie possesses an Enok, a special crystal that sounds a warning if Troy's enemy, Krangle the Skull Basher, is near. Troy's father, Grandpa Zelig, has an ancient ship called the *Anterias 1.*

On Evie's thirteenth birthday, Donna gave her a present Troy left for her — the crystal cube (Evie is the cube's source of energy). When Evie asks, "Will I ever see you?" Troy responds with, "I'm working on it very hard" (Anterias is still at war and Troy is needed). In the last first-run episode (5/26/91), Troy appeared on Earth again (via his Interplanetary Transport Booster) to surprise Evie on her eighteenth birthday. Troy, however, was transparent as a result of a malfunction in his rematerialization unit. The episode ended in a cliffhanger that was never resolved: Donna accidentally transported herself to Anterias, leaving Troy stranded on Earth.

Relatives: Tom Nolan (Donna's younger brother, *Mick Froelich,* a musician), Betsy Palmer (Donna's mother, *Barbara Froelich*), Tom Bosley (Troy's father, *Zelig*), Susan Bugg (Lindsey's mother, *Paula Selkirk*), Jack Lynch (Lindsey's brother, *Spencer Selkirk*).

Theme: An uncredited version of "Swinging on a Star" (Kevin Kiner receives music supervision billing).

545. *The Outsider*

NBC, 9/18/68 to 9/3/69

David Ross (Darren McGavin) is an embittered ex-con who now works as a private detective in Los Angeles. He lives in a moderately furnished apartment at 36841 Braxton. There is a refrigerator but no food (he seems to survive on the one bottle of milk in it). He drives a rather beat up sedan (license plate NEW 308) and makes "less than $10,000 a year." While he should look like a disheveled detective, to match the rest of his life-style, he is just the opposite: well dressed, charming and polite — or rugged and

two fisted, depending on the situation. Darren McGavin provides the narration as Ross strives to solve crimes.

Pete Rugolo composed the theme.

546. *Over My Dead Body*

CBS, 10/26/90 to 12/21/90
CBS, 6/6/91 to 6/20/91

Cast: Edward Woodward *(Maxwell Beckett),* Jessica Lundy *(Nikki Page).*

Facts: One night while nursing a bad cold, Nikki Page, a newspaper obituary writer, looks out her window and sees a man strangle a woman in the apartment across from hers. Nikki calls the police and rushes over to that apartment. However, before she or the police arrive, the killer removes his victim's body. The police arrive and see a hysterical Nikki dressed in a bathrobe and swinging an ax (she removed the ax from a fire box and was attempting to break through the apartment door); they conclude she is a flake when the apartment is searched and a body is not found.

The following day Nikki decides she needs a detective and hits on the idea of having her favorite mystery author, Maxwell Beckett, help her. When Nikki finds Maxwell, he is in a state of hysteria: his ex-wife is removing his furniture, and he is on the phone arguing with his never-seen publisher (it seems Beckett's last two books bombed because they had no grit. The publisher wants grit, not the drivel he just sent. "I'm out of grit," Beckett yells. "There is a shortage of grit this week"). Nikki manages to get a word in edgewise and tells Maxwell about the murder. "A window," he says. "Forget it; didn't you see *Rear Window?* They've done windows."

Although Maxwell dismisses Nikki, she is determined to have the former New Scotland Yard inspector help her solve the murder (and help her advance to a reporter's position on the paper).

The next day, while eating his breakfast, Maxwell is reading the paper when he sees that he has died (Nikki printed his obit). Maxwell rushes over to the paper. Nikki is almost fired when her editor finds out — but she accomplishes her goal and gets the burned-out writer to help her.

As they investigate, Maxwell finds that his creative juices have begun to flow again, and Nikki feels she has found her true calling as a crime reporter. Because each needs the other, they decide to remain a team after solving the murder (the girl, a hooker, was killed by an up and coming political figure who feared his affair with her would become a matter of public record).

Maxwell Beckett pretends to be a retired New Scotland Yard police inspector to give credibility to his books. He has written *All That Glitters* (four weeks on the best-seller list), *Hanging Crimes, The Five Confrontations, Taking the Heat, Hooker by Crook* and *Over My Dead Body.* Of the six books he has written, only three were a success. When Maxwell gets upset with his publisher (not named), he goes to the park to argue with himself.

Maxwell drives a Rolls Royce with the license plate 2915 AJ (mobile phone number 555-4242). His favorite restaurant is Alotta's, and his favorite charity is the Fog City Shelter. Maxwell was called "Beckett of the Yard" (or so he has led his readers to believe) and "the Catcher of Uncatchable Thieves, the Solver of Unsolvable Crimes." In 1981 he said he worked for the Anti-Terrorist Squad of the New Scotland Yard. Maxwell also wrote a series of children's books *(M. Mongoose)* under the pen name A.J. Edison.

Nikki Page, a Pisces, works under the name Miss Black. She is officially a journalist trainee for the San Francisco *Union*; her actual job is an entry level position writing the obituary column. She is a pretty, brash, street-smart young woman in her late twenties who aspires to bigger and better things. She rides a motorcycle (license plate not readable) and lives in Apartment 307 at 5045 Hode Street in San Francisco. Her unseen father, a football coach, leaves messages on her telephone answering service that predict her every move.

Relatives: Carolyn Seymour (Max's ex-wife, *Diane*; she has a dog named Woody).

Theme: "Over My Dead Body," by Lee Holdridge.

Note: A similar idea, originally titled "Love and Bullets," aired as the unsold pilot "Rewrite for Murder" on CBS (9/14/91). Carolyn Hudson (Pam Dawber) is a beautiful but uptight writer who created and scripts weekly episodes of the television series "Miss Markham Mysteries." Nick Bianco (George Clooney) is an ex-con (prison number 9736429) who, while serving time, created a detective called Biff Brannigan and featured him in three books: *Still on the Staircase, Corpse in the Kitchen* and *Kiss the Blood Off My Brannigan* (all published by Purity Press). When Carolyn's series takes a nosedive in the ratings, her producer, Buddy (Patrick Briscoe), hires Nick to spice up the show. Miss Markham ("I have no first name") is very prim and proper; Biff is rude, crude and streetwise. The characters are teamed and the series becomes "Love and Bullets." The proposed series was to relate Carolyn and Nick's adventures as television writers who become involved in real crimes, and their attempts to solve those crimes as their fictional characters would. Tim Scott composed the theme.

547. *Pacific Station*

NBC, 9/15/91 to 12/27/91

Robert ("Bob") Ballard (Robert Guillaume), Richard Capparelli (Richard Libertini), Sandy Callaway (Megan Gallagher) and Al Burkhardt (Ron Leibman) are police detectives based at Pacific Station in Venice, California (Room 112 is their headquarters). Bob has been a detective for 20 years and had six partners; he has a dog named Arsenio. Richard, a health food advocate, is now Bob's partner. His former partner was a police dog named Leo, and Richard is back on the force after a psychiatric leave. He was called "Donut" in high school and drives a 1962 Cadillac convertible. Al, who is partners with Sandy, reads the Victoria's Secret catalogue.

Ken Epstein (Joel Murray) is the captain. He worked previously as the mayor's press secretary. Ken has a major in journalism and a minor in criminology.

Grace Ballard (Pam Grier) is Bob's wife, and Dawn and Keith (Monica Calhoun and Leroy Edwards III) are his children. Judy Epstein (Janet Carroll) is Ken's wife; and Cassandra (Meredith Scott Lynn) is Richard's daughter (Richard had an affair at Woodstock in 1969 and didn't know he had a daughter until she looked him up).

Margo Thunder, Phaedra Butler and Rise Engerman sing the theme, "Rescue Me."

548. *Palace Guard*

CBS, 10/18/91 to 11/1/91

The cops say, "The guy is harder to find than a virgin in Vegas." The "guy" is Thomas ("Tommy") Logan (D.W. Moffett), a sophisticated thief whose specialty is robbing Palace Hotels all over the world. He is caught, however, robbing the New York Palace Hotel and sent to prison (Attica) for three years. After his release, Logan is approached by Arturo Taft (Tony LoBianco), the Palace Hotel chain owner. Taft hires Logan as his security chief—"Who better knows the hotel's weaknesses than a master thief." (Arturo attended Saint Martin's Academy. He is actually Tom's father, but Tom doesn't know it. Arturo learned about Tom two years ago from his first wife, who left him before she knew she was pregnant.)

Tom is officially the special head of security for the Palace Corporation (when there is a problem at any hotel, Logan is sent to resolve it). The hotel caters to the wealthiest and classiest people in the world. Assisting Logan is Christine ("Christy") Cooper (Marcy Walker), the vice president of publicity and public relations. She is a former actress (she starred in *Broken Arrows* and *Fool's Paradise*). Christy left the movie business because "I hated cattle calls and sleaze balls hitting on me all day." Her license plate reads XRZ 943.

Noelle Parker plays Melissa Taft, Arturo's 15-year-old daughter, and Dennis Boutsikaris was Christy's ex-husband, Marshall Lyons.

Mike Post composed the "Palace Guard Theme."

549. *Paper Dolls*

ABC, 9/23/84 to 12/25/84

A behind the scenes look at the world of modeling as seen through the experiences of two beautiful teenage high fashion models (called "paper dolls"), Taryn Blake (Nicollette Sheridan) and Laurie Caswell (Terry Farrell). Dinah Caswell (Jennifer Warren) is Laurie's overprotective mother, and Julia Blake (Brenda Vaccaro) is Taryn's ambitious and scheming mother.

The beautiful Racine (Morgan Fairchild), a former fashion model herself, now runs the Racine Model Agency. She is in direct competition with Grant Harper (Lloyd Bridges), the devious owner of the Harper World Wide Modeling Agency. Also vying for a piece of the money to be made from "paper dolls" are Colette Ferrier (Lauren Hutton), the owner of Ferrier Cosmetics; Mark Bailey (Roscoe Born), a fashion reporter for *Newsbeat Magazine*; and David Fenton (Richard Beymer), the owner of Tempus Sportswear.

John Bennett Perry played Dinah's husband, Michael Caswell; Dack Rambo was Grant's son, Wesley Harper; and Mimi Rogers was David's wife, Blair Fenton. In the television movie pilot, *Paper Dolls* (ABC, 5/4/83), Joan Collins was Racine; Darryl Hannah was Taryn; Alexandra Paul played Laurie; and Joan Hackett was Taryn's mother, Julia Blake.

Mark Snow composed the "Paper Dolls" theme.

550. *Paper Moon*

ABC, 9/12/74 to 1/2/75

Adelaide ("Addie") Loggins (Jodie Foster) is an 11-year-old girl who was raised by her mother, Essie Mae Loggins (not seen). Essie and Addie lived at 47 Bridge Corner in Ophelia, Kansas. Addie was born on November 19, 1922; Essie Mae was born in Oak View, Kansas. Addie is unaware of who her father is (Essie says only that he deserted her when Addie was born), but Addie suspects it is Moses ("Moze") Pray (Christopher Connelly), a man "who met my mother in a barroom." In 1933 Essie Mae is killed in a car accident. Moses reads about Essie's death and decides to pay his last respects. At the funeral service, Addie sees Moses and immediately believes that he is her father—"I look like you," she tells him, but Moses insists, "I don't look like you. I'm not your father." Addie's nearest living relative is her Aunt Billie in St. Joseph. When Essie's friend learns that Moses is headed for Missouri, she asks him to take Addie to her aunt. Though reluctant, Moses agrees. Addie is also reluctant to live with an aunt who doesn't want her when she can be with her father.

Moses is a con artist; en route, he pulls a con selling Bibles which involves Addie. The two work well as a team. Moses soon realizes that he can't get rid of Addie, for she is determined to stay with him. "I make all the decisions," he tells her. "You just have to look like a pretty little girl" (her part in scams). Stories follow their adventures as they travel throughout the Midwest during the Great Depression.

Moses is a salesman for the Dixie Bible Company, and he drives a 1931 Roadster with the license plate 68132. His favorite scam is the "Widow Business." (Moses reads the obituary columns to find grieving widows. He attempts to sell the wife a Bible supposedly ordered by her late husband for her. The widow feels obligated and buys the Bible.) Addie keeps her "treasures" in an old cigar box and cares for their finances (she keeps tabs on the money they make and spend and has a ten dollar bill put aside "for emergency use" only. "If it wasn't for me," Addie says, "we'd be broke all the time"). Moses has a false gold tooth that he uses when he sells Bibles and a deluxe edition Bible available with a person's name in gold lettering. Addie also calls herself Addie Pray. The series is based on the feature film of the same title (Moses was a salesman for the Kansas Bible Company here and Addie was nine years old).

Harold Arlen wrote the song, "Paper Moon," which is used as the theme.

Paradise see *Guns of Paradise*

551. *Parker Lewis Can't Lose*

Fox, 9/2/90 to 9/27/92

Cast: Corin Nemec (*Parker Lewis*), Maia Brewton (*Shelly Lewis*), Anne Bloom and Mary Ellen Trainor (*Judy Lewis*), Timothy Stack (*Martin Lewis*), William Jayne (*Mikey Randall*), Troy Slaten (*Jerry Steiner*), Melanie Chartoff (*Grace Musso*), Abraham Benrubi (*Larry Kubiac*), Taj Johnson (*Frank Lemmer*).

Facts: A comical depiction of life at Santo Domingo High School in California as seen through the eyes of three "best buds," Parker Lewis, Mikey Randall and Jerry Steiner.

Parker Lloyd Lewis is an enterprising student who simply can't lose—no matter what happens to him, he always comes out on top. He is the "cool" kid and has an ingenious plan for every situation; he resists authority and lives by his own rules. Parker, a sophomore, dreams of attending college and is a master of self-promotion. He records people on both audio- and videotape for "blackmail" purposes, and the earliest he has ever been at school is 7:52 A.M.

Parker and his friends watch movies at the Multi Plex Cinema. In the episode of 11/15/90, the best buds found the long abandoned underground school radio station, WFLM (89.8 FM). They reactivated "The Voice of Santo Domingo High" with Parker's call-in show, "Dr. Retro," with Jerry as the host of "The Freshman Show" and Mikey as the Iceman, the host of a rock and roll show. Parker's parents, Judy and Martin Lewis, own Mondo Video, a video rental store. Asking them for advice, Parker says "is like looking for gasoline with a match—you're lucky to get out alive." The only girl Parker fell head over heels in love with was Hayley Madison (April Lerman), a gorgeous schoolmate who nearly broke up the best buds. Parker's school headquarters is a small, abandoned room above the boys' gym. The buds eat at the Atlas Diner, and when they embark on a mission, Parker says, "Gentlemen, synchronize your Swatches" (each of the buds wears Swatch watch model 150M).

Michael Patrick ("Mikey") Randall, a sophomore, and Gerald ("Jerry") Steiner, a freshman, have been Parker's friends since childhood. Mikey is a Molly Ringwald fan, and the first song he wrote was a love sonnet to a girl named

Mary Lou (Alla Korot). When he wants to play the guitar, he goes into his parents' bathroom, gets in the tub and plays ("Great echo effects"). Mikey held a job in the mall at Dog on a Stick as a counterboy.

Jerry, the youngest of the best buds, calls Parker and Mikey "Sirs" and Mr. Lewis and Mr. Randall. He collects "Star Trek" figurines and possesses "The Musso Excuse File" (a listing of excuses Parker uses to get out of jams). Jerry carries a Big Bird thermos to school, has his coat Scotchguarded twice a month and "Eeeek!" is his expression when Ms. Musso, the principal, approaches. Jerry has a pet ant named Sparky and became very depressed when they discontinued Jetsons chewable vitamins. Jerry is addicted to computer games. It began with Candy Land, Chutes and Ladders and Monopoly board games. When Pac-Man came along he was hooked; he scored 3,000,020 points on his first try. He later joined Video Games-Anon to rid himself of the addiction. When Jerry would go to play a video game, the game would say "Oh no, Steiner, we surrender." In the third grade, Jerry carried a "Family Ties" lunchbox to school and was voted "Mr. Calculator" two years in a row.

Grace Musso, called Ms. Musso, is the stern, authoritarian principal who is out to get Parker. Her file number on Parker is SN2935-59. All Grace asks for "is a cup of coffee and a little peace and quiet in the morning" before she faces her nightmares—the students at Santo Domingo High. Parker calls Grace "more than a principal—a psychopath with tenure." Grace is feared by everyone and demands respect (her parents believe that a hunting lodge and rifle range is a good place for her to meet men). Her office phone number is KL5-4579; her mother's phone number is KL5-2739.

Grace earns $38,000 a year but lives in a $600,000 home—one of Parker's holds over her. She is very attractive and dresses to please no one but herself (her wardrobe is made up of tight skirts and blouses; she causes havoc when she attends basketball games as the boys leer at her and often lose the game). In 1969, when Grace was a junior at Santo Domingo High, she was an obedience helper to its principal; when she graduated in 1970, she was slimed with 60 gallons of lime Jell-O on the night of her senior prom (5/12/70). Grace owns a cabin at Sky Lake, and her detention room punishment is showing students a home video of her life—from infancy. Grace is Donny Osmond's number one fan (she has written thousands of letters to him since 1970). She also appeared on the television show "The Dating Connection" and mentioned that the Bee Gees and men with beards were her turn-ons. As of 10/13/91, Grace had had 1,357 blind dates; she has an account at the Santo Domingo Trust Bank.

Shelly Ann Lewis is Parker's 13-year-old sister. She is a freshman at Santo Domingo High and is following in the footsteps of her idol, Grace Musso (Shelly lives for the day when she can get the goods on Parker). Parker calls Shelly "Santo Domingo's hell cat" and is sure she is adopted (his nickname for her is "Shelly Belly").

Shelly, who weighs 77 pounds, is Grace's "pretty two-faced sugar plum freshman obedience trainee." Shelly is also a member of the snobbish Vogues, an all-girl club that is the terror of the school. (Called the "Glamour Girls of the Campus," they are selective in their associates and their signal to each other is air kisses. The rich and spoiled Melinda Harris [Brooke Theiss] is the chapter president.)

Shelly has an 11:00 P.M. curfew; if she helps Parker in any way, a red warning sign is flashed on the screen. Parker says, "Annie Riker [Tiffany Brissette] is the only friend Shelly ever had" and "My sister is capable of many things: humiliating me in public, reading my diary, selling my baby pictures, but getting a date, that's another story." Parker's effort to refine and bring out Shelly's natural beauty for her first date was called "Operation Pretty Woman—changing a 72 pound swamp monster into Julia Roberts."

Shelly's favorite movie is *Fatal Attraction* (she has seen it 15 times). She has "the largest collection of My Little Ponies on the continent" and developed a crush on Mikey in the episode of 10/14/90 (she drove him crazy by pretending to be "Breathless," his secret admirer). Shelly, who was named Janine in the original pilot, has a tattoo on her behind (its type was not revealed).

He believes that nine and a half years is almost a century and has been a junior at Santo Domingo for seven years. Lawrence ("Larry") Francis Kubiac is 20 years old, big (270 pounds, six feet seven inches tall), mean and "the most dangerous force ever to squeeze into a high school football uniform" (his jersey is number 77). Larry lives to eat and is very protective of his lunch (which he carries in a large paper bag with LARY'S LUNCH printed on it; Larry can't spell well). Anyone who messes with Larry's lunch is in for a beating. Although he appears menacing, he plays G.I. Joes with his little brother Bobby. Larry was said to have a police record, and when he gets upset he retreats to school bathroom Number 12—a forbidden area to other students—where Larry is king. Visitors, such as Parker, must get roughed up so Larry can maintain his image. When Larry is good, he is fed a fish. In the tenth annual District Science Fair, Larry won with his invention "Spud Light" (he stuffed the cylinder of a flashlight with a baked potato and the bulb lit). Larry's catchphrase is "Eat now?" He reads *Field and Heifer* magazine, has a job at the Smorgasbord Restaurant and is called "The Kube." In honor of Larry's tenth year at the school, the cafeteria named a sandwich after him: the Kube (pizza and french fries on sourdough bread).

Frank Lemmer is Grace's special guidance counselor (she summons him with a silent dog whistle). Frank has a pet piranha named Kathy and a subscription to *Soldier of Fortune* magazine, and when he attends the Soldier of Fortune Sleep Away Camp, he is voted "Most Likely to Be Killed by His Tentmates."

The Weekly Flamingo is the school newspaper; Grace's nemesis is Dr. Norman Pankow (Gerrit Graham), the principal at El Corrado High School. At Mondo Video, tapes rent for $2.99; TDK blank tape is sold and displayed. Cheerleader tryouts it the most eagerly awaited event at the school; the Golden Flamingo is the football team's mascot. Mikey keeps a jar of monkey brains on his desk (a buds' tradition); Jerry has a Spoons of the World collection; the local hangout is Sparky's Hamburgers.

Relatives: Wynn Irwin (Parker's uncle, *Bob*), Mina Kolb (Parker's aunt, *Celia*), Patrick J. O'Brien (*Larry's father*), Melanie MacQueen (*Larry's mother*), Zachary Bostrom (Larry's brother, *Bobby Kubiac*), Barbara Billingsley (*Grace's mother*), Andrea Elson (Grace's niece, *Denise Musso*), Jerry Mathers (Grace's brother, *Theodore Musso*), Sherry Rooney (*Mikey's mother*).

Flashbacks: Luke Edwards (*Jerry as a kid*).

Theme: "Parker Lewis Can't Lose," by Dennis McCarthy.

552. *The Partners*

NBC, 9/18/71 to 1/8/72

During the Korean War a bumbling private named Lennie Crooke (Don Adams) and a level-headed private named George Robinson (Rupert Crosse) became friends. A situation that would complicate their lives in later years—Lennie's knack for fouling everything up—began on the battlefields of Korea. While it is not made clear exactly what happened after the war, at some point they joined the Los Angeles Police Department.

When the series begins, Lennie and George are detectives with the 33rd Precinct. Lennie lives at 21 Ridge Canyon Road; George resides at 1103 West 4th Street, Apartment 302. Their car code is 8312. "They make a lot of mistakes" says their captain, Aaron William Andrews (John Doucette). "But they've been together a long time, and they always get the job done."

What Andrews, who has been captain of the 33rd Precinct for ten years, doesn't know is that it is George who saves the day by covering for Lennie. Despite the fact that Lennie is plagued by misfortune and doesn't always follow standard police procedure (he forgets), his foulups always seem to work for them (Lennie has a tendency to lose his gun, frisk furniture for concealed weapons, and arrest people without reading them their rights).

Dick Van Patten played Sergeant Nelson Higgenbottom, and Robert Karvelas was Freddie Butler, the man who confesses to every crime.

Lalo Schifrin composed the theme.

553. *Partners in Crime*

NBC, 9/22/84 to 12/29/84

Carole Stanwyck (Lynda Carter) is a beautiful brunette who measures 38-25-37. She was a debutante and a teabag heiress from New York who lost her money through bad investments. She now works as a freelance photographer. Carole wears a size medium dress, and her license plate reads IFL 896. She lives at 654 Veronna Drive.

Sydney Kovak (Loni Anderson) is a stunning blonde ("not my natural color") who measures 36-24-36. She grew up in the Mission District of San Francisco where she learned all

the tricks of the trade—from lock picking to picking pockets. She is now an aspiring but struggling musician (bass fiddle) who lives at 921 Hayworth Street (Apartment 3C). Sydney wears a size small dress, and her car license plate reads IPCE 467. She has a fake plaque that says SYDNEY KOVAK OF THE SAN FRANCISCO SYMPHONY ORCHESTRA (her dream is to play with the renowned orchestra). Sydney has been studying the bass for 20 years and has played professionally for 15.

Although strangers, Carole and Sydney have one thing in common: they were both married to Raymond Dashell Caulfield, a private detective who operates the Caulfield Detective Agency in San Francisco (also called the Raymond Dashell Caulfield Detective Agency). Carole was married to Raymond for three years, 1972–75, and was owed $62,000 in back alimony. Sydney was Raymond's second wife, 1976–78, and was owed $56,000 in back alimony. Ray proposed to both at the Top of the Mark Restaurant.

When Ray is killed during a case, Carole and Sydney inherit both his mansion and the detective agency. They solve Ray's murder and become "Partners in Crime" when they decide to remain a team and work as detectives.

Jeanine Caulfield (Eileen Heckart) is Ray's mother and Carole and Sydney's mutual mother-in-law. She is the unpublished author of 57 books and the owner of the Partners in Crime Book Store (later called Jeanine's Book Store). She lives in the mansion with Carole and Sydney. Harvey Shain (Walter Olkewicz) is their housekeeper (his claim to fame is that he met Rock Hudson on Fisherman's Wharf).

Cameron Mitchell appeared as Sydney's father, Duke Kovak.

Nathan Sassover and Ken Heller composed the "Partners in Crime" theme.

554. *The Partridge Family*

ABC, 9/25/70 to 8/31/74

Shirley Partridge (Shirley Jones) and her children, Keith (David Cassidy), Laurie (Susan Dey), Danny (Danny Bonaduce), Tracy (Suzanne Crough) and Chris (Jeremy Gelbwaks and Brian Forster), are the singing Partridge Family, a pop group managed by Reuben Kincaid (Dave Madden) but founded by Danny (who organized the family into a group, borrowed recording equipment from the school and convinced Reuben to take a chance on them).

The Partridges live at 698 Sycamore Road (also given as the 700 block on Vassario Road) in San Pueblo, California. They drive around the country in a psychedelic schoolbus with the license plate NLX 590 (and a "warning" sign on the back of the bus: CAREFUL. NERVOUS MOTHER DRIVING). The first song they performed on stage was "Together" (also their first hit single) in a Los Angeles show that was headlined by Johnny Cash. A picture of a partridge appeared on their first album, "The Partridge Family."

Keith and Laurie attend San Pueblo High School. Shirley's maiden name is Renfrew, and she worked at the

The Partridge Family. Front, left to right: Suzanne Crough, Shirley Jones and Susan Dey. Back, left to right: Brian Forster, David Cassidy and Danny Bonaduce.

Bank of San Pueblo before joining the group; the family has a dog named Simone.

Laurie is a teenage women's libber who sometimes feels bewildered and frustrated over all the attention girls bestow on Keith. Girls are a fringe benefit of the business and being a rock star, Keith found himself the object of many crushes. The first girl to develop a crush on him was Kathy (Claire Wilcox), a pretty teenager who thought it was an honor just to prepare the salad ("which Keith may eat") when Shirley invited her to dinner (she found her standing in the flower bed). Keith is a member of the school's basketball team and wears jersey number 15. His favorite foods are meatloaf and steak and potatoes. Keith writes the songs for the family and also plays the guitar. Laurie, who sometimes objects to Keith's lyrics (when she feels they are degrading to women), plays the keyboard. Danny plays guitar, Chris is the drummer and Tracy holds a tambourine. Shirley was reluctant to join the group at first, feeling she couldn't sing; Laurie convinced her that she has a sweet voice.

Danny attends San Pueblo Junior High. He is the schemer of the family and is always on the lookout for a way to make a dollar (for example, quitting school to become a business tycoon, and performing on his own as a standup comedian with an endless supply of old vaudeville jokes). Although Danny is only ten years old when the series begins, Reuben believes "he is a 40 year old midget."

Relatives: Rosemary DeCamp (Shirley's mother, *Amanda Renfrew*), Ray Bolger and Jackie Coogan (Shirley's father, *Walter Renfrew*), Margaret Hamilton *(Reuben's mother)*, Alan Bursky (Reuben's nephew, *Alan Kincaid*).

Performing Partridge Family Vocals: Shirley Jones, David Cassidy, Jackie Ward, Ron Hicklin and John and Tom Bahler.

Themes: "When We're Singing," by Wes Farrell and Diane Hildenbrand; and "Come On Get Happy," by Wes Farrell and Danny Janssen.

555. *The Patty Duke Show*

ABC, 9/18/63 to 8/31/66

Cast: Patty Duke *(Patty and Cathy Lane)*, William Schallert *(Martin Lane)*, Jean Byron *(Natalie Lane)*, Paul O'Keefe *(Ross Lane)*, Eddie Applegate *(Richard Harrison)*, Rita McLaughlin *(Patty when Patty Duke is Cathy; Cathy when Patty Duke is Patty)*.

Facts: The house at 8 Remsen Drive in Brooklyn Heights, New York, is a historic site. It was built in 1720 by Adam Prescott, whose son, Jonathan, served under General George Washington. Adam's daughter, Jane, offered the house to General Howe and charmed him in order to give Washington and his troops time to rest and regroup.

The current residents of 8 Remsen Drive are Martin Lane, his wife, Natalie, and their children Patty and Ross. Also living with them is Cathy Lane, Patty's sophisticated, lookalike cousin. The family dog is named Tiger, and their phone number is 624-1098.

Patricia ("Patty") Lane is the typical American teenage girl. She was born in December (Sagittarius is her birthsign), and she wears a size five dress. Patty wrote a book called *I Was a Teenage Teenager* ("Love, war, poverty, death and cooking recipes"). One hundred copies were published by Fyre Publishing (a vanity press). Patty also held a job as a waitress and singer at the Pink Percolator coffeehouse (where she worked under the name "Pittsburgh Patty"). Seventy-five kinds of coffee were served, and Patty's boyfriend, Richard Harrison, was the manager. Patty was editor of her high school newspaper, the *Bugle* (she patterned one issue after the New York *Query,* a paper that uses sensational headlines).

Catherine ("Cathy") Margaret Rollin Lane lived previously in Glasgow, Scotland. Her father is Kenneth Lane, a foreign correspondent for the New York *Chronicle*. Kenneth's assignments constantly uproot Cathy. To enable her to get her high school education, Kenneth arranged with his brother, Martin, to let Cathy live with him in Brooklyn.

Cathy wears a size five dress and attended Mrs. Tutles of Mountain Briar private school (where she was the debate champion) before coming to America. Her father calls her "Kit Kat," and she has a built-in lie detector: she gets the hiccups when she lies or tries to. Cathy is a member of the Literary Club at school.

Patty and Cathy attend Brooklyn Heights High School (they are both sophomores in first season episodes). The afterschool hangout is the Shake Shop (later Leslie's Ice Cream Parlor). They attempted to make money through some of Patty's harebrained schemes: the Worldwide Dress Company (selling Catnip dresses designed by Cathy for $9.95 each); Mother Patty's Preserves ("The Jam of Kings— King of the Jams," based on an apricot jam recipe Cathy found in a book of recipes from Charles III and packaged in jars purchased from the Fleming Bottle Company); and Doctors Baby Sitting Service (too many kids and no sitters closed the company after one day).

Patty Duke also played Betsy Lane, Patty's lookalike cousin from Atlanta, a Southern bombshell who took the boys of Brooklyn Heights by storm. While Patty called her a "Confederate Cleopatra," Betsy was, in reality, a lonely girl who desperately tried to get Cathy to leave so that she could stay with the Lanes (Betsy was ignored by her parents, who shipped her off to boarding schools, so they could devote full time to building up their business). Betsy's "security blanket" was her doll, Sara Jane.

Martin Lane is the managing editor of the New York *Chronicle*. He was captain of his college football team and married Natalie when she was 17 years old. They honeymooned at Lake George and have been married for 20 years (according to first season episodes). Ross attends P.S. 8 and has a weekly allowance of 50 cents; his birthsign is Taurus (Martin's is Virgo; Natalie's is Pisces). The New York *Record* is the paper in direct competition with the *Chronicle*.

In the episode "Fiancée for a Day," it is mentioned that Patty and Richard have been dating for five years. It is also mentioned that Richard's father is a banker; in another episode, he is a highway construction engineer. Lane family ancestors include Lieutenant Noah Lane, who was the first

Union officer captured at Bull Run, and Joshua Lane, who founded the first general store in Vermont. The school song of Brooklyn Heights High is sung to the tune of "O Tannenbaum"; the school colors are red and gold.

Relatives: William Schallert (Cathy's father, *Kenneth Lane*, and Martin's uncle, *Jed Lane*), Ilka Chase (Martin's aunt, *Pauline*), George Gaynes (Betsy's father, *Gaylord Lane*), Frances Heflin (Betsy's mother, *Cissy Lane*), David Doyle (Richard's father, *Jonathan Harrison*), Amzie Strickland (*Richard's mother*). Unseen relatives were Martin's Uncle Ben and Aunt Martha; his Aunt Kay (who sends him a basket of peaches every year from the farm), his niece, Ann, and his cousins, Clarence and Fran. Richard mentioned he had a cousin named Florence Lawrence.

Theme: "Theme from the Patty Duke Show," by Sid Ramin and Robert Wells.

556. *Peaceable Kingdom*

CBS, 9/20/89 to 11/15/89

Rebecca Cafferty (Lindsay Wagner) is the widowed mother of three children: Courtney (Melissa Clayton), Sam (Victor DiMattia) and Dean (Michael Manasseri). She lives in New York City (at 101 Park Avenue) but accepts a job in California to become the director of the Los Angeles County Zoo. Her dream is to turn the zoo into a model for promoting animal survival. Rebecca is assisted by her brother, Dr. Jed McFadden (Tom Wopat), the curator of mammals.

The Caffertys live in a special home that is located in the zoo and reserved for its director. Courtney and Dean attend Liberty High School (in New York, they were enrolled in the Marquis private school). Sam has a pet seal named Rover. Rebecca and Jed attended Madison High School. In the unaired pilot version of the series, Jed was Rebecca's love interest, not her brother.

"The Peaceable Kingdom Theme" was composed by David McHugh.

557. *The People's Choice*

NBC, 10/6/55 to 9/25/58

Cast: Jackie Cooper (*Sock Miller*), Patricia Breslin (*Mandy Peoples*), Margaret Irving (*Gus Bennett*), Paul Maxey (*John Peoples*), Dick Wesson (*Rollo*), Leonid Kinskey (*Pierre*), Mary Jane Croft (*Voice of Cleo*).

Facts: New City, California, is a city built in a hurry. It is famous for its lettuce crops, and it is near Los Angeles. Some people have streetlights, some have no sewers, some have terrible roads. Socrates ("Sock") Miller and his aunt, Augusta "Gus" Bennett, live in a trailer camp in New City's Paradise Park. Sock, who graduated from Cornell University (Phi Beta Kappa), was raised by his aunt following his parents' deaths when he was three years old. He served a

hitch in Korea (as a marine sergeant) and is now an ornithologist for the government's Bureau of Fish and Wildlife. His job is to "follow the birds" (he files reports on migratory birds, as their flights foretell climatic conditions and aid farmers when planting crops). When he was first introduced, Sock's assignment was to track the Yellow Necked Nuthatch. Since getting back from Korea, Sock has logged 80,000 miles following birds. There is one other resident living with Sock — his basset hound, Cleo. Cleo was six months old when Sock, a corporal at the time, won her in a crap game. Cleo, whose thoughts can be heard by voiceover dubbing, is glad that Sock can't talk for her — "If he could, I'd be off the show." As a puppy, Cleo liked to hang out at the camp's dynamite shed. Sock was the platoon's bayonet champion.

One day Sock befriends Amanda ("Mandy") Peoples, the pretty daughter of New City's mayor, John Peoples, when she becomes stranded on a country road and he stops to fix her flat tire. It seems like love at first sight. When Mandy discovers that Sock is being transferred to Ohio (to find out why the Rose Breasted Grosbeak is laying smaller eggs this season), she devises a plan to keep him in town (and with her).

Mandy feels that Sock is the right man to fill a city council vacancy. She delivers a television speech in which she urges voters to elect Sock as their 5th District councilman. If they want paved roads, sewers and streetlights, then Sock Miller is their man. (Sock ran on the platform that he refused Mandy's proposal of marriage and would not be in the mayor's back pocket.) Sock is overwhelmingly elected.

Sock is given an office on the first floor of the Municipal Building (the sign on his door reads SOCRATES MILLER — COUNCILMAN — 5TH DISTRICT). (Sock received special permission from the Department of Fish and Wildlife, Western Division, to remain in New City until his term of office is completed.)

Vickie Sommers (Joi Lansing) is blonde, shapely and very beautiful. She can also take shorthand and type 110 words a minute — and that is the reason Sock hires her as his secretary (at $250 a month). Mandy didn't believe it and became extremely jealous (Sock is reluctant to hire Mandy because she is the mayor's daughter). Although Sock hired Vickie, Mandy showed up for work the next day as Sock's new secretary (Mandy persuaded her father to find Vickie a better paying job — five dollars a week more with the Sanitation Department). Prior to Vickie, Sock's secretary was Gigi Carstairs (Tamar Cooper), who couldn't type or take shorthand and was given the job by the mayor because her wealthy father was one of his campaign supporters.

Two marriages resulted on the series. Aunt Gus married Mayor Peoples and Sock married Mandy in 1957. Shortly after his marriage, Sock applies for a position as a lawyer with Barker Amalgamated in New York City. They hire Sock — but as the sales manager for Barkerville, a housing development with 294 houses for sale "20 miles from nowhere." Houses sell for $15,995, and Sock and Mandy live rent free in the model house (number 119).

Valerie Delmar (Jean Porter) was Sock's girlfriend before Mandy; lawyer Roger Crutcher (John Stephenson) was Mandy's boyfriend prior to Sock. The mayor's phone extension at the Municipal Building is 40; Sock calls Mandy his "Ruby Throated Hummingbird" (in the book, *Birds of America*, this bird is described as "a dainty little atom possessing exquisite beauty"). At the annual county fair beauty contest, Mandy entered as "Miss New City" and won second place. She attended Valley Junior High School. John calls Sock "Nature Boy" and Gus "Mousey." He also owns part interest in a whaling ship in Seattle.

Hexley ("Hex") Rollo is a friend of Sock's from childhood who now resides in New City. They were in the marines together; when stationed at Fort Baxter, Rollo (who is cursed with bad luck) lost a 20 ton amphibious tank.

Pierre Quincy is Sock's friend, an eccentric painter. Sock calls him the "Michelangelo of Paradise Trailer Park." He is a member of the local Artists' Club and calls Cleo "Funny Face."

Theme: "The People's Choice," by Lou Kosloff.

558. *Perfect Strangers*

ABC, 3/25/86 to 9/11/92

Cast: Mark Linn-Baker (*Larry Appleton*), Bronson Pinchot (*Balki Bartokomous*), Melanie Wilson (*Jennifer Lyons*), Rebeca Arthur (*Mary Anne Spencer*).

Facts: In the Mediterranean there exists a small island called Mypos. Sheep herding is the number one occupation, and the Myposian national debt is $635. A picture of a cow graces Myposian money. When Balki Bartokomous discovers that he has an American cousin named Larry Appleton who is one-sixty-fourth Myposian, he sets out to find him. His search ends in Chicago at the Caldwell Hotel at 627 Lincoln Boulevard. In Apartment 203 (in some episodes Apartment E) lives his Wisconsin-born cousin and future roommate, Larry—who then offers to let Balki live with him. Balki's efforts to adjust to an American way of life are the focal point of the series.

Cousin Larry (as Balki calls him) and Balki first worked for Donald ("Twinkie") Twinkacetti (Ernie Sabella), the gruff owner of the Ritz Discount Store (they are also members of the Ritz Discount Royals softball team). In these first season episodes, Belita Moreno played Donald's wife, Edwina, Matthew Licht was their son, Donnie, and Erica Gayle was their daughter, Marie. The Twinkacettis lived at 2831 Garfield Street.

When Larry and Balki find better jobs at the Chicago *Chronicle* (Larry as an assistant to the city editor, Balki as a mailroom clerk), they quit their sales jobs at the Ritz and move to Apartment 209 at 711 Caldwell Avenue. The paper is located at 901 East Wacker Street, and Larry and Balki are members of the paper's Strike Force bowling team. Larry now has a steady girlfriend named Jennifer Lyons, and Balki dates her roommate, Mary Anne Spencer. Belita Moreno now plays Lydia Markham, a columnist ("Dear Lydia") who also did a television series based on her column called "Lydia Live."

Larry and Jennifer married in the episode of 9/27/91 and set up housekeeping on Elm Street—in a home they find they cannot afford. With three bedrooms and two and one half baths, they solve their money problems by renting the other bedrooms to Balki and Mary Anne (prior to the marriage, Balki called Jennifer "Future Cousin Jennifer"). On 4/18/92, Balki and Mary Anne married. Larry wrote a play called *Wheat*.

Balki takes night classes at Chicago Community College to improve his knowledge of America. His favorite television show is "Uncle Shaggy's Dog House," and he uses Mr. Ducky's Bubble Bath. Steve and Edie are the two pigeons who have made Balki's windowsill their home; Phil and Andy are the names Balki has given to his shoes. Balki has a parrot named Yorgi (named after his pet goat on Mypos), and as a kid he had a horse named Trodsky, a dog (Koos Koos) and a 300 pound turtle (Bibby). In one episode, he adopted a stray dog he called Super Dave. Balki's phone number (1992) is 555-9876.

Balki's favorite meal is eel wrapped in grape leaves and sheep-herder's bread with a side dish of Ding Ding Mac-Mood (pig snout). He eats yak links for breakfast. Balki is the best Bibibobacas baker in Mypos. The cream puff–like dessert can't be rushed; it has to be made slowly, or "the bib in the baca goes boom" (explodes). On Mount Mypos grows the Popadalupapadipu plant (it cures the common cold and Balki has one called Marge; the cold is cured by eating the pod, but the cure has a side effect on women—it grows mustaches, and the cold returns in two weeks when the effects wear off).

Balki's favorite singer is Wayne Newton. Balki rides Blue Thunder, the coin operated horse at the Shop and Save. He also draws a kids's comic for the *Chronicle* called "Dimitri's World" (about a cuddly little sheep; Dimitri is Balki's stuffed sheep). When someone lies, Balki fears the Gabuggies—the Myposian Fib Furies (Eva, Zsa Zsa and Magda; their god is Vertosh).

When Balki did volunteer work at Chicago General Hospital, he won the "Bed Changer of the Month" award. The episode of 2/15/91 saw Balki become a music star called Fresh Young Balki (he made a rap record for Knight Records called "Balki B"). Balki also ran for student body president of the college with the slogan "Pro Sheep, Anti Wolf."

Larry gargles to the tune of "Moon River." He was born in May, and as a kid in Madison, Wisconsin, he had a dog named Spot. Larry asked 12 girls to the senior prom. Thirteen girls turned him down (one came up to him and said, "Don't even think of asking me"). KYP 758 (later 993 753) is Larry's license plate, and "Oh, my Lord" is his catchphrase when something goes wrong. In the unaired pilot version, Louie Anderson played Cousin Larry.

Larry and Balki appeared on the television game show "Risk It All" (and lost everything) and bought a racehorse called Larry's Fortune; they also bought stock in Unicorn, Inc., the makers of Balki's favorite breakfast cereal, Raisin Puffs. When the Chicago Lotto hit $28 million, Balki played the following numbers: 15, 21, 27, 32, 37, 52. The winning numbers were 15, 21, 24, 32, 34, 52; they won $100.

Jennifer and Mary Anne have been friends since they were eight years old. They are both stewardesses for an unnamed airline. Mary Anne thinks that living with Jennifer is like living with a Barbie doll (she is too neat and perfect). Jennifer feels that Mary Anne is sloppy and hates it when she hogs the bathroom ("It takes her three hours to put on her makeup"). Jennifer was born in April in Iowa, where her parents own a corn canning business. Mary Anne was "Little Miss Gingivitis" in her sixth grade hygiene play.

Relatives: James Noble (*Larry's father*), Ted McGinley (Larry's brother, *Billy Appleton*), Sue Ball (Larry's sister, *Elaine Appleton*), John Anderson (Larry's grandfather, *Buzz Appleton*), Bronson Pinchot (*Balki's mother*; and Balki's cousin, *Bartok*), Marla Adams (Jennifer's mother, *Katherine Lyons*), Robert King (Jennifer's father, *Mr. Lyons*).

Theme: "Nothing's Gonna Stop Me Now," vocal by David Pomerantz.

Note: See also "Family Matters," the spinoff series.

559. *The Persuaders!*

ABC, 9/18/71 to 6/14/72

Cast: Roger Moore (*Brett Sinclair*), Tony Curtis (*Danny Wilde*), Laurence Naismith (*Judge Fulton*).

Facts: At the bar of the Hotel du Somme in France, Lord Brett Sinclair orders two Creole Screams. When the bartender does not know how to make the American drink Brett explains: "A jigger of white rum, a dash of bitters, chilled vermouth and a measure of grenadine. Then mix, stir in some crushed ice, shake, strain and pour. Top it off with one olive." Just then, Daniel ("Danny") Wilde, who is next to Brett, says, "Two. You were perfect up until the olives. Two olives. That way you can see them gently bounce up against each other." Brett, who couldn't care less if the olives gently bounce up against each other, insists on one. Danny insists on two. They can't agree and a fistfight ensues.

They are arrested—but instead of being sent to jail, they are brought to the hotel room of a retired judge named Fulton (no first name given). It seems that the judge had arranged for Brett and Danny to be at the hotel and knew they would get into trouble. Fulton explains that he was a judge for 15 years, and during that time he did his best to defend the innocent and punish the guilty: "The guilty ones that came to court, that is. One of the anomalies of the law is that in protecting the innocent, the guilty go free too. Since my retirement, I've done my best to redress that in my small private way. Now I have time to think, to study, to search for loopholes others might have overlooked."

The judge then gives them a choice: three months in jail or help him. "You are men with immense quality and potential and you fight—you fight over an olive. You are both docile and foolish and a useless waste of humanity. But you like to fight. All right, I'll give you a fight. I'll either make use of you or see that you are put away for

three months." When playboys Danny and Brett realize that it also means 90 nights, they agree to help the judge. Stories relate the globe-trotting exploits of Brett and Danny as they use their unique skills to help Judge Fulton bring criminals to justice.

Lord Brett Sinclair is a titled Englishman who was "born with a silver spoon in his mouth and all he does is lick the jam from it." Sinclair was once a proud and noble name that stood for justice and defended freedom—but that was before immense wealth changed it. Brett is a first class athlete, a connoisseur of the arts and a gourmet with a lusty taste in wine and women. He can speak seven languages, but all he uses them for is to order cocktails—"Your is the glib tongue at a hundred mindless parties," the judge says.

Danny Wilde is a multimillionaire who made and lost several fortunes. Making money has become so easy for him that he doesn't really bother anymore. But that wasn't always the case. He was born in the Bronx and lived in one of its poorest sections. His optimism, courage and a sense of humor pushed him to the top of the financial heap. He has a remarkable talent, but he just wastes it. "You just drift around the world gambling and womanizing. You were a nothing who became something. You are a nothing again," says Fulton.

Brett and Danny's favorite drink is the Creole Scream—whether with one or two olives: "Next to women and dogs, a man's best friend is a Creole Scream." The judge compares Brett and Danny to chemicals: "Take two relatively harmless compounds like nitro and glycerin. Mix them together and you have a very potent combination. Handle it carelessly and it can blow your head off. Nitro and glycerin—and I light the fuse." The stars are credited on screen by their last names only—Curtis (on top) and Moore (bottom).

Theme: "The Persuaders," by John Barry.

560. *Pete and Gladys*

CBS, 9/19/60 to 9/10/62

Cast: Harry Morgan (*Peter Porter*), Cara Williams (*Gladys Porter*).

Facts: In the opening theme, Cupid fires an arrow into a heart, where a married couple (Pete and Gladys) are seen arguing. When the arrow strikes the heart, they kiss and make up. Peter Porter, an insurance salesman for the Springer, Slocum and Klever Insurance Company in Los Angeles, and Gladys Hooper, a scatterbrained secretary, fell in love, eloped and married nine years earlier (1951) in the small town of Colbyville; they later set up housekeeping at 36 Bleecker Street in Westwood, California. Granite 5-5055 is their phone number. Their favorite restaurant is Petroni's (the song "Santa Lucia" is heard in the background when they go), and "Life Can Be a Problem" is their favorite television show.

Pete, who spent his military career as a clerk in a PX during World War II, told Gladys he was a hero (singlehandedly capturing a Japanese patrol). He has a hobby he doesn't want: restoring old cars (Gladys thought Pete needed a hobby so she bought him a 1924 Hutmobile Roadster, license plate JFH 647, for $20), and he puts up with all of Gladys's harebrained antics because "I've gotten used to her; I'm addicted to her."

"When strange things are looking to happen, somebody gives them Gladys's address," says Janet Colton (Shirley Mitchell), Gladys's friend, neighbor and cohort in misadventure.

Gladys is the entertainment chair of the Junior Matron's League of the Children's Hospital (she appeared as Mickey Rooney's "straightman" in the episode "Top Banana") and is a member of the Westwood Bowling League with friends Janet and Hilda Crocker (Verna Felton); they bowl with Sindler bowling balls. Gladys also appeared on the television show "Lucky Lady." When her audience ticket number (24931) was selected, she appeared on stage to relate a sad story in an attempt to win a trailer for a summer vacation (she won with a story that had Pete dying from an unknown disease; she later confessed to telling a lie, was given a stuffed penguin and told never to come back).

Barry Kelley appeared as Pete's boss, Barry Slocum; the series is a spinoff from "December Bride" (see entry), in which Gladys was never seen but was often talked about.

Relatives: Ernest Truex (Gladys's father, *Henry Hooper*), Bill Hinnant (Gladys's nephew, *Bruce*), Sue Randall (Gladys's cousin, *Helen Franklin*), Gale Gordon (Pete's uncle, *Paul Porter*; he gave Pete his first pair of roller skates; he believes Gladys is an idiot); Peter Leeds (Janet's husband, *George Colton*), Helen Kleeb (Barry's wife, *Laura Slocum*).

Theme: "Pete and Gladys," by Wilbur Hatch and Fred Steiner.

561. *Pete Kelly's Blues*

NBC, 4/5/59 to 9/4/59

The series is set in the 1920s and follows events in the life of Pete Kelly (William Reynolds), a cornet player and leader of the Big Seven, a band that plays regularly at 17 Cherry Street in Kansas City. Number 17 Cherry Street is also known as Lupo's and is a brownstone turned funeral parlor turned speakeasy. "It's a standard speakeasy," says Pete. "The booze is cut but the prices aren't. The beer is good, and the whisky is aged—if you get here later in the day. We play here from 10:00 P.M. to 4:00 A.M., with a pizza break at midnight. The hours are bad, but the music suits us."

George Lupo (Phil Gordon) is the owner of the speakeasy. "He was the only kid in Lanback County who got turned down for reform school," says Pete. "George later fought in the war with the 102nd Infantry and he pays scale—with a five dollar kickback."

Savannah Brown (Connee Boswell) is Pete's friend. "She sings at Fat Annie's on the Kansas side and says it's easy to sing the blues—all you need to do is be born when there is rain on the roof."

"There's one other thing about 17 Cherry Street," says Pete, "and that's trouble. You can get it by the yard, the pound, wholesale and retail. Like on Monday night..." (The episode would then begin.)

Johnny Cassiano (Anthony Eisley) is Pete's friend, an officer with the Kansas City Police Department; Dick Cathcart is the offscreen cornet player for Pete; and the Matty Matlock Combo provides the music for the club scenes.

Connee Boswell sings the theme, "Pete Kelly's Blues."

562. *Peter Gunn*

NBC, 9/22/58 to 9/27/60
ABC, 10/3/60 to 9/25/61

Peter Gunn (Craig Stevens) is a two fisted private detective who lives at 351 Ellis Park Road in Los Angeles; his home phone number is KR2-7056, and his mobile car number is JL1-7211. His romantic interest, Edith ("Edie") Hart (Lola Albright), is a singer at Mother's, a waterfront nightclub that was originally owned by a woman known only as Mother (Hope Emerson; later Minerva Urecal). Edie, who lives in Apartment 15 at the Bartell Hotel (1709 Ver Banna Street; phone number KL6-0699), later became the club owner and changed the name to Edie's.

Lieutenant Jacoby (Herschel Bernardi) of the 13th Precinct of the L.A.P.D. Homicide Squad, is Gunn's police department contact (366-2561 is his desk phone number). Babby (Billy Barty) is one of Gunn's snitches, a diminutive pool hustler (he tells Peter to "think tall"; when he sees that Gunn is in trouble he says, "You've got that eight ball look"). Wilbur (Herb Ellis) owns Cooky's, a beatnik coffeehouse; Emmett (Bill Chadney) plays the piano at Mother's.

Gunn pays his snitches ten dollars for information and frequents such "dives" as the Green Café and Natie's Hot Dogs (Ned Glass plays Natie). On 4/23/89, ABC presented the television movie *Peter Gunn*, with Peter Strauss as Peter Gunn in a story (set in 1964) that finds the private eye struggling to solve a mob connected murder. Barbara Williams played Edie Hart, Peter Jurasik was Lieutenant Jacoby, and Pearl Bailey was Mother.

Henry Mancini composed the series' jazz score and theme ("Peter Gunn") and the updated "Peter Gunn" theme for the movie.

563. *Peter Loves Mary*

NBC, 10/12/60 to 5/31/61

After 20 years on the road and living out of trunks, Peter Lindsey (Peter Lind Hayes) and his wife, Mary (Mary Healy), decide to give up show business and settle down. Peter, a comedian, singer and dancer, and Mary, a singer and dancer, and their children, Leslie (Merry Martin) and Steve

Pete and Gladys. **Harry Morgan and Cara Williams.**

(Gil Smith), move to 130 Maple Street in a small Connecticut town called Oakdale.

Peter and Mary performed in air force shows in the South Pacific during World War II, assisted Bob Hope with his USO tours, and appeared before royalty the world over. They always exited stage left, and the Porter Theatrical Agency represented them. Now, they seek only to settle down and enjoy life with their children (who attend the Oakdale School).

Mary is now a member of the P.T.A., the Garden Club and the Book Club. Peter, who has show business in his blood, performs at the Imperial Room in Manhattan but prefers "the living room circuit" (performing for their friends when Mary gives a party, which she does on a weekly basis). Peter is also president of the Keep Oakdale Beautiful Committee and chairman of the board of the High School Project (to finance the building of the community's first high school).

Bea Benaderet played Wilma, their housekeeper, and Wallace Ford appeared as Wilma's Uncle Charlie.

564. *Petticoat Junction*

CBS, 9/24/63 to 9/12/70

Cast: Bea Benaderet *(Kate Bradley)*, Edgar Buchanan *(Joe Carson)*, Jeannine Riley, Gunilla Hutton and Meredith MacRae *(Billie Jo Bradley)*, Pat Woodell and Lori Saunders *(Bobbie Jo Bradley)*, Linda Kaye Henning *(Betty Jo Bradley)*.

Facts: Kate Bradley is a widow and the mother of three beautiful daughters: Billie Jo, Bobbie Jo and Betty Jo. She owns the Shady Rest Hotel in Hooterville, a small farming community of 72 farms. Kate is assisted by her uncle, Joe Carson, the town's fire chief, who believes the hotel is haunted by the ghost of Chester W. Farnsworth, who was a guest at the hotel 50 years ago. When there is work to be done, Uncle Joe fakes an attack of lumbago; his favorite place at the hotel is the rocking chair on the front porch.

Billie Jo, the oldest of the Bradley girls, attends class at the Pixley Secretarial School; her first job was secretary to Oliver Fenton, an author whose books have been banned in Hooterville. Bobbie Jo and Betty Jo attend Hooterville High School. In one episode, the girls formed the singing group the Lady Bugs. Betty Jo, who had her first crush on Orville Miggs (who was more interested in cars than girls), married Steve Elliott (Mike Minor) in fourth season episodes. Steve was born in Seattle and became a cropduster when he was discharged from the air force. He crashed his plane in Hooterville when he saw the girls swimming in the water tower that feeds the local train, the Cannonball Express, and paid more attention to them than to where he was flying. Steve later became partners with Uncle Joe and formed the Carson-Elliott Cropdusting Company. Prior to his role as Steve, Mike Minor played Don Plout, the son of Kate's archenemy, Selma Plout (Virginia Sale).

Kate, who has a special recipe called "Bachelor Butter," was replaced as the mother figure on the show in 1968 by Dr. Janet Craig (June Lockhart); Bea Benaderet's death that year ended the Kate Bradley character. During Kate's illness, her Cousin Mae (Shirley Mitchell) and Aunt Helen (Rosemary DeCamp) cared for the family. Boy is the Bradley family dog (actually owned by Betty Jo, whom he followed home from school one day; press releases refer to Boy as the "Shady Rest Dog," played by Higgins).

Communities neighboring Hooterville are Pixley and Crabtree Corners. The Cannonball Express, an 1890s steam engine, coal car and combination mail/baggage/coach car, is owned by the C.F.&W. Railroad. (Railroad vice president Homer Bedloe, played by Charles Lane, is the valley's nemesis, as he seeks to scrap the ancient Cannonball.) Charley Pratt (Smiley Burnette) is the engineer, and Floyd Smoot (Rufe Davis) is the conductor. Three toots of the Cannonball's whistle alert the valley's children that it is time for their ride to school; Betty Jo's biggest thrill is driving the Cannonball.

The show's title refers to the Cannonball's watering stop at the Shady Rest Hotel. The Bradley girls swim in the tank on hot days—and their petticoats can be seen hanging over the top rim. In the original, unaired pilot version, Sharon Tate played Billie Jo (she was dropped by the producers of the family oriented show when they learned she had posed for a *Playboy* layout).

Don Ameche appeared as Steve's uncle, George, and twins Elaine and Danielle Hubbel played Betty Jo's daughter, Kathy Jo Elliott.

Theme: "Petticoat Junction," by Curt Massey.

Petticoat Junction. Pat Woodell, Jeannine Riley and Linda Kaye Henning.

565. *The Phil Silvers Show*

CBS, 9/20/55 to 9/11/59

Master Sergeant Ernest Bilko (Phil Silvers), serial number 10542699, is stationed at the Camp Freemont army base at Fort Baxter in Kansas (later episodes are set in Grove City, California). There, he is in charge of the 3rd Platoon of the Company B Motor Pool (24th Division), and he is totally dedicated to acquiring money by manipulating the U.S. Army for his own personal benefit.

Bilko, a master con artist, began his "career" during World War II. At that time he was with the 38th Division and stationed on New Guinea; he supplied the USO girls with something they desperately needed but were unable to get—nylons, at five dollars a pair. After the war, Bilko,

a master at pool and cards, was transferred to Fort Baxter where he now commands Company B: Privates Duane Doberman (Maurice Gosfield), Dino Paparelli (Billy Sands), Sam Fender (Herbie Faye), Fielding Zimmerman (Mickey Freeman), and Corporal Henshaw (Allan Melvin). The base cook, Rupert Ritzik (Joe E. Ross), is Bilko's main patsy. Ritzik eats Crispy Crunchies breakfast cereal, reads comic books and believes in flying saucers (he keeps a nightly watch in the hope of spotting one). His favorite television show is "Captain Dan, Space Man."

John T. ("Jack") Hall (Paul Ford) is the commanding officer. Other soldiers are: Corporal Rocco Barbella (Harvey Lembeck), Sergeant Francis Grover (Jimmy Little), Private Mullin (Jack Healy), Private Lester Mendelsohn (Gerald Hiken), Private Greg Chickeriny (Bruce Kirby) and Sergeant Stanley Sowicki (Harry Clark).

WAC Master Sergeant Joan Hogan (Elisabeth Fraser) is

Bilko's girlfriend; "Stacked" Stacy (Julie Newmar) is the waitress at the local diner; and George Kennedy played various MP (Military Police) roles.

Relatives: Beatrice Pons (Rupert's nagging wife, *Emma Ritzik*), Hope Sansbury (John's wife, *Nell Hall*), Sal Dano (Rocco's brother, *Angelo Barbella*), Betty Walker (Sam's wife, *Hattie Fender*), Toni Romer (Stanley's wife, *Agnes Sowicki*), George Richards (Stanley's son, *Stanley Jr.*), Doreen McLean *(Joan's mother)*, Harry Adams *(Joan's father)*. Not seen were Sam's kids: Raoul, Olivier, Benji, Claude, Cindy and Tab.

Theme: "Bilko's Theme," by John Strauss.

Note: The series was originally titled "You'll Never Get Rich" and is also known as "Sergeant Bilko." Phil Silvers attempted to recreate the success of Sergeant Ernie Bilko on two other occasions:

"The New Phil Silvers Show" (see entry).

"Eddie" (CBS, 9/5/71) was an unsold pilot in which Phil played Eddie Skinner, a patrolman with Pike's Private Patrol, a security service protecting the rich and famous. Like Sergeant Bilko, Eddie manipulated the company for his own gain. Fred Clark played Eddie's boss, Chief Pike. The pilot is also known as "Bel Air Patrol."

"At Ease" (ABC, 3/4/83 to 7/15/83) was an attempt to recreate a Sergeant Bilko type of character with comedian Jimmie Walker as Sergeant Tyrone Valentine, a conniving G.I. who was stationed at the Camp Tar Creek army base (Company A) in Texas. Like Bilko, Valentine sought easy money by manipulating the army for his own personal benefit. Private Tony Baker (David Naughton) was his cohort, Clarence Clapp (Roger Bowen) was the commanding officer and Major Hawkins (Richard Jaeckel) was the man out to bust Valentine. Jack Elliott composed the theme.

566. *Phyl and Mikhy*

CBS, 5/26/80 to 6/30/80

Phyllis ("Phyl") Wilson (Murphy Cross) is a pretty American track star for Pacific Western University (Pac West U for short). She lives with her father, Max Wilson (Larry Haines), at 11 Evergreen Place; Max is the track coach at Pac West U.

Mikhail ("Mikhy") Orlov (Rick Lohman) is a Russian track star who has come to the United States for a meet at Pac West U. He and Phyl meet and fall in love. Mikhy defects, and he and Phyl marry (they set up housekeeping in Phyl's room in Max's home). Stories follow the lives of the two young adults from different worlds as they attempt to make their marriage work.

Mikhy is a promising decathlon champion and a hope for the gold medal for the Soviet Union in the 1980 Olympics. He calls Phyl "Phyliska" and Max "Dead" (actually "Dad," but with his Russian accent it comes out "Dead"). Phyl calls Mikhy "my Russian Bear." She has a Creeping Charlie plant named Charlie. Mikhy earns $85 a week by caring for the lawn of the college president. When Mikhy upsets Max, Max goes on a milkshake drinking binge.

Eugene ("Truck") Morley (Jack Dodson) is Max's friend and the president of the Pac West U Alumni Association. He is "the number one distributor of fiberglass patio covers." Vladimir Gimenko (Michael Pataki) is the Soviet agent who is seeking to return Mikhy to the Motherland; Gwyn Bates (Rae Allen) is widower Max's romantic interest.

Rod Parker and Hal Cooper composed the "Phyl and Mikhy" theme.

567. *Picket Fences*

CBS, 9/18/92 to the present

Rome is a small town in Wisconsin. James ("Jimmy") Brock (Tom Skerritt) is the sheriff; Maxine ("Max") Stewart (Lauren Holly) and Kenny Lacos (Costas Mandylor) are his chief deputies.

Jimmy is married to Jill (Kathy Baker) and is the father of three children: Kimberly (Holly Marie Combs), Matthew (Justin Shenkarow) and Zachary (Adam Wylie). Jimmy was previously married to Kimberly's mother, Lydia (Cristine Rose), and moved to Rome 12 years ago (when he married Jill) "because it was safe." Jill is a private practice doctor who is also on call at Norwood Hospital. Kimberly is 16 years old and attends Rome High School. She plays the piano and has ambitions of being a singer. Matthew and Zachary attend the Fisher Elementary School. Matthew imagines himself as a detective; and the younger boy, Zachary, plays the trombone (Jimmy plays the saxophone). The Brocks are Protestant and live at 211 Willow Road.

The Sheriff's Department is located in the Rome City Hall Building. Max drives a squad car with the license plate 82203; Kenny was born in Illinois and was a Golden Gloves boxer. The license plate seen on the station house wall is Z82 7L3.

Other town residents are Carter Pike (Kelly Connell), the medical examiner ("chief pathologist") who yearns to become a detective (he seems to have an uncontrollable urge to perform autopsies); Douglas Wambaugh (Fyvush Finkel), the outspoken defense attorney (he will take any case "because Wambaugh is on the side of principle"); and Jenny (Zelda Rubinstein), the sheriff's office's nosy switchboard operator.

The *Herald* is the town newspaper, and Judge Henry Bone (Ray Walston) hears cases at the Hogan County Court House. The biggest event in town is the December Christmas Pageant (which officially starts the shopping season). At this time of year, Douglas organizes the "Multicultural Wambaugh Singers" to sing Christmas carols and bring people of all religions together.

But it is "what lies behind the picket fences"—the strange characters and unusual crimes—that makes for an interesting visit to Rome. There is "The Serial Bather" (a notorious criminal who breaks into people's homes when they are out in order to take a bath); K.C. McDonald (Jessica Tuck), "The Snake Lady" (she collects snakes and carries a boa with her at all times); Frank Tucker (David Proval), who carries a five pound bag of Idaho potatoes and is called "Frank the Potato Man"; and Louise Talbot (Natalija Nogulich), the town's transsexual schoolteacher (before her sex change, she was Walter Souder).

Richard Kiley appeared as Jill's father, Hayden Langston; Ann Guilbert was Douglas's wife, Miriam Wambaugh.

Stewart Levin composed the "Picket Fences Theme."

568. *Pistols 'n' Petticoats*

CBS, 9/17/66 to 8/26/67

Cast: Ann Sheridan (*Henrietta Hanks*), Carole Wells (*Lucy Hanks*), Douglas V. Fowley (*Andrew Hanks*), Ruth McDevitt (*Grandma Hanks*), Gary Vinson (*Harold Sikes*).

Facts: Wretched, Colorado, 1871, is a wild and woolly town plagued by outlaws, greedy land barons and constant Indian uprisings. Harold Sikes is the deputy sheriff. He is somewhat inept but strives to uphold the law. He has instituted "Wretched Beautiful" (an antilittering law where violators are fined 50 cents) and has a bulletin board with the latest in wanted posters. Laws also state that horses must be properly tied to hitching posts and shooting on Sunday is prohibited. The laws sound good, but Harold is simply incapable of enforcing them. He is clumsy, unable to shoot straight and plagued by guns that get stuck in his holster (making him slow on the draw). He trips a lot and has a white horse that he can't exactly ride (the horse always stops short and throws him off).

Coming to Harold's rescue (and the actual keepers of the peace) are the gun toting Hanks family. Henrietta, nicknamed "Hank," is an attractive widow "who could fire a gun with one hand milking a goat and hit a coyote on the run." Andrew, called "Grandpa," is Henrietta's father. He is a former Union Army private and is hopeless without his glasses (he can't see or shoot straight without them). He carries his former army rifle with him at all times; "he kept his gun in trim—nobody messed around with him." Andrew has a pet wolf named Bowzer and a mule named Molly.

Andrew's wife (name not mentioned; called "Honey" by Andrew) is a sweet looking elderly lady who "was best at shootin' buttons off a rustler's vest." Lucy, Henrietta's beautiful daughter, is very feminine and is in love with Harold. Although she rarely uses a gun, she is an expert shot and conceals one in a lacy garter she wears on her right thigh. Lucy has faith in Harold but can't convince her mother that "Harold can rescue people in distress and things like that." "Lucy, dear," responds Henrietta, "that's woman's work." Lucy and Harold enjoy sharing a vanilla malt when she comes to town (the Hanks live on a ranch on the outskirts of Wretched). Harold calls Lucy "Miss Lucy"; Grandma calls Harold "Harold Dear." As the theme says, "Chasing bandits to them was fun ... every outlaw in the West would run from Pistols and Petticoats."

Recurring Roles: Robert Lowery (*Bernard Courtney*, the land baron seeking to obtain the Hankses' ranch); Stanley Adams (*Jed Timmins*, the crooked lawyer); Lon Chaney, Jr.

Phyl and Mikhy. **Murphy Cross (bottom) and Rick Lohman.**

(*Eagle Shadow*, chief of the Kiowa Indians); Marc Cavell (*Gray Hawk*, Eagle Shadow's son); Jay Silverheels (*Great Bear*, chief of the Atona Indians); Alex Henteloff (*Little Bear*, Great Bear's son); Leo Gordon (*Cyrus Breech*, the gun smuggler); Gil Lamb (the unnamed town drunk); Bill Oberlin (the unnamed W.C. Fields type of character who hangs out at the Wretched saloon).

Theme: "Pistols 'n' Petticoats," by George Tibbles and Jack Elliott.

Note: In the original, unaired pilot film (produced in 1966), Chris Noel played Lucy Hanks and Joel D. McCrea was Sheriff Eric (the same type of role that later became that of Harold Sykes). The pilot film was titled "Quit Shootin' Folks, Grandma," and dealt with the Hankses' efforts to put down an Indian uprising.

569. *Planet of the Apes*

CBS, 9/13/74 to 12/27/74

Cast: Roddy McDowall (*Galen*), Ron Harper (*Alan Virdon*), James Naughton (*Peter Burke*), Mark Lenard (*Urko*), Booth Colman (*Zaius*).

Facts: A U.S. space capsule, launched in 1988, is approaching Alpha Centauri when it penetrates a radioactive turbulence area. The ship is propelled to Earth in the year

3881—a time when intelligent apes are ruling what is left of a world devastated by a holocaust sometime in the year 2000.

Two of the three astronauts aboard the ship—Colonel Alan Virdon and Captain Peter ("Pete") Burke—are captured by the ape leader Urko and imprisoned (the third astronaut, identified only as Jonesy, was killed on impact). The apes believe that simians have always ruled the world. There are humans in this time, but they are servants, laborers and farmers. Ape Prefect Zaius believes that Pete and Alan are a threat to their species because they have greater knowledge and abilities than the other humans; if it were known that there are intelligent humans, it would cause the apes' humans to revolt. Urko thinks that Pete and Alan should be killed before their presence becomes known. Zaius orders that the astronauts be kept alive, however, so their knowledge can be learned by the ape leaders. Urko disapproves.

Zaius's assistant, Galen, becomes intrigued by the astronauts' intelligence, and in seeking to learn more about them, he becomes their friend. One night, after Alan and Pete are fed, their cell door is left unlocked. As Pete and Alan emerge from their cell, Galen sees that Urko has set a trap to kill them. Galen yells, "Watch out!" to Pete and Alan; a fight ensues, and one of Urko's lieutenants is killed. Pete and Alan manage to escape, but Galen is caught and imprisoned—despite the fact that he accuses Urko of setting a trap. When Pete and Alan learn of Galen's imprisonment, they rescue him, and soon the three become fugitives from the state. Stories relate the trio's adventures as they seek a way to return to the Earth of the 1980s. Adapted from the feature film series of the same title.

Pete was born in New Jersey; Alan mentions that he has a wife and a child. They began their flight on August 19, 1988; the ship's time indicator read March 21, 3085 (they assume it stopped registering at this time; they have no idea what year they are actually in. In the opening theme, the last date on the meter reads October 14, 3881). Alan believes that their only hope of returning home is to use the ship's magnetic disk (which recorded the flight), find a computer and reverse the process. Their major problem: finding a computer and human intelligence enough to build a ship.

Pete and Alan crash-landed in California (San Francisco, Oakland and Malibu Beach are mentioned as areas they are in). The apes have renamed this area Central City, and it is ruled by the High Council. Humans are kept in small villages (such as Chailo, which is 30 miles south of Central City). Each village is ruled by a prefect, and finding food seems to be a major problem for some humans.

Where he is not known, Galen pretends to be Protus; Pete and Alan pose as his servants. Urko always assumes a human is lying—"It makes things easier." He has an unseen wife named Elta.

Theme: "Planet of the Apes," by Lalo Schifrin.

Note: In the animated series, "Return to the Planet of the Apes" (NBC, 9/6/75 to 9/4/76), astronauts Bill Hudson (voice of Richard Blackburn), Judy Franklin (Claudette Nevins) and Jeff Carter (Austin Stoker) are traveling aboard the NASA spacecraft *Venture* when they penetrate a time vortex and are hurled from present day Earth (1975) to Earth in the year 3979—a time when intelligent apes rule

the world. Their adventures as they seek a way to return to their time are depicted.

570. *Please Don't Eat the Daisies*

NBC, 9/14/65 to 9/2/67

At Ridgemont College in Ridgemont City, James ("Jim") Nash (Mark Miller), a teaching assistant, and Joan Holliday (Patricia Crowley), a journalism student, meet and fall in love. The time is 1952 and shortly after, Jim and Joan marry. They set up housekeeping in a small apartment on Second Street ("One flight up, first door on the left"). It was a struggle to make ends meet, and Jim was contemplating giving up teaching for a better paying job until Joan told him, "You love to teach and you've invested six years of your life into becoming a teacher. You love me and you want to do what is best for me. The best thing that ever happened to me was becoming Mrs. Jim Nash. And I love being married to a schoolteacher . . . If there are a few hardships along the way, that's fine and dandy. Because someday I'm going to be able to say, 'I want you to meet my husband, Professor James Nash.'"

On their tenth month anniversary, Jim surprises Joan with a puppy they later name Lad. Jim holds the dog and speaks for it: "Your husband informed me that I was to keep you company while he is away educating the youth of America. He has just been promoted to the position of instructor." It is at this time that Joan tells Jim she is pregnant (a baby they name Kyle is born seven months later).

When the series actually begins, Joan and Jim and their children, Kyle (Kim Tyler), Joel (Brian Nash) and twins Trevor (Jeff Fithian) and Tracy (Joe Fithian) live at 228 Circle Avenue in Ridgemont City. Jim is now an English professor at Ridgemont College and Joan, who works out of their home, is a freelance magazine writer who pens articles under the name Joan Holliday. Joel, Trevor and Tracy attend Ridgemont Grammar School, while 12-year-old Kyle is enrolled at Ridgemont Junior High. Before the birth of Kyle, Joan and Jim were contemplating the names David, Donald, Farley, Gregory and Winthrop (not one female name was mentioned). They decided on the name Kyle when Joan told Jim it was a name she once read in a novel and liked. Kyle weighed seven pounds, four ounces at birth. The kids mentioned their favorite television shows were "The Purple Avenger" (mythical) and "The Man from U.N.C.L.E."

It was mentioned that Joan's great-grandfather, Albert Tennyson Kerns, was a Civil War hero and the first man west of the Mississippi to own a bathtub. Ridgemont City is said to have a legend called "The Big Train," which is a mysterious storm that occurs every ten years and during which someone disappears.

King Donovan and Shirley Mitchell played the Nash's neighbors, Herb and Marge Thornton (who lived at 230

Circle Avenue); J. Pat O'Malley appeared as Joan's world-traveling father, Mr. Holliday. The series is based on the book by Jean Kerr.

Jeff Alexander composed the theme.

571. *Police Squad!*

ABC, 3/4/82 to 4/25/82
ABC, 7/22/82 to 8/5/82

Frank Drebin (Leslie Nielsen) is a detective lieutenant with the Police Squad, a special unit of the Police Department (headquartered at the police station of an unidentified city, "the tuba capital of the world"). Frank, who is based in the squad room, is also referred to as Captain Drebin. Too much caffeine makes Frank edgy, and Frank doesn't question the wives of murder victims until after they are dead. NAQ 758 is Frank's license plate in the opening theme; in the show it is YM4875 and TW4305. Frank lives at 14 Cherry Street at Galena Avenue next to the Military Millinery Store. His snitch is Johnny (William Duell), a shoeshine "boy" who knows everything about everything and spills his guts for a $20 bill (priests and fire captains are also seen using Johnny's services).

Captain Ed Hocken (Alan North) is Frank's superior; Officer Norberg (Peter Lupus) from the Undercover Unit, assists Frank; and Ted Olson (Ed Williams) is the sleazy police chemist who seems to delight in performing hazardous experiments on children (but is never given the chance—he is always interrupted by Frank).

Each episode has a special guest star (Lorne Greene, Georg Stanford Brown, Florence Henderson, William Shatner, Robert Goulet and William Conrad) who is killed off in the opening theme. "Rex Hamilton as Abraham Lincoln" is announced as a regular in the opening theme, but he never appears in the show. Ira Newborn composed the theme.

The series is based on the comedy and style of the movie *Airplane* (a subtle style of comedy that just didn't work on television—not in 1982 or when CBS rebroadcast five of the six episodes in 1991). The series did spawn two theatrical movies: *The Naked Gun* and *The Naked Gun 2½: The Smell of Fear.*

572. *Police Woman*

NBC, 9/13/74 to 8/30/78

Lee Ann ("Pepper") Anderson (Angie Dickinson) is a high fashion model turned police officer who quit her glamorous job when she became bored with it. Pepper first worked with the vice squad before being promoted to sergeant and assigned to the Criminal Conspiracy Division of the Los Angeles Police Department. Pepper, whose first name is also given as Suzanne, lives at 102 Crestview Drive

(514-7915 is her phone number). Her sister, Cheryl (Nicole Kallis), attends the Austin School for Learning Disabilities. Pepper's sedan license plate reads 635 CIN.

Pepper's co-workers are Sergeant William ("Bill") Crowley (Earl Holliman) and investigators Joseph ("Joe") Styles (Ed Bernard) and Peter ("Pete") Royster (Charles Dierkop). Bibi Besch appeared as Bill's ex-wife, Jackie; Keenan Wynn and Bettye Ackerman played Pepper's Uncle Ben and Aunt Helen Fletcher; Kandi Keith protrayed Joe's wife, Harriet.

In the original pilot, "The Gamble" (which aired on "Police Story" on 3/26/74), Angie Dickinson was Lisa Beaumont, a vice squad detective, and Bert Convy played Sergeant Bill Crowley. Morton Stevens composed the "Police Woman" theme.

Angie Dickinson next played Cassidy ("Cassie") Holland on the series "Cassie and Company" (NBC, 1/29/82 to 8/20/82). Cassie was a former L.A.P.D. officer turned private detective who now operates Holland Investigations. Next, Angie played Ann Cavanaugh, an officer with the San Diego Police Department, in the NBC television movie *Police Story: The Freeway Killings* (5/3/87), then Kelly Mulcahaney, a sergeant with the N.Y.P.D. in the NBC television movie *Prime Target* (9/29/89).

"Angie the Lieutenant" is an unsold ABC pilot (2/1/92) that failed to return Angie Dickinson to regular series work. Angie plays Angela ("Angie") Martin, a newly appointed lieutenant with the Metropolitan Division of the Washington, D.C., Police Department. She now heads an all-male division consisting of detectives Elliott Chase (Jesse Dabson), Carl Kanick (Michael MacRae), Ernesto Mendez (Geoffrey Rivas) and Oliver Jackson (Harold Sylvester). Angie's first and only case found her investigating the rape of a television anchorwoman.

The first attempt at a series featuring a policewoman was "Decoy" (syndicated, 1957-58). In it, Beverly Garland played Patricia ("Casey") Jones, a policewoman with the 16th Precinct of the Police Department of New York City. Casey lives at 110 Hope Street (Murray Hill 3-4643 is her phone number), wears badge number 300 and earns $75 a week.

573. *The Powers That Be*

NBC, 3/7/92 to 4/18/92
NBC, 11/7/92 to 1/9/93

Washington, D.C., is the setting for a comical look at the Powers, a dysfunctional political family: Senator William ("Bill") Franklin Powers (John Forsythe), his wife, Margaret (Holland Taylor), their married daughter, Caitlin Van Horne (Valerie Mahaffey) and Sophie Lipkin (Robin Bartlett), Bill's illegitimate daughter from a wartime romance (she now works for her father as a political aide).

Bill, a liberal Democrat, is 65 years old and has been a senator for 26 years. He and Margaret live at 2292 Applewood Drive. Bill is allergic to cold sesame noodles and has a martini, prepared each night by Caitlin, before dinner. Bill

Police Woman. Left to right: Angie Dickinson, Ed Bernard, Earl Holliman and Charles Dierkop.

had a dog named Little Dickens and is a big fan of Jerry Lewis films (*The Nutty Professor* is his favorite Lewis film; he and Caitlin have a tradition of seeing Jerry's movies together). Blueberry muffins are Bill's favorite food, and "Supercalafragalisticexpealadocious" is his favorite song.

Margaret is yearning to become a First Lady and is grooming Bill for the Oval Office. She is younger than Bill and is actively involved in the political arena (she becomes devastated if she is not invited to an important political function and dreads the thought of Bill performing his awful ventriloquist act at political functions). Margaret is famous for her chicken salad sandwiches and will join any charity to further Bill's political career.

Caitlin is very pretty, but also petty, self-serving and vain. She is married to the wimpy congressman Theodore Van Horne (David Hyde Pierce), who is unable to stand up to or overcome her dominance over him (he says simply, "Yes, dear," to everything she asks, and he appears to be on the brink of suicide). Caitlin had a fear of brunch (cured by

psychological counseling) and allows only "Mr. Sidney" to cut her hair. Caitlin and Theodore are the parents of young Pierce (Joseph Gordon-Levitt). Caitlin loves to wear pink and calls Margaret "Mummy." Before each political party, Caitlin buys a dress one size too small, then starves herself until she fits into it. Bill calls Caitlin "Cupcake" and "Princess"; Margaret calls her "Precious." Caitlin's favorite charity is the "Halfway House for Congressmen's Wives."

Jordan Miller (Eve Gordon) is Bill's legislative assistant (or press agent in some episodes) and Bill's mistress; she calls Bill "Button" (they have a secret rendezvous every Sunday morning; Margaret thinks Bill is at church). Bradley Grist (Peter MacNicol) is Bill's P.R. man, and Charlotte (Elizabeth Berridge) is the Powers' maid. She is famous for her crab cakes but is constantly belittled by Margaret and seems to live in fear of her. Charlotte and Theodore have a secret crush on each other (possibly the only thing that is keeping Theodore from killing himself).

Stephen Bishop sings the theme, "The Powers That Be."

574. *Primus*

Syndicated, 1971

Carter Primus (Robert Brown) is an ex–navy frogman turned troubleshooter who operates Primus, Inc., a Nassau-based company that tackles dangerous underwater assignments. Toni Hayden (Eva Renzi) is his beautiful, bikini-clad partner; and Charles Kingman (Will Kuluva) is his rugged assistant.

Tegtight is Carter's operational base in Nassau. *Dagat* is "the Mother Ship" (where he stores most of his equipment); the *Orka* is his patrol boat (for surface surveillance); the *Pegasus* is his underwater exploring vehicle; and *Big Kate* is his underwater robot.

Leonard Rosenman composed the theme.

575. *Princesses*

CBS, 9/27/91 to 10/25/91

Cast: Twiggy Lawson (*Georgy De La Rue*), Julie Hagerty (*Tracy Dillon*), Fran Drescher (*Melissa Kirshner*).

Facts: A luxurious apartment at 4107 5th Avenue in Manhattan is the rent-free residence of Princess Georgina ("Georgy") De La Rue, Tracy Dillon and Melissa ("Mel") Kirshner—three working girls who all dream of marrying wealthy men.

Tracy and Melissa met in college. Tracy planned to become a writer; Melissa sought to own her own cosmetics business. They vowed that when they reached age 28, they would meet handsome twins, get married and live next door to each other in Connecticut. They would each have two kids and maintain their careers. "What a pathetic illusion that was," says Mel, as they now share a small apartment in New York City and are struggling to make ends meet, Tracy as a creative writing teacher for adults at Manhattan College (she is later said to be teaching adult remedial English) and Mel as a cosmetics saleswoman at Macy's.

At this same time, but in another part of the world, the title of princess of Scilly (a small group of islands off the southwest coast of England) is bestowed upon 18-year-old Georgina De La Rue when she marries the older Prince Frederick. Some years later, a burst spleen kills Frederick, and Georgy inherits his money, but his family contests the will ("His stepchildren never accepted me as their mother"). Since Georgy was not born of royal blood, she is now penniless. With her only possessions (the clothes on her back and in several trunks), she accepts the offer of a friend to stay in his 5th Avenue apartment for one year while he is in Europe. Unknown to Georgy, her friend has also given the apartment as a wedding gift to Michael DeCrow (James Read), the man Tracy plans to marry.

At the apartment, Tracy and Mel meet Georgy. When Georgy learns that Michael was given the apartment first, she makes plans to leave. However, before she does, Tracy discovers that Michael has two ex-wives and cancels the wedding. Georgy receives the apartment and extends an invitation to Tracy and Mel: "Since I'm all alone with no friends and no family, how would you feel about moving in here and becoming my mates?" Tracy and Mel accept the offer.

The girls share the housework and each other's secrets, but mostly Georgy's fabulous wardrobe. Georgy was a British stage performer before she became a princess. She was tap dancing in the play *No, No, Prime Minister* when Frederick spotted her. He came backstage, they fell in love and married. Now, being an unemployed princess, Georgy seeks to become a dancer on Broadway, but can't seem to find anything—"If I wasn't meant to be a performer, why did God give me the talent to sing and dance a little? ... I'm just a simple princess looking for work." Georgy sings in the key of A and got a gig at the Blue Cord Club. She auditioned for the role of Hooker Number 2 in the play *Street Tango* and was the spokeswoman for Buckingham Airlines.

Tracy has to help a friend when they are in trouble ("It's my nature") and hates blind dates ("I feel so awkward and clumsy"). No additional information is given on Mel.

Relatives: Leila Kenzle (Mel's sister, *Debra Kleckner*), Richard Kind (Debra's husband, *Dr. Len Kleckner*).

Theme: "Some Day My Prince Will Come," vocal by the Roches.

576. *The Prisoner*

CBS, 6/1/68 to 9/21/68

Cast: Patrick McGoohan (*Number 6*), Angelo Muscat (*The Silent Butler*).

Facts: John Drake, a secret agent for the Ministry in England, allows a scientist he was ordered to find to defect when he discovers that the scientist is being sought for a deadly mind-transference device that he invented.

When Drake returns to the Ministry, he is reprimanded for his actions. Believing that what he did was right, Drake resigns—"It is a matter of principle."

Principle or not, someone else (assumed to be the Ministry) believes differently. At his home, Drake is packing his bags to leave London when an unknown man, dressed in black, places a nozzle in the keyhole of the front door. A gas is released and Drake is knocked unconscious.

Soon afterward, Drake awakens to find himself in a strange room. He discovers that he is no longer a man, but a number—Number 6—and the prisoner of a self-contained community known as the Village.

Continuing his investigation, Number 6 enters the Green Dome and meets one of the Village leaders, Number 2. Although he is unable to discover who his captors are or where the Village is, Number 6 learns the reason for his abduction: "It is a question of your resignation. A lot of people are curious about why you suddenly left. The information in your head is priceless. A man like you is worth a great deal on the open market. It is my job to check your motives."

Stories relate Number 6's efforts to discover who his captors are and his desperate attempts to escape from the Village. "We want information." "You won't get it." "By hook or crook we will." "Who is Number 1?" "You are Number 6." "I am not a number, I am a free man!"

The Village is a fantasy-like area bounded by mountains and ocean. It is a place from which there is no escape. Money is called units and stores have names that merely state their purpose (for example, the Café, the General Store). The symbol of the Village is a nineteenth-century bicycle (large front wheel, short back wheel). Names are forbidden in the Village, and questioning other residents of the Village is prohibited; prison is the penalty for answering questions. Rules prohibit animals (although Number 6 has a black cat he calls It; the cat, which mysteriously appears, is later said to belong to the female Number 2). The Village leaders have instructions "not to damage Number 6, but to get all he knows. He must be won over, not broken."

Number 6 is assumed to be John Drake, although his name is never revealed ("The Prisoner" is a continuation of the last episode of the series "Secret Agent," in which Patrick McGoohan played British intelligence agent John Drake). Before his abduction, Drake drove a car with the license plate KAR 120C. In the Village, Drake's I.D. card reads No. 6 (left side) and has his picture on the right side.

In the final episode, "Fall Out," Number 6 defeats Number 2. Unbroken by exhausting mind-bending experiments, Number 6 proves he is superior. He is led to an area below the Village. There he is presented to an assembly, recognized as an individual (a man superior to them) and given a choice: leave or remain and lead the people of the Village. Number 6 appears undecided. He is then met by his only friend, the Silent Butler, and led through a heavily guarded hallway to a room containing highly complex machinery that is designed to destroy him. When Number 6 discovers that it is a trap, he, the Silent Butler, and two rebels against the system, Number 2 (imprisoned for failing to break Number 6) and Number 48, join forces. The guards are overpowered and the machines are reset to self-destruct. The four escape in a truck through an underground tunnel as the Village is destroyed. The truck approaches London (indicating that the Village was within 50 miles of the city). Numbers 2 and 48 depart; Number 6, a free man, and the Silent Butler remain a team.

Colin Gordon, Clifford Evans, Mary Morris, John Sharpe, Peter Wyngarde, Guy Dolman and Leo McKern played Number 2 in various episodes. Alexis Kanner was Number 48, and Kenneth Griffith played the Village president.

Theme: "The Prisoner," by Ron Grainer.

577. *Prisoner: Cell Block H*

Syndicated, 1980

Cast: Peita Toppano (*Karen*), Kerry Armstrong (*Lynnette*), Val Lehman (*Bea*), Carol Burns (*Franky*), Colette Mann (*Doreen*), Margaret Laurance (*Marilyn*), Mary Ward (*Jeannie*), Sheila Florance (*Elizabeth*), Elspeth Ballantyne (*Meg*), Fiona Spence (*Vera*), Patsy King (*Erica*).

Facts: A harsh view of life in a women's prison (the Wentworth Detention Center) in Melbourne, Australia. See also "Women in Prison."

The Prisoners: Karen Angela Travers was born in Melbourne on 8/27/54. She has blue eyes and brown hair, weighs 118 pounds and is five feet three inches tall. Karen is a Roman Catholic and is also known as Karen Healey. She was a schoolteacher and was convicted of killing her brutal husband (she offered no defense at her trial, other than to claim she is innocent; she was given life). Her distinguishing marks are burns on her back.

Lynnette Jane Warner ws born in Melbourne on 9/7/59. She has blue eyes and brown hair, weighs 105 pounds and is five feet one inch tall. She is a Roman Catholic and has no distinguishing marks. Lynnette is a naïve country girl who was falsely convicted of kidnapping and attempting to murder her employer's child. She received a ten year sentence when she was unable to prove she was framed. Lynnette is single and was a professional nanny.

Bea Alice Smith, also known as Beatrice Carruthers, is a widow. She weighs 138 pounds, is five feet six inches tall, has brown eyes and gray hair and no distinguishing marks. Bea was born in Hobart on 2/2/38 and is a Methodist. She is a qualified hairdresser and was convicted, initially, of murdering a co-worker. She was released on parole after serving ten years but was later recommitted for killing her husband. She is the toughest of the women and the undisputed leader of the prison society.

Frieda ("Franky") Joan Doyle was born in Melbourne on 4/17/48. She weighs 147 pounds, is five feet six inches tall and has brown hair and green eyes. She is single, and her religion is Salvation Army. Franky was sentenced to life for armed robbery and murder. She is also a lesbian with an unrequited passion for Karen. Her distinguishing marks are tattoos of naked women on her breasts.

Doreen May Anderson, also known as Debbie Raye, is unmarried and the mother of a young son. She was born in Melbourne on 6/15/53. Doreen weighs 132 pounds, is five feet five and one-half inches tall, has blue eyes, black hair and no qualifications. Her religion is Salvation Army, and she has tattoos on her arms. Doreen was a battered child and is easily led into crime. She has many petty convictions, but was sentenced to four years for breaking and entering.

Marilyn Anne Mason, also known as Mandy, is a qualified fashion model; her religion is Church of England. Marilyn was born in Melbourne on 3/3/56. She weighs 112 pounds, is five feet four and one-half inches tall, and has blue eyes and blonde hair. Marilyn was sentenced to 12 years for soliciting. She has many such prior convictions and is known to have worked in a porno movie.

Jeannie ("Mum") Brooks was born in Melbourne on 5/17/18. She is a Presbyterian, weighs 97 pounds, has blue eyes and gray hair and is five feet two inches tall. She is also known as Jeannie Bradley and was sentenced to life for killing her husband. She spends much time tending the prison garden.

Elizabeth Josephine Birdsworth, also known as Lizzie Lee,

Prisoner: Cell Block H. Front: Colette Mann (left) and Sheila Florance. Center: Peita Toppano (left) and Patsy King. Back, left to right: Elspeth Ballantyne, Barry Quinn, Fiona Spence (near door).

was born in Perth on 11/5/08 and has four grown children. She is the oldest of the inmates. She has gray hair, green eyes, weighs 101 pounds and is five feet two inches tall. Her religion is Other Christian. She was given life for mass murder (she accidentally killed four sheep shearers by poisoning their food "to teach them a lesson"). She is obsessed with escaping.

Other Characters: Meg Jackson is the sympathetic prison guard, and she has a happy relationship with her husband, prison psychologist Bill Jackson (Don Baker).

Vera Bennett is the cruel and harsh prison guard who hopes her rule of iron will get her the prison governership. Vera is single and lives at home with her invalid mother. She has no social life and lives for her job at the prison.

Erica Davidson is the prison governor. She is capable of running the prison, but her approach keeps her remote and she fails to understand the frustrations of the prisoners.

Theme: "On the Inside," vocal by Lynne Hamilton.

Note: "Willow B: Women in Prison" is an ABC pilot film (6/29/80) that failed to generate an American version of "Prisoner: Cell Block H." Life in the El Camino Institution for Women was seen through the eyes of Kim Cavanaugh (Debra Clinger), a socialite who is convicted of felony manslaughter (driving while intoxicated and killing a pedestrian) and sentenced to section Willow B. Other prisoners are Chris Bricker (Trisha Noble), Claire Hastings (Carol Lynley), Kate Stewart (Sally Kirkland) and Sabrina Reynolds (Sarah Kennedy). Mrs. McCallister (Norma Donaldson) is the warden, and Sergeant Pritchett (Ruth Roman) is the sadistic guard.

578. *Private Benjamin*

CBS, 4/6/81 to 9/5/83

Judith ("Judy") Benjamin (Lorna Patterson) is the beautiful, spoiled daughter of a wealthy family. When her life-style becomes boring to her, she decides to join the army to find more excitement. She soon finds herself totally out of place as she discovers that the system does not exactly fulfill her needs. Judy's attempts to get the army to do things her way—and the army's efforts to turn her into a real soldier—are the focal point of the series.

Judy was originally stationed at Fort Trams. She was then transferred to Fort Bradley in Hobart, California ("The shoelace capital of the Northeast"). There, as part of the 2nd Platoon, B Company, Judy was a soldier in training for possible combat. When Judy graduated from boot camp (1/25/82), she was assigned to the Public Affairs Office as the administrative assistant to Captain Doreen Lewis (Eileen Brennan), later promoted to inspector general of Fort Bradley. (Judy's primary job is to issue press releases.)

Colonel Lawrence ("Ironman") Fielding (Robert Mandan) is the commanding officer; Sergeant Lucien C. Ross (Hal Williams) is Doreen's second in command.

Maria Gianelli (Lisa Raggio), Rayleen White (Joyce Little), Carol Winter (Ann Ryerson), Lu Ann Hubble (Lucy

Webb), Jackie Simms (Damita Jo Freeman) and Stacy Kouchalakas (Wendie Jo Sperber) are the other privates attached to Judy's company. (Jackie worked in the motor pool; Stacy, who has two pet turtles named Burt and Loni, works with Judy in the office.) Polly Holliday, as Major Amanda Allen, replaced Eileen Brennan in the last two episodes (Brennan was injured in a traffic accident). Based on the Goldie Hawn film of the same name.

Relatives: Barbara Barrie and K Callan (Judy's mother, *Harriet Benjamin*), William Daniels (Judy's father, *Ted Benjamin*), Stephanie Faracy (Judy's cousin, *Sherry Stern,* a clumsy army private), Arthur Peterson (Judy's grandfather, *Benjamin ["Ben"] Benjamin*).

Theme: "Judy's Song," by Madelyn Davis and Bob Carroll, Jr.

Note: ABC and NBC also produced pilots for a possible series based on the *Private Benjamin* feature film. ABC's attempt was "She's in the Army Now," which aired 5/20/81. The pilot, originally called "The Powder Puff Platoon," told the story of Cass Donner (Kathleen Quinlan), Rita Jennings (Jamie Lee Curtis), Sylvie Knoll (Melanie Griffith) and Yvette Rios (Julie Carmen) as privates with the U.S. Army's 3rd Platoon of Alpha Company at Fort Jackson.

"Wendy Hooper—U.S. Army" was NBC's attempt (8/14/81). Wendy Holcombe played Wendy Hooper, a pretty but naive Alabama girl who joins the army's communications center (at Fort Waco), thinking it will help her become a country and western singer. In the pilot, the truth dawns on Wendy, and she strives to do her best for the army. Michael Pataki was her sergeant, Michael Bruno; Dana Elcar was the C.O., Alfred Hubik; and Van Nessa Clarke and Carol Ann Susi were Wendy's friends, Diane Simpson and Theresa Pelligrini.

The *TV Guide* listing of 10/21/91 for "Major Dad" read "A perky but secretly self-serving sergeant (Lorna Patterson, promoted from 'Private Benjamin') performs perfectly as the new secretarial assistant, but she upstages Gunny (Beverly Archer)." Lorna was Sergeant Tammi Rae Perkins, who sought Gunny's job as secretary to Mac (Gerald McRaney).

579. *Private Secretary*

CBS, 2/1/53 to 9/10/57

International Artists, Inc., is a theatrical agency located on the twenty-second floor (Suite 2201) of a building at 10 East 56th Street in New York City. Peter Sands (Don Porter) is its founder; Susan ("Susie") Camille McNamara (Ann Sothern) is his private secretary; and Violet ("Vi") Praskins (Ann Tyrrell) is the agency's receptionist/switchboard operator.

Susie began working for Peter in 1945 (she previously served three years as a WAVE). She was born in Mumford, Indiana (her ancestors came from Scotland), and attended Mumford High School (in an early episode, Mumford is mentioned as being in Iowa). A big Saturday night in Mumford, Susie says, was to get all dressed up, go to the

City Hall and watch them polish the cannon. Susie is a Libra and incurably romantic. She types 65 words a minute and takes 125 words per minute by shorthand. Susie lives at the Brockhurst Apartments (Apartment H) on East 92nd Street in Manhattan. When Susie first came to work for Peter, he took her to the Penguin Club for lunch. Susie measures the milk for Peter's coffee with an eyedropper and makes two copies of each letter she types.

Peter was in the air force for four years before he established International Artists (the phone number is Plaza 5-1955). In high school, Peter was voted "Most Likely to Succeed," and in an early episode he referred to "a remarkable talent he discovered: Harriet Lake" (Ann Sothern's real name). Peter's birth sign is Aries, and he likes to look at women's legs—"I enjoy exercising that privilege." He calls Susie "the most faithful and loyal secretary I ever had."

Vi began working for Peter on 10/23/49; her birth sign is Scorpio, and she is interested in horoscopes (she reads *Advanced Astrology* magazine). Susie believes Vi is an old maid, but Vi feels she is not: "I'm still looking for Mr. Right."

Gloria Winters appeared as Susie's niece, Patty, and Alma Townsend was Peter's mother, Mrs. Sands. The series is also known as "Susie."

580. *Probe*

ABC, 3/7/88 to 4/14/88

Austin James (Parker Stevenson) is the "greatest scientific mind of the century." Serendip is his pet project, an organization that uses the latest scientific technology to solve problems. After establishing Serendip, Austin, the president, becomes bored with it and retreats to "The Batcave," an old warehouse where he now lives and conducts his scientific experiments.

Austin thinks while he sleeps (his bed is a sensory deprivation tank—"It helps me think"); has a pet spider (a tarantula called Steve) he lets roam around the lab; and an amazing photographic mind (he can retain and recall information faster than a computer). Stories relate Austin's exploits as he strives to solve extremely baffling crimes.

Michele ("Mickey") Castle (Ashley Crow) is Austin's pretty but batty secretary. Despite his photographic mind, he keeps Mickey around "to take notes" during his investigations. Mickey mentioned that she left her last job "because my boss said I could do the job better in the nude."

"We Can Do It" is Serendip's slogan, and Howard Millhouse (Jon Cypher) runs the company in Austin's absence (he also complains constantly that Austin runs up huge water and electric bills for his experiments). The series was cretaed by Isaac Asimov and Michael Wagner.

Sylvester Levay composed the theme.

Pros and Cons see *Gabriel's Fire*

581. *P.S.I. Luv U*

CBS, 9/15/91 to 1/4/92

Wanda Talbot (Connie Sellecca) is a beautiful girl who moves from town to town pulling cons. In New York City, Wanda is caught red-handed by Detective Joey Paciorek (Greg Evigan). Instead of booking her, Joey offers her a choice: help him bust a drug dealer or spend five years in jail. Wanda elects to help Joey. During the assignment, Wanda is exposed as an undercover agent and almost killed. The target escapes, but Wanda is now in jeopardy since she can testify against the mobster if he is ever caught. To protect Wanda, it is decided to give her a new identity and make her part of the witness protection program.

In Palm Springs, California, Wanda and Joey meet with Matthew Durning (Earl Holliman), a former Justice Department federal marshal, who gives them new identities: Wanda becomes Danielle ("Dani") Powell and Joey, who is assigned to guard her, becomes her husband, Cody Powell. Dani and Cody are given a small mobile home and must pretend to be married—despite the fact that they dislike each other. Matthew owns P.S.I. (Palm Springs Investigations, a private security firm) and puts Cody to work as a security guard. Dani finds employment as a receptionist for P.S.I. Stories relate Dani and Cody's misadventures as Dani uses cons to help Cody catch criminals. (Dani and Cody later move into the Packer mansion when the owners leave for Europe and entrust its security to P.S.I.)

Dani was born in the Bronx, and spending money is her favorite hobby. She loves clothes, especially dresses (size six, which she buys at a store called Crescendo's). Dani hates housework, cooking and children—"Kids are like fingernails on a blackboard. I can't take them." Dani learned the art of the con from her uncle, Ray Barkley (Patrick Macnee) and always carries a lock pick in her bra ("It's the safest place I know"). Dani's sports car license plate reads 2YAR 133; she later works as a case officer when she nails a big time mobster.

Cody, who had the badge number 346, was a street cop with the N.Y.P.D. for 12 years. His patrol car license plate reads 2DQ 1876, and his car code is PSI-5.

P.S.I.-LUVU (or 774-5888) is the telephone hotline number for Palm Springs Investigations. Jack Ging played Police Chief Hollings; Jayne Frazer was Jo Jo, the P.S.I. radio dispatcher; and Sonny Bono appeared as himself, the mayor of Palm Springs.

Greg Evigan and Suzanne Fountain sing the theme, "P.S., I Love You."

582. *Punky Brewster*

NBC, 9/16/84 to 9/7/86
Syndicated, 9/86 to 9/88

Cast: Soleil Moon Frye (*Punky Brewster*), George Gaynes (*Henry Warnimont*), Cherie Johnson (*Cherie Johnson*), Ami Foster (*Margaux Kramer*), Susie Garrett (*Betty Johnson*).

Punky Brewster. Back: Susie Garrett. Seated, left to right: Cherie Johnson, George Gaynes, Soleil Moon Frye.

Facts: When her husband walks out on her, and a young mother (Susan Brewster) feels no longer able to care for her seven-year-old daughter, she abandons the child and her dog, Brandon, in a Chicago shopping mall. The girl, Penelope ("Punky") Brewster, manages to make money by helping shoppers load groceries into their cars. She also finds a place to live—an empty apartment (2D) in a building managed by Henry Warnimont, a 60-year-old gruff widower.

One day, several weeks later, the adorable orphan is discovered by Henry. Punky takes an instant liking to Henry ("Well, Brandon," she says, "we gotta trust somebody sometime") and tells Henry what has happened, concluding with, "Maybe my mother just forgot about me; but one day she'll come back and we'll live happily ever after."

Henry hires a private detective to find Punky's mother. The days pass and Punky feels she has found a home—until Henry tells her the detective was unable to find her mother and that he is sending her to the Department of Children and Family Services. Feeling abandoned again, Punky packs her suitcase. "I must be a terrible person," she tells Henry. "First my father walks out on me, then my mother ditches me, then you try and get rid of me. Nobody wants me around. Well, that's okay, I don't need anybody. I can take care of myself." She leaves. Henry then realizes that his life has changed for the better since he met Punky and that he needs her as much as she needs him. He files a petition to adopt her. Social worker Randi Mitchell (Talia Balsam) is assigned to the case; Punky is sent to Fenster Hall (an adoption center) until the court hearing.

Case number 1143J, the temporary custody hearing of Penelope Brewster, begins. Despite the obvious affection between Henry and Punky and the fact that Punky "broke out" of Fenster Hall to be with Henry, the judge rejects Henry's petition, feeling Punky needs a more stable upbringing with a young couple. Just then, Randi asks the judge to reverse his decision—which he does when she tells him how Punky and Henry need each other.

Punky originally slept on the couch in the living room, until she asked Henry if she could use his study as her bedroom. She turned it into a "Funky" Brewster room. "The room would blind a Smurf," says Henry. "There are so many colors!" "I'm not nobody anymore," exclaims Punky. "I'm Punky Brewster!" Her bed is an old flower cart with a mattress attached; her window has the sun painted on it; the moon and stars are painted on her windowshade. Punky also has a Felix the Cat alarm clock.

Henry's fondest memory of Christmas is when he would go to Massachusetts to visit his grandfather and together they would go into the woods to chop down their tree. It changed when he was 12 years old—that was the year his grandfather was attacked by a moose and the tradition of buying store-bought trees began. Punky's most cherished Christmas memory is the warm feeling she got when her mother made cranberry pudding. On her first Christmas with Henry, Punky wished that Santa would reunite her with her mother. For Christmas, Punky gave Henry a homemade pipe; Henry gave Punky roller skates. While Punky did not get her wish (Henry made every attempt to grant it), Santa did leave her something: her mother's musical jewelry box; the gift Punky made for her mother, earrings, were gone. Was it a miracle? Punky thinks so, because "all you have to do is believe." Henry too had a dream that one day he would have a child; it came true when Punky came into his life (Henry was married many years ago to a woman named Claudia; she died a year after they were married).

Henry and Punky live in Apartment 2A at 2520 Michigan Avenue in Chicago. Henry is a photographer who owns the Warnimont Studios. The Waste Begone Company removes the building's trash.

Henry collects old National Geographic magazines (he feels they will be worth something someday). He drives a never-seen 1955 DeSoto and has an alarm in his wallet. Henry also received the Department of Motor Vehicles highway award: the Order of the Crosswalk. He was a merchant marine during World War II, and when he was a kid, Jack Benny (whom he listened to on radio) was his idol.

Henry says Punky has a marvelous imagination—"When I ask her to do chores, she comes up with brilliant excuses." Punky loves to wear miniskirts and believes that everything will be all right no matter how bad things look—"That's Punky power!" Punky eats Sugar Beasties cereal for breakfast and has a treehouse in the backyard; WATB is her favorite radio station (she says, "Rock and roll is the answer to everything").

As a young girl, Punky pretended she was Rapunzel and ran down the street with a bathroom tissue hanging from her head. She was also called "Gunky" Brewster when she first started school (not named).

In 1987, when Punky was 11, she had her first crush on a 16-year-old boy named Kevin Dowling (Dan Gauthier). Despite Henry's disapproval (he wants her to remain a tomboy for 30 or 40 more years), he let nature take its course. She dressed in orange (his favorite color), made him a chocolate cake with orange frosting and planned a romantic dinner for two (hamburgers by candlelight). When Kevin showed up with his girlfriend, Gina (Lisa Alpert), a broken hearted Punky realized that he was too old for her. At age 12, Henry had his first crush on the school nurse, Nurse Budnugger. He found a medical dictionary, came to her office every day with a new disease. She caught on when he got diseases in alphabetical order; she married the gym coach.

Cherie Johnson is Punky's best friend. She lives in Apartment 3A with her grandmother, Betty Johnson, a nurse at Cook County Hospital (Betty raised Cherie after her parents' deaths).

"I even look gorgeous when I'm nervous," says Margaux Kramer, Punky's very rich and very spoiled girlfriend. She lives on Oak Lane, and her telephone number is 555-RICH. She takes lessons from her mother on how to fire servants, had an extremely close call one day ("I almost got a snowflake in my hair") and "when it comes time for marriage, I'll look through *Who's Who* to see who has what."

Margaux's house "has so many rooms that you need a map to find your way around." Her room is in the east wing. There are metal detectors at the front door, and Margaux has her own masseuse, beautician and manicurist.

Margaux has a collection of dolls made by her personal doll maker; her most cherished is a dancing ballerina that plays the song "Beautiful Dreamer" ("She comforts me when I'm sad"). The closest Margaux ever comes to poverty is when she visits Punky at home (she considers it "the poverty pit").

To make money, Punky and Cherie sold Lady Contempo cosmetics door to door. At Camp Kookalookie, Punky, Cherie and Margaux shared Cabin 12 with a boy-crazy girl named Marcie (Tanya Fenmore); across the lake was the boys' camp, Camp Scratchanichee. Punky, Margaux and Cherie's homeroom is 103. In their first Christmas play, they starred in *The Saddest Raindrop* (about a raindrop [Punky] who is sad—until a winter wind turns her into a beautiful snowflake). The girls also entered the WHXY Old Time Radio Contest to win a free trip to Disneyland. They did "Gruesome Ghost Stories—"The Mystery of Horror House" and won first prize.

The real Punky Brewster, Peyton B. Rutledge, appeared in the episode of 11/10/85 ("The Search"). Peyton, known in her childhood as "Punky Brewster," is the daughter of the headmaster of the prep school that then–NBC president Brandon Tartikoff had attended. It was Tartikoff who remembered the name and suggested it for the title character.

A running gag on the show deals with Punky's dog, Brandon. He is made almost human (buys his own flea powder—Calvin Klein at $75—sends flowers, at $55, to his friend, Lady, and plays checkers; when Brandon is good, he gets an Oreo cookie).

Relatives: Loyita Chapel (*Margaux's mother*), Ernie Sabella (*Margaux's father*), Marilyn McCoo (Betty's younger sister, *Larnese Barker*).

Relatives Not Seen: Henry's aunt, Mabel; Punky's mother, Susan Brewster; Margaux's cousin, Millicent.

Theme: "Everytime You Turn Around," vocal by Gary Portnoy.

Note: An animated version of "Punky Brewster" appeared on NBC from 9/14/85 to 9/9/89 and continued to relate incidents in the lives of Punky, Henry, Margaux and Cherie (voices are by the same performers as in the taped series). An X-rated version, called "Funky Brewster," appeared on home video in 1985.

583. *Quantum Leap*

NBC, 3/26/89 to 5/5/93

Cast: Scott Bakula (*Sam Beckett*), Dean Stockwell (*Al Calavicci*).

Facts: Quantum Leap is a secret government project concerned with time travel (it is hidden in the desert 30 miles outside the town of Destiny County, New Mexico). When the government threatens to cut off its funding, quantum physics professor Dr. Samuel ("Sam") Beckett takes matters into his own hands and attempts to prove that a man can be sent into time. Sam steps into the unit's acceleration chamber and vanishes. He is sent back into time and can travel (leap) only within 30 years of his own lifetime, begin-

ning in 1953 (when he was born); however, a system malfunction traps Sam in time—where he is destined to remain until he can be retrieved. Through brainwave transmissions, Sam receives the holographic assistance of Al Calavicci, an admiral who is a project observer (and who can be seen and heard only by Sam).

While bouncing around in time, Sam assumes the identities of people he never knew to correct a mistake they made and set history straight (that is, according to what a computer named Ziggy deems it should be). The audience sees Sam in the various roles—but other people see the person Sam has become (when Sam looks into a mirror, he sees the person whose identity he has assumed; this person is transported to the "Waiting Room" at the Quantum Leap complex). When a mission has been completed, Sam is propelled (leaps) into another time period and the person—man or woman—is restored to his or her normal self. (Dogs, certain children and mentally unstable people can also see Al.)

Al, who carries a slightly defective miniature Ziggy (his hand link to the computer), has known Sam for many years. Al was born on June 15, 1945, and grew up in an orphanage (where he had a pet roach named Kevin). He ran away from the orphanage to join a circus and later enlisted in the navy (in 1957 he was an ensign and was called "Bingo" by his buddies). In 1969 Al married a girl named Beth (Susan Diol), the only girl, he says, he really loved. Al was next sent to Vietnam (at which time he began smoking cigars). He was later reported as missing in action and was assumed dead. When he was found in 1973 Beth had remarried, and Al never returned to her.

Sam was born and raised on a farm in Elkridge, Indiana, and developed a fear of heights at the age of nine (after seeing a Tarzan movie, he attempted and failed to swing from a homemade vine he rigged from the barn roof). He attended Elkridge High School and possesses seven degrees.

Sam built Ziggy as a parallel hybrid computer to run Quantum Leap. Sam gave Ziggy, which has a billion gigabyte capacity, Barbra Streisand's ego ("In my lab, Ziggy has a female voice"). Al's hologram is sent through time via the Imaging Chamber. Sam's romantic interest was a girl named Donna Alisi (Teri Hatcher and Mimi Kuzyk), a fellow scientist he worked with on the Star Bright Project in 1972. Sam's catchphrase is "Oh, boy" (which he says when he discovers who he has become or something goes wrong).

Relatives: Scott Bakula (Sam's father, *John Beckett*), Carolina Kava (Sam's mother, *Thelma Beckett*), Olivia Burnette (Sam's 13-year-old sister, *Katie Beckett*), David Newsom (Sam's brother, *Tom Beckett*).

Flashbacks: Jamie Walters (*Al in 1957*).
Theme: "Quantum Leap," by Mike Post.

584. *Quark*

NBC, 2/24/78 to 4/14/78

Cast: Richard Benjamin (*Adam Quark*), Tricia Barnstable (*Betty I*), Cyb Barnstable (*Betty II*), Tim Thomerson (*Jean/*

Gene), Richard Kelton (*Ficus*), Conrad Janis (*Otto Palindrome*), Alan Caillou (*The Head*), Bobby Porter (*Andy*), Misty Rowe (*Interface*).

Facts: The time: A.D. 2226. The premise: the voyages of a U.G.S.P. (United Galaxy Sanitation Patrol) garbage ship as it patrols the deep regions of space picking up the trash (for example, space Baggies) of the planets of the United Galaxies. The ship can hold 200,000 tons of compressed astro trash; floating garbage is retrieved by the auto grippers; the ship is set on Astro Track when a new garbage run is ordered.

Adam Quark is the ship's commander. "I myself am just an ordinary human, descended from planet Earth ... My ancestors were members of a subgroup called Americans." Adam also served in the military: he was captured in the Sagittarius Rebellion by the enemy—Solanites (slightly intelligent vegetables; Adam was taken prisoner by a unit of dissident potatoes). Adam has a pet alien creature called Ergo (he eats Heliobits Plasma pet food). Adam's thoughts (which the audience hears) are called Star Notes. His favorite meal is hearts of plankton, moon snails flambé, space biscuits and puree of astro germ.

Betty I and Betty II hold the joint position of second in command. "One of them is a clone," Adam says, "an artificial, laboratory created identical twin of the other. I'm extremely fond of Betty—if I only knew which Betty it is that I am extremely fond of." Both Bettys, blonde bombshells, are also in love with Adam, and each says she is the real Betty (the clone Betty was made from a cell taken from under the fingernail of the real Betty). In the pilot episode, the twins playing the role were credited as Tricia and Cibbie Barnett (the same actresses as in the series, only with shorter hair in the pilot).

Jean/Gene is the ship's chief engineer. She/he is a transmute and possesses a full set of female and male chromosomes. Jean/Gene unpredictably switches genders (via voice and actions; she/he always appears physically as a male), depending on the situations the ship encounters.

Ficus Panderato is the chief science officer. He is a plant in human form from the planet Vegeton. The character, a clone of Mr. Spock on "Star Trek," has a logical mind and finds humor against his nature.

Andy is a cowardly Servo Mechanical Android that Adam built and is still trying to perfect. Andy is primitively designed (a square Plexiglass head and a rectangular metal body), and the Load Control Box is his "girlfriend." In the pilot episode, Andy was created by O.B. Mudd (Douglas V. Fowley), an eminent scientist who was the ship's research and equipment specialist.

Dr. Otto Robert Palindrome is the always harassed superintendent and chief of Pera Base One, the base of the U.G.S.P.

The Head, distinguished by a very large forehead and apparently no body, is commander-in-chief of U.G.S.P. and "wrote a book on headaches."

Interface is a beautiful four handed girl who serves as an intergalactic telephone operator (one must contact Interface in order to speak to the Head). The pilot aired on May 7, 1977.

Theme: "Quark," by Perry Botkin, Jr.

The Queen and I see *The Gale Storm Show: Oh! Susanna*

585. *Quincy, M.E.*
NBC, 10/3/76 to 9/5/83

Dr. R. Quincy (Jack Klugman) is a medical examiner for the Los Angeles County Coroner's Office (he was a surgeon before becoming a pathologist; his specialty is now forensic pathology). Although he is a doctor, he has the mind of a detective and prefers to do his own investigating when necessary. Quincy lives on a boat (unnamed), which "I'm thinking of selling ... and moving into the lab" (where he spends most of his time). People call him Quincy or Dr. Quincy (a first name is never mentioned; the initial *R* came from a camera shot of his I.D. card); his coroner's station wagon license plate reads 899995. The coffee kitty in the lab asks for 25 cents per cup of coffee.

Quincy is a widower when the series begins. He and his first wife, Helen (Anita Gillette, in flashbacks) honeymooned at Lake Tahoe; she called him "Quince." Helen dreamed of having children—four boys and three girls—but Quincy, who had just started a practice, wanted to wait until they were more financially secure (he was afraid children would deny him his commitment to medicine). Helen died from a brain tumor before her dream could even begin to come true. Quincy's second wife, Emily Hanover (Anita Gillette), was a doctor Quincy married in the episode of 2/23/83; there was no mention of the fact that Emily was a dead ringer for Helen, and she too apparently never knew his first name (she called him "Honey," "Quince" and "Quincy") before and after they married. (Information on Helen appeared in the "Promises to Keep" episode of 3/1/79; Emily was first introduced in the episode "Rattlesnakes" on 9/29/82.)

Dr. Robert Asten (John S. Ragin) is Quincy's superior, the assistant deputy coroner; Dr. Sam Fugiyama (Robert Ito) is Quincy's assistant.

Danny Tovo (Val Bisoglio) owns the local bar hangout, Danny's Place; Frank Monahan (Garry Walberg) is a lieutenant with the Homicide Division of the L.A.P.D. (his car license plate reads 236 SXQ); Diane (Diane Markoff) is the waitress at Danny's Place; and Lee Potter (Lynnette Mettey) was Quincy's girlfriend in first season episodes (she is also the bikini-clad girl seen sharing a drink with Quincy on his boat in the opening theme).

Glen A. Larson composed the theme.

586. *Rachel Gunn, R.N.*
Fox, 6/28/92 to 9/4/92

The duplex in need of new plumbing at 668 Oak Street is owned by Rachel Gunn (Christine Ebersole), a pretty, middle aged nurse at Little Innocents Hospital. Rachel is in charge of the fourth floor nurses' station and is called the "Iron Nightingale" (she does have one problem, however— "I can't stand the sight of blood. I faint"). Rachel is brassy and cheap (she names her money and is obsessed with it). Rather than spend money for a vacation, she sits in her backyard with her feet in a plastic pool and pretends to be in Fiji. She keeps her lights off on Halloween so the UNICEF kids won't know she is home. Rachel feels nothing good ever happens to her. She hates doctors for all the attention they get and "all the nonattention nurses get." "Banana cream pie is my favorite dessert, but I also like coconut and strawberry cream pies—except for coconut and strawberries." Rachel's first job was that of Sherbet Girl at the Dip Queen Ice Cream Parlor, and as a kid she had a dog named Tuffy. Rachel's specialty is doing the voices from *The Wizard of Oz*; she has seen the film *Death Wish* 83 times.

Dave Dunkel (Kevin Conway) is the doctor who rents a room at Rachel's duplex. He has a dog named Spike and an ex-wife (Sheila) who took him for everything he had (he calls her "Cujo"). He plans to get even one day and become a rich doctor.

Rebecca Jo Fulbright (Megan Mullally), Zack (Bryan Brightcloud) and Dane (Dan Tullis, Jr.) are the other featured nurses. Sister Joan Ignatius (Kathleen Mitchell) is the Catholic nun assigned to Rachel's floor. She plays shortstop on the convent softball team, Nuns and Roses.

Jacqueline Donnelly played young Rachel in a flashback. The series was originally produced for CBS with K.T. Oslin as Rachel Gunn.

Christine Ebersole sings the theme, "Workin' for a Living."

587. *Rags to Riches*

NBC, 3/9/87 to 1/15/88

Nick Foley (Joseph Bologna) is a millionaire with a flamboyant life-style. He is the son of a bricklayer and made his fortune as the owner of the Foley Frozen Foods Company. His real name is Nicholas Folitini, and he is the foster father of five orphan girls: Diane (Bridget Michele), Rose (Kimiko Gelman), Marva (Tisha Campbell), Patti (Blanca DeGarr) and Mickey (Heidi Zeigler). (When his reputation began to affect his business dealings, Nick decided it was time to refine his life-style. He decided to take on responsibilities and began by adopting the girls.) The series is set in Los Angeles in 1962 and features musical numbers as it relates the adventures of five streetsmart girls who have vowed to remain a family.

Nick owns a mansion in Bel Air (address not given) and is a member of the Green Hills Country Club. Klondike 5-4023 is his home phone number, and RDH 352 is his license plate number.

Before their adoption, the girls lived in Room 204 of the Margaret Keating Home for Orphan Girls in Los Angeles. School names are not given for any of the girls. Rose and Marva work on their high school newspaper, the *Cougar*;

Patti hopes to become a writer; Marva seeks a career in the world of high finance; Diane drives a car with the license plate EZP 374; and Mickey, the youngest, has a pet guinea pig named Herbert. The girls buy their snack foods at Crawley's Market.

John Clapper (Douglas Seale), whom Nick calls Clapper, is Nick's butler and helps care for the girls. In the pilot episode, Heather McAdam played Nina, a sixth girl Nick had adopted; she was dropped when her mother came to reclaim her.

Gina Hecht appeared as Patti's mother, Gloria Lang; Joe Cortese was Nick's brother, Frankie Folitini; and Richard Grieco played Nick's godson, Billy Galanto.

Peter Robinson and Mark Miller composed the "Rags to Riches" theme.

588. *Raising Miranda*

CBS, 11/5/88 to 12/31/88

"My Life Story" was the original title of this bittersweet comedy about a father and daughter's relationship built on trust after the wife and mother deserts the family to search for her own identity.

Miranda Marshack (Royana Black) is the shy, sensitive and awkward 14-year-old girl; and Donald ("Don") Marshack (James Naughton) is her father, a boyish, charming contractor who is as much at home with Miranda as he is when he is out with the guys he works with. Miranda and Don find support from their neighbors, Bob and Joan Hoodenpyle (Steve Vinovich and Miriam Flynn), whose advice is most often off-target ("But they mean well," Don says). Adding to the calamity is Marcine Marie Lindquist (Amy Lynne), Miranda's best friend, a 14-year-old somewhat bossy girl who has taken Miranda under her wing; and Miranda's deadbeat uncle, Russell (Bryan Cranston), who offers his own brand of questionable support.

Miranda and Don live at 85 Muskeegan Road in Racine, Wisconsin. Their phone number is 555-5153, and Don works for the Big M Construction Company. Miranda and Marcine, who lives at 863 Fairview Lane, are freshmen at Racine High School. Miranda reads *Teen World* magazine, and at the end of each episode, she writes the day's activities in her diary. She concludes each entry with "Confidentially, Miranda."

Lee Garlington played Marcine's mother, Helen Lindquist. Martin Silvestri, Jeremy Stone and Joel Higgins composed the theme, "Raising Miranda."

589. *Rango*

ABC, 1/13/67 to 9/1/67

"From San Antone to the Rio Grande, on mountain peaks or desert sand, every outlaw fears the hand of danger from this Texas Ranger, Rango, Rango, Rango." (Rango (Tim Conway) is a Texas Ranger assigned to the Deep Wells Texas Ranger Station in Gopher Gulch, Texas (in the 1870s). He introduces himself by saying, "I'm Rango, just Rango, Texas Ranger." He believes "a law abiding town is a happy town" and tries to enforce that belief with proclamations (84 of them; number 1 is "No guns allowed in town," number 84 is "No whistling at girls on the street"). He is also bumbling, dim witted, slow on the draw, and a major headache to Ranger Captain Horton (Norman Alden): "Don't you think I would like to get rid of him? Don't you think I've tried to get rid of him? My hands are tied as long as his Uncle George is Commandant of the Rangers. I can't get rid of him."

Rango's assistant is Pink Cloud (Guy Marks), a "modernized" Indian who lives among savages but sees no need to go native. He doesn't talk or act like an Indian, and more often than not, he helps Rango outwit the bad guys.

In Gopher Gulch, the captain, who has a prized gun collection, refuses to let Rango carry a gun. He assigns Rango to cases that are so hopeless ordinary Rangers would quit in frustration. Rango, however, manages to overcome all obstacles and bring dignity to the Texas Rangers ("But," the captain says, "I'm still stuck with him!").

Frankie Laine sings the theme, "Rango."

590. *Raven*

CBS, 6/24/92 to 10/3/92

Jonathan Raven (Jeffrey Meek) is a private detective based in Oahu, Hawaii. He is a former ninja, trained by the deadly Black Dragon society, who is now searching for his long-lost son (he tends to get sidetracked by helping other people). Assisting Raven is Herman ("Ski") Jablonski (Lee Majors), a hard drinking security analyst, who now works as Jonathan's partner.

Jonathan was raised in Japan. His father worked for Interpol and was assigned to investigate drug trafficking by the Black Dragons. When he "got too close," he and his wife were killed by the society. Jonathan, a teenager at the time, became bitter and vowed to avenge their deaths. He infiltrated the cult and learned their deadly martial arts. When he felt the time was right, he killed those responsible for murdering his parents. He is now sought by the Black Dragons for betraying them. Before Jonathan left Japan, he had an affair with a Japanese girl named Aki Moshirho. Unknown to Jonathan, Aki was two months pregnant when he left Japan (he feared the Black Dragons would kill her). At seven months complications set in, and Aki died shortly after giving birth. Sometime later, Jonathan received a letter from a friend of Aki's telling him about the birth of his son, whom Aki named Hikatti ("Sparkling Light"), but not saying where he was. Jonathan is now in a desperate race to find his son before the Black Dragons do (who plan to kill him).

Jonathan drives a Jeep with the license plate R2H 103. He

also has a special talent for touching people on the back of the neck and instantly putting them to sleep. Big Kahuna's Bar is Jonathan and Ski's favorite hangout. Ski, a former special forces agent, has a boat called the *Brew-Ski,* which he docks at Big Kahuna's Diamond Head Marina (Pier G-22). Ski, who loves pastrami on rye, carries four guns (one on each side of his hips, one in his boot, one in the back of his belt), brass knuckles and a knife with him at all times.

Christopher Franke composed the theme.

591. *The Ray Milland Show*

CBS, 9/17/53 to 7/15/54
CBS, 9/16/54 to 9/30/55

Ray McNutley (Ray Milland) is a professor of English at the Lynnhaven College for Women in the town of Lynnhaven. Ray lives in a white frame house at 187 Maple Terrace with his wife, Peggy (Phyllis Avery); their phone number is Lynnhaven 3325. Their neighbors are Pete ("Petey") Thompson (Gordon Jones) and his wife, Ruth (Jacqueline DeWit). Pete is a real estate salesman (Thompson Real Estate), and he drives a green convertible with whitewalls and a locked trunk full of HOUSE FOR SALE signs. Pete calls Ray "Ray Boy," and together they purchased a used 32-foot fishing boat called the *Hesperus* (which previously sank twice and had an engine that blew up). Pete's phone number is Lynnhaven 2556, and he lives at 185 Maple Terrace. Minerva Urecal played Josephine Bradley, the college dean.

The series, also known as "Meet Mr. McNutley," changed formats for its second season. Ray and Peggy move to California when Ray becomes a drama professor at Comstock University, a coeducational college headed by Dean Dodsworth (Lloyd Corrigan). In this version of the series, the spelling of Ray's last name became "McNutly." David Stollery appeared as Peggy's boy-genius cousin, Grover. As is typical with many filmed series of this era, a theme composer is not credited.

592. *The Real McCoys*

ABC, 10/3/57 to 9/20/62
CBS, 9/24/62 to 9/22/63

Cast: Walter Brennan *(Amos McCoy)*, Richard Crenna *(Luke McCoy)*, Kathleen Nolan *(Kate McCoy)*, Lydia Reed *(Hassie McCoy)*, Michael Winkelman *(Little Luke McCoy)*, Tony Martinez *(Pepino Garcia)*.

Facts: Shortly after the death of his brother, Ben, Amos McCoy inherits his ranch in the San Fernando Valley in California. Amos, the cantankerous head of the clan; his grandson, Luke; Luke's wife, Kate; and Luke's sister and brother, Hassie and Little Luke, pack their belongings into their Model-T Ford ("Gertrude") and leave their dirt-poor farm in West Virginia to begin new lives in California.

When the McCoys arrive, they find the ranch is badly in need of repair but has good soil. They also find Pepino, Ben's Mexican ranchhand, whom Ben also willed to Amos.

Amos was born in Smokey Corners, West Virginia, in 1894. He and his wife (now deceased) honeymooned in "the best boardinghouse in town" (their bridal suite was next to the kitchen). Grandpa, as Amos is called, enjoys fishing, pitching horseshoes and playing the banjo. REST THY HEAD is embroidered on the headrest of Grandpa's favorite rocking chair in the living room. Amos is also a member of the Royal Order of the Mystic Nile Lodge.

Luke married Kate just before leaving West Virginia. They honeymooned at the Colonial Palms Motel and stayed in Room 204. "Margie" was the song to which Luke and Kate danced when they first met. Grandpa was upset with Luke for marrying Kate: "How could you marry a girl like Kate instead of Frank Goody's girl, Elviry . . . a 16-year-old girl who can lick two men in the morning and plow a field in the afternoon, and take up with a skinny woman past 20 . . . who said as bold as brass she didn't know how to shoe a mare? . . . I'd like to cry." "Kate," Luke says, "was brought up in a house of curtains; it ain't hardly her fault. She just takes gettin' used to." By the end of the first episode, when Kate embroiders the REST THY HEAD cloth for Grandpa's rocking chair, Amos accepts her. Luke calls Kate "Sugar Babe" ("Honey Babe" in the pilot).

Luke's parents are deceased. He and Kate care for his sister, Hassie, and his younger brother, Little Luke (Luke's parents were so excited when the baby was born they named him Luke—forgetting they already had a son named Luke). Thirteen-year-old Hassie attends Valley High School (Little Luke first attended Valley Elementary, then Valley High). Hassie is a member of the Alpha Beta Sigma sorority and has her hair done at Armand's Beauty Parlor (she was the first in her school to wear the latest craze from France—the Bouffant Beehive, which cost her $3.50). Pepino calls Amos "Señor Grandpa." The McCoys' phone number is Valley 4276, and they have a milk cow named Bessie. In 1962, after Kate's "death" (Kathleen Nolan left the series), Janet DeGore joined the cast as Louise Howard, a widow (and romantic interest for Luke) who purchased the farm next to the McCoys. Louise is the mother of a young boy named Gregg (Butch Patrick). Andy Clyde (as George MacMichael) is Amos's neighbor, who "owns the farm up the hill" from the McCoys. Madge Blake is Flora MacMichael, George's sister, who lives with him.

Relatives: Jack Oakie (Luke's uncle, *"Rightly" Ralph McCoy*), Nora Hayden (Amos's cousin, *Elviry Goody*), Joan Blondell (Louise's aunt, *Winifred Jordan*).

Theme: "The Real McCoys," by Harry Ruby.

593. *Reasonable Doubts*
NBC, 9/26/91 to 4/27/93

Tess Kaufman (Marlee Matlin) is a beautiful, hearing impaired prosecuting attorney for the Chicago District Attorney's Office. Richard ("Dicky") Cobb (Mark Harmon) is a tough detective with the Metropolitan Police Department, District 26. He is the only cop on the force who can read and speak in sign language (which he learned from his deaf father). Through a special arrangement with the D.A.'s office and the police department, Cobb is assigned to assist Tess in the field (as her investigator and interpreter) when she questions suspects in a case.

Tess lives at 1422 Barrington Avenue. Her phone number is 555-1311, and her license plate reads F4R 526. Cobb lives at 703 Beckman Place (Apartment 2) and has a dog named John. His license plate number is T5H 693. Tess and Cobb are members of the D.A.s (a softball team) and play at Longwood Park.

The Setup Bar, owned by Kay Lockman (Nancy Everhard) is Cobb's favorite watering hole. Kay, Cobb's romantic interest, was shot during a robbery of the bar in the episode of 9/29/92 ("Forever My Love"). Kay seemed to be recovering until a postoperative complication caused a massive stroke that left her brain dead. Cobb made the most difficult decision of his life when he turned off the respirator that kept her alive.

Margaret ("Maggie") Zombro (Kay Lenz) is a gorgeous and very expensive private practice attorney who most often defends the clients Tess is prosecuting. She is, as she says, "heartless and calculating and I know my way around a courtroom." Arthur Gold (William Converse-Roberts) is Tess's superior, the D.A.; Bruce Kaufman (Tim Grimm) is Tess's ex-husband.

Relatives: Bruce Kirby (Tess's father, *Don Morris*), Margaret Ladd (Tess's mother, *Libby Morris*), Glynnis O'Connor (Dicky's ex-wife, *Jo Cobb*), Nina Foch (Bruce's mother, *Carmela Kaufman*).

Theme: "Reasonable Doubts," by Brad Fiedel.

594. *The Rebel*
ABC, 10/4/59 to 9/24/61

The series is set in the post–Civil War West of 1867. Johnny Yuma (Nick Adams) is an embittered, leather-tough young ex–Confederate soldier who journeys west after the war to seek his own identity. He wears his Rebel uniform proudly wherever he goes; his saddle is his pillow, and he never stays in any one place long enough to call home— "The things I gotta learn about aren't here, just another stop in an off place." He keeps a diary of his travels, his "book," as he calls it, and he helps people in trouble—his strong sense of justice forces him into violent confrontations with those who oppose his beliefs.

Johnny was born in the town of Mason. He wanted to be a writer and work for the town newspaper, the Mason *Bulletin,* but he could never stay put; he ran away from home several times when he was 15 and joined the Confederate Army as a means of running away. Johnny's mother died when he was very young; his father, Ned Yuma, raised him. He now rides his late father's horse and carries his scattergun (Ned, the town sheriff, was killed in the line of duty).

The war may be over, but the hatred still exists. Johnny "packed no star as he wandered far, where the only law was a hook-and-a-draw." "Maybe I'll find my place one day," he says. In the opening theme, the left side profile of Johnny is branded on a piece of wood.

Johnny Cash sings the theme, "The Rebel—Johnny Yuma." Newly resyndicated episodes have a different (music only) opening and closing theme (not credited) as a result of copyright problems with the original theme. It is not widely known that Elvis Presley recorded the original theme for the pilot (which, for unknown reasons, was not used).

595. *Remington Steele*

NBC, 10/1/82 to 9/16/86

Cast: Stephanie Zimbalist *(Laura Holt),* Pierce Brosnan *(Remington Steele),* Doris Roberts *(Mildred Krebs).*

Facts: Remington Steele Investigations is a private detective organization located in suite 1157 of a building located at 606 West Beverly Boulevard in Los Angeles, California (its phone numbers are 555-9450, 555-3535 and 555-9548). Laura Holt is its founder, and Remingston Steele is her chief investigator.

Laura Holt weighs 110 pounds and lives at 800 Tenth Street, Apartment 3A, in a building owned by the Commercial Management Corporation. She has a cat named Nero, and her phone number is 555-6235. Laura's car license plate reads JEL 1525 (later 1E49463), and her mobile phone number is T7328. In college, Laura and three girlfriends were known as "The Four East" (they shared a fourth floor dorm room); Laura is plagued by the "Holt Curse"—a craving for chocolate candy. "Atomic Man" was Laura's favorite television show as a kid, and her nickname was "Binky."

After graduating from Stanford University, Laura got a job as an apprentice detective at the Havenhurst Detective Agency. She quit when she felt she could start her own company and opened Laura Holt Investigations. Her business immediately begins to fail. Figuring that perhaps "a female private investigator is too feminine," she invents a mythical boss named Remington Steele. She changes the company name to Remington Steele Investigations, and suddenly business is booming.

All this changes when Laura is hired to protect the Royal Lavulite Diamonds. A suave and sophisticated thief, who 12 years earlier was a boxer known as "The Kilkearney Kid," comes to Los Angeles to steal those jewels. When complications set in, the thief assumes the identity of Laura's Remington Steele to get himself out of a jam; he later convinces Laura to make him her partner.

"The Mysterious Remington Steele" is just that—mysterious. Born in Ireland and apparently an orphan, he was taught the fine art of crime by Daniel Chalmers (Efrem Zimbalist, Jr.), a master con artist. He now lives at 1594 Rossmore Street, Apartment 5A, and drives a 1936 Auburn, license plate R. STEELE, and a blue Mercedes with the license plate IDR 0373. "The Honeymooners" is his favorite television show, and he projects motion pictures onto real life, most often solving cases based on plots from old movies. On his living room wall are movie posters from *Casablanca, Hotel Imperial, The Thin Man* and *Notorious.*

Murphy Michaels (James Read) was Laura's original assistant (first season), and Bernice Foxx (Janet DeMay), whom Remington called "Miss Wolf," was her receptionist. Mildred Krebs, a former IRS auditor, replaced both characters from the second season on. Michael Constantine played George E. Mulch, the "idea man" who complicates Laura's life, and James Tolkan was Norman Keyes, the Vigilance Insurance Company detective who plagues Steele (seeking to uncover his true identity). The show's gimmick is the use of "Steele" in every episode title (for example, "Steele Sweet on You," "My Fair Steele" and "Women of Steele"). "Ben Pearson, from South Africa," was the first assumed name Remington used (all his assumed names are taken from the film characters of Humphrey Bogart).

Relatives: Beverly Garland (Laura's mother, *Abigail Holt*), Maryedith Burrell (Laura's sister, *Frances Piper*), Michael Durrell (Frances's husband, *Donald Piper*), Albert Macklin (Mildred's nephew, *Bernard*).

Theme: "Remington Steele," by Henry Mancini.

596. *The Reporter*

CBS, 9/25/64 to 12/25/64

"He's a man who cares about people, not a man who stands about with a notebook jotting down facts. He is a man standing up to his armpits in facts." He is Danny Taylor (Harry Guardino), an aggressive reporter for the *Globe,* a crusading New York newspaper. Danny, who lives at 63 East 46th Street in Manhattan, was a street-smart kid who used his knowledge of the streets to help him break into reporting. He works on open assignment under Lou Sheldon (Gary Merrill), the seasoned editor of the *Globe.* Although Danny is free to uncover his own stories, he often resents Lou's driving him "to the last heartbreaking expenditure of effort that only a champion in the making can give." Lou finds it necessary to act as Danny's trainer, taskmaster and conscience, for Danny is angry at the world's injustices. Once on a case, Danny becomes involved with his stories and will not rest until he has the facts that will bring justice.

The *Globe*'s city room is an exact duplicate of that of the New York *Mirror,* a tabloid that folded. Producer Keefe Brasselle purchased the *Mirror*'s entire "cluster" (from desks to typewriters) and reconstructed the city room for the series in a studio on mid–Manhattan's West Side.

Kenyon Hopkins composed the theme.

597. *Rescue 8*

Syndicated, 1958 to 1960

In 1958 Los Angeles had a population of five and one half million people. There were 27 rescue units (numbered 1 to 27) attached to the L.A. County Fire Department. When someone was trapped in a life and death situation, the men of these rescue units risked their lives to save them. "This program is dedicated to rescue teams throughout the U.S. and to the men who risk their lives daily to save others. And now, the stories behind rescues."

The series focuses on the rescues performed by one such unit—Rescue 8. Wes Cameron (Jim Davis) runs Rescue 8 out of Station 8. His "shotgun" (assistant) is Skip Johnson (Lang Jeffries). Wes is the veteran paramedic and is single. Skip is young and eager; he is a Korean War veteran and lives at 7023 Canyon Road with his wife, Patty (Nancy Rennick), and daughter, Susan (Mary K. Cleary).

Wes and Skip work with the odds stacked against them—"But what we're doing," Skip says, "someone's got to do." A Code R is a bad accident—"The kind of situation where death holds a stopwatch on us." Rescue 8 is also their mobile code to L.A. Base. Their original rescue truck license plate was 31459; it became 80448 in later episodes.

Douglas Heyes composed the theme.

The exploits of the paramedics of the L.A. County Fire Department were again depicted in the NBC series "Emergency" (1/22/72 to 12/31/78). Roy DeSoto (Kevin Tighe) and John Gage (Randolph Mantooth) were firemen with the Squad 51 Rescue Unit; they worked with Rampart Hospital personnel, doctors Kelly Brackett (Robert Fuller) and Joe Early (Bobby Troup) and Nurse Dixie McCall (Julie London). In the revised version (NBC, 6/26/79 to 7/3/79), Gage and DeSoto worked the paramedics Laurie Campbell (Deirdre Lenihan) and Gail Warren (Patricia McCormack) of the 87th Rescue Unit of the San Francisco Fire Department.

Rhoda see *The Mary Tyler Moore Show*

598. *Rhythm and Blues*

NBC 9/24/92 to 10/21/92

WBLZ radio is the voice of black Detroit. But the once profitable station has fallen on hard times through the mismanagement of Veronica Washington (Anna Maria Horsford), the wife of the late station owner, who took on the responsibility of running the station. Hoping to get the station back on its feet again, Veronica hires, sight unseen, Bobby Soul (Roger Kabler), a D.J. she believes is right for the job. Bobby, however, is white, but is talented and can sound like a black D.J. His efforts to prove he has the "Rhythm and Blues" and can help WBLZ make it back to the top are the focal point of the series.

Bobby's real name is Robert Botticher, Jr. He was born in Bloomfield Hills and wanted to be Bobby Soul, king of the D.J.s (as a kid, Bobby would listen to WBLZ on an inexpensive transistor radio and grew up loving black music). Bobby lives at the Liberty Hotel, later at the Fairview Apartments on Ridley Avenue. He has a cat (Gilligan), two fish (Shamoo and Tutu) and a canary (Aretha).

Collette Hawkins (Vanessa Bell Calloway) is WBLZ's beautiful program director. She is a graduate of Wellesley College and lives at 0730 Damon Street. When Collette had a dispute with Veronica, she went to work for WEZ radio. Don Phillips (Ron Glass) is the sales manager. He is a former singer and member of the Five Tops (Don threatened to leave unless he was made the lead singer; he wasn't, and they became the Four Tops). The Love Man (Troy Curvey, Jr.) hosts a program of romantic music and speaks in the third person ("The Love Man says...").

Veronica was married for 15 years; she lives in Highland Park: the station's slogan is "We play the hits"; WTRX is WBLZ's main competition. Mother Love played Veronica in the unaired pilot version of the series.

Monty Seward composed the "Rhythm and Blues" theme.

599. *Richard Diamond, Private Detective*

CBS, 7/1/57 to 9/23/57
CBS, 1/2/58 to 9/20/59
NBC, 10/5/59 to 1/25/60

Cast: David Janssen *(Richard Diamond)*, Mary Tyler Moore and Roxanne Brooks *(Sam)*.

Facts: "When I'm paid for a job I deliver," exclaims Richard Diamond, a handsome, two fisted private detective who operates out of New York City, then from Los Angeles. He lives at the Savoy Hotel (New York episodes) and charges $100 a day plus expenses; if it's a beautiful girl who is in trouble and she can't afford that, he lowers his price to $50 a day. Richard was formerly an officer with the N.Y.P.D. (5th Precinct), and he now operates out of office number 306 of an unnamed building (in Los Angeles, his office number is 117). He reads the New York *Chronicle*, doesn't come to the office on Tuesdays, and says, "A private detective is only as good as his snitch"; he pays his snitches as much as ten dollars for information.

"Oh that voice! And the only thing I know about her is what she tells me—and that ain't much!" Richard is referring to a girl known only as Sam, a beautiful, sexy-voiced telephone operator who owns the Hi Fi Answering Service. Sam (whom Richard calls "Samuel") operates from a small room. While Richard has never seen her (he says, on occasion, "You know, I've never even seen the girl"), viewers do. Sam is situated in a dimly lit room that is designed to accentuate her gorgeous long legs, slim waist and well developed bust. Sam's face is never clearly seen; she wears tight blouses or sweaters and slit skirts or dresses raised just enough to show the needed bit of thigh. She wears the then-famous "torpedo bra" (38B) and size ten stockings, medium length.

Sam answers Richard's office calls on the fourth ring. When she calls Richard she says, "It's me, Mr. D." Richard concluded his conversations with her with, "As usual, Samuel, thank you." Richard also receives clients from Sam ("Richard, I have a friend who needs help—a female friend"). Murray Hill 4-9099 was Sam's answering service number when Mary Tyler Moore played the role; OL 4-1654 was the phone number when Roxanne Brooks became Sam.

Richard's mobile phone number is ZM 1-2173 (also given as ZM 1-2713); he eats at the Lunch Counter and goes undercover (for example, as Fred Grebble) when he has to—"Because some people are allergic to my profession."

In New York episodes, Regis Toomey played Lieutenant Dennis ("Mac") McGough of the N.Y.P.D. 5th Precinct (Richard's former superior when he was on the force; he calls Diamond "Rick"). Russ Conway was Lieutenant Peter ("Pete") Kile in Los Angeles episodes. Barbara Bain played Karen Wells, Richard's girlfriend, in last season episodes; and Hillary Brooke, as Laura Renault, was Richard's most frequent client, a once famous movie star who had a knack for getting into perilous situations.

Theme: "Richard Diamond," by Pete Rugolo.

Note: The series is also known as "Call Mr. D." (its syndicated title in the 1960s). Under "Call Mr. D.," the theme and its entire musical background were changed. There is no credit for the "Call Mr. D" theme or its background music, only a credit for music supervision (Frank DeVol, Harry King). The opening visuals were also changed. In "Richard Diamond," Diamond is seen running here and there as the "sexy" theme plays; he then approaches the camera and lights a cigarette. In "Call Mr. D.," a figure is seen in a darkened alley; as the new theme plays, he walks forward and lights a cigarette; we see that it is Richard Diamond.

600. *Richie Brockelman, Private Eye*

NBC, 3/17/78 to 4/14/78

RICHARD BROCKELMAN—PRIVATE INVESTIGATOR is the name on his office door (number 24 in the Bromley Building at 4th and Alameda in Los Angeles); "Brockelman Detective Agency" is how his secretary, Sharon Peterson (Barbara Bosson), answers the phone. Richie Brockelman (Dennis Dugan) is 23 years old. He has more nerve than know-how and is listed in the Yellow Pages. "I charge $200 a day plus expenses, but I normally don't get it," he says. He drives a sedan with the license plate 238 PCE and lives

at 8410 North Turtle Dove Drive. If there is a problem at the office and Richie is not present, Sharon signals Richie by placing her fern on the fire escape (he has a back office with one window that leads to the fire escape). Richie's office is next to Chelsea Antiques and opposite the El Royale Motel.

Ted Coopersmith (Robert Hogan), whom Richie calls "Smitty," is the L.A.P.D. sergeant Richie involves in his cases; Ronnie (Melanie Chartoff) is Richie's police department information girl (Richie calls her Ronnie and she is credited as "Police Woman Ronnie").

Helen Page Camp plays Richie's mother; Norman Fell (pilot) and John Randolph play Richie's father.

The series is a spinoff from "The Rockford Files," and the pilot, "Richie Brockelman: Missing 24 Hours," aired on NBC on 10/27/76.

Stephen Geyes and Herb Pederson composed the theme, "School's Out."

601. *The Rifleman*

ABC, 9/30/58 to 7/1/63

The series is set in the 1860s in the town of North Fork, New Mexico. Four miles south of town is the old Dunlap Ranch, a 4,100-acre spread that is now owned by Lucas McCain (Chuck Connors) and his young son, Mark (Johnny Crawford). Lucas is a widower, and he left his home in "the Nations" to begin a new life after the death of his wife.

In the Nations, Lucas was called "the Rifleman," the fastest man with a .44-40 hair-trigger action rifle with a special hoop lever (which allows normal firing when a special screw is loose, rapid firing when the screw is tightened). In the opening theme, Lucas fires 12 shots; the rifle can fire eight times in two-and-a-half seconds. Lucas's horse is named Razor; Blue Boy is Mark's horse.

Micah Torrance (Paul Fix) is the town marshal; Eddie Holstead (John Harmon) owns the Madera House Hotel; Lou Mallory (Patricia Blair) owns the Mallory House Hotel; Millie Scott (Joan Taylor) runs the general store; and Sweeney (Bill Quinn) is the Last Chance Saloon bartender.

Relatives: Jerome Courtland (Lucas's brother-in-law, *Johnny Gibbs*), Thomas Gomez (Lucas's cousin by marriage, *Artemis Quarles*), Gloria DeHaven (Eddie's daughter, *Lillian Holstead*), Cheryl Holdridge (Millie's niece, *Sally Walker*).

Theme: "The Rifleman," by Herschel Burke Gilbert.

602. *Ripcord*

Syndicated, 1961

"This is the most danger-packed show on television. Every jump, every aerial maneuver is real, photographed just as it happened, without tricks or illusions. All that stands between a jumper and death is his Ripcord."

In this opening theme narration, the announcer is referring to James ("Jim") Buckley (Ken Curtis) and Theodore ("Ted") McKeever (Larry Pennell), daredevil skydivers for Ripcord, Inc., a combination sky diving school and charter service based at Brentwood Field in California. (The actual skydiving stunts were performed by Lyle Cameron.)

Jim and Ted are also trained smokejumpers and medics, and they assist authorities when skydiving into a disaster may be the only way to rescue people. "The Ripcord Plane," as Jim and Ted call it, has the I.D. number N32201. The plane's pilots were Chuck Lambert (Paul Comi) and, later, Charlie Kern (Shug Fisher), who called the plane "Old Betsy." (The actual pilot was real life pilot Cliff Winters).

Warren Barker composed the theme.

603. *Riptide*

NBC, 1/3/84 to 4/18/86
NBC, 8/22/86 (1 episode)

Pier 53 Investigations is a private detective company run by three friends: Cody Allen (Perry King), Nick Ryder (Joe Penny) and Murray ("Boz") Bozinsky (Thom Bray). It is located at Slip 7, Pier 56, in King Harbor in southern California. The agency is later called Riptide Investigations (a.k.a. the Riptide Detective Agency) to reflect the name of their houseboat and office, the *Riptide*). Their phone number is 555-8300. They also have a motorboat (*Ebbtide*) and a pink helicopter called the *Screaming Mimi* (I.D. Number N698). Murray has a robot called "The Roboz," and their friend, Mama Jo (Anne Francis) runs a cruise ship called *The Contessa*. The Straightaways Restaurant is the gang's hangout.

Ted Quinlan (Jack Ging, 1983–85) and Joanna Parisi (June Chadwick) are lieutenants with the King Harbor Police Department; Geena Davis plays Boz's sister, Melba Bozinsky.

Mike Post and Pete Carpenter composed the "Riptide" theme.

604. *The Roaring 20's*

ABC, 10/15/60 to 9/21/62

Cast: Dorothy Provine (*Pinky Pinkham*), Donald May (*Pat Garrison*), Rex Reason (*Scott Norris*), Gary Vinson (*Chris Higbee*), John Dehner (*Jim Duke Williams*), Mike Road (*Lieutenant Joe Switolski*).

Facts: Life in New York City during the 1920s (pinpointed as 1926 in one episode) as seen through the eyes of Pinky Pinkham, Pat Garrison and Scott Norris, three friends who live and work in Manhattan.

Pinky Pinkham, whose real first name is Delaware, is a beautiful singer who owns the Charleston Club, a hot nightspot on fashionable East 52nd Street. The club, which serves Highland Dew Scotch, is also called Pinky's and Pinky's Club. A life-size cardboard cutout of Pinky stands outside the club. She lives at the Grently Apartments (Room 21), and her telephone number is Skylar 2-098. Her normal wake-up time is 12:00 noon. When Pinky falls in love, the song "Someone to Watch Over Me" is heard playing in the background (Pinky has a tendency to fall for men with links to the criminal world). Pinky's backup singers are Cindy (Gayla Graves) and Dodie (Roxanne Arlen), who are billed as "the Girls" ("Pinky and the Girls"). Her musical backing is a group called the Playboys. Also seen at the Charleston Club are Dixie (Carolyn Komant), the hatcheck girl, and Andre (Gregory Gay), the maitre d'.

Scott Norris and Pat Garrison are newspaper reporters for the *Daily Record*. They both earn $40 a week (later $60) and strive to uncover stories by playing detective; their goal is to get the front page stories by putting the crooks and racketeers in jail. Their hangouts are Chauncey's (first season) and The Pit (second season). Wally Brown played Chauncey Kowalski, the bar owner; Chauncey's was located next door to the Record Building.

Reporter Scott Norris was dropped after the first season, and Jim Duke Williams was brought on to replace him. More than just a reporter, Duke also handled the city editor's job. Even though he worked for the *Record*, he used whatever means he could to get the stories before Pat.

Chris Higbee, who attended Cornell University and lived at the Hotel Hallmark, was originally the *Record*'s copy boy; he was made a cub reporter in second season episodes. Joe Switolski is a lieutenant with the 7th Precinct of the N.Y.P.D. (also seen as the Bell Street police station; Joe's direct telephone number is Spring 3-100); and Gladys (Louise Glenn) is the *Record*'s switchboard operator. The *Record*'s competition is the *Gazette*.

Theme: "The Roaring 20's," by Mack David and Jerry Livingston.

605. *Roc*

Fox, 8/25/91 to the present

Roc Emerson (Charles S. Dutton) is a garbage man. He quit his job on the docks for a position with the Baltimore Department of Sanitation. He is married to Eleanor (Ella Joyce) and lives with his widowed father, Andrew (Carl Gordon), and brother, Joseph ("Joey") Andrew Emerson (Rocky Carroll), at 864 Essex Street. Roc also has a dream: to own a semidetached house (his current, attached house, is furnished almost totally with "perks"—the items other people discard that Roc finds on his route).

Roc's newspapers are from the preceding day ("I read yesterday's news today"; the money he saves by not buying a daily paper is put into a jar for that dream house). When Roc does buy something, he will only buy it on sale (Eleanor is trying to get him to do the unusual—buy an item at list price). Roc has to empty 175,214 garbage cans to make $2,000. He has coffee at the Dump (the shop next to the depot; it was originally called the Landfill); his favorite watering hole is Charlene's Bar.

Eleanor is a nurse and works in Wing C of Harbor Hospital. Her favorite television show is "L.A. Law," and if she were to have an extramarital affair, it would be with Denzel Washington (Roc's affair would be with Dorothy Dandridge). Andrew, called "Pop" by Roc, was a porter on a train for 36 years; his late wife was named Loretta, and he has pictures of his hero, Malcolm X, on every wall in the house. Joey, a con artist, supposedly makes a living as a musician (he plays trumpet).

Richard Roundtree appeared as Andrew's brother, Russell Emerson; Rosalind Cash was Eleanor's mother, Margaret Carter. Second season episodes were broadcast live (and promoted as "Roc Live")—the first time a television sitcom had been broadcast live in more than 30 years.

Fred Tahler composed "Roc's Theme."

606. *Rock Candy*

Syndicated, 1987

Cast: Judy Landers (*Sherrie Waverly*), Audrey Landers (*Nicki Waverly*), Dick Van Patten (*Walter Waverly*), Debbie Milano (*Debbie Morton*).

Facts: Residing at 6753 Oakwood Drive in Sherman Oaks, California, are Walter Waverly, a widowed band leader, and his two beautiful daughters, Sherrie and Nicki, singers known as Rock Candy, who perform with a musical group called the Jaw Breakers.

In the 1940s Walter led an orchestra called The Waverly Dream Makers. As America's taste in music changed, the band changed with it: they became The Waves (1950s) and The Rough Waves (1960s), and are currently The Sounds of the Walter Waverly Orchestra, music geared to the older crowd.

Sherrie is a gorgeous, naive blonde who doesn't realize how sexy she is. She measures 37-24-36 and has many boyfriends, but says, "I don't know why. I guess they like my singing" (her Rock Candy wardrobe is a miniskirt, funky hair and a tight blouse). Sherrie works at whatever jobs she can get while she and Nicki wait for their big break. Sherrie and Nicki started Rock Candy in high school and worked with various groups before they met the Jaw Breakers. Sherrie loves fattening desserts but doesn't seem to gain an ounce.

Nicki is two years older than Sherrie and is just as gorgeous but not as busty. Nicki is also a blonde, but is level headed, intelligent and sometimes jealous of all the attention men give Sherrie. Nicki teaches piano lessons (her professional secret, she says, is earplugs). She and Sherrie (as well as Walter) are always in need of money; when it becomes tight, they "dine" at a chicken fast food place called Cluck for a Buck.

Debbie Morton is Sherrie's gorgeous friend. Debbie, who measures 36-24-36, was a topless dancer at the Viva Club in Las Vegas before she retired to marry Morton M. Morton

(Robert Pierce), the owner of a trendy fashion boutique called Morton's of Sherman Oaks. Debbie thinks "it was the biggest mistake of my life" and is now saddled with three kids: Morton II (Dana Darling), Morton III (Edith Conato) and Morton IV (Nicholas Lang). Nine-year-old Morton II seems to be the only normal one; Morton III is a very pretty 11-year-old girl who is having an identity crisis; and Morton IV, whom Debbie calls "the brat from hell," is only seven years old and is already feared by the entire neighborhood. To further complicate Debbie's life, she lives at 1115 Morton Drive, her license plate reads YO MORTON and her phone number is 555-MORT.

Theme: "Rock Candy," by the Jaw Breakers.

607. *The Rockford Files*

NBC, 9/13/74 to 7/25/80

James ("Jim") Rockford (James Garner) is an ex-con turned private investigator who operates the Rockford Private Detective Agency (a.k.a. the Rockford Agency) from his mobile home at the Paradise Cove Trailer Colony in Malibu Beach, California (address given as 29 Palm Road, 29 Cove Road and 2354 Pacific Coast). He charges $200 a day plus expenses and can be reached at 555-2368 (later 555-9000); his car license plate reads 853-CNG (later OK 6853).

Jim was falsely accused of robbery and sentenced to 20 years at San Quentin (he was released when new evidence cleared him). Jim stands six feet one inch tall (later six feet two inches tall) and weighs 200 pounds. He served in the army (as a corporal) during the Korean War and began the agency in 1968. Casa Tacos is his favorite eatery. The title refers to the original concept of the series: Jim's efforts to solve cases that are considered unsolvable and labeled inactive by the police. As the series progressed, he became the typical television private eye who took virtually any case that could make money.

Joseph ("Rocky") Rockford (Robert Donley in the pilot, then Noah Beery, Jr.) is Jim's father and occasional assistant; Dennis Becker (Joe Santos) is a sergeant with the Wilshire Division of the L.A.P.D.; Peggy Becker (Pat Finley) is Dennis's wife (she attends evening classes at UCLA); Beth Davenport (Gretchen Corbett) is Jim's lawyer friend; and Evelyn ("Angel") Martin (Stuart Margolin) is Jim's friend, a con artist who helps him when necessary.

Lance White (Tom Selleck) was Jim's rival, the mediocre private detective who did everything wrong but received more glory than Jim—who did everything right. An attempt was made to spin the character off into the series "Lance White," but it never materialized. Another recurring character, the budding gumshoe Richie Brockelman (Dennis Dugan), was spun off into the series "Richie Brockelman, Private Eye" (see entry).

Mike Post and Pete Carpenter composed the theme.

608. *Rocky and His Friends*

ABC, 11/19/59 to 9/23/61
NBC, 9/20/64 to 9/2/73

Voice Cast: June Foray *(Rocky and Natasha)*, Bill Scott *(Bullwinkle)*, Paul Frees *(Boris)*.

Facts: Frostbite Falls, Minnesota, population 29, is the setting for an insane battle of good against evil as seen through the animated adventures of Rocket J. ("Rocky") the Flying Squirrel and his dimwitted friend, Bullwinkle the Moose—the do-gooders who battle the evils of Boris Badenov and his assistant, Natasha Fataly.

Frostbite Falls is serviced by the Union Pathetic Railroad, and when the town's only movie theater, the Bijou, opened, the first picture they showed was *A Trolley Named Talullah*. Rocky and Bullwinkle attended Frostbite Falls High School and then Frostbite U. (where Bullwinkle was a "B.M.O.C."—Big Moose on Campus; he was also hoodwinked into playing football—jersey number 0—for Wossamatta U.). Red and purple were the Frostbite U. school colors. Each year Rocky and Bullwinkle vacation on an island called Moosylvania ("The wettest, soggiest, dreariest place on Earth") for one simple reason: after two weeks, any place on Earth looks like heaven. Moosylvania is located between the United States and Canada and has the distinction of being thought over by both countries (the U.S. believes Canada owns it; Canada believes it belongs to the United States).

Rocky, "The All-American Squirrel," wears an aviator's cap and says, "Hoakie smokes," when something goes wrong; his hero is Bullwinkle. Bullwinkle is "a moronic moose" whose claim to fame is an antigravity metal called Upsadaisium (which was founded by his uncle, Dewlop D. Moose on Mount Flatten). Bullwinkle, sometimes called Bullwinkle J. Moose, believes comic books are real life ("If you can't believe what you read in a comic book, what can you believe? It's enough to destroy a young moose's faith") and frequently asks the narrator for help with an episode ("It's difficult to follow the plot and be in it at the same time"). He also believes that he is the greatest actor since Elmo Lincoln (the screen's first Tarzan). His hero is Rocky.

The biggest event in Frostbite Falls is the yearly celebration of the Flotilla Festival (when all the kids go down to frolic at Veronica Lake and let the oldtimers enjoy a day of peace and quiet).

Boris Badenov, "International Bad Buy" and "the world's lowest snake in the grass," is, in some episodes, an international spy (from the country of Pottsylvania) and in others the vice president of Crime Syndicate. He is a member of both the Fetish of the Month Club and Local 12 (the Villains, Thieves and Scoundrels Union). He and Natasha operate from a house called "The Old Bleakley Place." Their superiors are Mr. Big (a midget who casts a large shadow) and Fearless Leader. Boris reads *Crime* magazine, and his hero is Fingers Scarenose, a notorious criminal.

Bullwinkle also appeared in filler segments called "Mr. Know-It-All" where he displayed his knowledge (his "bird's eye view with a brain to match").

Other Segments Include: "Dudley Do-Right of the Mounties" (see entry); "Peabody's Improbable History," with Mr. Peabody (voice of Bill Scott), the intelligent dog, and his boy, Sherman (voice of June Foray), traveling through time via the Way Back Machine to set history straight; and "Fractured Fairy Tales," with narrator Edward Everett Horton relaying slightly warped versions of classic stories.

The series originally aired on ABC as "Rocky and His Friends" and on NBC as "The Bullwinkle Show." William Conrad and Paul Frees did the narrating.

Theme: "Rocky's Theme," by Fred Steiner.

609. *Rocky Jones, Space Ranger*

Syndicated, 1954

The Space Rangers is a twenty-first century organization established to safeguard the planets of a united solar system from alien invaders. Rocky Jones (Richard Crane) is chief of the Space Rangers, and he pilots the rocketship *Orbit Jet* (later, the *Silver Moon*). Winky (Scotty Beckett) and later Biffen ("Biff") Cardoza (James Lydon) are Rocky's co-pilots. Vena Ray (Sally Mansfield) and Bobby (Robert Lyden) are Rocky's assistants. Secretary Drake (Charles Meredith) is the head of the Space Rangers, and Ranger Clark (William Hudson) operates refueling space station O.W.9.

XV-2 is Rocky's radio code (both ships), and the visograph permits the viewing of outer space from inside the ship. Apollo Minor is the supply satellite, and the Rangers have ray guns but rarely use them. SPACE RANGER is printed on the shoulder of ranger uniforms; a patch of the planet Saturn is on the right front side of the uniform. In the opening theme, when the show's title is seen, the *o* in "Rocky" is the planet Saturn and the *o* in "Jones" is the planet Earth.

Dian Fauntelle appeared as Yarra, ruler of the planet Medina; Walter Coy was Zorvac, king of the Moon Fornax; and Patsy Iannone played Volaca, Zorvac's daughter.

"Be with us again next week when we again take you into outer space with Rocky Jones, Space Ranger."

610. *Rocky King, Inside Detective*

DuMont, 1/14/50 to 12/26/54

Frank King (Roscoe Karns), nicknamed "Rocky," is a plainclothes inspector with the Homicide Division of the 24th Precinct of the N.Y.P.D. Rocky, who solves crimes by deductive reasoning, lives with his wife, Mabel (Grace Carney), at 836 Mead Street in Manhattan. Grace has trouble balancing her checkbook, owns 360 acres of oil land in Texas that has no oil (a gift from her great-grandfather), stock in the South Paw Safety Pin Company, and the gift of gab (Mabel is heard off-camera more often than she is seen). Rocky is assisted by Mabel's nephew, Dwight Hart (Todd Karns), a sergeant who helps Rocky solve crimes quite by accident (he has a knack for finding the crucial evidence Rocky needs).

Jack Ward composed the theme.

611. *Rod Brown of the Rocket Rangers*

CBS, 4/18/53 to 5/29/54

"CBS Television presents Rod Brown of the Rocket Rangers. Surging with the power of the atom, gleaming like great silver bullets, the mighty Rocket Rangers' spaceships, stand by for blastoff. [Rockets are seen blasting off.] Up, up, rockets blazing with white hot fury; the manmade meteors ride through the atmosphere, breaking the gravity barrier, pushing up and out, faster and faster and then outer space and high adventure for the Rocket Rangers."

In the twenty-second century, the planets of a United Solar System (Earth, Mercury, Jupiter, Mars and Venus) form the Rocket Rangers, an Earth-based defense organization designed to battle interplanetary evil and safeguard the universe. Stories relate the experiences of Rod Brown (Cliff Robertson), a Rocket Ranger who captains the ship the *Beta* (which blasts off from Orbit 4). Ranger Frank Boyle (Bruce Hall) assists Rod, and Ranger Wilbur ("Wormsey") Wormser (Jack Weston) is the navigator (he plots the *Beta's* course from the base). When something goes wrong, Wilbur exclaims, "Oh, great Jupiter!" Commander Swift (John Boruff), whom the rangers call "The Old Man," is head of the Rocket Rangers and commander of Omega Base, which is the rangers' headquarters.

There are no special codes or "lingo" for space transmissions. A typical sequence would play as follows: "Control tower to *Beta*." "*Beta* here, over." After the message is received by Rod, he simply says, "Check, over and out." When Rod has to call the control tower, he says, "Rocketship *Beta* calling Ranger Headquarters, Earth."

"Be sure to be with Rod Brown next week for another thrilling adventure in the far regions of outer space on 'Rod Brown of the Rocket Rangers'" (the uncredited theme would then play).

612. *Roller Girls*

NBC, 4/24/78 to 5/10/78

Selma ("Books") Cassidy (Joanna Cassidy), jersey number 9; Honey Bee Novak (Marcy Hanson), jersey number 12; Mongo Sue Lampert (Rhonda Bates), jersey number 1; Shana ("Pipeline") Akira (Marilyn Tokuda), jersey number 31; and J.B. Johnson (Candy Ann Brown), jersey number 68—these are the Pitts, a female roller derby team based in Pittsburgh.

Don Mitchell (Terry Kiser) is the team's sleazy owner. He had a dream of owning a roller girls team. Through manipulation, he managed to buy an arena and hire skaters: Selma, a professional; Honey Bee, a naive, former carhop; Mongo Sue, a farm girl turned professional skater (she and Selma were previously opponents; they rarely get along, and Mongo Sue constantly threatens to "take Books apart, page by page"); Shana, whose mother is Eskimo and father is Japanese, the wisecracking one of the group (she wears a T-shirt that reads SAVE THE WHALES); and J.B., the only black team member, who was formerly a waitress.

Don promised each of the girls a condo, but "they're not quite ready yet due to a lack of strategic materials—wood." He does keep his promise, however, and gives them a place to live—the back room of the locker room. He also gives them their uniforms: short shorts and tight, bosom-revealing tops. He calls them "The Dolls of the Roller Wheels." Honey Bee, the blonde bombshell of the group, loves the outfits ("They make me feel sexy"); Books calls herself "a vice squad candidate" in them; and Shana remarks, "We look like magazine centerfolds." Despite the uniforms, the lousy pay (which is always late) and the deplorable living conditions, the girls struggle to do their best and become the state champions.

James Murtaugh plays Howie Divine, the Pitts' rink announcers (he is a former FM radio opera announcer whom Don hoodwinked into working for him).

Shari Saba sings the theme, "Roller Girls."

613. *Room for Romance*

CBS, 7/27/90 to 8/24/90

The fashionable Upper East Side Manhattan apartment house is not named (nor is an exact address given; the awning number reads 223). The building has 97 apartments, 167 residents, 32 dogs "and an unknown number of cats." Caroline Gidot (Rebecca Harrell) appears to be the only regular tenant. She is a pretty "10 10/12" year old girl ("I'll be 11 in two months") who has very rich but never-seen parents. She was born on 9/5/79 at 7:32 A.M. and has a dog named Winnie. Her friend (and the only other series regular) is Ramon Carciofi (Dom Irrera), the building's nosy desk clerk. Through his and Caroline's observations, incidents in the lives of residents are seen.

In the original pilot (which aired as the last episode), Don Novello played Aldo Carciofi, the desk clerk (no relation mentioned to Ramon); Caroline appeared as she did in the series. While both Ramon and Dom wore a jacket with the building's name on it, it was just impossible to read due to camera angles or bright lighting.

Mark Snow composed the theme.

614. *Room for Two*

ABC, 3/24/92 to 4/29/92
ABC, 9/3/92 to 12/17/92

Kurland's Appliance World is a store owned by Lou Kurland (not seen) in Dayton, Ohio. The store's slogan was "If we don't have it, go somewhere else," and a clown named Blinky welcomed customers. Lou's wife, Edie (Linda Lavin), was "a wife, mother, president of the PTA and a good neighbor." Edie, however, was bored. When Lou dies, Edie sells the business and the house and moves to New York City to be near her daughter, Jill Kurland (Patricia Heaton), an up and coming television producer. When Edie attends a broadcast of Jill's show and speaks up against a fashion designer, Francine Luboff (Bonnie Bartlett), the executive producer, is impressed by her brashness and offers her a job on the show. Stories follow the relationship between the mother and daughter.

Edie was born in April and now lives in Apartment 4 above Dario's Italian Restaurant in Manhattan. Jill lives "across town from Edie" in Apartment 3 (address not given). Jill is the producer of "Wakeup, New York," an early morning show on WXOR-TV, Channel 3. Edie hosts the "Reality Check" segment (wherein she gives her honest opinions about life). Both Edie and Jill are allergic to shellfish.

Reid Ellis (Andrew Prine), the former star of the series "Cleavon, Commander of the Galaxy Squad," is the show's host; Diahann Beaudreaux (Paula Kelly) is the co-host. Ken Kazurinsky (Peter Michael Goetz) is Edie's across-the-hall neighbor; he runs a mail order business called The Kazurinsky Catalogue.

The "Room for Two" theme was composed by David Shire.

615. *Roomies*

NBC, 3/19/87 to 5/15/87

Cast: Burt Young (*Nick Chase*), Corey Haim (*Matthew Wiggins*).

Facts: Saginaw University is a small college in the town of Saginaw, New Jersey. In room 203 of the men's dorm live Nicholas ("Nick") Chase and Matthew Wiggins—two unlikely roomies.

Nick is a 20 year marine veteran who is seeking to better his life and acquire the college education he never achieved. He joined the marines because he thought his country needed him. He never married ("We move around too much in the Marine Corps. I never found a woman who wanted to live in a ditch").

Matthew is a whiz kid who entered high school at the age of 11 and now, at 14, is a college freshman. Fish are Matt's life. He studies them ("I believe fish are a sophisticated but legless society"), and Nick was the only person Matthew

could find who would share the room (there are fish tanks everywhere; the sound of the oxygen bubbles helps Nick to sleep at night). Matt got his first fish at F.W. Woolworth when he was a kid.

As a sergeant, Nick starred in the marine training film "Digging a Ditch" (Film number CIN 108). Matt was a D.J. on the college radio station (WSAG, 109 FM) where he was "Buddy Midnight" on a show that ran from midnight to 2:00 A.M. When Matt began to feel that he was not part of college life because of his fish, he joined the wrestling team "to become one of the guys" (he lost his first bout to a girl named Linda [Lana Cockrell]). Matt and Nick's favorite eatery is Pizza, Pizza, Pizza.

Other Roles: Kate Adler (Jane Daly), the abnormal psychology professor; Sheldon Paxton (Joshua Nelson), the dimwitted student; Jason (Michael Horton) and Carl (Sean Gregory Sullivan) are other students.

Relatives: Estelle Getty (*Nick's mother*), Candace Azzara (Nick's sister, *Josephine*), Bob Glavane (Nick's brother, *Charles Chase*), Nicholas Mele (Nick's brother, *Augie Chase*), Josephine Young (Nick's aunt, *Celia*), Bob Giovane (Josephine's husband, *Dominick*), Samantha Kaye (Josephine's daughter, *Gina*), Jay Ingram (*Matt's father*).

Theme: "Looking for Some Answers," vocal by Billy Vera.

The Ropers see *Three's Company*

616. *Roseanne*

ABC, 10/18/88 to the present

Cast: Roseanne Arnold (*Roseanne Conner*), John Goodman (*Dan Conner*), Lecy Goranson (*Becky Conner*), Sara Gilbert (*Darlene Conner*), Michael Fishman (*D.J. Conner*), Laurie Metcalf (*Jackie Harris*).

Facts: They met in Lanford High School. Dan Conner was an athlete (nicknamed "Yor") and a member of the school's football team. Roseanne Harris had dreams of becoming a writer and penning the great American novel. They dated through high school and married after graduation. They set up housekeeping at 714 Delaware Street in Lanford, Illinois. Roseanne became a housewife and the mother of three children (Becky, Darlene and D.J.); Dan founded his own company, 4 Aces Construction (his truck license plate reads 846 759C). The family sedan has the license plate 846 779, and Thursday is trash pickup day.

Roseanne buys her groceries at the Buy 'n' Bag Supermarket and held a number of jobs: assembly line worker at Wellman Plastics, telephone soliciter for Discount House Magazine, order taker at Divine Chicken, bartender at the Lobo Lounge, cleanup lady at Art's Beauty Parlor, and waitress at Rodbell's Luncheonette in the Lanford Mall.

Roseanne mentioned that her first date with Dan was on his motorcycle at the A & W Drive-In. On their second date, at the Blue Swan Café off Highway 72, Dan proposed to her (she had a New York steak; he had a shrimp cocktail). Roseanne and Dan have accounts at the Greyrock Bank; Dan calls her "Rosey." Roseanne gets annoyed by people who leave jelly in the peanut butter jar.

Dan reads the girlie magazine *Girls, Girls, Girls,* and his favorite watering hole is the Lobo Lounge. His most prized possession is his Harley-Davidson motorcycle, which he has had since he was 16 years old. In the episode of 9/17/91, Dan opened a new business called Lanford Custom Cycles, a motorcycle repair and sales shop. Cake is Dan's favorite dessert, and he is famous for his chocolate chip shake. He gets upset when the kids leave toast crumbs in the butter.

Becky, the oldest child (born 3/15/75) attends Lanford High School. She is sweet, very pretty and very feminine. She loves clothes and shopping at the mall and is closer to her mother than she is to Dan. Red is her favorite color; she eats Dannon yogurt, and she receives an allowance of ten dollars a week. When she first began to drive she got a $50 parking ticket for parking in a handicap zone, and she acquired her first job as a cashier at the Buy 'n' Bag Supermarket.

Darlene, the middle child, first attended South Elementary School, then Lanford Junior High and finally Lanford High School. She is a tomboy and nasty. She loves sports, helping her father put up drywall and is closer to her father than she is to Roseanne. Her allowance is five dollars a week, and she eats Fruit Rings and Frank 'n' Berries cereal for breakfast.

Both girls went through changes as the series progressed. Becky became more aggressive and independent and constantly defied parental authority. Darlene went from being a tomboy to a moody 14-year-old girl. She lost interest in sports, found an interest in boys and lived to some extent in her own dream world.

David Jacob, nicknamed D.J., is the youngest child, and he attends South Elementary School (later James Madison Elementary School). He has a collection of doll heads (Barbie, Cher and G.I. Joe) in one box and the body parts in another—both of which he hides under his bed. He also has a habit of getting his head stuck in drawers (how is not said—but Roseanne says, "He's got a gift for it." She "unsticks him" by putting oil on his head). Sal Barone played D.J. in the pilot episode.

Jacqueline ("Jackie") Harris is Roseanne's single sister. She lives in Apartment A (no address given) and first worked with Roseanne at Wellman Plastics. She later became an officer with the Lanford Police Department. She did her basic training in Springfield, but quit the force after she fell down the stairs while tackling a pervert (she sustained a herniated disc and was treated at Saint Joseph's Medical Center). Jackie then tried her hand at acting and joined the Lanford Theater Company (she starred in a production of *Cyrano de Bergerac*). When that failed, she became a perfume bottle squirter at the makeup counter at the mall. Jackie soon became bored by this and enrolled in a trucking school. She became a big rig driver in October 1991. As

kids, she and Roseanne attended the Wild Oaks Summer Camp.

Crystal Anderson (Natalie West) is Roseanne's best friend. She was married twice (to Rusty, then Travis; Travis was a welder, and when they divorced, he cut their trailer in half). In high school, Crystal was nicknamed "Too Easy"; she married Dan's father in the episode of 1/15/91.

Several changes occurred with the episode of 9/15/92. Dan loses the bike shop when he can't pay the mortgage. Roseanne loses her job when Rodbell's closes the luncheonette. Several weeks later (on 10/20/92), Dan and Roseanne become partners with Jackie and her friend Nancy (Sandra Bernhard) when they pool their resources to open a restaurant on Route 41 called the Lanford Lunch Box.

Becky leaves the family and moves to Minneapolis when she marries Mark (Glenn Quinn), a mechanic Dan had hired (when Dan let Mark go, Mark got a job from a friend in Minneapolis. Fearful of losing Mark, Becky eloped with him). Nancy revealed in the episode of 11/10/92 that she was a lesbian, making her the first such regular character on a sitcom (Morgan Fairchild played Nancy's lover, Marla, a cosmetics salesgirl at Rodbell's Department Store).

Relatives: John Randolph (Roseanne's father, *Al Harris*), Estelle Parsons (Roseanne's mother, *Beverly Harris*), Shelley Winters (Roseanne's grandmother, *Mary Harris*), Ann Wedgeworth (Dan's mother, *Audrey Conner*), Ned Beatty (Dan's father, *Ed Conner*).

Theme: "Roseanne," by Dan Foliart and Howard Pearl.

617. *The Rough Riders*

ABC, 10/2/58 to 9/24/59

"This is the story of three men who came to be known as the Rough Riders. Many years later and half a continent away that name was to win undying glory on the slopes of San Juan Hill. But our story is the beginning of the legend. Three men who came to be known in awe and admiration as the Rough Riders."

The three men the announcer speaks of in this opening theme narration are James ("Jim") Flagg (Kent Taylor), Colin Kirby (Jan Merlin) and Buck Sinclair (Peter Whitney)—two Union officers (Jim and Buck) and a Confederate (Colin) who team up after the surrender at Appomattox to journey west to begin new lives.

Jim was a captain, Buck a sergeant, and Colin a lieutenant. Jim is from a military family; Buck is an expert tracker (he can track through any terrain); and Colin is the son of a plantation owner. The men now look out for one another as they travel between the Great Smokies and the High Sierras during the mid-1860s. Their exploits, as they help "good people plagued by bandits," are the focal point of stories.

"Watch for our next story of these three men whose every path crossed adventure—adventures destined to create the adventures of the Rough Riders."

618. The Rousters

NBC, 10/1/83 to 7/21/84

Sladetown is a Los Angeles–based carnival with "Thrills, Chills and Spills. Providing Family Entertainment Since 1978." "Cactus" Jack Slade (Hoyt Axton) owns the carnival; his beautiful daughter, Ellen Slade (Mimi Rogers), handles the books and teaches school (five hours a day) for the carny kids. When trouble becomes apparent, Slade calls on the services of his security chief, Wyatt Earp III (Chad Everett), a descendant of the famous Old West lawman (1848–1929).

Wyatt hates his name (he has to show his I.D. when people don't believe him) and repeatedly says, "For 35 years I've heard all the bad jokes. So you can save yours." He believes the real Wyatt Earp was a drinker and a gambler and not the hero he was made out to be. Wyatt lives in a house trailer with his brother, Evan Earp (Jim Varney), his mother, Amanda ("Ma") Earp (Maxine Stuart), and his 14-year-old son, Michael Earp (Timothy Gibbs), whom Ma calls "Little Wyatt."

Evan claims, "I have a mind that is a natural resource. I see things in my sleep and my dreams come true." He has a dog named Lightning and is fascinated by engines (he thinks he can fix any engine, but in reality can't). He pokes his nose into everybody's business and has harebrained schemes to make money (for example, Earp Alert Burglar Alarms—mouse traps painted blue).

Ma carries a 12-gauge shotgun and is partners with Evan in the bounty hunting business. Ma believes the legend of Wyatt Earp is true and says, "We got the Earp tradition to live up to." Amanda is the "real" Wyatt Earp's sister-in-law; she has the trailer decorated with wanted posters she takes from the post office.

Every Saturday night Wyatt participates in "The Toughest Man Contest" (a boxing match); $500 is awarded to anyone who can beat Wyatt (with a ten dollar registration fee; one dollar admission). The Earps' phone number is 213-555-2318, and L569 317 is their pickup truck license plate number. Mickey is the carnival lion.

Ruta Lee played Jack's sister, Rowena Slade. At the height of ABC's "Love Boat" popularity, NBC decided to schedule "The Rousters" opposite it. "The Rousters" was doomed before it even premiered; even clever (and relentless) promos exclaiming, "The Rousters gonna sink the Love Boat!" couldn't save it.

Ronnie Milsap sings the theme, "Tough Enough."

619. Route 66

CBS, 10/7/60 to 9/18/64

Tod Stiles (Martin Milner) is the son of a wealthy man and was left penniless after his father's death. Buzz Murdock (George Maharis) was an employee of Tod's father who was abandoned as an infant and grew up in an orphanage

in New York's Hell's Kitchen. With undecided futures, Tod and Buzz pool their resources and purchase a 1960 Chevrolet (license plate 20-7876) and begin their travels along the highway of U.S. Route 66 seeking a place to settle down ("We're looking for a place with a nitch," says Buzz, "a place where we can really fit in"). (In 1963-64 episodes, Tod is partners with Linc Case, a Vietnam War veteran, played by Glenn Corbett.)

Tod's birthday was given as March 12, 1936; he married a woman named Mona (Barbara Eden) in the last episode. His unseen parents were named Lee and Martha; Beatrice Straight played his aunt, Kitty Chamberlain (his father's sister), in one episode. Buzz, social security number 100-20-0853, was born in September 1937. Linda Watkins played his mother in one episode; his father, Thomas, was not seen. Buzz's parents' home phone number in Landor, Texas, was (311) Klondike 5-2368.

Nelson Riddle composed the "Route 66" theme. In 1992, NBC produced an unaired pilot for a new version of "Route 66." A young man named Nick Lewis (Brent Fraser) learns that the father he never knew he had—Buzz Murdock—has just died. Nick heads for the Midwest to claim his inheritance: the gleaming, perfectly preservd 1960 red and white Chevrolet that his father once drove. With no particular destination in mind, he heads down the road. He stops to give a ride to a young hitchhiker named Arthur Clark (Andrew Lowery). The two become friends and begin their travels along the highway of Route 66.

Following the above format, but with James Wilder as Nick Lewis and Dan Cortese as Arthur Clark, NBC ran four episodes of a new "Route 66" from 6/8/93 to 7/6/93.

620. The Royal Family

CBS, 9/18/91 to 11/27/91
CBS, 4/8/92 to 5/13/92

Alfonso ("Al") Royal (Redd Foxx) and his wife, Victoria (Della Reese), have been married for 47 years. They live at 973 Glenview Avenue in Chamblee, Georgia (555-6739 is their phone number). After raising their family, Al and Victoria were looking forward to spending their golden years alone—until their newly divorced and homeless daughter, Elizabeth Royal (Mariann Aalda), and her children, Kim (Sylver Gregory), Hillary (Naya Rivera) and Curtis (Larenz Tate), shatter that dream by moving in with them. Al now seeks to regain his longed-for privacy by getting Elizabeth married and out of the house.

Al (who was called Alexander in the pilot) was the first black mailman in Atlanta (in some episodes Al is retired; in others he is working for the post office). All Al ever wanted to do was retire and live in peace with his wife. The last refuge Al now has is his workshop (he built, for example, a birdhouse with no door and a doghouse that collapsed). In his youth, Al was a baseball player for the Kansas City Monarchs. Al only went to school to the tenth grade, and his favorite television shows are "Sanford and Son" and wrestling. Pigs' feet, blackberry cobbler with ice cream and pecan waffles are Al's favorite foods.

On their first date, Al took Victoria to see *Casablanca*. Victoria, who has a dog named Dog, calls Al "Daddy." Al sleeps on the right side of the bed, and his mailman's motto for cold days is "Be it rain, sleet or snow, the people on my route can wait another day for their mail 'cause I'm freezing my stamps off."

Elizabeth is divorced (from the never-seen Dexter). She enrolled in night classes at the University of Georgia to become a doctor and earns money by selling Algon Cosmetics door to door. Sixteen year old Kim and Curtis, who is 15, attend Chamblee High School. Curtis works after school as a salesman at the Shoe Patrol. Four-year-old Hillary, whom Al calls "Puddin'," is enrolled in the Lakes and Flowers Preschool; her favorite sandwich is peanut butter and jelly (with the jelly on top and the peanut butter on the bottom).

In the episode of 11/27/91, Al has a heart attack while bowling in the Postman's Tournament (this reflects the real-life death of Redd Foxx a month earlier). Friends and family appeared to pay tribute to Al—as did Ruth (Jackee Harry), Victoria's younger and gorgeous half-sister, who came home after a 17 year absence to get her life back together and help Victoria raise the family. When the series returned (second date listing), Ruth Royal was now Victoria's man-crazy daughter (it was explained this time that Ruth ran away from home when she was 17 years old and has returned to settle down). Ruth, who is nicknamed "Coco," works part time at the men's cologne counter of Michaelson's Department Store.

David Allen Jones sings the theme, "We Are a Family."

621. *Sable*

ABC, 11/7/87 to 1/2/88

"I am Jon Sable. I play Nicholas Flemming," says Jon Sable (Lewis Van Bergen), a wanted murderer who establishes a new identity as children's book author Nicholas Flemming to enable him to come to terms with the death of his family by helping people in need. (Jon's past is a bit sketchy. It is only revealed that in South Africa Jon killed the man responsible for killing his wife and children. Jon fled Africa and established his new identity in Chicago.)

As Nicholas Flemming, who lives at 2435 Lincoln Park West, he enjoys great success as the author of *The Friends of B.B. Flemm,* a best-selling series of children's books, and as the creator of "Jon Sable, Freelance," a daily comic strip. Eden Kendall (Rene Russo) is the one who helped Jon Sable become Nicholas Flemming ("If it wasn't for me creating Nicholas Flemming, you would be dead," says Eden, who is also his literary agent and romantic interest). Sable disguises his face with makeup (stripes across his face; "He dresses like the Easter Bunny," Eden says), and he chooses his clients very carefully—"I have to. I have a price on my head." He's not a hired killer and takes cases when people are desperately in need of help. "If a case involves a kid, he gets crazy and careless," says Eden. "It's not going to bring

Route 66. George Maharis (l) and Martin Milner.

his family back, but he couldn't stand to see what happened to him happen to someone else."

Joseph ("Joe") Tyson (Ken Page), called "Cheesecake" by Sable, is Jon's blind information man. He is a computer whiz, hopes one day to become a standup comedian and loves cheesecake (strawberry is his favorite). Jon sends Joe a large strawberry cheesecake when he needs information (on the inside flap of the box is a message in braille). Joe lives in Apartment 6 at an unnamed address.

Myke Blackmon (Holly Fulger) is Nicholas's illustrator. "Great legs," Nicholas says of Myke, who is into the Flapper look and dresses like a girl living in the 1920s; Cynthia (Marge Kotlisky) is Nicholas's secretary.

Fern Parsons played Jon's stepmother, Rebecca Sable, in one episode; Michael Shreive composed the "Sable" theme.

622. *The Saint*

Syndicated, 1963 to 1966
NBC, 5/21/67 to 9/2/67
NBC, 2/18/68 to 9/14/68
NBC, 4/11/69 to 9/12/69

Cast: Roger Moore *(Simon Templar).*
Facts: Simon Templar, alias the Saint, "is a roaring adventurer who loves a fight; a dashing daredevil, imperturbable, debonair, preposterously handsome; a pirate or a philanthropist as the occasion demands. He lives for the pursuit of excitement . . . for the one triumphant moment that is his alone."

These words were used by "Saint" creator Leslie Charteris to describe his character when he first sold the rights to television in 1963. Simon, as portrayed on the small screen, "is lean, very tall and well able to look after himself. His voice and manners are deceptively lazy. He appeals to women and women appeal to him. The women he meets are the most glamorous in the world. They have luscious figures, provocative eyes and haunting voices. The stories are romantic adventures, covering a wide range of subjects and backgrounds. Simon is involved in every kind of adventure — from patching up a broken love affair to saving a beautiful women from a murderer to bringing fresh hope to a blind woman."

Simon is independently wealthy and a master among thieves. He is considered criminal by the police, but he assists them in his quest to help people in distress. In addition to cash, he carries a Diner's Club and an American Express card, an international driver's license and a passport wherever he goes. He drives a white Volvo 1800 with the license plate ST-1.

Roger Moore first played Simon Templar (dates above), with Ivor Dean as Claud Eustace Teal, the chief inspector of Scotland Yard. (Wensley Pithey and Norman Pitt played Teal in early, single episodes.)

Theme: "The Saint," by Edwin Astley (adapted from the original theme created by Leslie Charteris for films).

Note: Ian Ogilvy next played Simon Templar in "Return of the Saint" (CBS, 12/21/79 to 8/15/80), an update of the earlier series which continued to depict the global exploits of Simon Templar. Brian Dae composed "The New Saint Theme."

On June 12, 1987, CBS presented a 60 minute pilot called "The Saint," with Andrew Clark as Simon Templar. In the story, Simon helps a ballerina who is receiving mysterious threats. Mark Snow composed an adaptation of the original "Saint" theme.

Simon Templar's exploits again became a series called "The Saint" (syndicated, 10/89 to 1/90) in which Simon Dutton played the role. David Ryall was Inspector Claud Eustace Teal. Tony Britton composed the theme, a variation of the original "Saint" theme.

623. *Salvage 1*

ABC, 1/29/79 to 11/11/79

The *Vulture* is a homemade ten-feet wide by 30-feet high rocketship built by Harold ("Harry") Broderick (Andy Griffith), the owner of the Jettison Scrap and Salvage Company at 98 Ventura Boulevard in Los Angeles. Melanie ("Mel") Slozar (Trish Stewart) and Addison ("Skip") Carmichael (Joel Higgins) are Harry's partners in a unique service that guarantees to salvage anything anywhere or there is no fee.

The thought "of all that moon junk" the astronauts left on the moon started Harry thinking about salvaging it and selling it. He read the book *The Trans-Linear Vector Prin-*

ciple, by Skip Carmichael, which described a way of traveling to the moon using reduced speed and a special fuel. Skip is also an ex-astronaut, and Mel is an explosives and chemistry expert. Harry salvaged enough parts from NASA to build the *Vulture*; Mel developed the special fuel (Monohydrozyne) and Skip piloted the rocket (Mel was his co-pilot). Skip and Mel did the impossible: they landed on the moon (Mel became the first woman on the moon). They salvaged billions of dollars in "NASA junk" and returned to Earth. But they also upset the government, which says it is against federal law for a private citizen to own a rocket; flying it is another, more serious violation. They assign Department of Justice agent Jack Klinger (Richard Jaeckel) to keep tabs on Harry and his illegal flights.

Harry's Rolls Royce license plate is NNT 516, and 546-2144 is his mobile phone number. Skip worked as a used car salesman (company not named) before Harry found him; Mel adopted an orphan girl named Michele Ryan (Heather McAdam) in the last episode. Jacqueline Scott played Harry's ex-wife, Lorene. J. Jay Saunders was Harry's assistant, Mack.

Walter Scharf composed the "Salvage 1" theme.

624. *The Sandy Duncan Show*

CBS, 9/18/71 to 12/11/71
CBS, 9/17/72 to 12/31/72

Sandy Stockton (Sandy Duncan) lives at 130 North Weatherly Boulevard (Apartment 2A of the Royal Weatherly Hotel in Los Angeles). She previously lived in Illinois and has come to California to begin her career as a teacher. She is currently enrolled at UCLA as a student teacher and works part time as an actress for Maggie Prescott (Nita Talbot), the owner of the Prescott Advertising Agency on West Pico Street (telephone number 555-3174). In this version of the series ("Funny Face," first date listing), Sandy starred in two television commercials: "The Yummy Peanut Butter Girl" and spokesperson for "John E. Appleseed Used Cars, in the Heart of the San Fernando Valley." When the series returned as "The Sandy Duncan Show" in 1972, Sandy was still a student teacher at UCLA but was now a part time secretary for Bert Quinn (Tom Bosley), the senior member of the Quinn and Cohen Advertising Agency. The agency is located at 5099 Lincoln Boulevard, and Sandy's phone number was given as 555-3444 (she resides at the same address as in "Funny Face").

Jack Jones sings the theme, "The Kind of Girl She Is."

625. *Sanford and Son*

NBC, 1/14/72 to 9/2/77

Cast: Redd Foxx (*Fred Sanford*), Demond Wilson (*Lamont Sanford*), Dennis Burkley (*Cal Pettie*).

Facts: Sanford and Son Salvage is a junkyard located at

Salvage 1. Andy Griffith (front). Back, left to right: Joel Higgins, Trish Stewart and J. Jay Saunders.

9114 South Central in Los Angeles. Fred G. Sanford is the owner, a 65-year-old widower who refuses to retire; Lamont Sanford is his son, a 34-year-old bachelor who is dissatisfied with the business and seeks to better himself by beginning a life of his own—"You're holding me back here. I'll never get married. I'll wind up an old broken down junk dealer like you."

Fred has been a widower for 23 years when the series begins. Fred came from a very poor family in Georgia (they slept five to a room), and now he feels he is living in luxury, despite Lamont's feelings ("One of these days I'm gonna split this joint because I'm sick of doing all the work. I can't stand being poor like this").

Before retiring from show business to begin the Sanford Junk Empire, Fred was a dancer in vaudeville and was teamed with a girl named Juanita (played in old-age makeup by Ja'net DuBois).

Fred was married to a woman named Elizabeth. He is now ornery, cantankerous, set in his ways and distrustful of people. When Fred doesn't get his way, he feigns a heart attack ("I'm coming, Elizabeth; this is it, the big one"); he's had 15 major heart attacks by the end of the first episode. He also develops a sudden case of "arth-i-rit-is" when there is work to be done. His response to a smart aleck remark by Lamont (or anyone else) is "How would you like one across your lips?" (which he says making a fist). He also has a collection of eyeglasses, kept in a drawer in the living room which he rummages through when he needs to find a pair to read something.

Fred calls himself a junk dealer; Lamont, whom Fred calls "Dummy," considers himself a collector. When Lamont leaves the business in 1977 to work on the Alaska pipeline, Fred sells a share of the Sanford Empire to Cal Pettie, a not too bright friend of Lamont's, for $2000; thus was born the series "Sanford" (NBC, 3/15/80 to 7/10/81). While the house is the same and storylines still focus on two men operating a junk business, Fred's address was given as 4707 South Central in Watts. (Cal, an overweight Southerner, moved in with Fred and called him Mr. Sanford.)

Prior to "Sanford," the series "Sanford Arms" ran on NBC from 9/16/77 to 10/14/77. In it, Phil Wheeler (Theodore Wilson), a retired army man, purchased the Sanford and Son Junkyard (located at 9114 South Central) from Fred and turned it into the Sanford Arms Rooming House. He was assisted by his daughter, Angie Wheeler (Tina Andrews), and his son, Nat Wheeler (John Earl).

Other Regulars: Esther Anderson (LaWanda Page) is Fred's sister-in-law (usually called Aunt Esther). She is deeply religious and is constantly in verbal battles with Fred (whom she calls a heathen). Donna Harris (Lynn Hamilton) is Fred's first romantic interest (in "Sanford and Son"). She is much younger than Fred, but as Fred said—"I'm 65 and people say I look 55, and I look 45. I'd settle for 35, but you [Donna] make me feel 45." Evelyn Lewis (Marguerite Ray) is Fred's romantic interest in "Sanford" episodes. She is a wealthy woman (she lives at 77 Kantwell Drive in Beverly Hills) and didn't mind dating beneath her on the social scale.

Grady Wilson (Whitman Mayo) is Fred's longtime friend and neighbor; Julio Fuentes (Gregory Sierra) is the next door neighbor Fred disliked (he had a pet goat named Chico); Rollo Larson (Nathaniel Taylor) is Lamont's friend (together they managed an all-girl rock group called The Three Degrees); and patrol car officers "Swany" Swanhauser (Noam Pitlik), "Hoppy" Hopkins (Howard Platt) and "Smitty" Smith (Hal Williams) were the L.A.P.D. cops who were there to lend a hand when Fred needed help.

Relatives: Beah Richards (Fred's aunt, *Ethel*), Mary Alice (Fred's sister, *Frances Victor*), Allan Drake (Frances's husband, *Rodney Victor*), Raymond Allen (Esther's husband, *Woody Anderson*), Alma Beltran (Julio's sister, *Maria Fuentes*), Percy Rodrigues (Evelyn's brother, *Winston*), Suzanne Stone (Evelyn's daughter, *Cissy Lewis*).

Themes: "Sanford and Son," "Sanford" and "Sanford Arms," by Quincy Jones.

Spinoff Series: In addition to "Sanford" and "Sanford Arms," an original series called "Grady" aired for five episodes on NBC (12/4/75 to 3/4/76). In it, Fred's neighbor, Grady Wilson (Whitman Mayo) moves to Santa Monica (at 636 Carlisle Street) to live with his married daughter, Ellie Marshall (Carol Cole), her husband, Hal Marshall (Joe Morton), and their children, Laurie (Rosanne Katon) and Haywood (Haywood Nelson). John Addison composed the theme.

Note: "Sanford and Son" is based on the British series "Steptoe and Son" (about a team of "rag and bone men" [junk dealers]). Starring were Wilfrid Brambell as Albert Ladysmith Steptoe, the father, and Harry H. Corbett as his son, Harold Kitchener Steptoe. The series ran on the BBC from 1963 to 1973. While Fred and Lamont had a beat-up old pickup truck, Albert and Harold had two cart horses named Hercules and Delilah. In 1965 NBC produced an American version called "Steptoe and Son," with Lee Tracy as Albert and Aldo Ray as Harold; the pilot never aired. Prior to the pilot that sold "Sanford and Son," Norman Lear produced an unaired version with Barnard Hughes as the father and Paul Sorvino as his son.

626. *Saved by the Bell*

NBC, 8/20/89 to the present

Cast: Tiffani-Amber Thiessen *(Kelly)*, Elizabeth Berkley *(Jesse)*, Lark Voorhies *(Lisa)*, Leanna Creel *(Tori)*, Mark-Paul Gosselaar *(Zack)*, Dustin Diamond *(Screech)*, Mario Lopez *(Slater)*, Dennis Haskins *(Richard Belding)*.

Facts: Life at Bayside High School in fictional Palisades, California, as seen through the eyes of a group of students who are also best friends.

Kelly Kapowski, "the prettiest girl in the school," loves wind surfing and was voted Bayside Homecoming Queen. She is the head cheerleader (for the Bayside Tigers), captain of both the girls' softball and swim teams. Kelly first worked in the student bookstore, then as a waitress at the Max, the afterschool hamburger hangout. Kelly knows she is very beautiful but fears someone will discover she is not perfect (she wears a retainer at night). Her phone number is 555-4314; 141 is her locker number; and she scored 1100 on her SAT test. She lives at 3175 Fairfax Drive.

Jessica ("Jesse") Myrtle Spano is very pretty, very smart and sensitive to the fact that she is the tallest one of the group. Jesse is a talented dancer (she attended dance camp as a kid), a member of the Honors Society and is the student body president. She detests being called "chick," "babe" or any other slang term for a girl. She is for women's equality and hopes to attend Stanford University (she scored 1205 on her SAT exam and was accepted by Columbia University). Jesse won the French Award two years in a row, and her home phone number is 555-0635.

Lisa Marie Turtle is a stunning black girl who was the first one of the group to get her own credit card (and misuse it). She says, "I am beautiful, charming and always in fashion." Lisa loves shopping ("Lisa is my name, shopping is my game. If it's sold, I can find it"). She scored 1140 on the SAT test; her locker number is first 118, then 149. Lisa has the ability to guess correctly the contents of a gift package before she opens it. Her mother has a Mercedes with the license plate 2JE 025.

Tori Scott is a tough, biker-like girl with the beauty of Kelly and the liberalism of Jesse. Tori became a regular (9/19/92) when Kelly and Jesse were quietly dropped without explanation. Elizabeth Berkley's guest appearance on "Raven" on 10/3/92 ("The Death of Sheila"), would indicate that she, at least, left to pursue more adult roles (she played a high priced call girl and had what is by broadcast TV standards a nude scene—topless but seen from the back). Although it is difficult to tell the sisters apart, Leanna is the middle Creel triplet (her sisters are Joy and Monica, and they starred together in the Disney films *Parent Trap III* and *Parent Trap: Hawaiian Honeymoon*).

Zachary ("Zack") Morris is the preppy student and a natural-born con artist whose schemes most often backfire and land him in detention. Zack scored 1502 on his SAT exam (he hopes to attend Yale), and he has locker number 269. He and Kelly were "an item" in many episodes.

Samuel ("Screech") Powers lives at 88 Edgemont Road. He was fifth runner-up in an ALF lookalike contest, and he has a homemade robot named Kevin. He also has a dog (Hound Dog), a lizard (Oscar), a spider (Ted), two white rats (Spin and Marty), a roach (Herbert) and a mouse (Arnold). Screech wears a size 11 shoe, is a member of both the photography and the chess clubs and named his first zit Murray (he also invented Zit-Off, a blemish cream that removes pimples—but later turns the area on which the cream was used maroon). Screech has a crush on Lisa (a situation that makes her cringe). His only other girlfriend was Violet Bickerstaff (Tori Spelling), a very pretty "nerd girl" he called "My Heart." Violet has rich parents (as does Zack) and is very shy, and her goal in life is to blend in (she hides her beauty behind oversized eyeglasses and loose fitting clothes). She has a beautiful singing voice and is a member of the Glee Club. Screech scored 1200 on his SAT test and is also in charge of new membership in the Insect Club.

Albert Clifford ("A.C.") Slater, the school "hunk," is an army brat and was Zack's rival for Kelly before he and Jesse started dating (she calls him "Bubba"; he calls her "Mama"). Slater, as he is called, scored 1050 on the SAT test and won a wrestling scholarship to Iowa State College. He is captain of the wrestling and football teams and has a pet chameleon named Artie. He was the first one of the group to get his own car (license plate END 838).

Richard Belding is the school's principal. He served with the 55th National Guard in Indianapolis and won the 1963 Chubby Checker Twist Off. He calls Zack his "Zack Ache" and was himself a student at Bayside (he was a D.J. on the school's radio station and called himself "The Big Bopper").

The girls shop at the Palisades Mall. Kelly (the anchor) and Jesse and Lisa are also members of the swim team. When Zack hit on an idea to make money, he took pictures of the girls' swim team and put out "The Girls of Bayside High Swimsuit Calendar" (Kelly was "Miss November," Jesse was "Miss July" and Lisa became "Miss October." The photos led to a feature in *Teen Fashion* magazine in which Kelly was "The All-American Girl," Jesse, "The Studious, but Fashionable Girl," and Lisa, "The It's Happening Now Girl." The calendar sold for five dollars. With only 11 girls on the swim team, Zack had to improvise a Miss December; he spliced Belding's head onto Jesse's body—not a pretty sight!).

On Tiger Radio, Bayside's radio station (KKTY, 98.6 FM), Kelly had a show called "Kelly Desire" (romantic music), Jesse was the newscaster, Lisa hosted "The Galloping Gossip," Zack was the D.J. "Wolfman Zack," Screech hosted "Screech's Mystery Theater" and Slater was the sportscaster.

In another attempt to make money, Zack started "The Teen Line" (a phone number was not given for the advice line). Zack was "Nitro Man," Lisa pretended to be "Princess" and Screech was "Ant Man" (Kelly, Jesse and Slater were not involved).

In the "Miss Bayside Beauty Pageant" talent segment, Kelly sang (rather off-key) "Blue Moon," Jesse recited a poem about a butterfly, Lisa played the violin, and Screech, entered by Zack, did a magic act. Screech won the title "Miss Bayside" (as Lisa put it, "I can't believe it. I lost to a teenage mutant ninja geek").

Zack first formed Kelly, Lisa and Jesse into a sexy singing group called Hot Sundae (they sang "I'm Excited"). Zack next formed the band The Zack Attack, with himself on guitar, Kelly and Lisa (backup vocalists), Jesse (lead singer), Slater (drums) and Screech (keyboard). Two years later he reformed the group with Kelly (lead singer), Lisa (guitar), Screech (keyboard) and Slater (drums). Jesse was not a part of the group (no reason given). In 1992 Zack, Tori, Lisa, Screech and Slater were members of the Five Aces, a singing group Zack formed in his senior year. This same group attempted to make a million dollars by selling "Screech's Secret Sauce" (a spaghetti sauce recipe from his grandmother for three dollars a jar. Their slogan: "The sauce you gotta have. But the secret, she's-a-mine").

Episodes broadcast from 9/14/91 to 10/26/91 were set away from school and focused on the group's activities at the Malibu Sands Beach Club. Lisa is a member; Zack worked as the social director; Kelly and Slater were lifeguards; Jesse was the receptionist; and Screech was a waiter. Leon Corosi (Ernie Sabella) was the club owner, and his daughter, Stacey Corosi (Leah Remini), assisted him as the manager of summer help. In the annual "Fourth of July Miss Liberty Pageant," Kelly, Lisa, Jesse and Stacey entered; Kelly won, Stacey was runner-up. Leon calls Stacey "Honey Bunny"; Stacey calls her father "Papa Bear."

The series began as the NBC pilot "Good Morning, Miss Bliss" (7/11/87) in which Hayley Mills played Carrie Bliss, a sixth grade schoolteacher in Indianapolis (school name not given). Oliver Clark was the principal, Gerald Belding, and Wendy (Samantha Mills), Bobby (Jaleel White), Bradley (Gabriel Damon) and George (Matt Shakman) were the students.

In 1988 the Disney Channel aired "Good Morning, Miss Bliss," a series that eventually became "Saved by the Bell" on NBC. Hayley Mills was Carrie Bliss, an eighth grade teacher at J.F.K. Junior High School in Indiana. The students were Lisa Turtle (Lark Voorhies), Zack Morris (Mark-Paul Gosselaar), Screech Powers (Dustin Diamond), Nicole ("Nikki") Coleman (Heather Hopper) and Mickey (Max Battimo). Dennis Haskins was the principal, Richard Belding, and Tina Paladrino (Joan Ryan) was an English teacher. The hangout was a hamburger place called the Cosmos; the kids were in homeroom 103; Carrie, who was dropped for the NBC series, had been teaching history for 11 years. Robert Pine appeared as Zack's father, Peter Morris, in this version. The episodes have been retitled "Saved by the Bell" for syndication and begin with Zack appearing to tell viewers that this episode "is from our junior high days."

Relatives: Melody Rogers (Zack's mother, *Melody Morris*), John Sanderford (Zack's father, *Derek Morris*), Laura Mooney (Kelly's sister, *Nickki Kapowski*), John Mansfield (Kelly's father, *Frank Kapowski*), George McDaniel (Jesse's father, *David Spano*), Barbara Brighton (Jesse's stepmother, *Leslie Spano*), Josh Hoffman (Jesse's stepbrother, *Eric Tanner*), Ruth Buzzi (Screech's mother, *Roberta Powers*), Gerald Castillo (A.C.'s father, *Major Martin Slater*), Rana Haugen (A.C.'s sister, *J.B. Slater*), Jodi Peterson (Richard's niece, *Penny Belding*), Edward Blatchford (Richard's brother, *Rod Belding*), Susan Beaubian (Lisa's mother, *Dr. Judy Turtle*), Henry Brown (Lisa's father, *Dr. Turtle*).

Theme: "Saved by the Bell," vocal by Michael Damian.

Note: On 11/27/92, NBC presented *Saved by the Bell Hawaiian Style*, a two hour television movie featuring Kelly, Jesse, Lisa, Zack, Slater and Screech. The kids are invited to Hawaii by Kelly's grandfather, Harry Bannister (Dean Jones), who owns a hotel called the Hawaiian Hideaway. Their efforts to save the hotel from a ruthless land developer are the focal point of the movie.

After leaving the series, Tiffani-Amber Thiessen made a pilot film called "Just One of the Girls" (produced for CBS, but thus far unaired). Dr. Dorothy Loomis (Caroline McWilliams) is the headmistress of a private girls' school called Crawford Academy. The school has fallen on hard times, and one of the ways Dorothy sees to save the school is to enroll a boy—Robin McGuire (Michael Landes). She faces objections but is determined to stand by her decision. Tiffani-Amber Thiessen plays Allison Morgan, the most beautiful girl in the school; Leah Remini is student Didi DiConcini, a tough, streetwise Italian-American girl whose father is in the witness protection program; and T.C. Warner is Patti Hale, an insecure student who desperately wants to be liked. Diane Delano is Margaret Dezell, the uptight, volatile coach who refers to her girls as "little hoodlums"; she is desperate for Robin to break a rule so she can expel him.

627. *Scarecrow and Mrs. King*
CBS, 10/3/83 to 9/10/87

Lee Stetson (Bruce Boxleitner) is a U.S. government secret agent (for the Agency) who operates under the code name "Scarecrow." Amanda King (Kate Jackson) is a beautiful, divorced housewife and the mother of two sons, Philip (Paul Stout) and Jamie (Greg Morton). They are a team and work under William ("Billy") Melrose (Mel Stewart), the head of the Agency. (Lee was on assignment and being pursued by enemy agents when he ran into Amanda. He gave her a package to mail and later tracked her down. With her help, Lee plugged a security leak at the Agency. Although Amanda is an amateur, she is also an unknown, something Billy thinks the Agency needs, and he teams her with Lee.)

Amanda lives at 4247 Maplewood Drive in Arlington, Virginia (the Agency is located in Washington, D.C.). Amanda's telephone number is 555-3100; her children attend Calvin Elementary School; at the Agency, her security level is Fourth Level, 6SA. Lee lives at 46 Hamblin Boulevard, and his car license plate reads 3N6 105. He married Amanda in the episode of 2/13/87. The Agency, which was founded by Captain Harry V. Thornton (Howard Duff) in 1954, operates under the cover of International Federal Film).

Beverly Garland is Amanda's mother, Dotty West (she helps Amanda care for the kids); Martha Smith is Agency agent Francine Desmond; and Arlen Dean Snyder appeared as Lee's uncle, Colonel Robert Clayton. In flashback sequences, Bruce Boxleitner plays Lee's father, Major Stetson, and Wendie Malick is Lee's mother, Jennie Stetson.

Arthur B. Rubinstein composed the "Scarecrow and Mrs. King" theme.

628. *Scorch*
CBS, 2/28/92 to 3/13/92

A fire breathing dragon named Scorch goes to bed on the night of September 19, 1892—and wakes up 100 years later on September 19, 1992. It is a stormy night, and Scorch decides to stretch his wings and go flying. Scorch is over

New Haven, Connecticut, when he is struck by lightning and falls into the backyard of Brian Stevens (Jonathan Walker) and his 13-year-old daughter, Jessica (Rhea Silver-Smith).

Scorch is all alone in the world. Jessica is very lonely (her parents are divorced) and is always on the move as Brian seeks work. Brian and Jessica take pity on Scorch and decide to keep him.

The following day, Brian has no choice but to take Scorch (who is hidden in a tote bag) to an interview for a television weatherman. At the station, Brian is interviewed by the manager, Jack Fletcher (Todd Susman), but fails to get the job—until the talkative Scorch makes noises and Jack assumes Brian is a ventriloquist and Scorch is his dummy. Brian gets the job and Scorch agrees to help—as long as he can stay with him and Jessica.

Scorch (voice of Ronn Lucas) is 1,300 years old. He is four feet high and has a blue flame in his throat ("My pilot light"). Brian is the weatherman on "New Haven at Noon," which is broadcast over WWEN-TV. Allison King and Howard Gurman (Brenda Strong and John O'Hurley) are the co-anchors on the show.

Ray Colcord and Phyllis Katz composed the theme, "All the Time in the World."

629. *Sea Hunt*

Syndicated, 1957 to 1961

"Three-fifths of the world is covered by the sea, and most of us know little about it," says Michael ("Mike") Nelson (Lloyd Bridges), a navy frogman during World War II who now works as a freelance underwater troubleshooter (he accepts assignments from civilians, law enforcement agencies and the government). Mike is an expert at underwater demolition and also teaches sea diving. He has a Porta Sub (a hand-held scooter) for swift underwater movement, and a boat called the *Argonaut*. Ricou Browning stunt doubles for Lloyd; Zales Perry stunt doubles for female guest stars. Ray Llewellyn composed "The Sea Hunt Theme."

The series was updated for syndication (9/86 to 9/87), with Ron Ely as Mike Nelson and Kimber Sissons as his daughter, Jennifer Nelson, a beautiful marine biologist who assists him. Mike is an ex-navy frogman (Korean War), and he has a boat called the *Sea Hunt*. Melissa Sue Anderson was originally cast in the role of Jennifer. Braun Farnon and Fred Zurba composed "The New Sea Hunt Theme."

In 1960 "Sea Hunt" producer Ivan Tors attempted a similar series called "The Aquanauts" (CBS, 9/14/60 to 2/22/61) which dealt with the underwater adventures of Drake Andrews (Keith Larsen), Larry Lahr (Jeremy Slate) and Mike Madison (Ron Ely), professional salvage divers based in Honolulu. Drake, the head of the team, was an ex-navy frogman and had a boat called the *Atlantis*. David Buttolph composed "The Aquanauts Theme." The series was revamped as "Malibu Run" (CBS, 3/1/61 to 9/27/61). The locale was moved to Malibu Beach, California, and the

show followed the adventures of Larry Lahr (Jeremy Slate) and Mike Madison (Ron Ely), diving instructors and part time private investigators.

Also in 1960, the syndicated series "Assignment: Underwater" appeared. In it, Bill Greer (Bill Williams) was an ex-marine turned professional underwater diver. He works with his young daughter, Patty Greer (Diane Mountford) and operates a charter boat called the *Lively Lady* (WA7257 are its radio call letters). See also "Primus."

630. *Search*

NBC, 9/13/72 to 8/29/73

Hugh Lockwood (Hugh O'Brian), code name Probe One; Nicholas ("Nick") Bianco (Tony Franciosa), code name Omega Probe; and Christopher R. Grover (Doug McClure), code name Stand-by Probe, are three highly skilled investigators working for Probe, a supercomputerized detective agency that operates out of World Securities Corporation in Washington, D.C.

B.C. Cameron (Burgess Meredith) is the director of Probe Control, Unit 1. His Probe Control agents are: Gloria Harding (Angel Tompkins), Kuroda (Byron Chung), Miss Keach (Ginny Golden), Amy (Cheryl Ladd; worked under the name Cheryl Stoppelmoor), Griffin (Albert Popwell) and Harris (Tom Hallick). They are based in a secret room and monitor the on-assignment agents via elaborate, expensive and sophisticated equipment.

Lockwood, Grover and Bianco all have a superminiaturized transmitter-receiver surgically implanted in their ears (called an Ear Check); a sensing device is implanted in their bodies, and a body detector is implanted under their skin. It is through these multimillion dollar devices that Cameron can monitor his agents. Each agent also has an ultraminiaturized and ultrasensitive scanner (an amazing television camera that is about the size of a dime and can transmit a signal from any part of the world; its signal is picked up by "Tele Communications Trans Atlantic Net via Tracking Station Niner Grid Six" and then transmitted to Probe Control). The scanner also has a Spy Scope to X-ray items via Probe Control.

For nonverbal communications, field agents use their Dental Contact Switch (an implant in the upper jaw that is activated by pressing the lower teeth against the upper teeth; "beeps" are sent to Probe Control center; one beep means affirmative, two means negative).

The Medical Telepathy Body Implant is monitored 24 hours a day; it detects heartbeat, pulse, blood pressure, body temperature, respiration, brain waves and an EKG. A human cold is extremely dangerous as it causes a loss of audio and visual communications with Probe Control. All agents have a bottle of biohystodyne that they must take when they feel a cold coming on. Although Probe Control's giant television monitor is capable of amazing reception, it suffers visually if the agents are in poor reception areas (such as caves); picture breakup occurs if the scanner gets wet. A bright green signal from field agents means all systems are okay.

The Probe division specializes in the recovery of things that are missing (diamonds, people or money — "If you lose it, we find it"). Cameron calls it "Computerized Program Retrieval Operations." A Priority 3 Pass is needed to enter the computer rooms of Probe. When an agent gives Cameron a Code 10, it is a signal to Cameron that this agent must speak to him in extreme secrecy (Probe Control agents believe this code means "a wipe out" — the case is not solvable). Dogs pose a problem, as they can sense (hear) Probe agents' electronic transmissions; Probe Control must lower power output to keep dogs from barking and possibly drawing attention to their field agents. Field agents call B.C. "Cam."

The pilot, originally called "Probe" (now "Search"), aired on NBC on 2/21/72.

Theme: "Search," by Dominic Frontiere.

631. *Seinfeld*

NBC, 5/31/90 to the present

Cast: Jerry Seinfeld *(Himself)*, Julia Louis-Dreyfus *(Elaine Benes)*, Jason Alexander *(George Castanza)*, Michael Richards *(Kramer)*.

Facts: Jerry Seinfeld is a standup comedian who is plagued by life's everyday problems — and whose life unfolds each week in the format of a situation comedy. Jerry lives in Apartment 5A at 129 West 81st Street in Manhattan (although the building awning reads number 757; the building is across the street from Almo's Bar and Grill); 555-8383 is Jerry's phone number. While Jerry appears on various television shows, "The Tonight Show" is most often mentioned.

Elaine Marie Benes is Jerry's ex-girlfriend (although they are still close friends; Jerry claims the relationship broke up because there was no physical chemistry between them). Elaine works as a manuscript reader for Pendant Publishing. At the office Elaine has the nickname "Nip." (She distributed a Christmas card photo of herself without realizing that her blouse was open, exposing her nipple. Her friend Kramer took the photo, and Elaine says simply, "I missed buttoning a button.")

Kramer (no other name given) lives across the hall from Jerry in Apartment 5B (he previously lived at 18th Street on 3rd Avenue). He eats Kellogg's Double Dip Crunch cereal for breakfast and earns a living as a self-styled entrepreneur. He is a bit eccentric and seems to live in a world of his own. He once did an underwear ad for Calvin Klein and had a bit part on the television series "Murphy Brown." (After watching the film *30 Seconds Over Tokyo*, Kramer got the acting bug. He moved to Hollywood and took a shot at stardom. His only acting role was as Steve Snell, one of Murphy's wacky secretaries.) Kramer also appeared on one other series that is not a spinoff from "Seinfeld" — "Mad About You" (see entry for information).

George Castanza is Jerry's friend, a real estate broker for Rickbar Properties. When George was fired, Elaine got him a job as a proofreader for Pendant Publishing. In return, George bought Elaine a gift — a cashmere sweater marked down to $85 from $600 (because of a small red dot that marred it). George is attracted to "cleaning women and chamber maids"; he was fired shortly after for having sex on his desk with the office's cleaning woman. George later became Jerry's self-proclaimed agent to pursue a deal for Jerry when NBC expressed interest in giving Jerry his own show. George pretended to be a writer and convinced NBC to star Jerry in a show about nothing (events in his daily life). NBC offered $13,000 for a pilot episode, but George's greed got the best of him and NBC lowered the offer to $8,000. The deal also angered Joey DeVola (Peter Crombie), a psychotic who now stalks Jerry (he blames Jerry for ruining his deal with NBC). Jerry and George attended J.F.K. High School; their favorite eatery is a diner seen only as the Restaurant; the Improv is their favorite watering hole. The original pilot episode, titled "The Seinfeld Chronicles," aired on NBC on 7/5/89 (the same format and cast).

Relatives: Phil Bruns and Barney Martin (Jerry's father, *Morty Seinfeld*), Liz Sheridan (Jerry's mother, *Helen Seinfeld*), Len Lesser (Jerry's uncle, *Leo Seinfeld*), Magda Harout (Jerry's aunt, *Stella*), Ellen Gerstein (Jerry's cousin, *Carol*), Ron Steelman (Jerry's uncle, *Artie Levine*), Estelle Harris *(George's mother)*, Lawrence Tierney *(Elaine's father)*.

Theme: "Seinfeld's Theme," by Jonathan Wolff.

Sergeant Bilko see *The Phil Silvers Show*

632. *Sergeant Preston of the Yukon*

Syndicated, 1955

Just as William Preston (Richard Simmons) completes his college education in the United States, he receives word from Canada that his father has been killed in the Yukon by an evil criminal named Spike Wilson. The time is 1898, and to gain the legal authority to capture his father's killer, Preston joins the Royal Canadian Mounted Police. Following rigorous training, he is made a constable and assigned to capture Spike Wilson. After months of hardship and privation, traveling through a wind-swept wilderness, Preston comes to the end of his trail — the camp of Spike Wilson. A fight ensues, but Preston manages to apprehend his enemy; Spike is tried and sentenced to life imprisonment.

Shortly after, while on duty, Constable Preston intervenes in a lynx attack and rescues a husky puppy that has been raised by a female wolf. He names the dog Yukon King and teaches it to lead a sled team, respect good men and hate evil ones.

Months later, when Spike escapes from prison, Preston is again assigned to capture him. When he does, Preston is promoted to sergeant; Spike is sentenced to death. Stories, set in the early 1900s, relate Sergeant Preston's efforts to maintain law and order in the early Gold Rush days of the Yukon.

In addition to his dog, Yukon King, Preston also has a horse named Rex. In early episodes, the Mountie headquarters is in the town of Dawson; later it is at Lake La Barge.

Fred Foy did the announcing, and the Donna Diana Overture by Von Reznicek was used as the show's theme song.

633. *77 Sunset Strip*

ABC, 10/10/58 to 9/9/64

Cast: Efrem Zimbalist, Jr. *(Stuart Bailey)*, Roger Smith *(Jeff Spencer)*, Edward (Edd) Byrnes *(Kookie)*, Richard Long *(Rex Randolph)*, Jacqueline Beer *(Suzanne Fabray)*, Louis Quinn *(Roscoe)*, Robert Logan *(J.R. Hale)*, Byron Keith *(Lieutenant Roy Gilmore)*, Joan Staley *(Hannah)*.

Facts: Located at 77 Sunset Strip in Hollywood, California, are the offices of Stuart ("Stu") Bailey and Jeffrey ("Jeff") Spencer, suave and sophisticated private investigators who encounter mystery, intrigue, beautiful (sometimes treacherous) women and murder as they strive to solve crimes. Gerald Lloyd Kookson III, better known as Kookie, the parking lot attendant at Dino's Lodge, became their partner in later episodes, as did Rex Randolph (occupying office 104) when the series "Bourbon Street Beat" (see entry) folded.

It all began, Jeff says, when he arrived in Los Angeles and opened an office in Beverly Hills. While driving one Sunday afternoon, he got a flat tire. A kid in a hot rod named Kookie stopped and changed the tire for him. In gratitude, Jeff gave Kookie his business card and said, "If I can ever repay the favor, let me know." "Gee, a private investigator," remarks Kookie. "I'd like to go that route one day myself."

Meanwhile, it is learned that a detective named Stu Bailey had opened an office on the other side of town. While Jeff Spencer Investigations was a success, Bailey, Private Investigator, was on the skids.

When the Pacific Orient Insurance Company is unable to hire Jeff (he's too busy), they contact Stu to find the head of an auto theft ring. Shortly after, Pete (Brad Weston), a friend of Kookie's, tells him that he stumbled upon a car theft ring and that his sister Jo Ann (Carolyn Komant) has been kidnapped to keep him quiet. Kookie approaches Jeff to collect on the favor. Jeff and Kookie team, and in the process of investigating they meet Stu. The trio rescues the girl and breaks up the ring. Seeing how well Jeff and Stu work together causes Kookie to suggest that they work as a team. He tells them that offices are available next to Dino's at 77 Sunset Strip; Stu and Jeff open "Bailey and Spencer, Private Investigators." Both Stu and Kookie relate similar

stories as to how the Sunset Strip team was formed. In Stu's version, Jeff was on the skids and he was the success. It was Stu who got the flat tire, not Jeff. After Kookie helped Stu fix the flat, Stu gave him a business card and said, "If you ever need help, let me know." Meanwhile, Pacific Orient has hired Jeff to bust a car theft ring. Kookie calls in the favor from Stu to help rescue his friend's sister. The three meet and become friends.

Kookie tells it slightly differently: "If it hadn't been for me, they wouldn't have made the scene at all. It all started when my wheels went out on the blink. I was makin' with the tools when Jeff just happened to be driving by and stopped to help." Kookie said he would repay the favor. When his buddy gets mixed up in a car theft ring, Kookie figures to help Jeff by letting him in on the investigation ("I figured Jeff needed the publicity"). In the meantime, Stu has begun an independent investigation for Pacific Orient. The three meet, Kookie saves the day and tells them they make a great team, "and I've got just the place for you to get started—77 Sunset Strip." (Both Stu and Jeff, according to Kookie, were down on their luck until he came along.)

Stuart Bailey, who was in the OSS (Office of Strategic Services) for six years, has office number 101 at 77 Sunset Strip. He lives in Apartment 301 at the Sunset DeVilla, and his office phone number is Olympia 1-3792. His convertible license plate number is PAZ 184 (then AVE 424, JPN 300, RTU 020, and NPO 614). Stu's youngest client was Angel Conway (Evelyn Rudie), a very pretty nine-year-old girl who staged a jewel robbery to get publicity for her budding movie career.

Jeff Spencer has office number 102 and lives in Apartment 517 of an unidentified building. His license plate reads PYB 767 (later GBC 101). Girls often say, "You know, you're too cute to be a snoop." Jeff's office phone number is Olympia 6-1116. He reads *Playboy* magazine at home and at the office. Fifty dollars is the top price Jeff pays to a snitch for information.

Kookie, who lives at 18026 Valley Hart Drive, is the parking lot attendant at Dino's Lodge, the supperclub next to 77 Sunset Strip (a building number is not visible). His mother, Helen Margaret Kookson (not seen), is a public stenographer; his father (not named) is deceased. Kookie drives a hot rod with the license plate JOY 038 (later K-3400), and his favorite eateries are the Chez Paulette coffeehouse and the Cool Dragon. His favorite music group is the Mary Kaye Trio, and he uses expressions like "Squaresville, man," "Like, man, let's get out of here," "Hey, Dad" (his reference to both Stu and Jeff) and "I don't dig it." Trouble is "Troublesville"; pretty girls are "Dreamboats"; and he had a way of combing his hair that drove teenage girls crazy (the song "Kookie, Kookie, Lend Me Your Comb" became a hit). In fourth season episodes, Kookie quit the parking lot business to become partners with Jeff and Stu. Chic Hammons (Sue Randall), a beautiful, intellectual college girl (studying art), became, as Kookie said, "the only girl to appeal to my intellectual side" (he is usually seen with gorgeous girls who might today be called bimbos). J.R. Hale replaced him as the new parking lot attendant at Dino's.

Suzanne Fabray, a gorgeous French girl, operates the Sunset Answering Service from office 103 at 77 Sunset Strip. She is also a public stenographer (as seen on the lower left side of the door) and lives in Apartment 217 at 152½ North Maple Street (later 236 North Maple, Apartment B); her phone number is 354-4567. Olympia 4-0992 (later Olympia 5-1656) is the number one calls to reach Bailey and Spencer at 77 Sunset Strip via Suzanne. Kookie gives Suzanne two doughnuts and a cup of coffee "to refuel her energy." When Suzanne worked with Jeff on a case, Jeff proposed to her and said she was the only girl he ever proposed to (in the episode "Designing Eye," in which Suzanne went undercover as a swimsuit model at Rainbow Models to discover how designs were being stolen from Jeff's client, Surf 'n' Sun Styles). Suzanne refused Jeff's proposal; she mentioned having a brother named Marcel.

Roscoe (no last name given) was born in the Bronx and apparently makes a living as a stool pigeon, gambler and sometimes snoop for Stu and Jeff. He calls Suzanne "Frenchy" and bets often on the horses at Hollywood Park. He owned a greyhound racing dog named Genevieve (which he purchased for $500 in a claiming race), and his favorite drink is bourbon and ginger. To Roscoe, girls are "fillies."

Lieutenant Roy Gilmore, called "Gil" by Stu and Jeff, is with the Homicide Bureau of the L.A.P.D. He sometimes regrets the job and comments, "I should have taken my father's advice and studied air conditioning instead of Nick Carter books."

Stu and Jeff sometimes work for Pacific Casualty Insurance Company in San Francisco and Pacific Orient Insurance in Los Angeles. Dino's Lodge closes at 2:00 A.M. The Frankie Ortega Trio provides the music at Dino's Lodge (in the episode "Not an Enemy in the World," the trio plays the show's theme as part of the dance music). Kookie keeps a spare dinner jacket in the hatcheck room at Dino's for emergencies; in the back of the lodge is Dino's Poodle Palace (where the pampered poodles of patrons stay). In the episode "Six Superior Skirts," Kookie sings "Kookie's Love Song."

In last season episodes, the format changed to focus on Stu Bailey as a private detective on his own. Stu now has an office in downtown Los Angeles in the Bradford building. He has a secretary named Hannah (Joan Staley), and stories are told in a flashback format (as Stu talks to Hannah, flashbacks tell the story; when the flashback ends, Stu and Hannah return to sum up the case).

Themes: "77 Sunset Strip" (1958–63), by Mack David and Jerry Livingston; "The New 77 Sunset Strip Theme" (1963-64), by Bob Thompson.

Note: Two pilots were also produced: *Anything for Money* (ABC, 4/16/57, as a segment of "Conflict"), in which Stuart Bailey (Efrem Zimbalist, Jr.) is hired as a secret bodyguard to a yachtsman on a pleasure cruise to Havana.

Girl on the Run (ABC, 10/10/58). Stuart Bailey attempts to locate Kathy Allen (Erin O'Brien), a cabaret singer who witnessed the murder of a state witness, before the killer's hitman does. Edward Byrnes appeared as Kenneth Smiley, a killer; he became Kookie with the second episode of the series.

634. *Shades of L.A.*
Syndicated, 10/10/90 to 6/26/91

During a stakeout, Los Angeles homicide detective Michael Burton (John Di Aquino) is shot. "Suddenly I'm in kind of a strange limbo surrounded by ghosts. Some people call them Shades, as they are not quite alive and not quite dead but with unfinished business back in their lives." When the Shades discover that Michael is a detective, they feel he can help them. Suddenly, Michael wakes up in a hospital room (109). There, he learns that he had a mystical near death experience that has given him contact with the world beyond. Now the Shades appear to Michael seeking his help. Stories relate Burton's efforts to help the Shades complete their earthly missions and move on to their destinies. (The first Shade Michael helped was Chuck Yellin [Ben Murphy], a test pilot who was killed by his boss to cover up a flaw he discovered in a new plane.)

Michael is with the Los Angeles Metro Police Department, Westside Division. His badge number is 2147 (seen in opening theme) but is mentioned as 508. His car code is 2-Baker-3 and his license plate reads BLASTOFF. Michael attended Radford High School (class of '75), where he was called "Bare Butt Burton" (for mooning teachers). He now carries a small bullet fragment in his brain from the shooting—which Michael believes provides contact with the Shades.

Warren Berlinger plays Burton's superior, Lieutenant James ("Wes") Wesley. His favorite eatery is Henry's House of Cheese and Sausage; in his youth he was called "Wes the Mess" by women (he'd "mess with ladies' hearts"). Kenneth Mars plays Louis Burton, Michael's uncle, who owns Louie's Pick Parts Auto Junkyard.

At Christmastime, the precinct arranges to send gifts to Saint Luke's Children's Home.

Dana Kaproff composed the theme.

635. *Shannon's Deal*
NBC, 4/13/90 to 5/16/90
NBC, 3/23/91 to 6/5/91

John Francis ("Jack") Shannon (Jamey Sheridan) is a former corporate lawyer (with the firm of Coleman and Weiss) who is now struggling to make it on his own as a criminal lawyer (the sign on his office door, Room 406 [later Room 805], at 14 East Ashton Street, reads JOHN SHANNON—ATTORNEY AT LAW). He is divorced, addicted to gambling and is in serious debt to a bookie named Mr. Testa (Jack Orend), who is represented by his collector, Wilmer Slade (Richard Edson). Jack lives in Apartment 4B in a building at East 18th Street in Philadelphia. To help pay off some of his debts, Jack took a temporary job with the law firm of Bancroft and Sloane. His clients say, "Just make a deal with them, Mr. Shannon; they say you're good at that."

636. *Shazam!*; 637. *She-Wolf of London*

Neala Shannon (Jenny Lewis), Jack's pretty 15-year-old daughter, attends Westmuller Conservatory. She says, "Jack works on contingency—one third of the settlement fee; he likes it like that." In his office, Jack has a "swear bowl" (an old glass goldfish bowl). Every time he uses a "cuss word" he puts a quarter in it. Neala has to pay up every time she uses the word *putz*.

Lucy DaCosta (Elizabeth Pena) is Jack's attractive secretary. She says, "I work for the best lawyer in town," and appears to have a crush on him. (She receives little pay and sticks by him under all circumstances except one—"If you gamble, I go." Jack has not returned to gambling since; it's paying off his prior debts that is the problem.)

Relatives: Ralph Waite (Jack's father, *Harry Shannon*). Jack's late mother was named Grace, and Neala's unseen stepfather is named Jarrod.

Themes: "Shannon's Deal," by Mason Daring and John Sayles (first season); "The New Shannon's Deal," by Wynton Marsalis (second season, opening theme); and "Live and Learn," vocal by Diane Schuur, written by David Benoit and Alan and Marilyn Bergman (second season, closing theme).

636. *Shazam!*

CBS, 9/7/74 to 9/3/77

Billy Batson (Michael Gray), a young radio station broadcaster, is selected by the immortal Elders (Solomon, Hercules, Achilles, Zeus, Atlas and Mercury) for a neverending mission: to right wrongs. Billy is teamed with Mentor (Les Tremayne), a mysterious gray haired man who chauffeurs Billy "along the highways and byways of the land" in a 25 foot mobile home. In times of dire need, Billy has been given the power to summon awesome forces by uttering a single word: *Shazam!* When he does, the skies darken, a bolt of lightning strikes him and he is transformed into Captain Marvel (Jackson Bostwick, then John Davey), a heroic crime fighter who can fly, is impervious to harm and has superhuman strength.

The Elders appear in effective but cheaply animated segments (only their eyes and mouths move). The Elders can contact Billy through a magical dome shaped device that is inside the mobile home. Once Billy is contacted and speaks these words, "O, Elders, whose fate is strong and wise, appear before my eyes," the Elders appear and give him an assignment; Mentor can also contact the Elders by reciting the same phrase. Billy can also use the dome to call the Elders for advice.

If the Elders think Billy will need help to complete an assignment, they contact Mentor. He is given instructions to seek out Andrea Thomas (JoAnna Cameron), the California high school teacher who is secretly Isis, a gorgeous crime fighter who helps good defeat evil (for additional information, see "Isis"). Isis is first teamed with Captain Marvel in the episode "The Double-edged Sword."

The series is based on the comic book character created by

Ralph Daigh and Bill Parker. As originally conceived, Billy was a radio broadcaster for station WHIZ and Shazam was an aged wizard he found living in an abandoned subway tunnel. Shazam gave Billy the power to become Captain Marvel by shouting his name. The television version does not relate how Billy met Mentor or how Billy was selected by the Elders. *Shazam* is a combination of the first letters of each of the Elders' names.

Yvette Blais and Jeff Michael composed the theme.

637. *She-Wolf of London*

Syndicated, 10/9/90 to 3/1/91

Cast: Kate Hodge *(Randi Wallace)*, Neil Dickson *(Ian Matheson)*.

Trivia: Randi Wallace, a Los Angeles college student interested in mythology and disproving the supernatural, relocates to England to do research on her thesis. There, she begins classes at the University (as it is called) under Ian Matheson, a parapsychology professor.

Shortly after, while doing research on the Moors, Randi is attacked and bitten by a werewolf. Though she has deep scratches on the right side of her face, she appears to be recovering normally ("clean wounds, no residual scarring"). However, the first full moon brings about a dramatic change: the beautiful student becomes a hideous werewolf (in her first transformation, she chases Ian but does not kill him). When daylight breaks and she returns to her normal self, she finds herself naked and in search of clothes.

Randi has recollections of her transformations, and she asks Ian for help: "You and I can't explain what happened last night, so let's solve this thing together . . . Tomorrow is the first day of the rest of my curse." Stories relate Randi and Ian's involvement with supernatural creatures as they seek a cure for Randi.

Randi is marked by a pentagram (the sign of the wolf); just before she was attacked, Randi was reading a book called *The Face of Fear*, by Ian Matheson. The first thing Randi noticed different about herself after the attack was her craving for meat (which she had given up many years ago). Her first transformation took place in the University lab; she first "woke up" (became normal again) and found herself naked in the men's shower room of the University (one of the students was kind enough to give her a towel). Randi's favorite television show as a kid was "Beyond the Beyond" (a program like "Star Trek," about the explorations of the *Voyager*); she has seen each episode 100 times.

When Ian and Randi first met, Ian told her that in England her name means "erotically charged." When Ian discovers that Randi is unable to find a decent place to live (University residency problems), he gets her a room with his parents, who run the Matheson Bed and Breakfast Inn. To protect Randi on nights when the moon is full, Ian locks her in a cell in the basement of the inn.

Ian drives a car with the license plate JMW 346F and is the author of another book called *Satan's Sex Slaves* (a study of mythology). Ian is later promoted to the head of the Mythology Department of the University.

Pltak (Peter Lee Wilson) is the Gypsy werewolf who bit Randi. Although Pltak was killed in a car crash when Randi and Ian pursued him, Randi's curse was not lifted (legend states that killing the werewolf that caused the affliction will end the curse. This is true only if the werewolf killed is the source of the curse and the bloodline is ended). Dianne Youdale plays Randi as the werewolf in action scenes.

Ian is investigating unearthly happenings for book material; Randi is assisting him in the hope that one such occurrence will provide the cure she needs to end her affliction. If a cure other than the werewolf bloodline cannot be found, Randi's only release from her curse would be for Ian—who loves her—to kill her with a silver bullet.

Relatives: Jean Challis (Ian's mother, *"Mum" Matheson*), Arthur Cox (Ian's father, *"Dad" Matheson*), Dorothea Phillips (Ian's aunt, *Elsa Matheson*), Scott Fults (Ian's cousin, *Julian Matheson*).

Theme: "She-Wolf of London," by Steve Levine.

Note: See also "Love and Curses," the revised series title. Prior to "She-Wolf of London," Fox presented "Werewolf" (7/11/87 to 8/21/88), the first series to probe the folklore legend. While working on the fishing boat of Captain Janos Skorzeny (Chuck Connors), deckhand Ted Nichols (Raphael Sbarge) is bitten by a werewolf—Janos—and cursed to become a murderous creature by the light of the full moon. Hoping to end his curse, Ted gives his friend, Eric Cord (John J. York), a gun loaded with silver bullets and instructions to shoot him when the moon becomes full. Before Eric is able to kill Ted, he is attacked and bitten by Ted. Now, cursed, Eric begins a quest to find Janos and kill him to sever the original werewolf bloodline and end his curse. Eric's quest is hindered, however, by Alamo Joe (Lance LeGault), a bounty hunter who has seen Eric's transformations and now seeks to kill him (Joe's weapon is the .44-40 rifle Chuck Connors used on the series "The Rifleman"). Although Eric managed to find and kill Janos, his curse was not ended: Janos was only one of many werewolf pack leaders. The actual leader is Nicholas Remy (Brian Thompson), a 2,000-year-old werewolf he must now find and destroy. Sylvester Levay composed the theme.

On 2/24/91, the episode "Werewolf" was presented on "The Adventures of Superboy." In it, Paula Marshall, played by Christina Riley, was a young woman who was scratched by a werewolf; she sought Superboy's help to end the curse.

638. *Sheena, Queen of the Jungle*

Syndicated, 1956 to 1957

The series is set in Kenya, East Africa (although filmed in Mexico). Sheena (Irish McCalla) is a white jungle goddess who protects her adopted homeland from evil. She is 28

years old, weighs 141 pounds and measures 39½-24½-38. Sheena was born in 1928 and orphaned four years later when the plane on which she and her parents were traveling crashed in the dense jungle. She was found by the Inoma tribe and raised by its noble chief, Logi (Lee Weaver), who named her Sheena. Sheena learned to command the animals (which she does with a primitive horn), respect good men and hate bad ones. She is assisted by her chimpanzee, Chim, and helps Bob Rayburn (Christian Drake), a white trader who has made Kenya his home (he gets his supplies at the Evans Trading Post).

Anita Ekberg was first chosen to play Sheena but had to back out because of other commitments by the time the pilot was ready for shooting. The rare pilot was filmed in color; the series is in black and white. Mexican acrobat Raul Gaona was hired to perform the stunts when Irish injured her arm.

Eli Briskin composed the "Sheena" theme.

639. *Shell Game*

CBS, 1/8/87 to 6/17/87

"Solutions" is a consumer advocate program on KJME-TV, Channel 6, in Santa Ana, California. John Reid (James Read) is the producer, and Jennie Jerome (Margot Kidder) is his assistant. Reid, who was known as "Riley," and Jennie, also known as "Pocket," were partners in crime (con artists) before they split up to go their separate ways. John became legit; Jennie continued her previous ways. They became partners again when John helped Jennie out of a jam and she used a con to get John a story for his show. They now use their skills to investigate frauds and acquire stories for "Solutions."

Jennie lives in an apartment at 3613 Gantry Avenue, and John has an apartment at 17112 West Dawson Drive. Marg Helgenberger is Natalie Thayer, the station's newscaster, and Rod McCary is William Bauer, the host of "Solutions." Gene Barry appeared as Jennie's father, Jason Starr, from whom Jennie learned her trade (while it is not made perfectly clear, it appears that Jennie's real name is Pocket Starr).

Michel Colombier composed the theme.

640. *Sherlock Holmes*

Syndicated, 1954 to 1955

Cast: Ronald Howard *(Sherlock Holmes)*, H. Marion Crawford *(Dr. John H. Watson)*, Archie Duncan *(Inspector Lestrade)*.

Trivia: The series is set in London, England, in 1897. When John H. Watson, an army doctor stationed in Afghanistan, is wounded (shot in the shoulder), he is ordered to return home to England. While looking for a

Sheena, Queen of the Jungle. Irish McCalla with Christian Drake.

place to live, he runs into an old friend who tells him about "a chap named Sherlock Holmes" who is also seeking lodging. At the University Hospital, Watson first meets Sherlock Holmes. Holmes is working in a lab and tells Watson about a flat for rent at 221-B Baker Street (the first door up). "We examined the rooms," Dr. Watson says, "and we moved in the next day." (Their first case together: "To catch a murderer, of course," said Watson. The case was that of a girl accused of murdering her fiancé, in "The Case of the Cunningham Heritage.")

Sherlock Holmes is a consulting detective (he intervenes in baffling police matters), and Dr. Watson is his biographer (he writes of their experiences together and sells the stories to various magazines).

Holmes has a lab in the flat and conducts experiments (for example, on beneficial aspects of poison) and has begun investigating such unknown sciences as fingerprints and ink smudges. He solves cases by observation and deduction and says, "It is the little things that make the difference" (the seemingly insignificant pieces of evidence). Holmes plays the violin to think (he also has a fascination for the piano); smokes a pipe; and keeps his canister of tea at the end of a line of bottles of poison on a shelf. He doesn't care who gets the credit for solving a crime, but he takes pride in hearing Watson say, "Brilliant, Holmes, absolutely brilliant," after he solves a crime. Sherlock is also a member of the Saint Dennis Club, which forbids talking. He joined for triviality (a demerit is issued each time a member speaks inside the club; three demerits means expulsion).

Inspector Lestrade is with New Scotland Yard and likes his cases "fast and simple." He believes Sherlock's experiments are "nonsense" and is constantly amazed by Holmes's ability to solve a case using what he considers the insignificant. The series is based on the character created by Sir Arthur Conan Doyle and is also known as "The Casebook of Sherlock Holmes."

Theme: "Sherlock Holmes," by Paul Durand.

Note: Sherlock Holmes first appeared on television on 11/27/37 in an experimental 30 minute NBC drama called "The Adventure of the Three Garridebs." The story followed Sherlock Holmes (Louis Hector) and Dr. Watson (William Podmore) as they sought a man with the odd name of Garrideb to fill the conditions of an eccentric's will.

A 30 minute pilot (unaired) was produced in 1951, with John Longden as Holmes and Campbell Singer as Dr. Watson. In the episode, titled "The Man Who Disappeared," Holmes attempts to solve the mysterious disappearance of one of Dr. Watson's patients.

of two children. Hildy, a former deputy for two years, ten years ago, is appointed by the police commissioner to complete the term of office of her husband, Jim Granger. "She's prettier than Cagney and Lacey and as sexy as Pepper" ("Police Woman"'s Angie Dickinson), but is not as assertive or brash as her television counterparts. This is the basic plot, as Hildy, the county's first female sheriff, struggles to command an all-male force of deputies.

Hildy lives on the outskirts of the village at 3111 Pine Shadow Lane with her children, Allison (Nicky Rose) and Kenny (Taliesin Jaffe), and her widowed mother, Augusta ("Gussie") Holt (Pat Carroll). Their phone number is 555-1515. Hildy was born in Teaneck, New Jersey, and had the nickname "Pepper" Holt at Teaneck High. Her favorite television soap opera is "Doctors' Hospital," and she now commands the Lakes County Division of the Nevada County Sheriff's Department. On her first day on the job, Hildy captured a spy who was posing as a cuckoo clock repairman. Allison and Kenny attend the Lakes County Grammar School.

Other Regulars: Max Rubin (George Wyner) is the deputy who yearns for Hildy's job and schemes to get it by discrediting her; Deputy Dennis Putnam (Lou Richards) has a goldfish named Dwight; and deputies Hugh Mulcahy (Guich Koock) and Alvin Wiggins (Leonard Lightfoot).

Relatives: Jane Dulo (Hildy's aunt, *Jessie*), Kathleen Freeman (Hildy's aunt, *Bessie*), Eva La Rue (Alvin's wife, *Margaurite Wiggins*), Richard Erdman (Max's father, *Frank Rubin*).

Theme: "She's the Sheriff," by Bruce Miller.

Note: In the original, unaired pilot version of the series, Priscilla Barnes played Hildy. A similar pilot, called "Cass Molloy," aired on CBS on 7/21/82. In it, Cass Molloy (Caroline McWilliams), a widowed mother, is chosen by the police commissioner to fill the term of sheriff of Burr County, Indiana, when her husband, Big Jim Molloy, dies unexpectedly. While Hildy has two children, Cass had three: Colleen (Amanda Wyss), Nona (Heather Hobbs), and Little Big Jim (Corey Feldman). And like Hildy, Cass had George Wyner to contend with—this time as Max Rosencrantz, the deputy seeking her job. Lou Richards was also in the pilot, playing Deputy Dennis Little; Tom Wells composed the theme.

Though not a pilot for either of the above ideas, episode 57 of "Wild Bill Hickok" (1953, "The Sheriff Was a Redhead") featured Veda Ann Borg as Polly Loomis, a woman who takes over the job of sheriff of a town called Azalia when her husband is killed in the line of duty.

641. *She's the Sheriff*

Syndicated, 9/87

The headline of the local paper, the *Bugle,* read MRS. GRANGER TO FINISH LATE HUSBAND'S TERM. The term is that of sheriff of Lakes County, Nevada; the widow is Hildegarde ("Hildy") Granger (Suzanne Somers), the beautiful mother

642. *Shirley's World*

ABC, 9/15/71 to 1/5/72

Shirley Logan (Shirley MacLaine) is an ace photojournalist who juggles magazine deadlines and datelines in many different countries. It is because of this premise that there is virtually no trivia information. The program, however, is

Shirley MacLaine's first and only television series. Shirley, who works for the London-based *World Illustrated* magazine, is a beautiful woman with wanderlust, an insatiable curiosity and a warm hearted nature that involves her with other people's problems. She uses a black and silver Nikon 35mm camera and, more often than not, finds herself involved with the stories she is covering (thus leading to a mix of comedy and adventure in some of the world's most exotic locales—from Japan to Hong Kong to Spain).

Dennis Croft (John Gregson) is Shirley's editor, a strong willed but warm hearted man who is constantly upset by Shirley's antics.

John Barry composed the theme.

643. *Shotgun Slade*

Syndicated, 1959 to 1961

Cast: Scott Brady (*Shotgun Slade*), Monica Lewis (*Monica*).

Trivia: The time is the 1860s. A man known only as Mr. Slade to those who respect him (Slade to those who hate him), and as Shotgun to those who know him, is a private detective who hires out his services to people who require protection. Other than the nickname Shotgun, Slade has no other first name. When he first meets a client he says, "Call me Slade or Shotgun." Each episode begins with Slade's establishing his assignment. (For example, from the opening of "The Woman from Wyoming": "A client who I had never seen was arriving on the 2:10 from Casper, Wyoming. She was a woman and what she said in her letter, that her life was in danger, was enough for me. My name is Slade, Private Detective." The woman, Rebecca Howland [Sandra Marsh], feared someone was trying to cheat her out of an inheritance.)

Shotgun Slade wears a gun belt but carries his trademark—a unique two barreled sawed-off shotgun (which some people call "a cannon"); the right side of the belt contains 12 shotgun cartridges.

"Shotgun Slade . . . you're afraid that someday you'll be won by a woman, a dreamin' woman, maybe someone like me. Better run, Shotgun Slade, I'm the one, Shotgun Slade . . ." Monica is the "dreamin' woman" of the song she wrote about her friend, Shotgun Slade (Shotgun first heard the song when he met Monica, a dancehall girl who travels from town to town, in the town of Palimar). While it is not made perfectly clear, Shotgun and Monica were apparently lovers who drifted apart; she still carries a torch for him. They run into each other on occasion, and Shotgun always leaves by saying, "See you again, beautiful, in some other town."

Theme: "Shotgun Slade of the Two Barreled Gun." Gerald Fried performed the musical version (first season); Monica Lewis did the vocal (second season).

644. *Sibs*

ABC, 9/17/91 to 10/30/91
ABC, 4/15/92 to 4/29/92

"Grownups" was the original title for this series about the joys and sorrows of three adult sisters: Nora (Marsha Mason), who is happily married, and Audie (Margaret Colin) and Lily (Jami Gertz), who are miserably single.

Nora is married to Howard ("Howie") Ruscio (Alex Rocco), an eighth grade schoolteacher in Manhattan. Nora is the guiding star of the family, the one the others turn to for help. She was originally a bookkeeper for the Morris and Morris Business Management firm; she quit (second episode) to begin her own firm—Ruscio Management. Howie was born in Weehawken, New Jersey, and attended Rutgers University. He teaches civics and has a bumper sticker that reads TEACHERS DO IT WITH CLASS.

Audrey Elizabeth Wyler got her nickname "Audie" from Lily (as a baby she couldn't say Audrey; it came out "Audie"). Audie sells real estate. Three years ago she made $160,000; last year, $36,000; this year, nothing. Her credit cards were taken away and cut in half on her birthday. She owes $565 in unpaid parking tickets. She smokes, is in A.A. and delights in tormenting Lily. Audie watches old movies, takes a lot of baths, and cries a lot ("My way of dealing with a bad situation").

Lily works as a caterer and, as Nora says, "was good at being happy—until she broke up with her boyfriend and moved in with me." She is now indecisive and miserable. She wears a size four dress. The sisters' favorite watering hole is the bar on 4th Street.

George Clinton performs the theme, "Blood Is Thicker."

645. *Sigmund and the Sea Monsters*

NBC, 9/8/73 to 10/18/75

While playing on California's Cypress Beach, Johnny Stuart (Johnny Whitaker) and his brother, Scott Stuart (Scott Kolden), find Sigmund Ooz (Billy Barty), a lovable sea monster who was disowned by his family for his inability to scare humans. When Johnny and Scott learn that Sigmund has no place to go, they take him to their home at 730 Ocean Avenue (a.k.a. 1730 Ocean Avenue). Fearing that the authorities will take Sigmund away from them, they decide to hide him in their backyard clubhouse. Stories relate Sigmund's misadventures as he attempts to live a secret life with humans.

Johnny and Scott's parents are never seen (they are said to be away on business); the boys are cared for by housekeeper Zelda Marshall (Mary Wickes) and in last season episodes by Gertrude Gouch (Fran Ryan). Sigmund's family lives in a cave at Dead Man's Point on Cypress

Beach. Big Daddy Ooz (Van Snowden) and Sweet Mama Ooz (Sharon Baird) are Sigmund's parents, and Slurp (Paul Gale) and Blurp Ooz (Larry Larson) are Sigmund's brothers. The family pet is Prince, a barking lobster. Blurp and Slurp's favorite "shello-show" (they watch "shello-vision") is "The Cod Squad" (a takeoff on "The Mod Squad"). Sigmund was named after his rich great-uncle Sigmund ("Siggy") Ooz (from whom the Oozes hopes to inherit a fortune).

Last season episodes feature Sheldon the Sea Genie (Rip Taylor), whom Sigmund found in a seashell, and Shelby (Sparky Marcus), Sheldon's nephew. Characters are the creations of Sid and Marty Krofft.

Johnny Whitaker sings the theme.

646. *Silk Stalkings*

CBS, 11/7/91 to the present

"A lot of police work is a numbers game. A Code 5 is a stakeout; a 10-54 is a probable dead body. That usually means whoever found it was too spineless to find out for sure and called emergency instead, and 911 called the police." When such a 10-54 becomes a "silk stalking" (a society murder), sergeants Rita Lee Lance (Mitzi Kapture) and Chris Lorenzo (Rob Estes) of the Crimes of Passion Unit of the Palm Springs, Florida, Police Department, are assigned to the case.

Rita Lee and Chris are not just cops, they are best friends. Rita is a stunning girl who has a natural flair for impersonation (she pretends to be anyone she wants to get information from a suspect). Rita also suffers from an embolism in her brain which is located in a spot that is difficult to reach, and an operation could prove fatal. Since the swelling of the blood vessel is very minor, her doctors have told her that she can live a normal life, with medication (she has chosen not to have the operation as it will either kill her or paralyze her—"I'll take my chances. My philosophy is, you aren't sick unless you admit you are"). She hasn't told her captain, fearing she would be put on medical leave and be kept busy sweeping floors.

Mother Goose rhymes were Rita's favorite stories as a kid. She was born Rita Lee Fontana in 1965. Her mother died during childbirth; her father, the wealthy Donald Fontana, killed himself when he lost his millions. Rita was six years old and was adopted by Tom and Sue Lance; she took their last name because it meant so much to her. Rita worked with the vice squad when she first joined the force. She lives at 400 East Palm Drive; she attended Palm Beach High School and State College, and her phone number is 555-4793.

Chris, who lives at 4613 Fairway, drives a car with the license plate 284 736. "He always looks for the bad and the worst in each subject," says Rita. His dream car is a '55 Thunderbird, and he and Rita call each other "Sam" (they both love golf, and golfing great "Slammin'" Sammy Snead is their hero). While Chris calls high profile society murders

"silk stalkings," Rita calls them "bunker shots." They call autopsies "openings." One-X-Ray-8 is their car code.

Susan Horner (Susanna Thompson) is the Palm Beach D.A. Rita calls "a bitch—she makes me mad." While Susan does things strictly by the book, Rita takes a gung-ho approach to crime solving that Susan despises (as Susan says, "I gotta hand you one thing, Rita; God made you look good. Too bad He forgot to give you brains").

Ben Vereen appeared occasionally as Chris and Rita's boss, Captain "Hutch" Hutchinson. Hutch hates the FBI (which he calls Fumble, Bumble and Incompetent) for interfering in his department's cases. Alison Cuffe played Rita Lee as a six-year-old in a flashback sequence. The series is broadcast first on CBS, then is repeated three days later on the USA cable network.

Mike Post composed the "Silk Stalkings" theme.

647. *Silver Spoons*

NBC, 9/25/82 to 9/7/86
Syndicated, 9/86 to 9/88

Cast: Joel Higgins (*Edward Stratton III*), Erin Gray (*Kate Summers*), Ricky Schroder (*Ricky Stratton*), John Houseman (*Edward Stratton II*).

Trivia: Edward Stratton, III, a 32-year-old divorced millionaire who loves to play with toys, and his 12-year-old son, Ricky, a computer whiz, live at 123 Mockingbird Lane in Shallow Springs on Long Island; their phone number is 516-555-9898.

Edward, who attended Aspen Junior College, runs the Eddie Toys Company Division of Stratton Industries. (The company's first boardgame was called Endangered Species. The game sold only six of 50,000 units that were made—and two were returned.) As a kid, Edward had an invisible friend he called Clarence. Edward, who wears a size 10½ shoe, was married to Evelyn Bradford, a woman of social class and status. After six days the marriage broke up due to their social incompatibility. Edward rides a large scale-model train that is set up in the living room and once had a summer job as a counselor at Camp Al Bernstein.

Kate Sommers, who was born in Columbus, Ohio, worked as Edward's secretary before marrying him in episode 61 on 2/10/85. She has two cats, named Fluffy and Snickle Fritz. Kate, who is always fashionably dressed, is also a shoe nut—she worries about matching everything with her shoes ("I've always been a shoe worrier. I almost checked myself into the Buster Brown Clinic"). When Kate became an active part of Eddie Toys, the first toy that she marketed was the Berserk Warrior—a Viking doll with an attitude problem. On her first day in high school, a naive Kate was sold an elevator pass by the sophomores to an elevator that didn't exist. Edward had a life size Rudolph the Rednosed Reindeer on the front lawn. Kate thought it looked "too Christmassey" and had him remove it. A large plastic bullfrog now adorns the front lawn.

Richard ("Ricky") Stratton, who calls himself "The Ricker" (also his computer access code in later episodes), first attended the Burton Military Academy (at which time he was also a Muskrat with the Beaver Patrol Scouts). He later attends Fuller Junior High School and finally Buckminster Fuller High School (every last Friday of the month is Freaky Friday, when kids are allowed to dress as they want). When Rick first entered high school, Edward gave him the pencil he used in high school. Rick is the editor of the school newspaper, the Fuller *Flash,* and when he joined Eddie Toys (to form Stratton and Stratton), he tried to sell a board-game called Rock Express (about getting over obstacles to get to a rock concert; the game bombed).

Rick has a pet frog named Oscar (raised from a tadpole), and his hangouts are the Leave It to Burgers (a.k.a. Burgers) and The Bun and Run. While Rick was always "on the lookout for babes," he did have a semiregular girlfriend in 1986 — Tammy (Robyn Lively), who worked at the Atomic Burger Fast Food Store. At this same time, Rick had an afterschool job as a waiter at Chicken on a String. Before Edward married, he and Rick would dine at Rick's Café.

Edward Stratton II is Edward's father, the stern owner of Stratton Industries. As a young boy he had a pony named Patches. He claims that his father, Edward Stratton, was a "banana head" who became a millionaire by accident (one year before the invention of the car, Edward Stratton invented a rubber inner tube so he would not sink when he went to the beach. When Henry Ford invented the car a year later, he used Edward's invention — and thus the birth of Stratton Industries). Edward II is also the owner of the Big Enchilada Restaurant chain and is a member of the Barbarians Club (for wealthy businessmen).

Other roles: Dexter Stuffins (Franklyn Seales) is the treasurer of Eddie Toys; Alfonso Spears (Alfonso Ribeiro) is Dexter's nephew and attends the same high school as Ricky. Alfonso's never-seen mother is studying baboons in Kenya. Dexter, who cares for Alfonso, gives him a subscription to *The Wall Street Journal* for his birthday. Lulu Baker (Pearl Bailey) is Edward III's friend; she had a cooking show on television for Stratton Flour called "Cooking with Lulu." Derek Taylor (Jason Bateman) and Freddy Lippincottleman (Corky Pigeon) are Ricky's friends.

Relatives: Christina Belford (Edward's ex-wife, *Evelyn Stratton*; she is the author of a book called *Passion Parade*), Georgann Johnson and Gloria Henry (Kate's mother, *Marjorie Summers*), John Inge *(Kate's father),* Ray Walston (Kate's uncle, *Harry Summers*), Billie Bird (Kate's grandmother, *Pearl Summers*), Holland Taylor (Derek's mother, *Ruth Taylor*), Miriam Flynn (Freddy's mother, *Myrna Lippincottleman*), Earl Boen (Freddy's father, *Troy Lippincottleman*).

Theme: "Silver Spoons," by Rik Howard and Robert Wirth.

648. *The Simpsons*

Fox, 1/14/90 to the present

Voice Cast: Dan Castellaneta *(Homer Simpson),* Julie Kavner *(Marge Simpson),* Nancy Cartwright *(Bart Simpson),* Yeardley Smith *(Lisa Simpson),* Hank Azaria *(Moe).*

Trivia: An animated adult series about the Simpsons, an outrageous family who live in the town of Springfield, U.S.A. (which was founded by Jebediah Springfield in the 1840s).

Homer Simpson, the 34-year-old father, is a 239 pound safety inspector in Sector 7G of the Springfield Nuclear Power Plant. His watering hole is Moe's Tavern on Walnut Street (where Duff's beer is served), and pork chops are his favorite food. He has A-positive blood and was "Dancin' Homer," the mascot for the Isotopes baseball team. When Homer ran out of beer one night, he mixed leftover liquor with Krusty the Clown cough syrup, set it on fire and created a drink called Flaming Homer.

Marge, his wife, is a seemingly content blue haired housewife. She is 34 years old and wears a size 13AA shoe. Her favorite television show is "Search for the Sun," and in high school she had aspirations of being an artist (she was discouraged by her teacher and painted only one picture — her idol, Ringo Starr).

In 1974 Homer J. Simpson and Marjorie ("Marge") Bouvier were seniors at Springfield High School. One day Homer was caught smoking in the boys' bathroom and sent to detention (room 106 of the Old Building); at this same time, Marge was fighting for women's rights on campus and was sent to room 106 for burning her bra. Homer found Marge to be the woman of his dreams, and he attempted to impress her. After three weeks, Marge's dislike for Homer turned to love, and they married shortly after graduating. In another episode, it is 1980 when Homer and Marge began dating. Homer was working at the local fun center (he was 24 years old), and Marge was a waitress at Burgers Burgers. They had an affair in the castle on the miniature golf course. Marge became pregnant, and they married at Shotgun Pete's 24 Hour Chapel; it cost Homer $20 for the service. Homer and Marge then moved in with her family and into a home of their own when Homer acquired a job at the power plant. Their song was "You Light Up My Life."

Bartholomew J. ("Bart") Simpson is the oldest child, a ten-year-old wisecracking brat who is every parent's nightmare and "the bad boy of TV." Bart attends Springfield Elementary School (fourth grade), has a pet frog named Froggie and spends more time in detention hall and the principal's office than he does in classes (he is seen in the opening theme writing his punishment on the blackboard for something he did in class; for example, "I Did Not See Elvis," "I Shall Not Draw Naked Ladies in Class," "I Shall Not Torment the Emotionally Frail").

Bart, who has type double O-negative blood, is the undefeated champ of the video game "Slug Fest." He is allergic to butterscotch and has a dog named Santa's Little Helper. "Radio Active Man" is his favorite comic book and "Krusty the Clown" his favorite television show. (Krusty is a very nasty clown on whom Bart has based his whole life. Bart has badge number 16302 in the Krusty the Clown Fan Club. Krusty is Jewish and was born Herschel Krustofski.) Bart enjoys playing practical jokes (especially on Moe, the owner of Moe's Tavern), and his catchphrases are "Don't have a cow, man," and "My name is Bart Simpson; who the hell are you?"

Lisa, the middle child, attends the same school as Bart and is in the second grade. She is a budding saxophone player and the street musician Bleeding Gums Murphy is her inspiration. Lisa is precociously intelligent. "Casper, the Friendly Ghost" is her favorite comic book, and she reads the magazines *Teen Screen*, *Teen Dream* and *Teen Steam*. Lisa wears a size 4B shoe, and "The Itchy and Scratchy Show" (a violent cartoon) is her favorite television show; "The Broken Neck Blues" is her favorite song. Lisa entered the Little Miss Springfield Contest but quit when she discovered her sponsor was Laramie cigarettes.

Baby Maggie is the youngest and most content, calmly observing life while sucking her pacifier. Her favorite videocassette is "The Happy Little Elfs." In the opening theme, Maggie is passed over a supermarket checkout scanner; she costs $847.63.

Homer and Marge do not remember what Bart's first word was, but Homer always yearned for Bart to call him "Daddy" as an infant (Bart called him Homer). At this time, the family lived in a tiny apartment on the lower east side of Springfield. Before the birth of Lisa, Homer and Marge went shopping for their first home. They saw a houseboat, a home in a section called Rat's Nest and a house next to a hog fat recycling plant. When Marge saw and fell in love with the house they currently live in, Homer borrowed $15,000 from his father to buy it (it is financed by Lincoln Savings and Loan). Shortly after settling in, Marge gave birth to Lisa. The attention was now on Lisa, and Bart hated it. He did everything he could to get rid of her (for example, mailing her; shoving her through the neighbor's front door mail slot); despite this, Lisa admired him and *Bart* was her first word. She could say "Mommy" and "David Hasselhoff" but when she saw her father she said, "Homer." Again Homer was disappointed. In the episode of 12/3/92, Maggie spoke for the first time (via guest star Elizabeth Taylor). Homer put Maggie to bed and left the room. Maggie took the pacifier out of her mouth and said, "Daddy."

Other Characters: C. Montgomery Burns (Homer's boss), Millhouse Van Hatten (Bart's friend), Otto (the school bus driver).

Relatives (Voices): Danny DeVito (Homer's half-brother, *Herbert Powell*), Julie Kavner (Marge's sisters, *Patty* and *Selma*).

Theme: "The Simpsons," by Danny Elfman.

649. *Sister Kate*

NBC, 9/16/89 to 1/21/90
NBC, 7/16/90 to 8/5/90
NBC, 9/1/90 (1 episode)

In 1918 Redemption House, a Catholic residence for orphaned children, was established. Over the years, many children were given what was perhaps the only home they had ever known. On September 16, 1989, Sister Katherine

("Kate") Lambert (Stephanie Beacham) is appointed by the diocese to care for seven mischievous orphans who now reside at Redemption House: April Newberry (Erin Reed), Frederika ("Freddy") Marasco (Hannah Cutrona), Hilary Logan (Penina Segall), Eugene Colodner (Harley Cross), Violet Johnson (Alexaundria Simmons), Todd Mahaffey (Jason Priestley), and Neville Williams (Joel Robinson).

Seminars are held on Sundays to allow prospective parents to interview the children. Kate, however, knows her charges are rude and obnoxious and will never find a home ("I have nightmares that some poor parents will get stuck with them").

Little information is given about the children: April, who was born on June 2, 1974, is a stunning blonde who desperately hopes her mother, Julia Newberry (Sally Struthers) will overcome her affliction (clinical depression) and come back for her (following her husband's death, Julia retreated to her own world and now resides at the Brookhaven Mental Institution). April can cook Swedish meatballs—the only meal her mother was able to teach her to cook before tragedy struck.

Freddy, the victim of a broken home, has a tough exterior but longs for her father, Nick Marasco (Dan Hedaya), to clean up his act (he is a con artist) and return for her. Hilary, the handicapped girl (wheelchair bound) is desperately seeking love and knows, deep in her heart, that no one will adopt her. She struggles to be like the other kids and hides the hurt she feels with a cheerful attitude.

Violent, who had a doll named Oprah, is the most charming of the children and has the greatest chance for adoption. Just the opposite is Neville, whom Sister Kate believes is a devil in the guise of a little boy. He is from Jamaica and seems to despise females. He is nasty to everyone (even Sister Kate), disparages women, and is envious if a girl can do something he cannot. Without explanation (other than that the character was annoying), Neville was dropped and replaced by a cute orphan boy named Buster (Miko Hughes).

Lucas Underwood (Gordon Jump) is the field director of Diocesan Children's Services. He has the nickname "Spanky" and allows Kate $30 per month spending money. Laurel Adams played his wife, Sheila Underwood, and David Greenlee was his son, Kevin Underwood.

Theme: "The Sister Kate Theme," vocal by Amy Grant.

650. *Sisters*

NBC, 5/11/91 to the present

Cast: Patricia Kalember (*Georgie Reed-Whitsig*), Swoosie Kurtz (*Alex Reed-Halsey*), Sela Ward (*Teddy Reed-Margolis*), Julianne Phillips (*Frankie Reed*), Heather McAdam (*Cat Margolis*), Kathy Wagner and Ashley Judd (*Reed Halsey*), Garrett M. Brown (*John Whitsig*), Ed Marinaro (*Mitch Margolis*), David Dukes (*Wade Halsey*), Elizabeth Hoffman (*Beatrice Reed*).

Trivia: Events in the lives of four close sisters (Georgie,

Alex, Teddy and Frankie) who live in Winnetka, near Chicago. Flashbacks are used to a great extent to compare the sisters then and now ("We're more than sisters," Teddy says. "We're friends"). The girls attended West High School.

Georgiana ("Georgie") Reed-Whitsig is 35 years old, married to John and the mother of two boys: Trevor (Ryan Francis) and Evan (Dustin Berkovitz). Georgie is a real estate broker with Maple Leaf Realties and has become the main support of the family since John quit his job as a C.P.A. to become a singer (his dream is to release a television record album called "The Sound of Whitsig"). John made his nightclub singing debut at the Tropicabana Club as "The C.P.A. of Song."

Georgie has a Ph.D. in anthropology and drives a car with the license plate PC2 726; blueberry pancakes are her favorite breakfast (John eats Chocolate Warheads cereal for breakfast). Evan's plush rabbit is named Mr. Bigelow and he has a pet rat called Moriarty. Their house number is 844; 555-7842 is their phone number; and they have a dog named Watson. Georgie is a member of the Maple Leaf Rags bowling team (where she is called "Striker Whitsig"). The only holiday videotape Georgie has is the "Eight Is Enough" Christmas episode.

Alexandra ("Alex") Reed-Halsey is 39 years old and the miser of the family. She will drive 20 miles out of her way to save ten cents on an item (forgetting to figure on the gas and wear and tear on the car). She is organized, loves yard sales and is, in short, a shopaholic. Alex has been married to Wade, a plastic surgeon, for 15 years (the song played at their wedding was "Love for Just the Two of Us"). They have a teenage daughter named Reed. Wade's favorite breakfast is Peking duck pancakes, and to relax, he wears women's clothes ("It's something I like doing"). While Wade is primetime television's first cross-dresser, Alex was unaware of his secret life-style. (She discovered his secret when she thought he was having an affair and burst into his hotel room. "You're not the man I thought you were," said Alex, who had a difficult time accepting Wade's leisure time activity.) Alex has a shotgun under her bed for protection. Reed first attends an unnamed Catholic high school then a private school in Paris. When she is expelled for immoral conduct, Alex enrolls her in the Plumdale private school in Chicago.

In second season episodes, Wade leaves Alex for a younger woman. Alex had a fling with a younger man shortly after and had a lightning bolt tattooed on her right breast. Alex was in labor with Reed for 24 hours; she drives a car with the license plate 89F 890.

Theodora ("Teddy") Reed-Margolis is 37 years old, the mother of a rebellious 15-year-old girl named Cat, divorced from Mitch Margolis and a recovering alcoholic. Teddy is the unstable sister; she has a carefree attitude about her life and will go anywhere the wind blows when the mood strikes her. She holds whatever jobs she can and is a budding artist. When she and Mitch were married, Mitch would bring her a bouquet of lobsters ("We would eat them in bed and make love all night"; Teddy brags about having "25 orgasms at one time with Mitch"). Teddy worked in tele-

phone sales—555-MOAN—a line for men who feel lonely and need a woman to talk to (Teddy was Ramona, and the cost was five dollars for a three minute call). She then worked as a saleswoman for Wonderful You cosmetics and attempted her own line of clothes called Teddy Ware. Nude pictures of Teddy, taken by photographer Hank Seawell (Franc Luz) were displayed at the Douglas Gallery. Mitch owns Mitch's Catch of the Day, a fresh fish market; he has a pet lobster named Louie.

Francesca ("Frankie") Reed is the youngest sister. She is a marketing analyst for the firm of Fyre, Birnbaum and Coates (Teddy also worked there as a receptionist for a short time). Teddy calls Frankie "Stinkerbell." Frankie has been in love with Mitch since she was 12 years old; she went into the store to buy some sea bass, saw Mitch and fell in love with him. When Teddy divorced Mitch in 1988, Frankie began having an affair with him and married him in second season episodes.

Cat is Teddy's beautiful 15-year-old daughter. She is very close to her mother and longs for a stable home life (she and Teddy are living with Georgie). Cat likes clothes that are "stylin'," but around the house she parades around in her bra and panties—a habit Georgie is desperately trying to break.

Beatrice ("Bea") Reed is the mother of the four sisters. She is a widow (her late husband, Tom, was a doctor) and lives at the Regency Condo. In the backyard of her former home, she had four rosebushes that she named for each of her daughters (their father had hoped for boys, which is why they all have male names). Bea's license plate reads R3H 807. On each daughter's wedding day, Bea gave the bride a rose brooch.

Each episode opens with the four sisters talking to one another in a steam room. In the third episode, three of the sisters told the others which of the other's features they wished they had. Georgie would like Alex's legs, Alex wishes she had Teddy's "perfect breasts" and Frankie would like Georgie's eyes.

Flashbacks: Riff Regan (*young Georgie*), Alexondra Lee and Sharon Martin (*teenage Alex*), Sheridan Gayr (*young Alex*), Jill Novick and Devon Pierce (*teenage Teddy*), Rhianna Janette and Tasia Schutt (*little Frankie*), Annie Barker (*Frankie age 12*), Mark Patrick Gleason (*young Wade*). John McCann and Peter White (Bea's husband, *Dr. Thomas Reed*), Mary Ann Calder (*young Bea*), Josh Lozoff (*teenage Mitch*), Mike Simmrin (*young John*).

Relatives: Erica Yohn and Doris Belack (Mitch's mother, *Naomi Margolis*).

Theme: "Sisters," by Jay Gruska.

Note: CBS presented a similar series idea in the unsold pilot "Sisters" (5/24/90). The story focused on the lives of three sisters who squabble but help each other in times of duress. The sisters were Kate Morrison (Rita Wilson), the assistant D.A.; MacKenzie Morrison (Daphne Ashbrook), a fashion designer; and Ruth Morrison (Viveka Davis), a secretary.

The Six Million Dollar Man see *The Bionic Woman*

651. *The Six O'Clock Follies*

NBC, 4/24/80, 5/1/80, 8/2/80, 9/13/80

"The AFVN News and Sports" is a six o'clock news program produced by the Armed Forces Vietnam (TV) Network in wartime Saigon (1967) for American service personnel stationed in Vietnam. Because of the antics of the staff, the program is irreverently known as "The Follies."

Specialist Sam Paige (A.C. Weary) and Corporal Don ("Robby") Robinson (Laurence Fishburne) are the newscasters, but the most eagerly awaited segment begins when the beautiful, miniskirted Candi LeRoy (Aarika Wells) comes on screen and says, "Hi boys, this is Candi with the weather."

Specialist Midas Metcovich (Philip Charles MacKenzie) is the television director and wheeler-dealer who owns the local watering hole, the Midas Bar (it is insured by Mutual of Saigon and is covered by everything but sporadic gunfire). Colonel Harvey Marvin (Joby Baker) is the commanding officer. He was born in Baltimore and has been in the army for 18 years. Lieutenant Vaughn Beuhler (Randall Carver) is Marvin's aide, and Ho (George Kee Cheung) is the Vietnamese station janitor.

Joe Cocker sings the theme, "Home."

652. *Sky King*

NBC, 9/16/51 to 10/26/52
ABC, 11/8/52 to 9/12/54

"Out of the clear blue of the Western sky comes Sky King." Schuyler (pronounced Sky-ler) ("Sky") King is a former World War II naval aviator turned rancher who uses a plane to help maintain law and order in Arizona. Sky avoids violence when possible, uses a gun sparingly and never shoots to kill.

Sky (Kirby Grant) lives with his niece, Penny King (Gloria Winters), and nephew, Clipper King (Ron Hagerthy), on the Flying Crown Ranch outside of Grover City. Sky's plane, the *Songbird* (I.D. number N87832; later N5248A) is a Cessna P-50 in the first season, and a Cessna 310-B in the remainder of the series. It is a twin engine monoplane with fuel tanks in the wings for extended flights (up to 1,000 miles without refueling). In the 1952 episode "Designing Woman," Sky calls the plane *The Flying Arrow*. A crown with wings is the symbol of Sky's ranch and it appears in a decal on the side of the *Songbird*.

Ewing Mitchell plays the Grover City sheriff, Mitch Hargrove. Alec Compinsky composed the theme.

653. *Sledge Hammer*

ABC, 9/23/86 to 2/12/88

Cast: David Rasche (*Sledge Hammer*), Anne-Marie Martin (*Dori Doreau*), Harrison Page (*Captain Trunk*).

Trivia: The setting is an unidentified police department in an unspecified American city. Detective Sledge Hammer is the man with a badge (number 6316) and a gun (a .44 Magnum he speaks to and has named "Gun"). He is "dirtier than Harry, meaner than Bronson and makes Rambo look like Pee Wee Herman." The department considers him a menace (for example, he fires warning shots at jaywalkers), and his superior, Captain Trunk, gets migraines when he has to deal with Hammer; Trunk calls him "sadistic, barbaric, depraved and bloodthirsty."

His bumper sticker reads I LOVE VIOLENCE, and he does his target range practicing in his apartment (number 13, at 5517 Stafford Street). He carries a bazooka in his car's trunk (for taking out snipers), isn't too concerned about flesh wounds (except for the fact that they ruin good sport jackets) and his favorite charity is Toy Guns for Tots.

The trigger-happy Sledge Hammer believes "all other cops are wusses—except me. I never let my guard down." He doesn't care about police brutality—he'll do what is necessary to get confessions out of suspects (for instance, tying them to the back of his car and dragging them through the streets); if he feels he is being watched, he orders a suspect to beat himself up. His philosophy is, "The way to fight criminals is to be wilder than they are." He carries Gun with him everywhere he goes. If, for example, he has to do grocery shopping and runs into a holdup, he'll take the time to shoot the suspects, then go about his business—"What I did was absolutely necessary. I had no groceries."

Detective Dori Doreau, the young, beautiful girl who puts her life on the line each day, is Sledge's partner and believes what Sledge believes—"Trust me, I know what I'm doing." Dori is a police officer with a background in martial arts (top of her class in hand-to-hand combat) and an expert shot, and can handle herself quite impressively—so much so that Sledge has remarked, "I'd like to fight you sometime, Doreau." Dori has an apartment at 102 Las Palmas Drive.

Heather Lupton appeared as Sledge's ex-wife, Susan Hilton. They met via a computer dating service; she left him after three years of marriage "for a geek—someone who works for the Peace Corps."

Theme: "Sledge Hammer," by Danny Elfman.

654. *Small Wonder*

Syndicated, 9/85 to 9/89

Cast: Tiffany Brissette (*Vicki*), Dick Christie (*Ted Lawson*), Marla Pennington (*Joanie Lawson*), Jerry Supiran (*Jamie Lawson*).

Trivia: Ted Lawson, his wife, Joanie (a substitute school-teacher), their 11-year-old son, Jamie, and their robotic daughter, Vicki, live at 16 Maple Drive in Los Angeles (555-6606 is their phone number). Ted is a robotics engineer at United Robotronics. He created Vicki (Voice Input Child Identicate) as part of a secret experiment to help handicapped children. He must now mature her before she can be marketed; to do so, he passes her off as his adopted ten-year-old daughter so that she can interact with humans.

Vicki is made of a highly advanced, flexible plastic, transistors, wires and microchips. The Waffer Scale Integration System gives Vicki life. She generates FM radio waves and has a built-in microgenerator with a 440 volt capability (which provides electricity; for example, she can jump-start a car). Her control box is located in her back, and its logic code number is ML 5500. Vicki is basically always dressed in a cute red and white dress. She has a built-in tape recorder (she can be used like an answering machine) and the command "Stop" turns her off from whatever she is doing. Once Vicki does something (for example, climbing a ladder), she is programed to do it. Vicki takes everything people say literally—a problem Ted can't seem to resolve (for example, Jamie told Vicki to "go soak your head"; she did and blew three transistors). "It's not in my memory bank" is Vicki's response when someone says something she doesn't understand. Ted's sophisticated emotional computer program for Vicki is called LES (Logic and Emotional Stimulator), and Vanessa (also played by Tiffany Brissette) is Vicki's evil twin prototype. Vicki sleeps standing up in "Vicki's Closet" in Jamie's room. She has an electrical outlet under each of her arms, and she possesses incredible strength. Her brown eyes are solar cells and provide power. She and Jamie attend Washington Junior High School, later Grant Junior High School (where Joanie is also a teacher in later episodes). Jamie, who receives an allowance of three dollars a week, is a member of the Fearless Five Club and calls himself "The Big J." Vicki won the first runner-up title in the Little Miss Shopping Mall Contest (although Vicki was the most talented, Ellen Sue Beasley, the daughter of the mall owner, won).

Brandon Brindle (William Bogert), Ted's wimpy boss, his wife, Bonnie (Edie McClurg), and their daughter, Harriet (Emily Schulman), are the Lawsons' annoying neighbors. When Harriet first saw Vicki, Jamie said she was his cousin, who was brought up on a farm. When Bonnie sees that Vicki is living with the Lawsons, she reports it to the Department of Family Services. When Ted and Joanie are unexpectedly visited by a welfare worker and questioned about Vicki, they quickly concoct a story that Vicki's real name is Victoria Ann Smith and that her parents, Pat and Jim, were killed in an accident. Pat and Jim, they say, were good friends who made them Vicki's guardians if anything should ever happen to them. Strange as it seems, the welfare worker accepts the story and arranges for the Lawsons to adopt Vicki (in an episode prior to the adoption, Vicki was first Joanie's brother's daughter, then Ted's sister's daughter).

Joanie loves Vicki so much that she forgets she is not human ("I love every little microchip in her body") and gets highly emotional when something happens to her. She originally worked as a salesclerk at the Clothing Boutique. Joanie has dinner ready at 6:30 P.M. (she calls leftovers "reruns") and "That's nice" is her catchphrase (which she says when something strikes her as funny). As a kid Joanie had a canary named Tweet Tweet. Jamie's favorite food is chili dogs, and he attempted to make money with a business called I.B.M. (International Burrito Makers). The first child Vicki helped was Paula Preston (Emily Moultrie), who stuttered.

Harriet attends the same school as Jamie, has a typical store-bought robot named Rodney, two parrots (Polly and Waldo) and a turtle (Beatie). Harriet is a spoiled brat (as she calls herself) who puts on tantrums to get what she wants. She has a doll named Baby Puddles ("You squeeze her and she makes puddles") and believes that she is the most adorable girl in the world. She has a crush on Jamie and considers him "my main squeeze."

Bonnie, who annoys Joanie the most with her "No, no, no-no-no-no" catchphrase, was voted Miss Lettuce Head of the San Joaquin Valley. She greets people with "Hi-Yeeee" and makes it her business to know everyone else's business. Bonnie is also a member of the Gutter Gals bowling team; Brandon is a member of the Caribou Lodge.

Relatives: Jack Manning (Ted's father, *Bill Lawson*), Peggy Converse (Ted's mother, *Evelyn Lawson*), Alice Ghostley (Brandon's sister, *Ida Mae Brindle*), Leslie Bega (Harriet's cousin, *Mary*), David Glasser (Harriet's cousin, *Norman*).

Theme: "She's a Small Wonder," by Diane Leslie, Rod Alexander and Howard Leeds.

655. *Smilin' Ed's Gang*

NBC, 8/26/50 to 8/4/51
CBS, 8/11/51 to 12/53
ABC, 12/53 to 8/13/55

"Hi ya, kids," host Smilin' Ed McConnell would say. "You better come running, it's old Smilin' Ed and his Buster Brown Show." Ed and the gang (the studio audience) would then sing the theme (built around the show's sponsor, Buster Brown shoes): "I got shoes, you got shoes, everybody's got to have shoes, but there's only one kind of shoe for me—good old Buster Brown shoes!" (the gang cheers). "Thank you, buddies and sweethearts," Ed would say. "Good old Buster Brown shoes are on the air out here in Hollywood for another good old Saturday hullabaloo."

Children of all ages were then led into a world where the unreal became real. The set resembled a clubhouse, and Ed began each show seated in a large easy chair. He opened a rather big book called *Smilin' Ed's Stories,* and various filmed segments were shown (most often the serial-like adventures of "Ghanga Rama, the Elephant Boy"; these tales, set in Bakore, India, related the adventures of Ghanga Rama [Nino Marcel] and his friend, Charmer [Harry Stewart]).

Other segments were the antics of Midnight the Cat and Squeaky the Mouse (for example, Squeaky attempting to play "Oh Susannah" on his fiddle while Midnight accompanies him on a drum), Grandie the Talking Piano, the Buster Brown Jug Jingle (jingles sent in by viewers) and the most popular segment, Froggie the Gremlin, the mischievous, magical frog (a rubber toy that was eventually marketed).

Standing next to a grandfather clock, Ed would say, "Now Froggie, you better become visible. Plunk your magic twanger, Froggie" (at which time Froggie would become visible and say "Hi ya, kids, hi ya, hi ya, hi ya!"). After a brief conversation between Froggie and Smilin' Ed, the show's weekly guest star would come out (for example, Vito Scotti as Signor Pasta Fausuolo, the music teacher). Froggie would do his best to exasperate him to a point where he would just walk off the stage in disgust.

Ed McConnell and later Arch Presby and Frank Ferrin provided Froggie's gravel voice; June Foray was the voice of Midnight the Tabby Cat and Grandie. Jerry Marin played Buster Brown, and Bud Tollefson was the voice of his dog, Tige (while Buster Brown appeared only in the commercial segments, his well-known catchphrase was "That's my dog, Tige, he lives in a shoe. I'm Buster Brown, look for me in there too" [referring to the label inside the shoe]).

"Well, kids, old Smilin' Ed and the gang will be on television again next week at this same time. So be sure to invite your little pals over to see it. Now don't forget church or Sunday school. Now once again, we leave the air with this little song: "The happy gang of Buster Brown now leaves the air ... Watch for us Saturday when Buster Brown is on the air."

The series is based on the radio program of the same title. It was originally called "The Buster Brown TV Show, with Smilin' Ed McConnell and the Buster Brown TV Gang," and is also known as "Smilin' Ed McConnell and His Gang" and "Smilin' Ed's Buster Brown Gang." See also "Andy's Gang."

656. The Smothers Brothers Show

CBS, 9/17/65 to 9/9/66

Richard ("Dick") Smothers (himself) is an executive with Pandora Publications in Beverly Hills, California. He lives at 452 Vista Del Mar and is dating the boss's daughter. Life seems to be going well for him until his brother, Thomas ("Tom") Smothers (himself), decides to move in with him and turns his life upside down.

Tom is not your ordinary brother. Two years ago, "Tom was lost at sea without his waterwings" and drowned. He is now Probationary Angel Agent 009, a wingless apprentice angel who is assigned to the 11 eastern states and Alaska. His assignment is to help people in trouble to earn full angel status.

Tom's superior, who is not seen but who contacts Tom by phone, is named Ralph (the Temporary Assignment Angel). Dick's license plate reads PGL 175. Leonard J. Costello (Roland Winters) is Dick's boss; and Diane Costello (Marilyn Scott) is Leonard's daughter and Dick's romantic interest.

In the original, unaired pilot version of the series, Dick was an assistant administrative assistant at Amalgamated Consolidated, Inc. The boss, Leonard J. Costello, was played by Alan Bunce, and Julie Parrish played his daughter, Diane. In the series, Tom's first assignment was to spring a jailed marine so that he could marry his fiancée. In the unaired pilot, Tom's assignment was to break up a gambling ring of old ladies.

Tom and Dick Smothers sing "The Theme from the Smothers Brothers Show."

657. Snoops

CBS, 9/22/89 to 12/8/89
CBS, 6/22/90 (1 episode)

Chance Dennis (Tim Reid) is a criminology professor at Georgetown University in Washington, D.C. His wife, Micki Dennis (Daphne Maxwell Reid), is a protocol aide at the State Department. They are a perfectly matched couple with a penchant for solving crimes. Chance and Micki live at 30th Street in Georgetown and assist Sam Akers (John Karlen), a lieutenant with the Washington, D.C., Police Department; their phone number is 555-3111.

Katja Dennis (Tasha Scott) is Chance's daughter from a previous marriage. Denise Kendall (Lynn Whitfield) is Chance's sister, and Chance Dennis, Sr. (Moses Gunn), is Chance's father. General Ben Martin (Raymond St. Jacques) is Micki's father, and Virginia Martin (Barbara McNair) is Micki's mother. Christopher Babers played Chance as a boy in flashback sequence.

The theme, "Curiosity," is sung by Ray Charles.

658. So This Is Hollywood

NBC, 1/1/55 to 8/19/55

Queenie Dugan (Mitzi Green) and Kim Tracy (Virginia Gibson) share a room at the La Paloma Courts on Sweeter Street in Hollywood, California. Queenie is a stuntwoman, and Kim is an aspiring actress. Queenie frequently works with her boyfriend, stuntman Hubie Dodd (Gordon Jones). They work for Imperial Artists Studios and earn $70 a stunt; their claim to fame is that Queenie once doubled for Jeanette MacDonald and Hubie, a slight bumbler, once doubled for Nelson Eddy. Hollywood 2211 is the phone number for Imperial Artists Studios.

Kim acquires small roles in films. She got her big break when she was screen-tested for the role of the younger sister in the film *Dark Rapture* (the publicity department changed her name to Dale Vale for the project; they figured it was better sounding for theater marquees and newspaper ads).

Andrew ("Andy") Boone (James Lydon) is Kim's agent, who owns the Boone Theatrical Agency; Mr. Sneed (Raymond Hatton) is the girls' landlord; J.J. Carmichael (Paul Harvey) is the head of the studio (he plays golf at the Lakeside Golf Club); and Oliver Hampton (Victor Moore) is the retired actor who lives next door to Kim and Queenie (there are no numbers on the individual apartment doors). He drives a 1934 Rolls Royce and earns $350 a week as a stock performer. Oliver appeared in such films as *Flight Commander, The Last Chance* and *Wander Lust.*

William Lava composed the theme, "So This Is Hollywood."

659. *Something Is Out There*

NBC, 10/21/88 to 12/9/88

Cast: Joe Cortese *(Jack Breslin)*, Maryam D'Abo *(Ta'ra)*, Gregory Sierra *(Lieutenant Vic Maldonado)*.

Trivia: A series of unexplained killings—of a young female jogger and three construction workers—has the police baffled, especially Detective John ("Jack") Breslin of the L.A.P.D. The crimes are unusual in that the killer was able to throw his victims 50 yards from where they were attacked and perform surgery (removing vital organs) within a matter of seconds. At the site of a recent crime, Jack spots a girl he saw at one of the previous killings. Believing that she is a "kinko" and may know something, he attempts, but fails, to apprehend her. During the pursuit, the girl dropped an odd looking item, which Jack finds.

Later, when Jack enters his apartment, he senses the presence of an intruder. In the bedroom he again encounters the girl—who came to his apartment looking for the tracking device Jack found. He wrestles her to the floor, then places her under arrest. En route to the station, the girl pleads with Jack to listen to her story: "I'm from another star system. I was forced to crash my shuttle on your planet . . . I have proof, you cannot not believe me, I have no one else to convince." As Jack listens he learns that her name is Ta'ra and that her people are aware of Earth and have been studying it for some time. A still disbelieving Jack becomes a believer when Ta'ra takes him to the desert and he sees her shuttlecraft. She tells him that he must keep her secret and not tell anyone about her: "There will be worldwide announcements, research teams, scientists; we cannot tell them because of why I am here."

Ta'ra continues and tells Jack she was a med tech officer aboard a prison ship called the *Angelon.* "We had 212 convicted criminals aboard. We were well equipped to handle any prisoners, but not what we were trying to imprison at the end of D Block."

In D Block was a Zenamorph, a creature, not of her species (which resemble humans) that was thought to be extinct. "This one was discovered in the Centauri sector," she

tells Jack. "It is believed to be the only one left in the galaxy. It is a shape-changing alien form, a highly sophisticated cellular makeup.'

Through the power of mind control, the creature escaped from its cell (it willed a doctor to release the prisoners, who in turn released it). The Zenamorph, which resembles a giant scorpion in its natural form, then killed everyone on board except Ta'ra, for reasons she cannot explain (perhaps because she was behind a metal wall during the attack and the creature did not sense her). Following the creature's rampage, Ta'ra grabbed a tracker and a pulse rifle and pursued it. "What was I supposed to do," she asks, "let it escape, let it be unleashed on an unsuspecting planet? . . . I don't know how to exterminate it, but the pulse rifle at maximum setting can cause it great pain. The tracking unit is what I came to your apartment to get. All prisoners are injected with an isotope so they can always be tracked."

Ta'ra tells Jack that she believes the creature has been killing humans for scientific study, to learn how they are constructed so it can assimilate into the human environment—to reproduce itself and take over the planet.

She also tells him that "the long range transmitter on the *Angelon* was destroyed. I have no way of reaching my planet or telling anyone what has happened."

Unwilling to let the beautiful Ta'ra tackle the Zenamorph by herself, Jack volunteers to help her. After several unsuccessful attempts to kill it, Ta'ra believes that it has retreated to the safety of the prison ship. Because the prison ship has drifted into the Earth's atmosphere, Ta'ra can pursue the creature using her shuttlecraft. It is assumed that in the ensuing battle Jack and Ta'ra destroyed the creature. Stories follow Jack and Ta'ra's efforts to solve bizarre crimes.

Jack and Ta'ra live together in an apartment at the Oddfield Apartments (number 808 on the awning in front of the building). Ta'ra became Jack's roommate when his girlfriend, Mandy Estabrook (Kim Delaney), came over unexpectedly, saw a girl dressed in a T-shirt and became outraged. Jack quickly explained that the girl was his cousin from Milwaukee and that she has come to Los Angeles to work in the police crime lab (Mandy was later dropped from the series). Jack drives a sedan with the license plate IHTE-258 and has a pet parrot named Norton (who likes to sing along with the songs he hears on the radio).

The caffeine in coffee makes Ta'ra drunk; she was "turned on" on her unidentified planet by the Earth television show "Crime Story"; she can reads minds and knows what a bed is, but she sleeps in the nude ("I cannot sleep in garments; it would be unnatural and uncomfortable for me"). The two part television movie pilot aired on NBC on 5/8 and 5/9/88.

Theme: "Something Is Out There," by Sylvester Levay.

660. *Space: 1999*

Syndicated, 9/75 to 9/77

Cast: Martin Landau *(John Koenig)*, Barbara Bain *(Helena Russell)*, Catherine Schell *(Maya)*, Barry Morse

Space: 1999. **Left to right: Barbara Bain, Catherine Schell and Martin Landau.**

(Victor Bergman), Tony Anholt *(Tony Verdeschi)*, Zienia Merton *(Sandra Benes)*.

Trivia: In the year 1999, world governments unite to establish an early warning system on the moon to repel alien invaders. The dark side of the moon has been designated as a nuclear waste disposal area; the visible side be-

comes the headquarters for Moonbase Alpha and home to the 311 men and women assigned to operate it. On September 9, 1999, the Space Commission appoints John Koenig to the position of moonbase commander; his first assignment: to launch a probe to the planet Mecca to determine whether it can sustain human life. However, before he is able to do so, a leak is detected in waste disposal area two (atomic waste has become the Earth's biggest problem; storing that waste on the moon has solved it). The atomic radiation creates a series of magnetic chain reactions that cause the many storage containers to explode. Soon "the biggest bomb that man has ever made" explodes and causes the moon to dislodge itself from the Earth's orbit (the waste dumps act like a giant rocket motor and enable the moon to orbit on its own).

"Can we make it back to Earth?" asks a crew member. After a computer analysis, John responds, "Attention, all sections Alpha.... We have been completely cut off from planet Earth. As we are, we have power, environment and therefore the possibility of survival. If we should try to improvise a return to Earth ... it would be hopeless without full resources. It is my belief that we would fail. Therefore, in my judgment, we do not try."

Before Moonbase Alpha loses all contact with Earth, they hear from one final newscast that much death and destruction has occurred due to the sudden increase in gravity (basically from earthquakes) and that the International Lunar Commission holds little hope for the rescue of Moonbase Alpha because it has drifted to an area that is beyond the reach of current technology.

On September 13, 1999, the Moon begins its journey across the galaxy, seeking a new planet to which to affix itself. And, considered invaders by the inhabitants of other planets, the Earthlings struggle to combat the lifeforms of unknown worlds and the elements of outer space, and to sustain life on their new world.

Dr. Helena Russell is the chief medical officer; Professor Victor Bergman is the leading science officer; Tony Verdeschi is the head of security; and Sandra Benes is the chief communications officer.

In her opening narration for the first episode of the second season ("Metamorph"), Helena mentions that the moon has been drifting for 342 days and the population is now 297. She also explains that titanium is the one metal they need to sustain their life support systems. Finding it has become a vital concern. As the moon drifts, Moonbase Alpha receives a transmission from Mentor (Anouska Hempil), the ruler of the planet Psychon, who offers them all the titanium they require. The invitation becomes a nightmare when John and his crew discover that Mentor requires their minds to sustain his biological computer. They are saved by Maya, Mentor's beautiful daughter, when she discovers that her father's diabolical computer has been used to destroy life to sustain itself. Maya, who is opposed to killing, releases John, Helena and Tony. As John destroys the computer and the planet begins to explode, Mentor begs John to save Maya's life. John, his crew and Maya escape seconds before Psychon novas.

On Moonbase Alpha, John and Helena assure Maya that she has a home here: "We are all aliens until we get to know one another."

Maya has advanced scientific knowledge and the power of molecular transformation (the ability to transform herself into any living creature; on Psychon, she preferred to be a lion). Maya calls herself a Metamorph.

Aliens call the residents of Moonbase Alpha "Alphans." When the moon blasted out of the Earth's orbit, the situation was called "Operation Exodus." Besides ground defenses and laser guns (with settings for stun and kill), spaceships called Eagles are Moonbase Alpha's main weapons (there are Combat Eagles, Robot Eagles and Surveillance Eagles).

Theme: "Space: 1999," by Barry Gray.

661. *Space Patrol*

ABC, 3/13/50 to 2/26/55

"High adventure in the wild, vast regions of space. Missions of daring in the name of interplanetary justice. Travel into the future with Buzz Corry, commander-in-chief of the Space Patrol!" Buzz Corry (Ed Kemmer) is commander of the Space Patrol, a thirtieth-century, Earth-based organization that is responsible for the safety of the United Planets (Earth, Mars, Venus, Jupiter and Mercury). The United Planets measure seven and one third billion miles in diameter (it would take light, which travels at 186,000 miles per second, 11 hours to travel from one end of the galaxy to the other).

Cadet Happy (Lyn Osborn) is Buzz's co-pilot (and is famous for his catchphrase "Holy smokin' rockets," which he says when something goes wrong). Tonga (Nina Barra) is a Space Patrol ally; Carol Carlisle (Virginia Hewitt) is the daughter of the secretary-general of the United Planets; and Major "Robbie" Robertson (Ken Mayer) is the security chief of the Space Patrol.

The Space Patrol is based in the manmade city of Terra. Buzz's first ship was the *Battle Cruiser 100*; his second ship was the *Terra IV*; and finally, he commands the *Terra V* (equipped with a time drive and a paralyzer ray, it uses Star Drive to travel in deep space). The rocketship *XRC* (Experimental Rocket Ship), also known as the Rocket Cockpit Ship, is the only other patrol ship equipped with time traveling capabilities (via a magnetic time drive). When Cadet Happy was chosen to pilot the *XRC,* his first trip into time was to the New Mexico desert in 1956 at the site of an atomic bomb test. Space Cadets vacation at Lake Azur; they wear Space Patrol wristwatches; and Space Patrol flashlights are shaped like the *Terra V.* The Evil Price Bacarrati (Bela Kovacs) and Agent X (Norman Jolley) were two of Buzz's most diabolical enemies.

In 1950, when the series was seen locally in Los Angeles (over KCEA-TV), Kitt Corry (Glenn Denning), Buzz's brother, was head of the Space Patrol. In 1953, at the height of the 3-D craze, "Space Patrol" became the first series to present an episode in 3-D. In the episode "The Theft of the Rocket Cockpit," Carol mentions that the first Earth-to-moon flight occurred on October 23, 1966—an insignificant piece of dialogue that missed the actual date by less than three years. There is no credit for a theme composer listed on the screen.

662. *Spencer*

NBC, 12/1/84 to 1/12/85

Spencer Winger (Chad Lowe) is a slightly offbeat, girl-crazy 16-year-old boy who excels in finding trouble. Spencer lives with his mother, Doris (Mimi Kennedy), father, George (Ronny Cox), and sister, Andrea (Amy Locane), at 1901 Sunshine Place (city not identified). After six episodes, the format was revised and became "Under One Roof" (3/23/85 to 5/11/85). George Winger runs off with his 23-year-old bookkeeper and leaves Doris, Spencer (now played by Ross Harris) and Andrea to fend for themselves. The house at 1901 Sunshine Place becomes somewhat crowded when Doris's parents, Ben and Millie Sprague (Harold Gould and Frances Sternhagen), move in to help raise the children. While both formats followed Spencer's antics at school and home, the revised six episodes also focused on the problems of three generations living under one roof.

The Wingers' telephone number is 555-7588; Spencer and Andrea attend McKinley High School; Spencer's friend, Herbie Bailey (Dean Cameron), works at a fast food restaurant called Polly's Hot Dogs. Herbie claims, "My parents pay me to be normal in front of their friends." Ben and Millie have been married for 38 years; Doris has an unseen aunt named Shirley.

The "Spencer" theme was composed by Barry Goldberg.

663. *Square Pegs*

CBS, 9/27/82 to 9/12/83

"You know the feeling. The awkwardness, the tender times, the silly moments of being fourteen and not quite sure you've got what it takes to be popular. That's what 'Square Pegs' is all about. Join Patty and Lauren in the sights, sounds and songs of growing up in the eighties" (this is the CBS *TV Guide* ad for "Square Pegs" on 9/27/82). Patricia ("Patty") Greene (Sarah Jessica Parker) and Lauren Hutchinson (Amy Linker) are best friends. Patty is smart, thin, nearsighted and "waiting for cleavage." Lauren is also smart, but wears braces and is slightly overweight; she is "waiting for her first kiss." The girls, friends since Weemawee Grammar School, are now the square pegs in a round hole—Weemawee Central High School, the "in" high school in the town of Weemawee Heights. Patty lives at 98061 Walken Drive and Lauren next door at 98063 Walken. The girls are not preppies, eggheads or creeps—just awkward. Before entering high school they made a pledge to fit in. Now they are freshmen, and "all we have to do is click with the right clique," says Lauren. "We can have a social life that is worthy of us. This year we're gonna be popular, even if it kills us."

Other Students: Jennifer DiNuccio (Tracy Nelson) is the class beauty (she speaks Valley Girl style); Johnny ("Slash")

Lashawich (Merritt Butrick) is the New Wave freak (he drives a car called the Slashmobile and eats only junk food); Muffy Tepperman (Jami Gertz), the preppy cheerleader, is captain of the J.V. squad (she lives at 802 Grant Street); Marshall Blechtman (John Femia) is the class clown (he yearns to be a comedian); LaDonna Fredericks (Claudette Wells) is the fashion conscious student; and Vinnie Pasetta (Jon Caliri) is the class Romeo.

Dr. Winthrop Dingelman (Basil Hoffman) is the principal, and Rob Donovan (Steven Peterman) is the favorite teacher (history). Marj Dusay appeared as Muffy's mother, Beverly Tepperman.

The Waitresses sing the "Square Pegs" theme.

664. *Stand by Your Man*

Fox, 4/5/92 to 8/8/92

Rochelle Dumphy (Melissa Gilbert) lives with her husband, Roger (Sam McMurray), in a fashionable house at 866 Fairlawn Avenue in Paramus, New Jersey. Rochelle's sister, Lorraine Popowski (Rosie O'Donnell), and her husband, Artie (Rick Hall), reside in a less than desirable mobile home at the Camelot Court Trailer Park in New Jersey.

Roger owns a company called Prestige Patios and was voted "Builder of the Year" by *Porch and Patio News*. Artie assists him. Unknown to Rochelle and Lorraine, Prestige Patios is a front for illegal business operations (laundering money from the banks Roger and Artie rob). When Roger and Artie are finally caught (robbing the Franklin Heights Bank), they are sentenced to eight years in prison at the New Jersey State Penitentiary (Roger is prison number 42997; Artie is prisoner 01832).

Rochelle invites Lorraine to come and live with her, and stories follow their escapades as they try to live by Rochelle's belief that they should stand by their men during the lean times and help each other through the rough times ahead.

Rochelle, the younger and prettier of the two sisters, attended Paramus High School. She is sweet and very sexy, and believes she has the perfect marriage with the perfect man (she envisions herself five years from now with two children named Josh and Chelsey). Rochelle sleeps with her plush animal, Mr. Fluffy, and has a prized porcelain boy she calls Little Hans (which Roger gave to her when they moved into the house). Rochelle's car license plate reads 27AS943.

Lorraine, whose middle name is Marie, is the tough-as-nails older sister. She believes Rochelle is a bit naive (for example, Rochelle worked as the office manager for Prestige Patios and was unaware of what was going on) and acts and dresses like a Barbie doll. Lorraine has been working since she was 16 years old and now holds a job as a stock clerk at a discount store called Bargain Circus (Rochelle later works there as the manager). While Lorraine puts up with all of Rochelle's antics, she most objects to the "No-No Bottle" (when a house rule is broken, a quarter has to be put into a bottle; Rochelle's house rules include no slamming doors, wiping your shoes before entering the house, and "when you're done with food and drink, put your dishes in the sink").

Adrienne Stone (Miriam Flynn) is Rochelle's snooty, sex-crazy neighbor, and Stuart (George Wyner) is her husband, an attorney who is unaware of his wife's sexual activities. In the unaired pilot version of the series, Leila Kenzle played the Melissa Gilbert role as Cindy Dumphy.

Chuck Loeb composed the theme.

665. *Star Cops*

Syndicated, 1/91

In the early twenty-first century, the moon is colonized and Earth families begin to settle there. With the good comes the bad, and to battle crime the E.S.L. (European Space Liaison) funds a space police force called Star Cops to protect the settlers from outlaws.

Nathan Spring (David Calder) is appointed the commander, and inspectors Pal Kenzey (Linda Newton), David Thoreaux (Erick Ray Evans) and Colin Devis (Trevor Cooper) assist him. (Pal is the Australian member of the British team.)

The High Frontier is the most crime ridden area. The various colonies of the moon are called outposts (followed by a number). In references to the moon, the term *out there* is used, not *up there*. A Concord-like shuttle transports visitors from Earth to the moon. If an emergency arises on board, the stewardess uses the code "Will passenger Wilbur Force please report to the flight deck" to alert authorities and avoid a panic.

Moonbase One is the headquarters for Star Cops. Santatanian is the temporary waste disposal site (waste is transported from the Earth, stored on the moon, then sent into space). Nathan and David command Moon Rover 7, and both men like their coffee "black, no sweetness." Star Cops use laser pistols to battle outlaws. The Earth code to Moon Base One is 002-7373-155 (as seen on their television monitors; to activate televisions, one says, "Screen on," or "Screen off"). There are computer controlled pool games and two-way visual telephones, and it is mentioned that Venice, Italy, is now completely under water. For R & R, the Star Cops are sent to Earth.

While the British established Star Cops, they have no agreement with the United States, and they are not permitted to interfere in crimes that occur on U.S. space stations (for example, on the main American base, Space Station Ronald Reagan). The Americans, called "Yanks," by the British, are not in favor of international policing (which is the U.S. government's reason for not supporting Star Cops. Spring is trying to change the State Department's attitude, but with little luck. The Americans are in space only to do research). The Star Cops are called "Brits" by the Americans; Russians are called "Ruskies" by both countries.

Theme: "In the Shadow of the Moon," vocal by Justin Hayward.

666. *The Starlost*

Syndicated, 9/73 to 9/74

Cast: Keir Dullea (*Devon*), Gay Rowan (*Rachel*), Robin Ward (*Garth*).

Trivia: On Earth in the year 2285, a catastrophe of galactic proportions threatened all life on the planet. The Committee of Scientists and Philosophers set about selecting desirable elements of Earth life to seed other planets in an effort to save the legacy and culture of the human race. In order to do this, the committee built, between the Earth and the moon, the *Earth Ship Ark,* a spaceship 8,000 miles in character, which became the most monumental task humanity had ever undertaken. The *Ark* is an organic cluster of environmental domes called biospheres which are looped to one another through tubular corridors for life support and communications. In the biospheres are representative segments of Earth's population—three million beings in all. Whole, separate ecologies are sealed from one another and isolated to preserve their characteristics.

The *Ark* was launched that year and programed to find a solar system of a Class Six star. The *Ark* traveled for 100 years before it locked into a collision course with a Class G solar star. "No further data recorded."

The series is set in the year 2795; the only thing that is known about the *Ark* is that in the year 2790 it landed in a hilly area of a place called Cypress Corners. The area where the ship rests is now thought to be a place of evil by the inhabitants.

The people of Cypress Corners lead a simple life (much like the Amish). Devon is the village blacksmith. He is poor "and has nothing." Devon is in love with Rachel, a girl of higher social status, who is deemed unsuitable for him. Rachel has been promised to a man of equal status named Garth. Despite the fact that "the Creator" has deemed Devon's love for Rachel to be forbidden, he pursues Rachel and defies tradition. Devon is then said to be possessed by wickedness and is ordered killed as he is threatening genetic balance. When Devon overhears what is being planned for him, he takes refuge in the forbidden cave. There, as he enters the *Earth Ship Ark,* he is amazed to see a fabulous arena of controls. He accidentally touches one and activates a computer host named Mulander 165 (William Osler). It is through Mulander 165, "a visualization appropriate to preprogramed word replies," that Devon learns about the fate of the *Ark* (when he plays Cylinder 42 on the Playback Tray).

Devon leaves the safety of the *Ark* to find Rachel. In doing so, he is captured, imprisoned and sentenced to death. When Rachel visits Devon, he tells her about the wonders he has seen. Rachel professes her love for him and will return with him if he can escape. Shortly after, Garth helps Devon to escape so he will flee and leave Rachel alone. Rachel, however, joins Devon. As they journey to the *Ark,* they are followed by Garth. When Garth is unable to persuade Rachel to return with him, he decides to remain to protect her from Devon.

The series decpits their adventures as they explore the various biospheres, searching for someone or something to explain the mystery of the great catastrophe and save the remains of Earth life by finding the Class Six star—the Starlost. The *Ark* is now drifting in space and is on a collison course with a Class G solar star 5,000 miles in diameter. Should the collision occur, it would destroy all mankind. All systems aboard the *Ark* are functioning normally. Only navigation and propulsion ever required human control. The computer banks contain all the necessary information to save the *Ark*; however, Devon, Rachel and Garth are incapable of retrieving the relevant data from the computers; they are seeking someone who can reprogram the computers and reactivate the thermo-nuclear propulsion systems. If the propulsion systems can be restored, the *Ark* will continue on its preprogramed course to orbit a friendly environment where life can start afresh.

Other Roles: Walter Koenig (Oro, the alien from the planet Exar. He originally presented himself as an explorer whose spacecraft *Explorer Craft 531* crashed into the *Ark*. It was later learned that he is on a mission for his planet's leaders to seize the *Ark* and bring it into Exar's orbit at all costs. Oro is now a fugitive on the *Ark* and sought by Devon and Garth); Alexandra Bastedo (Idona. She is from the *Ark* biosphere Igret and is also known as 419B2. She was saved by Oro when he discovered her gasping for breath in her now contaminated biosphere. She now assists him).

Theme: "The Starlost," by Score Productions.

667. *Star of the Family*

ABC, 9/30/82 to 12/23/82

Sixteen-year-old Jennie Lee Krebs (Kathy Masinik) is a beautiful high school girl who aspires to be a singer. Her struggles up the rocky road to stardom are the focal point of the series.

Jennie, who attends Monroe High School in southern California, lives with her father, Leslie ("Buddy") Krebs (Brian Dennehy), and her brother, Douglas ("Douggie") Krebs (Michael Dudikoff), at 7136 La Salle Drive. Buddy is captain of Fire Company 64; and the not too bright Douggie also attends Monroe High. Judy ("Moose") Wells (Judy Pioli) is Jennie's manager; and Leo Feldman (Todd Susman), Max Hernandez (Danny Mora) and Frank Rosetti (George Deloy) are the firemen under Buddy's command.

Kathy Maisnik sings the theme, "Movin' Along."

668. *Step by Step*

ABC, 9/20/91 to the present

Cast: Suzanne Somers (*Carol Foster*), Patrick Duffy (*Frank Lambert*), Staci Keanan (*Dana Foster*), Angela Watson (*Karen Foster*), Christopher Castile (*Mark Foster*), Christine Lakin (*Alicia Lambert*), Brandon Call (*J.T. Lambert*), Josh Byrne (*Brendon Lambert*), Sasha Mitchell (*Cody Lambert*).

Trivia: Carol Foster is a widow with three children (Dana, Karen and Mark). She is a hairdresser and works out of her home at 201 Winslow Street in Port Washington, Wisconsin (population 9,338). Carol and her children are neat and tidy (for example, Carol alphabetizes the soup cans and irons Dana and Karen's lingerie). Carol first mentions her maiden name as being Baker; later it's Williams.

Franklin ("Frank") Delano Lambert is divorced and caring for his three children (Alicia [nicknamed Al], J.T. and Brendon). He is an independent contractor and owns the Lambert Construction Company. Frank and his children are untidy, or, as Carol says, "slobs." (Frank's wife ran off to become a lounge singer in Las Vegas.)

Carol and Frank are also married (they met when Frank came to her for a haircut; they were married at the Wedding Shack in Jamaica three months later). While Carol and Frank love each other, it is not a "Brady Bunch," as the kids despise one another and Carol's efforts to build a relationship step by step are the focal point of the series.

Carol is nervous about her new marriage and is afraid it is not gong to work. Frank takes the long term view: "A week ago you and I were raising our kids alone and we were sleeping alone; basically we were alone. Then fate threw us together . . . now we're not alone anymore . . . and you and I are going to be very happy because we love each other." Carol tries to run the house on a schedule, but it never works; she has breakfast ready at 7:30 A.M. and dinner at 6:30 P.M.; she buys food at the Port Washington Grocery. The simplest things about Carol impress Frank (for example, "She reads books—not just paperbacks, but hardbacks").

Frank's GMC pickup truck license plate number is 129-815 (later 52-7P9). He polishes the van only with Royal Carnuba Wax, which he buys at Auto World (for $15 a can). Frank's rules for doing the dishes are simple: "Don't leave a dish dirty for more than four days. After that, the Fruit Loops become like an unremovable glue." Frank isn't himself until he has his morning cup of coffee (for example, he calls Dana "Donna"). Frank, a member of the Mallard Lodge, uses a construction site story to explain aspects of life to the kids; Carol uses a beauty parlor story. In her youth Carol sang with a band; in 1971 she entered the Miss Small Curd Cottage Cheese Beauty Pageant and won first runner-up ("I lost to a girl with bigger curds"). In 1992 Carol and Karen entered the Mrs. Mom and Miss Mallard Beauty Pageant of the Mallard Lodge; they won with a snappy tap dancing act. In 1969 Frank was a member of the Sheboygan Super Bears team and was president of the Milwaukee Tile and Grout Association.

Dana, Karen and Al share a bedroom. Dana and Karen attend Port Washington High School; Al is enrolled at the Canyon Elementary School. Dana is Carol's oldest child (15). She is a straight-A student, always impeccably dressed and sensitive to the fact that she has a small bustline (as Al says, "You're smart and it's a good thing because you have no boobs"). Although Dana is very pretty, she is very selective about the boys she dates (J.T. calls her "Vampira" and "The Undatable"). Dana was an honors student at Lincoln Elementary School and writes for her high school newspaper, the *Wildcatter*. Dana was also assistant manager of The 50s Café (Karen worked there as the waitress Peggy Sue).

Karen is 14 years old and knows she is beautiful ("I'm what the guys call a babe"). She is very concerned about her appearance, especially her makeup ("A mirror is my best friend"). Karen is always fashionably dressed, adores shopping at the Port Washington Mall and worries constantly about zits (which she feels will be her downfall should she ever get one; she buys the giant size Clearasil). People often mistake Karen for a model ("I just look like one but I'm not"). Al calls Karen a "wuss" because everything frightens her. Carol believes that Karen's obsession started the day she gave her a Brooke Shields doll. Karen reads *Cosmopolitan* magazine and dreams of becoming a model (in second season episodes, she began part time modeling at Peterson's Department Store). Karen is also a cheerleader for the Wildcats.

Alicia is a very pretty 12-year-old tomboy. She is a catcher for the Beavers Little League team and a smart aleck. She always fears the worst in a situation and has a rattlesnake's head preserved in a jar; she also has a pet pig named Bullet. Dana thinks Al needs an attitude adjustment and was raised by wolves. "You little criminal" is one of Dana's "terms of endearment" for Al, "the son" Frank wishes he had (Al shows great potential for construction and "Lambert and Daughter Construction" is a dream Frank feels will never come true). When Frank and Carol returned from their honeymoon, Al was upset that they did not bring her back a voodoo doll. Al's study habits also upset Dana (she rents videos to do book reports). When Al first met Carol she called her a "bimbo." Al played drums in an all-girl rock band called Chicks with Attitudes (their first gig was at Greco's Bowl-a-Rama).

J.T., who attends Port Washington High (as did Frank), is on the school's track team. He is a walking disaster and has no flair for the construction business; he works on occasion as Carol's shampoo boy in the salon. His favorite meal is burritos; Dana calls him "a pea-brained idiot"; the Burger Palace is his afterschool hangout. Brendon, whose favorite snack is double stuffed Oreos (spaghetti and meatballs is his favorite dinner), and Mark, a brain who has a working model of the human intestine in his bedroom, attend Canyon Elementary School; their favorite hangout is the Burger Barn.

Cody Lambert is Frank's nephew. He works in demolition, lives in a van parked in the driveway and believes that he "is the coolest guy on the planet" ("No chick can resist my personal magnetism"). Dana believes he is "a brain-dead idiot." Cody eats ice cream for only one reason: "So I can get ice cream headaches." Cody rides a motorcycle and wears a leather jacket, but his idol is not Fonzie from "Happy Days"—"It's Ed, the attendant at the Texaco station." Cody thinks Dana is a hot babe—"If she were a prehistoric creature, she'd be a Babertooth Tiger." Cody and J.T. had a cable access television show called "J.T. and Cody's World." J.T. calls Cody "The Codeman."

Relatives: Peggy Rea (Carol's mother, *Ivy Baker*), Patrika Darbo (Carol's sister, *Penny Baker*), Richard Roat (Frank's father, *Bill Lambert*).

Theme: "The Second Time Around," vocal by Teresa James and Bennett Salvay.

669. *Steve Canyon*
NBC, 9/13/58 to 9/7/59

"Steve Canyon—a salute to the air force men of America. You are about to see an actual mission flown by the United States Air Force. All information, material and incidents contained herein are now declassified."

Steve Canyon (Dean Fredericks), serial number A0-041044, is a lieutenant colonel with the U.S. Air Force. Steve is first stationed at Edwards Air Force Base and in charge of the Air Force Flight Test Center (novice flyers are called "Jaybirds"). Steve flew a B-52 (I.D. number 53728) and has the air code Big Bear.

Beginning with the fifteenth episode (1/3/59), Steve became a troubleshooter and is transferred to Big Thunder Air Force Base in California. He pilots a jet fighter (I.D. number FW 754), and his air code is Blue Bird One. Steve waits for the last possible second before starting his jet—"Every minute of fuel burned on the ground costs you ten miles of air time." His jet is capable of cruising at 700 miles an hour.

Other Regulars: Major Willie Williston (Jerry Paris), Airman Abel Featherstone (Abel Fernandez), Police Chief Hagedorn (Ted DeCorsia) and Ingrid (Ingrid Goude), Steve's secretary. Based on the comic strip by Milton Caniff.

Walter Schumann composed the theme.

670. *Stingray*
NBC, 3/4/86 to 7/31/87

He is known only as Stingray or Ray. He helps people in deep trouble, people who are afraid to turn to the police. He asks no money for his help—only for a favor when he needs it. He is known by his trademark—the 1965 black Corvette Stingray he drives (license plate EGW 769; later STINGRAY). He can only be contacted through his newspaper ad, which he runs only on Friday: "'65 black Stingray for sale. Barter only. Call 555-7687." Nick Mancuso plays Ray; Mike Post and Pete Carpenter composed the theme, "Stingray."

671. *The Stockard Channing Show*
CBS, 3/24/80 to 6/28/80

"The Big Ripoff" is a consumer advocate program that airs locally in Los Angeles on West Hollywood station

KXLA. Susan Goodenow (Stockard Channing) is a pretty divorcée who assists Brad Franklin (Ron Silver), the program host. Susan dons various disguises, goes undercover to investigate ripoff artists and prepares each week's show. Brad gets the glory for a job well done by Susan.

Earline Cunningham (Sydney Goldsmith), the station's sexy but dim witted receptionist, says, "Susan's an attractive and successful girl and got a whole lot of class. I never knew nobody else who ate pizza with a knife and fork." Earline, who lives at 123 Morning Glory Circle, reads a gossip paper called *National Smarm* (title taken from a camera shot of the paper).

KXLA is owned by Gus Clyde (Max Showalter), a former actor who calls the station "The House That Gus Built." Susan, whose phone number is 555-3004, lives at 196 North Langley Drive.

Prior to this series, Stockard starred in "Stockard Channing in Just Friends" (CBS, 3/4/79 to 8/11/79). Channing was Susan Hughes, a girl on the rebound from a broken marriage, who becomes the assistant manager of the Fountain of Youth Health Spa in Beverly Hills. Sydney Goldsmith was Coral, the waitress at the spa's juice bar; Mimi Kennedy was Susan's married sister, Victoria Chasen; and Lou Criscuolo was Susan's boss, Milt DeAngelo. Lawrence Pressman appeared as Susan's ex-husband, Frank Hughes; Liz Torres was Milt's wife, Miranda DeAngelo; and Albert Insinnia was Milt's son, Angelo DeAngelo.

Delaney Bramlett composed the theme, "Stockard's Theme," for both versions.

672. *Strange Paradise*

Syndicated, 1969 to 1970

Maljardin is a forbidding island in the Caribbean. Its name, translated from the French, means "evil garden." The ocean surrounds the island, and poisonous weeds grow in its soil. The beautiful flowers that are seen are "flowers of evil." The mansion that stands on the island has been cursed for centuries by the "Curse of Maljardin." The lone inhabitants of the island are Jean Paul Desmond (Colin Fox), a wealthy financier, his new bride, Erica Carr (Tudi Wiggins), and their servants, Raxil (Cosette Lee) and Quito (Kurt Schiegl).

One year following their retreat to the island, Erica is stricken with an unknown disease and mysteriously dies. Jean Paul is unable to accept Erica's death and vows to bring her back to life. He places her body in a cryo capsule and preserves her through the process of cryogenics. Jean Paul begins by summoning Allison Carr (Dawn Greenhalgh), Erica's sister, to the island. Allison, a biochemist, is intrigued by Jean Paul's request and begins her experiments. However, when her chemicals fail to produce results, Jean Paul takes a drastic step: he summons the powers of darkness and breaks the ancient spell that has ruled the island and cursed his family when he conjures up the spirit of Jacques Eloi DeMonde (Colin Fox), an ancestor who lost his wife in the same manner 300 years before. To protect itself, the spirit takes refuge in the portrait of Jacques that hangs on the wall next to the fireplace. When Raxil, a priestess, discovers what Jean Paul has done, she vows to return Jacques to hell.

As the powers of evil begin to restore Erica's life, Raxil summons her friend Vangie (Angela Roland), a medium, to help her destroy Jacques.

Jean Paul's wish is granted shortly after when Erica is brought back to life. To celebrate her rebirth, Jean Paul invites several friends to the island: Dan Forest (Jon Granik); Tim Stanton (Bruce Gray), an artist he hires to paint Erica's portrait; Holly Marshall (Sylvia Feigel), a beautiful young heiress; Elizabeth Marshall (Paisley Maxwell), Holly's mother; and the Reverend Matthew Dawson (Dan McDonald).

To Jean Paul, Erica appears to be as beautiful as before—"I have my Erica back." What he can't see is the wickedness that is now Erica. She is suddenly afraid of fire, and there is an evil presence about her. To survive, Erica must use her powers of the dead to kill all who are on Maljardin. Holly is the one Erica has chosen for a special ceremony to ensure her immortality (Holly is the youngest; it is through her that Erica can live the longest). The instant Holly sees Erica, she becomes strangely attracted to her. Elizabeth fears for Holly—"My blood runs cold when I see you with her." "Erica is the most lovely and wonderful person I ever met," says Holly, "and I'd follow her to the deepest pit in hell."

Following the mysterious deaths of Vangie and Dan, Raxil discovers that Erica has caused them and vows to fight her by summoning the Power of the Serpent. But before Raxil can do anything, Erica's powers of evil destroy her secret temple of the serpent beneath the mansion.

There is no escape from the island, and additional murders are committed: Tim, Matthew and Allison. Elizabeth and Holly are left alone in the mansion when Jean Paul, Raxil and Quito rush to the boathouse to battle a fire started by Jacques. Holly, completely under Erica's control, is standing by her side. Erica needs to possess Holly's body to survive. To accomplish this, she must take Holly's soul to hell by piercing her heart with the Pin of Death. As Erica is about to stab Holly, Elizabeth sees what is happening and rushes down the staircase. She pushes Holly aside and is herself killed when she takes the pin meant for Holly. An exhausted Jean Paul enters the house and awakens Holly (who is taken to safety by Raxil and Quito). An angered Jean Paul sets the curtains on fire, then torches the portrait of Jacques. As the portrait burns, the flames engulf the house and Erica perishes.

Jean Paul, safely outside, looks back as the mansion burns. He hears the final words of Jacques echoing in the atmosphere: "Whether you live or die, Jean Paul Desmond, wherever you choose to run, your curse will follow you, and life for you will always be a Strange Paradise."

Score Productions is credited as the theme composer.

673. *Street Hawk*

ABC, 1/4/85 to 3/8/85

Cast: Rex Smith (*Jesse Mach*), Joe Regalbuto (*Norman Tuttle*).

Facts: Jesse Mach, a motorcycle officer with the Metropolitan Division of the L.A.P.D., is reckless and irresponsible, and he shows no regard for his equipment. Norman Tuttle, a research scientist for the Federal Government, has spent four years of his life on a project called "Operation Street Hawk," a top secret project concerned with law enforcement. Although Norman is reluctant to use Jesse because of his reckless nature, his superiors believe Jesse is what they are looking for—"a cop with a test pilot mentality who pushes himself beyond the limit." Jesse, however, refuses to join Norman's team—"I don't trust Feds. You never know whose side they're on."

Several days later, while testing his Honda cycle in an area called Devil's Kitchen, Jesse stumbles upon drug smugglers and is run down. How Jesse is found is not shown, but he is rushed to the hospital (he has a severe knee injury that makes him incapable of fighting street crime; he is later assigned to the public relations department).

Norman again approaches Jesse and tells him that a new prosthesis has been developed to repair his knee. It hasn't been approved by the F.D.A., and it involves a very expensive and complicated operation. When Jesse realizes that it is the only way he will ever be able to ride a bike again, he agrees to become Norman's test pilot.

Following the operation (at the Doctors Hospital of southern California), Norman takes Jesse to his base of operations—a lab that is hidden in a warehouse (Durrell's Bakers Supply Company). "It looks like the bridge of the Starship Enterprise," remarks Jesse when he sees Norman's command center (Norman can monitor the entire city from the main console).

Jesse then sees Street Hawk, a high tech motorcycle designed to battle crime ("Specifically," Norman says, "it's an all-terrain pursuit vehicle." "Whatever it is," responds Jesse, "I want to ride it"). (Street Hawk appears as a red blinking dot on Norman's map. To maintain his cover, Jesse wears a leg brace and continues working in the P.R. office.)

Street Hawk has a cruising speed of 200 mph. By incorporating four high volume air boxes and hyper thrust, the speed approaches 300 mph. Hyper speed is a computer assisted mode that Norman controls. Street Hawk is tied in by closed circuit audio and video. If anything should go wrong, Norman can shut down the bike to prevent disaster.

Street Hawk also has an aerodynamic coefficient of 0.05; thus friction is nontraceable. It also has a hydraulic suspension system that adjusts to off-road or street use. For braking, Norman redesigned the system to take advantage of negative airflow ("If necessary, you can stop on a dime"). A button on the handlebars controls the compressed air vertical lift system—which can propel Jesse 30 meters into the air.

The bike also has a high energy particle beam with two settings: maximum charge (which can immobilize a ten ton truck) or reduced power (which can stun and immobilize a suspect). There is only one hand weapon: a gun that fires a soft rubber slug.

The helmet is Jesse's nerve center. There are digital readouts in each corner. The left computes speed and RPMs; the right calibrates distance. Directly below that is the monicle targeting system. The helmet is also equipped with infrared detectors and light amplification for all-weather and night fighting capabilities. Anything Jesse sees, Norman sees, and it is automatically recorded.

Norman, who calls Street Hawk "My Baby," dreams of having such a bike in every police garage in the country. Right now Street Hawk must remain a secret "because people won't take it kindly to have an attack motorcycle patrolling their streets. It is being tested to see if it can be offered to local law enforcement agencies."

Jesse is then given a special racing suit, and the bike is programed to accept him (unauthorized personnel receive an electric charge if they attempt to use it).

Jesse first uses Street Hawk to find the drug smugglers who crippled him. Jesse won his first motorcycle race at age 14; at age 18 he won his first international race. He quit the racing circuit to become a cop.

Other Regulars: Jeannie Wilson (*Rachel Adams*; she is Jesse's superior and head of the P.R. department; Jayne Modean played the original head, Sandy McCoy, in the pilot); Richard Venture (*Police Commander Leo Altobelli*).

Theme: "Street Hawk," by Tangerine Dream.

674. *Street Justice*

Syndicated, 9/24/91 to the present

Adam Beaudreaux (Carl Weathers) is independently wealthy and partners with a beautiful woman known only as Molloy (Charlene Fernetz) in Molloy's Bar. Adam is also a sergeant with the Metropolitan Police Department of a Pacific Northwest city identified only as being in the "Beautiful Evergreen State." Adam, a Vietnam vet, works as a cop "to meet people and keep the trash off the streets."

Adam, badge number 2230, lives at 2731 West Bond Street and works with Grady Jamieson (Bryan Genesse), Molloy's bartender and a martial arts instructor at Chan's Dojo School, who uses his skills to help collar criminals. Adam's car code is 2-Henry-17 (also given as Unit 217); his license plate reads ISV 508 (later MZG 735); he was with the Special Forces in Vietnam. Adam's office is in Room 107 at the police department (located at 540 Remity Street). Molloy's bar is located at 843 Third Street. QXB 483 is Molloy's license plate, and 83-7201 is Grady's motorcycle license plate number (he lives in a room in back of the bar).

Sean O'Byrne appeared as Molloy's brother, Danny Molloy, and Devon LaChance played young Grady in a flashback sequence.

Lawrence Shragge composed the "Street Justice" theme.

675. *Strike Force*

ABC, 11/13/81 to 5/28/82

Room 414 of the Los Angeles Police Department is the headquarters of Strike Force, a special unit that is designed to battle the violent crimes that are considered too dangerous for ordinary police officers to handle. Frank Murphy (Robert Stack) is its captain; his team: Detective Rosie Johnson (Trisha Noble), Lieutenant Charlie Gunzer (Richard Romanus), Detective Paul Strobber (Dorian Harewood) and Detective Mike Osborn (Michael Goodwin). Their superior is Herbert Klein (Herb Edelman), the deputy police commissioner.

The team goes undercover when necessary; they kill when they have to—"This is what we do." Code Green indicates to the police that a case has been resolved by Strike Force. When the police commissioner wants Strike Force, they're on it—"Do it, Frank, just do it." When there is no time to find a pattern and a strike has to be made, Strike Force is sent into action—the reason why it was formed.

Frank, who lives in a rather untidy house at 36 Crest Drive, has a dog named Sam and drives a car with the license plate 376-42F. He has two large pink flamingo decorations on his front lawn and lives for his work (he is now divorced after being married eight years "to a tyrant named Donna"; in later episodes, she is called Eve).

Rosie, the team's only female member, is a gorgeous cop who lives in an apartment at 136 Shore Drive. Her car license plate reads 641-3FF, and she can be reached by telephone at 555-6162. When the series first began, Rosie, who is rather "well-built" (measurements not given), was part of the era of "jiggle TV" and dressed to accentuate her bosom. As the series progressed, Rosie did less running and dressed in less revealing blouses (even her running sequences from the opening theme were replaced). Rosie was only in love once—"With a Mr. Right. But he was lost in action in some dumb rice paddy I can't even pronounce."

Paul, the team's only black member, is married and has two kids (not seen). Charlie, who makes the office coffee (which Rosie dislikes), lives in Apartment 42 at 1908 Harbor View Drive; his license plate reads 183HYE.

Joanna Cassidy appeared as Frank's ex-wife, Eve Murphy. Dominic Frontiere composed the theme, "Strike Force."

676. *Struck by Lightning*

CBS, 9/19/79 to 10/3/79

The Bridgewater Inn is a decrepit Victorian lodge located off Highway 14 in Massachusetts. Following the death of its owner, Emil Stein, his grandson, Ted Stein (Jeffrey Kramer), a high school science teacher in Boston, inherits the inn. Ted, who "didn't know my grandfather was alive until he was dead," has no use for the inn and decides to sell it.

Ted's decision angers Frank (Jack Elam), the rather strange looking handyman. When Frank's efforts to scare Ted out of selling the inn fail, he takes Ted to a secret lab beneath the inn. Frank tells Ted that his real last name is Frankenstein and that his great-great-grandfather, Gustav Frankenstein, made him—"I'm the monster. Now I'm your monster." Frank then tells Ted that he needs a special serum, developed by Gustav, every 50 years to stay alive: "If I don't get it, my cells begin to disintegrate and the muscle tissue begins to go. I was created out of the graveyard. I'm 27 different parts trying to make it as one person." Unfortunately, Frank tells Ted, the original formula is gone, as Gustav ate it (Why? "Why does a 93-year-old man go skiing naked? Half the time he thought I was a chicken"). The only way to save Frank, who is now 230 years old, is to try to recreate the formula from Gustav's lab notes—something Frank cannot do, even though Ted thinks he is bright and eager ("I could have been a lot brighter. You should have seen the brain I almost had—if only that butterfingers Igor hadn't dropped it"). Realizing that he is Frank's only means of survival, Ted decides to continue in the tradition of the Frankenstein name and help Frank. Stories relate their efforts to find the elusive formula.

Nora Clavin (Millie Slavin) is the manager of the inn; Walt Clavin (Richard Stahl) is Nora's husband, a real estate salesman; and Brian Clavin (Jeff Cotler) is their son.

Frank hates rainy nights ("I get struck by lightning. Whoever said lightning doesn't strike twice in the same place is nuts. I got struck three times just tonight"). Nora calls him "a lightning rod." Frank fears fire ("You would too if you were chased by 300 screaming peasants carrying torches"). Ted's only two vices are "good cigars and the Boston Celtics."

An uncredited version of the song "You Are So Beautiful" is the opening theme; "Keep It Alive," by Alan Brackett and Joey Stec, is the closing theme.

677. *Sugar and Spice*

CBS, 3/30/90 to 5/25/90

Vickilyn and Loretta (Vickilyn Reynolds and Loretta Devine) are sisters. They live at 731 Oakwood Avenue in Ponca City, California, with their niece, Toby (LaVerne Anderson), a recent orphan whose parents were killed in a car accident. Stories follow the sisters' efforts to raise Toby.

Vickilyn and her neighbor, Bonnie Buttram (Stephanie Hodge), run a curio shop called Small World Miniatures. Loretta, a former singer with the group The Chevells, now works as a hostess at Café Jacques. Bonnie is married to Cliff Buttram (Gerrit Graham), a truck driver with an 18-wheeler he calls "Jolene" (he calls Bonnie "Prairie Blossom" and "Cuddle Buns"). Bonnie is an Elvis fan and president of the Truckers' Wives Auxiliary; she calls Cliff "Bunny Lips."

Toby and her wisecracking friend, Ginger (Dana Hill), attend Edison High School; Ginger has a goldfish named Freddie.

Leslie Pearl, Paul Solovay and Susan Spiegel Solovay composed the "Sugar and Spice" theme.

678. *Sugarfoot*

ABC, 9/17/57 to 9/13/60

Sugarfoot is a Western term for "a cowboy who is working his way up to be a tenderfoot." Tom Brewster (Will Hutchins) is considered a sugarfoot. He is peaceful, laid-back, idealistic and romantic—and looked upon as a gullible coward by the roughneck cowboys. Despite their belief, Tom is skilled with his gun, his fists and a knife—"Once you get his dander up, ain't no one who's quicker on the draw."

Tom was born in Oklahoma. When he was a child he was inspired by Judge Henry Davis (Harry Holcombe) to become a lawyer (the judge made decisions to help change the country; deciding, for example, that the Indian is a person as defined by the Constitution). He was a man who personified the law to Tom. When the series begins, Tom is a law school correspondence student who roams the West of the 1870s. He signed up "for some of them correspondence courses from Kansas City" (he is up to lesson seven in the pilot and carries the law book *Blackstone's Commentary*, volume 9). Tom plans to hang up his shingle in a place that needs him and which he needs.

Tom calls guns "tools of the devil." He wears his father's gun and believes that "shootin' ain't always the answer." He drinks sarsaparilla ("with a touch of cherry") and carries a HOME, SWEET HOME plaque with him as he wanders from town to town "tryin' to earn a little livin' money." While Tom struggled to avoid gunplay (he wanted only to study his law books), trouble was all that he found—whether as the sheriff of Blue Rock (his first job in the pilot, "Brannigan's Boots"), a substitute teacher in the town of Morgan or the ramrod of a cattle drive. His knowledge of the law and strong sense of justice helped him overcome difficult situations when defending clients.

In the town of Casa Grande, Arizona, Tom meets Toothy Thompson (Jack Elam), "a man with a face people distrust." When Tom gets Toothy acquitted of an attempted murder charge, he finds himself with a new friend and occasional companion on the trail. (Toothy, described as "kinda spooky looking, always smilin'," was so grateful for what Tom had done for him that he made himself Tom's best friend.)

In the episode "MacBrewster the Bold," three of Tom's Scottish relatives appear: Douglas MacBrewster (Robin Hughes), Angus MacBrewster (Tudor Owen) and Wee Rabbie MacBrewster (Alan Caillou). Will Hutchins also played his outlaw double, the Canary Kid, in several episodes.

Ray Heindorf, Max Steiner and Paul Francis Webster composed the "Sugarfoot" theme.

Sugar Time! **Top to bottom: Didi Carr, Barbi Benton, Marianne Black.**

679. *Sugar Time!*

ABC, 8/13/77 to 9/3/77
ABC, 4/10/78 to 5/29/78

Maxx Douglas (Barbi Benton), Diane Zuckerman (Didi Carr) and Maggie Barton (Marianne Black) are three starry eyed singers who perform as the group Sugar at the Tryout Room nightclub in Los Angeles.

The girls share a small apartment at 363 Lindhaven Street. Maxx, who teaches classes at The Health Spa, also held jobs as a model, hat-check girl at a fancy restaurant ("They paid me to check hats and coats even though people in California don't wear hats and coats") and as a go-go dancer ("Even though I didn't wear much and it looked like I didn't have clothes on, in my heart I had clothes on"). Maxx, the prettiest girl in the group, is a bit dense and mentioned that she was born in Cleveland (she mentions Texas in another episode).

Diane is 23 years old and works as a dental assistant to her boyfriend, Dr. Paul Landson (Mark Winkworth). She was born in the Bronx (lived on Jerome Avenue), and chocolate cake is her favorite dessert. She has the least self-confidence of the girls and feels that she can't make it—"I got one that moves better than me [Maxx] and one that stands better than me [Maggie]."

Maggie, the most logical one of the group, teaches dancing to children at the Willow Dancing School. She formed the group and believes they can make it to the big time (she met Maxx at The Health Spa and Diane when she came to have her teeth cleaned; she talked both into joining the group).

The first song that the group sang at the Tryout Room was "Goodbye, Eddie." Diane stands in the center; Maggie is on the left (of the screen) and Maxx on the right. Charles Fleischer plays Lightning Jack Rappaport, a struggling comedian at the Tryout Room, and Wynn Irwin is Al Marks, the club owner.

Barbi Benton, Didi Carr and Marianne Black sing the theme, "Girls, Girls, Girls."

680. *Sunday Dinner*

CBS, 6/2/91 to 7/7/91

Every Sunday evening in a house in Great Neck, Long Island, the Benedict family gathers for "great" family conversation and a dinner that is served at five o'clock sharp. Problem is, there is more arguing than conversation (or dinner), as the family members are always at odds with one another. When the audience is first permitted to attend dinner, they are introduced to the series' premise: a 56-year-old man (Ben) plans to marry a girl 26 years his junior (T.T.).

Benjamin ("Ben") Benedict (Robert Loggia) is the 56-year-old, a widowed father of three (Vicky, Diana and Kenneth) who lives with his sister, Martha Benedict (Marian Mercer), who prepares the Sunday dinners. Ben, whose late wife was named Jean, owns the Benedict Printing Company. He has been a widower for four years, and his favorite movie is *Animal Crackers,* with the Marx Brothers.

T.T. (Thelma Todd) Fagori (Teri Hatcher) is a beautiful 30-year-old environmental lawyer Ben met and fell in love with while on an assignment in Africa six months ago. T.T. believes she has a direct line to God, whom she calls "Chief" (when she is alone, she looks up and confides in Him — "Chief, have you got a minute?..."). T.T. does her best thinking in the bathtub. (In the last episode, T.T. set the wedding date for May 18, 1992.)

Victoria ("Vicky") Benedict (Martha Gehman) is Ben's oldest child (age 32). She has been married and divorced twice and is the mother of a 12-year-old girl named Rachel (Shiri Appleby). Vicky is a microbiologist and most opposed to her father's marriage plans. She is an atheist and also opposed to T.T. for her belief in God. Rachel attends public school and is living with Ben until her mother finishes her doctorate in microbiology. Vicky knows she is not as pretty as T.T. or her younger sister, Diana, and takes great pride in Rachel — "If one of us had to be beautiful," Vicky says, "I'm glad it was you, Rachel."

Diana Benedict (Kari Lizer) is Ben's 30-year-old daughter. She works as a fashion designer (of shoes and handbags) and is a bit of a flake. She sampled New Age religion as a way of finding herself; at age 16 she wanted to be a nun.

When she was 19, she fell in love with a rabbi. Diana then went to Murray the Mystic for a year. She has a guru and "has her aura changed once in a while." When she has to take aspirins, she drinks the water first, then takes the tablets ("I can't do it the other way"). Diana, who says, "I once had an out-of-body experience and couldn't get back in," is also opposed to Ben's marriage.

Kenneth Benedict (Patrick Breen) is Ben's 20-year-old son. He is an idea man with wild schemes he expects his father to finance. He is for his father's marriage and has a dog named Ivan Boesky.

Theme: "Love Begins at Home," vocal by Kim Carnes.

Note: An earlier series, originally titled "The Sunday Dinner" but changed to "The Montefuscos" (NBC, 9/4/75 to 10/23/75), dealt with a large Italian-American family that gathers every Sunday for dinner and conversation. The principals of the very large cast were Joseph Sirola and Naomi Stevens as the parents (Tony and Rose Montefusco), Ron Carey (their son, Frankie), John Aprea (their son, Joseph), Linda Dano (their married daughter, Angelina) and Sal Viscuso (their son, Nunzio).

681. *Sunset Beat*

ABC, 4/21/90 to 4/28/90

The abandoned firehouse on Sunset Boulevard in Los Angeles (the L.A. Hose Company) is the secret headquarters of a special unit of L.A.P.D. undercover cops who pose as rugged bikers. Their favorite eatery is Tail o' the Pup, and they ride Harley Davidson motorcycles.

Officer Chic Chesbro (George Clooney) has the code X-Ray 4309 and plays guitar in a band called Private Prayer. Officer Tim Kelly (Michael DeLuise) is a medical school dropout who is hiding the fact that he is a cop from his parents. Officer Bradley Coolidge (Markus Flanagan) teaches at Selmar City College in his spare time. Officer Tucson Smith (Erik King) landed a part in the adult film *Hot Coed Fever* when he went undercover to bust a porno producer. Captain Ray Parker (James Tolkan) is their superior.

Arlene Golonka played Ray's ex-wife, Harriet; Sydney Walsh was Chris's ex-wife, Holly; and Mark Hembrow and Kathy Karges appeared as Tim's father and mother.

The theme, "Sunset Beat," was composed by Clink Productions.

Superboy see *The Adventures of Superboy*

Superman see *The Adventures of Superman*

682. *Super Force*

Syndicated, 9/26/90 to 9/12/92

Cast: Ken Olandt (*Zack Stone*), Patrick Macnee (*E.B. Hungerford*), Larry B. Scott (*F.X. Spinner*), Lisa Niemi (*Carla Frost*), Musetta Vander (*Zander Tyler*).

Facts: It is the year 2020. The NASA spacecraft *Columbus* is returning to Earth after a two year mission to explore the planet Mars, when it is damaged by a meteor shower. To save the life of his crew, Commander Zachary ("Zack") Stone risks his life to jerry-rig the craft's drive shaft. The *Columbus* lands safely, and Zack is honored as a hero, "the man who risked his life to save his crew and the space program."

Shortly after, Zack learns that during his absence, his father has died and that his police officer brother, Frank Stone, has been killed in the line of duty. When he learns that Frank was believed to be on the take at the time, he joins the police force in an attempt to clear his name.

Zack graduates from the Metro Plex Police Academy in the summer of 2020. At this same time, Zack's adoptive uncle, E.B. Hungerford, the owner of Hungerford Industries, is shot. When Zack realizes that E.B. is not at his graduation ceremony, he leaves to find him. At the company lab, Zack befriends F.X. Spinner, the scientific genius E.B. employs. Together they search for and find E.B. in the parking lot garage. Although E.B. is dead, F.X. keeps him "alive" by programming his personality, achievements and voice patterns into a computer. E.B.'s image now appears on a computer screen and can function mentally as if he were actually alive (Zack later discovers that E.B. was shot by the same people who killed Frank—criminals who were programming young people to become violent on a moment's notice).

To help Zack battle crime, F.X. equips him with a variation on a space suit he was developing for Zack's next flight to Mars: a superstrong suit (black) equipped with the latest technology in weapons and tracking (his helmet, for example, shows weapons, range, charge and mode). Zack's secret identity as Super Force becomes known only to them (Zack rides a futuristic motorcycle, black with a green stripe).

Zack is assigned to the 33rd Division of the Metropolitan Police Department, a precinct whose main beat is the Crime Zone, the city's most notorious crime area; his badge number is 499. F.X., who shops at the Food Plex, has the Hungerford Industries I.D. number 36502007; as a kid, he was called "Cuddles." Captain Carla Frost is Zack's gorgeous, gutsy, no-nonsense superior at the police department. Zander Tyler is E.B.'s friend, an officer with the Esper (E.S.P.) Division of the police department. When a malfunction in Zack's Super Force helmet "kills" him, Zander uses her powers to go inside Zack's mind and bring him back from the dead (E.B. kept Zack alive via a neuro link until Zander was able to complete her mission). The experience gave Zack new powers: the ability to see something before it happens and the ability to sense danger. His strength has also increased (to that of 4.2 men), and he has heightened perception.

Addresses and phone numbers are not given. While license plates are seen, they are unreadable (all plates have bar codes—like those that appear on magazines for computer price scanning). Two former adult film actresses, Traci Lords and Ginger Lynn, appeared on the show: Traci, in the episode "Of Human Bondage" (wherein she played an unnamed alien seeking human specimens for a zoo); and Ginger, as Zack's girlfriend, Crystal, in "Come Under the Way," "There Is a Light," "Instant Karma" and "The Big Spin." Crystal's birthday was given as 12/14/95; Zack's birthday is 7/10/92.

Relatives: Marshall Teague (Zack's brother, *Frank Stone*), rap music stars Doctor Dre, Yo!, Mail Man and Brian Perry (F.X.'s cousins, *Otis Spinner, L.G. Spinner* and *R.X. Spinner*).

Theme: "Super Force," by Kevin Kiner.

683. *SurfSide 6*

ABC, 10/3/60 to 9/24/62

SurfSide 6 is the address of a houseboat moored on Indian Creek in Miami Beach, Florida. David ("Dave") Thorne (Lee Patterson), Kenneth ("Ken") Madison (Van Williams) and Sandor ("Sandy") Winfield (Troy Donahue) are its residents, three handsome young private detectives who operate an investigative service called the SurfSide 6 Agency. Dave is a former prosecutor from New York, Ken is a recent law school graduate (from Tulane University; the character first appeared on "Bourbon Street Beat"), and Sandy is a wealthy jet-setter. Each of the bachelors possesses a unique talent, which they pool to solve crimes.

Daphne ("Daphe") DeWitt Dutton (Diane McBain) is "the girl in the yacht next door" (at SurfSide 8), a beautiful jet-setter who is heir to Dutton Farms and the Dutton Racing Stables (she has a horse named Par-a-kee, which she raised from a colt). She also helps the guys when needed (for example, posing as a lingerie model when Sandy had to investigate a corrupt agency).

On Ocean Avenue is the famed Fontainebleau Hotel. Cha Cha O'Brien (Margarita Sierra) sings and dances (to the Latin beat) in the hotel's Boom Boom Room. (Cha Cha was born in Madrid, Spain, and has been singing and dancing since she was four years old).

Gene Plehn (Richard Crane) and Ray Snedigar (Donald Barry) are lieutenants with the Miami Police Department, Homicide Division; Mousie (Mousie Garner) is the Boom Boom Room waiter and SurfSide 6 information man.

Relatives: Raymond Bailey (Daphne's father, *Reginald Dutton*), Malachy McCourt (Cha Cha's cousin, *Dan O'Brien*), Mario Roccuzzo (Cha Cha's nephew, *Raphael*).

Theme: "SurfSide 6," by Mack David and Jerry Livingston.

684. *Suzanne Pleshette Is Maggie Briggs*

CBS, 3/4/84 to 4/15/84

Maggie Briggs (Suzanne Pleshette) is a hard news reporter for the City Side section of the New York *Examiner,* a daily newspaper that is in financial difficulty. Maggie attended Saint Barbara's High School. She is pretty, has street knowledge and valuable snitches. She covered fires, strikes, shootings and murders. After 15 years at the same desk in the same office, Maggie is reassigned to the feature department's *Modern Living* magazine in an attempt to breathe some life into the section and, it is hoped, improve circulation. After a succession of goodbyes, Maggie packs her office belongings and moves to her new job—a desk two away from her former desk.

The *Modern Living* magazine covers items like fashion, cooking and television reviews. Geoff Bennett (John Getz) heads the department; Walter Holden (Kenneth McMillan), Maggie's former editor ("I saw my first dead body with Walter," Maggie says) now edits *Modern Living*; Melanie Bitterman (Alison LaPlaca) is the fashion editor; Donny Bauer (Roger Bowen) is the religion editor; Leo Broadwater (Edward Edwards) reviews television shows; and Sherman Milslagle (Stephen Lee) is the food critic.

Connie Piscipoli (Shera Danese) is Maggie's friend, a lingerie model who designs clothes on the side. She has been Maggie's friend since the sixth grade and won't read the *Examiner*: "The ink comes off on my hands—can't you do something about that?" The bar hangout is the Pleez All Tavern, which is next door to the paper.

When her last boyfriend broke off their relationship, Maggie wore his cologne, "Lug Nut," for two years afterwards; Geoff was suspended from his junior year in college for cheating on his ethics exam; Maggie first became interested in journalism when a reporter named Walter Holden spoke at her school on career day.

Patrick Williams composed the "Maggie Briggs" theme.

685. *Swamp Thing*

USA, 8/17/90 to the present

Cast: Dick Durock *(Swamp Thing),* Mark Lindsay Chapman *(Dr. Arcane),* Carrell Myers *(Tressa Kipp),* Jesse Zeigler *(Jim Kipp),* Scott Garrison *(Will Kipp),* Kari Wuhrer *(Abigail).*

Facts: "The swamp is my world. It is where I am, it is what I am. I was once a man, I know the evil men do. Do not bring your evil here. I warn you—beware the wrath of Swamp Thing." The town of Huma, Georgia, is the setting. Dr. Alec Holland (Lonnie Smith), is a scientist who has been experimenting with a formula to arrest the aging process he calls the Restorative Formula (it permeates the

cellular structure, changing the DNA and rejuvenating the body's cells at such a vastly accelerated rate that, theoretically, no one will ever grow old). Dr. Anton Arcane is an evil scientist who has been experimenting with biogenetics in an attempt to bring his dead wife, Tatania (Heather Thomas), back to life through biogenetic transformation (Tatania died ten years ago and is now preserved in a glass coffin).

When Arcane learns about Alec's formula, he attempts to buy it from him; Alec refuses to sell it. One night Arcane breaks into Alec's lab to steal the formula. Alec, accompanied by his wife, Linda (Martha Smith), decides to go to the lab to finish an experiment. They encounter Arcane and his henchmen. A fight ensues between Alec and the henchmen (Anton is holding Linda). During the struggle, a fire starts and Alec is dowsed with the Restorative Formula. The formula ignites and sets Alec on fire. To save himself, Alec jumps into the swamp just outside the lab. As Arcane takes Linda to safety, the lab explodes and Alec is believed to have perished in the flames. Alec does not die, however; the swamp water reacts with the chemicals and turns Alec into a mutant plant and man called Swamp Thing. Stories relate Swamp Thing's efforts to stop Arcane from experimenting with biogenetics and creating hideous creatures called "Unmen" as he attempts to bring his wife back to life.

Alec and Linda were married on August 8; Linda called him "Einstein," and her maiden name was Mason. Sunlight provides Swamp Thing's strength (without it he will die). While Arcane seeks to kill Swamp Thing, Alec will not kill him ("To kill you is to become you"). Swamp Thing uses his plant power to turn his enemies into trees.

Tressa Kipp runs the Kipp Boat Rentals and Swamp Tours in Huma; Jim Kipp is Tressa's son and Swamp Thing's friend; Will Kipp is Tressa's stepson and aide to Swamp Thing; Abigail is one of Arcane's test tube creatures who was not mutated. She is beautiful, has special powers and now helps Swamp Thing. Patricia Helwick appeared as Tressa's mother, Savannah Langford.

Theme: "Swamp Thing," by Christopher L. Stone.

Note: An animated version, titled "Swamp Thing," appeared on Fox (4/20/91 to 5/18/91). The Louisiana swamplands are the background. Voices are Len Carlson (Swamp Thing), Don Francks (Anton Arcane), and Pauline Gillis (Abigail Arcane). Here, Dr. Alec Holland was experimenting with a growth formula to find a cure for world hunger. When Dr. Arcane learns of Alec's formula, he seeks it for the power it will give him. During Arcane's attempt to steal the formula, Alec is dowsed with the unstable Growth Formula and set on fire when it explodes. He escapes by jumping into the swamp. The swamp water reacts with the chemicals, and he becomes Swamp Thing. Stories relate Swamp Thing's efforts to protect the environment from Arcane as he ravages it to conduct his experiments. In this version, Abigail is Anton's niece; unknown to Arcane, she was Alec's friend and now possesses the vital diary Arcane needs to duplicate the Growth Formula (Alec gave it to her for safekeeping).

Both series are based on the *Swamp Thing* comic books, but most people readily associate it with the feature film *Swamp Thing* (the same basic format as the animated version, with the evil Arcane [Louis Jourdan] seeking the Growth Formula to become all-powerful. Dick Durock is Swamp Thing and Adrienne Barbeau is Alice Cable, the beautiful government agent Arcane uses to lure Swamp Thing out of the swamps. Alice became Abigail in both series; Linda was Alec's sister, not wife, in the film).

686. *Sweating Bullets*

CBS, 4/8/91 to the present

Cast: Rob Stewart *(Nick Slaughter)*, Carolyn Dunn *(Sylvie Girard)*, John David Bland *(Ian Stewart)*.

Facts: Nick Slaughter is the only private investigator on Key Mariah, in southern Florida. Sylvie Girard is a consultant for an exclusive travel agency. When a yacht left in her care disappears, Sylvie has no choice but to hire Nick to find the yacht and save her job. They solve the case (the yacht was being used by drug smugglers) and remain a team (Sylvie becomes his manager) when she is fired ("We don't want a yacht saboteur in our employ").

Nick was formerly a D.E.A. (Drug Enforcement Agency) cop stationed in Miami. Nick first said he was "laid off because they ran out of bad guys." In another episode he said he "got tired of seeing them railroad innocent people so some prosecutor could have an impressive record. When I tried to do something about it, I got fired." And, in still another episode he says, "I believed the suspect was being set up for something she didn't do. They had the frame so tight I couldn't break it. So I helped her get out of the country and was fired." He then became a P.I. (his shingle reads NICK SLAUGHTER — PRIVATE INVESTIGATOR). His office is in a building with the number 45; he charges $250 a day plus expenses; and his Jeep license plate reads NIR-548 (in the pilot, the plate reads B7N-N57). Nick was a cop for five years; he attended Lakeside High School and loves creole food.

Sylvie appointed herself as Nick's partner to organize and turn his pathetic life around. She receives 25 percent of what Nick makes each month and hates the "R" word (relationship). Her biggest challenge is to pay off Nick's huge I.R.S. bill and still keep their heads above water (Nick neglected to pay income tax for eight years and was caught). Sylvie doesn't trust Nick with sharp weapons and beautiful women. Nick calls her "the brains of the outfit"; her license plate reads J8E-731. In 1985 Sylvie was a contestant in the Miss Brick and Mortar Pageant (as a favor for her father, who owned a brick-laying company and needed a contestant).

Nick's friend, Ian Stewart, is a former rock star who now runs the Tropical Heat Bar on Key Mariah. Ollie Porter (Eugene Clark) is a sergeant with the Key Mariah P.D.

Theme: "Any Way the Wind Blows," by Fred and Larry Mollin.

687. *Sweet Surrender*

NBC, 4/18/87 to 5/16/87
NBC, 7/8/87 (1 episode)

Georgia (Dana Delany) and Ken Holden (Mark Blum) are a happily married couple who live at 1345 Bayridge Avenue in Philadelphia. Ken is an architect and works for the firm of Henderson and Associates; Georgia relinquished her career (type not mentioned) to marry and raise a family. Seven years later, they have two children, six-year-old Bartley ("Bart") Holden (Edan Gross) and one-year-old Lynnie (Rebecca and Sarah Simms), and a dog named Yoda. Although Georgia gave up her career, she loves being a housewife and mother—"I love being there when Bart comes home from school (an unnamed kindergarten) and being there when Lynnie wakes up from her nap." Georgia calls Bart "Lima Bean," "Pumpkin" and "Angel."

CAK (Catherine Antoinette Krowder) (Viveka Davis) is Georgia's baby-sitter; Francis (David Doyle) is Georgia's father; Joyce (Marjorie Lord and Jo de Winter) is Ken's mother.

Ray Colcord composed the theme.

688. *Switch*

CBS, 9/9/75 to 9/3/78

"They're the last hope you have. If they can't prove your innocence, no one can." They're Frank MacBride and Pete Ryan, private investigators who use cons to beat swindlers at their own game.

Frank ("Mac") MacBride (Eddie Albert) was a cop with the Central Division of the L.A.P.D. Twenty of his 25 years on the force were spent in the bunco division where he made an impressive number of arrests by posing as a mark and nabbing the country's most wanted felons.

Peterson ("Pete") T. Ryan (Robert Wagner) was, as Mac says, "The best con man I ever tried to catch." It was a battle of wits for ten years before Mac finally nabbed him (his shortcoming, Mac says, is that Pete always underestimates the police).

Mac retired from the force at just about the same time Pete was being released from serving a two year sentence at San Quentin. They decided to pool their talents and formed a private detective organization called MacBride-Ryan Investigations (also called the Ryan-MacBride Private Detective Organization), which is located at 1019 Florida Street in Los Angeles.

"I don't know why I just don't quit this screwy job," exclaims Maggie Philbin (Sharon Gless), the agency's pretty but naive secretary. Maggie took the job with a hope of learning the business and starting her own detective agency. Mac and Pete see her as their girl Friday and use her any way they can to assist in a con.

Ali McGinnis (Jaclyn Smith), who Pete says "can talk the

Switch. Eddie Albert, Robert Wagner, and Sharon Gless.

curves off a hockey puck," is a stunning brunette Pete uses to run interference during a con. Ali, a con artist herself, uses her beauty to accomplish her goals.

Malcolm Argos (Charlie Callas) is a friend of Pete's who runs the Bouziki Bar (the hangout). He too has a genius for the con and helps Mac and Pete when necessary. Revel (Mindi Miller) is the sexy waitress at the bar.

Jails still make Pete nervous. Pete's car license plate is 191 OJB; Mac's license plate reads 1409B; Maggie lives at 46710 Hillcrest Drive; and the agency phone number is 213-555-1678.

Glen A. Larson composed the "Switch" theme.

689. *Sword of Justice*

NBC, 9/10/78 to 12/31/78

Jack Martin Cole (Dack Rambo), vice president of Cole Industries, is framed and accused of embezzling $2.5

million from his late father's company. Innocent, but unable to prove it, Jack is found guilty of 25 counts of violating the federal penal code and sentenced to five years at the Louisiana Federal Penitentiary.

Bitter at the wrong done to him, Jack decides to get even and find the man responsible for framing him. With the help of his cellmate, Hector Ramirez (Bert Rosario), Jack is taught the tricks of the criminal trade: burglar alarms, precision acrobatics, second story work, electronic bugging and lock picking.

After three years, Jack is released for good behavior (as is Hector). With Hector's help, Jack finds the man responsible for framing him (Larry Hagman as Frank Blaine). Now, operating as a team, Jack and Hector anonymously fight crime by helping the authorities get the goods on white collar criminals.

In prison Jack was called the "Park Avenue Kid" and had the I.D. number 193325. Hector, who had the I.D. number 13344, was sentenced for three and a half years for stealing a car (he stole a car to see his girlfriend in a hospital and was arrested for transporting stolen goods across state lines).

Jack, who lives off a trust fund set up by his mother, resides at 636 Park Avenue, Apartment 6F, in Manhattan; he poses as a New York playboy as a cover for his crime fighting activities. Jack helps Arthur Woods (Alex Courtney), a former attorney who is now an agent with the Federal Task Force. Jack's trademark is the three of spades playing card. The three represents the time he served in prison, the spade indicates that his task has been completed (the back of the card is inscribed with these words: "The spade is the Sword of Justice. Its rapier marks the end").

June Lockhart appeared as Jack's mother, Mrs. Cole. John Andrew Tartaglia composed the "Sword of Justice" theme.

690. *Sydney*

CBS, 3/21/90 to 8/6/90

Cast: Valerie Bertinelli *(Sydney Kells)*, Rebeccah Bush *(Jill)*, Craig Bierko *(Matt Keating)*, Matthew Perry *(Billy Kells)*, Barney Martin *(Ray O'Shaughnessey)*.

Facts: Sydney Kells lives at 1144 Oliphant Street in Los Angeles. She is a beautiful 25-year-old single girl who works as an investigator for the law firm of Fenton, Benton and Sloane in Century City. Sydney has brown eyes and brown hair, is five feet five inches tall and weighs 110 pounds. Her right thumbprint appears on the right side of her private investigator's license (number M83456).

Sydney is a sloppy housekeeper and has a cat named Calvin. Hershey Bars with almonds on white bread is her favorite sandwich, and chocolate milk is her favorite drink. About the only nutritional meal she has is when she has dinner with her mother on Thursday nights. The Blue Collar Bar is her favorite hangout, and she first cried when Dick Sargent replaced Dick York on "Bewitched." In the episode of 4/25/90 ("Georgie"), Valerie was reunited with her former "One Day at a Time" co-star, Pat Harrington, Jr., in a story that found Sydney working with a 1940s-style private eye named Georgie Garrity. The Los Angeles *Times* printed a story on Sydney called "A Week in the Life of Sydney Kells."

Sydney's friend, Jill, is a model for Contemporary Fashions. At age 12, she shared her first secret with Sydney—that Mighty Mouse was her hero. Jill likes to lounge around in a bathrobe and wear a lacy push-up bra under her pajama tops.

Billy Kells is Sydney's brother, a police officer with the L.A.P.D. (his favorite candy is Lemon Heads); Matt Keating is Sydney's boss; and Ray O'Shaughnessey owns the Blue Collar Bar.

Georgia Brown appeared as Sydney's mother, Linda Kells, and Jane Milmore was Matt's girlfriend, Claire (who believes Sydney is "a fat, middleaged bald man").

Valerie Bertinelli selected the theme, "Finish What Ya Started," by Eddie Van Halen (her husband).

Tabitha see *Bewitched*

691. *Tales of the Gold Monkey*

ABC, 9/22/82 to 7/21/83

The setting is the South Pacific island of Bora Gora in 1938. Jake Cutter (Stephen Collins) is a cargo pilot based on the French-owned island. He has a one-eyed dog named Jack and a sea plane he calls *Cutter's Goose* (a.k.a. the *Grumman Goose*). Jake, who suffers from bouts of malaria, is assisted by Corky (Jeff MacKay), a former alcoholic who now works as Jake's mechanic and assistant. Corky was the chief mechanic for Pan Pacific Airlines and was a top notch mechanic who was fired for drinking. Jake won't let Corky touch any hard liquor—only beer, and he restricts that. Two barks from Jack means yes when he is asked something. Corky is always joking—even in tight situations—and never loses his sense of humor.

Bon Chance Louie (Ron Moody and Roddy McDowall) is the magistrate of justice and the owner of the Monkey Bar and Hotel. Sarah Stickney-White (Caitlin O'Heaney) is an American spy who poses as a singer at the Monkey Bar. She is the daughter of an archaeologist and an expert shot ("I never miss"). Princess Kogi (Marta DuBois) is the evil Eurasian seeking the Gold Monkey (an idol that is supposedly worth a fortune and said to be guarded by giant monkeys). She is based on the Japanese island of Matuka.

Mike Post and Pete Carpenter composed "The Tales of the Gold Monkey Theme."

692. *Tales of Wells Fargo*

NBC, 3/18/57 to 9/8/62

The series is set in the town of Gloribee (near San Francisco) during the 1860s, where the gold transporting company, Wells Fargo, Inc., has established a base. James ("Jim") Whitcomb Hardie (Dale Robertson) is its chief agent and troubleshooter who risks his life to protect gold shipments from outlaws. Shipments are made via Wells Fargo stages; the Overland Stage Lines and the Denver and Rio Grande Railroad service the area.

Jim also owns the Haymaker Farm, a cattle ranch near Salt Canyon. Jebediah ("Jeb") Ganes (William Demarest) is Jim's foreman; Beau McCloud (Jack Ging) is Jim's assistant; and the Widow Ovie (Virginia Christine) is Jim's neighbor. The Widow Ovie's two daughters, Tina (Lory Patrick) and Mary Gee Ovie (Mary Jane Saunders), buy their clothes at the Dress Shop in Gloribee. Mary Gee, the younger sister, has a crush on Jim and riles Jeb by using the ranch as a riding stable. Jeb's prize palomino is named Snowball. Hal Humphrey (Steve Darrell) is the town's sheriff. The pilot episode, "A Tale of Wells Fargo," aired on "The Schlitz Playhouse of Stars" on 12/14/56.

Harry Warren composed the theme, "Tales of Wells Fargo."

693. *Tammy*

ABC, 9/17/65 to 7/15/66

Tambry ("Tammy") Tarleton (Debbie Watson) is a pretty bayou girl who lives with her grandfather, Mordecai Tarleton (Denver Pyle), and her uncle, Lucius Tarleton (Frank McGrath), on the *Ellen B,* a riverboat that is moored on the Louisiana shore in Ducheau County. Tammy is a very sweet and trusting girl. She is 18 years old and was raised by her grandfather, "with a little help from her Uncle Lucius," after the death of her parents when she was just a child. Tammy possesses enthusiasm and the ability to overcome adverse situations through her philosophy of love and understanding. The Tarletons are a poor family, and "if we don't have anything else," Grandpa says, "we have self-respect." Tammy is an excellent cook and famous for her "river vittles" (for example, hog liver soup, poke weed salad, stuffed catfish and mustard greens). Delilah is the Tarletons' dog; Beulah is their cow; and Nan is Tammy's pet goat.

When the series begins, Tammy is seen returning from secretarial school (she previously completed special courses at nearby Seminole College) and applying for a position as the personal secretary to John Brent (Donald Woods), a wealthy widower who owns Brent Enterprises (which he runs from his home at Brentwood Hall). Tammy's ability to type 200 words a minute causes friction when she is offered the job over another applicant, Gloria Tate (Linda Marshall). Gloria's mother, Lavinia (Dorothy Green), had hoped that Gloria would get the job and thus increase her own chances of marrying Gloria's new boss. Lavinia's efforts to discredit Tammy (in the hope of getting her fired) is a recurring aspect of the series. Tammy also has an amazing ability to add (she can do it faster than an adding machine: "It sort of comes naturally to me — like smelling to a skunk."

The Tates are a wealthy high society family. Lavinia is divorced and has made it her goal to marry John Brent. She has a prized dog named King Alfonse of Normandy and despises Tammy's "sweetness" and her language, which she calls "river talk." When Tammy causes a setback in Lavinia's plans, it is typical for Lavinia to say, "I'm sick and tired of that water nymph pushing me into the backwoods with Mr. Brent," and then devise a plan to get Tammy fired. Gloria looks up to her mother ("You're so devious, cunning and underhanded; I'm so proud of you") and wants to follow in her footsteps. While Lavinia has Tammy to contend with, Gloria has the unwanted romantic attentions of Tammy's cousin, Cletus Tarleton (Dennis Robertson). Cletus has made it his goal to convince Gloria that he is the man for her. He serenades her, calls her "my darlin'" and "wants a kiss from her ruby lips." Gloria calls Cletus "an oaf" and "a bumpkin" (the "term of endearment" he prefers). The series is based on the novels *Tammy Out of Time* and *Tammy Tell Me True,* by Cid Ricketts Sumner; the books were also made into the 1957 movie *Tammy and the Bachelor,* with Debbie Reynolds as Tammy.

Relatives: Jeanette Nolan (Tammy's aunt, *Hannah*), Jay Sheffield (John's son, *Steven Brent*), Doris Packer (John's Mother *Brent*), David Macklin (Lavinia's son, *Peter Brent*), Sal Ponti (Lavinia's cousin, *Beauregard Bassett*), Jeff York (Lavinia's cousin, *Grundy Tate*), Bella Bruck (Grundy's wife, *Sybelline Tate*).

Theme: "Tammy," by Jay Livingston and Ray Evans.

694. *The Tammy Grimes Show*

ABC, 9/8/66 to 9/29/66

Tamantha ("Tammy") Ward (Tammy Grimes) is young, beautiful and single. She is an heiress, but cannot collect her multimillion dollar inheritance until she reaches the age of 30 — a condition of her late parents' will that her guardian, her uncle, Simon Grimsley (Hiram Sherman), strictly enforces. Stories follow Tammy's misadventures as she devises elaborate schemes to finance her expensive tastes.

Tammy lives at 365 Central Park West in New York City (476-7671 is her phone number). She works for her Uncle Simon, the president of Perpetual Savings Bank ("The Bank with a Heart") as its customer service relations officer. Tammy's twin brother, Terence Ward (Dick Sargent), is a bank vice president and lives at 51 Gramercy Place. While Tammy is wild and extravagant, Terence is laid back and stingy and opposed to the way Tammy schemes to get money. Only four of ten produced episodes aired.

Johnny Williams composed "The Theme from the Tammy Grimes Show."

695. *Tarzan*

Syndicated, 9/28/91 to 9/12/92

A plane, carrying a family of three, crashes in the African jungle. The lone survivor, a young boy, is found by Kala, the great ape, and raised as Tarzan, Lord of the Jungle. The series is set many years later when Tarzan is an adult. Tarzan (Wolf Larson) and his companion, Cheetah the chimp, live in a treehouse by the Great River; their struggle to protect the animals in their jungle paradise from environmental wrongdoers is the focal point of this adaptation of the Edgar Rice Burroughs character.

Jane Porter (Lydie Denier) is a beautiful French research scientist who maintains a compound near Tarzan's home. She works for the Wildlife Institute to save endangered species. She is assisted by Roger Taft (Sean Roberge), the son of Roger Taft, Sr. (Chuck Shamota), the man who funds Jane's research. Simon Gaubier (Malick Bowens), a native African, looks out for both of them.

Prior to Cheetah, Tarzan's chimp was Maya; Juma is Tarzan's lion and Tantor his elephant. XADAC is the I.D. on Simon's plane. Details are not related as to how Tarzan learned to speak English or how he met Jane (in the episode of 12/14/91, "Tarzan's Christmas," Jane mentions that she has been in Africa for one year).

Tammy. **Left to right: Frank McGrath, Denver Pyle and Debbie Watson.**

Marsha Pare appeared as Jane's cousin, Patrice Porter. Robert O. Ragland composed the "Tarzan" theme.

An earlier "Tarzan" series aired on NBC (9/8/66 to 9/13/68), with Ron Ely as Tarzan (there was no Jane in this version). Ron Ely made a guest appearance on the above "Tarzan" series as Gordon Shaw in the episode of 11/2/91 ("Tarzan the Hunted"). In it, Shaw was a hunter who sought human prey—Tarzan.

696. *Tate*

NBC, 6/8/60 to 9/28/60

He is known only as Tate (David McLean). During the Battle of Vicksburg in May 1863, his left arm was smashed ("I didn't run fast enough"), and it is now preserved in a black leather casing. The Civil War toughened him ("He's ugly as ever and twice as mean looking"); he is now a gunfighter who wanders from town to town siding with justice against criminal elements. Despite his handicap, he is lightning fast "and can shoot five times without reloading."

Tate was a hard nosed kid. He was born in Kansas City and had the nickname "Curley" ("You're too ugly to be called that now," folks say). His one and only love was a girl named Mary Ellen (not seen; she is mentioned as having died in the 1850s when Tate was a young man). When Tate returned to his hometown and ate at the Kansas City Steak House, pie was six cents a slice, coffee ten cents a cup and a sandwich 12 cents.

Irving Friedman composed the theme.

697. *Taxi*

ABC, 9/12/78 to 6/10/82
NBC, 9/30/82 to 7/13/83

Cast: Judd Hirsch (*Alex Reiger*), Marilu Henner (*Elaine Nardo*), Tony Danza (*Tony Banta*), Danny DeVito (*Louie DePalma*), Christopher Lloyd (*Jim Ignatowski*), Jeff Conaway (*Bobby Wheeler*), Andy Kaufman (*Latka Gravas*), Carol Kane (*Simka Gravas*).

Facts: The Sunshine Cab Company is a Manhattan-based taxi service in New York City. Rates are 75 cents for the first mile and ten cents for each additional tenth of a mile (later 90 cents, then one dollar for each mile; 15 cents for each additional mile; 555-6328 is the company's phone number). The cabs are washed at Cars-a-Poppin' (located at 23rd Street between 5th and 6th avenues), and a notice is posted in the garage: DAYLINE DRIVERS MUST REPORT OR PHONE IN BY 6 A.M. NIGHTLINE DRIVERS MUST REPORT OR PHONE IN BY 3 P.M. Cab 804, driven by virtually every cabbie, holds the record of one-half million miles; Cab 413 is known as "the Widow Maker," and Cab 704 as "the Memory Cab." According to Louie DePalma, the nasty dispatcher (whose office is called "the cage"), all his drivers are losers, people who will never amount to anything. The only cabbie to make it out without returning was James Caan—"But he'll be back. They all come back." The cabbies' hangout is Mario's (a bar-restaurant). The vending machine in the garage dispenses hot coffee, chocolate or soup for 25 cents.

Louie, who lives for his job at the company, has been working there for 15 years—first as a driver, then as a dispatcher. With regard to his cabbies, only three things will make him happy: "Keep bookings high, call 24 hours in advance if you can't work and never, never, but never say the word *accident*." Louie, who worships money, is lecherous and mean. He considers himself a ladies' man and will pursue any woman he thinks is worthy of him. He had a brief romance with Zina Sherman (Rhea Perlman), the candy vending-machine delivery girl.

Alex Reiger, the oldest of the cabbies and the one the others turn to for help and advice, lives in Apartment 2A (address not given) and has a dog named Buddy. Alex best describes Louie: "If God had a reason for creating snakes, lice and vermin, He had a reason for creating Louie."

Elaine Nardo, the divorced mother of two children (Jennifer and Jason), works part time as a cabbie and part time in an unidentified art gallery. Elaine is the only female cabbie with a speaking part (others are seen lingering in the background) and is thus a natural target for Louie's lecherous ways (he refers to her breasts as "headlights" and has even made a peephole so he can watch Elaine undress in the ladies' room). Elaine, whose maiden name is O'Connor, attended Eastside High School and lives with her kids in Apartment 6A (address not given); Jennifer (Melanie Gaffin) and Jason (David Mendenhall) attend P.S. 33 in Manhattan.

Tony Banta, the cabbie who aspires to become a world champion boxer, is a middleweight boxer (who loses most of his matches). He served in Vietnam and has two goldfish named George and Wanda.

Bobby Wheeler, the aspiring actor, made his television debut on the soap opera "For Better, for Worse" as "Skip"; he also made a television pilot (title not given) but didn't win the role (the producers told him he wasn't sexy enough). Bobby also starred in the one-man play "Charles Darwin Tonight."

Latka Gravas, the alien from an unidentified country, is the garage mechanic. He married Simka, a girl from his homeland, and has an alter ego named Vic Ferrari, a playboy who speaks perfect, unaccented English. Latka's attempt to make money was the ill-fated Grandma Latka's Cookies (which tasted great—but were laced with drugs). While Simka is normally very romantic and very moody, she becomes a beast when her monthly *crimpka poosh* time arrives.

James Ignatowski, who is nicknamed "Iggie," is the spaced out cabbie who still lives in the 1960s. Jim was a studious, intelligent Harvard man before he turned to drugs (via "funny brownies") and ruined his life. He changed his name from James Caldwell to Jim Ignatowski because he thought *Ignatowski* was "Star Child" spelled backward. His heroes are Saint Thomas Aquinas, Alan Alda and Louie DePalma. *Star Wars* and *E.T.* are Jim's favorite movies; he was arrested at the 1968 Democratic Convention for stealing decorations. Jim bought a racehorse he named Gary for $10,000 and lives in a condemned building in Manhattan. When the building was torn down, Jim went to live with Louie. Jim left a beanbag on the stove, the apartment burned, and it cost Jim's wealthy father $29,542 to replace Louie's "stuff." When Jim inherited his father's money, he bought the hangout, Mario's, and changed the name to Jim's Mario's. Jim doesn't put the cap back on the toothpaste tube and screams for several hours in his sleep. He was also ordained as a minister in the Church of the Peaceful in 1968, and he is sometimes called Reverend Jim.

In the episode "On the Job," the Sunshine Cab Company temporarily goes broke and the cabbies are forced to look for other work. The jobs they found were as a stockbroker on Wall Street (Louie); night watchman in an office building (Alex); secretary for an unnamed company (Elaine); collector for a bookie (Tony); party entertainer for kids (Bobby); and door to door encyclopedia salesman (Jim—although he thought he was selling vacuum cleaners). In the closing theme, Cab 804 is seen. When the scene changes to show the cab at a different angle, Cab 734 (later 239) is seen (9207TI is its license plate).

Relatives: Jack Gilford (Alex's father, *Joe Reiger*), Joan Hackett (Alex's sister, *Charlotte*), Louise Lasser (Alex's ex-wife, *Phyllis Reiger*), Talia Balsam (Alex's daughter, *Cathy Reiger*), Julie Kavner (Tony's sister, *Monica Douglas*), Donnelly Rhodes (Tony's father, *Angie Banta*), Richard Foronjy (Louie's brother, *Nick DePalma*), Julia DeVito (Louie's mother, *Gabriella DePalma*), Victor Buono (Jim's father, *Mr. Caldwell*), Walter Olkewicz (Jim's brother, *Tom Caldwell*), Barbara Deutsch (Jim's sister, *Lila Caldwell*), Susan Kellerman (Latka's mother, *Greta Gravas*), Mark Blankfield (Simka's cousin, *Zifka*).

Theme: "Theme from Taxi," by Bob James.

698. *The Ted Knight Show*

CBS, 4/8/78 to 5/13/78

With a dream of starting his own escort service, Roger Dennis (Ted Knight) convinces his wealthy brother, Burt Dennis (Normann Burton), to finance the business. In return, Roger agrees to repay the loan and hire Dottie (Iris Adrian), Burt's cranky and inefficient sister-in-law, as his secretary.

From his apartment at 136 East 46th Street in Manhattan, Roger operates his business—the Mr. Dennis Escort Service (telephone 555-DATE). In addition to his son, Winston (Thomas Leopold), who attends NYU, Roger's "family" is made up of the alluring girls who work for him and make the agency successful: the sweet but zany Graziella (Cissy Colpitts), the shy Irma (Ellen Regan), the flirtatious Honey (Fawne Harriman), sexy Cheryl (Janice Kent), the beautiful Philadelphia ("Phil") Brown (Tanya Boyd) and the sweet and adoring Joy (Deborah Harmon).

The agency's slogan is "We never let a client down." While the agency is basically set up for women to escort men, Roger broke the rules to escort Victoria Diamond (Sara Slack), a pretty teenage girl who likes older men, to her sweet sixteen birthday party. Claude Stroud had a recurring role as Hobart Nalven, the elderly mailman.

Michael Leonard composed the theme.

699. *Teech*

CBS, 9/18/91 to 10/16/91

David Gibson (Phill Lewis), nicknamed "Teech," is a black music teacher at the prestigious Winthrop Academy, an exclusive all-white private boarding school. Teech was formerly a South Philadelphia Public School system music teacher who applied for the position after he was laid off. Cassie Lee (Maggie Han) is the assistant headmaster (the only female on the show). The main students who delight in mischief and put Teech to the test are: George Dubeck, Jr. (Curnal Achilles Aulisio), Boyd Askew (Ken Lawrence Johnston), Alby Nichols (Jason Kristofer) and Kenny Freedman (Joshua Hoffman). The students share Room 34 in the dorm. Franco's Pizza Parlor is the hangout.

B.B. King performs the theme, "Teech."

700. *Ten Speed and Brown Shoe*

ABC, 1/27/80 to 6/27/80

Lionel Whitney (Jeff Goldblum) is a reserved stockbroker with the Los Angeles firm of Grey, Johnson and Smith. He has few pleasures in life but finds adventure by reading private detective books called *A Mark Savage Mystery,* by Stephen J. Cannell (the show's producer). Lionel attended Pomona College (where he had the nickname "Bunky" and was a member of the Pistol Range Club). Lionel drives a blue Datsun, is bored with the stock market and is engaged to marry the boss's daughter, Bunny LaCrosse (Simone Griffeth).

E.L. Turner (Ben Vereen) is an ingenious, streetwise con artist. His ability to impersonate others is his key to getting himself out of jams. E.L. is nicknamed Ten Speed and claims that the *E.L.* stands for "Early LeRoy" (he was born in the taxi cab that was taking his mother to the hospital). E.L. studied law at Yale but was expelled after two years for rigging student elections and skipping off to Tijuana with the funds.

Lionel and E.L. meet at San Francisco International Airport when a plan by E.L. to heist gangland money backfires and he uses Lionel as a pawn to smuggle the money into L.A. In Los Angeles, E.L. involves Lionel with the underworld when he tries to retrieve the money. The adventures that follow as they try to elude mobsters give Lionel the feeling of excitement he has longed for, but has only been able to get by reading books. When a con by E.L. allows the police to catch the mobsters, Lionel quits his job (he was up for promotion to head institutional sales), and he and E.L. open their own detective firm: the Lionel Whitney Agency (also called Whitney Investigations). Stories follow their case investigations. E.L. calls Lionel a "Brown Shoe"—"a guy in a three-piece suit with brown shoes, a square, a Dow Jones." (When Bunny discovered that Lionel quit his job, she called off the wedding. They were to be married at Saint Veronica's Church and to live in an apartment at University Park.) *The Screaming Dead Man* was the title of *A Mark Savage Mystery* given in the pilot.

John Hillerman and Dana Wynter played Lionel's parents, William and Harriet Whitney.

"The Theme from Ten Speed and Brown Shoe" was composed by Mike Post and Pete Carpenter.

701. *Tequila and Bonetti*

CBS, 1/17/92 to 4/24/92

Nico Bonetti (Jack Scalia) is a cop with the N.Y.P.D. 62nd Precinct in Brooklyn. During an assignment, Nico was faced with a life-and-death situation: kill or be killed by a 12-year-old girl. The Firearms Control Board called it a justifiable shooting, but Nico was shattered by it. To help him over the ordeal, his supervisors lend Nico to the South Coast Police Department in California. There he is teamed with Angela Garcia (Mariska Hargitay), a very pretty rookie police officer, and Officer Tequila, a burrito loving dog whose commentary regarding Nico and Angela is heard only by the audience (Brad Sanders provides Tequila's voice). Stories follow their case investigations.

Nico, who owns a 1957 dusty rose–colored classic Cadillac

convertible (license plate BX2 100LB), drove from New York to Los Angeles in 37 hours and 14 minutes. He lives at 41445 Brooke Avenue in Bensonhurst's Bay Parkway section; he now resides at 2291 Pacific Way, the address of a former dance studio. His superior, Captain Midian Knight (Charles Rocket), calls him "Visiting Detective Bonetti." Midian, who served with Bravo Company, Fifth Marines, in Vietnam, hates to be called "Captain Midnight." His license plate reads CAP MID, and he frequents a restaurant called Finocci's. As a kid he had a dog named Scruffy and an imaginary girlfriend named Sophia; he also had a plush dog named Little Gino.

Angela is "the best-darned rookie that has come through here in years," says Knight, and he wants Nico to teach her the ropes. Angela is a widow (her husband, Officer Paulie Garcia, was killed in the line of duty) and the mother of a young daughter named Teresa (Noley Thornton). Angela lives at 36112 Parker Drive; on special occasions, she and Teresa have backwards dinners (the dessert first, then the meal). IB 896 is Angela's license plate number, and she orders pizza from a shop called Tootsie's. Angela attended Long Beach State College (where she met Paulie); the car code for her and Nico is K-1-9.

Tequila, a brown dog, is a graduate of the L.A. Canine Academy. He is not much on looks but he has more busts than most cops—"Tequila will cover your butt better than any cop." Tequila dreams of poodles, calls Angela "Sweet Pea," Nico "B" and crooks "Dirt Bags." Tequila lives with Nico as part of department regulations. Tequila is a Leo, and when he rescued a baby from a burning building he was called "Wonder Dog" and became the "spokesdog" for Gold Badge Security Systems.

Elena Stiteler appeared as Nico's ex-wife, Terry Bonetti, a former Rockette dancer; Carol Lawrence played Nico's mother, Rose Bonetti. The series was originally produced as "Tequila and Boner," with Rick Rossovich as T.T. Boner, a hip, new wave cop, who is teamed with a police dog named Tequila (voice of Pat Corley).

Mike Post composed the theme.

702. *Terry and the Pirates*

Syndicated, 1952 to 1953

Air Cathay is a small Singapore based cargo airline run by Chopstick Joe (Jack Reitzen). Terry Lee (John Baer), a former U.S. Air Force colonel, and his partner, Charles C. Charles (William Tracy), better known as "Hot Shot Charlie" and "Chazz," are the airline's pilots. They fly both a DC-3 and a C-47 (two-engine propellor planes). Terry's code to Chopstick Joe is "Flight Lee"; Joe's code for Terry is "Air Cathay Base."

Burma (Sandra Spence), "the gal who's always around," is Terry's friend, a beautiful freelance reporter (most often for the Affiliated News Service) who finds trouble wherever she goes. Lai Choi San, alias the Dragon Lady (Gloria Saunders), is "the femme fatale of the Far East," an evil Eurasian

who has her hand in all the illegal deals. Terry calls her "D.L." (she calls Terry "Golden One"). Hot Shot Charlie calls Chopstick Joe "Chops."

Mari Blanchard played Burma in the pilot episode, and Jack Kruschen was Hot Shot Charlie in the pilot (by the time the series was sold, after the pilot was made, Mari had been signed by Universal Pictures and Jack was busy with other commitments). There is no theme credit, only music supervision by Edward Haire.

703. *That Girl*

ABC, 9/8/66 to 9/10/71

Cast: Marlo Thomas (*Ann Marie*), Ted Bessell (*Don Hollinger*).

Facts: Ann Marie is a pretty small-town girl (from Brewster, New York) who moves to New York City to fulfill her dream of becoming an actress. Her greatest hope is to purchase the rights to the book *A Woman's Story*, by Joseph Nelson, and star in the movie version of it (every actress's dream). Ann was a member of her college drama club, the Brewster Community Playhouse, and as a kid she won a medal for best actress at Camp Winnepoo.

Ann lives at 344 West 78th Street (Apartment 4D; sometimes seen as Apartment D); she later resides at 627 East 54th Street, Apartment 2C. She is a member of the Benedict Workshop of the Dramatic Arts, and to support herself between acting jobs she takes whatever work she can find. Ann's temporary jobs have included roving model at Sardi's Restaurant (she performed scenes from movies while modeling), spokesgirl ("Miss Chicken Big") for the fast food chain Chicken Big, Inc. ("We Fry Harder"), door-to-door salesgirl for Smart and Stunning Shoes, perfume salesclerk at Macy's and model to British photographer Noel Prince (Gary Marshall). Ann worked as a meter maid before leaving Brewster.

Ann made her television debut on an unnamed show (she played a bank teller who gets killed; her end credit read "The Girl . . . Ann Marie"). She understudied famous Broadway actress Sandy Stafford (Sally Kellerman) in an unnamed play. Her most embarrassing moment occurred when, on live television, she played a corpse—and opened her eyes on camera.

Donald ("Don") Hollinger, born in Toledo, Ohio, is Ann's boyfriend, a reporter for *Newsview* magazine. He is a sloppy housekeeper and lives in Apartment 1 (address not given), and his home phone number is Bryant 9-9970. He and Ann frequent Nino's Italian Restaurant.

Ann's parents are Lou and Helen Marie (Lew Parker and Rosemary DeCamp). Lou owns the La Parisienne Restaurant and is a member of the Shriners' Club and the Brewster Country Club (where each year during its annual show he performs the song "Minnie the Moocher"). Lou dislikes Ann in long earrings and short skirts and doesn't really approve of her becoming an actress (the first sign of approval he gave Ann was to let her direct the club's annual show). Lou calls Don "Hollinger," and his competition is Tony's Restaurant. Frank Faylen and Mabel Albertson played Don's parents, Bert and Mildred Hollinger.

Ann is represented by the Gilliam and Norris Theatrical Agency; her agents are Sandy Stone (played by Morty Gunty), George Lester (George Carlin), Harvey Peck (Ronnie Schell) and Seymour Schwimmer (Don Penny). Billy DeWolfe plays Jules Benedict, Ann's dramatic coach (the sign on his office door reads NEVER ENTER HERE); Cloris Leachman appeared as Don's sister, Sandi. In one episode, Ann, who was told she had "a rotten name for an actress" (most producers ask, "Ann Marie who?"), contemplated changing her name to Marie Brewster, combining her last name and her hometown, but she never did.

In the original, unaired pilot (produced in 1965), Marlo Thomas played Ann Marie; Ted Bessell was her boyfriend, Don Bluesky, a writer for *Newsview* magazine; and Harold Gould and Penny Santon played Ann's mother and father.

Theme: "That Girl," by Earle Hagen and Sam Denoff.

704. *That's My Boy*

CBS, 4/10/54 to 1/1/55

John ("Jarrin' Jack") Jackson (Eddie Mayehoff) is the perennial college boy who fears growing old. He lives for the trophies he earned as a football star at Rossmore College. He is the school's most famous alumnus and played quarterback; he earned the nickname "Jarrin' Jack" for his philosophy of "hitting them hard, fast and low. And if they get up, hit 'em again." He wore jersey number 66.

Jack lives at 734 Appletree Lane in Rossmore, Ohio. He is married to Alice (Rochelle Hudson), a former tennis star, and is the father of an 18-year-old son named Jack Jackson, Jr. (Gil Stratton, Jr.). Jarrin' Jack yearns to relive his college days through his son. He had high hopes of Junior's becoming the next great football star at Rossmore, but he found only disappointment: Junior Jackson, as he is called, is a weakling and has no interest in sports; he'd rather be attending the engineering school at MIT. Jack's efforts to instill Junior with the sports spirit are the focal point of the series.

Jack heads an engineering firm called Jackson and Patterson. Henrietta Patterson (Mabel Albertson) is the wife of Jack's partner (who is not seen). Jack gives orders to his employees in the same way he used to give signals on the football field. Jack's grandfather attended Rossmore College and built the stadium. Since Jack was a nine-letter man and Alice is a former athlete, Jack has trouble understanding how Junior could be theirs—"Is there nothing to this heredity business? Could the hospital have made a mistake?" Alice assures Jack that "Junior is ours; he was born at home."

Junior wears glasses, is clumsy and allergic to strawberries. He also suffers from hay fever and is prone to sinus attacks. He wears Dr. Denton pajamas ("In case I get a chill") and size nine shoes. When Junior was six years old, Jack bought him the finest gym equipment; when he was ten, Jack bought him the best football equipment—but it never interested Junior, who fears he will not be able to fill his father's shoes: "They're too big and I keep tripping over them." The series is based on the feature film of the same title.

Bill Goodwin does the announcing, and Leith Stevens provides the show's bridge music.

705. *They Came from Outer Space*

Syndicated, 10/9/90 to 9/16/91

Cast: Stuart Fratkin *(Abe)*, Dean Cameron *(Bo)*.

Facts: Like most parents, Mr. and Mrs. Osceack believe their sons Ablerama ("Abe") and Boximaxio ("Bo") need a year of college to teach them responsibility. Although they live on the planet Crouton, Abe and Bo decide to attend Earth's Cambridge University in England. En route to Earth, Bo begins to read his favorite Earth girlie magazine, *Baby Doll* (borrowed from the Crouton Public Library), and he becomes fascinated with a bikini-clad girl named Tammy. When he reads that Tammy sunbathes in the nude, he goes wild and convinces Abe that they should make California their home, not musty old England. Just as Abe programs California on their intergalactic travel guide, their spaceship enters the Earth's atmosphere. Before Abe can lower the ship's sunscreen, the rays damage the craft, and it crash-lands in an auto junkyard in California.

With their arms linked (to activate their power of object transfer), Abe and Bo transform several junk cars into a brand new '57 red Corvette (license plate RWE 2KL). They equip their car with the communication devices from their ships and decide to travel across the United States for their college education. (Bo believes that he has solved the problem of what to do when the year is up: actually go to England, call their parents and tell them that someone stole the saucer.)

As Bo and Abe begin their "Route 66" travels, Colonel Barker (Allan Royal) and Lieutenant Wilson (Christopher Carroll) of the air force, begin a search to find them (Crouton's previous Earth visitors, the Petulas sisters, were captured and then mysteriously disappeared; they were exposed by the *National Tipster*).

Bo and Abe are 6.5 light years from home. Crouton was voted "Most boring planet in the universe." On Crouton, Bo and Abe, who studied advanced math for 11 years, frequented Blocknick's Burgertorium ("The best hamburgers on Crouton"). On Earth, they find fresh air, sunshine and doughnuts to be a perfect morning (on Crouton, they preferred Ziedel dumplings).

Bo and Abe support themselves by taking various jobs. They can mind-speak, have enormous appetites and can become part of an inanimate object via inanimate projection (but only for one minute at a time; any longer and they become stuck in that position for ten hours). They also feel each other's pain (for example, if Bo gets punched, Abe feels the pain; if Abe gets drunk, Bo has the hangover). They both like chasing beautiful women (Bo's career ambition), eating licorice ripple ice cream and watching the Crouton television show "The Fungal Gourmet." Bo also mentioned his favorite television shows as being "Daffy Duck," "Wrestling" and "My Friend Flicka" (which he picked up from Earth transmissions); his favorite cake is chocolate butterscotch with chicken liver filling. Abe mentioned his favorite movie as being *A Yogurt for Hymie* (about a man who is forced to eat dairy products).

In the episode of 11/13/90, Bo and Abe did manage to attend Cambridge—the Cambridge School for Girls, that is, when they stumble upon the college, which has just gone coed. They stayed only long enough to show their parents a report card from Cambridge.

Barker and Wilson are with the Extraterrestrial Investigation Unit of the Air Force. Their Dodge van license plate is J9485, and the Alien Hot Line is 1-800-555-1221 (as seen on wanted posters). Barker calls his gun "Bertha."

Relatives: Rosalee Mayeux *(Bo and Abe's mother)*, Victor Brandt *(Bo and Abe's father)*.

Theme: "They Came from Outer Space," by Gary Stockdale.

706. *Thicker Than Water*

ABC, 6/13/73 to 8/8/73

Cast: Julie Harris *(Nellie Paine)*, Richard Long *(Ernie Paine)*, Malcolm Atterbury *(Jonas Paine)*.

Facts: In 1910 an enterprising young man named Jonas Paine established a business called Paine's Pure Pickles. He instituted some rules (for instance, "Never let your cucumber crumble; nobody likes a soggy pickle," and "Remember the gherkin rule—no cucumber bigger than your finger"). In 1911 he won the gold medal for his gherkins at the American Grain Exhibition.

In 1933 his daughter, Nellie, was born; in 1937 his wife, Frances, gave birth to a boy they named Ernie. Jonas became a widower in 1955, and in 1963 he became chronically ill. In 1965 Ernie left home, and Nellie, who became a spinster, remained behind to run the family pickle works and to care for her father, "an old codger who just won't kick the bucket."

In 1973, at age 82, Jonas takes another turn for the worse. As Nellie enters the room, we discover what Jonas wants most: "Ernie, is that you?" "No, Pop," responds Nellie, "it's not Ernie." "But your shoes squeaked just like Ernie's," says Jonas. "It's been eight years, Pop. Ernie is no good, he never has been and he never will be." "You'll see, he'll be back. Blood's thicker than water."

Then one day, shortly after, Bert Taylor (Pat Cranshaw), the pickle factory foreman, finds Ernie, now a penniless playboy. When Ernie learns of Jonas's condition, he realizes there is money at stake and rushes back home.

The meeting between Ernie and Nellie is anything but happy, for they despise each other. Nellie is bitter because Ernie left her to care for Pop; Ernie insists there is nothing wrong with Jonas ("He's been in that bedroom too long and needs a change of scenery").

After eight years of constantly asking for Ernie, Jonas is about to get his wish—or is he? Ernie enters the room. "Ernie, is that you?" "Hey Pop!" "Who is it?" "It's me." "Well, who the hell is me?" "Pop, don't you recognize me? ... It's me, Ernie." "How do I know it's Ernie? Maybe you're just out to steal the secret of my gherkins." "Gherkins! Who wants your gherkins, you silly old codger." Jonas yells, "Ernie!" and they both hug.

With the family reunited, Jonas reveals the conditions of his will: Ernie and Nellie will each receive $75,000, "the money to be paid you five years from today, provided you both operate the family pickle works and live together in the family residence." Ernie and Nellie begin bickering; Jonas interrupts: "Now stop it! You've got to. All you've got left is each other." Reluctantly, Nellie and Ernie agree to Pop's conditions and struggle to care for him and the pickle plant—and each other.

Klondike 5-3061 is the Paines' home phone number (an address is not given). Jonas gets his medication from Pike's Pharmacy, and almost every home in town (unnamed) has a jar of Paine's Pickles. While Jonas did build the pickle factory up from nothing, he also invested in such losing propositions as a dude ranch in Chicago and electric fishing poles.

Ernie left home because he couldn't stand the smell of pickles. In school, the kids called Ernie "Ernie Gherkin" and Nellie was called "Nellie, Nellie, Pickle Belly." Nellie, who sees a need to save money, buys her clothes at Harrison's Discount Store (35–45 percent off). Ernie entertains his ladies at Vito's Atomic Bar (if he gets lucky, it's off to the Hideaway Motel); his favorite bar hangouts are the Purple Cow and the Golden Slipper. Ernie studiously avoids work, drinks, chases women and has a talent for getting the prize out of the Crackerjack box without opening it. When they were children, Nellie gave Ernie a doll that looked so much like him they called it the "Ernie Doll."

Relatives: Jessica Myerson (Nellie's first cousin, *Lily Paine*), Lou Fant (Lily's husband, *Walter Paine*).

Theme: No credit appears for the show's only music, the "Thicker Than Water" theme.

707. *The Thin Man*

NBC, 9/20/57 to 6/26/59

Cast: Peter Lawford *(Nick Charles)*, Phyllis Kirk *(Nora Charles)*.

Facts: Nick Charles is a former private detective (Nicholas Charles—Confidential Investigations) turned mystery editor for an unnamed publishing house in New York City. He is married to Nora, a beautiful but trouble prone girl who has a knack for stumbling upon and involving him in crimes. They married in 1950 and honeymooned at the

The Thin Man. **Peter Lawford and Phyllis Kirk (holding Asta).**

Ambassador Hotel (stayed in Room 3C), and each year on the twenty-eighth (month not named) they celebrate "Asta Day"—the day their pet dog brought them together.

It all began in San Francisco when a Colonel McCarra (Charles Watts) hired Nick to find Randy Watts (William Hudson), the man who ran out on his daughter. During his investigation, Nick discovers that Randy went to the Bay City Kennel Club with a wealthy woman named Nora Clair-idon. Nick attempts to question Nora, but she refuses to talk to him. In an attempt to acquire information, Nick decides to charm Nora. That too fails—until he follows her to a pet shop and sees her admiring a wirehaired terrier puppy. Nick approaches Nora and begins to admire the dog. He learns that as a kid she had a wirehaired that she called Asta, but this particular dog has been sold. As they con-

tinue to talk, Nick tricks Nora into giving him the information he needs to find Randy. At a restaurant, where they had made dinner plans, Nora realizes what Nick has done, slaps his face and leaves. Later that night, Nora is awakened from her sleep when the doorbell rings. She slips on a robe, answers the door and is surprised (and delighted) to find that it is the puppy she had admired. She calls Nick; they eventually marry and move to New York.

Nick and Nora live in an apartment in Greenwich Village (Regent 4-4598 is their phone number); Nick's license plate reads NICK I; and he uses the "Laundry List" method to solve crimes (Nick relates the facts, Nora writes them down). When someone takes a shot at Nick, he falls down so as not to disappoint the shooter—"It also prevents them from taking another shot." Nick calls Nora "Tiger"; Nora calls Nick "Nickie." Nora is extremely jealous and becomes very upset when beautiful girls start "making goo-goo eyes at him." At such times she calls Nick "Nicholas!" Nora wears a size eight dress and is a member of both the Junior Matrons' Breakfast Club and a charity organization called the Junior Guild. Nora never thinks in emergencies—"I only have hunches."

Nick calls Asta their "child" because of the way Nora babies him. Even though the dog is a male, Nora gave him a girl's name, based on her Uncle Harry's theory that a sissy name will make a man out of a boy. In the opening theme, Nick and Nora are seen driving on a darkened road. The road sign that is seen reads CURVES AHEAD.

Beatrice Dean (Nita Talbot) is a beautiful con artist who goes by the alias Blondie Collins. "Blondie has a knack for larceny," says Nick, who has arrested her on several occasions (she serves time at the Elmsville Prison for Women). When Blondie is in trouble, she considers the Charleses' home a port of call and retreats to it for help (and Nick's affections). Despite Nora's jealousy, Nick can't resist "a gorgeous doll" and always helps Blondie.

Blondie calls Nick "Nickie Lover" or "Nickie Darling" and Nora "That Woman" (because she feels Nora "is trying to horn in on me and Nickie"). Despite Blondie's dislike for Nora (for being married to Nick), Blondie knows she needs Nora and uses sob stories to get her on her side. Doris Packer and Maurice Manson appeared as Blondie's Aunt Della and Uncle Wallace.

Hazel (Patricia Donahue) is Nora's friend, an attractive single girl who has a crush on Nick and flirts with him at every opportunity (she lives in the brownstone next to Nick and Nora's; in second season episodes, Nick and Nora appear to live in a brownstone rather than in an apartment as evidenced by outside scenes).

Ralph Raines (Stafford Repp) and Harry Evans (Jack Albertson) are lieutenants with the N.Y.P.D. Homicide Bureau who "assist" Nick in solving crimes.

Themes: "The Thin Man" (1957–58), by Johnny Greene, and "The Thin Man Theme" (1958–59), by Pete Rugolo.

Note: On 3/4/75, ABC presented a pilot called "Nick and Nora," with Craig Stevens (Nick Charles) and Jo Ann Pflug (Nora Charles), in an unsold series idea based on the characters created by Dashiell Hammett. (In the story, Nick and Nora investigate a murder in a luxurious Los Angeles hotel.)

708. *This Is Alice*

Syndicated, 1958 to 1959

River Glen, "a good place to live," is a small town in New Jersey. It has a population of 24,695, and its elevation is 322 feet. Alice Holliday (Patty Ann Gerrity) is a bright and bubbly nine-year-old who lives at 857 Elm Street with her father, Chet (Tommy Farrell), her mother, Clarissa Mae (Phyllis Coates), and her grandfather (Clarissa's father), Colonel Dixon (Lucien Littlefield). Alice also has an infant brother named Junior, but no screen credit is given.

Alice attends the River Glen Elementary School with her friends Clarence ("Soapy") Weaver (Stephen Wootton), Susan Gray (Nancy DeCarl) and Stingy Jones (Jimmy Baird). Their classes are held in room 4B. Alice is president of the All for One Club ("Friends to the end" is their slogan"); Susan is vice president. Alice is allowed to have as many pets as she wants—as long as she keeps them out of the house. She has many pets that she keeps in the garage, but only a few are given names: Pegasus (a pony), Rudolph (a frog) and Henry and Madeline (flies). Alice also had a pet elephant named Cuddles, whom she bought for 55 cents from a bankrupt carnival. Alice also has a little problem—a compulsion to help people in trouble, whether they want her help or not.

Chet works as a reporter for the local newspaper, the *Star Herald*; Clarissa Mae was born in Georgia, where her family owns a peanut plantation. Henry Weaver (Benny Baker) is Soapy's father; John Gray (Russell Arms) is Susan's father; and Mrs. Porter (Amy Douglas) is Susan's grandmother.

E.C. Norton is credited as the music supervisor; no credit is given for the "This Is Alice" theme composer.

Three's a Crowd see *Three's Company*

709. *Three's Company*

ABC, 3/15/77 to 9/18/84

Cast: John Ritter (*Jack Tripper*), Joyce DeWitt (*Janet Wood*), Suzanne Somers (*Chrissy Snow*), Jenilee Harrison (*Cindy Snow*), Priscilla Barnes (*Terri Alden*), Richard Kline (*Larry Dallas*), Norman Fell (*Stanley Roper*), Audra Lindley (*Helen Roper*), Don Knotts (*Ralph Furley*).

Facts: Janet Wood, Chrissy Snow and Eleanor Garvey (Marianne Black) live in Apartment 201 at the Ropers' Apartment House in Santa Monica, California (the locale is also given as Los Angeles). Following a wild going-away party for Eleanor, Janet and Chrissy find Jack Tripper, a guy who came to the party with a friend who knew one of the gate-crashers, sleeping in their bathtub. Like Janet, who got so drunk on Chrissy's punch that she attempted a striptease, Jack can't remember how he wound up in the bathtub. Jack, a cooking student (specializing in French cuisine) who is staying at the Y.M.C.A., can't afford an apartment of his own; Janet and Chrissy, who can neither cook nor afford the $300-a-month rent, agree to let Jack rent Eleanor's old room (the one to the right of the living room) for $100 a month. To convince their landlords, Stanley and Helen Roper, that theirs will be a platonic relationship, Janet tells Stanley that Jack is gay—a charade Jack must live out through the entire series run in order to stay with the girls. (Patricia Crawford, played by Kit McDonough, was the one who answered the ad for a roommate before the girls asked Jack; Eggs Madeira was the first meal Jack prepared for Janet and Chrissy.)

Three's Company. Norman Fell, left. Center (bottom to top): Suzanne Somers, John Ritter, Joyce DeWitt. Right: Audra Lindley.

Jack attended San Diego High School and later served a hitch in the navy. As the result of a reunion celebration with his navy buddies, Jack got a tattoo of a heart on his behind which says THE LOVE BUTT. After graduating from the Los Angeles Technical School ("You're looking at the Galloping Gourmet of 1980"), Jack becomes a chef at Angelino's Italian Restaurant, then opens his own French eatery called Jack's Bistro (located at 834 Ocean Vista in Los Angeles; about one mile from the Ropers' Apartment House).

Janet, who was born in Massachusetts, is a salesgirl (later manager) of the Arcade Florist Shop. She has a tendency to nag a lot and usually gets her way (people give in "just to shut her up"). Janet, who is small busted, contemplated a breast enlargement to get attention (but later backed down) and wore a blonde wig to see if blondes really do have more fun (she found they did; but she also found the wig was changing her personality and so she discarded it).

Christmas ("Chrissy") Snow was born on December 25. She is a beautiful blonde bombshell who is a bit naive at times (she has a habit of turning men on and not realizing she is doing it). Chrissy is very sweet and trusting and works as a secretary for an unnamed company. She also had a part time job selling Easy Time cosmetics door to door.

Cynthia ("Cindy") Snow is Chrissy's beautiful cousin who moved in when Suzanne Somers left the series. Cindy is a student at UCLA and earns money both by working as a secretary and by hiring herself out as a maid. She is very clumsy and accident prone (Jack is most often on the receiving end of her mishaps).

Terri Alden, who was born in Indiana, is a nurse at Wilshire Memorial Hospital in Los Angeles (her character replaced Cindy's when Jenilee Harrison left the series). Terri is a warm, caring and sensitive girl who became a true friend to Jack and Janet despite the fact that Terri and Jack disliked each other when they first met (Jack cut himself and needed a tetanus shot; he felt intimidated when Terri was assigned to take care of "the big baby").

Larry Dallas, Jack's playboy friend, is a rather dishonest used-car salesman (company not named) who is always in need of money.

The gang's hangout is the Regal Beagle, a bar styled after a British pub. Greedy Gretchen (Teresa Ganzel) is the girl of Jack's dreams. In 1978, Ralph Furley, who believes he is a ladies' man, becomes the new landlord when his rich brother, Bart (Hamilton Camp), buys the Ropers' Apartment House and hires him to manage the building. Helen and Stanley move to a condominium at 46 Peacock Drive in Chevia Hills, California, and thus was born the spinoff series "The Ropers" (3/13/79 to 5/22/80). Helen and Stanley live at the Royal Condominium townhouse complex; their phone number is 555-3099. Their neighbors, at 44 Peacock Drive, are Jeffrey Brookes III (Jeffrey Tambor), a real estate salesman, his beautiful wife, Anne (Patricia McCormack), and their son, David (Evan Cohen). Helen, who was a USO entertainer during the war, has a dog named Muffin and a parakeet named Stanley. Helen's mother (Lucille Benson) calls Stanley "Herbert."

While returning home from a business trip in San Fran-

cisco (on flight 701), Jack, who has an acute fear of flying, makes a spectacle of himself when the plane encounters turbulence. Victoria ("Vicky") Bradford (Mary Cadorette) is the stewardess who comes to Jack's assistance. Jack's tendency to become clumsy when he gets nervous involves them in several mishaps and produces the unexpected—a mutual attraction.

When Jack returns home, he is surprised by two announcements: Janet has accepted the marriage proposal of her boyfriend (Philip Dawson, played by David Ruprecht), and Terri has accepted a job in Hawaii. Shortly after Janet returns from her honeymoon in Acapulco, Jack asks Vicky to marry him. She refuses: "It frightens me. I lived through my parents' marriage and divorce. I used to lie awake listening to them fight . . . I still have nightmares about it." She then suggests that she and Jack live together, and the spinoff series "Three's a Crowd" (9/18/84 to 9/17/85) begins. Jack and Vicky move into Apartment 203 over Jack's Bistro at 834 Ocean Vista in Ocean Vista, California (altered slightly from the earlier series). Vicky is a flight attendant for Trans-Allied Airlines; her divorced parents are James (Robert Mandan) and Claudia Bradford (Jessica Walter). James is Jack's landlord and owner of Allied Waste Disposal, the company that removes the Bistro's trash. The series is also known as "Three's Company, Too."

"Three's Company" is based on the British series "Man About the House"; "The Ropers" is adapted from the British series "George and Mildred"; and "Three's a Crowd" is based on the British series "Robin's Nest."

Relatives: Dick Shawn (Jack's father, *Jack Tripper, Sr.*), Georgann Johnson (*Jack's mother*), Edward Andrews (Jack's *Grandpa Tripper*), John Getz (Jack's brother, *Lee Tripper*), John Ritter (Jack's brother, *Tex Tripper*), Peter Mark Richman (Chrissy's father, *the Reverend Luther Snow*), Priscilla Morrill (*Chrissy's mother*), Jay Garfield (Chrissy's cousin, *Daniel Trent*), Paula Shaw (Janet's mother, *Ruth Wood*), Devon Ericson (Janet's sister, *Jenny Wood*), Macon McCalman (Janet's father, *Roland Wood*), Mina Kolb (*Terri's mother*), Jennifer Walker (Terri's sister, *Samantha Alden*), Alan Manson (*Terri's father*), Sue Ane Langdon (Cindy's aunt, *Becky Madison*), Lucinda Dooling (Larry's sister, *Diane Dallas*), Brian Robbins (Ralph's nephew, *Marc Furley*), Christina Hart (Stanley's niece, *Karen*), Irene Tedrow (Helen's *Aunt Martha*).

Theme: "Three's Company," vocal by Julia Rinker and (The Other) Ray Charles.

710. *The Thunderbirds*

Syndicated, 1968

Voice Cast: Peter Dyneley (*Jeff Tracy*), Shane Rimmer (*Scott Tracy*), David Holliday (*Virgil Tracy*), Matt Zimmerman (*Alan Tracy*), David Graham (*Gordon Tracy*), Ray Barrett (*John Tracy*), Sylvia Anderson (*Lady Penelope*), Ray Barrett (*The Hood*).

Facts: International Rescue (I.R.) is a global organization

The Ropers. Evan Cohen (bottom), Norman Fell and Audra Lindley (center). Patricia McCormack and Jeffrey Tambor (back).

dedicated to rescuing people trapped in unusual predicaments. Their base is a remote Pacific island; all characters are marionettes.

Jeff Tracy is the head of I.R. He is a former astronaut and has named his five sons, all members of I.R., after American astronauts.

Scott Tracy is the oldest son. He is fast talking and quick thinking and pilots *Thunderbird I*, a fast scout vehicle that speeds to the crisis area. It can reach speeds of 7,000 miles an hour and can take off vertically for speed. It also has retractable wings, booster and downward firing rockets, which allow it to land vertically without the need for wheels.

Virgil Tracy is reliable and steady and the pilot of *Thunderbird II*, a freighter that handles the priceless rescue equipment. It has rollers instead of wheels to allow the craft's body to land on the ground. Hydraulic legs then lift the fuselage off the ground so that the rescue equipment can be lowered. It is the only armed craft (being slower, it is more vulnerable to attack).

Alan Tracy is the most romantic of the sons and the pilot of *Thunderbird III*, which is capable of space flight. It possesses laser radio scanners that alert the base of its location.

Gordon Tracy is young, enthusiastic and a joker; he operates *Thunderbird IV*, the underwater vehicle (which is contained in the pod of *Thunderbird II*).

John Tracy, the youngest of the brothers, commands *Thunderbird V*, the satellite base of I.R. It possesses the most advanced scientific equipment, the most ingenious of which is the Interpreter, which can immediately translate any language into English.

Lady Penelope Creighton-Ward is I.R.'s glamorous London agent. She is adventurous and daring—a female James Bond. She owns an exotic wardrobe and a shocking pink Rolls Royce with the license plate FAB I. The car's wheels rotate sideways so that it can be parked crabwise; all wheels have retractable studs for snow and ice; and, at the press of a button, pointed end rods shoot out to form a tire slasher. A machine gun is hidden in the radiator, and the car can reach speeds of up to 200 miles per hour. In addition to bulletproof glass and a steel canopy, the car has its back seat with retractable handcuffs and a chestband to subdue prisoners.

The Hood is the enemy of International Rescue and is dedicated to discovering the secrets of its operations. He lives in an exotic eastern temple and practices "Hoodoo" (spells that control people for his purposes).

Theme: "The Thunderbirds," by Barry Gray.

Time for Beany see *The Beany and Cecil Show*

711. *The Time Tunnel*

ABC, 9/9/66 to 9/1/67

Cast: James Darren *(Tony Newman)*, Robert Colbert *(Doug Phillips)*, Whit Bissell *(Heywood Kirk)*.

Facts: The time: 1968. The place: Tic Toc Base, a secret government base in the middle of the Arizona desert. The project: The Time Tunnel, a seven and one-half billion dollar experiment concerned with time displacement.

General Heywood ("Woody") Kirk is the project supervisor. He and Douglas ("Doug") Phillips, a doctor of electrophysics, have been working on the project since 1958. They were joined in 1965 by Anthony ("Tony") Newman, an eager young electrophysicist (born in 1938) who has made great strides in accomplishing the impossible: traveling in time. Dr. Anne McGregor (Lee Meriwether), an electromicrobiologist, and Dr. Raymond Swain (John Zaremba), a man with the finest electronics mind in the country, supervise the electrical operations of the project (which include history computers, tracking, freezing time and telecontrol, an amazing portal through which events of the past can be viewed as they happened). And, ramrod of the Tunnel's security force, is Master Sergeant Jiggs (Wesley Lau).

The Time Tunnel itself is located more than 800 floors beneath the surface of the desert. It takes but a mere ten seconds to travel by elevator from the surface to the Tunnel.

A visitor passes through areas of massive atomic turbines (needed to supply the Tunnel's power) and rows of the most highly sophisticated computers before facing the Time Tunnel, an oval, psychedelic portal through which scientists hope to achieve the most valuable treasure that humanity will ever find—the control of time.

A car, carrying Senator LeRoy Clark (guest star Gary Merrill) approaches the base. "Mobile Tic Toc One" is his code to the base, "Red Line One." Once this is confirmed, an entrance to the base appears, then disappears after the car enters (like a zipper opening and closing).

Clark meets with Kirk, Tony and Doug and tells them that the government is seriously considering scrapping the project. In its ten year history, scientists have succeeded only in sending mice and monkeys back in time; however, they have not been able to retrieve them. The retrieval process is the major stumbling block facing the scientists.

Concerned only with results, not problems, the senator gives Kirk an alternative: send a man in time now or "I will either write you a blank check or cut off your umbilical cord."

That night, Tony decides to take matters into his own hands. He activates the Time Tunnel and enters its chamber. An explosion is seen and a red alert is sounded. Engineers rush to their terminals. Anne sees that Tony is suspended in motion in a blue mist inside the tunnel. She gives the signal for a 16 second countdown to remove him. At zero, an explosion is heard and Tony vanishes into time: "Yesterday, today, tomorrow—or a million years from now."

The blue mist was a radioactive bath Tony had developed to enable Time Tunnel personnel to locate a traveler in time via a magnetic fix. While engineers struggle to track him, Tony falls through the swirling infinite corridors of time to April 13, 1912—as an unregistered passenger on the *Titanic*, one day before its fatal encounter with an iceberg.

When computers reveal that Tony has been sent back in time less than 100 years, "a mere heartbeat in the countless billions of years of time," they pinpoint him. Tony's immediate environment is realized through the Time Tunnel's recorders and reproduced via the telecontrol's image area. Tony can be seen, but he can't see them. Even though Tony lives in the present, he is affected by events of the past or future; if, for example, Tony is aboard the *Titanic* when it sinks, he will become one of its victims.

With the Time Tunnel engineers unable to control Tony's destiny or return him to the present, Doug believes the only way to save Tony is to go back and help him (Tony is now a prisoner and locked in the hull that is first ripped open by the iceberg; Tony's attempts to convince the captain of impending doom failed, and he was locked up as a stowaway).

Doug dresses for the era and brings a newspaper dated April 15, 1912—the day after the disaster. The 16 second countdown begins and Doug is sent to the *Titanic* (he "lands" on a pile of coal in the engine room; Tony "landed" on the deck). Doug finds Tony, but he too is unable to convince the captain (who tossed the newspaper out of a porthole) of the impending tragedy. At 11:40 P.M., as history had recorded, the *Titanic* strikes an iceberg. As the ship begins to sink, Time Tunnel engineers freeze Tony and Doug. They accelerate power and transport them to another time.

The Time Tunnel receives its funding. "We are perfecting our apparatus and techniques every day," Kirk tells Clark as he leaves, "It's just a matter of time [before we retrieve Tony and Doug]."

Stories depict Tony and Doug's experiences as travelers lost in time. In the unaired pilot version, coming attractions placed their second adventure in a world of prehistoric monsters. In the network version, Tony and Doug's next adventure placed them as unknown passengers aboard a primitive NASA rocket.

Theme: "The Time Tunnel," by John Williams.

712. *T.J. Hooker*

ABC, 3/13/82 to 5/4/85
CBS, 9/25/85 to 9/17/87

L.C. City, California, is the locale. T.J. Hooker (William Shatner) is a police officer dedicated to upholding law and order. He is a sergeant with the Academy Precinct of the L.C.P.D. and holds the record for the most damaged or destroyed police cars. His car code is 4-Adam-30, and 115 (also seen as 141) is his badge number. Hooker wears a Magnum Body Armor bulletproof vest and resides in a messy room at the Safari Inn. Fran Hooker (Leigh Christian and Lee Bryant) is Hooker's ex-wife (she calls him Hooker,

as does everybody else; what "T.J." stands for is not mentioned). Chrissy (Nicole Eggert and Jenny Beck), Cathy (Susan McClung) and Tommy (Andre Gower) are Fran and T.J.'s children. Fran works as a nurse at Memorial Hospital in L.C. City (what "L.C." stands for is not given).

Officer Stacey Sheridan (Heather Locklear), badge number 280, lives in an apartment at the Marina Club. She and her partner, Officer Jim Corrigan (James Darren), ride in a car with the code 4-Adam-16. Jim was born in San Francisco. Officer Vince Romano (Adrian Zmed), Hooker's partner, was born in South Philadelphia and as a kid had a dog named Bear.

In ABC episodes, the hangout is the Mid-City Bar; it's Sherry's Bar in CBS episodes. Vince's favorite afterhours hangout is Adrienne's Bar.

Captain Dennis Sheridan (Richard Herd) is Stacey's father, and John Hooker (John McLiam) is T.J.'s father.

Mark Snow composed the "T.J. Hooker" theme.

713. *To Rome with Love*
CBS, 9/28/69 to 9/1/71

Michael Endicott (John Forsythe), a widower, and his three daughters, Alison (Joyce Menges), Penelope ("Penny") (Susan Neher) and Jane ("Pokey") (Melanie Fullerton), leave Iowa and relocate to Italy when Michael, an English professor, is hired to teach at the American School in Rome.

The Endicotts acquire a new home at the Rome Hotel and Apartments (a.k.a. Mama Vitale's Boarding House) in the town of Trastavity. Stories relate their adventures as they attempt to adjust to a new homeland.

Gino Mancini (Vito Scotti), a con artist who runs a taxi service called Gino's Taxi Stand, and Mama Vitale (Peggy Mondo), Michael's landlady, quickly become friends. Other businesses on the block are Giotto's Bakery, Martinelli's Grocery and Butcher Shop, Cartorchello's Pizza Shop and Mrs. Strait's Restaurant. In one episode, Alison, the oldest of the girls, was picked by Gino to represent his company as "Miss Gino's Taxi" in the town's first beauty contest, the Pageant of Trastavity (she won best historical costume and best formal costume and was crowned Miss Trastavity). Mike also took a temporary job as the manager of the Catnip Club, a night spot in Rome for swingers.

In first season episodes, Walter Brennan played Michael's father-in-law, Andy Pruitt (who lived with them at Mama Vitale's). Kay Medford as Mike's sister, Harriet Endicott, joined the family for second season episodes.

Jay Livingston and Ray Evans composed the theme, "To Rome with Love."

714. *Together We Stand*
CBS, 9/22/86 to 10/29/86

At 37 Brookfall Road in Portland, Oregon, lives the Randall family: parents Lori (Dee Wallace Stone) and David

T.J. Hooker. **Clockwise from top center: James Darren, Adrian Zmed, William Shatner, Heather Locklear.**

(Elliott Gould) and their children, Amy (Katie O'Neill), Jack (Scott Grimes), Sam Vu Tron (Ke Huy Quan) and Sally (Natasha Bobo). When Lori learned that she would not be able to have children, she and David adopted Amy (now 15) when she was an infant (her mother left her on the doorstep of an orphanage). A year later, Lori became pregnant. After giving birth to Jack, Lori was told "the miracle can never happen again." Years later, when Lori and David learn that two children at the orphanage, 13-year-old Sam (who is Oriental) and six-year-old Sally (who is black), are "having a difficult time finding someone to love them," they adopt them also. Sam's father is an unknown U.S. serviceman who was stationed in the Mekong Delta in Vietnam; his mother was killed in the last days of the war in the bombing. Sam was found alive with two other babies in a chicken coop. Sally was abandoned by her mother at an early age.

David played basketball for Oregon State (jersey number 18) and was known as "Dunkin' Dave." He then became a basketball coach (for the Portland Trail Blazers) and now owns the Randall Sporting Goods Store in the local mall. Amy, who won the Portland Science Fair for her replica of the human brain (made by gluing 71 different-colored

sponges together) attends Mid Central High School. She is very pretty, hates her hair ("It's too flat and blah") and thinks she is too perfect. Amy does have a perfect attendance record (the school gives "Amy Awards" to students who maintain good attendance records). To "tarnish" her "goody-goody" image, she cut class one day "to run amok through the city" ("I wanted to be normal and imperfect"; Amy spent her time at the library—"Well, I had no place else to go").

Jack, the schemer of the family, and Sam, the worrier, attend Gregory Heights Junior High School. Sally, who is very close to Sam, attends an unnamed grammar school.

The Randalls' car license plate is NE8 396, and 555-3117 is their telephone number. Michael Jacobs, Al Burton, Sherwood Schwartz and David Kurtz composed the theme, "Together We Stand."

The series disappeared after four episodes. When it returned as "Nothing Is Easy" (CBS, 2/8/87 to 4/24/87), it is learned that David was killed in a car accident and Lori is now a working mother (her alarm clock rings at 7:00 A.M.). Lori's exact job is not revealed (in one episode it is assumed she is a secretary when she mentions getting her hair caught in a typewriter; no mention is made of the sporting goods store). Lori also attends an unnamed night school, where she is studying to become a court stenographer. New to the cast is Julia Migenes as Marion Simmons, Lori's bubbly neighbor, who is studying to become a bartender. She is divorced (from "the Bum," as she calls him) and is the mother of an eight-year-old nightmare named Chuckie. Chuckie is never seen and appears to be the child every parent dreads. He is extremely mischievous, so much so that Marian has a chain on her bedroom door to keep Chuckie out. One of the few ways Marian finds to keep Chuckie busy is telling him to watch for UFOs ("He's not to move until he sees one"). Amy was put in charge of the laundry; Sam handles the mail ("I sort everything so there is no confusion").

Al Burton, Dee Wallace Stone and David Kurtz composed the "Nothing Is Easy" theme.

Both series are based on an unsold pilot called "Kelly's Kids" (ABC, 1/4/74, on "The Brady Bunch"). In it, Ken Kelly (Ken Berry) and his wife, Kathy (Brooke Bundy), a childless couple, adopt three children of different ethnic backgrounds: Matt (Todd Lookinland), a Caucasian; Steve (Casey Wong), an Oriental; and Dwayne (William Attmore), a black. Their efforts to become a family despite racist neighbors were the focal point of the story.

To Rome with Love. John Forsythe and Joyce Menges.

715. *Tom Corbett, Space Cadet*

CBS, 10/2/50 to 12/29/50
ABC, 1/1/51 to 9/26/52
NBC, 7/7/51 to 9/8/51
DuMont, 8/29/53 to 5/22/54
NBC, 12/11/54 to 6/25/55

"Space Academy, U.S.A. in the world beyond tomorrow. Here the Space Cadets train for duty on distant planets. In roaring rockets they blast through the millions of miles from Earth to far-flung stars and brave the dangers of cosmic frontiers, protecting the liberties of the planets, safeguarding the cause of universal peace in the age of the conquest of space." The year is A.D. 2350. War as we know it no longer exists; guns are outlawed. Men no longer wear suits (their everyday clothes are made in one piece); women wear short skirts, "with the well-formed feminine knee in full view." Navigators have been replaced by astrogators, and nucleonics have replaced engineers. The planets Earth, Mars, Venus and Jupiter have all been colonized and now form the Solar Alliance—a group of planets protected by the Solar Guards, a celestial police force that is based at Space Academy, U.S.A., a training school for aspiring Solar Guards.

Frankie Thomas plays Cadet Tom Corbett; Jan Merlin is Cadet Roger Manning; Astro, the Venusian, is played by Al Markim; and Margaret Garland (later Patricia Ferris) plays Dr. Joan Dale.

Tom's ship is the *Polarus*; other Space Academy ships are the *Orion*, the *Vega*, the *Falcon*, the *Sirius* and the *Hydro*. The most common weapon is the Paralo-Ray (which causes temporary paralysis) and is only used when Solar Guards set out to explore new areas of the universe. Mercury, the smallest of the planets, has not yet been explored and is not part of the Solar Alliance. Pilots use Tele-Transceivers for visual communication with Space Academy and Strato-Screen for visual space exploration. There is no credit for theme music; as Tom would say in early episodes, "So long for now, and spaceman's luck to all of you."

716. *The Tom Ewell Show*

CBS, 9/27/60 to 7/18/61

The Potter Real Estate Company on Main Street and the home at 611 Elm Street in Las Palmas, California, are owned by Thomas ("Tom") Potter (Tom Ewell), the lone male in a house full of women: his wife, Frances ("Fran") Potter (Marilyn Erskine), their children, Carol (Cindy Robbins), Debbie (Sherry Alberoni) and Cissy (Eileen Chesis), and Fran's mother, Irene Brady (Mabel Albertson). Tom's efforts to cope with life at work and home are the focal point of the series.

Tom has a secret recipe for barbecuing ("Flip the burgers counterclockwise") and a method for avoiding problems ("Honey, I've got to go to work"). While Tom says, "The Potter family has three wonderful girls, each a queen in her own right," he also calls Carol, Debbie and Cissy "The Three Golddiggers" when they ask him for money. He calls Irene "Mother Brady."

Carol is the oldest child (17 years old) and attends Las Palmas High School. She is smart, fashion conscious and interested in makeup, boys and dating. Her favorite television show is "Teenage House Hop"; her first job was baby-sitting Jeffrey (Billy Mumy), "the neighborhood monster."

Debbie is 11 years old and the middle child. She attends the Richmond Street Elementary School and rarely enters the house through the front door. She prefers entering through the window on the right side of the door (viewed from the living room). She then does a cartwheel and goes up the stairs to her room (Tom says she is the only one of the girls who can do cartwheels). Debbie's first job was delivering newspapers for the Las Palmas *Gazette*. She also launched "The Debbie Daily," a neighborhood gossip sheet Tom helped her print and distribute.

Cissy, whose real name is Catherine, is six years old and attends the same school as Debbie. "She is sweet, adorable and huggable" and had a first job walking the neighbor's dog, Bismark (Bismark was much bigger than Cissy and walked her—through bushes that tore her dresses; Tom found it was costing him more for Cissy to have a job than to give her an increase in her allowance). In some episodes, Cissy is blonde, like her sisters; in others she has black, possibly dark brown, hair (the series is in black and white).

Theme: "Theme from the Tom Ewell Show," by Jerry Fielding.

Note: In the late 1960s, the series was retitled "The Trouble with Tom" for syndication purposes.

717. *Too Close for Comfort*

ABC, 11/11/80 to 9/15/83
Syndicated, 4/84 to 3/86

Cast: Ted Knight *(Henry Rush)*, Nancy Dussault *(Muriel Rush)*, Deborah Van Valkenburgh *(Jackie Rush)*, Lydia Cornell *(Sarah Rush)*, JM J Bullock *(Monroe Ficus)*, Deena Freeman *(April Rush)*.

Facts: The red Victorian two-family house on Buena Vista Street in San Francisco was once a famous brothel. It has long since lost that reputation and is now owned by Henry and Muriel Rush, the overprotective parents of two beautiful girls, Jackie and Sarah. In order to keep tabs on his daughters, Henry rents them the downstairs apartment for $300 a month.

Henry is the creator and artist of the comic strip "Cosmic Cow" (a space crime fighter; his biggest challenge "is to draw an udder so it is not offensive"). He first worked as an artist by painting turtles. "Cosmic Cow" is published by Random Comics, a division of Wainwright Publishing. Henry gives Muriel $150 a week to run the house. Muriel is a freelance photographer. Before marrying Henry, she was Muriel Martin, a singer with Al Crowler and His Orchestra. Henry and Muriel honeymooned at the Golden Pines Hotel, and in each episode Henry is seen wearing a different college sweatshirt.

Jacqueline, nicknamed Jackie, is the older sister (22). She is first a teller at the Bay City Bank, then a salesgirl at Balaban's Department Store and finally a fashion designer. She wears a size 32A bra, is excessively neat and jealous of women with fuller figures.

Sarah, a freshman at San Francisco State College, takes various part time jobs to earn her half of the rent money. Her first job was as a "wench waitress" at the Fox and Hound Bar (she got the job because she has a figure that fit the available uniform). She then became a teller at Jackie's bank, the local weather forecaster for KTSF-TV's "Dawn in San Francisco" program and a businesswoman who attempted to market Cosmic Cow Cookies. Sarah, who considers herself a "ten," wears a size 36C bra, is somewhat lazy and a sloppy housekeeper. The constant attention men give Sarah makes Jackie extremely jealous.

Monroe Ficus was originally a friend of Sarah's who attended State College and sort of just attached himself to her. His major was communications, with a minor in journalism; he later became a security guard at the Riverwood Shopping Mall. He earns $200 a week, rents a converted attic apartment from Henry for $300 a month and was once named Security Guard of the Month (Officer April) for catching a lady taking pantyhose out of the egg; he has a pet hamster named Spunky.

April Rush, Henry's niece, appeared for one season and was a free spirited musician who hung out with a character named Moonbeam.

In April 1986 the series became "The Ted Knight Show" (later retitled "Too Close for Comfort" after the initial run). Henry and Muriel relocate to Marin County, California, after Jackie and Sarah move away. Henry becomes co-owner (49 percent) of the weekly paper, the *Marin Bugler*, with Hope Stinson (Pat Carroll), who owns 51 percent. Norris J. Stinson (not seen), Hope's late husband, founded the paper 35 years ago. Brutus is the name of the dog on the paper's masthead. Monroe is now Henry's assistant at the paper. He hopes to become a standup comic and performs as Buddy Ficus at the Comedy Shack. Henry and Muriel's son, Andrew (an infant on the earlier series) is now five years old and is played by Joshua Goodwin. Lisa Antille plays the Rushes' maid, Lisa, and Leah Ayres appeared as Hope's niece, Jennifer.

Relatives: Audrey Meadows (Muriel's mother, *Iris Martin*), Ray Middleton (Henry's father, *Huey Rush*), Robert Mandan (Henry's brother, *Bill Rush*), Pat Paulsen (Monroe's father, *Benjamin Ficus*). Twins Eric and Jason Wells and William and Michael Cannon play Henry and Muriel's infant son, Baby Andrew.

Theme: "Too Close for Comfort," by Johnny Mandel.

Note: "Too Close for Comfort" is based on the British series "Keep It in the Family." It is the story of Dudley Rush (Robert Gillespie), a strip cartoonist (of "Barney, the Bionic Bulldog"), and his wife, Muriel (Pauline Yates), as they struggle to keep tabs on their daughters, Jacqui (Jenny Quayle) and Susan (Stacy Dorning), when they move into the basement apartment of the Rush home.

Too Close for Comfort. **Left to right: Deena Freeman, Deborah Van Valkenburgh, Ted Knight, JM J Bullock, Nancy Dussault, Lydia Cornell.**

718. *Top of the Heap*

Fox, 4/14/91 to 6/9/91

Apartment 3A at 116 East Hampton in Chicago is the residence of Charles ("Charlie") Verducci (Joseph Bologna) and his son, Vincent ("Vinnie") Verducci (Matt Le Blanc), two men who are poor and looking for the perfect way to get rich quick.

Charlie, the building's super, is a former marine who dreams that the "Verducci Master Plan" (finding Vinnie a rich girl to marry and living on easy street) will one day come true. Vinnie, who has a cat named Mr. Fluffy, is a former boxer who now works at the Rolling Hills Country Club. Vinnie was hired by Alixandra ("Alix") Stone (Rita Moreno), the club manager, "to keep the ladies off my back." His favorite ice cream is macadamia nut.

Mona Mullins (Joey Adams) is the Verduccis' ultrasexy neighbor. She is 16 years old and considers herself "sen-

suous, desirous and sexy." Mona is obsessed with Vinnie and wants to have his children. Vinnie finds it difficult to resist her, but does — "Mona, you're 16 and jailbait. I'll wind up with other guys who might want me." Mona's idol is Kelly Bundy (from "Married . . . with Children"), whom she calls "The Queen of Love." When Mona met Kelly (Christina Applegate), Kelly signed her bubble gum wrapper with "Wait until you're married to get fat. Kelly Buddy" (Kelly doesn't know there is an *n* in *Bundy*).

Lupe Hernandez (Irene Olga Lopez) is the complaining tenant (Charlie doesn't ignore tenants' complaints, he just doesn't listen to them), and Emmet Lefebvre (Leslie Jordan) is the "Rolling Hills Security Force."

Kenny Yarbrough sings the theme, "Puttin' on the Ritz." The series is a spinoff from "Married . . . with Children" (the pilot aired as the episode of 4/7/91, "Top of the Heap"). See also "Vinnie and Bobby."

719. *Topper*

CBS, 10/9/53 to 9/30/55

George and Marian Kerby (Robert Sterling and Anne Jeffreys) are celebrating their fifth wedding anniversary in Switzerland when they are killed in an avalanche during a ski trip. Perishing with them was a booze consuming Saint Bernard Marian named Neil (after George's cousin, whom the dog resembles).

Three months later in New York, the henpecked Cosmo Topper (Leo G. Carroll) and his wife, Henrietta (Lee Patrick), purchase the $27,000 Kerby home (at 101 Maple Drive) for $16,000. Along with the house, Cosmo inherits the fun loving ghosts of George, Marian and Neil, who now try to bring some joy into his dull life.

Topper, a bank vice president (with a bank account of $3,500.27), does his business entertaining at Club 22 in Manhattan. Over the course of the series, Topper is employed by the following banks: National Security Bank, City Bank, Gotham Trust Company and City Trust and Savings Bank. Humphrey Schuyler (Thurston Hall) is the bank president (all banks listed), and Kathleen Freeman (1953-54) and Edna Skinner (1954-55) are the Toppers' maids, Katie and Maggie. Neil was played by two Saint Bernards raised by Beatrice Knight of the Sanctuary Kennels in Oregon. The series is based on the feature film of the same title.

Two pilots were also made: "Topper Returns" (NBC, 4/19/73), and "Topper" (ABC, 11/9/79). In the first one, Roddy McDowall is Cosmo's nephew, Cosmo Topper, Jr., who inherits his uncle's possessions, including the ghosts of George and Marian Kerby (John Fink and Stefanie Powers). In the second pilot, Cosmo Topper (Jack Warden) is a lawyer who inherits the ghosts of George and Marian Kerby (Andrew Stevens and Kate Jackson) after they are killed in a car crash. Rue McClanahan was Cosmo's wife, Clara, and the Kerbys had a dog named Sam.

720. *The Torkelsons*

NBC, 9/21/91 to 6/20/92

The house (number 855) off Farm Route Two in the small town of Pyramid Corners, Oklahoma, is home to the Torkelson family: Millicent (Connie Ray), the divorced mother of five children, Dorothy Jane (Olivia Burnette), Ruth Ann (Anna Slotky), Mary Sue (Rachel Duncan), Steven Floyd (Aaron Michael Metchik) and Chuckie Lee (Lee Norris). They are a proud but poor family, and to help meet expenses Millicent takes in a boarder named Wesley Hodges (William Schallert), a retired salesman who pays her $125 a month rent for a basement room; he is affectionately called "Boarder Hodges." The family attends the Pyramid Corners Community Church on Sundays and has a dog named Fred.

Millicent is a very attractive woman who devotes all her energies to raising her family. She has not dated since her ex-husband, Randall (Gregg Henry), walked out on her. Millicent speaks her mind on everything. If she can make it she will (for example, clothes for everybody); she hates hearing the term *store bought*. Millicent runs a small business (Millicent Torkelson—Custom Upholstering and Design) from her home and is famous for her pickled vegetables, a recipe begun by her grandmother and handed down by her mother. Dorothy Jane is next in line to receive it. Each autumn Millicent opens up the Torkelson's roadside stand and sells Torkelsons' Treats for one dollar a jar (homemade jellies, jams and the famous pickled vegetables). Millicent attended Will Rogers Junior High and Pyramid Corners High School. Her maiden name is Dowd.

Dorothy Jane is the oldest child (age 14) and longs "for a life of poetry, romance and beauty." She believes her family is weird and is convinced that she was switched at birth and that her real family lives in Palm Springs. The only sanctuary she has is her bedroom (the tower room with a wraparound balcony that overlooks the street); she calls it her "santuary from the storm."

Dorothy Jane is a freshman at Pyramid Corners High School. She is the only kid in her class who wears clothes that were once something else (for example, Millicent made curtains into a dress for her). Dorothy Jane confides her dreams, joys, sorrows and ambitions to the Man in the Moon. She is very pretty but shy and desperately wants to become an adult ("Dear Man in the Moon, the nightmare continues. Here sits the soul of a woman trapped in the shell of a child"). While Dorothy Jane could have the pick of any boy she wants, she finds herself being wooed by Kirby Scroggins (Paige Gosney), the boy who lives next door whom she despises (his biggest thrill was seeing Dorothy Jane in her towel before taking a shower). Dorothy Jane played Juliet in her high school production of *Romeo and Juliet*. She is head over heels in love with Riley Roberts (Michael Landers), a boy four years her senior. Riley, however, feels Dorothy Jane is too young for him and neglects her. When Dorothy Jane felt she needed to change her wholesome image to attract boys, she modeled herself after Callie Kimbrough (Amy Hathaway), "a highly sculptured ice princess." Dorothy Jane discarded her intellectual side for that of a ditz. She dyed her hair blonde (Playful Minx shade) and became "Dottie. I'm not a young lady anymore. I'm a teenage bombshell." Dorothy Jane achieved her goal and had the boys in a dither over her, but went back to her old self "because it felt goofy being someone else."

Ruth Ann attends Will Rogers Junior High and plays the French horn in the school band. She believes she is beauty pageant material ("I've got legs that go on forever") and entered herself in the Junior Miss Oklahoma Pageant (but never actually participated).

Mary Sue is the youngest child (6) and has two dolls: Martha Sue and Elmo (the muppet from "Sesame Street"). Millicent calls her "Pumpkin," and her favorite sandwich is bologna. Schools for Mary Sue, Chuckie Lee and Steven

Floyd are not given. Chuckie Lee likes to hang out with the school custodian; Mary Sue enjoys going to Crawford's Pet Shop to pet the hamsters; and Dorothy Jane and Steven Floyd enjoy ice cream and hamburgers at the Frostee King.

In the episode "Return to Sender" (11/24/91), William Schallert and Patty Duke were reunited (he played Patty's father, Martin Lane, on "The Patty Duke Show"). Patty was Catherine Jeffers, the wife of Wesley's late son, Michael (Catherine lives at 37 Martin Lane in Philadelphia).

Ronnie Claire Edwards appeared occasionally as Millicent's mother-in-law, Bootsie Torkelson (she owns Bootsie's Beauty Shop). In the pilot episode, Elizabeth Poyer played Ruth Ann and Benji Thall was Steven Floyd. The town newspaper is the *Signal*. Drew Carey appeared as Kirby's uncle, Herb Scroggins; Connie Ray played her aunt, Jimmie Sissy Dowd.

Naomi and Wynonna Judd sing the theme, "Everything Will Be All Right."

721. *The Tortellis*

NBC, 1/22/87 to 5/12/87

A spinoff from "Cheers." Nick Tortelli (Dan Hedaya) is Carla's ex-husband. He is now married to the beautiful Loretta (Jean Kasem) and has a business at 171 Hope Drive called "Nick's Talent Emporium (phone number 609-555-4397). Loretta is his main client, a singer with a group called the Grinning Americans (the group is later called the Lemon Sisters). With his business failing, Nick and Loretta decide to begin new lives in Las Vegas, where Loretta has high hopes of becoming a showgirl. Nick and Loretta, as well as Nick's son, Anthony (Timothy Williams), and Anthony's wife, Annie (Mandy Ingber), move to Nevada and into the home of Loretta's sister, Charlotte Cooper (Carlene Watkins), and her young son, Mark (Aaron Moffatt). Charlotte lives at 6531 Veronna Street and is a substitute schoolteacher for the Nevada public school system. While Loretta struggles to achieve her dream, Nick sets up a new business called Tortelli's TV Hospital, which he operates from Charlotte's garage (the business phone number is 555-4768).

Perry Botkin composed "The Tortellis Theme."

722. *A Touch of Grace*

ABC, 1/20/73 to 6/16/73

"You're never too old for love . . . Never say no to love . . . Until the twilight comes, we'll take what time allows. . ." The theme lyric speaks of the love between two elderly people: Grace Simpson (Shirley Booth), a 65-year-old widow who lost her husband, Henry, two years ago, and Herbert Morrison (J. Pat O'Malley), a widowed 70-year-old gravedigger—two lonelyhearts who met and fell in love when Grace first came to tend Henry's grave. Stories ten-

derly relate the aspects of their courtship and eventual marriage.

Grace, a member of the Over 60s Club, lives with her married daughter, Myra Bradley (Marian Mercer), and her husband, Walter ("Wally") Bradley (Warren Berlinger), at 103 Court Street. Myra feels that Herbert is just not right for her mother and objects to their relationship: "What's the hurry? It took her 20 years to find my dad—and only two years to find this gravedigger. What kind of life is she going to have with this man? He makes less money than my dad did. She's entitled to have a little fun." Wally, the manager of the Penny Mart Supermarket, feels that Grace and Herbert are good for each other. He convinces Myra of this on the day Herbert proposes to Grace: "Myra, those people like each other an awful lot and getting married will make your mother very happy. The fact is, Grace will have more fun becoming 70 with Mr. Morrison than anything else." "So now you know, you're never too old for love, believe it's true, because I'm so in love with you" (as Grace sang in the episode, "The Proposal"). Had the series been renewed, it would have continued to focus on the lives of an elderly married couple. Herbert mentioned that he was with the Lancaster Light Infantry in 1917 and that the carpets in his room (address not given) came from the Chapel of the Repose Church. Based on the British series, "For the Love of Ada."

Pete Rugolo composed the theme, "You're Never Too Old for Love."

723. *Trackdown*

CBS, 10/4/57 to 9/23/59

Porter County, Texas, during the early 1870s is the setting. When the town's sheriff is killed, Hoby Gilman (Robert Culp), a Texas Ranger with the Frontier Company A, is assigned the job of temporary sheriff. Hoby is two fisted, fast on the draw and hard to figure. In some episodes he appears bloodthirsty and wants the outlaw to use his gun—"'Cause I gotta have a reason to kill ya" (he will never shoot an unarmed man)—while in others he seems to have compassion for outlaws (he saves their lives from vengeful people).

Henrietta Porter (Ellen Corby), the founder of the town, now publishes the town's only newspaper, the *Enterprise*. Aaron Adams (James Griffith) is Hoby's friend, the barber; Penny Adams (Gail Kobe) is Aaron's younger sister (she has eyes for Hoby). Ralph (Norman Leavitt) is Hoby's deputy.

While most businesses in town carry the name Porter before them (such as the Porter Hotel, the Porter Barber Shop, the Porter Bank), the local watering hole has a name all its own: the Buckhorn Saloon. Early episodes (before Hoby's appointment) relate his efforts to track down outlaws throughout Texas. See also "Wanted: Dead or Alive."

Herschel Burke Gilbert composed the "Trackdown" theme.

724. *The Trials of Rosie O'Neill*

CBS, 9/17/90 to 12/19/91
CBS, 4/11/92 to 5/30/92

Cast: Sharon Gless (*Rosie O'Neill*), Lisa Rieffel (*Kim Ginty*), Ed Asner (*Walter Kovatch*), Georgann Johnson (*Charlotte O'Neill*), Lisa Banes (*Doreen Morrison*), Dorian Harewood (*Hank Mitchell*), Ron Rifkin (*Ben Meyer*).

Facts: "I'm 43 years old and divorced," says Fiona Rose ("Rosie") O'Neill in television and radio ads. "He [Patrick Ginty] got the law practice, the house, the classic Mercedes, the dog and a girl young enough to be his daughter. I got a job in the public defender's office." In printed ads, Rosie was quoted as saying, "I'm 43 years old and divorced. He got the law practice, our house, our Mercedes and the dog. It's only natural I'm bitter. I really liked that dog."

In the series, Rosie is 43 years old and in the process of getting a divorce from Patrick (who ran off with a young girl named Bridget). Patrick did get their Beverly Hills home (no mention of a dog), but Rosie kept the car (which cost $80,000). Rosie now lives in Santa Monica (house number 418; telephone number 555-2363). She left the law practice she and Patrick shared to become a lawyer in the Central Felonies Division of the Los Angeles County Public Defenders Office (Rosie parks the car five blocks from the office—"Do you think the guys I work with can afford a Mercedes?"). In Beverly Hills, Rosie would help her rich clients get richer; she now feels she can do something she always wanted to do—help people who actually need her.

Rosie grew up in Waco, Texas. She attended Brownie camp when she was in the fourth grade, and in high school, she liked history, gym and lunch; "I hated algebra." She was sophomore class president, captain of the swimming and diving teams and "a porker." Her best friend since the second grade was Victoria Lindman (Tyne Daly), who is now a famous Broadway star (she called Rosie "Lumpy"). In high school, Rosie played Julie Jordan in *Carousel* (the school review read, "Rosie O'Neill is a triple threat on stage: She can't act, can't sing and can't dance").

Rosie later moved to the classy Hancock Park section of Beverly Hills and graduated fifth in her class at Wellesley College. She worked as a lawyer for 16 years before going out on her own. Rosie is an idealist and says, "My real first name is Fiona, but it sounds too soft and dreamy—like a fairy tale princess. I think my mother must have been expecting something else."

Before Rosie and Patrick broke up, Rosie ordered 800 checks; Patrick left her 285. (Rosie has had a checking account since she was 15. When she first got the account, she went to Jergenson's Bakery and bought $30 worth of éclairs. She likes the idea of checks: "You give someone a worthless piece of paper and they give you something.")

Rosie's Mercedes was serviced by Sierra Motors before it was destroyed by fire; she replaced it with an average car (license plate 2URH 134). Rosie wears a perfume called Temptation, and her co-workers say that when she wears red "it washes her out." Patrick is now a private practice attorney, and Bridget Kane (Helen Hunt) is the young woman he left Rosie for. Each episode relates Rosie's efforts to get her life back together again. She talks to an unseen psychiatrist at the beginning of each episode. Rosie's remarks from the first episode were quite unexpected and gathered much publicity the next day: "I'm thinking maybe of having my tits done. I may not want them any bigger; they're a nice size already. I just thought maybe I'd have them fluffed up a bit..." She also mentioned, "I've been wearing a lot of red lately. Patrick hated me in red. For ten years I never wore it; now everything I buy is red."

Kimberly ("Kim") Ginty is Rosie's pretty 16-year-old stepdaughter. She attends Beverly Hills High (later Taylor High School) and desperately wants to live with Rosie (she is unhappy at home; in second season episodes she gets her wish). Kim, whom Rosie calls "Kimmer," has an afterschool job as a waitress in a coffee house called Topaz.

Walter Kovatch is Rosie's investigator in second season episodes. He was a cop for 35 years and was arrested for breaking into his apartment after being evicted for nonpayment of rent (Rosie was assigned as his defense lawyer. She needed an investigator; he needed a job to stay out of jail). Walter never sits in a chair when in Rosie's office (when he left the force he vowed never to sit in a city-issued chair again). When they are on a case, Walter does the driving, Rosie does the talking.

Charlotte O'Neill is Rosie's 64-year-old mother. She is a snob and wishes Rosie would move back to Beverly Hills. Doreen Morrison is Rosie's married sister (to the unseen Doug). She drives a station wagon (license 2SVA 737) and lives in a ranch-style home at 684 LaMasa Drive. Hank Mitchell is a public defender who works with Rosie, and Ben Meyer is Rosie's superior.

Coffee dues at the office are two dollars a week; Rosie's father (deceased) was named Bill and was a lawyer with the firm of O'Neill, Watson, Stamford and Brown. In the opening theme, the book, *California Reporter,* is opened to page 548; a copy of *The Merchant of Venice* is seen on a table; and two antique dolls are shown.

Relatives: David Rasche (Rosie's ex-husband, *Patrick Ginty*), Kevin Davis (Hank's brother, *Willie Mitchell*).

Theme: "I Wish I Knew," vocal by Melissa Manchester (written by Carole King, who sings it in the episode "Reunion").

725. *Trouble with Father*
ABC, 10/21/50 to 4/13/55

Hamburgers were 25 cents; milk was 10 cents a quart; and eggs were 25 cents a dozen. The time is the early 1950s, and the place is Hamilton, a small town in Anywhere, U.S.A. At 143 Melville Avenue lives the Erwin family: parents Stu (Stu Erwin) and June (June Collyer Erwin) and their daughters, Joyce (Ann Todd and Merry Anders) and Jackie (Sheila James).

Stu and June have been married 19 years when the series begins. They eloped ("We were young and romantic and it was spring"), and on their honeymoon June made golden crust fried chicken—a tradition she still observes once a week (when they were dating, Stu was crazy about June's guava jelly sandwiches). Stu was originally a teacher at Alexander Hamilton High School and is now the principal (he also teaches night classes in civics for adults and is a member of the University Club—where he goes for peace and quiet). June, who pays two dollars for a pair of nylons, is a member of the Women's Club (which sends packages to Care once a month). She has the family's clothes cleaned at Ling Ying's Laundry; Stu's license plate reads IT 2N 514; he reads a newspaper called the *Daily Star.* June reads *Woman's Home Companion* magazine.

Joyce and Jackie share a bedroom. Joyce is the older daughter and attends Hamilton High (State College in 1954, when Merry Anders took over the role). She is very pretty and is described as "the perfect lady" (but, as Joyce says, "I wasn't always. I was a tomboy and got into fights with boys. I was the terror of the neighborhood. It all changed when I fell in love. I was 11. His name was Freddy. All I remember about him is that he had big ears"). Joyce wears a perfume called Divine Scent. Her allowance is one dollar a week, and her favorite dinner is fried chicken and candied yams.

Jacqueline, nicknamed Jackie, first attended Hamilton Elementary School, then Hamilton High (1954). She receives an allowance of 50 cents a week. She is a tomboy, "collects bugs, bottles, beetles and butterflies." "There are a lot of nice little girls for her to play with," says June, "but she doesn't want to." Stu wishes that she would change her ways—"But she just won't," he says. Jackie has off-camera fights with boys—"Mostly sticking up for Joyce when they insult her for mooning over boys." Jackie has a pet frog named Elmer ("He's trained. He can do somersaults and everything"). Freshly made strawberry jam is her favorite dessert, and she likes eating dinner in the kitchen—"It's closer to second helpings." Biff's Ice Cream Parlor is the afterschool hangout for both girls. Jackie is president of the Secret Six Club, and wrestling is her favorite television program.

In high school, Jackie joined the boys' basketball team when the coach discovered she was "a natural-born sharpshooter." (While Jackie did have the ability to sink every shot, she actually joined to be near a fellow student named Glen [Dwayne Hickman]; five years later, Sheila and Dwayne would become famous as Zelda Gilroy and Dobie Gillis.)

Willie (Willie Best) is a Baptist from North Carolina who works as the school's custodian, basketball team equipment manager and handyman for Stu around the house. Drexell Potter (Martin Milner) is Joyce's boyfriend (also a student at Hamilton High). They appeared together on "The TV Amateur Hour" in an elopement skit written by Drexell.

The series is also known as "Life with the Erwins," "The Stu Erwin Show" and "The New Stu Erwin Show."

The Trouble with Tom see The Tom Ewell Show

726. The Trouble with Tracy

Syndicated, 1971

"The two principal characters in this story are not fictitious. Very often I wish they were. Any similarity to persons alive or on videotape is purely intentional." Douglas Young (Steve Weston) is the "I" of this opening speech from the series' first episode. The other principal character is his wife, Tracy Young (Diane Nyland).

Douglas is a young, level-headed executive with the advertising firm of Hutton, Dutton and Norris in Toronto, Canada. Tracy is pretty, a bit forgetful and somewhat scatterbrained. She can be brilliant when she wants to (as long as she is coached first) and she has an uncanny knack for turning her blunders into lifesavers (for example, scheduling a party but forgetting to tell Doug, who is bringing an important client home. The client thinks the party is for her—and becomes a new account, thanks to Tracy). Doug and Tracy live at 3110 Crescent Street, and their phone number is Plaza 9-3123. Tracy is also famous for her malapropisms (for instance, "If I'm wrong, I'm not far from it," or "You've got to take the bitter with the batter"). Doug has autographed photos of Annette Funicello and Frankie Avalon (from the *Beach Party* films) and of Goodman and Jane Ace, who were the stars of his favorite radio series, "Easy Aces."

Also plaguing Doug's life is Tracy's brother, Paul Sherwood (Franz Russell), an unemployed moocher who constantly borrows money from Doug in the hope of investing in something that is going to put him on easy street. "Unfortunately," Doug says, "Paul has yet to find that investment. He keeps track of every cent I loan him; or, should I say, the track keeps every cent of it." Paul is an active member of the Free Al Capone Peace Movement (they are trying to raise $100,000 despite the fact that no one in the group knows that, in 1971, Capone has been dead for more than 20 years). Paul also fills out income tax returns—even though he doesn't work ("The boys [his friends] were filling them out, so I decided to fill one out myself"). For his 1970 return, Paul gave himself a $15,000 salary, and "it was tough cutting corners and making Tracy a dependent." He wound up owing the government $250.

At work, the seemingly always harassed Douglas finds more hassles from his boss, Jonathan Norris (Ben Lennick), who "believes a man's best friend is his motto" and stresses that point every time he speaks (for example, "Douglas the early bird catches the worm, I always say"). Like most television bosses, Norris takes the credit for the good that results from Doug's hard work—and blames Doug for the things that go wrong when a client is unhappy. Sandra Scott appeared as Jonathan's wife, Margaret Norris.

Tracy's best friend, Sally Anderson (Bonnie Brooks), is Doug's man-crazy secretary. Sally lives at a singles complex called the Happy Hunting Grounds Apartments, and her phone number is Plaza 9-6712. She reads *Confidential Confessions* and *Spy Secrets* magazines, and she is also "a single, uncomplicated girl who enjoys reading, browsing through museums, dabbling in finger painting, crossword puzzles, wood work, ping pong, pool, water skiing, karate, ballet, touch football, classical music, Western movies, dominos, darts, dancing and drag racing." She is also captain of the Y.W.C.A. volleyball team.

The series is created and written by Goodman Ace and is based on his radio (1930–48) and television (1949–50) series, "Easy Aces" (wherein Goodman played the long suffering husband of his scatterbrained wife, Jane).

727. *True Blue*

NBC, 12/3/89 to 2/16/90
NBC, 7/5/91 (1 episode)

Officers Frankie Avila (Eddie Velez), Robert ("Bobby") Traverso (John Bolger), Jessica ("Jessy") Haley (Ally Walker), Casey Pierce (Grant Show) and Mike Duffy (Dick Latessa) are members of the E.S.U. (Emergency Services Unit) of the N.Y.P.D. Sergeant Skiboss ("Ski") Wojeski (Timothy Van Patten) is their superior.

The team is attached to the Truck One Station, based on Bleecker Street in Manhattan. The unit's dog is named Bird, and the E.S.U. Standard Automated Robot is nicknamed Sam. Jessy, chosen from 287 applicants, is a registered nurse with psychological training. Her mobile code is Charlie One, and her truck license plate reads 8324. Boy One is Frankie's mobile code; 9465 is Mike's truck license plate.

Yuri (Elya Baskin) is the amateur news photographer who drives a cab (license plate T48611T) and frequently plagues the team as he attempts to capture rescues on tape; Tess (Suzanne Gregard) is Bobby's ex-wife; Judy (Brit Hammer) is Ski's wife; Lou Servino (Victor Arnold) is the police chief of the 8th Precinct; and Sophie Zackalakis (Mimi Cechini) is the elderly woman who lives across the street from Truck One.

Shawnee Jackson sings the theme, "True Blue."

728. *True Colors*

Fox, 9/2/90 to 8/23/92

Cast: Stephanie Faracy (*Ellen Davis-Freeman*), Brigid Conley Walsh (*Katie Davis*), Frankie Faison and Cleavon Little (*Ron Freeman*), Claude Brooks (*Terry Freeman*), Adam Jeffries (*Lester Freeman*), Nancy Walker (*Sara Bower*).

Facts: When Ellen Davis cracks a tooth while eating a muffin (she bit into a walnut), she is referred by her boss, Herschel Freeman, to his brother Richard, a dentist. While looking in the phone book, Ellen sees R. Freeman and calls for an appointment. Ellen is white, divorced and the mother of a teenage daughter (Katie). The R. Freeman turns out to be Ron Freeman, who is black, a widower and the father of two sons (Terry and Lester). It's love at first sight, and a year later they marry and set up housekeeping at 218 Bratner Boulevard in Baltimore, Maryland.

Ellen and Ron are married two months when the series begins. Ellen is a bit neurotic, intense and excessively neat. She has been a kindergarten teacher since 1978, and she always feels compelled to accomplish something. Ellen, whose maiden name is Bower, was married to Leonard Davis for six years. Leonard is a writer whose latest book is *Life Is Meaningless* (the dedication reads, "To my daugher, Katie, the one reason why this book may be wrong"). Ellen later works as a substitute teacher at Cortez Junior High, then as housemother at the Alpha Kappa fraternity house of Marshall College, before she turns to her true love of painting.

Ron, whose favorite singer is Lena Horne, has an office in the basement of his home. Ron believes he is very handy around the house; so much so that Ellen suggested he get the book *Home Repair for Idiots*.

Katie was born on October 9, 1974, and attends John Marshall High School. Her hero is Penelope Atwater ("one of the greatest philanthropists in the world"), and she is an animal rights activist (for example, she is a member of the Save the Flipper Crab movement). Katie insists that the family recycle and has a plush dog she calls Mr. Snoofus. She loves serious films like *Scenes from a Marriage*.

Terry, age 17, attends Marshall High, and 13-year-old Lester is enrolled in Marshall Junior High (he later attends Marshall High). Terry is the bright one. He is on the school's football team, and his lucky charm is his high school T-shirt. He later attends Marshall State College and is a member of the varsity football team (jersey number 22) and the Alpha Kappa fraternity. In early 1992, Terry, who is majoring in business, began an internship at the brokerage house of Haywood, Bates and Hamilton. Lester, who had a pet turkey named Ray, loves movies with violence and gore. He wears a size 10½ shoe, and calls Terry "Tee."

Sara Bower, Ellen's mother, also lives with the family. She considers herself "the only ray of sunshine in this whole house." She nags, is somewhat opposed to her daughter's marriage and is having a difficult time accepting Ron as her son-in-law. When Ellen was young, Sara scared away her prom date, embarrassed her at graduation and criticized her taste in men. This can be attributed, Sara says, to the fact that she has been suffering for 40 years from an impacted wisdom tooth (Ron finally pulled it; her previous dentist never took X-rays and never noticed it). She calls Katie "Pumpkin" and Terry "Butch."

Relatives: Paul Sand (Ellen's ex-husband, *Leonard Davis*), Michele Scarabelli (Ellen's sister, *Connie Bower*), Frances Bay (Ellen's aunt, *Sylvia*), Ja'net DuBois (Ron's mother, *Mae Freeman*), Bill Cobbs (Ron's father, *Bernard Freeman*), Kathleen Mitchell (Ron's cousin, *Toby*), Sam McMurray (Sara's nephew, *Marvin*).

Flashbacks: Cyndi James Gossett (Ron's wife, *Renee*

Freeman), Jason Bosesmith (*Terry as a boy*), Joseph J. Bryant (*Lester as a boy*).

Theme: "True Colors," by Lennie Niehaus.

Note: In the original, unaired pilot version, Joan McMurtrey played Ellen and Brigid Conley Walsh played Ellen's daughter, Steffi (not Katie).

729. *Tucker's Witch*

CBS, 10/6/82 to 8/8/83

Tucker and Tucker, Inc., is a Los Angeles–based private detective organization at 7000 Vista Del Mar Drive. Amanda Tucker (Catherine Hicks) and her husband, Rick (Tim Matheson), operate the agency. Amanda and Rick are not a typical couple: Amanda is a beautiful apprentice witch and is still in the process of perfecting her powers (witchcraft runs in her family, although it skips every tenth generation; girls born in the "off generation" do not inherit the powers of witchcraft). Rick is a typical mortal trying to cope with an unusual wife.

Amanda and Rick are also part time investigators for the Sandrich Insurance Company. They live on a farm in Laurel Canyon's Mill Valley (555-4616 is their phone number). Amanda has a Siamese cat named Dickens (after her favorite writer, Charles Dickens) and a goat named Myra. Their office phone number is 555-6111, and 555-8734 is Amanda's mobile phone number.

Also living with Amanda and Rick is Amanda's mother, Ellen Hobbes (Barbara Barrie). Ellen is not a witch as she was born in the "off generation." In the original, unaired pilot version, "The Good Witch of Laurel Canyon," Kim Cattrall played Amanda Tucker and Art Hindle was Rick.

Brad Fiedel composed the "Tucker's Witch" theme.

Tugboat Annie see *The Adventures of Tugboat Annie*

730. *21 Jump Street*

Fox, 4/12/87 to 9/17/90
Syndicated, 9/90 to 9/91

In an attempt to curtail the rising crime rate in high schools, a secret undercover unit called Jump Street Chapel (located in an abandoned chapel at 21 Jump Street and 6th Avenue) is established by the Metropolitan Police Department. The unit takes young looking cops and teaches them to be teenagers. Stories relate the exploits of officers Tom Hanson (Johnny Depp), Judy Hoffs (Holly Robinson), H.T. (Harry Truman) Ioki (Dustin Nguyen) and Doug Penhall (Peter DeLuise) as they infiltrate high schools to battle juvenile crime.

Thomas ("Tom") Hanson is 21 years old and the son of a cop. When he first became an officer, he was assigned to patrol car duty with the Metro Police Department (he rode in Car 25, and his code was 1-Zebra-6). Tom graduated with top honors in his class at the academy; his license plate reads LCH 937. His first assignment was at Amhurst High School. Friday night is bowling night for Tom and his team, the King Pins.

Judith ("Judy") Marie Hoffs is a gorgeous black cop and was first assigned to the vice squad where she worked undercover as a hooker. In high school in Chicago, Judy was a three time all-city guard on her basketball team; on Wednesday nights she does counseling at the West Side Rape Crisis Clinic (she herself having once been a victim of rape). Judy does her banking at First City State Savings and Loan, and her car license plate reads DVL 737. She drinks Ocean Spray Cranberry Juice (brick pack) and was assigned to show newcomer Hanson the ropes (on his first time out, Tom paid $200 for a pair of socks he thought were filled with drugs).

H.T. Ioki is a Vietnamese refugee. On his first time out, he bought a gram of baby laxative for $100 thinking it was cocaine. He drinks Coca-Cola Classic. Ioki's real name is Vinh Von Tran. He was born in Saigon and lived on Kanot Street. In April 1975, when he was 14 years old, the Vietcong invaded his city. He fled Saigon and found himself in St. Louis, where he was raised by a woman named Bessy Mason. He was the first Vietnamese refugee in St. Louis. He learned to speak English by watching "Sesame Street" and loved cop shows ("S.W.A.T." was his favorite); they instilled in him a desire to become a cop. After high school graduation, he went to San Francisco and posed as a reporter for a college paper to gain access to death records. He took the name H.T. Ioki, enrolled in the police academy, finished fifth in his class and was assigned to the Jump Street unit by Captain Jenko.

Douglas ("Doug") Penhall is five feet ten inches tall, weighs 165 pounds; he was born on March 1, 1964, and lives at 8137 Juniper Street. His driver's license number is 71-6583.

Other Regulars: Captain Richard Jenko (Frederic Forrest). He calls Tom "Sport" and plays lead guitar Saturday nights with a band called the Bunco Dudes (his idol is Jimi Hendrix; his license plate reads 9486-EO). Captain Adam Fuller (Steven Williams) replaced Jenko when he was killed in a hit and run accident. He attended the University of Toronto and goes undercover as a teacher when necessary.

Officer Joey Penhall (Michael DeLuise) is Doug's brother; his first undercover assignment was infiltrating the religious cult Heaven's Gate. Kati Rocky (Alexandra Powers) was a federal agent who worked briefly as a Jump Street cop; she had a cat named Bugsy. Sal ("Blowfish") Banducci (Sal Jenco) is the Chapel's maintenance man.

Detective Dennis Booker (Richard Grieco) was spun off into his own series, "Booker" (Fox, 9/24/89 to 8/26/90), when Dennis leaves the Jump Street Chapel to become the head investigator of the Teshima Corporation, a Los Angeles–based, Japanese-owned insurance company located in the Teshima Building. Marcia Strassman is Alicia Rudd, vice president in charge of corporate acquisitions, and Lori Petty is Booker's assistant, Suzanne Dunne. Booker's license plate reads DVP762; Suzanne's license plate is PX29190; and Billy Idol sings the theme, "Hot in the City."

At Jump Street Chapel, soda is contained in a gas station–like pump which has the slogan on it, ROAR WITH GILMORE GASOLINE. In the opening theme, when "21 Jump Street" is spray-painted, the paint runs on the letters *J* and *S*.

Relatives: Dom DeLuise (Doug's uncle, *Nick Penhall*), Marcia Rodd (Tom's mother, *Margaret Hanson*), Mindy Cohn *(Sal's wife)*, David Raynr (Adam's son, *Kip Fuller*), Lillian Lehman (Judy's mother, *Dolores Hoffs*), Robert Hooks (Judy's father, *Robert Hoffs*).

Flashbacks: Luke Edwards *(Tom as a boy)*, R.J. Williams *(Doug as a boy)*, Michael DeLuise *(Doug as a teenager)*, Larenz Tate *(Adam as a boy)*, Keone Young *(Ioki's father)*, Haunani Minn *(Ioki's mother)*.

Theme: "21 Jump Street," vocal by Holly Robinson.

731. *Twin Peaks*

ABC, 4/8/90 to 4/18/91

Cast: Sheryl Lee *(Laura Palmer)*, Kyle MacLachlan *(Dale Cooper)*, Michael Ontkean *(Harry Truman)*, Peggy Lipton *(Norma Jennings)*, Ray Wise *(Leland Palmer)*, Joan Chen *(Josie Packard)*.

Due to the confusing nature of this surreal series, information has been limited to what can be reported without confusion—the aspects of the Laura Palmer murder case.

Facts: Twin Peaks, population 51,201, is a Northwestern lumber town located five miles south of the Canadian border. Big Ed's Gas Farm sells Indian Head Gasoline. The Double R Restaurant, owned by Norma Jennings, offers coffee for 25 cents a cup (free refills). One-Eyed Jack's is the local casino and brothel. The local department store is Horne's; Callahan General is the town's hospital; and the Ghostwood Country Club and Estates is where the wealthy frolic. The Roadhouse is the local bar.

The Packard Saw Mill stands on land near Black Lake. The mill is owned by Jocelyn ("Josie") Packard, who is struggling to save it from the Ghostwood Land Developers who seek the land for a new club. Early one morning, Pete Martell, the mill foreman, decides to go fishing. While walking to his favorite spot, he finds the body of a 17-year-old girl named Laura Palmer. The mystery surrounding Laura's death becomes the focal point of first season episodes.

"Laura Palmer was bright, beautiful and charming. She was impatient for life to begin, for life to catch up with her dreams." It is estimated that Laura died between midnight and 4:00 A.M. from a loss of blood. Her nude body was wrapped in plastic and shallow wounds (like bite marks) were found on her neck and shoulders. Her wrists showed evidence of being tied before she was killed.

Laura attended Twin Peaks High School. She was voted homecoming queen and worked at the perfume counter of Horne's Department Store. She was the typical high school girl until she joined the Heavenly Choir, a cult group that changed her life. Laura was suddenly into drugs. She posed for the girlie magazine *Flesh World* and worked as a call girl at One-Eyed Jack's. The last entry found in her diary read, "Feb. 23, 1990. Asparagus for dinner again. I hate asparagus."

Laura was brought to Callahan General, where an autopsy revealed the following: 1. Cocaine was found in her system; 2. Rope fibers were found embedded in her wrists and upper arms; 3. She was tied twice on the night she died; 4. Clawlike marks were found on her neck and back (later found to be bird pecks); 5. A small piece of plastic with the letter *J* on it was found in her stomach; 6. Industrial strength soap residue was found on the back of her head (it is assumed she was killed near the railroad yards where the soap is used); 7. On the night she was murdered, Laura had sexual relations with three men.

Shortly after, FBI agent Dale Cooper, who has been investigating a similar case elsewhere, is called in to assist Twin Peaks sheriff Harry S. Truman. Cooper, who loves coffee ("Black as midnight on a moonless night") and cherry pie, examines Laura's body and finds an additional clue: a letter *R* on a small piece of paper under the nail of her ring finger. The remainder of the episodes kept viewers curious—but also confused many as to what was happening as Cooper began his investigation.

In the second season premiere, it was revealed that "Bob" killed Laura Palmer. But who is Bob? Based on the episode of 11/10/90, Bob was a menacing figure from Laura's past. An evil alter ego of Bob possessed Laura's father, attorney Leland Palmer, and forced him to kill his daughter (it is possible, however, to interpret a different ending based on one's own viewing of the series).

Other Characters: Sarah Palmer (Grace Zabriskie) is Laura's mother; she seems to possess psychic powers. Madeline Ferguson (Sheryl Lee) is Leland's niece and Laura's exact double. Bobby Briggs (Dana Ashbrook) is Laura's boyfriend. Donna Hayward (Lara Flynn Boyle) is Laura's girlfriend. Ben Horne (Richard Beymer) owns the Lamplighter Inn. Audrey Horne (Sherilyn Fenn) is Ben's daughter. Pete Martell (Jack Nance) is the mill foreman. Katherine Martell (Piper Laurie) is Pete's wife. And the Log Lady (Catherine Coulson) is the woman who carries a log and has a weakness for saplings and rugged, good looking men.

Theme: "Falling, the Theme from Twin Peaks," by Angelo Badalamenti (Julee Cruse sings the theme on a commercial release of the song).

Note: The original concept of the series is an unaired pilot called "Northwest Passage," which was produced for ABC in 1989. There was no Laura Palmer and no confusion; it was a mystery that dealt with crime prevention in a small Pacific Northwest town. Harry S. Truman (Michael Ontkean) was the sheriff, and Dale Cooper (Kyle MacLachlan) the FBI agent who comes to town to help him find a serial killer. Also cast were Richard Beymer (as Ben Horne), Brad Dourif (Jerry Horne), Joan Chen (Josie Packard), Piper Laurie (Katherine Packard), Lara Flynn Boyle (Donna Hayward) and Dana Ashbrook (Bobby Briggs).

732. *240-Robert*

ABC, 8/28/79 to 8/23/80
ABC, 3/7/81 to 9/19/81

Morgan Wainwright (Joanna Cassidy), Dwayne L. ("Thib") Thibideaux (Mark Harmon) and T.R. (Theodore Roosevelt) ("Trap") Applegate III (John Bennett Perry) are deputies for the E.S.D. (Emergency Service Detail) of the Los Angeles County Sheriff's Department. They operate under the overall code 240-Robert. Dwayne, who sings in his spare time, wrote the song "Saddle My Dream" and rides with T.R. in car 240-R-2 (license plate 280 648). Morgan pilots the unit's helicopter, 240-R-A (Robert Air), I.D. number N506. In second season episodes, Pamela Hensley replaced Joanna Cassidy as Deputy Sandy Harper; and Stephan Burns replaced Mark Harmon as Deputy Brett Cueva.

The theme, "240-Robert," was composed by Mike Post and Pete Carpenter.

733. *Two Girls Named Smith*

ABC, 1/20/51 to 10/13/51

Barbara ("Babs") Smith (Peggy Ann Garner and Marcia Henderson) and her cousin, Frances ("Fran") Smith (Peggy French), are two small town girls from Omaha, Nebraska, who move to New York City to further their career ambitions: Babs, an aspiring model (when Peggy Ann Garner played the role, a singer-actress when Marcia Henderson took over), and Fran, an aspiring artist (later a hopeful fashion designer). The girls live together in a small Manhattan apartment at 514 East 51st Street (Plaza 3-0707 is their phone number). Jeffrey Carter (Kermit Kegley) is a lawyer and Fran's boyfriend; Mr. Basmany (Joseph Buloff) is a bohemian poet who calls himself Babs and Fran's "friend, companion and philosopher." In the final episode, Babs gets her big break when she replaces Janice Avery (Gloria Stroock) as the lead in the Broadway play, *Stairway to Venus*.

Jacques Press composed the theme, "Two Girls Named Smith."

734. *The Two of Us*

CBS, 4/6/81 to 8/10/82

A brownstone on East 23rd Street in New York City is home to Nanette ("Nan") Gallagher (Mimi Kennedy) and her daughter, Gabrielle ("Gabby") Gallagher (Dana Hill). Nan, the co-host of a local television show called "Mid-Morning Manhattan," lived previously in Ohio, where she was the host of a morning show called "Wake Up, Cleveland." She moved to New York when the opportunity arose

The Two of Us. **Dana Hill (left) and Mimi Kennedy.**

to host a major market series, but the move resulted in a divorce (details are not related; Nan mentioned her husband was named Marty and that he divorced her—"And I've been losing ground ever since"). Nan is a Gemini, an art lover and a music buff, and she majored in English at Ohio State University. Marty kept her life in order; without him, she is totally lost when it comes to organization. She does a lot of research, and as a result books and papers are scattered all over the house. She and Gabby (who attends Saint Bernadette's Grammar School) eat whatever they can find, with nutrition being a secondary consideration.

On a suggestion from her agent, Cubby Royce (Oliver Clark), Nan advertises for a housekeeper. Robert Brentwood (Peter Cook), a spit and polish British butler, answers the ad, thinking the English major mentioned in her ad meant he would be working for a British major—not a woman who used the term to refer to her education.

Brentwood is a gentleman's gentleman and previously worked for the British cultural attaché to the United Nations (he became unemployed when the attaché was killed trying to ride a mechanical bull). Brentwood dislikes Americans, but finds Nan fascinating, despite the fact "that you have a child." He sees Nan as a challenge: "You're such a helpless wreck of a woman, that's why I accept the job." He also prefers to be called by his surname: "My name is Robert Brentwood, Madam. I am known as Brentwood." Stories follow his efforts to care for Nan and Gabby.

Patrick Williams composed the theme.

735. *2000 Malibu Road*

CBS 8/23/92 to 9/9/92

Two thousand Malibu Road is the address of a luxurious beachfront house on Malibu Beach in California. It is owned by Jade O'Keefe (Lisa Hartman), a beautiful high-priced call girl. Because of the recession, Jade finds it difficult to meet her monthly rent payments and takes in three roommates: Lindsay Wallace (Drew Barrymore), a gorgeous but unknown actress; Joy Wallace (Tuesday Knight), her plain looking sister and agent; and Perry Quinn (Jennifer Beals), an attractive criminal attorney. Stories follow events in their lives.

Jade can command as much as $4,000 a night. Her real name is Victoria Page Tremont, and she is the daughter of the influential Tremonts of Virginia (who have a net worth of $500 million). Victoria wanted no part of the life her parents had chosen for her (who to marry and how many children to have) and ran away from home when she was 17 years old. Becoming a prostitute was the only way she found to support herself. That is the true story. Victoria, who changed her name to Jade O'Keefe to break ties with the family, tells a different tale: "I was dirt-poor and hungry and became a prostitute to survive. I thought I could sell my body without selling my soul, but it doesn't work that way. There is still enough of me left to fight for something better." She is now hoping to do just that—without help from her family.

Lindsay is an aspiring actress who appears to have little confidence in her abilities. She is busty and accentuates her breasts with low cut blouses (her sister thinks the sexier she is, the better her chances of getting work). While Lindsay is absolutely gorgeous, she believes that "there are thousands of girls who are a lot prettier and a lot bustier than I am." While Lindsay is very sweet and trusting, Joy is deceitful and devious. She has a gift for telling pathetic stories about herself or Lindsay and having people believe her to get what she wants. Joy is also "far out" and believes in psychic powers, tarot cards and Ouija boards. She is very nosy and pries into everyone's business (information she uses to blackmail people into helping Lindsay). Joy calls Lindsay "Honey Bunny" and through blackmail got Lindsay the role of the younger daughter on the DBS network television series "The Jessica Rolley Show" (Sally Kellerman played Jessica, a neurotic superstar who was taking her first plunge into television).

Lindsay works under the professional name of Lindsay Rule. (Joy's snooping led her to uncover an affair DBS-TV executive Scott Sterling [Scott Bryce] was having with a married woman; Joy threatened to expose him unless he got Lindsay the role. Scott's license plate reads NETWORK I). Joy claims that she is "going to make Lindsay Rule the biggest name in show business." Lindsay is afraid to fall in love again; she was stood up at the altar by her high school sweetheart. She is now being romanced by Eric Adler (Brian Bloom), an independent filmmaker who wants her to star in his movie about the homeless. Eric has a dog named Allie.

Perry is a private practice criminal lawyer with a honest compassion for her clients. Other than Perry's late husband being named Mitch (a cop with the South Central Precinct who was killed in the line of duty), no additional information is given.

Constance Towers plays Victoria's mother, Camilla Tremont, and Mitchell Ryan is her stepfather, Porter Tremont.

James Newton Howard composed the theme, "2000 Malibu Road."

736. *227*

NBC, 9/14/85 to 7/28/90

Cast: Marla Gibbs (*Mary Jenkins*), Hal Williams (*Lester Jenkins*), Regina King (*Brenda Jenkins*), Jackee Harry (*Sandra Clark*), Helen Martin (*Pearl Shay*), Alaina Reed Hall (*Rose Holloway*), Paul Winfield (*Julian Barlow*).

Facts: Events in the lives of a group of people who live at 227, an apartment building in Washington, D.C. (an exact address is not given).

Mary Jenkins, a housewife, lives in Apartment E with her husband, Lester, an engineer for Stumer and Nathan Construction, and her daughter, Brenda, who attends Wendell Willkie High School. Mary first came to 227 when she was pregnant with Brenda. She worked as a counter girl at the Burger Barge and is president of the Tenants Association. Mary, whose maiden name is Hurley, attempted to market "Mary's Secret Cookies," a delicious cookie that was made from flour, sugar, water, salt, nutmeg, eggs, butter, nuts and the family's secret ingredient (which was not revealed). Mary also held a job at the Winslow Travel Agency.

Brenda Marie Jenkins originally attended Waverly High School and she receives an allowance of five dollars a week; her first job was burger bagger at Billy Bob's Burger Barge. Mary and Lester pay $39 a month for cable television, and in later episodes, Countess Vaughn played Alexandria DeWitt, the college student (and genius) who lived with the Jenkins.

Sandra Clark, who lives in Apartment J, is a very beautiful woman who is a threat to other men's wives (they "are jealous of my sexy walk, the way I act and the way I flaunt what I have"). Sandra calls her stunning figure, especially her breasts (which she proudly displays in low cut dresses), "her equipment." Her favorite letter of the alphabet is *M* ("for money, men and me"). She uses her feminine wiles to get men to do what she wants them to do—no matter what they want. Sandra first came to 227 when she was in college; her nickname at the time was "Sparkles." Sandra's jobs include the following: receptionist for an unnamed talent agency, receptionist for the Stumer and Nathan Construction Company, salesclerk at Benson's Department Store, door-to-door salesgirl for Luscious Lingerie, commercial television model for tuna fish (she was "The Tuna Lady," but only her hands were seen as she opened a can of tuna), travel agent for Winslow Travel (at the same time as Mary; their boss, Bob Winslow, was played by Garrett Morris). Sandra also had a brief stint as a television weather forecaster on Channel 87.

When Sandra feels sick, she goes shopping ("It makes me feel better"), and she doesn't like to be yelled at ("Don't yell at me, I'm sensitive"). Sandra and Mary appeared on the television game shows "Family Feud" and "Wheel of Fortune." For their "Wheel of Fortune" prizes, Mary received a case of wood varnish, and Sandra got a case of Oodles of Noodles soup.

Rose Holloway was the owner of 227 when the series began (she inherited it from the original owner, Herb Calloway [not seen], who died suddenly and left it to her "because it was his and he liked my apple pies"). Rose first came to 227 during the 1960s. In last season episodes, Julian c. Barlow became the new building owner when he bought it from Rose. Julian uses a lowercase c in his name because his mother thought it would make him humble. He is not as rich as he pretends to be, reads *High Finance* magazine and calls 227 the Beverly Barlow Hotel.

Pearl Shay is the elderly busybody tenant who is friends with Mary, Sandra and Rose. She was one of the first tenants at 227, having moved there when she was a teenager in the early 1940s. When the Lotto hit $3.5 million, Pearl, Mary and Rose saw a newspaper headline that read SENATOR, 34 [sic], LEAVES WIFE OF 8 YEARS FOR GIRL 19. REASON: 36-24-35. They played these numbers: 8, 19, 24, 34, 35, 36. The numbers came out, but 13,257 people won—each of whom got $267.01.

Other Regulars: Toukie A. Smith (*Eva Rawley,* Mary's not too bright friend, works at an art gallery called Gallery Moderne. Eva is from Lubbock, Texas, and yearns to design a footstool for the Lincoln Memorial: "Abe looks so uncomfortable," she says); Stoney Jackson (*Travis Filmore*); Barry Sobel *(Dylan McMillan).* Travis and Dylan share Apartment L with Pearl's grandson, Calvin. Travis owns the one-car Fillmore Limo Service; Dylan is a public school teacher.

Relatives: Whitman Mayo (Mary's father, *Henry Hurley*), Beah Richards, (Mary's mother, *Carolyn Hurley*), Harrison Page (Mary's brother, *Louis Hurley*), John Hacker (Mary's uncle, *Al*), Virginia Capers (Mary's aunt, *Gwen*), Brian Mitchell (Mary's cousin, *Ed*), Vanessa Bell (Ed's wife, *Sherry*), Kim Fields (Mary's niece, *Donna Denton*), George Kirby (Lester's father, *Milton Jenkins*), Nipsey Russell (Lester's uncle, *Edmund*), Gary Grubbs (Lester's distant cousin, *Chester Jenkins*), Brandis Kemp (Lester's distant cousin, *Amy Jo Jenkins*), Robina Ritchie (Lester's distant cousin, *Bonnie Bell Jenkins*), Della Reese (Sandra's mother, *Rita Clark*), Jackee Harry (Sandra's cousin, *Conchita Clark*), Curtis Baldwin (Pearl's grandson, *Calvin Dobbs*), Rick Fitts *(Calvin's father),* Charlotte Rae (Dylan's mother, *Millie McMillan*), Reid Shelton (Dylan's father, *Buster McMillan*), Kia Goodwin (Rose's daughter, *Tiffany Holloway*). Lester mentioned his late mother's name as being Ruby.

Flashbacks: Stephanie Covington (*Pearl as a teenager*).
Theme: "There's No Place Like Home," vocal by Marla Gibbs.

Note: An attempt was made to spin the Sandra Clark character into a show of her own, but only a pilot episode resulted ("Jackee," NBC, 5/11/89). In it, Sandra leaves 227 to move to New York to take a job as a fashion designer for Midway Productions. When she discovers that Midway produces X-rated films, she turns down the job. Shortly after, she becomes the assistant manager of the Sensations Health and Fitness Health Club. Stories were to relate her misadventures as she attempts to run the club.

737. *U.F.O.*

Syndicated, 9/72 to 9/73

Cast: Ed Bishop *(Edward Straker),* George Sewell *(Alec Freeman),* Michael Billington *(Paul Foster),* Gabrielle Drake *(Gay Ellis),* Dolores Montez *(Nina Barry),* Antoni Ellis *(Joan Harrington).*

Facts: The series is set eight years into the future: 1980. It is a time when the world has progressed greatly since the landing on the moon in 1969. It is also a time of great danger from the unknown—a menace from outer space called U.F.O. (unidentified flying object).

To deal with the problem of U.F.O.s, world governments unite, and a multibillion dollar, highly organized defense organization called SHADO (Supreme Headquarters Alien Defense Organization) is established and guarded under a veil of deep secrecy (a worldwide panic is feared if it were known that Earth is battling aliens).

A bona fide feature film studio called Harlington-Straker is established in England as a front for SHADO control (which is housed beneath it). A base is established on the moon, and the most advanced weapons and equipment become part of SHADO's defense force. Who are they? Where do they come from? And what do they want? SHADO operatives seek answers to these questions as they strive to protect the Earth from the unknown.

Edward Straker is the commander of SHADO. He was an air force colonel for ten years, possesses a degree in astrophysics and studied lunar science for two years at MIT. He is assisted by Colonel Alec Freeman and Colonel Paul Foster (a pilot for eight years, a test pilot for two years; he tested the Ventura XV104 before joining SHADO). Leaders at SHADO must pass "the stiffest medical exam ever experienced. They must have weeks of computer and psychoanalytical tests and a training course that will tear your guts out."

"The most glamorous girls to be seen on television screens" are part of Moon Base. Lieutenant Gay Ellis is the commander of Moon Base. She is assisted by lieutenants Nina Barry and Joan Harrington. Together they operate as one team of Space Trackers. Like all the women of Moon Base, they have purple hair, and they wear sexy one-piece silver uniforms. Leisure clothes for these well-endowed girls (seemingly a requirement) are bosom-revealing short dresses (usually metallic blue). Those based on Earth must comply with a stricter dress code: one piece white (and tight) jean/shirt combinations; hair color is optional. Commander Straker's normal attire is a beige Nehru-like suit. Astronauts wear silver space suits with tan helmets; Interceptor pilots wear blue, one piece uniforms with white belts; there are no female interceptor pilots. The logo for SHADO appears on a patch worn on the right shoulder of all operatives: A white circle is outlined in black; a figure is shown casting a shadow, and SHADO is printed in red (all stated colors are based on pristine prints).

Newly developed technology in lightweight but durable high tech metals enabled the building of Skydiver, a unique sea and air vehicle (a submarine with tail wings that houses *Sky 1*, an attack jet that can be launched from under the sea to intercept a U.F.O. that has entered the Earth's atmosphere). Georgianna Moon plays the Skydiver commander (no name given). She and the women in her crew have auburn hair and wear two piece uniforms: light brown fish net–like see-through blouses and medium brown pants with a white belt.

S.I.D. (Space Intruder Detector) is a satellite that is white with red striping, and it constantly maintains a scan for U.F.O.s (it can detect U.F.O.s 32 million miles from Moon Base). When a U.F.O. is detected, S.I.D. sounds a red alert. Within two minutes, the Interceptors are launched (same coloring as S.I.D.). Each Interceptor contains only one weapon: a missile in its nose that is capable of destroying a U.F.O. Once it has discharged its missile, the Interceptor becomes useless and must return to Moon Base.

While it is not specifically stated, all the U.F.O.s apparently come from the same unknown planet (they are all black and shaped like a Frisbee on the bottom with an eggshell top; separating the two shapes is the rotating sphere that powers the craft). In one episode, it was said that the aliens are seeking humans for experimentation and body parts. Since they appear in human form, SHADO has concluded that human parts are being used in alien bodies.

The series features a very large cast (mostly unnamed pilots, navigators and other SHADO personnel). Other key roles: Miss Eland (Norma Ronald), Edward's secretary; Colonel Virginia Lake (Wanda Ventham); Captain Peter Karlen (Peter Gordino); General James Henderson (Grant Taylor); and pilots Lew Waterman (Garry Myers) and Mark Bradley (Harry Baird). The Century 21 Fashions (as they are credited) were created by Sylvia Anderson.

Relatives: Suzanne Neve (Ed's ex-wife, *Mary Rutland*), Barnaby Shaw (Ed's son, *John Rutland*).

Theme: "U.F.O.," by Barry Gray.

738. *Uncle Buck*

CBS, 9/10/90 to 11/23/90
CBS, 1/26/91 to 3/9/91

Cast: Kevin Meaney (*Buck Russell*), Dah-ve Chodan (*Tia Russell*), Sarah Martineck (*Maizy Russell*), Jacob Gelman (*Miles Russell*).

Facts: Five months after the death of his brother (Bobby) and his sister-in-law (Margaret), Buck Russell, an insensitive, uncouth and ill-mannered man, becomes the guardian of his brother's three children, Tia, Maizy and Miles. Stories relate Buck's efforts to raise the Russell children despite his total lack of preparedness.

Buck, who tends to solve family problems by accident, drives a beatup, muffler smoking sedan with the license plate 521-214. His hangout is Rafe's Place ("Pool, Food, Friendship"), and he is a Chicago Cubs fan (he wears a Cubs jersey and in one episode did the guest announcing at Wrigley Field on a television show called "Call an Inning with Harry"). As a kid Buck would cut classes to learn the art of the con from Pete O'Halahan (Art Carney), who hung out at the local drugstore and taught Buck how to work scams, from three-card monte to handicapping. Buck was expelled from high school for planting cherry bombs in the bathroom. Buck stays in room 13 of the Stark Weather Lodge in Wisconsin when he goes on his yearly fishing trip.

Tia, the eldest child (age 16) has a fake I.D. (saying she is 21), likes to date older guys and dresses "too damn sexy" to suit Buck. The boy-crazy Tia receives a weekly allowance of ten dollars and attends Monroe High School. She drinks Minute Maid orange juice (brick packs), wants to become a model and held her first job as a salesgirl at the French Collection, a boutique in the mall. Tia feels she has every technical skill to be a model right now: "I can walk and wear lip gloss at the same time." Her best friend is Lucy (Rachel Jacobs).

Maizy, who is seven years old, is a very pretty and adorable girl with a smart mouth. She attends the Livingston Avenue Grammar School and receives an allowance of 50 or 60 cents a week (Buck isn't quite sure). She was first a Blue Bell, then a Tulip in the Girl Scouts (Tia was a Blue Bell also), and she calls her brother, Miles, a "wuss" (because of a birthmark on his behind, Miles calls Maizy "Freckle Butt"). Maizy is on the girls' basketball team, the Pigtails (her jersey number is 11); she wants to be a doctor when she grows up because she cares about people. Maizy has a *Jetsons: The Movie* poster on her bedroom wall. Maizy and Tia are very close sisters; Maizy is the only person to whom Tia can't lie. Tia calls Maizy "Sprout"; Buck calls Maizy "Maze."

Ten-year-old Miles attends the same school as Maizy and receives an allowance of one dollar a week (again, Buck is not sure, "but it is easier to give the kid a buck and shut him up"). He is a smark aleck and always in trouble. He and Maizy (sometimes Tia) eat Kellogg's Corn Flakes for breakfast. His ambition is to become manager of the Chicago Cubs when he grows up.

Other Regulars: Audrey Meadows (*Margaret Hogoboom*; she is the children's grandmother and lived in Southbrook, Indiana, before her house burned down); Laurel Diskin (*Darlene*; she is Maizy's friend and stays with her a lot "because the longer I'm out of the house, the better chance my mother has of getting through tomorrow"); Dennis Cockrum (*Bruno ["Shank"] Shankowski* is Buck's uncouth friend; he works in a slaughterhouse). The series is based on the motion picture of the same title.

Theme: "Uncle Buck," vocal by Ronnie Milsap.

739. *Undercover*

ABC, 1/7/91 to 2/16/91

Cast: Linda Purl (*Kate Del'Amico*), Anthony John Denison (*Dylan Del'Amico*), John Rhys-Davies (*Flynn*), Kasi Lemmons (*Alex*), Josef Sommer (*Stuart Merriman*).

Facts: The series, originally called "The Company," relates the adventures of agents attached to the N.I.A. (National Intelligence Agency) of the U.S. Government. The N.I.A.'s concerns are truth, detail and the why of a case (the reason behind an agent's decision to take a case); an agent's concerns are the money, glamour and temptations associated with a case.

The Task Force Agents: Kate and Dylan Del'Amico are married and the parents of three children: Megan (Arlene Taylor), Emily (Marne Patterson) and Marlon (Adam Ryen). They live in suburban Maryland (house number 2037), and Dylan's license plate reads KXB 808.

Kate, the only child of Edmond and Margaret Singleton, was born in Europe in 1955. She attended the Concord Boarding School in Boston and later became the first woman operative of the C.I.A. Her skills are risk management, damage control, interrogation, role playing and master recruiting. Kate can also speak Chinese and Russian. She is a voracious reader, has a tendency to lose her keys and her favorite drink is Scotch on the rocks. She will kill only in self-defense and will not under any circumstances participate in a sexual liaison. Her Achilles' heel is Dylan, whom she married in 1980. In 1982 Kate quit the agency to raise her natural children, Emily and Marlon, and her stepdaughter, Megan. She returned to active duty in 1990.

Dylan was 20 years old when he joined the N.I.A. in 1975. He is a "fallen Catholic" and drives a red vintage Corvette. He is a Yankees fan (he hates the Dodgers), speaks Russian and Italian and loves action and fun (he enjoys setting people up for practical jokes). He values loyalty and does things his own way. He drinks brandy, and his cover is that of a security consultant for a company called Langley (Kate's cover is that she works for the State Department). Dylan was raised in the Bronx, attended Fordham University and had a job as an insurance agent. When he saw the inscription on the Lincoln Memorial, he believed the words and wanted to make a difference; he then joined the N.I.A. (his father was a street cop in New York City).

For Kate and Dylan, the most distressing part of their jobs is having to lie to their children about their true occupations. Megan is 16 years old and full of resentment and angry that her father is continually absent from her life. She also harbors resentment for Kate, whom she blames for taking Dylan away from her natural mother, Molly (Mariangela Pino). Emily is nine years old and loves to play soccer; seven-year-old Marlon is shy and a member of a Little League baseball team called the Dodgers.

Flynn is an agent who has no first name (his file lists "NFN"—No First Name Flynn). He requests that he be called just Flynn. He is a womanizer, and the N.I.A. is his family. Flynn is a killer and understands the world in Euro-pean style. He has been with the N.I.A. for 20 years and sees things that others do not; he is a weapons man who doesn't get into fights. His cover: Chameleon (always changing roles).

Stuart Merriman is the chief of the task force agents. He is married, a good father to his kids, an excellent chess player and a master manipulator. He has a hardened sense of reality, and nothing escapes his notice. Stuart has a martini every day at 5:00 P.M. and was formerly a banker.

Alex is a beautiful N.R. (New Recruit). She is young, just out of college, athletic, smart and intelligent. She expects to be on the fast track and will do anything it takes to win the game. Alexandria understands her sexual attractiveness and will do nothing to discourage it.

Theme: "Undercover," by Cameron Allen.

740. *Unsub*

NBC, 2/3/89 to 4/14/89

The fictional Behavioral Science Unit of the U.S. Department of Justice is a special investigative team that incorporates forensic technology to help various police forces solve baffling crimes. When a culprit cannot be determined, they refer to him or her as "Unsub" (unknown subject). The team prefers to investigate a crime scene that is "sealed up tight—no one touching it before they do." They approach each crime scene wearing hospital gowns and slippers, "so nothing gets disturbed." Team director Wes Grayson (David Soul) explains: "We had a case last year. We found a hair, one red hair. Spectral analysis told us that the host body hadn't eaten for a couple of days and we discovered that the folicle had been washed with a chemical compound we later identified as a rare French shampoo. We traced the store that sold the shampoo, put out 30 feds on the street with a criminal profile, all looking for a thin red haired killer. It was my wife! The hair had come from my coat. She had been dieting and using a French shampoo that her sister sent her for Christmas. That's why we're careful."

In addition to Wes, the team consists of Ann Madison (Jennifer Hetrick), an RNDSC (a registered nurse who is also a doctor of psychology) who gives them their psychological killer profiles. Ned Platt (M. Emmet Walsh) is "one of the best old time feds who ever walked. Ned knows more tricks about solving cases than you and I put together," says Wes.

Allen McWhirter (Kent McCord) is "a forensic scientist. He can make a crime scene talk." Jimmy Bello (Richard Kind) has a degree in advanced hypnotic therapy and uses hypnosis to make witnesses recall something they never remember seeing. Wes keeps Jimmy around "because he is so uncomplicated; he helps the rest of the team when they become eaten by crimes."

Tony D'Agostino (Joe Maruzzo) is the rebellious member of the team and is constantly at odds with Wes. Wes is opposed to Tony's tardiness but needs his unique ability to approach a crime scene and psychologically become the Unsub.

Through Tony, the team learns the sometimes elusive motive behind a crime.

Jimmy calls Wes "Skipper." Wes was born in Key Largo, Florida. Ned likes to talk to people around the crime scene to feel them out. When they are at their base in Washington, D.C., the team has a sedan with the license plate 37242.

Kerry Sandomirsky played Tony's sister, Janice D'Agostino. Mike Post composed the theme.

741. *The Untouchables*

ABC, 10/15/59 to 9/10/63

Cast: Robert Stack *(Eliot Ness)*, Jerry Paris *(Martin Flaherty)*, Abel Fernandez *(William Youngfellow)*, Steve London *(Jack Rossman)*, Nicholas Georgiade *(Enrico Rossi)*, Paul Picerni *(Lee Hobson)*, Anthony George *(Cam Allison)*, Peter Leeds *(Lamar Kane)*, Eddie Firestone *(Eric Hanson)*, Walter Winchell *(Narrator)*.

Facts: Chicago, 1929: "By law the country was dry. Through conveyance with Al Capone, Chicago was wet—helped by corrupt officials and a public that was indifferent." Eliot Ness, a 26-year-old Prohibition agent, is summoned to the office of Beecher Asbury, the U.S. district attorney, to discuss a way of stopping Al Capone and the seemingly endless supply of bootlegged beer. "We have 300 agents in Chicago," Ness says. "Of those 300 men, some can be bought ... What if you have a special squad, small, operating on its own; every man thoroughly investigated; brought in from all parts of the country. Men who'll spit on Capone's graft; just a few he can't buy."

June 28, 1929: Eliot Ness arrives in Washington, D.C., with full access to all agents' files. His task: find six or seven men who are reliable, courageous, dedicated and honest—"six or seven of the most honest men."

July 5, 1929: Office 208 in the Federal Building in Chicago. The men who would become the Federal Special Squad, dubbed "The Untouchables" by the press (they "can't be touched by the mob"), meet for the first time: Martin Flaherty, a former Boston police officer with an outstanding record of arrests. William Longfellow, a full blooded Cherokee Indian, second team, All-American in 1924; largely responsible for the breakup of the Oklahoma booze ring. Jack Rossman, a former New York telephone company lineman, now a wiretap expert. Enrico Rossi, a barber who witnessed a hit by Frank Nitti (Bruce Gordon) that killed an innocent 17-year-old girl; angered and wanting "to stop those butchers," he became a material witness against the mob, and later an agent for Ness. Lamar Kane of the Richmond Bureau, a law school graduate, married with two kids. Eric Hanson of the San Francisco Bureau, a former guard at San Quentin's Death Row.

Additional agents (pilot episode): Tom Kopka (Robert Osterloh) of the Sacramento Bureau, a former Pennsylvania State Trooper and World War I hero. Joe Fuscelli (Keenan Wynn), who "knows every street and alley in the city; best

driving hands in Chicago; speaks the Sicilian and Neapolitan dialects." He also spent five years in prison for robbery. (Joe was killed off and Kopka was not used in the series; they were replaced by agents Lee Hobson and Cam Allison).

March 13, 1930: Al Capone (Neville Brand) returns to Chicago after serving time for a gun violation. A room above the Montmartre Café becomes his headquarters. "Seven honest men against the underworld empire of Al Capone": The Untouchables worked for 18 months to bring Capone to justice, eventually nailing him on an income tax evasion charge (for which he got 11 years in the Atlanta State Penitentiary; Capone, prison number 40886, was sentenced to Cell 39, Block D).

"And so Al Capone disappeared from view, to be replaced by other racketeers—more subtle and even more destructive. Against this new breed of racketeer ... Eliot Ness fought until his death in 1957 ... But the struggle between the Capones and the Nesses goes on and on and on."

In the opening theme, the book *The Untouchables*, by Eliot Ness and Oscar Fraley is seen in the center of the screen. Two guns are on the left side of the book; a box of bullets with 13 visible shells is on the right side. Eliot's office phone number is Superior 7-599. In the pilot episode (CBS, 4/20 and 4/27/59, on "Desilu Playhouse"), Eliot dated Betty Anderson (Patricia Crowley) and married her in November 1929; her phone number was Superior 2-198. The pilot also featured Bill Williams as Martin Flaherty, Paul Dubov as Jack Rossman and Paul Picerni as Tom Lugari.

Theme: "The Untouchables," by Nelson Riddle.

Note: On 11/10/91, NBC aired *The Return of Eliot Ness*, a two-hour television movie in which Robert Stack reprised his role as Eliot Ness. The story is set in Chicago in 1947. When former Untouchable Marty Labine is killed in what appears to be a cop-on-the-take situation, Ness, who has been living in Ohio, returns to the Windy City to prove Marty's death was a set-up by the mob. He teams with Marty's son, police sergeant Gil Labine (Jack Coleman) and proves that Madeline Whitfield (Lisa Hartman), the girlfriend of mobster Art Malto (Philip Bosco) was responsible for the frame in order to further her position in the Malto mob.

In 1993 "The Untouchables" returned to television via first-run syndication. Eliot Ness (Tom Amandes) is now head of the Federal Task Force and married to the former Catherine Staley (Nancy Everhard). His Untouchables are Mike Malone (John Rhys-Davies), Paul Robbins (David James Elliott), George Steelman (Michael Horse) and Tony Pagano (John Haymes Newton). Eliot was born in Chicago and attended Fenger High School and the University of Chicago. After college Eliot acquired a job with the Perennial Insurance Company. When Eliot and Catherine witnessed a gangland hit in which an innocent bystander was killed, Eliot quit his job to become a law enforcer. Catherine attended Jefferson High School and met Eliot in college.

Mike is an embittered ex-cop and explosives expert. Paul was an army fighter pilot then attorney before joining the Treasury Department. George is a full-blooded Cherokee

Indian. He is an ex–Carlyle University football star and worked out of the Omaha office. Tony, who hails from the Detroit office, has an outstanding arrest record and drives midget race cars.

The focal point of the series is Ness's efforts to free prohibition era Chicago from the reign of terror imposed by mobster Al Capone (William Forsythe). Eliot and his team are based at 4478 Racine—in a brewery once occupied by Capone. Joel Goldsmith composed the new "Untouchables" theme.

Valerie see *The Hogan Family*

742. *Vinnie and Bobby*

Fox, 5/30/92 to 9/5/92

A revamped version of "Top of the Heap," which continues to depict events in the life of Vincent ("Vinnie") Caulfield Verducci (Matt LeBlanc), a former boxer who is now a construction worker for Rand Construction. Vinnie shares Apartment 3B at 623 Cypress Avenue in Chicago with Robert ("Bobby") Grazzo (Robert Torti), a not too bright construction worker who considers himself the consummate ladies' man. The only other character salvaged from the original series is Mona Mullins (Joey Adams), Vinnie's beautiful and sensuous 17-year-old downstairs neighbor. Mona still craves Vinnie and can't wait until she turns 18. (She has given Vinnie a "Mona Countdown to Heaven Calendar." "I circled my eighteenth birthday; it's our wedding day." The calendar contains sexy, bikini-clad poses of Mona.) Vinnie still thinks Mona is too young for him ("jailbait") and avoids her like the plague ("Mona, you're like my kid sister, and we're never getting married"; Mona insists he is wrong). Mona's favorite television show is "Beverly Hills 90210."

Vinnie and Bobby have been friends since Bobby gave Vinnie the mumps in kindergarten. Bobby also gave Vinnie poison sumac at Sleepaway Camp, ran over his foot when he first learned to drive and tried to fix Vinnie's chipped tooth with Crazy Glue when he broke it. Vinnie attends night classes at Dick Butkus Community College (the only school that would accept him with a *D* average; Vinnie hopes to become a businessman with his name on the door).

Mona calls Vinnie "Heartthrob" and Bobby "Heartache." Vinnie wishes Mona would be nicer to Bobby, but she'll only do that if Vinnie is nicer to her ("I'm as nice as I can be," says Vinnie, "to a 17-year-old girl whose father owns a gun shop"). When Mona gets upset she cuts the heads off her Ken dolls.

Bobby is most concerned about his hair and uses the Omni Magnum 2000, the world's most powerful hair dryer. When he flexes his muscles, he talks to his arms (which turns off Mona; when Vinnie flexes his muscles, he calls

them Thunder and Lightning). According to Vinnie, Bobby has only been right about something once in his life: "predicting that 'Cop Rock' wouldn't last the season." Bobby has a little black book he calls his "Chickonary"; Vinnie has an American Express credit card ($500 credit limit) and a motorcycle he calls Ruby. They frequent Martino's Restaurant and pick up girls at Smoke's, a pool hall and bar.

William ("Billy") Melvin Belly (John Pinette) is the overweight, jovial construction worker who works with Vinnie and Bobby. Pizza is his favorite food, and he believes that Hoss Cartwright (on "Bonanza") was the only man on television who knew what to do when the dinner bell rang. Bill greets people with "Hi, I just ate, but I'll be hungry soon." Bill also believes he is an amateur detective (he reads *Shameless Shamus* magazine) and frequents Martino's Pizza Parlor. Julie Uribe played Bill's ex-wife, Shelley Belly.

Jimmy Thrill Quill and Danny Harvey sing the theme, "Vinnie and Bobby."

743. *Voyage to the Bottom of the Sea*

ABC, 9/14/64 to 9/15/68

Off the southern coast of California is located the N.I.M.R. (Nelson Institute for Marine Research), a government organization that does oceanic research. Five hundred feet beneath the institute is a top secret base, carved out of solid rock, which houses the *Seaview,* an awesome, atomic powered submarine.

"The *Seaview* is the most extraordinary submarine in all the seven seas. Its public image is that of an instrument of marine research; in actuality it is the mightiest weapon afloat and is secretly assigned the most dangerous missions against the enemies of mankind."

Harriman Nelson (Richard Basehart), an admiral in the U.S. Navy, is the creator and designer of the sub; he is also in charge of the scientific projects the *Seaview* will undertake. Lee Crane (David Hedison) is the sub's captain. He is a by-the-books commander and once before served under Nelson when he captained the submarine *Nautilus*. Chip Morton (Bob Dowdell) is the skipper, and Chief Petty Officer Curley Jones (Henry Kulky), Chief Francis Sharkey (Terry Becker) and "Ski" Kowalski (Del Monroe) are the featured crew members.

The *Seaview* can take depths up to 3,600 feet (anything deeper strains the hull and could cause the sub to explode). Code 452 is the *Seaview*'s code to the White House; Code 777 is the sub's code to the Pentagon. In the original, unaired pilot version (filmed in December 1963), the sub's commander was John Phillips (a credit was not given). "The *Seaview*'s job is never finished," says Nelson, "as long as there are evil forces active in the world."

Paul Sawtell composed the theme.

744. *Voyagers!*

NBC, 10/3/82 to 7/31/83

Cast: Jon-Erik Hexum *(Phineas Bogg),* Meeno Peluce *(Jeffrey Jones).*

Facts: A Voyager is a traveler in time who helps correct history's mistakes. Voyagers travel through time using the power of an Omni, a compasslike device that is inscribed with the words TIME WAITS FOR NO MAN. When an Omni flashes a red light, it indicates that history is wrong; a green light means that all is normal in a historical period.

Phineas Bogg is a seventeenth-century pirate who was "plucked out of time" to become a Voyager. Following the deaths of his parents, Bill and Cathy, 11-year-old Jeffrey Jones is sent to live with his aunt, Elizabeth (Janie Bradley), in Manhattan. As Bogg is traveling in time, his Omni, which had been programed only up to 1970, malfunctions and sends him to 1982. Phineas "falls to earth" on the window ledge of Jeffrey's high rise apartment building bedroom. Bogg breaks the window and enters the room. Jeffrey's dog, Ralph, grabs Bogg's guidebook and a struggle ensues. As Jeffrey is attempting to get the book from Ralph, he accidentally falls out the window. Phineas jumps out after him. He grabs Jeffrey, touches his Omni and the two are sent safely into time (1450 B.C. Egypt). Because of the setting on his Omni, Bogg is unable to return Jeffrey to his time and is forced to become his guardian.

Bogg attended Voyager School but was more interested in watching the girls in his class than in learning about history; he is therefore lost without his guidebook. Jeffrey, who is destined to become a Voyager, is a history buff and soon himself becomes Bogg's "guidebook." Together they set out to correct history's mistakes. (A split second before Phineas and Jeffrey met, the camera showed two books on Jeffrey's shelf: *Pirates and History* and *The Man Out There,* both of which refer to Phineas.)

Phineas has an eye for the ladies of the eras he visits. He calls Jeffrey "Kid" and remarks, "Smart kids give me a pain." He uses the catchphrase "Bat's breath" when something goes wrong. Jeffrey, whose father was a history professor, calls Phineas "Bogg" and poses as his son or his nephew depending on the situation. Tracy Brooks Swope plays Voyager Olivia Dunn (class of '97), and Stephen Liska is Drake, the renegade Voyager (he has a model 31650 Open-Time Calibrated Omni). Anne Lockhart and John O'Connell appeared as Jeffrey's great-grandparents, Amy and Steven Jones, in the episode "Merry Christmas, Bogg."

Theme: "Voyagers!" by Jerrold Immel.

Note: In 1985 MCA Home Video released *Voyager from the Unknown* and everything changed: "Far out in the cosmos there exists a planet known as Voyager, where the mystery of travel into space and through time has been solved. It is inhabited by a race who call themselves Voyagers. Their purpose is to keep constant surveillance on history... These people have a time-machine device, the Omni, which will take them into the past, present or future. As each Voyager graduates ... he is given an Omni

and a guidebook. One such graduate was Phineas Bogg, who was assigned as a field worker to operate in certain time zones..." (The History Surveillance Unit, a computer complex, keeps track of Voyagers during their assignments.)

The 91-minute movie was re-edited from the pilot and the "Voyagers of the *Titanic*" episodes of the series. The year in which Jeffrey and Phineas met has been changed to 1984; the Omni now buzzes when opened (instead of sounding a bell); and they now travel through time in computer guided space hoops (instead of by quasi-free flight through space as in the series).

745. *Walter and Emily*

NBC, 11/16/91 to 2/22/92

Walter and Emily Collins (Brian Keith and Cloris Leachman) have been married for 38 years. (Forty years ago in Chicago, Emily was working in the millinery department of the Marshall Field Department Store. Walter was a salesman and they accidentally bumped into each other. He bought her a turkey sandwich and they fell in love. Two years later they married—on the day Count Turf won the Kentucky Derby.)

When their son, Matt (Christopher McDonald), gets a divorce, Walter and Emily decide to move in with him and help him raise their 11-year-old grandson, Zack (Matthew Lawrence).

Matt is a sportswriter for the San Francisco *Examiner* and is constantly on the road. Walter, a salesman for 40 years, had a part time job as a tour guide on the *Harbor Princess,* a ferry that tours San Francisco Bay. Walter's favorite watering hole is the Bridge Café. Walter and Emily once took a cruise—the ferry to Alcatraz. Emily was the spelling bee champion of 1939 and is now a member of the Conservative Club. The family heirloom is a 1932 Joe ("Ducky") Medwick baseball card. Matt attended San Francisco State College.

Jeff Andrew Koz composed the theme, "It's Never Too Late for Love."

746. *The Waltons*

CBS, 9/14/72 to 8/20/81

Cast: Ralph Waite *(John Walton),* Michael Learned *(Olivia Walton),* Will Geer *(Zeb Walton),* Ellen Corby *(Esther Walton),* Richard Thomas and Robert Wightman *(John-Boy Walton),* Judy Norton-Taylor *(Mary Ellen Walton),* Mary Elizabeth McDonough *(Erin Walton),* Kami Cotler *(Elizabeth Walton),* John Walmsley *(Jason Walton),* Eric Scott *(Ben Walton),* David W. Harper *(Jim-Bob Walton).*

Facts: With only an ax, a plow and a mule to his name, a pioneer named Rome Walton settled in the Blue Ridge

Mountains of Virginia. The year was 1789 (another episode mentions 1796). He fought wars there (disease, cold, fire and flood) and raised a family there. The area came to be known as Waltons' Mountain (they don't own it but "sort of hold it in trust").

The series itself is set much later, beginning in 1931. The area surrounding Waltons' Mountain is now Jefferson County, and the current Waltons are John, his wife, Olivia, and their children, John-Boy (John Walton, Jr.), Mary Ellen, Erin, Elizabeth, Jason, Ben, and Jim-Bob. Also living with them is John's father, "Grandpa" Zebulon ("Zeb") Walton, and his wife, "Grandma" Esther Walton. The times are difficult, the country being in the midst of the Depression, and the family earns a living by operating a sawmill.

John and Olivia married in 1916 and established the mill in 1931 (1935 in another episode). Although Olivia's parents disliked John because they were Baptists and he was "a heathen," she and John still married (they eloped and were married by Preacher Hicks). John, a dedicated, hard working family man, would do what he could to provide for his family. According to the narration of series creator Earl Hamner, Jr., John passed away in 1965 (1969 in another episode). Olivia, who is known for her applesauce cake, was replaced by her cousin Rose Burton (Peggy Rea) when Olivia left to work as a nurse in an army hospital during World War II (this was the off-screen explanation as to what happened to Olivia when Michael Learned asked to be released from her contract in 1980).

Zeb's bones give him the weather forecast: "They feel one way for good weather, another way for bad weather." He calls Olivia "Livie" and "Daughter." In November 1976, Ellen Corby was forced to give up the role of Grandma when she had a stroke; in the March 30, 1978, episode she returned. It was explained that Esther had had a stroke and had been hospitalized. As a result of the illness, Grandma (and Ellen) were victims of aphasia (speech difficulty).

John-Boy, the oldest child, keeps a journal about his family and longs to be a writer. He attended Boatwright University and established his own newspaper, the Blue Ridge *Chronicle* (his printing press was a 1912 Champlin-Price, which he purchased from Professor Ames at Boatwright). His first serious love affair was with Jenny Pendleton (Sian Barbara Allen), a runaway the Waltons took in. John-Boy left Waltons' Mountain to pursue his career in New York as a writer (there he befriended a Broadway dancer named Daisy Garner [Deirdre Lenihan]). After having his first novel published, he became a reporter for a national wire service. He later married and raised a family in California.

Mary Ellen, the oldest girl, became a nursing student and married Dr. Curtis Willard (Tom Bower and Scott Hylands). They had a son they named John Curtis Walton Willard (Marshall and Michael Reed; John Friedman). Mary Ellen later married Arlington ("Jonesy") Westcott (Richard Gilliland). When Mary Ellen was a youngster and got upset, she would go into the barn and hug a cow to feel better.

Erin, the second oldest girl, worked as an operator at the Jefferson County Phone Company and later at the Pickett Metal Products Company. Her first boyfriend, George

("G.W.") Haines (David Doremus) enlisted in the army (World War II) and was killed in action. She later married Paul Northridge (Morgan Stevens).

Jason, the second oldest son, is seeking musical fame (he wrote the song "Will You Be Mine"). He studied at the Clyneburg Conservatory and played with the Bobby Bigelow and His Hayseed Gang band. Jason also played in a band called the Rhythm Kings and sang with the WQSR (radio) Gospelites. He also had an afterschool job at the Jarvis Used Car Lot and worked as a musician (playing guitar) at the Dew Drop Inn.

Ben, the third oldest son, took over the family sawmill business and turned it into the Walton Lumber Mill. He married Cindy Brunson (Leslie Winston) and had a daughter they named Virginia (Angela Rhodes).

Elizabeth and Jim-Bob are the youngest Walton children. Elizabeth was carefree and anxious to grow up and had a sleepwalking problem because of a subconscious fear of a carnival ferris wheel. Jim-Bob was a twin; his brother, Joseph Zebulon, died (possibly at birth). He is a loner and constantly lost in his dreams. Jim-Bob wanted to be an airline pilot but couldn't because of astigmatism.

Family pets are Reckless (a dog), Chance (a cow), Blue (a mule), Myrtle (a goat), Calico (a cat), and Rover (a peacock). Charlottesville is the nearest major city, and neighboring towns are Hickory Creek (six miles away) and Waynesboro. The White Arrow Bus Lines services the area.

On Christmas Eve in 1931, as the family gathered in front of the tree, Elizabeth yawned and was about to say goodnight when Mary Ellen interrupted: "Don't say goodnight yet. Wait until we're all in bed and the last light is out." Thus began the program's traditional closing, with the Waltons wishing one another goodnight.

Other Regulars: Ike Godsey (Joe Conley), the owner of Ike Godsey's General Merchandise Store (the phone rings three shorts, one long; Ike keeps the keys to the store in the coffee grinder); Corabeth Walton (Ronnie Claire Edwards) is John's spinster cousin from Doe Hills (she married Ike in the episode of 1/9/75).

Aimee Godsey (Rachel Longaker and DeAnna Robbins) is Ike and Corabeth's adopted daughter (and Elizabeth's best friend). Mamie Baldwin (Helen Kleeb) and Emily Baldwin (Mary Jackson) are two spinster sisters who are famous for "Papa's Recipe" (a home brewed liquor); they are referred to as "Miss Emily" and "Miss Mamie," and they own a cottage at Virginia Beach. Miss Emily was born on October 19.

Marmaduke Ephraim ("Ep") Bridges (John Crawford) is the local sheriff; Patsy Brimmer (Eileen McDonough and Debbie Gunn) was Jim-Bob's first girlfriend; Ruby Davis (Heather Totten) was Ben's first girlfriend; Matthew Fordwick (John Ritter) is the town's preacher; and Rosemary Fordwick (Mariclare Costello) is Matthew's wife.

Other Relatives: Linda Purl (Curt's sister, *Vanessa*), Beulah Bondi (John's 90-year-old aunt), Martha Nix (Rose's granddaughter, *Serena*), Keith Mitchell (Rose's grandson, *Jeffrey*).

Pilot Episode Roles: ("The Homecoming," CBS, 12/19/71): Patricia Neal (*Olivia Walton*), Andrew Duggan (*John Walton*), Edgar Bergen (*Zeb Walton*), Woodrow

Parfrey *(Ike Godsey)*, David Huddleston *(Ep Bridges)*, Josephine Hutchinson *(Miss Mamie)*, Dorothy Stickney *(Miss Emily)*.

Theme: "The Waltons," by Alexander Courage.

Note: Three NBC television movies appeared: *A Wedding on Waltons' Mountain* (2/22/82; Erin's marriage to Paul); *Mother's Day on Waltons' Mountain* (5/9/82; Olivia returns to help her chidren: Mary Ellen, who learns she cannot have children after a car accident; Ben, whose marriage is failing; and Elizabeth, who is fighting to grow up); and *A Day for Thanks on Waltons' Mountain* (11/22/82; Elizabeth's efforts to reunite her family for Thanksgiving Day in 1947).

747. *Wanted: Dead or Alive*

CBS, 9/6/58 to 3/29/61

Cast: Steve McQueen *(Josh Randall)*, Wright King *(Jason Nichols)*.

Facts: On March 7, 1957, "The Bounty Man" aired on the CBS series "Trackdown." It introduced viewers to a bounty hunter named Josh Randall and spawned the successful series "Wanted: Dead or Alive." While millions of people saw the episode, only potential sponsors saw the show's sales pitch (which played right before the closing theme). It went like this:

Hi, my name is Steve McQueen. I hope you liked what you just saw. Kind of a new approach to Westerns. I hope you liked Josh Randall. Oh, he's not a lawman, but he's got a lot of friends who are. And they like him because he respects them and their jobs. Since Josh doesn't wear a badge, he can take the shortest distance between two people. On these occasions, his lawmen friends kinda turn their heads and wish they could use the same methods. The stories on "Wanted: Dead or Alive" are about the people of the times; their dreams, their problems, their happiness ... There are a lot of stories on "Wanted: Dead or Alive" and they all have one thing in common—they all happen to people ... Any way you slice it, "Wanted: Dead or Alive" is a good show, full of action, drama and adventure. Good entertainment for the whole family—and that's what'll sell any product ... See y'all now.

The time is the 1870s, and being a bounty hunter "wasn't a bad way to live. You got to see a lot of the country and meet a lot of people. It was a living and now and then a good one." Josh Randall liked the life "and it seemed to like him." Though the world may be big and men can easily hide from the law, Josh finds that not a problem— "He's a man; there's nowhere he can lay down his feet that I can't walk—I'll find him." Josh's motto: "If he's got a price on his head, I've got an empty pocket."

Josh is a compassionate bounty hunter and sometimes finds himself in the position of protector, struggling to safeguard his prisoners from the less scrupulous bounty hunters. Josh carries a .30-40 caliber sawed-off carbine he calls his "Mare's leg": "It's kinda like a hog's leg but not

quite as mean. If I have to use it, I want to get the message across."

Josh's occasional assistant is Jason Nichols, a bounty hunter who travels with an unnamed mutt he calls "Hey, Dog."

The first person Josh tracked was Nate Phillips (George Niese), a killer with a $500 price tag who was wanted for murder in Texas.

Theme: "Wanted: Dead or Alive Theme," by Rudy Schrager.

748. *War of the Worlds*

Syndicated, 10/8/88 to 9/30/89
Syndicated, 10/89 to 9/90

Cast: Jared Martin *(Harrison Blackwood)*, Lynda Mason Green *(Suzanne McCullough)*, Richard Chaves *(Paul Ironhorse)*, Philip Akin *(Norton Drake)*, Rachel Blanchard *(Debi McCullough)*.

Facts: In 1953 (as depicted in the film, *War of the Worlds*), the Earth is invaded by Martians, who begin an unprovoked attack on humanity, whose weapons are useless against their destructive rays and dome-protected ships. It seemed that the Earth was doomed until the smallest of things, the bacteria in the air, to which humans have become immune, killed the Martians.

In 1988 it is learned that the aliens' remains have been stored in metal containers. A group of aliens is revived by a nuclear accident when radioactive waste contacts one of the storage containers. They soon begin to revive others of their kind. To protect themselves from Earthly viruses, the aliens must inhabit human bodies.

Their leaders (now from the planet Mortex, not Mars) are called the Advocacy. When the U.S. government learns what has happened, it suppresses the information and creates the Blackwood Project, a secret army to battle the aliens. Dr. Harrison Blackwood is the leader; Dr. Suzanne McCullough, Colonel Paul Ironhorse and Norton Drake are his key assistants.

Blackwood's team is based in a secret government safe house (Cottage 348) on 25 secured acres of land. Blackwood's army is called the Omega Squad; Suzanne, who is divorced (her maiden name is Baxter), lives on the base with her teenage daughter, Debi (who has a dog named Guido). Norton Drake, a crippled computer expert, calls his voice activated wheelchair Gertrude. Harrison's aunt is Sylvia Van Buren, who witnessed the original 1953 invasion as a girl and can now sense when the aliens are near (because of the traumatic shock she suffered, she now resides at the Westwood Mental Health Center). Before a dramatic storyline change, Elaine Giftos was introduced as Katara, the Synth from the planet Qar'to. Katara, a beautiful killing android, was sent to Earth to aid Blackwell, destroy the Mortex and save mankind for Katara's people's more sinister purpose—to use Earth as a food source.

When the series returned for its second season (10/89 to 9/90), the format was revamped in an effort to improve the show. It is now set in a time called Almost Tomorrow. When the planet Morthrai is destroyed, survivors journey to Earth and take over the war begun by the Mortex—with a goal of making Earth their new Morthrai. In a fierce battle among the three different lifeforms, the Mortex are destroyed and the Earth is heavily damaged. Surviving Earthlings unite in an effort to defeat their new enemy. Adrian Paul as John Kincaid joins Suzanne, Debbie and Blackwood when Ironhorse and Drake are killed in the battle. The new aliens are led by the Eternal; Catherine Disher (Mana) and Denis Forest (Malzor) are the two Morthrai aliens who serve the Eternal.

Relatives: Ann Robinson (Harrison's aunt, *Sylvia Van Buren*), Michael Parks (Suzanne's ex-husband, *Cash McCullough*).

Theme: "War of the Worlds," by Bill Thorpe.

749. *Waterfront*

Syndicated, 1954

John Herrick (Preston Foster) works for the Wellington Towing Company in San Pedro, California. He is captain of the tugboat *Cheryl Ann,* which he docks in Berth 14 of the San Pedro Harbor. John was born in San Pedro (he lived at 91 Surf Street in an area called the Wharf) and married his first and only sweetheart, May (Lois Moran), whom he calls "Mom" (she is famous for her lemon pies). John's telephone number is Terminal 5-6741, and he buys his gear from a store called Bailey's; he does his fishing off Bell Point.

John and May's son, Carl Herrick (Douglas Dick) is captain of the tugboat *Belinda* (docked in Berth 5). His friend Dan Cord (Ramon Vallo) captains the tugboat *Isabel* (all tugs owned by Wellington are named after women), and his friend Max Benson (George Chandler) runs the Lobster Claw Restaurant.

Zachary Morgan (Ralph Dumke) is John's boss and the owner of Wellington Towing. John's oldest son, Dave Herrick (Carl Betz), is a detective with the San Pedro Police Department. The wealthy Terry Van Buren (Kathleen Crowley), who lives in the influential Crown Hill section of town, is Carl's fiancée (Frank Wilcox and Frieda Inescort appeared as Terry's parents, Henry and Emily Van Buren).

Alexander Laszlo composed the "Waterfront" theme.

750. *We Got It Made*

NBC, 9/8/83 to 3/30/84
Syndicated, 9/87 to 9/88

Mickey MacKenzie (Teri Copley) is a blonde bombshell. She measures 36-24-34 and has a Marilyn Monroe–like aura about her (her speech, facial expressions and walk are reminiscent of Marilyn's). "That," she says, "is how men see me. But they don't see *me*." The "me" Mickey is referring to is the sweet, innocent and rather sensitive girl she really is, a girl who is very shy and afraid to take a chance. "All my life I've been afraid to take a chance. I didn't go out for cheerleading, I didn't apply to college, I didn't even take the Pepsi Challenge. I never took a risk and I never lost. I never did anything exciting." After high school, Mickey held jobs as a dancer and as a movie theater usherette. Her life changed suddenly when she began working for a company called American Fryer and found a boyfriend who seemed to like her for her real self. When her boyfriend ran off with her mother, Mickey quit her job and moved to New York City to escape her past. Only hours after arriving in Manhattan, she saw an ad for a housekeeper's position and applied for it. David Tucker (Matt McCoy) and Jay Bostwick (Tom Villard) are the men who placed the ad—two sloppy bachelors who share Apartment 9A at 1054 West 61st Street. Jay hires Mickey the instant he sees her ("Boy, is she gorgeous!"). Although Mickey has no experience as a professional housekeeper, she applied for the job to take a chance, "to try something different and make people happy. It's good, honest work."

As the series progressed, Mickey also had a chance to realize a lifelong ambition by moonlighting at "the hottest spot in town"—a strip joint called Marcel's Club Marcel (where Mickie worked, not as a stripper but as an awful standup comic). David and Jay first paid her $75, then $150 a week.

David is a private practice attorney, and Jay is an idea man who imports seemingly useless gag items. Claudia Evans (Stepfanie Kramer), a salesclerk at Bloomingdale's Department Store in Manhattan, is David's girlfriend; Beth Sorenson (Bonnie Urseth), a kindergarten teacher at the Ridgeway School, is Jay's girlfriend (she was previously a WAC and had dreams of becoming a stripper; she was too shy, however, "to take it off" when it came time to perform). Beth and Claudia are also best friends and take aerobics classes at the Manhattan Health Club.

In the syndicated version, John Hillner played David (now a lawyer employed by Herbert Foley [John O'Leary]). Beth and Claudia were dropped and replaced by Jay and David's neighbors, Max Papavasilios, Sr. (Ron Karabatsos), and his son, Max Jr. (Lance Wilson-White).

Relatives: Elaine Joyce (Mickey's mother, *Arlene MacKenzie*), Teri Copley (Mickey's Southern cousin, *Lucy MacKenzie*), David Knell (David's brother, *Rick Tucker*).

Theme: "We Got It Made," by Tom Wells (NBC) and Score Productions (syndicated version).

751. *W.E.B.*

NBC, 9/13/78 to 10/5/78

The experiences of Ellen Cunningham (Pamela Bellwood), an up and coming programing executive for T.A.B. (the Trans-Atlantic Broadcasting Company) in New York

City (in the pilot episode, T.A.B. stood for the Trans-American Broadcasting Company). Ellen was originally assistant to the head of daytime programing. When she saves the network's fall season by re-editing "Our America," a 30 hour miniseries, she is promoted to director of the Department of Special Events. ("Our America" was a negative look at the United States and deemed unsuitable for airing. Ellen cut the negative aspects, added narration and stills and saved the first three weeks of T.A.B.'s fall season; the miniseries also won the network several Emmy Awards for outstanding program.)

The role of Board Chairman Harry Brooks was played by John Colicos in the pilot and by Stephen McNally in the series. The only relatives seen were Joyce Gittlin as Yetta Pearlstein, the wife of Research Director Harvey Pearlstein (Lee Wilkof), Barbara Babcock as Claire Kiley, the wife of Programing Chief Jack Kiley (Alex Cord) and Katy Kurtzman as Jackie Kiley, Jack's daughter.

The title refers to a television network, not some company whose initials are W.E.B. (Periods were probably used in the title to distinguish this series from two earlier anthology series called "The Web" (CBS, 1950–54; NBC, 1957).

David Rose composed the theme.

752. *Webster*

ABC, 9/16/83 to 9/11/87
Syndicated, 9/87 to 1/88

Cast: Susan Clark (*Katherine Papadopolis*), Alex Karras (*George Papadopolis*), Emmanuel Lewis (*Webster Long*), Henry Polic II (*Jerry Silver*), Cathryn Damon (*Cassie Parker*), Eugene Roche (*Bill Parker*), Ben Vereen (*Phillip Long*).

Facts: During an ocean voyage, Katherine Calder-Young and George Papadopolis meet, fall in love and marry. During the ceremony (held aboard the ship), a storm began to develop. The boat was rocked back and forth by 12 foot swells, the minister kept losing his place while reading the wedding vows, and when he said "Do you," Katherine did, "right out the porthole window."

Two weeks later, when Katherine and George return home (to George's apartment), George learns that his best friends, Travis and Gert Long, have been killed in a car accident. Shortly thereafter, George receives a telegram saying that he has been appointed the guardian of Webster Long, Travis and Gert's seven-year-old black son (George is Webster's godfather). Stories relate Webster's efforts to adjust to a new life with white parents, and George and Katherine's efforts to adjust to parenthood.

Webster, who attends Clemens Elementary School, has a teddy bear he calls Teddy and keep his "menstoes" (mementos) in an old cigar box. He calls "George, "George" and Katherine "Mam" (it sounds like "Mom" to him). Webster has two pet frogs (Fred and Peggy), a pet snake he calls Dr. Plotsman and a homemade robot called Mr.

Spielberg. Webster's favorite number is three, and for breakfast he eats Sugar Sweeties and Farina Pops cereal. When Webster was a member of the Boy Braves Scout Troop, he earned a merit badge by helping the Great Walnutto (Harold Gould) make a comeback (he was a famous radio magician in the 1940s). For a fourth grade social sciences project, his class was paired off into couples to understand what married life is about. Webster (who had number B-7) was paired with Annette (Mya Akerling), who was number G-7. They were given an egg, which they named Chester, to care for as if it were a real baby.

Webster plays the triangle in his school band and enjoys feeding pigeons in the park (his favorite one is Charlie). In one episode, Webster accidentally killed a mother bird while playing with his BB gun. He cared for the eggs that were in the nest (hatching them in the school incubator) and named the babies, George, Mam and Webster. His favorite television show is "Don't Jump" (a mythical game).

Katherine Papadopolis is 37 years old and was originally a consumer advocate for the mayor's office in Chicago. She later attended the University of Chicago with the hope of becoming a child psychologist (as a present for her first anniversary at college, Webster gave Katherine a hideous Eiffel Tower dress that lights up). As a kid, Katherine had a horse named Binky ("His real name was Mortimer but we called him "Binky") and two dogs named Farnsworth and Derek. She also attended Camp Kitchecuwowa, and at age 12, when she had to give the Valedictorian's speech at her school (unnamed), she got so nervous that she lost her voice (all was fine until she learned that a representative of her dream college, Radcliffe, was present. She got up to the podium, forgot her speech, related the terms of her Bloomingdale's charge card, then lost her voice).

On Valentine's Day, Katherine hopes George will give her a large, heart-shaped box of chocolates—"the 50,000 calorie kind. But what do I get? Sensible gifts, like a Water Pik." In one third season episode, Katherine lied about her age on a Lotto ticket (she put 36 instead of 39) and lost the family one million dollars when five of the numbers Webster chose (3, 6, 8, 9, 43) came out. The sixth winning number was 39. Katherine developed a love for the ballet when she was a child (her butler, Chives, would perform *Swan Lake* for her).

George Papadopolis, a 41-year-old former pro football player, now works as a sportscaster for WBJX-TV, Channel 6 (he is the host of "Papadopolis on Sports"). George's old jersey number was 71, and he attempted to make a comeback via the Warriors football team; he found he was too old to play again. As a kid, George attended the Tumbleweed Ranch in Arizona and stayed in bunkhouse number 7. George wears white socks with black shoes and calls Webster "Web," and he and Webster eat chili cheese dogs at Sloppy Eddie's and pizza at Angelo's Pizza. George calls Katherine "Jelly Bean" and "Love Breath" (she calls George "Cuddle Bunny"). When George gets excited or upset, he sings songs from "Carmen."

Jerry Silver was originally Katherine's assistant, then owner of Jerry Silver's Health Club and Spa. He also does volunteer work at the Oak Sure Hospital.

Webster. **Left to right: Alex Karras, Emmanuel Lewis and Susan Clark.**

Cassandra ("Cassie") Parker and her husband, Bill, are George and Katherine's landlords in later episodes. They have been married for 25 years (1986 episodes) and spent their honeymoon at the Venus Arms Motel in Chicago. Bill and Cassie spent their first romantic Valentine's Day seeing the movie *The Attack of the 50 Foot Woman* (which is now their movie).

Phillip Long is Webster's uncle (his brother, Travis, was Webster's father). Although Philip is a blood relative, Travis and Gert believed that if anything happened to them, Webster would be better off with George (Philip is a dancer and has an unstable life). Although Philip petitioned the courts to raise Webster, he withdrew the petition when he realized that George and Katherine could provide a better life for Webster than he could. Although their relationship got off to a rocky start, Philip, George and Katherine became good friends. Philip calls Webster "Baby," and in one episode Philip created a work of art called "Sea Harvest" (made of old soda and beer cans) as a statement about the need to save the planet.

Maurice (Richard Karron) is a former football player and friend of George's who now owns the Trocadero Diner.

George, Katherine and Webster first lived in Apartment 14B at 534 Steiner Boulevard; their phone number was

555-8775. After a fire destroyed the apartment, they moved into the home of Cassie and Bill Parker (an address was not given), where they rented the upstairs apartment. Cindy (Jennifer Ann Ursitti) is Webster's baby-sitter. She earns $1.50 an hour, eats ice cream and has the cold cuts finished before George and Katherine are out of the driveway.

Relatives: Neva Patterson (Katherine's mother, *Emily Calder-Young*), Gwen Verdon (Katherine's aunt, *Charlotte*), John Astin (Katherine's uncle, *Charles*), Jack Kruschen (George's father, *George ["Papa"] Papadopolis, Sr.*; he owns a shop called "Papa Papadopolis You Break It, I Fix It Shop"), Jennifer Holmes (Bill and Cassie's daughter, *Maggie Parker*), Jamie McEnnan (Maggie's son, *Max*), Dan Frishman (Cassie's nephew, *Skippy Loomis*), Lu Leonard (Maurice's sister, *Babe*).

Flashbacks: Harrison Page (Webster's father, *Travis Long*; he called Webster his "Little Quarterback" and had the jersey number 26).

Theme: "Then Came You," by Steve and Madeline Sunshine.

753. *Wendy and Me*

ABC, 9/14/64 to 9/6/65

Cast: George Burns *(Himself)*, Connie Stevens *(Wendy Conway)*, Ron Harper *(Jeff Conway)*, James Callahan *(Danny Adams)*, J. Pat O'Malley *(Mr. Bundy)*.

Facts: The Sunset de Ville is an apartment complex at 4820 Highland in Los Angeles that is owned by George Burns, a former vaudeville, movie, radio and television star turned landlord ("Well, here I am doing a weekly television series again. I didn't want to do it. I told the network not a chance. They said, 'George, we'll let you sing all you want.' I said, 'Where do I sign?'").

George lives in Apartment 104 and is the only one who is aware of a viewing audience. He speaks directly to them, relates monologues and sings whenever the occasion allows (much as he did on "The George Burns and Gracie Allen Show"). George practices singing five or six hours a day: "I want to be ready in case somebody gives a party . . . I love to sing. I'd rather sing than eat. Some of my friends who heard me sing say they'd rather eat." George was a tenant and had to buy the building in order to sing: "I have it in the tenants' leases that they cannot evict the landlord."

George's favorite tenants are Wendy and Jeff Conway, a married couple who live in Apartment 217. Wendy was an airline stewardess and Jeff was a pilot for TGA (Trans Globe Airlines). Wendy was assigned to his flight and spent 20 minutes trying to fasten his seat belt before he could explain he was the pilot. "Having Wendy help you," George says, "is like being lost in the desert for four days and then having someone give you a glass of sand." After their first flight together, Jeff asked Wendy out on a date. He took her to an unnamed French restaurant and proposed. Wendy accepted, the waiter spilled wine on her dress and she and Jeff were married three weeks later. (In another episode,

Wendy says she was a stewardess assigned to a Honolulu flight; Jeff was a pilot assigned to a Chicago flight. Wendy boarded the wrong plane and met Jeff when she tried to tell him that he was going in the wrong direction.)

Wendy and Jeff have been married one year when the series begins. Wendy is blonde, beautiful and totally scatterbrained. "People gave up wondering why Wendy does things a long time ago. I'm glad I own the building. People can go to Wendy's apartment, get confused and come to my apartment to hear me sing."

Wendy is always leaving Jeff notes; she loves him very much and wants "him to know where I am even when we're together" (for example, "Dear Jeff. I've gone downstairs to pick up the mail. I should be back by the time you finish reading this. Your loving wife, Wendy." She told Jeff she left the note because "I didn't want you to think I was out when I was gone."). Wendy has an organized type of mind—"She never knows what she is going to say even after she says it." She celebrates everything (such as the day she met Jeff, the day she first put sugar in Jeff's coffee, and March 23, "the day nothing happened"). In the annual airline show, which George emceed, Wendy and George performed the song "If I Could Be with You."

Living across the hall from the Conways in Apartment 219 is Danny Adams, Jeff's co-pilot. Danny is a ladies' man and can't go 24 hours without a woman (he gets withdrawal pains; if things become desperate, he walks past beauty parlors until someone whistles). Danny has a little black book, and a red one called "The Red Star Edition."

Mr. Bundy is George's janitor (his favorite eatery is Jenny's Tea Room); Bob Hunter (playing himself) is George's piano player ("He's out of the Juilliard School of Music. When they found out he was working for me, the next day he was out").

Relatives: Sheila Bromley (Jeff's aunt, *Harriet*), Walter Sande (Jeff's uncle, *Benson Conway III*), Amzie Strickland (Danny's sister, *Mary Jo Adams*).

Theme: "Wendy and Me," by George Duning.

Werewolf see *She-Wolf of London*

754. *The Westerner*

NBC, 9/30/60 to 12/30/60

Cast: Brian Keith *(Dave Blassingame)*, John Dehner *(Burgundy Smith)*.

Facts: He rides a spotted horse, has a dog named Brown and a 405 Winchester repeating rifle with a telescopic sight. He can't read or write, he tends to get drunk and is often defeated in fist fights. He wanders through the West of the 1890s looking for work, most often as a ranchhand or as a wrangler with a cattle drive. "He's a cheap tin horn with a two bit reputation who doesn't have enough guts to wear a gun." This is one description of Dave Blassingame, a man who once had a dream of settling down and starting a ranch but was dealt a cruel hand by fate. He can "break broncs with the best of 'em," rides "'cause it's a big country" and has the utmost respect for women ("Women must be God's favorites," Dave says, "because he made 'em finer than anything in creation").

Little is revealed about Dave's past. In the episode "Jeff," information about Dave's desire to become a rancher is mentioned when he meets a "ghost" from his past, a now beautiful woman named Jeff (Diana Millay). Dave was dismayed to find Jeff (no other name given) had drifted into the world of prostitution, but he remembered her as she was, "a young girl he helped raise and loved like she was his own blood." They met again by chance, but how they drifted apart or how Jeff began working the cathouse circuit is not mentioned.

The pilot episode, "Trouble at Tres Cruces," reveals that Dave has an uncle named Adam Brown (Ted DeCorsia) "who raised him when they were breaking ground around Coleman." It also learned throughout the series that Dave first rode a horse when he was eight years old and that Brown is his own dog. Dave picked Brown up to feed him and has been with him ever since. He calls the dog Brown "cause he's a big brown dog." The pilot episode also mentions that Dave's rifle is a .95 Winchester repeating rifle (the bullets are more than double the size of the standard .44-40 rifle; Dave later mentions that the rifle is a 405 Winchester when he is asked what kind it is).

"Burgundy Smith is a reptile, a no good, low down, cheatin' rattlesnake," says Dave about Burgundy Smith, the snazzy dresser who riles Dave no end. They met on a friendly note—until Smith took a fancy to Brown and tried to steal him. They are now rivals at everything and constantly bicker whenever they meet.

Theme: "The Westerner," by Herschel Burke Gilbert.

Note: The original pilot, "Trouble at Tres Cruces," aired on "The Zane Grey Theater" on 3/26/59 (the proposed series title at the time was "Winchester"). In 1963 (1/15) on "The Dick Powell Show," a pilot called "The Losers" aired. It was an unsold attempt to revise "The Westerner" series, with Lee Marvin as Dave Blassingame and Keenan Wynn as Burgundy Smith, drifters of the Old West who help people in trouble.

755. *What a Country*

Syndicated, 9/86 to 9/87

Room 107 of Los Angeles High School is "home" to a group of foreign students studying for their citizenship tests. Taylor Brown (Garrett M. Brown) is their English teacher, and the students are Nikolai Rostopovich (Yakov Smirnoff), Maria Conchata Lopez (Ada Maris), Yung Hee (Leila Hee Olsen), Laslo Garbo (George Murdock), Victor Ortega (Julian Reyes), Robert·Moboto (Harry Waters, Jr.),

Inga Berstrom (Donna Dixon) and Ali Nadeem (Vijay Amritraj). Joan Courtney (Gail Strickland) was the original principal; she was replaced by Don Knotts as F. Jerry ("Bud") McPherson. Dani (Elaine Giftos) owns the afterschool hangout, Dani's Diner.

Taylor, who lives at 36 Whitney Way, is from Dakota and originally came to California to find a job as a high school coach. Joan first hired him as a one night substitute teacher for the citizenship class; he became the permanent teacher when the earlier one resigned. Joan lived at 71306 Harper Valley Drive, and Bud, who fancied himself a rugged sportsman, lived at 11 Fairlawn Street.

Nikolai was born in Russia and now drives a taxi cab; he is hoping to open his own retail appliance store. The gorgeous Spanish-born Maria lives in Beverly Hills and is the maid to Lenny Feldman (Larry Gelman), the owner of Feldman's Sofa Village. Yung Hee is a very beautiful but very shy Chinese woman. She is hoping to become a nurse, and her name means "petal of wildflower blossoming in sun. Then withers and dies and is gone forever."

Robert is an African prince ("of all one can envision") and the son of Julius Moboto, the ousted king of Africa. Inga is a Swedish bombshell who has the male students in a fog. Laslo is from Hungary; Ali was born in Pakistan; and Victor is from Puerto Rico.

Relatives: Audrey Meadows (Taylor's mother, *Millie Brown*), Gordon Jump (Taylor's father, *Ed Brown*), William Marshall (Robert's father, *King Julius Moboto*).

Theme: "I Want to Be an American," vocal by Richard De Benedictis.

Note: Prior to "What a Country," NBC aired the pilot "Almost American" (4/1/81), which dealt with a group of foreign students preparing for their naturalization tests. Catherine Armstrong (Maureen McNamara) was the teacher. The school was not named, and the students were Milosh Dubrowski (Bob Ari), Ming-Lee Chang (Rosalind Chao), Kwame Botulo (Ernie Hudson), Rudy (Richard Yniquez) and Kristen (Ann Bjorn). Classes were held in room 104. Had the series sold, it would have been called "Night School." Both versions are based on the British series "Mind Your Language."

756. *What a Dummy*

Syndicated, 9/28/90 to 9/7/91

Cast: Annabel Armour *(Polly Brannigan)*, David Doty *(Ed Brannigan)*, Stephen Dorff *(Tucker Brannigan)*, Joshua Rudoy *(Cory Brannigan)*, Jeanna Michaels *(Maggie Brannigan)*, Kaye Ballard *(Treva Travalony)*, Loren Freeman *(Voice of Buzz)*.

Facts: Shortly after the death of their great-uncle, Jackie Brannigan, a 99-year-old vaudeville performer, Ed and Polly Brannigan and their children, Tucker, Cory and Maggie, inherit his possessions, including an old trunk. While looking through the trunk, Cory finds Buster ("Buzz") Brannigan, the dummy Jackie used in his act Brannigan and Buzz.

Buzz, however, is no ordinary ventriloquist's dummy—he is alive and can talk (he's been in the trunk for 50 years, is full of wisecracks and has a lot to say; details are not given as to how he came to life). Stories revolve around Buzz's antics and the Brannigans' efforts to keep him a secret.

The Brannigans live at 912 Lincoln Drive in Secaucus, New Jersey. Ed, who wears Beast aftershave lotion, owns Brannigan's Seafood Restaurant. Ed and Polly have been married for 17 years when the series begins (their most romantic dates involved horror movies; Polly would get scared and put her arms around Ed). Wednesday night is "whoopie night" for Ed and Polly. Polly's mother was in labor with her for 22 hours, and Polly "washes eggs before she uses them because of where they have been." Ed has a classic Mustang (not seen) he calls "Mary Lee." The family goldfish is named Spotty.

Tucker, whose middle name is Humphrey, attends Seabury High School. He believes the future is a new breakfast cereal, and on the school radio station, WXRB, he had a show called "Talking with Tucker." Tucker's heroes are the Three Stooges, especially Curly; he claims to have every film they made on videotape.

Cory is the brightest of the children and is easily exasperated. He attends Daniel Boone Elementary School, and Tucker calls him "Nerd," "Dweeb," "Wuss" and "Geek." He calls Tucker "Airhead."

Margaret ("Maggie") Michelle Brannigan is six years old and also attends the Daniel Boone School (she is called "The Rock" at school for her nerves of steel). She likes to eat raw cookie dough and has dolls named Helen, Mary, Brian and Susan.

Buzz first mentioned he was made of redwood; later he said he was made of oak and was in love with Effie Klinker (Edgar Bergen's dummy) but it didn't work: "She was made of mahogany and I was made of oak." Buzz mentioned that his mother died of Dutch elm disease. His favorite color is green, and he reads *Variety* and a magazine called *Turf Today*. His biggest weakness is pepperoni pizza; he can't resist a straight line and he can recite the Gettysburg Address in pig latin.

Treva Ann Maria Travalony is the Brannigans' nosy neighbor. She is a psychic and says she was such a beautiful baby that she "was in diaper ads." She was married a number of times (the third time at the Lucky Horse Shoe Wedding Chapel in Atlantic City).

Relatives: Shelley Berman (Ed's father, *Sam Brannigan*), Michelle Mann (Treva's niece, *Chris Travalony*).

Theme: "What a Dummy," by L.A. Aprino.

757. *What's Happening!!*

ABC, 8/5/76 to 4/28/79

Roger ("Raj") Thomas (Ernest Thomas), Dwayne Clemens (Haywood Nelson) and Frederick ("Freddie") Stubbs (Fred Berry) are three black teenagers and friends who attend Jefferson High School in southern California. Roger, the most studious of the group, lives with his mother, Mabel Thomas (Mabel King), and his smart aleck, obnoxious sister, Dee Thomas (Danielle Spencer), at 1147 Central Avenue. Mabel, called "Mama," is a "supervisor of domestic maintenance in private residences" (a maid). Dee first attends an unnamed grammar school, then Jefferson High; she receives an allowance of one dollar a week, and a strawberry milkshake is her favorite drink.

Roger yearns to be a writer. He was editor of the Jefferson High *Gazette* and was paid $35 by *Little Miss Muffet* magazine for a story he wrote called "Mr. Beaver Builds a Dam and Saves the Town of Gum Drop Falls." He also worked briefly as a writer on the television series "Central Avenue" (about three black teenagers), started an underground high school newspaper (not named) and worked as a delivery boy for Pronson's Market.

"Hey, what's happening!!" is the catchphrase Freddie uses when he greets his friends. He is nicknamed "Rerun" (for his habit of repeating in summer school what he should have learned during the school year). He was a member of the music group the Rockets and in last season episodes was a page at KABC-TV in Los Angeles. Roger and Rerun later shared an apartment (3A). Dwayne, who lives at 534 Oakmont, is the typical girl-crazy student.

Rob's Place, located on Second Avenue in Los Angeles, is the afterschool hamburger joint hangout. Shirley Wilson (Shirley Hemphill), a Leo, is the wisecracking, overweight waitress, and Rob (Earl Billings) is the owner. Earl Barrett, Jr. (David Hollander), called "Little Earl," is the nine-year-old white boy with a crush on Dee.

Relatives: Thalmus Rasulala (Mabel's ex-husband, *Bill Thomas*), Lee Chamberlain (Bill's second wife, *Lee Thomas*), Chip Fields (Rerun's married sister, *Donna*; later Shirley's sister, *Norma Wilson*); Nathaniel Taylor (Donna's husband, *Ike*), Greg Morris (Dwayne's father, *Lawrence Clemens*).

Theme: "What's Happening!!" by Henry Mancini.

Note: See also "What's Happening Now!!"

758. *What's Happening Now!!*

Syndicated, 9/85 to 9/87

A continuation of "What's Happening!!" which follows further events in the lives of Roger ("Raj") Thomas (Ernest Thomas), Dwayne Clemens (Haywood Nelson) and Freddie ("Rerun") Stubbs (Fred Berry).

Roger is now a newlywed, married to a beautiful social worker named Nadine (Anne-Marie Johnson). They live at 1147 Central Avenue in what is now Roger's home (his mother, Mabel, remarried, moved to Arizona and sold Roger the house). Dee Thomas (Danielle Spencer), Roger's sister, is attending an unnamed college and appears in some episodes.

Dwayne now works for Milster Computers, and Rerun

(who now lives with Dwayne) is a used car salesman for K-Doe's OK Cars (he appears as "Swami Stubbs" in television commercials). Dwayne mentioned that he joined the army after high school and learned about computers. Roger is now a struggling writer (his first novel, *The Kremlin Dimension,* sold 25 copies; his second book, *Fateful Harvest,* was published by Ballard Publishing. He also wrote a play called *It's Nothing Personal* and a movie script titled *The Great Cleveland Jewel Heist*).

Nadine's specialty is working with troubled children. She posed nude for art classes in college and met Roger on a New York subway (she changed seats to get away from a wino); their first date was seeing the Broadway play *A Chorus Line*; they honeymooned in Maine.

When Roger sees Shirley for the first time in six years, he learns that their former hangout, Rob's Place, has been closed and is slated for demolition. Shirley, who worked at Rob's for 11 years, convinces Roger to join her in purchasing the diner. They save a memory and become business partners in the new Rob's Place. (Roger did a television commercial for Rob's Place as Mr. Good Chef on Channel 77; the diner sponsors a Little League team called the Rangers. In addition to working in the restaurant business, Shirley wrote the "Dear Al" advice column for the Los Angeles *Gazette*.)

Shortly after, a little girl named Carolyn Williams (Regina King) runs away from an orphanage and "camps out" in front of Rob's Place. When Nadine discovers that she is a runaway, she and Roger take her in for the weekend; they later adopt her.

During second season episodes, the character of Rerun was dropped when Fred Berry demanded a large raise. Martin Lawrence was brought on as Maurice Waterfield, the waiter at Rob's Place, to replace him.

Relatives: Thalmus Rasulala (Roger's father, *Bill Thomas*), Roger Thomas (Roger's criminal cousin, *"Wee Willie" Thomas*), Lillian Lehman (Nadine's mother, *Yvonne Hudson*), Al Fann (Shirley's father, *Roscoe Wilson*).

Theme: "What's Happening Now!!" by Henry Mancini (actually the exact same theme as used in "What's Happening!!").

759. *Whirlybirds*

Syndicated, 1954 to 1957

Whirlybirds, Inc., is a helicopter charter service located at Longwood Field in California. Chuck Martin (Kenneth Tobey) and P.T. Moore (Craig Hill) are the pilots of Bell Ranger helicopters N975B and N2836B; their air code is Seven-Five-Bravo. Janet Culver (Sandra Spence) was their original ground assistant; she was replaced by Helen Carter (Nancy Hale). Al (Joe Perry) is the base mechanic. There is no credit for a theme; only music supervision by Ed (E.C.) Norton.

760. *The Whiz Kids*

CBS, 10/5/83 to 6/2/84

Computer whiz kids Richard ("Richie") Adler (Matthew Laborteaux), Alice Tyler (Andrea Elson), Jeremy Saldino (Jeffrey Jacquet) and Hamilton ("Ham") Parker (Todd Porter) attend Canyon High School in California. Richie has a "home brewed" 64K computer named Ralph, a roving robot called Herman and a dog named Rabies, and Alice works after school as an order taker at the Burger Barn; they are also members of the Canyon High Computer Club. Richie, Alice, Ham and Jeremy use their skills to help the authorities solve crimes, most notably Lew Farley (Max Gail), a reporter for the Los Angeles *Gazette*; Carson Marsh (Dan O'Herlihy), the head of the Athena Society (an intelligence agency), and Neal Quinn (A Martinez), a detective with the L.A.P.D.

Irene Adler (Madelyn Cain) is Richie's divorced mother, and Cheryl Adler (Melanie Gaffin) is Richie's younger sister (they live at 601 North Canyon Drive).

Relatives: Jim McMullan (Richie's father, *Don Adler*), Michael Boyle (Alice's father, *David Tyler*), Wayne Norton (Ham's father, *Lew Parker*), Barbara Brownell (Ham's mother, *Aggie Parker*).

Theme: "The Whiz Kids," by Paul Chihara.

761. *Who's the Boss?*

ABC, 9/20/84 to 9/10/92

Cast: Tony Danza *(Tony Micelli)*, Judith Light *(Angela Bower)*, Alyssa Milano *(Samantha Micelli)*, Katherine Helmond *(Mona Robinson)*, Danny Pintauro *(Jonathan Bower)*.

Facts: At a summer camp called Cataba, Tony Micelli and a girl named Ingrid become friends. They shared their first kiss at Kissing Rock. Unknown to Tony, the girl was afraid to use her real name of Angela Robinson; she would later become Angela Bower, and Tony's boss when she hires him as her live-in housekeeper.

Tony, the widowed father of a young girl (Samantha), tends house for Angela (a divorcée), her son, Jonathan, and Angela's mother, Mona Robinson. They live at 3344 Oak Hill Drive (also given as 3334 Oaks Hills Drive) in Fairfield County, Connecticut; their phone number is KL5-6218.

Tony, whose middle name is Morton, was born on April 23, 1952. He is a Catholic, attended P.S. 86 and was an altar boy at the Blessed Sacrament Church. At Brooklyn's Pitkin High School, he was a member of a band called the Dreamtones. After a hitch in the navy, Tony played second base for two seasons with the St. Louis Cardinals. When an injury ended his career, he returned to Brooklyn where he acquired a job as a fish truck driver. Several years later, following the death of his wife, Tony applied for a job as Angela's housekeeper in an attempt to give Samantha a better life.

Who's the Boss? **Front, left to right: Alyssa Milano, Tony Danza, Danny Pintauro. Back: Judith Light (left) and Katherine Helmond.**

When Samantha enrolls in college, Tony decides to complete his education and begins to take night courses in business at Ridgemont College. As the series progressed, Tony changed his major to education and soon became a substitute teacher at the Nelson Academy for Boys (he teaches English, history and science, and his classes are held in room 103). Tony also taught history and was the baseball coach at Wells College in Iowa.

Tony, who scored a 545 on his college entrance exams, became a legend at Ridgemont when he "liberated the monkeys from the bio lab." He was also the manager of a softball team called Tony's Tigers (red jerseys) and did the sportscasting on the Ridgemont College Sports Channel. With a ten handicap, Tony plays golf at the Ridgemont Golf Club, is a member of a bowling team (Dr. Whittier's Drill Team) and posed as "Mr. November" for a calendar. He first had a 1967 Chevy van (license plate 780 AGN), then a black Jeep Cherokee (plate PH 3925) and finally a sedan (plate 518 G8Q). Tony does his grocery shopping at Food Town and proposed to Angela in the episode of 11/16/91.

Samantha, affectionately called Sam, receives an allow-ance of $15 a week. She has a teddy bear named Freddy Fuzzy Face and wears a size 5½ hockey skate. French toast (which she calls "Mr. Frenchie") is her favorite breakfast, and pasta she calls "Mr. Linguini" is her favorite dinner.

Sam's tomboyish ways came to an end when she became 12 and wanted her first bra, "the one with the little pink bow." Thinking he knows better, that Sam wouldn't want little pink bows, Tony bought her the no frills "My Training Bra" (model number 0134). Angela and Mona stepped in when they saw the disappointment on Sam's face and took her to Bloomingdale's. The tomboy returned as a beautiful young lady.

Samantha attended P.S. 86 (in Brooklyn) and in Connecticut, Fairfield Junior High, Fairfield High (where she skipped her senior year) and Ridgemont College (she also applied to Tate, Winnetka, Ryerson, Marston and Northeastern). While she desperately wanted to attend Tate College in California, she didn't meet its requirements and so she chose to attend Ridgemont in order to be near home. In the episode of 10/16/90, Sam moved into the college dorm, which is two miles from her home; she shares room 214 with Melinda (Andrea Elson). In 1992, Sam married Hank

Tomopopolus (Curnal Aulisio), a would-be puppeteer (Candice Azzara and Vic Poliza appeared as Hank's parents, Fran and Joe Tomopopolus).

Samantha was a member of the Bulldogs baseball team, and her first job experience was as Angela's girl Friday at her ad agency. She then had a job as a waitress at the Yellow Submarine (a hamburger joint). Her first car was a yellow 1968 Olds (license plate SAM'S CAR) with red reflectors on the sides, five rear brake lights and an old tire on the rear bumper (Sam called it her "yellow nightmare").

Bonnie Munson (Shana Lane-Block) is Sam's best friend. They met while waiting in the milk line in sixth grade: Bonnie cut in, Sam pushed her to the ground and called her a "chowderhead." They then became the best of friends. Bonnie calls herself and Sam "The Three Musketeers" (Sam doesn't understand it either); their hangout is the Burger Palace.

Angela, formerly the president of the Wallace and McQuade Advertising Agency in New York City, later began her own company, the Angela Bower Agency, at 323 East 57th Street in Manhattan. Angela was born on October 16 (no year given) and attended the Montague Academy for Girls and later Harvard Business School (where she was a member of the singing group, the Curlets). At Montague, Angela was, as she called herself, a geek and was jealous because she was not as busty as the other girls in her class. She attempted to become one of the cool kids by stuffing her bra with tissues, but she was still rejected. She drowned her sorrows in food (for example, she had three chocolate puddings with lunch) and became overweight before she cleaned up her act and learned to accept herself. Angela, who is in the 39 percent tax bracket, also managed a softball team called John's Giants (blue jerseys). Her first job was rowboat manager of the Fairfield Boat Club.

Mona, Angela's ultrasexy mother, works as Angela's assistant at the ad agency. She is very proud of her large bust (her mother calls her "all boobs and no brains") and is constantly reminding Angela that she lacks cleavage. Mona, who seems to have had many affairs, appeared in a sexy pose on the cover of *Mature Woman* magazine. She has a dog named Grover, and when Angela was a kid, she discouraged her from playing the cello (Angela was so bad that Mona hid the cello in the attic).

Jonathan, who has a pet snake named Wilbur, first attends Oak Valley Grammar School, then Fairfield High School. He has a complete Lawrence Welk record collection and loves the accordion (which he is attempting to learn to play).

In the episode of 10/23/90, when elderly neighbor Mrs. Napoli (Vera Lockwood) falls ill and is unable to care for her grandson, Billy (Jonathan Halyalkar), she asks Tony to care for him. Billy, a very annoying character, just didn't fit the show and was dropped after one season.

Relatives: James Naughton (Angela's ex-husband, *Michael Bower*), James Coco (Tony's father-in-law, *Nick Milano*), Ana Obregon (Tony's cousin, *Anna*), Vito Scotti (Tony's uncle, *Aldo*), Richard Grieco (Tony's cousin, *Maurio Micelli*), Tony Danza *(Tony's grandfather)*, Antonia Ray (Tony's aunt, *Rosa Micelli*), Louis Guss (Tony's cousin,

Dominic Micelli), Gordon Jump (Mona's brother, *Archie Rockwell*), James B. Sikking (Mona's brother, *Cornelius Rockwell*), Efrem Zimbalist, Jr. (Mona's late husband, *Robert*, in a ghost sequence), Marian Seldes (Mona's mother, *"Nana" Reynolds*).

Flashbacks: Danny Geuis *(Tony as a boy)*, Kenny Morrison *(Tony as a teenager)*, Lani Golay *(Angela as a girl)*, Candace Cameron *(Mona as a girl)*.

Theme: "Brand New Life," vocal by Rick Riso.

Note: See also "Living Dolls," the spinoff series.

762. *Who's Watching the Kids?*

NBC, 9/22/78 to 12/15/78

Stacy Turner (Caren Kaye) and Angie Vitola (Lynda Goodfriend) are two beautiful showgirls who work at the Sand Pile, a seedy Las Vegas night club Angie says is "a garbage pile with a liquor license." The girls live in a spacious apartment (number 23) at 86 Desert Way. Also living with them are Melissa Turner (Tammy Lauren), Stacy's pretty nine-year-old sister, and Frankie Vitola (Scott Baio), Angie's wisecracking 15-year-old brother. Melissa is sweet and feminine; she is an *A* student and a chess expert, and enjoys balancing the checkbook (she came to live with Stacy after their parents were killed in a car accident). Frankie is a smart aleck and calls himself "Frankie the Fox." Like Angie, Frankie was born in South Philadelphia. His mother felt he had the potential to become a juvenile delinquent and sent him to live with Angie in the hope of straightening him out. Frankie, who is not as bright as Melissa, needs help with his school work, but insists, "I don't need no tutor." Their parents own a grocery store in Philadelphia.

Larry Parnell (Larry Breeding) is Stacy and Angie's neighbor (there is no number on the door to his one room apartment). Larry is a newscaster for KVGS-TV, "The Voice of the Desert" (he is a field reporter and anchors the six o'clock "KVGS News Watch"; the show is broadcast from "The KVGS News Action Center"). Larry is from the East, and his hero is David Brinkley (he has his poster on his kitchen door). His family owns a business called Parnell Paints ("Semi-Gloss for a Better Nation"). His father wanted him to go into the business after college (studying journalism), but after six months he left "to cover the news, not walls." Larry answered an ad in *Broadcasting* magazine, "and here I am in Las Vegas trying to make it on my own." His field minicam operator is Burt Gunkle (James Belushi) who despises being called "Gunk" ("Don't call me Gunk. The name is Gunkle, it rhymes with *uncle*").

"A Parnell promise is like Parnell Paints—it sticks" Larry says. Larry begins his newscasts by saying, "Good evening. From the sun-baked desert to the snow-capped mountains, this is Larry Parnell, K-Vegas News, your voice of the desert."

Angie best sums up what the series title means: "We

[Stacy and Angie] work all night. Larry works during the day. He can look in on the kids for us while we work. It ain't a bad trade—dinner for baby-sitting." This sounds good in theory and it usually works; the comedy stems from the complications that set in when it doesn't work (for instance, when Larry has to leave Frankie in charge because he has to cover a fastbreaking story).

Memphis (Lorrie Mahaffey), Cochise (Shirley Kirkes) and Bridget (Elaine Bolton) are the showgirls who work with Stacy and Angie. Mitzi Logan (Marcia Lewis) is the landlady who yearns to be a comedian. The pilot episode, "Legs," aired on ABC on 5/19/78.

Charles Bernstein composed the theme, "Who's Watchin'?"

763. *Wild Bill Hickok*

Syndicated, 1951 to 1956

The West of the 1870s is the setting for a series that relates the exploits of Marshal James Butler ("Wild Bill") Hickok (Guy Madison) and his sidekick, Deputy Jingles P. Jones (Andy Devine), as they strive to maintain law and order. Bill is agile, fast on the draw and quick with his fists; Jingles is somewhat overweight, easily scared, a bit clumsy, superstitious and an expert marksman; together they form a unique team of undercover agents for the federal government.

Fort Larabee is their regional headquarters; Bill's horse is named Buckshot and Joker is Jingles's horse (which he bought from an Indian). Jingles has a two-bit Confederate coin that he carries as a good luck charm, and he mentioned he had an uncle named Petey ("a mountain man who got chewed up by a grizzly"). Being the comedy foil, Jingles receives the worst assignments. Bill feels he overplays roles and complains, but "when I play a part I get into it," says Jingles.

In the opening theme, the *W* in "Wild," the *B* in "Bill" and the *H* in "Hickok" are made with double horseshoes. Both men are seen riding. After Jingles yells, "Hey, Wild Bill, wait for me!" Bill fires six shots into the camera; Jingles fires one shot (after Bill first fires two). John Cannon and Charles Lyon did the announcing (there are no music credits).

764. *Wild Jack*

NBC, 1/15/89 to 7/9/89

"Wild" Jack McCall (John Schneider) is a wilderness guide in Skagway, Alaska. One of his clients, who became a dear friend, was Winston Fielding (Mel Ferrer). When Winston dies, Jack inherits Fielding's multimillion dollar broadcasting empire, FCI Communications, in Los Angeles. Winston believed that his company needed to be run by a

decent and honest man; Wild Jack was the only person Winston knew who could meet those requirements.

In California, Jack becomes chairman of the board of FCI, but he gives Winston's daughter, Constance Fielding (Carol Huston), the power to run the company. To feel more at home, Jack begins his own side business, Tracking Unlimited, through which, with the help of his pet wolf, Denali (the Great One), he helps people in trouble. Jack's 4 × 4 has the license plate 2LK-G497; Constance was born on August 27, 1957.

The series is also known as "McCall" and "McCall of the Wild." Phil Marshall composed the theme, "Wild Jack."

765. *The Wild Wild West*

CBS, 9/17/65 to 9/19/69

Cast: Robert Conrad *(Jim West)*, Ross Martin *(Artemus Gordon)*.

Facts: The series is set in the 1870s. An 1860 2-4-0 steam engine (number 3), a coal car and a luxurious passenger coach called "The Nimrod," constitutes the mobile base of operations of Major James T. ("Jim") West, an underground intelligence officer (Secret Service) for the president (Ulysses S. Grant) of the United States, and his partner, Artemus ("Artie") Gordon, a brilliant actor turned agent who uses the wizardry of his craft (disguises) to help Jim apprehend criminals who pose a threat to the safety of the country.

Jim had been in the cavalry for ten years before he was selected by President Grant (James Gregory and Roy Engel) for the assignment. His mobile base is a government loan; but as far as the outside world is concerned, the train is the sole property of Jim West, a big spender from the East who is known as "The dandiest dude who ever crossed the Mississippi in his own train."

The Nimrod has an assortment of weapons (rifles, guns, knives and explosives), a secret wardrobe for Jim's undercover assignments and a pool table for relaxation. The car also contains several cages that house Artie's homing pigeons (Henry, Henrietta, Anabella and Arabella). The marker lights at the tail end of the coach actually serve two purposes: an alert for other trains on the same track and a signal that something is wrong (for example, if Artie is out of the car and Jim is in trouble, Jim switches on the lights). Artie, whose favorite color is red, gets the less glamorous assignments—nondescript characters who are there to help Jim. Artie can read and write in English, Latin, Greek, German, Chinese and braille; he can't read Russian but can speak it. Artie's everyday wardrobe accommodates smoke bombs, putty explosives and knock-out powders. Jim has pop-out guns up his sleeves, a tiny derringer is concealed in two parts in the heels of his boots, a skeleton key hides behind his lapel, a sword is kept in his pool cue and smoke bombs are located under his holster.

While Jim and Artie battled many notorious villains (in some cases using surveillance techniques that had not yet been invented), their most diabolical enemy was Dr.

Miguelito Coyote Loveless (Michael Dunn), an evil scientist who owed his villainy "to the curse of my midget size." He also believed the U.S. government took the country away from his grandmother, and so getting back at the government was his number one goal.

Tennison (Charles Davis) was Jim's manservant on the train; Voltaire (Richard Kiel) and Antoinette (Phoebe Dorin) were two of Loveless's assistants; and Jeremy Pike (Charles Aidman), Frank Harper (William Schallert) and Bosley Cranston (Pat Paulsen) also appeared as Jim's assistants in various episodes.

The series was originally titled "The Wild West" (same music and characters; title graphics are the only difference).

Theme: "The Wild Wild West," by Richard Markowitz.

Note: Two pilots (now seen as television movies) were also produced: "The Wild Wild West Revisited" (CBS, 5/9/79), and "More Wild Wild West" (CBS, 10/7 and 10/8/80). In the first story, set in 1890, Jim (who had retired to Mexico) and Artie (who began his own road company, The Deadwood Strolling Players Traveling Tent Show; his play: "The Society Lady's Revenge") are reunited by Robert T. Malone (Harry Morgan), the head of the Secret Service, to stop Miguelito Loveless, Jr. (Paul Williams), the son of their old adversary, from controlling the world with perfect clones of heads of state, "people" who will be responsible only to him. In the second story, Jim and Artie battle Professor Albert Paradine II (Jonathan Winters), a daft megalomaniac who seeks to rule the world with his diabolical weapons of doom.

766. *Wings*

NBC, 4/19/90 to the present

Joseph ("Joe") Hackett (Timothy Daly) and his brother, Brian Hackett (Steve Weber) run Sandpiper Air, a one plane airline based at the Tom Nevers Field in Nantucket, a rustic island off the coast of Massachusetts. Their plane, a Cessna 402, has the I.D. number N121PP and the radio call letters Sandpiper 28. Joe started Sandpiper Air with $5,700 and a lot of sweat; Brian joined him as a partner after flying for Iguana Air ("We're ugly, but we get you there"). When Joe was a baby, his mother would put brandy in his milk to make him sleep; when he was older he developed an interest in airplanes and cleaning. Brian and Joe grew up in a house at 427 Madigan Way.

Helen Chappel (Crystal Bernard), the gorgeous airport lunch counter operator, is a musician and hopes to one day play the cello with the Cambridge Symphony Orchestra. (Her big break almost came when she auditioned for and got a job with the Maine State Symphony Orchestra. The orchestra, however, lost its funding and Helen lost her job.) Helen was born in Texas, wears Tahitian Rose lip gloss and Dusty Roads blush. As kids Joe, Brian and Helen were friends when they lived in Boston. Joe accidentally saw Helen in the nude when she was ten years old (how was not mentioned), and they didn't speak to each other for two

The Wild Wild West. **Ross Martin (left) and Robert Conrad.**

years. Although it is hard to believe, Helen said she "was once as big as a whale." When she lived in Boston, her hangout was the South Bay Fudge Factory; she was such a good customer that one Christmas, the staff made a life size statue of Helen in fudge; she ate it in half an hour. Helen's Jeep license plate reads CELLO; she and the brothers' favorite watering hole is the Club Car.

Roy Biggins (David Schramm) is the owner of the rival six-plane Aeromass Airline. Faye Evelyn Cochran (Rebecca Schull) is the reservations clerk; Faye's favorite color is blue. She is a member of the Quilting Club, and she claims that when she was a stewardess, she was the first one to use the emergency exit gestures.

Kim Ulrich appeared as Brian's ex-wife, Carol, and Barbara Babcock played Joe and Brian's mother, Mae Hackett. In a flashback sequence, Valri Jackson was Joe and Brian's mother; Granville Ames was their father; Adrian Arnold was young Joey; Spencer Vrooman was young Brian; and actress Valentino was young Helen.

A public domain piece by Franz Schubert is credited as "The Wings Theme."

767. *WIOU*

CBS, 10/24/90 to 3/19/91

WNDY, Channel 12, is a local Midwest television news station that is better known, because of its financial position, as WIOU. It is housed in a rundown building with the street number 6000 (an actual address is not given), and the N in the WNDY neon sign on the outside of the station has a tendency to go on the blink.

Hank Zaret (John Shea) began his career at WNDY as an intern and is now the station's news director. His goal is to make "News 12" number one in the ratings (right now it is tied for fourth place with reruns of "Mr. Ed").

Kelly Robinson (Helen Shaver) is the beautiful co-anchor of "News 12." She is 37 years old and desperately seeking to protect her job from the younger, glamourous reporters who are seeking it. Kelly has been in local television news for 12 years, and now, at WNDY, she feels she can grab the brass ring and become an anchor. Kelly and Hank are former lovers, and she has been at WNDY for two years. Kelly keeps her Christmas cards in her lingerie drawer. She is also worried about her biological clock and desperately wants a baby.

Ann Hudson (Jayne Brook) is a 25-year-old field producer who has a nose for news. She has a tendency to freeze up on the air if a technical mishap causes a graphics problem when she is reading copy (she does the "Newsbreak 12" reports). Ann wants to be taken seriously and to become an on-the-air reporter.

Elizabeth ("Liz") McVay (Mariette Hartley) is the executive producer of "News 12" and second in command in the newsroom. She very much wants to be the news director but has been passed over for the job three times in the past year.

Neal Frazier (Harris Yulin) is the anchor of "News 12" and he earns $1.3 million a year. He left his job at the network (which is assumed to be CBS) for the job. He also brought his network sized ego with him. The fiftyish anchor is fond of younger women, and Kelly calls him "the most lecherous anchorman in America."

Floyd Graham (Dick Van Patten) is the station's veteran weatherman. He takes advantage of his celebrity status by promoting his restaurant ("Floyd's Restaurant") on the show. He caters to senior citizens, who he feels "are his numbers."

Taylor Young (Kate McNeil) is the newest member of WNDY (she joined shortly after Hank). She is determined to replace Kelly and become the co-anchor. Taylor knows her beauty gets her numbers and she uses her sexuality to acquire ratings.

Lenny Lubinsky (Kevin Conroy) is WNDY's sportscaster. His claim to fame is having been the only white player on the local N.B.A. team's roster (though he never played more than the last 15 seconds of a game).

Grant Gelt played Elizabeth's son, Daniel McVay (he attends Saint Patrick's Grammar School); Eddie Jones appeared as Hank's father, Gus Zaret; and Rita Wilson played Hank's ex-wife, Ellen Zaret.

Gary Chang composed the theme.

768. *WKRP in Cincinnati*
CBS, 9/18/78 to 9/20/82

Cast: Loni Anderson (*Jennifer Marlowe*), Gordon Jump (*Arthur Carlson*), Howard Hesseman (*Dr. Johnny Fever*),

Tim Reid (*Venus Flytrap*), Richard Sanders (*Les Nessman*), Frank Bonner (*Herb Tarlek*), Jan Smithers (*Bailey Quarters*), Gary Sandy (*Andy Travis*).

Facts: WKRP is a 5,000 watt AM radio station (1530 on the dial) that signed on the air on December 7, 1941. It is located in Suite 1412 (on the ninth floor) of the Flem Building in downtown Cincinnati, Ohio. It is the number 16 station in a 18 station market. Its mascot is a fish (a carp), and 555-WKRP is its phone number. Snooky's Bar is the staff's watering hole. The first rock song played on the station was "Queen of the Forest" from the *Stranglehold* album by Ted ("The Sledge") Nugent.

Arthur Carlson is the manager of WKRP (he has held the job since 1955, and his forbidding mother, "Mama" Carlson, owns the station). Arthur is a family man (he has been married to Carmen for 27 years) and is active in his church. He tends to shun station responsibility and resorts to playing with toys or practicing fishing or golf in his office. His favorite reading matter is the magazine *Ohio Fisherman*. Employee Herb Tarlek calls him "Big Guy." When Arthur ran for city council, he used the slogan "A big guy for a big job." In his youth Arthur was a ballplayer and had the nickname "Moose."

Jennifer Elizabeth Marlowe is the ultrasexy receptionist. She is the highest paid employee at WKRP and earns $24,000 a year. She will not take dictation or make coffee. Jennifer wears tight skirts and low cut blouses and knows she is, as she says, "a very sexy and desirable woman."

Other women describe Jennifer as "the best-looking woman I have ever seen." She dates wealthy, older men because she feels safer and more secure with them. Jennifer won't lend money to men or do any favors for them, yet they buy her things: "cars, acoustical ceilings, microwaves and appliances." Jennifer, who was born in Rock Throw, West Virginia, lives in a gorgeous apartment (number 330; address not given) that is filled with appliances. Her doorbell plays the song "Fly Me to the Moon," and she has box seats at Cincinnati Reds' games (season tickets). In later episodes, Jennifer moves to a Victorian house in the town of Landersville (its location is given as across the lake) for which she paid $125,000. Her former boyfriend from Rock Throw is T.J. Watson (Hoyt Axton).

Bailey Quarters, the only other female employee at the station, majored in journalism in college and first did continuity work before becoming a member of the news staff (she does two of the ten daily "WKRP News Roundup" broadcasts).

Lester ("Les") Nessman is the news director of WKRP. He is a graduate of Xavier University and uses his motor scooter as the WKRP mobile news unit. Les is the proud recipient of the Silver Sow Award (for his hog reports) and has also won the Buckeye Newshawk Award for his news broadcasts. In his youth (he was born in Dayton, Ohio), Les took up playing the violin and was pretty handy around the house until he tried to make a footstool and blew out the back of the garage. Les, the self-proclaimed "Information Beacon of the Ohio Valley," has a nasty dog named Phil and has only one record in his collection—"Chances Are," by Johnny Mathis. His favorite topic as chairman and speechmaker at the Cricket Club is "The Red Menace in Our Backyard." His favorite music is Beethoven's Ninth Symphony, and when he works in a large room with Bailey and Herb Tarlek, he has imaginary walls and an office door that all the staff respect. Les's news shows begin with a deep-voiced announcer saying: "London! Madrid! Bangkok! Moscow! Cincinnati! From the four corners of the world; from the news capitals at home and abroad; the day's headlines brought into focus. The issues and events that shape our times. WKRP, information bureau of the Ohio Valley, presents Les Nessman and the News." He ends each news broadcast with "Good day and may the good news be yours."

Dr. Johnny Fever, whose real name is Johnny Caravella, is the spaced-out disc jockey who earns $17,500 a year. He was fired from a Los Angeles station for using the word *booger* on the air, and he has a photo of himself taken with Mick Jagger. He is addicted to gambling and is often in need of money.

Venus Flytrap, whose real name is Gordon Simms, is the night disc jockey. He went AWOL after serving ten months and 29 days in the army and has been in hiding ever since. Though it is against the rules, he makes the most of his job by romancing his many women friends with candlelight and wine in the broadcast booth.

Herb Tarlek, the obnoxious sales manager, has been married to his wife, Lucille, for 12 years and is the father of two children, Herb III and Bunny. Although he has "the hots" for Jennifer, she won't give him the time of day. Herb's catchphrase is "O.K., fine."

Andy Travis, the station's program director, has a dog named Pecos Bill (he found him on Mount Baldy) and is the only one at WKRP who realizes the station will never do any better than number 14 (which it did achieve in one ratings period). The love of Andy's life is Linda Taylor, a singer played by Barrie Youngfellow.

The show's gimmick was a bandage that Les wore in each episode—but always in a different location (it was a reminder of an injury Sanders received on the first day of shooting). The weather director was the unseen Skivvy Nelson. Carlson once hired Sparky Anderson (in a guest role) to do a sports show called "In the Bullpen." The three singers heard during the Sunday morning religious programming are the Three Merciful Sisters of Melody. WPIG is WKRP's main competition. The most embarrassing incident at WKRP occurred during the Thanksgiving Giveaway Gimmick of 1978. A helicopter flew over the Pine Dale Shopping Mall with a banner saying HAPPY THANKSGIVING. The copter circled the parking lot, and Carlson started dropping live turkeys from 2,000 feet. Shoppers started running for their lives as the turkeys hit the ground like wet bags of cement. "As God is my witness," Arthur said, "I thought turkeys could fly."

Relatives: Sylvia Sidney and Carol Bruce (Arthur's mother, *Mama Carlson*), Allyn Ann McLerie (Arthur's wife, *Carmen Carlson*), Sparky Marcus (Arthur's son, *Arthur Carlson, Jr.*; Herb calls him "Little Big Guy"), Ruth Silveira (Johnny's ex-wife, *Paula*), Patrie Allen (Johnny's daughter, *Lori Caravella*), Allison Argo (Andy's sister, *Carol Travis*), Edie McClurg (Herb's wife, *Lucille Tarlek*), Stacey Heather

Tolkin (Herb's daughter, *Bunny Tarlek*), N.P. Soch (Herb's son, *Herb Tarlek III*), Bert Parks (Herb's father, *Herb Tarlek, Sr.*).

Theme: "WKRP in Cincinnati," by Tom Wells.
Note: See also "The New WKRP in Cincinnati."

769. *Wolf*

CBS, 9/13/89 to 11/14/89

Anthony ("Tony") Wolf (Jack Scalia) is a former San Francisco police department sergeant who now works as an investigator for Dylan Elliott (Nicolas Surovy), a high priced criminal attorney. Tony, who wears a San Francisco Giants jacket, lives on a boat called the *Sea Wolf* with his father, Salvatore ("Sal") Lupo (Joseph Sirola); Tony uses the English translation of his Italian last name for business. Tony was married to a woman named Renee (not seen) and is now romantically involved with Connie Bacarri (Mimi Kuzak), a single mother with a teenage daughter named Angeline (J.C. Brandy). Connie owns Bacarri's Bar, and Angeline, a member of the Bellas softball team, attends Pertola High School (Tony calls her "Angel"). Sal's late wife was named Laura.

Karen Kondazian appeared as Connie's aunt, Gina, and Judith Hoag played Elliott's sister, Melissa Shaw Elliott. In the original, unaired pilot version of the series, Jack Scalia played Nick Wolf.

Artie Kane composed the "Wolf" theme.

770. *Women in Prison*

Fox, 10/11/87 to 4/2/88

Cast: Julia Campbell (*Vicki Springer*), Peggy Cass (*Eve Shipley*), Antoinette Byron (*Bonnie Harper*), C.C.H. Pounder (*Dawn Murphy*), Wendie Jo Sperber (*Pam Norwell*), Denny Dillon (*Meg Bando*), Blake Clark (*Cliff Rafferty*).

Facts: A comical look at life in a women's prison, as seen through the experiences of Victoria ("Vicki") Springer, a pampered, naïve and rich woman who is set up on a shoplifting charge by her husband and convicted of grand larceny. She is sent to the Bass Women's Prison in Wisconsin and assigned to Cell Block J.

Vicki can't file or type; she can cross her legs and show a little bit of thigh. For this talent, prison warden Cliff Rafferty, who majored in hotel management in college, appoints her as his secretary. Vicki, who believes she is "very sexy and the most attractive woman in captivity," was voted "Most likely to be pictured running naked in slow motion on a beach." She held the title of Miss Dairyland in 1984 and 1985, and her résumé lists "soft, mysterious and feminine" as her qualifications. Vicki wears a size 34B bra and a size seven shoe; she will allow only her hairdresser,

Women in Prison. Bottom, left to right: Wendie Jo Sperber, Antoinette Byron, Denny Dillon. Back, left to right: C.C.H. Pounder, Peggy Cass, Blake Clark, and Julia Campbell.

Mr. Joey, "to cut my gorgeous hair." Vicki's prison number is 659142.

Eve Shipley is a gun moll serving a life sentence for robbery and murder; her prison number is 00023. Bonnie Harper is a coquettish lesbian who was arrested for soliciting (prison number 563478). She wears a 34C bra, a size seven shoe and a streetwalker-like wardrobe; she also yearns to make love to Vicki (who wants nothing to do with her).

Dawn Murphy, prison number 447210, is the toughest of the women and commands respect through fear; she was convinced of murder. Pam Norwell is a computer whiz who was arrested for embezzling; her prison number is 519731. While Vicki, Bonnie, Eve and Dawn share a cell, Pam has her own cell, complete with computer, a shade for privacy and furnishings.

Meg Bando is the nasty prison guard who delights in tormenting the prisoners, especially Vicki. Her favorite pastime is going down to Death Row and fiddling with the dimmer switch.

In the pilot episode, the prisoners had the following numbers: Vicki, 689055; Eve, 628524; Bonnie, 856095; Dawn, 526482; and Pam, 596085.

Relatives: Thomas Callaway (Vicki's low-life husband, *Philip Springer*), Arlen Dean Snyder (Eve's husband, *Charlie Shipley*).

Theme: "Women in Prison," by Ray Colcord and Phyllis Katz.

771. *Wonder Woman*

ABC, 11/7/75 (pilot)
ABC, 3/31/76 to 7/30/77
CBS, 9/23/77 to 2/19/79

Cast: Lynda Carter (Diana Prince/Wonder Woman), Lyle Waggoner *(Steve Trevor/Steve Trevor, Jr.)*, Debra Winger *(Drusilla/Wonder Girl)*.

Facts: In the year 200 B.C., the rival gods Mars and Aphrodite ruled the Earth. When Aphrodite failed to defeat Mars, she created a race of superwomen called Amazons and established a home for them on a still uncharted land mass in the Bermuda Triangle. There, the goddess Hippolyta became their queen and named their home Paradise Island ("There are no men here. It is free of their wars and barbaric ways. We live in peace and sisterhood"). As the war continued, Mars resorted to skulduggery and used Hippolyta's own weapon of love to defeat her. To receive forgiveness, Hippolyta fashioned a small statue out of clay and offered it to Aphrodite. Aphrodite brought the statue to life as the baby Diana. Diana grows into a beautiful young woman as the centuries pass and is being raised by Hippolyta to become a ruler.

In 1942, the idyllic life of Paradise Island is shattered when man once again threatens its serenity. U.S. fighter pilot Steven ("Steve") Leonard Trevor is on a mission to intercept a Nazi plane (en route to bomb the Brooklyn ship-

yards) when his plane is hit by gunfire. Though wounded, Steve manages to eject from the plane, and his parachute lands on a beach near a cave on Paradise Island. There, he is found by the Princess Diana and nursed back to health. When Diana learns from Steve that the world is engaged in a war and that the Allies are battling a fierce enemy called Nazis, she asks her Queen Mother for permission to use her great abilities to help America. Hippolyta is reluctant at first, until Diana proves herself superior in an Olympic contest (number XXXIII) to determine which Amazon should take Steve back to America.

Diana stands before Hippolyta and receives a gold belt to retain her cunning, strength and immortality away from Paradise Island. Hippolyta then gives her a magic lariat, which is "made of an indestructible material" and compels people to tell the truth. To signify Diana's allegiance to freedom and democracy, Diana is given a red, white and blue costume made by Hippolyta from that same indestructible material. Diana also receives a gold tiara (with a red star in the middle) and a set of gold bracelets, which are made of a rare metal, found only on Paradise Island, called Feminum. The bracelets are capable of deflecting bullets ("The Amazon mind is conditioned for athletic ability and academic learning. Only we have the speed and coordination to attempt bullets and bracelets").

As Diana prepares to leave, she faces her mother one last time. "Go in peace, my daughter. And remember, in a world of ordinary mortals, you are a Wonder Woman." "I will make you proud of me and of Wonder Woman," Diana tells Hippolyta as she leaves to fly Steve back to Washington, D.C., in her invisible plane. Diana brings Steve to the Armed Services Hospital and leaves. Steve, who is still very ill, has no memory of Paradise Island (he was given a special drug from the Hybernia Tree to erase his memory of Diana and the island).

After acquainting herself with the American way of life, Wonder Woman adopts the alias Diana Prince and secures a position as a navy yeoman. She is assigned to the War Department as Major Steve Trevor's secretary.

When the need arises for Diana to use her superpowers, the plain looking Diana does a twirling striptease that transforms her into the gorgeous Wonder Woman. Diana lives at 2890 West 20th Street; her phone number is Capitol 7-362. She works with Steve in the Military Building (Air Corps Intelligence Division) on D Street. In addition to strength, Wonder Woman possesses the ability to impersonate any voice and to run and jump at an accelerated speed.

Wonder Woman's sexy costume is a strapless one piece bathing suit ("her satin tights," as the theme says) which has a blue bottom with white stars and a red with gold (around the bustline) top. For modesty, Hippolyta also fashioned a removable blue and white skirt, which Diana rarely wears.

When Hippolyta feels that Diana has spent enough time in America, she sends her gorgeous younger daughter, Drusilla, to bring Diana home (Diana has to start assuming her role as heiress to the throne). Drusilla, however, becomes fascinated by the American way of life and talks

Diana into letting her stay with her. Drusilla, as Wonder Girl, possesses the same powers as Diana, but her costume is different. It is a bit less revealing (red top with white stars over the right shoulder strap and breast; a gold belt and blue bottom). Dru, as Diana calls her, takes on the guise of a 15-year-old girl to conceal her true identity. She finds ice cream the most fascinating part of American culture and can't get enough of it.

The first commandment of Paradise Island is never to tell anyone about it. Paradise Island is not charted and is not on any map. Refraction of light prevents the island from being seen (Diana and Dru can find it "because we know where it is"). The unknown metal, Feminum, can only be found on Paradise Island and is mined on a remote side of the island. The Nazis believe that Wonder Woman is a top secret U.S. weapon. Steve's office safe combination is 24-36-33. The ABC version ended with Steve and Diana battling Nazism in 1945. It is assumed that Diana returned to Paradise Island when the war ended. General Philip Blankenship (Richard Eastham) is Steve's superior, and Yeoman Etta Candy (Beatrice Colen) is Philip's secretary. While Wonder Woman's measurements were not given, publicity information first said Lynda Carter was 38-20-37 and got the role not only because of her stunning looks but because "she could fill Wonder Woman's 38-inch breastplate." A year later (1977), her measurements were listed as 37½-25-37, which are supposedly Lynda's actual measurements at the time.

The CBS Version: In 1977 a sabotaged plane lands on Paradise Island. By coincidence, Steve Trevor, Jr., the son of the major Diana helped 35 years ago, is aboard. When Diana learns that the modern world is threatened by evil, she again receives permission from her Queen Mother to save the free world from its enemies. Diana uses her invisible plane to guide the jet back to Washington, D.C. There, she again adopts the disguise of Diana Prince and gets a job as Steve's assistant at the I.A.D.C. (Inter-Agency Defense Command). The I.A.D.C.'s computer (voiced by Tom Kratichzil) is named Ira; addresses and phone numbers are not given for Steve or Diana. Joe Atkinson (Normann Burton) is their superior. When Diana is Wonder Woman, she can be seen in high heeled boots. During a running sequence, the boots have flat heels; they switch back to high heels when the running sequence is over. The only other person Diana revealed her true identity to was Tina (Julie Ann Haddock), a pretty girl from the undersea kingdom of Ilandia. The series is also known as "The New, Original Wonder Woman" (ABC) and "The New Adventures of Wonder Woman" (CBS).

In 1968, 20th Century–Fox produced the first known "Wonder Woman" pilot, with Ellie Wood Walker as Diana Prince/Wonder Woman. In this unaired version, Diana is 27 million years old and lives in a modern-day apartment with her domineering mother (Maudie Prickett). Diana appears to be misadventure prone (for example, she falls off her chair while reading the newspaper) and is very vain. She is not as busty or gorgeous as Lynda Carter's Wonder Woman, but wears a similar outfit (a bosom-revealing red and gold top and a blue bottom with white stars). Diana

loves to look at herself in a mirror and admire her figure. "She knows she has the strength of Hercules, the wisdom of Athena, the speed of Mercury—and she thinks she has the beauty of Aphrodite."

Mother is worried that she has "an unmarried daughter Diana's age" and fears what the neighbors are saying about the situation. She refuses to let Diana go out of the house in bad weather or become Wonder Woman on an empty stomach ("Where do you think all that strength comes from? Those gods? From my cooking! Eat first, save the world later"). When Diana decides to fight crime and become Wonder Woman, she takes her blue bracelets out of a dresser drawer, approaches a wall and pushes it. The wall revolves to reveal Diana's secret dressing room. When she emerges as Wonder Woman, she admires herself in the mirror, climbs out the window and says, "Away, away, you vision of enchantment, you've got a job to do." She is then able to fly by her own power. When Diana admires herself, the song "Oh, You Beautiful Doll" is played in the background. "Ellie Wood Walker as Wonder Woman" is the only screen credit.

In 1974 Warner Brothers adapted the comic strip to television with Cathy Lee Crosby as Diana Prince/Wonder Woman. On Paradise Island, the beautiful Diana is instructed by her Queen Mother (Charlene Holt) to leave the serenity of the island and assist the world in its battle against crime. Diana adopts the alias Diana Prince and gets a job as secretary to Steve Trevor (Kaz Garas), a U.S. government agent in Washington, D.C. Only a pilot episode called "Wonder Woman" resulted (ABC, 3/12/74). In this pilot, set in modern times, Wonder Woman wears a very conservative costume: a blue blouse (with white stars on the sleeve) and blue pants. Over this she wears a red blouse/skirt outfit.

Relatives: Cloris Leachman and Carolyn Jones (Diana's *Queen Mother* on ABC), Beatrice Straight (Diana's *Queen Mother* on CBS).

Theme: "Wonder Woman," vocal by the Charles Fox Singers.

772. *The Wonder Years*
ABC, 1/31/88 to 5/12/93

Cast: Fred Savage *(Kevin Arnold)*, Dan Lauria *(Jack Arnold)*, Alley Mills *(Norma Arnold)*, Olivia D'Abo *(Karen Arnold)*, Jason Hervey *(Wayne Arnold)*, Danica McKellar *(Winnie Cooper)*, Josh Saviano *(Paul Pfeiffer)*, Crystal McKellar *(Becky Slater)*, Daniel Stern *(Narrator)*.

Facts: A nostalgic look at life in the late 1960s and early 1970s as recalled by the narration of the adult Kevin Arnold, but seen through his eyes as a preteen (age 12) and teenager.

Kevin was born on March 18, 1956, and attended Hillcrest Grammar School, Robert F. Kennedy Junior High School, (he graduated in June 1971) and William McKinley High School (beginning in fall 1971). He hopes to become a

The Wonder Years. Left to right: Jason Hervey, Dan Lauria, Olivia D'Abo, Alley Mills and Fred Savage.

writer, a center-fielder for the San Francisco Giants or an astronaut (and become a member of the first manned flight to Mars). Kevin, a member of the rock band the Electric Shoes, keeps a picture of Raquel Welch on his locker door at Hillcrest and wears a New York Jets football jacket. He was also a member of the Kennedy Junior High Glee Club (they sang "Stout Hearted Men" for the 1970 Spring Sing).

The Pizza Barn is Kevin's hangout and his allowance was 50 cents a week in 1969, $2.50 in 1970 and $3.00 in 1971. He first held a job as a caddy ($20 a game), then as a stock clerk at Harris and Sons Hardware Store. Kevin has a dog named Buster, and he and his friends skate at the Moonlight Roller Rink. Kevin's first secret crush was in the seventh grade on his English teacher, Miss White (Wendel Meldrum).

Gwendolyn ("Winnie") Cooper, the pretty girl next door, is Kevin's on and off girlfriend. She likes to read, dance and play tennis. Winnie was a member of the Kennedy Junior High cheerleading team (for the Wildcats) and starred in the school's production of *Our Town* (Kevin worked the spotlight). She and Kevin shared their first kiss while sitting on a rock in Harper's Woods. Classmate Becky Slater is the girl Kevin turns to when he and Winnie have a falling out. At age 12 Kevin was (and still is) confused by girls. When he broke up with both Winnie and Becky (who punched his lights out), Kevin had a "Star Trek" dream in which he was

Captain Kirk and Winnie was a beautiful alien with long hair and a short skirt ("Hey, it's my fantasy. I figured I might as well do it right"). Even as Kirk, Kevin still couldn't understand girls.

In the spring of 1970, Winnie moves to a new home (four miles away; their house, number 525, was sold by Arbor Lynn Real Estate) and enrolls in Lincoln Junior High. Although her relationship with Kevin seems lost, Kevin explains that "I'm a part of Winnie and Winnie is a part of me. For as long as I live I will never let her go." In the fall of 1971, Winnie enrolls at McKinley High. Although she and Kevin now attend the same school, they have grown apart (but Kevin still holds a torch for her).

During the summer of 1969, when Kevin and his family vacationed in Ocean City, Kevin met an "older woman," a 15-year-old girl named Teri (Holly Sampson). She called him Brown Eyes, and it appeared that they had a crush on each other. When it came time to part and she returned to New Mexico, she said she would write. She wrote only once, however ("I keep that letter in an old shoebox now"). On Labor Day in 1970, at the Norcom Annual Picnic, Kevin developed a crush on Mimi Detweiler (Soleil Moon Frye), a former childhood friend who had the nickname "The Stick." When Kevin saw how she developed, he went "gaga" over her. In the summer of 1971 during the family vacation at Lake Winahatchie, Kevin fell in love with a girl named Cara (Lisa Gerber), whom he had to give up when the vacation ended. Julie Aidem (Wendy Cox) is a stunning girl who attached herself to Kevin when he and Winnie split (for the umpteenth time) in 1972. Julie had a dog named Poo Poo and smothered Kevin, so much so that after three weeks he broke off the relationship. The following week, Kevin and Winnie were back together again.

Jack Arnold, Kevin's father, was born on November 6, 1927. He served in Korea and is now the manager of distribution and product support services for Norcom Enterprises, a government company. He gets up at five in the morning, fights traffic, "busts his hump all day," comes home and pays taxes. His ritual the night before paying his income taxes is to watch the news on television and hope to see someone who is worse off than he is. His Chevrolet Impala license plate reads GPE 385 (later BEQ 326); XDH 975 is the plate of the family's station wagon. In 1972 they had an Oldsmobile with the license plate QGF 846.

Norma Arnold, Kevin's mother, keeps the family together. She and Jack married in 1949 and spent their honeymoon in Ocean City. They have lived in their current house (number 516; street and city not given) for 17 years. As a teenager, Norma was sent to the principal's office for smoking, and she dreamed of becoming a singer after high school (she even auditioned for a radio show). In the episode of 3/20/91, Norma enrolled in River Community College to improve her secretarial skills after she was discharged for poor typing and dictation at Kennedy Junior High (where she worked in the attendance room).

Karen, Kevin's rebellious 16-year-old sister, is the typical flower child of the 1960s. She attended the same schools as Kevin, and in 1971 (1991 episodes) she enrolled in "McKinley College up north." In the episode of 4/29/92, Karen married Michael (David Schwinmer) and moved to Alaska.

Wayne is Kevin's obnoxious older brother (he attended the same schools as Kevin) and delights in annoying him (he calls Kevin "Butthead"). The only thing he and Kevin ever agreed on was that for Christmas 1969 they wanted a color television set (which they didn't get until 1971).

Paul Pfeiffer is Kevin's best friend. He attended the same schools as Kevin until fall 1971 (1991 episodes) when his parents sent him to the Allenwood Academy Prep School (a year later, Paul is suddenly Kevin's classmate again and attending McKinley High). Paul finds schoolwork a breeze and suffers from a number of allergies. He and his family are members of the Fairlawn Country Club. During the summer of 1972, Paul and Kevin worked at Mr. Chung's Chinese Restaurant.

Relatives: David Huddleston (Jack's father, *Albert Arnold*), Lynn Milgrim *(Winnie's mother)*, H. Richard Greene *(Winnie's father)*, John C. Moskoff (Paul's father, *Alvin Pfeiffer*), Stephanie Satie (Paul's mother, *Ida Pfeiffer*), Torrey Anne Cook (Paul's sister, *Debbie Pfeiffer*), Philip Sterling (Paul's *Grandpa Pfeiffer*), Arlen Dean Snyder (Jack's cousin, *Lloyd Arnold*), Helen Page Camp (Jack's cousin, *Opal Arnold*), John Brandon (Jack's cousin, *Philip Arnold*), Danny Breen (Jack's cousin, *Ray McKinney*). Winnie's older brother, Brian (Bentley Mitchell) was killed in Vietnam.

Flashbacks: Zachary Benjamin *(young Kevin)*, Jodie Rae *(young Karen)*, Benjamin Daskin *(young Paul)*.

Theme: "With a Little Help from My Friends," vocal by Joe Cocker.

773. *Woops!*

Fox, 9/27/92 to 12/6/92

During a parade in which new missiles from Fort Pratt are being displayed, the frequencies from remote control cars being played with by some kids activate the nuclear missiles. The missiles hit assigned targets in foreign countries. Enemy nations retaliate and the world is destroyed—except for six survivors who must build a new society. They each manage to stumble upon an untouched farmhouse, which becomes their new home.

Alice McConnell (Meagan Fay) was the owner of Every Woman's Book Store. She was at the cash register when the tape ran out. Alice went to the basement to get a new register tape when it happened.

Curtis Thorpe (Lane Davies) was a stockbroker, a corporate giant with an office on the sixty-third floor of the International Trade Building in New York. He ran Thorpe, Inc., and was in the company's vault when the missiles struck.

Suzanne Skillman (Marita Geraghty) was a manicurist at Antoine's (how she survived is not mentioned). She is a bit ditsy and can't quite understand what has actually happened; she still dreams of becoming a hairdresser. She had a pony named Ben as a kid and was a cheerleader at Marshall Schrum High School.

Jack Connors (Fred Applegate) was a carpenter for 15 years. The stock market took a turn for the worse. He lost his wife and became homeless, living in a cardboard refrigerator box under the interstate highway, where he was when the disaster happened. Jack attended Harvard Business School.

Dr. Frederick Ross (Cleavant Derricks) is apparently the only black survivor. A pathologist, he was working two stories below ground in the morgue when it happened.

Mark Braddock (Evan Handler) was a teacher at Jefferson Elementary School. He was in his Volvo at an automated teller machine when the missiles hit.

The first other lifeform the group encountered was a turkey, which appeared at Thanksgiving, but grew to an enormous size. Santa Claus (Stuart Pankin) was the first additional human survivor they found (stuck in their chimney and depressed; they restored his faith, which enabled him to search the world for other survivors).

Alice was the first to be physically affected by the results of the accident: she found a crystal that dramatically increased the size of her breasts (the effects wore off after she discarded the crystal). Frederick was next: an electrical storm temporarily turned him into a kid again (played by Jimmy Lee Newman, Jr.). While it seemed that most food was not affected (the group has its own farm), certain foods, like berries, cause intoxicating side-effects when eaten.

GNG Music is credited as the theme composer.

774. *Working Girl*

NBC, 4/16/90 to 7/30/90

Tess McGill (Sandra Bullock) is the working girl of the title. She works for Trask Industries in Manhattan as the junior marketing executive for Bryn Newhouse (Nana Visitor), the marketing head. Tess began working for Trask on April 13, 1989, as a secretary. A year later, when she felt she was qualified to become Bryn's assistant (though lacking a college degree), Tess submitted a report to Bryn under the name Fred McDonald. The report impressed Bryn and got Tess the job. Tess was born on Staten Island on January 25, 1965. She attended Island High School, and Adorable is her favorite perfume. Bryn, a Yale graduate, was a member of the Kappa Gamma sorority. She lives in Manhattan at 63 East 63rd Street, a two block walk from Trask (located at 165 East 65th Street).

Tess and her girlfriend, Lana (Judy Prescott), a secretary in accounting at Trask, shoot pool at Nick's Pool House. Tess's parents, Joe and Fran McGill (David Schramm and B.J. Ward), run McGill's Deli on Staten Island, where Tess also lives in Apartment 210 (address not given). In the original, unaired pilot film (produced in 1989), Nancy McKeon played Tess and Holly Fulger was Lana. Based on the feature film of the same title.

Carly Simon sings the theme, "Let the River Run."

775. *Working It Out*

NBC, 8/22/90 to 12/26/90

Cast: Jane Curtin *(Sarah Marshall)*, Stephen Collins *(David Stuart)*, Kyndra Joy Casper *(Molly Marshall)*, David Garrison *(Stan Rice)*, Mary Beth Hurt *(Andrea Kristoli)*, Robin Lange *(Jodie Stuart)*.

Facts: Sarah Marshall, a divorcée with a nine-year-old daughter (Molly), and David Stuart, a divorced man with a 17-year-old daughter (Jodie), meet at Mr. G's Cooking School (both are taking the course "Italian Cooking for Beginners"). They find an attraction but neither is willing to make a serious commitment. Stories relate their attempts to work out their differences and begin a serious relationship (they have the same sense of humor and the same tastes, but nothing else in common).

Sarah, who loves anything Italian, is the assistant manager of the Bennington Hotel in Manhattan and lives in Apartment 9G at 654 West 54th Street. "The Twilight Zone" is her favorite television show; *The Ghost and Mrs. Muir* is her favorite movie. Sarah's ex-husband, Joe, was a tennis pro who couldn't make it ("Neither could our marriage"); now Joe is a schoolteacher in Hawaii. For her divorce present, Sarah gave herself a rafting trip down the Colorado River. Molly, Sarah's daughter, carries a Barbie lunchbox to school; she eats Oat Puffs cereal for breakfast and is allergic to green beans.

David is a freelance photographer who runs Stuart Photography from his apartment at 36 West 72nd Street. He is allergic to mustard, and "The Twilight Zone" is his favorite television show also. His daughter, Jodie, attends Lincoln High School.

Andrea ("Andy") Kristoli, Sarah's neighbor (Apt. 9B), is a book editor (company not named). Her husband, Charlie (not seen), lists her as "the Little Woman" on their income tax return. Stan is Stuart's agent and assistant. He attended Camp Kawani as a kid and mentioned that every time Stuart breaks up with a girl, he enrolls in a class to forget his troubles.

Theme: "Working It Out," by John Leffler.

Note: In the original unaired pilot, "The Jane Curtin Show," Jane Curtin was Jane Marshall; Stephen Collins was Dan Stuart; David Garrison was Steve Rice; and Randy Graff was Jean (the role that became Andy).

776. *World of Giants*

Syndicated, 1959

Cast: Marshall Thompson *(Mel Hunter)*, Arthur Franz *(Bill Winters)*, Marcia Henderson *(Miss Brown)*.

Facts:

You are about to see one of the most closely guarded secrets and one of the most fantastic series of events ever recorded in the annals of counterespionage. This is my story, the story of Mel Hunter, who lives in your world—a world of giants.

Down through history, man's survival has been dependent upon his adaptability. You learn fast when your life is at stake. No one knows this better than I. My own life is in jeopardy 24 hours a day. Still, in the six months since my accident, I've learned to get up in the morning as if nothing had actually happened.

The Federal Bureau of Investigation guards many fantastic secrets—but none perhaps as unusual as that of Mel Hunter. It all began six months ago in Europe when FBI counterespionage agents Mel Hunter and his partner, Bill Winters, infiltrated a secret missile launching site behind the Iron Curtain. During an experiment to test a new type of fuel, one of the rockets blew up. Mel was in exposure radius of the blast. At first the exact nature of his illness was not known; he seemed simply to be suffering from shock, accompanied by a loss of appetite. Bill managed to get Mel back to the States when it started to happen: some unknown ingredient in the rocket fuel began to affect Mel's molecular structure. Fourteen doctors and 17 scientists watched as Mel began to shrink. In less than a month, Mel was reduced to a height of six inches. While his physical appearance remained the same, a medical report stated that he now possesses "superhuman manual dexterity coupled with agility and reflexes many times faster than normal: somewhere between a hummingbird and a mongoose."

Mel is the first such case known to medical history and has scientists stumped; they are unable to determine what ingredient caused the shrinkage or how to reverse the process. Thus Mel's condition is classified top secret. "There are hundreds of people working in this country on new fuel for rockets. Can you imagine the panic that would ensue if Mel's story became public? The problem is to keep him classified and alive," says Commissioner H.G. Hall (John Gallaudet), Mel and Bill's superior (whom they call "Chief").

Mel was originally six feet two inches tall; he is now six inches tall and lives with Bill in Apartment 3B at 37 Lynley Drive in Washington, D.C. Things most people wouldn't notice (such as a pencil falling off a desk) could mean death for Mel. He has to be careful 3,600 seconds of every hour. When Mel travels, he does so in a specially constructed black attaché case. He has a special chair inside the case, which Bill chains to his wrist. There are four airholes (two on each side of the case) and one door, which is disguised as one of the bottom airholes. "In a world of giants," Mel says, "strapping myself in my special chair is the safest way to travel."

Mel and Bill are assisted by Miss Brown, a pretty FBI agent who works with them out of Bill's apartment (she is always called Miss Brown). The special telephone code Bill and Mel use to contact Hall in an emergency is 342. In his spare time, Mel, a jazz music expert, plays the drums. In the opening theme, the series is referred to as "WOG." A pair of scissors is dropped, a man's shoe is seen stepping down, and a cup filled with a liquid falls and breaks.

There are no screen credits for theme or music.

777. *Yancy Derringer*

CBS, 10/2/58 to 9/24/59

Cast: Jock Mahoney *(Yancy Derringer)*, X Brands *(Pahoo)*, Kevin Hagen *(John Colton)*, Frances Bergen *(Mme. Francine)*.

Facts: In a hotel room in New Orleans, Louisiana (1868), John Colton, the city administrator, meets with Marchancy ("Yancy") Derringer, a former Confederate soldier who owns both a riverboat and a plantation:

Since becoming administrator of this city, I've come across a very astonishing fact. In the highest to the lowest places, particularly the lowest, your name has always been spoken with the greatest respect. I want you to work for me . . . The war is over. New Orleans has become a treasure chest; the fortune hunters of the world are here. I want a man who loves this city, loves the South, who will work without pay, without portfolio, without protection as my personal agent. I want a black angel who will be on the inside before something happens, a man who will do anything for law and order—anything and get away with it. Because if that man were caught, I might be compelled to hang him.

"What you want," replies Yancy, "is a rogue, scoundrel, gentleman, smuggler, gambler and fool . . . Well, Mr. Colton, I guess I'm your Huckleberry." Yancy's adventures as

he helps Colton institute a system of law and order are depicted. Yancy is assisted by a nonspeaking Pawnee Indian named Pahoo-Ka-Ta-Wah ("Wolf Who Stands in Water"). (Pahoo saved Yancy's life at some point within the last eight years. He went against his faith saving a white man and is now responsible for Yancy's life.) Pahoo carries a shotgun with him at all times.

The only background information on Yancy is that he was born in New Orleans. He left in 1860, joined the Confederacy, was shot during the Battle of Cold Harbor and spent one year in a Yankee prison. When he got out (possibly in 1865), he went out West to strike it rich but didn't (it was probably at this time that Pahoo saved Yancy's life). Yancy then returned to Louisiana to pick up where he left off. Old Dixie is Yancy's dog, the *Sultana* is his riverboat and Waverly Plantation is the place of his birth and is his home. Yancy indeed carries a derringer, in his hat, up his sleeve, in his belt and in his boot. He owns a silver mine in Virginia City, Nevada, and buys his fancy "duds" at Devereaux's Gentlemen's Apparel.

Mme. Francine is Yancy's love interest; Mai Ling Mandarin (Lisa Lu), Yancy's friend, runs the Sazarack Restaurant; and Captain Billy (J. Pat O'Malley) is the skipper of the *Sultana*. The Central Pacific Railroad was mentioned as laying track in New Orleans.

Relatives: Noreen Marsh (John's sister, *Agatha Colton*), Victor Sen Yung (Mai Ling's cousin, *Hon Lee*; he owns the Green Dragon Café in San Francisco).

Theme: "Yancy Derringer," by Don Quinn and Henry Russell.

778. *You Take the Kids*

CBS, 12/15/90 to 1/12/91

Cast: Nell Carter *(Nell Kirkland)*, Roger E. Mosley *(Michael Kirkland)*, Caryn Ward *(Lorette Kirkland)*, Trent Cameron *(Nathaniel Kirkland)*, Marlon Taylor *(Peter Kirkland)*, Dante Beze *(Raymond Kirkland)*.

Facts: Michael Kirkland, a school bus driver, and his wife, Nell, a piano teacher, live at 830 Fairview Lawn (in Pittsburgh) with their children, Lorette, Raymond, Nathaniel and Peter. Their house reflects their interest in recycling: in their kitchen are bins for cans, bottles and plastic. The kids eat Wheaties for breakfast; the family's station wagon, painted "Exotic Emerald Enchantment" (green), has the license plate number IO43.

Nell and Michael have been married 17 years. Michael earns $18,000 a year, and in high school (where he met Nell) he and his three best friends were called "The Love Surgeons."

Raymond, the oldest son (16), thinks "he's pretty." He is a *D* student and a member of the school's basketball team. His favorite eatery is the Wiener Schnitzel.

Lorette is 13 years old and "desperately wants breasts, to become popular." (She stuffs her bra with Raymond's multicolored wool socks. Nell calls the socks "Lorette's two friends," and despite Lorette's complaints—"I'm the only girl in my class who hasn't developed yet"—Nell continually takes them away from her. She is a *C* student at school and appeared in the plays *The Fantasticks, Oklahoma* and *My Fair Lady*. Lorette eats Dipples brand potato chips, and for a school social studies project, when she had to care for three eggs as if they were children, she named them Sally, Jessy and Raphael.

Peter, who is 12 years old, is the studious one and wants to become a doctor. He is an *A* student, and his "disease," as he calls it, is being excessively neat.

Nathaniel is 10 years old and has a pet goldfish named Dirt Bag. He has a job as a delivery boy at Mr. Stereo, is a *C* student at school and Raymond calls him "Squirt."

Schools for the kids are not mentioned; the last episode, scheduled to air on 1/19/91, never ran due to coverage of the Persian Gulf War.

Relatives: Leila Danette (Nell's mother, *"Mama" Helen*).
Theme: "Nobody's Got It Easy," vocal by Nell Carter.

You'll Never Get Rich see *The Phil Silvers Show*

779. *The Young Pioneers*

ABC, 4/2/78 to 4/16/78

On April 8, 1873, 16-year-old Molly Foster (Linda Purl) and 18-year-old David Beaton (Roger Kern) marry. With a dream of becoming homesteaders, Molly and David leave their home in Indian Falls, Iowa, and head for Dakota in their horse-drawn wagon (pulled by their Morgan horses, Star and Whitefoot). In Yankton, Dakota, David files a claim for 160 acres of farmland (on which they are to plant wheat and corn) and five extra acres for planting trees. The cost is $18: $14 down and the balance to be paid after homesteading for five years. Through Molly's narration, their struggles are chronicled. (Molly records her and David's adventures in her diary, which she keeps in a seashell-decorated box that David gave to her.)

Molly and David lived alone in the wilderness when they first homesteaded; they were closest to the town of Wildrose and eventually acquired some neighbors: Dan Gray (Robert Hays), and the pioneering Peters family, a man (Robert Donner) and his three children, Nettie (Mare Winningham), Flora (Michelle Stacy) and Charlie (Jeff Cotler). Mr. Peters (no first name given) owns the claim next to the Beatons'. During the harsh winter months, David earns money by working as a hauler for the Chicago and Northwestern Railroad (later the Dakota Southern Railroad) or as a hand at the Roslyn Feed Mill. Wood is said to be very scarce and valuable.

In the first pilot (ABC, 3/1/76), Shelly Juttner played Nettie, and a son, Little Davy, is born to Molly on January 18, 1874 (the infant is not credited). In the second pilot, "Young Pioneers' Christmas" (ABC, 12/17/76), Kay Kimler played Nettie, Sherri Wagner was Flora and Brian Melrose was Charlie. (In the story, Molly and David lose little Davy to a high fever in June 1874 and struggle to put aside their grief to extend the gift of friendship at Christmas time.)

Charles Tyner played David's father, Mr. Beaton, in the first pilot.

Laurence Rosenthal composed "The Young Pioneers Theme."

780. *The Zoo Gang*

NBC, 7/16/75 to 8/6/75

Steve Halliday (Brian Keith), Manouche Roget (Lilli Palmer), Tom Devon (John Mills) and Alec Marlowe (Barry Morse) are former World War II resistance fighters known as "The Zoo Gang." The Fox (Steve), the Leopard (Manouche), the Elephant (Tom) and the Tiger (Alec) reunite 33 years later (1975) to battle crime in Europe. Steve has become an antiques dealer, Manouche owns the Les Pêcheurs Bar in France (their headquarters), Tom is a jeweler and Alec is a mechanic. Jill Barton (Seretta Wilson) is Tom's niece; Police Lieutenant Georges Roget (Michael Petrovitch) is Manouche's son.

"The Zoo Gang Theme" was composed by Paul and Linda McCartney.

781. *Zorro*

ABC, 10/10/57 to 9/24/59
ABC, 10/30/60 to 4/2/61

Cast: Guy Williams *(Don Diego/Zorro)*, Gene Sheldon *(Bernardo)*, George J. Lewis *(Don Alejandro)*, Henry Calvin *(Sergeant Garcia)*, Britt Lomond *(Captain Monasterio)*, Peter Adams *(Captain Pollidano)*.

Facts: "Out of the night when the full moon is bright, comes the horseman known as Zorro. This bold renegade carves a *Z* with his blade, a *Z* that stands for Zorro." The series is set in Spanish California in 1820. On a ship bound for Old Los Angeles, we first meet Don Diego de la Vega, a Spanish nobleman who is returning to his home in Monterey after three years of study at the University of Spain. He has been summoned by his father to help fight a tyrant, the new *comandante*, Enrique Monasterio, who has imposed harsh laws and taxes on the people in his quest to become the richest man in California.

In his cabin, Don Diego tells his mute servant, Bernardo, that he must find a way to deal with Monasterio without arousing the suspicion that his father has summoned him home. Bernardo uses sign language to suggest force—"No, Bernardo. I'm dealing with a powerful enemy. We must play another game." Just then Diego recalls a proverb:

"When you cannot clothe yourself in the skin of a lion, put on that of a fox." This gives him an idea for a plan: "I must convince the new *comandante* that I am perfectly harmless ... Instead of a man of action, I shall be a man of letters, an innocent scholar interested only in the arts and sciences." Fearing that he will be searched in Los Angeles, Diego has Bernardo burn his father's letter and discard his fencing trophies from the university.

As Diego adopts his new character (he wears a maroon-front jacket with gold braid and carries a walking stick), Bernardo motions that he wants to help: "Very well, you shall play the fool. You shall be the eyes and ears behind my back. You cannot only not speak, you hear nothing."

As Diego suspected, he is searched when he arrives in Old Los Angeles. He has fooled Monasterio's soldiers; now he must fool his father, Don Alejandro de la Vega.

That night, Don Alejandro tells his son about the intolerable conditions that exist: "We must get rid of him ... Someone must do something." Diego responds: "I'm going to sit down and write a detailed letter of complaint to the governor." This angers Alejandro, who "hardly expected such discretion" from his son and vows to take action himself. While Diego accomplished one goal, convincing his father that he is a coward, he must now find a way to protect Don Alejandro from Monasterio. Recalling the proverb about the lion and the fox, Diego tells Bernardo, "From now on I shall be el Zorro—the Fox" (he draws his sword and carves his first *Z* on a sheet of music on the piano). He then chooses a black mask and outfit to disguise his true identity.

The following morning, Diego and Bernardo are seen in a hilly area of the de la Vega ranch. Diego whistles and a black horse comes into view. "I've brought you here to meet a third member ... Tornado. An old shepherd has been keeping him for me. He was a colt when I left ... Even my father would not recognize this horse." (Diego, as himself, is seen riding a tan and white horse named Phantom.)

The de la Vegas are the most important family in southern California. Zorro's base is a secret cave below his hacienda in Monterey. (The entrance is through the fireplace. Diego found it as a boy and believes it was built by his grandfather as a means of escaping Indian raids.) Zorro's trademarks are the carved sign of the *Z*, his black hat, mask and cape. He carries both a sword and a whip, and in the opening theme Zorro leaves a warning for Monasterio—"Beware, Comandante. My sword is a flame, to right every wrong. So hold well my name—Zorro." Monasterio has posted the following: REWARD. 1000 PESOS WILL BE PAID FOR THE CAPTURE—DEAD OR ALIVE—OF THE BANDIT WHO CALLS HIMSELF ZORRO.

While Zorro is an expert swordsman, Don Diego pretends to be inexperienced at fencing (at the university, Diego was the fencing champion). To further cover his tracks when he is Zorro, Diego teaches Bernardo to play the guitar (to make it appear that Diego is in his room practicing when in reality he is out as Zorro). Although Zorro helps the people, he is considered a criminal by the authorities. Zorro, "a friend of the people," is "the defender of the oppressed" and "the champion of justice."

Captain Enrique Monasterio is the real threat to Zorro (he is based in the Pueblo de Los Angeles, which was founded in 1781). When the viceroy (John Dehner) arrives to inspect the Pueblo and discovers that Enrique is corrupt, he arrests him. Enrique's second in command, the bumbling and dimwitted Sergeant Garcia, is appointed the temporary *comandante*. In the episode of 3/20/58, Captain Arturo Pollidano becomes the new *magistrato*—and an enemy of Zorro's.

Sergeant Demetrio Lopez Garcia is a soldier of the king of Spain (the king's Lancers); in second season episodes, the overweight Garcia becomes the acting *comandante* when Arturo is dropped. "How did one so stupid become a sergeant?" "It was easy. I was a private for a long time. Then one day I saw the *comandante* kissing the *magistrato*'s wife, and the next thing you know, I am a sergeant ... because I possess the natural qualities of leadership." The Pasada de Los Angeles is his favorite watering hole; Garcia and the other lancers are paid every six months.

Cresencia (Penny Santon) is the de la Vega maid; Anna Maria Verdugo (Jolene Brand) is Diego's romantic interest; Ricardo Delano (Richard Anderson) is Don Diego's rival for Anna Maria's hand. In episode 52 ("Amnesty for Zorro," 1/1/59), Don Alejandro learns that his son is Zorro (he prevents Diego from dueling with Delano for the hand of Anna Maria so he can fight on for the liberation of the peasants). (Eduard Franz appeared as Anna Maria's father, Señor Verdugo.)

Señor Esteban de la Cruz (Cesar Romero) is Don Diego's playboy uncle on his mother's side; Lieutenant Rafael Santos (Carlos Romero) is another "badman" who plagued Zorro; Ignacio ("Nacio") Torres (Jan Arvan) is Diego's neighbor (Eugenia Paul played his daughter, Elena Torres); and Father Felipe (Joseph Calleia) is the padre at the Mission de San Gabriel and Diego's friend (he is unaware that Diego is Zorro).

Annette Funicello appeared in both versions of the series, but in different roles. In 1959, in half hour episodes, Annette played Anita Cecilia Isabella Cabrillo, a beautiful girl from Spain who journeys to Los Angeles to find her father, Don Miguel Cabrillo (Arthur Space). Immediately, upon inquiring about him, she finds that no one has ever heard of him. Don Diego takes an interest in the matter, and with Zorro's help Anita discovers that her father is Gonzales, the stable master (he was ashamed to let her know that he was only "a servant of horses").

In the third hour-long episode, "The Postponed Wedding" (1/1/61), Annette is Constansia de la Torres, a girl Don Diego and Sergeant Garcia have known since she was a child. Constansia lives in Santa Clara and comes to Los Angeles to marry Miguel Serano (Mark Oamo), a scoundrel Diego (as Zorro) exposes as a fortune hunter after Constansia's money.

In addition to 78 half-hour shows, four one-hour episodes were produced and aired on ABC's "Walt Disney Presents" on the following dates: 10/30/60 ("El Bandito"), 11/6/60 ("Adiós el Cuchillo"), 1/1/61 ("The Postponed Wedding") and 4/2/61 ("Auld Acquaintance"). Guy Williams, Henry Calvin and George J. Lewis repeated their roles.

Theme: "Zorro," vocal by Henry Calvin (backed by a male chorus).

Note: A satirical version of "Zorro" called "Zorro and Son" ran on CBS for six episodes (4/6/83 to 6/1/83). The new series is set in 1845, 25 years after Don Diego first became Zorro. Don Diego (Henry Darrow) is still defending the people of Old Los Angeles from their oppressors, but "the old gray fox isn't what he used to be" and his inability to perform prompts Bernardo (Bill Dana), Diego's faithful servant, to send to Spain for Diego's son, Don Carlos de la Vega (Paul Regina), in the hope that the young man may help his father. When Don Carlos arrives in California and discovers that the new *comandante,* Paco Pico (Gregory Sierra), is unfairly imposing his law on the citizens, he is inspired with a desire to help them. Seeing this, Diego reveals to his son his other identity, and begins a quest to train his son as the new Zorro. Zorro's horse is Tornado; Bernardo, who could talk in this version, has a donkey named Rosita.

A third version, called "The New Zorro," premiered on cable's Family Channel on 1/5/90. The series follows the format of the ABC version with Duncan Regehr as Don Diego/Zorro; Efrem Zimbalist, Jr., and Henry Darrow as his father, Don Alejandro; Patrice Camhi as Victoria Escalante, Diego's love interest and owner of the Pueblo's tavern; Michael Tylo as Louis Ramon, the corrupt Alcalde; James Victor as Sergeant Mendoza; and Juan Diego Botto as Felipe, Diego's confederate (replacing Bernardo; Felipe, like Bernardo, was mute but not deaf, but he pretended to be both).

Index

References are to entry numbers, not pages. Titles in **bold** refer to the series that are chronicled in this book. Titles in *italics* indicate programs (series and pilot films) that are detailed within bold face titles. Titles seen in quotes indicate alternative series titles, original series titles or mythical shows contained within bold face entries. SMALL CAP names refer to characters in shows.

A

The A-Team 1
AAAA Painting 117
Aames, Angela 63
Aames, Willie 111, 112, 196, 529
The Abbott and Costello Show 2
Abbott, Bruce 144
Abbott, Bud 2
Abbott, James 118
ABERNATHY, BILL 16
ABERNATHY, LILLIAN 16
ABERNATHY, STEVE 26
ABERNATHY, VAL 26
ABRAMS, SOL 106
Abrell, Sarah 169, 221, 486
Academy for Gifted Babies 36
Ace, Goodman 726
Ace Comics 69
Ackroyd, David 93
Acme Bird Seeds 125
Acme Bowling Alley 317
"Active 8 News" 174
ADAMA 46
Adams Apple 394
"Adams Apples" 330
Adams, Beverly 97, 250
ADAMS, CRUNCH 141
ADAMS, DOC 277
Adams, Don 246, 552
Adams, Jane 18
Adams, Joey (actress) 441, 718, 742
Adams, Julie 128
Adams, Marla 280, 558
Adams, Mason 378
Adams, Nick 594
Adams, Sari 141
Adams, Stanley 568
ADAMS, TURK 188

ADAMS, WILLARD 12
Adamson, Harold 96
The Addams Family 3
ADDAMS, GOMEZ 3
ADDAMS, MAUMUD KALI PASHU 3
ADDAMS, MORTICIA 3
ADDAMS, PANCHO 3
ADDAMS, PUGSLEY 3
ADDAMS, WEDNESDAY 3
ADDISON, DAVID 478
Addison, John 192
ADDISON, KAY 469
ADDISON, ROGER 469
ADLER, RICHIE 760
Adventures in Dairyland 462
Adventures in Paradise 4
Adventures of Clint and Mack 462
The Adventures of Superboy 5
The Adventures of Superman 6
The Adventures of Tugboat Annie 7
"Advice Radio" 416
Aeromass Airlines 766
Africa 3, 32, 136, 139, 695
"AFVN News and Sports" 651
AGARN, RANDOLPH 205
The Agency 627
AGENT 44 246
AGENT 13 246
Aidman, Charles 765
Ainley, Anthony 171
Air Cathay 702
Airwolf 8
AKALINO, ETHEL 65
Akerling, Mya 269, 354, 752
Akers, Andrea 502
"The Alan Brady Show" 162
Alaska 80, 377, 764
The Alaskans 377
Alberoni, Sherry 168

Albert, Eddie 270, 688
Albert, Edward 50, 275
Albertson, Frank 146
Albertson, Jack 304, 469, 707
Albertson, Mabel 6, 19, 56, 512, 703, 704, 716
ALBRIGHT, JOAN 133
Albright, Lola 80, 562
ALBRIGHT, MARGIE 493
ALBRIGHT, VERN 493
Alda, Alan 447
Alda, Robert 447
Alden, Norman 218, 269, 500, 588
ALDEN, TERRI 709
ALDER, DIANE 301
ALDER, LARRY 301
ALDER, RUTHIE 301
Aldred, Sophie 171
Aletter, Frank 84, 107, 342
Alexander, Erika 136
Alexander, Sandra 174
ALF 9
Ali, Tatyana M. 235
Alice 10
Alice, Mary 163
Alien Nation 11
All in the Family 12
All Sports Cable Network 262
Alldredge, Michael 212
ALLEN, AMY 1
ALLEN, BARRY 225
Allen, Chad 170, 541
Allen, Debbie 68
ALLEN, EVE 225
Allen, Gracie 243
ALLEN, HENRY 225
ALLEN, JAY 225
ALLEN, LORI BETH 280
ALLEN, MAJOR AMANDA 578